Map pages south

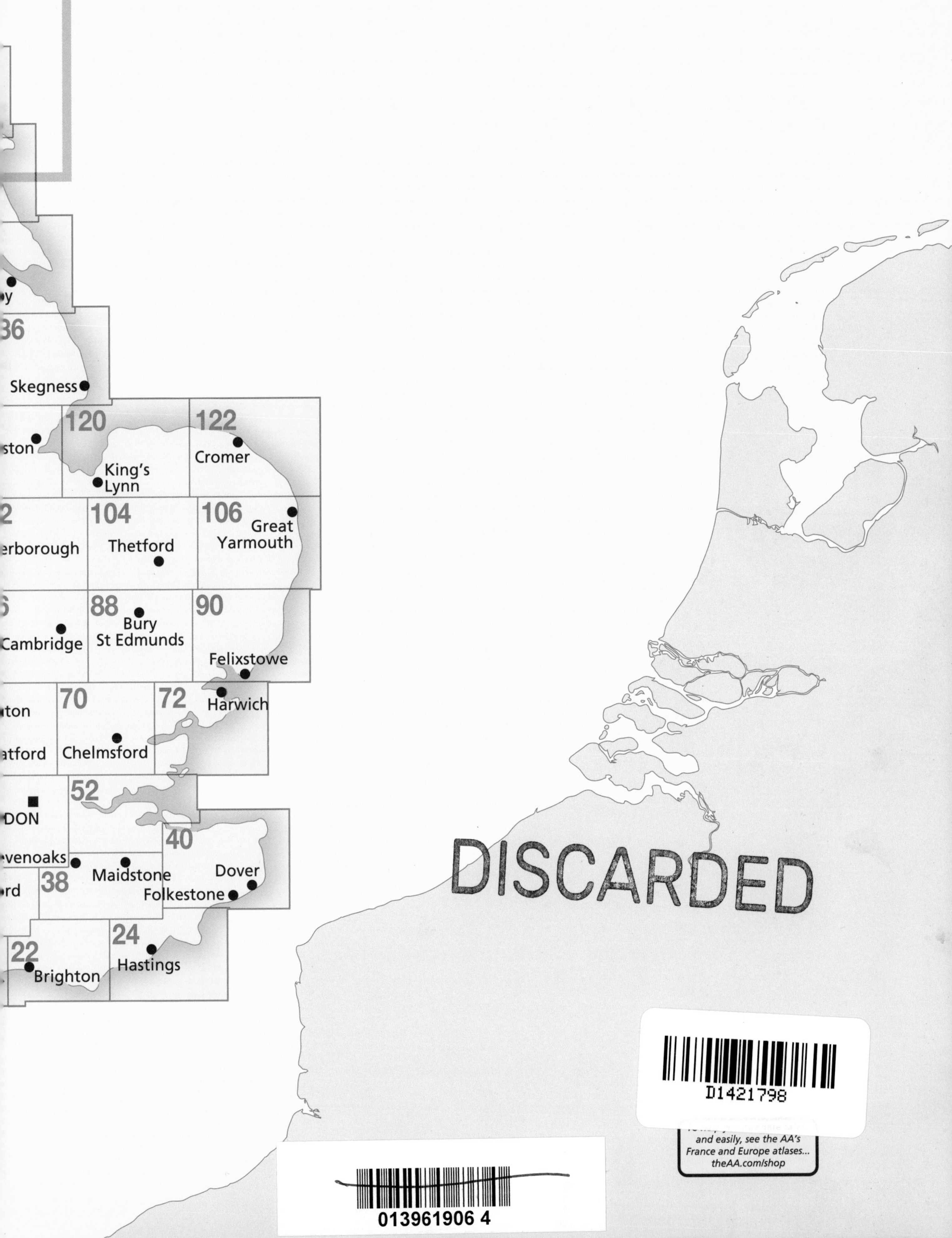

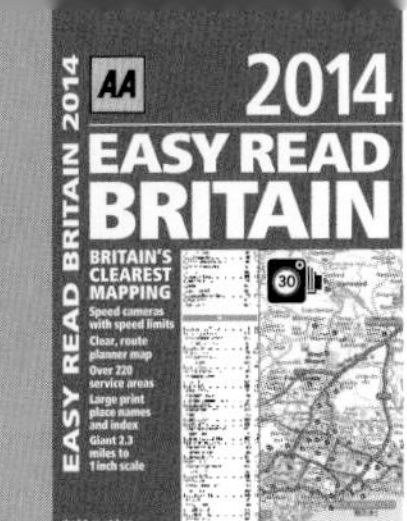

Atlas contents

Scale 1:148,000 or 2.34 miles to 1 inch

Section	Pages
Map pages south	inside front cover
Route planner	**II–VII**
Atlas symbols	**VIII–1**
Road maps 1:148,000 scale	**2–283**
Channel Islands 1:100,000 scale	9
Isle of Man 1:200,000 scale	154
Orkney Islands 1:450,000 scale	275
Shetland Islands 1:450,000 scale	281
Western Isles 1:480,000 scale	282–283
Restricted junctions	**284–285**
Index to place names	**286–368**
County, administrative area map	286–287
Map pages north	inside back cover

14th edition July 2013

Original edition printed 2000.

Cartography:
All cartography in this atlas edited, designed and produced by the Mapping Services Department of AA Publishing (A05051).

Publisher's notes:
Published by AA Publishing (a trading name of AA Media Limited, whose registered office is Fanum House, Basing View, Basingstoke, Hampshire RG21 4EA, UK. Registered number 06112600).

ISBN: 978 0 7495 7452 9. A CIP catalogue record for this book is available from The British Library.

Disclaimer:
The contents of this atlas are believed to be correct at the time of the latest revision, it will not contain any subsequent amended, new or temporary information including diversions and traffic control or enforcement systems. The publishers cannot be held responsible or liable for any loss or damage occasioned to any person acting or refraining from action as a result of any use or reliance on material in this atlas, nor for any errors, omissions or changes in such material. This does not affect your statutory rights.

The publishers would welcome information to correct any errors or omissions and to keep this atlas up to date. Please write to the Atlas Editor, AA Publishing, The Automobile Association, Fanum House, Basing View, Basingstoke, Hampshire RG21 4EA, UK. E-mail: *roadatlasfeedback@theaa.com*

Acknowledgements:
AA Publishing would like to thank the following for their assistance in producing this atlas:

RoadPilot® Information on fixed speed camera locations provided by and © 2013 RoadPilot® Driving Technology.
Crematoria data provided by Cremation Society of Great Britain. Cadw, English Heritage, Forestry Commission, Historic Scotland, Johnsons, National Trust and National Trust for Scotland, RSPB, The Wildlife Trust, Scottish Natural Heritage, Natural England, The Countryside Council for Wales.

Printer:
Printed in China by Leo Paper Products

REPUBLIC OF IRELAND

DUBLIN
Dún Laoghaire
(Mar–Sept)
Rosslare Harbour

Holyhead
Anglesey
Llandudno
Colwyn Bay
Rhyl
Bangor
Conwy
Abergele
Holywell
Bethesda
Caernarfon
Denbigh
Mold
Ruthin
SNOWDONIA
Betws-y-coed
Wrexham
Pwllheli
Porthmadog
Abersoch
Llangollen
Bala
Oswestry
Barmouth
Dolgellau
Welshpool
Shrewsbury
Machynlleth
Cardigan Bay
Aberystwyth
WALES
Newtown
Llangurig
Rhayader
Aberaeron
Tregaron
Llandrindod Wells
Lampeter
Builth Wells
Cardigan
Newcastle Emlyn
Fishguard
St David's
PEMBROKESHIRE COAST
Haverfordwest
Milford Haven
Pembroke Dock
Pembroke
Tenby
Carmarthen
St Clears
Llandovery
Llandeilo
Brecon
BRECON BEACONS
Hay-on-Wye
Llanelli
Swansea
Neath
Port Talbot
Bridgend
Pontypridd
Merthyr Tydfil
Abergavenny
Cwmbran
Newport
CARDIFF
Cardiff

Formby
Ormskirk
Skelmersdale
Bolton
Bury
Crosby
Wigan
St Helens
LIVERPOOL
Birkenhead
Warrington
Widnes
John Lennon
Runcorn
Knutsford
Ellesmere Port
Northwich
Queensferry
Chester
Crewe
Nantwich
Newcastle-under-Lyme
Whitchurch
Market Drayton
Newport
Telford
Church Stretton
WOLVERHAMPTON
Bridgnorth
Stourbridge
Kidderminster
Ludlow
Knighton
Bromsgrove
Leominster
Worcester
Kington
Great Malvern
Hereford
Ledbury
Ross-on-Wye
Gloucester
Monmouth
Chepstow
Stroud
Avonmouth
Clevedon
BRISTOL
Bristol
Weston-super-Mare
Bath
Cheddar
Wells
Frome
Shepton Mallet
Glastonbury

Bristol Channel
Lundy
Ilfracombe
Lynton
Minehead
EXMOOR
Barnstaple
Bridgwater
Bideford
Great Torrington
South Molton
Taunton
Wincanton
Yeovil
Sherborne
Shaftesbury
Ilminster
Chard
Crewkerne
Blandford Forum
Bude
Hatherleigh
Tiverton
Holsworthy
Crediton
Okehampton
Exeter
Honiton
Axminster
Bridport
Lyme Regis
Dorchester
Weymouth
Fortuneswell
Launceston
DARTMOOR
Exmouth
Dawlish
Teignmouth
Newton Abbot
Torquay
Paignton
Wadebridge
Tavistock
Bodmin
Newquay
Liskeard
Buckfastleigh
Plymouth
Lostwithiel
Saltash
PLYMOUTH
Totnes
Torpoint
St Austell
Dartmouth
Kingsbridge
Redruth
Truro
Camborne
Penzance
Land's End
Helston
Falmouth
Lizard

Santander (Mar–Oct)
Roscoff
St Malo (Nov–Mar)
Guernsey
Jersey
St-Malo
Guernsey
Jersey
St-Malo
ENGLISH

Route planner

Motorway
Toll motorway
Primary route dual carriageway
Primary route single carriageway
Other A roads
Vehicle ferry
Fast vehicle ferry or catamaran

0 10 20 30 miles
0 10 20 30 40 kilometres

To help you navigate safely and easily, see the AA's France and Europe atlases... theAA.com/shop

NORTHERN IRELAND

REPUBLIC OF IRELAND

IRISH SEA

LOCH LOMOND AND THE TROSSACHS

LAKE DISTRICT

SNOWDONIA

Firth of Forth

Firth of Clyde

Solway Firth

Isle of Man

Anglesey

Colonsay
Jura
Islay
Arran

EDINBURGH
GLASGOW
BELFAST
DUBLIN
LIVERPOOL

St Andrews, Crieff, Auchterarder, Cupar, Inveraray, Callander, Dunblane, Kinross, Glenrothes, Alloa, Stirling, Dunfermline, Kirkcaldy, Lochgilphead, Helensburgh, Rosyth, Falkirk, Dunbar, Dunoon, Dumbarton, Port Askaig, Greenock, Airdrie, Livingston, Dalkeith, Tarbert, Kennacraig, Largs, Paisley, Motherwell, East Kilbride, Port Ellen, Ardrossan, Kilwinning, Strathaven, Lanark, Peebles, Irvine, Kilmarnock, Galashiels, Troon, Prestwick, Biggar, Kelso, Ayr, Selkirk, Campbeltown, Cumnock, Jedburgh, Hawick, Maybole, Moffat, Girvan, Thornhill, Langholm, Lockerbie, Cairnryan, New Galloway, Dumfries, Newton Stewart, Longtown, Stranraer, Castle Douglas, Annan, Brampton, Larne, Carlisle, Alston, Maryport, Cockermouth, Penrith, Workington, Keswick, Egremont, Ambleside, Ravenglass, Windermere, Ramsey, Kendal, Sedbergh, Peel, Millom, Kirkby Lonsdale, Douglas, Castletown, Isle of Man (Ronaldsway), Barrow-in-Furness, Morecambe, Heysham, Lancaster, Fleetwood, Clitheroe, Blackpool, Preston, Southport, Ormskirk, Bolton, Formby, Skelmersdale, Wigan, Crosby, St Helens, Warrington, Birkenhead, Widnes, John Lennon, Runcorn, Llandudno, Colwyn Bay, Rhyl, Holywell, Ellesmere Port, Holyhead, Dún Laoghaire, Bangor, Conwy, Abergele, Queensferry, Northwich, Bethesda, Denbigh, Mold, Chester, Caernarfon, Ruthin, Crewe, Betws-y-coed, Wrexham, Nantwich, Newcastle-under-Lyme, Llangollen, Whitchurch, Pwllheli, Porthmadog, Bala, Abersoch, Oswestry, Market Drayton, Newport, Barmouth, Dolgellau, Shrewsbury, Welshpool, Telford

(Mar–Oct) (Apr–Sept) (Nov–Mar) (Mar–Oct) (Apr–Sept) (Mar–Sept)

To help you navigate safely and easily, see the AA's Ireland atlases... theAA.com/shop

Motorway
Toll motorway
Primary route dual carriageway
Primary route single carriageway
Other A roads
Vehicle ferry
Fast vehicle ferry or catamaran
0 10 20 30 miles
0 10 20 30 40 kilometres
Eyemouth
Berwick-upon-Tweed
Wooler
Alnwick
Amble
Ashington
Morpeth
Newcastle
Tynemouth
North Shields
South Shields
Amsterdam (IJmuiden)
Gateshead
NEWCASTLE UPON TYNE
SUNDERLAND
Consett
Chester-le-Street
Durham
Hartlepool
Bishop Auckland
Barnard Castle
Stockton-on-Tees
Middlesbrough
Darlington
Durham Tees Valley
Guisborough
Whitby
Scotch Corner
Richmond
NORTH YORK MOORS
Northallerton
Scarborough
Leyburn
Thirsk
Pickering
Helmsley
Filey
Ripon
Easingwold
Malton
Bridlington
Driffield
Harrogate
York
Wetherby
Market Weighton
Otley
Leeds Bradford
Keighley
LEEDS
BRADFORD
Selby
Beverley
Halifax
KINGSTON UPON HULL
Pontefract
Goole
Killingholme
Immingham
Wakefield
Huddersfield
Thorne
Scunthorpe
Humberside
Grimsby
Cleethorpes
Rotterdam (Europoort)
Zeebrugge
Barnsley
Oldham
Doncaster
Brigg
Robin Hood Doncaster Sheffield
Rotherham
Glossop
Bawtry
Market Rasen
Stockport
SHEFFIELD
Gainsborough
Louth
PEAK DISTRICT
Retford
Mablethorpe
Worksop
Buxton
Chesterfield
Lincoln
ENGLAND
Bakewell
Horncastle
Skegness
Mansfield
Matlock
Alfreton
Leek
Newark-on-Trent
Sleaford
STOKE-ON-TRENT
Ashbourne
Ilkeston
Boston
The Wash
Sheringham
Cromer
Hunstanton
Stone
Uttoxeter
DERBY
NOTTINGHAM
Grantham
North Walsham
Long Eaton
Aylsham
Fakenham
East Midlands
Stafford
Burton upon Trent
Loughborough
Spalding
King's Lynn
Rugeley
Melton Mowbray
Bourne
Dereham
Norwich
Caister-on-Sea
THE BROADS
Lichfield
Oakham
Stamford
Wisbech
Swaffham
Great Yarmouth
LEICESTER

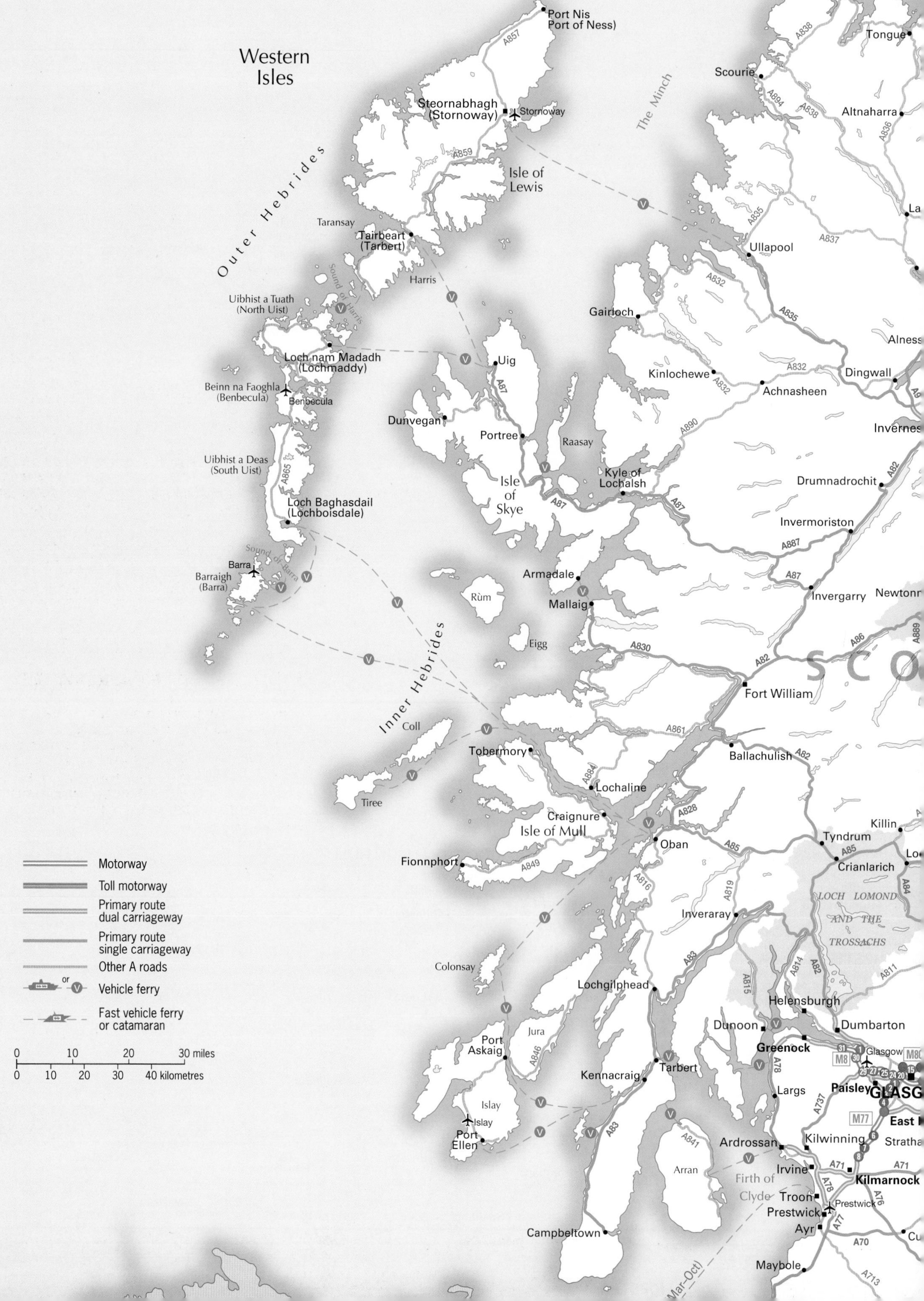
Western Isles
Outer Hebrides
Inner Hebrides
The Minch
Port Nis (Port of Ness)
Steornabhagh (Stornoway)
Stornoway
Isle of Lewis
Taransay
Tairbeart (Tarbert)
Harris
Sound of Harris
Uibhist a Tuath (North Uist)
Loch nam Madadh (Lochmaddy)
Beinn na Faoghla (Benbecula)
Benbecula
Uibhist a Deas (South Uist)
Loch Baghasdail (Lochboisdale)
Sound of Barra
Barra
Barraigh (Barra)
Uig
Dunvegan
Portree
Raasay
Isle of Skye
Kyle of Lochalsh
Armadale
Mallaig
Rùm
Eigg
Coll
Tiree
Tobermory
Lochaline
Craignure
Isle of Mull
Fionnphort
Oban
Colonsay
Jura
Port Askaig
Islay
Port Ellen
Kennacraig
Tarbert
Lochgilphead
Inveraray
Campbeltown
Arran
Firth of Clyde
Scourie
Tongue
Altnaharra
Ullapool
Gairloch
Kinlochewe
Achnasheen
Dingwall
Alness
Inverness
Drumnadrochit
Invermoriston
Invergarry
Newtonmore
Fort William
Ballachulish
Tyndrum
Killin
Crianlarich
LOCH LOMOND AND THE TROSSACHS
Helensburgh
Dunoon
Dumbarton
Greenock
Glasgow
Paisley
GLASG
East
Largs
Kilwinning
Ardrossan
Irvine
Kilmarnock
Troon
Prestwick
Ayr
Maybole
SCO
Motorway
Toll motorway
Primary route dual carriageway
Primary route single carriageway
Other A roads
Vehicle ferry
Fast vehicle ferry or catamaran
0 10 20 30 miles
0 10 20 30 40 kilometres

FERRY INFORMATION

Hebrides and west coast Scotland

calmac.co.uk	0800 066 5000
skyeferry.co.uk	01599 522 236
western-ferries.co.uk	01369 704 452

Orkney and Shetland

northlinkferries.co.uk	0845 6000 449
pentlandferries.co.uk	0800 688 8998
orkneyferries.co.uk	01856 872 044
shetland.gov.uk/ferries	01595 743 970

Isle of Man

steam-packet.com	08722 992 992

Ireland

irishferries.com	08717 300 400
poferries.com	08716 642 020
stenaline.co.uk	08447 70 70 70

North Sea (Scandinavia and Benelux)

dfdsseaways.co.uk	08715 229 955
poferries.com	08716 642 020
stenaline.co.uk	08447 70 70 70

Isle of Wight

wightlink.co.uk	0871 376 1000
redfunnel.co.uk	0844 844 9988

Channel Islands

condorferries.co.uk	0845 609 1024

Channel hopping (France and Belgium)

brittany-ferries.co.uk	0871 244 0744
condorferries.co.uk	0845 609 1024
eurotunnel.com	08443 35 35 35
ldlines.co.uk	0844 576 8836
dfdsseaways.co.uk	08715 229 955
poferries.com	08716 642 020
transeuropaferries.com	01843 595 522
myferrylink.com	0844 2482 100

Northern Spain

brittany-ferries.co.uk	0871 244 0744
poferries.com	08716 642 020

EMERGENCY DIVERSION ROUTES

In an emergency it may be necessary to close a section of motorway or other main road to traffic, so a temporary sign may advise drivers to follow a diversion route. To help drivers navigate the route, black symbols on yellow patches may be permanently displayed on existing direction signs, including motorway signs. Symbols may also be used on separate signs with yellow backgrounds.

For further information see *www.highways.gov.uk, trafficscotland.org* and *traffic-wales.com*

Atlas symbols

Motoring information

Symbol	Meaning
M4	Motorway with number
T4 Toll / Toll	Toll motorway with toll station
11	Motorway junction with and without number
3	Restricted motorway junctions
S Fleet	Motorway service area
	Motorway and junction under construction
A3	Primary route single/dual carriageway
11	Primary route junction with and without number
3	Restricted primary route junctions
S	Primary route service area
BATH	Primary route destination
A1123	Other A road single/dual carriageway
B2070	B road single/dual carriageway
	Minor road more than 4 metres wide, less than 4 metres wide
	Roundabout
	Interchange/junction
	Narrow primary/other A/B road with passing places (Scotland)
	Road under construction/ approved
	Road tunnel
Toll	Road toll
	Steep gradient (arrows point downhill)
30	Speed camera site (fixed location) with speed limit in mph
40	Section of road with two or more fixed speed cameras, with speed limit in mph
50 50	Average speed (SPECS™) camera system with speed limit in mph
V	Fixed speed camera site with variable speed limit
5	Distance in miles between symbols
or V	Vehicle ferry
	Fast vehicle ferry or catamaran
	Railway line, in tunnel
	Railway station and level crossing
	Tourist railway
	Airport, heliport
F	International freight terminal
H	24-hour Accident & Emergency hospital
C	Crematorium
P+R	Park and Ride (at least 6 days per week)
	City, town, village or other built-up area
628 ▲	Spot height in metres
637 Lecht Summit	Mountain pass
	Sandy beach
	National boundary
	County, administrative boundary

Touring information

To avoid disappointment, check opening times before visiting.

- Scenic route
- Tourist Information Centre
- Tourist Information Centre (seasonal)
- Visitor or heritage centre
- Picnic site
- Caravan site (AA inspected)
- Camping site (AA inspected)
- Caravan & camping site (AA inspected)
- Abbey, cathedral or priory
- Ruined abbey, cathedral or priory
- Castle
- Historic house or building
- Museum or art gallery
- Industrial interest
- Aqueduct or viaduct
- Garden
- Arboretum
- Vineyard
- Country park
- Agricultural showground
- Theme park
- Farm or animal centre
- Zoological or wildlife collection
- Bird collection
- Aquarium
- RSPB site
- National Nature Reserve (England,Scotland, Wales)
- Local nature reserve
- Wildlife Trust reserve
- Forest drive
- National trail
- Viewpoint
- Hill-fort
- Roman antiquity
- Prehistoric monument
- 1066 Battle site with year
- Steam railway centre
- Cave
- Windmill
- Monument
- Golf course (AA listed)
- County cricket ground
- Rugby Union national stadium
- International athletics stadium
- Horse racing
- Show jumping/equestrian circuit
- Motor-racing circuit
- Air show venue
- Ski slope (natural)
- Ski slope (artificial)
- National Trust property
- National Trust for Scotland property
- English Heritage site
- Historic Scotland site
- Cadw (Welsh heritage) site
- Other place of interest
- Boxed symbols indicate attractions within urban areas
- World Heritage Site (UNESCO)
- National Park
- National Scenic Area (Scotland)
- Forest Park
- Heritage coast
- Major shopping centre

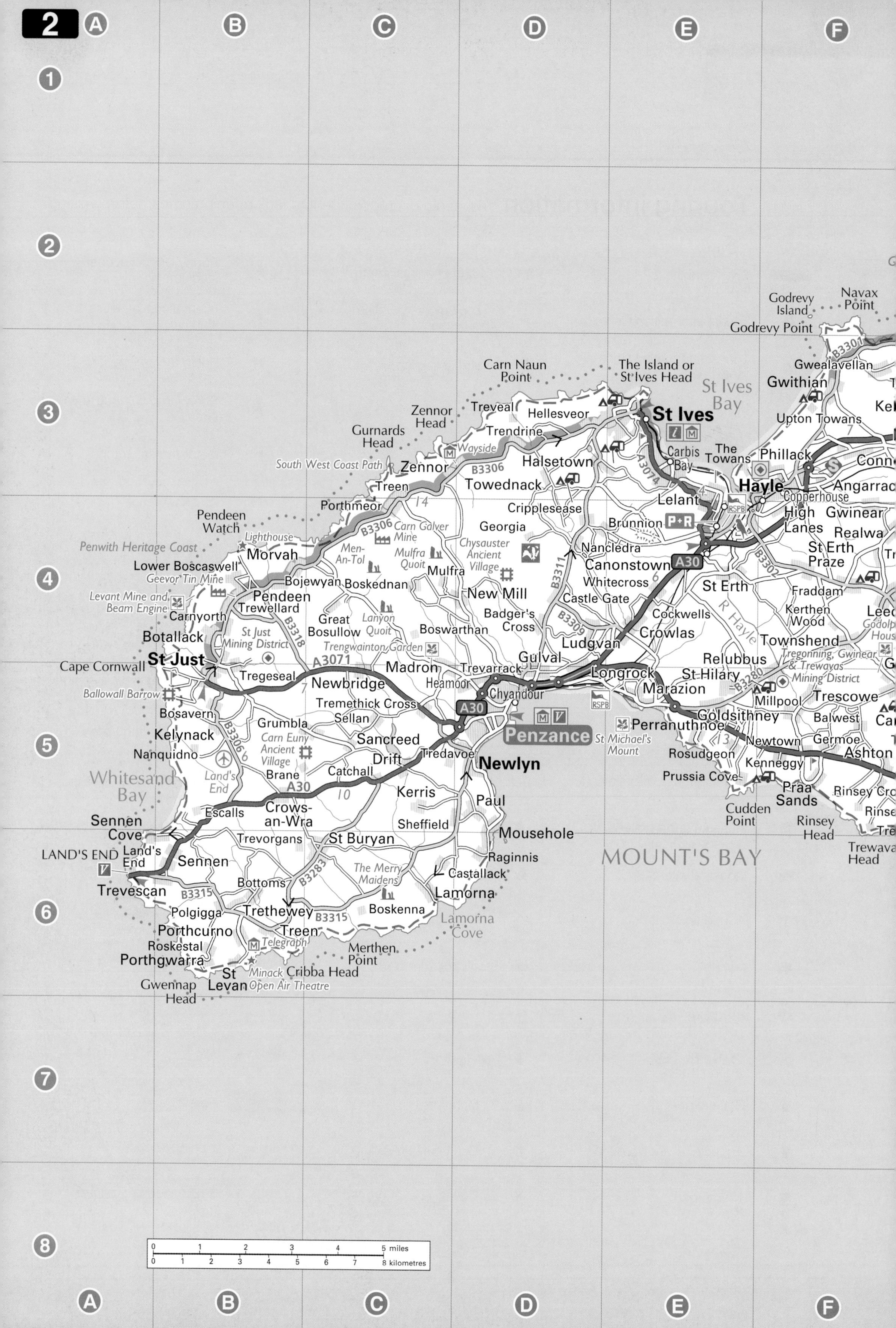
A
B
C
D
E
F
1
2
3
4
5
6
7
8
Godrevy Island
Navax Point
Godrevy Point
B3301
Gwealavellan
Gwithian
Upton Towans
St Ives Bay
Carn Naun Point
The Island or St Ives Head
St Ives
Zennor Head
Treveal
Hellesveor
Trendrine
Gurnards Head
Wayside
Halsetown
Carbis Bay
The Towans
Phillack
South West Coast Path
Zennor
B3306
Towednack
A3074
Hayle
Copperhouse
Angarrack
Treen
Lelant
Porthmeor
Cripplesease
RSPB
High Lanes
Gwinear
Pendeen Watch
Carn Galver Mine
Georgia
Brunnion
P+R
Realwa
Lighthouse
Men-An-Tol
Chysauster Ancient Village
Nancledra
St Erth Praze
Penwith Heritage Coast
Morvah
Mulfra Quoit
B3311
A30
B3302
Lower Boscaswell
Geevor Tin Mine
Mulfra
Canonstown
Bojewyan
Boskednan
Whitecross
St Erth
Fraddam
Levant Mine and Beam Engine
Pendeen
New Mill
Castle Gate
Trewellard
Carnyorth
Great Bosullow
Lanyon Quoit
Badger's Cross
B3309
Cockwells
Kerthen Wood
B3318
Boswarthan
Crowlas
R Hayle
Botallack
St Just Mining District
Trengwainton Garden
Ludgvan
Townshend
Tregonning, Gwinear & Trewavas Mining District
St Just
A3071
Gulval
Relubbus
Cape Cornwall
Madron
Trevarrack
St Hilary
Tregeseal
Longrock
B3280
Ballowall Barrow
Newbridge
Heamoor
Marazion
Chyandour
Millpool
Trescowe
Tremethick Cross
RSPB
Bosavern
Sellan
Goldsithney
Balwest
Grumbla
Perranuthnoe
Kelynack
B3306
Carn Euny Ancient Village
Sancreed
Penzance
St Michael's Mount
Newtown
Germoe
Ashton
Nanquidno
Drift
Tredavoe
Rosudgeon
Land's End
Newlyn
Kenneggy
Whitesand Bay
Brane
Catchall
Prussia Cove
Praa Sands
Rinsey Cross
A30
Kerris
Paul
Cudden Point
Rinsey Head
Escalls
Crows-an-Wra
Sennen Cove
Sheffield
Mousehole
Trevorgans
St Buryan
LAND'S END
Land's End
Sennen
Raginnis
MOUNT'S BAY
Trewavas Head
The Merry Maidens
Castallack
Bottoms
B3283
Trevescan
B3315
Lamorna
Polgigga
Trethewey
Boskenna
B3315
Lamorna Cove
Porthcurno
Treen
Roskestal
Telegraph
Merthen Point
Porthgwarra
St Levan
Minack Open Air Theatre
Cribba Head
Gwennap Head
0 1 2 3 4 5 miles
0 1 2 3 4 5 6 7 8 kilometres

Cligga Point
Goonhavern
Brighton
Carland
Trevellas Downs
Cocks
Perranwell
Perranzabuloe
St Agnes Heritage Coast
ST AGNES HEAD
Cross Coombe
Penhallow
St Agnes
Mithian
Callestick
Zelah
St Allen
Trispen
Trelassick
Ladock
New Mills
Wheal Coates
Barkla Shop
Marazanvose
Goonvrea
Goonbell
St Agnes Mining District
Coldharbour
Silverwell
Treworgan
St Erme
Treverbyn
Allet Common
Porthtowan
Mount Hawke
Shortlanesend
Idless
Probus
South West Coast Path
Three Burrows
Tresillian
Mawla
Menagissey
P+R
Kenwyn
Tresawle
Portreath
Cambrose
Wheal Peevor
Wheal Rose
Blackwater
A390
Threemilestone
Truro
Merther
Portreath Heritage Coast
Illogan
North Country
Chacewater
Saveock
Higher Town
St Clement
Tehidy Park
Paynter's Lane End
A30
Scorrier
Newbridge
Tregenna
South Tehidy
Bottom
Mount Ambrose
Gwennap Mining District
Baldhu
Kea
Calenick
Malpas
St Michael Penkevil
Ruan Lanihorne
East Pool Mine
St Day
Cross Lanes
Killiow
Porthkea
Skadinnick
Redruth
Twelveheads
Chyeowling
Playing Place
Old Kea
Lamorran
Tuckingmill
Pool
A3047
Carharrack
Frogpool
Bissoe
Carnon Downs
Coombe
Trelissick Garden
Trelissick
Treworga
Philleigh
Carn Brea
Trevarth
Gwennap
Penelewey
Roseworthy
Camborne
Lanner
A393
Perranwell
Devoran
Treworthal
Treworlas
Penponds
Carnkie
Perranarworthal
A39
Penpol
Trevilla
Bolenowe
Four Lanes
Penhalurick
Kennall Vale
Devoran & Perran
Feock
Treluggan
Barripper
Troon
Penhalvean
Perran Wharf
Angarrick
Trewithian
Carnhell Green
Hendra
Ponsanooth
Restronguet
Cargurrel
Gerrans Bay
Croft Mitchell
Mylor Bridge
Rosevine
Stithians
Burnthouse
Lower Treluswell
St Just-in-Roseland
Praze-an-Beeble
Tregolls
Trelew
Portscatho
Carrick Roads
Burras Farm Common
St Gluvia's
Mylor
Blackrock
Carnkie
Longdowns
Tregew
Gerrans
Mabe Burnthouse
Penryn
Flushing
Crowan
Porkellis
Rame
Lezerea
Edgcombe
Greeb Point
Castle
St Mawes
Trenoweth
Budock Water
Releath
Wendron Mining District
Argal & College Water Park
Pendennis Castle
Trenwheal
Nancegollan
Bohortha
Trenear
Poldark Mine
Treverva
Falmouth
Prospidnick
Wendron
A394
Seworgan
Lamanva
South West Coast Path
Pendennis Point
Crowntown
Manhay
Penjerrick
ZONE POINT
Sithney Green
Lower Town
Coverack Bridges
High Cross
Bareppa
Sithney
Brill
Carlidnack
Maenporth
Falmouth Bay
Mawnan Smith
Trewennack
Constantine
Trebah
Sithney Common
Helston
Porth Navas
Carwinion
ROSEMULLION HEAD
Gweek
Glendurgan Garden
Helford Passage
Durgan
Mawnan
Mellangoose
Flambards
Seal Sanctuary
Helford River
Helford
St Anthony
Porthleven
Mawgan
Gear
Manaccan
Gillan
Nare Point
Higher Pentire
A3083
Trelowarren
Carne
Lestowder
Garras
St Martin
Roskorwell
Chyvarloe
Halliggye Fogou
Tregidden
Gunwalloe
Berepper
Tregarne
Porthallow
Chyanvounder
White Cross
Newtown-in-St Martin
Trenance
Porthoustock
Treleague
Manacle Point
Cury
Traboe
Rosenithon
Cross Lanes
B3293
St Keverne
The Lizard
Zoar
Angrouse
Poldhu Point
Trewoon
Marconi Memorial
GOONHILLY DOWNS
Trelan
Lowland Point
B3296
Mullion
Mullion Cove
Penhale
Ponsongath
North Corner
Mullion Island
Coverack
Ruan Major
Gwenter
Trewillis
Predannack Head
Predannack Wollas
Kuggar
Treleaver
South West Coast Path
St Ruan
Poltescoe
Black Head
Mount Hermon
Vellan Head
Ruan Minor
The Lizard
Grade
Cadgwith
The Lizard Heritage Coast
Devil's Frying Pan
Lizard Head
Kynance Cove
Church Cove
Lizard
Bass Point
LIZARD POINT
Lizard Lighthouse & Heritage Centre
G
H
J
K
L
M
1
2
3
4
5
6
7
8

4
A
B
C
D
E
F
1
2
3
4
5
6
7
8
Porthcothan
St Issey
Little Petherick
Trenance
Park Head
Treburrick
Penrose
10
St Ervan
Rumford
Tredinnick
Engollan
Trelow
St Jidgey
Bedruthan Steps
Carnewas
Downhill
St Eval
Crealy Great Adventure Park
Trenance
Nine Maidens
B3274
Berryls Point
Mawgan Porth
A39
Griffins Point
Trevarrian
B3276
Vale of Mawgan
St Mawgan
Carloggas
Talskiddy
Watergate Bay
Tregurrian
Newquay
Gluvian
St Wenn
Reterth
Towan Head
Newquay Bay
St Columb Minor
A3059
St Columb Major
Newquay
Porth
30
Tregaswith
Castle-an-Dinas
Fistral Bay
Trevithick
A3058
Trebudannon
Colan
Black Cross
West Pentire
Pentire
Kelsey Head
Bosoughan
Ruthvoes
Holywell Bay
Treninnick
Mountjoy
Trevarren
Crantock
Lane
Quintrell Downs
A392
Toldish
Trenowah
Trevemper
Enniscaven
Penhale Point
Tresean
Rosecliston
Kestle Mill
St Columb Road
B3279
Carne
Holywell
Treveal
Retyn
Indian Queens
Fraddon
Ligger Point
Trevoll
Dairyland Farm World
Troan
Penhale
Blue Anchor
Cubert
Trerice
Gummow's Shop
St Enoder
St Dennis
Ligger or Perran Bay
Newlyn East
A3058
A30
Mount
Lappa Valley
Summercourt
Treviscoe
Rejerrah
Burthy
A3075
Trevilson
Rose
A3076
Chapel Town
Melbur
Fiddlers Green
Scarcewater
Perranporth
Mitchell
Trethosa
Goonhavern
Cligga Point
B3285
Carland Cross
Brighton
A3058
High Street
Bolingey
St Stephen
Trevellas Downs
Cocks
Carnkiet
B3285
Trendeal
Gwindra
St Agnes Heritage Coast
Perranwell
Trelassick
Trelion
ST AGNES HEAD
Cross Coombe
Perranzabuloe
Zelah
New Mills
St Agnes
Penhallow
St Allen
A39
Coombe
Ladock
Wheal Coates
Mithian
Callestick
Trispen
Barkla Shop
Goonvrea
Marazanvose
Grampound Road
Treverbyn
Goonbell
3
Coldharbour
Treworgan
St Erme
St Agnes Mining District
Silverwell
B3275
Allet Common
Probus
A390
B3277
B3284
Grampound
Porthtowan
Mount Hawke
Shortlanesend
Idless
Creed
Mawla
Menagissey
Three Burrows
Tresillian
B3287
West Path
P+R
Tresawle
Tucoyse
Cambrose
Wheal Peevor
Wheal Rose
Blackwater
A390
Threemilestone
Kenwyn
River Fal
B3300
Polmassick
Truro
Illogan
North Country
Chacewater
Saveock
40
H
Merther
Trevithick
A30
Higher Town
40
Tregony
Paynter's Lane End
Scorrier
Newbridge
St Clement
Park Bottom
Gwennap Mining District
Baldhu
Tregenna
Mount Ambrose
Kea
Calenick
Malpas
A3078
Pool Mine
St Day
Cross Lanes
St Michael Penkevil
Ruan Lanihorne
St Michael Caerhays
Killiow
Porthkea
Redruth
Twelveheads
Chyeowling
Pool
A3047
Playing Place
Lamorran
Portholland
Carharrack
Old Kea
Carn Brea
Frogpool
Bissoe
3
Carnon Downs
Coombe
Ruan High Lanes
Veryan Green
30
Carn Brea
Trevarth
B3298
Trelissick Garden
Treworga
Treviskey
Camborne
Carnkie
Gwennap
Penelewey
Trelissick
Philleigh
Lanner
A393
Perranwell
Devoran
Treworthal
Veryan
Portloe
Bolenowe
B3297
Perranarworthal
A39
Penpol
Trevilla
V
B3289
Treworlas
Four Lanes
Penhalurick
Kennall Vale
Devoran & Perran
Feock
Penhalvean
Perran Wharf
Treluggan
Carne
Hendra
Angarrick
Trewithian
The Roseland Heritage Coast
Croft Mitchell
Ponsanooth
Cargurrel
Stithians
Mylor Bridge
Restronguet
Gerrans Bay
Burnthouse
Lower Treluswell
St Just-in-Roseland
Rosevine
Nare Head
Tregolls
B3280
B3297
Trelew
Portscatho
Burras Farm Common
St Gluvia's
Carnkie
Longdowns
40
Mylor
Carrick Roads
Percuil R
Gerrans
Tregew
Mabe Burnthouse
Penryn
Porkellis
Flushing
Rame
A39
Lezerea
Edgcombe
Castle
Greeb Point
Trenoweth
St Mawes
Wendron Mining District
Argal & College Water Park
Budock Water
Pendennis Castle
3
Trenear
Poldark Mine
Bohortha
Treverva
Falmouth
Wendron
A394
Sewargan
Lamanva
Pendennis Point
South West Coast Path
Manhay
60
Penjerrick
Penjerrick
ZONE POINT
Coverack Bridges
Brill
High Cross
Bareppa
Falmouth Bay
Carlidnack
Maenporth

Egloshayle
St Breock
Sladesbridge
Treneague
Burlawn
Hay
Polbrock
Brocton
Camel Valley
Ruthernbridge
Tregawne
Withiel
Withielgoose
Tremore
Retire
Lamorick
Tredethy
Pencarrow
Hellandbridge
Colquite
Washaway
Helland
Lane End
Dunmere
Boscarne
Nanstallon
St Lawrence
Bodmin
Tregullon
Lanivet
Waterloo
Millpool
Cardinham
Mount
Cooksland
Fletchersbridge
Bodmin & Wenford Railway
Warleggan
St Neot
Pantersbridge
Tredinnick
Lampen
Ley
Carnglaze Caverns
Doublebois
Golitha Falls
King Doniert's Stone
Caradon Mining District
Minions
Common Moor
Darite
Trethevy Quoit
Tremar
St Cleer
Trembraze
Dobwalls
Moorswater
Lamellion
Trevelmond
St Pinnock
Paul Corin's Magnificent Music Machines
St Keyne
Herodsfoot
Duloe
Widegates
Tredinnick
Sandplace
Morval
Muchlarnick
Pelynt
St Martin
Trelawne
Looe
Portlooe
Porthallow
Looe or St George's Island
Talland Bay
Polperro
Crumplehorn
Model Village
Trenewan
Lansallos
Lantivet Bay
Pencarrow Head
Lantic Bay
South West Coast Path
Gribbin Head - Polperro Heritage Coast
West Taphouse
Middle Taphouse
East Taphouse
Braddock 1643
Boconnoc
Cutmadoc
Lanhydrock
Trebyan
Sweetshouse
Restormel Castle
Lostwithiel
Penhale
Castle
Milltown
Couch's Mill
Porfell Wildlife Park
Bocaddon
Lerryn
Lanreath
St Veep
Penpoll
Golant
Lanteglos Highway
Bodinnick
Polruan
Fowey
St Catherine's Castle
Menabilly
Polkerris
Gribbin Head
Polmear
Torfrey
Treesmill
Tywardreath
Penpillick
Tywardreath Highway
Eden Project
Luxulyan
Luxulyan Valley
Lanlivery
Tredinnick
Helman Tor
Bokiddick
Lockengate
Bodwen
Criggan
Higher Town
Victoria
Roche
Carbis
Bugle
Rosevean
Carnsmerry
Whitemoor
Treverbyn
Stenalees
Carthew
Wheal Martyn
Penwithick
Trethurgy
Ruddlemoor
Carclaze
Tregrehan Mills
St Blazey
St Blazey Gate
Par
Biscovey
Carlyon Bay
Boscoppa
St Austell
Trewoon
Holmbush
Charlestown
Polgooth
Mewan
Tregorrick
Porthpean
St Austell Bay
Sticker
London Apprentice
Levalsa Meor
Trenarren
Black Head
Towan
Rescorla
Lost Gardens of Heligan
Pentewan
Mevagissey Bay
Kestle
Tregiskey
Penare Point
Mevagissey
Portmellon
Chapel Point
Gorran High Lanes
Gorran Churchtown
Gorran Haven
Treveor
Maenease Point
Penare
Dodman Point
A30
A38
A389
A390
A391
A3082
A387
B3268
B3269
B3274
B3273
B3359
B3254
B3252
B3253
0 1 2 3 4 5 miles
0 1 2 3 4 5 6 7 8 kilometres
G
H
J
K
L
M
1
2
3
4
5
6
7
8
9
10
11

6
A
B
C
D
E
F
1
2
3
4
5
6
7
8
Cheesewring
Upton
Plushabridge
South Hill
Downgate
Chilsworthy
Gulworthy
The Hurlers Stone Circles
Caradon Town
Kelly Bray
Coxpark
St Ann's Chapel
Gunnislake
Minions
Sterts Open-Air Theatre
Trewoodloe
Kit Hill
Caradon Mining District
Downgate
Golberdon
Harrowbarrow
Morwellham Quay
11
12
Common Moor
Darite
Crow's Nest
Pensilva
Trevigro
Haye
Dupath Well
Norris Green
Albaston
Horrabridge
Trethevy Quoit
Middlehill
Charaton
Callington
Metherell
The Garden House
King Doniert's Stone
Gang
Frogwell
St Dominick
Cotehele
Calstock
Golitha Falls
Tremar
Calstock Viaduct
Buckland Monachorum
St Cleer
St Ive
Buckland Abbey
B3254
Merrymeet
Cadson Bury
Burraton
Bohetherick
Tamar Valley Mining District
St Ive Cross
Bealbury
St Mellion
Bere Alston
Milton Combe
Trembraze
A390
Newton Ferrers
Dobwalls
Halton Quay
Cotts
Liskeard
Pengover Green
Quethiock
Weir Quay
Moorswater
Pillaton
A388
Trehunist
Maristow
Trevelmond
Lamellion
Trewint
Pillatonmill
Cargreen
Bere Ferrers
St Pinnock
A38
Menheniot
Blunts
Hatt
Moorswater
R Tiddy
Cuttivett
Paul Corin's Magnificent Music Machines
Landulph
Tamerton Foliot
Roborough
5
Doddy Cross
Tideford Cross
Botusfleming
River Tamar
St Keyne
Plymouth
Cutmere
Carkeel
Horningtops
Tideford
Notter
B3252
B3251
B3254
Saltash
Budge's Shop
Landrake
Trewidland
Toll
Crownhill
Duloe
St Erney
Trematon
Widegates
South Pill
Shorta Cross
Trerulefoot
Markwell
Tredinnick
B3249
Trehan
St Budeaux
Tredinnick
St Germans
St Stephens
Egg Buckland
Sandplace
Churchtown Farm Community
Antony House
Hessenford
Morval
W Looe R
No Man's Land
Trelowia
Polbathic
B3253
Narkurs
Pelynt
Monkey Sanctuary
St Martin
Sheviock
A374
Devonport
Antony
Torpoint
Trelawne
B3247
Seaton
Crafthole
St John
A387
St John's Lake
Stonehouse
Looe
Downderry
Cremyll
Portwrinkle
Model Village
Looe Bay
Penhale
Smeaton's Tower
Mountbatten Centre
Portlooe
Higher Tregantle
Insworke
Mount Edgcumbe
Turnchapel
Porthallow
Looe or St George's Island
Freathy
Millbrook
Anderton
The Sound
Talland Bay
Whitsand Bay
South West Coast Path
Kingsand
Gribbin Head - Polperro Heritage Coast
Cawsand
Cawsand Bay
Down Thomas
Rame
Heybrook Bay
RAME HEAD
Penlee Point
Rame Head Heritage Coast
Santander (Mar-Oct)
Roscoff St-Malo (Nov-Mar)
0 1 2 3 4 5 miles
0 1 2 3 4 5 6 7 8 kilometres

DARTMOOR NATIONAL PARK
Plymouth
Plympton
Ivybridge
Buckfastleigh
Ashburton
Kingsbridge
Salcombe
Bigbury Bay
South Devon Heritage Coast
Walkhampton
Dousland
Yelverton
Sheepstor
Meavy
Hoo Meavy
Clearbrook
Goodameavy
Shaugh Prior
Bickleigh
Wotter
Lee Moor
Lutton
Hemerdon
Sparkwell
Venton
Cornwood
Harford
Cheston
Wrangaton
Bittaford
Lee Mill
Ermington
Modbury
Ugborough
South Brent
Brent Mill
Aish
Didworthy
Harbourneford
Dean Prior
Deancombe
Holne
Michelcombe
Scorriton
Buckfast
Hele
Rew
Woodland
Denbury
Landscove
Staverton
Rattery
Avonwick
Diptford
North Huish
Harberton
Harbertonford
Totnes
Halwell
Moreleigh
Brownston
Loddiswell
Woodleigh
Aveton Gifford
Churchstow
Bigbury
Bigbury-on-Sea
Burgh Island
Bantham
Thurlestone
South Milton
West Alvington
Malborough
Hope
Bolt Tail
Bolberry
Collaton
Soar
Rickham
Bolt Head
East Portlemouth
Prawle Point
East Prawle
Chillington
Frogmore
Stokenham
Yealmpton
Brixton
Elburton
Newton Ferrers
Noss Mayo
Holbeton
Kingston
Ringmore
Mothecombe
A38
A379
A381
A385
A3121
B3196
B3392
B3186
B3213
B3417
B3212

8 Devon Riviera
Newton Abbot
Ashburton
Knighton
Highweek
Netherton
Coombe Cellars
Ringmore
R Teign
Shaldon
Combeinteignhead
Stokeinteignhead
Middle Rocombe
Lower Gabwell
Higher Gabwell
Maidencombe
Coffinswell
Daccombe
Watcombe
Barton
Coombe
Pafford
Model Village
Babbacombe Bay
Goodstone
West Ogwell
East Ogwell
Wolborough
Bradley Manor
Wildlife Hospital
Abbotskerswell
Kingskerswell
North Whilborough
Dainton
Two Mile Oak Cross
Denbury
Woodland
Hele
Hembury Castle
Rew
Thornecroft
Forder Green
Torbryan
Ipplepen
Landscove
Woolston Green
Broadhempston
Butterfly Farm & Otter Sanctuary
Dean
Staverton
Combe Fishacre
South Devon Railway
Compton
Castle
Edginswell
Shiphay
St Marychurch
Babbacombe
Ellacombe
TORQUAY
Cockington
Marldon
Hopes Nose
Rockend
Pennywell Farm
West Combe
Dartington
R Dart
Littlehempston
Afton
Hollicombe
Preston
Week
Shinnersbridge
Cott
Berry Pomeroy
Berry Pomeroy Castle
Westerland
Rattery
Mill Cross
Long Cause
Castle
Tigley
Blagdon
Paignton
Tor Bay
Blakemore
Belsford
Totnes
Longcombe
Collaton St Mary
Harberton
Aish
Yalberton
Goodrington
East Leigh
Sharpham
Luscombe
Diptford
Ashprington
Stoke Gabriel
Waddeton
Brixham
Bow
Tuckenhay
Galmpton
Harbour
BERRY HEAD
Yetson
Cornworthy
Harbertonford
Washbourne
Dittisham
Churston Ferrers
St Mary Bay
East Cornworthy
Greenway
Higher Brixham
Sharkham Point
Curtisknowle
Allaleigh
Capton
Paignton & Dartmouth Railway
Hillhead
Halwell
Woodhuish
Moreleigh
Dartmouth
Woodlands
Coleton Fishacre
Scabbacombe Head
Hendham
Bugford
Woodford
Bayard's Cove Fort
Kingswear
Dartmouth Castle
Blackawton
Hutcherleigh
Warfleet
Woodleigh
Millcombe
Ash
Eastdown
Bowden
Abbotsleigh
Stoke Fleming
Burlestone
East Allington
Blackpool
Cole's Cross
Ledstone
Goveton
Strete
South Devon Heritage Coast
Buckland-Tout-Saints
Harleston
Slapton
Start
Dodbrooke
Sherford
Frittiscombe
Start Bay
East Charleton
Chillington
Stokenham
Charleton
Frogmore
Torcross
Kingsbridge Estuary
Kernborough
Beeson
Lincombe
South Pool
Ford
Beesands
Batson
Salcombe
Chivelstone
Kellaton
Hallsands
East Portlemouth
Bickerton
South Allington
South West Coast Path
Lighthouse
Start Point
East Prawle
Prawle Point
0 1 2 3 4 5 miles
0 1 2 3 4 5 6 7 8 kilometres
A385
A381
A380
A379
A3022
B3060
A3122
B3205
A384

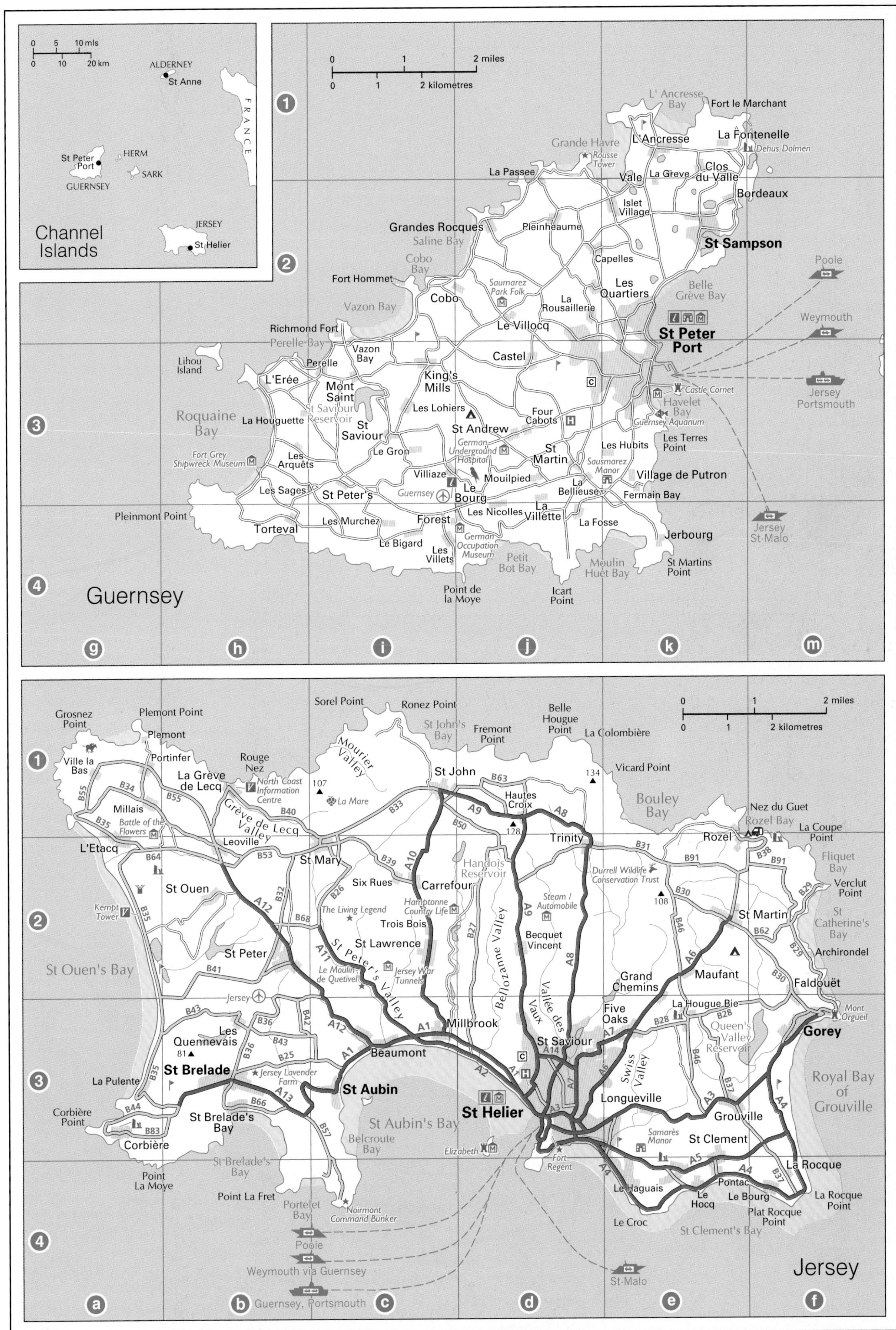

0 5 10 mls
0 10 20 km
ALDERNEY
St Anne
FRANCE
St Peter Port
HERM
SARK
GUERNSEY
Channel Islands
JERSEY
St Helier
0 1 2 miles
0 1 2 kilometres
L' Ancresse Bay
Fort le Marchant
La Fontenelle
Dehus Dolmen
Grande Havre
Rousse Tower
L'Ancresse
La Passee
Vale
La Greve
Clos du Valle
Bordeaux
Islet Village
Grandes Rocques
Saline Bay
Pleinheaume
St Sampson
Cobo Bay
Capelles
Poole
Fort Hommet
Cobo
Saumarez Park Folk
Les Quartiers
Belle Grève Bay
Vazon Bay
La Rousaillerie
Weymouth
Richmond Fort
Le Villocq
St Peter Port
Perelle Bay
Vazon Bay
Lihou Island
Perelle
Castel
L'Erée
Mont Saint
King's Mills
Castle Cornet
Jersey Portsmouth
Roquaine Bay
St Saviour Reservoir
Les Lohiers
Four Cabots
Havelet Bay
La Houguette
St Saviour
St Andrew
Guernsey Aquarium
Les Terres Point
Fort Grey Shipwreck Museum
Les Arquêts
Le Gron
German Underground Hospital
St Martin
Les Hubits
Sausmarez Manor
Villiaze
Village de Putron
Mouilpied
Les Sages
St Peter's
Guernsey
Le Bourg
La Bellieuse
Fermain Bay
Pleinmont Point
Les Murchez
Forest
Les Nicolles
La Villette
La Fosse
Torteval
Jersey St-Malo
Le Bigard
German Occupation Museum
Jerbourg
Les Villets
Petit Bot Bay
Moulin Huet Bay
St Martins Point
Point de la Moye
Icart Point
Guernsey
g h i j k m
Grosnez Point
Plemont Point
Sorel Point
Ronez Point
Belle Hougue Point
Fremont Point
St John's Bay
La Colombière
0 1 2 miles
0 1 2 kilometres
Plemont
Mourier Valley
Ville la Bas
Portinfer
Rouge Nez
St John
134
Vicard Point
La Grève de Lecq
North Coast Information Centre
107
La Mare
B63
B34
B55
B40
B33
Hautes Croix
Bouley Bay
Millais
B55
A9
A8
Nez du Guet
Battle of the Flowers
Grève de Lecq Valley
B50
128
Rozel Bay
La Coupe Point
B35
Leoville
Trinity
L'Etacq
B53
St Mary
B31
Rozel
B64
B39
A10
Handois Reservoir
B91
B38
B91
Fliquet Bay
Durrell Wildlife Conservation Trust
Six Rues
Carrefour
Verclut Point
St Ouen
B26
B30
B29
Kempt Tower
B35
B32
Hamptonne Country Life
Steam / Automobile
108
The Living Legend
A9
St Martin
St Catherine's Bay
A12
B68
Trois Bois
Bellozanne Valley
B46
B62
St Lawrence
B27
Becquet Vincent
A8
Archirondel
St Ouen's Bay
St Peter
A11
St Peter's Valley
A6
B29
B41
Le Moulin de Quetivel
Jersey War Tunnels
Grand Chemins
Maufant
B30
Faldouët
Jersey
Vallée des Vaux
La Hougue Bie
Five Oaks
B43
B36
B42
A12
A1
Millbrook
B28
B28
Queen's Valley Reservoir
Mont Orgueil
Les Quennevais
Gorey
81
B43
A1
St Saviour
A7
B25
Beaumont
A14
B46
B36
Swiss Valley
St Brelade
A2
A6
B35
Jersey Lavender Farm
A1
A7
B37
Royal Bay of Grouville
La Pulente
A13
St Aubin
A3
A4
B44
St Helier
Longueville
Corbière Point
B66
Grouville
B83
St Brelade's Bay
St Aubin's Bay
B57
Samarès Manor
St Clement
Corbière
Belcroute Bay
Elizabeth
A5
Fort Regent
A4
La Rocque
A4
St Brelade's Bay
Pontac
Point La Moye
B37
Le Haguais
La Rocque Point
Point La Fret
Le Hocq
Le Bourg
Portelet Bay
Noirmont Command Bunker
Plat Rocque Point
Le Croc
St Clement's Bay
Poole
Weymouth via Guernsey
St-Malo
Jersey
Guernsey, Portsmouth
a b c d e f
1 2 3 4

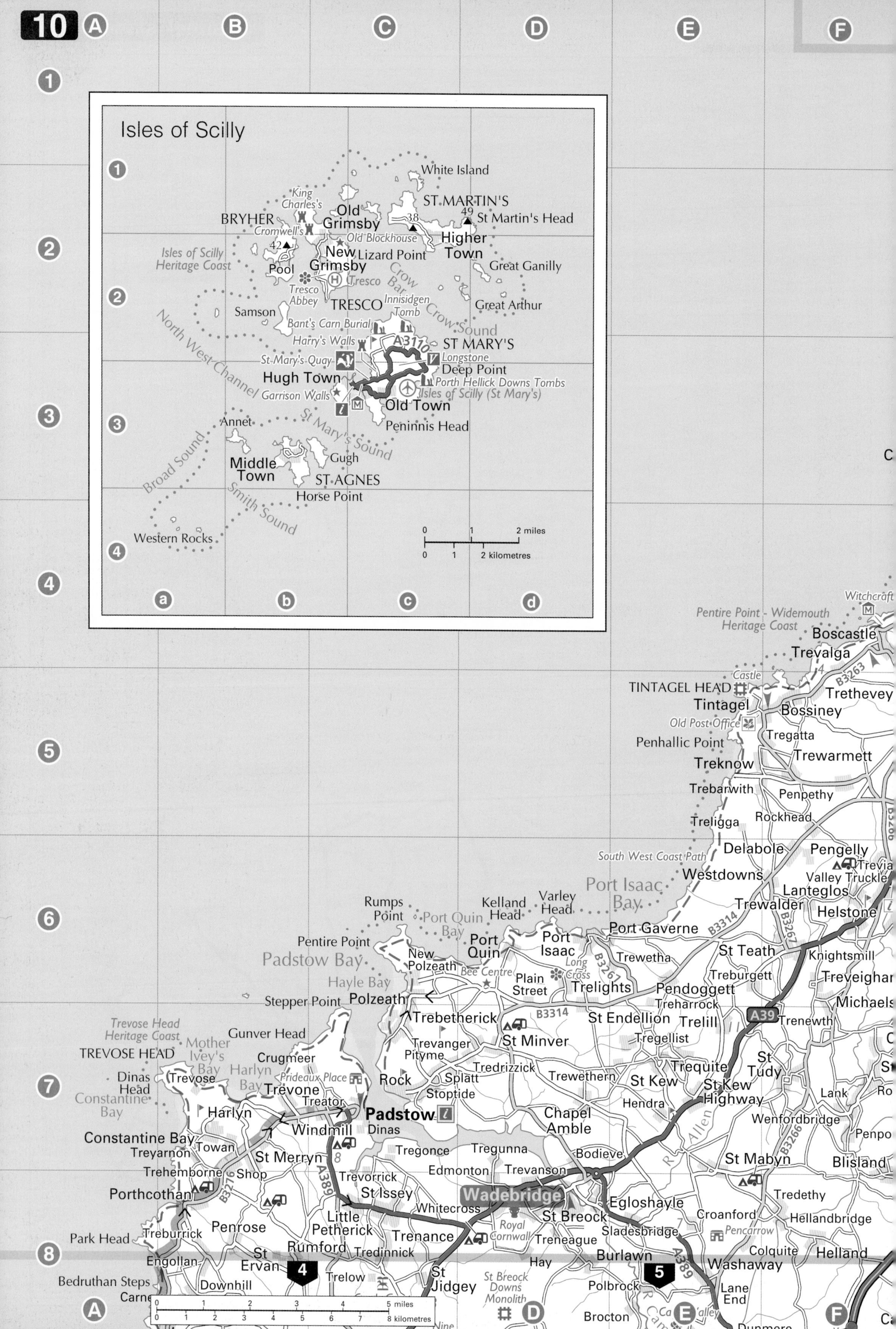
Isles of Scilly
White Island
ST MARTIN'S
St Martin's Head
Higher Town
BRYHER
King Charles's
Old Grimsby
Cromwell's
Old Blockhouse
New Grimsby
Lizard Point
Isles of Scilly Heritage Coast
Pool
Tresco
Tresco Abbey
TRESCO
Innisidgen Tomb
Great Ganilly
Great Arthur
Crow Bar
Crow Sound
Samson
Bant's Carn Burial
Harry's Walls
ST MARY'S
Longstone
Deep Point
St Mary's Quay
Hugh Town
Porth Hellick Downs Tombs
Isles of Scilly (St Mary's)
Garrison Walls
Old Town
Peninnis Head
North West Channel
Annet
St Mary's Sound
Gugh
Middle Town
ST AGNES
Broad Sound
Horse Point
Smith Sound
Western Rocks
2 miles
2 kilometres
Pentire Point - Widemouth Heritage Coast
Witchcraft
Boscastle
Trevalga
Castle
TINTAGEL HEAD
Tintagel
Trethevey
Bossiney
Old Post Office
Tregatta
Penhallic Point
Trewarmett
Treknow
Trebarwith
Penpethy
Treligga
Rockhead
South West Coast Path
Delabole
Pengelly
Westdowns
Trevia
Valley Truckle
Lanteglos
Port Isaac Bay
Trewalder
Helstone
Rumps Point
Kelland Head
Varley Head
Port Quin Bay
Port Gaverne
Pentire Point
Port Quin
Port Isaac
St Teath
Padstow Bay
New Polzeath
Trewetha
Knightsmill
Bee Centre
Long Cross
Treburgett
Treveighan
Hayle Bay
Plain Street
Trelights
Pendoggett
Stepper Point
Polzeath
Treharrock
Michaelstow
Trebetherick
St Endellion
Trelill
Trenewth
Trevose Head Heritage Coast
Gunver Head
Mother Ivey's Bay
Trevanger
St Minver
Tregellist
TREVOSE HEAD
Crugmeer
Pityme
Harlyn Bay
Tredrizzick
Trewethern
Trequite
St Tudy
Dinas Head
Trevose
Prideaux Place
Rock
Splatt
St Kew
St Kew Highway
Trevone
Constantine Bay
Treator
Stoptide
Hendra
Lank
Harlyn
Padstow
Chapel Amble
Windmill
Dinas
Wenfordbridge
Constantine Bay
Towan
Tregonce
Tregunna
Penpont
Treyarnon
St Merryn
Bodieve
St Mabyn
Trehemborne
Shop
Edmonton
Trevanson
Blisland
Trevorrick
St Issey
Porthcothan
Wadebridge
Egloshayle
Tredethy
Whitecross
Little Petherick
St Breock
Croanford
Hellandbridge
Penrose
Royal Cornwall
Park Head
Treburrick
Trenance
Treneague
Sladesbridge
Pencarrow
Rumford
Tredinnick
Colquite
Helland
Engollan
St Ervan
Burlawn
Washaway
Hay
Trelow
St Jidgey
St Breock Downs Monolith
Bedruthan Steps
Downhill
Polbrock
Lane End
Carne
Brocton
Dunmere
5 miles
8 kilometres
Nine
A39
A389
A3110
B3314
B3267
B3266
B3263
B3276
4
5

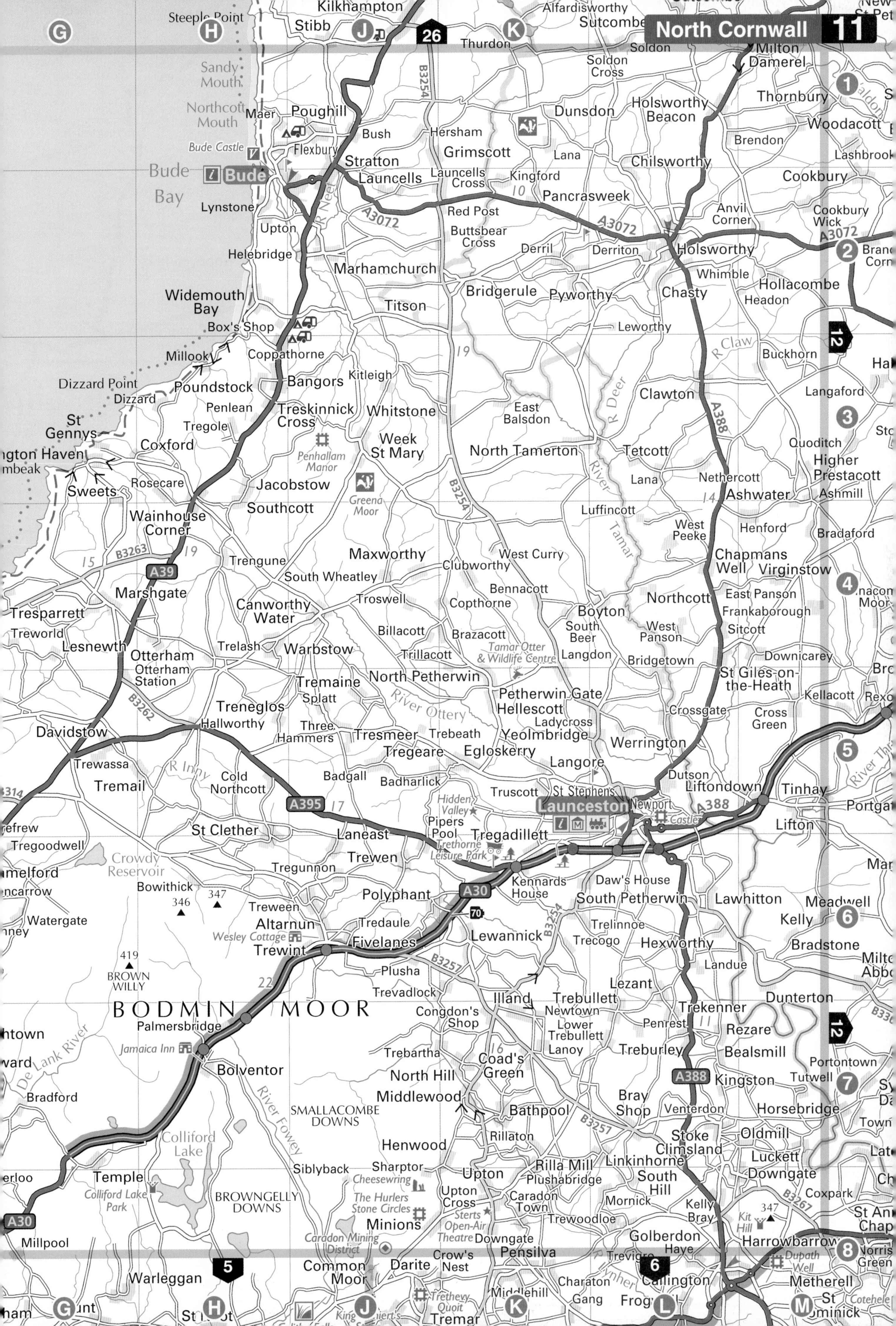
Kilkhampton
Steeple Point
Stibb
Alfardisworthy
Sutcombe
Thurdon
Soldon
Milton Damerel
Soldon Cross
Sandy Mouth
Northcott Mouth
Maer
Poughill
Bush
Hersham
Dunsdon
Holsworthy Beacon
Thornbury
Woodacott
Bude Castle
Flexbury
Grimscott
Brendon
Lana
Lashbrook
Bude Bay
Bude
Stratton
Launcells
Launcells Cross
Kingford
Chilsworthy
Cookbury
Lynstone
Pancrasweek
Red Post
Anvil Corner
Cookbury Wick
Upton
Buttsbear Cross
Derril
Derriton
Holsworthy
Helebridge
Marhamchurch
Whimble
Hollacombe
Headon
Widemouth Bay
Titson
Bridgerule
Pyworthy
Chasty
Box's Shop
Leworthy
Millook
Coppathorne
R Claw
Buckhorn
Dizzard Point
Dizzard
Poundstock
Bangors
Kitleigh
Clawton
Langaford
St Gennys
Penlean
Tregole
Treskinnick Cross
Whitstone
East Balsdon
R Deer
Coxford
Week St Mary
North Tamerton
Tetcott
Quoditch
Higher Prestacott
Penhallam Manor
Lana
Nethercott
Ashwater
Ashmill
Sweets
Rosecare
Jacobstow
Greena Moor
River Tamar
Southcott
Luffincott
Wainhouse Corner
West Peeke
Henford
Bradaford
B3263
A39
Trengune
Maxworthy
West Curry
Chapmans Well
Virginstow
South Wheatley
Clubworthy
Bennacott
Marshgate
Troswell
Copthorne
Boyton
Northcott
East Panson
Frankaborough
Tresparrett
Canworthy Water
South Beer
West Panson
Sitcott
Treworld
Billacott
Brazacott
Lesnewth
Trelash
Warbstow
Tamar Otter & Wildlife Centre
Langdon
Bridgetown
Downicarey
Otterham
Otterham Station
Trillacott
Tremaine
North Petherwin
St Giles-on-the-Heath
Splatt
River Ottery
Petherwin Gate
Kellacott
Treneglos
Hellescott
Ladycross
Crossgate
Cross Green
Davidstow
Hallworthy
Three Hammers
Tresmeer
Trebeath
Yeolmbridge
Werrington
B3262
Trewassa
Tregeare
Egloskerry
Langore
R Inny
Cold Northcott
Badgall
Badharlick
Dutson
Tremail
Liftondown
Tinhay
Truscott
St Stephens
A395
Launceston
Newport
Castle
A388
Hidden Valley
Pipers Pool
Tregadillett
Lifton
St Clether
Laneast
Trethorne Leisure Park
Tregoodwell
Crowdy Reservoir
Trewen
Tregunnon
Kennards House
Daw's House
Bowithick
347
346
Polyphant
A30
South Petherwin
Lawhitton
Meadwell
Treween
Kelly
Watergate
Altarnun
Tredaule
Trelinnoe
Wesley Cottage
Lewannick
Trecogo
Hexworthy
Bradstone
Trewint
Fivelanes
B3254
Landue
419
BROWN WILLY
Plusha
B3257
Lezant
Trevadlock
BODMIN MOOR
Congdon's Shop
Illand
Trebullett
Newtown
Lower Trebullett
Lanoy
Trekenner
Dunterton
Penrest
Rezare
Palmersbridge
Treburley
Bealsmill
Jamaica Inn
Trebartha
Coad's Green
Portontown
De Lank River
Bolventor
North Hill
A388
Kingston
Tutwell
Bradford
Middlewood
Bray Shop
Venterdon
Horsebridge
River Fowey
SMALLACOMBE DOWNS
Bathpool
Rillaton
B3257
Stoke Climsland
Oldmill
Colliford Lake
Henwood
Sharptor
Rilla Mill
Linkinhorne
Luckett
Temple
Siblyback
Cheesewring
Upton
Plushabridge
South Hill
Downgate
Colliford Lake Park
The Hurlers Stone Circles
Upton Cross
Caradon Town
Mornick
Coxpark
B3267
BROWNGELLY DOWNS
Sterts Open-Air Theatre
Kelly Bray
Kit Hill
347
Minions
Trewoodloe
Golberdon
Haye
Harrowbarrow
A30
Millpool
Caradon Mining District
Downgate
Pensilva
Crow's Nest
Darite
Trevigro
Common Moor
Warleggan
Charaton
Callington
Dupath Well
Metherell
Middlehill
Gang
Frogwell
Trethevy Quoit
Tremar
St Dominick
Cotehele
Rexon
Portgate
Milton Abbot
Mar
26
12
5
6
12
G
H
J
K
L
M
1
2
3
4
5
6
7
8
10
19
14
15
19
17
22
16
11

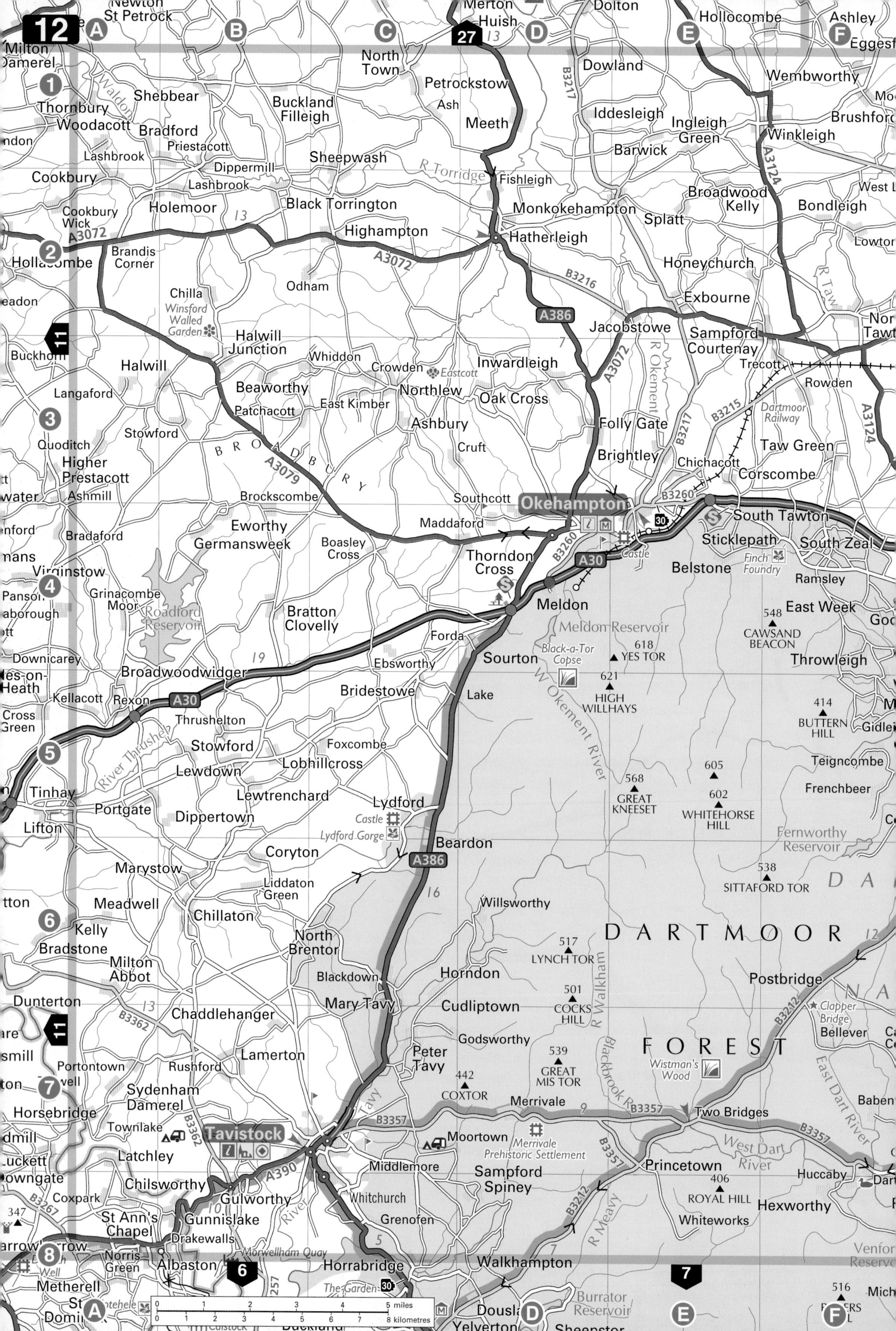
12
A
B
C
D
E
F
27
Newton St Petrock
Merton
Huish
Dolton
Hollocombe
Ashley
Eggesford
Milton Damerel
North Town
Petrockstow
Dowland
Wembworthy
Shebbear
Buckland Filleigh
Ash
Iddesleigh
Ingleigh Green
Winkleigh
Brushford
Thornbury
Woodacott
Bradford
Meeth
Waldon
Priestacott
Barwick
Lashbrook
Sheepwash
A3124
Cookbury
Dippermill
R Torridge
Fishleigh
Lashbrook
West Lowton
Broadwood Kelly
Bondleigh
Cookbury Wick
Holemoor
Black Torrington
Monkokehampton
Splatt
A3072
Highampton
Hatherleigh
Lowton
Hollacombe
Brandis Corner
A3072
Honeychurch
B3216
R Taw
Odham
Exbourne
Chilla
Winsford Walled Garden
A386
North Tawton
Jacobstowe
Sampford Courtenay
11
Buckhorn
Halwill Junction
Halwill
Whiddon
Crowden
Eastcott
Inwardleigh
Trecott
R Okement
A3072
Rowden
Langaford
Beaworthy
Northlew
Oak Cross
Patchacott
East Kimber
Dartmoor Railway
B3215
Ashbury
Folly Gate
B3217
A3124
Quoditch
Stowford
Cruft
Taw Green
BROADBURY
Higher Prestacott
A3079
Brightley
Chichacott
Corscombe
Ashmill
Brockscombe
Southcott
Okehampton
B3260
South Tawton
Bradaford
Maddaford
30
Eworthy
Germansweek
Boasley Cross
Thorndon Cross
B3260
Castle
A30
Sticklepath
South Zeal
Finch Foundry
Belstone
Virginstow
Ramsley
Grinacombe Moor
Meldon
Pancrasweek
Roadford Reservoir
Bratton Clovelly
East Week
548
CAWSAND BEACON
Meldon Reservoir
Forda
Downicarey
19
618
YES TOR
Black-a-Tor Copse
Sourton
Throwleigh
Ebsworthy
621
HIGH WILLHAYS
Heath
Broadwoodwidger
Kellacott
Rexon
A30
Bridestowe
Lake
W Okement River
414
BUTTERN HILL
Gidleigh
Cross Green
Thrushelton
River Thrushel
Stowford
Foxcombe
Lobhillcross
Lewdown
605
568
GREAT KNEESET
Teigncombe
Tinhay
Lewtrenchard
602
WHITEHORSE HILL
Frenchbeer
Portgate
Dippertown
Lydford
Castle
Lydford Gorge
Lifton
Beardon
Fernworthy Reservoir
Coryton
A386
Marystow
Liddaton Green
538
SITTAFORD TOR
16
Meadwell
Willsworthy
Chillaton
Kelly
DARTMOOR
Bradstone
North Brentor
517
LYNCH TOR
Milton Abbot
Blackdown
Horndon
Postbridge
R Walkham
Dunterton
13
B3362
Chaddlehanger
Mary Tavy
Cudliptown
501
COCKS HILL
Clapper Bridge
B3212
Bellever
Godsworthy
FOREST
Lamerton
Peter Tavy
539
GREAT MIS TOR
Blackbrook R
Wistman's Wood
East Dart River
Portontown
Rushford
442
COXTOR
Sydenham Damerel
Merrivale
Horsebridge
R Tavy
B3357
B3357
Two Bridges
Townlake
B3362
Tavistock
Moortown
Merrivale Prehistoric Settlement
West Dart River
Latchley
Middlemoor
Princetown
Chilsworthy
A390
Sampford Spiney
Huccaby
B3357
Whitchurch
406
ROYAL HILL
Hexworthy
Coxpark
Gulworthy
B3212
347
St Ann's Chapel
Gunnislake
Grenofen
Whiteworks
Drakewalls
Tavy River
R Meavy
Venford Reservoir
Norris Green
Morwellham Quay
Albaston
Horrabridge
Walkhampton
Metherell
6
The Garden
30
7
516
Burrator Reservoir
St Dominick
Cotehele
Dousland
Yelverton
Buckland
0 1 2 3 4 5 miles
0 1 2 3 4 5 6 7 8 kilometres
A
D
E
F

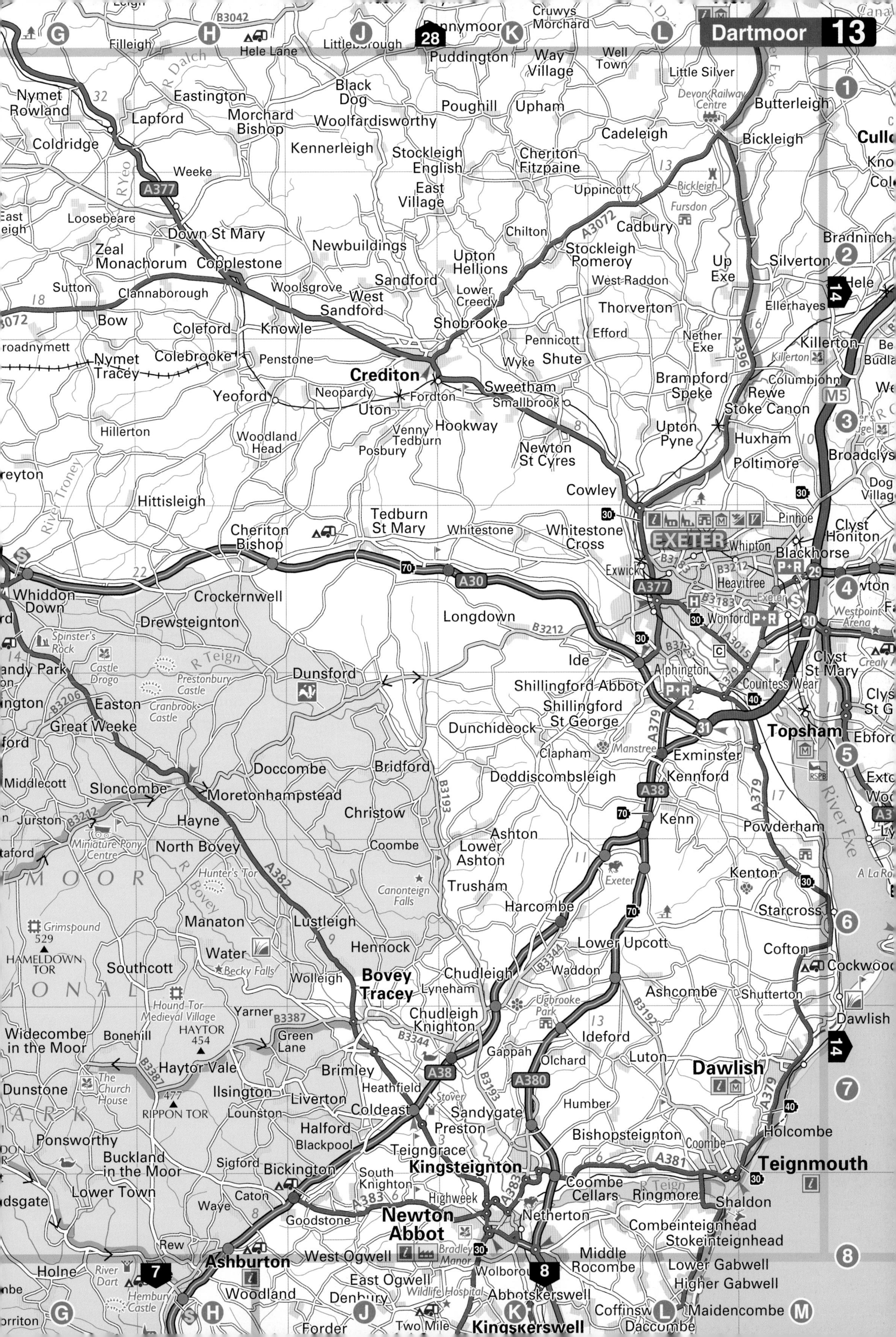

Crediton
Exeter
Topsham
Dawlish
Teignmouth
Newton Abbot
Ashburton
Bovey Tracey
Moretonhampstead
Kingsteignton
Kingskerswell
Copplestone
Cheriton Bishop
Tedburn St Mary
Dunsford
Chudleigh
Exminster
Starcross
Thorverton
Silverton
Bradninch
Cullompton
Stoke Canon
Shaldon
Widecombe in the Moor
Haytor Vale
Lustleigh
Manaton
Drewsteignton
Whiddon Down
Dartmoor National Park

14
A
B
C
D
E
F
29
30
13
1
2
3
4
5
6
7
8
Ash Thomas
Willand
Smithincott
Coldharbour Mill
Ashill
Abbey
Bolham R
Madford
Smeatharpe
Marsh
River Exe
Canal
Diggerland
Blackborough
Bradfield
Butterleigh
Kentisbeare
Northcott
Sheldon
Slade
Madford River
River Culm
Cullompton
Cullompton
Cullompton
Saint Hill
Dunkeswell
Upottery
Luppitt
Rawridge
A303
Yarcombe
Knowle
Colebrook
Dulford
Kerswell
Wolford Chapel
Beacon
Stockland Hill
Stockland
Millhayes
Westcott
Mutterton
Bradninch
Norman's Green
Colliton
A373
Broadhembury
Hembury Castle
Wick
Langford
Plymtree
Upton
Godford Cross
Combe Raleigh
A30
Monkton
Hele
Luton
Lower Tale
Payhembury
Ellerhayes
Cotleigh
Ham
Killerton
Beare
Budlake
Clyst Hydon
Aunk
Colestocks
Buckerell
Awliscombe
Weston
Dalwood
Wilmington
Columbjohn
Talaton
Feniton
Offwell
A35
Westwood
Clyst St Lawrence
Newtown
Honiton
Widworthy
M5
R Clyst
Marker's Cottage
Higher Burrowton
Knowle Cross
Larkbeare
Fenny Bridges
Escot
Gittisham
Alfington
Offwell Brook
Shute
Broadclyst
Lower Burrowton
Whimple
Fairmile
Gosford
Church Green
Dog Village
Jack-in-the-Green
Hand and Pen
Taleford
Cadhay
B3177
Ottery St Mary
Northleigh
Pinhoe
Farway
Whitford
Clyst Honiton
Rockbeare
Allercombe
A375
Woodbridge
Colyton
Blackhorse
Exeter
West Hill
Southleigh
R Coly
P+R
Sowton
Marsh Green
Fluxton
Wiggaton
Blackbury Camp
Colyford
Exeter
Aylesbeare
B3184
B3180
Farringdon
Tipton St John
Coombe
Westpoint Arena
Perkins Village
Venn Ottery
Sidbury
A3052
Seaton
Clyst St Mary
Crealy Adventure Park
RSPB
Southerton
Harpford
Bowd
Sidford
Harcombe
Bulstone
B3174
Countess Wear
Woodbury Salterton
Hawkerland
Stowford
The Donkey Sanctuary
The Old Bakery
Beer
Pecorama
Beer
Clyst St George
B3178
Newton Poppleford
B3176
Woolbrook
Street
Salcombe Regis
Weston
Vicarage
Topsham
Ebford
B3179
Kingston
Colaton Raleigh
Branscombe
South West Coast Path
Woodbury
Sidmouth
Jurassic Coast World Heritage Site
Exton
Pinn
Yettington
Bicton Park
River Otter
Woodmanton
Otterton
East Devon Heritage Coast
A376
East Budleigh
Powderham
Lympstone
Bystock
Otterton Mill
Dalditch
Ladram Bay
A La Ronde
Bystock
Knowle
Hulham
Kersbrook
Starcross
Littleham
Budleigh Salterton
Cofton
Exmouth
Cockwood
Model Railway
World of Country Life
Dawlish Warren
Dawlish
A379
Holcombe
Teignmouth
0
1
2
3
4
5 miles
0
1
2
3
4
5
6
7
8 kilometres

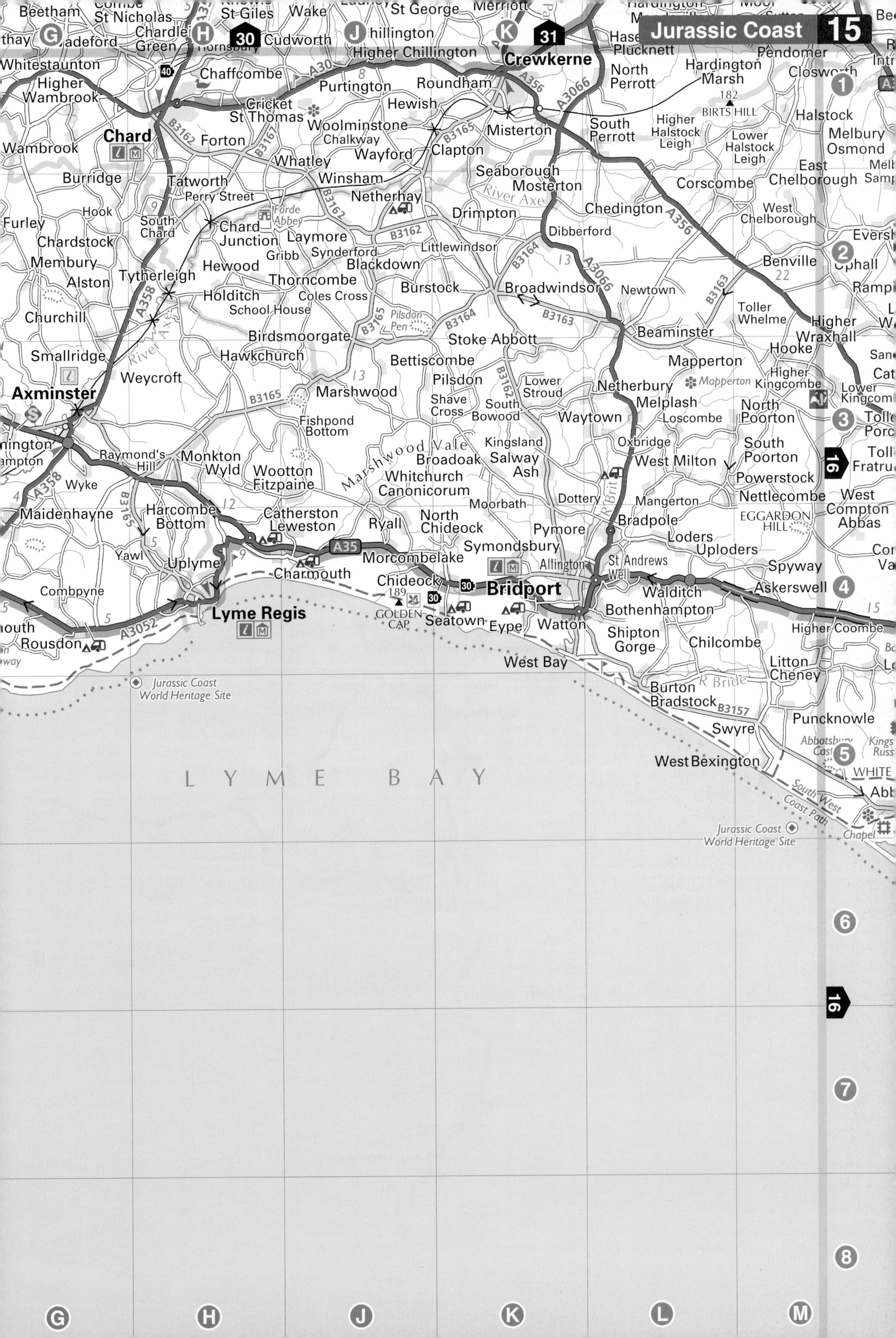
Crewkerne
Chard
Axminster
Lyme Regis
Bridport
Charmouth
Chideock
Seatown
Eype
West Bay
Beaminster
Broadwindsor
Netherbury
Burton Bradstock
Swyre
West Bexington
Puncknowle
Litton Cheney
Askerswell
Uploders
Loders
Bradpole
Powerstock
Morcombelake
Whitchurch Canonicorum
Marshwood
Hawkchurch
Uplyme
Rousdon
Combpyne
Tytherleigh
Chardstock
Membury
Misterton
Mosterton
Drimpton
Thorncombe
Winsham
Golden Cap
Jurassic Coast World Heritage Site
South West Coast Path
L Y M E B A Y
G H J K L M

16
A
B
C
D
E
F
31
32
Beer Hackett
Knighton
Boys Hill
Crouch Hill
King's Stag
Fifehead Common
Okeford Fitzpaine
Pendomer
Ryme Intrinseca
Yetminster
Sandhills
Packers Hill
Kingston
Closworth
A37
Hamlet
Holnest
East Pulham
Hazelbury Bryan
Fifehead St Quintin
Belchalwell
Belchalwell Street
Halstock
Drive End
Leigh
B3146
Glanvilles Wootton
Pulham
Melbury Osmond
Chetnole
Middlemarsh
West Pulham
Wonston
Droop
Ibberton
Stockwood
Hermitage
B3143
Brockhampton Green
Woolland
East Chelborough
Melbury Sampford
Melbury Bubb
Duntish
Westfields
Bulbarrow Hill
Lyon's Gate
Stoke Wake
Hilfield
Sharnhill Green
Mappowder
West Chelborough
Batcombe
Buckland Newton
Winterborne Houghton
Evershot
Holywell
Minterne Magna
Minterne House
Higher Ansty
Ansty Cross
Henley
Minterne Parva
Lower Ansty
Hilton
Uphall
Alton Pancras
Melcombe Bingham
Up Cerne
Rampisham
Frome St Quintin
Cerne Giant
Plush
Milton
Bingham's Melcombe
Milton Abbas
Lower Wraxhall
Up Sydling
Higher Wraxhall
Cerne Abbas
Chalmington
Hooke
Sandhills
Higher Kingcombe
Cattistock
Sydling St Nicholas
Piddletrenthide
Cheselbourne
Bingham
Lower Kingcombe
White Lackington
Chilfrome
Nether Cerne
PUDDLETON DOWN
Dewlish
A354
Toller Porcorum
A356
Maiden Newton
Godmanstone
Piddlehinton
Milborne St Andrew
Toller Fratrum
Hog Cliff
R Cerne
A352
Higher Waterston
Cruxton
A37
Frampton
Forston
Lower Waterston
Athelhampton
Tolpuddle
West Compton Abbas
Wynford Eagle
Charlton Down
B3143
B3142
Puddletown
A35
Southover
Grimstone
Burleston
Affpuddle
Compton Valence
Stratton
YELLOWHAM HILL
Athelhampton
Spyway
Muckleford
Charminster
Hardy's Cottage
Briantspuddle
Bradford Peverell
A35
Kingston Russell
Burton
Higher Bockhampton
Ilsington
Tincleton
Pallington
B3390
Winterbourne Abbas
Dorchester
Stinsford
Higher Coombe
Barrows
B3150
Woodsford
Clouds Hill
Litton Cheney
Long Bredy
The Nine Stones
A35
Kingston Maurward
West Stafford
Hurst
River Frome
B3159
Poundbury
B3147
Winterbourne Steepleton
Martinstown
Winterborne Came
Moreton
Littlebredy
Maiden Castle
Whitcombe
Puncknowle
Valley of Stones
West Knighton
Crossways
Bovington
Abbotsbury Castle
Kingston Russell
Hardy Monument
Winterborne Monkton
Winterborne Herringston
A354
Giddy Green
WHITE HILL
Portesham
Friar Waddon
Broadmayne
Warmwell
Waddon
A352
Abbotsbury
Owermoigne
A352
South West Coast Path
Upwey
Bincombe
White Horse
East Knighton
Abbey Remains
Coryates
Poxwell
Rodden
Chapel
Swannery
Sutton Poyntz
Osmington
Winfrith Newburgh
Broadwey
Holworth
Nottington
A353
East Chaldon (Chaldon Herring)
Langton Herring
Buckland Ripers
Overcombe
Upton
West Chaldon
Preston
B3157
P+R
Jordan Hill
Osmington Mills
CHALDON DOWN
Lulworth Camp
RSPB
Chesil Beach
The Fleet
Chickerell
B3155
Weymouth Bay
Ringstead Bay
West Lulworth
Fleet
Putton
Lulworth Cove
Water Gardens
Durdle Door
Chesil Bank and The Fleet
Charlestown
Weymouth
Westham
B3156
Sea Life Tower
Nothe Fort
Lulworth Cove
Wyke Regis
Portland Harbour
A354
Portland Castle
Castletown
West Bay
Fortuneswell
Grove
Easton
Guernsey
Jersey
St-Malo
PORTLAND
Weston
Portland
Southwell
Portland Bill Lighthouse
PORTLAND BILL
1
2
3
4
5
6
7
8
15

South Dorset
17
32
33
18
A354
St Michael
Tarrant Hinton
Cripplestyle
Stourpaine
Ash
Pimperne
Tarrant Launceston
Long Crichel
Tarrant Monkton
Gussage All Saints
Moor Crichel
Knowlton
B3078
B3081
Romford
Verwood
Harbridge
Ellingham
Blashford
Whitmore
Woodlands
Horton
B3072
Royal Signals
Bryanston
Blandford Camp
Tarrant Rawston
Manswood
New Town
Witchampton
Chalbury
Uppington
Chalbury Common
Crab Orchard
Mannington
Three Legged Cross
Ringwood
Blandford St Mary
Langton Long Blandford
Tarrant Rushton
Hinton Martell
Gaunt's Common
Holt Heath
Lower Mannington
Moors Valley
Ashley Heath
St Leonards
St Ives
Ashley
Littleton
Charlton Marshall
Charlton on the Hill
Tarrant Keyneston
Stanbridge
Pig Oak
Holt
West Moors
Moor
Badbury Rings
Honeybrook
Tarrant Crawford
Thornicombe
B3082
Clapgate
Furzehill
Broom Hill
A31
Avon Heath
Higher Whatcombe
Spetisbury
Kingston Lacy
Hillbutts
Merry Field Hill
Pilford
Colehill
Ferndown
FOXBURY HILL
Lower Whatcombe
A350
Shapwick
Abbott Street
Canford Bottom
Trickett's Cross
B3075
Sturminster Marshall
Winterborne Whitechurch
Pamphill
Stapehill
Knoll
A338
Wimborne Minster
Leigh Park
Oakley
Hampreston
Almer
Lower Street
Winterborne Tomson
Winterborne Zelston
Ashington
Sleight
Merley
Canford Magna
Longham
Dudsbury
East Parley
Bournemouth
Avon
Combe Almer
Knighton
West Parley
Hurn
B3073
Aviation
Anderson
B3074
A349
A341
Kinson
Parley Green
Adventure Wonderland
West Morden
Corfe Mullen
Bearwood
Cudnell
Red Hill
Morden
West Howe
Ensbury
Newport
Broadstone
A348
A347
Throop
Bloxworth
East Morden
Lytchett Matravers
Upton Heath
East Howe
Moordown
A3060
East Bloxworth
Post Green
Waterloo
Canford Heath
A3049
Wallisdown
Winton
A35
Sherford
Slepe
Talbot Village
Iford
Upton
Newtown
Branksome
Pokesdown
Morden Bog
Organford
Lytchett Minster
B3068
B3061
A3040
Boscombe
River Piddle or River Trent
A351
Hamworthy
Parkstone
Westbourne
Lake
Branksome Park
Holton Heath
Lower Hamworthy
Lilliput
BOURNEMOUTH
POOLE
Poole Harbour
Sandford
B3369
B3065
Monkey World
Arne
Canford Cliffs
Northport
RSPB
POOLE BAY
Stokeford
Binnegar
Brownsea Island
Worgret
Wareham
Sandbanks
Bindon
East Stoke
Stoborough
Ridge
Toll
West Holme
East Holme
Stoborough Heath
Stoborough Green
Purbeck Heritage Coast
Cherbourg (Mar-Oct)
Coombe Keynes
Hartland Moor
ISLE OF PURBECK
Studland Bay
B3070
Creech
The Blue Pool
East Creech
P+R
Studland
THE FORELAND
East Lulworth
Corfe Castle
Purbeck Hills
Swanage Railway
B3351
Church Knowle
Harman's Cross
Ulwell
Ballard Point
Guernsey Jersey St-Malo
Tyneham Village
Steeple
Swanage Bay
Kingston
Worbarrow Bay
Kimmeridge
B3069
Herston
Swanage
Kimmeridge Bay
South West Coast Path
Acton
Langton Matravers
Durlston
DURLSTON HEAD
Jurassic Coast World Heritage Site
Chapman's Pool
Worth Matravers
Anvil Point
ST ALDHELM'S OR ST ALBAN'S HEAD
5 miles
8 kilometres
G
H
J
K
L
M
1
2
3
4
5
6
7
8

Fordingbridge
Upper Burgate
Godshill
Stuckton
Blissford
Frogham
Bickton
Hyde
Hungerford
Harbridge Green
33
North Gorley
South Gorley
Harbridge
Ibsley
Ibsley Common
Mockbeggar
Linwood
Rockford Common
Ellingham
Rockford
Blashford
North Poulner
Linford
Ringwood
Poulner
Shobley
Picket Post
Ashley Heath
Hightown
Burley Street
St Ives
Ashley
Liberty's Owl, Raptor & Reptile Centre
Moortown
Crow
Burley Lawn
North Kingston
Kingston Great Common
Kingston
MARKWAY HILL
Burley
Sandford
Bisterne
FOXBURY HILL
North Ripley
Thorney Hill
Avon Heath
Ripley
Bournemouth
Avon
Bransgore
North Bockhampton
Neacroft
Hurn
Sopley
Mid Bockhampton
Adventure Wonderland
Godwinscroft
Hinton Admiral
South Bockhampton
Winkton
Throop
Burton
Iford
Somerford
Christchurch
Tuckton
Pokesdown
Wick
Mudeford
Boscombe
Southbourne
Christchurch Bay
HENGISTBURY HEAD
BOURNEMOUTH
POOLE BAY
17
Bramshaw
Fritham
Furzley
Newbridge
Paultons Park
Brook Hill
Brook
Rufus Stone
Upper Canterton
Stoney Cross
Furzey
Minstead
Newtown
NEW FOREST NATIONAL PARK
Emery Down
Bank
Lyndhurst
Clayhill
Rhinefield Ornamental Drive
Balmerlawn
Brockenhurst
Setley
Wootton
Sway
Tiptoe
Battramsley Cross
Bashley
Beckley
Sammy Miller Motorcycle
New Milton
Hinton
Walkford
Ashley
Hordle
Upper Pennington
Pennington
Everton
Highcliffe
Highcliffe Castle
Barton-on-Sea
Downton
Braxton
Milford on Sea
Lower Pennington
Keyhaven
Hurst Castle
Wigley
Ower
Stonyford
Copythorne
Calmore
Winsor
Cadnam
34
Netley Marsh
Totton
Bartley
Woodlands
Foxhills
Ashurst
Longdown Activity Farm
New Forest Wildlife Park
Beaulieu River
Beaulieu Road Station
Upton
Rownhams
Nursling
Hillstreet
Testwood
Shirley
Millbrook
Eling
Toll
SOUTHAMPTON
Marchwood
Dibden Purlieu
National Motor Museum
Beaulieu
Hill Top
Hatchet Gate
Bucklers Hard
East Boldre
Boldre
Pilley Bailey
Pilley
Norleywood
Spinners
Portmore
South Baddesley
Buckland
East End
Walhampton
Lymington
Woodside
Sconce Point
Yarmouth
Bouldnor
Hamstead
Cranmore
Newtown
Thorley
Ningwood
Colwell Bay
Norton
Totland
Totland Bay
Norton Green
Thorley Street
Wellow
Freshwater
Afton
Chessell Pottery Barns
Alum Bay
Needles Park
Dimbola
Freshwater Bay
THE NEEDLES
Needles Old Battery & New Battery
Compton Bay & Downs
Compton Bay
Shalcombe
Brook
Hulverstone
Hanover Point
Tennyson Heritage Coast
Mottistone
Chilton Chine
A31
A35
A337
A338
A336
A3060
B3078
B3079
B3081
B3347
B3058
B3055
B3073
B3056
B3054
B3322
B3399
B3401
M27
M271
0 1 2 3 4 5 miles
0 1 2 3 4 5 6 7 8 kilometres
A B C D E F
1 2 3 4 5 6 7 8

Southampton
Itchen Valley
Heath
Palace
Durley
Waltham Chase
Shirrell Heath
Clanfield
Moorgreen
Long Common
Boorley Green
Curdridge
Soberton Heath
Hambledon
Catherington
Blendworth
West End
Bitterne
Botley
Shedfield
35
Newtown
Hoe Gate
Anthill Common
Horndean
Lovedean
Thornhill
Row Ash
Wickham
Kingsmead
Denmead
Anmore
Finchdean
Northam
Hedge End
Manor Farm
Worlds End
Furzeley Corner
Soake
Sholing
Curbridge
North Boarhunt
Cowplain
Woolston
Lower Swanwick
Burridge
Knowle Village
Whiteley
WATERLOOVILLE
Southwick
Stakes
Bursledon
Swanwick
Funtley
Boarhunt
Netley
Sarisbury
Park Gate
Ports Down
Purbrook
Royal Armouries Fort Nelson
Royal Victoria
Locks Heath
Titchfield Common
Titchfield Abbey
Wallington
Widley
Bedhampton
Hythe
Hamble-le-Rice
Warsash
Catisfield
Cosham
Drayton
Fleetend
Brockhampton
Buttsash
Southampton Water
Hook
Titchfield
FAREHAM
Portchester
Farlington
Langstone
Hardley
Little Posbrook
Castle
Port Solent
20
Fawley
Ashlett
Stubbington
Peel Common
Portsmouth Harbour
Hilsea
North Hayling
Bridgemary
Calshot Castle
Hill Head
Whale Island
Langstone Harbour
Stoke
Ower
Activities Centre
Fort Brockhurst
Elson
Continental Ferry Terminal
North End
Calshot
Langley
Rowner
Hardway
GOSPORT
Portsea
Fratton
Stanswood Bay
Lee-on-the-Solent
Exbury
Spinnaker Tower
Lower Exbury
West Town
Isle of Wight Ferry Terminal
Southsea
Lepe
Stokes Bay
Alverstoke
Fort Cumberland
Eastney
Needs Ore Point
SOLENT
PORTSMOUTH
Hayling Bay
Cowes
Gilkicker Point
Gurnard Bay
Osborne
East Cowes
Spitbank Fort
Gurnard
Osborne House
Osborne Bay
SPITHEAD
Rew Street
Thorness Bay
Hillis Corner
Northwood
Whippingham
Cherbourg (May-Sept)
Le Havre (Mar-Sept)
Wootton Bridge
Fishbourne
Ryde
R Medina
Seaview Wildlife Encounter
Puckpool Point
Porchfield
Mark's Corner
Wootton
Quarr Hill
Binstead
Brickfields Horse Country
Nettlestone Point
Seaview
Cherbourg
Guernsey
Jersey
St-Malo
Caen (Ouistreham)
Bilbao (Mar-Nov)
Le Havre
Santander
Old Town Hall
Locksgreen
Forest Side
Wootton Common
Smithecloses
Rosemary
Havenstreet
Nettlestone
Colemans
Butterfly & Fountain World
Isle of Wight Steam Railway
Little Whitefield
St Helens
Cross Lane
Staplers
The Duver
Carisbrooke
Newport
Robin Hill
East Ashey
Bembridge
Shide
Downend
Castle
Shipwreck Centre
Nunwell
Brading
Bembridge Windmill
Lifeboat Station
FORELAND
ISLE OF WIGHT
Steyne Cross
Calbourne
Bowcombe
Arreton
Yarbridge
Bembridge Down
BRIGHSTONE DOWN
Blackwater
Newchurch
Alverstone
Whitecliff Bay
Horringford
Morton
Dinosaur Isle
Rowborough
Gatcombe
Merstone
Queen's Bower
Yaverland
Culver Cliff
Chillerton
Moortown
Cheverton
Rookley
Winford
Lake
Sandown
Limerstone
Shorwell
Rookley Green
Branstone
Sandown Bay
Apse Heath
Model Village
Sandford
Yafford
Kingston
Godshill
Whiteley Bank
Shanklin
Old Smithy & Gardens
Shanklin Chine
Little Atherfield
Chale Green
Roud
Luccombe Village
Wroxall
Luccombe Chine
Atherfield Green
St Catherine's Down
Southford
Appuldurcombe House
Ventnor Downs
Atherfield Point
Bierley
Nettlecombe
DUNNOSE
Chale
St Catherine's Oratory
Steephill
Bonchurch
Whale Chine
Whitwell
Ventnor
Blackgang Chine
Niton
IOW Glass
Botanic Garden
Blackgang
Rocken End
Knowles Farm
St Lawrence
The Undercliffe
ST CATHERINE'S POINT
St Catherine's Lighthouse
Binnel Bay
G
H
J
K
L
M

20
A
B
C
D
E
F
Kitwood
East Tisted
Charlwood
Newton Valence
White
B3006
Empshott
Empshott Green
Colemore
Greatham
A3
Conford
Longmoor Camp
Griggs Green
Old Thorns
Liphook
Shottermill
B2131
Linchmere
Ansteadbrook
Haste Hill
Gospel Green
Kingsley Green
Black Down
280
BLACKDOWN HILL
Hawkley
Liss Forest
Langley
Hollycombe Steam
Burgates
Liss
B2070
Fernhurst
Lurgashall
Hillgrove
Filmore Hill
Bailey Green
High Cross
Oakshott
East Liss
Rake
Milland
Dial Green
Privett
Stoner Hill
Milland Marsh
Woodmansgreen
A286
West Meon Hut
Steep
Hill Brow
Lickfold
Lurgashall
Redford
Henley
Bexleyhill
A272
Froxfield Green
Borden
Tote Hill
Sheet
Bell Hill
Eastshaw
Langrish
Rogate
Fyning
Petersfield
Chithurst
Iping
Woolbeding
Lodsworth
River
Stroud
SOUTH DOWNS
Ramsdean
R Rother
East Meon
Causeway
Habin
Trotton
Stedham
Easebourne
Halfway Bridge
Weston
Nyewood
36
Midhurst
Coombe Cross
Nursted
West Harting
NATIONAL PARK
Minsted
Selham
233
271
BUTSER HILL
B2146
Buriton
Elsted
West Lavington
South Ambersham
Coulter
Cocking Causeway
South Harting
East Harting
War Down
Didling
Hoyle
Queen Elizabeth
Treyford
Chidden
249
Bepton
Cocking
Upper Norwood
Duncton
LINCH DOWN
Uppark House & Garden
Heyshott
Clanfield
South Downs Way
Graffham
Duncton Hill
Butser Ancient Farm
North Marden
East Lavington
Chalton
A3
255
DUNCTON HILL
LEVIN DOWN
170
B2141
Chilgrove
35
Compton
Up Marden
East Marden
Catherington
West Marden
Singleton
Blendworth
West Dean
Horndean
Lovedean
Denmead
Anmore
Finchdean
Forestside
Charlton
East Dean
Upwaltham
Weald & Downland Open Air
Goodwood
Deanlane End
Stoughton
B2149
A285
Soake
Cowplain
Bow Hill
The Trundle
206
THE TRUNDLE
Halnaker Hill
Rowland's Castle
Kingley Vale
144
NORE HILL
Walderton
Lordington
Eartham
WATERLOOVILLE
A3(M)
B2150
Staunton
B2148
Aldsworth
B2146
Woodend
West Stoke
East Lavant
Waterbeach
Denmans Garden
Funtington
Mid Lavant
Stakes
Westbourne
Goodwood
Strettington
Halnaker
Fontwell
Widley
HAVANT
Woodmancote
West Ashling
East Ashling
Westerton
Priory
Bedhampton
B2147
Summersdale
Boxgrove
Crockerhill
Hambrook
A27
B2178
Goodwood
Tangmere
Norton
Drayton
B2177
A259
Southbourne
Broadbridge
Nyton
Brockhampton
Hermitage
Westhampnett
Aldingbourne
Farlington
Langstone
Emsworth
Prinsted
Nutbourne
Roman Palace
Shopwyke
Walton
Oving
Westergate
Eastergate
A3023
Northney
Fishbourne
Chichester
Woodgate
Hilsea
Chidham
Bosham
Dell Quay
Apuldram
Merston
Barnham
A2030
THORNEY ISLAND
Colworth
North Hayling
Tye
Bosham Hoe
A259
North End
Stoke
HAYLING ISLAND
West Thorney
Donnington
Runcton
Shripney
Langstone Harbour
B2201
North Mundham
Elbridge
North Bersted
Fleet
West Itchenor
Hunston
Birdham
B2166
Flansham
19
Fratton
Chichester Harbour
A286
Sidlesham Common
South Mundham
South Bersted
Fisher
Shipton Green
West Town
South Hayling
Street End
Southsea
Sidlesham
Rose Green
B2179
Fort Cumberland
Somerley
Eastney
A288
Hayling Bay
West Wittering
Highleigh
Nyetimber
Aldwick
BOGNOR
PORTSMOUTH
Almodington
Pagham Harbour
Pagham
East Wittering
B2198
B2145
Earnley
Bracklesham
Church Norton
Bracklesham Bay
Selsey
SELSEY BILL
1
2
3
4
5
6
7
8

Horsham
Billingshurst
Southwater
Pulborough
West Chiltington
Storrington
Henfield
Steyning
Upper Beeding
Arundel
Angmering
Rustington
Littlehampton
East Preston
Ferring
Sompting
Lancing
Shoreham-by-Sea
Portslade-by-Sea
Southwick
WORTHING
Petworth
Kirdford
Wisborough Green
Slinfold
Itchingfield
Cowfold
Bolney
Hickstead
Poynings
Findon
Washington
Amberley
Bury
Houghton
Burpham
Clapham
Patching
Goring-by-Sea
Durrington
Broadwater
South Downs Way
Widening in progress

Faygate
Horsham
St Leonards Forest
Colgate
Pease Pottage
Tilgate Forest Row
Balcombe
Handcross
Slaugham
Staplefield
Southwater
Warnham
Broadbridge Heath
Itchingfield
Christ's Hospital
Manning's Heath
Lower Beeding
Monk's Gate
Nuthurst
Warninglid
Cowfold
Bolney
Crabtree
Maplehurst
Copsale
Cuckfield
Haywards Heath
Lindfield
Ardingly
West Hoathly
Sharpthorne
Highbrook
Horsted Keynes
Danehill
Scayne's Hill
Wivelsfield
Burgess Hill
Hurstpierpoint
Hassocks
Keymer
Ditchling
Plumpton
Henfield
Partridge Green
West Grinstead
Shipley
Coolham
Dial Post
Thakeham
Ashurst
Steyning
Upper Beeding
Bramber
Washington
Findon
Sompting
Lancing
Shoreham-by-Sea
Southwick
Portslade-by-Sea
HOVE
BRIGHTON
WORTHING
Rottingdean
Peacehaven
Lewes
Falmer
Pyecombe
Poynings
Fulking
Edburton
Small Dole
Albourne
Twineham
Hickstead
Clayton
Patcham
Woodingdean
Saltdean
Telscombe
Kingston near Lewes
Offham
SOUTH DOWNS NATIONAL PARK
DITCHLING BEACON
Widening in progress
5 miles
8 kilometres

21
37
38

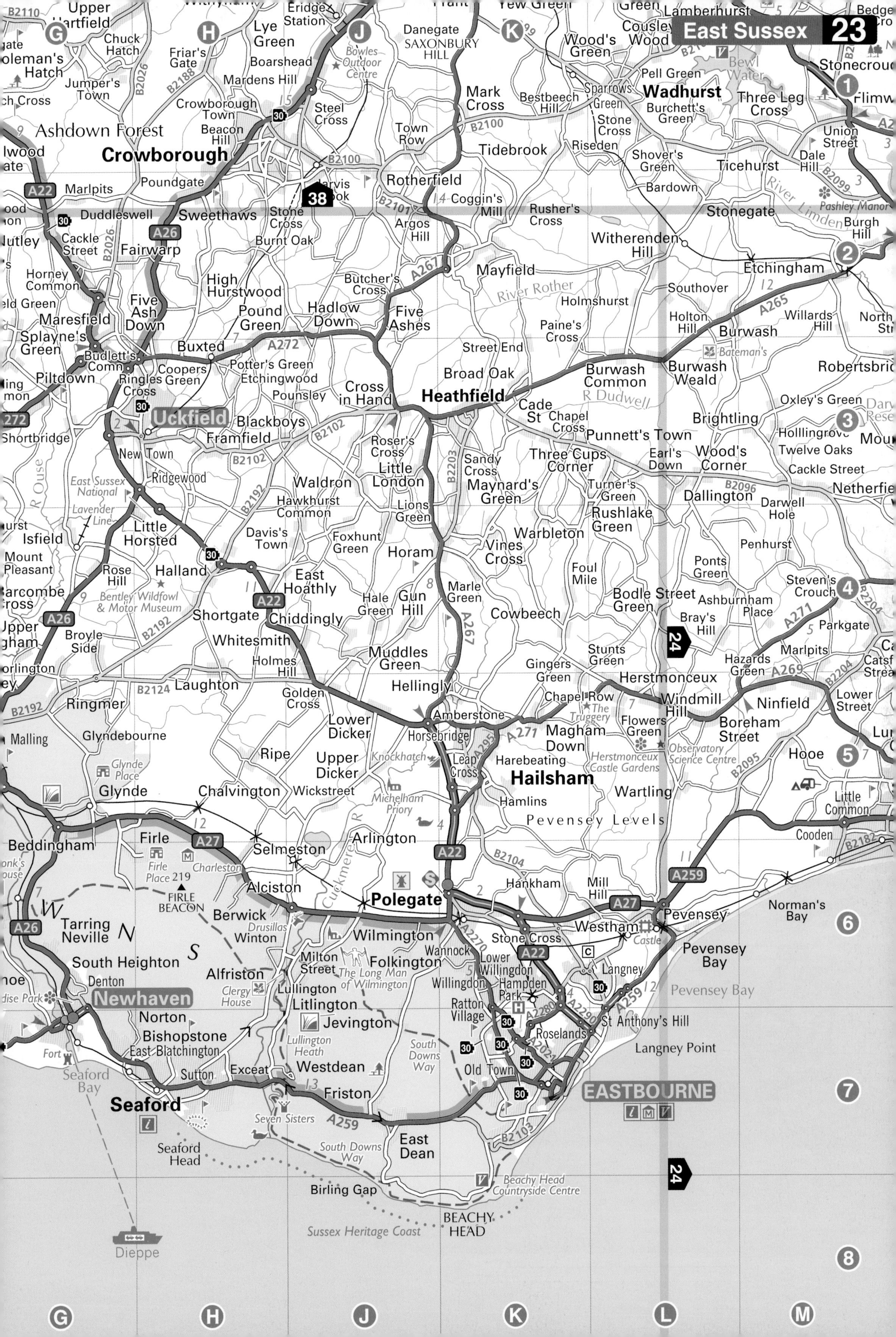

Upper Hartfield
Chuck Hatch
Coleman's Hatch
Jumper's Town
Friar's Gate
Lye Green
Eridge Station
Boarshead
Mardens Hill
Bowles Outdoor Centre
Danegate
SAXONBURY HILL
Wood's Green
Cousley Wood
Lamberhurst
Bewl Water
Pell Green
Stonecrouch
Ashdown Forest
Crowborough
Crowborough Town
Beacon Hill
Steel Cross
Town Row
Mark Cross
Bestbeech Hill
Sparrows Green
Wadhurst
Burchett's Green
Three Leg Cross
Stone Cross
Union Street
Tidebrook
Riseden
Shover's Green
Ticehurst
Dale Hill
Marlpits
Poundgate
Jarvis Brook
Rotherfield
Coggin's Mill
Rusher's Cross
Bardown
Stonegate
River Limden
Pashley Manor
Burgh Hill
Duddleswell
Sweethaws
Stone Cross
Burnt Oak
Argos Hill
Witherenden Hill
Etchingham
Nutley
Cackle Street
Fairwarp
Horney Common
High Hurstwood
Butcher's Cross
Mayfield
River Rother
Southover
Holmshurst
Maresfield
Five Ash Down
Pound Green
Hadlow Down
Five Ashes
Holton Hill
Burwash
Willards Hill
Splayne's Green
Budlett's Common
Buxted
Paine's Cross
Street End
Bateman's
Coopers Green
Potter's Green
Etchingwood
Burwash Common
Burwash Weald
Robertsbridge
Piltdown
Ringles Cross
Pounsley
Cross in Hand
Broad Oak
Heathfield
Cade St
Chapel Cross
R Dudwell
Oxley's Green
Uckfield
Blackboys
Framfield
Roser's Cross
Punnett's Town
Brightling
Hollingrove
Twelve Oaks
Shortbridge
New Town
Ridgewood
Little London
Sandy Cross
Three Cups Corner
Earl's Down
Wood's Corner
Cackle Street
East Sussex National
R Ouse
Waldron
Maynard's Green
Turner's Green
Dallington
Netherfield
Lavender Line
Hawkhurst Common
Lions Green
Darwell Hole
Rushlake Green
Isfield
Little Horsted
Davis's Town
Foxhunt Green
Horam
Warbleton
Vines Cross
Penhurst
Mount Pleasant
Rose Hill
Halland
East Hoathly
Foul Mile
Ponts Green
Steven's Crouch
Barcombe Cross
Bentley Wildfowl & Motor Museum
Hale Green
Gun Hill
Marle Green
Bodle Street Green
Ashburnham Place
Bray's Hill
Parkgate
Upper Wellingham
Broyle Side
Shortgate
Chiddingly
Cowbeech
Whitesmith
Muddles Green
Stunts Green
Marlpits
Hazards Green
Catsfield Stream
Holmes Hill
Gingers Green
Herstmonceux
Laughton
Hellingly
Golden Cross
Chapel Row
The Truggery
Windmill Hill
Ninfield
Lower Street
Ringmer
Amberstone
Lower Dicker
Horsebridge
Flowers Green
Boreham Street
Malling
Glyndebourne
Magham Down
Leap Cross
Ripe
Upper Dicker
Knockhatch
Harebeating
Herstmonceux Castle Gardens
Observatory Science Centre
Hooe
Glynde Place
Glynde
Chalvington
Wickstreet
Michelham Priory
Hailsham
Hamlins
Wartling
Little Common
Pevensey Levels
Cuckmere R
Beddingham
Firle
Selmeston
Arlington
Cooden
Firle Place 219
Charleston
Alciston
Hankham
Mill Hill
FIRLE BEACON
Polegate
Berwick
Drusillas
Pevensey
Norman's Bay
Tarring Neville
Winton
Wilmington
Westham
Stone Cross
Castle
Wannock
Pevensey Bay
South Heighton
Milton Street
Folkington
The Long Man of Wilmington
Lower Willingdon
Langney
Denton
Alfriston
Clergy House
Lullington
Willingdon
Hampden Park
Newhaven
Litlington
Ratton Village
St Anthony's Hill
Norton
Jevington
Roselands
Bishopstone
East Blatchington
Lullington Heath
South Downs Way
Langney Point
Fort
Seaford Bay
Sutton
Exceat
Westdean
Old Town
Friston
Seaford
EASTBOURNE
Seven Sisters
East Dean
Seaford Head
South Downs Way
Birling Gap
Beachy Head Countryside Centre
BEACHY HEAD
Sussex Heritage Coast
Dieppe
A22
A26
A267
A272
A265
A271
A269
A27
A259
A2270
A2280
A2290
A2021
A295
B2110
B2026
B2188
B2100
B2101
B2102
B2192
B2203
B2096
B2204
B2124
B2104
B2095
B2182
B2103
B2099
38
24
G
H
J
K
L
M
1
2
3
4
5
6
7
8

A
B
C
D
E
F
1
2
3
4
5
6
7
8
Yew Green
Lamberhurst Down
Bedgebury Cross
Bedgebury National Pinetum
Hartley
Goddard's Green
Parkgate
Wood's Green
Cousley Wood
Bewlbridge
Bewl Water
Stonecrouch
A229
Benenden
Beacon Hill
Pell Green
Wadhurst
Sparrows Green
Burchett's Green
Bestbeech Hill
Stone Cross
Three Leg Cross
Flimwell
High Street
Gill's Green
Iden Green
Gun Green
B2086
Strood
The C.M Booth Collection of Historic Vehicles
Rolvenden
Dingleden
Mark Cross
B2100
Tidebrook
Riseden
Shover's Green
Union Street
A268
Highgate
Hawkhurst
Standen Street
Dale Hill
Ticehurst
B2099
Four Throws
Rolvenden Layne
Heathfield
Coggin's Mill
Bardown
Rusher's Cross
River Limden
Pashley Manor
39
The Moor
Sandhurst
A28
Kent & East Sussex Railway
Stonegate
Burgh Hill
Merriments
Kent Ditch
Linkhill
Newenden
Witherenden Hill
Hurst Green
B2244
Sandhurst Cross
Great Dixter House & Gardens
Mayfield
Etchingham
A21
River Rother
Southover
Bodiam
Bodiam Castle
Holmshurst
A265
Willards Hill
Northbridge Street
Salehurst
Ewhurst Green
Northiam
Four Oaks
Paine's Cross
Holton Hill
Burwash
Bateman's
B2088
Street End
Broad Oak
Burwash Common
Burwash Weald
Robertsbridge
Staple Cross
Millcorner
Beckley
B2165
Clayhill
Peasmarsh
Cripp's Corner
Collier's Green
Horns Cross
Cade Street
R Dudwell
Oxley's Green
Darwell Reservoir
Chapel Cross
Brightling
John's Cross
Punnett's Town
Holllingrove
Mountfield
Vinehall Street
B2089
Chitcombe
Sandy Cross
Three Cups Corner
Earl's Down
Wood's Corner
Twelve Oaks
Goatham Green
Broad Oak
R Tillingham
B2203
Maynard's Green
Turner's Green
Cackle Street
A2100
Scrays
Cackle Street
Broadland Row
B2096
Netherfield
Udimore
Dallington
Darwell Hole
Whatlington
Rushlake Green
Sedlescombe
Brede
River Brede
Warbleton
Lidham Hill
Broad Street
Vines Cross
Penhurst
Battle
Kent Street
Icklesham
Foul Mile
Ponts Green
New Cut
Steven's Crouch
Starr's Green
Guestling Thorn
A267
Bodle Street Green
Ashburnham Place
B2204
1066
Three Oaks
Westfield
Cowbeech
Bray's Hill
A271
Parkgate
B2095
A259
23
Stunts Green
Marlpits
Catsfield
Guestling Green
Gingers Green
Hazards Green
Catsfield Stream
Baldslow
Herstmonceux
A269
B2093
RSPB
Chapel Row
Windmill Hill
Lower Street
Crowhurst
Bachelor's Bump
The Truggery
Ninfield
Henley's Down
St Helens
Amberstone
Flowers Green
Boreham Street
B2092
B2159
Green Street
Hellingly
Magham Down
Observatory Science Centre
Lunsford's Cross
A2101
Ore
Fairlight
Harebeating
Herstmonceux Castle Gardens
Hooe
St Leonards
Lower Cross
Hailsham
B2095
HASTINGS
Wartling
Sidley
A2036
Bulverhythe
Hamlins
Little Common
30
40
Pevensey Levels
Cooden
A22
B2104
B2182
Bexhill
Hankham
A259
Mill Hill
A27
Norman's Bay
Pevensey
Westham
Castle
Stone Cross
A22
Polegate
A2270
Pevensey Bay
Lower Willingdon
Langney
Willingdon
Hampden Park
Pevensey Bay
Ratton Village
A2280
A2290
St Anthony's Hill
Roselands
Langney Point
A2021
Old Town
EASTBOURNE
B2103
Beachy Head Countryside Centre
BEACHY HEAD
0 1 2 3 4 5 miles
0 1 2 3 4 5 6 7 8 kilometres

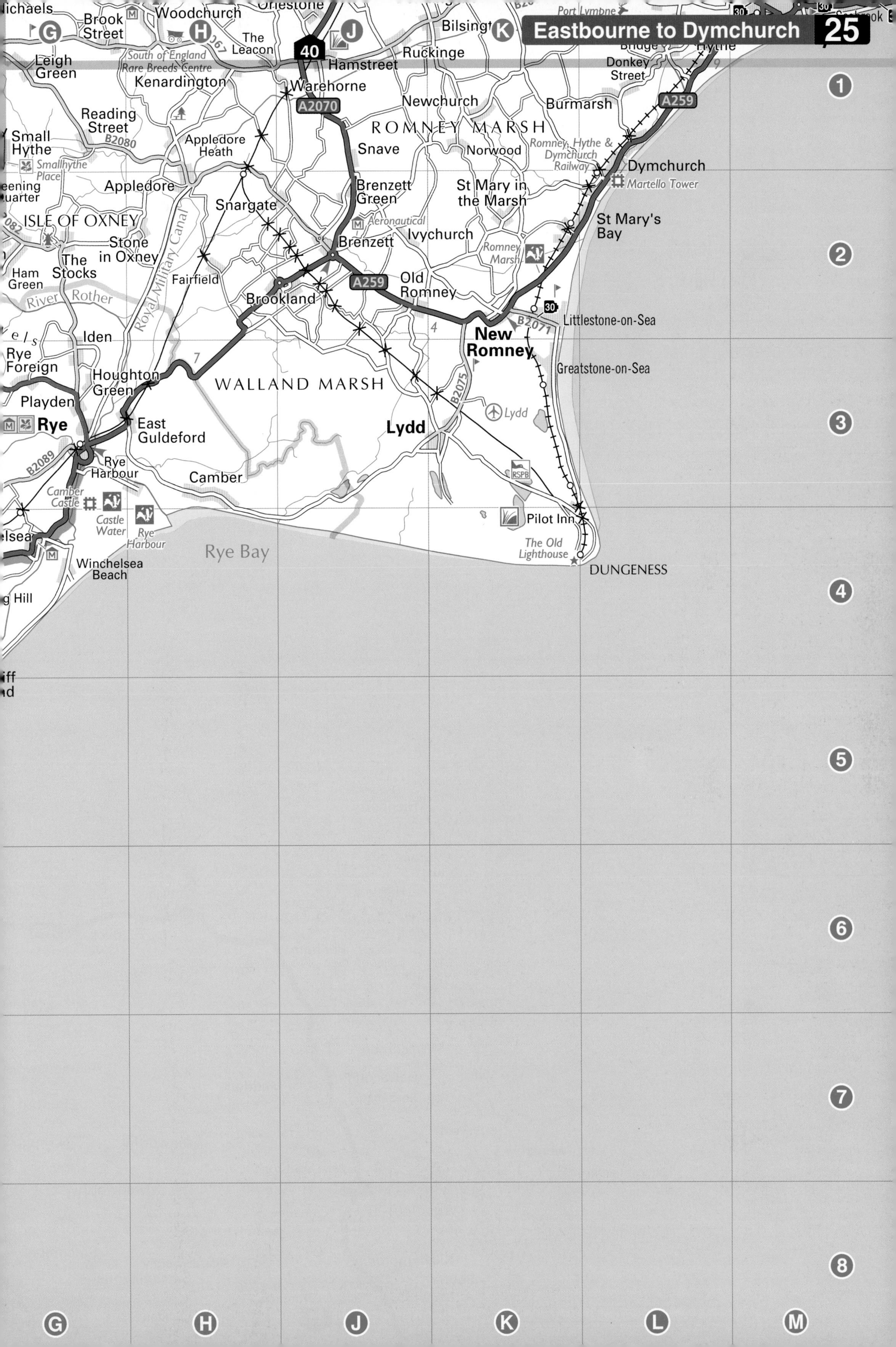
Brook Street
Woodchurch
The Leacon
Bilsington
Port Lympne
Leigh Green
South of England Rare Breeds Centre
Hamstreet
Ruckinge
Donkey Street
Hythe
Kenardington
Warehorne
A2070
Newchurch
Burmarsh
A259
Reading Street
B2080
ROMNEY MARSH
Small Hythe
Smallhythe Place
Appledore Heath
Snave
Norwood
Romney, Hythe & Dymchurch Railway
Dymchurch
Martello Tower
Appledore
Brenzett Green
St Mary in the Marsh
Snargate
ISLE OF OXNEY
Aeronautical
Ivychurch
St Mary's Bay
Stone in Oxney
Royal Military Canal
Brenzett
Romney Marsh
Ham Green
The Stocks
Fairfield
A259
Old Romney
River Rother
Brookland
B2071
Littlestone-on-Sea
Iden
New Romney
Rye Foreign
Greatstone-on-Sea
Houghton Green
WALLAND MARSH
B2075
Playden
Lydd
Rye
East Guldeford
Lydd
B2089
Rye Harbour
Camber
RSPB
Camber Castle
Castle Water
Rye Harbour
Pilot Inn
Rye Bay
The Old Lighthouse
Winchelsea Beach
DUNGENESS
1
2
3
4
5
6
7
8
G
H
J
K
L
M

A
B
C
D
E
F
1
2
3
4
5
6
7
8
North West Point
Lundy Heritage Coast
LUNDY
142
Marisco
Surf Point
Shutter Point
BARNSTAPLE
OR
BIDEFORD BAY
HARTLAND POINT
Shipload Bay
Titchberry
Damehole Point
Hartland Abbey & Gardens
Brownsham
Stoke
Hartland Quay
B3248
Velly
Clovelly
Hartland
B3237
Higher Clovelly
Buck's Mills
Spekes Mill Mouth
Milford
Docton Mill Gardens
Philham
Milky Way
Buck's Cross
A39
Elmscott
Edistone
Woolfardisworthy
Hardisworthy
Tosberry
Cranford
South Hole
Welcombe
Ashmansworth
Mead
Darracott
Meddon
East Putford
Gooseham Mill
Woolley
Gooseham
Eastcott
East Youlstone
Dinworthy
Gnome Reserve
Morwenstow
Higher Sharpnose Point
West Youlstone
Colscott
Shop
A39
Bradworthy
South West Coast Path
Woodford
Lower Sharpnose Point
Tamar Lakes
Kimworthy
Kilkhampton
Alfardisworthy
Sutcombe
Steeple Point
Stibb
Sutcombemill
Thurdon
Soldon
Soldon Cross
11
5 miles
8 kilometres

Ilfracombe
Hele
Combe Martin
Berrynarbor
Mortehoe
Woolacombe
Morte Bay
Trimstone
West Down
Bittadon
Kentisbury
Parracombe
Martinhoe
Trentishoe
Arlington
Loxhore
Shirwell
Muddiford
Marwood
Georgeham
Croyde
Croyde Bay
Saunton
Braunton
Wrafton
Chivenor
Ashford
Pilton
Goodleigh
Barnstaple
Landkey
Swimbridge
Fremington
Yelland
Instow
Appledore
Northam
Westward Ho!
Abbotsham
Bideford
East-the-Water
Westleigh
Eastleigh
Horwood
Tawstock
Bishop's Tawton
Newton Tracey
Alverdiscott
Landcross
Littleham
Monkleigh
Frithelstock
Great Torrington
Little Torrington
Weare Giffard
Huntshaw
Yarnscombe
Atherington
Umberleigh
Chittlehampton
Chittlehamholt
Satterleigh
Kings Nympton
High Bickington
St Giles in the Wood
Kingscott
Roborough
Beaford
Burrington
Ashreigney
Riddlecombe
Dolton
Merton
Huish
Petrockstow
Peters Marland
Langtree
Stibb Cross
Newton St Petrock
Buckland Brewer
Eggesford
Ashley
Hollocombe
Dowland
Filleigh
Brayford
Stoke Rivers
Bratton Fleming
River Taw
Barnstaple & Bideford

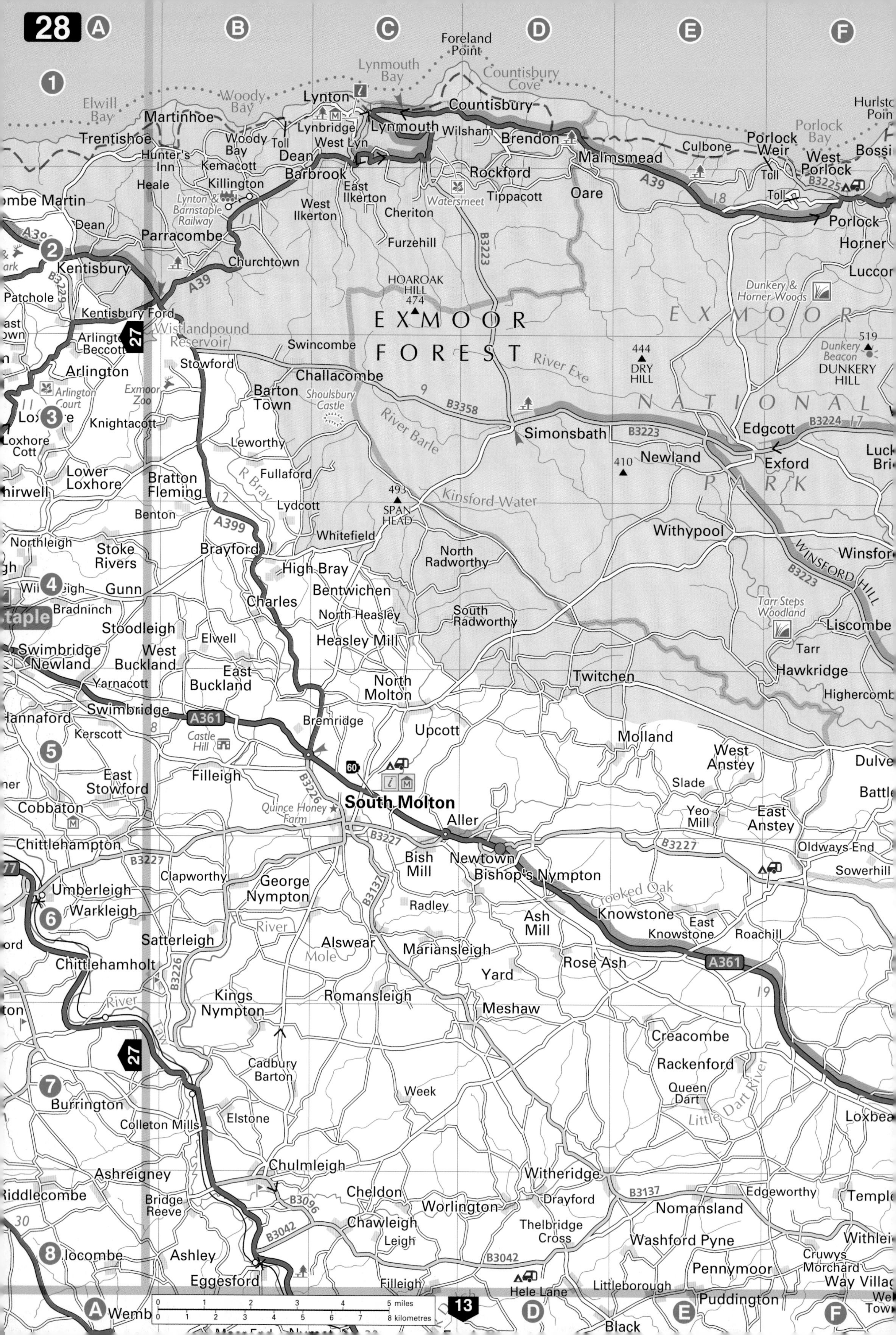

A
B
C
D
E
F
1
2
3
4
5
6
7
8
Foreland Point
Lynmouth Bay
Countisbury Cove
Elwill Bay
Woody Bay
Lynton
Countisbury
Hurlstone Point
Porlock Bay
Martinhoe
Trentishoe
Woody Bay
Lynbridge
Lynmouth
Wilsham
Brendon
Culbone
Porlock Weir
West Porlock
Bossington
Hunter's Inn
West Lyn
Dean
Malmsmead
Kemacott
Barbrook
Rockford
Heale
Killington
Combe Martin
Lynton & Barnstaple Railway
East Ilkerton
West Ilkerton
Watersmeet
Tippacott
Oare
A39
B3225
Toll
Porlock
Cheriton
Dean
Parracombe
Horner
Furzehill
B3223
Kentisbury
Churchtown
Luccombe
Dunkery & Horner Woods
HOAROAK HILL 474
Patchole
B3229
Kentisbury Ford
EXMOOR FOREST
EXMOOR NATIONAL PARK
Wistlandpound Reservoir
Arlington Beccott
27
Swincombe
444 DRY HILL
519 Dunkery Beacon
DUNKERY HILL
Stowford
River Exe
Arlington
Challacombe
Arlington Court
Exmoor Zoo
Barton Town
Shoulsbury Castle
B3358
Loxhore
Knightacott
River Barle
Simonsbath
B3223
Edgcott
B3224
Loxhore Cott
Leworthy
Newland
Exford
410
Lower Loxhore
Bratton Fleming
Fullaford
Shirwell
R Bray
493 SPAN HEAD
Kinsford Water
Lydcott
Benton
A399
Whitefield
Withypool
Northleigh
Stoke Rivers
Brayford
North Radworthy
Winsford
WINSFORD HILL
High Bray
Gunn
Bentwichen
Bradninch
Charles
North Heasley
South Radworthy
Tarr Steps Woodland
Liscombe
Stoodleigh
Barnstaple
Elwell
Heasley Mill
Tarr
Swimbridge Newland
West Buckland
East Buckland
Hawkridge
Yarnacott
North Molton
Twitchen
Highercombe
Swimbridge
A361
Hannaford
Bremridge
Upcott
Molland
Kerscott
Castle Hill
West Anstey
Dulverton
60
East Stowford
Filleigh
Slade
Battleton
B3226
South Molton
Yeo Mill
East Anstey
Cobbaton
Quince Honey Farm
Aller
Chittlehampton
B3227
Oldways End
Bish Mill
Newtown
Bishop's Nympton
Sowerhill
Clapworthy
George Nympton
Umberleigh
B3137
Radley
Crooked Oak
Warkleigh
Ash Mill
Knowstone
East Knowstone
Roachill
River Mole
Alswear
Satterleigh
Mariansleigh
Rose Ash
Chittlehamholt
Yard
B3226
Kings Nympton
Romansleigh
Meshaw
River Taw
Creacombe
Cadbury Barton
Rackenford
Queen Dart
Little Dart River
Burrington
Week
Colleton Mills
Elstone
Loxbeare
Chulmleigh
Ashreigney
Witheridge
Cheldon
Drayford
B3137
Edgeworthy
Templeton
Riddlecombe
Bridge Reeve
B3096
Worlington
Nomansland
Chawleigh
Thelbridge Cross
B3042
Leigh
Washford Pyne
Witheridge
Dolcombe
Ashley
B3042
Cruwys Morchard
Pennymoor
Eggesford
Filleigh
Hele Lane
Littleborough
Way Village
Puddington
Wembworthy
Black
13
0 1 2 3 4 5 miles
0 1 2 3 4 5 6 7 8 kilometres

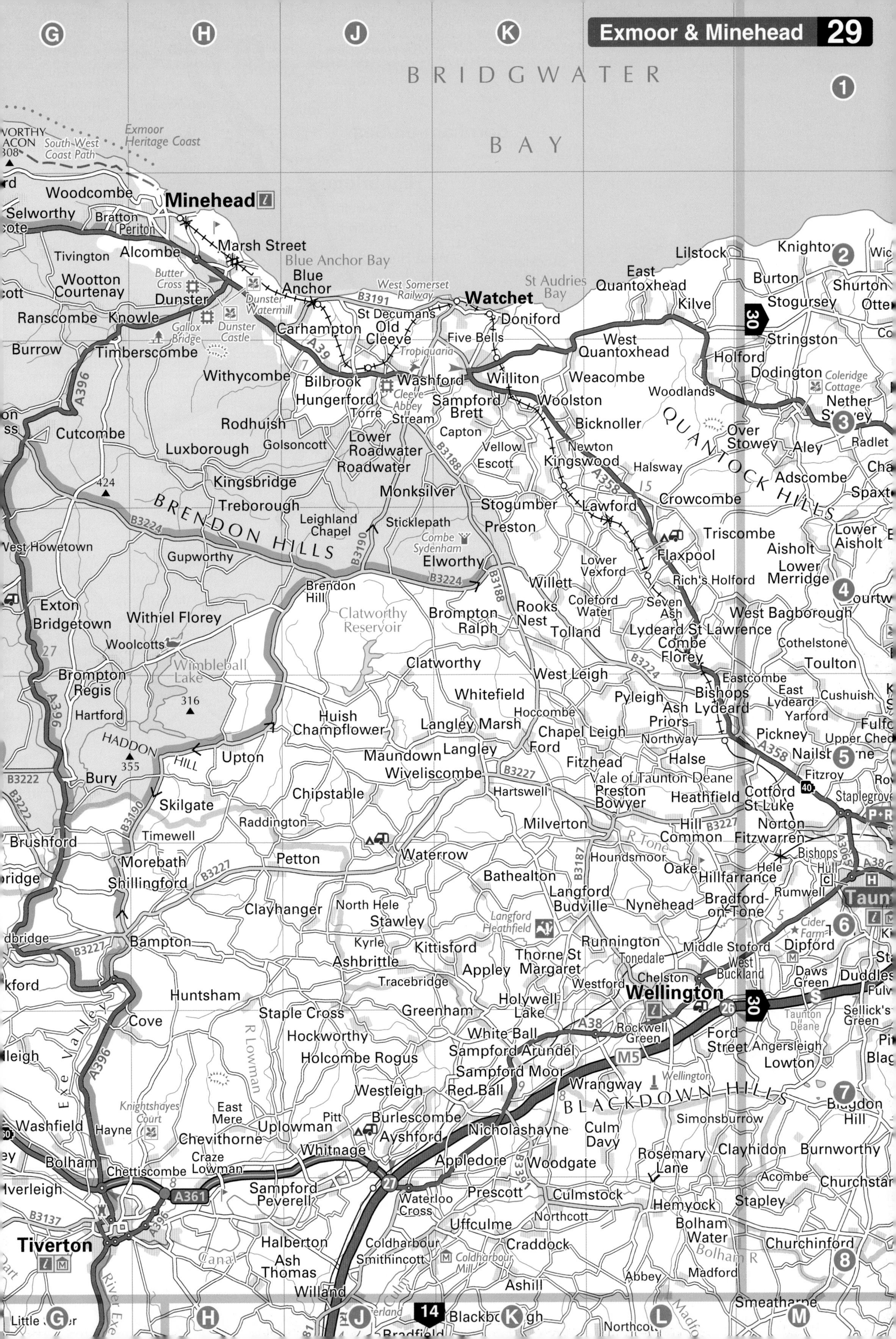
G
H
J
K
BRIDGWATER
BAY
1
Exmoor Heritage Coast
South West Coast Path
Woodcombe
Minehead
Selworthy
Bratton
Periton
Marsh Street
Blue Anchor Bay
Tivington
Alcombe
Blue Anchor
Butter Cross
Wootton Courtenay
Dunster
Dunster Watermill
West Somerset Railway
B3191
Watchet
St Audries Bay
East Quantoxhead
Lilstock
Knighton
2
Burton
Shurton
Kilve
Stogursey
30
Ranscombe
Knowle
Gallox Bridge
Dunster Castle
Carhampton
St Decumans
Old Cleeve
Doniford
Five Bells
West Quantoxhead
Stringston
Holford
Burrow
Timberscombe
A39
Tropiquaria
Dodington
Coleridge Cottage
Withycombe
Bilbrook
Washford
Williton
Weacombe
Woodlands
A396
Hungerford
Cleeve Abbey
Sampford Brett
Woolston
Nether Stowey
Torre
Stream
Bicknoller
3
Radlet
Cutcombe
Rodhuish
Capton
QUANTOCK HILLS
Over Stowey
Aley
Golsoncott
Lower Roadwater
Yellow
Newton
Luxborough
Roadwater
B3188
Escott
Kingswood
Halsway
Adscombe
424
Kingsbridge
A358
Monksilver
Stogumber
Crowcombe
Spaxton
BRENDON HILLS
Treborough
Lawford
B3224
Leighland Chapel
Sticklepath
Preston
Triscombe
Lower Aisholt
West Howetown
Combe Sydenham
Aisholt
Gupworthy
B3190
Elworthy
Flaxpool
Lower Merridge
Brendon Hill
Willett
Lower Vexford
Rich's Holford
4
Exton
Clatworthy Reservoir
Brompton Ralph
Rooks Nest
Coleford Water
Seven Ash
West Bagborough
Bridgetown
Withiel Florey
Tolland
Lydeard St Lawrence
Woolcotts
Combe Florey
Cothelstone
27
Clatworthy
Toulton
Wimbleball Lake
West Leigh
Eastcombe
Brompton Regis
Whitefield
Pyleigh
Bishops Lydeard
East Lydeard
Cushuish
316
Ash Priors
Yarford
Hartford
Huish Champflower
Hoccombe
Langley Marsh
Chapel Leigh
HADDON HILL
Ford
Pickney
355
Maundown
Langley
Northway
Upton
Fitzhead
Halse
Nailsbourne
5
B3222
Bury
Wiveliscombe
B3227
Vale of Taunton Deane
Fitzroy
Skilgate
Chipstable
Hartswell
Preston Bowyer
Heathfield
Cotford St Luke
40
Staplegrove
Raddington
Milverton
Hill Common
Norton Fitzwarren
Brushford
Timewell
Waterrow
R Tone
Bishops Hull
Morebath
Petton
B3187
Houndsmoor
Oake
Hele
Shillingford
Bathealton
Hillfarrance
A38
Langford Budville
Rumwell
Taunton
Clayhanger
North Hele
Nynehead
Bradford-on-Tone
Stawley
Langford Heathfield
Cider Farm
6
Bampton
Kyrle
Runnington
Middle Stoford
Dipford
Kittisford
Thorne St Margaret
Tonedale
West Buckland
Ashbrittle
Appley
Chelston
Daws Green
Dudderidge
Huntsham
Tracebridge
Westford
Wellington
Holywell Lake
26
Staple Cross
Greenham
Taunton Deane
Sellick's Green
Cove
R Lowman
Hockworthy
White Ball
Rockwell Green
Ford Street
Angersleigh
Exe Valley
Holcombe Rogus
Sampford Arundel
M5
Lowton
Sampford Moor
Wellington
Wrangway
Westleigh
Red Ball
BLACKDOWN HILLS
7
Blagdon Hill
Knightshayes Court
East Mere
Pitt
Burlescombe
Simonsburrow
Washfield
Hayne
Uplowman
Culm Davy
Chevithorne
Ayshford
Nicholashayne
Whitnage
Rosemary Lane
Clayhidon
Burnworthy
Craze Lowman
Bolham
Chettiscombe
Appledore
Woodgate
A361
Acombe
Churchstanton
Sampford Peverell
Prescott
Culmstock
B3391
Waterloo Cross
Hemyock
Stapley
B3137
Northcott
Uffculme
Bolham Water
Tiverton
Halberton
Craddock
Churchinford
Coldharbour
Canal
Ash Thomas
Smithincott
Coldharbour Mill
Bolham R
8
Abbey
Madford
River Exe
Willand
Ashill
Little
14
Blackborough
Smeatharpe
Northcott
L
M

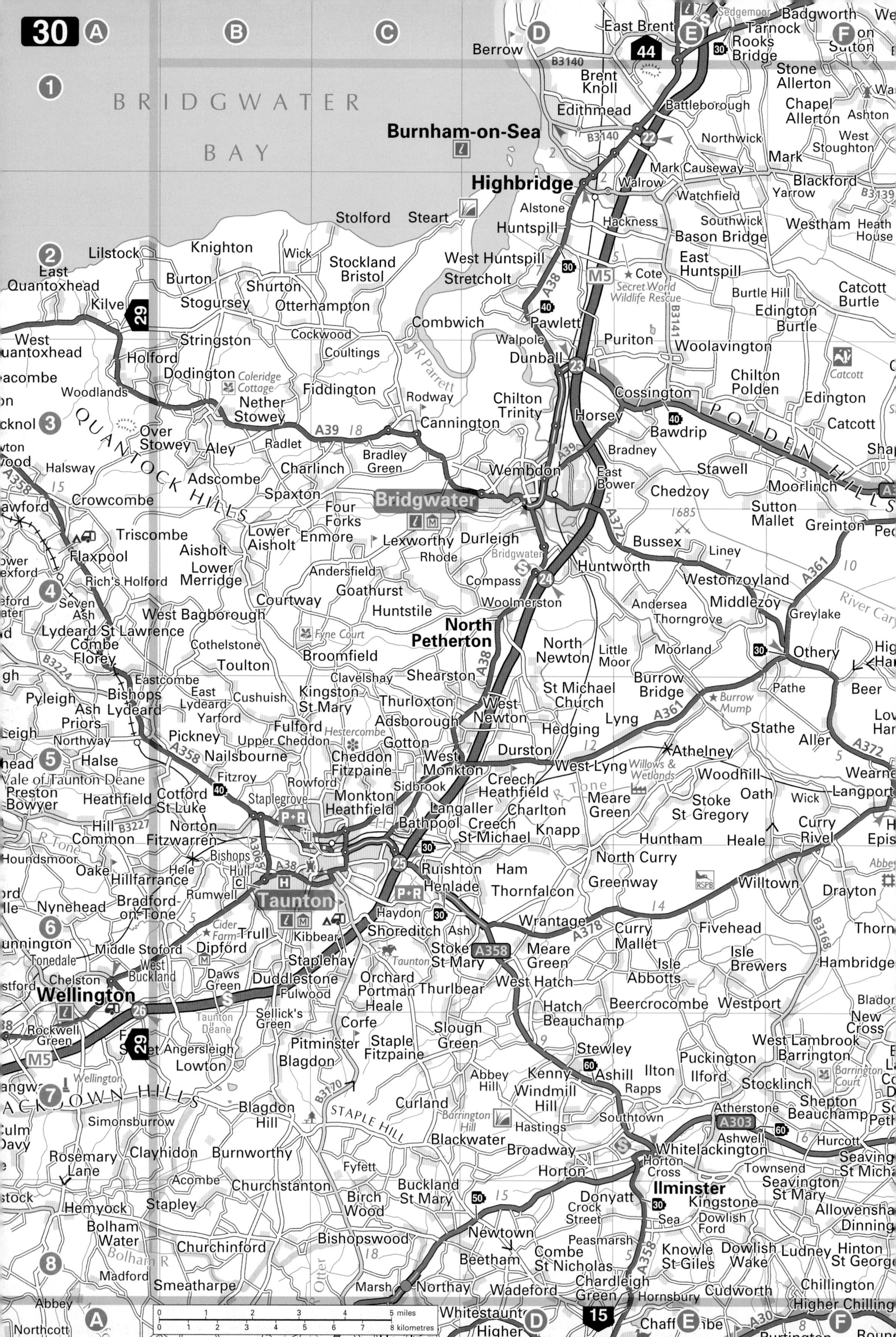

30
A
B
C
D
E
F
1
2
3
4
5
6
7
8
BRIDGWATER
BAY
Berrow
East Brent
Sedgemoor
Badgworth
Tarnock
Rooks Bridge
44
B3140
Brent Knoll
Edithmead
Stone Allerton
Chapel Allerton
Ashton
Battleborough
Burnham-on-Sea
B3140
22
Northwick
West Stoughton
Mark
Mark Causeway
Blackford
Yarrow
Highbridge
Walrow
Watchfield
Alstone
Hackness
Southwick
Westham
Heath House
Huntspill
Bason Bridge
Stolford
Steart
Lilstock
Knighton
Wick
Stockland Bristol
West Huntspill
East Huntspill
East Quantoxhead
Burton
Shurton
Stretcholt
M5
Cote
Secret World Wildlife Rescue
Burtle Hill
Catcott Burtle
Kilve
29
Stogursey
Otterhampton
Pawlett
Edington Burtle
Combwich
B3141
West Quantoxhead
Stringston
Cockwood
Walpole
Puriton
Woolavington
Holford
Coultings
Dunball
23
Dodington
Coleridge Cottage
R Parrett
Chilton Polden
Catcott
Woodlands
Nether Stowey
Fiddington
Rodway
Chilton Trinity
Cossington
Edington
Over Stowey
QUANTOCK HILLS
A39
Cannington
Horsey
Bawdrip
POLDEN HILLS
Catcott
Aley
Radlet
Bradley Green
Bradney
Halsway
Charlinch
Wembdon
Stawell
Adscombe
East Bower
Moorlinch
A358
Crowcombe
Spaxton
Bridgwater
Chedzoy
Sutton Mallet
Four Forks
1685
Greinton
Triscombe
Lower Aisholt
Enmore
Lexworthy
Durleigh
A372
Bussex
Flaxpool
Aisholt
Rhode
Bridgwater
Liney
Lower Merridge
Andersfield
Huntworth
A361
Westonzoyland
Rich's Holford
Compass
24
Seven Ash
Goathurst
Middlezoy
Courtway
Woolmerston
Andersea
River Cary
West Bagborough
Huntstile
Thorngrove
Greylake
Lydeard St Lawrence
North Petherton
Combe Florey
Cothelstone
Fyne Court
North Newton
Little Moor
Moorland
Othery
Broomfield
B3224
Toulton
A38
Eastcombe
Clavelshay
Shearston
Burrow Bridge
Pyleigh
Bishops Lydeard
East Lydeard
Cushuish
Kingston St Mary
St Michael Church
Pathe
Beer
Ash Priors
Thurloxton
West Newton
Burrow Mump
Yarford
Adsborough
Lyng
Northway
Pickney
Fulford
Hestercombe
Hedging
Stathe
Aller
Halse
A358
Nailsbourne
Upper Cheddon
Gotton
Durston
Athelney
A372
Vale of Taunton Deane
Fitzroy
Cheddon Fitzpaine
West Monkton
West Lyng
Willows & Wetlands
Woodhill
Langport
Preston Bowyer
Heathfield
Cotford St Luke
Rowford
Sidbrook
Creech Heathfield
R Tone
Meare Green
Oath
Wick
Staplegrove
Monkton Heathfield
Langaller
Charlton
Stoke St Gregory
Curry Rivel
Hill Common
B3227
Norton Fitzwarren
P+R
Bathpool
Creech St Michael
Knapp
Huntham
Heale
R Tone
Houndsmoor
A3065
Bishops Hull
Ruishton
Ham
North Curry
Oake
Hele
A38
25
Henlade
Thornfalcon
Greenway
Willtown
Drayton
Hillfarrance
Rumwell
Taunton
P+R
RSPB
Bradford-on-Tone
Haydon
Nynehead
Cider Farm
Trull
Kibbear
Shoreditch
Ash
Wrantage
A378
Curry Mallet
Fivehead
B3168
Middle Stoford
Dipford
Stoke St Mary
A358
Meare Green
Isle Brewers
Tonedale
Staplehay
Taunton
Hambridge
West Buckland
Chelston
Daws Green
Duddlestone
Orchard Portman
Thurlbear
West Hatch
Isle Abbotts
Wellington
Fulwood
Heale
Hatch Beauchamp
Beercrocombe
Westport
New Cross
Taunton Deane
Sellick's Green
Corfe
Rockwell Green
26
Slough Green
West Lambrook
Barrington
Pitminster
Staple Fitzpaine
M5
29
Angersleigh
Stewley
Lowton
Blagdon
Puckington
Barrington Court
Wellington
Abbey Hill
Kenny
Ashill
Ilton
Ilford
Stocklinch
Windmill Hill
Rapps
BLACKDOWN HILLS
B3170
Curland
Atherstone
Shepton Beauchamp
Blagdon Hill
STAPLE HILL
Barrington Hill
Southtown
A303
Simonsburrow
Hastings
Ashwell
Hurcott
Blackwater
Broadway
Whitelackington
Seavington St Michael
Rosemary Lane
Clayhidon
Burnworthy
Horton Cross
Townsend
Fyfett
Horton
Acombe
Churchstanton
Buckland St Mary
Ilminster
Seavington St Mary
Hemyock
Stapley
Birch Wood
Donyatt
Kingstone
Crock Street
Allowenshay
Bolham Water
Sea
Dowlish Ford
Dinnington
Newtown
Peasmarsh
Churchinford
Bishopswood
Combe St Nicholas
Knowle St Giles
Dowlish Wake
Ludney
Hinton St George
Bolham R
Otter
A358
Beetham
Madford
Smeatharpe
Marsh
Northay
Wadeford
Chardleigh Green
Chillington
Cudworth
Hornsbury
Abbey
Higher Chillington
Whitestaunton
15
Northcott
Higher
A30
0 1 2 3 4 5 miles
0 1 2 3 4 5 6 7 8 kilometres

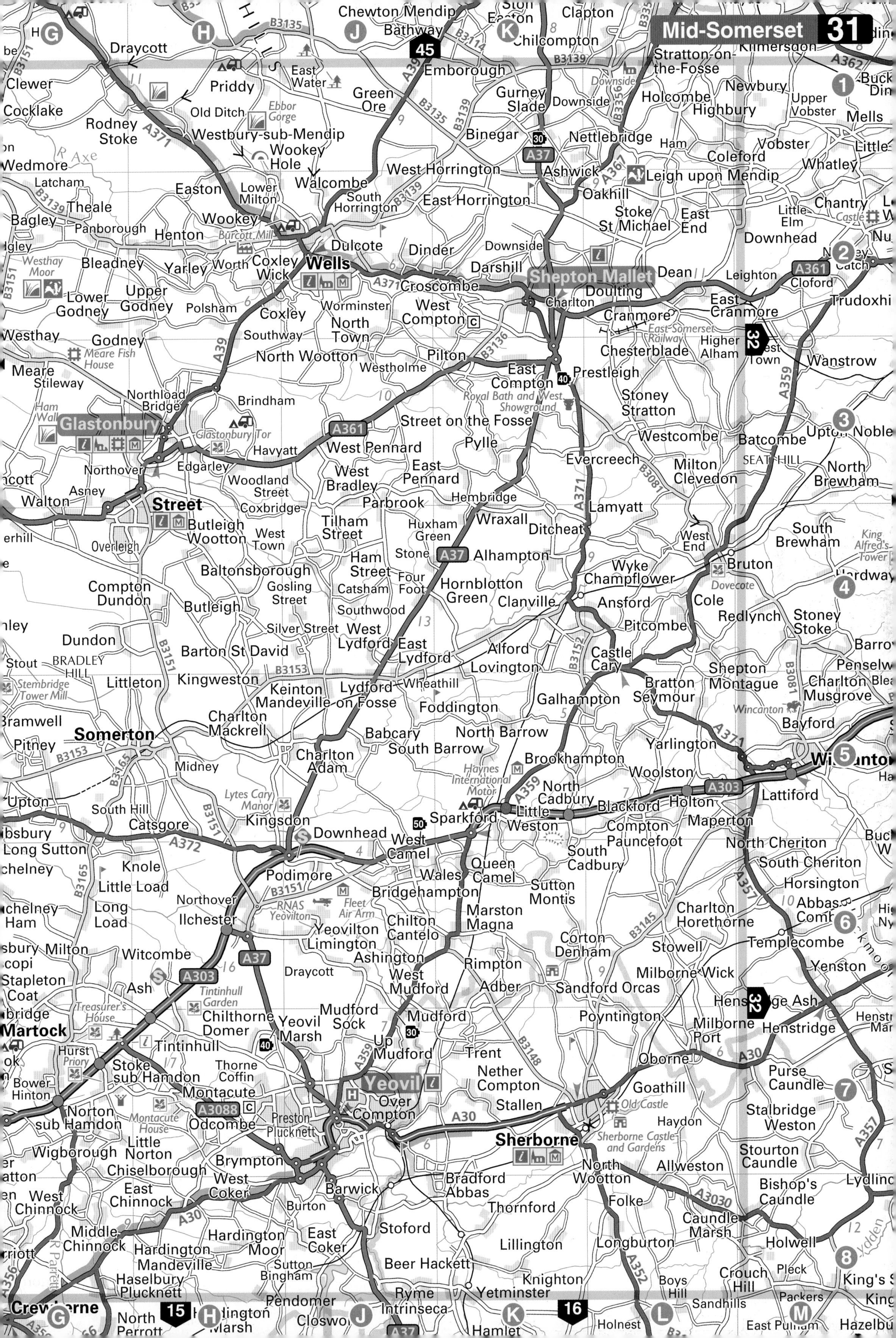

Chewton Mendip, Bathway, Emborough, Chilcompton, Clapton, Stratton-on-the-Fosse, Kilmersdon, Draycott, Priddy, East Water, Green Ore, Gurney Slade, Downside, Holcombe, Newbury, Highbury, Upper Vobster, Mells, Clewer, Cocklake, Rodney Stoke, Old Ditch, Ebbor Gorge, Westbury-sub-Mendip, Wookey Hole, Binegar, Nettlebridge, Ham, Coleford, Vobster, Whatley, Wedmore, Latcham, Theale, Bagley, Panborough, Easton, Lower Milton, Walcombe, West Horrington, South Horrington, East Horrington, Ashwick, Oakhill, Leigh upon Mendip, Chantry, Little Elm, Wookey, Henton, Burcott Mill, Dulcote, Dinder, Downside, Stoke St Michael, East End, Downhead, Westhay Moor, Bleadney, Yarley, Worth, Coxley Wick, Wells, Darshill, Shepton Mallet, Dean, Leighton, Cloford, Lower Godney, Upper Godney, Polsham, Coxley, Worminster, Croscombe, West Compton, Charlton, Doulting, Cranmore, East Cranmore, Trudoxhill, Westhay, Godney, Meare Fish House, Southway, North Town, East Somerset Railway, Chesterblade, Higher Alham, West Town, Wanstrow, Meare, Stileway, North Wootton, Westholme, Pilton, East Compton, Prestleigh, Northload Bridge, Brindham, Royal Bath and West Showground, Stoney Stratton, Ham Wall, Glastonbury, Glastonbury Tor, Havyatt, West Pennard, Street on the Fosse, Pylle, Westcombe, Batcombe, Upton Noble, Northover, Edgarley, Woodland Street, West Bradley, East Pennard, Evercreech, Milton Clevedon, Seat Hill, North Brewham, Walton, Asney, Street, Coxbridge, Parbrook, Hembridge, Lamyatt, Butleigh Wootton, Overleigh, West Town, Tilham Street, Huxham Green, Wraxall, Ditcheat, West End, South Brewham, King Alfred's Tower, Stone, Alhampton, Wyke Champflower, Bruton, Dovecote, Compton Dundon, Baltonsborough, Gosling Street, Ham Street, Catsham, Four Foot, Hornblotton Green, Clanville, Ansford, Cole, Redlynch, Stoney Stoke, Hardway, Butleigh, Southwood, Pitcombe, Dundon, Silver Street, West Lydford, East Lydford, Alford, Barton St David, Lovington, Castle Cary, Shepton Montague, Stout, Bradley Hill, Littleton, Kingweston, Keinton Mandeville, Lydford-on-Fosse, Wheathill, Bratton Seymour, Charlton Musgrove, Stembridge Tower Mill, Galhampton, Wincanton, Bayford, Bramwell, Charlton Mackrell, Foddington, Somerton, Babcary, North Barrow, South Barrow, Yarlington, Pitney, Charlton Adam, Midney, Brookhampton, Woolston, Haynes International Motor Museum, North Cadbury, Upton, Lytes Cary Manor, Kingsdon, South Hill, Catsgore, Sparkford, Little Weston, Blackford, Holton, Lattiford, Maperton, Compton Pauncefoot, Downhead, West Camel, Long Sutton, Queen Camel, South Cadbury, North Cheriton, South Cheriton, Knole, Little Load, Podimore, Wales, Bridgehampton, Sutton Montis, Horsington, Long Load, Northover, RNAS Yeovilton, Fleet Air Arm, Marston Magna, Charlton Horethorne, Abbas Combe, Ilchester, Yeovilton, Limington, Chilton Cantelo, Corton Denham, Stowell, Templecombe, Witcombe, Draycott, Ashington, Rimpton, Milborne Wick, Yenston, Stapleton, Ash, Tintinhull Garden, West Mudford, Adber, Sandford Orcas, Henstridge Ash, Treasurer's House, Chilthorne Domer, Yeovil Marsh, Mudford Sock, Mudford, Poyntington, Milborne Port, Henstridge, Martock, Tintinhull, Up Mudford, Trent, Oborne, Hurst Priory, Stoke sub Hamdon, Thorne Coffin, Nether Compton, Purse Caundle, Bower Hinton, Montacute, Yeovil, Over Compton, Goathill, Stallen, Old Castle, Norton sub Hamdon, Montacute House, Odcombe, Preston Plucknett, Haydon, Stalbridge Weston, Sherborne, Sherborne Castle and Gardens, Little Norton, Wigborough, Chiselborough, Brympton, Stourton Caundle, North Wootton, Allweston, West Coker, Bradford Abbas, Lydlinch, Bishop's Caundle, East Chinnock, West Chinnock, Barwick, Burton, Thornford, Folke, Caundle Marsh, Middle Chinnock, Hardington Moor, East Coker, Stoford, Lillington, Longburton, Holwell, Hardington Mandeville, Sutton Bingham, Beer Hackett, Knighton, Crouch Hill, Pleck, King's Stag, Haselbury Plucknett, Yetminster, Boys Hill, Ryme Intrinseca, Sandhills, Packers Hill, Crewkerne, Pendomer, Hardington Marsh, Closworth, Hamlet, Holnest, East Pulham, Hazelbury, North Perrott

45 · 32 · 15 · 16

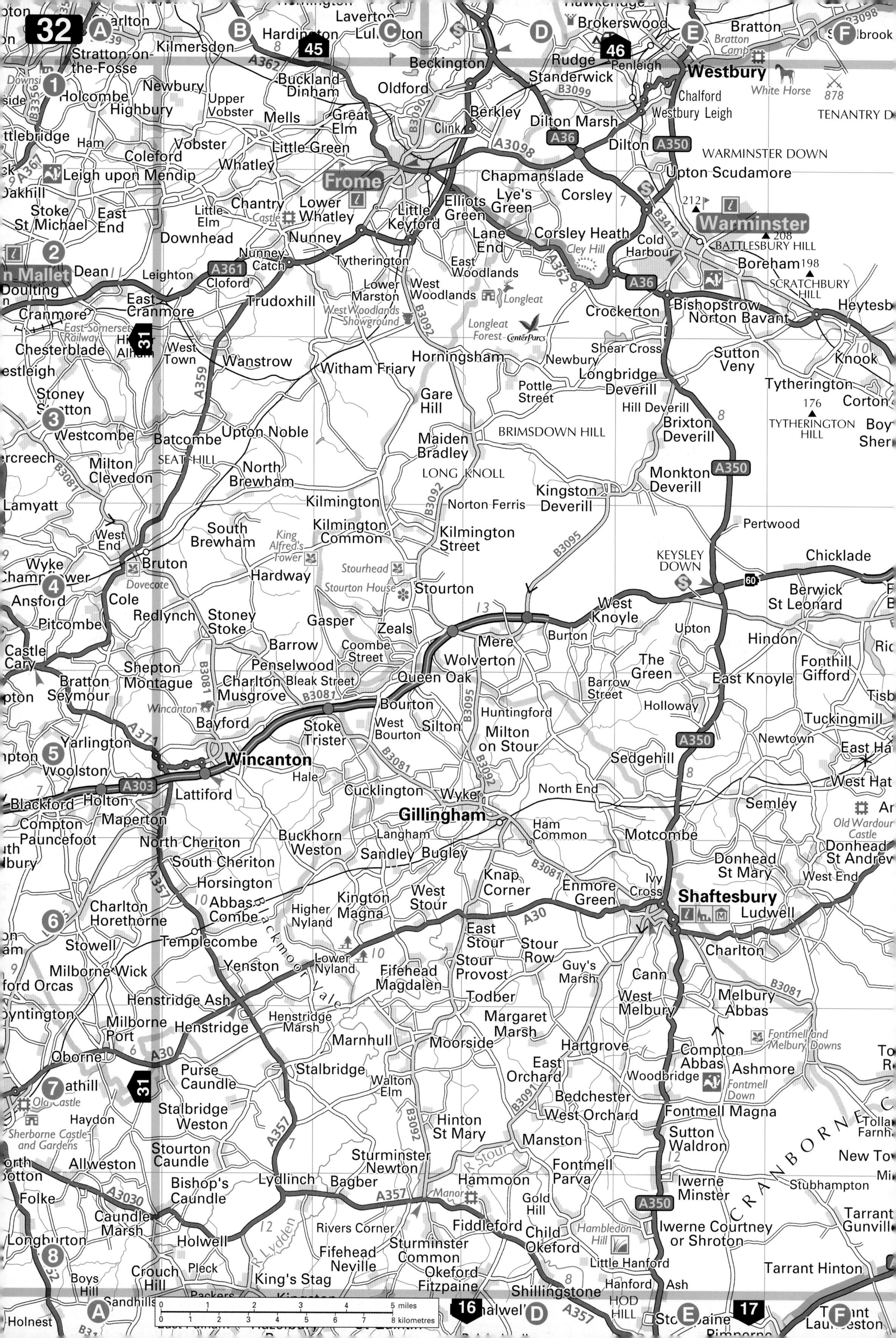
A
B
C
D
E
F
Kilmersdon
Hardington
Laverton
Lullington
Brokerswood
Bratton
Bratton Camp
45
46
Stratton-on-the-Fosse
A362
Beckington
Rudge
Penleigh
Westbury
White Horse
878
Holcombe
Newbury
Upper Vobster
Buckland Dinham
Oldford
Standerwick
B3099
Chalford
Westbury Leigh
TENANTRY D
Highbury
Mells
Great Elm
Berkley
Dilton Marsh
Ham
Vobster
Little Green
Clink
A36
Dilton
A350
Coleford
Whatley
A3098
WARMINSTER DOWN
Leigh upon Mendip
Frome
Chapmanslade
Upton Scudamore
Stoke St Michael
East End
Little Elm
Chantry
Castle
Lower Whatley
Little Keyford
Elliots Green
Lye's Green
Corsley
B3414
Warminster
Downhead
Nunney
Lane End
Corsley Heath
Cold Harbour
208
BATTLESBURY HILL
Dean
Nunney Catch
Tytherington
Cley Hill
A362
Boreham
198
Leighton
A361
Cloford
East Woodlands
Lower Marston
West Woodlands
Longleat
SCRATCHBURY HILL
Doulting
East Cranmore
Trudoxhill
West Woodlands Showground
B3092
Crockerton
Bishopstrow
Heytesb
Cranmore
East Somerset Railway
Longleat Forest
Center Parcs
Norton Bavant
31
Chesterblade
West Town
Wanstrow
Witham Friary
Horningsham
Shear Cross
Newbury
Sutton Veny
Knook
Stoney Stratton
A359
Gare Hill
Pottle Street
Longbridge Deverill
Tytherington
Corton
176
Westcombe
Batcombe
Upton Noble
Maiden Bradley
Hill Deverill
Brixton Deverill
BRIMSDOWN HILL
TYTHERINGTON HILL
SEAT HILL
North Brewham
LONG KNOLL
Milton Clevedon
B3081
Monkton Deverill
Kilmington
Norton Ferris
Kingston Deverill
Lamyatt
South Brewham
King Alfred's Tower
Kilmington Common
Kilmington Street
Pertwood
West End
B3095
Bruton
KEYSLEY DOWN
Chicklade
Wyke Champflower
Hardway
Stourhead
Dovecote
Stourton House
Stourton
60
Berwick St Leonard
Ansford
Cole
Redlynch
Stoney Stoke
Gasper
Zeals
West Knoyle
Pitcombe
Barrow
Coombe Street
Mere
Burton
Upton
Hindon
Castle Cary
Shepton Montague
Penselwood
Wolverton
The Green
Fonthill Gifford
Bratton Seymour
B3081
Charlton Musgrove
Bleak Street
Queen Oak
Barrow Street
East Knoyle
Wincanton
Bourton
Huntingford
Holloway
Tuckingmill
Bayford
Stoke Trister
West Bourton
Silton
Milton on Stour
A350
Newtown
A371
Yarlington
Wincanton
Sedgehill
Woolston
Hale
B3092
Lattiford
A303
Cucklington
Wyke
North End
Semley
Blackford
Holton
Gillingham
Ham Common
Old Wardour Castle
Compton Pauncefoot
Maperton
Buckhorn Weston
Langham
Motcombe
Donhead St Andrew
North Cheriton
Sandley
Bugley
Donhead St Mary
South Cheriton
A357
Horsington
Knap Corner
B3081
Enmore Green
Ivy Cross
West End
Shaftesbury
Charlton Horethorne
Abbas Combe
Blackmore Vale
Higher Nyland
Kington Magna
West Stour
A30
Ludwell
Stowell
Templecombe
East Stour
Stour Row
Charlton
Yenston
Lower Nyland
Fifehead Magdalen
Stour Provost
Guy's Marsh
Cann
Milborne Wick
B3081
Henstridge Ash
Todber
West Melbury
Melbury Abbas
Henstridge Marsh
Margaret Marsh
Milborne Port
Henstridge
Marnhull
Moorside
Hartgrove
Fontmell and Melbury Downs
Oborne
A30
Compton Abbas
Purse Caundle
Stalbridge
East Orchard
Ashmore
Walton Elm
Woodbridge
Fontmell Down
Old Castle
Haydon
Stalbridge Weston
B3091
Bedchester
West Orchard
Fontmell Magna
Sherborne Castle and Gardens
A357
B3092
Hinton St Mary
Sutton Waldron
Manston
CRANBORNE
Stourton Caundle
R Stour
Allweston
Sturminster Newton
Fontmell Parva
New To
Bishop's Caundle
Lydlinch
Bagber
Hammoon
Iwerne Minster
Stubhampton
A3030
A357
Manor
Gold Hill
A350
Tarrant Gunville
Caundle Marsh
Rivers Corner
Fiddleford
Child Okeford
Hambledon Hill
Iwerne Courtney or Shroton
R Lydden
Holwell
Fifehead Neville
Sturminster Common
Little Hanford
Longburton
Pleck
King's Stag
Okeford Fitzpaine
Tarrant Hinton
Boys Hill
Crouch Hill
Hanford
Ash
Shillingstone
Sandhills
0 1 2 3 4 5 miles
0 1 2 3 4 5 6 7 8 kilometres
16
HOD HILL
A357
17
Holnest

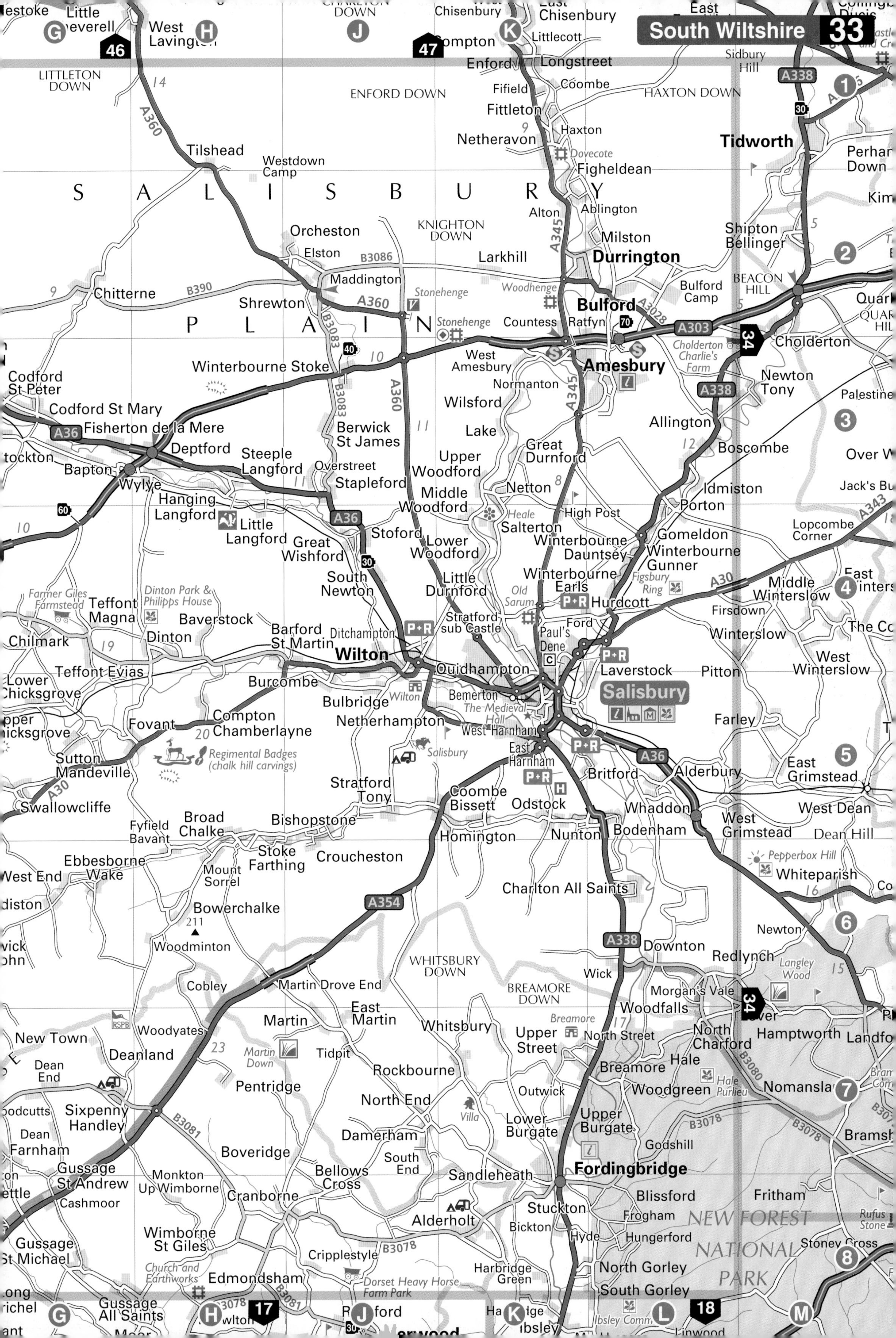

46
47
34
17
18
LITTLETON DOWN
ENFORD DOWN
HAXTON DOWN
West Lavington
Chisenbury
East Chisenbury
Littlecott
Enford
Longstreet
Coombe
Fifield
Fittleton
Haxton
Netheravon
Dovecote
Figheldean
Sidbury Hill
Tidworth
Perham Down
Tilshead
Westdown Camp
SALISBURY PLAIN
Alton
Ablington
Milston
Durrington
Orcheston
KNIGHTON DOWN
Elston
B3086
Larkhill
Shipton Bellinger
BEACON HILL
Bulford Camp
Maddington
Stonehenge
Woodhenge
Chitterne
B390
Shrewton
A360
Bulford
A3028
Ratfyn
Countess
A303
Cholderton
Cholderton Charlie's Farm
West Amesbury
Amesbury
B3083
Winterbourne Stoke
Codford St Peter
Codford St Mary
Normanton
A345
A338
Newton Tony
Palestine
Wilsford
A36
Fisherton de la Mere
Berwick St James
Lake
Allington
Deptford
Upper Woodford
Great Durnford
Boscombe
Over Wallop
Bapton
Steeple Langford
Overstreet
Stapleford
Wylye
Netton
Idmiston
Porton
Jack's Bush
Hanging Langford
Middle Woodford
Heale
High Post
Salterton
Little Langford
Stoford
Lower Woodford
Winterbourne Dauntsey
Gomeldon
Winterbourne Gunner
Lopcombe Corner
A343
Great Wishford
South Newton
Little Durnford
Winterbourne Earls
Figsbury Ring
A30
Middle Winterslow
East Winterslow
Farmer Giles Farmstead
Teffont Magna
Dinton Park & Philipps House
Old Sarum
Hurdcott
Firsdown
Baverstock
Stratford sub Castle
Ford
Paul's Dene
Winterslow
The Common
Chilmark
Dinton
Barford St Martin
Ditchampton
Wilton
Quidhampton
Laverstock
Pitton
West Winterslow
Teffont Evias
Lower Chicksgrove
Burcombe
Bemerton
Salisbury
Bulbridge
The Medieval Hall
Upper Chicksgrove
Fovant
Compton Chamberlayne
Netherhampton
West Harnham
Farley
Regimental Badges (chalk hill carvings)
East Harnham
Britford
Alderbury
East Grimstead
Sutton Mandeville
Swallowcliffe
Stratford Tony
Coombe Bissett
Odstock
Whaddon
West Dean
West Grimstead
Fyfield Bavant
Broad Chalke
Bishopstone
Homington
Nunton
Bodenham
Dean Hill
Ebbesborne Wake
Stoke Farthing
Croucheston
Pepperbox Hill
Whiteparish
West End
Mount Sorrel
Charlton All Saints
Bowerchalke
A354
Newton
Woodminton
Downton
Redlynch
Langley Wood
WHITSBURY DOWN
Wick
Cobley
Martin Drove End
BREAMORE DOWN
Morgan's Vale
Woodfalls
East Martin
Martin
Breamore
Upper Street
North Street
North Charford
Hamptworth
New Town
Woodyates
Whitsbury
Deanland
Martin Down
Tidpit
Breamore
Hale
B3080
Dean End
Rockbourne
Hale Purlieu
Pentridge
Woodgreen
Nomansland
Outwick
North End
Villa
Sixpenny Handley
B3081
Lower Burgate
Upper Burgate
B3078
Bramshaw
Dean
Damerham
Godshill
Farnham
Boveridge
Gussage St Andrew
South End
Bellows Cross
Sandleheath
Fordingbridge
Monkton Up Wimborne
Cranborne
Blissford
Fritham
Cashmoor
Stuckton
Frogham
NEW FOREST NATIONAL PARK
Alderholt
Bickton
Rufus Stone
Wimborne St Giles
Hyde
Hungerford
Stoney Cross
Gussage St Michael
Cripplestyle
Church and Earthworks
Harbridge Green
North Gorley
Edmondsham
Dorset Heavy Horse Farm Park
South Gorley
Gussage All Saints
Ibsley
Linwood

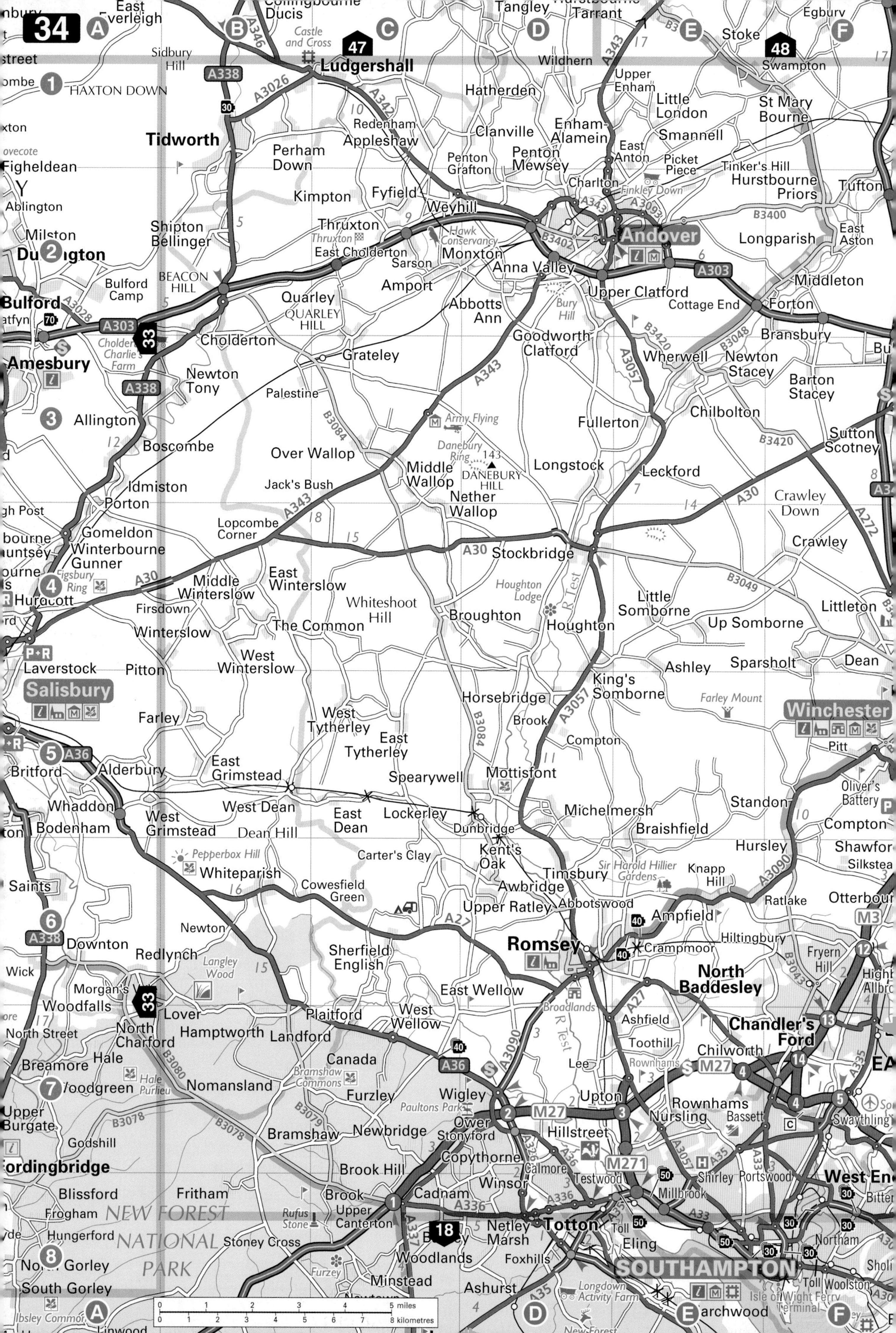
East Everleigh
Collingbourne Ducis
Castle and Cross
47
Ludgershall
Tangley
Tarrant
Wildhern
Egbury
Stoke
48
Swampton
Sidbury Hill
A338
A3026
A346
A342
HAXTON DOWN
Tidworth
Redenham
Appleshaw
Hatherden
Clanville
Enham-Alamein
Upper Enham
Little London
St Mary Bourne
Smannell
East Anton
Picket Piece
Tinker's Hill
Hurstbourne Priors
Tufton
Perham Down
Penton Grafton
Penton Mewsey
Charlton
Finkley Down
Figheldean
Ablington
Kimpton
Fyfield
Weyhill
Hawk Conservancy
Thruxton
East Cholderton
Sarson
Monxton
Anna Valley
Andover
B3400
Longparish
East Aston
Milston
Shipton Bellinger
Bulford Camp
BEACON HILL
Amport
Abbotts Ann
Upper Clatford
Cottage End
A303
Middleton
Forton
Bulford
Quarley
QUARLEY HILL
Bury Hill
Goodworth Clatford
Bransbury
Amesbury
Cholderton
Grateley
A343
Wherwell
Newton Stacey
Barton Stacey
A3057
B3420
B3048
Newton Tony
Palestine
B3084
Chilbolton
Allington
Army Flying
Fullerton
Sutton Scotney
Boscombe
Over Wallop
Danebury Ring
143
DANEBURY HILL
Middle Wallop
Nether Wallop
Longstock
Leckford
Idmiston
Porton
Jack's Bush
Crawley Down
A30
A272
Lopcombe Corner
Gomeldon
Winterbourne Gunner
Stockbridge
Crawley
Figsbury Ring
Middle Winterslow
East Winterslow
Whiteshoot Hill
Houghton Lodge
R Test
Little Somborne
B3049
Hurdcott
Firsdown
The Common
Broughton
Houghton
Up Somborne
Littleton
Winterslow
West Winterslow
Ashley
Sparsholt
Dean
Laverstock
Pitton
Salisbury
King's Somborne
Farley Mount
Winchester
Horsebridge
Brook
Farley
West Tytherley
East Tytherley
Compton
Pitt
A36
Britford
Alderbury
East Grimstead
Spearywell
Mottisfont
Oliver's Battery
Whaddon
West Dean
East Dean
Lockerley
Michelmersh
Standon
Bodenham
West Grimstead
Dean Hill
Dunbridge
Braishfield
Compton
Kent's Oak
Hursley
Shawford
Pepperbox Hill
Carter's Clay
Timsbury
Sir Harold Hillier Gardens
Knapp Hill
Silkstead
Saints
Whiteparish
Cowesfield Green
Awbridge
A3090
Ratlake
Otterbourne
Upper Ratley
Abbotswood
Ampfield
M3
A27
Newton
Hiltingbury
Downton
Redlynch
Sherfield English
Romsey
Crampmoor
Fryern Hill
Langley Wood
North Baddesley
Wick
Morgan's Vale
33
East Wellow
Woodfalls
Lover
Plaitford
West Wellow
Broadlands
Ashfield
Chandler's Ford
North Street
North Charford
Hamptworth
Landford
Toothill
Chilworth
Canada
Rownhams
M27
Breamore
Hale
Lee
Woodgreen
Hale Purlieu
Nomansland
Bramshaw Commons
Furzley
Wigley
Upton
Rownhams
Paultons Park
Upper Burgate
B3078
B3079
Ower
Nursling
Bassett
Swaythling
Hillstreet
Godshill
Bramshaw
Newbridge
Stonyford
Copythorne
A326
M271
A35
Fordingbridge
Brook Hill
Calmore
Testwood
Shirley
Portswood
West End
Blissford
Fritham
Brook
Winsor
Millbrook
Cadnam
A336
Frogham
NEW FOREST NATIONAL PARK
Rufus Stone
Upper Canterton
Netley Marsh
Totton
Toll
A33
Hungerford
Stoney Cross
A337
18
Eling
Northam
North Gorley
Woodlands
Foxhills
SOUTHAMPTON
Sholing
South Gorley
Furzey
Minstead
Ashurst
Longdown Activity Farm
Toll
Woolston
Isle of Wight Ferry Terminal
Ibsley Common
Linwood
Marchwood
0 1 2 3 4 5 miles
0 1 2 3 4 5 6 7 8 kilometres

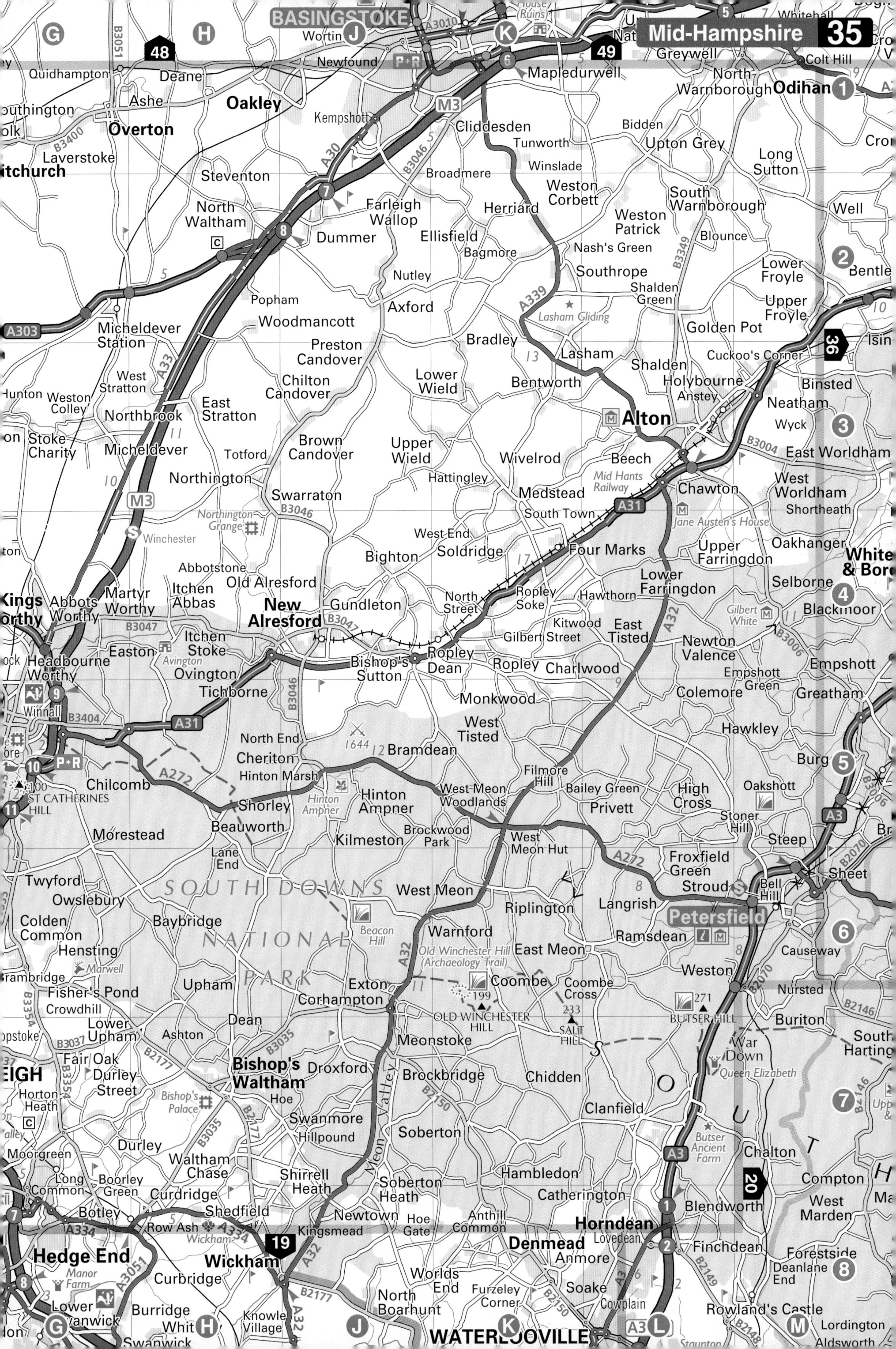
BASINGSTOKE
Wortin
Newfound
Quidhampton
Deane
Ashe
Oakley
Overton
Laverstoke
Whitchurch
Mapledurwell
Greywell
North Warnborough
Odiham
Colt Hill
Kempshott
Cliddesden
Tunworth
Bidden
Upton Grey
Long Sutton
Winslade
Broadmere
Steventon
North Waltham
Farleigh Wallop
Dummer
Herriard
Weston Corbett
South Warnborough
Weston Patrick
Well
Ellisfield
Bagmore
Nash's Green
Blounce
Southrope
Lower Froyle
Upper Froyle
Nutley
Popham
Axford
Shalden Green
Lasham Gliding
Golden Pot
Micheldever Station
Woodmancott
Preston Candover
Bradley
Lasham
Shalden
Cuckoo's Corner
Isington
West Stratton
Chilton Candover
Lower Wield
Bentworth
Holybourne
Anstey
Binsted
Neatham
Hunton
Weston Colley
Northbrook
East Stratton
Alton
Wyck
Stoke Charity
Micheldever
Totford
Brown Candover
Upper Wield
Wivelrod
Beech
East Worldham
West Worldham
Shortheath
Northington
Hattingley
Mid Hants Railway
Medstead
Chawton
Swarraton
Northington Grange
Winchester
South Town
Jane Austen's House
West End
Bighton
Soldridge
Four Marks
Upper Farringdon
Oakhanger
Abbotstone
Old Alresford
Lower Farringdon
Selborne
Kings Worthy
Abbots Worthy
Martyr Worthy
Itchen Abbas
New Alresford
Gundleton
North Street
Ropley Soke
Hawthorn
Gilbert White
Blackmoor
Headbourne Worthy
Easton
Itchen Stoke
Avington
Kitwood
East Tisted
Gilbert Street
Newton Valence
Ovington
Tichborne
Bishop's Sutton
Ropley Dean
Ropley
Charlwood
Empshott
Empshott Green
Colemore
Greatham
Winnall
Monkwood
West Tisted
Hawkley
North End
Bramdean
1644
Cheriton
Hinton Marsh
Burgate
Chilcomb
Filmore Hill
Bailey Green
Oakshott
ST CATHERINES HILL
West Meon Woodlands
Privett
High Cross
Shorley
Hinton Ampner
Beauworth
Brockwood Park
Stoner Hill
Morestead
Kilmeston
West Meon Hut
Steep
Lane End
Froxfield Green
Sheet
Twyford
SOUTH DOWNS
West Meon
Stroud
Bell Hill
Owslebury
Riplington
Langrish
Petersfield
Colden Common
Baybridge
NATIONAL
Beacon Hill
Warnford
Ramsdean
Hensting
Old Winchester Hill (Archaeology Trail)
East Meon
Causeway
Marwell
PARK
Weston
Brambridge
Fisher's Pond
Upham
Exton
Coombe
Coombe Cross
Nursted
Crowdhill
Corhampton
199
233
271
Lower Upham
Dean
OLD WINCHESTER HILL
SALT HILL
BUTSER HILL
Buriton
Ashton
South Harting
Meonstoke
War Down
Fair Oak
Queen Elizabeth
Durley Street
Bishop's Waltham
Droxford
Brockbridge
Chidden
Horton Heath
Hoe
EASTLEIGH
Bishop's Palace
Swanmore
Clanfield
Hillpound
Meon Valley
Soberton
Butser Ancient Farm
Durley
Moorgreen
Waltham Chase
Chalton
Long Common
Boorley Green
Shirrell Heath
Hambledon
Compton
Soberton Heath
Curdridge
Catherington
West Marden
Botley
Shedfield
Newtown
Blendworth
Anthill Common
Row Ash
Hoe Gate
Wickham
Kingsmead
Horndean
Lovedean
Finchdean
Hedge End
Denmead
Anmore
Forestside
Deanlane End
Manor Farm
Curbridge
Worlds End
Soake
Furzeley Corner
Cowplain
Rowland's Castle
Lower Swanwick
Burridge
Whiteley
Knowle Village
North Boarhunt
WATERLOOVILLE
Lordington
Aldsworth
Swanwick
M3
A30
A303
A33
A339
A31
A32
A272
A3
A334
A3051
B3051
B3400
B3046
B3349
B3047
B3404
B3004
B3006
B2070
B2146
B2177
B2150
B2149
B2148
B3035
B3037
B3354
48
49
36
20
19
G
H
J
K
L
M
1
2
3
4
5
6
7
8

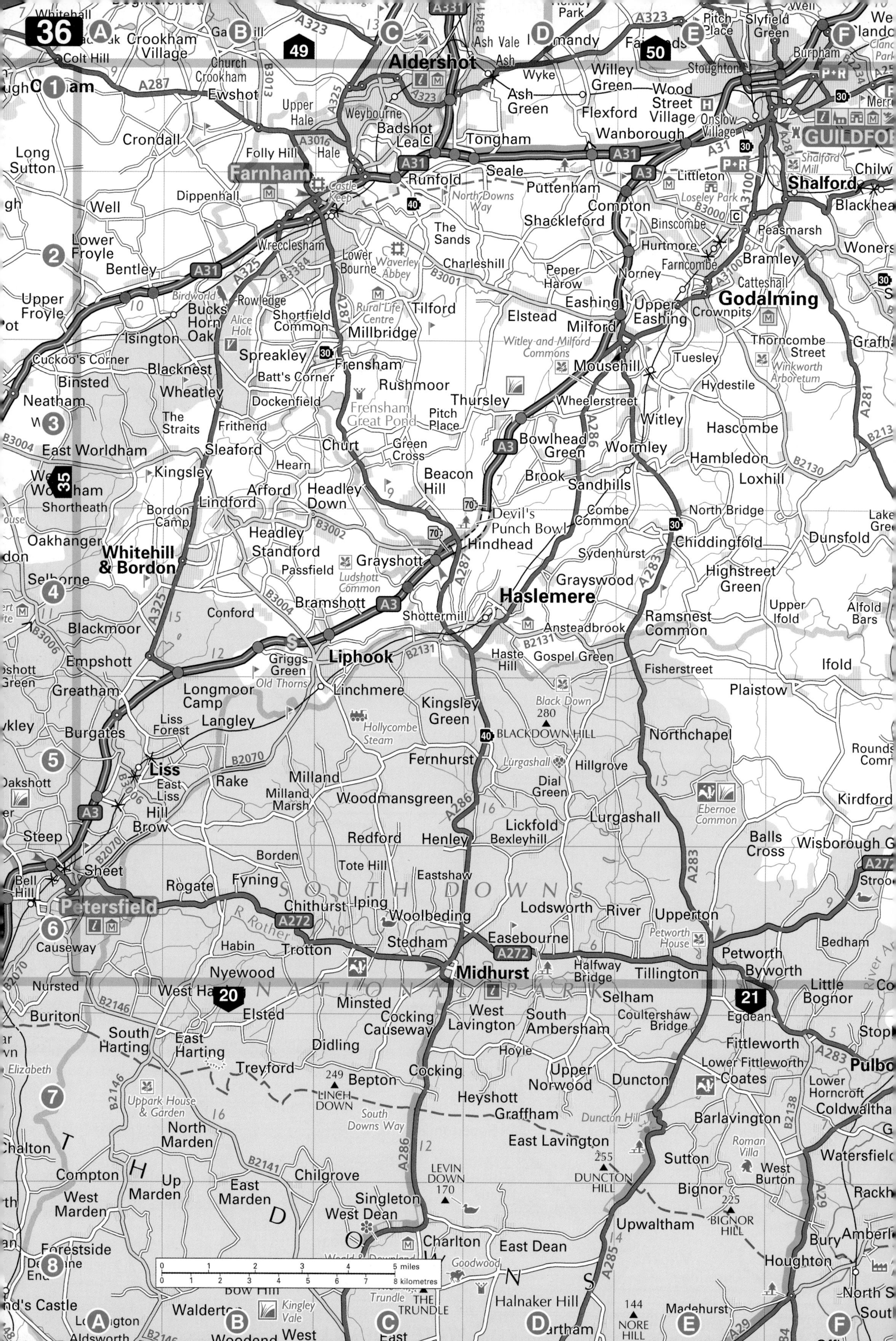
A
B
C
D
E
F
1
2
3
4
5
6
7
8
49
50
35
20
21
Crookham Village
Church Crookham
Ewshot
A287
B3013
A323
A325
Aldershot
Ash Vale
Ash
Wyke
Ash Green
Willey Green
Wood Street Village
Flexford
Wanborough
Pitch Place
Slyfield Green
Burpham
Stoughton
Onslow Village
GUILDFORD
Colt Hill
Upper Hale
Weybourne
Badshot Lea
Tongham
Crondall
Long Sutton
Folly Hill
Hale
A3016
A31
Farnham
Castle Keep
Runfold
Seale
Puttenham
North Downs Way
Compton
Littleton
Loseley Park
B3000
Shalford
Shalford Mill
Chilworth
Blackheath
Dippenhall
Well
Lower Froyle
Bentley
Wrecclesham
Lower Bourne
Waverley Abbey
The Sands
Charleshill
Shackleford
Binscombe
Hurtmore
Farncombe
Peasmarsh
Bramley
Wonersh
Peper Harow
Norney
Catteshall
Godalming
B3001
Upper Froyle
Isington
Birdworld
Alice Holt
Rowledge
Bucks Horn Oak
Shortfield Common
Rural Life Centre
Tilford
Millbridge
Elstead
Eashing
Upper Eashing
Milford
Crownpits
Thorncombe Street
Witley and Milford Commons
Mousehill
Tuesley
Winkworth Arboretum
Cuckoo's Corner
Spreakley
Batt's Corner
Frensham
Binsted
Blacknest
Wheatley
Neatham
Rushmoor
Hydestile
Thursley
Dockenfield
Frensham Great Pond
Pitch Place
Wheelerstreet
Witley
Hascombe
The Straits
Frithend
Churt
Green Cross
Bowlhead Green
Wormley
Hambledon
East Worldham
B3004
Sleaford
Hearn
Kingsley
Beacon Hill
Brook
Sandhills
Loxhill
B2130
Shortheath
Lindford
Arford
Headley Down
Bordon Camp
Devil's Punch Bowl
Combe Common
North Bridge
Oakhanger
Headley
B3002
Hindhead
Dunsfold
Whitehill & Bordon
Standford
Grayshott
Sydenhurst
Chiddingfold
Passfield
Ludshott Common
Highstreet Green
Selborne
Grayswood
A283
A286
Haslemere
Bramshott
A3
Conford
Shottermill
Upper Ifold
Alfold Bars
Ansteadbrook
Ramsnest Common
Blackmoor
B3006
Liphook
B2131
Haste Hill
Gospel Green
Fisherstreet
Ifold
Empshott
Griggs Green
Old Thorns
Greatham
Longmoor Camp
Linchmere
Plaistow
Black Down
280
Kingsley Green
Liss Forest
Langley
Burgates
Hollycombe Steam
BLACKDOWN HILL
Northchapel
Liss
B2070
Fernhurst
Lurgashall
Hillgrove
Rounds Common
East Liss
Rake
Milland
Dial Green
Oakshott
Milland Marsh
Woodmansgreen
Ebernoe Common
Kirdford
Hill Brow
Lickfold
Lurgashall
Steep
Redford
Henley
Bexleyhill
Balls Cross
Wisborough Green
Borden
Tote Hill
Eastshaw
Sheet
Bell Hill
Rogate
Fyning
SOUTH DOWNS
Petersfield
Chithurst
Iping
Lodsworth
River
Upperton
A272
R Rother
Woolbeding
Petworth House
Bedham
Causeway
Habin
Trotton
Stedham
Easebourne
Petworth
Nyewood
Midhurst
Halfway Bridge
Tillington
Byworth
Nursted
West Harting
NATIONAL PARK
Selham
Little Bognor
B2146
Minsted
West Lavington
Cocking Causeway
South Ambersham
Coultershaw Bridge
Egdean
Buriton
South Harting
East Harting
Didling
Hoyle
Fittleworth
A283
Stopham
Pulborough
Lower Fittleworth
Coates
Treyford
249
Bepton
Cocking
Upper Norwood
Duncton
Lower Horncroft
Uppark House & Garden
LINCH DOWN
South Downs Way
Heyshott
Graffham
Duncton Hill
Barlavington
Coldwaltham
B2138
North Marden
East Lavington
Chalton
Roman Villa
Sutton
Watersfield
Compton
Up Marden
B2141
Chilgrove
LEVIN DOWN
255
DUNCTON HILL
West Burton
East Marden
Singleton
170
Bignor
225
Rackham
West Marden
West Dean
BIGNOR HILL
Upwaltham
A29
Forestside
Charlton
East Dean
Bury
Amberley
Houghton
Goodwood
A285
miles
kilometres
Trundle
THE TRUNDLE
Halnaker Hill
144
NORE HILL
Madehurst
North Stoke
South Stoke
Kingley Vale
Walderton
Woodend
West
East
Aldsworth
Lordington
Boxgrove
Eartham

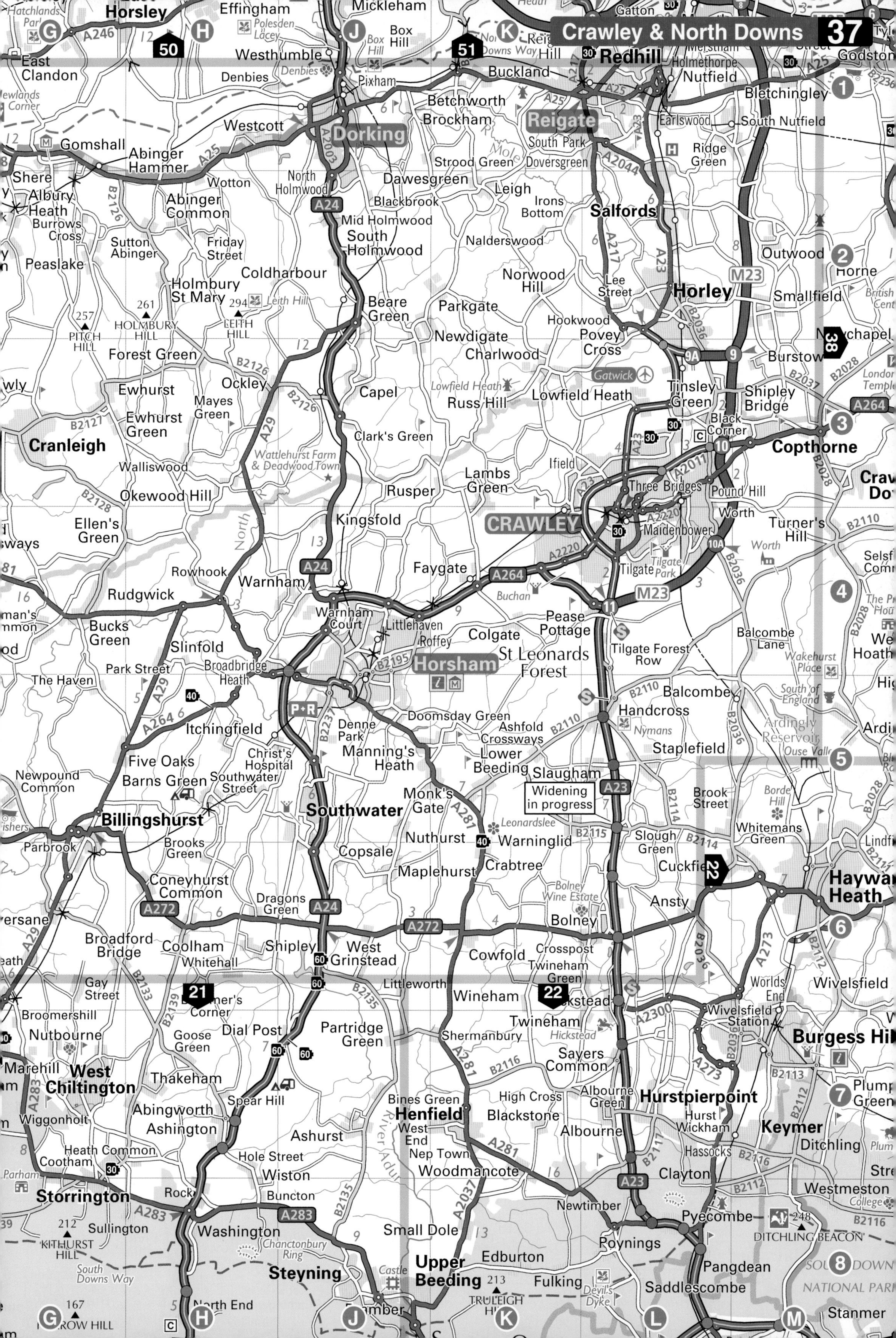

Crawley & North Downs
37
Horsley
Effingham
Mickleham
Gatton
Polesden Lacey
Box Hill
Reigate Hill
Redhill
Godstone
East Clandon
Westhumble
Denbies
Pixham
Buckland
Nutfield
Bletchingley
Betchworth
Brockham
Reigate
Earlswood
South Nutfield
Gomshall
Westcott
Dorking
South Park
Ridge Green
Abinger Hammer
Shere
Albury Heath
Wotton
North Holmwood
Strood Green
Doversgreen
Dawesgreen
Leigh
Abinger Common
Blackbrook
Irons Bottom
Salfords
Burrows Cross
Mid Holmwood
South Holmwood
Nalderswood
Sutton Abinger
Friday Street
Outwood
Horne
Peaslake
Coldharbour
Norwood Hill
Lee Street
Holmbury St Mary
Leith Hill
Horley
Smallfield
Beare Green
Parkgate
Hookwood
Povey Cross
Newdigate
Charlwood
Burstow
Forest Green
Gatwick
Ockley
Ewhurst
Capel
Lowfield Heath
Russ Hill
Tinsley Green
Shipley Bridge
Mayes Green
Ewhurst Green
Clark's Green
Black Corner
Copthorne
Cranleigh
Wattlehurst Farm & Deadwood Town
Walliswood
Lambs Green
Ifield
Three Bridges
Pound Hill
Okewood Hill
Rusper
Kingsfold
CRAWLEY
Worth
Turner's Hill
Ellen's Green
Maidenbower
Tilgate
Tilgate Park
Rowhook
Warnham
Faygate
Buchan
Rudgwick
Bucks Green
Warnham Court
Littlehaven
Roffey
Colgate
Pease Pottage
Slinfold
St Leonards Forest
Tilgate Forest Row
Balcombe Lane
Wakehurst Place
Park Street
Broadbridge Heath
Horsham
The Haven
Balcombe
Handcross
Nymans
Itchingfield
Denne Park
Doomsday Green
Ashfold Crossways
Christ's Hospital
Manning's Heath
Lower Beeding
Staplefield
Five Oaks
Barns Green
Southwater Street
Slaugham
Newpound Common
Widening in progress
Monk's Gate
Brook Street
Billingshurst
Southwater
Leonardslee
Nuthurst
Warninglid
Whitemans Green
Parbrook
Brooks Green
Slough Green
Copsale
Crabtree
Cuckfield
Maplehurst
Coneyhurst Common
Bolney Wine Estate
Haywards Heath
Dragons Green
Ansty
Bolney
Broadford Bridge
Coolham
Shipley
West Grinstead
Cowfold
Crosspost
Twineham Green
Whitehall
Gay Street
Littleworth
Wineham
Hickstead
Wivelsfield
Worlds End
Wivelsfield Station
Broomershill
Dial Post
Partridge Green
Twineham
Nutbourne
Goose Green
Shermanbury
Burgess Hill
Marehill
West Chiltington
Thakeham
Sayers Common
Spear Hill
Bines Green
High Cross
Albourne Green
Hurstpierpoint
Wiggonholt
Abingworth
Henfield
Blackstone
Hurst Wickham
Keymer
Ashington
Ashurst
West End
Albourne
Ditchling
Heath Common
Cootham
Hole Street
Nep Town
Hassocks
Wiston
Woodmancote
Clayton
Parham
Storrington
Rock
Buncton
Westmeston
Newtimber
Pyecombe
Sullington
Washington
Small Dole
DITCHLING BEACON
Kithurst Hill
Chanctonbury Ring
Poynings
Edburton
South Downs Way
Steyning
Upper Beeding
Pangdean
Fulking
Devil's Dyke
Saddlescombe
South Downs National Park
Truleigh Hill
North End
Bramber
Stanmer

38
A
B
C
D
E
F
Croydon
Addington
New Addington
Keston
Locksbottom
Farnborough
Chelsfield
Lullingstone Roman Villa
Parkgate
Eynsford
Eynsford Castle
Brands Hatch
West Yoke
New Ash Green
Ash
Purley
Selsdon
Nash
Farthing Street
Green Street Green
Maplescombe
West Kingsdown
Lullingstone
Preston Hill
Pratt's Bottom
Badgers Mount
Hutchinson's Bank
Leaves Green
Down House
Downe
Romney Street
Stansted
Fairseat
Sanderstead
Farleigh
Fickleshole
Biggin Hill
Cudham
Halstead
Shoreham
Knockmill
Kenley
Single Street
Lett's Green
M25
Otford
Woodlands
Hamsey Green
Biggin Hill
Berry's Green
Knockholt Pound
Crowdleham
Wrotham
Whyteleafe
Chelsham
Aperfield
Kemsing
Heaverham
Warlingham
Horn's Green
Knockholt
52
M26
Borough Green
Tatsfield
North Downs Way
Chevening
Dunton Green
Sevenoaks
Noah's Ark
Seal
Fuller Street
Ightham
Longford
Chipstead
St Johns
Oldbury
Riverhead
A25
Woldingham
B2024
Brasted
Westerham
Stone Street
Basted
Caterham
Titsey
Sundridge
Knole
Bitchet Green
Ivy Hatch
Old Soar Manor
Clacket Lane
51
Brasted Chart
Limpsfield
Hosey Hill
Whitley Row
Sevenoaks
Plaxtol
Ightham Mote
Dunk's Green
M25
Moorhouse Bank
French Street
A21
Brewer Street
Tylers Green
Under River
Shipbourne
Oxted
Emmetts Garden
Godstone
51
Hurst Green
Limpsfield Chart
Toy's Hill
Ide Hill
Goathurst Common
Bayley's Hill
Four
Chartwell
Oakhurst
Pitt's Wood
Bletchingley
Tandridge
Crockham Hill
Cooper's Corner
Sevenoaks Weald
Fletcher Green
South Nutfield
Pooting's
Mapleton
Winkhurst Green
Hildenborough
Parkers Green
South Godstone
Marlpit Hill
Four Elms
Hilden Park
Higham
Crowhurst Lane End
Crowhurst
Chiddingstone Causeway
Crough House Green
Leigh
Tonbridge
Haysden
Blindley Heath
Edenbridge
Bough Beech
Penshurst Station
Barden Park
Outwood
Haxted Mill
Haxted
Haysden
R Eden
Hever
Chiddingstone
Horne
Marsh Green
Lingfield
Penshurst Place
Croch
Smallfield
British Wildlife Centre
Penshurst
Bidborough
A26
A21
Markbeech
Cowden Pound
Stockland Green
Newchapel
Lingfield Park
Dormans Land
Smart's Hill
Southborough
Felcourt
Cowden Station
Burstow
Poundsbridge
Speldhurst
High Brooms
London Temple
Dormans Park
Cowden
Fordcombe
Shipley Bridge
Felbridge
Walters Green
Lower Green
Langton Green
A264
Baldwin's Hill
Ashurst
Rusthall
Copthorne
Hammerwood
Holtye
Stone Cross
Royal Tunbridge Wells
East Grinstead
Crawley Down
Groombridge Place
Spa Valley Railway
37
Ashurstwood
Balls Green
Groombridge
A26
Turner's Hill
Saint Hill Manor
Hartfield
Eridge Green
Park Corner
Forest Row
Gallypot Street
Bells Yew Green
Saint Hill
Standen
Frant
Worth
Selsfield Common
Upper Hartfield
Withyham
Eridge Station
B2110
Weirwood Reservoir
Highgate
Chuck Hatch
Lye Green
Danegate
Saxonbury Hill
The Priest House
Coleman's Hatch
Friar's Gate
Bowles Outdoor Centre
Boarshead
West Hoathly
Sharpthorne
Jumper's Town
Mardens Hill
Mark Cross
Wych Cross
Crowborough Town
Balcombe Lane
Wakehurst Place
Steel Cross
Highbrook
Ashdown Forest
Beacon Hill
Town Row
South of England
Birchgrove
Chelwood Gate
Crowborough
Tidebrook
Ardingly
Ardingly Reservoir
Horsted Keynes
Marlpits
Poundgate
Jarvis Brook
Rotherfield
Ouse Valley
Chelwood Common
Duddleswell
Sweethaws
Stone Cross
Coggin's Mill
Bluebell Railway
22
23
Danehill
Nutley
Cackle Street
A26
Burnt Oak
Argos Hill
Borde Hill
Fairwarp
Furner's Green
Horney Common
High Hurstwood
Butcher's Cross
Mayfield
Whitemans Green
Lindfield
Sheffield Green
Five Ash Down
Hadlow Down
River Rother
Maresfield
Pound Green
Five Ashes
Haywards Heath
Buxted
A272
Street End
Scaynes Hill
Fletching
Uckfield
Coopers Green
Potter's Green
Etchingwood
Broad Oak
A272
Grisling Common
Piltdown
Ringles Cross
Pounsley
Cross in Hand
Heathfield
0 1 2 3 4 5 miles
0 1 2 3 4 5 6 7 8 kilometres

Snodland
Aylesford
Ditton
MAIDSTONE
Bearsted
Coxheath
East Peckham
Paddock Wood
Marden
Staplehurst
Headcorn
Cranbrook
Tenterden
Wadhurst
Hawkhurst
Lamberhurst
Goudhurst
Sissinghurst
Biddenden
Hollingbourne
Harrietsham
Lenham
West Malling
Wateringbury
Mereworth
Yalding
Teston
Loose
Boughton Monchelsea
Sutton Valence
Frittenden
Rolvenden
Northiam
Robertsbridge
Bodiam
Wittersham
Smarden
Egerton
Ticehurst
Burwash
Etchingham
Flimwell
Horsmonden
Brenchley
Matfield
Sandhurst
Newenden
Benenden

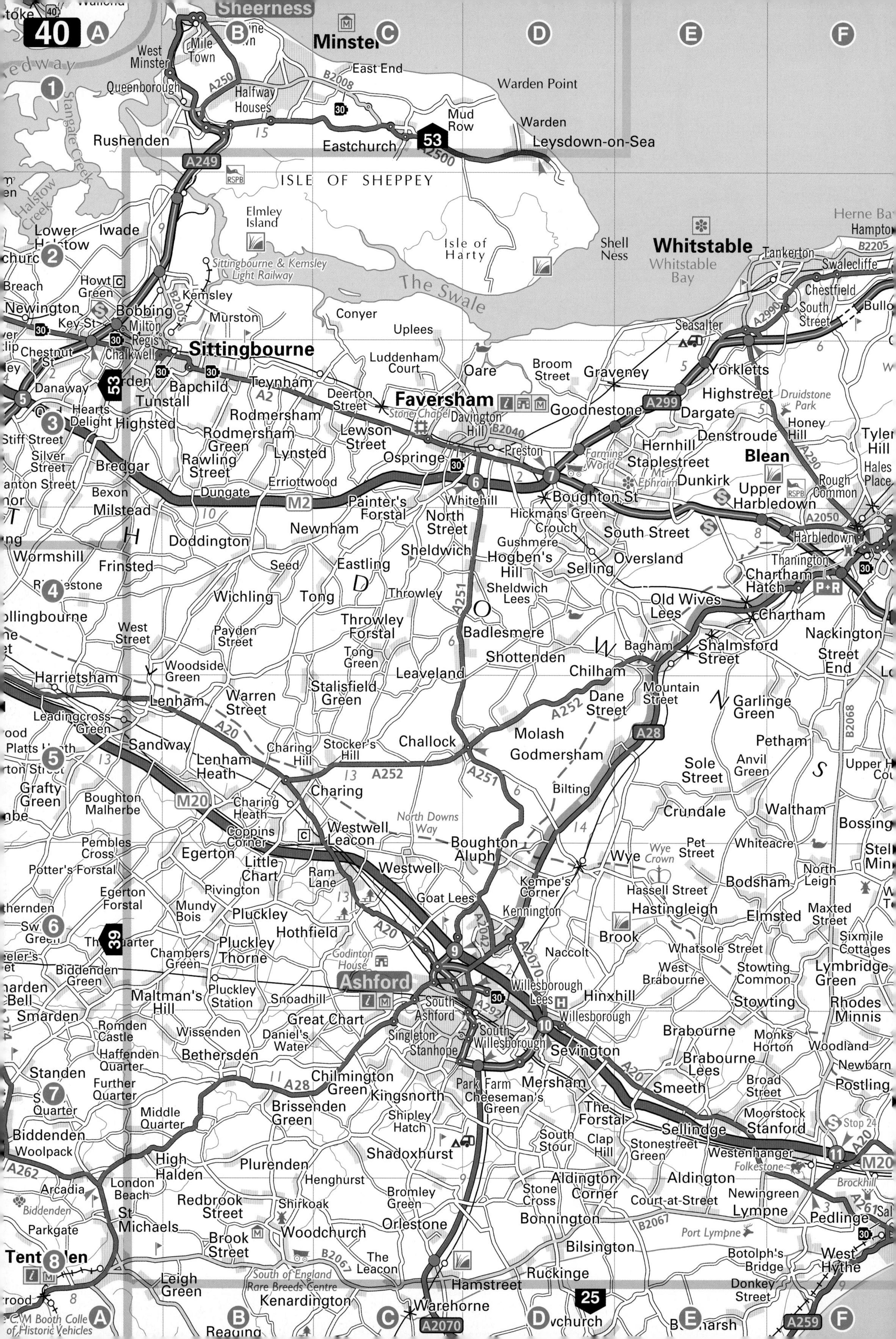

40
A
B
C
D
E
F
Sheerness
Minster
West Minster
Mile Town
Queenborough
A250
Halfway Houses
East End
B2008
Warden Point
Mud Row
Warden
53
Leysdown-on-Sea
Eastchurch
A2500
Rushenden
A249
ISLE OF SHEPPEY
Elmley Island
Isle of Harty
Shell Ness
Whitstable
Whitstable Bay
Herne Bay
Tankerton
B2205
Swalecliffe
Chestfield
South Street
Sittingbourne & Kemsley Light Railway
The Swale
Lower Halstow
Iwade
Howt Green
Kemsley
Murston
Bobbing
Newington
Key St
Milton Regis
Chalkwell
Sittingbourne
Conyer
Uplees
Seasalter
Yorkletts
Luddenham Court
Oare
Broom Street
Graveney
Teynham
Bapchild
Tunstall
Danaway
Hearts Delight
Highsted
Rodmersham
Deerton Street
Faversham
Stone Chapel
Davington Hill
Goodnestone
A299
Highstreet
Druidstone Park
Dargate
Rodmersham Green
Lewson Street
B2040
Preston
Hernhill
Denstroude
Honey Hill
Tyler Hill
Rawling Street
Lynsted
Ospringe
Farming World
Staplestreet
Mt Ephraim
Blean
Hales Place
Stiff Street
Silver Street
Bredgar
Erriottwood
Dunkirk
Rough Common
Upper Harbledown
Bexon
Dungate
M2
Painter's Forstal
Whitehill
Boughton St
Hickmans Green
A2050
Harbledown
Milstead
North Street
Crouch
South Street
Doddington
Newnham
Gushmere
Wormshill
Frinsted
Seed
Eastling
Sheldwich
Hogben's Hill
Selling
Oversland
Thanington
Chartham Hatch
Wichling
Tong
Throwley
Sheldwich Lees
Old Wives Lees
Chartham
West Street
Payden Street
Throwley Forstal
Badlesmere
Nackington
Bagham
Shalmsford Street
Street End
Harrietsham
Woodside Green
Tong Green
Leaveland
Shottenden
Chilham
Mountain Street
Lenham
Warren Street
Stalisfield Green
Dane Street
Garlinge Green
Leadingcross Green
Sandway
A20
A252
A28
Molash
B2068
Platts Heath
Lenham Heath
Charing Hill
Stocker's Hill
Challock
Godmersham
Petham
Upper Hardres Court
Sole Street
Anvil Green
Grafty Green
Boughton Malherbe
M20
Charing Heath
Charing
A251
Bilting
Crundale
Waltham
Bossingham
North Downs Way
Coppins Corner
Westwell Leacon
Pembles Cross
Egerton
Boughton Aluph
Wye
Wye Crown
Pet Street
Whiteacre
Stelling Minnis
Potter's Forstal
Little Chart
Ram Lane
Westwell
Kempe's Corner
Bodsham
North Leigh
Pivington
Hassell Street
Egerton Forstal
Mundy Bois
Pluckley
Goat Lees
Kennington
Hastingleigh
Elmsted
Maxted Street
Hothfield
Brook
Pluckley Thorne
Naccolt
Whatsole Street
Sixmile Cottages
Chambers Green
Godinton House
A2042
A2070
Stowting Common
Lymbridge Green
Biddenden Green
West Brabourne
Ashford
Willesborough Lees
Hinxhill
Maltman's Hill
Pluckley Station
Snoadhill
South Ashford
Stowting
Rhodes Minnis
Smarden
Willesborough
Romden Castle
Great Chart
A292
South Willesborough
Brabourne
Monks Horton
Woodland
Wissenden
Daniel's Water
Singleton
Stanhope
Sevington
Haffenden Quarter
Bethersden
Brabourne Lees
Newbarn
Standen
Further Quarter
Chilmington Green
Park Farm
Mersham
Smeeth
Broad Street
Postling
Kingsnorth
Cheeseman's Green
Middle Quarter
Brissenden Green
The Forstal
Moorstock
Shipley Hatch
Stanford
Stop 24
Biddenden
Sellindge
South Stour
Clap Hill
Stonestreet Green
Woolpack
High Halden
Shadoxhurst
Westenhanger
Folkestone
A262
Plurenden
Aldington Corner
Aldington
Brockhill
Arcadia
London Beach
Henghurst
Stone Cross
Newingreen
A261
Redbrook Street
Bromley Green
Court-at-Street
Lympne
Pedlinge
Parkgate
St Michaels
Shirkoak
Bonnington
B2067
Woodchurch
Orlestone
Port Lympne
Brook Street
Bilsington
Botolph's Bridge
West Hythe
Tenterden
The Leacon
Ruckinge
Leigh Green
South of England Rare Breeds Centre
Hamstreet
Donkey Street
25
Kenardington
Warehorne
C M Booth Collection of Historic Vehicles
Reading
A2070
A259
39

MARGATE
Foreness Point
Westgate on Sea
Westbrook
Cliftonville
Kingsgate
NORTH FORELAND
Northdown
Reading Street
Lighthouse
Minnis Bay
Herne Bay
Reculver Towers & Roman Fort
Reculver
Bishopstone
Hillborough
Beltinge
Eddington
Broomfield
Herne
Highstead
Potten Street
Brooks End
Birchington
Garlinge
Hornby
Westwood
St Peter's
Broadstairs
ISLE OF THANET
Lydden
Acol
RAF Manston
Haine
Manston
Dumpton
Hereson
Kent International
St Nicholas at Wade
Boyden Gate
Maypole
Sarre
Monkton
Way
Durlock
St Lawrence
Ramsgate
Chislet
Gore Street
Hoo
Cliffsend
Hoath
Hicks Forstal
Upstreet
West Stourmouth
Plucks Gutter
Minster
St Augustine's Cross
Viking Ship 'Hugin'
Pegwell
Pegwell Bay
Oostende
Hersden
Grove
R Stour
East Stourmouth
Westmarsh
Preston Street
Paramour Street
Goldstone
Richborough Roman Fort
Westbere
Elmstone
Preston
Stodmarsh
Cop Street
Cooper Street
Sandwich Bay
Town Hall
Walmestone
Hoaden
Weddington
Great Stonar
Fordwich
Wickhambreaux
Littlebourne
Wingham
Shatterling
Ash
Sandwich
Canterbury
Seaton
Ickham
Royal St Georges
Durlock
Guilton
Wingham
Marshborough
Stone Cross
Toll
Howletts
Bekesbourne Hill
Bramling
Twitham
Staple
Barnsole
Woodnesborough
Statenborough
Worth
Bekesbourne
Goodnestone
Eastry
Patrixbourne
Heronden
Ham
Hacklinge
Adisham
Ratling
Chillenden
West Street
Finglesham
Knowlton
The Downs
Bishopsbourne
Aylesham
Nonington
Marley
Sholden
North Downs Way
Easole Street
Betteshanger
Northbourne
Deal
Out Elmstead
Kingston
Womenswold
Holt St
Tilmanstone
Great Mongeham
Upper Deal
Plant Centre
Frogham
Elvington
Little Mongeham
Ripple
Marley
Barham
Lower Eythorne
Walmer
Castle
Woolage Village
Barfrestone
Sutton
Derringstone
Woolage Green
Eythorne
East Studdal
Ringwould
East Kent Railway
Shepherdswell
Ashley
Sutton Downs
Kingsdown
Breach
Bladbean
North Downs Way
West Langdon
Martin
Lydden Hill
Coldred
Denton
Lydden
East Langdon
Wingmore
Wootton
Whitfield
St Margaret's at Cliffe
Selsted
Temple Ewell
Guston
St Margaret's Bay
North Elham
Ewell Minnis
Kearsney
West Cliffe
The Pines
Swingfield Minnis
Chilton
River
SOUTH FORELAND
Lighthouse
South Foreland Heritage Coast
Swingfield Street
World of Butterflies
Wolverton
Buckland
Castle
The White Cliffs of Dover
Ridge Row
Densole
Alkham
St Radigunds
Maxton
South Alkham
Upper Standen
Hawkinge
Drellingore
West Hougham
Dunkerque
Calais
Lower Standen
Farthingloe
DOVER
Channel Tunnel Terminal
Battle of Britain
Capel-le-Ferne
Satmar
Peene
Samphire Hoe
Dover - Folkestone Heritage Coast
Channel Tunnel (Rail)
Cheriton
Morehall
East Wear Bay
Horn Street
Sandgate
FOLKESTONE
Seabrook
Hythe
A299
A28
A253
A291
A256
A257
A258
A2
A260
A20
A259
A254
A255
B2051
B2052
B2048
B2190
B2046
B2011
5 miles
8 kilometres

A
B
C
D
E
F
Godre'r-graig
Ynysmeudwy
Hir Fynydd
Glas
Pont Walby
Rhigos
Hirwaun
Penywaun
A465
Tre-Gibbon
Llwydcoed
Aber-nant
Llangiwg
Cilybebyll
Gellinudd
Crynant
Mynydd March Hywel
Blaengwrach
Cwmgwrach
B4242
A4059
Cwmdare
Trecynon
Aberdare
(Aberdâr)
Rhos
Abergarwed
Vale of Neath
River Neath
383
RESOLVEN MOUNTAIN
600
CRAIG-Y-LLYN
A4061
Fforest Gôch
A474
River Dulais
Resolven
Melin Cwrt Waterfalls
Melincourt
B4434
Mynydd Ystradffernol
Aberaman
Cilfrew
Cadoxton Juxta-Neath
Clyne
493
MOEL-YR-HYRDDAD
Blaenrhondda
Cwmaman
Tin Works and Waterfall
Aberdulais
Blaen-y-cwm
Tynewydd
Abercwmboi
A4233
Tonna
Cefn Mawr
Glyncorrwg
60
Treherbert
Maerdy
Neath
(Castell-nedd)
Cefn Morfydd
Afan Forest Park
Ynyswen
478
Blaenllechau
Skewen
A465
Abercregan
Blaengwynfi
Rhondda Valley
Treorchy
Ferndale
Cimla
B4287
Tonmawr
Cymer
A4107
Abergwynfi
Cwmparc
Pentre
Ystrad
Cynonville
Duffryn
Croeserw
571
WERFA
Gelli
Tylorstown
Pontygwaith
Briton Ferry
Efail-fach
Pont-rhyd-y-fen
Afan Forest Park
Foel y Dyffryn
Caerau
556
MYNYDD CAERAU
B4223
A4119
FOEL MYNYDDAU
A4107
371
MOEL TRAWSNANT
Dyffryn
Nant-y-moel
Clydach Vale
Llwynypia
Trealaw
Brynbryddan
371
Pwll-y-glaw
Rock
Wyndham
Mynydd Llangeinwyr
Price Town
B4278
Baglan
B4282
Nantyffyllon
Blaengarw
A48
B4286
Cwmafan
Bryn
Maesteg
Pontycymer
Tonypandy
Dinas
A4058
Penygraig
Glanllynfi
Pant-y-gog
A4061
Williamstown
Trebanog
Aberavon
A4241
57
Garth
A4064
Ogmore Vale
Gilfach Goch
B4564
B4278
Cwmfelin
Mynydd Margam
Port Talbot
Pont Rhyd-y-cyff
Pont-yr-Rhyl
Bryn Golau
Taibach
Llangynwyd
Llangeinor
A4093
Lewistown
A4093
Ty'n-y-bryn
Rhiwinder
Stones Museum
321
MOEL TON-MAWR
Betws
Margam
A4063
A4064
Blackmill
A4241
Margam
Bryngarw
Coytrahen
Brynmenyn
A4061
Mynydd Maendy
B4283
A48
Tondu
Abergarw
Heol-y-Cyw
M4
Water Street
Cefn Cribwr
Aberkenfig
Sarn
Bryncethin
Brynna Woods
Ynysmaerdy
Afon Kenfig
Pant-ffrwyth
Brynna
Llanharan
Sarn Park
B4280
Talbot Green
Pyle
Kenfig Hill
B4281
Cefn Cross
Pen-y-fai
Litchard
Castle
Pendre
Pencoed
Mawdlam
North Cornelly
Bridgend
Hendre
A473
Llanilid
Bryncae
Pontyclun
Kenfig
(Pen-y-Bont-ar-Ogwr)
Coity
Llanharry
Brynsadler
South Cornelly
Laleston
A4061
B4181
M4
A4229
NEWTON DOWN
A473
Old Castle
A473
Coychurch
A4222
Rest Bay
Nottage
A4106
Tythegston
A48
Priory
St Mary Hill
City
Ystradowen
Merthyr Mawr
Treoes
Llangan
Llansannor
Newton
Candleston
Castle
Corntown
Craig Penllyn
Trerhyngyll
Prisk
Porthcawl
Ogmore
Ewenny
A48
Penllyn
Pen-y-lan
Porthcawl Point
Maendy
B4265
St Quentin's Castle
Ogmore-by-Sea
St Bride's Major
Colwinston
Pentre Meyrick
B4268
Aberthin
B4524
Pitcot
Llysworney
Cowbridge
Southerndown
Llandow
B4270
Llanblethian
Llandough
Llanmihangel
St Hilary
Old Beaupre Castle
Wick
Sigingstone
Llandow
Monkton
St Mary Church
Broughton
B4270
Flemingston
Monknash
B4265
Llanmaes
Marcross
Eglwys-Brewis
St Donats
Llantwit Major
St Athan
B4265
Nash Point
Gileston
Glamorgan Heritage Coast
West Aberthaw
Limpert Bay
Aberthaw
Breaksea Point
1
2
3
4
5
6
7
8
0 1 2 3 4 5 miles
0 1 2 3 4 5 6 7 8 kilometres

Merthyr Tydfil
(Merthyr Tudful)
Rhymney
Pontlottyn
Fochriw
Waunlwyd
Cwm
Ebbw Valley
West Bank
Cwmtillery
Abertillery
(Abertyleri)
Tal-y-Waun
Abersychan
Garnclochdy
Penperlleni
Pen-groes-oped
Rhymney Valley
Sirhowy Valley
Abertysswg
Manmoel
Pentrebach
Troedrhiwfuwch
Parc Cwm Darran
Tirphil
Dyffryn
Troedyrhiw
New Tredegar
Deri
Bedlinog
Brithdir
Hollybush
Markham
Aberbeeg
Six Bells
St Illtyd
Brynithel
Llanhilleth
Hafod-y-coed
Pen-twyn
Pentre-piod
Wainfelin
Croes-y-pant
Mamhilad
Little Mill
Monkswood
Glascoed
Trevethin
Pontnewynydd
Pontypool
(Pont-y-Pŵl)
Pontypool Road
Sowhill
Griffithstown
New Inn
Sebastopol
Aberfan
Merthyr Vale
Cwmfelin
Aberbargoed
Bargoed
(Bargod)
Bedwellty
Pen-y-fan Pond
Argoed
Pen-twyn
Trinant
Swffryd
Pantygaseg
Hafodyrynys
Newtown
Llancaiach Fawr
Penpedairheol
Gilfach
Oakdale
Crumlin
Mynydd Maen
Treharris
Pengam
Penmaen
Blackwood
Pontllanfraith
Newbridge
The Square
Gelligaer
Trelewis
Quaker's Yard
Nelson
Edwardsville
Fleur-de-lis
Pentwynmawr
Celynen
Greenmeadow Community Farm
Lowlands
Pontnewydd
Croesyceiliog
Llandegveth
Forge Hammer
Cwmbran
(Cwmbrân)
Hengoed
Maesycwmmer
Gelligroes
West End
Abercarn
Cwmcarn
Cwmcarn Forest Drive
Gelli
Llantarnam
Croes-y-mwyalch
Ponthir
Abercynon
Ynysybwl
Ystrad Mynach
Ynysddu
Mynydd Lan
Pontywaun
Crosskeys
Risca
Castell-y-bwch
Henllys
Malpas
Bettws
Mynydd Eglwysilan
Senghenydd
Cilfynydd
Cwmfelinfach
Wattsville
Machen
Llanbradach
Bedwas
Abertridwr
Trethomas
Chatham
Ty'n-y-coedcae
Lower Machen
Rogerstone
Rhiwderyn
Bassaleg
Cefn
Maindee
Christchurch
Glyntaff
Rhydyfelin
Trefforest
Hawthorn
Groes-Wen
Pandy
Castle
R. Rhymney
Caerphilly
(Caerffili)
Rudry
Draethen
Pentre-poeth
Pillgwenlly
Transporter Bridge
Maes-glas
Llantwit Fardre
Church Village
Ton-teg
Upper Boat
Nantgarw
Thornhill
Parc Cefn Onn
Michaelstone-y-Fedw
Tredegar House
Coedkernew
Nash
Solutia
Saltmarsh
Tyn-y-nant
Efail Isaf
Glan-y-llyn
Castell Coch
Llantrisant
Soar
Taff's Well
Tongwynlais
Lisvane
Cardiff Gate
Began
Castleton
Rhiwsaeson
Cross Inn
Creigiau
Pentyrch
Rhiwbina
Llanishen
Llanedeyrn
St Mellons
Marshfield
St Brides Wentlooge
Groes-faen
Capel Llanilltern
Morganstown
Radyr
Whitchurch
Birchgrove
Llanrumney
Rumney
CARDIFF
Peterstone Wentlooge
Cardiff West
St y-Nyll
St Brides super-Ely
St Fagans
National History
Llandaff
Roath
Pengam
Newton
Fairwater
River Ely
Canton
Ely
Splottlands
Peterston-super-Ely
St George's
Caerau
CARDIFF
(CAERDYDD)
St Nicholas
Greenway
Leckwith
Michaelston-le-Pit
Bonvilston
Twyn-yr-Odyn
Tinkinswood
Llandough
Llantrithyd
St Lythans
Wenvoe
Penarth Head
Aubrey
Dyffryn
Burial Chamber
Eastbrook
Cogan
St Andrew's Major
Penarth
Walterston
Dinas Powys
Westra
Lower Penarth
Pancross
Moulton
Penmark
Welsh Hawking Centre
Merthyr Dyfan
Cadoxton
Palmerstown
Cosmeston Lakes & Medieval Village
Lavernock
Fonmon
Font-y-gary
Cardiff
Barry
(Y Barri)
Sully
Swanbridge
Lavernock Point
Sully Island
Porthkerry
Rhoose
Barry Island
Cold Knap Point
Flat Holm
Sand Point
Sand Bay
Kewstoke
SEVERN
M4
A48(M)
A4060
A469
A4048
A4046
A4054
A470
A4059
A472
A4049
A4042
A467
A4051
A4058
A4119
A4161
A4232
A4160
A468
A4050
A4231
A4055
A4226
A4262
A4267
A4596
A4237
B4251
B4254
B4255
B4257
B4263
B4273
B4471
B4511
B4591
B4595
B4600
B4623
B4236
B4239
B4487
B4562
B4267
61
62
44

A
B
C
D
E
F
Pontywaun
Crosskeys
Risca
Machen
Lower Machen
Chatham
Ty'n-y-coedcae
Rogerstone
Rhiwderyn
Bassaleg
Draethen
Rudry
Pentre-poeth
Parc Cefn Onn
Michaelstone-y-Fedw
Began
Lisvane
Cardiff Gate
Llanedeyrn
St Mellons
Llanrumney
Rumney
Pengam
Roath
Newton
Splottlands
CARDIFF
(CAERDYDD)
CARDIFF
Castleton
Marshfield
St Brides Wentlooge
Peterstone Wentlooge
Coedkernew
Tredegar House
Pont-Ebbw
Maes-glas
Pillgwenlly
Transporter Bridge
Cwmcarn Forest Drive
Croes-y-mwyalch
Llantarnam
Llanfrechfa
Castell-y-bwch
Henllys
Bettws
Malpas
Cefn
Maindee
Castle
Christchurch
Caerleon
Celtic Manor
Cat's Ash
Garth
Coed-y-caerau
Llandevaud
Llanbeder
Penhow
Parc Seymour
Llanvaches
Llanvair Discoed
Five Lanes
Carrow Hill
Roman Town
Caerwent
Runston Chapel
St Brides Netherwent
Highmoor Hill
Langstone
Milton
Llanmartin
Bishton
Llanwern
Liswerry
NEWPORT
(CASNEWYDD-AR-WYSG)
Llandevenny
Wilcrick
Magor
Llanfihangel Rogiet
Rogiet
Ifton
Toll
Undy
Magor Marsh
Redwick
Whitson
Pye Corner
Nash
Goldcliff
Solutia
Saltmarsh
SEVERN ESTUARY
Penarth Head
Penarth
Lower Penarth
Cosmeston Lakes Medieval Village
Lavernock
Lavernock Point
Flat Holm
Steep Holm
Battery Point
Portishead
Weston-in-Gordano
Clapton-in-Gordano
Walton-in-Gordano
Walton Park
Clevedon Court
Middletown
Cadbury Camp
East Clevedon
Clevedon
Tickenham
Stone-edge-Batch
Nailsea
Wain's Hill
R Kenn
Kenn
West End
St Mary's Grove
Chelvey
Woodspring Bay
Kingston Seymour
Sand Point
Wick St Lawrence
North End
Claverham
Horsecastle
Icelton
East Hewish
Yatton
Cleeve
Sand Bay
Ebdon
Bourton
Norton
West Hewish
Hewish
R Yeo
Congresbury
Kewstoke
St Georges
Puxton
Wrington
Toll
Milton
Worle
Rolstone
East Rolstone
Ashcombe
Stock
Blackmoor
WESTON-SUPER-MARE
West Wick
Way Wick
Brinsea
Langford
Stonebridge
Sandford
Churchill
Lower Langford
Locking
Hutton
Lower Canada
Upper Canada
Banwell
Upper Langford
Burrington
Brean Down
Uphill
Tropical Bird Garden
Oldmixon
Bleadon Hills
Star
Rowberrow
Walborough
Yarborough
Sidcot
Winscombe
Shipham
Brean
Bleadon
Hamwood
Christon
Shiplate
Loxton
Compton Bishop
King John's Hunting Lodge
Charterhouse
Batch
Webbington
Cheddar Gorge & Caves
Eastertown
Cross
Axbridge
Lympsham
Biddisham
Lower Weare
Cheddar Resr
Cheddar
Edingworth
Sedgemoor
Badgworth
Weare
Tarnock
East Brent
Rooks Bridge
Alston Sutton
Hythe
Berrow
Brinscombe
Stone Allerton
Brent
Clewer
Battleborough
Chapel
Cocklake
A467
A468
A4042
A48
B4245
B4596
B4591
M4
B4237
A48(M)
B4562
B4487
B4239
A470
B3124
M5
B3133
A370
B3440
A371
A368
A38
B3140
B3151
62
43
30
0 1 2 3 4 5 miles
0 1 2 3 4 5 6 7 8 kilometres
1
2
3
4
5
6
7
8

Chepstow
(Cas-Gwent)
Thornbury
Yate
Chipping Sodbury
BRISTOL
Keynsham
BATH
Radstock
Midsomer Norton
Pucklechurch
Long Ashton
Easton-in-Gordano
Severn Bridge
Portskewett
Sudbrook
Aust
Olveston
Almondsbury
Filton
Patchway
Kingswood
Saltford
Chew Magna
Chew Valley Lake
Blagdon
Marshfield
Tormarton
Dyrham
Wickwar
Hawkesbury
Timsbury
Paulton
Chilcompton
Stratton-on-the-Fosse

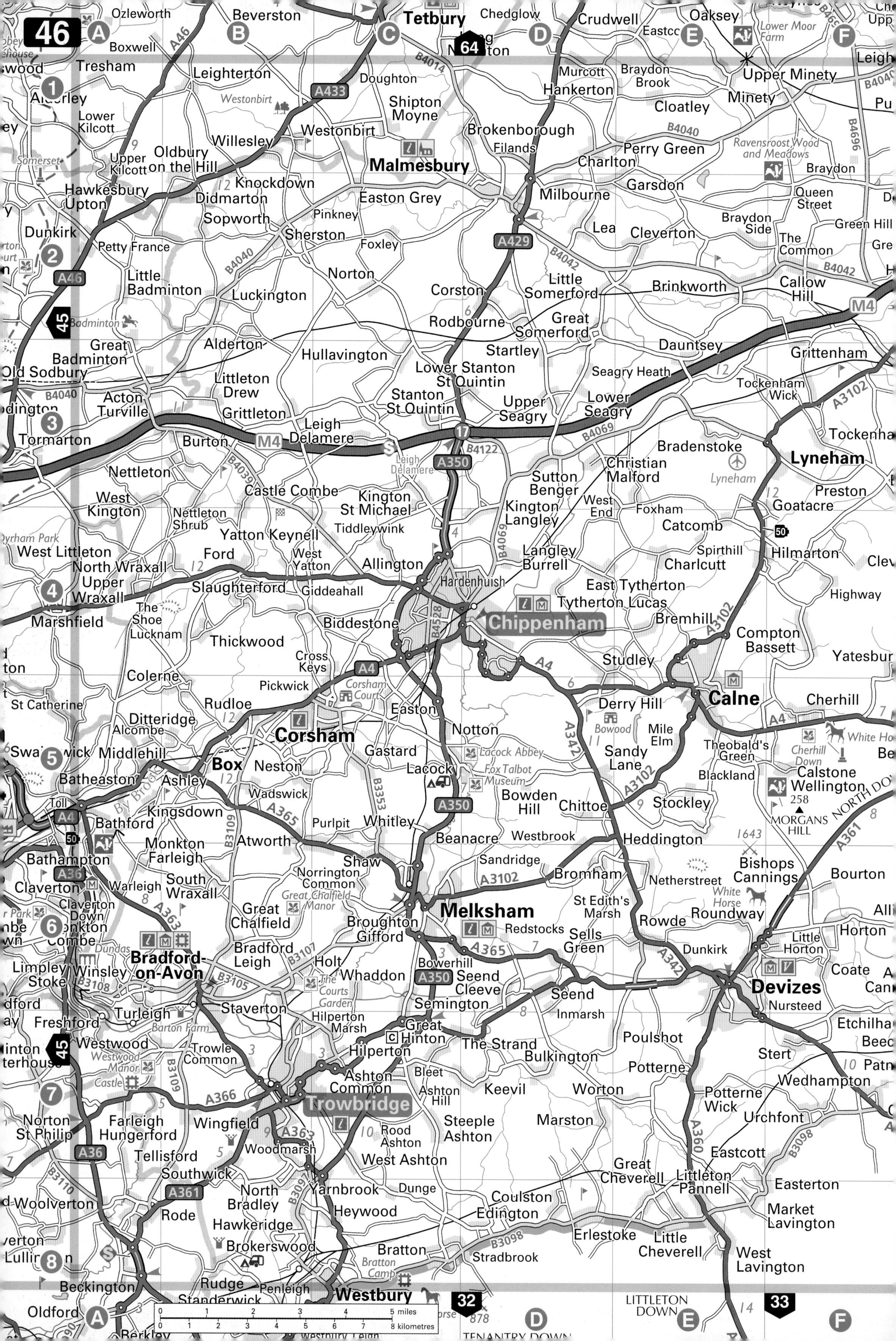
Tetbury
Malmesbury
Chippenham
Calne
Lyneham
Corsham
Melksham
Devizes
Bradford-on-Avon
Trowbridge
Westbury
Box
Hardenhuish
M4
A350
A429
A4
A46
A36
A365
A3102
A342
A361
A360
A366
A363
A433
B4040
B4042
B3098

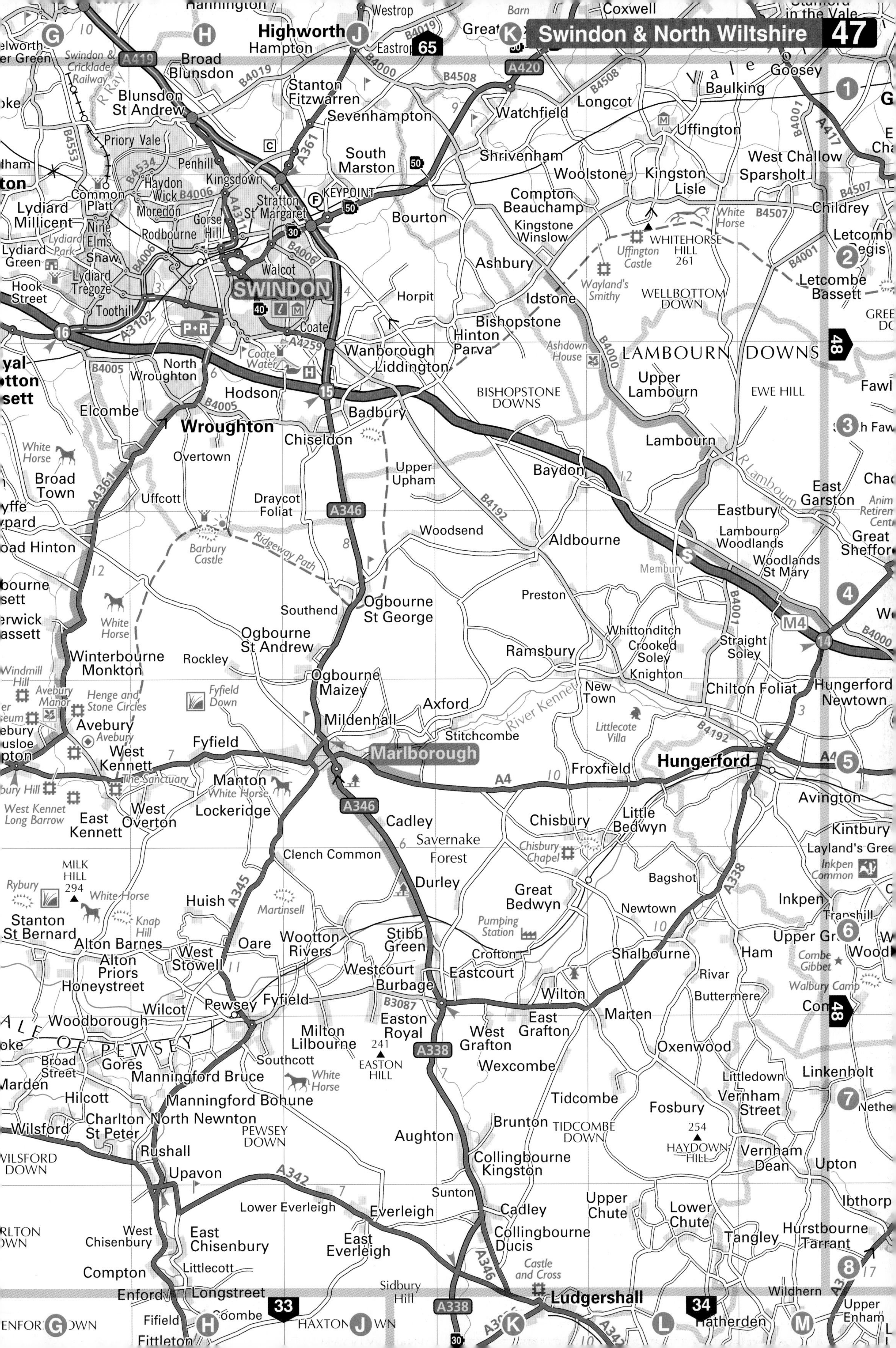
Highworth
Hampton
Westrop
Eastrop
Coxwell
Broad Blunsdon
Blunsdon St Andrew
Stanton Fitzwarren
Sevenhampton
Watchfield
Longcot
Goosey
Baulking
Uffington
Swindon & Cricklade Railway
Priory Vale
Penhill
Kingsdown
South Marston
Shrivenham
Woolstone
Kingston Lisle
West Challow
Sparsholt
Childrey
Common Platt
Haydon Wick
Stratton St Margaret
Compton Beauchamp
Kingstone Winslow
KEYPOINT
Lydiard Millicent
Moredon
Gorse Hill
Bourton
Nine Elms
Rodbourne
Lydiard Park
Lydiard Green
Shaw
Walcot
Ashbury
Uffington Castle
WHITEHORSE HILL 261
White Horse
Letcombe Regis
Letcombe Bassett
Hook Street
Lydiard Tregoze
SWINDON
Wayland's Smithy
WELLBOTTOM DOWN
Toothill
Horpit
Idstone
Coate
Bishopstone
Hinton Parva
Wanborough
Liddington
Coate Water
P+R
North Wroughton
Ashdown House
LAMBOURN DOWNS
Upper Lambourn
EWE HILL
Hodson
Elcombe
Wroughton
Badbury
Chiseldon
BISHOPSTONE DOWNS
Lambourn
Overtown
White Horse
Broad Town
Upper Upham
Baydon
R Lambourn
East Garston
Uffcott
Draycot Foliat
Eastbury
Woodsend
Lambourn Woodlands
Great Shefford
Barbury Castle
Ridgeway Path
Aldbourne
Membury
Woodlands St Mary
Preston
Southend
Ogbourne St George
Ogbourne St Andrew
Whittonditch
Crooked Soley
Straight Soley
Winterbourne Monkton
Rockley
Ramsbury
Knighton
Windmill Hill
Avebury Manor
Henge and Stone Circles
Fyfield Down
Ogbourne Maizey
Chilton Foliat
New Town
Hungerford Newtown
Avebury
Axford
Mildenhall
River Kennet
Littlecote Villa
Stitchcombe
Marlborough
West Kennett
Fyfield
The Sanctuary
Manton
White Horse
Froxfield
Hungerford
West Kennet Long Barrow
East Kennett
West Overton
Lockeridge
A4
Avington
Cadley
Little Bedwyn
Chisbury
Savernake Forest
Chisbury Chapel
Kintbury
Clench Common
Layland's Green
Inkpen Common
MILK HILL 294
Rybury
White Horse
Durley
Bagshot
Huish
Great Bedwyn
Stanton St Bernard
Knap Hill
Martinsell
Newtown
Inkpen
Pumping Station
Alton Barnes
Oare
Wootton Rivers
Stibb Green
Upper Green
Ham
Combe Gibbet
Alton Priors
West Stowell
Crofton
Shalbourne
Honeystreet
Westcourt
Eastcourt
Rivar
Walbury Camp
Burbage
Wilton
Buttermere
Wilcot
Pewsey
Fyfield
Woodborough
Easton Royal
Marten
East Grafton
West Grafton
VALE OF PEWSEY
Milton Lilbourne
241 EASTON HILL
Oxenwood
Broad Street
Gores
Southcott
White Horse
Wexcombe
Manningford Bruce
Littledown
Linkenholt
Marden
Hilcott
Manningford Bohune
Tidcombe
Vernham Street
Fosbury
Charlton St Peter
North Newnton
PEWSEY DOWN
Brunton
TIDCOMBE DOWN
254 HAYDOWN HILL
Wilsford
Aughton
Vernham Dean
Upton
WILSFORD DOWN
Rushall
Collingbourne Kingston
Upavon
Sunton
Upper Chute
Lower Chute
Ibthorpe
Lower Everleigh
Everleigh
Cadley
West Chisenbury
East Chisenbury
East Everleigh
Collingbourne Ducis
Tangley
Hurstbourne Tarrant
Compton
Littlecott
Castle and Cross
Enford
Longstreet
Sidbury Hill
Ludgershall
Wildhern
Upper Enham
Fifield
Coombe
Athenden
Fittleton
HAXTON DOWN
ENFORD DOWN
A419
A420
A361
A4311
A3102
A4259
A346
A345
A338
A342
A4
M4
B4019
B4000
B4508
B4534
B4006
B4553
B4005
B4192
B4507
B4001
B4087
B3087
B4000
B4192
65
48
33
34
30
40
50
16
15
14

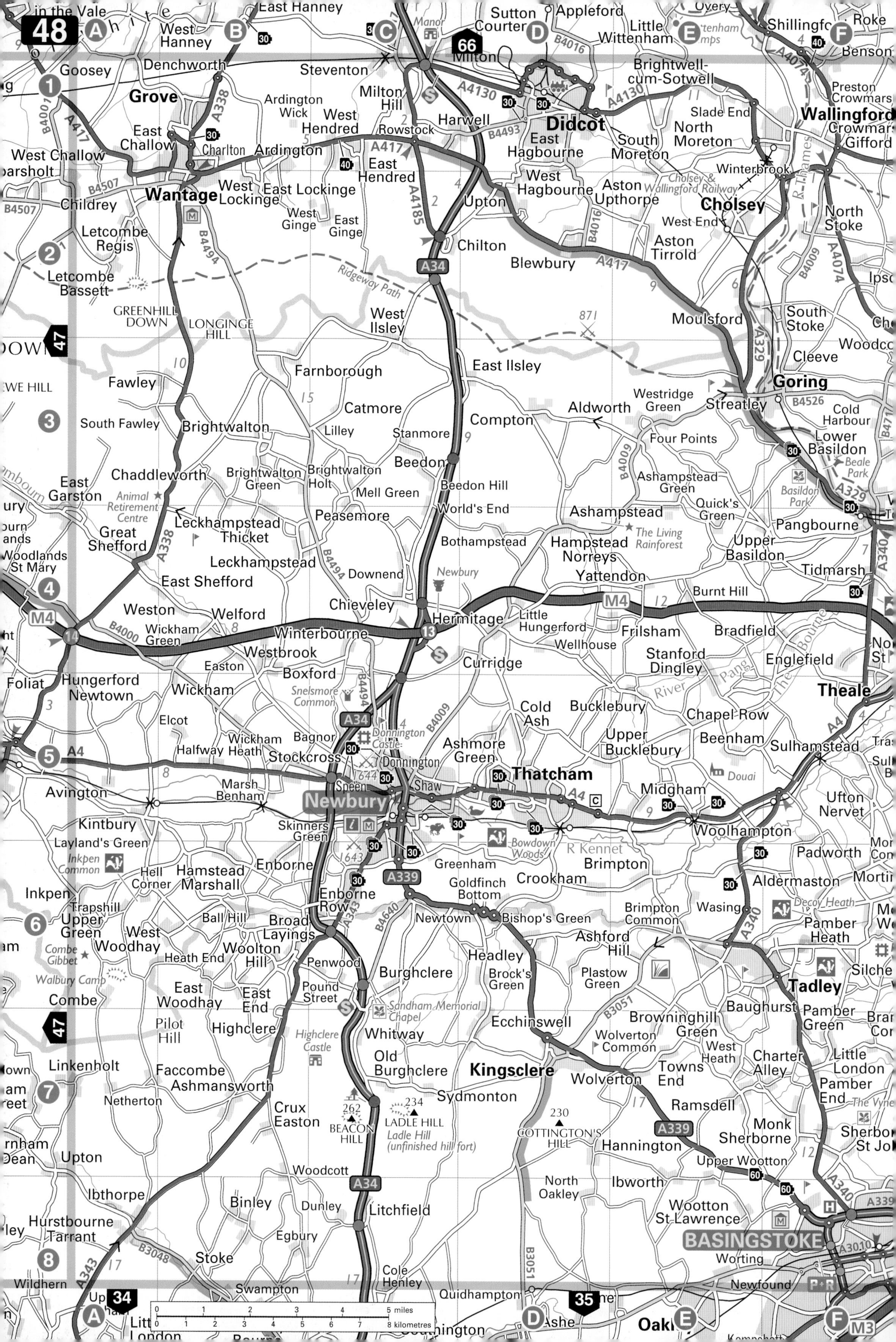

66
47
34
35
A
B
C
D
E
F
1
2
3
4
5
6
7
8
in the Vale
West Hanney
East Hanney
Sutton Courtenay
Appleford
Little Wittenham
Shillingford
Roke
Benson
Goosey
Denchworth
Steventon
Milton
Manor
Brightwell-cum-Sotwell
Preston Crowmarsh
Wallingford
Crowmarsh Gifford
Grove
Ardington Wick
West Hendred
Milton Hill
Harwell
Didcot
Slade End
North Moreton
South Moreton
East Challow
Charlton
Ardington
Rowstock
East Hagbourne
West Challow
Wantage
West Lockinge
East Lockinge
East Hendred
West Hagbourne
Aston Upthorpe
Cholsey & Wallingford Railway
Winterbrook
Cholsey
North Stoke
Childrey
West Ginge
East Ginge
Upton
West End
Letcombe Regis
Chilton
Aston Tirrold
Blewbury
Letcombe Bassett
Ridgeway Path
GREENHILL DOWN
LONGINGE HILL
West Ilsley
871
Moulsford
South Stoke
Cleeve
Woodcote
Fawley
Farnborough
East Ilsley
Goring
South Fawley
Catmore
Brightwalton
Lilley
Stanmore
Compton
Aldworth
Westridge Green
Streatley
Cold Harbour
Lower Basildon
Beale Park
Four Points
Beedon
East Garston
Chaddleworth
Brightwalton Green
Brightwalton Holt
Mell Green
Beedon Hill
Ashampstead Green
Basildon Park
Animal Retirement Centre
World's End
Quick's Green
Ashampstead
Great Shefford
Leckhampstead Thicket
Peasemore
Bothampstead
Hampstead Norreys
The Living Rainforest
Pangbourne
Upper Basildon
Woodlands St Mary
Leckhampstead
East Shefford
Downend
Newbury
Yattendon
Tidmarsh
Burnt Hill
Weston
Welford
Chieveley
Hermitage
Little Hungerford
Wickham Green
Winterbourne
Frilsham
Bradfield
Wellhouse
Westbrook
Easton
Curridge
Stanford Dingley
Englefield
Boxford
River Pang
The Bourne
Hungerford Newtown
Wickham
Snelsmore Common
Cold Ash
Bucklebury
Chapel Row
Theale
Foliat
Elcot
Donnington Castle
Ashmore Green
Upper Bucklebury
Beenham
Sulhamstead
Wickham Heath
Bagnor
Halfway
Stockcross
Donnington
Thatcham
Douai
Speen
Shaw
Midgham
Avington
Marsh Benham
Newbury
Ufton Nervet
Kintbury
Skinners Green
Woolhampton
Layland's Green
Bowdown Woods
R Kennet
Inkpen Common
Greenham
Brimpton
Padworth
Hell Corner
Hamstead Marshall
Enborne
Goldfinch Bottom
Crookham
Aldermaston
Inkpen
Enborne Row
Brimpton Common
Wasing
Decoy Heath
Trapshill
Upper Green
Ball Hill
Broad Layings
Newtown
Bishop's Green
Pamber Heath
West Woodhay
Ashford Hill
Combe Gibbet
Heath End
Woolton Hill
Penwood
Burghclere
Headley
Brock's Green
Plastow Green
Silchester
Walbury Camp
Tadley
East Woodhay
East End
Pound Street
Sandham Memorial Chapel
Combe
Baughurst
Pamber Green
Pilot Hill
Highclere
Ecchinswell
Brown in ghill Green
Wolverton Common
Highclere Castle
Whitway
West Heath
Charter Alley
Little London
Linkenholt
Old Burghclere
Kingsclere
Towns End
Faccombe
Ashmansworth
Wolverton
Pamber End
Netherton
Crux Easton
262
BEACON HILL
234
LADLE HILL
Ladle Hill (unfinished hill fort)
Sydmonton
230
COTTINGTON'S HILL
Ramsdell
Monk Sherborne
Sherborne St John
Upton
Hannington
Woodcott
Upper Wootton
North Oakley
Ibworth
Ibthorpe
Binley
Dunley
Litchfield
Wootton St Lawrence
Hurstbourne Tarrant
Egbury
BASINGSTOKE
Worting
Stoke
Cole Henley
Newfound
Wildhern
Swampton
Quidhampton
Oakley
Ashe
Little London
M4
M3
A34
A4130
B4016
A4074
B4001
A417
A338
B4493
A4185
B4507
B4494
B4016
B4009
A329
A4074
B4526
B4009
B4000
A4
A340
A339
A343
B4640
B3051
B3048
A3010
0 1 2 3 4 5 miles
0 1 2 3 4 5 6 7 8 kilometres

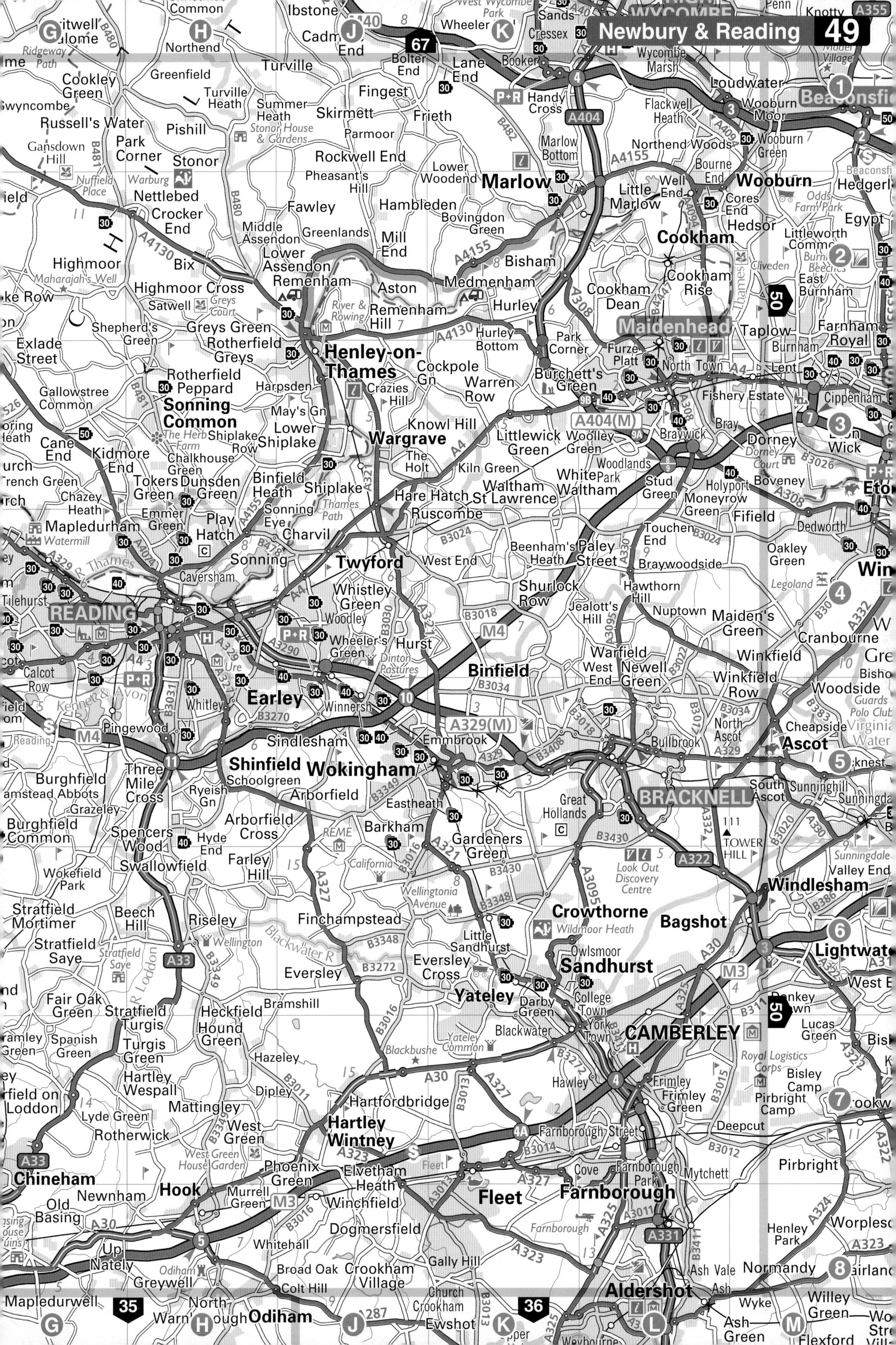
Common
Ibstone
Northend
Cadmore End
Wheeler End
Lane End
Bolter End
Cressex
Booker
Handy Cross
Wycombe Marsh
Loudwater
Model Village
Ridgeway Path
Cookley Green
Greenfield
Turville
Turville Heath
Summer Heath
Fingest
Skirmett
Frieth
Flackwell Heath
Wooburn Moor
Wooburn Green
Northend Woods
Russell's Water
Pishill
Stonor House & Gardens
Parmoor
Gansdown Hill
Park Corner
Stonor
Rockwell End
Marlow Bottom
Nuffield Place
Warburg
Pheasant's Hill
Lower Woodend
Marlow
Little Marlow
Well End
Bourne End
Wooburn
Hedgerley
Nettlebed
Crocker End
Fawley
Hambleden
Bovingdon Green
Cores End
Odds Farm Park
Egypt
Middle Assendon
Greenlands
Mill End
Hedsor
Cookham
Littleworth Common
Highmoor
Bix
Lower Assendon
Bisham
Cliveden
Burnham Beeches
Maharajah's Well
Remenham
Aston
Medmenham
Cookham Rise
East Burnham
Highmoor Cross
Greys Court
Satwell
River & Rowing
Remenham Hill
Hurley
Cookham Dean
Shepherd's Green
Greys Green
Hurley Bottom
Maidenhead
Taplow
Farnham Royal
Exlade Street
Rotherfield Greys
Henley-on-Thames
Park Corner
Furze Platt
Burnham
Rotherfield Peppard
Harpsden
Cockpole Gn
Warren Row
Burchett's Green
North Town
Lent
Gallowstree Common
Sonning Common
Crazies Hill
Fishery Estate
Cippenham
May's Gn
The Herb Farm
Shiplake Row
Lower Shiplake
Knowl Hill
Littlewick Green
Woolley Green
Braywick
Bray
Dorney
Eton Wick
Cane End
Kidmore End
Chalkhouse Green
Wargrave
The Holt
Kiln Green
Woodlands Park
Dorney Court
Tokers Green
Dunsden Green
Binfield Heath
Shiplake
White Waltham
Stud Green
Holyport
Boveney
Chazey Heath
Emmer Green
Play Hatch
Sonning Eye
Thames Path
Hare Hatch
Waltham St Lawrence
Moneyrow Green
Eton
Mapledurham
Watermill
Ruscombe
Fifield
Dedworth
Charvil
Touchen End
Caversham
Sonning
Twyford
Beenham's Heath
Paley Street
Braywoodside
Oakley Green
West End
Shurlock Row
Hawthorn Hill
Legoland
Tilehurst
READING
Whistley Green
Woodley
Jealott's Hill
Nuptown
Maiden's Green
Cranbourne
Wheeler's Green
Hurst
Warfield
West End
Newell Green
Winkfield
Calcot Row
Ure
Dinton Pastures
Binfield
Winkfield Row
Woodside
Guards Polo Club
Kennet & Avon
Whitley
Earley
Winnersh
North Ascot
Cheapside
Virginia Water
Pingewood
Emmbrook
Bullbrook
Ascot
Sindlesham
Three Mile Cross
Shinfield
Wokingham
Burghfield
Schoolgreen
Ryeish Gn
Arborfield
BRACKNELL
South Ascot
Sunninghill
Sunningdale
Grazeley
Eastheath
Great Hollands
Burghfield Common
Spencers Wood
Arborfield Cross
REME
Barkham
Tower Hill
Hyde End
Gardeners Green
Wokefield Park
Swallowfield
Farley Hill
California
Look Out Discovery Centre
Valley End
Windlesham
Wellingtonia Avenue
Stratfield Mortimer
Beech Hill
Riseley
Finchampstead
Crowthorne
Wildmoor Heath
Bagshot
Wellington
Blackwater R
Little Sandhurst
Lightwater
Stratfield Saye
Owlsmoor
Sandhurst
Eversley
Eversley Cross
Yateley
College Town
West End
Fair Oak Green
Stratfield Turgis
Heckfield
Bramshill
Darby Green
Donkey Town
Spanish Green
Hound Green
Blackwater
York Town
CAMBERLEY
Lucas Green
Turgis Green
Hazeley
Blackbushe
Yateley Common
Royal Logistics Corps
Bisley Camp
Hartley Wespall
A30
Hawley
Frimley
Dipley
Frimley Green
Pirbright Camp
Lyde Green
Mattingley
Hartfordbridge
Deepcut
West Green
Hartley Wintney
Farnborough Street
Rotherwick
West Green House Garden
Chineham
Phoenix Green
Elvetham Heath
Fleet
Cove
Farnborough Park
Mytchett
Pirbright
Newnham
Hook
Murrell Green
Winchfield
Fleet
Farnborough
Old Basing
Dogmersfield
Farnborough
Worplesdon
Up Nately
Whitehall
Henley Park
Greywell
Odiham
Broad Oak
Crookham Village
Gally Hill
Ash Vale
Normandy
Colt Hill
Church Crookham
Aldershot
Ash
Wyke
Willey Green
Mapledurwell
North Warnborough
Odiham
Ewshot
Ash Green
Flexford
35
36
50

50
A
B
C
D
E
F
68
49
36
37
Penn
Knotty Green
Chalfont St Giles
Seer Green
Chalfont Common
Maple Cross
Batchworth
Batchworth Heath
Eastbury
Northwood
Hatch End
Harrow Weald
Stanmore
Wycombe Marsh
Forty Green
Bekonscot Model Village
Jordans
Chalfont St Peter
West Hyde
Harefield
Ruislip Woods
Pinner Green
Pinner
Wealdstone
Harrow
Loudwater
Flackwell Heath
Wooburn Moor
Beaconsfield
Layter's Green
Gerrards Cross
Denham Green
Bayhurst Wood
Eastcote
Harrow on the Hill
Northend Woods
Wooburn Green
Bourne End
Wooburn
Hedgerley
Hedgerley Gn
Denham
Newyears Green
Ruislip
Cores End
Odds Farm Park
RSPB
Egypt
Hedsor
Cookham
Cookham Rise
Littleworth Common
Burnham Beeches
Farnham Common
Fulmer
New Denham
Ickenham
Sudbury
Cliveden
East Burnham
Stoke Poges
Black Park
Uxbridge
North Hillingdon
Northolt
Perivale
Maidenhead
Taplow
Wexham Street
Iver Heath
Farnham Royal
Burnham
Stoke Green
Wexham
Cowley
Hayes End
Wood End
Yeading
Greenford
North Town
Lent
SLOUGH
Shreding Green
George Green
Iver
Yiewsley
Hayes
Fishery Estate
Cippenham
Chalvey
Upton
Richings Park
West Drayton
Southall
Norwood Green
Hanwell
Ealing
Bray
Dorney
Eton Wick
Dorney Court
Langley
Thorney
Harmondsworth
Harlington
Heston
Osterley Park
Brentford
Holyport
Boveney
Eton
Stud Green
Moneyrow Green
Fifield
Dedworth
Datchet
Colnbrook
Poyle
Sipson
Longford
Heathrow
Cranford
Osterley
Syon
Touchen End
Frogmore House
Horton
Oakley Green
Windsor
Old Windsor
Stanwell Moor
Stanwell
West Bedfont
Hatton
Hounslow
Isleworth
Twickenham
Braywoodside
Legoland
Wraysbury
East Bedfont
Hawthorn Hill
Nuptown
Maiden's Green
Windsor Great Park
Cranbourne
Runnymede
Hythe End
Feltham
Winkfield
Egham
Ashford
Lower Feltham
Hampton
Teddington
Winkfield Row
Bishops Gate
Savill Garden
Englefield Green
Thorpe Lea
STAINES UPON-THAMES
Queen Mary Resr
Felthamhill
Hanworth
Kempton Park
Woodside
Guards Polo Club
Egham Wick
Valley Gardens
Virginia Water
Cheapside
North Ascot
Ascot
Thorpe
Laleham
Charlton
Sunbury
Hampton Wick
Bullbrook
Blacknest
Stroude
Thorpe Park
Littleton
Upper Halliford
Hampton Court Palace
Surbiton
Sunninghill
Wentworth
Trumpsgreen
Shepperton Green
West Molesey
East Molesey
BRACKNELL
South Ascot
Sunningdale
Broomhall
Lyne
Lower Halliford
Walton-on-Thames
Thames Ditton
Long Ditton
Knowle Hill
Chertsey
Shepperton
Tower Hill
Sunningdale
Valley End
Great Cockcrow
Addlestonemoor
Thames Path
Oatlands Park
Sandown Park
Hinchley Wood
Windlesham
Longcross
Addlestone
Weybridge
Hersham
West End
Esher
Claygate
Bagshot
Chobham Common
Ottershaw
Row Town
New Haw
Burrowhill
Claremont Landscape Garden
Lightwater
Chobham
Woodham
St George's Hill
Whiteley Village
Chessington
West End
Anthonys
Castle Green
West Byfleet
Byfleet
Fairmile
Oxshott Heath
Malden Rushett
Camberley
Donkey Town
Sheerwater
Cobham
Oxshott
Lucas Green
Bisley
Maybury
Painshill Park
Royal Logistics Corps
Bisley Camp
Knaphill
Horsell
Pyrford
Wisley
Semaphore Tower
Downside
Frimley
Frimley Green
Pirbright Camp
Goldsworth Park
WOKING
RHS Wisley
Martyr's Green
May's Green
Stoke D'Abernon
Brookwood
St Johns
Cobham
Leatherhead
Deepcut
Mayford
Old Woking
Ripley
Ockham
Fetcham
Mytchett
Pirbright
Fox Corner
Send
Send Marsh
Little Bookham
Great Bookham
Farnborough
Burntcommon
Bocketts
Sutton Green
Henley Park
Worplesdon
Jacobs Well
West Horsley
East Horsley
Norbury Park
Effingham
Hatchlands Park
Pitch Place
Slyfield Green
West Clandon
Ash Vale
Normandy
Fairlands
Polesden Lacey
Clandon Park
Burpham
Westhumble
Aldershot
Ash
Willey
Stoughton
East Clandon
Denbies
Merrow
0 1 2 3 4 5 miles
0 1 2 3 4 5 6 7 8 kilometres

LONDON
Camden Town
Islington
Hackney
Hammersmith
Westminster
Greenwich
Woolwich
Barking
Lewisham
Bromley
Croydon
Sutton
Orpington
Banstead
Biggin Hill
New Addington
Caterham
Westerham
Limpsfield
Oxted
Redhill
Southwark
Lambeth
Wimbledon
Putney
Wandsworth
Stratford
Walthamstow
Tottenham
Edmonton
Finchley
Hendon
Hampstead
Highgate
Kensington
Chelsea
Fulham
Brixton
Peckham
Eltham
Sidcup
Bexley
Purley
Coulsdon
Kenley
Whyteleafe
Warlingham
Merstham
Godstone
Tandridge
Nutfield
Downe
Knockholt
Chelsfield
Farnborough
Keston
Hayes
Beckenham
Penge
Streatham
Mitcham
Morden
Cheam
Ewell
Epsom Downs
Tadworth
Kingswood
Chipstead
Hooley
Woldingham
Titsey
Chaldon
Bletchingley

Havering-atte-Bower
Havering
Harold Hill
Brook Street
Wickford
Ingrave
Little Burstead
Great Burstead
Crays Hill
Hainault
Collier Row
Herongate
Thorndon N
Little Warley
Noak Bridge
Barkingside
Gidea Park
Harold Wood
Great Warley
Thorndon S
Dunton Wayletts
BASILDON
Newbury Park
Chadwell Heath
Romford
West Horndon
Laindon
Seven Kings
Goodmayes
Rush Green
Hornchurch
Cranham
Lee Chapel
Vange
Ilford
Eastbrookend
Upminster
Dry Street
Langdon
One Tree Hill
Becontree
Elm Park
Corbets Tey
North Ockendon
Bulphan
Langdon Hills
Barking
Dagenham
Hornchurch
Hacton
Fobbing
South Hornchurch
Horndon on the Hill
Corringham
Rainham
Belhus Woods
South Ockendon
Orsett
Stanford le Hope
LONDON GATEWAY TERMINAL
Wennington
Baker Street
Thamesmead
North Stifford
Mucking
Aveley
Linford
Rainham Marshes
Thurrock
Woolwich
Abbey Wood
River Thames
Lakeside
Chafford Hundred
Chadwell St Mary
West Tilbury
Muckingford
Plumstead
Belvedere
Erith
Low Street
Purfleet
West Thurrock
South Stifford
Grays
Little Thurrock
East Tilbury
East Wickham
Slade Green
Dartford Crossing
Queen Elizabeth Bridge
Coalhouse Fort
Barnehurst
Tilbury
Tilbury Fort
Welling
Bexleyheath
Crayford
Tolls
Greenhithe
West Street
Red House
Hall Place
Stone
Knockhall
Swanscombe
Northfleet
Church Street
Milton
Blackfen
Bexley
Dartford
Bluewater
Swanscombe Skull
Ebbsfleet International
Denton
Chalk
Lower Higham
New Eltham
North Cray
GRAVESEND
Joyden's Wood
Wilmington
Stonewood
Higham
Sidcup
Bean
Lane End
Green Street Green
Hook Green
Betsham
Southfleet
Singlewell
Thong
Shorne Woods
Shorne
Foots Cray
Hawley
Hextable
Clement St
Darenth
Chislehurst
Ruxley Corner
Sutton at Hone
South Darenth
Westwood
Istead Rise
Nash Street
Owletts
Cobham
Strood
ROCHESTER
Upper Hockenden
Swanley Village
Swanley
Dean Bottom
Grubb Street
Longfield
New Barn
Round Street
Sole Street
St Paul's Cray
St Mary Cray
Petts Wood
Crockenhill
Horton Kirby
Hartley Green
Hartley
Meopham Station
Rochester Castle
Farningham
Upper Bush
Orpington
Wested
Fawkham Green
Meopham
Henley Street
Cuxton
Eynsford
Lullingstone Roman Villa
Eynsford Castle
Brands Hatch
West Yoke
Meopham Green
Foxendown
Luddesdown
North Halling
North Downs Way
Chelsfield
Well Hill
Parkgate
New Ash Green
David Street
Upper Halling
Farnborough
Lullingstone
Maplescombe
South Street
Priestwood Green
Wouldham
Green Street Green
West Kingsdown
Ash
Ridley
Halling
Preston Hill
Hodsoll Street
Harvel
Pratt's Bottom
Badgers Mount
Culverstone Green
Paddlesworth
Holborough
Romney Street
Stansted
Snodland
Burham
Shoreham
Fairseat
Vigo
Ham Hill
Knockmill
Trosley
Birling
Halstead
Cudham
Trottiscliffe
Ryarsh
New Hythe
Eccles
Lett's Green
Otford
Woodlands
Crowdleham
Wrotham
Lunsford
Aylesford
Knockholt Pound
Heaverham
Addington
Larkfield
Kemsing
Leybourne
Knockholt
Borough Green
Wrotham Heath
West Malling
Ditton
Horn's Green
Dunton Green
Sevenoaks
Noah's Ark
Mill Street
Chevening
Longford
Seal
Fuller Street
Ightham
Platt
Little Comp
Great Comp
Kings Hill
St Leonard's Street
East Malling
British Legion Village
Chipstead
St Johns
Riverhead
Oldbury
Stone Street
Basted
Crouch
Claygate Cross
Herne Pound
East Malling Heath
MAIDSTONE
Westerham
Brasted
Sundridge
Knole
Bitchet Green
Ivy Hatch
Old Soar Manor
Old Soar
Mereworth
Kent Street
Waterlingbury
Barming Heath
East Barming
Teston
Hosey Hill
Brasted Chart
Whitley Row
Sevenoaks
Ightham Mote
Plaxtol
Dunk's Green
Roughway
Nettlestead
East Farleigh
French Street
Chartwell
Toy's Hill
Ide Hill
Common
Hill
West Peckham
Nettlestead Green
West Farleigh
Four Wents
Goose Green
Pitt's Wood
Hadlow
Oakhurst
Sevenoaks Weald
Coopers Corner
Fletcher
East
Yalding
Coxheath
5 miles
8 kilometres
70
71
51
38
39

Rawreth
Hockley
Ashingdon
Paglesham
FOULNESS ISLAND
Potton Is
Hawkwell
Rayleigh
Great Stambridge
Rochford
Stroud Green
R Roach
Barling
New Thundersley
Thundersley
Daws Heath
Little Wakering
Great Wakering
Eastwood
Prittlewell
Hadleigh
Bournes Green
Hadleigh Castle
Leigh-on-Sea
Westcliff-on-Sea
Southchurch
North Shoebury
Shoeburyness
Thorpe Bay
Leigh Beck
Canvey Point
SOUTHEND-ON-SEA
Shoebury Ness
Canvey Island
THAMES ESTUARY
Allhallows-on-Sea
St Mary's Hoo
Allhallows
Isle of Grain
Cooling
Lower Stoke
Grain
Wallend
High Halstow
Fenn Street
Middle Stoke
Stoke
Sheerness
Marine Town
Minster
Sharnal Street
North Street
Mile Town
West Minster
East End
Hoo St Werburgh
River Medway
Queenborough
Halfway Houses
Warden Point
Broad Street
Lower Upnor
Upnor Castle
Upper Upnor
The Historic Dockyard, Chatham
Rushenden
Eastchurch
Mud Row
Warden
Leysdown-on-Sea
Fort Amherst
Ham Green
Stangate Creek
ISLE OF SHEPPEY
Brompton
Grange
Riverside
Lower Rainham
Wetham Green
Halstow Creek
Elmley Island
GILLINGHAM
East Rainham
Lower Halstow
Iwade
Isle of Harty
Luton
Upchurch
Sittingbourne & Kemsley Light Railway
Darland
Otterham Quay
Breach
Howt Green
The Swale
Rainham
Wigmore
Moor Street
Newington
Bobbing
Kemsley
Murston
Conyer
Capstone
Hempstead
Hartlip
Lower Hartlip
Key St
Milton Regis
Uplees
Meresborough
Chestnut St
Chalkwell
Sittingbourne
Luddenham Court
Oare
Faversham
Lidsing
Chesley
Hill Green
Danaway
Borden
Bapchild
Teynham
Deerton Street
Lords Wood
Guildstead
Tunstall
Stone Chapel
Davington Hill
Goodnestone
Bredhurst
Kemsley Street
Oad St
Hearts Delight
Rodmersham
Lewson Street
Preston
Westfield Sole
Dunn Street
Stockbury
Stiff Street
Rodmersham Green
Lynsted
Ospringe
Silver Street
Rawling Street
Erriottwood
Boxley
South Green
Bredgar
Swanton Street
Bexon
Dungate
Painter's Forstal
Whitehill
Boughton
Kent Event Centre
Bicknor
Milstead
North Street
Hickmans Green
White Horse Wood
Newnham
Detling
Hucking
Doddington
Sandling
Thurnham
Sheldwich
Hogben's Hill
Selling
Ware Street
Wormshill
Frinsted
Seed
Eastling
Broad Street
Bearsted
Ringlestone
Grove Green
Wichling
Tong
Throwley
Sheldwich Lees
Sutton Street
Hollingbourne
Badlesmere
Willington
Eyhorne Street
West Street
Payden Street
Throwley Forstal
Shottenden
Otham
Leeds
Tong Green
Chilham
Shepway
Woodside Green
Leaveland
Otham Hole
Harrietsham
Stalisfield Green
Warren Street
Leeds
Broomfield
Lenham
Boughton Green
Langley
Leadingcross Green
Molash
Cock St
Chart Corner
Five Wents
Kingswood
Challock
Platts Heath
Sandway
Charing Hill
Stocker's Hill
Boughton Monchelsea
Chart Sutton
Liverton Street
Bapchild

A
B
C
D
E
F
1
2
3
4
5
6
7
8
Porthgain
Abereiddy
Berea
Llanrhian
Mathry
Llangloffan
Jordanston
Castle Morris
B4331
Llangloffan Fen
A487
Square & Compass
Croes-goch
Tretio
Treglemais
Treffynnon
Letterston
Welsh Hook
ST DAVID'S HEAD
Treleddyd-fawr
Carnhedryn
Cerbyd
B4330
Rhodiad-y-brenin
Whitesand Bay
Caer Farchell
River Solva
Llandeloy
Tancredston
Pont-yr-hafod
Wolf's Castle
B4583
Bishop's Palace
Whitchurch
Middle Mill
Treffgarne Owen
Hayscastle
Hayscastle Cross
St David's
74
RAMSEY ISLAND
Ramsey Sound
RSPB
Nine Wells
Solva
Treffgarne
Pen-y-cwn
178
DUDWELL MT
Leweston
St David's Peninsula Heritage Coast
Newgale
Western Cleddau
Roch
Wolfsdale
PEMBROKESHIRE COAST NATIONAL PARK
Roch Gate
Simpson Cross
Camrose
A40
Rickets Head
Keeston
Pembrokeshire County
Nolton Haven
Nolton
Tangiers
St Brides Bay
St Brides Bay Heritage Coast
Pelcomb Cross
Pelcomb
Lambston
Glanafon
Pelcomb Bridge
Druidston
Sutton
Haroldston West
Portfield Gate
B4341
Broad Haven
Broadway
B4327
Dreen Hill
Merlin's Bridge
A4076
Little Haven
Walton West
Lower Freystrop
Pembrokeshire Coast Path
Solbury
Freystrop
Talbenny
Tiers Cross
Johnston
St Brides
Walwyn's Castle
Wooltack Point
SKOMER ISLAND
Hasguard
Marloes
A477
St Ishmael's
Sandy Haven
Thornton
Broad Sound
Herbrandston
Steynton
Honeyborough
Hubberston
Waterston
Marloes and Dale Heritage Coast
Dale
Hakin
Great Castle Head
Llanstadwell
B4325
Westdale Bay
Dale Point
SKOKHOLM ISLAND
Milford Haven
Milford Haven (Aberdaugleddau)
Pembroke Dock (Doc Penfro)
Angle
Angle Bay
Pwllcrochan
Rhoscrowther
St Anns Head
B4320
Rosslare Harbour
Hundleton
Castlemartin Brook
Freshwater West
B4319
Castlemartin
St Twynnells
Warren
Merrion
Linney Head
PEMBROKESHIRE COAST NATIONAL PARK
Bosherston
Pembrokeshire Coast Path
0 1 2 3 4 5 miles
0 1 2 3 4 5 6 7 8 kilometres

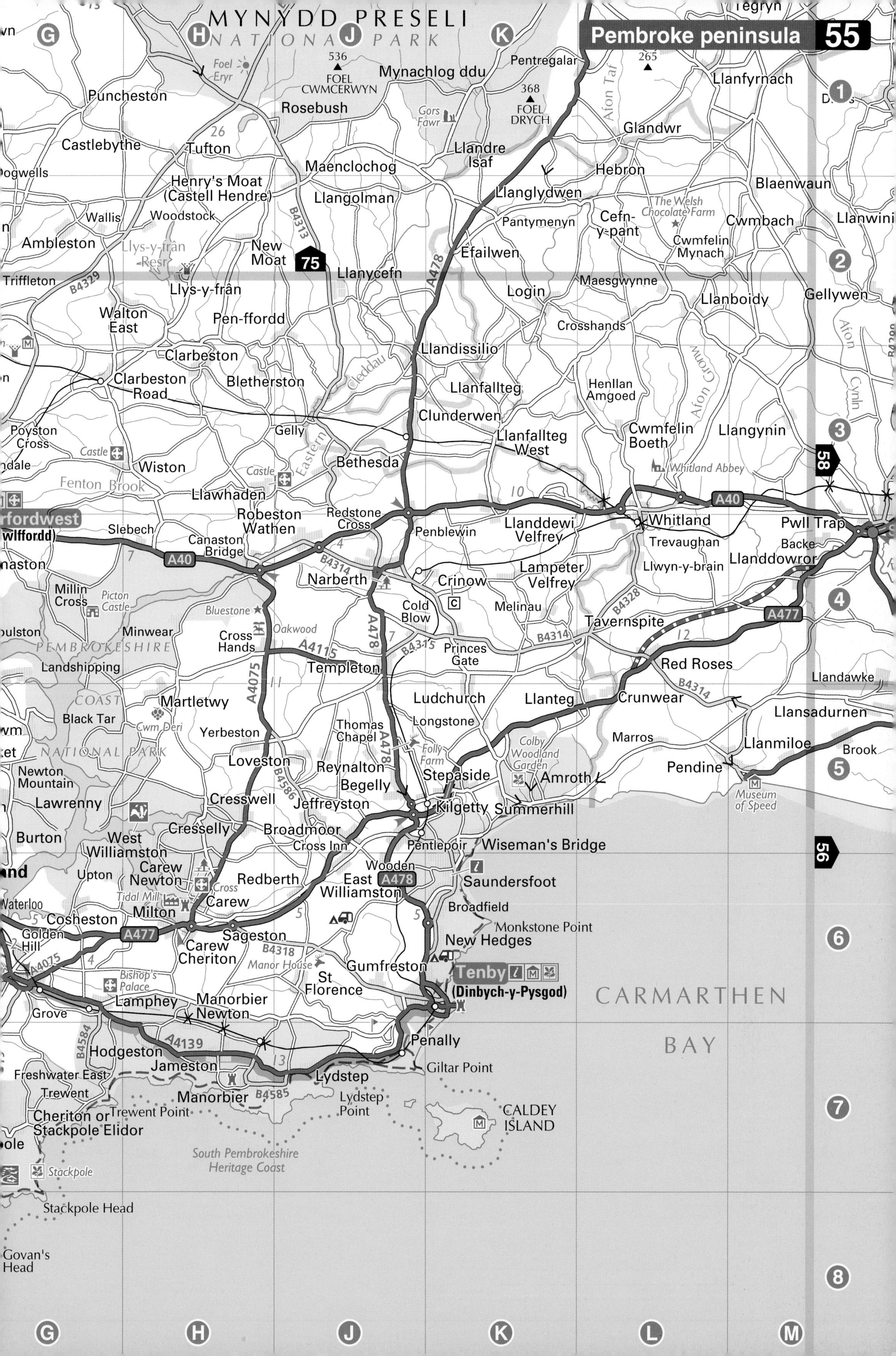
MYNYDD PRESELI
NATIONAL PARK
Foel Eryr
536
FOEL CWMCERWYN
Mynachlog ddu
Pentregalar
Tegryn
265
Llanfyrnach
368
FOEL DRYCH
Gors Fawr
Puncheston
Rosebush
Afon Taf
Glandwr
Castlebythe
Tufton
Llandre Isaf
Maenclochog
Hebron
Henry's Moat (Castell Hendre)
Llangolman
Llanglydwen
Blaenwaun
B4313
The Welsh Chocolate Farm
Wallis
Woodstock
Pantymenyn
Cefn-y-pant
Cwmbach
Llanwini
Ambleston
Llys-y-frân Resr
New Moat
75
Efailwen
Cwmfelin Mynach
Triffleton
B4329
Llanycefn
A478
Maesgwynne
Llys-y-frân
Login
Llanboidy
Gellywen
Walton East
Pen-ffordd
Crosshands
Llandissilio
Clarbeston
Afon Gronw
Afon Cynin
Clarbeston Road
Bletherston
Cleddau
Llanfallteg
Henllan Amgoed
Clunderwen
Poyston Cross
Gelly
Eastern
Cwmfelin Boeth
Llangynin
Llanfallteg West
Castle
Wiston
Bethesda
Whitland Abbey
58
Fenton Brook
Castle
Llawhaden
10
A40
rfordwest
Robeston Wathen
Redstone Cross
Whitland
Pwll Trap
Slebech
wlfford)
Canaston Bridge
Penblewin
Llanddewi Velfrey
Trevaughan
Backe
A40
B4314
Lampeter Velfrey
Llwyn-y-brain
Llanddowror
Narberth
Crinow
Millin Cross
Picton Castle
Bluestone
Cold Blow
Melinau
B4328
A477
Oakwood
Taverspite
Minwear
Cross Hands
A478
B4314
PEMBROKESHIRE
A4115
B4315
Princes Gate
12
Red Roses
Landshipping
Templeton
A4075
B4314
Llandawke
COAST
Martletwy
Ludchurch
Llanteg
Crunwear
Black Tar
Cwm Deri
Yerbeston
Thomas Chapel
Longstone
Llansadurnen
NATIONAL PARK
Colby Woodland Garden
Marros
Llanmiloe
Brook
Newton Mountain
Loveston
Folly Farm
Reynalton
Pendine
B4586
Begelly
Stepaside
Amroth
Lawrenny
Cresswell
Jeffreyston
Museum of Speed
Kilgetty
Summerhill
West Williamston
Cresselly
Broadmoor
Burton
Cross Inn
Pentlepoir
Wiseman's Bridge
56
Carew Newton
Wooden
Upton
Redberth
East Williamston
A478
Saundersfoot
Cross
Tidal Mill
Carew
Waterloo
Milton
Broadfield
Cosheston
5
Monkstone Point
A477
Sageston
Golden Hill
Carew Cheriton
New Hedges
B4318
A4075
Manor House
Gumfreston
Tenby
Bishop's Palace
St Florence
(Dinbych-y-Pysgod)
CARMARTHEN
Grove
Lamphey
Manorbier Newton
BAY
B4584
A4139
Penally
Hodgeston
Jameston
13
Giltar Point
Freshwater East
Lydstep
Trewent
Manorbier
B4585
Lydstep Point
CALDEY ISLAND
Cheriton or Stackpole Elidor
Trewent Point
South Pembrokeshire Heritage Coast
Stackpole
Stackpole Head
Govan's Head
G
H
J
K
L
M
1
2
3
4
5
6
7
8

56
Meidrim
Merthyr
Carmarthen
(Caerfyrddin)
Tre-Vaughan
White Mill
Abergwili
Nantgaredig
Llangunnor
Capel Dewi
Llanarthne
Tre-gynwr
Johnstown
Llanllwch
United Counties
Nant-y-caws
Llangynin
Sarnau
Bancyfelin
Pwll Trap
St Clears
Backe
Llanddowror
Croesyceiliog
Llangain
Idole
Cwmffrwd
Llanddarog
Cwmisfael
Bancycapel
Llangendeirne
Crwbin
Drefach
Cwmmawr
Llangynog
Llanybri
Pontantwn
Bancffosfelen
Laugharne
Llandawke
Llansteffan
Llandyfaelog
Pontyberem
Meinciau
Ferryside
Broadlay
Broadway
Llansadurnen
Brook
Llanmiloe
Museum of Speed
Wharley Point
Ginst Point
River Towy
River Taf
Afon Cywyn
Four Roads
Pontyates
Ponthenry
Cynheidre
Mynyddgarreg
Llansaint
Llangadog
Mynydd Sylen
R Gwendraeth
Kidwelly
(Cydweli)
Carway
Ffos Las
Five Roads
Horeb
Trimsaran
Pinged
Pen-y-Mynydd
Pembrey
Ffrwd Farm Mire
Cwm Capel
Cwm-bach
Archddu
Felinfoel
Furnace
Dafen
Dyfatty
Pwll
Burry Port
Llanelli
Millennium Coastal Park
Machynys
CARMARTHEN
BAY
Burry Inlet
Salthouse Point
Crofty
Whiteford Burrows
Wernffrwd
Broughton Bay
Llanmadoc
Landimore
Weobley Castle
Burry Holms
Cheriton
Llangennith
Oldwalls
Burry Green
Llanrhidian
Arthur's Stone
Hillend
Rhossili Bay
Rhossili Downs
Burry
Reynoldston
Cefn-y-Bryn
Llanddewi
Rhossili
Knelston
Penmaen
Scurlage
Nicholaston
Visitor Centre
Middleton
Penrice
WORMS HEAD
Oxwich
Pilton Green
Horton
Gower Coast
Paviland
Port Eynon
Oxwich Green
Oxwich Castle
Overton
Culver Hole
Port Einon Point
Port Einon Bay
GOWER
A40
A48
A484
A4066
A477
A4118
B4298
B4299
B4300
B4310
B4306
B4312
B4309
B4317
B4308
B4311
B4304
B4247
58
55
0 1 2 3 4 5 miles
0 1 2 3 4 5 6 7 8 kilometres
A B C D E F
1 2 3 4 5 6 7 8

Fawr
A40
Dinefwr Park & Castle
Llandeilo
Capel Gwynfe
Cilsan
Ffairfach
Neuadd
Aberglasney
Dryslwyn
Castle
River Towy
B4300
Gelli Aur
Golden Grove
Trapp
Carreg Cennen Castle
CARMARTHEN VAN
BLACK MOUNTAIN
618 CARREG LWYD
Glyntawe
558 CARREG GOCH
Dan-yr-Ogof
National Showcaves Centre for Wales
River Tawe
River Twrch
River Giedd
B4297
Carmel
Derwydd
Llandyfan
Llyn Llech Owain
Pentre-Gwenlais
Llandybie
A476
Gorslas
B4556
Cae'r bryn
Brynamman
A4068
Cefn-bryn-brain
Ynyswen
Abercraf
Glanaman
Penygroes
Saron
Pontamman
Garnant
A474
A4069
Penller-Fedwen
Cwmllynfell
Cross Hands
Ammanford (Rhydaman)
59
Gwaun-Cae-Gurwen
Pen Rhiwfawr
Cwm-twrch Uchaf
Cwmgiedd
Caehopkin
Cae'r-bont
Cefn Byrle
A4221
A483
Betws
Capel Hendre
Tycroes
Pantyffynnon
Cwmgors
Cwm-twrch Isaf
Penrhos
Onllwyn
Ystradgynlais
Ystradfawr
A48
Garnswllt
Gurnos
Glan-rhyd
Dyffryn Cellwen
Seven Sisters
River Loughor
Mynydd-y-Gwair
Lower Clydach River
River Egel
Ystalyfera
339 MYNYDD ALLT-Y-GRUG
354 FARTEG HILL
B4599
A4109
A4067
B4297
Llanedi
Craig-Fawr
Godre'r-graig
Cilmaengwyn
Ynysmeudwy
Hir Fynydd
Morfa
Glan-yr-afon
Llangiwg
Rhydyfro
Gelligron
Craig Llangiwg
Cilybebyll
Gellinudd
60
Crynant
B4242
A465
B4306
Fforest
Hendy
213 CEFN DRUM
Cwm Dulais
Pontardawe
Mynydd March Hywel
Trebanos
RSPB
Craig-y-Duke
Alltwen
Rhos
River Dulais
Abergarwed
Vale of Neath
River Neath
Resolven
Melin Cwrt Waterfalls
Melincourt
Pontarddulais
Craigcefnparc
Felindre
Fagwyr
Faerdre
B4603
Fforest Gôch
A474
B4434
Waungron
Clydach
Cilfrew
Clyde
Grovesend
M4
Swansea (West)
Pant-lasau
Ynystawe
A4067
Glais
Cadoxton
Juxta-Neath
Aberdulais
Tin Works and Waterfall
Pontlliw
Cwmrhydyceirw
Ynysforgan
B4291
Bryn-côch
Rhydding
Gorseinon
Penllergaer
Heol-las
Birchgrove
Tonna
Cefn Morfydd
Llwchwr
Loughor
A4240
Kings Bridge
Llangyfelach
Mynydd-Bach
Morriston
Llansamlet
Lôn-las
Neath (Castell-nedd)
A484
B4620
Cadle
B4489
Winshwen
A465
Skewen
Cimla
B4287
Abercregan
Tonmawr
Duffryn
B4295
Fforest Fach
Landore
A4217
Llandarcy
Cynonville
Gowerton
Waunarlwydd
Cockett
Cwmdu
Bon-y-maen
Pentre-chwyth
Crymlyn Bog
Jersey Marine
Efail-fach
Pont-rhyd-y-fen
Afan Forest Park
Foel y Dyffryn
A4107
371 MOEL TRAWSNANT
B4296
Three Crosses
Dunvant
A4118
A4216
Port Tennant
A483
B4290
Briton Ferry
FOEL MYNYDDAU
Brynbryddan 371
Pwll-y-glaw
Rock
Killay
Sketty
Brynmill
National Waterfront
Baglan
B4282
Bryn
Swansea
Upper Killay
A4067
SWANSEA (ABERTAWE)
A48
B4286
Cwmafan
Maesteg
Mayals
Black Pill
Aberavon
A4241
42
Bishopston
Kittle
West Cross
Northway
Norton
Swansea Bay
Port Talbot
Mynydd Margam
Cwmfelin
Oystermouth
Pennard
Taibach
Llangynwyd
Caswell Bay
Langland
B4593
B4433
The Mumbles
Mumbles Head
Margam
Stones Museum
321 MOEL TON-MAWR
Pwlldu Head
Margam
B4283
Afon Kenfig
Water Street
Pyle
B4281
Kenfig Hill
Mawdlam
North Cornelly
Kenfig
South Cornelly
NEWTON
G
H
J
K
L
M

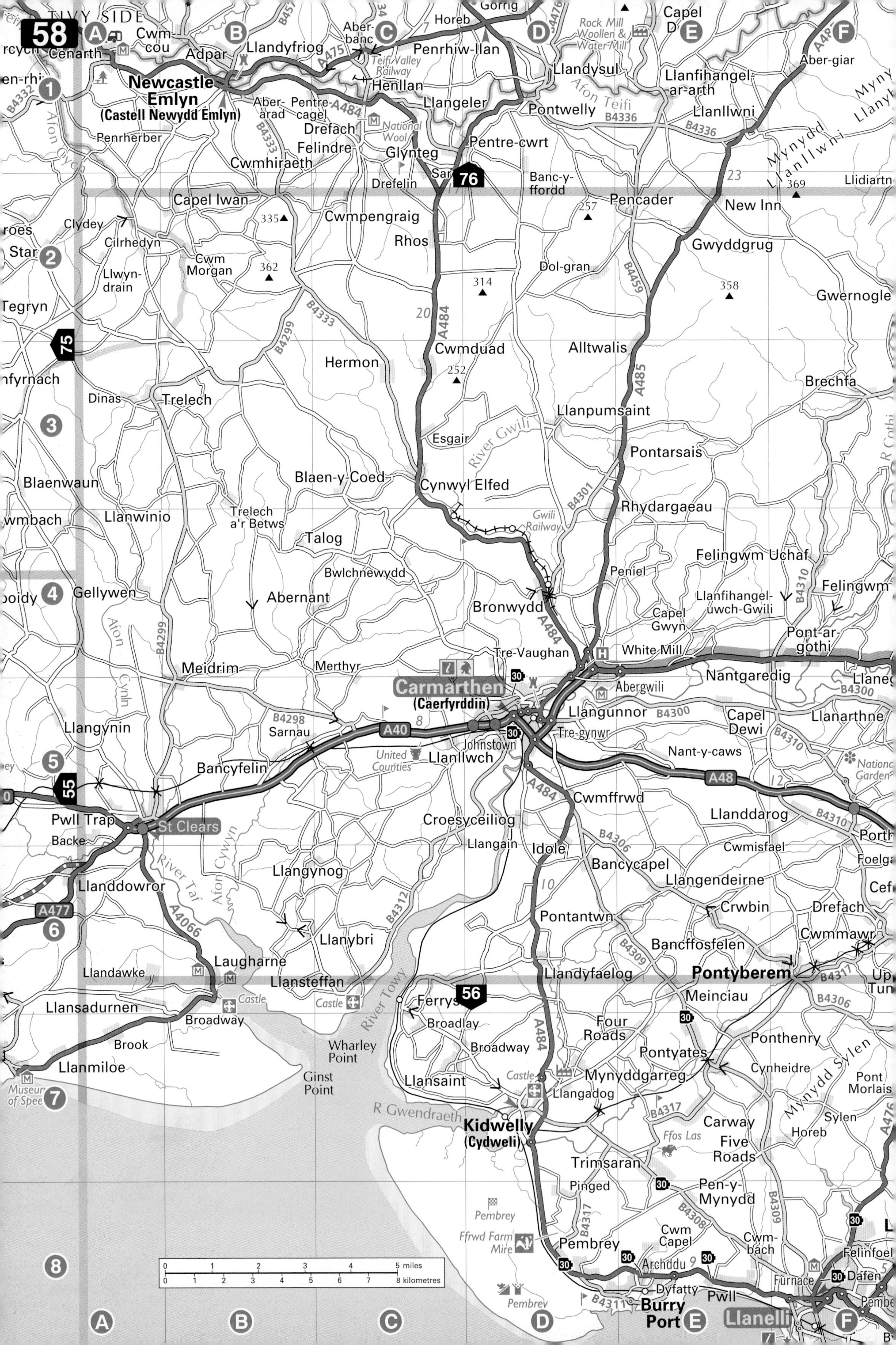

TIVY SIDE
Cenarth
Cwm-cou
Adpar
Llandyfriog
Aber-banc
Horeb
Penrhiw-llan
Gorrig
Rock Mill Woollen & Water Mill
Capel Dewi
Aber-giar
Newcastle Emlyn
(Castell Newydd Emlyn)
Teifi Valley Railway
Henllan
Llandysul
Llanfihangel-ar-arth
Afon Teifi
Llangeler
Pontwelly
B4336
Llanllwni
Aber-arad
Pentre-cagel
A484
Drefach
National Wool
Felindre
Glynteg
Pentre-cwrt
Mynydd Llanllwni
Penrherber
Afon Cych
Cwmhiraeth
Sarn
76
Banc-y-ffordd
Drefelin
Pencader
New Inn
369
Llidiartnenog
Capel Iwan
335
257
Clydey
Cwmpengraig
Rhos
Gwyddgrug
Cilrhedyn
Star
Cwm Morgan
362
Llwyn-drain
Dol-gran
B4459
314
358
Tegryn
Gwernogle
B4333
20
A484
B4299
75
Cwmduad
Alltwalis
Hermon
252
A485
Brechfa
Dinas
Trelech
Llanpumsaint
Esgair
River Gwili
Pontarsais
Blaenwaun
Blaen-y-Coed
Cynwyl Elfed
B4301
Rhydargaeau
Trelech a'r Betws
Llanwinio
Gwili Railway
Talog
Felingwm Uchaf
Bwlchnewydd
Peniel
B4310
Gellywen
Abernant
Llanfihangel-uwch-Gwili
Felingwm
Bronwydd
Capel Gwyn
Afon Cynin
B4299
Pont-ar-gothi
Tre-Vaughan
White Mill
Meidrim
Merthyr
Carmarthen
(Caerfyrddin)
Abergwili
Nantgaredig
B4300
B4298
Sarnau
A40
8
Llangunnor
Capel Dewi
Llanarthne
Llangynin
Tre-gynwr
Johnstown
B4310
Nant-y-caws
United Counties
Llanllwch
National Garden
Bancyfelin
55
A48
12
A484
Cwmffrwd
Pwll Trap
St Clears
Croesyceiliog
Llanddarog
B4310
Backe
Afon Cywyn
Llangain
Idole
B4306
Cwmisfael
River Taf
Llangynog
Bancycapel
Llanddowror
Llangendeirne
10
A477
A4066
B4312
Crwbin
Drefach
Pontantwn
Cwmmawr
Llanybri
B4309
Bancffosfelen
Laugharne
Llandawke
Llansteffan
Llandyfaelog
Pontyberem
B4317
56
Ferryside
Meinciau
Castle
Llansadurnen
B4306
Broadway
River Towy
Broadlay
A484
Four Roads
Ponthenry
Brook
Wharley Point
Broadway
Pontyates
Cynheidre
Mynydd Sylen
Llanmiloe
Ginst Point
Llansaint
Castle
Mynyddgarreg
Pont Morlais
Museum of Speed
Llangadog
B4317
R Gwendraeth
Kidwelly
(Cydweli)
Carway
Sylen
Horeb
Ffos Las
Five Roads
Trimsaran
Pinged
Pen-y-Mynydd
Pembrey
B4317
B4308
B4309
Ffrwd Farm Mire
Cwm Capel
Cwm-bach
Pembrey
Archddu
9
Felinfoel
Furnace
Dafen
Dyfatty
Pwll
Pembrey
B4311
Burry Port
Llanelli
5 miles
8 kilometres

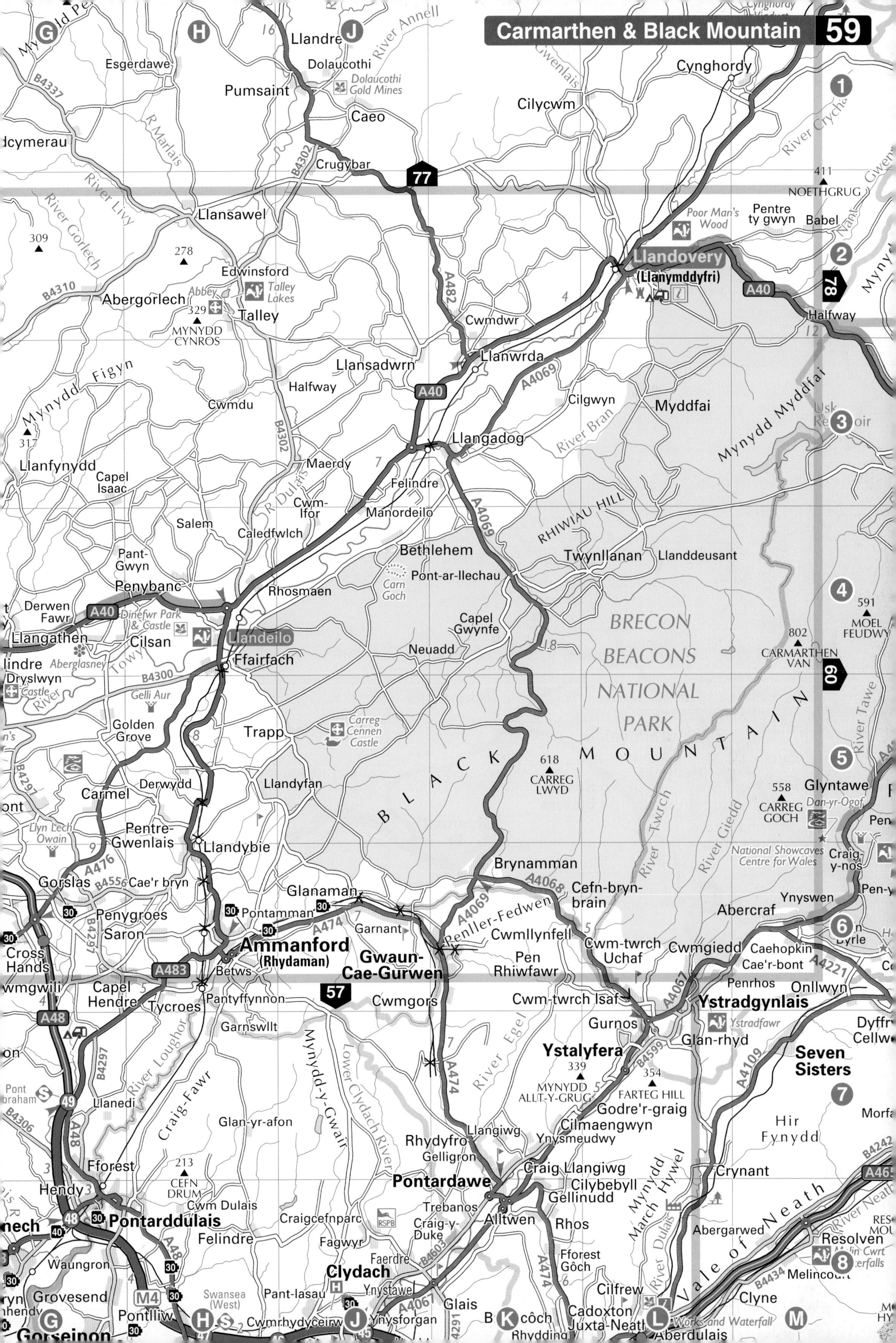
Llandre
Dolaucothi
Dolaucothi Gold Mines
Esgerdawe
Pumsaint
Caeo
Cynghordy
Cilycwm
Crugybar
77
Llansawel
Poor Man's Wood
Pentre ty gwyn
Babel
NOETHGRUG
Llandovery
(Llanymddyfri)
78
Halfway
Edwinsford
Talley Lakes
Abergorlech
Talley
MYNYDD CYNROS
Cwmdwr
Llanwrda
Llansadwrn
Halfway
Cilgwyn
Myddfai
Mynydd Myddfai
Cwmdu
Mynydd Figyn
Llangadog
Llanfynydd
Capel Isaac
Maerdy
Felindre
Cwm-Ifor
Manordeilo
Salem
Caledfwlch
RHIWIAU HILL
Bethlehem
Twynllanan
Llanddeusant
Pant-Gwyn
Pont-ar-llechau
Carn Goch
Penybanc
Rhosmaen
Derwen Fawr
Dinefwr Park & Castle
Llangathen
Cilsan
Llandeilo
Capel Gwynfe
BRECON BEACONS NATIONAL PARK
MOEL FEUDWY
CARMARTHEN VAN
Neuadd
Ffairfach
Aberglasney
Dryslwyn Castle
Gelli Aur
60
Golden Grove
Trapp
Carreg Cennen Castle
BLACK MOUNTAIN
CARREG LWYD
Derwydd
Llandyfan
Carmel
Glyntawe
CARREG GOCH
Dan-yr-Ogof
Llyn Llech Owain
Pentre-Gwenlais
Llandybie
National Showcaves Centre for Wales
Craig-y-nos
Brynamman
Gorslas
Cae'r bryn
Glanaman
Cefn-bryn-brain
Penygroes
Pontamman
Abercraf
Ynyswen
Saron
Garnant
Penller-Fedwen
Cwmllynfell
Cross Hands
Ammanford
(Rhydaman)
Gwaun-Cae-Gurwen
Pen Rhiwfawr
Cwm-twrch Uchaf
Cwmgiedd
Caehopkin
Cae'r-bont
Capel Hendre
Betws
Tycroes
57
Pantyffynnon
Cwmgors
Cwm-twrch Isaf
Penrhos
Onllwyn
Ystradgynlais
Ystradfawr
Gurnos
Garnswllt
Glan-rhyd
Mynydd-y-Gwair
Lower Clydach River
River Egel
Ystalyfera
Seven Sisters
MYNYDD ALLT-Y-GRUG
FARTEG HILL
Godre'r-graig
Llanedi
Craig-Fawr
Glan-yr-afon
Cilmaengwyn
Hir Fynydd
Llangiwg
Ynysmeudwy
Rhydyfro
Gelligron
Fforest
CEFN DRUM
Craig Llangiwg
Crynant
Hendy
Pontardawe
Cilybebyll
Gellinudd
Mynydd March Hywel
Cwm Dulais
Trebanos
Pontarddulais
Craigcefnparc
Alltwen
Rhos
Vale of Neath
Resolven
Felindre
Craig-y-Duke
Abergarwed
Fagwyr
Waungron
Faerdre
Fforest Gôch
Clydach
Melincourt
Grovesend
Ynystawe
Cilfrew
Clyne
Swansea (West)
Pant-lasau
Glais
Pontlliw
Cwmrhydyceirw
Ynysforgan
Cadoxton Juxta-Neath
Aberdulais
Works and Waterfall
Gorseinon
Rhyddings

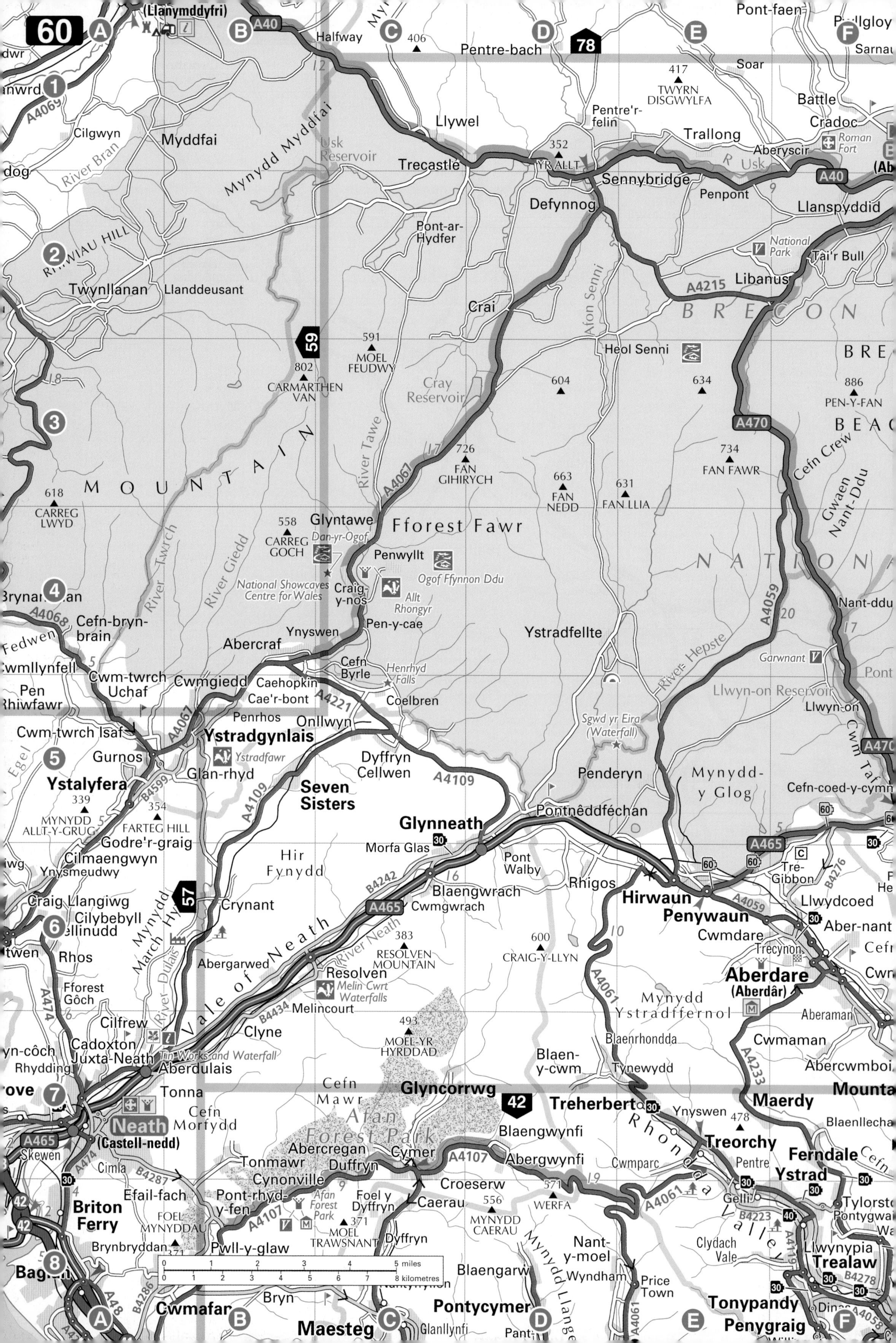
Llandovery (Llanymddyfri)
Halfway
Pentre-bach
Pont-faen
Pwllgloyw
Sarnau
Soar
TWYRN DISGWYLFA
Battle
Cradoc
Llywel
Pentre'r-felin
Trallong
Roman Fort
Cilgwyn
Myddfai
Mynydd Myddfai
Usk Reservoir
Trecastle
YR ALLT
Aberyscir
R Usk
Sennybridge
Penpont
River Bran
Defynnog
Llanspyddid
Pont-ar-Hydfer
National Park
Tai'r Bull
Libanus
Twynllanan
Llanddeusant
Crai
Afon Senni
BRECON
Heol Senni
MOEL FEUDWY
CARMARTHEN VAN
Cray Reservoir
PEN-Y-FAN
MOUNTAIN
River Tawe
FAN GIHIRYCH
FAN FAWR
Cefn Crew
FAN NEDD
FAN LLIA
CARREG LWYD
Glyntawe
CARREG GOCH
Dan-yr-Ogof
Fforest Fawr
Gwaen Nant-Ddu
Penwyllt
Ogof Ffynnon Ddu
NATIONAL
River Twrch
River Giedd
National Showcaves Centre for Wales
Craig-y-nos
Allt Rhongyr
Nant-ddu
Cefn-bryn-brain
Yynyswen
Pen-y-cae
Ystradfellte
Abercraf
Cwmllynfell
Cwm-twrch Uchaf
Cwmgiedd
Caehopkin
Cae'r-bont
Cefn Byrle
Henrhyd Falls
Coelbren
River Hepste
Garwnant
Llwyn-on Reservoir
Llwyn-on
Pen Rhiwfawr
Penrhos
Onllwyn
Cwm-twrch Isaf
Ystradgynlais
Ystradfawr
Sgwd yr Eira (Waterfall)
Gurnos
Dyffryn Cellwen
Penderyn
Mynydd-y Glog
Cefn-coed-y-cymmer
Ystalyfera
Glan-rhyd
Seven Sisters
MYNYDD ALLT-Y-GRUG
FARTEG HILL
Glynneath
Pontnêddféchan
Godre'r-graig
Morfa Glas
Pont Walby
Cilmaengwyn
Hir Fynydd
Ynysmeudwy
Rhigos
Hirwaun
Tre-Gibbon
Craig Llangiwg
Blaengwrach
Cwmgwrach
Penywaun
Llwydcoed
Cilybebyll
Rhyd-y-fro
Crynant
Aber-nant
Vale of Neath
Cwmdare
Trecynon
Rhos
Mynydd March Hywel
RESOLVEN MOUNTAIN
CRAIG-Y-LLYN
Abergarwed
River Neath
Resolven
Aberdare (Aberdâr)
Fforest Gôch
Melin Cwrt Waterfalls
Melincourt
Mynydd Ystradffernol
Aberaman
Cilfrew
River Dulais
Clyne
MOEL-YR HYRDDAD
Cwmaman
Cadoxton Juxta-Neath
Tin Works and Waterfall
Blaenrhondda
Rhydding
Aberdulais
Blaen-y-cwm
Tynewydd
Abercwmboi
Tonna
Cefn Mawr
Glyncorrwg
Treherbert
Maerdy
Neath (Castell-nedd)
Cefn Morfydd
Afan Forest Park
Ynyswen
Treorchy
Blaenllechau
Skewen
Abercregan
Blaengwynfi
Rhondda Valley
Cimla
Tonmawr
Duffryn
Cymer
Abergwynfi
Cwmparc
Pentre
Ferndale
Ystrad
Cynonville
Croeserw
Efail-fach
Briton Ferry
Pont-rhyd-y-fen
Afan Forest Park
Foel y Dyffryn
Caerau
WERFA
Gelli
Tylorstown
FOEL MYNYDDAU
MOEL TRAWSNANT
MYNYDD CAERAU
Clydach Vale
Llwynypia
Brynbryddan
Pwll-y-glaw
Dyffryn
Mynydd Llangeinor
Nant-y-moel
Trealaw
Baglan
Blaengarw
Wyndham
Price Town
Tonypandy
Cwmafan
Bryn
Pontycymer
Penygraig
Maesteg
Garnlllynfi
Pant
0 1 2 3 4 5 miles
0 1 2 3 4 5 6 7 8 kilometres

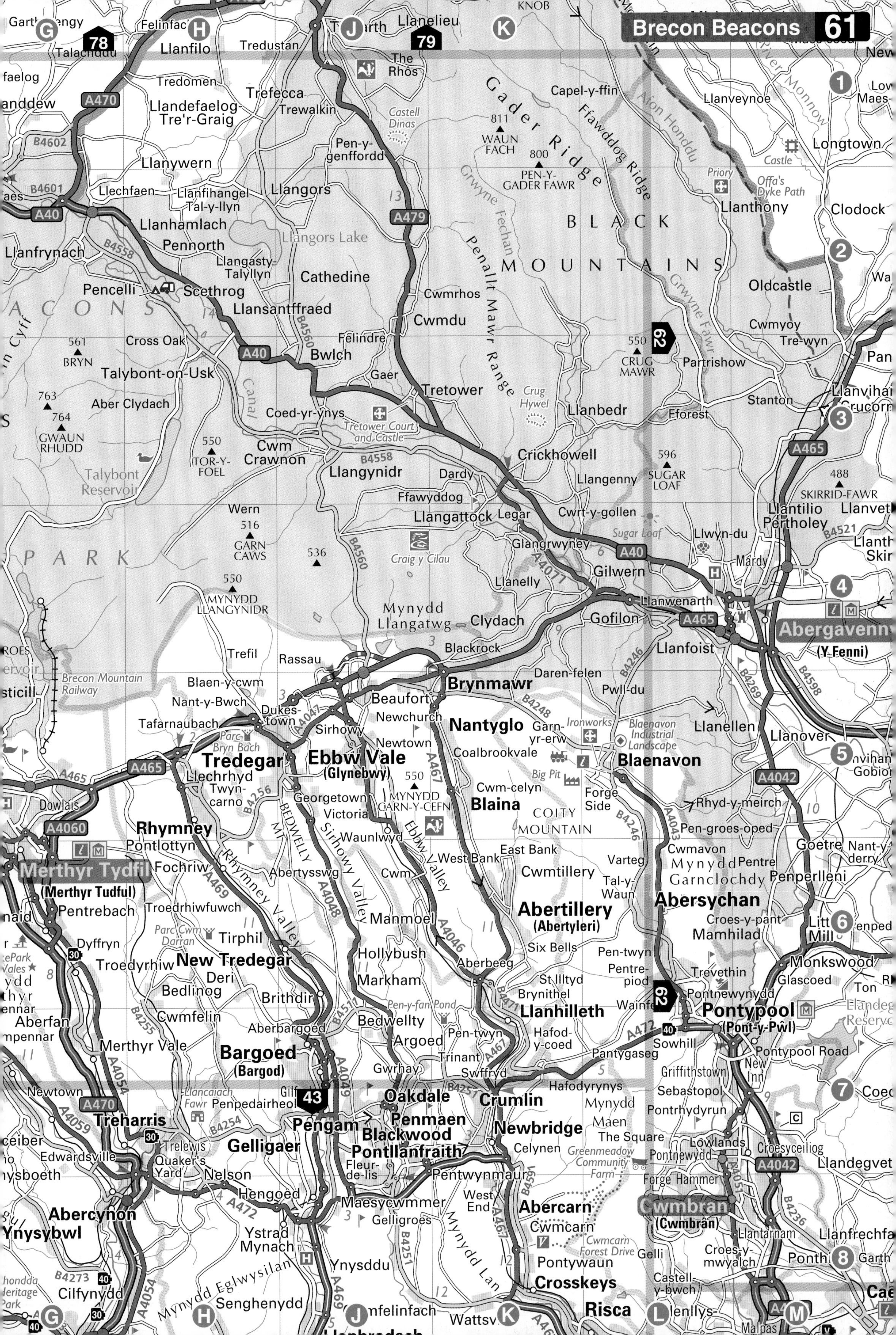

Garth
Felinfach
Talachddu
Llanfilo
Tredustan
Talgarth
Llanelieu
The Rhôs
KNOB
faelog
Tredomen
Trefecca
Trewalkin
Llandefaelog-Tre'r-Graig
anddew
A470
B4602
Castell Dinas
811
WAUN FACH
Gader Ridge
Capel-y-ffin
Ffawddog Ridge
Afon Honddu
800
PEN-Y-GADER FAWR
Pen-y-genffordd
Llanywern
B4601
Llechfaen
Llanfihangel Tal-y-llyn
Llangors
A40
A479
Llanhamlach
Llangors Lake
Grwyne Fechan
BLACK MOUNTAINS
Penallt Mawr Range
Llanfrynach
B4558
Pennorth
Llangasty-Talyllyn
Cathedine
Pencelli
Scethrog
Llansantffraed
Cwmrhos
Cwmdu
B4560
Felindre
Cross Oak
561
BRYN
Talybont-on-Usk
Bwlch
Gaer
Tretower
Crug Hywel
550
CRUG MAWR
Grwyne Fawr
Partrishow
763
764
Aber Clydach
GWAUN RHUDD
Canal
Coed-yr-ynys
Tretower Court and Castle
Llanbedr
Efforest
550
TOR-Y-FOEL
Cwm Crawnon
Llangynidr
Dardy
Crickhowell
596
SUGAR LOAF
Llangenny
Talybont Reservoir
Ffawyddog
Llangattock
Legar
Cwrt-y-gollen
Sugar Loaf
Wern
516
GARN CAWS
536
B4560
Craig y Cilau
Glangrwyney
A4077
Gilwern
Llwyn-du
PARK
550
MYNYDD LLANGYNIDR
Llanelly
Mardy
Mynydd Llangatwg
Clydach
Gofilon
Llanwenarth
A465
Blackrock
Llanfoist
Abergavenny
(Y Fenni)
B4598
Trefil
Rassau
Brecon Mountain Railway
Blaen-y-cwm
Brynmawr
Daren-felen
B4246
Pwll-du
B4269
Nant-y-Bwch
Dukestown
Beaufort
Tafarnaubach
Parc Bryn Bach
A4047
Sirhowy
Newchurch
Nantyglo
B4248
Garn-yr-erw
Ironworks
Blaenavon Industrial Landscape
Llanellen
Llanover
Tredegar
Ebbw Vale
(Glynebwy)
Newtown
Coalbrookvale
Blaenavon
A465
Llechrhyd
Twyn-carno
Georgetown
550
MYNYDD GARN-Y-CEFN
A467
Big Pit
Cwm-celyn
Forge Side
Rhyd-y-meirch
A4042
Dowlais
B4256
Victoria
Blaina
COITY MOUNTAIN
A4043
Pen-groes-oped
A4060
Rhymney
Pontlottyn
BEDWELLTY
Sirhowy Valley
Waunlwyd
Ebbw Valley
Cwmavon
Mynydd Garnclochdy
Pentre
Goetre
Merthyr Tydfil
(Merthyr Tudful)
Fochriw
A469
Rhymney Valley
Abertysswg
A4048
Cwm
West Bank
East Bank
Cwmtillery
Varteg
Tal-y-Waun
Penperlleni
Pentrebach
Troedrhiwfuwch
Manmoel
Abertillery
(Abertyleri)
Abersychan
Croes-y-pant
Mamhilad
Parc Cwm Darran
Tirphil
A4046
Six Bells
Pen-twyn
Dyffryn
Hollybush
Little Mill
Troedyrhiw
New Tredegar
Aberbeeg
Pentre-piod
Trevethin
Monkswood
Deri
Markham
St Illtyd
Glascoed
Bedlinog
Brithdir
Brynithel
Pontnewynydd
Aberfan
Cwmfelin
B4255
B4511
Pen-y-fan Pond
Bedwellty
Llanhilleth
Wainfelin
Pontypool
(Pont-y-Pŵl)
Aberbargoed
Pen-twyn
Hafod-y-coed
Sowhill
Merthyr Vale
Bargoed
(Bargod)
Argoed
A472
Pantygasag
Pontypool Road
A4054
Trinant
New Inn
Gwrhay
Swffryd
Griffithstown
A4049
Hafodyrynys
Newtown
A470
Llancaiach Fawr
Pengam
Oakdale
Crumlin
Sebastopol
Pontrhydyrun
Treharris
Penpedairheol
Penmaen
Mynydd Maen
Blackwood
Newbridge
The Square
A4059
Gelligaer
Pontllanfraith
Celynen
Greenmeadow Community Farm
Lowlands
Croesyceiliog
Llandegveth
Edwardsville
Trelewis
Quaker's Yard
Fleur-de-lis
Pentwynmawr
Pontnewydd
Forge Hammer
A4042
Nelson
Hengoed
B4254
Maesycwmmer
West End
Abercarn
Cwmbran
(Cwmbrân)
Abercynon
Ystrad Mynach
Gelligroes
Mynydd Lan
Cwmcarn
Cwmcarn Forest Drive
Llantarnam
Llanfrechfa
Ynysybwl
B4251
A467
Gelli
Croes-y-mwyalch
Ponthir
Garth
B4273
Ynysddu
Pontywaun
Cilfynydd
Mynydd Eglwysilan
A469
Crosskeys
Castell-y-bwch
Senghenydd
Cwmfelinfach
Wattsville
Risca
Henllys
Malpas
Llanthony
Priory
Offa's Dyke Path
Longtown
Castle
Llanveynoe
River Monnow
Clodock
Oldcastle
Cwmyoy
Tre-wyn
Stanton
Llanvihangel Crucorney
A465
488
SKIRRID-FAWR
Llantilio Pertholey
B4521

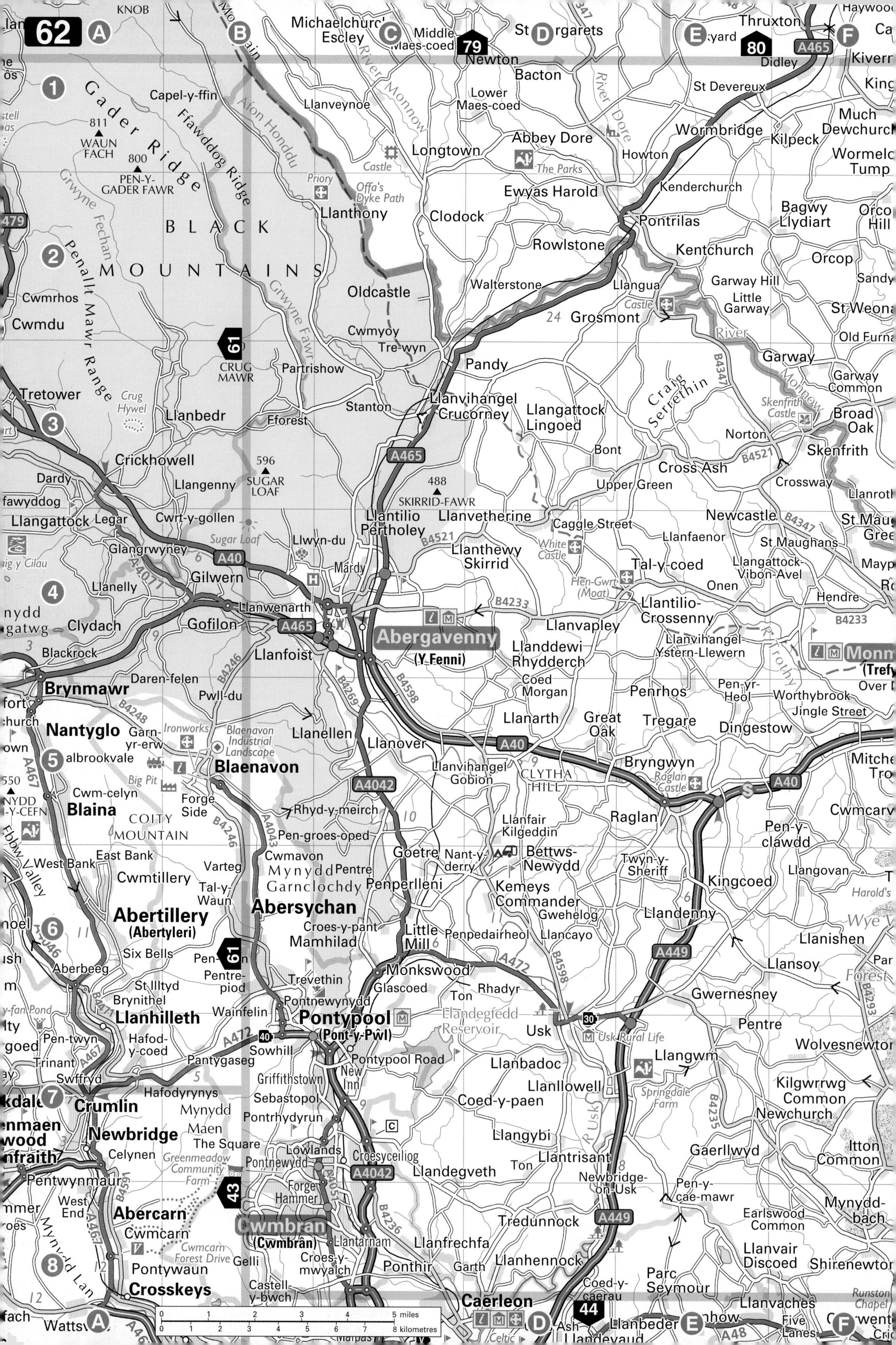
62
A
B
C
D
E
F
79
80
1
2
3
4
5
6
7
8
KNOB
Michaelchurch Escley
Middle Maes-coed
St Margarets
Thruxton
Haywood
Kiverr
Didley
A465
Newton
Bacton
St Devereux
King
Capel-y-ffin
Gader Ridge
Ffawddog Ridge
Afon Honddu
River Monnow
River Dore
811
WAUN FACH
800
PEN-Y-GADER FAWR
Llanveynoe
Lower Maes-coed
Wormbridge
Kilpeck
Much Dewchurch
Wormelo Tump
Longtown
Castle
Abbey Dore
The Parks
Howton
Priory
Offa's Dyke Path
Grwyne Fechan
Ewyas Harold
Kenderchurch
BLACK MOUNTAINS
Llanthony
Clodock
Pontrilas
Bagwy Llydiart
Orcop Hill
Rowlstone
Kentchurch
Orcop
Penallt Mawr Range
Walterstone
Llangua
Garway Hill
Sandy
Little Garway
Cwmrhos
Oldcastle
Castle
Grosmont
24
St Weona
Cwmdu
Grwyne Fawr
Cwmyoy
River
Old Furna
Tre-wyn
61
CRUG MAWR
Partrishow
Pandy
B4347
Garway
Craig Serrethin
Monnow
Garway Common
Tretower
Crug Hywel
Stanton
Llanvihangel Crucorney
Llangattock Lingoed
Skenfrith Castle
Broad Oak
Llanbedr
Eforest
Norton
Skenfrith
A465
Bont
B4521
Cross Ash
Crickhowell
596
SUGAR LOAF
488
SKIRRID-FAWR
Upper Green
Crossway
Dardy
Llangenny
Llanroth
fawyddog
Llangattock
Legar
Cwrt-y-gollen
Llantilio Pertholey
Llanvetherine
Caggle Street
Newcastle
B4347
St Maug
Sugar Loaf
Llwyn-du
White Castle
Llanfaenor
St Maughans
Gree
Glangrwyney
A40
6
B4521
Llanthewy Skirrid
Mardy
Tal-y-coed
Llangattock-Vibon-Avel
Mayp
A4077
Gilwern
Hen-Gwrt (Moat)
Onen
Llanelly
B4233
Llantilio-Crossenny
Hendre
Llanwenarth
Clydach
Gofilon
A465
Abergavenny
(Y Fenni)
Llanvapley
B4233
9
B4246
Llanvihangel-Ystern-Llewern
Monm
(Trefy
3
Blackrock
Llanfoist
Llanddewi Rhydderch
R Trothy
Over
Brynmawr
Daren-felen
B4269
B4598
Coed Morgan
Penrhos
Pen-yr-Heol
Worthybrook
Pwll-du
Jingle Street
B4248
Llanarth
Great Oak
Tregare
Dingestow
Nantyglo
Garn-yr-erw
Ironworks
Blaenavon Industrial Landscape
Llanellen
Llanover
A40
Bryngwyn
Mitchel Tro
A467
albrookvale
Blaenavon
Llanvihangel Gobion
CLYTHA HILL
Raglan Castle
A40
550
NYDD Y-CEFN
Big Pit
A4042
Cwm-celyn
Forge Side
Raglan
Cwmcarv
Blaina
COITY MOUNTAIN
A4043
Rhyd-y-meirch
10
Llanfair Kilgeddin
Pen-y-clawdd
B4246
Pen-groes-oped
Ebbw Valley
East Bank
Cwmavon
Goetre
Nant-y-derry
Bettws-Newydd
Twyn-y-Sheriff
Llangovan
West Bank
Cwmtillery
Varteg
Mynydd Garnclochdy
Pentre
Penperlleni
Kemeys Commander
Kingcoed
Harold's
Tal-y-Waun
Abersychan
Gwehelog
Llandenny
Wye
Abertillery
(Abertyleri)
11
Croes-y-pant
Little Mill
Pendedairheol
Llancayo
A449
Llanishen
Mamhilad
B4598
Par
Six Bells
61
Pentre-piod
A472
Llansoy
Forest
Aberbeeg
Monkswood
Glascoed
Trevethin
St Illtyd
Brynithel
Rhadyr
Ton
Gwernesney
B4293
Pontnewynydd
Llandegfedd Reservoir
Llanhilleth
Wainfelin
Pontypool
(Pont-y-Pŵl)
Usk
30
Pentre
Usk Rural Life
Pen-twyn
Hafod-y-coed
A472
Sowhill
Wolvesnewton
Trinant
A467
Pantygaseg
Pontypool Road
Llanbadoc
Llangwm
Swffryd
5
New Inn
Llanllowell
Kilgwrrwg Common
Hafodyrynys
Griffithstown
Springdale Farm
Crumlin
Sebastopol
Coed-y-paen
Newchurch
Mynydd Maen
Pontrhydyrun
R Usk
B4235
Newbridge
The Square
Llangybi
Itton Common
Celynen
Greenmeadow Community Farm
Lowlands
Croesyceiliog
Gaerllwyd
Pentwynmaur
B4591
Pontnewydd
A4042
Llandegveth
Ton
Llantrisant
8
43
Forge Hammer
A4051
Newbridge-on-Usk
Pen-y-cae-mawr
West End
Abercarn
Tredunnock
Earlswood Common
Mynydd-bach
Mynydd Lan
A467
Cwmbran
(Cwmbrân)
B4236
A449
Cwmcarn
Llantarnam
Llanfrechfa
Llanvair Discoed
Cwmcarn Forest Drive
Gelli
Croes-y-mwyalch
Llanhennock
Shirenewton
Pontywaun
12
Ponthir
Garth
Parc Seymour
Crosskeys
Castell-y-bwch
Coed-y-caerau
Runston Chapel
12
Caerleon
Llanvaches
44
Wattsv
Ash
Llanbedr
Five Lanes
A48
Llandevaud
Celtic
Malpas
0 1 2 3 4 5 miles
0 1 2 3 4 5 6 7 8 kilometres

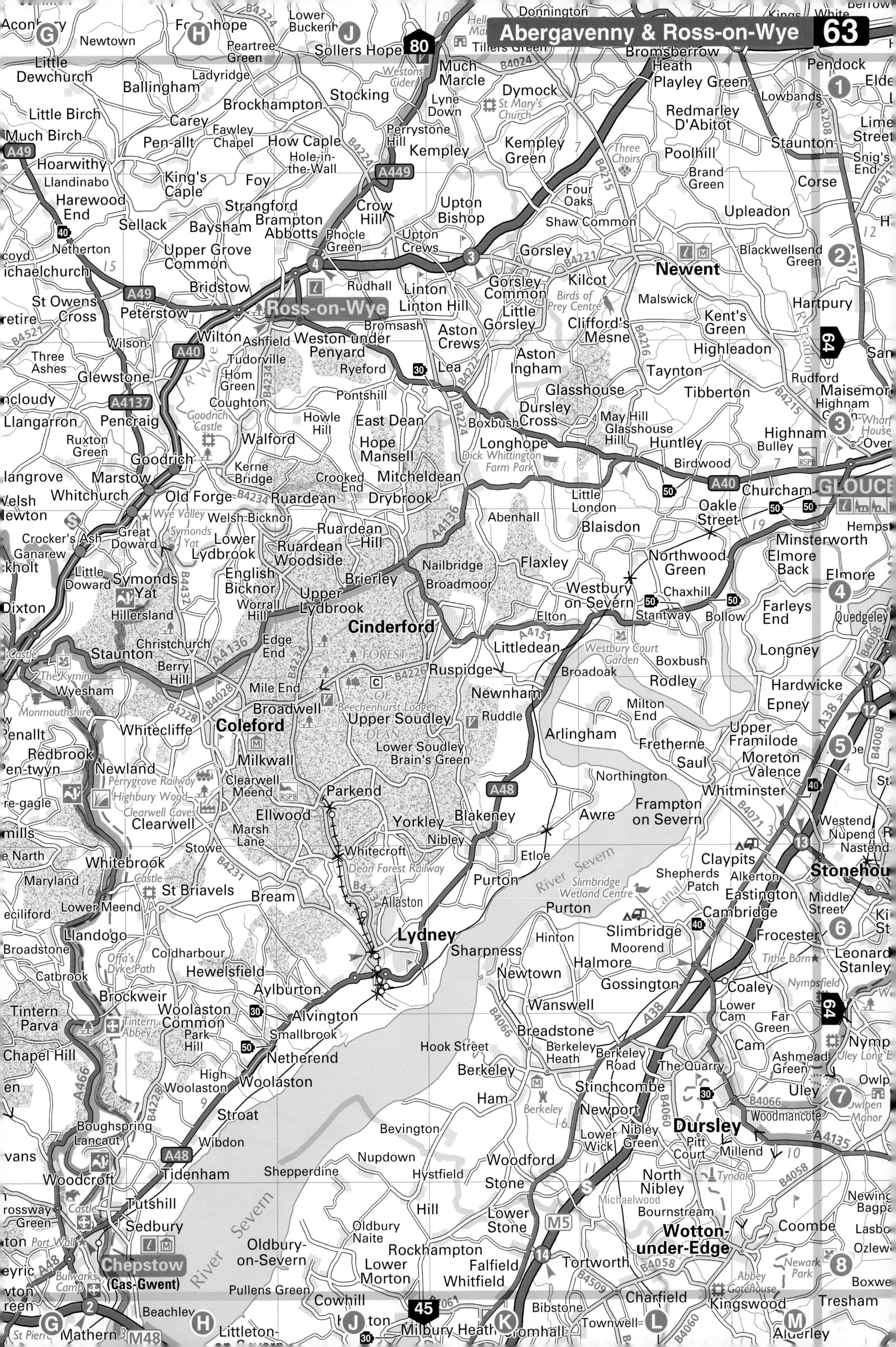
Donnington
Lower Buckenhill
Fownhope
Newtown
Peartree Green
Sollers Hope
80
Much Marcle
Westons Cider
Tillers Green
Bromsberrow Heath
Pendock
Little Dewchurch
Ballingham
Ladyridge
Stocking
Lyne Down
Dymock
St Mary's Church
Playley Green
Lowbands
Little Birch
Brockhampton
Carey
Perrystone Hill
Redmarley D'Abitot
Much Birch
Fawley Chapel
Pen-allt
How Caple
Kempley
Kempley Green
Three Choirs
Poolhill
Staunton
Corse
Hoarwithy
Llandinabo
Hole-in-the-Wall
King's Caple
Foy
A449
Brand Green
Four Oaks
Harewood End
Strangford
Crow Hill
Upton Bishop
Upleadon
Sellack
Baysham
Brampton Abbotts
Phocle Green
Upton Crews
Shaw Common
Netherton
Upper Grove Common
Gorsley
Blackwellsend Green
Michaelchurch
Newent
Bridstow
Rudhall
Linton
Gorsley Common
Kilcot
Malswick
Hartpury
St Owens Cross
Peterstow
Ross-on-Wye
Linton Hill
Birds of Prey Centre
Little Gorsley
Kent's Green
Clifford's Mesne
Bromsash
Weston under Penyard
Aston Crews
Wilton
Ashfield
Wilson
Three Ashes
Glewstone
Tudorville
Hom Green
Ryeford
Lea
Aston Ingham
Highleadon
Taynton
Rudford
Maisemore
Pontshill
Glasshouse
Tibberton
Highnam
Coughton
Goodrich Castle
Howle Hill
East Dean
Dursley Cross
Llangarron
Pencraig
Boxbush
May Hill
Glasshouse Hill
Ruxton Green
Walford
Hope Mansell
Longhope
Huntley
Highnam
Bulley
Goodrich
Dick Whittington Farm Park
Birdwood
Kerne Bridge
Crooked End
Mitcheldean
Marstow
Whitchurch
Old Forge
Ruardean
Drybrook
Little London
Churcham
Oakle Street
Welsh Newton
Wye Valley
Welsh Bicknor
Abenhall
Blaisdon
Great Doward
Symonds Yat
Ruardean Hill
Minsterworth
Crocker's Ash
Lower Lydbrook
Ruardean Woodside
Flaxley
Northwood Green
Elmore Back
Ganarew
Little Doward
Symonds Yat
English Bicknor
Brierley
Nailbridge
Broadmoor
Westbury on Severn
Chaxhill
Elmore
Dixton
Worrall Hill
Upper Lydbrook
Stantway
Bollow
Farleys End
Hillersland
Cinderford
Elton
Quedgeley
Christchurch
Edge End
Littledean
Westbury Court Garden
Longney
Staunton
Berry Hill
Forest of Dean
Ruspidge
Broadbush
Boxbush
The Kymin
Wyesham
Mile End
Rodley
Hardwicke
Monmouthshire
Broadwell
Beechenhurst Lodge
Newnham
Milton End
Epney
Penallt
Whitecliffe
Coleford
Upper Soudley
Ruddle
Arlingham
Upper Framilode
Redbrook
Newland
Lower Soudley
Brain's Green
Fretherne
Moreton Valence
Pen-twyn
Milkwall
Saul
Perrygrove Railway
Clearwell Meend
Northington
Whitminster
Highbury Wood
Parkend
A48
Clearwell Caves
Ellwood
Frampton on Severn
Clearwell
Yorkley
Blakeney
Awre
Westend
Marsh Lane
Nupend
Nastend
Whitecroft
Nibley
Stowe
Etloe
Whitebrook
Dean Forest Railway
Claypits
River Severn
Stonehouse
Maryland
Castle
St Briavels
Shepherds Patch
Alkerton
Purton
Slimbridge Wetland Centre
Bream
Eastington
Middle Street
Lower Meend
Allaston
Purton
Cambridge
Slimbridge
Llandogo
Lydney
Hinton
Frocester
Broadstone
Offa's Dyke Path
Coldharbour
Sharpness
Moorend
Tithe Barn
Leonard Stanley
Catbrook
Hewelsfield
Newtown
Halmore
Nympsfield
Gossington
Coaley
Aylburton
Brockweir
Tintern Parva
Woolaston Common
Alvington
Wanswell
Lower Cam
Far Green
Tintern Abbey
Park Hill
Smallbrook
Breadstone
River Wye
Chapel Hill
Hook Street
Berkeley Heath
Berkeley Road
Cam
Netherend
Berkeley
Ashmead Green
Uley Long Barrow
High Woolaston
Woolaston
The Quarry
Stinchcombe
Uley
Berkeley
Ham
Newport
Owlpen Manor
Stroat
Woodmancote
Boughspring
Bevington
Nibley Green
Dursley
Lancaut
Lower Wick
Pitt Court
Millend
Wibdon
Nupdown
Woodford
Woodcroft
Tidenham
Shepperdine
Hystfield
Stone
North Nibley
Tyndale
Tutshill
Michaelwood
Newington Bagpath
Castle
Hill
Lower Stone
Bournstream
Coombe
Sedbury
M5
Wotton-under-Edge
Oldbury Naite
Port Wall
Rockhampton
Tortworth
Ozleworth
Chepstow
(Cas-Gwent)
Oldbury-on-Severn
Lower Morton
Falfield
Whitfield
Newark Park
Bulwarks Camp
River Severn
Abbey Gatehouse
Pullens Green
Cowhill
Charfield
Boxwell
Kingswood
Tresham
Beachley
Bibstone
Mathern
St Pierre
M48
Littleton-
Milbury Heath
Cromhall
Townwell
Alderley
45
64

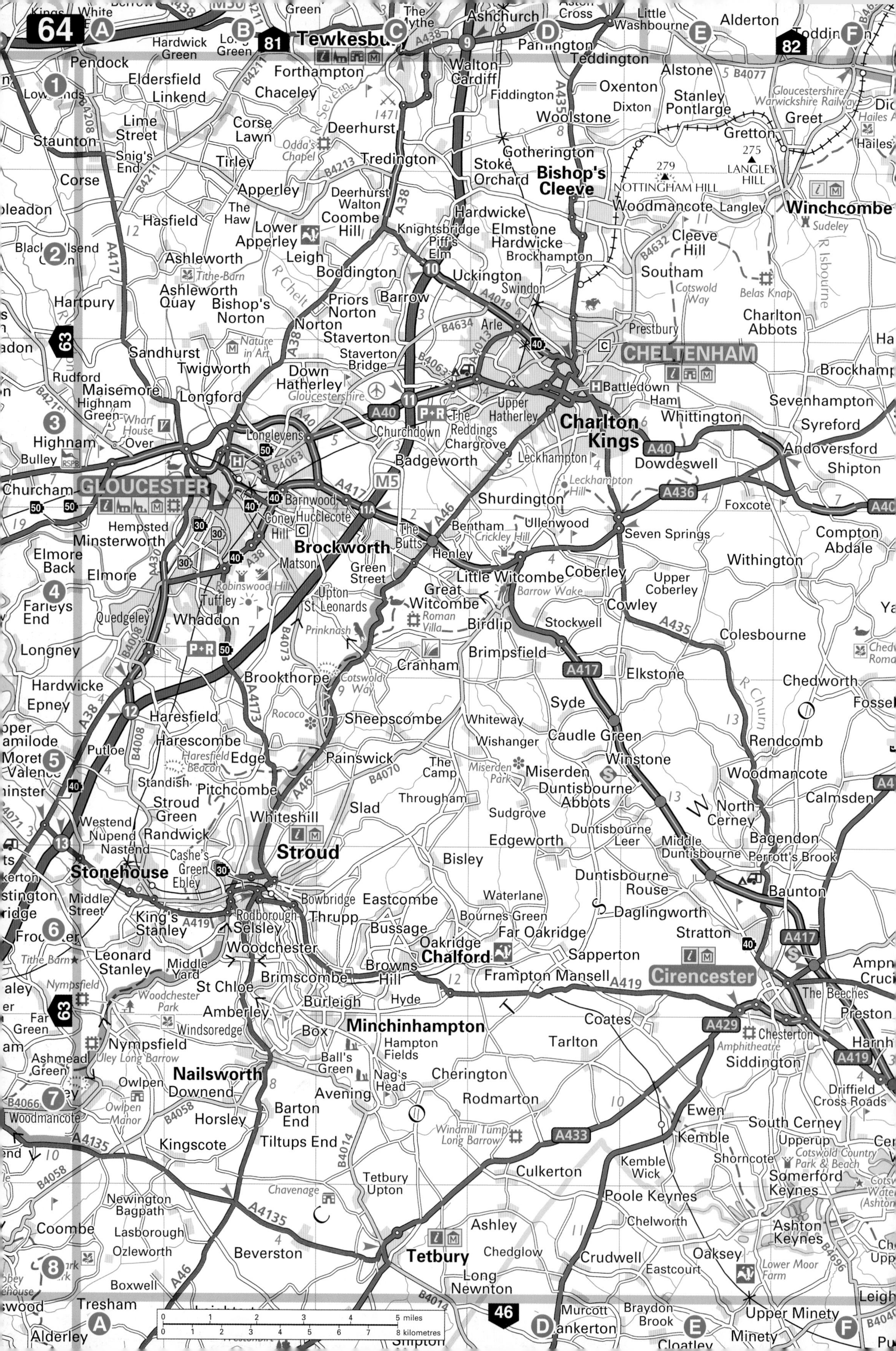

64
A
B
C
D
E
F
81
82
Tewkesbury
Kings
White
Hardwick
Long Green
Green
The Mythe
Ashchurch
Cross
Little Washbourne
Alderton
Toddington
Pendock
Forthampton
Walton Cardiff
Pamington
Teddington
Alstone
B4077
Eldersfield
Chaceley
Fiddington
Oxenton
Stanley Pontlarge
Gloucestershire Warwickshire Railway
Lowlands
Linkend
Dixton
Woolstone
Greet
Lime Street
Corse Lawn
Deerhurst
Gretton
Staunton
Odda's Chapel
Gotherington
Hailes
Snig's End
Tirley
Tredington
Stoke Orchard
Bishop's Cleeve
279
275
LANGLEY HILL
NOTTINGHAM HILL
Corse
Apperley
Deerhurst Walton
Woodmancote
Langley
Winchcombe
Sudeley
Pleadon
The Haw
Coombe Hill
Hardwicke
Hasfield
Lower Apperley
Knightsbridge
Elmstone Hardwicke
Cleeve Hill
Piff's Elm
Brockhampton
Blackwellsend Green
Ashleworth
Leigh
Boddington
Uckington
Southam
Tithe Barn
Swindon
Cotswold Way
Belas Knap
R Isbourne
Hartpury
Ashleworth Quay
Bishop's Norton
Priors Norton
Barrow
A4019
Charlton Abbots
63
Norton
Staverton
B4634
Arle
Prestbury
Sandhurst
Nature in Art
CHELTENHAM
Twigworth
Staverton Bridge
Brockhampton
Rudford
Down Hatherley
Battledown
Maisemore
Gloucestershire
Ham
Sevenhampton
Highnam Green
Longford
Upper Hatherley
Whittington
Wharf House
Over
The Reddings
Charlton Kings
Syreford
Highnam
Longlevens
Churchdown
Chargrove
Andoversford
Bulley
RSPB
Badgeworth
Leckhampton
Dowdeswell
Shipton
Churcham
GLOUCESTER
M5
Leckhampton Hill
A436
Barnwood
Shurdington
Foxcote
Hempsted
Hucclecote
Coney Hill
Bentham
Ullenwood
Compton Abdale
Minsterworth
The Butts
Seven Springs
Brockworth
Henley
Crickley Hill
Elmore Back
Matson
Withington
Elmore
Green Street
Little Witcombe
Coberley
Upper Coberley
Robinswood Hill
Upton St Leonards
Great Witcombe
Barrow Wake
Farleys End
Tuffley
Cowley
Quedgeley
Whaddon
Roman Villa
Birdlip
Stockwell
Colesbourne
Prinknash
A435
Longney
P+R
Cranham
Brimpsfield
A417
Elkstone
Chedworth Roman Villa
Hardwicke
Brookthorpe
Chedworth
Epney
Syde
Haresfield
Rococo
Sheepscombe
Whiteway
Fosse
R Churn
Caudle Green
Rendcomb
Putloe
Harescombe
Wishanger
Haresfield Beacon
Edge
Painswick
The Camp
Miserden Park
Miserden
Winstone
Woodmancote
Moreton Valence
Standish
Pitchcombe
Duntisbourne Abbots
Calmsden
Stroud Green
Throughham
B4070
Slad
Sudgrove
North Cerney
Westend
Whiteshill
Randwick
Duntisbourne Leer
Nupend
Middle Duntisbourne
Bagendon
Nastend
Stroud
Edgeworth
Perrott's Brook
Cashe's Green
Bisley
Stonehouse
Ebley
Duntisbourne Rouse
Baunton
Middle Street
Bowbridge
Eastcombe
Waterlane
King's Stanley
Rodborough
Thrupp
Bournes Green
Daglingworth
Stratton
A419
Selsley
Bussage
Far Oakridge
Frocester
Woodchester
Oakridge
Chalford
Sapperton
Tithe Barn
Leonard Stanley
Browns Hill
Cirencester
Middle Yard
Brimscombe
Frampton Mansell
Nympsfield
St Chloe
Hyde
The Beeches
Woodchester Park
Burleigh
Amberley
Coates
Preston
Windsoredge
Box
Minchinhampton
A429
Chesterton
Far Green
Nympsfield
Hampton Fields
Tarlton
Amphitheatre
Uley Long Barrow
Ball's Green
Siddington
Ashmead Green
Nailsworth
Nag's Head
Cherington
Owlpen
Downend
Avening
Rodmarton
Driffield Cross Roads
B4066
Owlpen Manor
Barton End
Ewen
Woodmancote
B4058
Horsley
South Cerney
A4135
Kingscote
Tiltups End
Windmill Tump Long Barrow
A433
Kemble
Upperup
B4014
Shorncote
Cotswold Country Park & Beach
Kemble Wick
Culkerton
Somerford Keynes
B4058
Tetbury Upton
Chavenage
Poole Keynes
Newington Bagpath
Coombe
Chelworth
Ashton Keynes
Lasborough
Ashley
Ozleworth
Beverston
Chedglow
Crudwell
Oaksey
Tetbury
Lower Moor Farm
Boxwell
Long Newnton
Eastcourt
B4696
46
Tresham
Murcott
Braydon Brook
Upper Minety
Leigh
Alderley
Hankerton
Minety
Cloatley
0 1 2 3 4 5 miles
0 1 2 3 4 5 6 7 8 kilometres

Snowshill
Cotswold Lavender
Batsford
Lemington
Cotswold Falconry Centre
Four Shire Stone
Barton-on-the-Heath
Compton
Bourton-on-the-Hill
Moreton-in-Marsh
Taddington
Bourton Downs
Sezincote
Kitebrook
Swerford
Great Rollright
Little Rollright
Rollright Stones
Cutsdean
Longborough
Chastleton
Little Compton
Ford
Condicote
Evenlode
Salford
Over Norton
Dunthrop
Temple Guiting
Donnington
Chastleton House
Broadwell
Adlestrop
Heythrop
Cotswold
Stow-on-the-Wold
Upper Swell
Lower Swell
Cornwell
The Common
Chipping Norton
Daylesford
Barton
Oddington
Maugersbury
Kingham
Churchill
Enstone
Naunton
Upper Slaughter
Dean
Lower Slaughter
Wyck Rissington
Icomb
Bledington
Sarsden
Chadlington
Taston
Foscot
Spelsbury
Bourton-on-the-Water
Aylworth
Miniatures
Model Village
Westcote
Nether Westcote
Foxholes
Lyneham
Greenend
Bruern Abbey
Notgrove
Motor & Toy
Little Rissington
Upper Rissington
Idbury
Fifield
Chilson
Hazleton
Cold Aston
Clapton-on-the-Hill
Ascott Earl
Ascott-under-Wychwood
Turkdean
Milton-under-Wychwood
Shipton-under-Wychwood
Wychwood
Finstock
Great Rissington
R Windrush
Langley
Ramsden
Farmington
Habber Gallows Hill
Fullbrook Hill
Leafield
Northleach
Sherborne
Great Barrington
Taynton
Whiteoak Green
Delly End
World of Mechanical Music
Eastington
Windrush
Fordwells
North Leigh
Little Barrington
Upton
Fulbrook
Asthall Leigh
Crawley
Hailey
Swinbrook
Minster Lovell
Minster Lovell Hall
Coln St Dennis
Burford
Asthall
Witney
Charterville Allotments
Calcot
Westwell
Signet
Coln Rogers
Aldsworth
Cotswold Wildlife Park
Holwell
Shilton
Winson
Cogges
Curbridge
Ablington
R Leach
Brize Norton
Ducklington
Arlington
Bibury
Carterton
Lew
Coln St Aldwyns
Hatherop
Eastleach Turville
Eastleach Martin
Kencot
Alvescot
Yelford
Filkins
Black Bourton
Quenington
Broughton Poggs
Broadwell
Aston
Bampton
Cote
Ampney St Mary
Southrop
Weald
Fairford Park
Langford
Little Clanfield
Clanfield
Fairford
Little Faringdon
Poulton
Milton End
Grafton
Chimney
Horcott
Lechlade on Thames
Radcot
R Thames
Meysey Hampton
Whelford
Kelmscott
Thrup
Carswell Marsh
Inglesham
Hinton Waldrist
Buscot
Thames Path
Eaton Hastings
Buckland
Marston Meysey
Dunfield
Cotswold Water Park (Fairford/Lechlade)
Littleworth
Down Ampney
Kempsford
R Cole
Buscot Park
Pusey
Upper Inglesham
Faringdon
Charney Bassett
Latton
Castle Eaton
Hannington Wick
Badbury Hill
Hatford
Great Coxwell Barn
Coleshill
Little Coxwell
Calcutt
Hannington
Westrop
Stanford in the Vale
Highworth
Great Coxwell
Shellingford
Hampton
Eastrop
Fernham
Swindon & Cricklade Railway
Broad Blunsdon
Vale of White Horse
Goosey
Stanton Fitzwarren
Baulking
Blunsdon
Longcot

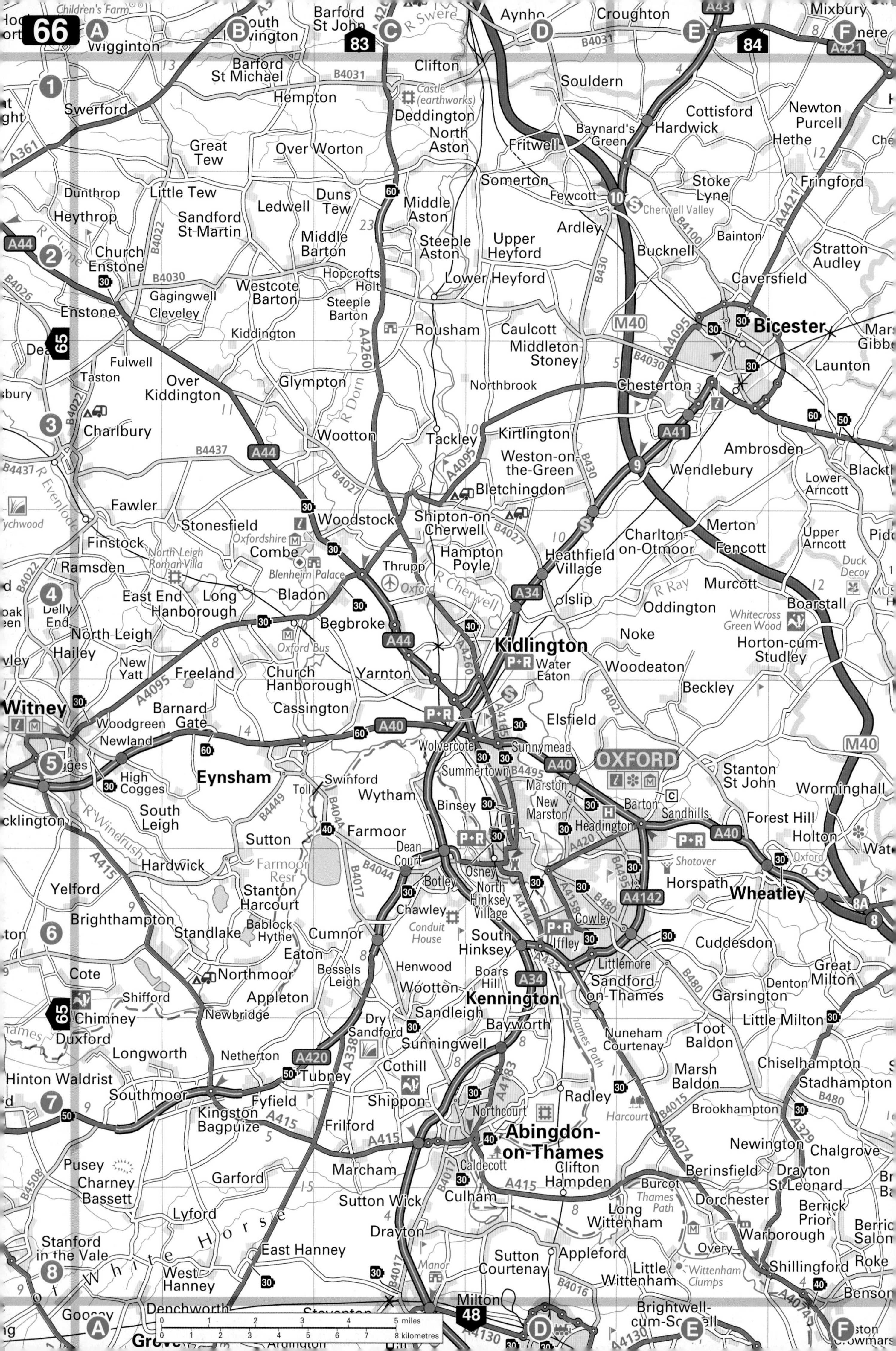

66
83
84
65
48
Children's Farm
Wigginton
South Newington
Barford St John
Barford St Michael
R Swere
Aynho
Croughton
Mixbury
Clifton
Souldern
Swerford
Hempton
Castle (earthworks)
Deddington
Cottisford
Hardwick
Newton Purcell
Hethe
Great Tew
Over Worton
North Aston
Fritwell
Baynard's Green
Dunthrop
Little Tew
Ledwell
Duns Tew
Middle Aston
Somerton
Fewcott
Stoke Lyne
Fringford
Heythrop
Sandford St Martin
Middle Barton
Steeple Aston
Upper Heyford
Ardley
Cherwell Valley
Bainton
Church Enstone
Bucknell
Stratton Audley
Westcote Barton
Hopcrofts Holt
Steeple Barton
Lower Heyford
Caversfield
Enstone
Gagingwell
Cleveley
Kiddington
Rousham
Caulcott
Middleton Stoney
Bicester
Launton
Fulwell
Taston
Over Kiddington
Glympton
R Dorn
Northbrook
Chesterton
Charlbury
Wootton
Tackley
Kirtlington
Ambrosden
Weston-on-the-Green
Wendlebury
Lower Arncott
Blackthorn
Fawler
Woodstock
Bletchingdon
Shipton-on-Cherwell
Stonesfield
Oxfordshire Museum
Combe
Finstock
North Leigh Roman Villa
Blenheim Palace
Hampton Poyle
Heathfield Village
Charlton-on-Otmoor
Merton
Fencott
Upper Arncott
Ramsden
Thrupp
Oxford
R Cherwell
Murcott
Duck Decoy
East End
Long Hanborough
Bladon
Islip
Oddington
R Ray
Boarstall
Whitecross Green Wood
Delly End
North Leigh
Begbroke
Noke
Horton-cum-Studley
Hailey
Oxford Bus
Kidlington
Water Eaton
New Yatt
Freeland
Church Hanborough
Yarnton
Woodeaton
Beckley
Witney
Woodgreen
Barnard Gate
Cassington
Elsfield
Newland
Eynsham
Wolvercote
Sunnymead
OXFORD
Summertown
Stanton St John
High Cogges
Swinford
Toll
Wytham
Marston
New Marston
Barton
Sandhills
Worminghall
South Leigh
Binsey
Headington
Forest Hill
Holton
Sutton
Farmoor
Dean Court
Shotover
Wheatley
R Windrush
Hardwick
Farmoor Resr
Botley
Osney
North Hinksey Village
Horspath
Yelford
Stanton Harcourt
Chawley
Cowley
Conduit House
Brighthampton
Standlake
Bablock Hythe
Cumnor
South Hinksey
Iffley
Cuddesdon
Eaton
Littlemore
Great Milton
Cote
Bessels Leigh
Henwood
Boars Hill
Sandford-on-Thames
Denton
Garsington
Shifford
Northmoor
Wootton
Kennington
Chimney
Appleton
Newbridge
Sandleigh
Little Milton
Duxford
Dry Sandford
Bayworth
Toot Baldon
Thames Path
Nuneham Courtenay
Longworth
Netherton
Sunningwell
Chiselhampton
Cothill
Marsh Baldon
Hinton Waldrist
Tubney
Stadhampton
Southmoor
Fyfield
Shippon
Radley
Kingston Bagpuize
Northcourt
Harcourt
Brookhampton
Frilford
Abingdon-on-Thames
Newington
Chalgrove
Pusey
Garford
Marcham
Caldecott
Clifton Hampden
Berinsfield
Drayton St Leonard
Charney Bassett
Culham
Burcot
Sutton Wick
Dorchester
Berrick Prior
Lyford
Long Wittenham
Warborough
Stanford in the Vale
Drayton
Vale of White Horse
East Hanney
Appleford
Overy
Wittenham Clumps
Shillingford
West Hanney
Manor
Sutton Courtenay
Little Wittenham
Benson
Goosey
Denchworth
Milton
Brightwell-cum-Sotwell
Grove
M40
A44
A4260
A4095
A34
A40
A420
A415
A4074
A4142
A41
A43
A421
A4421
A338
A4183
A4130
B4030
B4031
B4027
B4022
B4437
B4449
B4044
B4017
B4495
B4015
B480
B4016
B4100
B430
B4508
0 1 2 3 4 5 miles
0 1 2 3 4 5 6 7 8 kilometres

84
49
68
Bletchley
Newton Longville
Little Brickhill
Great Brickhill
Potsgrove
Gawcott
Singleborough
Great Horwood
Little Horwood
Padbury
Adstock
Drayton Parslow
Stoke Hammond
Preston Bissett
Hillesden
Addington
Winslow
Mursley
Heath and Reach
Steeple Claydon
Middle Claydon
Twyford
Shipton
Hollingdon
Swanbourne
Soulbury
Clipstone
Stewkley
Claydon House
East Claydon
Hoggeston
Linslade
Leighton Buzzard
Calvert
Granborough
Dunton
Botolph Claydon
Burcott
Littleworth
Stanbridge
Edgcott
North Marston
Cublington
Wing
Ascott
Grove
Finemere Wood
Little Billington
Ledburn
186
QUAINTON HILL
Oving
Whitchurch
Slapton
R Ray
Grendon Underwood
Aston Abbotts
Pitchcott
Nup End
Mentmore
Northall
Quainton
Crafton
Kingswood
Woodham
Buckinghamshire Railway Centre
Hardwick
Wingrave
Horton
Grand Union Canal
Ludgershall
Westcott
Waddesdon
Weedon
Rowsham
Cheddington
Wotton Underwood
Hulcott
Ivinghoe
Waddesdon Manor
Bierton
Long Marston
Rushbeds Wood
Upper Winchendon
Burcott
Puttenham
Astrope
Marsworth
Dorton
Upper Pollicott
Ashendon
Aylesbury
Broughton
Wilstone
Bulbourne
R Thame
Wilstone Green
Tringford
Lower Pollicott
Nether Winchendon
Stone
Lower Hartwell
Buckland
Tring Wharf
New Mill
Chilton
Southcourt
Aston Clinton
Drayton Beauchamp
Tring
Cuddington
Sedrup
Stoke Mandeville
Upton
Dinton
Weston Turville
Chearsley
Westlington
Bucks Goat Centre
Halton
Dancersend
Easington
Long Crendon Courthouse
Bishopstone
Hastoe
Wigginton
Wigginton Bottom
Long Crendon
Haddenham
Ford
Marsh
North Lee
Worlds End
Ridgeway Path
Lower End
Tiggywinkles Wildlife Hospital
Kimble Wick
Nash Lee
Wendover
Buckland Common
Aston Sandford
Little Kimble
Church End
St Leonards
Shabbington
Thame
Kingsey
Owlswick
Meadle
Butler's Cross
Cholesbury
Ellesborough
Rycote
Askett
Great Kimble
Kingsash
Ilmer
Pulpit Hill
Lee
Rycote Chapel
Towersey
Longwick
Monks Risborough
Dunsmore
The Lee
Clump
Bellingdon
Whiteleaf
Little Hampden
Moreton
Cross (hill carving)
Lee Common
Milton Common
Skittle Green
Pitch Green
Princes Risborough
Hunts Green
Ballinger Common
Emmington
Henton
Great Hampden
Potter Row
Tetsworth
Horsenden
Sydenham
Bledlow
Saunderton
South Heath
Latchford
Chalford
Kingston Stert
Chinnor & Princes Risborough Railway
Loosley Row
Hyde Heath
Postcombe
Oakley
Chinnor
Lacey Green
Great Missenden
Adwell
209
LODGE HILL
Prestwood
Crowell
Bryant's Bottom
Image
Rout's Green
Speen
Heath End
Wheatfield
Kingston Blount
Aston Rowant
Walter's Ash
Little Kingshill
Little Missenden
Radnage
Hughenden Valley
Great Kingshill
Amersham
South Weston
Lewknor
Bennett End
Bledlow Ridge
Amersham Old Town
Cryers Hill
Holmer Green
The City
Bradenham
Pyrton
Naphill
Penn Street
Cuxham
Shirburn
Stokenchurch
Beacon's Bottom
Hell-Fire Caves
Hughenden Manor
Widmer End
Hazlemere
West Wycombe
Downley
Brightwell Upperton
Watlington
Horsley's Green
Piddington
Winchmore Hill
Tylers Green
Christmas Common
West Wycombe Park
High Wycombe
Penn
Ibstone
Knotty Green
Britwell Salome
Wheeler End
Sands
Cadmore End
Cressex
Forty Green
Wycombe Marsh
Northend
Ridgeway Path
Bolter End
Lane End
Booker
Turville
Cookley Green
Loudwater
Fingest
Handy
M40
A40
A41
A413
A418
A421
A4010
A4128
A4129
A4146
A5
A329
A355
A404
B4033
B4032
B4034
B4009
B4012
B4443
B4444
B4445
B482
B480
B485
B488
B489
B474
B4635

68
A
B
C
D
E
F
85
86
Brickhill
Woburn
Park
Berry End
Church End
Pulloxhill
Westoning
Hanscombe
Higham Gobion
Shillington
Apsley End
Holwell
Burge End
Little Brickhill
Woburn Abbey
Church End
Tingrith
Westoning Woodend
Harlington
Barton-le-Clay
Pirton
Ickleford
Great Brickhill
Potsgrove
Milton Bryan
Sharpenhoe
Hexton
Pegsdon
Hitchin
Stockgrove
King's Wood
A5
Toddington
Barton Hills
Ravensburgh Castle
Sundon Hills
Heath and Reach
Battlesden
Upper Sundon
Streatley
Little Offley
Charlton
Chalgrave
Fancott
Well Head
Hockliffe
Tebworth
Lower Sundon
Warden Hill
Great Offley
Clipstone
Chalton
Marsh Farm
Lilley
Linslade
Eggington
Wingfield
Sundon Park
A6
Limbury
Leygreen
Leighton Buzzard
Tilsworth
Houghton Regis
Mangrove Green
Stanbridge
Leagrave
Stopsley
Cockernhoe
Littleworth
A505
Ascott
Grove
Billington
Sewell
Totternhoe
Wandon End
Darleyhall
Little Billington
Eaton Green
Round Green
Ledburn
Slapton
Eaton Bray
Chaul End
LUTON
Breachwood Green
Whitwell
Church End
Stockwood
Luton
Mentmore
Northall
Moor End
Dunstable
Someries
Crafton
Horton
Edlesborough
Tree Cathedral
Church End
Caddington
Chiltern Green
Peter's Green
Wingrave
Kensworth Common
Slip End
Ivinghoe Aston
Whipsnade
Pepperstock
East Hyde
Cheddington
Woodside Farm & Leisure Park
West Hyde
Blackmore End
ZSL Whipsnade
Holywell
Ivinghoe
Kinsbourne Green
Thrales End
Long Marston
Dagnall
Studham
Markyate
Cold Harbour
Windmill
Clement's End
Flamstead
Batford
Astrope
Pitstone
Harpenden
Marshall's Heath
Wilstone
Marsworth
Ringshall
Little Gaddesden
Jockey End
Trowley Bottom
Wheathampstead
Bulbourne
Herts County
Hatching Green
Wilstone Green
Tringford
Bridgewater
Hudnall
Gaddesden Row
Amwell
Tring Wharf
New Mill
Ashridge Estate
Redbourn
Drayton Beauchamp
Tring
Aldbury
Great Gaddesden
Church End
Childwick Green
Water End
Dancersend
Wigginton
Nettleden
Piccotts End
Childwick Bury
Halton
Dudswell
Frithsden
Ridgeway Path
Hastoe
Castle
Potten End
M1
ST ALBANS
Wigginton Bottom
Wendover
Buckland Common
Northchurch
HEMEL HEMPSTEAD
Marshalswick
Berkhamsted
Adeyfield
Theatre
Clock Tower
St Leonards
Leverstock Green
Old Gorhambury House
Bourne End
Boxmoor
Cholesbury
Hawridge
A41
A414
Tyttenhanger
Kingsash
Ashley Green
Whelpley Hill
Two Waters
Bellingdon
Lee
Potters Crouch
The Lee
Clump
Felden
Gardens of the Rose
Asheridge
Chiswell Green
Park Street
Lee Common
Chartridge
Lye Green
Bovingdon
Bedmond
A405
Hunts Green
Kings Langley
Ballinger Common
Chesham
Bulstrode
Potter Row
South Heath
Botley
Abbots Langley
Bricket Wood
Colney Street
Ley Hill
Garston
Shenley
Great Missenden
Hyde Heath
Waterside
Chipperfield
Hunton Bridge
Flaunden
Bucks Hill
Studio Tour
Radlett
Belsize
M25
Heath End
Chesham Bois
Sarratt
Little Kingshill
Amersham
Latimer
Aldenham
Round Bush
Little Missenden
Amersham on the Hill
Micklefield Green
Chandler's Cross
Letchmore Heath
Great Kingshill
Chenies
Amersham Old Town
Amersham Common
Cryers Hill
Holmer Green
Little Chalfont
Chorleywood
WATFORD
Patchetts Green
Chorleywood West
Borehamwood
Penn Street
Croxley Green
Bushey
Hazlemere
Rickmansworth
Coleshill
Winchmore Hill
Tylers Green
Heronsgate
Chiltern Open Air
Oxhey
Bushey Heath
Merry Hill
HIGH WYCOMBE
Penn
Knotty Green
Chalfont St Giles
Batchworth
Maple Cross
Horn Hill
Beaconsfield Model Village
Forty Green
Seer Green
Chalfont Common
Batchworth Heath
Eastbury
Stanmore
Wycombe Marsh
West Hyde
50
Hatch End
5 miles
8 kilometres

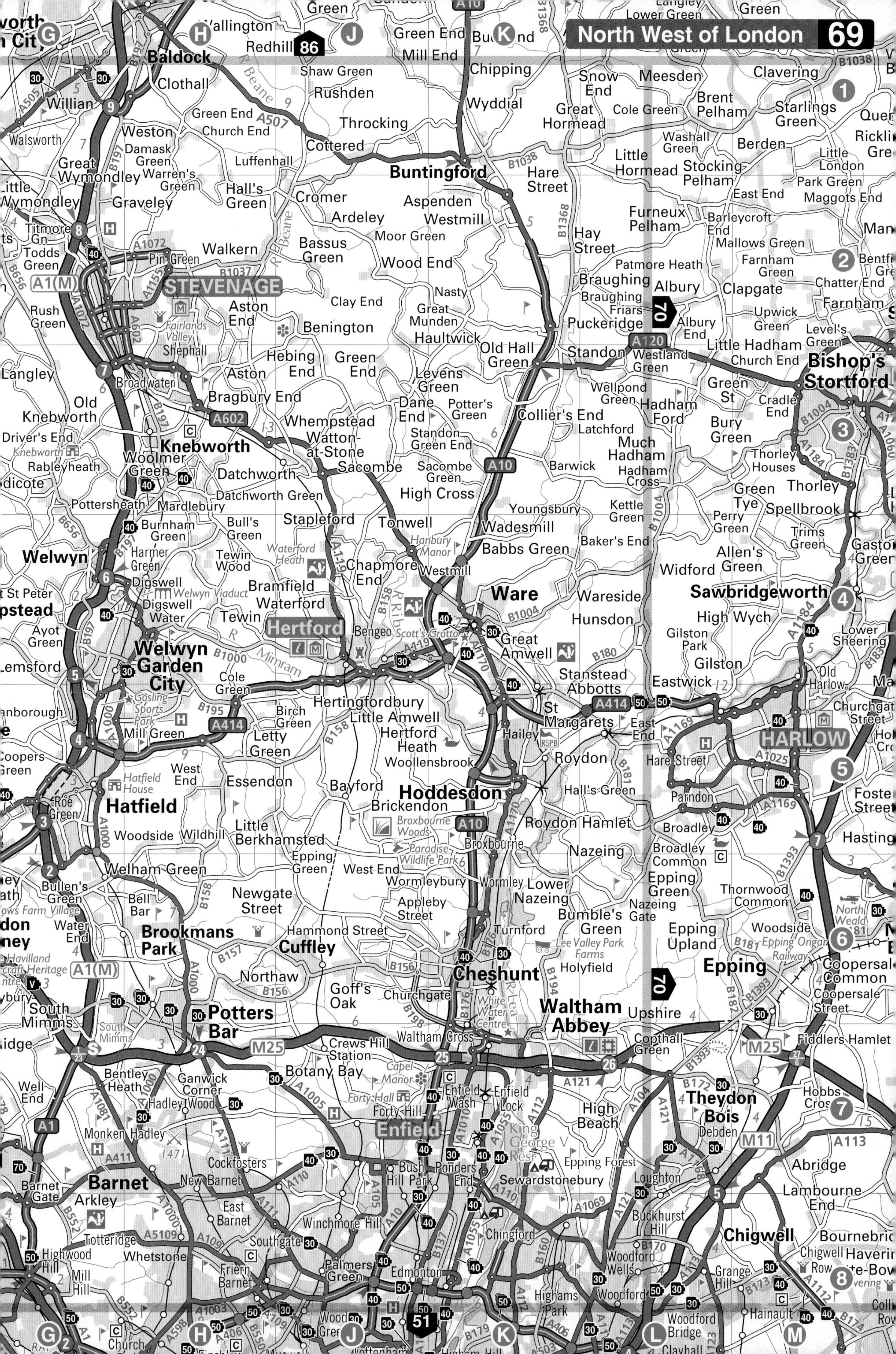

Baldock
Wallington
Redhill
Clothall
Willian
Walsworth
Weston
Great Wymondley
Little Wymondley
Graveley
Titmore Gn
Todds Green
STEVENAGE
Rush Green
Langley
Old Knebworth
Driver's End
Knebworth
Woolmer Green
Rableyheath
Codicote
Pottersheath
Welwyn
Harmer Green
Digswell
Digswell Water
Ayot Green
Lemsford
Welwyn Garden City
Mill Green
Roe Green
Hatfield
Woodside
Welham Green
Bullen's Green
Bell Bar
Water End
Brookmans Park
South Mimms
Potters Bar
Bentley Heath
Ganwick Corner
Hadley Wood
Monken Hadley
Barnet
Barnet Gate
Arkley
Totteridge
Whetstone
Highwood Hill
Mill Hill
Cockfosters
New Barnet
East Barnet
Southgate
Friern Barnet
Shaw Green
Rushden
Throcking
Cottered
Luffenhall
Hall's Green
Cromer
Ardeley
Walkern
Bassus Green
Aston End
Benington
Clay End
Aston
Hebing End
Bragbury End
Datchworth
Datchworth Green
Mardlebury
Burnham Green
Bull's Green
Tewin Wood
Tewin
Bramfield
Waterford
Hertford
Bengeo
Cole Green
Letty Green
Birch Green
Hertingfordbury
Essendon
West End
Little Berkhamsted
Wildhill
Newgate Street
Cuffley
Northaw
Goff's Oak
Crews Hill Station
Botany Bay
Enfield
Forty Hill
Bush Hill Park
Winchmore Hill
Palmers Green
Edmonton
Buntingford
Chipping
Wyddial
Aspenden
Westmill
Moor Green
Wood End
Nasty
Great Munden
Haultwick
Green End
Levens Green
Dane End
Potter's Green
Standon Green End
Watton-at-Stone
Whempstead
Sacombe
Sacombe Green
High Cross
Stapleford
Tonwell
Chapmore End
Wadesmill
Babbs Green
Ware
Great Amwell
Stanstead Abbotts
St Margarets
Hailey
Little Amwell
Hertford Heath
Woollensbrook
Hoddesdon
Bayford
Brickendon
Broxbourne
West End
Wormleybury
Wormley
Appleby Street
Hammond Street
Turnford
Cheshunt
Churchgate
Waltham Cross
Enfield Wash
Enfield Lock
Sewardstonebury
Chingford
Highams Park
Woodford Wells
Woodford
Great Hormead
Hare Street
Hay Street
Braughing
Braughing Friars
Puckeridge
Standon
Old Hall Green
Collier's End
Youngsbury
Barwick
Latchford
Much Hadham
Hadham Cross
Kettle Green
Baker's End
Widford
Wareside
Hunsdon
Eastwick
Roydon
Hall's Green
Roydon Hamlet
Nazeing
Lower Nazeing
Bumble's Green
Holyfield
Waltham Abbey
Upshire
Copthall Green
High Beach
Loughton
Buckhurst Hill
Snow End
Meesden
Clavering
Brent Pelham
Starlings Green
Berden
Little Hormead
Stocking Pelham
Furneux Pelham
Barleycroft End
Patmore Heath
Albury
Albury End
Little Hadham
Hadham Ford
Bury Green
Green Tye
Perry Green
Allen's Green
Sawbridgeworth
High Wych
Gilston Park
Gilston
HARLOW
Hare Street
Parndon
Broadley Common
Epping Green
Nazeing Gate
Epping Upland
Epping
Thornwood Common
Theydon Bois
Debden
Abridge
Lambourne End
Chigwell
Grange Hill
Hainault
Woodford Bridge
Bishop's Stortford
Thorley
Thorley Houses
Spellbrook
Trims Green
Farnham
Farnham Green
Clapgate
Upwick Green
Mallows Green
Maggots End
Little London
Park Green
East End
Washall Green
Cole Green
Wellpond Green
Westland Green
Cradle End
Green St
Lower Sheering
Old Harlow
Churchgate Street
Foster Street
Hastingwood
North Weald
Woodside
Coopersale Common
Coopersale Street
Fiddlers Hamlet
Hobbs Cross
Epping Ongar Railway
Lee Valley Park Farms
Epping Forest
King George V Res
Paradise Wildlife Park
Broxbourne Woods
Hanbury Manor
Scott's Grotto
Waterford Heath
Fairlands Valley
Shephall
Broadwater
Pin Green
Gosling Sports Park
Hatfield House
Welwyn Viaduct
Capel Manor
Forty Hall
White Water Centre

87 88 69 52

A B C D E F

Anstey, Lower Green, Green, Roast Green, Stickling Green, Newport, Howlett End, Debden, Thaxted

Mill End, Chipping, Wyddial, Snow End, Meesden, Brent Pelham, Clavering, Wicken Bonhunt, Rickling, Widdington, Debden Green

Great Hormead, Cole Green, Starlings Green, Quendon, Hamperden End, Cutler's Green, Bardfield End Green

Buntingford, Hare Street, Little Hormead, Washall Green, Berden, Stocking Pelham, Little London, Rickling Green, Henham, R Cam

Aspenden, Westmill, Green, Hay Street, Furneux Pelham, Barleycroft End, East End, Park Green, Maggots End, Ugley, Ugley Green, Woodend Green, Monk Street, Sibley's Green

Mallows Green, Manuden, Pledgdon Green, Broxted, Duton Hill, Tilty, Lindsell

Patmore Heath, Braughing, Albury, Farnham Green, Clapgate, Bentfield Green, Elsenham, Fuller's End, Gaunt's End, Brick End, Great Easton

Nasty, Great Munden, Braughing Friars, Chatter End, Farnham, Tye Green, Molehill Green

Haultwick, Puckeridge, Albury End, Upwick Green, Level's Green, Stansted Mountfitchet, Burton End, Little Easton

Old Hall Green, Standon, Westland Green, Little Hadham, Church End, Birchanger, Stansted, Bamber's Green, Great Dunmow

Levens Green, Wellpond Green, Green St, Cradle End, Bishop's Stortford, Takeley, Smith's Green, Little Canfield

Potter's Green, Collier's End, Hadham Ford, Bury Green, Takeley St, Brewers End, Birchanger Green, Hatfield Forest, Hope End Green, Barnston

Stand Green End, Latchford, Much Hadham, Thorley Houses, Great Hallingbury, Philpot End, Wellstye Green

Sacombe Green, Barwick, Hadham Cross, Thorley, Little Hallingbury, Great Canfield

High Cross, Youngsbury, Kettle Green, Green Tye, Spellbrook, Perry Green, Hatfield Broad Oak, Taverners Green, High Roding, Bishop's Green

Wadesmill, Hanbury Manor, Baker's End, Trims Green, Wright's Green, Broad Street, R Roding

Babbs Green, Allen's Green, Gaston Green, Aythorpe Roding, THE RODINGS

Westmill, Widford, Hatfield Heath

Ware, Wareside, Sawbridgeworth, Roundbush Gn

Hunsdon, High Wych, Ardley End, White Roding, High Easter

Scott's Grotto, Great Amwell, Gilston Park, Lower Sheering, Sheering, Leaden Roding, Clatterford End

Gilston, Old Harlow, Newman's End, Manwood Green, Margaret Roding, Good Easter

Stanstead Abbotts, Eastwick, Matching Tye, Matching, Nether Street

Amwell, St Margarets, East End, Churchgate Street, Carters Green, Matching Green, Abbess Roding, Pepper's Green, Farnham End

Hertford Heath, Hailey, RSPB, HARLOW, Hobbs Cross, Beauchamp Roding

Hoddesdon, Roydon, Hare Street, Threshers Bush, Little Laver, Birds Green

Hall's Green, Parndon, High Laver, Norwood End, Miller's Green, Shellow Bowells

Broxbourne Woods, Roydon Hamlet, Broadley, Foster Street, Magdalen Laver, Fyfield, Willingale, Cooksmill Green

Paradise Wildlife Park, Broxbourne, Nazeing, Broadley Common, Hastingwood, Moreton

Wormleybury, Wormley, Lower Nazeing, Epping Green, Thornwood Common, Tyler's Green, Bobbingworth, Shelley, Norton Mandeville, Radley Green

Appleby Street, Bumble's Green, Nazeing Gate, North Weald, Bovinger, Norton Heath

Turnford, Lee Valley Park Farms, Epping Upland, Woodside, Epping Ongar Railway, North Weald Bassett, High Ongar

Cheshunt, Holyfield, Epping, Coopersale Common, Wooden Church, Greensted, Chipping Ongar, Blackmore

Waltham Abbey, Upshire, Coopersale Street, Toot Hill, Marden Ash, Paslow Wood Common, Stondon Massey, Mill Green

White Water Centre, Waltham Cross, Copthall Green, Fiddlers Hamlet, Stanford Rivers, Hook End, Fryerning

Enfield Lock, High Beach, Theydon Bois, Hobbs Cross, Stapleford Tawney, Hare Street, Doddinghurst, Wyatt's Green, Heybridge

Nuclear Bunker, Passingford Bridge, Kelvedon Hatch, Fox Hatch, Swallows Cross

King George V Res, Debden, Navestock, Navestock Side, Mountnessing

Epping Forest, Ponders End, Sewardstonebury, Loughton, Abridge, Sabine's Green, Crow Green, Pilgrims Hatch

Lambourne End, R Rom, Wattons Green, Coxtie Green, Shenfield

Chingford, Buckhurst Hill, Chigwell, Stapleford Abbotts, South Weald, BRENTWOOD, Hutton

Edmonton, Woodford Wells, Bournebridge, Noak Hill, Brook Street

Highams Park, Woodford, Grange Hill, Chigwell Row, Havering-atte-Bower, Harold Hill

Hainault, Collier Row, Ingrave, Thorndon Little Warley

0 1 2 3 4 5 miles

0 1 2 3 4 5 6 7 8 kilometres

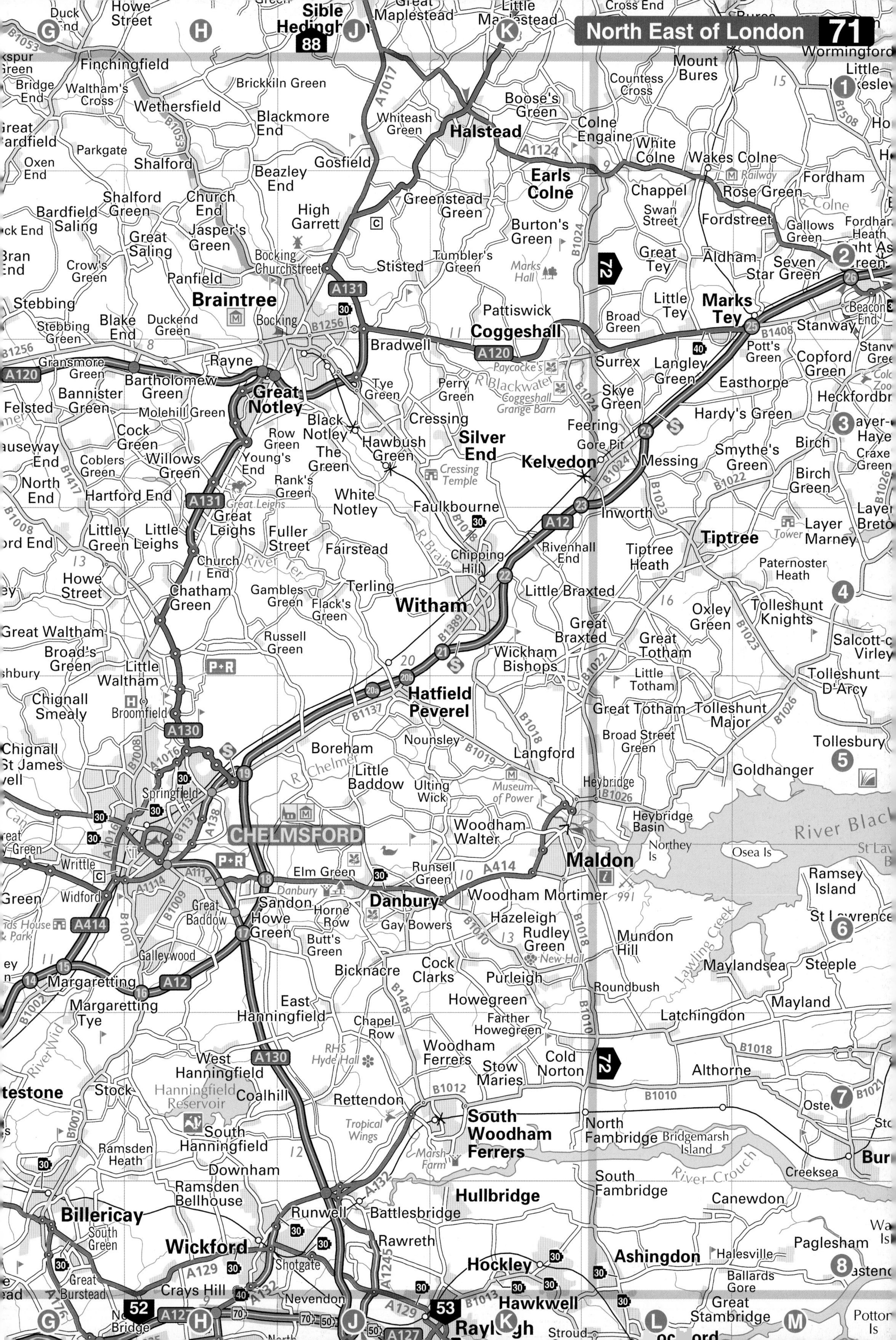
Duck End
Howe Street
Sible Hedingham
88
Great Maplestead
Little Maplestead
Cross End
Wormingford
Finchingfield
Little Horkesley
Mount Bures
Countess Cross
Brickkiln Green
Bridge End
Waltham's Cross
Wethersfield
Boose's Green
Great Bardfield
Blackmore End
Whiteash Green
Halstead
Colne Engaine
White Colne
Wakes Colne
Parkgate
A1124
Oxen End
Shalford
Gosfield
Beazley End
Earls Colne
Chappel
Fordham
Railway
Rose Green
R Colne
Shalford Green
Church End
Greenstead Green
Bardfield Saling
High Garrett
Swan Street
Fordstreet
Gallows Green
Fordham Heath
Jasper's Green
Great Saling
Burton's Green
Great Tey
Aldham
Seven Star Green
Bran End
Crow's Green
Bocking Churchstreet
Stisted
Tumbler's Green
Marks Hall
72
Panfield
A131
Little Tey
Marks Tey
Braintree
Stebbing
Pattiswick
Broad Green
Stanway
Beacon End
Stebbing Green
Blake End
Duckend Green
Bocking
B1256
Coggeshall
B1408
Bradwell
A120
Pott's Green
Copford Green
Gransmore Green
Rayne
Surrex
Langley Green
Paycocke's
R Blackwater
Bartholomew Green
Easthorpe
Bannister Green
Great Notley
Tye Green
Perry Green
Coggeshall Grange Barn
Skye Green
Heckfordbridge
Felsted
Molehill Green
Black Notley
Cressing
Feering
Hardy's Green
Cock Green
Row Green
Hawbush Green
Silver End
Gore Pit
Birch
Messing
Smythe's Green
Causeway End
Willows Green
Young's End
The Green
Kelvedon
Coblers Green
Cressing Temple
Birch Green
B1022
North End
Rank's Green
White Notley
Hartford End
Great Leighs
Faulkbourne
Inworth
B1023
Layer Marney
Tiptree
Tower
Great Leighs
A12
Littley Green
Little Leighs
Fuller Street
Fairstead
R Brain
Rivenhall End
Tiptree Heath
Paternoster Heath
Chipping Hill
Church End
River Ter
Howe Street
Witham
Little Braxted
Chatham Green
Gambles Green
Terling
Flack's Green
Oxley Green
Tolleshunt Knights
Great Braxted
Great Waltham
Russell Green
B1389
Great Totham
Salcott-cum-Virley
Broad's Green
Wickham Bishops
Little Waltham
P+R
Little Totham
Tolleshunt D'Arcy
Chignall Smealy
Broomfield
Hatfield Peverel
B1137
Great Totham
Tolleshunt Major
A130
Nounsley
B1018
B1026
Chignall St James
Boreham
B1019
Langford
Broad Street Green
Tollesbury
Springfield
Little Baddow
R Chelmer
Heybridge
Goldhanger
Ulting Wick
Museum of Power
Woodham Walter
Heybridge Basin
River Blackwater
CHELMSFORD
Northey Is
Osea Is
Writtle
Maldon
A414
Elm Green
Runsell Green
Ramsey Island
Danbury
Woodham Mortimer
Widford
Sandon
Great Baddow
Horne Row
Howe Green
Gay Bowers
Hazeleigh
St Lawrence
Hylands House & Park
B1007
B1009
B1010
Rudley Green
Mundon Hill
Butt's Green
New Hall
Lawling Creek
Galleywood
Bicknacre
Cock Clarks
Purleigh
Maylandsea
Steeple
Margaretting
Roundbush
Howegreen
Mayland
Margaretting Tye
East Hanningfield
B1418
Latchingdon
Chapel Row
Farther Howegreen
RHS Hyde Hall
Woodham Ferrers
B1018
Stow Maries
Cold Norton
Althorne
West Hanningfield
Ingatestone
Stock
Hanningfield Reservoir
Coalhill
Rettendon
B1012
South Woodham Ferrers
B1010
Oster
B1021
South Hanningfield
Tropical Wings
North Fambridge
Bridgemarsh Island
Ramsden Heath
Marsh Farm
Burnham
Creeksea
Downham
South Fambridge
River Crouch
Ramsden Bellhouse
Hullbridge
Canewdon
Billericay
Runwell
Battlesbridge
A132
South Green
Wickford
Rawreth
Paglesham
Ashingdon
Halesville
Great Burstead
Shotgate
Hockley
Ballards Gore
A129
A1245
Crays Hill
Nevendon
Hawkwell
Great Stambridge
52
53
Noak Bridge
A127
Rayleigh
Stroud Green
Potton Island
B1013
B1002
A176
B1008
B1417
B1053
A1017
A1016
A138
A1114
B1024

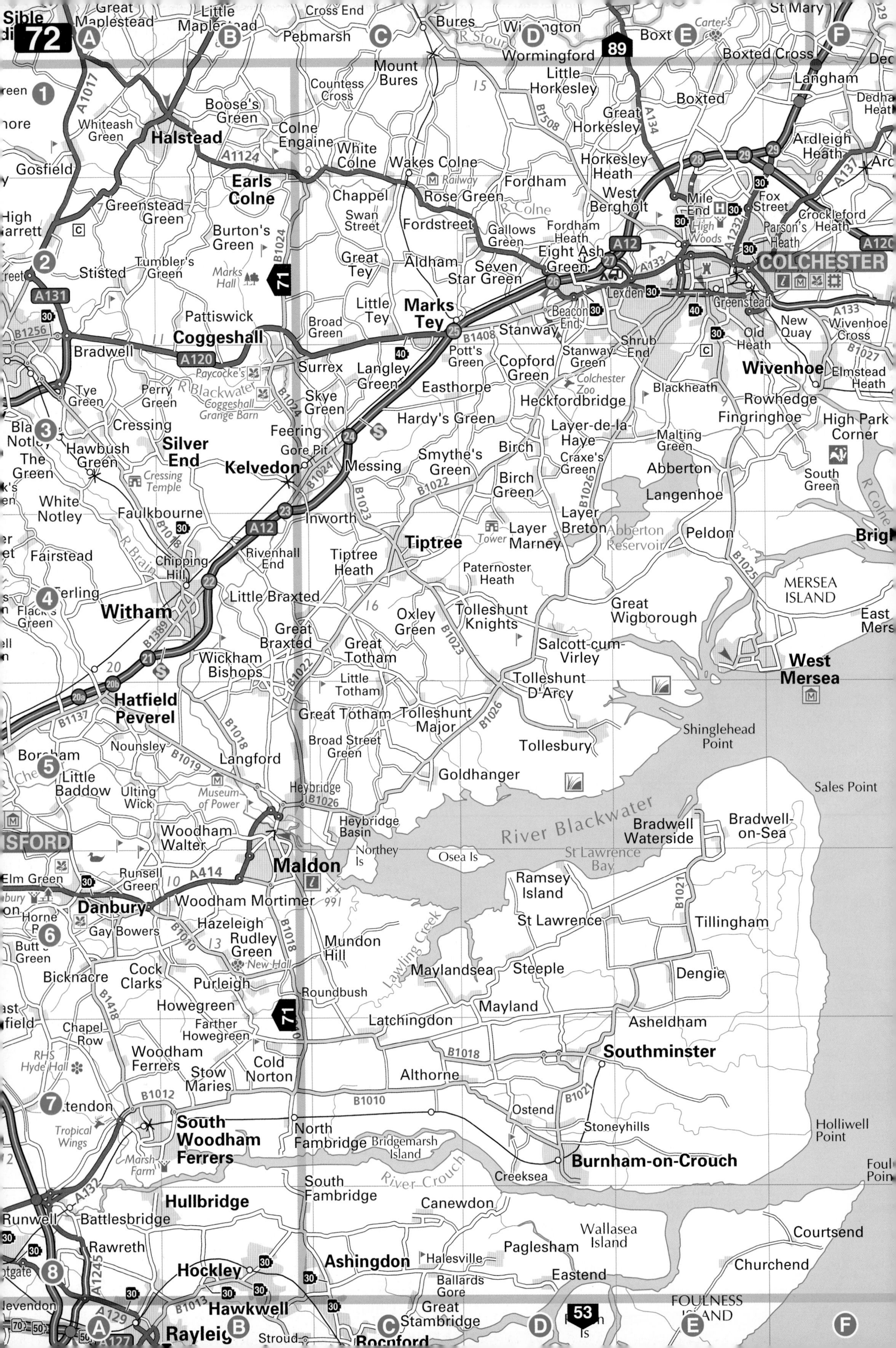

72
Great Maplestead
Little Maplestead
Cross End
Pebmarsh
Bures
Wormingford
R Stour
89
Boxted
Carter's
St Mary
Boxted Cross
Langham
Mount Bures
Countess Cross
Little Horkesley
Great Horkesley
B1508
A134
A1017
Whiteash Green
Halstead
Boose's Green
Colne Engaine
White Colne
Wakes Colne
Railway
A1124
Earls Colne
Gosfield
Greenstead Green
Chappel
Swan Street
Rose Green
Fordham
Horkesley Heath
West Bergholt
Ardleigh Heath
A137
Mile End
High Woods
Fox Street
Crockleford Heath
Parson's Heath
A1232
Fordstreet
R Colne
Gallows Green
Fordham Heath
Eight Ash Green
A12
A133
COLCHESTER
Burton's Green
B1024
Marks Hall
71
Stisted
Tumbler's Green
Great Tey
Aldham
Seven Star Green
Lexden
Greenstead
A131
Pattiswick
Little Tey
Marks Tey
Broad Green
Beacon End
Stanway
B1256
Coggeshall
Bradwell
A120
B1408
Pott's Green
Stanway Green
Shrub End
Old Heath
New Quay
Wivenhoe Cross
B1027
Wivenhoe
Elmstead Heath
Paycocke's
R Blackwater
Coggeshall Grange Barn
Surrex
Langley Green
Copford Green
Colchester Zoo
Heckfordbridge
Blackheath
Rowhedge
Fingringhoe
High Park Corner
Tye Green
Perry Green
Cressing
Skye Green
Easthorpe
Hardy's Green
Layer-de-la-Haye
Malting Green
Black Notley
Hawbush Green
The Green
Silver End
Feering
Gore Pit
Kelvedon
Messing
Smythe's Green
Birch
Birch Green
Craxe's Green
Abberton
Langenhoe
South Green
R Colne
Cressing Temple
B1024
B1022
B1023
B1026
White Notley
Faulkbourne
Inworth
Layer Marney
Tower
Layer Breton
Abberton Reservoir
Peldon
R Brain
B1018
A12
Rivenhall End
Tiptree
Fairstead
Chipping Hill
Tiptree Heath
Paternoster Heath
B1025
MERSEA ISLAND
Terling
Flack's Green
Witham
Little Braxted
Oxley Green
Tolleshunt Knights
Great Wigborough
East Mersea
B1389
Great Braxted
Great Totham
Salcott-cum-Virley
Wickham Bishops
West Mersea
Hatfield Peverel
B1137
Little Totham
Tolleshunt D'Arcy
Great Totham
Tolleshunt Major
Shinglehead Point
Boreham
Nounsley
B1019
Langford
Broad Street Green
Tollesbury
Little Baddow
Ulting Wick
Museum of Power
Heybridge
Goldhanger
Sales Point
Heybridge Basin
River Blackwater
Bradwell Waterside
Bradwell-on-Sea
Woodham Walter
Northey Is
Osea Is
St Lawrence Bay
Elm Green
Runsell Green
A414
Maldon
Ramsey Island
B1021
Danbury
Woodham Mortimer
Hazeleigh
St Lawrence
Tillingham
Gay Bowers
B1010
Rudley Green
Lawling Creek
Mundon Hill
New Hall
Bicknacre
Cock Clarks
Purleigh
Maylandsea
Steeple
Dengie
B1418
Roundbush
Howegreen
Mayland
Farther Howegreen
Latchingdon
Asheldham
Chapel Row
B1018
Southminster
RHS Hyde Hall
Woodham Ferrers
Stow Maries
Cold Norton
Althorne
B1012
B1010
Ostend
Tropical Wings
South Woodham Ferrers
North Fambridge
Bridgemarsh Island
Stoneyhills
Holliwell Point
Marsh Farm
Burnham-on-Crouch
River Crouch
Creeksea
A132
South Fambridge
Hullbridge
Canewdon
Runwell
Battlesbridge
Wallasea Island
Courtsend
Rawreth
A1245
Paglesham
Hockley
Ashingdon
Halesville
Churchend
Eastend
Ballards Gore
B1013
Hawkwell
Great Stambridge
FOULNESS ISLAND
53
A129
A127
Rayleigh
Stroud
Rochford

Brantham
Cattawade
Mistley Towers
Mistley
Manningtree
New Mistley
Holbrook
90
River Stour
Wrabness
RSPB
Mistley Heath
Bradfield
B1352
Ramsey
Parkeston Quay
Parkeston
Street
Shotley Gate
International Ferry Terminal
The Redoubt
Bath Side
Harwich Harbour
Landguard Fort
Landguard Point
Upper Dovercourt
Dovercourt
Harwich
Little Bromley
Horsleycross Street
Bradfield Heath
A120
Wix
Little Oakley
Horsley Cross
Wix Green
Great Oakley
Pennyhole Bay
Hoek van Holland
Esbjerg
Great Bromley
Little Bentley
Tendring Heath
Stones Green
Tendring Green
B1414
Goose Green
Hare Green
Beaumont
Horsey Island
A133
Tendring
B1035
Thorpe Green
Thorpe-le-Soken
Tower
The Naze
Kirby le Soken
Frating
Great Bentley
Weeley
B1033
B1034
Walton on the Naze
Weeley Heath
Kirby Cross
B1441
Aingers Green
Thorrington
Frinton-on-Sea
Cook's Green
Samson's Corner
Little Clacton
Great Holland
B1442
B1032
Hurst Green
Great Clacton
Holland-on-Sea
B1027
St Osyth
Rush Green
Point Clear
CLACTON-ON-SEA
Jaywick
Colne Point
0 1 2 3 4 5 miles
0 1 2 3 4 5 6 7 8 kilometres
G H J K L M
1 2 3 4 5 6 7 8

A
B
C
D
E
F
1
2
3
4
5
6
7
8
Rosslare Harbour
STRUMBLE HEAD
Carregwa
Pen Brush
Llanwnda
Pwll Deri
Goodwick
Ocean
Pembrokeshire Coast Path
Trefasser
Manorowen
St Nicholas
Panteg
Ynys Daullyn
Granston
Scledd
Carreg Sampson
Abercastle
A40
Llangloffan
Jordanston
Porthgain
Trefin
Mathry
Castle Morris
16
A487
B4331
Abereiddy
Llanrhian
Square & Compass
Llangloffan Fen
Berea
Croes-goch
Ne
Tretio
Treffynnon
Letterston
ST DAVID'S HEAD
Treleddyd-fawr
Treglemais
Welsh Hook
Carnhedryn
Cerbyd
B4330
Whitesand Bay
Rhodiad-y-brenin
Caer Farchell
River Solva
Llandeloy
B4583
Tancredston
Pont-yr-hafod
Wolf's Castle
Bishop's Palace
Whitchurch
Middle Mill
Treffgarne Owen
RAMSEY ISLAND
St David's
Hayscastle
Hayscastle Cross
Nine Wells
Solva
A487
Treffgarne
RSPB
Ramsey Sound
Pen-y-cwn
54
178
DUDWELL MT
Leweston
St David's Peninsula Heritage Coast
Newgale
16
Western Cleddau
Roch
Wolfsdale
PEMBROKESHIRE COAST NATIONAL PARK
Roch Gate
Simpson Cross
A40
Camrose
Rickets Head
Keeston
Pembrokeshire County
Nolton Haven
Nolton
A487
Tangiers
0 1 2 3 4 5 miles
0 1 2 3 4 5 6 7 8 kilometres
Pelcomb Cross
Pelcomb
St Brides Bay Heritage Coast
St Brides Bay
Lambston
Glanafon
Pelcomb Bridge
Druidston
Sutton

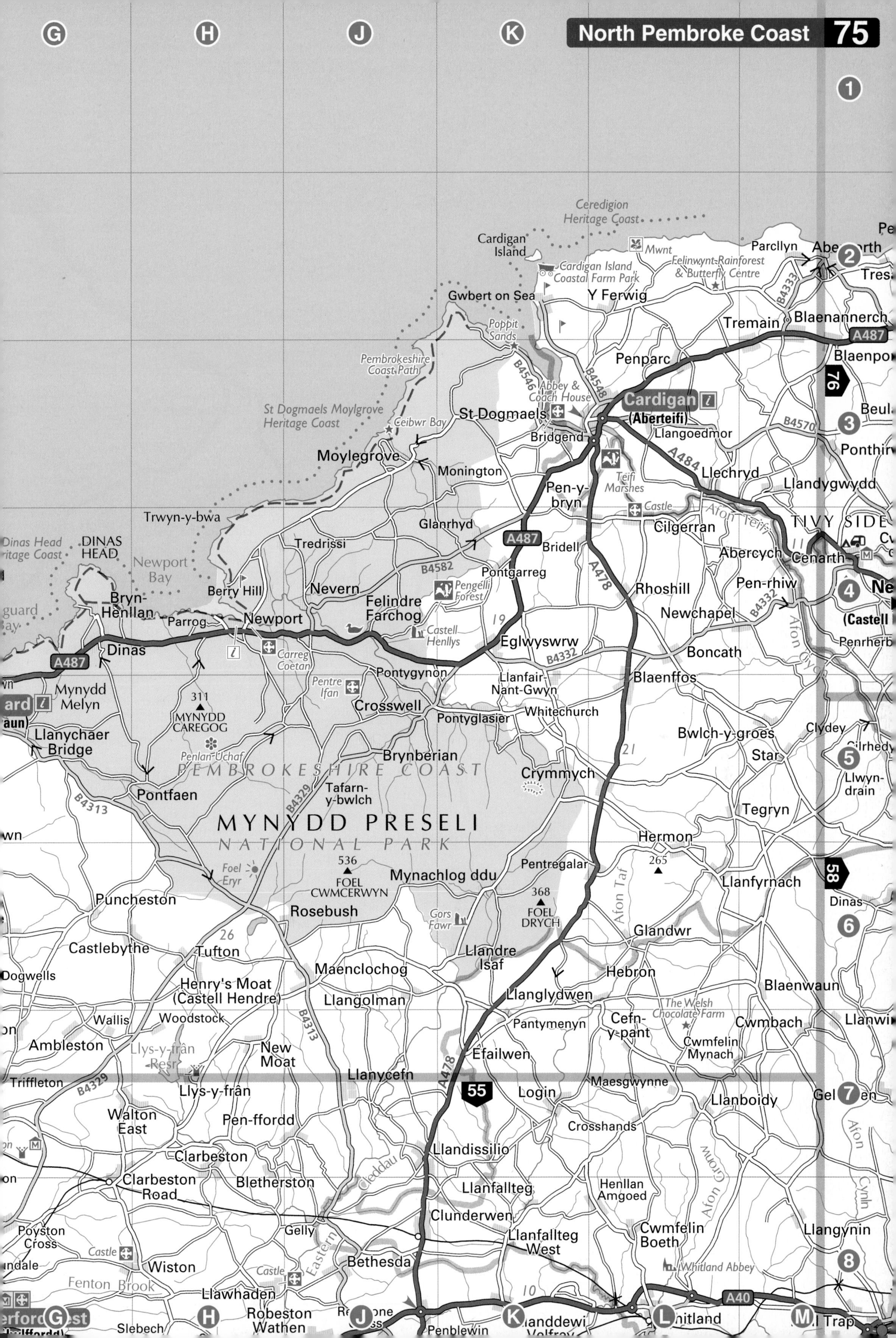
MYNYDD PRESELI
NATIONAL PARK
PEMBROKESHIRE COAST
Cardigan
(Aberteifi)
Newport
Nevern
Felindre Farchog
Eglwyswrw
Crymmych
St Dogmaels
Moylegrove
Cilgerran
Newchapel
Boncath
Blaenffos
Rosebush
Maenclochog
Llangolman
Puncheston
Castlebythe
Tufton
Henry's Moat
(Castell Hendre)
Llys-y-frân
Clarbeston Road
Llandissilio
Clunderwen
Llanfallteg
Bethesda
Llawhaden
Efailwen
Llanglydwen
Login
Llanboidy
Crosshands
Hermon
Llanfyrnach
Glandwr
Hebron
Blaenwaun
Cwmbach
Tegryn
Llechryd
Llandygwydd
Abercych
Cenarth
Penparc
Tremain
Blaenannerch
Y Ferwig
Gwbert on Sea
Cardigan Island
Mwnt
Dinas
Pontfaen
Mynydd Melyn
Llanychaer Bridge
A487
A478
A484
A40
B4582
B4332
B4329
B4313
B4546
B4548
B4570
B4333
55
58
76

A
B
C
D
E
F
1
2
3
4
5
6
7
8
Ceredigion Heritage Coast
Llanrhystud
A487
Llansantffraid
Llanon
Rhos Haminiog
Aberarth
Aberaeron
Pennant
Monachty
Llyswen
Llanerchaeron
New Quay
Foss-y-ffin
Llanina
Cilcennin
Newbridge
A482
Afon Aeron
Llwyncelyn
Gilfachrheda
Maen-y-groes
Cwmtydu
Cross Inn
Llanarth
Oakford
Ciliau-Aeron
A486
B4342
B4339
Nanternis
Ystrad Aeron
Ynys-Lochtyn
Caerwedros
Dihewyd
Llwyndafydd
Mydroilyn
Pentre'rbryn
Synod Inn
Temple Bar
Llangrannog
Pontgarreg
B4321
B4334
Morfa
Plwmp
Penbryn
Ffynnonddewi
B4338
Cae Hir
311
Parcllyn
Aberporth
Pentregat
Tresaith
Sarnau
Brynhoffnant
Talgarreg
Gorsgoch
Criby
324
Blaenannerch
Tan-y-groes
Bwlchyfadfa
Glynarthen
Capel Cynon
Blaenporth
Clettwr Fawr
B4459
B4337
Rhydlewis
Cwrt-newydd
Ffostrasol
Llanwnnen
75
Bettws Evan
Hawen
Pontshaen
Beulah
B4571
Cwmsychbant
Drefach
Alltyblaca
B4570
Troedyraur
Penrhiw-pal
A475
Ponthirwaun
Brongest
Coed-y-Bryn
Maesllyn
Tre-groes
Pren-gwyn
Llanwenog
Rhydowen
B4333
Llandygwydd
Croes-lan
Llanybydder
Llangynllo
Rhuddlan
258
Gorrig
TIVY SIDE
Horeb
B4476
Capel Dewi
Cwm-cou
Aber-banc
Rock Mill Woollen & Water Mill
Cenarth
Adpar
Llandyfriog
Penrhiw-llan
A485
Aber-giar
Teifi Valley Railway
Llandysul
Afon Teifi
Llanfihangel-ar-arth
Newcastle Emlyn
(Castell Newydd Emlyn)
Henllan
Aber-arad
Pentre-cagel
A484
Llangeler
Pontwelly
B4336
Llanllwni
B4332
Drefach
National Wool Museum
Penrherber
Felindre
Glynteg
Pentre-cwrt
Mynydd Llanllwni
Cwmhiraeth
Saron
Banc-y-ffordd
Drefelin
23
369
Llidiartnenog
Capel Iwan
58
257
Pencader
New Inn
335
Cwmpengraig
Clydey
Rhos
Gwyddgrug
Cilrhedyn
Cwm Morgan
Dol-gran
Llwyn-drain
362
314
358
Gwernogle
0 1 2 3 4 5 miles
0 1 2 3 4 5 6 7 8 kilometres
B4299
Cwmduad
Alltwalis
Hermon
252

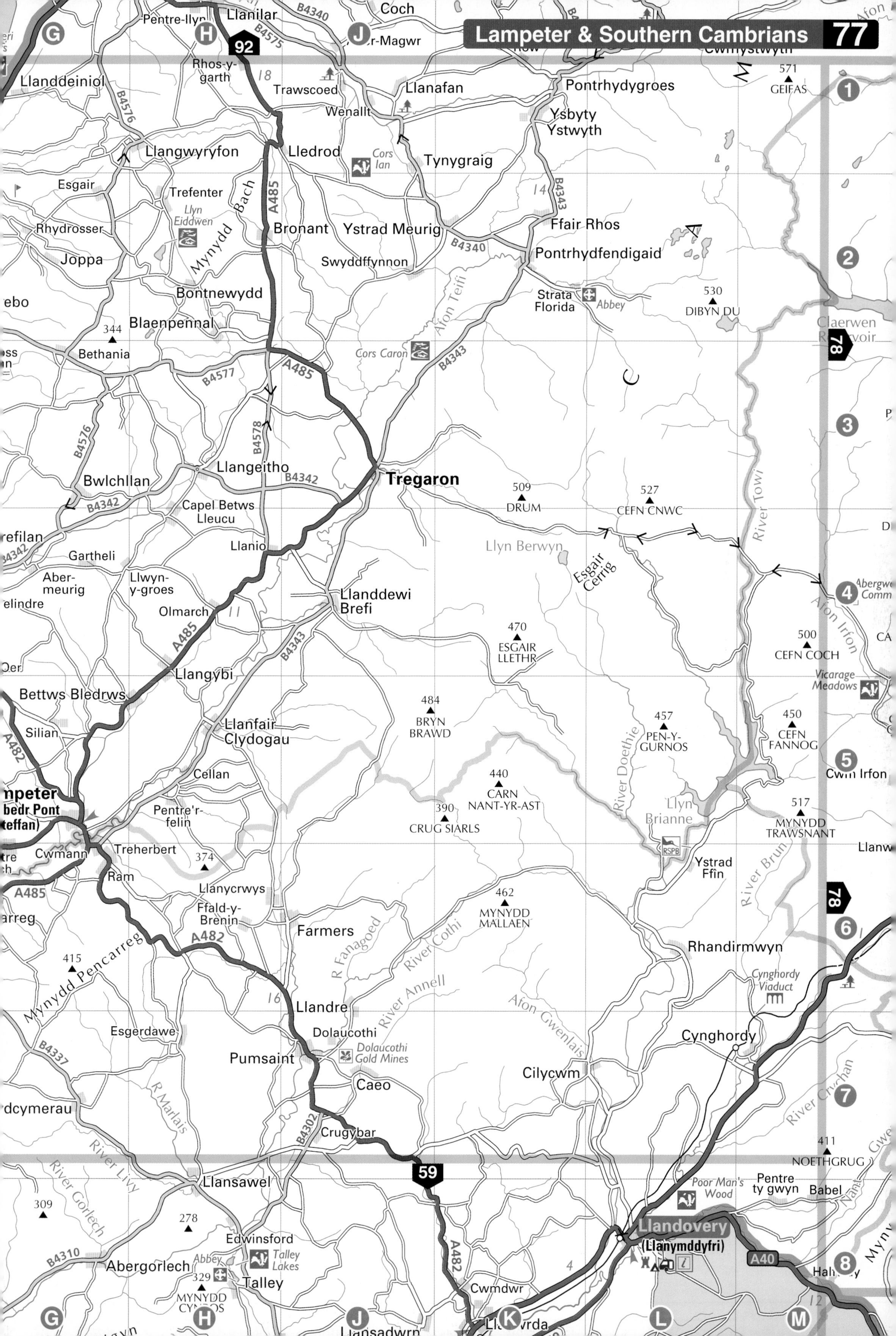
G
H
J
92
Pentre-llyn
Llanilar
B4340
Coch
B4575
Pontrhydygroes
Rhos-y-garth
Trawscoed
Llanafan
571
GEIFAS
1
Llanddeiniol
B4576
Wenallt
Ysbyty Ystwyth
Llangwyryfon
Lledrod
Cors Ian
Tynygraig
Esgair
Trefenter
A485
B4343
Llyn Eidwen
Mynydd Bach
Ffair Rhos
Rhydrosser
Bronant
Ystrad Meurig
B4340
Pontrhydfendigaid
2
Joppa
Swyddffynnon
Bontnewydd
Afon Teifi
Strata Florida
Abbey
530
DIBYN DU
Claerwen
344
Bethania
Blaenpennal
Cors Caron
B4343
78
A485
B4577
3
B4576
B4578
Llangeitho
B4342
Tregaron
509
DRUM
527
CEFN CNWC
River Towi
Bwlchllan
B4342
Capel Betws Lleucu
Llanio
Llyn Berwyn
Gartheli
Esgair Cerrig
Aber-meurig
Llwyn-y-groes
Llanddewi Brefi
4
Olmarch
A485
B4343
470
ESGAIR LLETHR
500
CEFN COCH
Afon Irfon
Vicarage Meadows
Llangybi
Bettws Bledrws
484
BRYN BRAWD
457
PEN-Y-GURNOS
450
CEFN FANNOG
Silian
Llanfair Clydogau
River Doethie
5
A482
Cwm Irfon
Cellan
440
CARN NANT-YR-AST
Llyn Brianne
517
MYNYDD TRAWSNANT
Pentre'r-felin
390
CRUG SIARLS
RSPB
Treherbert
Cwmann
374
Ystrad Ffîn
Ram
River Brun
A485
Llanycrwys
462
MYNYDD MALLAEN
Ffald-y-Brenin
78
A482
Farmers
R Fanagoed
River Cothi
6
Rhandirmwyn
415
Mynydd Pencarreg
Cynghordy Viaduct
Llandre
River Annell
Afon Gwenlais
Esgerdawe
Dolaucothi
Cynghordy
B4337
Pumsaint
Dolaucothi Gold Mines
Caeo
Cilycwm
R Marlais
River Crychan
7
dcymerau
Crugybar
B4302
411
NOETHGRUG
River Livy
River Gorlech
Llansawel
59
Poor Man's Wood
Pentre ty gwyn
Babel
309
278
Edwinsford
Llandovery
(Llanymddyfri)
A40
B4310
Abbey
Talley Lakes
A482
8
Abergorlech
329
MYNYDD CYNROS
Talley
Cwmdwr
G
H
J
K
L
M
Llansadwrn

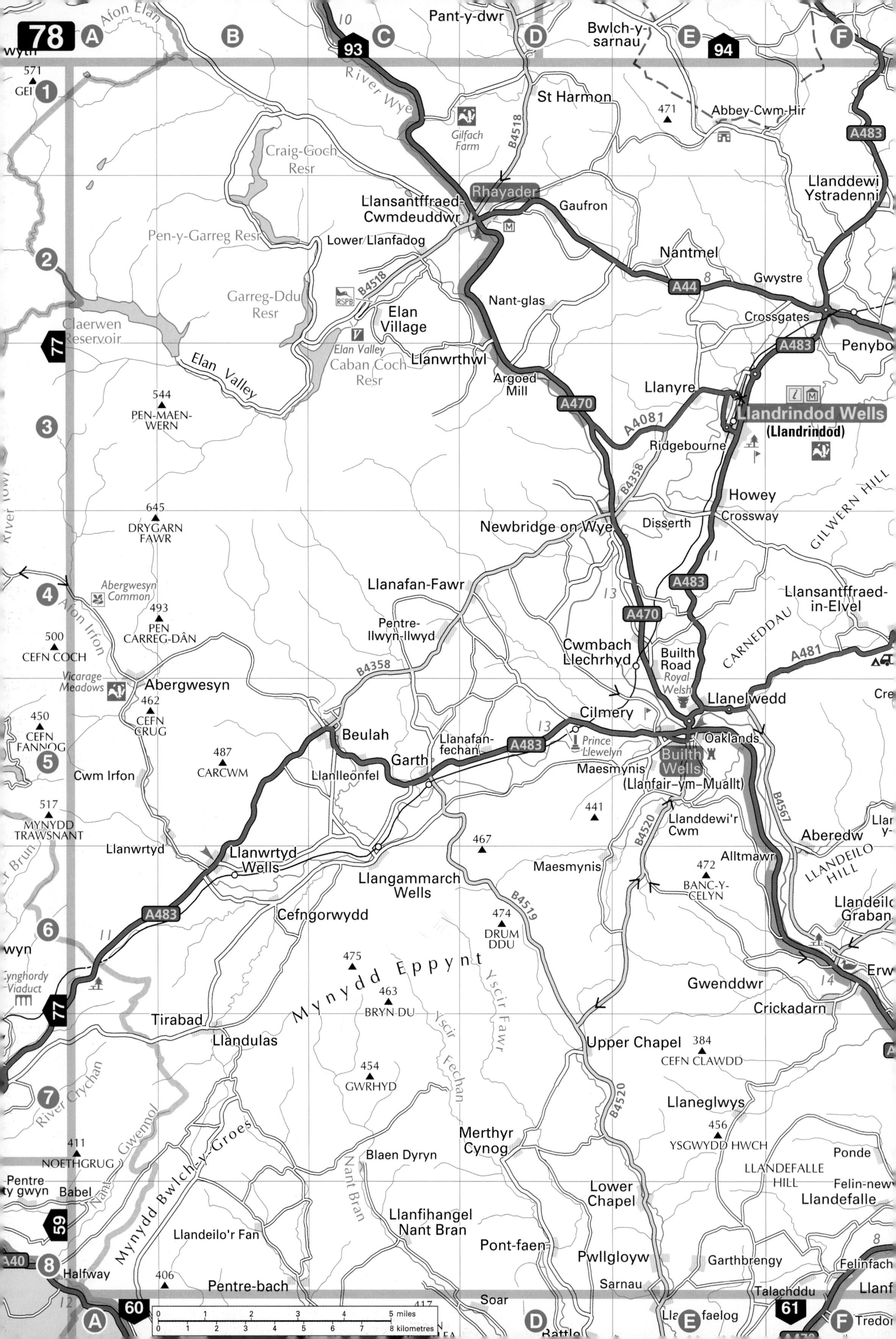
93
94
77
59
60
61
A
B
C
D
E
F
1
2
3
4
5
6
7
8
Afon Elan
Pant-y-dwr
Bwlch-y-sarnau
River Wye
St Harmon
471
Abbey-Cwm-Hir
A483
Gilfach Farm
B4518
Craig-Goch Resr
Rhayader
Llansantffraed-Cwmdeuddwr
Gaufron
Llanddewi Ystradenni
Pen-y-Garreg Resr
Lower Llanfadog
Nantmel
Garreg-Ddu Resr
B4518
RSPB
A44
Gwystre
Elan Village
Nant-glas
Crossgates
Claerwen Reservoir
Elan Valley
Caban Coch Resr
Llanwrthwl
Penybo
Elan Valley
Argoed Mill
Llanyre
A470
Llandrindod Wells
(Llandrindod)
544
PEN-MAEN-WERN
A4081
Ridgebourne
B4358
Howey
645
DRYGARN FAWR
Newbridge on Wye
Disserth
Crossway
GILWERN HILL
Abergwesyn Common
Afon Irfon
Llanafan-Fawr
A483
Llansantffraed-in-Elvel
493
PEN CARREG-DÂN
500
CEFN COCH
Pentre-llwyn-llwyd
A470
CARNEDDAU
Cwmbach Llechrhyd
Builth Road
Royal Welsh
A481
Vicarage Meadows
B4358
Abergwesyn
462
CEFN CRUG
Llanelwedd
450
CEFN FANNOG
Cilmery
Beulah
Llanafan-fechan
A483
Prince Llewelyn
Oaklands
487
CARCWM
Garth
Maesmynis
Builth Wells
(Llanfair-ym-Muallt)
Cwm Irfon
Llanlleonfel
517
MYNYDD TRAWSNANT
441
B4567
Llanddewi'r Cwm
B4520
467
Aberedw
Llanwrtyd
Llanwrtyd Wells
Maesmynis
472
BANC-Y-CELYN
Alltmawr
LLANDEILO HILL
Llangammarch Wells
Llandeilo Graban
A483
Cefngorwydd
B4519
474
DRUM DDU
475
Mynydd Eppynt
463
BRYN-DU
Ysgir Fechan
Ysgir Fawr
Gwenddwr
Cynghordy Viaduct
Erw
Crickadarn
Tirabad
Llandulas
Upper Chapel
384
CEFN CLAWDD
454
GWRHYD
River Crychan
B4520
Llaneglwys
Gwennol
456
YSGWYDD HWCH
Merthyr Cynog
411
NOETHGRUG
Blaen Dyryn
Ponde
Nant Bran
LLANDEFALLE HILL
Felin-newydd
Pentre-ty gwyn
Babel
Mynydd Bwlch-y-Groes
Lower Chapel
Llandefalle
Llanfihangel Nant Bran
Llandeilo'r Fan
Pont-faen
A40
Pwllgloyw
Garthbrengy
Halfway
406
Felinfach
Pentre-bach
Sarnau
Soar
Talachddu
Llanf
417
Tredu
Battle
5 miles
8 kilometres

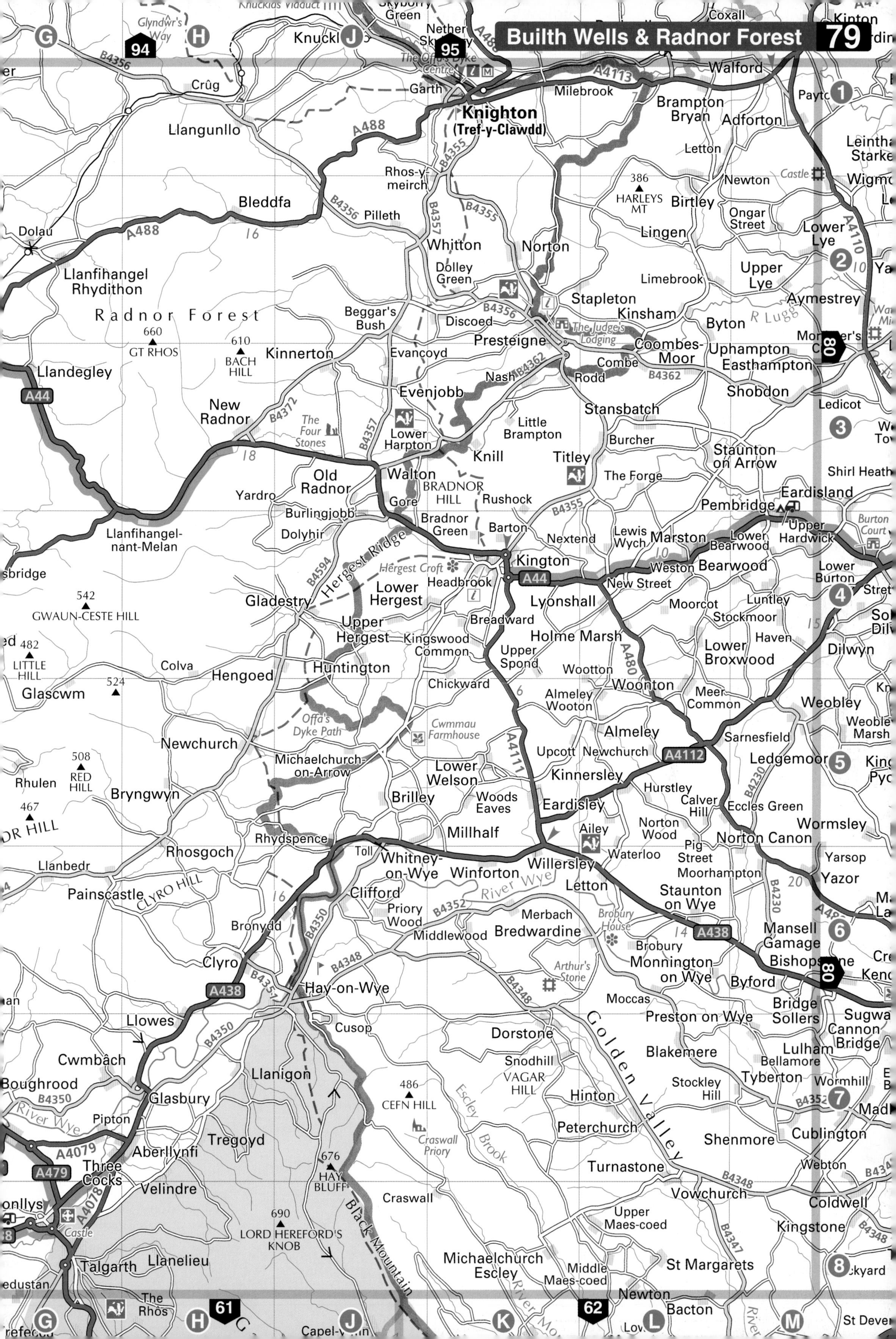
Knighton
(Tref-y-Clawdd)
Radnor Forest
Presteigne
Kington
Hay-on-Wye
Golden Valley
Black Mountain
Llangunllo
Bleddfa
Llanfihangel Rhydithon
Llandegley
New Radnor
Old Radnor
Gladestry
Huntington
Newchurch
Clyro
Glasbury
Talgarth
Whitney-on-Wye
Eardisley
Weobley
Pembridge
Shobdon
Titley
Dorstone
Peterchurch
Michaelchurch Escley
Hergest Ridge
Offa's Dyke Path
River Wye
The Judge's Lodging
Hergest Croft
The Four Stones
Cwmmau Farmhouse
Arthur's Stone
Craswall Priory
HAY BLUFF
LORD HEREFORD'S KNOB
CEFN HILL
GT RHOS
BACH HILL
A44
A438
A4111
A480
A4112
A488
A4113
B4356
B4355
B4357
B4362
B4350
B4348
B4352
94
95
80
61
62

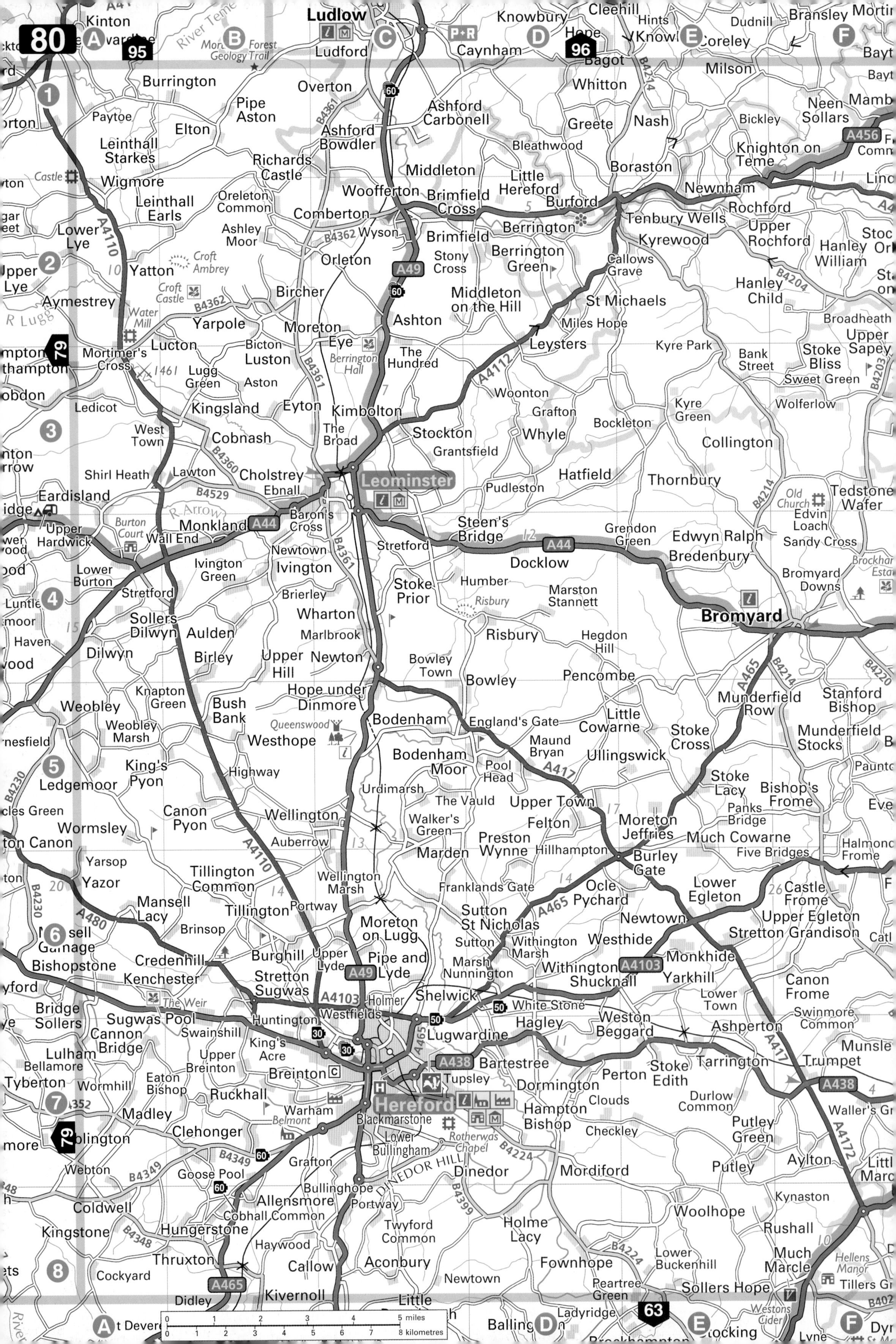

80
95
96

A B C D E F

Kinton
Aymestrey
River Teme
Mortimer Forest Geology Trail
Ludlow
Ludford
Caynham
P+R
Knowbury
Cleehill
Hints
Hope Bagot
Knowle
Coreley
Dudnill
Bransley
Milson
Burrington
Overton
Whitton
Pipe Aston
Paytoe
Elton
Ashford Carbonell
Greete
Nash
Bickley
Neen Sollars
Ashford Bowdler
Leinthall Starkes
Richards Castle
Bleathwood
Knighton on Teme
A456
Castle
Wigmore
Middleton
Little Hereford
Boraston
Newnham
Leinthall Earls
Orleton Common
Woofferton
Brimfield Cross
Burford
Rochford
Lower Lye
Ashley Moor
Comberton
Berrington
Tenbury Wells
Upper Rochford
A4110
B4362
Wyson
Brimfield
Kyrewood
Hanley William
Upper Lye
Yatton
Croft Ambrey
Orleton
Stony Cross
Berrington Green
Callows Grave
Hanley Child
B4204
Croft Castle
Bircher
A49
Middleton on the Hill
St Michaels
Aymestrey
R Lugg
Water Mill
B4362
Yarpole
Moreton
Ashton
Miles Hope
Broadheath
Upper Sapey
Eye
Berrington Hall
Leysters
Kyre Park
Bank Street
Stoke Bliss
79
Mortimer's Cross
Lucton
Bicton
Luston
The Hundred
Sweet Green
1461
Lugg Green
Aston
A4112
Woonton
B4203
Ledicot
Kingsland
Eyton
B4361
Kimbolton
Grafton
Kyre Green
Wolferlow
West Town
Cobnash
The Broad
Stockton
Whyle
Bockleton
Collington
Grantsfield
Shirl Heath
Lawton
B4360
Cholstrey
Leominster
Hatfield
Thornbury
Eardisland
B4529
Ebnall
Pudleston
Old Church
Tedstone Wafer
R Arrow
Baron's Cross
B4214
Edvin Loach
Upper Hardwick
Burton Court
Monkland
A44
Steen's Bridge
Grendon Green
Edwyn Ralph
Wall End
Stretford
Sandy Cross
Newtown
B4361
A44
Bredenbury
Brockhampton Estate
Lower Burton
Ivington Green
Ivington
Docklow
Bromyard Downs
Stretford
Stoke Prior
Humber
Marston Stannett
Brierley
Risbury
Bromyard
Sollers Dilwyn
Aulden
Wharton
Risbury
Hegdon Hill
Marlbrook
Dilwyn
Birley
Upper Hill
Newton
Bowley Town
Pencombe
A465
B4214
B4220
Bowley
Munderfield Row
Stanford Bishop
Weobley
Knapton Green
Bush Bank
Hope under Dinmore
Weobley Marsh
Dinmore
Bodenham
England's Gate
Little Cowarne
Munderfield Stocks
Queenswood
Westhope
Maund Bryan
Stoke Cross
Bodenham Moor
Pool Head
A417
Ullingswick
Ledgemoor
King's Pyon
Highway
Stoke Lacy
Bishop's Frome
B4230
Urdimarsh
The Vauld
Upper Town
Panks Bridge
Canon Pyon
Wellington
Walker's Green
Felton
Moreton Jeffries
Wormsley
Auberrow
Marden
Preston Wynne
Much Cowarne
Hillhampton
Burley Gate
Five Bridges
Yarsop
Yazor
Tillington Common
A4110
Wellington Marsh
Franklands Gate
Ocle Pychard
Lower Egleton
Castle Frome
Mansell Lacy
Tillington
Portway
Moreton on Lugg
Sutton St Nicholas
A465
Newtown
Upper Egleton
A480
Brinsop
Stretton Grandison
Mansell Gamage
Sutton
Withington Marsh
Westhide
Bishopstone
Credenhill
Burghill
Upper Lyde
Pipe and Lyde
Marsh
Monkhide
A49
Nunnington
Withington
A4103
Kenchester
Stretton Sugwas
Shucknall
Yarkhill
Canon Frome
Bridge Sollers
The Weir
A4103
Holmer
Shelwick
White Stone
Lower Town
Swinmore Common
Sugwas Pool
Huntington
Westfields
Lugwardine
Hagley
Weston Beggard
Ashperton
Munsley
Cannon Bridge
Swainshill
King's Acre
A465
A417
Lulham
Bellamore
Upper Breinton
A438
Bartestree
Tarrington
Trumpet
Breinton
Tupsley
Stoke Edith
Tyberton
Wormhill
Eaton Bishop
Ruckhall
Dormington
Perton
A438
Hereford
Clouds
Durlow Common
Waller's Green
B4352
Madley
Warham
Belmont
Blackmarstone
Hampton Bishop
Putley Green
79
Kingstone
Clehonger
Rotherwas Chapel
Checkley
A4172
Webton
Lower Bullingham
B4224
B4349
Grafton
Dinedor
Putley
Aylton
Little Marcle
B4349
Goose Pool
DINEDOR HILL
Mordiford
Bullinghope
Coldwell
Allensmore
B4399
Kynaston
Portway
Woolhope
Cobhall Common
Twyford Common
Holme Lacy
Rushall
Kingstone
Hungerstone
B4348
Haywood
B4224
Lower Buckenhill
Much Marcle
Helens Manor
Thruxton
Callow
Aconbury
Fownhope
Cockyard
Newtown
Peartree Green
Tillers Green
A465
Sollers Hope
Westons Cider
Didley
Kivernoll
Little
Ladyridge
63
B4024
St Devereux
Ballingham
Brockhampton
Stocking
Dymock
Lyne

0 1 2 3 4 5 miles
0 1 2 3 4 5 6 7 8 kilometres

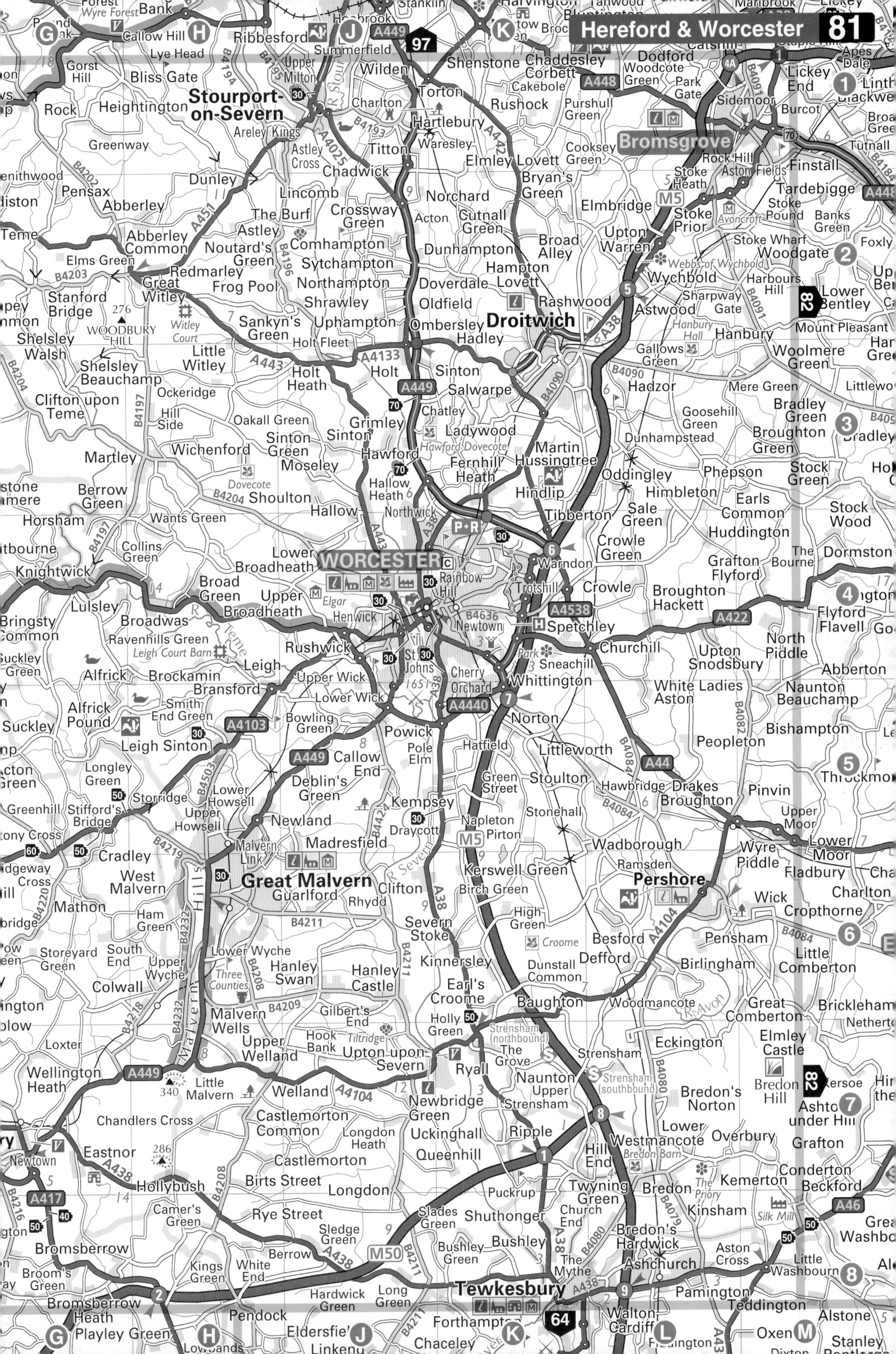
Wyre Forest
Bank
Callow Hill
Ribbesford
Habberley
Summerfield
Stanklin
Harvington
Chaddesley Corbett
Dodford
Woodcote Green
Park Gate
Lickey End
Apes Dale
Linthurst
Lye Head
Gorst Hill
Bliss Gate
Upper Milton
Wilden
Shenstone
Cakebole
Rock
Heightington
Stourport-on-Severn
Charlton
Torton
Rushock
Purshull Green
Sidemoor
Burcot
Areley Kings
Hartlebury
Waresley
Bromsgrove
Greenway
Astley Cross
Titton
Cooksey Green
Rock Hill
Tutnall
Chadwick
Elmley Lovett
Aston Fields
Finstall
Stoke Heath
Tardebigge
Pensax
Dunley
Lincomb
Bryan's Green
Abberley
Norchard
Elmbridge
Stoke Prior
Stoke Pound
Banks Green
The Burf
Crossway Green
Acton
Cutnall Green
Avoncroft
Astley
Abberley Common
Noutard's Green
Comhampton
Dunhampton
Broad Alley
Upton Warren
Stoke Wharf
Woodgate
Foxlydiate
Elms Green
Sytchampton
Hampton Lovett
Webbs of Wychbold
Redmarley
Northampton
Doverdale
Wychbold
Harbours Hill
Great Witley
Frog Pool
Stanford Bridge
Shrawley
Oldfield
Rashwood
Sharpway Gate
Lower Bentley
Astwood
Woodbury Hill
Witley Court
Sankyn's Green
Uphampton
Ombersley
Droitwich
Hanbury Hall
Hanbury
Mount Pleasant
Shelsley Walsh
Holt Fleet
Hadley
Gallows Green
Woolmere Green
Little Witley
Shelsley Beauchamp
Holt Heath
Holt
Sinton
Salwarpe
Hadzor
Mere Green
Littleworth
Ockeridge
Clifton upon Teme
Chatley
Goosehill Green
Bradley Green
Hill Side
Oakall Green
Grimley
Ladywood
Martin Hussingtree
Dunhampstead
Broughton Green
Wichenford
Sinton Green
Sinton
Hawford Dovecote
Hawford
Fernhill Heath
Martley
Moseley
Oddingley
Phepson
Stock Green
Dovecote
Shoulton
Hallow Heath
Hindlip
Himbleton
Berrow Green
Hallow
Northwick
Sale Green
Earls Common
Stock Wood
Horsham
Wants Green
Tibberton
Huddington
Collins Green
Crowle Green
Knightwick
Lower Broadheath
WORCESTER
Warndon
Grafton Flyford
The Bourne
Dormston
Rainbow Hill
Trotshill
Crowle
Broughton Hackett
Broad Green
Upper Broadheath
Elgar
Lulsley
Henwick
Flyford Flavell
Bringsty Common
Broadwas
Newtown
Spetchley
North Piddle
Ravenhills Green
Leigh Court Barn
Rushwick
Churchill
Upton Snodsbury
Sneachill
Abberton
Alfrick
Brockamin
Leigh
St Johns
Cherry Orchard
Whittington
White Ladies Aston
Naunton Beauchamp
Bransford
Upper Wick
Lower Wick
Alfrick Pound
Smith End Green
Bowling Green
Powick
Norton
Bishampton
Suckley
Leigh Sinton
Pole Elm
Hatfield
Littleworth
Peopleton
Callow End
Longley Green
Deblin's Green
Green Street
Stoulton
Hawbridge
Drakes Broughton
Pinvin
Throckmorton
Storridge
Lower Howsell
Kempsey
Stonehall
Upper Moor
Stifford's Bridge
Upper Howsell
Newland
Draycott
Napleton
Pirton
Lower Moor
Cradley
Malvern Link
Madresfield
Wadborough
Wyre Piddle
Ramsden
Fladbury
West Malvern
Great Malvern
Kerswell Green
Pershore
Charlton
Clifton
Birch Green
Guarlford
Rhydd
Mathon
Wick
Cropthorne
Ham Green
High Green
Severn Stoke
Pensham
Croome
Besford
Defford
Little Comberton
Storeyard Green
South End
Upper Wyche
Lower Wyche
Hanley Swan
Hanley Castle
Kinnersley
Birlingham
Three Counties
Dunstall Common
Colwall
Earl's Croome
Baughton
Woodmancote
Great Comberton
Bricklehampton
Malvern Wells
Gilbert's End
Holly Green
Strensham (northbound)
Elmley Castle
Loxter
Hook Bank
Tiltridge
Upper Welland
Upton upon Severn
Ryall
The Grove
Strensham
Eckington
Wellington Heath
Little Malvern
Welland
Naunton
Upper Strensham
Strensham (southbound)
Bredon's Norton
Bredon Hill
Kersoe
Ashton under Hill
Chandlers Cross
Castlemorton Common
Newbridge Green
Longdon Heath
Uckinghall
Ripple
Lower Westmancote
Overbury
Eastnor
Newtown
Queenhill
Castlemorton
Hill End
Bredon Barn
Grafton
Conderton
Hollybush
Birts Street
Longdon
Puckrup
Twyning Green
Bredon
The Priory
Kemerton
Beckford
Camer's Green
Rye Street
Slades Green
Shuthonger
Church End
Kinsham
Silk Mill
Bromsberrow
Sledge Green
Bushley Green
Bushley
Bredon's Hardwick
Aston Cross
Great Washbourne
Broom's Green
Kings Green
White End
Berrow
The Mythe
Ashchurch
Little Washbourne
Hardwick Green
Long Green
Tewkesbury
Pamington
Bromsberrow Heath
Pendock
Teddington
Playley Green
Eldersfield
Forthampton
Walton Cardiff
Alstone
Oxenton
Stanley Pontlarge
Chaceley
Fiddington
A449
A448
A442
A451
A443
A4133
A4025
A38
A4538
A422
A44
A4103
A4440
A4104
A438
A417
A46
M5
M50
B4194
B4195
B4193
B4196
B4202
B4203
B4197
B4204
B4090
B4091
B4184
B4636
B4084
B4082
B4503
B4219
B4220
B4232
B4218
B4208
B4209
B4211
B4424
B4080
B4079
B4216
276
340
286
97
82
64
G
H
J
K
L
M
1
2
3
4
5
6
7
8

98

81

65

A B C D E F

1 2 3 4 5 6 7 8

Lickey Rock
Staple Hill
Barnt Green
Arrowfield Top
Hopwood Park
Weatheroak Hill
Tanner's Green
Forshaw Heath
Terry's Green
Earlswood
Four Ashes
Darley Green
Chessetts Wood
Fen End
Chadwick End
Lickey End
Apes Dale
Withybed Green
Alvechurch
Linthurst
Portway
Wood End
Hockley Heath
Packwood House
Baddesley Clinton
Sidemoor
Blackwell
Burcot
Broad Green
Rowney Green
Heath Gn
Branson's Cross
Aspley Heath
Tanworth in Arden
Kingswood
Lapworth
Grand Union Canal
Wroxall
Kingswood Brook
Kemps Green
Tutnall
Finstall
Rock Hill
Aston Fields
Beoley
Holt End
Trap's Green
Danzey Green
Turner's Green
Rowington
M40
M42
Tardebigge
Stoke Pound
Avoncroft
REDDITCH
Forge Mill
Banks Green
Blunts Green
Lowsonford
High Cross
Ullenhall
Shrewley
Little Shrewley
Stoke Wharf
Woodgate
Foxlydiate
Webheath
Headless Cross
Outhill
Buckley Green
Kite Green
Preston Bagot
Holywell
Harbours Hill
Upper Bentley
Lower Bentley
Callow Hill
Crabbs Cross
Mappleborough Green
Henley-in-Arden
Beaudesert
Lye Green
Pinley Green
Tarpway Gate
Green Lane
Oldberrow
Preston Green
Walkwood
Studley
Studley Common
Hanbury
Mount Pleasant
Hunt End
Ham Green
Wootton Wawen
Claverdon
Hampton on the Hill
Lower Norton
Stratford-upon-Avon Canal
Colmere Green
Thomas Town
Spernall
Shelfield
Langley
Wolverton
Norton Lindsey
Astwood Bank
Littleworth
Mere Green
Bradley Green
Feckenham
Edgiock
Sambourne
Ridgeway
Coughton Court
Little Alne
Edstone
Langley Green
Shelfield Green
Bearley Cross
Bearley
Pigeon Green
Heath End
Broughton Green
Bradley
Shurnock
New End
Coughton
Great Alne
Aston Cantlow
Snitterfield
Phepson
Stock Green
Holberrow Green
Mary Arden's Farm
Bouts
King's Coughton
Earls Common
Stock Wood
Cladswell
Cookhill
Alcester
Kinwarton Dovecote
Walcot
Pathlow
Wilmcote
Huddington
Inkberrow
Arrow
Upton
Haselor
Hampton Lucy
Grafton Flyford
The Bourne
Dormston
Oversley Green
Bishopton
Alveston
Abbots Morton
Weethley
Exhall
Red Hill
Billesley
Kington
Temple Grafton
Tiddington
Flyford Flavell
Goom's Hill
Ragley Hall
Wood Bevington
Wixford
Shottery
Anne Hathaway's Cottage
Stratford-upon-Avon
North Piddle
Rous Lench
Dunnington
Broom
Ardens Grafton
Upton Snodsbury
Abberton
Cock Bevington
Bidford-on-Avon
Cranhill
Binton
Luddington
Butterfly Farm
Naunton Beauchamp
Church Lench
Iron Cross
Welford-on-Avon
Weston-on-Avon
Clifford Chambers
Bishampton
Ab Lench
Salford Priors
Atherstone on Stour
Peopleton
Atch Lench
Abbot's Salford
Barton
Marlcliff
Preston on Stour
Throckmorton
Dorsington
Willicote
Pinvin
Harvington
Cleeve Prior
Long Marston
Wimpstone
Upper Moor
Norton
R Avon
Lower Quinton
Alderminster
Lenchwick
North Littleton
Pebworth
Crimscote
Wyre Piddle
Lower Moor
Offenham
Middle Littleton
Fladbury
Chadbury
Tithe Barn
Broad Marston
Newbold on Stour
Wick
Charlton
South Littleton
Upper Quinton
Admington
Cropthorne
Evesham
Aldington
Bretforton
Honeybourne
Armscote
Pensham
Little Comberton
Bengeworth
The Fleece Inn
Mickleton
Kiftsgate Court
Hidcote Bartrim
Blackwell
Hampton
Badsey
Vale of Evesham
Aston-sub-Edge
Hidcote Manor Garden
Ilmington
Great Comberton
Bricklehampton
Netherton
Hidcote Boyce
Darlingscott
Elmley Castle
Hinton Green
Wickhamford
Weston-sub-Edge
Ebrington
Bredon Hill
Kersoe
Murcot
Willersey
Saintbury
Charingworth
Hinton on the Green
Ashton under Hill
Childswickham
Chipping Campden
Stretton on Fosse
Overbury
Grafton
Aston Somerville
Cotswold Way
Tidmington
Sedgeberrow
Broad Campden
Paxford
Conderton
Kemerton
Beckford
Wormington
Broadway
Silk Mill
Dumbleton
Rectory
Buckland
Broadway Tower
Blockley
Draycott
R Stour
Todenham
Great Washbourne
Laverton
Aston Magna
Aston Cross
Little Washbourne
Alderton
Stanton
Snowshill
Snowshill Manor
Cotswold Lavender
Batsford
Lower Lemington
Alstone
Toddington
Dorn
Teddington
Stanway
Cotswold Falconry Centre
Four Shire Stone
Oxenton
Bourton-on-the-Hill
Sezincote
Moreton-in-Marsh
Warwickshire Railway
Didbrook
Snowshill Didbrook

0 1 2 3 4 5 miles
0 1 2 3 4 5 6 7 8 kilometres

Green
Crackley
Spring
Coventry
Baginton
Ryton-on-Dunsmore
Bilton
Cawston
RUGBY
Kilsby
Stoneleigh
Bubbenhall
Stretton-on-Dunsmore
Bourton on Dunsmore
Dunchurch
Thurlaston
Toft
Barby
Windy Arbour
Stareton
National Agricultural Centre
Princethorpe
Weston under Wetherley
Wappenbury
Frankton
Draycote
Ashow
Leek Wootton
Old Milverton
Cubbington
Eathorpe
Marton
Birdingbury
Draycote Water
Kites Hardwick
Woolscott
Oxford Canal
Willoughby
Ashby St Ledgers
ROYAL LEAMINGTON SPA
Hunningham
Leamington Hastings
Hill
Grandborough
Braunston
Warwick
Milverton
Offchurch
Long Itchington
Sawbridge
Wolfhampcote
Newbold Comyn
Broadwell
Nethercote
Grand Union Canal
Bascote
Stockton
Radford Semele
Whitnash
Warwickshire Exhibition Centre
R Itchen
Tomlow
Flecknoe
Longbridge
Lower Shuckburgh
Southam
Bascote Heath
Staverton
Ufton
Napton on the Hill
Napton Hill
Sherbourne
Bishop's Tachbrook
Harbury
Barford
Chapel Green
Lower Catesby
Upper Catesby
Newnham
Wasperton
Chesterton
Ladbroke
Priors Marston
Hellidon
Badby
Ashorne
Chesterton Green
Warwick
Newbold Pacey
Bishop's Itchington
Windmill
Charlecote
Moreton Morrell
Lighthorne
Lighthorne Heath
Priors Hardwick
Fawsley
Charwelton
Preston Capes
Wellesbourne
Wellesbourne Mountford
Moreton Paddox
Heritage Motor Centre
Knightcote
Wormleighton
Upper Boddington
Canal
Walton
Compton Verney
Gaydon
Northend
Wharf
Westhorp
Byfield
Woodford Halse
Chadshunt
Burton Dassett
Magpie Hill
Fenny Compton
Lower Boddington
West Farndon
Canons Ashby
Combrook
Kineton
Burton Dassett
Avon Dassett
Claydon
Aston le Walls
Eydon
Moreton Pinkney
Butlers Marston
Little Kineton
Edgehill 1642
Farnborough
Farnborough Hall
Pillerton Hersey
Radway
Arlescote
Edgehill
Warmington
Chipping Warden
Pillerton Priors
Edgehill
Ratley
Mollington
Culworth
The National Herb Centre
Wardington
Edgcote 1469
Fullready
Oxhill
Shotteswell
Cropredy
Upper Wardington
Thorpe Mandeville
Whatcote
Lower Tysoe
Hornton
Great Bourton
Williamscot
Idlicote
Upton House & Gardens
Middle Tysoe
Chacombe
Upper Tysoe
Horley
Little Bourton
Ettington
Alkerton
Hanwell
Honington
Shenington
Drayton
Middleton Cheney
Thenford
Great
Balscote
Marston St Lawrence
Aston on Stour
Winderton
Wroxton
Overthorpe
Lower Middleton Cheney
Shutford
Upper Brailes
Epwell
Farthinghoe
Barcheston
Lower Brailes
North Newington
Warkworth
Banbury
Great Purston
Cross
Willington
Burmington
Swalcliffe
Broughton
Tadmarton
Bodicote
Upper Astrop
Newbottle
Sutton-under-Brailes
Cherington
Sibford Gower
Sibford Ferris
Stourton
King's Sutton
Hinton-in-the-Hedges
Lower Tadmarton
Astrop
Adderbury
Little Wolford
Ascott
Bloxham
Milton
Walton Grounds
Charlton
Waterfowl Sanctuary & Children's Farm
Milcombe
Whichford
Barford St John
R Swere
Aynho
Croughton
Hook Norton
South Newington
Long Compton
Barton-on-the-Heath
Wigginton
Barford St Michael
Clifton
Souldern
Swerford
Hempton
Castle (earthworks)

84
100
A
B
C
D
E
F
Thornby
Lamport
Lamport Hall
Winwick
Cottesbrooke
Cottesbrooke Hall
M1
A428
18
Crick
West Haddon
Guilsborough
Hollowell
Creaton
Hanging Houghton
Old
Walg
DIRFT Logistics Park
Kilsby
M45
Coton Manor
Coton
Scaldwell
Brixworth
Hannington
Barby
17
Ravensthorpe
Teeton
Spratton
Holcot
Oxford Canal
Ashby St Ledgers
Watford
B5385
East Haddon
A5199
Brixworth
Pitsford Reservoir
A361
Watford Gap
Northampton & Lamport Railway
Pitsford
Willoughby
Long Buckby
Holdenby House
Holdenby
Braunston
Welton
Chapel Brampton
A508
Moulton
Sywe
fhampcote
Great Brington
Boughton
Overst
Whilton
Church Brampton
Daventry
Little Brington
Althorp Park
Harlestone
A5076
Fleckno
83
B4036
Kingsthorpe
Boothville
Norton
Nobottle
Kingsley Park
New Duston
Dallington
Brockhall
Queen's Park
Great Bill
Staverton
Daventry
A5
NORTHAMPTON
Weston Favell
Little Billing
M1
Harpole
Duston
Abington
A45
Dodford
Flore
Upper Heyford
A4500
St James's End
Little Houghton
Upper Catesby
Newnham
16
A43
B4037
Weedon
Upton
Far Cotton
R Nene
Stowehill
Kislingbury
A5076
1460
Hellidon
Little Everdon
Upper Weedon
Lower Weedon
Nether Heyford
Great Houghton
Badby
Eleanor Cross
Windmill
Church Stowe
Hunsbury Hill
Hardingstone
Great Everdon
Bugbrooke
Northampton
15A
A45
Fawsley
Upper Stowe
Rothersthorpe
Wootton
Preston Deanery
Preston Capes
Farthingstone
Gayton
Collingtree
A361
A5
Milton Malsor
15
Quinton
Pattishall
Little Preston
Litchborough
Eastcote
Piddington
Grimscote
Cold Higham
Blisworth
Quinton Green
Byfield
A43
Woodford Halse
Maidford
Astcote
Courteenhall
B526
West Farndon
70
Tiffield
Roade
Adstone
Quinbury End
Foxley
Duncote
Canons Ashby
Blakesley
M1
Caldecote
Stoke Bruerne
Hartwell
Ey
5
Canons Ashby
Moreton Pinkney
Shutlanger
Greens Norton
The Canal
A508
Ashton
Woodend
Stoke Park Pavilions
Bradden
Long Street
Plumpton
Towcester
R Tove
Grafton Regis
Culworth
Weedon Lois
Slapton
Edgcote 1469
Weston
Alderton
Milthorpe
Foscote
Hanslope
Wood Burcote
Thorpe Mandeville
Abthorpe
Paulerspury
Sulgrave
Yardley Gobion
Wappenham
Pury End
A5
6
Helmdon
Plumpton End
Grand Union Canal
Castlethorpe
Haversh
B4525
Silverstone
Whittlebury
Falcut
Potterspury
Furtho
Greatworth
Syresham
A43
Silverstone
A413
Cosgrove
Marston St Lawrence
Crowfield
Brackley Hatch
Puxley
Old Wolverton
Pimlico
Lillingstone Lovell
Old Stratford
Farthinghoe
Halse
Radstone
Lillingstone Dayrell
Deanshanger
Wolver
Stony Stratford
7
Biddlesden
Passenham
A422
Whitfield
Wicken
Calverton
MILTON KEYNES
Brackley
Turweston
Dadford
Stowe Gardens
A422
Newbottle
Upper Weald
Shalstone
Leckhampstead
Akeley
Hinton-in-the-Hedges
Beachampton
Maids Moreton
Charlton
Chackmore
Westbury
A422
Evenley
Water Stratford
Thornton
R Great Ouse
A43
Buckingham
Croughton
Mixbury
Radclive
Nash
8
B4031
Finmere
Tingewick
A421
Thornborough
Souldern
66
67
Gawcott
Singleborough
Great Horwood
A421
5 miles
8 kilometres

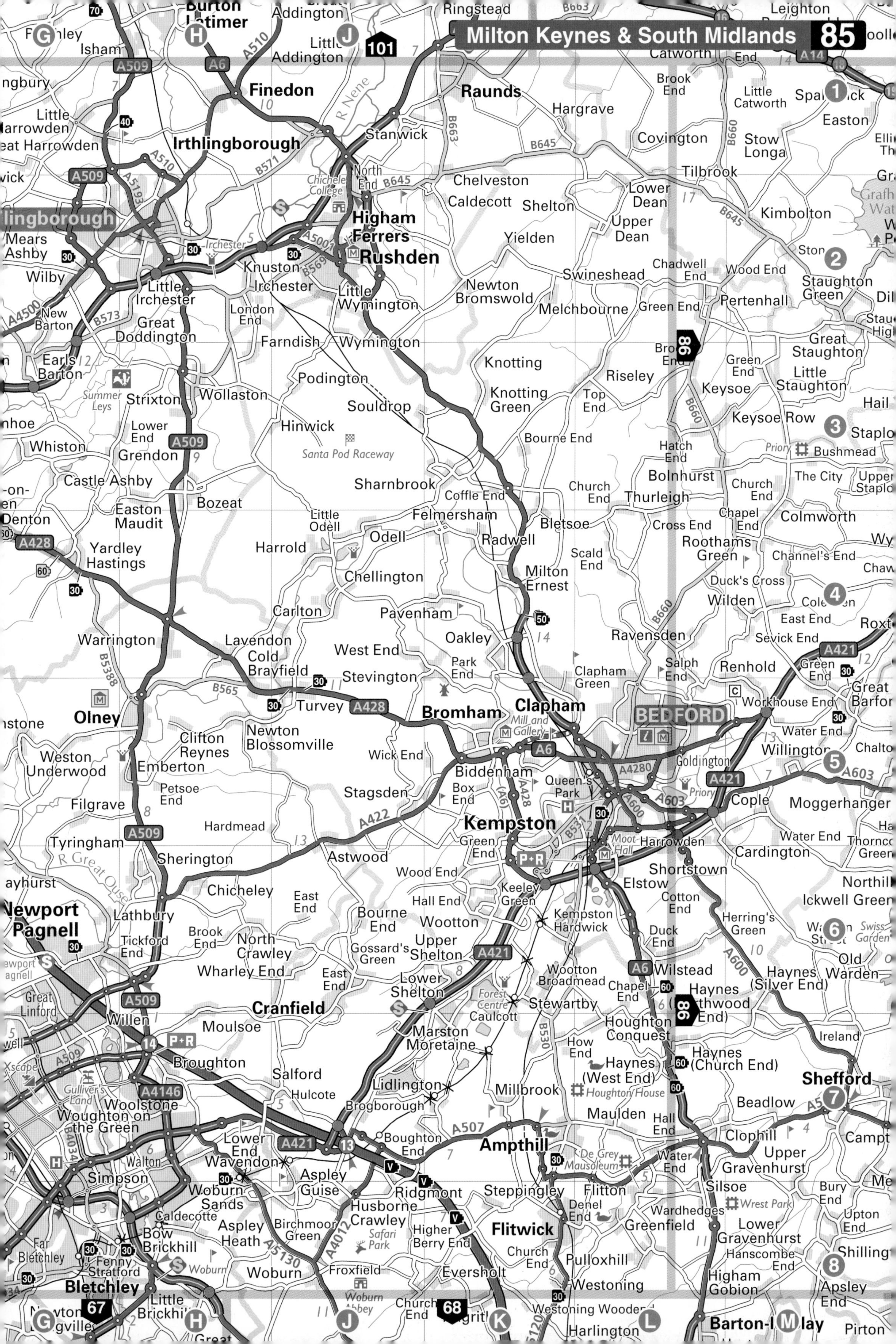
Burton Latimer
Addington
Little Addington
Ringstead
Finedon
Raunds
Irthlingborough
Stanwick
Hargrave
Covington
Tilbrook
Kimbolton
Chelveston
Caldecott
Shelton
Lower Dean
Upper Dean
Higham Ferrers
Rushden
Yielden
Knuston
Irchester
Little Irchester
Little Wymington
Wymington
Newton Bromswold
Swineshead
Melchbourne
Pertenhall
Staughton Green
Great Staughton
Little Staughton
Great Doddington
Earls Barton
Farndish
Podington
Knotting
Knotting Green
Riseley
Keysoe
Keysoe Row
Wollaston
Strixton
Souldrop
Hinwick
Santa Pod Raceway
Bourne End
Bolnhurst
Thurleigh
Grendon
Castle Ashby
Bozeat
Sharnbrook
Coffle End
Felmersham
Bletsoe
Colmworth
Easton Maudit
Odell
Radwell
Harrold
Yardley Hastings
Chellington
Milton Ernest
Roothams Green
Carlton
Pavenham
Oakley
Ravensden
Wilden
Warrington
Lavendon
Cold Brayfield
West End
Stevington
Turvey
Bromham
Clapham
BEDFORD
Renhold
Olney
Clifton Reynes
Newton Blossomville
Emberton
Weston Underwood
Biddenham
Kempston
Stagsden
Goldington
Willington
Cople
Moggerhanger
Cardington
Filgrave
Tyringham
Sherington
Astwood
Harrowden
Shortstown
Elstow
Newport Pagnell
Chicheley
Lathbury
Wootton
Kempston Hardwick
Cranfield
Stewartby
Houghton Conquest
Haynes
Marston Moretaine
Willen
Moulsoe
Broughton
Salford
Lidlington
Millbrook
Maulden
Clophill
Shefford
Woolstone
Woughton on the Green
Brogborough
Ampthill
Wavendon
Aspley Guise
Ridgmont
Husborne Crawley
Steppingley
Flitton
Silsoe
Simpson
Woburn Sands
Flitwick
Greenfield
Bow Brickhill
Aspley Heath
Woburn
Eversholt
Pulloxhill
Westoning
Bletchley
Fenny Stratford
Little Brickhill
Harlington
Barton-le-Clay
Higham Gobion
Pirton

86
A
B
C
D
E
1
2
3
4
5
6
7
8
102
85
68
69
Huntingdon
Catworth
Church End
Leighton Bromswold
Woolley
Great Stukeley
Sapley
Green End
St Peter's Hill
Hartford
Wyton
Hemingford Abbots
Houghton Mill
Brook End
Little Catworth
Spaldwick
Easton
Ellington
Huntingdon
Hinchingbrooke
Brampton
Godmanchester
Hargrave
Covington
Stow Longa
Ellington Thorpe
Grafham
Tilbrook
Chelveston
Caldecott
Shelton
Lower Dean
Upper Dean
Kimbolton
Grafham Water
West Perry
Grafham Exhibition Centre
Buckden
Stirtloe
Offord Cluny
Offord D'Arcy
Yielden
Stonely
East Perry
Diddington
Newton Bromswold
Swineshead
Chadwell End
Wood End
Staughton Green
Dillington
Melchbourne
Green End
Pertenhall
Staughton Highway
Duck End
Papworth St Agnes
Great Staughton
Southoe
Great Paxton
Graveley
Knotting
Brook End
Green End
Little Staughton
R Great Ouse
Riseley
Keysoe
Knotting Green
Top End
Hail Weston
Little Paxton
Toseland
Yelling
Bourne End
Keysoe Row
Staploe
Duloe
St Neots
Croxton
Priory
Bushmead
Hatch End
Bolnhurst
Church End
The City
Upper Staploe
Eaton Ford
Eaton Socon
Eynesbury
Eltisley
Church End
Thurleigh
Chapel End
Colmworth
Bletsoe
Cross End
Radwell
Roothams Green
Channel's End
Wyboston
Little Barford
Abbotsley
Great Gransden
Scald End
Chawston
Milton Ernest
Duck's Cross
Wilden
Colesden
East End
Roxton
Tempsford
Waresley
Little Gransden
Oakley
Ravensden
Sevick End
Park End
Clapham Green
Salph End
Renhold
Green End
Church End
Gamlingay Cinques
Waresley and Gransden Woods
Clapham
BEDFORD
Workhouse End
Great Barford
Gamlingay Great Heath
Gamlingay
Mill and Gallery
Water End
Blunham
Everton
Biddenham
Goldington
Willington
Chalton
Cockayne Hatley
East Hatley
Box End
Queen's Park
Priory
Cople
Moggerhanger
Girtford
Sandy
Potton
Kempston
Harrowden
Hatch
Stratford
Wrestlingworth
Green End
Moot Hall
Water End
Thorncott Green
Beeston
Sutton
Brook End
Cardington
Lower Caldecote
Tadlow
Shortstown
Upper Caldecote
Eyeworth
Keeley Green
Elstow
Northill
R Cam or Rhee
Cotton End
Ickwell Green
Biggleswade
Kempston Hardwick
Herring's Green
Warden Street
Swiss Garden
Shuttleworth Collection
Great Green
Duck End
Newton
Dunton
Old Warden
Guilden Morden
Wootton Broadmead
Wilstead
Haynes (Silver End)
Old Warden
Broom
Forest Centre
Chapel End
Haynes (Northwood End)
Southill
Stewartby
Caulcott
Houghton Conquest
Ireland
Langford
Edworth
Ashwell End
How End
Haynes (Church End)
Stanford
Hinxworth
Ashwell
Haynes (West End)
Shefford
Clifton
Houghton House
Beadlow
Astwick
Maulden
Henlow
Caldecote
Odsey
Hall End
Ampthill
Clophill
Campton
Church End
Stotfold
Baldock
Newnham
Upper Gravenhurst
De Grey Mausoleum
Water End
Meppershall
Arlesey
Steppingley
Flitton
Silsoe
Bury End
Upper & Lower Stondon
Radwell
Bygrave
Denel End
Wardhedges
Wrest Park
Norton
Flitwick
Greenfield
Lower Gravenhurst
Upton End
Church End
Pulloxhill
Hanscombe End
Shillington
Letchworth Garden City
Wallington
Holwell
Westoning
Higham Gobion
Apsley End
Burge End
Lower Green
Baldock
Redhill
Harlington
Icklefor
A1
A14
A6
A421
A428
A603
A600
A4280
A507
A505
A1198
A6001
B645
B660
B661
B1514
B1043
B1040
B1046
B1428
B1042
B658
B659
B656
B530
0 1 2 3 4 5 miles
0 1 2 3 4 5 6 7 8 kilometres

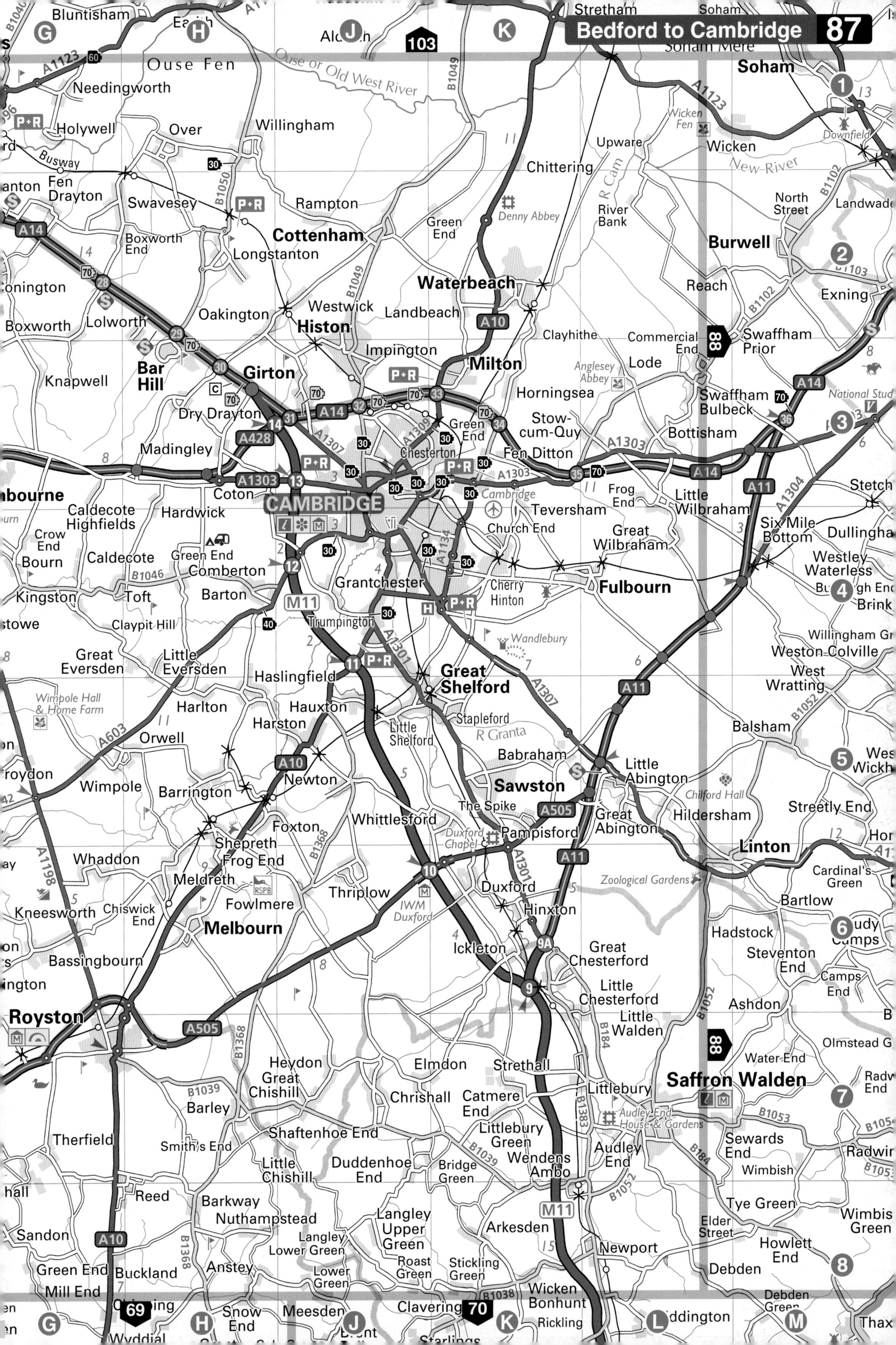
Bluntisham
Ouse Fen
Ouse or Old West River
Stretham
Soham
Soham Mere
Soham
Needingworth
Holywell
Over
Willingham
Wicken Fen
Wicken
Downfield
New River
Busway
Fen Drayton
Swavesey
Rampton
Chittering
Upware
R Cam
River Bank
North Street
Landwade
Boxworth End
Longstanton
Cottenham
Denny Abbey
Green End
Burwell
Conington
Waterbeach
Reach
Exning
Boxworth
Lolworth
Oakington
Westwick
Histon
Landbeach
Clayhithe
Commercial End
Swaffham Prior
Knapwell
Bar Hill
Girton
Impington
Milton
Anglesey Abbey
Lode
Horningsea
Swaffham Bulbeck
National Stud
Dry Drayton
Green End
Stow-cum-Quy
Bottisham
Madingley
Chesterton
Fen Ditton
Coton
CAMBRIDGE
Cambridge
Frog End
Little Wilbraham
Stetchworth
Caldecote Highfields
Hardwick
Teversham
Six Mile Bottom
Dullingham
Crow End
Bourn
Caldecote
Green End
Comberton
Church End
Great Wilbraham
Westley Waterless
Kingston
Toft
Barton
Grantchester
Cherry Hinton
Fulbourn
Brink
Claypit Hill
Trumpington
Wandlebury
Willingham Green
Great Eversden
Little Eversden
Haslingfield
Great Shelford
Weston Colville
West Wratting
Wimpole Hall & Home Farm
Harlton
Hauxton
Harston
Stapleford
Little Shelford
R Granta
Balsham
Orwell
Babraham
Little Abington
Wimpole
Barrington
Newton
Sawston
Chilford Hall
Hildersham
Streetly End
The Spike
Great Abington
Foxton
Whittlesford
Duxford Chapel
Pampisford
Linton
Shepreth
Whaddon
Frog End
Meldreth
Thriplow
Duxford
Zoological Gardens
Cardinal's Green
Bartlow
Kneesworth
Chiswick End
Fowlmere
IWM Duxford
Hinxton
Melbourn
Ickleton
Hadstock
Bassingbourn
Great Chesterford
Steventon End
Camps End
Little Chesterford
Ashdon
Royston
Little Walden
Olmstead Green
Heydon
Elmdon
Strethall
Water End
Great Chishill
Littlebury
Saffron Walden
Radwinter End
Barley
Chrishall
Catmere End
Audley End House & Gardens
Therfield
Smith's End
Shaftenhoe End
Littlebury Green
Sewards End
Little Chishill
Duddenhoe End
Bridge Green
Wendens Ambo
Audley End
Radwinter
Wimbish
Reed
Barkway
Tye Green
Nuthampstead
Langley Upper Green
Arkesden
Elder Street
Wimbish Green
Sandon
Langley Lower Green
Newport
Howlett End
Green End
Buckland
Anstey
Lower Green
Roast Green
Stickling Green
Debden
Mill End
Wicken Bonhunt
Debden Green
Snow End
Meesden
Clavering
Rickling
Thaxted
Wyddial
Starlings
A1123
A14
A10
A428
A1303
A1307
A1309
A1134
A1301
M11
A603
A505
A11
A1304
A1198
B1050
B1049
B1046
B1368
B1039
B1383
B1184
B1052
B1053
B1038
B1102
B1103

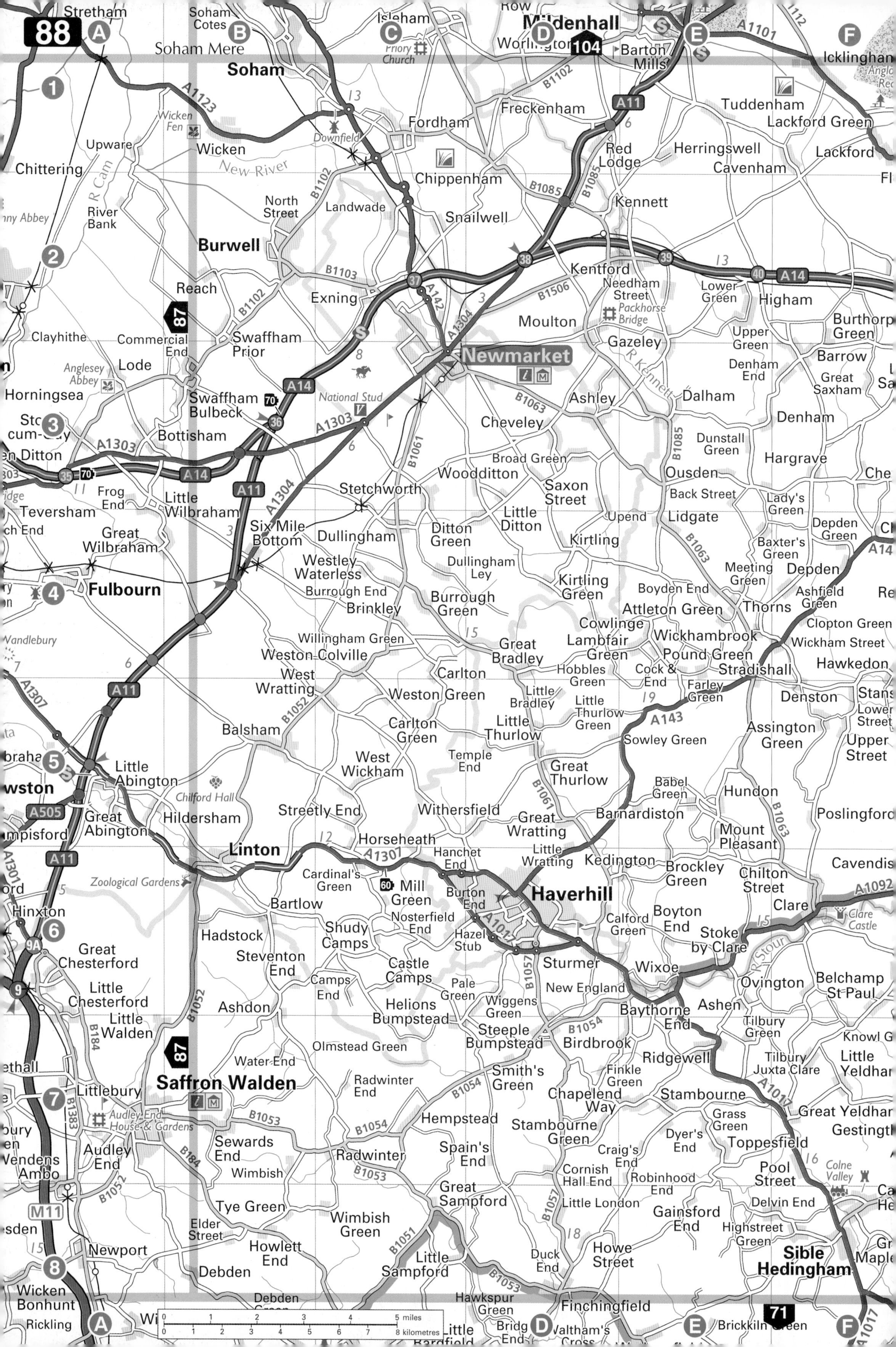
88
A
B
C
D
E
F
1
2
3
4
5
6
7
8
Stretham
Soham Cotes
Soham Mere
Soham
Isleham
Priory Church
Mildenhall
Worlington
104
Barton Mills
A1101
Icklingham
A1123
Wicken Fen
Upware
Wicken
New River
Chittering
R Cam
River Bank
Downfield
Fordham
Freckenham
B1102
A11
Tuddenham
Lackford Green
Lackford
Red Lodge
Herringswell
Cavenham
Chippenham
Landwade
North Street
B1085
Kennett
Snailwell
Burwell
Reach
B1103
Exning
37
A142
38
Kentford
Needham Street
Packhorse Bridge
39
40
A14
Lower Green
Higham
B1506
Moulton
Burthorpe Green
87
B1102
Clayhithe
Commercial End
Swaffham Prior
A1304
Newmarket
Gazeley
Upper Green
Barrow
Anglesey Abbey
Lode
Denham End
Great Saxham
R Kennett
Dalham
Horningsea
Swaffham Bulbeck
70
National Stud
B1063
Ashley
36
A1303
Cheveley
Denham
Bottisham
A1303
B1061
Dunstall Green
Ditton
35
A14
Broad Green
B1085
Hargrave
Frog End
Wood Ditton
Saxon Street
Ousden
Teversham
Little Wilbraham
A11
Stetchworth
Back Street
Lady's Green
Great Wilbraham
Six Mile Bottom
Dullingham
Ditton Green
Little Ditton
Upend
Lidgate
Depden Green
Kirtling
Baxter's Green
B1063
A14
Westley Waterless
Dullingham Ley
Meeting Green
Depden
Fulbourn
Burrough End
Kirtling Green
Boyden End
Ashfield Green
Brinkley
Burrough Green
Attleton Green
Thorns
Cowlinge
Clopton Green
Wandlebury
Willingham Green
Great Bradley
Lambfair Green
Wickhambrook
Wickham Street
Weston Colville
Pound Green
Hobbles Green
Cock & End
Stradishall
Hawkedon
A1307
West Wratting
Carlton
Little Bradley
Farley Green
Denston
Weston Green
Little Thurlow Green
A143
B1052
Carlton Green
Little Thurlow
Sowley Green
Assington Green
Balsham
Upper Street
Little Abington
West Wickham
Temple End
Great Thurlow
Babel Green
Hundon
Chilford Hall
B1061
A505
Great Abington
Hildersham
Streetly End
Withersfield
Great Wratting
Barnardiston
B1063
Poslingford
Mount Pleasant
A1301
Linton
Horseheath
A1307
Hanchet End
Little Wratting
Kedington
Brockley Green
Cavendish
A11
Zoological Gardens
Cardinal's Green
60
Mill Green
Burton End
Haverhill
Chilton Street
A1092
Hinxton
Bartlow
Nosterfield End
Calford Green
Boyton End
Clare
Clare Castle
Hadstock
Shudy Camps
A1017
Hazel Stub
Stoke by Clare
Great Chesterford
Steventon End
Castle Camps
Sturmer
Wixoe
R Stour
Little Chesterford
Camps End
Pale Green
B1057
New England
Ovington
Belchamp St Paul
Ashdon
Helions Bumpstead
Wiggens Green
Baythorne End
Ashen
Little Walden
B1184
B1054
Tilbury Green
B1052
Olmstead Green
Steeple Bumpstead
Birdbrook
Knowl Green
87
Water End
Smith's Green
Ridgewell
Tilbury Juxta Clare
Little Yeldham
Saffron Walden
Radwinter End
Finkle Green
Littlebury
B1054
Chapelend Way
Stambourne
A1017
B1383
Audley End House & Gardens
B1053
Hempstead
Grass Green
Great Yeldham
Stambourne Green
Dyer's End
Gestingthorpe
Audley End
Sewards End
B1054
B184
Spain's End
Craig's End
Toppesfield
Wendens Ambo
Wimbish
Radwinter
Cornish Hall End
Pool Street
B1052
B1053
Robinhood End
Colne Valley
Tye Green
Great Sampford
Little London
Delvin End
M11
B1057
Gainsford End
Highstreet Green
Elder Street
Wimbish Green
Newport
B1051
Howlett End
Duck End
Howe Street
Sible Hedingham
Little Sampford
B1053
Debden
Wicken Bonhunt
Debden Green
Hawkspur Green
Finchingfield
71
Rickling
Little Bardfield
Bridge End
Waltham's Cross
Brickkiln Green
A1017
0 1 2 3 4 5 miles
0 1 2 3 4 5 6 7 8 kilometres

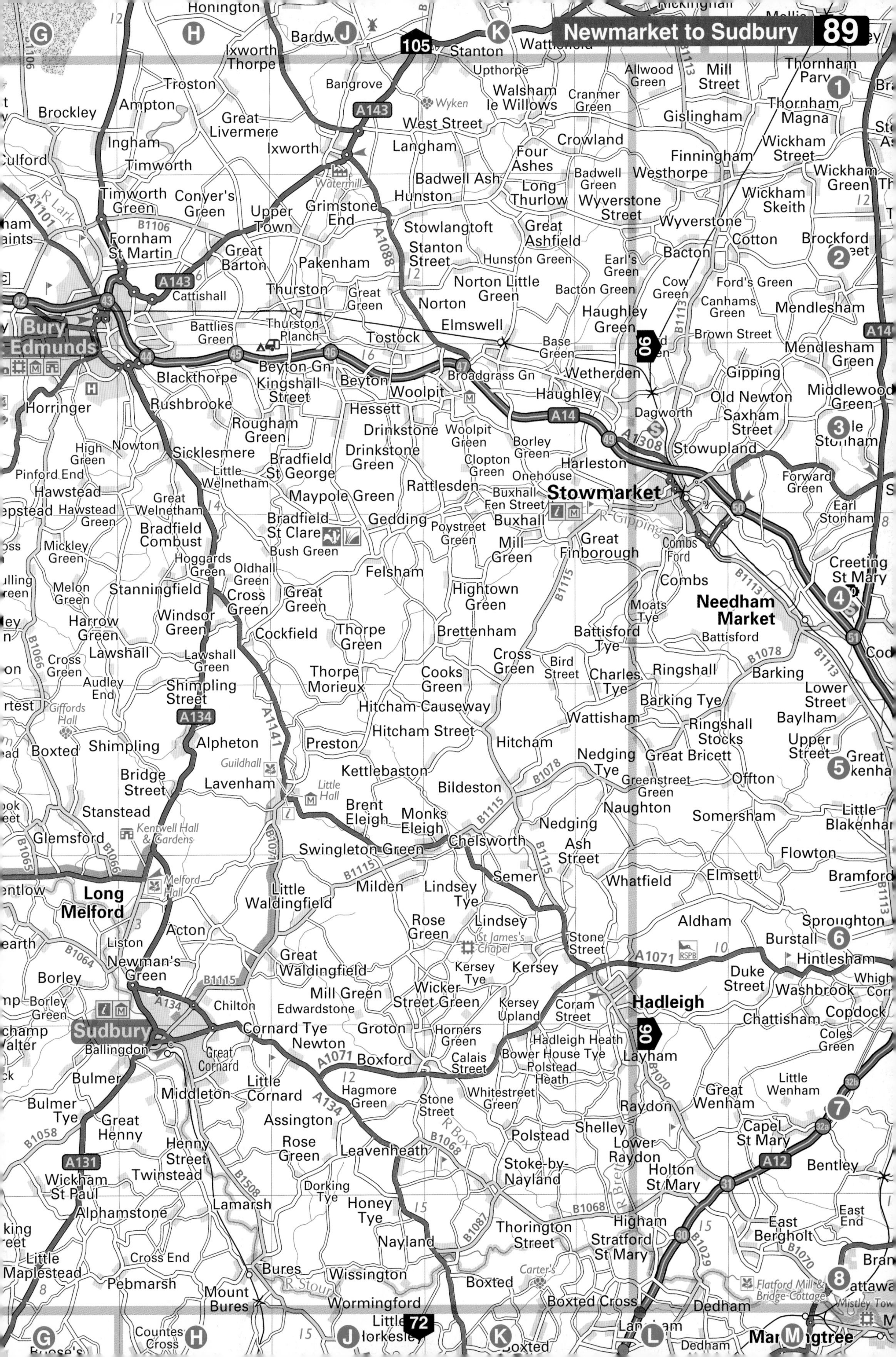

Bury St Edmunds
Stowmarket
Needham Market
Hadleigh
Long Melford
Sudbury
Lavenham
Ixworth
Woolpit
Elmswell
Thurston
Pakenham
Stanton
Walsham le Willows
Mendlesham
Bildeston
Boxford
Nayland
Bures
Dedham
Manningtree
Stoke-by-Nayland
Polstead
Kersey
Hitcham
Glemsford
Cavendish
Clare

105
90
72

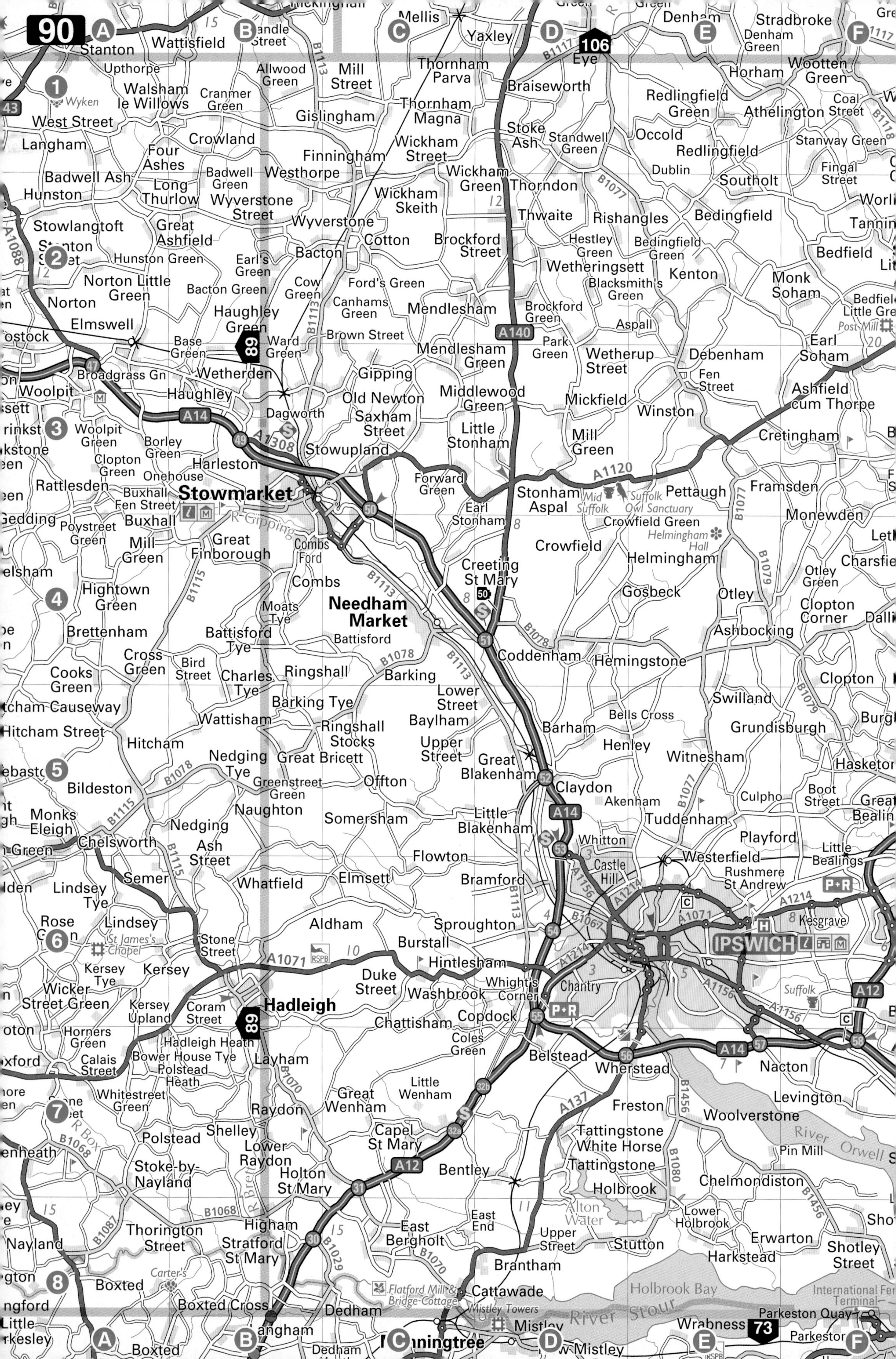
A
B
C
D
E
F
106
89
73
1
2
3
4
5
6
7
8
Stanton
Wattisfield
Sandle Street
Mellis
Yaxley
Eye
Denham
Stradbroke
Denham Green
Upthorpe
Wyken
Allwood Green
Mill Street
Thornham Parva
Braiseworth
Horham
Wootten Green
Walsham le Willows
Cranmer Green
Thornham Magna
Redlingfield Green
Athelington
Coal Street
West Street
Gislingham
Stoke Ash
Standwell Green
Occold
Langham
Crowland
Wickham Street
Redlingfield
Stanway Green
Four Ashes
Finningham
Dublin
Fingal Street
Badwell Ash
Badwell Green
Westhorpe
Wickham Green
Thorndon
Southolt
Hunston
Long Thurlow
Wyverstone Street
Wickham Skeith
Stowlangtoft
Great Ashfield
Wyverstone
Thwaite
Rishangles
Bedingfield
Stanton Street
Hunston Green
Earl's Green
Bacton
Cotton
Brockford Street
Hestley Green
Bedingfield Green
Bedfield
Norton Little Green
Wetheringsett
Kenton
Norton
Bacton Green
Cow Green
Ford's Green
Blacksmith's Green
Monk Soham
Bedfield Little Green
Haughley Green
Canhams Green
Mendlesham
Brockford Green
Elmswell
Ward Green
Brown Street
Aspall
Post Mill
Base Green
Mendlesham Green
Park Green
Wetherup Street
Debenham
Earl Soham
Broadgrass Gn
Wetherden
Gipping
Fen Street
Woolpit
Haughley
Old Newton
Middlewood Green
Mickfield
Ashfield cum Thorpe
Dagworth
Saxham Street
Winston
Woolpit Green
Borley Green
Little Stonham
Mill Green
Cretingham
Stowupland
Clopton Green
Harleston
Forward Green
Rattlesden
Onehouse
Stowmarket
Stonham Aspal
Mid Suffolk Owl Sanctuary
Pettaugh
Framsden
Buxhall Fen Street
Earl Stonham
Crowfield Green
Monewden
Gedding
Poystreet Green
Buxhall
R Gipping
Helmingham Hall
Mill Green
Great Finborough
Combs Ford
Creeting St Mary
Crowfield
Helmingham
Charsfield
Otley Green
Hightown Green
Combs
Gosbeck
Otley
Needham Market
Moats Tye
Clopton Corner
Brettenham
Battisford Tye
Battisford
Ashbocking
Coddenham
Hemingstone
Cross Green
Bird Street
Charles Tye
Ringshall
Barking
Cooks Green
Lower Street
Clopton
Swilland
Bells Cross
Barking Tye
Baylham
Wattisham
Ringshall Stocks
Barham
Grundisburgh
Hitcham Street
Hitcham
Upper Street
Henley
Nedging Tye
Great Bricett
Great Blakenham
Witnesham
Hasketon
Bildeston
Greenstreet Green
Offton
Claydon
Akenham
Culpho
Boot Street
Monks Eleigh
Naughton
Somersham
Little Blakenham
Tuddenham
Nedging
Playford
Chelsworth
Ash Street
Whitton
Westerfield
Little Bealings
Semer
Flowton
Castle Hill
Rushmere St Andrew
Lindsey Tye
Whatfield
Elmsett
Bramford
Rose Green
Lindsey
Aldham
Sproughton
Kesgrave
St James's Chapel
Stone Street
Burstall
IPSWICH
Kersey Tye
Kersey
A1071
RSPB
Hintlesham
Duke Street
Whight's Corner
Chantry
Wicker Street Green
Kersey Upland
Coram Street
Hadleigh
Washbrook
P+R
Suffolk
Horners Green
Hadleigh Heath
Chattisham
Copdock
Coles Green
Calais Street
Bower House Tye
Polstead Heath
Layham
Belstead
Wherstead
Nacton
Whitestreet Green
Great Wenham
Little Wenham
Levington
Stone Street
Raydon
Freston
Woolverstone
Polstead
Shelley
Capel St Mary
Tattingstone White Horse
River Orwell
Lower Raydon
Pin Mill
Stoke-by-Nayland
Holton St Mary
Bentley
Tattingstone
Chelmondiston
R Brett
Holbrook
Alton Water
Lower Holbrook
Thorington Street
Higham
East Bergholt
East End
Upper Street
Stutton
Erwarton
Shotley Street
Nayland
Stratford St Mary
Harkstead
Brantham
Boxted
Carter's
Flatford Mill & Bridge Cottage
Cattawade
Holbrook Bay
International Ferry Terminal
Boxted Cross
Dedham
Mistley Towers
River Stour
Parkeston Quay
Langham
Mistley
Wrabness
Parkeston
Boxted
Manningtree
New Mistley
A14
A140
A1120
A12
A137
A1088
A1156
A1214
A1071
B1113
B1117
B1077
B1078
B1079
B1115
B1068
B1070
B1087
B1029
B1456
B1080
B1067
B1118

Huntingfield
Walpole
Blackheath
Bramfield
Thorington
107
B1117
B1387
A12
A144
Laxfield
Heveningham
Ubbeston Green
Pouy Street
High Street
Darsham
Suffolk Coast
Dunwich
Grey Friars
Owl's Green
Sibton
Peasenhall
Goddard's Corner
A1120
Yoxford
Westleton
Capon's Green
Badingham
B1122
Middleton
Minsmere
Dunwich Heath
Middleton Moor
Dennington
Bruisyard
North Green
B1120
Eastbridge
Brabling Green
Bruisyard Street
Theberton
East Green
Poplar Street
Cransford
Rendham
Kelsale
Leiston Abbey
Castle
Shawsgate
B1119
Carlton
Saxmundham
Swefling
Sizewell
North Green
Great Glemham
Benhall Street
Benhall Green
Knodishall
Leiston
Mill Green
Sternfield
Coldfair Green
Aldringham
B1116
Stratford St Andrew
50
Friday Street
B1121
B1353
Thorpe Ness
Parham
Silverlace Green
Farnham
Friston
Knodishall Common
Hacheston
Snape
A1094
Thorpeness
Easton
Gromford
Snape Street
Marlesford
Little Glemham
Snape Maltings
Aldeburgh
Lower Hacheston
Blaxhall
B1069
Wickham Market
Iken
Campsea Ash
Pettistree
Tunstall
High Street
Aldeburgh Bay
Rendlesham
B1078
River Alde
Upper Ufford
Ufford
A1152
Sudbourne
Chillesford
Lower Ufford
Friday Street
Eyke
B1438
Melton
Bromeswell
B1084
Butley
B1084
Castle
Orford
Woodbridge
Butley High Corner
Capel Green
Orford Ness
Sutton Hoo
B1083
Capel St Andrew
RSPB
Sutton
Boyton
Orfordness-Havergate
Waldringfield
River Ore
Suffolk Heritage Coast
Shottisham
Hollesley
North Weir Point
Newbourne
B1083
Hollesley Bay
Hemley
Ramsholt
Shingle Street
River Deben
Alderton
Kirton
Bawdsey
Falkenham
Trimley St Mary
59
Felixstowe Ferry
Walton
Old Felixstowe
61
Felixstowe
Landguard Fort
Landguard
0 1 2 3 4 5 miles
0 1 2 3 4 5 6 7 8 kilometres
G H J K L M
1 2 3 4 5 6 7 8

A
B
C
D
E
F
110
1
2
3
4
5
6
7
8
Barmouth Bay
Fairbourne & Barmouth Steam Railway
Fairbourne
Friog
Arthog
SNOWDONIA NATIONAL PARK
CADER IDRIS 892
621
Tal-y-llyn
Llwyngwril
Llangelynin
Llanfihangel-y-pennant
Castell y Bere
Afon Dysynni
Tal-y-llyn
King Arthur's & Corris Cr
Abergynolwyn
667
Rhoslefain
A493
Peniarth
Llanegryn
Dolgoch
Tal-y-Llyn Railway
Ton fanau
Bryncrug
B4405
Dolgoch Falls
633
TAREN HENDRE
Aber Dysynni
Pandy
Ynysymaengwyn
Rhyd-yr-onnen
Tywyn
Pennal
Cwrt
Dovey
Cors Dyfi
Aberdovey
Aberdyfi
A493
Glandyfi
Eglwys Fach
Ynys-hir
Ysgubor-y-Coed
Furnace
Afon Dyfi (River Dovey)
447
PEN CARREG-C
A487
Dyfi Furnace
Ynyslas
B4353
Cwm Clettwr
Llancynfelyn
Tre'r-ddol
Tre Taliesin
Borth
Staylittle
Tal-y-bont
Upper Borth
B4353
Dolybont
Ceredigion Heritage Coast
Llandre
Bont-goch or Elerch
Pen-y-garn
Rhyd-y pennau
Bow Street
B4572
Clarach Bay
Clarach
Salem
Penrhyncoch
Garth
Penrhyncoch
Pen-bont Rhydybeddau
A4159
Cliff Railway
Bwlch Nant yr Arian
Aberystwyth
Waunfawr
Capel-Dewi
Llanbadarn Fawr
Dollwen
Capel Bangor
Goginan
Penparcau
Blaengeufforddd
Cwmbrwyno
Rheidol power station
Rhydyfelin
Moriah
Capel Seion
Aberffrwd
Coed Penglanowen
12
A4120
Vale of Rheidol
Llanfarian
Pisgah
Mynydd Buch
Gors
New Cross
Llanfihangel-y-Creuddyn
A485
Capel Trisant
Blaenplwyf
Afon Ystwyth
Cnwch Coch
B4340
Llanilar
Pentre-llyn
B4575
Aber-Magwr
0 1 2 3 4 5 miles
0 1 2 3 4 5 6 7 8 kilometres
Ceredigion Heritage Coast
Rhos-y-garth
77
Trawsco
Llanafan

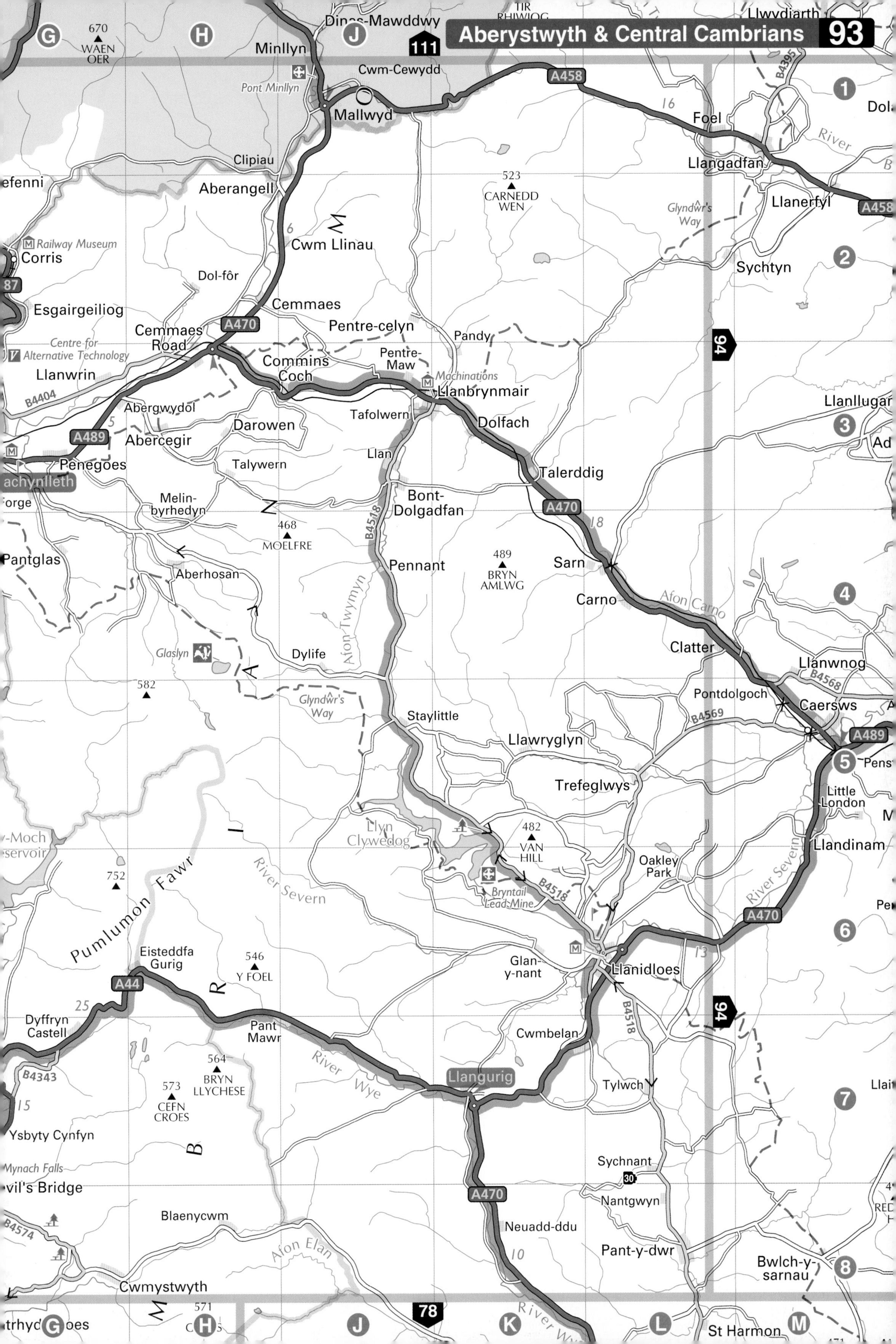
Minllyn
Dinas-Mawddwy
111
Cwm-Cewydd
Pont Minllyn
Mallwyd
A458
Foel
Llangadfan
Llanerfyl
Clipiau
Aberangell
523
CARNEDD WEN
Glyndŵr's Way
Railway Museum
Corris
Cwm Llinau
Sychtyn
Dol-fôr
Esgairgeiliog
Cemmaes
Cemmaes Road
A470
Pentre-celyn
Pandy
Centre for Alternative Technology
Llanwrin
Commins Coch
Pentre-Maw
Machinations
Llanbrynmair
94
B4404
Abergwydol
Darowen
Tafolwern
Dolfach
Llanllugan
A489
Abercegir
Penegoes
Talywern
Llan
Talerddig
achynlleth
Melin-byrhedyn
Bont-Dolgadfan
468
MOELFRE
B4518
Pennant
489
BRYN AMLWG
Sarn
Pantglas
Aberhosan
Carno
Afon Carno
Afon Twymyn
Clatter
Llanwnog
B4568
Glaslyn
Dylife
582
Pontdolgoch
Caersws
B4569
Staylittle
Llawryglyn
Trefeglwys
Little London
Llyn Clywedog
482
VAN HILL
Llandinam
Oakley Park
River Severn
752
Bryntail Lead Mine
A470
Pumlumon Fawr
Glan-y-nant
Llanidloes
Eisteddfa Gurig
546
Y FOEL
A44
B4518
Dyffryn Castell
Pant Mawr
Cwmbelan
B4343
564
BRYN LLYCHESE
River Wye
Llangurig
Tylwch
573
CEFN CROES
Ysbyty Cynfyn
Mynach Falls
Sychnant
vil's Bridge
A470
Nantgwyn
Blaenycwm
Neuadd-ddu
B4574
Afon Elan
Pant-y-dwr
Bwlch-y-sarnau
Cwmystwyth
78
571
St Harmon

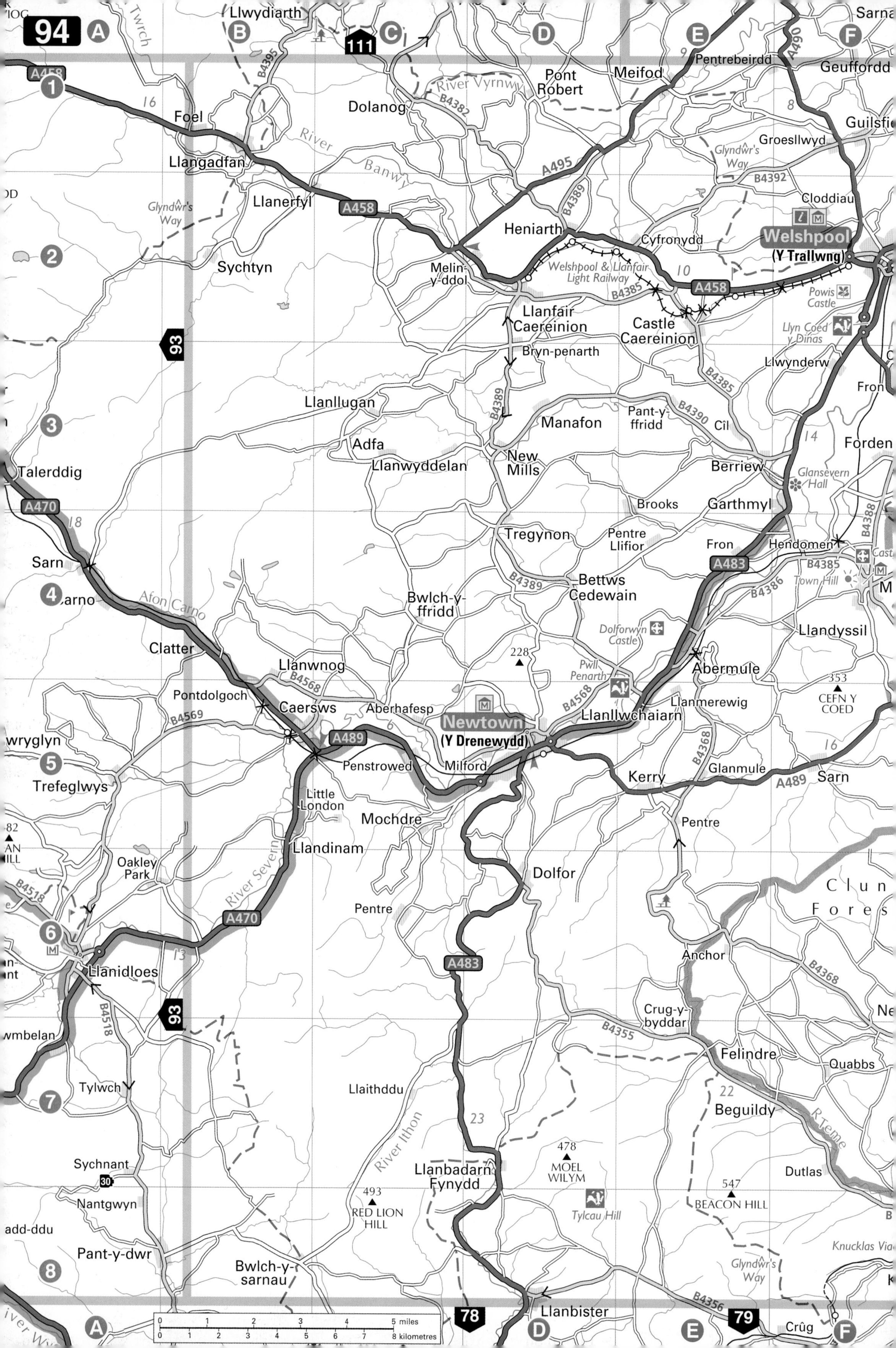
A
B
C
D
E
F
111
Llwydiarth
Twrch
B4395
A458
1
16
Foel
Llangadfan
Llanerfyl
Glyndŵr's Way
River Banwy
A458
Dolanog
River Vyrnwy
B4382
Pont Robert
Meifod
Pentrebeirdd
A490
Geufford
Guilsfield
8
Groesllwyd
A495
B4389
B4392
Cloddiau
Welshpool
(Y Trallwng)
Heniarth
Cyfronydd
2
Sychtyn
Melin-y-ddol
Welshpool & Llanfair Light Railway
10
B4385
A458
Powis Castle
Llanfair Caereinion
Castle Caereinion
Llyn Coed y Dinas
93
Bryn-penarth
Llwynderw
B4385
Llanllugan
B4389
Pant-y-ffridd
B4390
Cil
Fron
3
Manafon
Adfa
14
Forden
Talerddig
Llanwyddelan
New Mills
Berriew
Glansevern Hall
A470
18
Brooks
Garthmyl
Tregynon
Pentre Llifior
Fron
Hendomen
B4388
Sarn
A483
B4385
4
Carno
Afon Carno
B4389
Bettws Cedewain
B4386
Town Hill
Bwlch-y-ffridd
Llandyssil
Clatter
Dolforwyn Castle
228
Llanwnog
Pwll Penarth
Abermule
353
B4568
CEFN Y COED
Pontdolgoch
Caersws
Aberhafesp
Llanmerewig
B4569
B4568
Llanllwchaiarn
Newtown
(Y Drenewydd)
A489
6
B4368
16
Trefeglwys
5
Penstrowed
Milford
Kerry
Glanmule
A489
Sarn
Little London
Mochdre
Pentre
Llandinam
Oakley Park
River Severn
Dolfor
Clun Forest
B4518
Pentre
A470
6
Llanidloes
13
A483
Anchor
B4368
B4518
93
Crug-y-byddar
B4355
Tylwch
Felindre
Quabbs
7
Llaithddu
22
Beguildy
23
River Ithon
R Teme
478
MOEL WILYM
Sychnant
30
Llanbadarn Fynydd
Dutlas
493
RED LION HILL
547
BEACON HILL
Tylcau Hill
Nantgwyn
Pant-y-dwr
Bwlch-y-sarnau
Glyndŵr's Way
Knucklas Viaduct
8
B4356
78
Llanbister
79
Crûg
0 1 2 3 4 5 miles
0 1 2 3 4 5 6 7 8 kilometres

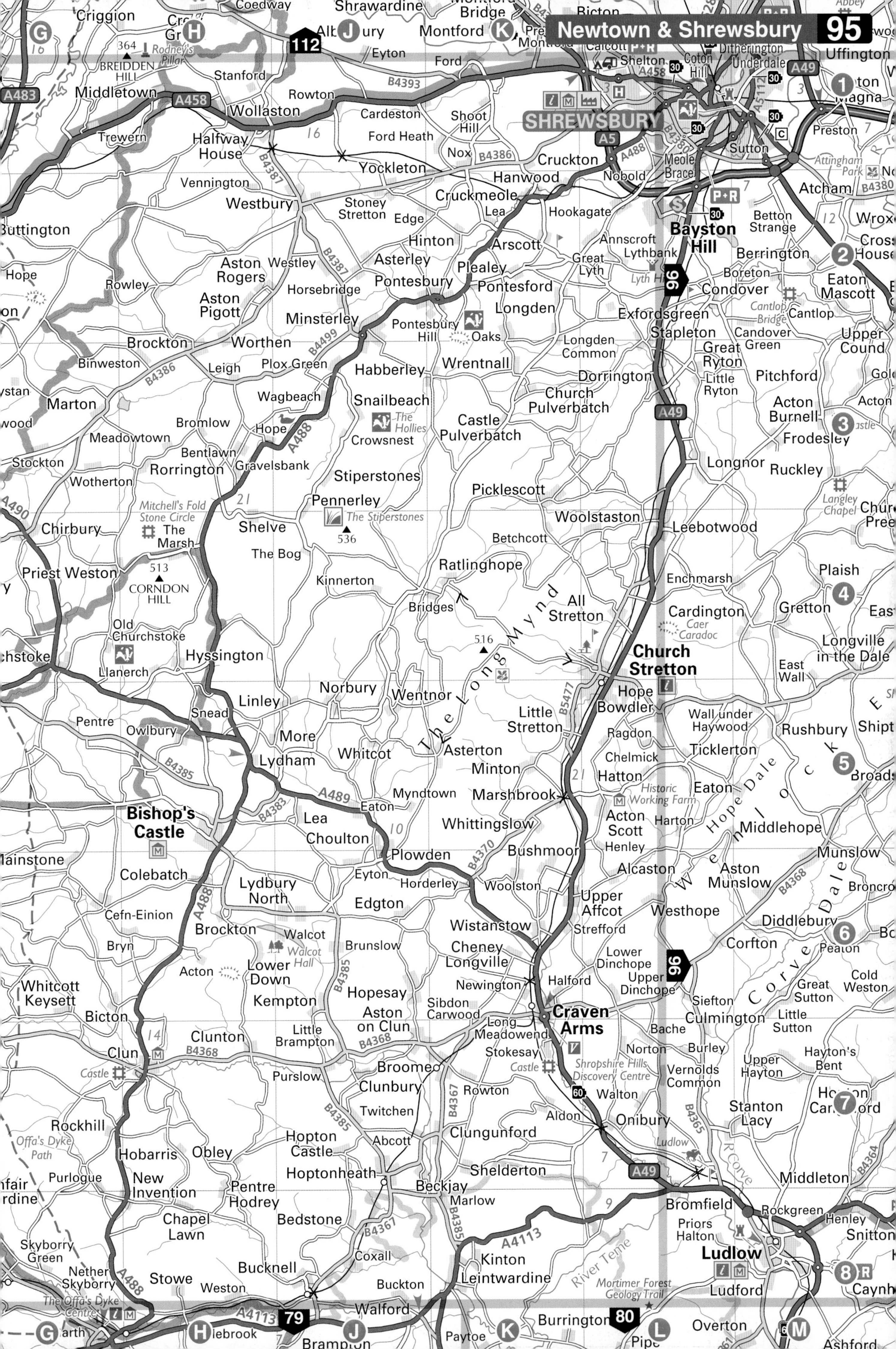
SHREWSBURY
Criggion
Coedway
Shrawardine
Montford Bridge
Bicton
Montford
Alberbury
Eyton
Ford
Shelton
Coton Hill
Ditherington
Uffington
Underdale
BREIDDEN HILL
Rodney's Pillar
Middletown
Stanford
Rowton
Wollaston
Cardeston
Shoot Hill
Ford Heath
Trewern
Halfway House
Nox
Cruckton
Meole Brace
Sutton
Preston
Attingham Park
Atcham
Yockleton
Hanwood
Nobold
Vennington
Westbury
Stoney Stretton
Edge
Cruckmeole
Lea
Hookagate
Bayston Hill
Betton Strange
Wroxeter
Cross Houses
Buttington
Hinton
Arscott
Annscroft
Lythbank
Great Lyth
Lyth Hill
Berrington
Hope
Aston Rogers
Westley
Asterley
Plealey
Boreton
Eaton Mascott
Rowley
Aston Pigott
Horsebridge
Pontesbury
Pontesford
Condover
Cantlop Bridge
Cantlop
Minsterley
Pontesbury Hill
Oaks
Longden
Exfordsgreen
Stapleton
Candover Green
Upper Cound
Brockton
Worthen
Longden Common
Great Ryton
Binweston
Leigh
Plox Green
Habberley
Wrentnall
Dorrington
Little Ryton
Pitchford
Marton
Wagbeach
Snailbeach
Church Pulverbatch
Acton Burnell
Hope
The Hollies
Castle Pulverbatch
Frodesley
Bromlow
Meadowtown
Crowsnest
Bentlawn
Rorrington
Gravelsbank
Stiperstones
Longnor
Ruckley
Stockton
Wotherton
Picklescott
Langley Chapel
Mitchell's Fold Stone Circle
The Marsh
Pennerley
The Stiperstones
Chirbury
Shelve
Woolstaston
Leebotwood
The Bog
Betchcott
Priest Weston
CORNDON HILL
Kinnerton
Ratlinghope
Enchmarsh
Plaish
Bridges
All Stretton
Cardington
Caer Caradoc
Gretton
Old Churchstoke
The Long Mynd
Church Stretton
Longville in the Dale
Hyssington
Llanerch
East Wall
Norbury
Wentnor
Hope Bowdler
Linley
Snead
Little Stretton
Wall under Haywood
Pentre
Owlbury
More
Ragdon
Rushbury
Lydham
Whitcot
Asterton
Ticklerton
Chelmick
Minton
Hatton
Historic Working Farm
Eaton
Myndtown
Marshbrook
Bishop's Castle
Lea
Eaton
Acton Scott
Harton
Wenlock Edge
Hope Dale
Middlehope
Choulton
Whittingslow
Henley
Plowden
Bushmoor
Munslow
Colebatch
Eyton
Alcaston
Aston Munslow
Lydbury North
Horderley
Woolston
Upper Affcot
Edgton
Westhope
Broncroft
Cefn-Einion
Diddlebury
Corve Dale
Brockton
Walcot
Wistanstow
Strefford
Corfton
Peaton
Bryn
Brunslow
Cheney Longville
Lower Dinchope
Walcot Hall
Acton
Lower Down
Upper Dinchope
Cold Weston
Whitcott Keysett
Hopesay
Newington
Halford
Great Sutton
Kempton
Sibdon Carwood
Siefton
Bicton
Aston on Clun
Craven Arms
Culmington
Little Sutton
Clunton
Little Brampton
Long Meadowend
Bache
Clun
Castle
Stokesay Castle
Norton
Burley
Hayton's Bent
Purslow
Broome
Shropshire Hills Discovery Centre
Vernolds Common
Upper Hayton
Clunbury
Rowton
Walton
Twitchen
Aldon
Onibury
Stanton Lacy
Hopton Cadford
Rockhill
Hopton Castle
Abcott
Clungunford
Ludlow
Offa's Dyke Path
Hobarris
Obley
Hoptonheath
Shelderton
River Corve
Purlogue
New Invention
Pentre Hodrey
Beckjay
Middleton
Marlow
Bromfield
Rockgreen
Henley
Chapel Lawn
Bedstone
Priors Halton
Snitton
Skyborry Green
Coxall
Kinton
River Teme
Ludlow
Nether Skyborry
Stowe
Bucknell
Leintwardine
Mortimer Forest Geology Trail
Ludford
Caynham
The Offa's Dyke Centre
Weston
Buckton
Walford
Burrington
Overton
Brampton
Paytoe
Pipe
Ashford
A483
A458
A5
A488
A49
A490
A489
A4113
A5112
B4393
B4386
B4387
B4380
B4499
B4385
B4383
B4370
B4477
B4368
B4367
B4365
B4364
B4361
112
96
79
80
364
513
536
516

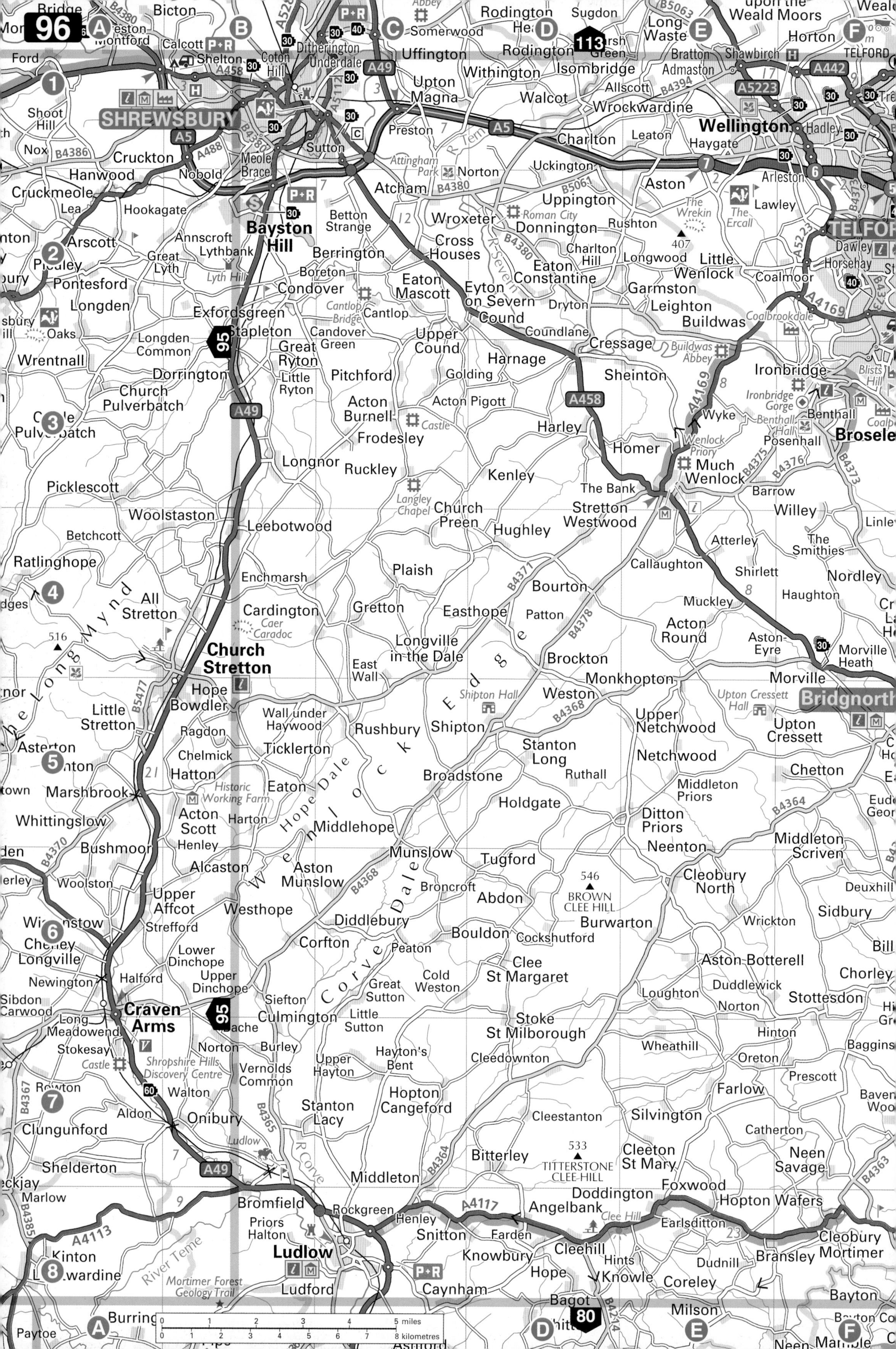

96
Bicton
Calcott
Shelton
Coton Hill
Ditherington
Underdale
Somerwood
Rodington
Rodington Heath
Sugdon
Long Waste
Weald Moors
Horton
TELFORD
Ford
Uffington
Withington
Isombridge
Bratton
Admaston
Shawbirch
SHREWSBURY
Upton Magna
Walcot
Allscott
Wrockwardine
Shoot Hill
Preston
Charlton
Leaton
Wellington
Hadley
Haygate
Nox
Cruckton
Meole Brace
Sutton
Attingham Park
Norton
Uckington
Hanwood
Nobold
Atcham
Aston
Arleston
Cruckmeole
Lea
Hookagate
Bayston Hill
Betton Strange
Wroxeter
Roman City
Uppington
Donnington
Rushton
The Wrekin
The Ercall
Lawley
Arscott
Annscroft
Lythbank
Cross Houses
407
Dawley
Great Lyth
Berrington
Charlton Hill
Longwood
Little Wenlock
Horsehay
Pontesford
Lyth Hill
Boreton
Eaton Constantine
Eaton Mascott
Condover
Eyton on Severn
Garmston
Coalmoor
Longden
Cantlop Bridge
Cantlop
Dryton
Leighton
Buildwas
Oaks
Exfordsgreen
Cound
Coalbrookdale
Stapleton
Candover Green
Coundlane
Longden Common
Great Ryton
Upper Cound
Cressage
Buildwas Abbey
Wrentnall
Harnage
Dorrington
Little Ryton
Pitchford
Golding
Sheinton
Ironbridge
Church Pulverbatch
Ironbridge Gorge
Acton Burnell
Acton Pigott
Wyke
Benthall
Castle Pulverbatch
Castle
Harley
Benthall Hall
Frodesley
Wenlock Priory
Posenhall
Broseley
Longnor
Ruckley
Homer
Much Wenlock
Kenley
Picklescott
The Bank
Barrow
Langley Chapel
Church Preen
Stretton Westwood
Willey
Woolstaston
Leebotwood
Hughley
Betchcott
Atterley
The Smithies
Ratlinghope
Plaish
Callaughton
Shirlett
Nordley
Enchmarsh
Bourton
All Stretton
The Long Mynd
Muckley
Haughton
516
Cardington
Gretton
Easthope
Patton
Acton Round
Caer Caradoc
Aston-Eyre
Morville Heath
Church Stretton
Longville in the Dale
Brockton
Morville
East Wall
Monkhopton
Hope Bowdler
Shipton Hall
Weston
Upton Cressett Hall
Bridgnorth
Little Stretton
Wall under Haywood
Rushbury
Shipton
Upper Netchwood
Upton Cressett
Ragdon
Stanton Long
Asterton
Chelmick
Ticklerton
Netchwood
Hatton
Broadstone
Ruthall
Chetton
Historic Working Farm
Eaton
Middleton Priors
Marshbrook
Wenlock Edge
Hope Dale
Holdgate
Acton Scott
Harton
Ditton Priors
Whittingslow
Middlehope
Henley
Neenton
Middleton Scriven
Bushmoor
Alcaston
Munslow
Tugford
Aston Munslow
546
Woolston
Broncroft
Abdon
Cleobury North
Deuxhill
BROWN CLEE HILL
Upper Affcot
Westhope
Sidbury
Wistanstow
Diddlebury
Burwarton
Wrickton
Strefford
Corfton
Bouldon
Cockshutford
Cheney Longville
Lower Dinchope
Peaton
Aston Botterell
Corve Dale
Clee St Margaret
Chorley
Halford
Newington
Upper Dinchope
Cold Weston
Great Sutton
Duddlewick
Stottesdon
Sibdon Carwood
Siefton
Loughton
Norton
Craven Arms
Culmington
Little Sutton
Long Meadowend
Bache
Stoke St Milborough
Hinton
Shropshire Hills Discovery Centre
Stokesay Castle
Burley
Hayton's Bent
Wheathill
Baggins
Cleedownton
Vernolds Common
Upper Hayton
Oreton
Rowton
Walton
Prescott
Farlow
Hopton Cangeford
Aldon
Onibury
Stanton Lacy
Cleestanton
Silvington
Clungunford
Catherton
Ludlow
R Corve
533
Cleeton St Mary
Shelderton
Bitterley
TITTERSTONE CLEE HILL
Neen Savage
Middleton
Foxwood
Marlow
Doddington
Hopton Wafers
Bromfield
Rockgreen
Angelbank
Priors Halton
Henley
Clee Hill
Earlsditton
Snitton
Farden
Cleobury Mortimer
Kinton
River Teme
Ludlow
Cleehill
Bransley
Knowbury
Hints
Dudnill
Leintwardine
Mortimer Forest Geology Trail
Hope
Knowle
Coreley
Ludford
Caynham
Bayton
Bagot
Milson
Burrington
Paytoe
Neen
Marble
A
B
C
D
E
F
1
2
3
4
5
6
7
8
95
113
80
0 1 2 3 4 5 miles
0 1 2 3 4 5 6 7 8 kilometres

Woodcote
Great Chatwell
Orslow
Mitton
Heath Hill
Lilleshall Abbey
Chadwell
Brineton
114
Marston
Bickford
Whiston
Penkridge
Lilyhurst
Weston Heath
Shropshire Union Canal
Congreve
Huntington
Hednesford
Granville
Sheriffhales
Blymhill
Wheaton Aston
Lapley
Green Heath
Cannock Chase
Church Hill
Blymhill Lawn
Stretton
Water Eaton
High Town
Burlington
Weston-under-Lizard
Crackleybank
A5
Gailey
Hatherton
Weston Park
Bishop's Wood
Shutt Green
Horsebrook
Kiddemore Green
Crateford
Telford
A41
Boscobel House
Four Ashes
Four Crosses
CANNOCK
Norton Canes
M54
Tong Norton
Great Saredon
Haughton
Shifnal
White Ladies Priory
Brewood
Standeford
Little Saredon
Littlewood
Tong
Lower Green
Shareshill
Cheslyn Hay
Great Wyrley
The Wyke
Shackerley
Coven
Slade Heath
Chillington
Little Wyrley
Cosford
Sydnal Lane
Coven Heath
Cross Green
Featherstone
Upper Landywood
Evelith
Royal Air Force
Codsall Wood
Codsall
Hilton Park
Pelsall
Newtown
Kemberton
Albrighton
Kingswood Common
Bilbrook
Moseley Old Hall
Springhill
Essington
Brockton
Grindle
Whiston Cross
Lane Green
Wallington Heath
Little Bloxwich
Ryton
Oaken
Bushbury
Wood Hayes
Blakenall Heath
Sutton Maddock
Boningale
Oxley
Bloxwich
Beckbury
Wood End
Short Heath
Burnhill Green
Wrottesley
Wergs
Stockwell End
Roughwood
Harden
Tettenhall
Wednesfield
Lane Head
Coal Pool
Badger
Pattingham
Nurton
Perton
Tettenhall Wood
WOLVERHAMPTON
Heath Town
Willenhall
Kingslow
Wightwick
Portobello
Stableford
Ackleton
Moseley
Caldmore
Trescott
Monmore Green
Darlaston Green
Chesterton
Wightwick Manor
Merryhill
Blakenhall
Palfrey
Catstree
Lower Penn
Ettingshall
Darlaston
Allscott
Worfield
Shipley
Penn
Bilston
King's Hill
Wyken
Hilton
Upper Ludstone
Orton
Wednesbury
Burcote
Hopstone
Seisdon
Bradley
Swancote
The Bratch
Gospel End
Cinder Hill
Coseley
Friar Park
Roughton
Aston
Trysull
Sedgley
Ocker Hill
Golds Green
Hill Top
Woundale
Draycott
Ounsdale
Baggeridge
Hurst Hill
Tipton
Claverley
Wombourne
Wrens Nest
Tipton Green
Swan Village
Upper Farmcote
Heathton
Himley Hall Park
Dudley Port
Danesford
Halfpenny Green
Smestow
Farmcote
Lower Beobridge
Swindon
Himley
Lower Gornal
WEST BROMWICH
Quatford
Wolverhampton Halfpenny Green
Bobbington
DUDLEY
Mose
Hinksford
Wall Heath
Six Ashes
Highgate Common
Kingswinford
Pensnett
Rounds Green
Dudmaston
Quatt
Brockmoor
Oldbury
Bromley
Netherton
Portway
Four Ashes
Ashwood
Rowley Regis
Tuckhill
Wordsley
Merry Hill
Hampton Loade
Primrose Hill
Coxgreen
Enville
Brierley Hill
Prestwood
Audnam
Blackheath
Hampton
Staffs & Worcs Canal
Amblecote
Cradley Heath
Coombeswood
Bearwood
Turleygreen
Birdsgreen
Compton
Quarry Bank
Stourton
Alveley
Lye
Cradley
Quinton
Woodhill
Dunsley
Wollaston
Severn Valley
Potter's Cross
Old Swinford
Woodgate Valley
Highley
Romsley
Kinver
Wollescote
HALESOWEN
Moor Street
Stanley
STOURBRIDGE
Hasbury
Woodgate
Fenn Green
Pedmore
Hayley Green
Lutley
Netherton
River Severn
Whittington
Illey
Bartley Green
Nash End
Bodenham Arboretum
Kingsford
Hagley
Hunnington
Upper Arley
Blakeshall
The Falconry Centre
Hagley Hall
Frankley
Coppicegate
Shatterford
Caunsall
Islandpool
West Hagley
Lower Clent
Clent Hills
Drakelow
Cookley
Romsley
Severn Valley Railway
Wolverley
Churchill
Clent
Axborough
Broome
Holy Cross
Dayhouse Bank
Pound Green
Blakedown
Newtown
Trimpley
Low Habberley
Franche
Broadwaters
Hackman's Gate
Bell End
Bell Heath
Windmill Hill
Buttonoak
Yieldingtree
Habberley
Stoneybridge
Wyre Forest
Blakebrook
Belbroughton
Rubery
Rednal
Eachway
KIDDERMINSTER
Drayton
Bewdley
Wribbenhall
Stone
Broom Hill
Wildmoor
Lydiate Ash
Cofton Hackett
Lem Hill
Far Forest
West Midland
Hillpool
Woodrow
Fairfield
Long Bank
Stanklin
Harvington
Tanwood
Marlbrook
Lickey
Wyre Forest
Bluntington
Upper Catshill
Pound Bank
Callow Hill
Hoobrook
Mustow Green
Brockencote
Bournheath
Lickey Rock
Barnt Green
Ribbesford
Catshill
Staple Hill
Gorst Hill
Lye Head
Summerfield
Chaddesley Corbett
Dodford
Apes Dale
Upper Milton
Wilden
Shenstone
Woodcote Green
Lickey End
Linthurst
Bliss Gate
Stourport-
81
Torton
Blackwell

Penkridge
114
Pye Green
Forest Centre
Upper Longdon
Brereton
Armitage
115
A515
Rileyhill
Overley
Alrewas
Fradley
A449
A460
A51
Longdon
Congreve
Lapley
Huntington
Hednesford
Cannock Chase
Green Heath
Hazelslade
Castle Ring
Longdon Green
Cannock Wood
Rawnsley
Church Hill
Stonywell
Elmhurst
Stretton
Water Eaton
High Town
Littleworth
Gentleshaw
Farewell
Hilliard's Cross
Lichfield
Heath Hayes & Wimblebury
Chorley
Gailey
Hatherton
Creswell Green
Streethay
Horsebrook
A5192
Crateford
Chase Terrace
Boney Hay
Burntwood Green
Leomansley
A5
CANNOCK
A5190
Four Ashes
Four Crosses
Woodhouses
Darnford
Great Saredon
Norton Canes
Burntwood
Standeford
Little Saredon
Chasewater Railway
Chasetown
Pipehill
Whittington
Littlewood
Hammerwich
Letocetum Baths
Lower Green
Shareshill
Great Wyrley
Cheslyn Hay
Staffordshire Regiment
Coven
Slade Heath
Wall
A5148
Little Wyrley
Brownhills
A38
Coven Heath
Cross Green
97
Featherstone
Hilton Park
Upper Landywood
Summerhill
Chesterfield
M54
Pelsall Wood
Clayhanger
Springhill
Lynn
Shenstone
Hopwas
Newtown
Pelsall
Shire Oak
Stonnall
Lower Stonnall
Weeford
Moseley Old Hall
Essington
Springhill
Wallington Heath
Little Bloxwich
Walsall Wood
A461
Thornes
Hints
Brookhouse Lane Green
Bushbury
Wood Hayes
Blakenall Heath
Shelfield
Little Hay
Oxley
Bloxwich
Stockwell End
Wood End
Short Heath
Roughwood
Rushall
Stubbers Green
Leighswood
Mill Green
M6 Toll
Wednesfield
Harden
Lane Head
Coal Pool
Daw End
Shenstone Woodend
WOLVERHAMPTON
M6
A454
Aldridge
A453
Heath Town
Portobello
Willenhall
Little Aston
Mere Green
Moseley
Monmore Green
Darlaston Green
Caldmore
WALSALL
Hardwick
Four Oaks
Middleton
Blakenhall
Ettingshall
Palfrey
Streetly
Doe Bank
Ash End House
Merryhill
Bilston
Darlaston
Barr Beacon
Stoke End
Whitehouse Common
Allen End
Penn
King's Hill
Wednesbury
Yew Tree
Sutton Park
SUTTON COLDFIELD
Maney
A446
Bradley
Great Barr
Kingstanding
Over Green
Gospel End
Cinder Hill
Coseley
Friar Park
Queslett
New Oscott
Boldmere
Wylde Green
Wishaw
Sedgley
Ocker Hill
Walmley
A463
Hurst Hill
Golds Green
Hill Top
Newton
Hamstead
Tipton
Walmley Ash
Curdworth
Baggeridge
Himley
Tipton Green
Wrens Nest
Churchfield
Short Heath
Himley Hall Park
Dudley Port
Swan Village
Sandwell Valley
Alexander Stadium
Perry
Erdington
Water Orton
Minworth
Himley
Lower Gornal
WEST BROMWICH
Brown's Green
Perry Barr
Witton
Gravelly Hill
Tyburn
Castle Bromwich
DUDLEY
Handsworth
Birchfield
A38(M)
Washwood Heath
Wall Heath
Rounds Green
Kingswinford
Pensnett
Oldbury
Aston
Ward End
Shard End
Kingshurst
Brockmoor
Bromley
Netherton
Portway
Smethwick
Saltley
Stechford
Kitt's Green
Wordsley
Rowley Regis
Merry Hill
Brierley Hill
Primrose Hill
Ladywood
BIRMINGHAM
Tile Cross
Chelmsley Wood
Wollaston
Audnam
Amblecote
Blackheath
Coombeswood
Bearwood
Small Heath
Yardley
Lyndon Green
Marston Green
Quarry Bank
Cradley Heath
Cradley
Lye
Sheldon
Birmingham
Stourbridge
Old Swinford
Wollescote
HALESOWEN
Quinton
Woodgate Valley
Harborne
Edgbaston
Balsall Heath
Tyseley
Sparkhill
Acock's Green
A45
Elmdon
Moor Street
Woodgate
Bournebrook
Moseley
Wake Green
Sarehole Mill
Hasbury
Hayley Green
A456
Lutley
Pedmore
Illey
Bartley Green
Selly Oak
Stirchley
Cadbury World
Bournville
Olton
Ulverley Green
Bickenhill
Hagley
Hagley Hall
Hunnington
Frankley
Cotteridge
King's Heath
Alcester Lane End
Lifford
Hall Green
Elmdon Heath
Lode Heath
The Falconry Centre
West Hagley
Lower Clent
Clent Hills
Clent
Romsley
Frankley
Northfield
King's Norton
Maypole
Yardley Wood
Highter's Heath
Sharman's Cross
SOLIHULL
Broome
Holy Cross
A491
Dayhouse Bank
Newtown
Bell End
M5
West Heath
Walker's Heath
Shirley
Major's Green
Belbroughton
Yieldingtree
Bell Heath
Windmill Hill
Longbridge
Rubery
Rednal
Headley Heath
Hollywood
Dickens Heath
Monkspath
Tilehouse Green
Bentley Heath
Drayton
Hillpool
Woodrow
Broom Hill
Wildmoor
Stoneybridge
Eachway
Lydiate Ash
Cofton Hackett
Hopwood
Forhill
A435
Whitlock's End
Wythall
Tidbury Green
Cheswick Green
Harvington
Tanwood
Fairfield
Bluntington
Marlbrook
Lickey
Arrowfield Top
Barnt Green
Hopwood Park
Tanner's Green
Earlswood
Four Ashes
Upper Catshill
Bournheath
Catshill
Lickey Rock
Staple Hill
Weatheroak Hill
Forshaw Heath
Terry's Green
Chessetts Wood
Chaddesley Corbett
Dodford
Woodcote Green
Apes Dale
Withybed Green
M42
82
Alvechurch
Portway
Wood End
Hockley Heath
Cakebole
0 1 2 3 4 5 miles
0 1 2 3 4 5 6 7 8 kilometres

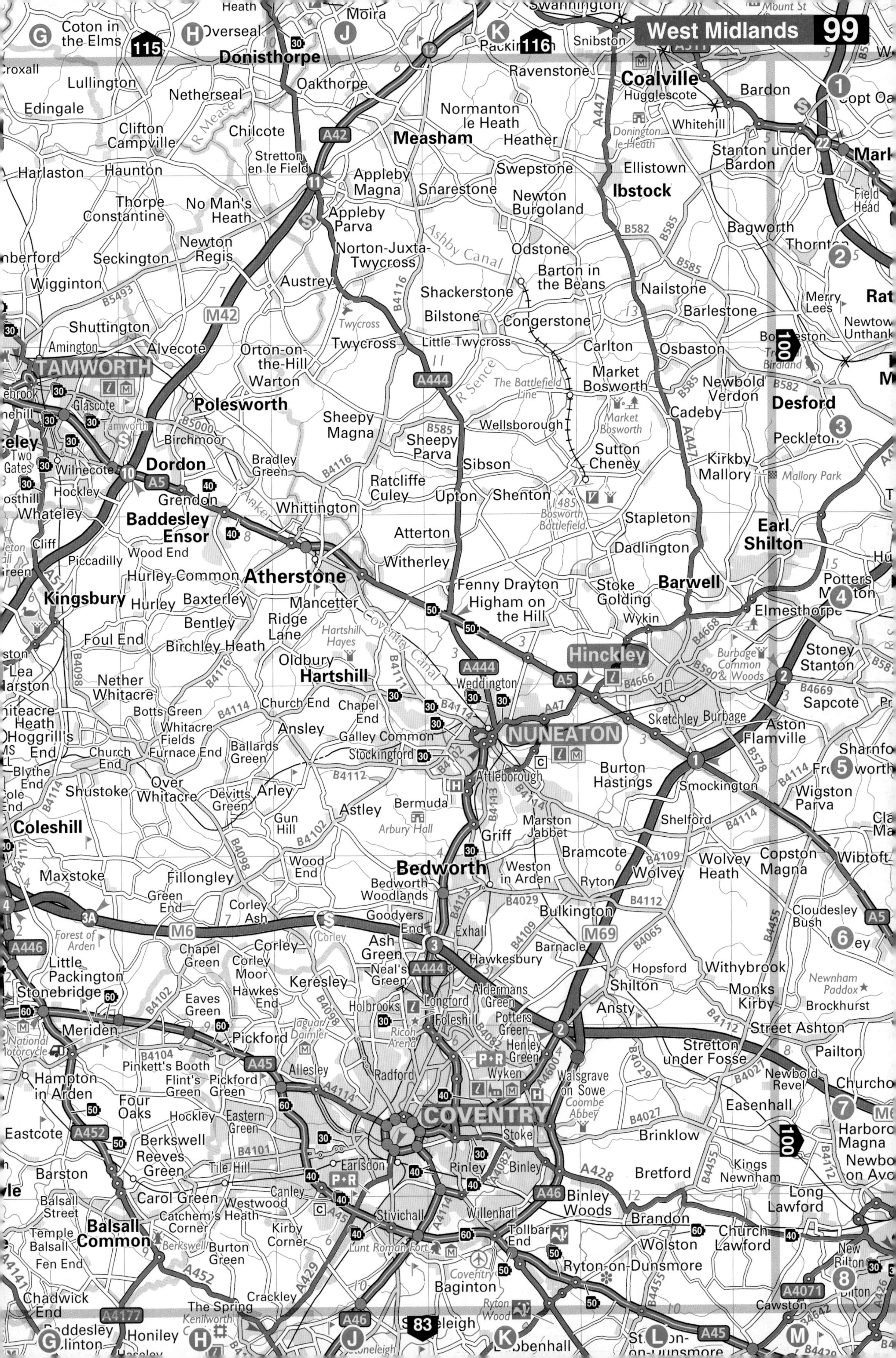
Coton in the Elms
Overseal
Moira
Packington
Swannington
Snibston
Donisthorpe
115
116
Croxall
Lullington
Netherseal
Oakthorpe
Ravenstone
Coalville
Hugglescote
Bardon
Copt Oak
Edingale
Clifton Campville
Chilcote
R Mease
Normanton le Heath
Measham
Heather
Whitehill
Donington le Heath
Stanton under Bardon
Markfield
Harlaston
Haunton
Stretton en le Field
Appleby Magna
Snarestone
Swepstone
Ellistown
Ibstock
Field Head
Thorpe Constantine
No Man's Heath
Appleby Parva
Newton Burgoland
Bagworth
Thornton
Newton Regis
Seckington
Norton-Juxta-Twycross
Ashby Canal
Odstone
Barton in the Beans
Nailstone
Wigginton
Austrey
Shackerstone
Merry Lees
Ratby
Bilstone
Congerstone
Barlestone
Newtown Unthank
Shuttington
Twycross
Amington
Alvecote
Orton-on-the-Hill
Little Twycross
Carlton
Osbaston
Botcheston
Tropical Birdland
TAMWORTH
Warton
The Battlefield Line
Market Bosworth
Newbold Verdon
Desford
Glascote
Polesworth
R Sence
Sheepy Magna
Wellsborough
Cadeby
Peckleton
Tamworth
Birchmoor
Sheepy Parva
Sutton Cheney
Two Gates
Wilnecote
Dordon
Bradley Green
Sibson
Kirkby Mallory
Mallory Park
Hockley
Grendon
Ratcliffe Culey
Upton
Shenton
1485 Bosworth Battlefield
Whateley
Baddesley Ensor
R Anker
Whittington
Stapleton
Earl Shilton
Atterton
Cliff
Wood End
Dadlington
Piccadilly
Witherley
Hurley Common
Atherstone
Fenny Drayton
Stoke Golding
Barwell
Potters Marston
Kingsbury
Hurley
Baxterley
Mancetter
Higham on the Hill
Elmesthorpe
Bentley
Ridge Lane
Wykin
Foul End
Birchley Heath
Hartshill Hayes
Coventry Canal
Hinckley
Stoney Stanton
Oldbury
Burbage Common & Woods
Lea Marston
Hartshill
Nether Whitacre
Weddington
Sapcote
Whiteacre Heath
Church End
Chapel End
Botts Green
Whitacre Fields
Ansley
Galley Common
NUNEATON
Sketchley
Burbage
Aston Flamville
Hoggrill's End
Church End
Furnace End
Ballards Green
Stockingford
Burton Hastings
Sharnford
Blythe End
Attleborough
Smockington
Frolesworth
Shustoke
Over Whitacre
Devitts Green
Arley
Wigston Parva
Coleshill
Gun Hill
Astley
Bermuda
Arbury Hall
Marston Jabbet
Shelford
Griff
Bramcote
Wolvey
Wolvey Heath
Copston Magna
Wibtoft
Maxstoke
Fillongley
Wood End
Bedworth
Weston in Arden
Ryton
Bedworth Woodlands
Green End
Corley Ash
Goodyers End
Bulkington
Cloudesley Bush
Forest of Arden
Chapel Green
Corley
Exhall
Barnacle
Little Packington
Corley Moor
Ash Green
Hawkesbury
Withybrook
Stonebridge
Hawkes End
Keresley
Neal's Green
Hopsford
Shilton
Monks Kirby
Newnham Paddock
Brockhurst
Eaves Green
Holbrooks
Longford
Aldermans Green
Ansty
Meriden
Pickford
Jaguar Daimler
Ricoh Arena
Foleshill
Potters Green
Henley Green
Street Ashton
National Motorcycle
Stretton under Fosse
Pailton
B4104
Pinkett's Booth
Allesley
Radford
Wyken
Walsgrave on Sowe
Newbold Revel
Churchover
Hampton in Arden
Flint's Green
Pickford Green
Coombe Abbey
Easenhall
Four Oaks
Hockley
Eastern Green
COVENTRY
Eastcote
Berkswell
Stoke
Brinklow
Harborough Magna
Reeves Green
Tile Hill
Earlsdon
Binley
Pinley
Bretford
Kings Newnham
Newbold on Avon
Barston
Carol Green
Canley
Binley Woods
Long Lawford
Balsall Street
Westwood
Catchem's Corner
Stivichall
Willenhall
Brandon
Temple Balsall
Balsall Common
Berkswell
Burton Green
Kirby Corner
Lunt Roman Fort
Tollbar End
Wolston
Church Lawford
New Bilton
Fen End
Coventry
Ryton-on-Dunsmore
Chadwick End
The Spring
Crackley
Baginton
Cawston
Kenilworth
Ryton Wood
Baddesley Clinton
Honiley
Stoneleigh
Stretton-on-Dunsmore
83
Bubbenhall
100
M42
M6
M69
A5
A42
A444
A447
A45
A46
A452
A446
A4177
A4071
A428

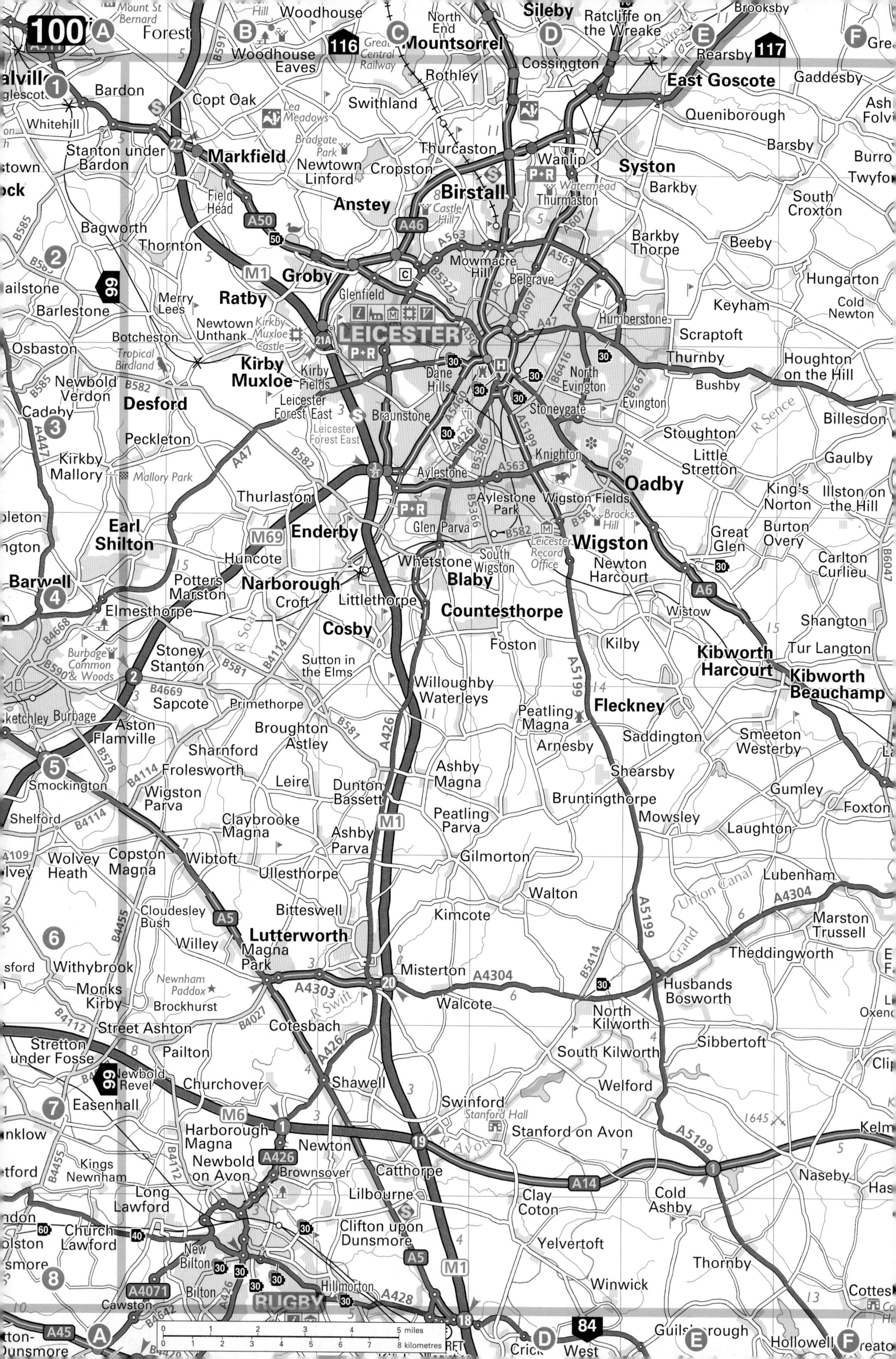
100
116
117
99
84
Mount St Bernard
Forest
Woodhouse
Woodhouse Eaves
Great Central Railway
North End
Mountsorrel
Sileby
Ratcliffe on the Wreake
Brooksby
R Wreake
Rearsby
Cossington
Rothley
East Goscote
Gaddesby
Bardon
Copt Oak
Lea Meadows
Swithland
Queniborough
Whitehill
Stanton under Bardon
Markfield
Bradgate Park
Newtown Linford
Cropston
Thurcaston
Wanlip
Syston
Barsby
Field Head
Anstey
Birstall
Watermead
Thurmaston
Barkby
South Croxton
Castle Hill
Bagworth
Thornton
A50
A46
A563
A607
Barkby Thorpe
Beeby
Groby
Mowmacre Hill
Belgrave
Hungarton
Ratby
Merry Lees
Glenfield
Keyham
Cold Newton
Barlestone
Newtown Unthank
Kirby Muxloe Castle
LEICESTER
Humberstone
Scraptoft
Botcheston
Tropical Birdland
Osbaston
Kirby Muxloe
Kirby Fields
Dane Hills
North Evington
Thurnby
Houghton on the Hill
Bushby
Newbold Verdon
Desford
Leicester Forest East
Braunstone
Evington
Stoneygate
Cadeby
R Sence
Billesdon
Peckleton
Kirkby Mallory
Mallory Park
Stoughton
Little Stretton
Gaulby
Knighton
Aylestone
Thurlaston
Oadby
King's Norton
Illston on the Hill
Earl Shilton
Aylestone Park
Wigston Fields
Brocks Hill
Burton Overy
Enderby
Glen Parva
Leicester Record Office
Wigston
Great Glen
Huncote
Whetstone
South Wigston
Newton Harcourt
Carlton Curlieu
Barwell
Potters Marston
Narborough
Blaby
Croft
Littlethorpe
Countesthorpe
Wistow
Elmesthorpe
Cosby
Foston
Kilby
Shangton
Kibworth Harcourt
Tur Langton
Kibworth Beauchamp
Burbage Common & Woods
Stoney Stanton
Sutton in the Elms
Fleckney
Sapcote
Primethorpe
Willoughby Waterleys
Peatling Magna
Saddington
Smeeton Westerby
Hinckley
Burbage
Aston Flamville
Broughton Astley
Arnesby
Sharnford
Ashby Magna
Shearsby
Gumley
Frolesworth
Leire
Dunton Bassett
Bruntingthorpe
Foxton
Smockington
Wigston Parva
Peatling Parva
Mowsley
Laughton
Shelford
Claybrooke Magna
Ashby Parva
Gilmorton
Wolvey Heath
Copston Magna
Wibtoft
Ullesthorpe
Lubenham
Walton
Grand Union Canal
Bitteswell
Kimcote
Marston Trussell
Cloudesley Bush
Lutterworth
Theddingworth
Willey
Magna Park
Withybrook
Misterton
Husbands Bosworth
Newnham Paddox
Monks Kirby
Brockhurst
A4303
A4304
R Swift
Walcote
North Kilworth
Street Ashton
Cotesbach
Sibbertoft
Stretton under Fosse
Pailton
South Kilworth
Newbold Revel
Churchover
Shawell
Welford
Easenhall
Swinford
Stanford Hall
1645
Harborough Magna
Stanford on Avon
Newton
R Avon
A5199
Kings Newnham
Newbold on Avon
Brownsover
Catthorpe
Naseby
Long Lawford
Lilbourne
A14
Clay Coton
Cold Ashby
Church Lawford
Clifton upon Dunsmore
New Bilton
Yelvertoft
Thornby
Bilton
Hillmorton
Winwick
A4071
Cawston
RUGBY
A428
A45
M1
M6
M69
A5
A426
A6
A47
B582
Crick
West
Guilsborough
Hollowell
Cottesbrooke
0 1 2 3 4 5 miles
0 1 2 3 4 5 6 7 8 kilometres

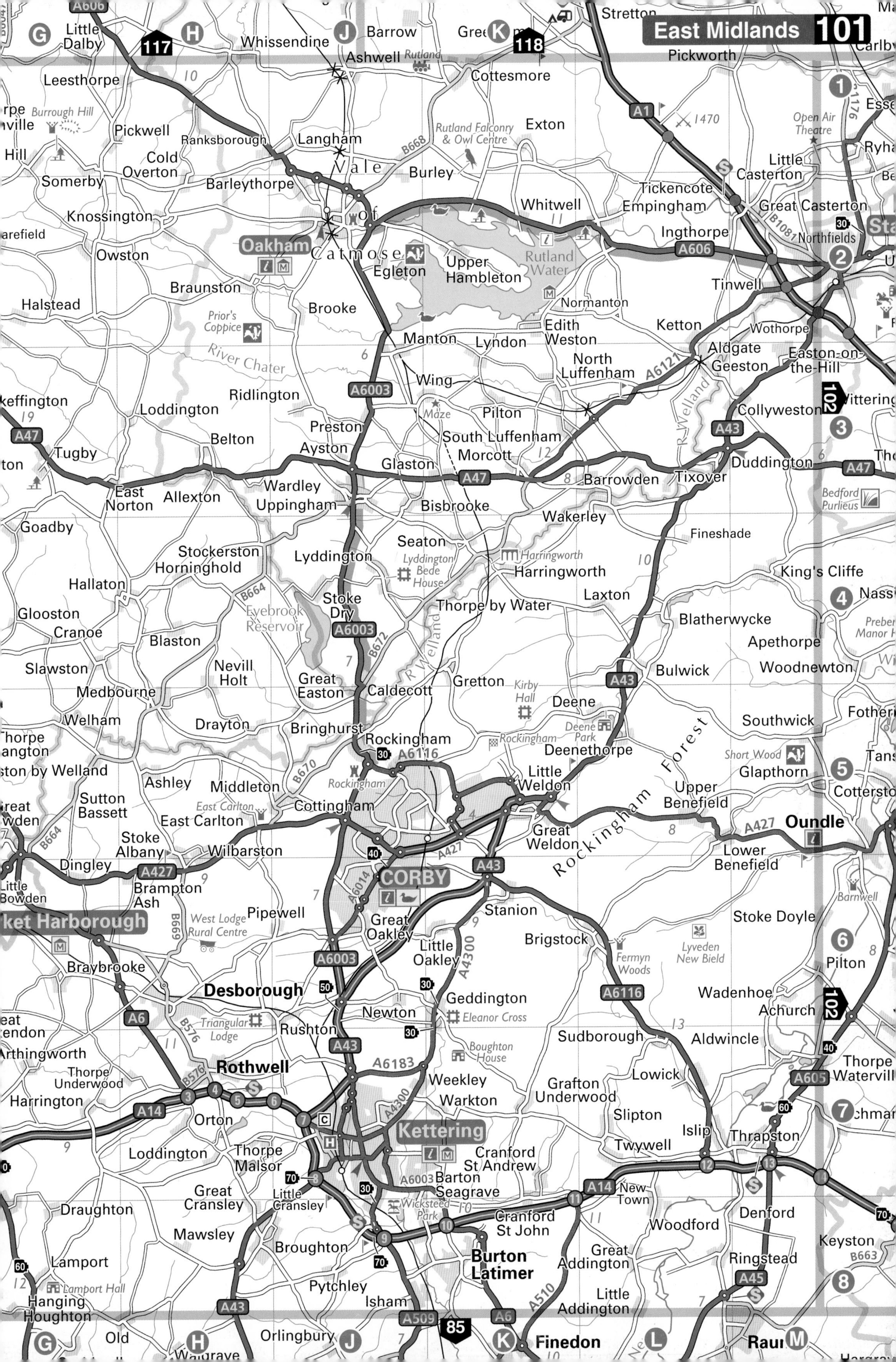
Little Dalby
Whissendine
Barrow
Stretton
Pickworth
Ashwell
Rutland
Cottesmore
Leesthorpe
Burrough Hill
Pickwell
Ranksborough
Langham
Rutland Falconry & Owl Centre
Exton
1470
Open Air Theatre
Cold Overton
Somerby
Barleythorpe
Vale of Catmose
Burley
Little Casterton
Tickencote
Empingham
Whitwell
Great Casterton
Knossington
Ingthorpe
Northfields
Owston
Oakham
Egleton
Upper Hambleton
Rutland Water
Tinwell
Braunston
Normanton
Halstead
Brooke
Prior's Coppice
Ketton
Wothorpe
Manton
Lyndon
Edith Weston
Aldgate
Geeston
Easton-on-the-Hill
River Chater
North Luffenham
Wing
R Welland
Ridlington
Loddington
Maze
Pilton
Collyweston
Preston
South Luffenham
Belton
Ayston
Morcott
Tugby
Glaston
Barrowden
Tixover
Duddington
East Norton
Allexton
Wardley
Uppingham
Bisbrooke
Bedford Purlieus
Goadby
Wakerley
Fineshade
Seaton
Stockerston
Horninghold
Lyddington
Lyddington Bede House
Harringworth
King's Cliffe
Hallaton
Laxton
Stoke Dry
Eyebrook Reservoir
Thorpe by Water
Glooston
Cranoe
Blatherwycke
Blaston
Apethorpe
Slawston
Nevill Holt
Bulwick
Woodnewton
Medbourne
Great Easton
Caldecott
Gretton
Kirby Hall
Deene
Welham
Southwick
Drayton
Bringhurst
Rockingham
Deene Park
Deenethorpe
Short Wood
Glapthorn
Ashley
Middleton
Little Weldon
Rockingham Forest
Upper Benefield
Sutton Bassett
East Carlton
Cottingham
Great Weldon
Oundle
Stoke Albany
Wilbarston
Lower Benefield
Dingley
Brampton Ash
CORBY
Barnwell
Little Bowden
West Lodge Rural Centre
Pipewell
Stanion
Stoke Doyle
Great Oakley
Brigstock
Little Oakley
Fermyn Woods
Lyveden New Bield
Pilton
Braybrooke
Desborough
Geddington
Wadenhoe
Newton
Eleanor Cross
Achurch
Triangular Lodge
Rushton
Sudborough
Aldwincle
Boughton House
Rothwell
Lowick
Thorpe Waterville
Thorpe Underwood
Weekley
Grafton Underwood
Harrington
Orton
Warkton
Slipton
Kettering
Islip
Thrapston
Loddington
Thorpe Malsor
Twywell
Cranford St Andrew
Great Cransley
Little Cransley
Barton Seagrave
New Town
Draughton
Wicksteed Park
Cranford St John
Denford
Woodford
Mawsley
Keyston
Broughton
Burton Latimer
Great Addington
Ringstead
Lamport
Lamport Hall
Little Addington
Hanging Houghton
Pytchley
Isham
Old
Orlingbury
Finedon
Walgrave

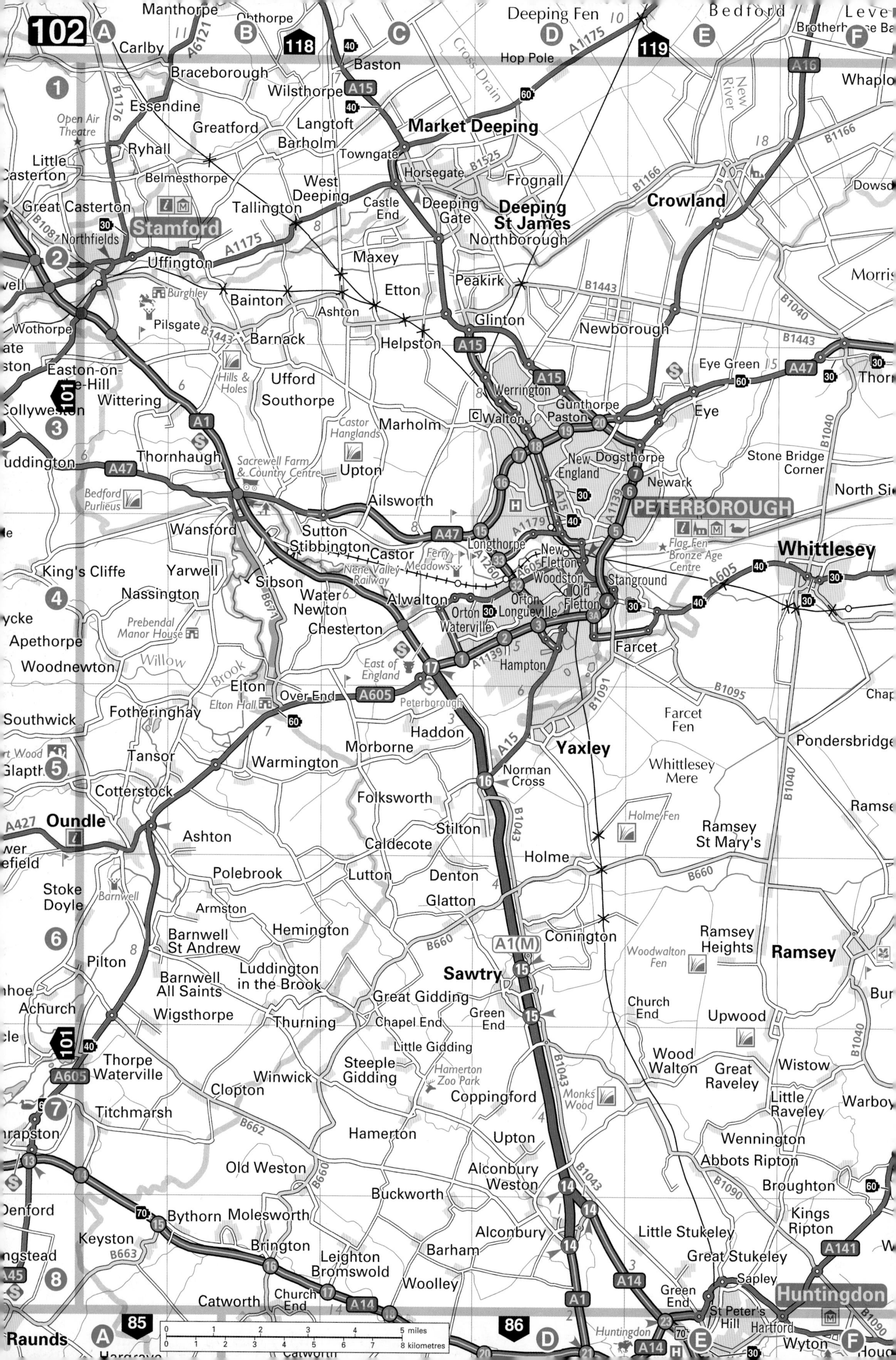

102
A
B
C
D
E
F
118
119
Manthorpe
Obthorpe
Carlby
A6121
Deeping Fen
A1175
Bedford
Brotherhouse Bar
Hop Pole
A16
Baston
Braceborough
Wilsthorpe
A15
Cross Drain
New River
Whaplode
1
Essendine
B1176
Open Air Theatre
Greatford
Langtoft
Market Deeping
B1166
Ryhall
Barholm
Towngate
Little Casterton
Horsegate
B1525
Belmesthorpe
Frognall
West Deeping
Dowsdale
Great Casterton
Tallington
Castle End
Deeping Gate
Deeping St James
Crowland
B1081
Northfields
Stamford
A1175
Northborough
2
Uffington
Maxey
Morris
Burghley
Bainton
Etton
Peakirk
B1443
Wothorpe
Ashton
Pilsgate
Glinton
B1040
Barnack
Helpston
Newborough
A15
Easton-on-the-Hill
B1443
Hills & Holes
Ufford
Eye Green
A47
101
Wittering
Southorpe
Werrington
A15
Thorney
Collyweston
Castor Hanglands
Marholm
Walton
Gunthorpe
Paston
Eye
3
A1
B1040
Duddington
Thornhaugh
Sacrewell Farm & Country Centre
New England
Dogsthorpe
Stone Bridge Corner
A47
Upton
Newark
Bedford Purlieus
North Side
Ailsworth
A1139
PETERBOROUGH
Wansford
Sutton
A47
Longthorpe
A1179
Stibbington
Castor
Ferry Meadows
New Fletton
Flag Fen Bronze Age Centre
Whittlesey
King's Cliffe
Yarwell
Nene Valley Railway
A1260
A605
Woodston
Stanground
Sibson
Old Fletton
A605
4
Nassington
Water Newton
Alwalton
Orton
Orton Waterville
Orton Longueville
Prebendal Manor House
B671
Chesterton
Apethorpe
Farcet
A1139
Hampton
Woodnewton
Willow Brook
East of England
Elton
Over End
A605
B1091
B1095
Chapel End
Elton Hall
Peterborough
Southwick
Fotheringhay
Farcet Fen
Haddon
Yaxley
Tansor
Morborne
A15
Whittlesey Mere
Pondersbridge
5
Warmington
Norman Cross
Cotterstock
Folksworth
B1040
Ramsey
A427
Oundle
B1043
Holme Fen
Ashton
Stilton
Ramsey St Mary's
Caldecote
Holme
Polebrook
Lutton
Denton
B660
Stoke Doyle
Barnwell
Glatton
Armston
Hemington
Barnwell St Andrew
Conington
Ramsey Heights
6
B660
A1(M)
Woodwalton Fen
Ramsey
Pilton
Luddington in the Brook
Sawtry
Barnwell All Saints
Great Gidding
Church End
Achurch
Wigsthorpe
Thurning
Chapel End
Green End
Upwood
Little Gidding
B1040
Thorpe Waterville
Wood Walton
Wistow
101
Steeple Gidding
Hamerton Zoo Park
Great Raveley
A605
Winwick
Clopton
Coppingford
B1043
Monks Wood
Little Raveley
Warboys
7
Titchmarsh
B662
Thrapston
Hamerton
Upton
Wennington
Abbots Ripton
Old Weston
B660
Alconbury Weston
B1043
Buckworth
B1090
Broughton
Denford
Bythorn
Molesworth
Kings Ripton
Keyston
Alconbury
Little Stukeley
A141
B663
Brington
Barham
Great Stukeley
Ringstead
A45
8
Leighton Bromswold
Sapley
Woolley
A14
Catworth
Church End
A14
A1
Green End
Huntingdon
St Peter's Hill
Hartford
B1090
85
86
Raunds
Huntingdon
Wyton
Houghton
A14
0 1 2 3 4 5 miles
0 1 2 3 4 5 6 7 8 kilometres

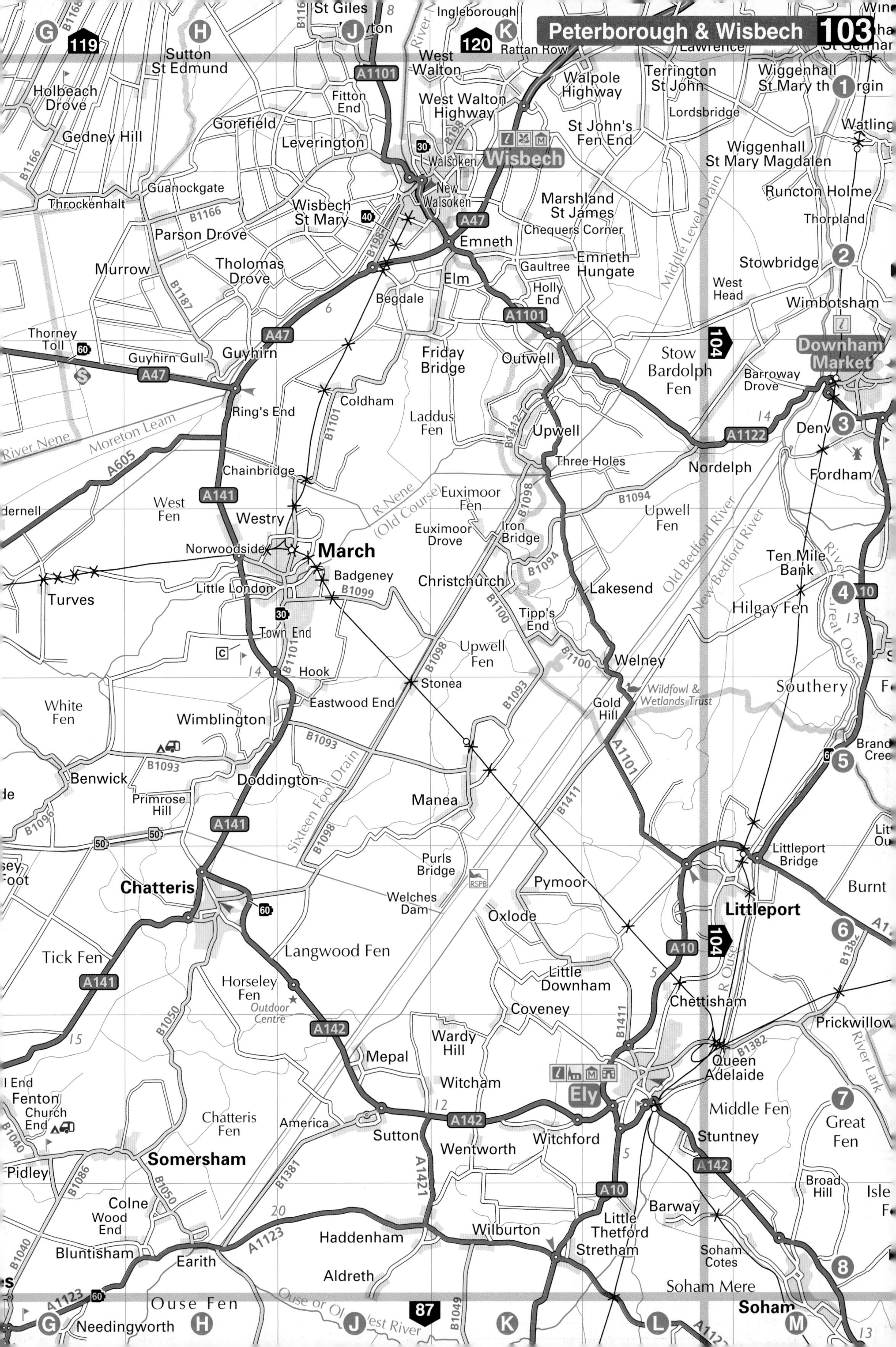
Peterborough & Wisbech
103
119
120
104
87
Sutton St Edmund
Holbeach Drove
Gedney Hill
Gorefield
Leverington
Fitton End
West Walton
West Walton Highway
Walsoken
Wisbech
New Walsoken
Walpole Highway
Terrington St John
Lordsbridge
St John's Fen End
Wiggenhall St Mary Magdalen
Runcton Holme
Thorpland
Stowbridge
Wimbotsham
Downham Market
Barroway Drove
West Head
Stow Bardolph Fen
Guanockgate
Throckenhalt
Wisbech St Mary
Parson Drove
Murrow
Tholomas Drove
Emneth
Marshland St James
Chequers Corner
Emneth Hungate
Gaultree
Holly End
Elm
Begdale
Thorney Toll
Guyhirn Gull
Guyhirn
Friday Bridge
Outwell
Upwell
Coldham
Laddus Fen
Ring's End
Moreton Leam
River Nene
R. Nene (Old Course)
Middle Level Drain
Three Holes
Nordelph
Denver
Fordham
Chainbridge
West Fen
Westry
March
Norwoodside
Badgeney
Little London
Turves
Town End
Euximoor Fen
Euximoor Drove
Iron Bridge
Upwell Fen
Christchurch
Lakesend
Tipp's End
Old Bedford River
New Bedford River
Ten Mile Bank
Hilgay Fen
River Great Ouse
Hook
Stonea
Upwell Fen
Welney
Wildfowl & Wetlands Trust
Gold Hill
Southery
White Fen
Wimblington
Eastwood End
Benwick
Primrose Hill
Doddington
Manea
Sixteen Foot Drain
Purls Bridge
RSPB
Welches Dam
Pymoor
Oxlode
Littleport Bridge
Littleport
Chatteris
Tick Fen
Langwood Fen
Horseley Fen
Outdoor Centre
Little Downham
Coveney
Chettisham
Prickwillow
River Lark
Wardy Hill
Mepal
Witcham
Queen Adelaide
Ely
Middle Fen
Great Fen
Fenton
Church End
Chatteris Fen
America
Sutton
Wentworth
Witchford
Stuntney
Pidley
Somersham
Colne
Wood End
Bluntisham
Earith
Haddenham
Aldreth
Wilburton
Little Thetford
Stretham
Barway
Soham Cotes
Broad Hill
Soham Mere
Soham
Ouse Fen
Needingworth
Ouse or Old West River
A47
A1101
A141
A605
A142
A10
A1122
A1123
A1421
B1166
B1187
B1101
B1099
B1098
B1094
B1100
B1093
B1096
B1050
B1086
B1040
B1381
B1411
B1382
B1049
B1412

104
120
121
103
88
Downham Market
Littleport
Ely
Soham
Mildenhall
Brandon
Feltwell
Lakenheath
Beck Row
Watlington
Marham
Shouldham
Stoke Ferry
Methwold
Hilgay
Denver
Southery
Welney
Upwell
Wereham
Oxborough
Narborough
Wormegay
Stow Bardolph
Wimbotsham
Crimplesham
Weeting
Eriswell
Isleham
Prickwillow
Chettisham
Stuntney
Witchford
0 1 2 3 4 5 miles
0 1 2 3 4 5 6 7 8 kilometres

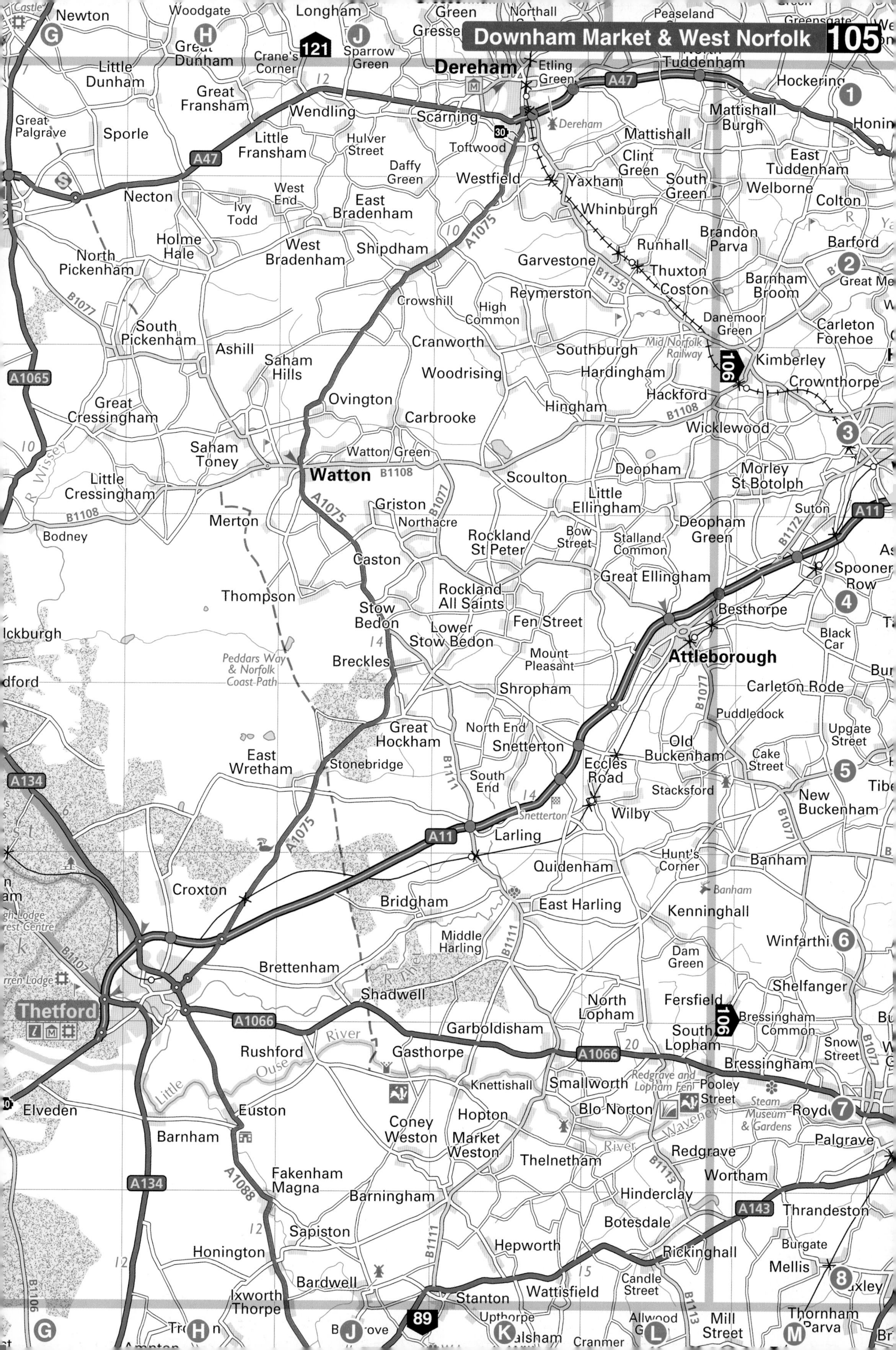
Newton
Woodgate
Longham
Great Dunham
Little Dunham
Crane's Corner
Sparrow Green
121
Dereham
Etling Green
A47
Tuddenham
Hockering
Great Fransham
Wendling
Scarning
Dereham
Mattishall Burgh
Great Palgrave
Sporle
Little Fransham
Hulver Street
30
Toftwood
Mattishall
East Tuddenham
A47
Daffy Green
Westfield
Clint Green
Yaxham
South Green
Welborne
Necton
West End
Ivy Todd
East Bradenham
Whinburgh
Colton
Holme Hale
A1075
Brandon Parva
Barford
North Pickenham
West Bradenham
Shipdham
Garvestone
Runhall
Thuxton
Barnham Broom
B1077
Crowshill
Reymerston
B1135
Coston
High Common
Danemoor Green
Carleton Forehoe
South Pickenham
Ashill
Cranworth
Southburgh
Mid Norfolk Railway
Saham Hills
Woodrising
Hardingham
106
Kimberley
A1065
Crownthorpe
Ovington
Hackford
Great Cressingham
Carbrooke
Hingham
B1108
Wicklewood
Saham Toney
Watton Green
R. Wissey
Watton
B1108
Scoulton
Deopham
Morley St Botolph
Little Cressingham
Little Ellingham
A1075
Griston
B1077
Suton
A11
B1108
Merton
Northacre
Rockland St Peter
Bow Street
Stalland Common
Deopham Green
B1172
Bodney
Caston
Great Ellingham
Spooner Row
Thompson
Rockland All Saints
Stow Bedon
Besthorpe
Lower Stow Bedon
Fen Street
Black Car
Attleborough
Peddars Way & Norfolk Coast Path
Breckles
Mount Pleasant
Shropham
Carleton Rode
B1077
Puddledock
Great Hockham
North End
Upgate Street
East Wretham
Snetterton
Old Buckenham
Stonebridge
Eccles Road
Cake Street
A134
B1111
South End
Stacksford
New Buckenham
Snetterton
Wilby
B1077
A1075
A11
Larling
Quidenham
Hunt's Corner
Banham
Croxton
Banham
Bridgham
East Harling
Kenninghall
Middle Harling
B1111
Winfarthing
B1107
Dam Green
Brettenham
R. Thet
Shelfanger
Thetford
Shadwell
North Lopham
Fersfield
106
Bressingham Common
A1066
Garboldisham
South Lopham
Rushford
River
Gasthorpe
A1066
Snow Street
B1077
Little Ouse
Bressingham
Knettishall
Smallworth
Redgrave and Lopham Fen
Pooley Street
Steam Museum & Gardens
Elveden
Euston
Blo Norton
Hopton
Royden
Waveney
Coney Weston
Market Weston
River
Barnham
Thelnetham
Redgrave
Palgrave
B1113
Wortham
A134
A1088
Fakenham Magna
Hinderclay
Barningham
A143
Thrandeston
Botesdale
Sapiston
Burgate
Hepworth
Rickinghall
Mellis
Honington
B1111
Bardwell
Candle Street
Wattisfield
B1106
Ixworth Thorpe
Stanton
B1113
Thornham Parva
89
Upthorpe
Allwood Green
Mill Street
Cranmer

106
A
B
C
D
E
F
Peaseland Green
Greensgate
Weston Longville
Wensum
122
Thorpe Marriott
A140
Horsham St Faith
Spixworth
Rackheath
Green
North Tuddenham
Drayton
Aviation
A47
Hockering
Ringland
Taverham
Norwich
New Rackheath
1
Mattishall Burgh
Costessey
Hellesdon
Old Catton
Sprowston
Thorpe End
Dereham
Mattishall
Honingham
A1042
NORWICH
Clint Green
East Tuddenham
Easton
New Costessey
Plumstead
Yaxham
South Green
Welborne
Royal Norfolk
Thorpe St Andrew
Whinburgh
Colton
Marlingford
A1074
B1140
Brandon Parva
Bowthorpe
Runhall
Barford
Yare
Bawburgh
B1108
Earlham
A1242
2
Thuxton
B1108
Little Melton
Colney
Whitlingham
Coston
Barnham Broom
Great Melton
A47
New Lakenham
Norfolk Ski Centre
B1135
Wramplingham
Lynch Green
Cringleford
Eaton
Trowse Newton
Kirby Bedon
Danemoor Green
High Green
Old Lakenham
A146
Carleton Forehoe
Arminghall
Southburgh
Mid-Norfolk Railway
Hethersett
Keswick
Framingham Pigot
Hardingham
Kimberley
Kidd's Moor
B1172
Caistor St Edmund
Framingham Earl
Hackford
Crownthorpe
Ketteringham
Caistor Roman Town
Yelverton
Hingham
B1108
Swardeston
Dunston
Upper Stoke
3
Wicklewood
East Carleton
Poringland
B1113
Alpington
Deopham
105
Morley St Botolph
Wymondham
Mulbarton
Swainsthorpe
Stoke Holy Cross
B1332
Little Ellingham
A140
Howe
Suton
A11
Wreningham
Bracon Ash
Hawe's Green
Shotesham
Deopham Green
Silfield
Newton Flotman
Stubbs Green
Bow Street
Stalland Common
B1172
Toprow
Saxlingham Thorpe
Ashwellthorpe
Saxlingham Nethergate
Great Ellingham
Spooner Row
Fundenhall
Flordon
4
Hapton
Tasburgh
Saxlingham Green
Street
Besthorpe
Low Tharston
Tacolneston
Upper Tasburgh
Black Car
Tharston
Hempnall
Mount Pleasant
Attleborough
Forncett End
Stratton St Michael
Bunwell
Forncett St Mary
B1527
Carleton Rode
Road Green
B1113
Fritton
B1077
Forncett St Peter
Hempnall Green
Topcroft
Puddledock
Bunwell Hill
Pottergate Street
Upgate Street
Morningthorpe
Lundy Green
Topcroft Street
Old Buckenham
Cake Street
Wacton
Long Stratton
Shelton
Upgate Street
Eccles Road
Hargate
5
Great Moulton
Shelton Green
Stacksford
Tibenham
Aslacton
New Buckenham
Wilby
Sneath Common
High Green
Hardwick
Great Green
B1077
A140
Snetterton
Pristow Green
Colegate End
Hunt's Corner
B1134
Quidenham
Banham
North Green
Denton
Tivetshall St Margaret
Bush Green
Banham
Alburgh
East Harling
Kenninghall
Gissing
Pulham Market
Pulham St Mary
105
Tivetshall St Mary
Wortwell
6
Winfarthing
Starston
Hom
Dam Green
Mill Green
Garlic Street
Redenhall
Shelfanger
Shimpling
15
North Lopham
Fersfield
Rushall
Harleston
Burston
Bressingham Common
Mendham
South Lopham
Needham
20
A1066
Snow Street
Walcot Green
Dickleburgh
B1123
Withersdale Street
Bressingham
B1077
Thelveton
Thorpe Abbotts
Weybread
Redgrave and Lopham Fen
Smallworth
Pooley Street
Diss
Upper Street
Brockdish
Metfield
Steam Museum & Gardens
7
Norton
Roydon
Scole
Weybread Street
Waveney
Upper Weybread
River
Palgrave
A143
Billingford
Syleham
Thelnetham
Redgrave
B1118
B1116
Fressingfield
Hoxne
Stuston
Wingfield Green
Wingfield
Wortham
B1113
Oakley
College
Little Whittingham Green
Hinderclay
Cross Street
A143
40
Thrandeston
Brome Street
Chickering
Broad Road
Botesdale
Brome
Heckfield Green
Silverley Green
Burgate
Langton Green
Dove
South Green
Pixey Green
Rickinghall
Mellis
Denham
Stradbroke
Ashfield Green
8
Candle Street
B1117
Denham Green
Yaxley
Wattisfield
B1117
Eye
Thornham
Wootten Green
Russel's Green
Allwood Green
90
Horham
B1116
Cranmer
Redlingfield
Wilby
0 1 2 3 4 5 miles
0 1 2 3 4 5 6 7 8 kilometres

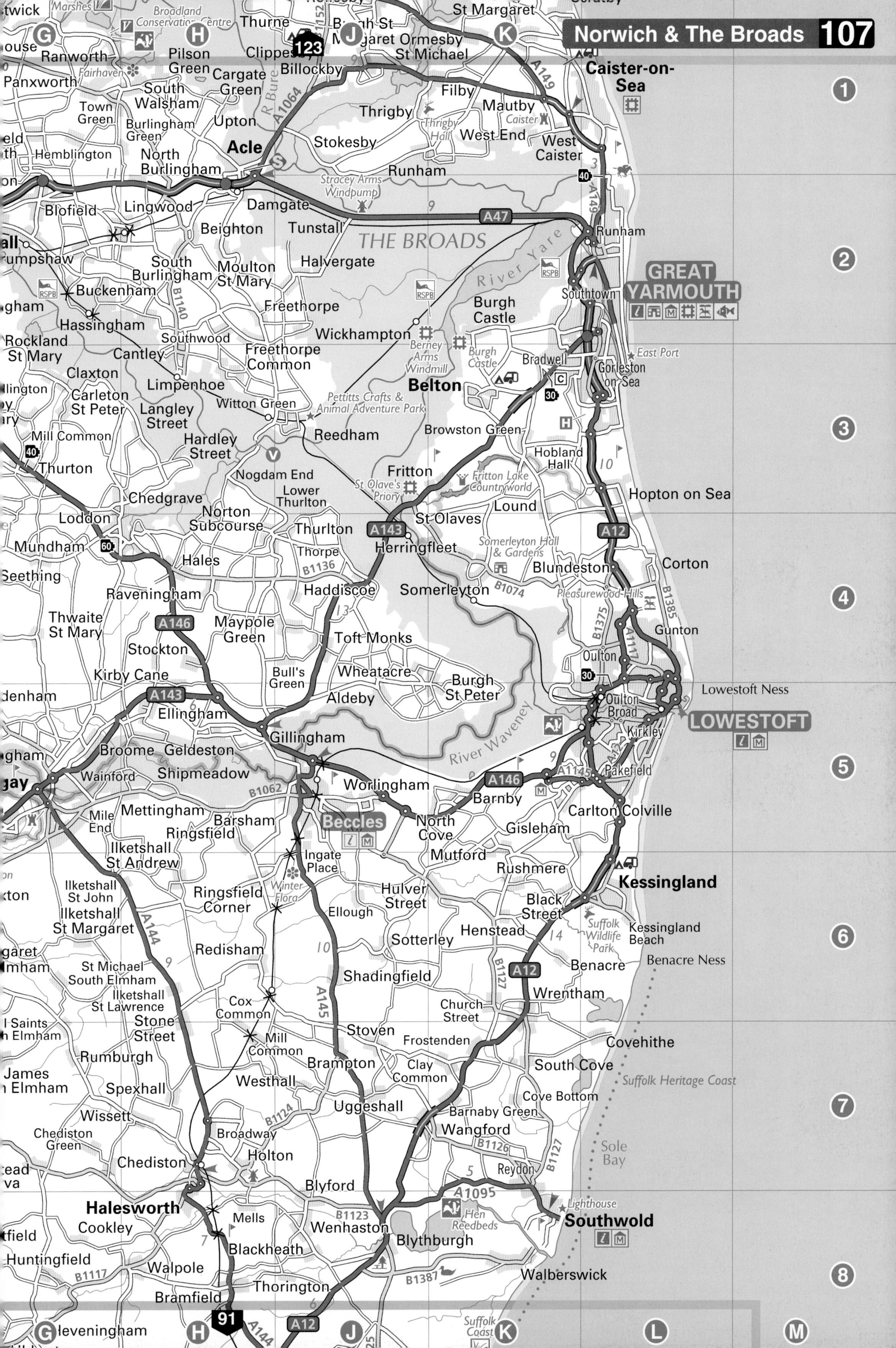
Broadland Conservation Centre
Thurne
St Margaret
Ranworth
Pilson Green
Clippesby
Billockby
Ormesby St Michael
Caister-on-Sea
Fairhaven
Panxworth
South Walsham
Cargate Green
R Bure
A1064
Filby
A149
Town Green
Burlingham Green
Upton
Thrigby
Thrigby Hall
Mautby
Caister
West End
West Caister
Hemblington
North Burlingham
Acle
Stokesby
Runham
Stracey Arms Windpump
Blofield
Lingwood
Damgate
A47
Tunstall
Beighton
THE BROADS
River Yare
Runham
Rumpshaw
South Burlingham
Moulton St Mary
Halvergate
GREAT YARMOUTH
RSPB
Buckenham
B1140
Freethorpe
Burgh Castle
Southtown
Hassingham
Wickhampton
Berney Arms Windmill
Burgh Castle
Bradwell
East Port
Rockland St Mary
Southwood
Cantley
Freethorpe Common
Gorleston on Sea
Claxton
Limpenhoe
Belton
Carleton St Peter
Langley Street
Witton Green
Pettitts Crafts & Animal Adventure Park
Mill Common
Hardley Street
Reedham
Browston Green
Hobland Hall
Thurton
Nogdam End
Fritton
Fritton Lake Countryworld
Lower Thurlton
St Olave's Priory
Hopton on Sea
Chedgrave
Norton Subcourse
Lound
Loddon
St Olaves
Thurlton
A143
Herringfleet
Somerleyton Hall & Gardens
A12
Mundham
Hales
Thorpe
B1136
Blundeston
Corton
Seething
Haddiscoe
Somerleyton
B1074
Pleasurewood Hills
Raveningham
B1385
Thwaite St Mary
A146
Maypole Green
B1375
A1117
Gunton
Stockton
Toft Monks
Oulton
Kirby Cane
Bull's Green
Wheatacre
Burgh St Peter
Lowestoft Ness
Ellingham
Aldeby
Oulton Broad
Gillingham
River Waveney
LOWESTOFT
Kirkley
Broome
Geldeston
Wainford
Shipmeadow
Worlingham
A1145
Pakefield
B1062
Barnby
Mile End
Mettingham
Barsham
Ringsfield
Beccles
North Cove
Carlton Colville
Gisleham
Ilketshall St Andrew
Ingate Place
Mutford
Rushmere
Ilketshall St John
Ilketshall St Margaret
Ringsfield Corner
Winter Flora
Ellough
Hulver Street
Kessingland
Black Street
Suffolk Wildlife Park
Kessingland Beach
A144
Redisham
Sotterley
Henstead
B1127
Benacre
Benacre Ness
St Michael South Elmham
Ilketshall St Lawrence
Shadingfield
Wrentham
Cox Common
A145
Church Street
Stone Street
Covehithe
Rumburgh
Mill Common
Stoven
Frostenden
Brampton
Clay Common
South Cove
Suffolk Heritage Coast
Spexhall
Westhall
Cove Bottom
Wissett
Uggeshall
Barnaby Green
B1124
Chediston Green
Broadway
Wangford
B1126
Sole Bay
Chediston
Holton
Reydon
Blyford
A1095
Lighthouse
Halesworth
Hen Reedbeds
Southwold
Cookley
Mells
B1123
Wenhaston
Blythburgh
Huntingfield
Blackheath
B1117
Walpole
B1387
Walberswick
Bramfield
Thorington
Suffolk Coast
Heveningham
123
91
A12
A144

A B C D E F
1 2 3 4 5 6 7 8
CAERNARFON BAY
Lleyn Heritage Coast
Tre
564
YR EIF
Trwyn y Grolech
B4417
Llithfa
Porth Nefyn
Carreg Ddu
Pistyll
Morfa Nefyn
Llw
Nefyn
Porth Dinllaen
Groesffordd
Fron
Edern
Bodfuan
Porth Ysgaden
Rhos-y-llan
Llanr
Tudweiliog
A497
LLEYN
Efailne
Dinas
Porth Colman
371
Carn Fadrun
B4415
Denio
Bryn-mawr
Llaniestyn
Rhyd-y-clafdy
Pen-y-graig
B4417
Garnfadryn
A499
Penrhos
Llangwnnadl
Meyllteyrn
Llanbedrog
Sarn
Botwnnog
B4413
Mynytho
Nanhoron
Bryncroes
Porthoer
Trwyn Llanbedr
Llandegwning
Rhydlios
Rhoshirwaun
St Tudwal's Road
Plas yn Rhiw
Llangian
B4413
Anelog
Penycaerau
Abersoch
Y Rhiw
Llanengan
Sarn Bach
Aberdaron
Llanfaelrhys
Porth Neigwl or Hell's Mouth
St Tudwal's Island East
Uwchmynydd
Porth Ysgo
Bwlchtocyn
Marchros
Aberdaron Bay
St Tudwal's Island West
Bardsey Sound
Porth Geiriad
Lleyn Heritage Coast
St Mary's
Ynys Enlli
BARDSEY ISLAND
0 1 2 3 4 5 miles
0 1 2 3 4 5 6 7 8 kilometres

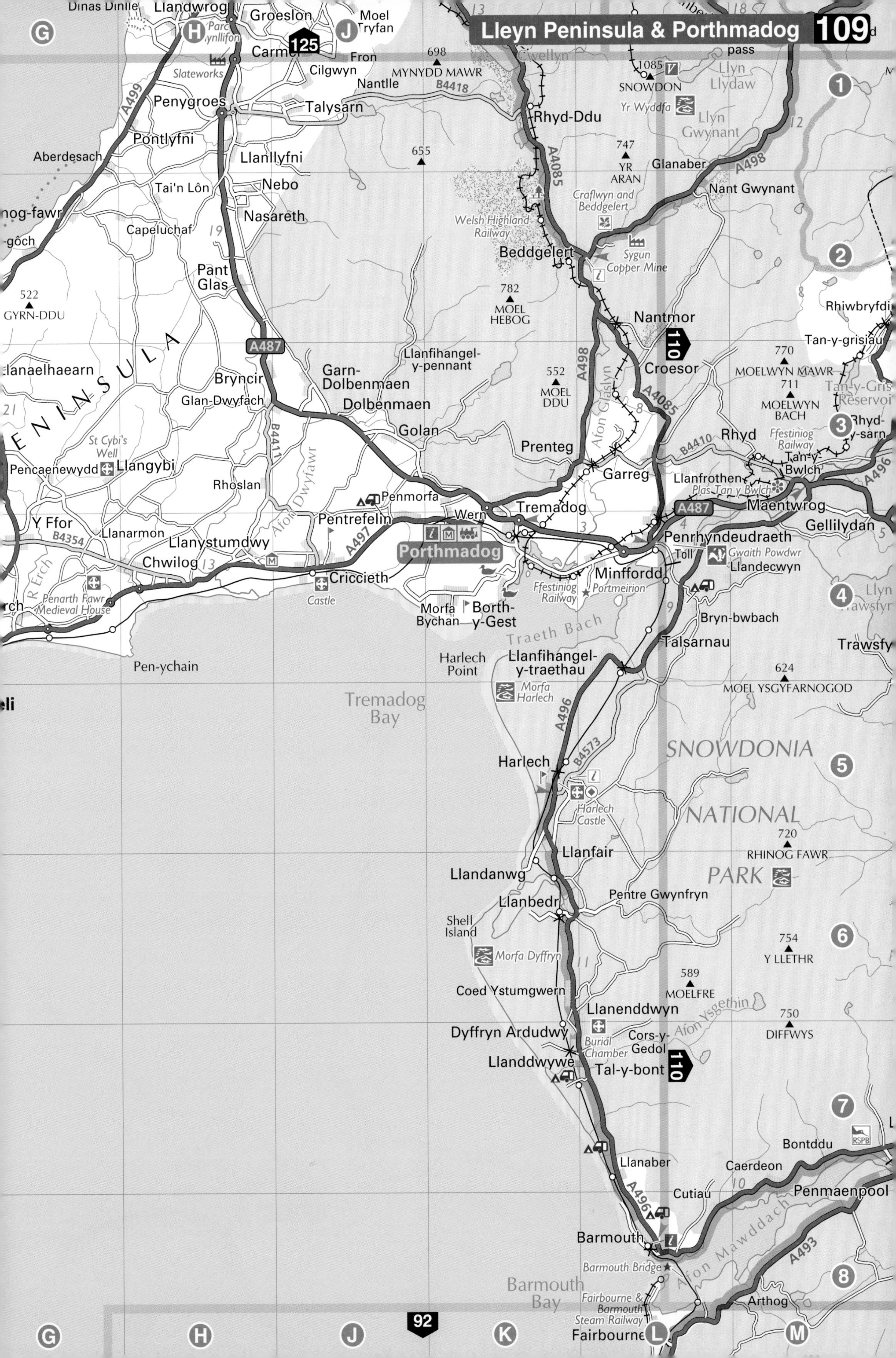
Dinas Dinlle
Llandwrog
Groeslon
Moel Tryfan
Parc Glynllifon
125
Carmel
Fron
698
MYNYDD MAWR
Cilgwyn
Nantlle
B4418
Slateworks
A499
Penygroes
Talysarn
Pontlyfni
Aberdesach
Llanllyfni
655
Tai'n Lôn
Nebo
Nasareth
Capeluchaf
19
Pant Glas
522
GYRN-DDU
A487
PENINSULA
Llanaelhaearn
Bryncir
Glan-Dwyfach
B4411
St Cybi's Well
Pencaenewydd
Llangybi
Rhoslan
Afon Dwyfawr
Y Ffor
B4354
Llanarmon
Llanystumdwy
Chwilog
13
R Erch
Penarth Fawr Medieval House
Pen-ychain
Garn-Dolbenmaen
Dolbenmaen
Golan
Llanfihangel-y-pennant
Penmorfa
Pentrefelin
A497
Wern
Porthmadog
Criccieth
Castle
Morfa Bychan
Borth-y-Gest
Tremadog Bay
Harlech Point
Cwellyn
1085
SNOWDON
Yr Wyddfa
Llyn Llydaw
Llyn Gwynant
Rhyd-Ddu
A4085
747
YR ARAN
Glanaber
A498
Nant Gwynant
Craflwyn and Beddgelert
Welsh Highland Railway
Beddgelert
Sygun Copper Mine
782
MOEL HEBOG
Nantmor
110
Croesor
552
MOEL DDU
Afon Glaslyn
Prenteg
Garreg
Tremadog
Minffordd
Ffestiniog Railway
Portmeirion
Traeth Bach
Llanfihangel-y-traethau
Morfa Harlech
Penrhyndeudraeth
Toll
Gwaith Powdwr
Llandecwyn
Bryn-bwbach
Talsarnau
Rhyd
B4410
Llanfrothen
Plas Tan y Bwlch
Tan-y-Bwlch
Maentwrog
Gellilydan
Ffestiniog Railway
Rhiwbryfdir
Tan-y-grisiau
770
MOELWYN MAWR
711
MOELWYN BACH
Tan-y-Grisiau Reservoir
Rhyd-y-sarn
A496
Llyn Trawsfynydd
Trawsfynydd
624
MOEL YSGYFARNOGOD
SNOWDONIA NATIONAL PARK
Harlech
B4573
Harlech Castle
A496
720
RHINOG FAWR
Llanfair
Llandanwg
Llanbedr
Pentre Gwynfryn
Shell Island
Morfa Dyffryn
754
Y LLETHR
589
MOELFRE
Coed Ystumgwern
Llanenddwyn
Afon Ysgethin
750
DIFFWYS
Dyffryn Ardudwy
Burial Chamber
Cors-y-Gedol
Llanddwywe
Tal-y-bont
110
RSPB
Bontddu
Llanaber
Caerdeon
Cutiau
Penmaenpool
Barmouth
Barmouth Bridge
Afon Mawddach
A493
Barmouth Bay
Fairbourne & Barmouth Steam Railway
Arthog
Fairbourne
92
G
H
J
K
L
M
1
2
3
4
5
6
7
8

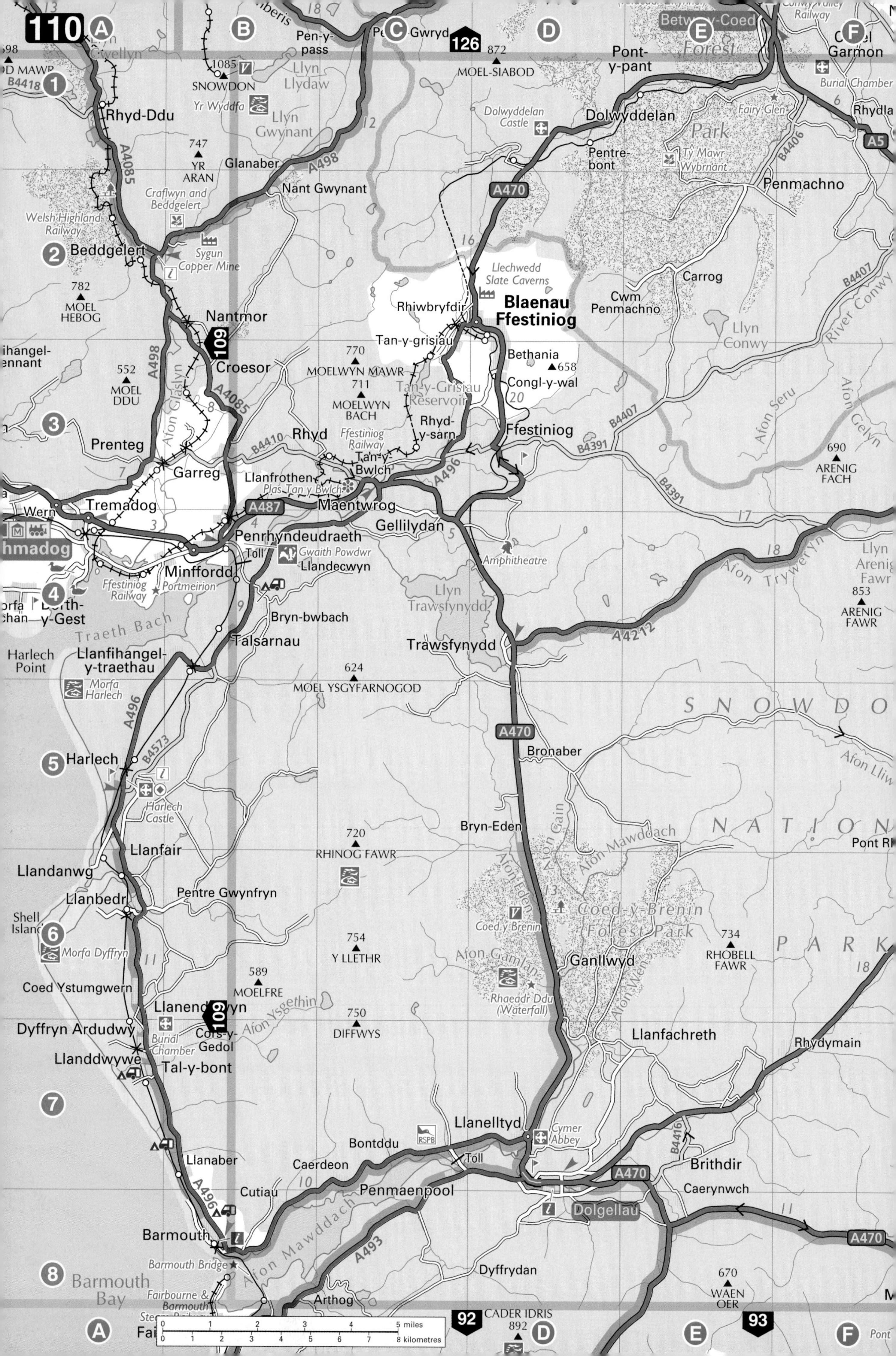

Rhyd-Ddu
Beddgelert
Welsh Highland Railway
Craflwyn and Beddgelert
Sygun Copper Mine
SNOWDON
Yr Wyddfa
1085
Llyn Llydaw
Llyn Gwynant
Pen-y-pass
Glanaber
Nant Gwynant
747
YR ARAN
782
MOEL HEBOG
Nantmor
Croesor
552
MOEL DDU
Afon Glaslyn
Prenteg
Garreg
Tremadog
Wern
Penrhyndeudraeth
Minffordd
Toll
Ffestiniog Railway
Portmeirion
Traeth Bach
Harlech Point
Llanfihangel-y-traethau
Morfa Harlech
Talsarnau
Bryn-bwbach
Llandecwyn
Gwaith Powdwr
Llanfrothen
Plas Tan y Bwlch
Maentwrog
Tan-y-Bwlch
Rhyd
Rhyd-y-sarn
Ffestiniog Railway
770
MOELWYN MAWR
711
MOELWYN BACH
Tan-y-Grisiau Reservoir
Tan-y-grisiau
Rhiwbryfdir
Blaenau Ffestiniog
Llechwedd Slate Caverns
Bethania
658
Congl-y-wal
Ffestiniog
Gellilydan
Amphitheatre
Llyn Trawsfynydd
Trawsfynydd
624
MOEL YSGYFARNOGOD
Dolwyddelan
Dolwyddelan Castle
Pentre-bont
MOEL-SIABOD
872
Pont-y-pant
Betws-y-Coed
Forest
Park
Fairy Glen
Ty Mawr Wybrnant
Penmachno
Carrog
Cwm Penmachno
Llyn Conwy
River Conwy
Afon Serw
Afon Gelyn
690
ARENIG FACH
Afon Tryweryn
Llyn Arenig Fawr
853
ARENIG FAWR
Conwy Valley Railway
Capel Garmon
Burial Chamber
Rhydlanfair
Harlech
Harlech Castle
Llanfair
Llandanwg
Llanbedr
Shell Island
Morfa Dyffryn
Pentre Gwynfryn
Coed Ystumgwern
Llanenddwyn
Dyffryn Ardudwy
Burial Chamber
Cors-y-Gedol
Llanddwywe
Tal-y-bont
Afon Ysgethin
589
MOELFRE
720
RHINOG FAWR
754
Y LLETHR
750
DIFFWYS
Bronaber
Bryn-Eden
SNOWDONIA NATIONAL PARK
Afon Mawddach
Afon Cain
Afon Eden
Coed y Brenin
Coed-y-Brenin Forest Park
Afon Gamlan
Rhaeadr Ddu (Waterfall)
Ganllwyd
Afon Wen
734
RHOBELL FAWR
Llanfachreth
Rhydymain
Afon Lliw
Pont Rhyd-y-Fen
Llanelltyd
Cymer Abbey
Bontddu
RSPB
Caerdeon
Toll
Llanaber
Cutiau
Penmaenpool
Barmouth
Barmouth Bridge
Barmouth Bay
Fairbourne & Barmouth Steam Railway
Afon Mawddach
Arthog
Dyffrydan
Dolgellau
Brithdir
Caerynwch
670
WAEN OER
CADER IDRIS
892
0 1 2 3 4 5 miles
0 1 2 3 4 5 6 7 8 kilometres
109
126
92
93

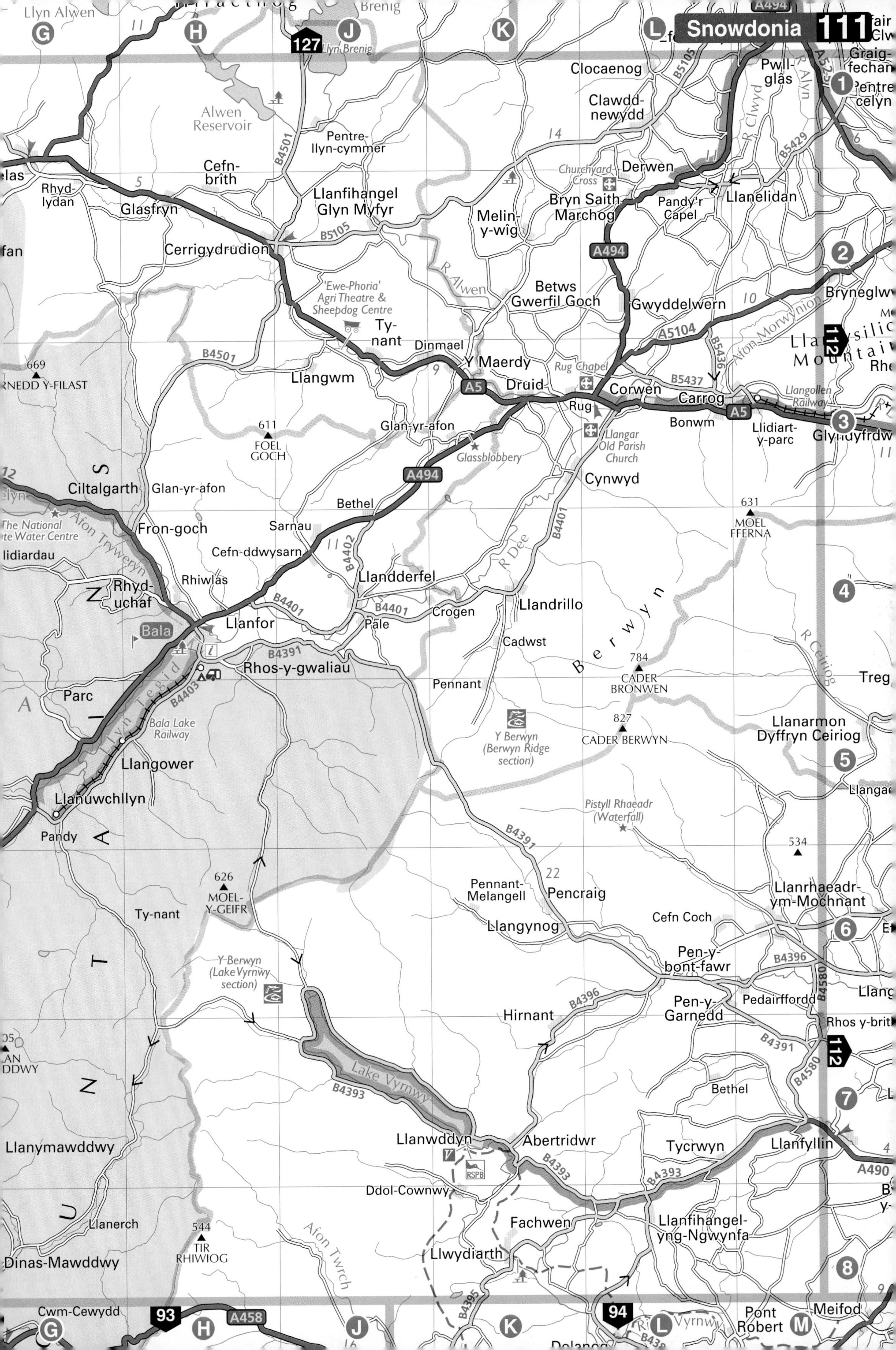
Llyn Alwen
Brenig
127
Llyn Brenig
Alwen Reservoir
Clocaenog
Pwll-glâs
Graig-fechan
Pentre-celyn
Clawdd-newydd
Pentre-llyn-cymmer
Cefn-brîth
Rhyd-lydan
Glasfryn
Llanfihangel Glyn Myfyr
Churchyard Cross
Derwen
Bryn Saith Marchog
Pandy'r Capel
Llanelidan
Melin-y-wîg
Cerrigydrudion
'Ewe-Phoria' Agri Theatre & Sheepdog Centre
Betws Gwerfil Goch
Gwyddelwern
Bryneglwys
Ty-nant
Dinmael
Y Maerdy
Rug Chapel
Druid
Corwen
Carrog
Llangollen Railway
Llangwm
Rug
Bonwm
Llidiart-y-parc
Glyndyfrdwy
669
CARNEDD Y-FILAST
611
FOEL GOCH
Glan-yr-afon
Glassblobbery
Llangar Old Parish Church
Cynwyd
Ciltalgarth
Glan-yr-afon
Bethel
The National White Water Centre
Afon Tryweryn
Fron-goch
Sarnau
631
MOEL FFERNA
Cefn-ddwysarn
Rhyd-uchaf
Rhiwlas
Llandderfel
Llandrillo
Bala
Llanfor
Pale
Crogen
Berwyn
Cadwst
Rhos-y-gwaliau
784
CADER BRONWEN
Treg
Parc
Llyn Tegid
Bala Lake Railway
Pennant
Y Berwyn (Berwyn Ridge section)
827
CADER BERWYN
Llanarmon Dyffryn Ceiriog
R Ceiriog
Llangower
Llanuwchllyn
Pandy
Pistyll Rhaeadr (Waterfall)
534
626
MOEL-Y-GEIFR
Pennant-Melangell
Pencraig
Llanrhaeadr-ym-Mochnant
Ty-nant
Llangynog
Cefn Coch
Y-Berwyn (Lake Vyrnwy section)
Pen-y-bont-fawr
Pen-y-Garnedd
Pedairffordd
Hirnant
Rhos y-brithdir
112
Lake Vyrnwy
Bethel
Llanwddyn
Abertridwr
Tycrwyn
Llanfyllin
Llanymawddwy
RSPB
Ddol-Cownwy
Fachwen
Llanfihangel-yng-Ngwynfa
Llanerch
544
TIR RHIWIOG
Afon Twrch
Llwydiarth
Dinas-Mawddwy
Cwm-Cewydd
93
A458
94
Pont Robert
Meifod
A5
A494
A5104
B4501
B5105
B4401
B4402
B4391
B4403
B4393
B4396
B4580
B5437
B5436
B5429
B4395
A490

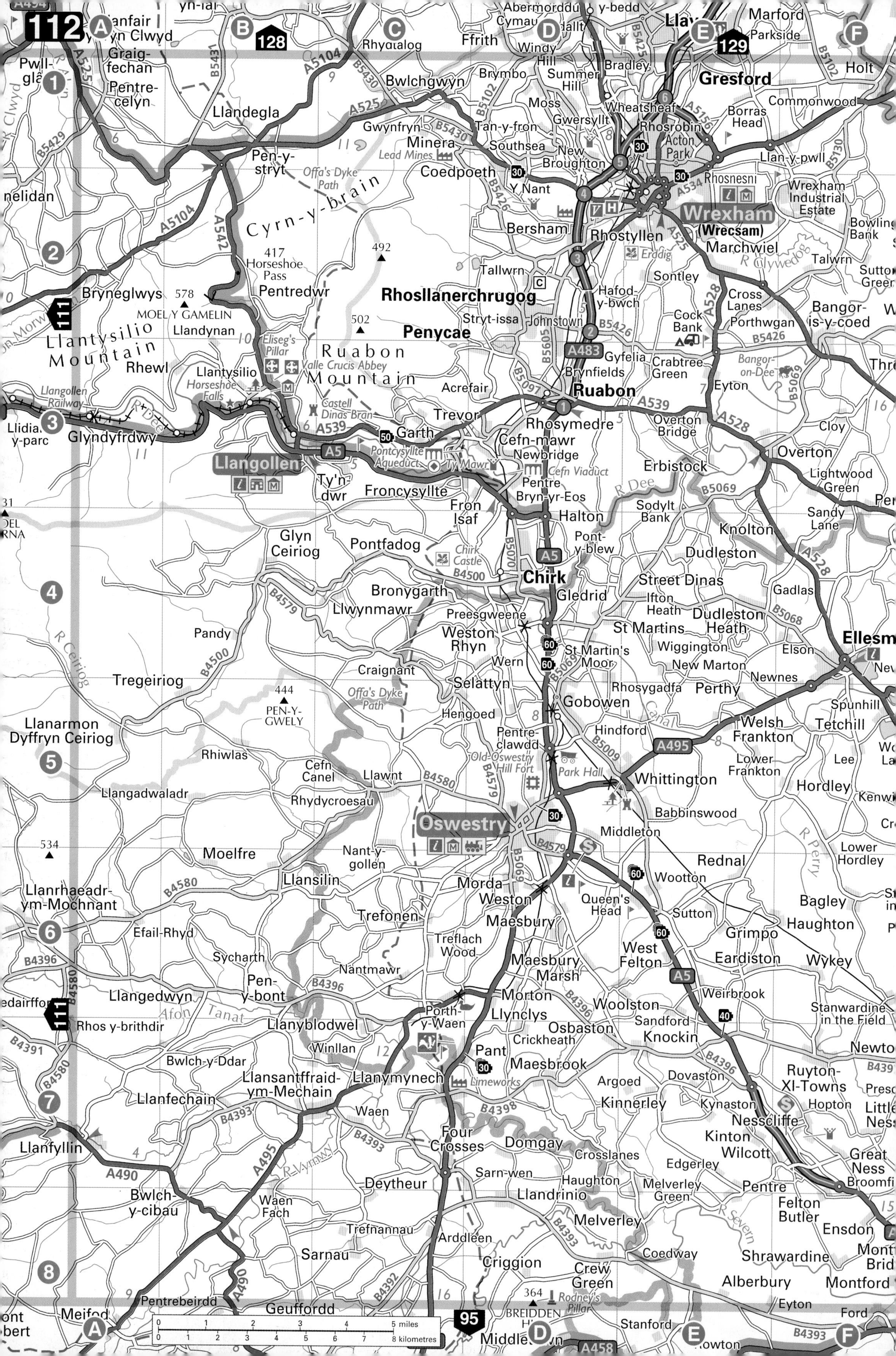

112
A
B
C
D
E
F
128
129
1
2
3
4
5
6
7
8
111
111
95
Gresford
Holt
Marford
Parkside
Commonwood
Borras Head
Llan-y-pwll
Wrexham
(Wrecsam)
Wrexham Industrial Estate
Bowling Bank
Rhosnesni
Acton Park
Rhosrobin
Wheatsheaf
Bradley
Gwersyllt
Summer Hill
Moss
Windy Hill
Ffrith
Rhydtalog
Bwlchgwyn
Brymbo
Tan-y-fron
Southsea
New Broughton
Minera
Lead Mines
Gwynfryn
Coedpoeth
Y Nant
Bersham
Rhostyllen
Erddig
Marchwiel
Talwrn
R Clywedog
Llandegla
Pen-y-stryt
Offa's Dyke Path
Cyrn-y-brain
Graig-fechan
Pentre-celyn
Bryneglwys
MOEL Y GAMELIN
Llandynan
Llantysilio Mountain
Rhewl
Llantysilio
Horseshoe Falls
Eliseg's Pillar
Valle Crucis Abbey
Ruabon Mountain
Castell Dinas Bran
Horseshoe Pass
Pentredwr
Llangollen Railway
Glyndyfrdwy
Llidiart y-parc
Llangollen
Garth
Trevor
Pontcysyllte Aqueduct
Ty Mawr
Froncysyllte
Ty'n dwr
Tallwrn
Rhosllanerchrugog
Penycae
Stryt-issa
Johnstown
Hafod-y-bwch
Sontley
Cross Lanes
Bangor-is-y-coed
Cock Bank
Porthwgan
Gyfelia
Crabtree Green
Bangor-on-Dee
Brynfields
Ruabon
Eyton
Acrefair
Rhosymedre
Cefn-mawr
Newbridge
Cefn Viaduct
Pentre
Bryn-yr-Eos
Overton Bridge
Overton
Cloy
Erbistock
Lightwood Green
Sandy Lane
Fron Isaf
Halton
Sodylt Bank
Knolton
Glyn Ceiriog
Pontfadog
Chirk Castle
Chirk
Pont-y-blew
Dudleston
Street Dinas
Gadlas
Bronygarth
Llwynmawr
Gledrid
Ifton Heath
Dudleston Heath
St Martins
Ellesmere
Preesgweene
Weston Rhyn
Wern
St Martin's Moor
Wiggington
New Marton
Elson
Newnes
Pandy
R Ceiriog
Tregeiriog
Craignant
Selattyn
Rhosygadfa
Perthy
PEN-Y-GWELY
Hengoed
Gobowen
Hindford
Welsh Frankton
Spunhill
Tetchill
Llanarmon Dyffryn Ceiriog
Rhiwlas
Pentre-clawdd
Old Oswestry Hill Fort
Park Hall
Whittington
Lower Frankton
Lee
Hordley
Cefn Canel
Llawnt
Rhydycroesau
Llangadwaladr
Oswestry
Babbinswood
Middleton
Moelfre
Nant-y-gollen
Llansilin
Rednal
Lower Hordley
Wootton
Morda
Weston
Queen's Head
Sutton
Bagley
Llanrhaeadr-ym-Mochnant
Efail-Rhyd
Trefonen
Maesbury
Grimpo
Haughton
Treflach Wood
West Felton
Eardiston
Wykey
Sycharth
Pen-y-bont
Nantmawr
Maesbury Marsh
Llangedwyn
Morton
Weirbrook
Woolston
Stanwardine in the Field
Afon Tanat
Rhos y-brithdir
Porth-y-Waen
Llynclys
Osbaston
Sandford
Llanyblodwel
Knockin
Winllan
Crickheath
Pant
Bwlch-y-Ddar
Maesbrook
Ruyton-XI-Towns
Llansantffraid-ym-Mechain
Llanymynech
Limeworks
Argoed
Dovaston
Llanfechain
Kinnerley
Kynaston
Hopton
Waen
Nesscliffe
Four Crosses
Domgay
Kinton
Wilcott
Great Ness
Llanfyllin
Crosslanes
Edgerley
Sarn-wen
R Vyrnwy
Deytheur
Haughton
Melverley Green
Pentre
Llandrinio
Felton Butler
Bwlch-y-cibau
Waen Fach
Melverley
R Severn
Ensdon
Trefnannau
Arddleen
Sarnau
Coedway
Shrawardine
Criggion
Crew Green
Alberbury
Montford
364
Rodney's Pillar
BREIDDEN HILL
Eyton
Ford
Pentrebeirdd
Meifod
Geufford
Stanford
Middletown
417
492
502
578
444
534
A5
A483
A495
A490
A525
A528
A539
A542
A5104
A534
A458
B5102
B5430
B5426
B5069
B5070
B4500
B4579
B4580
B4396
B4398
B4393
B4392
B5009
B5068
B4391
B5097
B5605
B5130
B5431
B5429
B5425
B5156
0 1 2 3 4 5 miles
0 1 2 3 4 5 6 7 8 kilometres

Chowley
Harthill
Higher Burwardsley
Peckforton
Haughton Moss
Barbridge
Radmore Green
Clutton
Broxton
Barnhill
Bulkeley
Ridley Green
Reaseheath
Wistaston Green
Crewe Green
Barton
Fuller's Moor
Gallantry Bank
A534
Faddiley
Burland
A51
Wistaston
Wells Green
Gresty Green
Stretton
Bickerton
Croxton Green
Acton
Willaston
Shavington
A41
Cholmondeley Castle
Duckington
Gradeley Green
Nantwich
A500
Weston
Tilston
Edge Green
A49
Stoneley Green
Hough
Horton Green
Hampton Green
Hetherson Green
Chorley
Ravensmoor
Butt Green
Haymoor Green
Chorlton
Wybunbury
Shocklach
Ebnal
Hampton Heath
Bickley Moss
Stapeley Water
Stapeley
Hack Green
Walgherton
Chorlton Lane
Bickley
Norbury Common
Wrenbury
Secret Bunker
Malpas
No Man's Heath
Sound
Hatherton
Bradley Common
Norbury
Gaunton's Bank
Pinsley Green
A530
Broomhill Green
Hunsterson
Checkley
Marbury
Aston
Upper Threapwood
Oldcastle Heath
Marley Green
Newhall
Hankelow
Bridgemere
Tallarn Green
Hollyhurst
Bell o' th' Hill
Dodd's Green
Audlem
Higher Wych
Wirswall
Royal's Green
Buerton
Canal
Grindley Brook
Whitchurch
Burleydam
Lightwood Green
Kinsey Heath
Eglwys Cross
The Chequer
Coxbank
Woore
Broughall
Wilkesley
Dorrington
Catteralslane
Knighton
Redbrook
Bearstone
Bronington
Ash Magna
Adderley
Arowry
A495
Alkington
Ash Parva
Ightfield
A529
Shropshire Union Canal
Norton in Hales
Tilstock
Prees Heath
Calverhall
Platt Lane
Steel Heath
Betton
Prees Higher Heath
Welsh End
Hollinwood
Longslow
Sandylane
A53
Bettisfield
Whixall
B5476
Moreton Say
Almington
Hookgate
Balmer Heath
Coton
A49
A41
Sandford
Longford
Blore
Prees
Bletchley
Market Drayton
Hales
Northwood
Quina Brook
Darliston
Lyneal
Paddolgreen
Prees Lower Heath
Fauls
Ternhill
The Fouralls
Newtown
Edstaston
Marchamley Wood
Prees Green
Sutton
Lostford
Woodseaves
Ryebank
Old Colehurst Manor
Wolverley
Lowe
Creamore Bank
B5065
Hawkstone
Wollerton
Cheswardine
Lipley
Horton
Weston-under-Redcastle
Marchamley
Hodnet
Stoke Heath
Wistanswick
Brownheath
Loppington
Great Soudley
Wixhill
Lockleywood
Wem
Aston
Hodnet Hall
Heathcote
Noneley
Goldstone
Little Soudley
Commonwood
Barkers Green
Bury Walls
Millgreen
A528
Stoke upon Tern
Lee Brockhurst
Moston
Sleap
Hungryhatton
Ellerton
Booley
Preston Brockhurst
High Hatton
Ollerton
Hinstock
A53
Besford
Child's Ercall
Stanford Bridge
Clive
Stanton upon Hine Heath
Peplow
Sambrook
Myddle
Alderton
Grinshill
Howle
Eyton
Newton on the Hill
Moreton Corbet
Castle
Ellerdine Heath
Eaton upon Tern
Yorton Heath
Moretonmill
A442
Harmer Hill
Shawbury
Edgebolton
Cold Hatton
Great Bolas
Chetwynd
Old Woods
Merrington
Meeson
Edgmond Marsh
Preston Gubbals
Hadnall
Little Wytheford
Cold Hatton Heath
Rowton
Tibberton
Cherrington
Bomere Heath
Great Wytheford
Waters Upton
Edgmond
Walford Heath
Astley
Bings
B5062
Leaton
Albrighton
Poynton Green
Walton
Moortown
Adeney
Fitz
Battlefield
Poynton
High Ercall
Crudgington
Longford
Church Aston
A5124
Cotwall
Tern
Kynnersley
Haughton
Rosehill
Harlescott
Roden
Longdon upon Tern
Sleapford
Eyton upon the Weald Moors
Preston upon the Weald Moors
A518
Haughmond Abbey
Bicton
Rodington Heath
Sugdon
Long Waste
Hoo Farm
Somerwood
Horton
Muxton
Calcott
Shelton
Ditherington
Marsh Green
Rodington
Bratton
Shawbirch
TELFORD
Donnington
Underdale
Uffington
Admaston
Lilyhurst
A458
Coton Hill
Withington
Upton Magna
Walcot
A5223
Trench
Granville

114
A
B
C
D
E
F
Haslington
Alsager
130
Church Lawton
Mount Pleasant
Harriseahead
Newchapel
End
Greenway
Black Bull
Leek
Dunwood
Ladderedge
Longsdon
Crewe Green
Oakhanger
A534
B5077
A5077
B5078
A5011
Packmoor
Kidsgrove
Brown Edge
Endon Bank
A53
Ladderedge
1
Gresty Green
A5020
Talke
Parrot's Drumble
Talke Pits
Goldenhill
Great Chell
Ball Green
Horsebridge
Endon
Flint Mill
Deep Hayes
A500
16
Weston
Barthomley
Shavington
Stockton Brook
Stanley
Hough
Engleseabrook
Norton in the Moors
Stanley Moor
Tompkin
Cheddleton
Audley
Butters Green
Red Street
Tunstall
Bradeley
Baddeley Green
Balterley Green
Boon Hill
B5500
Smallthorne
Baddeley Edge
Bagnall
A520
Churnet Valley Railway
Chorlton
Balterley Heath
Balterley
Wood Lane
Crackley
Ceramica
Burslem
Milton
Wybunbury
Shraleybrook
Chesterton
Buddileigh
Halmer End
Porthill
Cobridge
Northwood
Armshead
Wetley Rocks
Consall
Walgherton
Betley
A531
Alsagers Bank
Broad Meadow
B5376
Wolstanton
Central Forest Park
2
Blakenhall
A51
Wrinehill
Scot Hay
NEWCASTLE-UNDER-LYME
May Bank
Hanley
Werrington
Cellarhead
M6
Leycett
Etruria
Bucknall
A52
Blakeley Lane
Checkley
Madeley Heath
Silverdale
Knutton
Hulme
Bridgemere
Checkley Green
Little Madeley
Hartshill
P+R
STOKE-ON-TRENT
113
Middle Madeley
Keele
Keele University
Stoke-upon-Trent
Fenton
A50074
Keele
Madeley
A5272
Weston Coyney
Cookshill
Dilhorne
Bridgemere Garden World
Seabridge
A50
Longton
Caverswall
A525
A519
Trent Vale
B5490
A53
Dresden
Meir
Foxfield Light Railway
3
Onneley
15
Butterton
A521
Woore
Pipe Gate
Aston
Hanford
Blurton
Forsbrook
Dorrington
Whitmore
A5182
Acton
Hanchurch
Lightwood
Blythe Bridge
Blythe Marsh
Knighton
Baldwin's Gate
A5035
Trentham
The Wedgwood Story
B5029
Meir Heath
Shelton Under Harley
Bearstone
Dorothy Clive
Hill Chorlton
Rough Close
Stallington
Blackbrook
Stableford
Cresswell
Norton in Hales
Maer
Beech
Barlaston
A520
Fulford
Saverley Green
Mucklestone
Chapel Chorlton
Tittensor
Downs Banks
Knenhall
Crossgate
4
Ashley
Upper Hatton
Lower Hatton
B5026
B5415
Loggerheads
Cranberry
Swynnerton
Oulton
Moddershall
Middleton Green
Podmore
Bowers
Cotes Heath
Meaford
Cotwalton
Hookgate
Standon
Hilderstone
1459
Blore
Cotes
Stone
Chatcull
Little Stoke
Garshall Green
Hales
Broughton
Wetwood
Walford
Millmeece
Croxtonbank
Aspley
Coldmeece
Yarnfield
B5027
Dayhills
Fairoak
Croxton
Slindon
Walton
Milwich
Woodwall Green
Little Sugnall
Brockton
Stafford (northbound)
Stafford (southbound)
Fradswell
5
Chipnall
Sugnall
Cheswardine
Lipley
Outlands
Bishop's Offley
Pershall
Sturbridge
Norton Bridge
Aston-by-Stone
B5066
Hartley Green
R. Sow
R. Trent
Burston
Sandon
Great Soudley
Doley
Shallowford
Offleymarsh
Copmere End
Chebsey
A34
Enson
Eccleshall
A5013
Izaak Walton's Cottage
Sandon Bank
A51
Gayton
Goldstone
Adbaston
Whitgreave
Little Soudley
Tunstall
Wootton
Walton
Marston
Salt
Knighton
Whitley Heath
Little Bridgeford
Amerton
Ellenhall
Great Bridgeford
Hopton
6
Ellerton
High Offley
Woodseaves
Weston
Hinstock
Shebdon
Lawnhead
14
A513
Staffordshire County
Weston Jones
Seighford
Holmcroft
A518
Pasturefields
Sambrook
Knightley
B5405
Ranton
STAFFORD
Ingestre
Norbury
Norbury Junction
Ranton Green
Coton Clanford
Aston
Doxey
A41
Pickstock
Knightley Dale
Littleworth
Tixall
Oulton
Derrington
Puleston
Long Compton
Forebridge
Weeping Cross
Shugborough
R. Meese
113
Sutton
Chetwynd
Aqualate Mere
Gnosall
Audmore
Shut Heath
Edgmond Marsh
Forton
A518
Rickerscote
Milford
7
B5062
Haughton
Walton-on-the-Hill
Newport
A518
Coton
Gnosall Heath
Allimore Green
Billington
Hyde Lea
Brocton
Edgmond
Coppenhall
Apeton
Acton Trussell
Outwoods
Longford
Bradley
Little Heath
Dunston
13
CANNOCK CHASE
Chetwynd Aston
Bromstead Heath
Wood Eaton
Church Aston
Church Eaton
Bednall
Moreton
Pave Lane
Levedale
Dunston Heath
Stockton
A518
High Onn
Lynn
Newport upon the Weald Moors
Lilleshall
Woodcote
Orslow
Longridge
M6
A34
Mitton
Great Chatwell
8
Honnington
A449
Heath Hill
Muxton
Lilleshall Abbey
Bickford
Whiston
Penkridge
Donnington
Chadwell
Brineton
Lilyhurst
Congreve
97
Lapley
Huntington
Shropshire
R. Penk
Granville
Trench
5 miles
8 kilometres

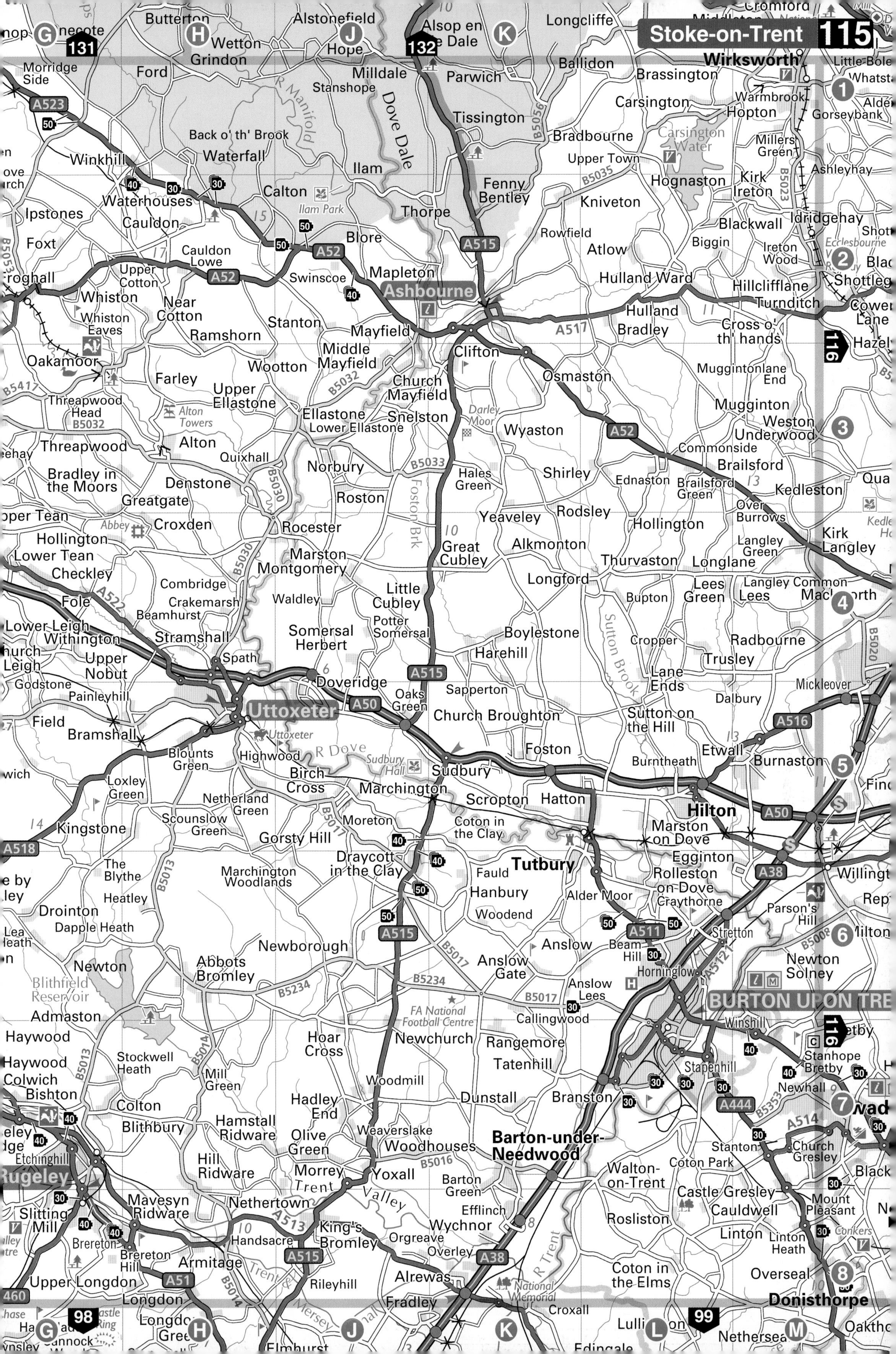

Butterton
Alstonefield
Alsop en le Dale
Longcliffe
Cromford
Wetton
Hope
Grindon
Morridge Side
Ford
Milldale
Stanshope
Parwich
Ballidon
Brassington
Wirksworth
Little Bolehill
Whatstandwell
Carsington
Warmbrook
Hopton
Alderwasley
Gorseybank
Tissington
R Manifold
Dove Dale
Back o' th' Brook
Bradbourne
Carsington Water
Millers Green
Winkhill
Waterfall
Ilam
Upper Town
Kirk Ireton
Ashleyhay
Fenny Bentley
Hognaston
Calton
Ilam Park
Thorpe
Kniveton
Waterhouses
Ipstones
Cauldon
Blackwall
Idridgehay
Foxt
Cauldon Lowe
Blore
Rowfield
Atlow
Biggin
Ireton Wood
Ecclesbourne Valley Railway
Shottle
Froghall
Upper Cotton
Swinscoe
Mapleton
Ashbourne
Hulland Ward
Hillcliffane
Turnditch
Cowers Lane
Whiston
Near Cotton
Hulland
Whiston Eaves
Stanton
Mayfield
Bradley
Cross o' th' hands
Ramshorn
Clifton
Oakamoor
Middle Mayfield
Wootton
Osmaston
Muggintonlane End
Farley
Threapwood Head
Upper Ellastone
Church Mayfield
Mugginton
Alton Towers
Ellastone
Snelston
Darley Moor
Wyaston
Weston Underwood
Lower Ellastone
Commonside
Threapwood
Alton
Quixhall
Norbury
Brailsford
Bradley in the Moors
Denstone
Hales Green
Shirley
Ednaston
Brailsford Green
Kedleston
Roston
Foston Brk
Greatgate
Yeaveley
Rodsley
Over Burrows
Upper Tean
Abbey
Croxden
Rocester
Hollington
Hollington
Great Cubley
Alkmonton
Langley Green
Kirk Langley
Lower Tean
Marston Montgomery
Thurvaston
Longlane
Checkley
Longford
Combridge
Langley Common
Fole
Crakemarsh
Waldley
Little Cubley
Bupton
Lees Green
Lees
Mackworth
Beamhurst
Potter Somersal
Lower Leigh
Withington
Stramshall
Somersal Herbert
Boylestone
Cropper
Radbourne
Church Leigh
Upper Nobut
Spath
Harehill
Sutton Brook
Trusley
Lane Ends
Godstone
Doveridge
Sapperton
Mickleover
Painleyhill
Oaks Green
Dalbury
Uttoxeter
Church Broughton
Sutton on the Hill
Field
Bramshall
Uttoxeter
Etwall
Blounts Green
Highwood
R Dove
Sudbury Hall
Foston
Burnaston
Birch Cross
Sudbury
Burntheath
Loxley Green
Marchington
Scropton
Hatton
Hilton
Netherland Green
Moreton
Coton in the Clay
Marston on Dove
Kingstone
Scounslow Green
Gorsty Hill
Draycott in the Clay
Tutbury
Egginton
The Blythe
Marchington Woodlands
Fauld
Rolleston on Dove
Willington
Heatley
Hanbury
Alder Moor
Craythorne
Repton
Drointon
Parson's Hill
Dapple Heath
Woodend
Stretton
Milton
Anslow
Beam Hill
Newborough
Anslow Gate
Horninglow
Newton Solney
Newton
Abbots Bromley
Blithfield Reservoir
Anslow Lees
Burton upon Trent
Admaston
FA National Football Centre
Callingwood
Winshill
Bretby
Haywood
Hoar Cross
Newchurch
Rangemore
Stockwell Heath
Stanhope Bretby
Great Haywood
Colwich
Mill Green
Tatenhill
Stapenhill
Newhall
Woodmill
Bishton
Hadley End
Dunstall
Branston
Colton
Hamstall Ridware
Blithbury
Olive Green
Weaverslake
Barton-under-Needwood
Stanton
Church Gresley
Woodhouses
Hill Ridware
Morrey
Yoxall
Walton-on-Trent
Coton Park
Etchinghill
Rugeley
Trent Valley
Barton Green
Castle Gresley
Slitting Mill
Mavesyn Ridware
Nethertown
Efflinch
Cauldwell
Mount Pleasant
Rosliston
Wychnor
King's Bromley
Handsacre
Orgreave
Linton
Linton Heath
Conkers
Brereton
Brereton Hill
Armitage
Overley
R Trent
Upper Longdon
Rileyhill
Alrewas
Coton in the Elms
Overseal
National Memorial Arboretum
Longdon
Fradley
Donisthorpe
Croxall
Castle Ring
Longdon Green
Mersey
Lullington
Netherseal
Oakthorpe
Elmhurst
Edingale
A523
A52
A515
A517
A522
A50
A518
A516
A38
A511
A5121
A444
A514
A513
A51
B5053
B5056
B5035
B5023
B5417
B5032
B5033
B5030
B5020
B5017
B5013
B5014
B5234
B5016
B5008
B5353
131
132
116
98
99
G
H
J
K
L
M
1
2
3
4
5
6
7
8

116
A
B
C
D
E
F
Alfreton
Ashfield
133
28
South Wingfield
Derwent Valley Mills
Crich
Carr
Wingfield Manor
Oakerthorpe
Upper Birchwood
Lower Birchwood
Pinxton
Kirkby Woodhouse
Ravenshead
Belehill
Little Bolehill
Whatstandwell
Park Head
Swanwick
Somercotes
Selston
Nuncargate
Annesley
Annesley Woodhouse
Newstead Abbey
Newstead
Alderwasley
Gorseybank
Fritchley
Pentrich
Bullbridge
Riddings
Pye Bridge
Woodnook
Dove Green
Butterley
Ironville
Midland
Jacksdale
Westwood
Bagthorpe
Linby
Papplewick
Ambergate
Toadmoor
Lower Hartshay
Golden Valley
Nether Heage
Heage
Ripley
New Brinsley
Friezeland
Underwood
Hucknall
Butler's Hill
Bestwood Village
Millers Green
Ashleyhay
Belper Lane End
Upper Hartshay
Codnor
Hobsick
Brinsley
Idridgehay
Shottle
Mount Pleasant
Greenhillocks
Street Lane
Peasehill
Cross Hill
Loscoe
Aldercar
Marehay
Denby Potteries
Ecclesbourne Valley Railway
Blackbrook
Belper
Whitemoor
Moorgreen
Greasley
Broom Hill
Shottlegate
Openwoodgate
Smithy Houses
Denby Bottles
Langley Mill
Eastwood
Newthorpe
Watnall
Turnditch
Cowers Lane
Farnah Green
Bargate
Denby
Heanor
Langley
New Eastwood
Giltbrook
Kimberley
Hazelwood
Holbrook Moor
Milford
Holbrook
Lower Kilburn
Kilburn
Horsley Woodhouse
Marlpool
Shipley
Awsworth
Nuthall
Bulwell
Old Basford
Makeney
Horsley
Smalley
Smalley Green
Stanley Common
Woodside
Cotmanhay
Mapperley
Babbington
Cossall Marsh
Cossall
Duffield
Little Eaton
Coxbench
Smalley Common
Ilkeston
Bilborough
Whitemoor
Strelley
Weston Underwood
Quarndon
West Hallam Common
Morley
West Hallam
Kirk Hallam
Little Hallam
Trowell
Old Radford
Kedleston
Kedleston Hall
Kirk Langley
Allestree
Breadsall
Stanley
Hallam Fields
Wollaton
Wollaton Hall
Lenton
Darley Abbey
Oakwood
DERBY
Dale
Stanton by Dale
Stapleford
Bramcote
Markeaton
Langley Common
Mackworth
Chaddesden
Spondon
Ockbrook
Risley
Sandiacre
Beeston
Chilwell
Rylands
Borrowash
Mickleover
Littleover
Normanton
Crewton
Alvaston
Shacklecross
Breaston
Toton
Attenborough
Clifton
Barton in Fabis
Allenton
Draycott
Long Eaton
Ruddington
Elvaston
Sunnyhill
Sinfin
Stenson Fields
Shelton Lock
Thulston
Church Wilne
Sawley
Trentlock
Findern
Great Central (Nottingham) Railway
Thrumpton
Chellaston
Shardlow
Trent & Mersey Canal
Gotham
Aston-upon-Trent
Lockington
Ratcliffe on Soar
Willington
Barrow upon Trent
Swarkestone
Weston-upon-Trent
Hemington
Kingston on Soar
Repton
Ingleby
Stanton by Bridge
Castle Donington
Kegworth
West Leake
East Leake
Parson's Hill
Milton
Foremark
King's Newton
Donington Park
Grand Prix Collection
East Midlands
Sutton Fields
Newton Solney
Melbourne
Diseworth
Sutton Bonington
Isley Walton
Long Whatton
Wilson
Donington Park
Rempstone
BURTON UPON TRENT
Bretby
Stanhope Bretby
Ticknall
Calke Abbey
Breedon on the Hill
Tonge
Zouch
Normanton on Soar
Calke
Hathern
Stanford on Soar
Hartshorne
Newhall
Swadlincote
Heath End
Staunton Harold Church
Worthington
Cotes
Belton
Shepshed
Lount
Thorpe Acre
Loughborough
Church Gresley
Woodville
Smisby
Newbold
Osgathorpe
Blackfordby
Outwoods
Griffydam
Peggs Green
Nanpantan
Mount Pleasant
Norris Hill
Ashby-de-la-Zouch
Coleorton
Thringstone
Woodthorpe
Linton Heath
Conkers
Castle
Farm Town
New Swannington
Charnwood Forest
Quorn
Moira
Swannington
Mount St Bernard
Beacon Hill
Woodhouse
Over
Whitwick
Great Central Railway
Mountsorrel
Donisthorpe
Packington
Snibston
Woodhouse Eaves
99
100
Coalville
Hugglescote
Ravenstone
Bardon
Copt Oak
Swithland
Measham
Normanton
miles
kilometres
M1
A38
A6
A52
A50
A42
A453
A511
A512
A514
A516
A5111
A609
A610
A608
A6096

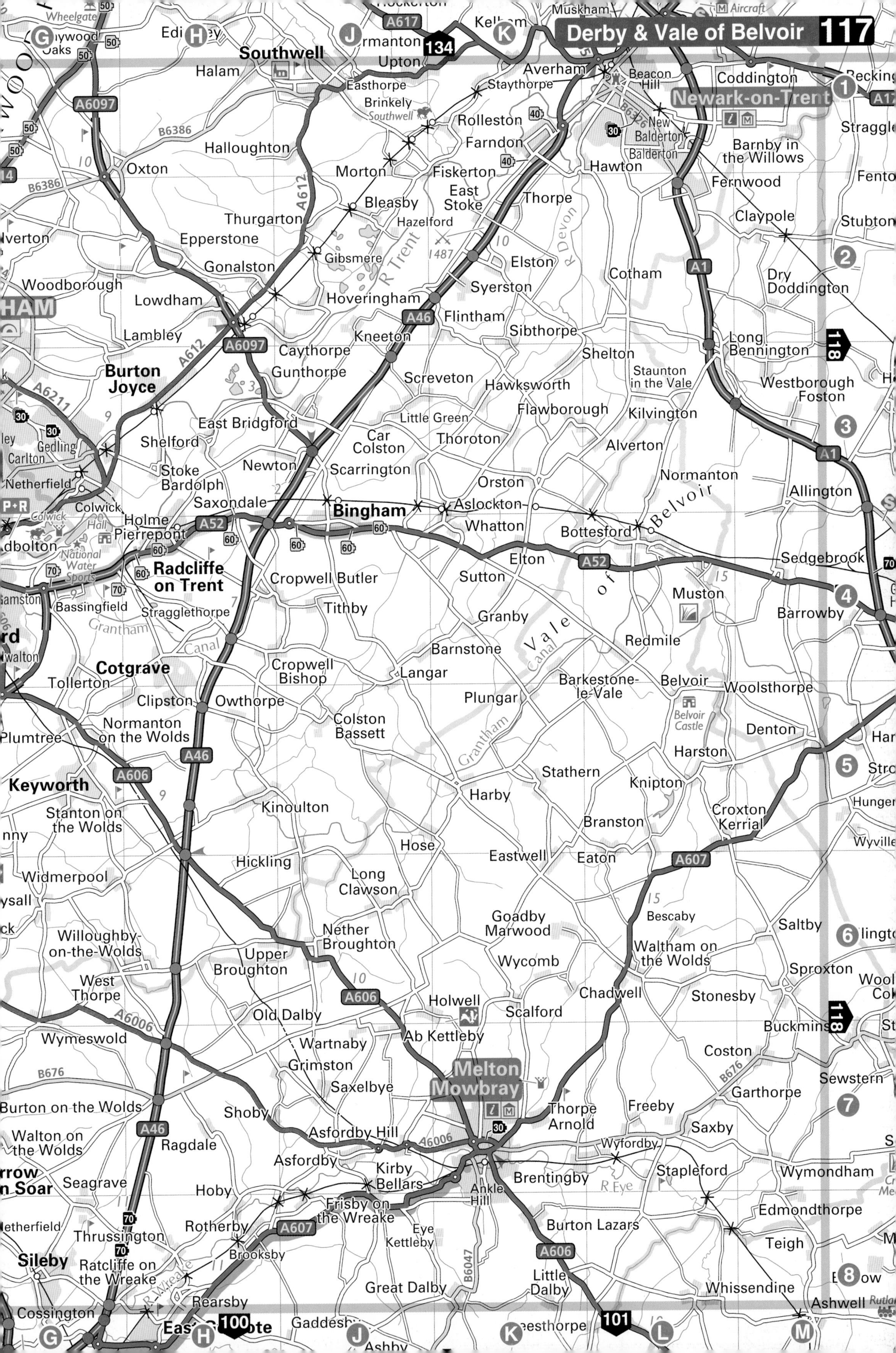
Southwell
Halam
Upton
Averham
Beacon Hill
Coddington
Newark-on-Trent
Easthorpe
Brinkely
Staythorpe
Rolleston
New Balderton
Balderton
Farndon
Halloughton
Oxton
Morton
Fiskerton
Hawton
Barnby in the Willows
Fernwood
East Stoke
Thorpe
Bleasby
Hazelford
Thurgarton
Epperstone
Gibsmere
R Trent
Claypole
Stubton
Gonalston
Elston
Cotham
Dry Doddington
Woodborough
Lowdham
Syerston
Hoveringham
Flintham
Lambley
Kneeton
Sibthorpe
Caythorpe
Long Bennington
Shelton
Gunthorpe
Staunton in the Vale
Burton Joyce
Screveton
Hawksworth
Westborough
Foston
Flawborough
Kilvington
East Bridgford
Little Green
Gedling
Carlton
Shelford
Car Colston
Thoroton
Alverton
Netherfield
Stoke Bardolph
Newton
Scarrington
Normanton
Allington
Orston
Colwick
Saxondale
Aslockton
Vale of Belvoir
Holme Pierrepont
Bingham
Whatton
Bottesford
National Water Sports
Elton
Sedgebrook
Radcliffe on Trent
Cropwell Butler
Sutton
Muston
Bassingfield
Stragglethorpe
Tithby
Granby
Barrowby
Grantham Canal
Redmile
Barnstone
Cotgrave
Cropwell Bishop
Langar
Barkestone-le-Vale
Belvoir
Woolsthorpe
Tollerton
Clipston
Owthorpe
Plungar
Belvoir Castle
Normanton on the Wolds
Colston Bassett
Denton
Plumtree
Harston
Stathern
Keyworth
Knipton
Harby
Stanton on the Wolds
Kinoulton
Croxton Kerrial
Branston
Hose
Eastwell
Eaton
Hickling
Widmerpool
Long Clawson
Bescaby
Saltby
Goadby Marwood
Nether Broughton
Willoughby-on-the-Wolds
Waltham on the Wolds
Upper Broughton
Wycomb
Sproxton
West Thorpe
Chadwell
Stonesby
Holwell
Scalford
Old Dalby
Buckminster
Wymeswold
Ab Kettleby
Wartnaby
Coston
Grimston
Melton Mowbray
Sewstern
Saxelbye
Garthorpe
Burton on the Wolds
Shoby
Thorpe Arnold
Freeby
Walton on the Wolds
Asfordby Hill
Saxby
Ragdale
Wyfordby
Asfordby
Kirby Bellars
Stapleford
Wymondham
Seagrave
Brentingby
R Eye
Hoby
Ankle Hill
Frisby on the Wreake
Edmondthorpe
Rotherby
Eye Kettleby
Burton Lazars
Thrussington
Teigh
Sileby
Brooksby
Ratcliffe on the Wreake
R Wreake
Little Dalby
Great Dalby
Whissendine
Rearsby
Ashwell
Cossington
East Goscote
Gaddesby
Ashby
A617
A6097
A612
A46
A1
A52
A6211
A606
A6006
A607
B6386
B676
B6047
134
118
100
101

A
B
135
C
D
Ashby de la Launde
E
Rowston
Walcot
F
136
Beckingham
Brant Broughton
Welbourn
Bloxholm
Digby
Billinghay
A17
Stragglethorpe
Dorrington
Leadenham
B1188
Ruskington
Fenton
A17
Cranwell
RAF College (Cranwell)
Anwick
Fulbeck
Caythorpe
Stubton
B1429
Leasingham
Brandon
Frieston
Dry Doddington
B1209
Evedon
A17
A607
North Rauceby
Holdingham
Sleaford
Kirkby la Thorpe
Ewerby
Hough-on-the-Hill
Normanton
B6403
South Rauceby
Gelston
Carlton Scroop
Asgarby
117
Westborough
Hougham
Sudbrook
Ancaster
B1517
Quarrington
Heckington
Marston
A153
Honington
Wilsford
A15
Foston
Heckington
A1
Barkston
Kelby
Silk Willoughby
Burton Pedwardine
Syston
Swarby
Allington
Belton
Culverthorpe
Scredington
Aswarby
Great Gonerby
Belton House
Oasby
Heydour
Aunsby
B1394
A607
Aisby
Sedgebrook
Londonthorpe
Osbournby
Spanby
B1174
Welby
Swaton
Gonerby Hill Foot
Manthorpe
B6403
Dembleby
Scott Willoughby
Barrowby
Grantham
A52
Newton
Haceby
Threekingham
New Somerby
Braceby
Walcot
Horbling
A52
Ropsley
Sapperton
Pickworth
Billingborough
B1174
Little Ponton
Old Somerby
Humby
Folkingham
Birthorpe
Sempringham
Denton
Harlaxton
Laughton
A15
Hanby
B1176
Boothby Pagnell
Pointon
Stroxton
Great Ponton
B6403
Aslackby
Hungerton
Scotland
Lenton
Milthorpe
Ingoldsby
Graby
Wyville
Bitchfield
A1
Keisby
Dowsby
R Witham
Rippingale
Hall
Bassingthorpe
Hawthorpe
Stoke Rochford
Easton
Burton Coggles
Irnham
Kirkby Underwood
B1177
Saltby
Skillington
B1176
Dunsby
Woolsthorpe Manor
Corby Glen
Bulby
Stainfield
Sproxton
A151
Hacconby
Woolsthorpe-by-Colsterworth
Colsterworth
Hanthorpe
117
Birkholme
Morton
Buckminster
Stainby
Twyford
Elsthorpe
North Witham
Swayfield
Grimsthorpe
Dyke
B6403
Swinstead
Edenham
Sewstern
Gunby
A15
B1176
Scottlethorpe
Bourne
A151
Creeton
B1193
Eastgate
South Witham
R Glen
Castle Bytham
Little Bytham
Wymondham
Cribbs Meadow
A151
Lound
Thistleton
Northorpe
Edmondthorpe
Witham on the Hill
Toft
R Glen
Clipsham
Careby
Thurlby
Teigh
Market Overton
Stretton
Manthorpe
Obthorpe
Barrow
Greetham
Aunby
A6121
Carlby
Ashwell
Rutland
Pickworth
Baston
A
101
D
Braceborough
102
E
Wilsthorpe
A15
F
0 1 2 3 4 5 miles
0 1 2 3 4 5 6 7 8 kilometres

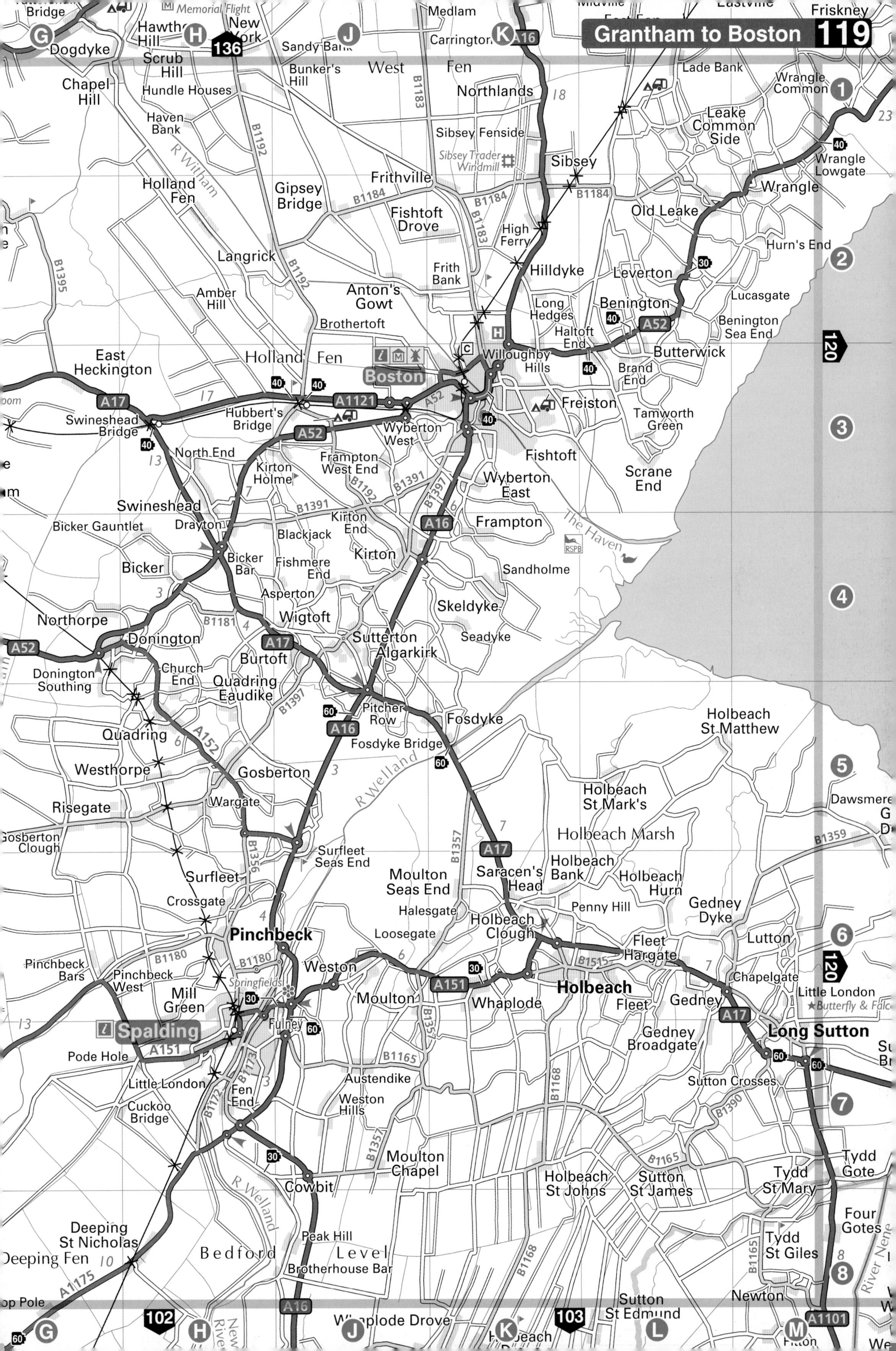
Boston
Spalding
Holbeach
Long Sutton
Pinchbeck
Sibsey
Wrangle
Old Leake
Leverton
Benington
Butterwick
Freiston
Fishtoft
Frampton
Kirton
Sutterton
Algarkirk
Swineshead
Donington
Quadring
Gosberton
Surfleet
Weston
Moulton
Whaplode
Fleet
Gedney
Cowbit
Moulton Chapel
Holbeach St Johns
Sutton St James
Tydd St Mary
Tydd St Giles
Holbeach St Matthew
Holbeach St Mark's
Holbeach Marsh
Fosdyke
Skeldyke
Wigtoft
Bicker
Dogdyke
Frithville
Gipsey Bridge
Langrick
Holland Fen
Anton's Gowt
Hilldyke
Northlands
Sibsey Trader Windmill
Butterfly & Falconry
A16
A17
A52
A151
A1121
A1101
A1175
A152
B1184
B1192
B1183
B1391
B1397
B1181
B1357
B1356
B1180
B1515
B1165
B1168
B1390
B1359
B1172
B1173
B1395
R Witham
R Welland
The Haven
Bedford Level
136
120
102
103

120
137
119
103
104
THE WASH
Friskney
Wrangle Lowgate
Wrangle
Hunstanton
Old Hunstanton
Holme Dunes
Ringstead
Heacham
Norfolk Lavender
Sedgeford
Snettisham
Park Farm
Southgate
Ingoldisthorpe
Dersingham
Dersingham Bog
Doddshill
Wolferton
Babingley River
Castle Rising
North Wootton
South Wootton
Congham
Roydon
Gaywood
King's Lynn
Fairstead
Bawsey
Gayton
Pott Row
Brow-of-the-Hill
Ashwicken
Fair Green
East Winch
Middleton
Blackborough End
North Runcton
West Winch
Setchey
Saddle Bow
Wiggenhall St Germans
Great Ouse
West Lynn
Tilney All Saints
Clenchwarton
African Violet Centre
Terrington St Clement
Little London
The Wash
Walpole Cross Keys
Walpole St Andrew
Walpole St Peter
Hay Green
Tilney High End
Tilney St Lawrence
St John's Highway
Ingleborough
Rattan Row
West Walton
River Nene
Dawsmere
Gedney Drove End
Little London
Butterfly & Falconry Park
Long Sutton
Sutton Bridge
Tydd Gote
Tydd St Mary
Four Gotes
Tydd St Giles
Fitton
A17
A47
A10
A148
A149
A1078
B1359
B1440
B1439
B1145

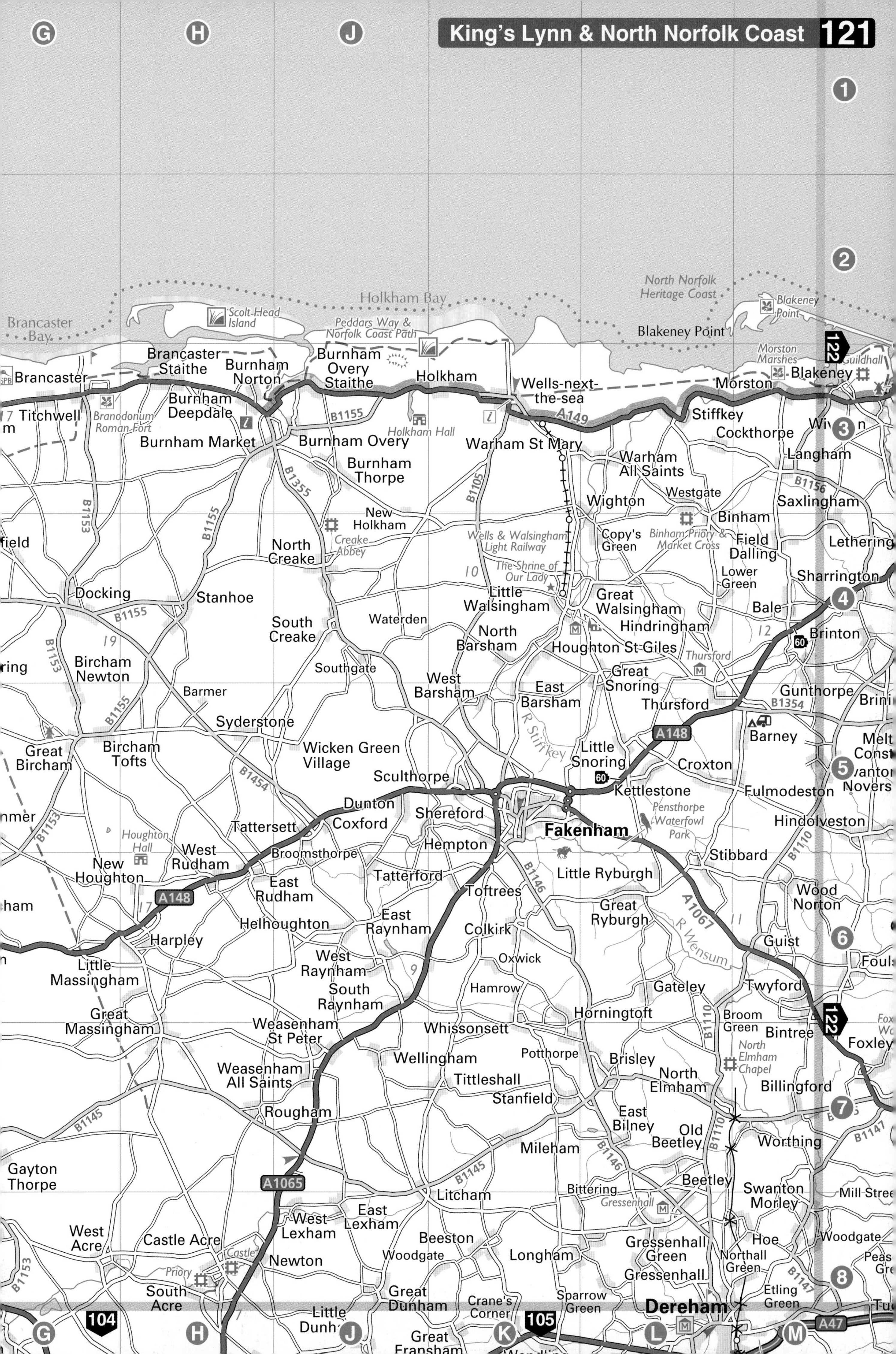
Brancaster Bay
Scolt Head Island
Holkham Bay
Peddars Way & Norfolk Coast Path
North Norfolk Heritage Coast
Blakeney Point
Morston Marshes
Brancaster
Brancaster Staithe
Burnham Norton
Burnham Overy Staithe
Holkham
Wells-next-the-sea
Morston
Blakeney
Guildhall
Titchwell
Branodunum Roman Fort
Burnham Deepdale
Burnham Market
Burnham Overy
Holkham Hall
Warham St Mary
Stiffkey
Cockthorpe
Langham
Burnham Thorpe
Warham All Saints
Wighton
Westgate
Saxlingham
New Holkham
Creake Abbey
North Creake
Wells & Walsingham Light Railway
Copy's Green
Binham
Binham Priory & Market Cross
Field Dalling
Letheringsett
Docking
Stanhoe
The Shrine of Our Lady
Little Walsingham
Great Walsingham
Lower Green
Sharrington
South Creake
Waterden
North Barsham
Hindringham
Bale
Brinton
Bircham Newton
Southgate
Houghton St Giles
Thursford
West Barsham
East Barsham
Great Snoring
Barmer
Syderstone
Gunthorpe
Great Bircham
Bircham Tofts
Wicken Green Village
R Stiffkey
Little Snoring
Barney
Croxton
Sculthorpe
Kettlestone
Fulmodeston
Hindolveston
Dunton
Shereford
Tattersett
Coxford
Fakenham
Pensthorpe Waterfowl Park
Houghton Hall
West Rudham
Hempton
Stibbard
New Houghton
Broomsthorpe
East Rudham
Tatterford
Little Ryburgh
Toftrees
Wood Norton
Great Ryburgh
East Raynham
Helhoughton
Colkirk
R Wensum
Harpley
Guist
West Raynham
Oxwick
Little Massingham
South Raynham
Hamrow
Gateley
Twyford
Great Massingham
Weasenham St Peter
Whissonsett
Horningtoft
Broom Green
Bintree
Foxley
Wellingham
Potthorpe
Brisley
North Elmham Chapel
Weasenham All Saints
Tittleshall
North Elmham
Billingford
Stanfield
Rougham
East Bilney
Old Beetley
Worthing
Mileham
Gayton Thorpe
Beetley
Swanton Morley
Litcham
Bittering
Gressenhall
Mill Street
West Acre
Castle Acre
Castle
West Lexham
East Lexham
Beeston
Hoe
Woodgate
Gressenhall Green
Longham
Newton
Priory
Northall Green
Gressenhall
South Acre
Great Dunham
Crane's Corner
Sparrow Green
Etling Green
Dereham
Little Dunham
Great Fransham
A149
A148
A1067
A1065
A47
B1155
B1355
B1105
B1153
B1156
B1354
B1454
B1110
B1146
B1145
B1147
122
104
105
G
H
J
K
L
M
1
2
3
4
5
6
7
8

Blakeney Point
Morston Marshes
Guildhall
Cley Marshes
Blakeney
Cley next the Sea
Muckleburgh Collection
Sheringham
West Runton
East Runton
Cromer
Salthouse
Weybourne
Sheringham Park
Newgate
Wiveton
Kelling
Upper Sheringham
Beeston Regis
Norfolk Shire Horse Centre
Langham
Glandford
A1082
A149
A148
Overstrand
B1156
Saxlingham
R Glaven
North Norfolk Railway
High Kelling
Bodham
Aylmerton
Felbrigg
Sidestrand
Holt
Letheringsett
West Beckham
East Beckham
Felbrigg Hall
Northrepps
Crossdale Street
B1436
Sharrington
Little Thornage
Baconsthorpe Castle
Gresham
Holt Lowes
Bessingham
Sustead
Metton
Southrepps
Gimingham
Bale
B1110
Hempstead
Baconsthorpe
Roughton
Thornage
Hanworth
Brinton
Hunworth
Plumstead
Thurgarton
Alby Hill
A140
Thorpe Market
Lower Street
Trunch
Stody
Edgefield Green
Plumstead Green
Matlask
Gunthorpe
Briningham
Edgefield
Aldborough
Bradfield
B1354
Little Barningham
Wickmere
Antingham
Old Hall Street
Barney
Melton Constable
B1149
Erpingham
Suffield
Calthorpe
Colby
Swafield
Briston
Mannington Gardens
Wolterton Park
North Walsham
Swanton Novers
Craymere Beck
Saxthorpe
Itteringham
Fulmodeston
R Bure
Banningham
B1145
Hindolveston
Corpusty
Ingworth
Nethergate
Blickling
Blickling Estate
Tungate
Thurning
Norton Corner
Oulton
Felmingham
Silvergate
Wood Norton
Oulton Street
Tuttington
Skeyton Corner
Westwick
Heydon
Aylsham
Wood Dalling
Guestwick
Burgh next Aylsham
Skeyton
B1150
Salle
Southgate
Foulsham
Bure Valley Railway
Swanton Abbott
Twyford
Themelthorpe
Oxnead
Cawston
Marsham
Lamas
Scottow
Brampton
Bintree
Foxley Wood
Reepham
Little Hautbois
Foxley
Eastgate
Whitwell Street
Buxton Heath
Westgate Street
Buxton
Sco Ruston
Billingford
Great Witchingham
Brandiston
Stratton Strawless
St James
Bawdeswell
Hevingham
Sparham
Norfolk Wildlife Park
Waterloo
Worthing
B1147
Alderford
Swannington
Horstead
Coltishall
Sparhamill
A1067
Felthorpe
Hainford
Belaugh
Lyng
Dinosaur
Frettenham
Swanton Morley
Mill Street
Lenwade
Upgate
Wroxham
Elsing
Morton on the Hill
Horsford
Newton St Faith
Hillside
Hoe
Woodgate
Primrose Green
Attlebridge
A1151
Peaseland Green
R Wensum
Crostwick
Greensgate
Weston Longville
Thorpe Marriott
Horsham St Faith
Etling Green
North Tuddenham
Ringland
Taverham
Aviation
Spixworth
Drayton
Rackheath
Norwich
New Rackheath
106
0 1 2 3 4 5 miles
0 1 2 3 4 5 6 7 8 kilometres

G
H
J
K
1
2
3
4
5
6
7
8
Mundesley
Paston
B1159
Bacton
Walcott
Pollard Street
Witton
Ridlington
Ridlington Street
Happisburgh
Whimpwell Green
Crostwight
Happisburgh Common
Eccles on Sea
Hempstead
Lessingham
Ingham Corner
B1159
Sea Palling
East Ruston
Ingham
Waxham
Stalham
Calthorpe Street
Dilham
Stalham Green
Hickling
Low Street
A149
Horsey Corner
Sutton
Hickling Green
Horsey
Pennygate
Barton Turf
Wood Street
Hickling Heath
Hill Common
Hickling Broad
Horsey Windpump
Barton Broad
Neatishead
Catfield
Catfield Common
Irstead
East Somerton
Potter Heigham
West Somerton
Threehammer Common
Sharp Green
R Ant
Winterton-on-Sea
Ludham
Martham
BeWILDerwood
Johnson's Street
Bastwick
A1062
Cess
Hemsby Hole
Hemsby
R Thurne
Newport
Horning
Ormesby Broad
Upper Street
Repps
Rollesby
Ormesby St Margaret
Scratby
Bure Marshes
Broadland Conservation Centre
B1152
Thurne
Burgh St Margaret
Ormesby St Michael
California
Ranworth
Pilson Green
Clippesby
Fairhaven
Billockby
A149
Caister-on-Sea
Cargate Green
107
South Walsham
Filby
Bure
Mautby
L
M

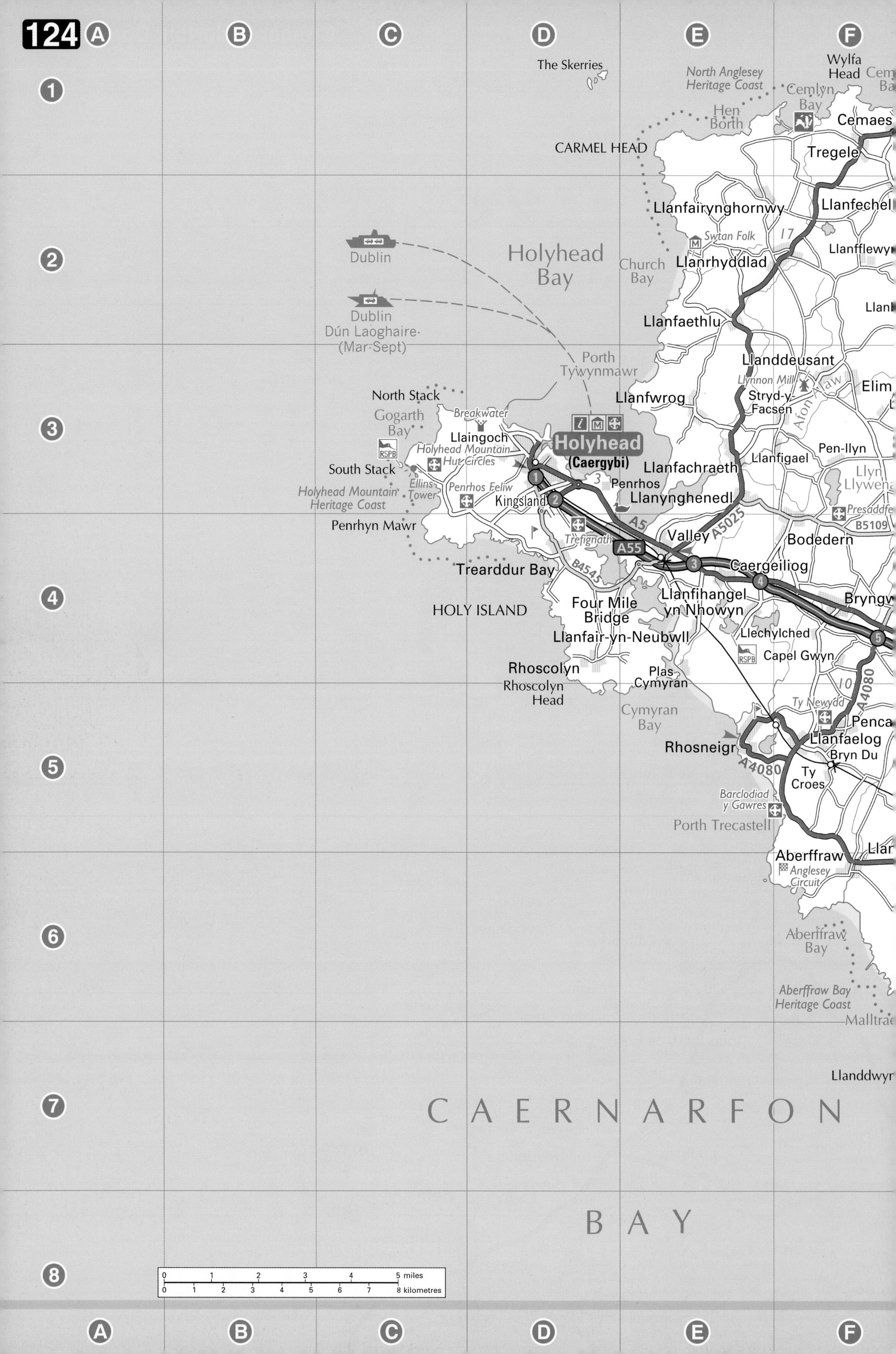
A B C D E F
1 2 3 4 5 6 7 8
The Skerries
Wylfa Head
North Anglesey Heritage Coast
Cemlyn Bay
Hen Borth
Cemaes
CARMEL HEAD
Tregele
Llanfairynghornwy
Llanfechell
Swtan Folk
Dublin
Holyhead Bay
Church Bay
Llanrhyddlad
Dublin
Dún Laoghaire (Mar-Sept)
Llanfaethlu
Porth Tywynmawr
Llanddeusant
Llynnon Mill
Elim
North Stack
Llanfwrog
Stryd-y-Facsen
Afon Alaw
Gogarth Bay
Breakwater
Llaingoch
Holyhead
(Caergybi)
Holyhead Mountain Hut Circles
Pen-llyn
South Stack
Llanfigael
Llanfachraeth
Llyn Llywenan
Ellins Tower
Penrhos Feliw
Penrhos
Holyhead Mountain Heritage Coast
Kingsland
Llanynghenedl
Presaddfed
Penrhyn Mawr
A5
A5025
B5109
Trefignath
Valley
Bodedern
A55
Trearddur Bay
B4545
Caergeiliog
HOLY ISLAND
Four Mile Bridge
Llanfihangel yn Nhowyn
Bryngwran
Llanfair-yn-Neubwll
Llechylched
Rhoscolyn
Capel Gwyn
Rhoscolyn Head
Plas Cymyran
A4080
Cymyran Bay
Ty Newydd
Penca
Rhosneigr
Llanfaelog
Bryn Du
A4080
Ty Croes
Barclodiad y Gawres
Porth Trecastell
Aberffraw
Anglesey Circuit
Aberffraw Bay
Aberffraw Bay Heritage Coast
Malltraeth
Llanddwyn
CAERNARFON BAY
0 1 2 3 4 5 miles
0 1 2 3 4 5 6 7 8 kilometres

Amlwch
Bull Bay
Point Lynas
Llaneilian
Burwen
Pengorffwysfa
Pentrefelin
Rhosbeirio
Bodewryd
Penysarn
Nebo
Dulas
Gadfa
Rhosybol
City Dulas
Dulas Bay
Capel Parc
Seawatch Centre
Brynrefail
Rhôs Lligwy
Llyn Alaw
Moelfre
Din Lligwy
Llanallgo
Llandyfrydog
Marian-glas
Maenaddwyn
Llannerchymedd
Hebron
Bachau
Capel Coch
Brynteg
Tynygongl
Benllech
Red Wharf Bay
Puffin Island
Penmon Priory
Black Point
Caim
Toll
Penmon
Glan-yr-afon
Llanbedrgoch
Tregaian
Llanddona
Llangoed
Llanddyfnan
Pentraeth
Llangwyllog
Rhosmeirch
Cefni Reservoir
Oriel Ynys Môn
Talwrn
Rhoscefnhir
Llanfaes
Gaol
Beaumaris Castle
Beaumaris
Llansadwrn
Courthouse
Bodffordd
Gwalchmai
Heneglwys
Llangefni
Ceint
Llanfairfechan
Penmaenmawr
Llandegfan
Menai Bridge (Porthaethwy)
Bangor
Penmynydd
Cerrigceinwen
Llangristiolus
Anglesey Column
Llanfair P G
Penrhyn
Gorddinog
Abergwyngregyn
Henblas
Pentre Berw
Gaerwen
Llandygai
Capel Mawr
Trefdraeth
Afon Cefni
Bryn Celli Ddu
Britannia Bridge
Penrhos garnedd
Plas Newydd
Coedydd Aber
Tal-y-bont
Aber Falls
Llanddaniel Fab
Malltraeth
Capel-y-graig
Llanllechid
Moel Winion
Bodowyr Burial Chamber
Afon Braint
Waen-wen
Glasinfryn
Llangaffo
Caer Lêb
Y Felinheli
Greenwood Forest Park
Rhyd-y-groes
Pentir
Tregarth
Rachub
Bethesda
Y Drosgl
Brynsiencyn
Llanidan
Sling
Castell Bryn Gwyn
Seion
Waen-pentir
Gerlan
Dwyran
Bethel
Llanddeiniolen
Afon Caseg
Ogwen Bank
Anglesey Sea Zoo
Newborough
Saron
Rhiwlas
Mynydd Llandygai
Pen-lôn
Foel Farm Park
Penisarwaun
Carnedd Llewelyn
Waterloo Port
Llanrug
Rhiwen
Deiniolen
Caernarfon
Pont-rug
Carnedd Dafydd
Segontium
Clwt-y-bont
Caernarfon Castle
Brynrefail
Gallt-y-foel
Caeathro
Cwm-y-glo
Llyn Padarn
Dinorwic
Elidir Fawr
Ceunant
Padarn
Llanberis Lake Railway
Pont Pen-y-benglog
Llyn Ogwen
Welsh Highland Railway
Abermenai Point
Llanberis
National Slate
Gypsy Wood
Groeslon
Y Garn
Foryd Bay
Electric Mountain
Dolbadarn Castle
Llyn Peris
Bontnewydd
Y Tryfan
Airworld Aviation
Saron
Waunfawr
Nant Peris
Gwastadnant
Glyder Fawr
Glyder-Fach
Morfa Dinlle
Llanwnda
Rhostryfan
Betws Garmon
Moel Eilio
Snowdon Mountain Railway
Pass of Llanberis
Rhosgadfan
Penyffridd
Dinas Dinlle
Llandwrog
Groeslon
Moel Tryfan
Parc Glynllifon
Llyn Cwellyn
Pen-y-pass
Pen-y-gwryd
Carmel
Fron
Mynydd Mawr
Snowdon
Llyn Llydaw
Nantlle
Slate works
A55
A5
A5025
A5114
A4080
A4087
A545
A487
A4086
A4085
A4244
A4244
B5111
B5110
B5108
B5109
B5420
B4422
B4419
B4421
B4366
B4547
B4409
B4418
126
109
580
757
1062
1044
923
946
917
1001
994
726
442
698
1085

A
B
C
D
E
F
1
2
3
4
5
6
7
8
Dulas Bay
Seawatch Centre
Moelfre
Llanallgo
Marian-glas
125
B5108
Benllech
Red Wharf Bay
Red Wharf Bay
Pentraeth
A5025
B5109
Llanddona
Glan-yr-afon
Caim
Penmon Priory
Toll
Penmon
Puffin Island
Black Point
Llangoed
B5109
Llanfaes
Gaol
Beaumaris
Beaumaris Castle
Courthouse
Llansadwrn
Llandegfan
A545
Menai Bridge (Porthaethwy)
Anglesey Column
Bangor
Penrhyn
Llandygai
Britannia Bridge
Penrhos garnedd
Bryn Celli Ddu
Plas Newydd
Capel-y-graig
A4087
A55
A5
Y Felinheli
GreenWood Forest Park
B4547
Waen-wen
Pentir
Rhyd-y-groes
Glasinfryn
Tregarth
Sling
Waen-pentir
Seion
Bethel
Llanddeiniolen
Saron
B4366
Penisarwaun
A4244
Rhiwlas
Llanrug
Rhiwen
Deiniolen
Mynydd Llandygai
Pont-rug
Caeathro
Cwm-y-glo
Brynrefail
Clwt-y-bont
Gallt-y-foel
Dinorwic
Llyn Padarn
Padarn
Llanberis Lake Railway
National Slate
442
Llanberis
Electric Mountain
Dolbadarn Castle
Groeslon
A4085
Waunfawr
Betws Garmon
726
MOEL EILIO
Snowdon Mountain Railway
Rhosgadfan
Penyffridd
Llyn Cwellyn
698
Fron
Nantlle
B4418
Llyn Peris
Pass of Llanberis
Nant Peris
Gwastadnant
A4086
1085
Pen-y-pass
Pen-y-Gwryd
923
ELIDIR FAWR
Pont Pen-y-benglog
946
Y GARN
1001
GLYDER FAWR
994
GLYDER-FACH
917
Y TRYFAN
Llyn Ogwen
1044
CARNEDD DAFYDD
1062
CARNEDD LLEWELYN
Ogwen Bank
Gerlan
B4409
Bethesda
Rachub
Llanllechid
580
MOEL WINION
757
Y DROSGL
Tal-y-bont
Abergwyngregyn
Coedydd Aber
Afon Anafon
Aber Falls
Afon Caseg
942
FOEL-FRAS
Afon Dulyn
Llyn Eigiau
Llyn Cowlyd
Afon Ddu
Llanfairfechan
Gorddinog
Nant-y-pandy
Garizim
Penmaenan
Penmaenmawr
Dwygyfylchi
SNOWDONIA NATIONAL PARK
610
TAL-Y-FAN
Capelulo
Conwy
Conwy Castle
Henryd
Rowen
B5106
Ty'n-y-Groes
Caerhun
Castell
Llanbedr-y-Cennin
Tal-y-Bont
Dolgarrog
Pont Dolgarrog
R Conwy
Vale of Conwy
Trefriw Woollen Mills
Trefriw
Llanrhychwyn
Llanrwst
Llyn Crafnant
Llyn Geirionydd
Gwydir Uchaf Chapel
The Ugly House (Ty Hyll)
Gwydyr
Capel Curig
National Mountain Centre (Plas y Brenin)
Pont Cyfyng
Swallow Falls (Rhaeadr Ewynnol)
Betws-y-Coed
Forest
Pont-y-pant
872
MOEL-SIABOD
110
Conwy Bay
Great Orme Heritage Coast
GREAT ORMES HEAD
Llandudno
Llanrhos
Deganwy
A546
B5115
0 1 2 3 4 5 miles
0 1 2 3 4 5 6 7 8 kilometres

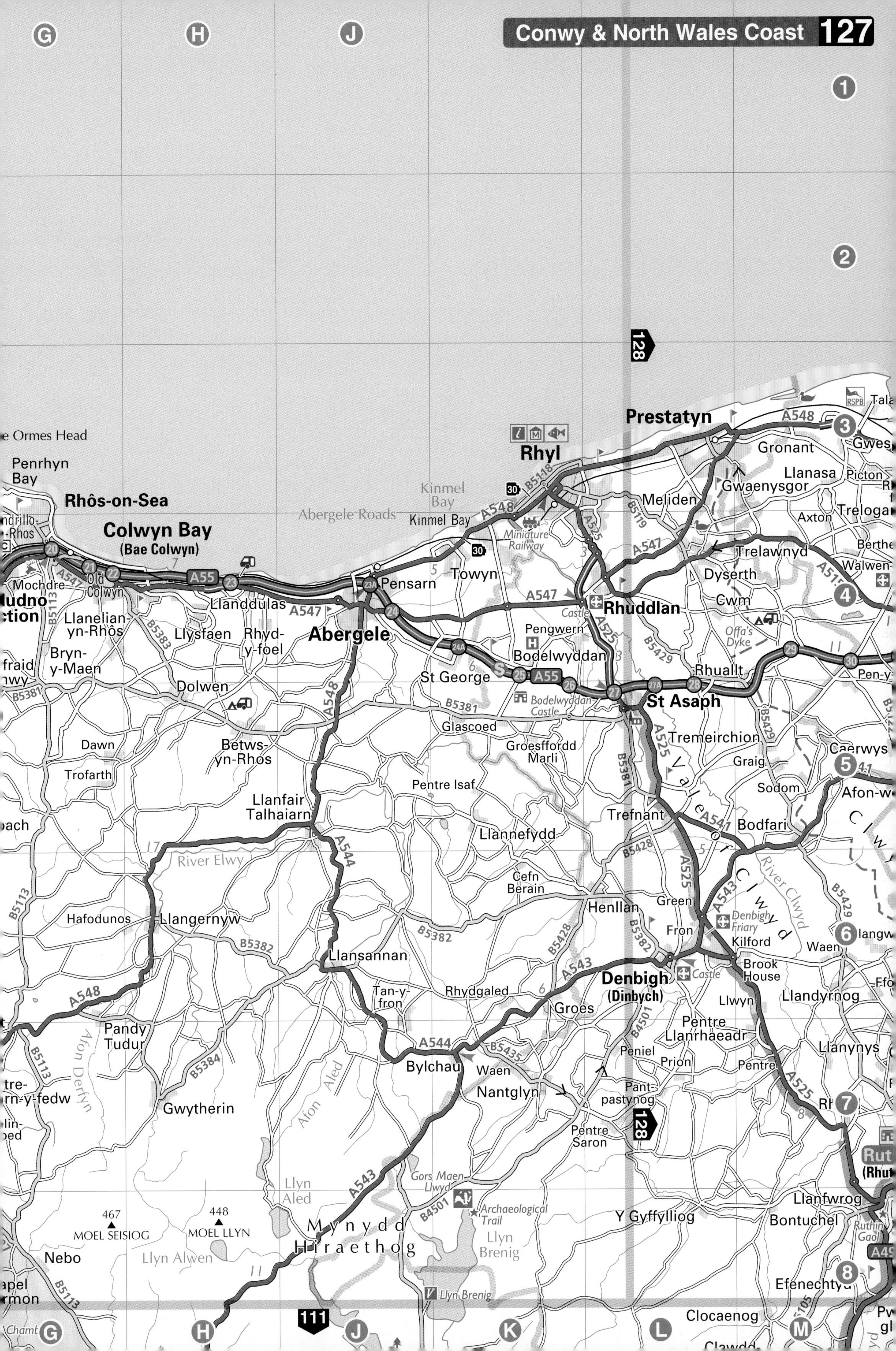
Prestatyn
Rhyl
Rhôs-on-Sea
Colwyn Bay
(Bae Colwyn)
Abergele
Rhuddlan
St Asaph
Denbigh
(Dinbych)
Penrhyn Bay
Kinmel Bay
Abergele Roads
Towyn
Pensarn
Llanddulas
Llysfaen
Old Colwyn
Mochdre
Llanelian-yn-Rhôs
Bryn-y-Maen
Rhyd-y-foel
Dolwen
Betws-yn-Rhos
Dawn
Trofarth
St George
Bodelwyddan
Pengwern
Glascoed
Groesffordd Marli
Pentre Isaf
Llanfair Talhaiarn
Llannefydd
Trefnant
Tremeirchion
Meliden
Gronant
Gwaenysgor
Llanasa
Picton
Axton
Trelawnyd
Dyserth
Cwm
Rhuallt
Graig
Sodom
Bodfari
Caerwys
Henllan
Cefn Berain
Green
Fron
Kilford
Waen
Brook House
Llangernyw
Hafodunos
River Elwy
Llansannan
Tan-y-fron
Rhydgaled
Groes
Llwyn
Pentre Llanrhaeadr
Peniel
Prion
Pentre
Llandyrnog
Llanynys
Pandy Tudur
Afon Derfyn
Gwytherin
Bylchau
Waen
Nantglyn
Pant-pastynog
Pentre Saron
Afon Aled
Llyn Aled
Gors Maen Llwyd
Archaeological Trail
Llyn Brenig
Mynydd Hiraethog
Y Gyffylliog
Llanfwrog
Bontuchel
Ruthin Gaol
Efenechtyd
Clocaenog
MOEL SEISIOG
467
MOEL LLYN
448
Llyn Alwen
Nebo
Ormes Head
Miniature Railway
Bodelwyddan Castle
Denbigh Friary
Castle
Offa's Dyke
Vale of Clwyd
River Clwyd
A55
A547
A548
A544
A543
A525
A541
B5381
B5382
B5383
B5384
B5113
B5428
B5429
B5435
B4501
B5119
B5118
A5151
128
111

A
B
C
D
E
F
1
2
3
4
5
6
7
8
Great Meols
Hoylake
Royal Liverpool
Hilbre Island
Red Rocks Marsh
Middle Eye
Little Eye
West Kirby
Grange
B5140
Caldy
Thurstaston
127
Point of Ayr
Talacre
RSPB
River Dee
Prestatyn
A548
Rhyl
Gronant
Gwespyr
Ffynnongroyw
Kinmel Bay
Roads
Kinmel Bay
30
B5118
Llanasa
Picton
Rhewl-fawr
Gwaenysgor
Meliden
B5119
Trelogan
Rhewl Mostyn
Mostyn
Axton
Tre-Mostyn
Glan-y-don
Berthengam
Buarth-draw
Miniature Railway
A525
A547
Trelawnyd
Walwen
Maen Achwyfan Cross
Downing
Towyn
Dyserth
A5151
Whitford
Basingwerk Abbey
Pensarn
A547
Rhuddlan
Cwm
Greenfield Valley
Greenfield
Castle
Lloc
Gorsedd
Carmel
Walwen
Pengwern
Offa's Dyke
Holway
Whelston
Bodelwyddan
B5429
A5026
Pentre Bach
St George
A55
Rhuallt
Pantasaph
St Winefride's Well
Holywell (Treffynnon)
Bagillt
Bodelwyddan Castle
St Asaph
Pen-y-cefn
Calcot
Milwr
B5381
Glascoed
Brynford
Tremeirchion
Babell
Dolphin
Flint (Y Fflint)
Groesffordd Marli
B5122
Myndd-llan
A5026
Caerwys
B5121
Graig
A541
Pentre Isaf
B5381
Ysceifiog
Lixwm
Pentre Halkyn
Sodom
Afon-wen
Rhes-y-cae
Halkyn
Catch
Trefnant
Vale of Clwyd
Ddol
Walwen
A5119
Llannefydd
Bodfari
Clwydian Range
B5428
Pen-y-felin
Nannerch
A55
Cefn Berain
A525
River Clwyd
Wern-y-gaer
Northop
B5429
Hendre
Henllan
Green
B5123
Rhosesmor
A543
Denbigh Friary
Rhydymwyn
B5382
B5428
Fron
Kilford
Llangwyfan
B5382
Waen
Llyn-y-pandy
Fawnog
Brook House
A541
New Brighton
A543
Denbigh (Dinbych)
Castle
Tan-y-fron
Rhydgaled
Ffordd-las
Cilcain
Gwernaffield
Groes
Llwyn
Llandyrnog
Offa's Dyke Path
Pant-y-mwyn
Mold (Yr Wyddgrug)
B4501
Pentre Llanrhaeadr
A544
Llangynhafal
Cadole
B5435
Loggerheads
Bylchau
Peniel
Llanynys
Gellifor
555
MOEL FAMAU
Waen
Prion
Pentre
Tafarn-y-Gelyn
Gwernymynydd
Nantglyn
Pant-pastynog
Rhos
A525
Moel Famau
Rhewl
Hirwaen
Llanferres
Maeshafn
Nercwys
Pentre Saron
Llanbedr-Dyffryn-Clwyd
Ruthin (Rhuthun)
A494
Gors Maen Llwyd
Top-y-rhos
B4501
Archaeological Trail
Llanfwrog
Eryrys
Y Gyffylliog
Bontuchel
B5429
Ruthin Gaol
B5430
Llyn Brenig
Llanarmon-yn-Ial
Graianrhyd
A494
Llanfair Dyffryn Clwyd
Efenechtyd
Llyn Brenig
Graig-fechan
B5431
A5104
B5430
111
112
Pentre-
Rhydt
0 1 2 3 4 5 miles
0 1 2 3 4 5 6 7 8 kilometres

EURO RAIL TERMINAL
BOOTLE
Knowsley
Haydock
Eccleston
Earlestown
LIVERPOOL
Prescot
Burtonwood
Norris Green
Croxteth Hall
Knowsley Safari Park
West Derby
Kirkdale
Anfield
Everton
New Brighton
WALLASEY
Liscard
Egremont
Poulton
Seacombe
Mersey Tunnels
Albert Dock
Bidston
Claughton
BIRKENHEAD
Tranmere
Rock Ferry
Toxteth
Dingle
Allerton
Aigburth
Grassendale
Garston
Knotty Ash
Roby
Huyton
Whiston
Rainhill
Rainhill Stoops
Sutton Manor
Clock Face
Childwall
National Wildflower Centre
Whitefield Lane End
Cronton
Upton
Farnworth
Bold Heath
Penketh
WIDNES
Woolton
Tarbock Green
Halewood
Hough Green
Appleton
Cuerdley Cross
Hunt's Cross
Speke
Speke Hall
John Lennon
Oglet
Hale Bank
Hale
DITTON
West Bank
Catalyst
RUNCORN
Halton
Norton
Weston
River Mersey
ELLESMERE PORT
Manchester Ship Canal
Prenton
Thingwall
Storeton
Port Sunlight
New Ferry
Bebington
Spital
Bromborough
Eastham Ferry
Eastham
Barnston
Brimstage
Thornton Hough
Raby
Hooton
Parkgate
Neston
Little Neston
Ness
Ness Botanic Gardens
Willaston
Childer Thornton
Overpool
Little Sutton
Great Sutton
Whitby
Ince
Elton
Elton Green
Sutton Weaver
Frodsham
Newtown
Overton
Fivecrosses
Helsby
Newton
Kingsley
Hapsford
Alvanley
Thornton-le-Moors
Stoak
Ledsham
Whitbyheath
Blue Planet
Backford Cross
Little Stanney
Capenhurst
Dunkirk
Burton
Puddington
Shotwick
Backford
Wervin
Picton
Bridge Trafford
Dunham-on-the-Hill
Manley
Mouldsworth
Hatchmer
Commonside
Birch Hill
Cookson Green
Great Saughall
Mollington
Connah's Quay
Garden City
Little Saughall
Upton Heath
Upton
Mickle Trafford
Plemstall
Long Green
Little Barrow
Ashton
Delamere Forest Park
Blakemere
Blacon
Newton
Guilden Sutton
Hollowmoor Heath
Great Barrow
Tarvin Sands
Kelsall
Willington Corner
Shotton
Queensferry
Pentre
Sandycroft
Aston
Ewloe Castle
Ewloe Green
Mancot
Little Mancot
CHESTER
Littleton
Christleton
Stamford Bridge
Tarvin
Oscroft
Quarrybank
Ewloe
Hawarden
Handbridge
Castle
Brown Heath
Duddon Common
Duddon
Utkinton
Burton
Clotton
Drury
Broughton
Bretton
Saltney
Huntington
Rowton
Waverton
Spon Green
Lower Kinnerton
Eccleston
Saighton
Hargrave
Huxley
Birch Heath
Tarporley
Penymynydd
Gorstella
Penyffordd
Dodleston
Hatton Heath
Gates Heath
Shropshire Union Canal
Higher Kinnerton
Kinnerton Green
Cuckoo's Nest
Aldford
Bruera
Brassey Green
Hand Green
Tiverton
Coed Talon
Tir-y-fron
Hope
Golly
Broadoak
Pulford
Lavister
Burton Green
Milton Green
Tattenhall
Newton
Beeston
Bunbury Heath
Caergwrle
Darland
Rossett
Trevalyn
Handley
Aldersey Green
Burwardsley
Spurstow
Cefn-y-bedd
Abermorddu
Cymau
Sydallt
Llay
Marford
Parkside
Churton
Chowley
Coddington
Harthill
Higher Burwardsley
Peckforton
Ffrith
Windy Hill
Summer Hill
Farndon
Clutton
Broxton
Barnhill
Bulkeley
Gresford
Holt
Barton
Gallantry Bank
Ridley
Commonwood

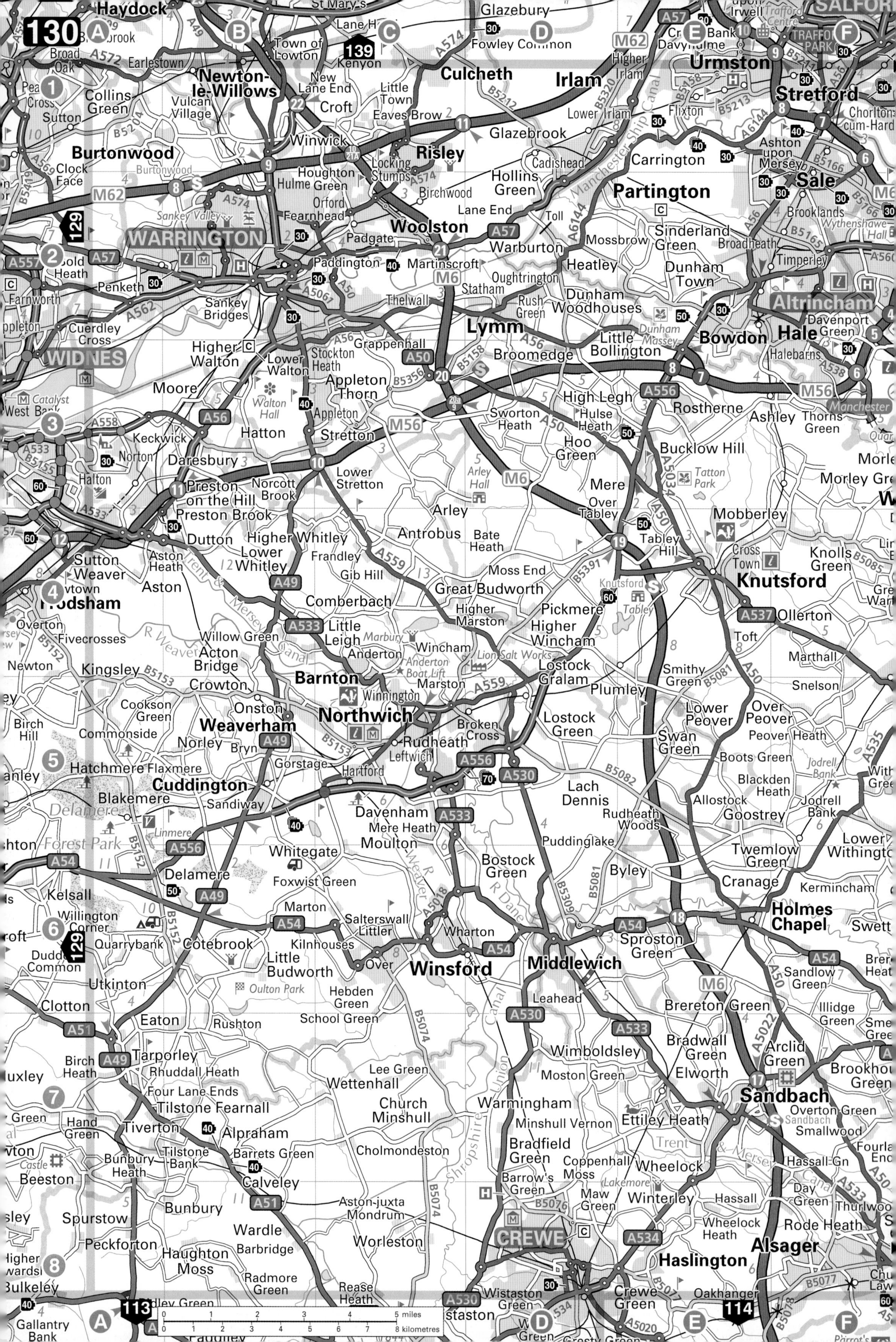

130
A
B
C
D
E
F
Haydock
St Mary's
Glazebury
Lane Head
Town of Lowton
139
Kenyon
Fowley Common
Irwell
Trafford Centre
SALFORD
Trafford Park
Broad Oak
Earlestown
Newton-le-Willows
Culcheth
Irlam
Higher Irlam
Davyhulme
Urmston
Stretford
Peasley Cross
Collins Green
Vulcan Village
New Lane End
Croft
Little Town
Eaves Brow
Lower Irlam
Flixton
Chorlton-cum-Hardy
Sutton
Winwick
Glazebrook
Ashton upon Mersey
Burtonwood
Risley
Cadishead
Carrington
Sale
Clock Face
Houghton Green
Locking Stumps
Hollins Green
Hulme
Birchwood
Partington
M62
Sankey Valley
Orford
Fearnhead
Lane End
Toll
Brooklands
WARRINGTON
Padgate
Woolston
Mossbrow
Sinderland Green
Broadheath
Wythenshawe Hall
Bold Heath
Penketh
Paddington
Martinscroft
Warburton
Heatley
Dunham Town
Timperley
Farnworth
Sankey Bridges
Thelwall
Statham
Oughtrington
Rush Green
Dunham Woodhouses
Altrincham
Cuerdley Cross
Lymm
Dunham Massey
Bowdon
Hale
Davenport Green
WIDNES
Higher Walton
Lower Walton
Stockton Heath
Grappenhall
Little Bollington
Broomedge
Halebarns
Moore
Appleton Thorn
High Legh
Rostherne
Catalyst
West Bank
Walton Hall
Appleton
Hulse Heath
Ashley
Thorns Green
Manchester
Keckwick
Hatton
Stretton
Swarton Heath
Hoo Green
Bucklow Hill
Norton
Daresbury
Halton
Lower Stretton
Arley Hall
Tatton Park
Morley Green
Preston on the Hill
Norcott Brook
Mere
Over Tabley
Preston Brook
Arley
Mobberley
Dutton
Higher Whitley
Antrobus
Bate Heath
Tabley Hill
Sutton Weaver
Aston Heath
Lower Whitley
Frandley
Cross Town
Knolls Green
Aston
Gib Hill
Moss End
Knutsford
Frodsham
Comberbach
Great Budworth
Tabley
Overton
Little Leigh
Higher Marston
Pickmere
Ollerton
Fivecrosses
Willow Green
Marbury
Higher Wincham
Toft
Acton Bridge
Anderton
Wincham
Lion Salt Works
Newton
Kingsley
Anderton Boat Lift
Lostock Gralam
Marthall
Crowton
Barnton
Marston
Smithy Green
Snelson
Cookson Green
Onston
Winnington
Plumley
Lower Peover
Over Peover
Birch Hill
Weaverham
Northwich
Broken Cross
Lostock Green
Swan Green
Commonside
Norley
Bryn
Rudheath
Peover Heath
Leftwich
Boots Green
Jodrell Bank
Hatchmere
Flaxmere
Gorstage
Hartford
Blackden Heath
Cuddington
Lach Dennis
Blakemere
Sandiway
Davenham
Allostock
Goostrey
Delamere
Mere Heath
Rudheath Woods
Delamere Forest Park
Linmere
Moulton
Puddinglake
Twemlow Green
Lower Withington
Whitegate
Bostock Green
Foxwist Green
Byley
Cranage
Kermincham
Kelsall
Marton
Holmes Chapel
Willington Corner
Salterswall
Littler
Wharton
Sproston Green
Quarrybank
Cotebrook
Kilnhouses
Little Budworth
Over
Winsford
Middlewich
Sandlow Green
Dudden Common
Utkinton
Oulton Park
Hebden Green
Leahead
Clotton
School Green
Brereton Green
Illidge Green
Eaton
Rushton
Bradwall Green
Arclid Green
Birch Heath
Tarporley
Wimboldsley
Elworth
Brookhouse Green
Rhuddall Heath
Lee Green
Moston Green
Sandbach
Wettenhall
Four Lane Ends
Tilstone Fearnall
Church Minshull
Warmingham
Overton Green
Hand Green
Tiverton
Alpraham
Minshull Vernon
Ettiley Heath
Smallwood
Tilstone Bank
Barrets Green
Cholmondeston
Bradfield Green
Beeston Castle
Beeston
Bunbury Heath
Calveley
Coppenhall Moss
Wheelock
Hassall Green
Barrow's Green
Lakemore
Spurstow
Bunbury
Aston juxta Mondrum
Maw Green
Winterley
Hassall
Day Green
Wardle
CREWE
Wheelock Heath
Rode Heath
Peckforton
Barbridge
Worleston
Haslington
Alsager
Haughton Moss
Radmore Green
Rease Heath
Bulkeley
Crewe Green
Oakhanger
Wistaston Green
Wistaston
Gallantry Bank
113
114
0 1 2 3 4 5 miles
0 1 2 3 4 5 6 7 8 kilometres

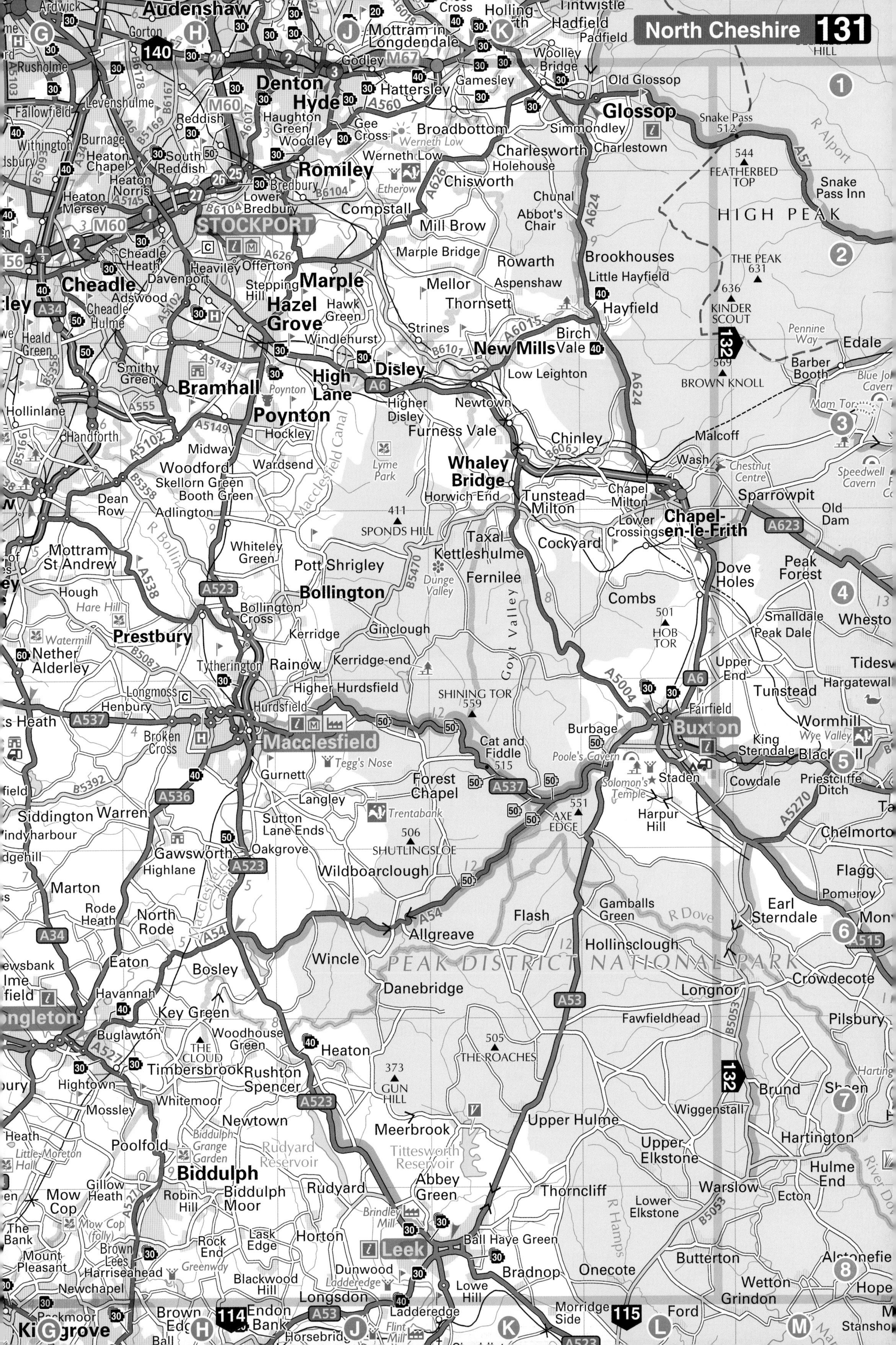

Audenshaw
Ardwick
Gorton
140
Mottram in Longdendale
Hollingworth
Tintwistle
Hadfield
Padfield
Rusholme
Levenshulme
Fallowfield
Withington
Burnage
Heaton Chapel
Heaton Norris
Heaton Mersey
Reddish
South Reddish
Denton
Hyde
Godley
Hattersley
Gamesley
Woolley Bridge
Old Glossop
Glossop
Haughton Green
Woodley
Gee Cross
Broadbottom
Werneth Low
Simmondley
Charlestown
Charlesworth
Holehouse
Snake Pass 512
Snake Inn
R Alport
FEATHERBED TOP
HIGH PEAK
Romiley
Bredbury
Lower Bredbury
Etherow
Chisworth
Chunal
Abbot's Chair
Compstall
Mill Brow
STOCKPORT
Cheadle Heath
Cheadle
Offerton
Heaviley
Davenport
Marple Bridge
Rowarth
Brookhouses
Little Hayfield
THE PEAK 631
KINDER SCOUT
Adswood
Cheadle Hulme
Stepping Hill
Marple
Mellor
Aspenshaw
Thornsett
Hayfield
Hazel Grove
Hawk Green
Strines
Birch Vale
Pennine Way
Edale
Windlehurst
New Mills
132
Heald Green
Smithy Green
Bramhall
Disley
High Lane
Low Leighton
BROWN KNOLL
Barber Booth
Blue John Cavern
Hollinlane
Poynton
Higher Disley
Newtown
Mam Tor
Handforth
Hockley
Furness Vale
Chinley
Malcoff
Midway
Wardsend
Lyme Park
Whaley Bridge
Wash
Chestnut Centre
Speedwell Cavern
Woodford
Skellorn Green
Booth Green
Macclesfield Canal
Horwich End
Tunstead Milton
Chapel Milton
Sparrowpit
Dean Row
Adlington
SPONDS HILL
Taxal
Lower Crossings
Chapel-en-le-Frith
Old Dam
R Bollin
Kettleshulme
Cockyard
Mottram St Andrew
Whiteley Green
Pott Shrigley
Dove Holes
Peak Forest
Fernilee
Dunge Valley
Goyt Valley
Hough
Bollington
Combs
Hare Hill
Bollington Cross
HOB TOR
Smalldale
Peak Dale
Whesto
Watermill
Prestbury
Kerridge
Ginclough
Nether Alderley
Kerridge-end
Upper End
Tidesw
Rainow
Tytherington
Higher Hurdsfield
SHINING TOR 559
Hargatewal
Tunstead
Longmoss
Henbury
Hurdsfield
Fairfield
Wormhill
Heath
Broken Cross
Macclesfield
Cat and Fiddle 515
Burbage
Buxton
Wye Valley
King Sterndale
Blackwell
Tegg's Nose
Poole's Cavern
Staden
Solomon's Temple
Cowdale
Priestcliffe Ditch
Gurnett
Forest Chapel
Siddington
Warren
Langley
AXE EDGE 551
Harpur Hill
Windyharbour
Sutton Lane Ends
Trentabank
SHUTLINGSLOE 506
Chelmorto
Gawsworth
Oakgrove
Highlane
Wildboarclough
Flagg
Pomeroy
Marton
Rode Heath
North Rode
Earl Sterndale
Flash
Gamballs Green
R Dove
Allgreave
Hollinsclough
Monya
Wincle
Eaton
Bosley
PEAK DISTRICT NATIONAL PARK
Danebridge
Crowdecote
Longnor
Havannah
Key Green
Fawfieldhead
Pilsbury
Congleton
Buglawton
Woodhouse Green
THE CLOUD
Heaton
505 THE ROACHES
Timbersbrook
Rushton Spencer
GUN HILL 373
Hightown
Whitemoor
Brund
Sheen
Mossley
Newtown
Wiggenstall
Meerbrook
Upper Hulme
Poolfold
Biddulph Grange Garden
Rudyard Reservoir
Tittesworth Reservoir
Upper Elkstone
Hartington
Little Moreton Hall
Biddulph
Abbey Green
Hulme End
Gillow Heath
Mow Cop
Robin Hill
Biddulph Moor
Rudyard
Thorncliff
Warslow
Ecton
Lower Elkstone
R Hamps
The Bank
Mow Cop (folly)
Brindley Mill
Rock End
Lask Edge
Horton
Ball Haye Green
Leek
Mount Pleasant
Brown Lees
Harriseahead
Greenway
Butterton
Alstonefield
Onecote
Bradnop
Dunwood
Ladderedge
Newchapel
Blackwood Hill
Lowe Hill
Wetton
Hope
Grindon
Packmoor
Longsdon
Kidsgrove
Brown Edge
114
Endon Bank
Horsebridge
Flint Mill
Morridge Side
115
Ford
Stanshope

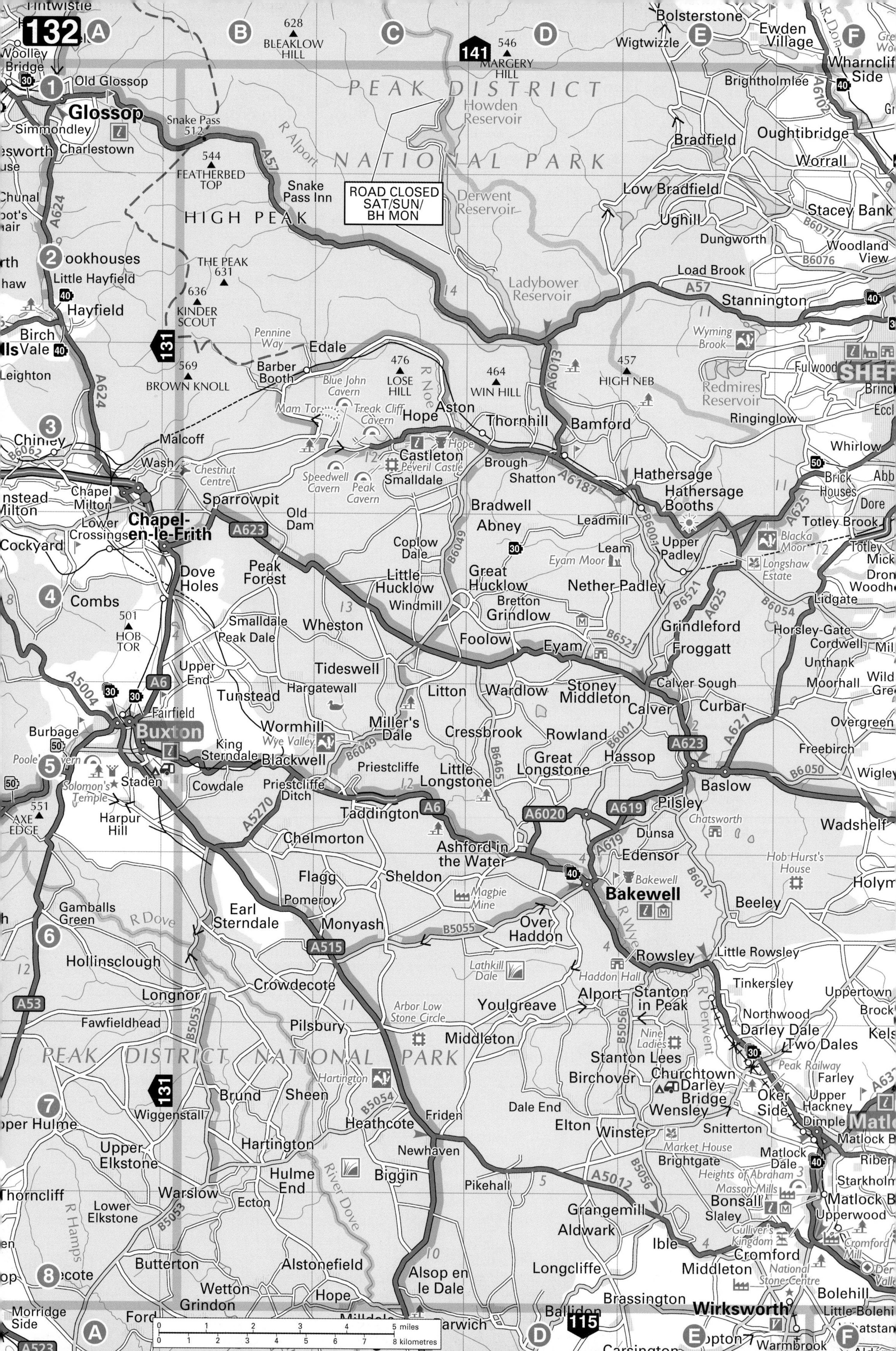

132
141
131
115
PEAK DISTRICT NATIONAL PARK
HIGH PEAK
ROAD CLOSED SAT/SUN/ BH MON
Glossop
Old Glossop
Simmondley
Charlestown
Snake Pass 512
FEATHERBED TOP
Snake Pass Inn
BLEAKLOW HILL
MARGERY HILL
Howden Reservoir
Derwent Reservoir
Ladybower Reservoir
KINDER SCOUT
THE PEAK
Hayfield
Little Hayfield
Birch Vale
Edale
Barber Booth
BROWN KNOLL
LOSE HILL
WIN HILL
HIGH NEB
Hope
Aston
Thornhill
Bamford
Castleton
Peveril Castle
Blue John Cavern
Treak Cliff Cavern
Speedwell Cavern
Peak Cavern
Mam Tor
Smalldale
Brough
Shatton
Hathersage
Hathersage Booths
Chapel-en-le-Frith
Chapel Milton
Chinley
Malcoff
Sparrowpit
Dove Holes
Combs
Peak Forest
Bradwell
Abney
Great Hucklow
Little Hucklow
Grindlow
Foolow
Eyam
Tideswell
Wheston
Litton
Wardlow
Stoney Middleton
Calver
Curbar
Froggatt
Grindleford
Buxton
Fairfield
Burbage
King Sterndale
Blackwell
Wormhill
Miller's Dale
Cressbrook
Great Longstone
Little Longstone
Hassop
Baslow
Pilsley
Chatsworth
Edensor
Bakewell
Ashford in the Water
Taddington
Chelmorton
Flagg
Sheldon
Monyash
Over Haddon
Earl Sterndale
Hollinsclough
Longnor
Crowdecote
Rowsley
Haddon Hall
Alport
Stanton in Peak
Youlgreave
Middleton
Pilsbury
Arbor Low Stone Circle
Stanton Lees
Birchover
Darley Dale
Two Dales
Matlock
Matlock Bath
Cromford
Wirksworth
Hartington
Sheen
Brund
Biggin
Hulme End
Warslow
Alstonefield
Alsop en le Dale
Wetton
Grindon
Butterton
Winster
Elton
Grangemill
Aldwark
Brassington
Longcliffe
Bradfield
Low Bradfield
Oughtibridge
Stannington
Bolsterstone
Ewden Village
Wharncliffe Side
Worrall
Stacey Bank
Dungworth
Ringinglow
Whirlow
Totley Brook
Longshaw Estate
Wyming Brook
Redmires Reservoir
Fulwood
Lidgate
Freebirch
Beeley
A57
A624
A623
A6
A515
A5004
A5270
A6187
A6013
A625
A621
A619
A6020
A53
A5012
B6049
B6001
B6465
B5055
B5053
B5056
B5054
B6050
B6054
B6521
B6012
B6062
B6077
B6076
0 1 2 3 4 5 miles
0 1 2 3 4 5 6 7 8 kilometres

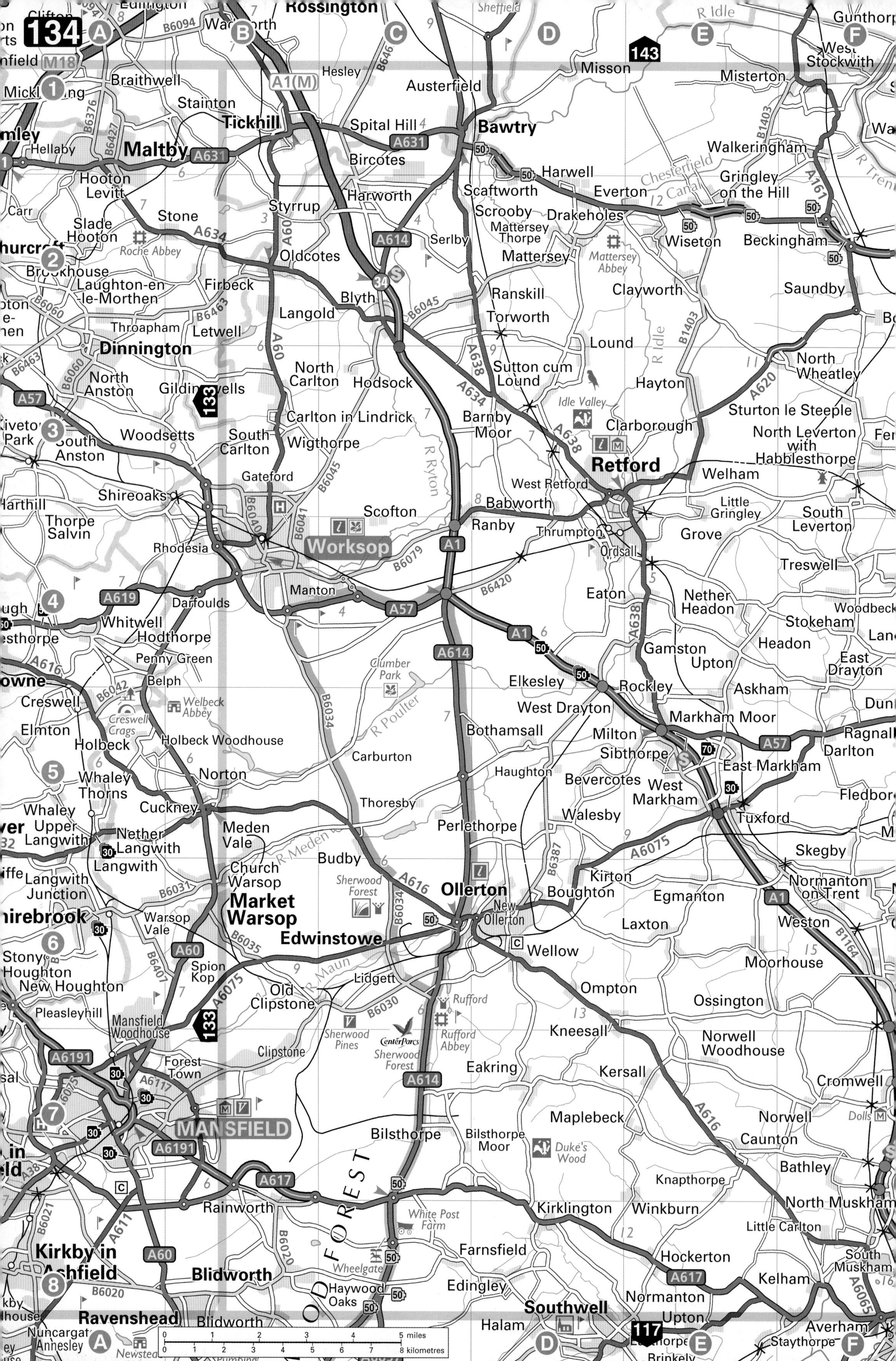

134
143
133
117
Rossington
Bawtry
Tickhill
Maltby
Misson
Misterton
West Stockwith
Austerfield
Spital Hill
Bircotes
Harworth
Styrrup
Oldcotes
Blyth
Langold
Serlby
Scaftworth
Scrooby
Mattersey Thorpe
Mattersey
Mattersey Abbey
Harwell
Everton
Drakeholes
Wiseton
Gringley on the Hill
Walkeringham
Beckingham
Saundby
Clayworth
Ranskill
Torworth
Lound
Sutton cum Lound
Hayton
North Wheatley
Sturton le Steeple
North Leverton with Habblesthorpe
Clarborough
Idle Valley
Retford
Welham
West Retford
Babworth
Ranby
Thrumpton
Ordsall
Little Gringley
Grove
South Leverton
Treswell
Eaton
Nether Headon
Stokeham
Headon
Gamston
Upton
East Drayton
Askham
Rockley
Elkesley
West Drayton
Markham Moor
Milton
Sibthorpe
East Markham
Darlton
Ragnall
Bothamsall
Haughton
Bevercotes
West Markham
Walesby
Tuxford
Fledborough
Perlethorpe
Kirton
Boughton
Egmanton
Skegby
Normanton on Trent
Laxton
Weston
Ollerton
New Ollerton
Wellow
Ompton
Moorhouse
Ossington
Kneesall
Norwell Woodhouse
Kersall
Cromwell
Norwell
Caunton
Maplebeck
Bathley
Eakring
Bilsthorpe
Bilsthorpe Moor
Duke's Wood
Knapthorpe
North Muskham
Kirklington
Winkburn
Little Carlton
Farnsfield
Hockerton
South Muskham
Kelham
Edingley
Normanton
Southwell
Upton
Averham
Staythorpe
Halam
Brinkely
Hesley
Braithwell
Stainton
Hellaby
Hooton Levitt
Stone
Slade Hooton
Roche Abbey
Brookhouse
Laughton-en-le-Morthen
Firbeck
Throapham
Letwell
Dinnington
North Anston
Gildingwells
North Carlton
Hodsock
Carlton in Lindrick
South Carlton
Wigthorpe
Woodsetts
South Anston
Gateford
Shireoaks
Thorpe Salvin
Rhodesia
Scofton
Worksop
Manton
Darfoulds
Whitwell
Hodthorpe
Penny Green
Belph
Welbeck Abbey
Clumber Park
Creswell
Creswell Crags
Elmton
Holbeck
Holbeck Woodhouse
Carburton
Whaley Thorns
Whaley
Norton
Cuckney
Thoresby
Upper Langwith
Nether Langwith
Langwith
Meden Vale
Church Warsop
Budby
Sherwood Forest
Langwith Junction
Shirebrook
Warsop Vale
Market Warsop
Edwinstowe
Spion Kop
Stony Houghton
New Houghton
Pleasleyhill
Old Clipstone
Lidgett
Rufford
Rufford Abbey
Sherwood Pines
Center Parcs Sherwood Forest
Mansfield Woodhouse
Clipstone
Forest Town
MANSFIELD
Rainworth
White Post Farm
Kirkby in Ashfield
Blidworth
Wheelgate
Haywood Oaks
Ravenshead
Annesley
Newstead
SHERWOOD FOREST
R Idle
R Ryton
R Poulter
R Meden
R Maun
Chesterfield Canal
A1(M)
A1
A57
A60
A614
A616
A619
A620
A631
A634
A638
A6075
A6191
A6117
A617
A611
A38
A161
A6065
B6094
B6376
B6427
B6060
B6463
B6045
B6040
B6041
B6079
B6420
B6042
B6034
B6031
B6035
B6407
B6030
B6020
B6021
B6387
B1403
B1164
M18
0 1 2 3 4 5 miles
0 1 2 3 4 5 6 7 8 kilometres

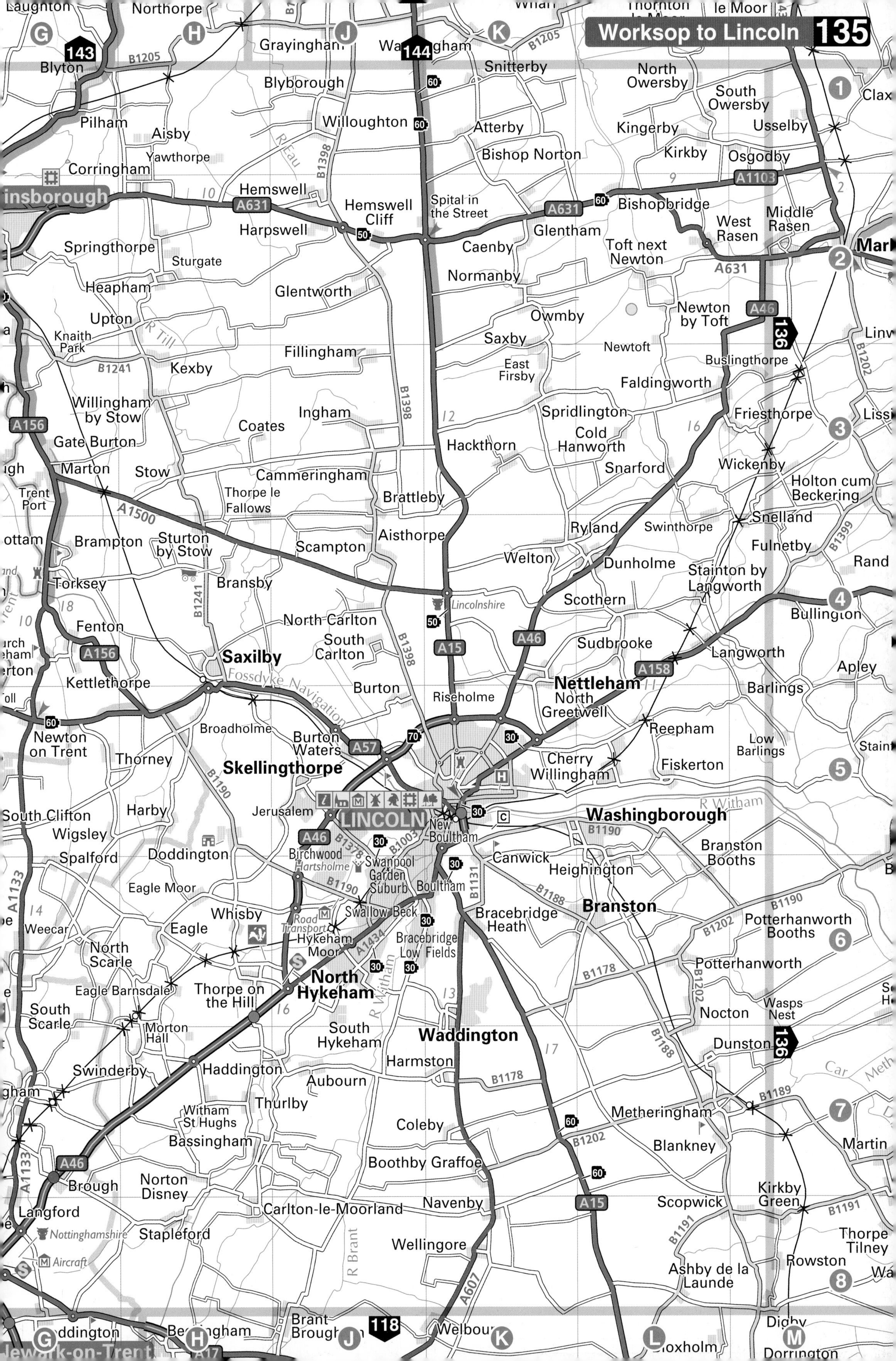
Worksop to Lincoln
135
143
144
136
118
Blyton
Northorpe
Grayingham
Snitterby
North Owersby
South Owersby
Blyborough
Willoughton
Atterby
Kingerby
Usselby
Pilham
Aisby
Yawthorpe
Corringham
Bishop Norton
Kirkby
Osgodby
Hemswell
Hemswell Cliff
Spital in the Street
Bishopbridge
West Rasen
Middle Rasen
Harpswell
Glentham
Toft next Newton
Springthorpe
Sturgate
Caenby
Normanby
Heapham
Glentworth
Upton
Owmby
Newton by Toft
Knaith Park
Saxby
Newtoft
Buslingthorpe
Kexby
Fillingham
East Firsby
Faldingworth
Willingham by Stow
Ingham
Spridlington
Friesthorpe
Coates
Cold Hanworth
Gate Burton
Hackthorn
Wickenby
Marton
Stow
Cammeringham
Snarford
Holton cum Beckering
Trent Port
Thorpe le Fallows
Brattleby
Snelland
Brampton
Sturton by Stow
Aisthorpe
Ryland
Swinthorpe
Scampton
Welton
Dunholme
Fulnetby
Rand
Stainton by Langworth
Torksey
Bransby
Scothern
Bullington
Fenton
North Carlton
South Carlton
Lincolnshire
Sudbrooke
Langworth
Saxilby
Fossdyke Navigation
Burton
Riseholme
Nettleham
Apley
Kettlethorpe
North Greetwell
Barlings
Newton on Trent
Broadholme
Burton Waters
Reepham
Low Barlings
Thorney
Skellingthorpe
Cherry Willingham
Fiskerton
LINCOLN
Jerusalem
Harby
South Clifton
Wigsley
New Boultham
R Witham
Washingborough
Branston Booths
Spalford
Doddington
Birchwood
Hartsholme
Swanpool Garden Suburb
Boultham
Canwick
Heighington
Eagle Moor
Swallow Beck
Bracebridge Heath
Branston
Weecar
Whisby
Eagle
Road Transport
Hykeham Moor
Bracebridge Low Fields
Potterhanworth Booths
North Scarle
Potterhanworth
Eagle Barnsdale
Thorpe on the Hill
North Hykeham
Nocton
Wasps Nest
South Scarle
Morton Hall
South Hykeham
Waddington
Dunston
Swinderby
Haddington
Harmston
Aubourn
Thurlby
Metheringham
Witham St Hughs
Coleby
Bassingham
Blankney
Martin
Boothby Graffoe
Brough
Norton Disney
Kirkby Green
Scopwick
Langford
Carlton-le-Moorland
Navenby
Nottinghamshire
Stapleford
Thorpe Tilney
Wellingore
Aircraft
R Brant
Rowston
Ashby de la Launde
Brant Broughton
Digby
Dorrington
A631
A1103
A46
A1500
A156
A15
A158
A57
B1241
B1398
B1205
B1202
B1399
B1190
B1188
B1178
B1131
B1003
B1378
B1189
B1191
A1434
A1133
A607
R Till
R Eau

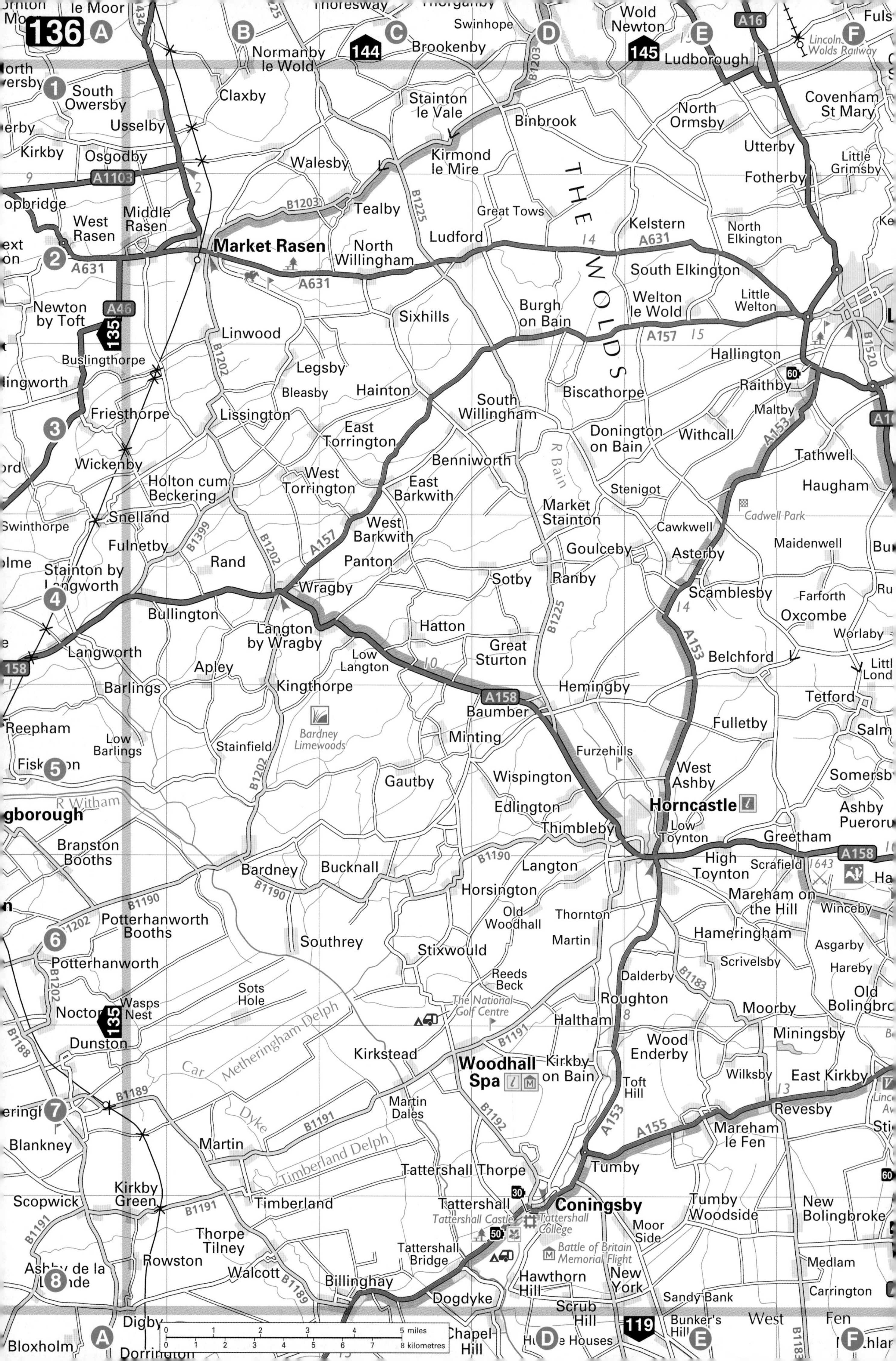
136
144
145
135
119
A
B
C
D
E
F
1
2
3
4
5
6
7
8
le Moor
Swinhope
Wold Newton
Brookenby
Normanby le Wold
Ludborough
Lincolnshire Wolds Railway
South Owersby
Claxby
Stainton le Vale
Binbrook
North Ormsby
Covenham St Mary
Usselby
Kirkby
Osgodby
Walesby
Kirmond le Mire
Utterby
Little Grimsby
Fotherby
A1103
Middle Rasen
West Rasen
B1203
Tealby
Great Tows
THE WOLDS
Kelstern
North Elkington
Market Rasen
North Willingham
Ludford
A631
South Elkington
Newton by Toft
A46
Linwood
Sixhills
Burgh on Bain
Welton le Wold
Little Welton
A157
Buslingthorpe
Legsby
Hallington
B1202
B1225
B1520
Bleasby
Hainton
South Willingham
Biscathorpe
Raithby
Friesthorpe
Lissington
East Torrington
Donington on Bain
Withcall
Maltby
A153
Wickenby
Benniworth
R Bain
Tathwell
Holton cum Beckering
West Torrington
East Barkwith
Stenigot
Haugham
Snelland
West Barkwith
Market Stainton
Cawkwell
Cadwell Park
Swinthorpe
Fulnetby
B1399
Rand
Panton
Goulceby
Asterby
Maidenwell
Stainton by Langworth
Wragby
Sotby
Ranby
Scamblesby
Farforth
Bullington
Langton by Wragby
Hatton
Oxcombe
Worlaby
Langworth
Low Langton
Great Sturton
Belchford
Apley
A158
Barlings
Kingthorpe
Hemingby
Tetford
Baumber
Reepham
Bardney Limewoods
Minting
Fulletby
Low Barlings
Stainfield
Furzehills
West Ashby
Fiskerton
Gautby
Wispington
Somersby
R Witham
Edlington
Horncastle
Ashby Puerorum
Thimbleby
Low Toynton
Greetham
Branston Booths
B1190
Langton
High Toynton
Scrafield
Bardney
Bucknall
Horsington
Mareham on the Hill
Winceby
Potterhanworth Booths
Old Woodhall
Thornton
Martin
Hameringham
Southrey
Asgarby
Potterhanworth
Stixwould
Scrivelsby
Hareby
Reeds Beck
Dalderby
B1183
Sots Hole
Roughton
Old Bolingbroke
Wasps Nest
Nocton
The National Golf Centre
Moorby
Metheringham Delph
Haltham
Miningsby
B1188
Dunston
B1191
Wood Enderby
Kirkstead
Woodhall Spa
Kirkby on Bain
Car Dyke
Wilksby
East Kirkby
Toft Hill
B1189
Martin Dales
Revesby
B1192
A155
Mareham le Fen
Blankney
Martin
Timberland Delph
Tattershall Thorpe
Tumby
Kirkby Green
Scopwick
Timberland
Tattershall
Coningsby
Tumby Woodside
New Bolingbroke
Tattershall Castle
Tattershall College
Moor Side
Thorpe Tilney
Battle of Britain Memorial Flight
Rowston
Tattershall Bridge
Medlam
Walcott
Hawthorn Hill
New York
Billinghay
Carrington
Dogdyke
Sandy Bank
Scrub Hill
Digby
Bunker's Hill
West Fen
Chapel Hill
Bloxholm
Dorrington
1643
60
30
50
5 miles
8 kilometres

145
Somercotes
Church End
Skidbrooke North End
Saltfleet
South Somercotes
Skidbrooke
Saltfleetby St Clement
North Cockerington
South Cockerington
North End
Saltfleetby All Saints
Saltfleetby St Peter
Theddlethorpe St Helen
B1200
A1031
Theddlethorpe All Saints
Manby
Little Carlton
Great Carlton
Legbourne
Great Eau
Mablethorpe
North Reston
Gayton le Marsh
A157
South Reston
Strubby
A1104
Trusthorpe
Thorpe
A52
Sutton on Sea
Withern
Maltby le Marsh
Sandilands
Tothill
Authorpe
B1373
Woodthorpe
Hagnaby
A1111
Beesby
Claythorpe
Hannah
Belleau
Saleby
Watermill & Wildfowl Gardens
Markby
Asserby Turn
Asserby
White Pit
Swaby
Aby
Thoresthorpe
South Thoresby
Ailby
Huttoft
Bilsby
Thurlby
Anderby Creek
Calceby
Haugh
Alford
B1449
Anderby
Rigsby
B1196
Farlesthorpe
Mumby
Authorpe Row
Driby
A1104
Well
Cumberworth
Chapel Point
Mawthorpe
Helsey
Ulceby
Bonthorpe
Hogsthorpe
Chapel St Leonards
Sutterby
Willoughby
A1028
Claxby
Slackholme End
Langton
Sloothby
Dalby
Skendleby
Hasthorpe
Fantasy Island
Habertoft
Addlethorpe
Sausthorpe
Grebby
Ingoldmells
Partney
Welton le Marsh
Ingoldmells Point
Scremby
R Lymn
Candlesby
Raithby
A16
Ashby by Partney
Gunby
Orby
Spilsby
Hundleby
Monksthorpe
Winthorpe
Halton Holegate
Burgh le Marsh
Great Steeping
Toynton All Saints
A158
Bratoft
Northcote
B1195
Halton Fenside
Skegness
East Keal
Irby in the Marsh
Toynton St Peter
Little Steeping
Firsby
Seacroft
Keal Cotes
Toynton Fen Side
Croft
Fendike Corner
Thorpe St Peter
Wainfleet Haven
Wainfleet Bank
Wainfleet All Saints
Gibraltar
New Leake
Wainfleet St Mary
A52
Gibraltar Point
Eastville
Friskney
East Fen
Friskney Eaudike
Lade Bank
119
120
G
H
J
K
L
M
1
2
3
4
5
6
7
8

138
BLACKPOOL
Shore
Hoohill
Highcross
Newt
Staining
147
Thistleton
Roseacre
Wharles
Medlar
Catforth
Model Village
Great Marton
Mythop
Weeton
M55
Corner Row
Moor Side
Swillbrook
South Shore
Little Plumpton
Great Plumpton
Wesham
Treales
Common Edge
A583
Kirkham
Dowbridge
Westby
Ribby
Peel
Lower Ballam
Wrea Green
Blackpool
Higher Ballam
Hall Cross
Newton with Scales
Clifton
Hey Houses
Moss Side
Bryning
St Anne's
Kellamergh
A584
Freckleton
Ansdell
Saltcotes
Warton
Royal Lytham & St Annes
Fairhaven
River Ribble
Lytham St Anne's
Lytham
RSPB Discovery Centre
Longton
Walmer Bridge
Hesketh Bank
West Lancashire Light Railway
Hundred End
Becconsall
Banks
Tarleton
Marshside
Crossens
A565
SOUTHPORT
New Pleasureland
P+R
Churchtown
Mere Brow
Sollom
A59
Leisure Lakes
Blowick
Holmeswood
Rufford
Windmill Animal Farm
Birkdale
Brown Edge
Snape Green
Tarlscough
The Royal Birkdale
Wildfowl & Wetlands Trust
Scarisbrick
Burscough Bridge
Shirdley Hill
Ainsdale-on-Sea
A570
Bescar
New Lane
Ainsdale
Pinfold
Heaton's Bridge
Woodvale
Hurlston Green
Halsall
Ring o'Bells
Ainsdale Sand Dunes
Primrose Hill
Burscough
Newburgh
Leeds & Liverpool Canal
Barton
Bangor's Green
Cabin Hill
Freshfield
Haskayne
Ormskirk
A577
Westhead
Formby
Downholland Cross
Scarth Hill
Formby Point
Little Altcar
Aughton Park
Blaguegate
Great Altcar
Town Green
Skelmersdale
Aughton
Stanley Gate
M58
North End
Holt Green
Bowker's Green
Hightown
Lydiate
Ince Blundell
Bickerstaffe
Homer Green
Maghull
Moss Side
Royal Oak
Dublin
Lunt
Kennessee Green
Barrow Nook
Little Crosby
Melling Mount
Thornton
Sefton
Douglas
(Mar-Oct)
Melling
Sefton Town
Waddicar
LIVERPOOL BAY
Blundellsands
KIRKBY
Brighton le Sands
CROSBY
Aintree
Belfast
Waterloo
Litherland
Seaforth
EURO RAIL TERMINAL
Orrell
A580
Fazakerley
(Nov-Mar)
Douglas
Croxteth
Knowsley
BOOTLE
M57
129
Green
0 1 2 3 4 5 miles
0 1 2 3 4 5 6 7 8 kilometres

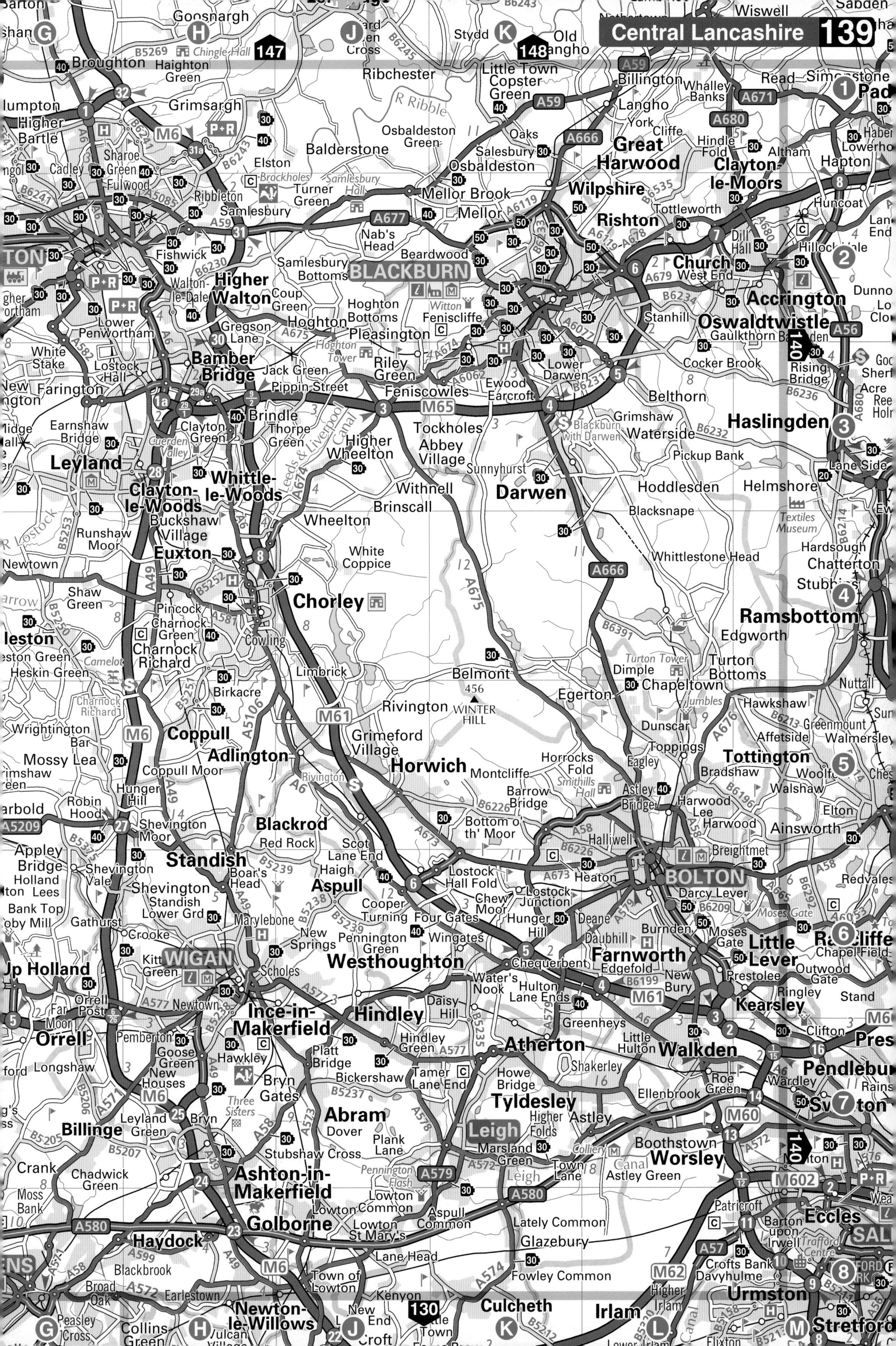
Goosnargh
Broughton
Haighton Green
Grimsargh
Ribchester
Stydd
Little Town
Copster Green
Billington
Whalley
Langho
Great Harwood
Clayton-le-Moors
Read
Simonstone
Altham
Hapton
Huncoat
Balderstone
Osbaldeston
Samlesbury
Mellor Brook
Mellor
Wilpshire
Rishton
Tottleworth
Fulwood
Ribbleton
Fishwick
Higher Walton
BLACKBURN
Church
Accrington
Oswaldtwistle
Beardwood
Lower Penworth
Gregson Lane
Hoghton
Pleasington
Feniscliffe
White Stake
Lostock Hall
Bamber Bridge
Riley Green
Lower Darwen
Farington
Jack Green
Pippin Street
Feniscowles
Ewood
Belthorn
Haslingden
Rising Bridge
Brindle
Clayton Green
Tockholes
Grimshaw
Waterside
Earnshaw Bridge
Leyland
Higher Wheelton
Abbey Village
Sunnyhurst
Pickup Bank
Whittle-le-Woods
Clayton-le-Woods
Withnell
Darwen
Hoddlesden
Helmshore
Brinscall
Blacksnape
Buckshaw Village
Wheelton
Runshaw Moor
Euxton
White Coppice
Whittlestone Head
Hardsough
Chatterton
Newtown
Shaw Green
Chorley
Pincock
Charnock Green
Charnock Richard
Ramsbottom
Edgworth
Cowling
Heskin Green
Limbrick
Belmont
Turton Tower
Dimple
Chapeltown
Turton Bottoms
Birkacre
Egerton
Nuttall
Rivington
WINTER HILL
Hawkshaw
Wrightington Bar
Coppull
Grimeford Village
Dunscar
Greenmount
Affetside
Walmersley
Mossy Lea
Adlington
Horwich
Tottington
Toppings
Eagley
Coppull Moor
Horrocks Fold
Montcliffe
Bradshaw
Walshaw
Hunger Hill
Robin Hood
Barrow Bridge
Astley Bridge
Harwood Lee
Harwood
Elton
Shevington Moor
Blackrod
Bottom o' th' Moor
Ainsworth
Red Rock
Halliwell
Breightmet
Appley Bridge
Shevington Vale
Standish
Scot Lane End
Haigh
Lostock Hall Fold
Heaton
BOLTON
Redvales
Shevington
Aspull
Lostock Junction
Darcy Lever
Standish Lower Grd
Cooper Turning
Four Gates
Chew Moor
Deane
Burnden
Moses Gate
Gathurst
Marylebone
New Springs
Pennington Green
Wingates
Hunger Hill
Daubhill
Little Lever
Radcliffe
Crooke
WIGAN
Westhoughton
Farnworth
Edgefold
Chapel Field
Kitt Green
Scholes
Chequerbent
Outwood Gate
Up Holland
Prestolee
Water's Nook
Hulton Lane Ends
New Bury
Ringley
Newtown
Ince-in-Makerfield
Hindley
Daisy Hill
Kearsley
Stand
Orrell
Orrell Post
Pemberton
Greenheys
Clifton
Hindley Green
Atherton
Little Hulton
Walkden
Goose Green
Platt Bridge
Tamer Lane End
Shakerley
Pendlebury
Longshaw
Hawkley
Bickershaw
Howe Bridge
Ellenbrook
Roe Green
New Houses
Bryn Gates
Tyldesley
Wardley
Abram
Higher Folds
Astley
Swinton
Billinge
Leyland Green
Bryn
Dover
Plank Lane
Leigh
Boothstown
Worsley
Marsland Green
Crank
Stubshaw Cross
Chadwick Green
Ashton-in-Makerfield
Town Lane
Astley Green
Moss Bank
Lowton
Lowton Common
Aspull Common
Patricroft
Eccles
Golborne
Haydock
Lowton St Mary's
Lately Common
Barton upon Irwell
Glazebury
Blackbrook
Lane Head
Crofts Bank
Davyhulme
Urmston
Town of Lowton
Fowley Common
Broad Oak
Earlestown
Kenyon
Higher Irlam
Culcheth
Irlam
Newton-le-Willows
Stretford
Peasley Cross
Collins Green
Flixton
Kirk
M6
M61
M65
M60
M62
M602
A59
A666
A677
A675
A6
A49
A580
A579
A58
A577
A572
A574
A56
A680
A671
A679
A5209
R Ribble
Leeds & Liverpool Canal
147
148
130
140

140
148
149
139
131
Wiswell
Sabden
Fence
Higham
Read
Simonstone
Padiham
Gawthorpe Hall
Whalley Banks
A671
A680
Hindle Fold
Altham
Clayton-le-Moors
Hapton
Habergham
Lowerhouse
Huncoat
Lane Ends
Hillock Vale
Dill Hall
West End
Accrington
Oswaldtwistle
Gaulkthorn
Baxenden
Cocker Brook
Rising Bridge
Haslingden
Dunnockshaw
Love Clough
Goodshaw
Goodshaw Fold
Goodshaw Chapel
Sherfin
Acre
Reeds Holme
Crawshawbooth
Water
Dean
Constable Lee
Rawtenstall
Lumb
Forest of Rossendale
Broad Clough
Edgeside
Bacup
Rockliffe
Britannia
Stacksteads
Lane Side
Helmshore
Textiles Museum
East Lancashire Railway
Ewood Bridge
Cowpe
Boarsgreave
Hardsough
Chatterton
Stubbins
Edenfield
Turn
Shuttleworth
Ramsbottom
Edgworth
Turton Bottoms
Nuttall
Summerseat
Hawkshaw
Greenmount
Affetside
Walmersley
Tottington
Woolfold
Walshaw
Harwood Lee
Harwood
Elton
Ainsworth
Breightmet
BOLTON
Darcy Lever
Moses Gate
Little Lever
Radcliffe
Chapel Field
Outwood Gate
Prestolee
Ringley
Stand
Kearsley
Clifton
Walkden
Pendlebury
Wardley
Roe Green
Swinton
Rainsough
Monton
Worsley
Patricroft
Eccles
Barton upon Irwell
Trafford Centre
Weaste
SALFORD
TRAFFORD PARK
Urmston
Davyhulme
Marsden Height
Brierfield
Catlow
Lane Bottom
Forest of Trawden
BOULSWORTH HILL
518
459
Haggate
Harle Syke
Thursden
Widdop
Wadsworth Moor
Stanbury
Marsh
Shaw
Oxenhope
BURNLEY
Rose Hill
Worsthorne
Hurstwood
Mereclough
Towneley Hall
Walk Mill
Holme Chapel
Heptonstall Moor
Colden
Slack
Blackshaw Head
Heptonstall
Mytholm
Charlestown
Hebden Bridge
Mytholmroyd
Pecket Well
Old Town
Chisley
Cornholme
Portsmouth
Lydgate
Sharneyford
Holden Gate
Clough Foot
Shade
Todmorden
Pennine Way
Stoodley Pike
Mankinholes
Lumbutts
Knowle Wood
Walsden
Trough Gate
Bottoms
Shawforth
Warland
Facit
Millgate
Whitworth
Calderbrook
Wardle
Shore
Caldermoor
Summit
Rishworth Moor
Rishworth
Ripponden
Soyland Town
Luddenden
Boulder Clough
Steep Lane
Catley Lane Head
Broadley
Syke
Healey
Dearnley
Smallbridge
Durn
Lydgate
Littleborough
Hollingworth Lake
Saddleworth Moor
381
463
Red Lumb
Wolstenholme
Norden
Shawclough
Cutgate
Smithy Bridge
Rakewood
ROCHDALE
Bamford
Firgrove
Milnrow
Moss Moor
Higher Ogden
Limefield
Chesham
BURY
Hooley Bridge
Sudden
Crimble
Lower Place
Newhey
Balderstone
Haugh
Close Moor
Heywood
Castleton
Burnedge
Crompton Fold
Denshaw
Slackcote
Hopwood
Slattocks
Summit
Tandle Hill
Shaw
Royton
Clough Grains
Bar
Delph
Harrop Dale
Diggle
Hollins
Birch
Top of Hebers
Heyside
Moorside
New Delph
Dobcross
Whitefield
Chadderton Fold
Langley
Long Sight
Thurston Clough
Besses o' th' Barn
Simister
Chadderton
Austerlands
Scouthead
Uppermill
Heaton Hall
MIDDLETON
Lees
OLDHAM
Grotton
Grasscroft
Greenfield
Prestwich
Blackley
Alt
Pitses
Sedgley Park
Crumpsall
Moston
Failsworth
Park Bridge
Mossley
Cheetham Hill
Harpurhey
Bardsley
Broughton
Newton Heath
Woodhouses
Daisy Nook
Luzley
Charlestown
Strangeways
Miles Platting
Ashton-under-Lyne
Hazelhurst
Heyrod
Carrbrook
Millbrook
MANCHESTER
Droylsden
Guide Br
Stalybridge
Copley
Ardwick
Audenshaw
Dukinfield
Roe Cross
Hollingworth
Hulme
Gorton
Mottram in Longdendale
Old Trafford
Rusholme
Godley
Gamesley
Denton
Hyde
Hattersley
M65
M66
M60
M602
M62
M67
A627(M)
A682
A646
A56
A58
A57
A6033
A671
A681
A680
A672
A640
A669
A62
A635
A6104
A664
A663

Cullingworth
Cottingley
Moorhead
Shipley
Wilsden
149
Frizinghall
Greengates
Eccleshill
150
Bagley
Rodley
Moorside
Bramley
Kirkstall
Woodhouse
LEEDS
Sandy Lane
Heaton
Manningham
Woodhall Hill
Undercliffe
Farsley
Stanningley
Hare Croft
Lingbob
Denholme
Wells Head
Girlington
Allerton
Thornton
Thornbury
Laisterdyke
Fartown
Hough End
Armley
Sheepscar
Osmondthorpe
Keelham
Clough
Great Horton
School Green
Tyersal
Pudsey
Farnley
Wortley
Clayton
BRADFORD
Little Horton
Bowling
Dudley Hill
Yews Green
West Bowling
Tong
New Farnley
Upper Moor Side
Beeston
Hunslet
Cross Green
Stourton
Ogden
Mountain
Westgate Hill
Cockersdale
Gildersome
Churwell
Bradshaw
Ambler Thorn
Queensbury
Wibsey
Buttershaw
Odsal
East Bierley
Drighlington
Moor Head
White Rose
Middleton Railway
Middleton
Rothwell
Holdsworth
Illingworth
Holmfield
Shibden Head
Shelf
Low Moor
Oakenshaw
Birkenshaw
Adwalton
Daisy Hill
Robin Hood
Catherine Slack
Stone Chair
Norwood Green
Swincliffe
Morley
Thorpe on the Hill
Carlton
Ovenden
Northowram
Booth Town
Hunsworth
Wyke
Oakwell Hall
Bruntcliffe
Birks
Ouzlewell Green
Wheatley
Priestley Green
Lower Wyke
Scholes
Spen
Gomersal
Ardsley East
Lofthouse
HALIFAX
Shibden Hall
Birstall
Upper Batley
Tingley
Hipperholme
Bank Top
Hove Edge
Bailiff Bridge
Hartshead Moor
Cleckheaton
Heckmondwike
Woodkirk
Carr Gate
Lower Soothill
Beggarington Hill
Thornhills
Liversedge
Norristhorpe
Hanging Heaton
Chidswell
Newton Hill
Southowram
Clifton
Roberttown
Batley
Kirkhamgate
Wrenthorpe
Norland Town
Copley
Brighouse
Rastrick
Hartshead
Crossley
Dewsbury
Gawthorpe
Greetland
Elland
Lower Edge
Bradley
Dewsbury Moor
Earlsheaton
Alverthorpe
Flanshaw
Elland
Mirfield
Ravensthorpe
Northorpe
Savile Town
Ossett
Flushdyke
Holywell Green
Broad Carr
Netheroyd Hill
Sheepridge
Colne Bridge
Thornhill Lees
Healey
Hall Cliffe
Lupset
Stainland
Clough Head
Birchencliffe
Fartown
Upper Heaton
Upper Hopton
Thornhill
South Ossett
Horbury
Thornes
Sowood
Outlane
Lindley
HUDDERSFIELD
Kirkheaton
Whitley Lower
Coxley
Calder Grove
Mount
Edgerton
Hill Side
Middlestown
Durkar
Crigglestone
Scapegoat Hill
Moldgreen
National Coal Mining Museum
Houses Hill
Grange Moor
Overton
Netherton
Great Cliffe
Pole Moor
Golcar
Greenside
Cowmes
Fenay Bridge
Flockton Green
Bolster Moor
Lower Houses
Almondbury
Lepton
Newmillerdam
Linthwaite
Crosland Hill
Berry Brow
Newsome
Rowley Hill
High Green
Flockton
Midgley
West Bretton
Emley Moor
Woolley Edge
Netherton
Armitage Bridge
Dogley Lane
Highburton
Emley
Notton
Blackmoorfoot
Woolley
Hill Top
South Crosland
Roydhouse
Yorkshire Sculpture Park
Helme
Crosland Edge
Honley
Farnley Tyas
Kirkburton
Kirklees Light Railway
Staincross
Marsden
Meltham Mills
Shelley
Skelmanthorpe
Clayton West
High Hoyland
Darton
Meltham
Brockholes
Thurstonland
Shelley Far Bank
Lower Cumberworth
Scissett
Kexbrough
Mapplewell
Wilshaw
Fulstone
Shepley
Cannon Hall Open Farm
Cawthorne
Barugh
Smithies
Netherthong
New Mill
Upperthong
Wooldale
Upper Cumberworth
Denby Dale
Barugh Green
Gawber
Holmfirth
Scholes
Birds Edge
Lower Denby
Higham
Austonley
Jackson Bridge
High Flats
Upper Denby
Tivy Dale
Holmbridge
Hepworth
Silkstone
Holme
Longley
Noblethorpe
Dodworth
Victoria
Ingbirchworth
Hoyland Swaine
Dodworth Green
Dodworth Bottom
582 BLACK HILL
525
Holme Moss
Hade Edge
Crow Edge
Thurlstone
Silkstone Common
Winscar Reservoir
Carlecotes
Millhouse Green
Spring Vale
Four Lane End
Stainborough
Worsbrough Bridge
Townhead
Penistone
Hood Green
Wentworth Castle
Pennine Way
Dunford Bridge
Oxspring
Crane Moor
Cubley
Thurgoland
Hermit Hill
Birdwell
Langsett
Snowden Hill
Dean Head
Pilley
Crowden
450
Woodhead
Upper Midhope
Finkle Street
Wortley
Green Moor
Midhopestones
Garden Village
Howbrook
Bromley
High Green
PEAK DISTRICT NATIONAL PARK
Howden Moors
Stocksbridge
Deepcar
Chapeltown
Bolsterstone
628 BLEAKLOW HILL
Ewden Village
Greno Woods
546 MARGERY HILL
Wigtwizzle
Wharncliffe Side
Burncross
132
Glossop
Brightholmlee
Whitley
Howden Reservoir
Grenoside
R. Don
R. Calder
A629
A644
A647
A641
A58
A6036
A643
A62
A638
A653
A650
A6025
A6026
B6113
A640
A642
A636
A637
A635
A616
A628
A6024
A629
A61
A6102
B6105
B6106
B6107
B6108
B6116
B6118
B6117
B6128
B6449
B6462
B6124
B6123
B6154
B6144
B6145
B6141
B6269
B6481
B6428
M606
M621
M62
M1
142
G
H
J
K
L
M
1
2
3
4
5
6
7
8

A
B
C
D
E
F
150
151
141
133
Barwick in Elmet
Scholes
Seacroft
Saxton
Scarthingwell
Cawood
Church Fenton
Barkston Ash
Wistow
Lotherton Hall
Manston
Cross Gates
Austhorpe
Sheepscar
Halton
Osmondthorpe
Whitkirk
Colton
Hollingthorpe
Temple Newsam
Swillington
Cross Green
Hunslet
Stourton
Garforth
East Garforth
Micklefield
Newthorpe
Sherburn in Elmet
Little Fenton
Biggin
South Milford
Thorpe Willoughby
Brayton
Hambleton
Monk Fryston
Steeton Hall Gatehouse
Lumby
Kippax
Little Preston
Great Preston
Ledston Luck
Ledsham
Ledston
Woodlesford
Rothwell
Oulton
Bower's Row
Allerton Bywater
Fairburn
Hillam
Gateforth
Burton Salmon
Birkin
Chapel Haddlesey
Selby Canal
Carlton
Ouzlewell Green
Wood Row
Methley
Mickletown
New Fryston
Water Fryston
Wheldale
Castleford
Brotherton
West Haddlesey
Beal
Kellington
Lofthouse
Lofthouse Gate
Methley Junction
Diggerland
Glass Houghton
Cutsyke
Xscape
Whitwood
Ferrybridge
Sutton
Knottingley
Hut Green
Wakefield Europort
Outwood
Newton Hill
Stanley Ferry
Stanley
Altofts
Hopetown
Normanton
Eggborough
Wrenthorpe
WAKEFIELD
Woodhouse
Ackton
Featherstone
Pontefract
High Eggborough
Whitley
Cridling Stubbs
Kirkthorpe
Warmfield
New Sharlston
Heath
Carleton
Darrington
Purston Jaglin
Sharlston Common
Sharlston
Nostell Priory
High Ackworth
East Hardwick
Womersley
Belle Vue
Thornes
Sandal Magna
Crofton
Foulby
Hessle
Low Ackworth
Little Smeaton
Walden Stubbs
Balne
Milnthorpe
Durkar
Crigglestone
Walton
New Crofton
Braken Hill
Wragby
Ackworth Moor Top
Wentbridge
Kirk Smeaton
Norton
Pledwick
Overtown
Hill Top
Wintersett
Fitzwilliam
Thorpe Audlin
Newmillerdam
Ryhill
Kinsley
Badsworth
Upton
Wrangbrook
Barnsdale Bar
Campsall
Askern
Notton
Cold Hiendley
Havercroft
South Hiendley
Hemsworth
North Elmsall
Skelbrooke
Sutton
Haywood
Applehaigh
Felkirk
Royston
Shafton
Brierley
South Elmsall
Moorthorpe
Burghwallis
Trumfleet
Staincross
Owston
Carlton
Shafton Two Gates
South Kirkby
Moorhouse
Hampole
Skellow
Thorpe in Balne
Mapplewell
Blacker
Sid Cop
Upper Cudworth
Grimethorpe
Carcroft
New Lodge
Monk Bretton
Cudworth
Adwick Le Street
Hooton Pagnell
Shaftholme
Almholme
Barugh
Smithies
Clayton
Woodlands
Toll Bar
BARNSLEY
Monk Bretton Priory
Great Houghton
Brodsworth
Hall & Gardens
Pickburn
Highfields
Scawthorpe
Arksey
Hoyle Mill
Stairfoot
Little Houghton
Thurnscoe
Hickleton
Bentley
Dodworth
Dodworth Bottom
Ardsley
Middlecliffe
Billingley
Marr
Scawsby
Wheatley Hills
Darfield
Millhouses
DONCASTER
Worsbrough Dale
Low Valley
Broom Hill
Bolton Upon Dearne
Goldthorpe
Barnburgh
Worsbrough Bridge
Wombwell
High Melton
Hexthorpe
Wentworth Castle
Worsbrough
Harlington
Blacker Hill
Hemingfield
West Melton
Adwick upon Dearne
Sprotbrough
Doncaster Carr
Birdwell
Jump
Brampton
DONCASTER RAILPORT
Hoyland Common
Hoyland Nether
Wath upon Dearne
Mexborough
Warmsworth
Cadeby
Pilley
Wortley
Tankersley
Elsecar
Elsecar Workshops
Balby
Upper Tankersley
Denaby
Denaby Main
Castle
Bromley
Harley
Wentworth
Swinton
New Edlington
High Green
Hood Hill
Upper Haugh
Conisbrough
Loversall
Chapeltown
Barley Hole
Nether Haugh
Kilnhurst
Old Edlington
Thorpe Hesley
Rawmarsh
Thrybergh
Clifton
Wadworth
Burn Cross
Scholes
Sandhill
Hooton Roberts
Whitley
Greasbrough
Ravenfield
Thorpe
Braithwell
Grenoside
Ecclesfield
Micklebring
Dalton Parva
Stainton
R Aire
R Went
R Dearne
R Don
Ferrybridge
M1
M62
M18
M621
A1(M)
A1
A63
A64
A19
A61
A58
A6120
A642
A639
A645
A628
A638
A655
A6021
A635
A633
A6195
A6023
A6022
A630
A60
A6182
A616
B1217
B1222
B6137
B6134
B6136
B6378
B6428
B6132
B6273
B6474
B6422
B6411
B6096
B6098
B6097
B6089
B6090
B6094
B6376
B1220
A1246
A656
RSPB
0 1 2 3 4 5 miles
0 1 2 3 4 5 6 7 8 kilometres

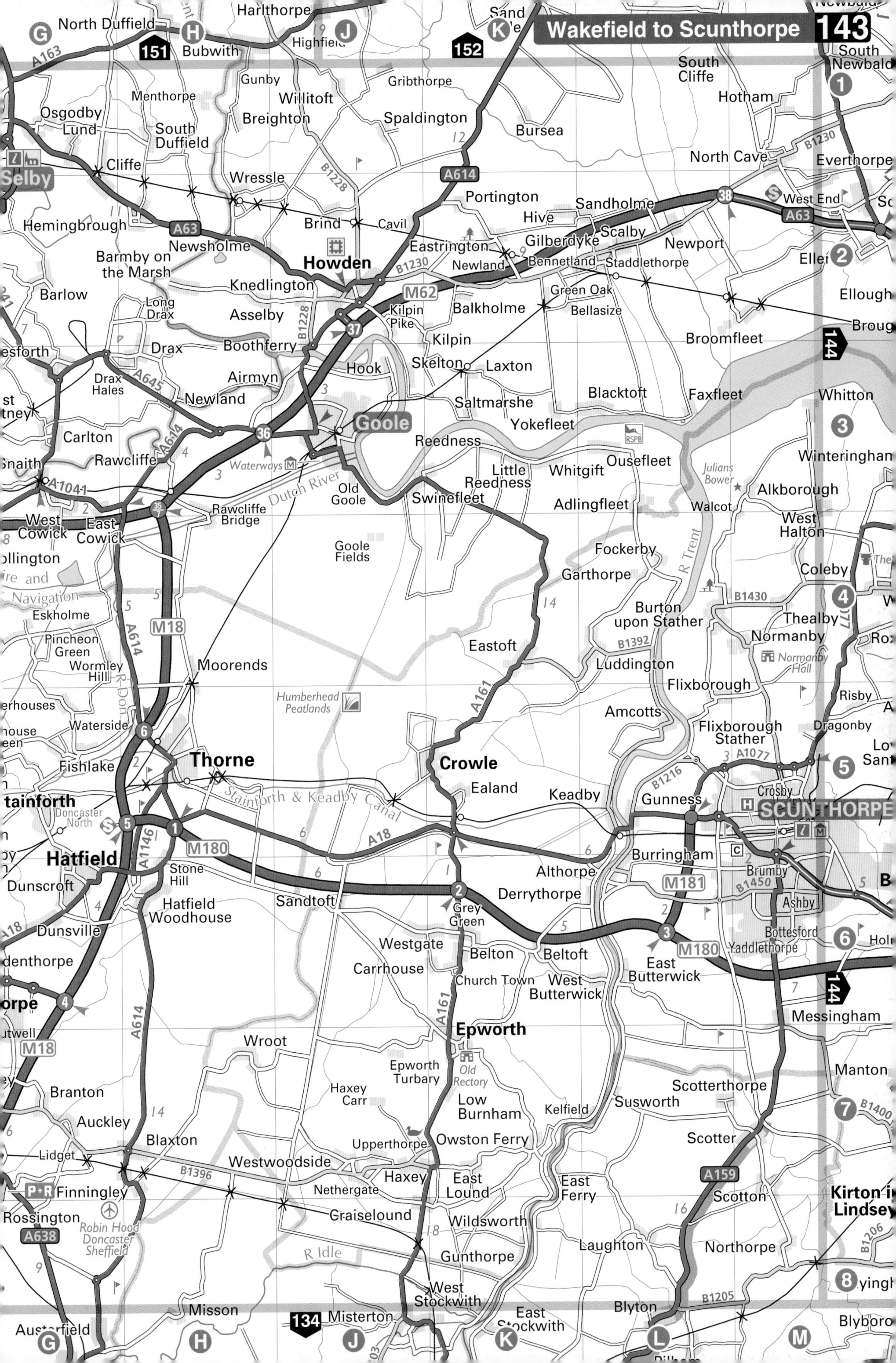
North Duffield
Bubwith
Harlthorpe
Highfield
Gunby
Willitoft
Gribthorpe
Spaldington
Bursea
South Cliffe
Hotham
South Newbald
Everthorpe
North Cave
Menthorpe
Osgodby
Lund
South Duffield
Breighton
Cliffe
Selby
Wressle
Hemingbrough
Brind
Cavil
Portington
Hive
Sandholme
Gilberdyke
Scalby
Newport
West End
Newsholme
Barmby on the Marsh
Howden
Eastrington
Newland
Bennetland
Staddlethorpe
Ellerker
Elloughton
Barlow
Knedlington
Green Oak
Bellasize
Long Drax
Asselby
Kilpin Pike
Balkholme
Kilpin
Broomfleet
Drax
Boothferry
Hook
Skelton
Laxton
Drax Hales
Airmyn
Newland
Saltmarshe
Blacktoft
Faxfleet
Whitton
Goole
Yokefleet
Carlton
Reedness
Rawcliffe
Waterways
Dutch River
Little Reedness
Whitgift
Ousefleet
Julians Bower
Winteringham
Old Goole
Swinefleet
Adlingfleet
Alkborough
Walcot
Rawcliffe Bridge
West Cowick
East Cowick
West Halton
Goole Fields
Fockerby
Garthorpe
Coleby
R Trent
Navigation
Eskholme
Burton upon Stather
Thealby
Normanby
Normanby Hall
Pincheon Green
Wormley Hill
Moorends
Eastoft
Luddington
Flixborough
Risby
Humberhead Peatlands
Amcotts
Waterside
Flixborough Stather
Dragonby
Fishlake
Thorne
Crowle
Stainforth & Keadby Canal
Ealand
Keadby
Gunness
Crosby
SCUNTHORPE
Stainforth
Doncaster North
Hatfield
Stone Hill
Burringham
Althorpe
Brumby
Dunscroft
Sandtoft
Derrythorpe
Grey Green
Ashby
Hatfield Woodhouse
Dunsville
Bottesford
Yaddlethorpe
Westgate
Belton
Beltoft
East Butterwick
Carrhouse
Church Town
West Butterwick
Messingham
Epworth
Wroot
Epworth Turbary
Old Rectory
Manton
Branton
Haxey Carr
Low Burnham
Kelfield
Susworth
Scotterthorpe
Auckley
Upperthorpe
Owston Ferry
Scotter
Blaxton
Lidget
Westwoodside
Haxey
East Lound
East Ferry
Finningley
Nethergate
Scotton
Rossington
Graiselound
Wildsworth
Robin Hood Doncaster Sheffield
Laughton
Northorpe
Kirton in Lindsey
R Idle
Gunthorpe
West Stockwith
Misson
Blyton
Austerfield
Misterton
East Stockwith
Blyborough
A163
A63
A614
B1228
B1230
M62
A645
A1041
A18
A614
M18
A161
B1392
B1430
A1077
B1216
M180
A1146
M181
B1450
B1396
A159
A638
B1400
B1206
B1205
RSPB
151
152
144
134

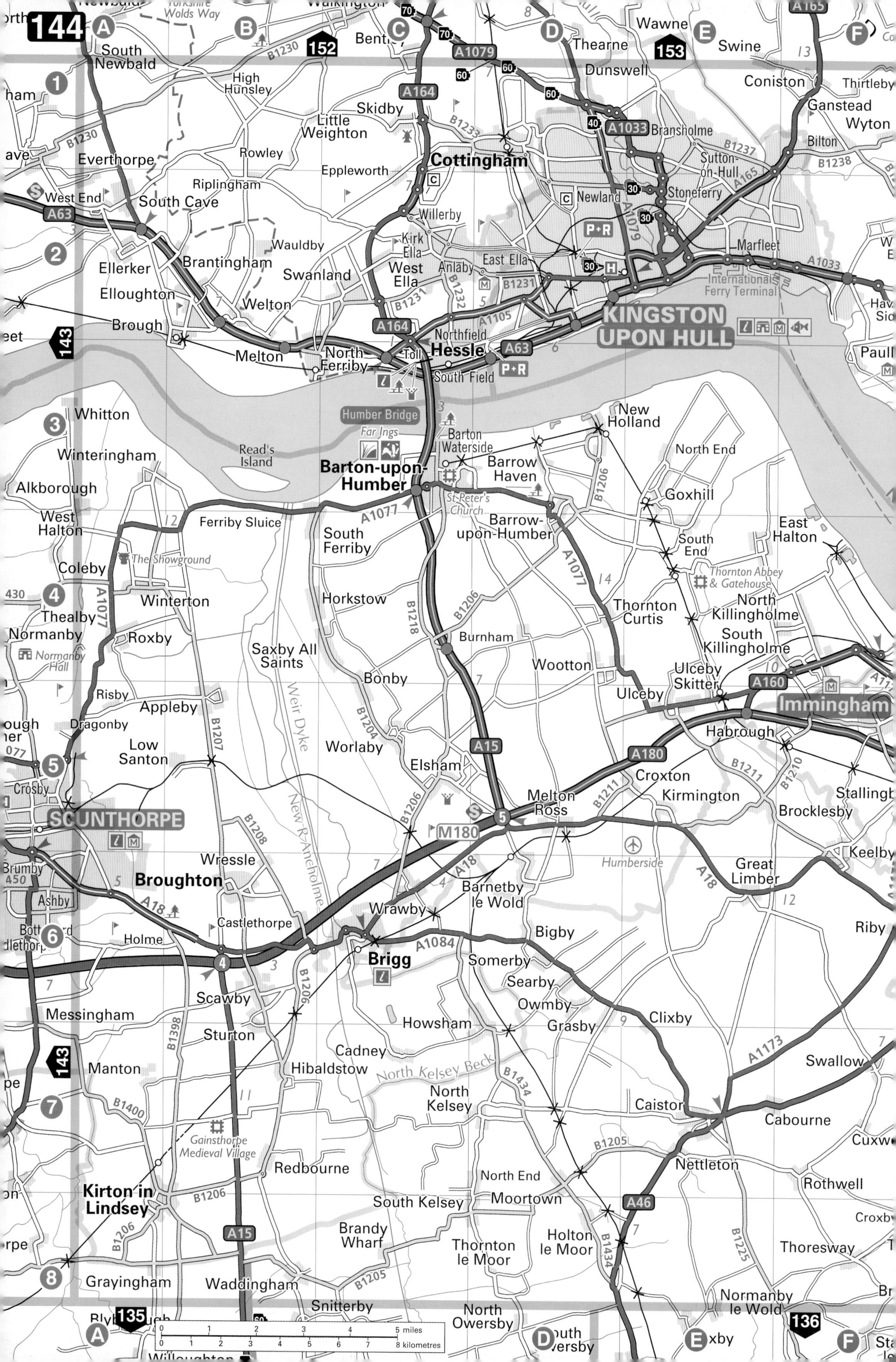

144
152
153
143
135
136
A
B
C
D
E
F
1
2
3
4
5
6
7
8
Yorkshire Wolds Way
South Newbald
High Hunsley
Bentley
Walkington
Thearne
Wawne
Swine
Dunswell
Coniston
Thirtleby
Ganstead
Wyton
Bilton
Skidby
Little Weighton
Rowley
Everthorpe
Eppleworth
Cottingham
Riplingham
West End
South Cave
Willerby
Newland
Bransholme
Sutton-on-Hull
Stoneferry
Wauldby
Kirk Ella
West Ella
Anlaby
East Ella
Marfleet
Ellerker
Brantingham
Swanland
Elloughton
Welton
Brough
Melton
North Ferriby
Hessle
Northfield
Toll
South Field
KINGSTON UPON HULL
International Ferry Terminal
Paull
Humber Bridge
Far Ings
Whitton
Winteringham
Read's Island
Barton Waterside
Barton-upon-Humber
Barrow Haven
New Holland
North End
Goxhill
Alkborough
West Halton
Ferriby Sluice
South Ferriby
St Peter's Church
Barrow-upon-Humber
South End
East Halton
The Showground
Coleby
Winterton
Thealby
Normanby
Normanby Hall
Roxby
Horkstow
Thornton Abbey & Gatehouse
Thornton Curtis
North Killingholme
South Killingholme
Saxby All Saints
Burnham
Wootton
Bonby
Ulceby Skitter
Ulceby
Immingham
Risby
Appleby
Dragonby
Weir Dyke
Habrough
Low Santon
Worlaby
Elsham
Croxton
Kirmington
Stallingborough
Crosby
SCUNTHORPE
Melton Ross
Brocklesby
New R. Ancholme
Humberside
Keelby
Brumby
Wressle
Broughton
Barnetby le Wold
Great Limber
Ashby
Wrawby
Castlethorpe
Holme
Bottesford
Brigg
Bigby
Riby
Somerby
Searby
Scawby
Owmby
Messingham
Grasby
Clixby
Howsham
Sturton
Cadney
Swallow
Manton
Hibaldstow
North Kelsey Beck
North Kelsey
Caistor
Cabourne
Gainsthorpe Medieval Village
Cuxwold
Nettleton
Redbourne
North End
Rothwell
Kirton in Lindsey
Moortown
South Kelsey
Croxby
Brandy Wharf
Holton le Moor
Thornton le Moor
Thoresway
Grayingham
Waddingham
Snitterby
Normanby le Wold
North Owersby
South Owersby
Blyborough
Usselby
Stainton le Vale
Willoughton
A63
A164
A1079
A1033
A1105
B1230
B1231
B1232
B1233
B1237
B1238
A165
A15
A1077
A160
A180
A18
M180
A1084
A1173
A46
B1206
B1207
B1208
B1218
B1204
B1211
B1210
B1398
B1400
B1434
B1205
B1225
P+R
5 miles
8 kilometres

Newton
Garton
Grimston
Fitling
Humbleton
Hilston
Owstwick
Tunstall
Elstronwick
Danthorpe
North End
Burton Pidsea
Roos
Waxholme
Rimswell
Owthorne
Burstwick
West End
Withernsea
East End
Thorngumbald
Halsham
Keyingham
Hollym
Ryehill
Ottringham
Winestead
Holmpton
Patrington
Out Newton
Patrington Haven
Welwick
Weeton
Easington
Sunk Island
Skeffling
South End
Spurn Heritage Coast
Kilnsea
HUMBER
SPURN HEAD
GRIMSBY
West Marsh
Cleethorpes
Great Coates
Little Coates
Old Clee
Thrunscoe
The Jungle
Pleasure Island
Rotterdam (Europoort)
Zeebrugge
Nunsthorpe
Bradley
Laceby
Scartho
Humberston
New Waltham
Waltham
Waltham Windmill
Holton le Clay
Barnoldby le Beck
Tetney Lock
Brigsley
North End
Beelsby
Ashby cum Fenby
Hatcliffe
Tetney
North Cotes
Waithe
West Ravendale
Grainsby
Marshchapel
East Ravendale
North Thoresby
Eskham
Donna Nook
Churchthorpe
West End
Grainthorpe
North Somercotes
Fulstow
Wold Newton
Conisholme
Lincolnshire Wolds Railway
Canal
Ludborough
Covenham St Bartholomew
Church End
Skidbrooke North End
South Somercotes
A180
A1033
A46
A16
A1098
A1031
A18
B1362
B1242
B1445
B1219
B1203
B1201
153
136

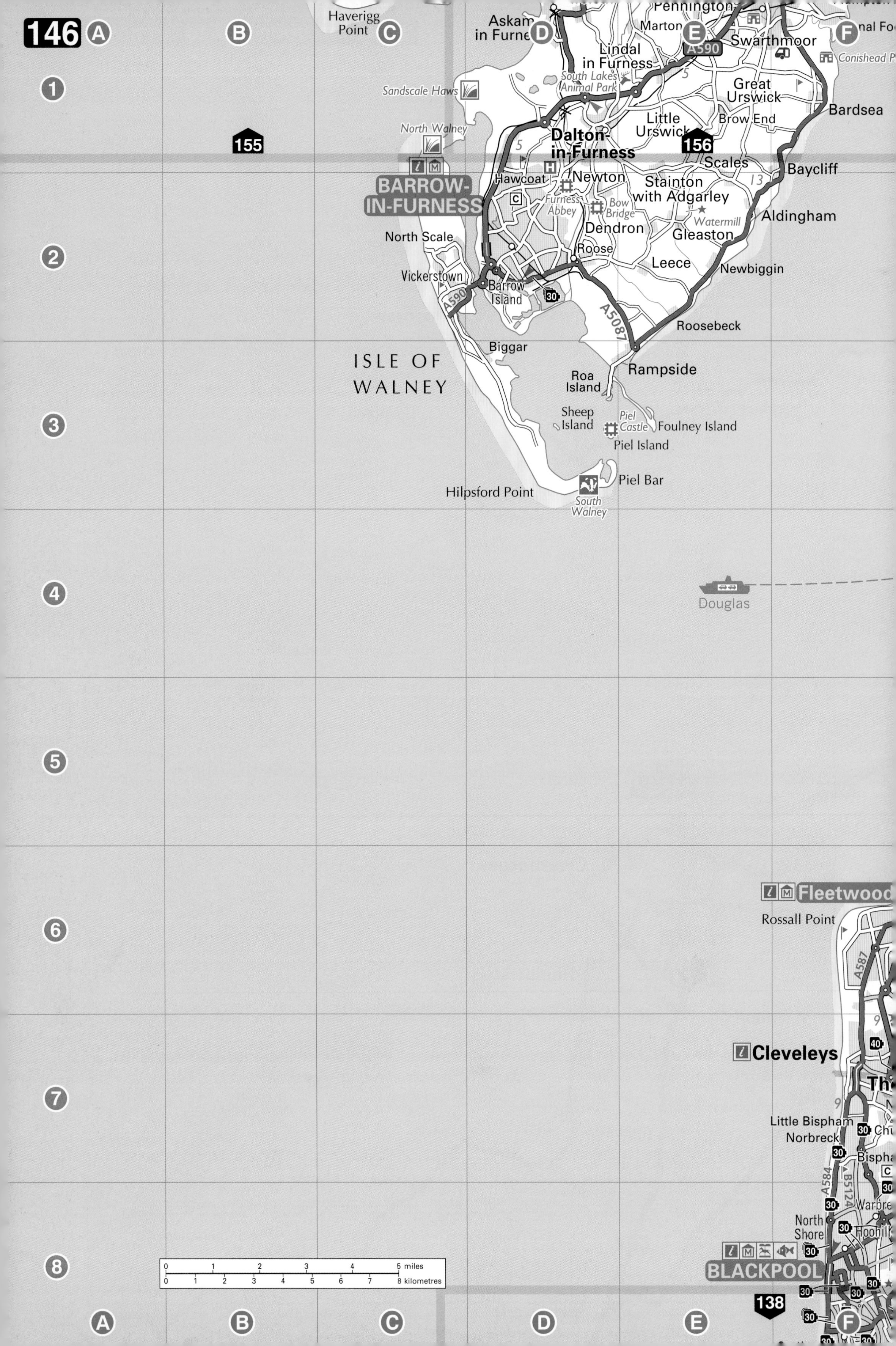
A
B
C
D
E
F
1
2
3
4
5
6
7
8
Haverigg Point
Askam in Furne
Pennington
Marton
Swarthmoor
Conishead P
Lindal in Furness
A590
South Lakes Animal Park
Sandscale Haws
Great Urswick
Bardsea
North Walney
155
Dalton-in-Furness
Little Urswick
Brow End
156
Scales
Baycliff
Hawcoat
Newton
Stainton with Adgarley
BARROW-IN-FURNESS
Furness Abbey
Bow Bridge
Watermill
Aldingham
North Scale
Dendron
Gleaston
Roose
Leece
Newbiggin
Vickerstown
Barrow Island
A5087
Roosebeck
Biggar
ISLE OF WALNEY
Rampside
Roa Island
Sheep Island
Piel Castle
Foulney Island
Piel Island
Piel Bar
Hilpsford Point
South Walney
Douglas
Fleetwood
Rossall Point
A587
Cleveleys
Little Bispham
Norbreck
A584
B5124
North Shore
BLACKPOOL
138
0 1 2 3 4 5 miles
0 1 2 3 4 5 6 7 8 kilometres

MORECAMBE BAY
Grange-over-Sands
Allithwaite
Kents Bank
Humphrey Head
Arnside Knott
Silverdale
Jack Scout
Yealand Storrs
Yealand Redmayne
Leighton Hall
Crag Foot
Yealand Conyers
Heald Brow
Warton
Old Rectory
Millhead
Carnforth
Bolton le Sands
Hest Bank
Morecambe
Bare
Torrisholme
Skerton
Sandylands
Lower Heysham
Heysham
Higher Heysham
Lancaster
Aldcliffe
Heaton
Scotforth
Middleton
Stodday
Overton
Sunderland
Glasson
Conder Green
River Lune
Cockersand
Galgate
Ellel
Smith Green
Bailrigg
Hampson Green
Bay Horse
Potters Brook
Forton
Cockerham
Pilling Lane
Pilling
Preesall
Fisher's Row
Cockerham Moss
Winmarleigh
Cabus
Garstang
Nateby
Bowgreave
Churchtown
Catterall
Bonds
Burton-in-Kendal
Dalton
Whittington
Newton
Docker
Priest Hutton
Borwick
Capernwray
Arkholme
Gressingham
Over Kellet
Nether Kellet
Bolton Town End
Slyne
Aughton
Claughton
Halton
Halton Green
Caton
River Lune Millennium Park
Caton Green
Brookhouse
Crossgill
Quernmore
Hornby
Wray
Farleton
Tatham
Wennington
Melling
Wrayton
Tunstall
Cantsfield
Burrow
Lower Salter
Middle Salter
High Salter
Ward's Stone
Ortner
Abbeystead
Dolphinholme
Street
Hollins Lane
Hawthornthwaite Fell
Forest of Bowland
Scorton
Calder Fell
Oakenclough
Calder Vale
Bleasdale
Fairsnape Fell
Parlick
Totridge Fell
Chipping
Beacon Fell
Claughton
White Chapel
Inglewhite
Hesketh Lane
Longridge
Knowle Green
Goosnargh
Bilsborrow
Brock
Barton
Newsham
Broughton
Chingle Hall
Haighton Green
Ribchester
Ward Green Cross
Myerscough
St Michael's on Wyre
Great Eccleston
Little Singleton
Singleton
Poulton-le-Fylde
Hambleton
Stanah
Little Thornton
Stalmine
Stalmine Moss Side
Moor End
Staynall
Hale Nook
Sower Carr
Hambleton Moss Side
Out Rawcliffe
Moss Edge
Ratten Row
Whin Lane End
Larbreck
Copp
Lane Heads
Inskip Moss Side
Inskip
Cuddy Hill
Elswick
Thistleton
Roseacre
Esprick
Wharles
Greenhalgh
Staining
Medlar
Lewth
Catforth
Moor Side
Woodplumpton
Weeton
Eagland Hill
Ford Green
Stake Pool
Small Wood Hey
M6
M55
A6
A683
A589
A588
A586
A585
B5272
B6430
B5269
B6254
A687
138
139
148
157

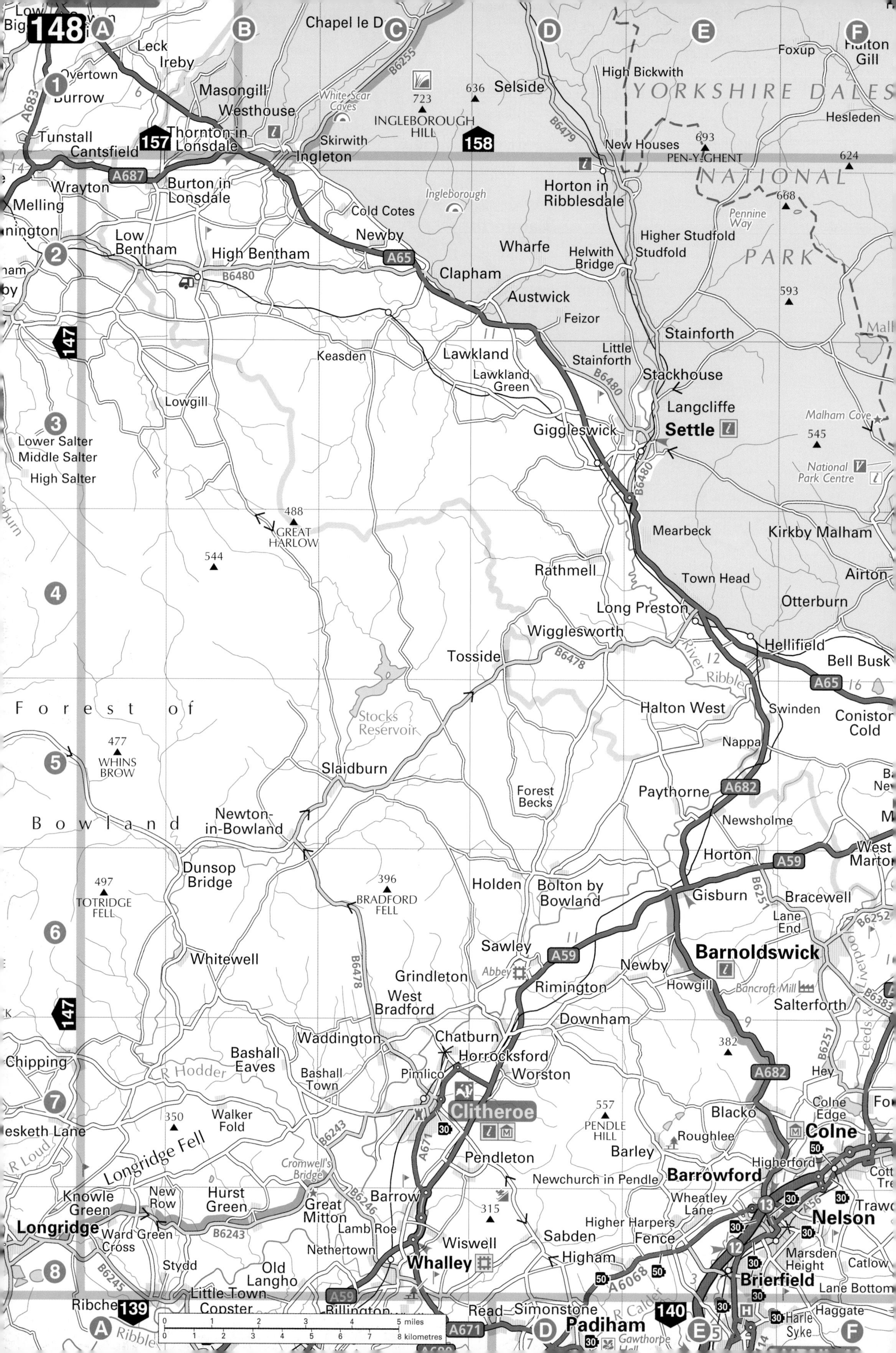
148
A
B
C
D
E
F
Leck
Ireby
Overtown
Burrow
Masongill
Westhouse
Thornton-in-Lonsdale
157
Tunstall
Cantsfield
Chapel le Dale
B6255
White Scar Caves
723
INGLEBOROUGH HILL
636
158
Selside
High Bickwith
YORKSHIRE DALES
NATIONAL
PARK
Foxup
Halton Gill
Hesleden
693
PEN-Y-GHENT
624
New Houses
B6479
Skirwith
Ingleton
A683
A687
Wrayton
Melling
Burton in Lonsdale
Ingleborough
Cold Cotes
Horton in Ribblesdale
668
Pennine Way
Low Bentham
High Bentham
Newby
A65
Wharfe
Helwith Bridge
Higher Studfold
Studfold
B6480
Clapham
Austwick
Feizor
593
147
Keasden
Lawkland
Lawkland Green
Little Stainforth
Stainforth
Stackhouse
Langcliffe
Settle
Giggleswick
Malham Cove
545
National Park Centre
Lowgill
Lower Salter
Middle Salter
High Salter
488
GREAT HARLOW
544
Mearbeck
Kirkby Malham
Rathmell
Town Head
Airton
Long Preston
Otterburn
Wigglesworth
Hellifield
Bell Busk
Tosside
B6478
River Ribble
A65
Stocks Reservoir
Halton West
Swinden
Conistone Cold
Forest of Bowland
477
WHINS BROW
Nappa
Slaidburn
Forest Becks
Paythorne
A682
Newton-in-Bowland
Newsholme
Horton
A59
West Marton
Dunsop Bridge
497
TOTRIDGE FELL
396
BRADFORD FELL
Holden
Bolton by Bowland
Gisburn
B6251
Bracewell
Lane End
B6252
Sawley
Barnoldswick
Whitewell
Grindleton
Abbey
Rimington
Newby
Howgill
Bancroft Mill
Salterforth
West Bradford
Downham
Leeds & Liverpool
B6383
Waddington
Chatburn
Horrocksford
382
Chipping
Bashall Eaves
R Hodder
Bashall Town
Pimlico
Worston
A682
Hey
Clitheroe
557
PENDLE HILL
Blacko
Colne Edge
Colne
Roughlee
350
Walker Fold
Hesketh Lane
Longridge Fell
B6243
A671
Pendleton
Barley
R Loud
Cromwell's Bridge
Higherford
Newchurch in Pendle
Barrowford
Knowle Green
New Row
Hurst Green
Great Mitton
B6246
Barrow
315
Wheatley Lane
A56
Trawden
Nelson
Longridge
Ward Green Cross
B6243
Lamb Roe
Higher Harpers
Sabden
Fence
Wiswell
Nethertown
Whalley
Higham
Marsden Height
Catlow
Stydd
Old Langho
B6245
A6068
Brierfield
Lane Bottom
Little Town
Ribchester
139
Copster
Billington
Read
Simonstone
Padiham
R Calder
140
Haggate
Harle Syke
Gawthorpe Hall
A671
Ribble
0 1 2 3 4 5 miles
0 1 2 3 4 5 6 7 8 kilometres

Buckden
617
TOR MERE TOP
605
LITTLE WHERNSIDE
Scar House Reservoir
Angram Reservoir
River Nidd
Grewelthorpe
Carlesmoor
Laverton
starbotton
River Wharfe
704
GREAT WHERNSIDE
159
Stean
Middlesmoor
Lofthouse
Nidderdale
Greygarth
Dallow
Low Grantley
High Grantley
Arncliffe
Kettlewell
Hawkswick
Arncliffe Cote
575
MEUGHER
496
CONISTONE MOOR
Bouthwaite
Ramsgill
Gouthwaite Reservoir
Wath
Heathfield
150
B6265
Kilnsey
Kilnsey Park & Trout Farm
Conistone
532
Grass Wood
Bordley
B6160
Pateley Bridge
Bridgehouse Gate
Bewerley
Glasshouses
Wilsill
Brimham Rock formation
Smelthouses
Grimwith Reservoir
Greenhow Hill
New House Farm
Threshfield
Grassington
Linton
Hebden
Stump Cross Caverns
B6165
New York
Summerbridge
Hartwith
Dacre Banks
Heyshaw
359
Thorpe
Burnsall
Parcevall Hall
Threapland
Cracoe
506
Appletreewick
Skyreholme
485
SIMON'S SEAT
Dacre
Darley
Darley Head
Padside
Birstwith
Hetton
Rylstone
Drebley
Bramley Head
Thornthwaite
Thruscross Reservoir
Kettlesing Bottom
Winterburn
Barden Tower
West End Outdoor Centre
B6451
Forest Moor
433
Flasby
Blubberhouses
Eastby
Halton East
Bolton Abbey
Bolton Priory
A59
22
Fewston Reservoir
Fewston
Swinsty Res
409
Thorlby
Stirton
Embsay
Bolton Bridge
Timble
Draughton
Embsay & Bolton Abbey Steam Railway
Beamsley
Jack Hill
Langbar
A6069
Skipton
A65
Broughton
A6131
Addingham
Nesfield
Middleton
Denton
Askwith
Clifton
Elslack
High Bradley
A6034
Carleton
Cringles
Lindley
Low Bradley
Rombalds Moor
Farnley
Weston
A629
Swartha
Silsden
Ilkley
Ben Rhydding
Cononley
Brunthwaite
Stead
Newall
A660
Otley
Lothersdale
Kildwick
Becks
Burley in Wharfedale
Wedding Hall Fold
Dale End
Glusburn
Cross Hills
River Aire
403
Burley Wood Head
Chevin Forest Park
A6038
Lane Ends
Sutton-in-Craven
Eastburn
Steeton
Airedale
Menston
East Carlton
Cowling
Ellers
West Morton
Guiseley
Ickornshaw
New Road Side
Utley
Riddlesden
East Riddlesden Hall
East Morton
KEIGHLEY
A650
Braithwaite
Micklethwaite
Hawksworth
Park Gate
Lund's Tower
Wainman's Pinnacle
Laycock
Thwaites
Yeadon
A6068
Fell Lane
Thwaites Brow
Cross Flatts
Eldwick
Esholt
Exley Head
Baildon
Little London
Keighley & Worth Valley Railway
Bingley
Baildon Green
Charlestown
Sympson Green
Wycoller
443
B6143
Ingrow
Hainworth
Gilstead
Saltaire
Thackley
Apperley Bridge
Keighley Moor
Oakworth
Oldfield
Lees
Barcroft
B6429
Idle
Calverley
Haworth
Cullingworth
Harden
Shipley
Stanbury
Cottingley
Moorhead
Greengates
Forest of Trawden
Penistone Hill
Flappit Spring
B6144
Hewenden
Wilsden
B6269
Wrose
Frizinghall
Eccleshill
Woodhall Hills
518
Marsh
Heaton
BOULSWORTH HILL
140
459
Shaw
Hare Croft
Lingbob
Sandy Lane
141
Manningham
Oxenhope
Denholme
Girlington
A629
A658

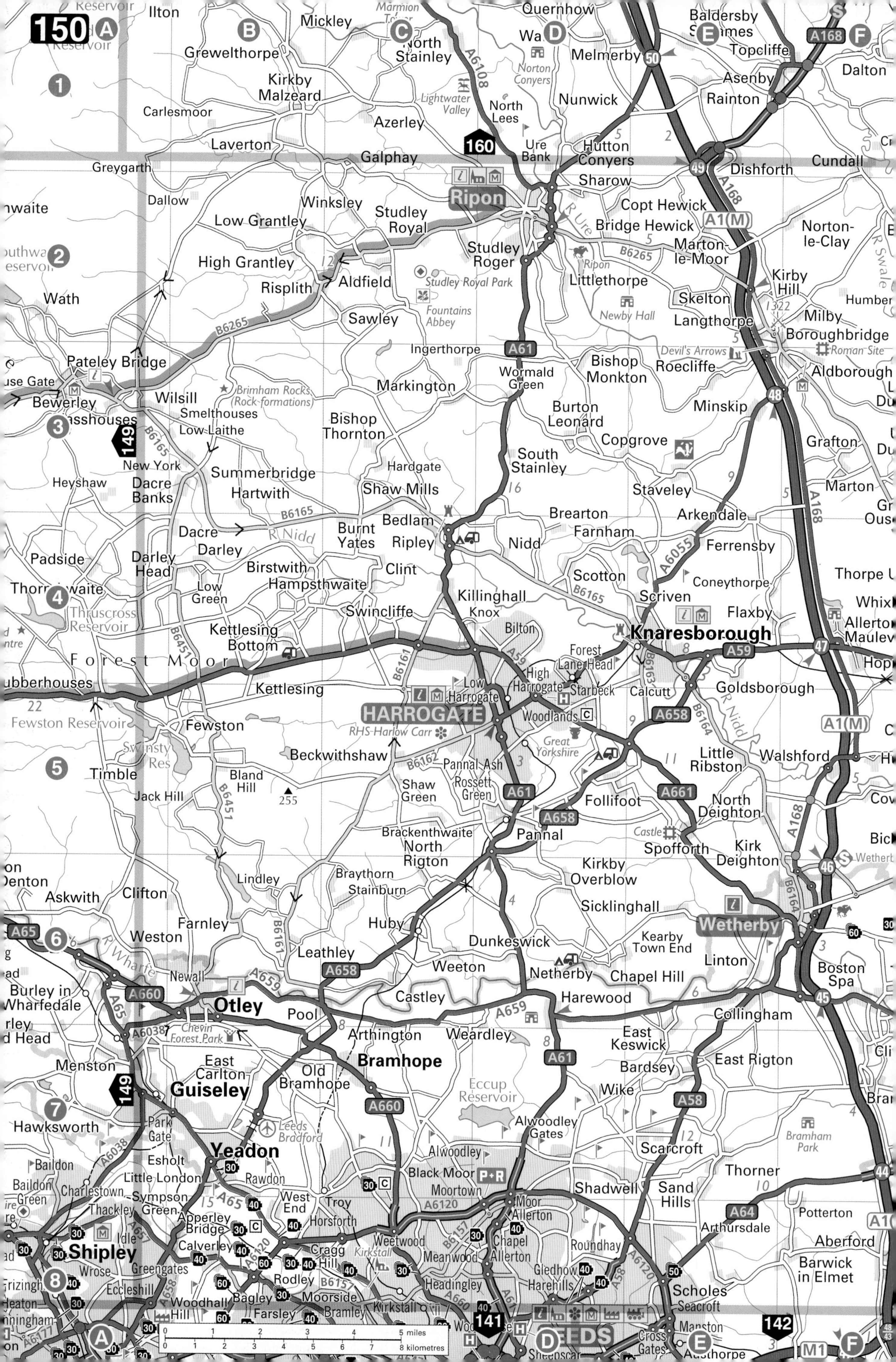
Ilton
Mickley
Marmion Tower
Quernhow
Baldersby St James
Wath
Melmerby
Topcliffe
Dalton
Grewelthorpe
North Stainley
A6108
Norton Conyers
Asenby
Rainton
Kirkby Malzeard
Lightwater Valley
Nunwick
Carlesmoor
Azerley
North Lees
160
Ure Bank
Hutton Conyers
Laverton
Galphay
Cundall
Greygarth
Dishforth
Sharow
Ripon
A168
Dallow
Winksley
Copt Hewick
Low Grantley
Studley Royal
Bridge Hewick
A1(M)
Norton-le-Clay
Studley Roger
B6265
Marton-le-Moor
High Grantley
Ripon
Littlethorpe
Kirby Hill
Risplith
Aldfield
Studley Royal Park
Humberton
Wath
Fountains Abbey
Skelton
Sawley
Newby Hall
Langthorpe
Milby
B6265
Boroughbridge
Ingerthorpe
A61
Devil's Arrows
Roman Site
Pateley Bridge
Bishop Monkton
Roecliffe
Wormald Green
Aldborough
Bewerley
Brimham Rocks (Rock formations)
Markington
Wilsill
Smelthouses
Burton Leonard
Minskip
Low Laithe
Bishop Thornton
149
B6165
Copgrove
Grafton
South Stainley
New York
Heyshaw
Dacre Banks
Summerbridge
Hardgate
Marton
Hartwith
Shaw Mills
Staveley
B6165
Brearton
Arkendale
Bedlam
Burnt Yates
Dacre
R Nidd
Farnham
Ferrensby
Ripley
Nidd
A6055
Padside
Darley
Darley Head
Birstwith
Clint
Scotton
Thorpe Underwood
Hampsthwaite
Coneythorpe
Thornthwaite
Low Green
Killinghall
B6165
Scriven
Thruscross Reservoir
Swincliffe
Knox
Flaxby
Kettlesing Bottom
Bilton
Knaresborough
B6451
Forest Moor
A59
Forest Lane Head
Hopperton
Kettlesing
B6161
High Harrogate
Starbeck
Calcutt
Goldsborough
Low Harrogate
Harrogate
Woodlands
A658
B6164
Fewston Reservoir
Fewston
RHS Harlow Carr
Great Yorkshire
R Nidd
A1(M)
Swinsty Res
Beckwithshaw
Little Ribston
Walshford
B6162
Pannal Ash
Timble
Bland Hill
Shaw Green
Rossett Green
A61
A661
Jack Hill
255
Follifoot
North Deighton
B6451
A658
Brackenthwaite
Pannal
Castle
Spofforth
North Rigton
Kirk Deighton
Braythorn
Kirkby Overblow
Lindley
Stainburn
Askwith
Clifton
Sicklinghall
Wetherby
Farnley
Huby
B6161
A65
Weston
R Wharfe
Dunkeswick
Kearby Town End
Leathley
Linton
Boston Spa
Newall
A658
Weeton
Netherby
Chapel Hill
Burley in Wharfedale
A660
A659
Otley
Castley
Harewood
A65
Pool
A659
Collingham
Chevin Forest Park
A6038
Arthington
Weardley
East Keswick
Menston
East Carlton
Bramhope
A61
Bardsey
East Rigton
Old Bramhope
Guiseley
149
Eccup Reservoir
A660
Wike
A58
Hawksworth
Park Gate
Leeds Bradford
Alwoodley Gates
Bramham Park
Esholt
Yeadon
Alwoodley
Scarcroft
Baildon
A6038
Little London
Rawdon
Black Moor
P+R
Thorner
Charlestown
Moortown
Shadwell
Sand Hills
Baildon Green
Sympson Green
A65
West End
Troy
Moor Allerton
Thackley
Apperley Bridge
A6120
Potterton
A64
Horsforth
Arthursdale
A657
A6120
Idle
Calverley
Weetwood
Chapel Allerton
Aberford
Shipley
Greengates
Cragg Hill
B6157
Roundhay
Kirkstall
Meanwood
A6120
Barwick in Elmet
Wrose
Rodley
Gledhow
Eccleshill
B6157
Headingley
Harehills
A58
Scholes
Woodhall Hill
Bagley
Moorside
Bramley
Kirkstall
A660
A61
Seacroft
Farsley
141
Manston
142
Cross Gates
Austhorpe
Leeds
M1
Sheepscar
miles
kilometres

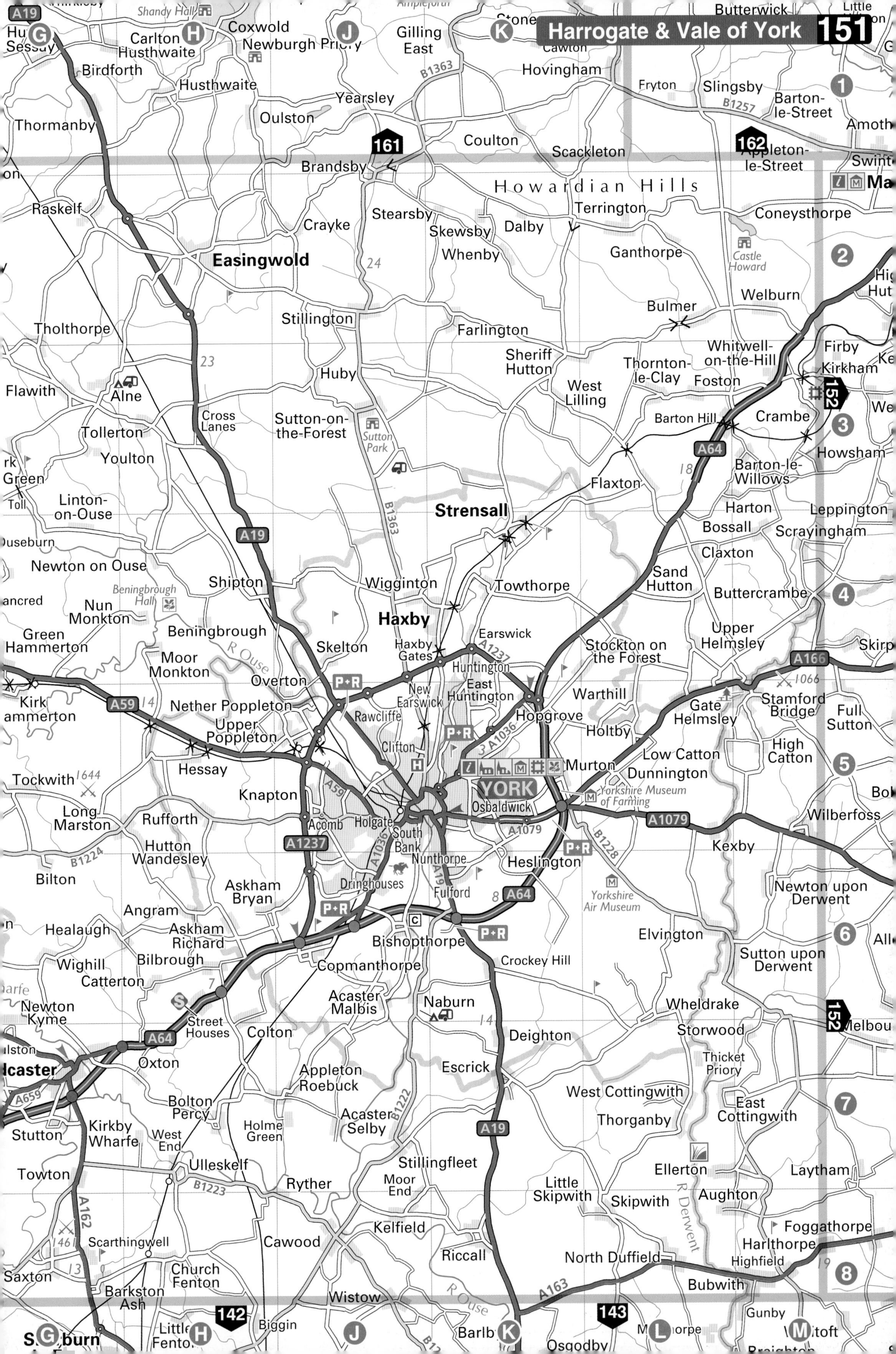

Shandy Hall
Coxwold
Newburgh Priory
Gilling East
Butterwick
Carlton Husthwaite
Birdforth
Husthwaite
B1363
Hovingham
Fryton
Slingsby
Barton-le-Street
B1257
Yearsley
Oulston
Thormanby
161
Coulton
Scackleton
162
Appleton-le-Street
Brandsby
Howardian Hills
Terrington
Coneysthorpe
Raskelf
Crayke
Stearsby
Skewsby
Dalby
Whenby
Ganthorpe
Castle Howard
Easingwold
24
Welburn
Bulmer
Stillington
Farlington
Tholthorpe
Sheriff Hutton
Whitwell-on-the-Hill
Firby
Kirkham
23
Thornton-le-Clay
Foston
Huby
West Lilling
Flawith
Alne
152
Cross Lanes
Sutton-on-the-Forest
Sutton Park
Barton Hill
Crambe
Tollerton
A64
Howsham
Youlton
Barton-le-Willows
18
Flaxton
Linton-on-Ouse
Strensall
Harton
Leppington
B1363
Bossall
Scrayingham
A19
Newton on Ouse
Claxton
Sand Hutton
Shipton
Beningbrough Hall
Wigginton
Towthorpe
Buttercrambe
Nun Monkton
Haxby
Beningbrough
Earswick
Upper Helmsley
Green Hammerton
Skelton
Haxby Gates
A1237
Stockton on the Forest
Moor Monkton
R Ouse
Huntington
A166
Overton
P+R
East Huntington
Warthill
1066
Kirk Hammerton
A59
14
Nether Poppleton
New Earswick
Gate Helmsley
Stamford Bridge
Full Sutton
Rawcliffe
Hopgrove
Upper Poppleton
A1036
Holtby
Clifton
High Catton
Low Catton
Hessay
Murton
Tockwith
1644
Dunnington
Knapton
YORK
Yorkshire Museum of Farming
Long Marston
A59
Osbaldwick
Rufforth
Acomb
Holgate
South Bank
A1079
A1079
Wilberfoss
Hutton Wandesley
A1237
A1036
Nunthorpe
B1228
Kexby
B1224
Heslington
Bilton
Askham Bryan
Dringhouses
Fulford
8
A64
Yorkshire Air Museum
Newton upon Derwent
Angram
Healaugh
Askham Richard
Bishopthorpe
Elvington
Crockey Hill
Sutton upon Derwent
Bilbrough
Copmanthorpe
Wighill
Catterton
7
Acaster Malbis
Naburn
Newton Kyme
Wheldrake
Street Houses
Colton
14
Deighton
Storwood
A64
152
Oxton
Thicket Priory
Escrick
Appleton Roebuck
West Cottingwith
Bolton Percy
East Cottingwith
A659
Thorganby
Acaster Selby
B1222
Kirkby Wharfe
Holme Green
A19
Stutton
West End
Stillingfleet
Towton
Ulleskelf
Ellerton
Laytham
Little Skipwith
Skipwith
Ryther
B1223
Moor End
Aughton
R Derwent
A162
1461
Kelfield
Foggathorpe
Scarthingwell
Cawood
Harlthorpe
Riccall
North Duffield
Highfield
13
19
Church Fenton
Saxton
Bubwith
Barkston Ash
A163
Wistow
R Ouse
Gunby
142
143
Biggin
Osgodby

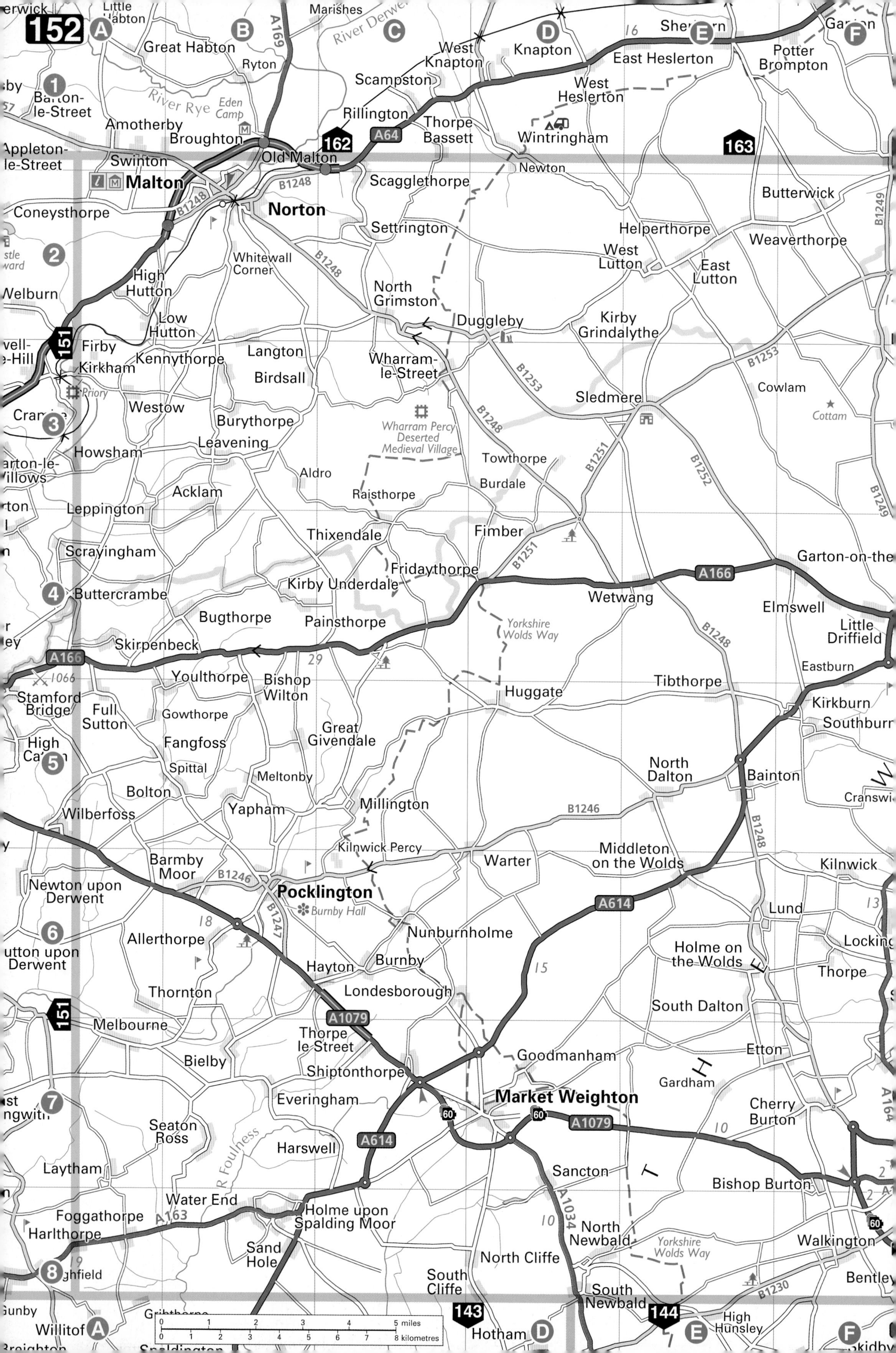

152
A
B
C
D
E
F
Little Habton
Great Habton
Ryton
Marishes
River Derwent
A169
West Knapton
Knapton
Sherburn
East Heslerton
Potter Brompton
Scampston
West Heslerton
Barton-le-Street
River Rye
Eden Camp
Amotherby
Broughton
Rillington
Thorpe Bassett
Wintringham
A64
162
163
Appleton-le-Street
Swinton
Old Malton
Newton
Malton
B1248
Scagglethorpe
Butterwick
Norton
Coneysthorpe
Settrington
Helperthorpe
Weaverthorpe
B1249
Whitewall Corner
West Lutton
East Lutton
High Hutton
North Grimston
Welburn
Low Hutton
Duggleby
Kirby Grindalythe
151
Firby
Kirkham
Kennythorpe
Langton
Birdsall
Wharram-le-Street
B1253
Priory
Westow
Sledmere
Cowlam
Cottam
Burythorpe
Wharram Percy Deserted Medieval Village
Howsham
Leavening
Aldro
Towthorpe
B1251
B1252
Acklam
Raisthorpe
Burdale
Leppington
Thixendale
Fimber
Scrayingham
Fridaythorpe
Garton-on-the
Kirby Underdale
A166
Buttercrambe
Wetwang
Elmswell
Bugthorpe
Painsthorpe
Yorkshire Wolds Way
Little Driffield
Skirpenbeck
1066
Youlthorpe
Bishop Wilton
29
Huggate
Tibthorpe
Eastburn
Stamford Bridge
Full Sutton
Gowthorpe
Kirkburn
Southburn
Great Givendale
High Catton
Fangfoss
Spittal
Meltonby
North Dalton
Bainton
Bolton
Cranswick
Wilberfoss
Yapham
Millington
B1246
Kilnwick Percy
Middleton on the Wolds
Barmby Moor
Warter
Kilnwick
Newton upon Derwent
Pocklington
Burnby Hall
A614
Lund
B1247
18
Allerthorpe
Nunburnholme
Sutton upon Derwent
Holme on the Wolds
Lockington
Hayton
Burnby
15
Thorpe
Thornton
Londesborough
South Dalton
Melbourne
A1079
Thorpe le Street
Bielby
Goodmanham
Etton
Shiptonthorpe
Gardham
Everingham
Market Weighton
Cherry Burton
Seaton Ross
60
R Foulness
Harswell
10
Laytham
Sancton
Bishop Burton
A1034
Water End
Foggathorpe
A163
Holme upon Spalding Moor
North Newbald
Harlthorpe
Sand Hole
Walkington
North Cliffe
South Cliffe
Bentley
South Newbald
B1230
Gunby
Willitoft
143
Hotham
144
High Hunsley
0 1 2 3 4 5 miles
0 1 2 3 4 5 6 7 8 kilometres

Hunmanby
Fordon
Reighton
Speeton
Flamborough Head Heritage Coast
Bempton Cliffs
RSPB
Thornwick Bay
Wold Newton
163
Buckton
Bempton
Burton Fleming
North Landing
Grindale
A165
Selwicks Bay
FLAMBOROUGH HEAD
Lighthouse
Marton
B1255
Flamborough
Sewerby
B1229
B1259
B1253
Bondville Miniature Village
Boynton
Rudston
Monolith
Bridlington
BRIDLINGTON BAY
Bessingby
Hilderthorpe
Carnaby
Haisthorpe
Kilham
Thornholme
Burton Agnes
Norman Manor House
Harpham
Lowthorpe
Fraisthorpe
A614
Nafferton
Little Kelk
Gransmoor
Great Kelk
Lissett
Barmston
B1242
Wansford
Gembling
Ulrome
Cruckley Animal Farm
Foston on the Wolds
Castle
Skipsea
Skerne
B1249
Brigham
Beeford
Upton
Skipsea Brough
North Frodingham
Dunnington
Rotsea
Atwick
Hempholme
Nunkeeling
Bewholme
Honeysuckle Farm
Hornsea Mere
Hornsea
Burshill
Brandesburton
Seaton
B1244
Aike
Sigglesthorne
Rolston
Leven
Catwick
Goxhill
Arram
Little Catwick
Mappleton
Little Hatfield
Mappleton Sands
Great Hatfield
Long Riston
B1243
Routh
A1035
Rise
Great Cowden
North End
Tickton
Arnold
Withernwick
New Ellerby
Meaux
Mount Pleasant
Weel
Skirlaugh
Marton
Aldbrough
A1174
Woodmansey
Old Ellerby
West Newton
East Newton
R Hull
B1238
Wawne
Burton Constable Hall
Flinton
Thearne
Swine
Garton
Dunswell
Grimston
144
Coniston
Thirtleby
145
Humbleton
1
2
3
4
5
6
7
8
G
H
J
K
L
M

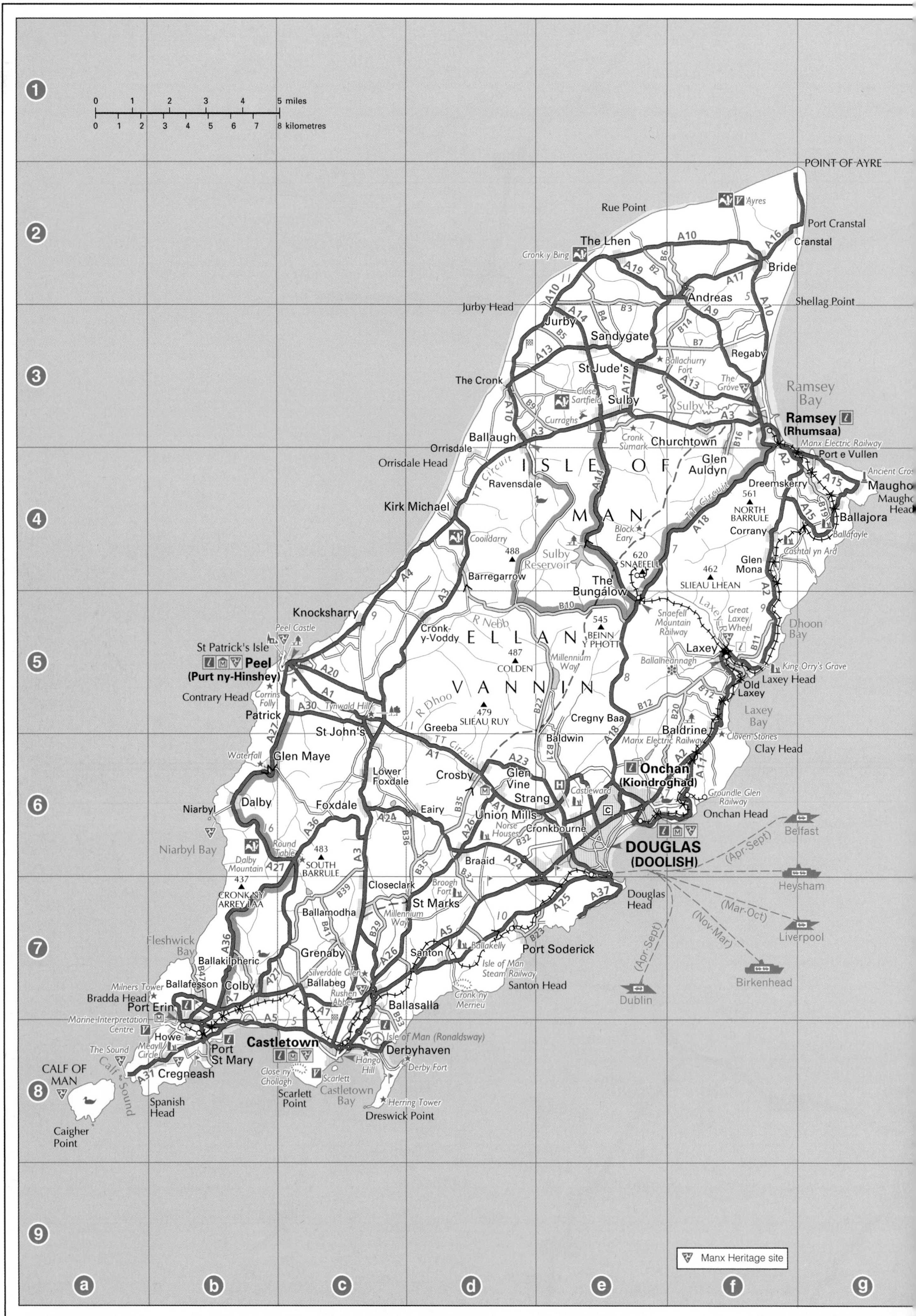

ISLE OF MAN
ELLAN VANNIN
DOUGLAS
(DOOLISH)
Ramsey
(Rhumsaa)
Peel
(Purt ny-Hinshey)
Castletown
Onchan
(Kiondroghad)
Port Erin
Port St Mary
Laxey
Ramsey Bay
Point of Ayre
Rue Point
Jurby Head
Orrisdale Head
Kirk Michael
Snaefell
Calf of Man
Belfast
Heysham
Liverpool
Birkenhead
Dublin
(Apr-Sept)
(Mar-Oct)
(Nov-Mar)
0 1 2 3 4 5 miles
0 1 2 3 4 5 6 7 8 kilometres
Manx Heritage site

St Bees
Egremont
Wilton
164
PILLAR
Seath
HAYCOCK
KIRK FELL
GREAT
Worm Gill
Coulderton
Thornhill
Carleton
Middletown
Haile
Wasdale Head
River Bleng
691
SEATALLAN
Nethertown
Blackbeck
978
964
SCAFELL
Beckermet
Calder Bridge
Braystones
Wast Water
Ponsonby
Nether Wasdale
Burnmoor Tarn
R Ehen
Cross
Wellington
Calder
R Irt
Gosforth
B5343
R Mite
156
Santon
Santon Bridge
Hardknott Fort
Boot
Eskdale Green
Beckfoot
Seascale
Hallsenna Moor
Eskdale
Drigg
Holmrook
652
HARTER FELL
Muncaster Mill
Ravenglass and Eskdale Railway
River Esk
Devoke Water
Saltcoats
LAKE DISTRICT
Muncaster
Hall Dunnerdale
Ravenglass
Roman Bath House
A595
Broad Oak
NATIONAL
Newbiggin
Waberthwaite
573
WHITFELL
PARK
Corney
Broughton Mills
Loganbeck
Hycemoor
Beckfoot
Lower Hawthwaite
Selker Bay
Duddon Bridge
Swinside Stone Circle
Hyton
Bootle
A595
Lady Hall
Foxfie
Annaside
600
BLACK COMBE
Hallthwaites
Arnaby
Bridge End
Whitbeck
The Green
Gutterby Spa
The Hill
Whicham
A5093
Sand Side
Silecroft
156
Soutergate
Kirksanton
Millom
Steel Green
Borwick Rails
RSPB
Haverigg
Haverigg Point
Askam in Furness
Sandscale Haws
South
North Walney
Dalton in-Fu
146
Hawcoat
BARROW-IN-FURNESS
Furness Abbey
North Scale
Vickerstown
0 1 2 3 4 5 miles
0 1 2 3 4 5 6 7 8 kilometres
G H J K L M

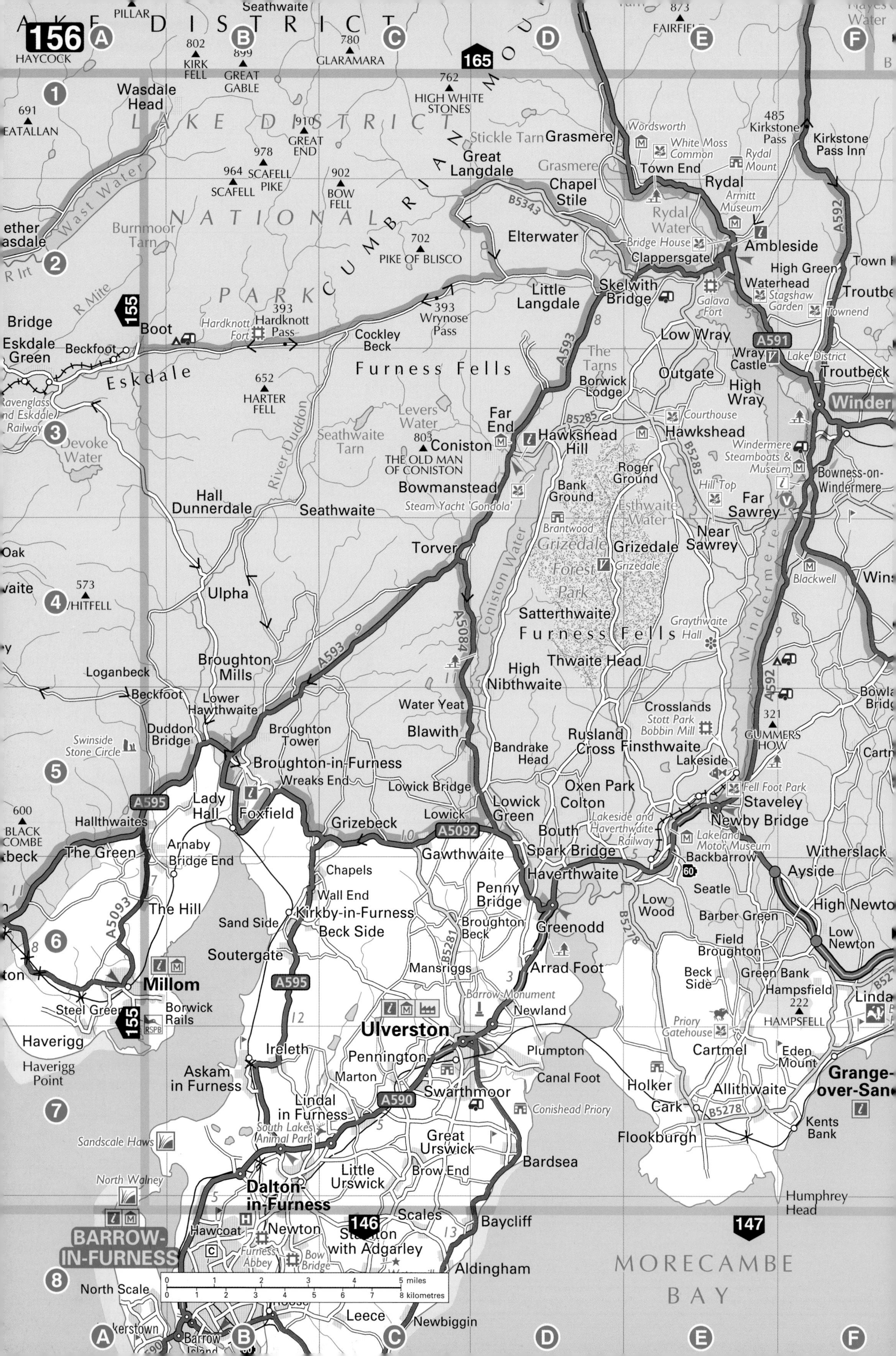

156
LAKE DISTRICT
PILLAR
Seathwaite
HAYCOCK
802
KIRK FELL
899
GREAT GABLE
780
GLARAMARA
165
873
FAIRFIELD
Hayes Water
Wasdale Head
691
SEATALLAN
LAKE DISTRICT
910
GREAT END
762
HIGH WHITE STONES
978
SCAFELL PIKE
964
SCAFELL
902
BOW FELL
Wast Water
Nether Wasdale
Burnmoor Tarn
NATIONAL
PARK
CUMBRIAN MOUNTAINS
702
PIKE OF BLISCO
Stickle Tarn
Grasmere
Great Langdale
Chapel Stile
B5343
Elterwater
Wordsworth
White Moss Common
Town End
Rydal Mount
Rydal
Armitt Museum
Rydal Water
Bridge House
Clappersgate
Ambleside
485
Kirkstone Pass
Kirkstone Pass Inn
A592
High Green
Town End
Waterhead
Stagshaw Garden
Townend
Troutbeck
R Irt
R Mite
155
Bridge
Boot
Eskdale Green
Beckfoot
Eskdale
Hardknott Fort
393
Hardknott Pass
393
Wrynose Pass
Cockley Beck
Little Langdale
Skelwith Bridge
Galava Fort
Low Wray
Wray Castle
A591
Lake District
Troutbeck
Ravenglass and Eskdale Railway
652
HARTER FELL
Furness Fells
A593
The Tarns
Borwick Lodge
Outgate
High Wray
Windermere
Devoke Water
River Duddon
Levers Water
Seathwaite Tarn
803
THE OLD MAN OF CONISTON
Coniston
Far End
B5285
Hawkshead Hill
Courthouse
Hawkshead
B5285
Windermere Steamboats & Museum
Bowness-on-Windermere
Hall Dunnerdale
Seathwaite
Bowmanstead
Steam Yacht 'Gondola'
Bank Ground
Roger Ground
Brantwood
Esthwaite Water
Hill Top
Far Sawrey
Near Sawrey
Grizedale Forest Park
Grizedale
Torver
Coniston Water
Windermere
Blackwell
Oak
573
WHITFELL
Ulpha
A5084
Satterthwaite
Furness Fells
Graythwaite Hall
Broughton Mills
A593
High Nibthwaite
Thwaite Head
A592
Loganbeck
Beckfoot
Lower Hawthwaite
Water Yeat
Crosslands
Stott Park Bobbin Mill
321
GUMMERS HOW
Bowland Bridge
Swinside Stone Circle
Duddon Bridge
Broughton Tower
Blawith
Rusland Cross
Finsthwaite
Bandrake Head
Broughton-in-Furness
Lakeside
Wreaks End
A595
Lady Hall
Foxfield
Lowick Bridge
Lowick Green
Oxen Park
Colton
Fell Foot Park
Staveley
600
BLACK COMBE
Hallthwaites
Grizebeck
Lowick
A5092
Bouth
Lakeside and Haverthwaite Railway
Newby Bridge
Lakeland Motor Museum
Witherslack
The Green
Arnaby
Bridge End
Gawthwaite
Spark Bridge
Backbarrow
Haverthwaite
Ayside
Chapels
Penny Bridge
60
Seatle
A5093
The Hill
Wall End
Kirkby-in-Furness
Broughton Beck
Low Wood
High Newton
Sand Side
Beck Side
Greenodd
B5278
Barber Green
Low Newton
Field Broughton
B5281
Soutergate
Mansriggs
Arrad Foot
Beck Side
Green Bank
Millom
A595
Barrow Monument
Newland
Hampsfield
222
HAMPSFELL
Lindale
Steel Green
Borwick Rails
RSPB
Priory Gatehouse
Haverigg
Ulverston
Ireleth
Pennington
Plumpton
Cartmel
Eden Mount
Haverigg Point
Askam in Furness
Marton
Canal Foot
Holker
Grange-over-Sands
Lindal in Furness
A590
Swarthmoor
Conishead Priory
Cark
Allithwaite
B5278
Sandscale Haws
South Lakes Animal Park
Great Urswick
Flookburgh
Kents Bank
Bardsea
North Walney
Little Urswick
Brow End
Dalton-in-Furness
Humphrey Head
BARROW-IN-FURNESS
Hawcoat
Newton
146
Stainton with Adgarley
Scales
Baycliff
147
Furness Abbey
Bow Bridge
MORECAMBE BAY
Aldingham
North Scale
0 1 2 3 4 5 miles
0 1 2 3 4 5 6 7 8 kilometres
Leece
Newbiggin
Barrow Island
A B C D E F
1 2 3 4 5 6 7 8

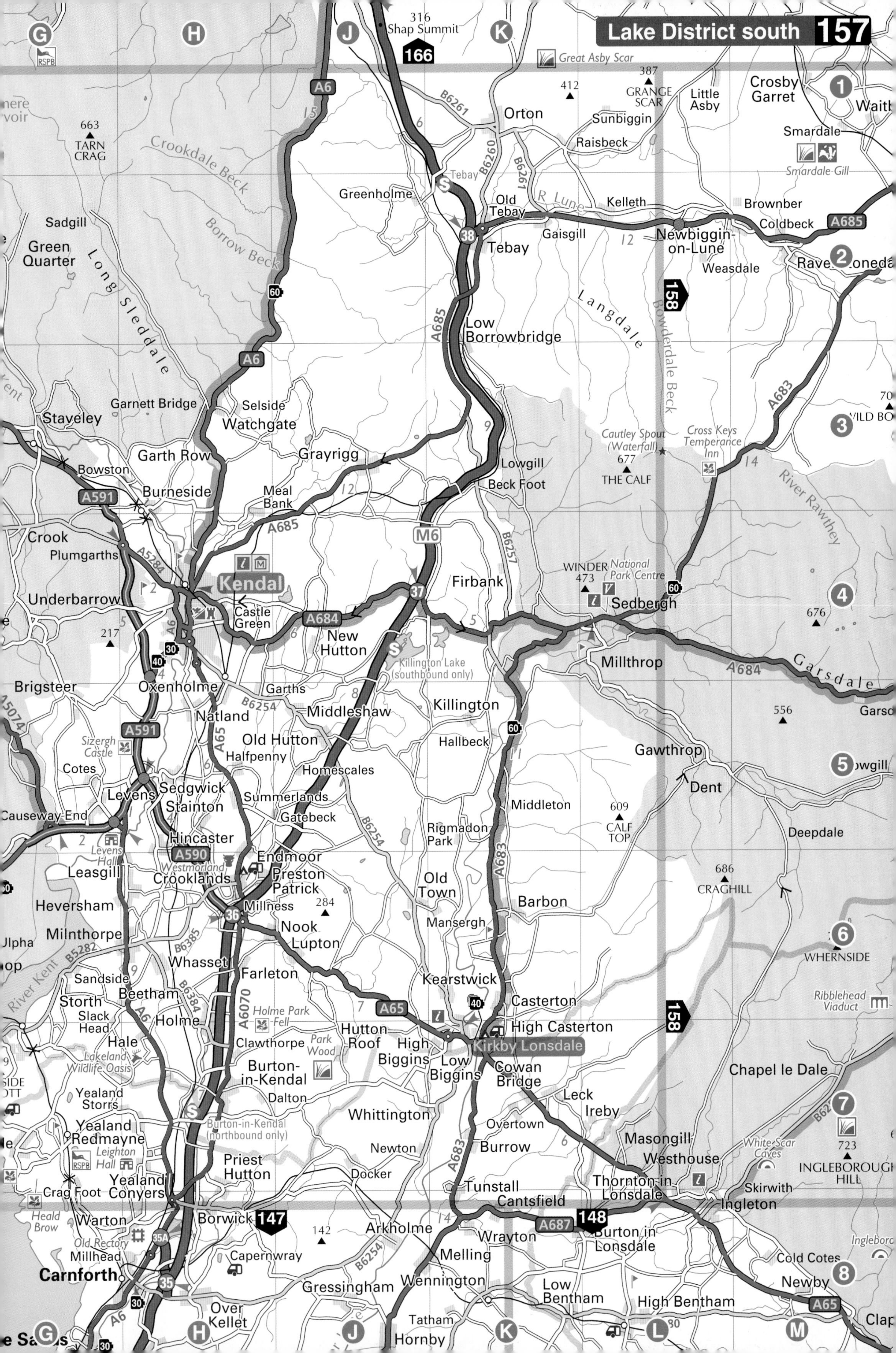
Shap Summit
316
166
Great Asby Scar
Crosby Garret
Little Asby
GRANGE SCAR
387
412
Orton
Sunbiggin
Raisbeck
Smardale
Smardale Gill
Waitby
663
TARN CRAG
Crookdale Beck
Borrow Beck
Greenholme
Tebay
Old Tebay
R. Lune
Kelleth
Brownber
Coldbeck
Gaisgill
Newbiggin-on-Lune
Weasdale
Ravenstonedale
Sadgill
Green Quarter
Long Sleddale
Langdale
Bowderdale Beck
158
Low Borrowbridge
A685
A683
A6
A591
M6
Garnett Bridge
Selside
Watchgate
Staveley
Cautley Spout (Waterfall)
Cross Keys Temperance Inn
677
THE CALF
Garth Row
Grayrigg
Lowgill
Beck Foot
River Rawthey
Bowston
Burneside
Meal Bank
Crook
Plumgarths
A5284
B6257
Kendal
WINDER
473
National Park Centre
Firbank
Underbarrow
Castle Green
A684
New Hutton
Sedbergh
676
217
Killington Lake (southbound only)
Millthrop
Garsdale
Brigsteer
Oxenholme
Garths
B6254
Middleshaw
Killington
556
Natland
Sizergh Castle
Old Hutton
Halfpenny
Hallbeck
Gawthrop
A65
Cotes
Homescales
Dent
Levens
Sedgwick
Stainton
Summerlands
Middleton
609
CALF TOP
Causeway End
Gatebeck
Rigmadon Park
Deepdale
Hincaster
Levens Hall
A590
Westmorland
Endmoor
Leasgill
Crooklands
Preston Patrick
Old Town
686
CRAGHILL
Heversham
Millness
284
Barbon
Nook
Lupton
Mansergh
Milnthorpe
B6385
B5282
River Kent
WHERNSIDE
Whasset
Farleton
Sandside
Kearstwick
Storth
Beetham
B6384
Casterton
Ribblehead Viaduct
Slack Head
Holme
A6070
Holme Park Fell
Hale
Hutton Roof
High Biggins
High Casterton
Kirkby Lonsdale
Lakeland Wildlife Oasis
Clawthorpe
Park Wood
Low Biggins
Cowan Bridge
Chapel le Dale
Burton-in-Kendal
Yealand Storrs
Dalton
Leck
Ireby
Whittington
Overtown
Yealand Redmayne
Burton-in-Kendal (northbound only)
Masongill
White Scar Caves
Leighton Hall
Newton
Burrow
Westhouse
723
INGLEBOROUGH HILL
Priest Hutton
Yealand Conyers
Docker
Tunstall
Thornton in Lonsdale
Skirwith
Crag Foot
Cantsfield
Ingleton
Heald Brow
Warton
Borwick
147
148
A687
Burton in Lonsdale
Old Rectory
142
Arkholme
Wrayton
Millhead
Capernwray
Melling
Ingleborough
Cold Cotes
Carnforth
Gressingham
Wennington
Low Bentham
High Bentham
Newby
Over Kellet
Tatham
Hornby
Clapham

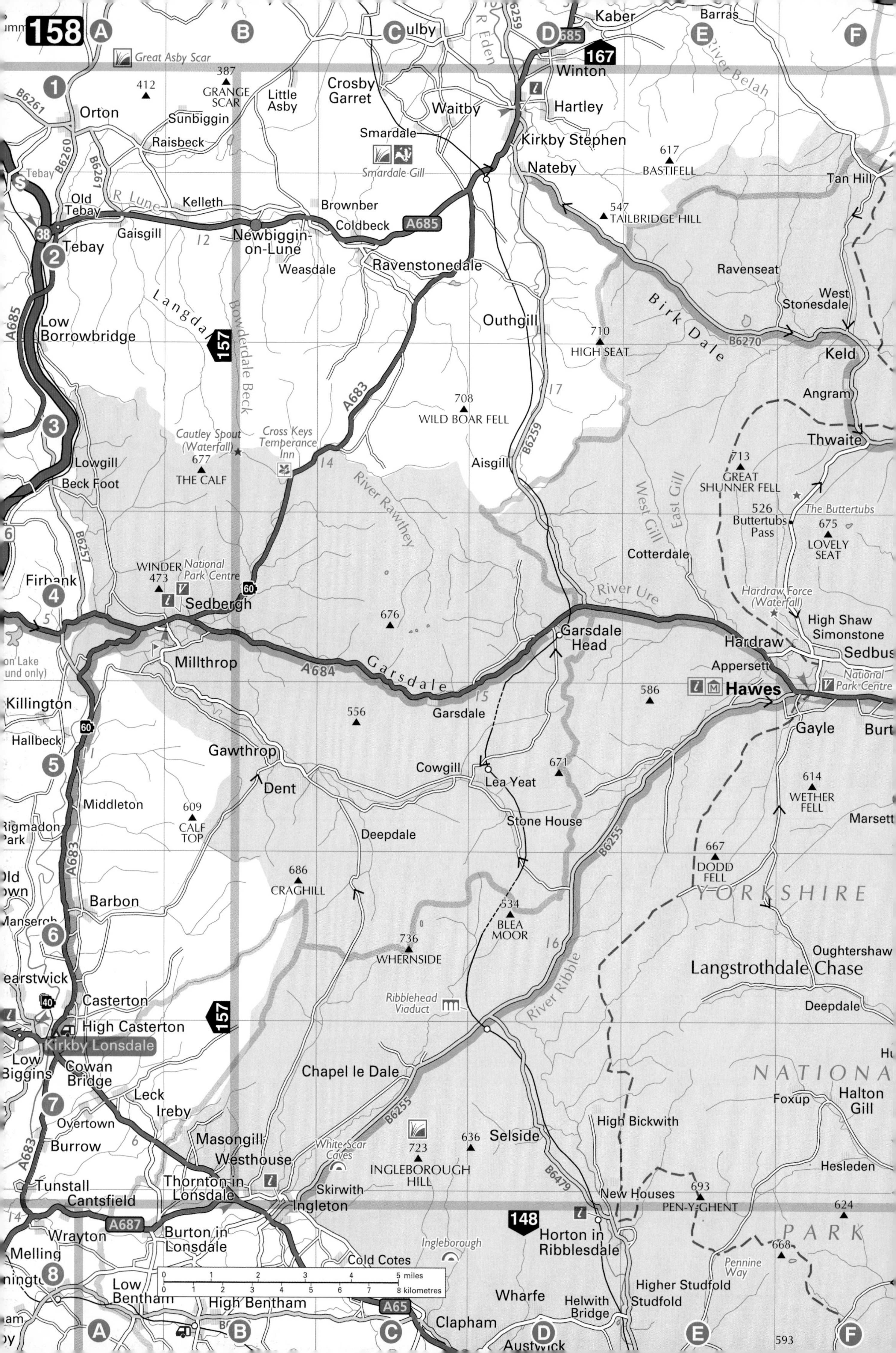

158
A
B
C
D
E
F
1
2
3
4
5
6
7
8
167
157
148
Great Asby Scar
387
GRANGE SCAR
412
Little Asby
Crosby Garret
Culby
R Eden
B6259
Kaber
Barras
685
River Belah
Winton
Hartley
Waitby
Smardale
Smardale Gill
Kirkby Stephen
617
BASTIFELL
Nateby
Tan Hill
547
TAILBRIDGE HILL
B6261
Orton
Sunbiggin
Raisbeck
B6260
Tebay
Old Tebay
R Lune
Kelleth
Brownber
Coldbeck
A685
38
Gaisgill
12
Newbiggin-on-Lune
Weasdale
Ravenstonedale
Ravenseat
West Stonesdale
Langdale
Bowderdale Beck
Outhgill
710
HIGH SEAT
Birk Dale
B6270
Keld
Angram
Thwaite
Low Borrowbridge
A683
708
WILD BOAR FELL
17
B6259
Aisgill
Cautley Spout (Waterfall)
677
THE CALF
Cross Keys Temperance Inn
14
River Rawthey
713
GREAT SHUNNER FELL
The Buttertubs
526
Buttertubs Pass
675
LOVELY SEAT
West Gill
East Gill
Cotterdale
Lowgill
Beck Foot
B6257
Firbank
WINDER
473
National Park Centre
60
Sedbergh
676
River Ure
Hardraw Force (Waterfall)
High Shaw
Simonstone
Garsdale Head
5
Millthrop
A684
Garsdale
Hardraw
Appersett
Sedbus
Hawes
National Park Centre
586
on Lake
und only)
Killington
556
15
Garsdale
Gayle
Burt
Hallbeck
11
Gawthrop
Dent
Cowgill
Lea Yeat
671
614
WETHER FELL
Middleton
609
CALF TOP
Stone House
Marsett
Rigmadon Park
Deepdale
B6255
667
DODD FELL
Old Town
686
CRAGHILL
YORKSHIRE
Barbon
534
BLEA MOOR
Mansergh
736
WHERNSIDE
16
River Ribble
Oughtershaw
Langstrothdale Chase
Hearstwick
Casterton
40
Ribblehead Viaduct
Deepdale
High Casterton
Kirkby Lonsdale
Low Biggins
Cowan Bridge
NATIONAL
Hu
Chapel le Dale
Leck
Ireby
Overtown
Foxup
Halton Gill
High Bickwith
6
Burrow
Masongill
White Scar Caves
723
INGLEBOROUGH HILL
636
Selside
Westhouse
Hesleden
B6479
Tunstall
Thornton in Lonsdale
Skirwith
Cantsfield
693
PEN-Y-GHENT
New Houses
624
Ingleton
A687
Horton in Ribblesdale
PARK
Wrayton
Burton in Lonsdale
Ingleborough
668
Pennine Way
Melling
Cold Cotes
0 1 2 3 4 5 miles
0 1 2 3 4 5 6 7 8 kilometres
Low Bentham
High Bentham
Wharfe
Helwith Bridge
Higher Studfold
Studfold
A65
Clapham
Austwick
593

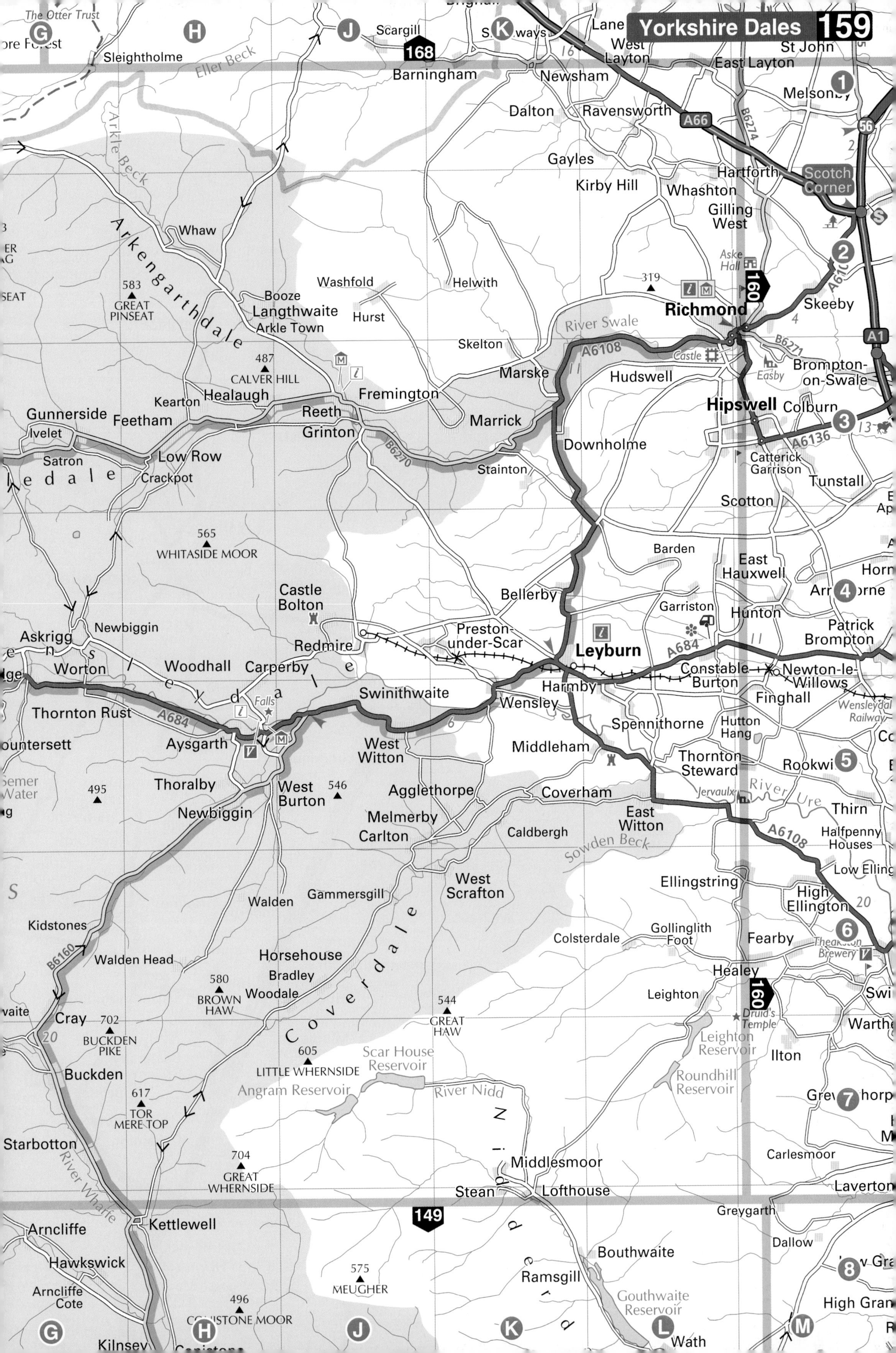

The Otter Trust
Sleightholme
Scargill
Barningham
Newsham
Dalton
Ravensworth
Gayles
Kirby Hill
Whashton
Hartforth
Gilling West
Scotch Corner
Aske Hall
Richmond
Skeeby
River Swale
A6108
Castle
Brompton-on-Swale
Easby
Hudswell
Hipswell
Colburn
Catterick Garrison
A6136
Tunstall
Downholme
Scotton
Barden
East Hauxwell
Garriston
Hunton
Patrick Brompton
Bellerby
Leyburn
Preston-under-Scar
Redmire
Castle Bolton
Constable Burton
Newton-le-Willows
Harmby
Finghall
Wensleydale Railway
Wensley
Spennithorne
Hutton Hang
Middleham
Thornton Steward
Rookwith
Jervaulx
River Ure
Thirn
Coverham
East Witton
Caldbergh
Sowden Beck
Halfpenny Houses
Low Ellington
High Ellington
Ellingstring
Colsterdale
Gollinglith Foot
Fearby
Theakston Brewery
Healey
Leighton
Druid's Temple
Leighton Reservoir
Roundhill Reservoir
Ilton
Carlesmoor
Laverton
Greygarth
Dallow
High Grantley
Bouthwaite
Ramsgill
Gouthwaite Reservoir
Wath
Middlesmoor
Lofthouse
Stean
Nidderdale
River Nidd
Scar House Reservoir
Angram Reservoir
Whaw
Arkengarthdale
583 GREAT PINSEAT
Booze
Langthwaite
Arkle Town
Arkle Beck
Eller Beck
Washfold
Hurst
Helwith
Skelton
Marske
487 CALVER HILL
Healaugh
Kearton
Fremington
Reeth
Grinton
B6270
Marrick
Stainton
Gunnerside
Feetham
Ivelet
Satron
Low Row
Crackpot
565 WHITASIDE MOOR
Askrigg
Newbiggin
Worton
Woodhall
Carperby
Wensleydale
Falls
Swinithwaite
Thornton Rust
A684
Aysgarth
West Witton
Countersett
Semer Water
495
Thoralby
West Burton
546
Agglethorpe
Newbiggin
Melmerby
Carlton
West Scrafton
Walden
Gammersgill
Coverdale
Kidstones
B6160
Walden Head
Horsehouse
Bradley
Woodale
580 BROWN HAW
544 GREAT HAW
Cray
702 BUCKDEN PIKE
Buckden
605 LITTLE WHERNSIDE
617 TOR MERE TOP
Starbotton
River Wharfe
704 GREAT WHERNSIDE
Kettlewell
Arncliffe
Hawkswick
Arncliffe Cote
575 MEUGHER
496 CONISTONE MOOR
Kilnsey
319
168
160
149
A66
B6274
B6271
A1
Lane
West Layton
East Layton
St John
Melsonby

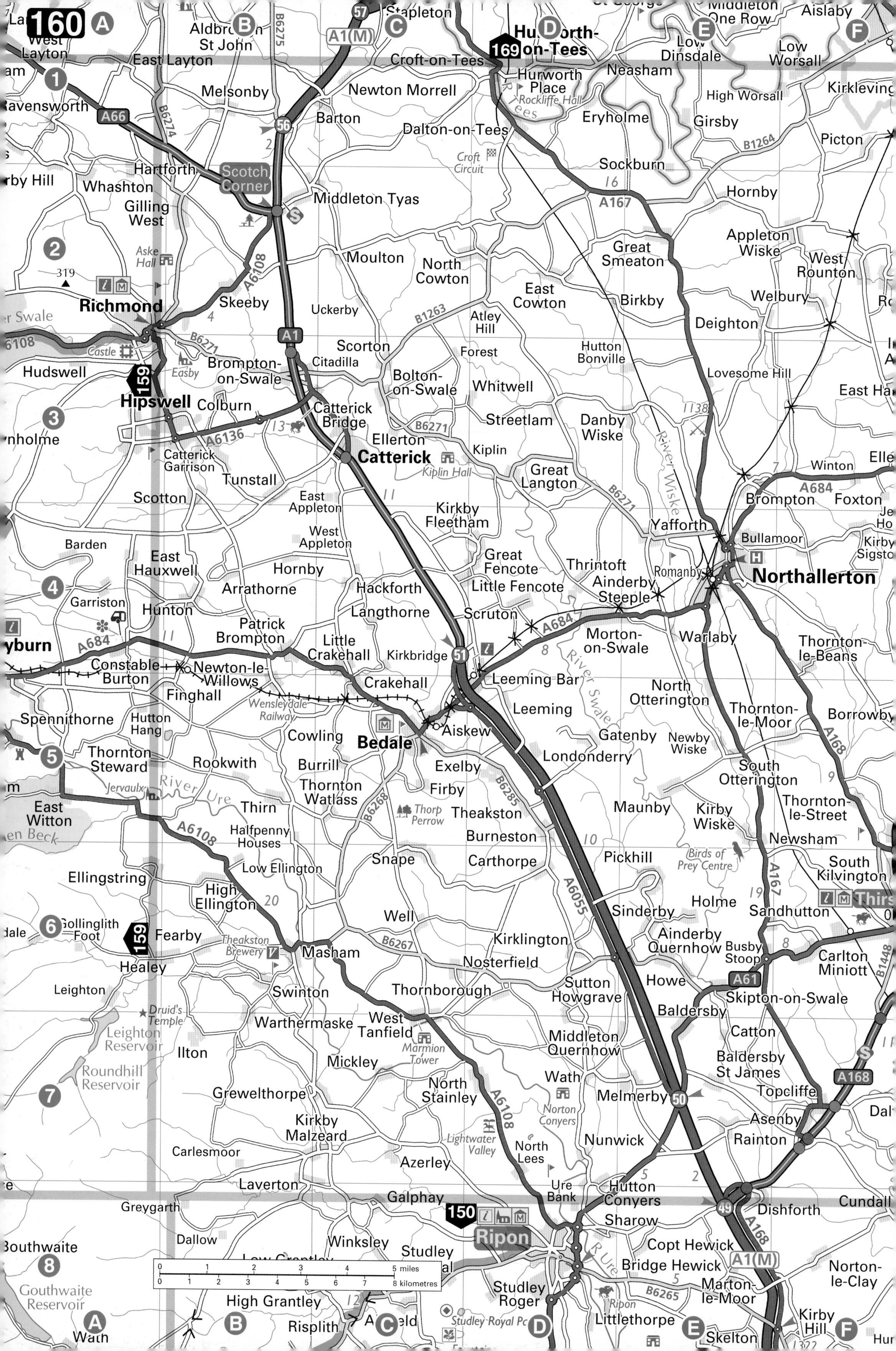

A
B
C
D
E
F
West Layton
Aldbrough St John
B6275
A1(M)
57
Stapleton
Hurworth-on-Tees
169
Middleton One Row
Aislaby
East Layton
Croft-on-Tees
Hurworth Place
Neasham
Low Dinsdale
Low Worsall
1
Melsonby
Newton Morrell
Rockliffe Hall
R Tees
High Worsall
Kirkleving
Ravensworth
A66
Barton
56
Eryholme
Girsby
B6274
Dalton-on-Tees
Croft Circuit
Picton
B1264
Hartforth
Scotch Corner
Sockburn
Whashton
Gilling West
Middleton Tyas
16
A167
Hornby
2
Aske Hall
Moulton
North Cowton
Great Smeaton
Appleton Wiske
West Rounton
319
A6108
East Cowton
Birkby
Welbury
Richmond
Skeeby
Uckerby
Atley Hill
Deighton
Swale
B1263
A1
Castle
B6271
Scorton
Forest
Hutton Bonville
Hudswell
159
Easby
Brompton-on-Swale
Citadilla
Bolton-on-Swale
Whitwell
Lovesome Hill
Hipswell
Colburn
Catterick Bridge
East Ha
3
A6136
13
Streetlam
Danby Wiske
1138
Ellerton
River Wiske
Catterick Garrison
Catterick
Kiplin
Kiplin Hall
Winton
Tunstall
Great Langton
A684
Brompton
Foxton
East Appleton
11
Kirkby Fleetham
Scotton
Yafforth
West Appleton
Bullamoor
Barden
East Hauxwell
Great Fencote
Thrintoft
Romanby
Northallerton
Hornby
Arrathorne
Hackforth
Little Fencote
Ainderby Steeple
4
Garriston
Hunton
Langthorne
Scruton
Patrick Brompton
Little Crakehall
Kirkbridge
51
Morton-on-Swale
Warlaby
Thornton-le-Beans
Constable Burton
Newton-le-Willows
Crakehall
Leeming Bar
8
Finghall
Wensleydale Railway
Leeming
North Otterington
Thornton-le-Moor
Borrowby
Spennithorne
Hutton Hang
Aiskew
Cowling
Bedale
River Swale
Gatenby
Newby Wiske
5
Thornton Steward
Rookwith
Burrill
Exelby
Londonderry
South Otterington
A168
Jervaulx
River Ure
Thornton Watlass
Firby
B6285
9
East Witton
Thirn
B6268
Thorp Perrow
Theakston
Maunby
Kirby Wiske
Thornton-le-Street
A6108
Halfpenny Houses
Burneston
Newsham
10
Snape
Carthorpe
Pickhill
Birds of Prey Centre
Ellingstring
Low Ellington
A6055
South Kilvington
A167
High Ellington
20
19
Sinderby
Holme
Sandhutton
Well
6
Gollinglith Foot
159
Fearby
Kirklington
Ainderby Quernhow
Busby Stoop
Carlton Miniott
B1448
Theakston Brewery
Masham
B6267
Nosterfield
Healey
A61
Leighton
Swinton
Thornborough
Sutton Howgrave
Howe
Skipton-on-Swale
Druid's Temple
Warthermaske
West Tanfield
Baldersby
Leighton Reservoir
Catton
Ilton
Marmion Tower
Middleton Quernhow
Baldersby St James
Roundhill Reservoir
Mickley
Wath
A168
North Stainley
Melmerby
50
Topcliffe
7
Grewelthorpe
Norton Conyers
Asenby
Kirkby Malzeard
A6108
Lightwater Valley
Nunwick
Rainton
North Lees
Carlesmoor
Azerley
Laverton
Ure Bank
Hutton Conyers
Galphay
Cundall
Greygarth
150
Ripon
Sharow
49
Dishforth
Dallow
Winksley
Copt Hewick
A168
Studley
Bridge Hewick
A1(M)
Southwaite
8
Studley Roger
Marton-le-Moor
Norton-le-Clay
High Grantley
B6265
Gouthwaite Reservoir
Risplith
Studley Royal Pc
Ripon
Littlethorpe
Kirby Hill
Wath
Skelton
0 1 2 3 4 5 miles
0 1 2 3 4 5 6 7 8 kilometres

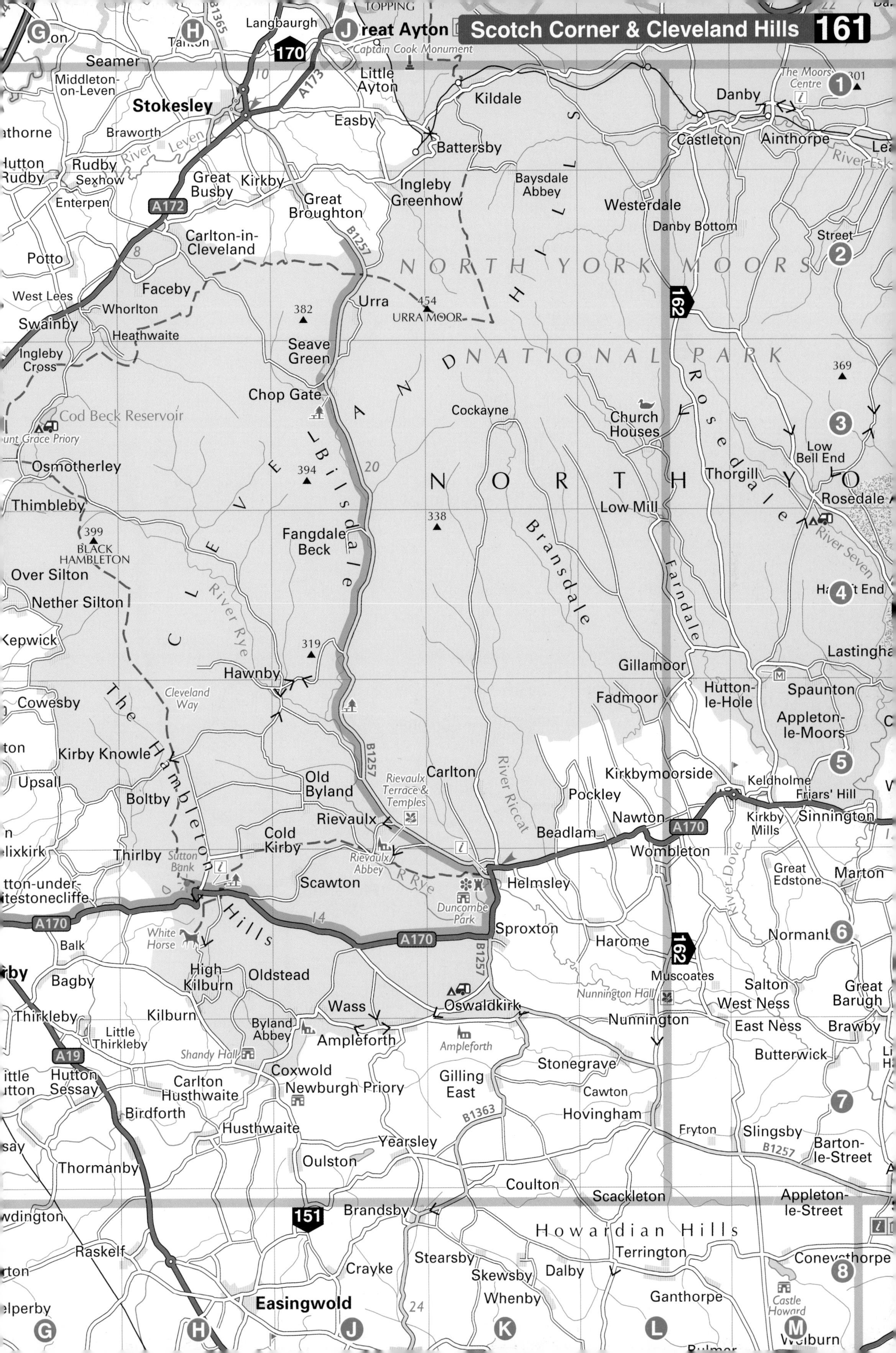
Great Ayton
Captain Cook Monument
Langbaurgh
170
Seamer
Middleton-on-Leven
Stokesley
Little Ayton
Kildale
Danby
The Moors Centre
Castleton
Ainthorpe
River Esk
Easby
Braworth
River Leven
Battersby
Hutton Rudby
Rudby
Sexhow
Great Busby
Kirkby
Ingleby Greenhow
Baysdale Abbey
Westerdale
Enterpen
Great Broughton
A172
A173
B1365
B1257
Danby Bottom
Carlton-in-Cleveland
Street
Potto
NORTH YORK MOORS
Faceby
West Lees
Whorlton
Urra
URRA MOOR
454
382
Swainby
Heathwaite
162
Seave Green
NATIONAL PARK
369
Ingleby Cross
Chop Gate
Cockayne
Cod Beck Reservoir
Church Houses
Osmotherley
Low Bell End
394
Bilsdale
Thorgill
Rosedale
Thimbleby
Low Mill
399
BLACK HAMBLETON
338
Fangdale Beck
Bransdale
Farndale
River Seven
Over Silton
Nether Silton
River Rye
CLEVELAND HILLS
Kepwick
319
Lastingham
Hawnby
Gillamoor
Cleveland Way
Cowesby
Fadmoor
Hutton-le-Hole
Spaunton
Appleton-le-Moors
The Hambleton Hills
Kirby Knowle
Carlton
River Riccal
Kirkbymoorside
Keldholme
Upsall
Old Byland
Pockley
Friars' Hill
Boltby
Rievaulx Terrace & Temples
Rievaulx
Nawton
A170
Kirby Mills
Sinnington
Beadlam
Cold Kirby
Thirlby
Sutton Bank
Rievaulx Abbey
Wombleton
River Dove
Great Edstone
Marton
Scawton
R Rye
Helmsley
Duncombe Park
Sproxton
Harome
White Horse
Balk
High Kilburn
Oldstead
Muscoates
Salton
Great Barugh
Bagby
Oswaldkirk
Nunnington Hall
West Ness
Thirkleby
Kilburn
Wass
Nunnington
East Ness
Brawby
Little Thirkleby
Byland Abbey
Ampleforth
A19
Shandy Hall
Butterwick
Coxwold
Stonegrave
Hutton Sessay
Carlton Husthwaite
Newburgh Priory
Gilling East
Cawton
Birdforth
B1363
Hovingham
Husthwaite
Fryton
Slingsby
Barton-le-Street
Yearsley
Thormanby
Oulston
Coulton
Scackleton
Appleton-le-Street
151
Brandsby
Howardian Hills
Raskelf
Stearsby
Terrington
Conevthorpe
Crayke
Skewsby
Dalby
Ganthorpe
Castle Howard
Whenby
Easingwold
G
H
J
K
L
M
1
2
3
4
5
6
7
8
10
14
20
24

162
A
Commondale
B
C
D
171
Dunsley
E
F
Raithwaite
Newholm
Barnby
Hutton Mulgrave
1
Kildale
The Moors Centre
301
Danby
Stonegate
A171
Aislaby
Briggswath
Battersby
Castleton
Ainthorpe
Lealholm
Lealholm Side
Sleights
River Esk
Egton
The Green
Iburndale
Baysdale Abbey
Westerdale
Glaisdale
Esk Dale
Grosmont
Danby Bottom
Egton Bridge
A169
Littlebeck
Street
Key Green
2
NORTH YORK MOORS
Beck Hole
326
PIKE HILL
Goathland
161
369
NATIONAL PARK
North Yorkshire Moors Railway
292
Cockayne
3
Church Houses
Rosedale
Wheeldale Roman Road
Eller Beck
Low Bell End
NORTH YORK MOOR
Thorgill
Low Mill
Rosedale Abbey
Newtondale Forest Drive
Bransdale
290
Stape
20
River Seven
Hole of Horcum
North Riding Forest Park
4
Farndale
Hartoft End
Newton Dale
Levisham
Bridestones (Rock Formation)
Lastingham
Gillamoor
Newton-on-Rawcliffe
Dalby Forest Drive
Hutton-le-Hole
Spaunton
Lockton
Fadmoor
239
Appleton-le-Moors
Cawthorn
Cropton
North Riding
5
Staindale Beck
River Riccal
Kirkbymoorside
Keldholme
Wrelton
Toll
Dalby Forest
Pockley
Friars' Hill
Aislaby
Nawton
A170
Kirkby Mills
Sinnington
Middleton
New Bridge
A169
Beadlam
13
Wombleton
Keld Head
Castle
River Dove
Helmsley
Great Edstone
Marton
Wilton
Pickering
A170
Thornton le Dale
Duncombe Park
161
6
Sproxton
Normanby
Allerston
B1415
Harome
B1257
Flamingo Land
Muscoates
Salton
Little Barugh
Great Barugh
Nunnington Hall
Oswaldkirk
West Ness
Kirby Misperton
High Marishes
8
Nunnington
East Ness
Brawby
Ampleforth
Low Marishes
B1258
Butterwick
River Derwent
Stonegrave
Little Habton
Gilling East
Cawton
A169
7
Great Habton
West Knapton
Hovingham
Ryton
Fryton
Slingsby
Scampston
Barton-le-Street
River Rye
Eden Camp
B1257
Rillington
Amotherby
Thorpe Bassett
Coulton
Broughton
A64
Scackleton
Appleton-le-Street
Old Malton
151
Swinton
152
Howardian Hills
Malton
Scagglethorpe
B1248
Terrington
B1248
Coneysthorpe
Norton
8
Dalby
Settrington
Whenby
Ganthorpe
Castle Howard
Whitewall Corner
B1248
High Hutton
North Grimston
Welburn
C
D
E
F
0 1 2 3 4 5 miles
0 1 2 3 4 5 6 7 8 kilometres

High Hawsker
Ness Point or North Cheek
Robin Hood's Bay
Raw
Fylingthorpe
Robin Hood's Bay
Old Peak or South Cheek
Ravenscar
Staintondale
Shire Horse Centre
Hayburn Wyke
Cloughton Newlands
Harwood Dale
Cloughton
Cloughton Wyke
Cromer Point
Burniston
Broxa
Silpho
Suffield
Cleveland Way
Hackness
Newby
Scalby
Scarborough
Castle
Wrench Green
Everley
Sea Cut
Falsgrave
Hatherleigh Deep Sea Trawler
River Derwent
Oliver's Mount
Bee Dale
A170
A165
West Ayton
East Ayton
Eastfield
Osgodby
Cayton Bay
Irton
Hutton Buscel
Ruston
Crossgates
High Killerby
Seamer
The Wyke
Wykeham
Cayton
Brompton-by-Sawdon
Lebberston
Filey Brigg
Gristhorpe
A1039
R. Hertford
Filey
A64
Folkton
Muston
Willerby
Flixton
West Flotmanby
Staxton
Filey Bay
Sherburn
Ganton
Yorkshire Wolds Way
Hunmanby
Flamborough Head Heritage Coast
East Heslerton
Potter Brompton
Fordon
Reighton
Speeton
Bempton Cliffs
Wold Newton
Foxholes
Buckton
Bempton
153
Burton Fleming
Butterwick
Grindale
Helperthorpe
Weaverthorpe
Thwing
Octon
East Lutton
Bondville

A
B
C
D
E
F
176
1
2
3
4
5
6
7
8
Wolsty
Beckfoot
Pelutho
Highlaws
B5300
Newtown
Tarns
Holme St Cuthbert
B5301
Mawbray
Salta
Dubmill Point
Edderside
New Cowper
13
Westnewton
Allonby
Allonby Bay
Hayton
Aspatria
A596
Prospect
B5300
Allerby
Arkleby
Crosscanonby
Parsonby
Crosby
Crosby Villa
Bullgill
Gilcrux
B5301
Fort
River Ellen
Greengill
Maryport
Dearham
Townhead
Ellenborough
Risehow
A594
Tallentire
Woodside
Fothergill
7
Bridekirk
Flimby
Broughton Moor
6
Standingstone
Dovenby
A595
St Helens
Great Broughton
Little Broughton
Papcastle
Siddick
High Seaton
Camerton
Seaton
Great Clifton
A66
Brigham
8
North Side
Bridgefoot
Greysouthen
Lakeland Sheep Wool Centre
Stainburn
Workington
Little Clifton
Eaglesfield
A596
Mossbay
Moss Bay
9
Westfield
4
Deanscales
Salterbeck
High Harrington
A595
Winscales
Low Lorton
Harrington
Branthwaite
Dean
Mosser Mains
Grayson Green
A597
Pardshaw
Ullock
Distington
C
Mockerkin
Common End
B5306
Gilgarran
Waterend
A5086
Pica
40
Howgate
Kidburngill
Lowca
Low Moresby
R Keekle
16
Loweswater
Parton
Brownrigg
Lamplugh
572
A595
Asby
Moresby Parks
Arlecdon
Rowrah
Kirkland
Whitehaven
Hensingham
High Leys
Kells
Frizington
Winder
Saltom Bay
615
636
B5295
B5294
H
Mirehouse
Cleator Moor
Ennerdale Water
Sandwith
6
Moor Row
Ennerdale Bridge
River Ehen
Sandwith Newtown
B5345
Rottington
St Bees Head
RSPB
Cleator
River Calder
Bigrigg
St Bees Head Heritage Coast
533
LANK RIGG
St Bees
Egremont
0 1 2 3 4 5 miles
0 1 2 3 4 5 6 7 8 kilometres
Wilton
155
Worm Gill
Thornhill
Carleton
Haile
691

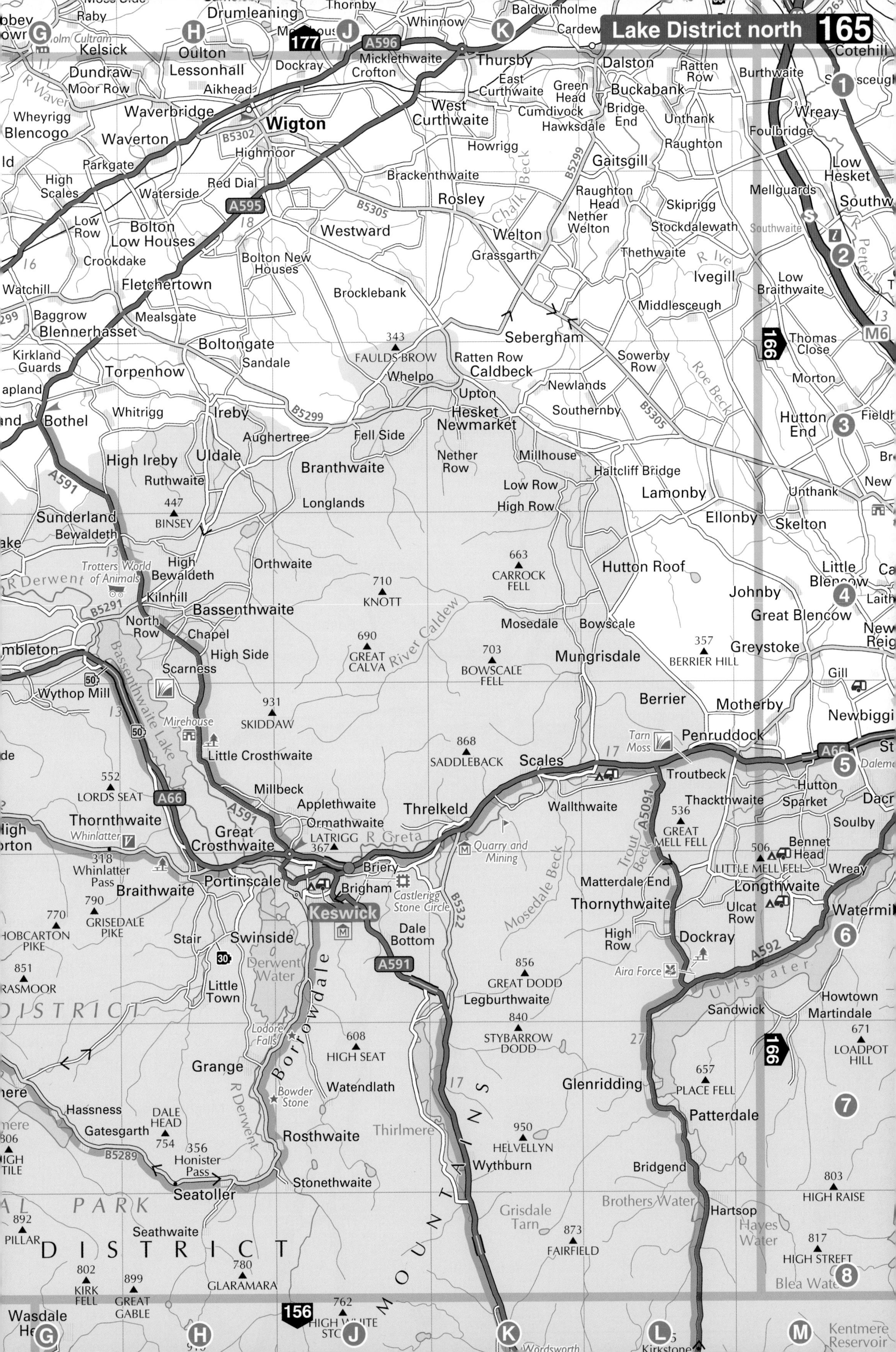

Lake District north
165
Raby
Drumleaning
Thornby
Baldwinholme
Whinnow
Cardew
177
A596
Kelsick
Oulton
Micklethwaite
Thursby
Dalston
Ratten Row
Burthwaite
Cotehill
Dundraw
Lessonhall
Dockray
Crofton
East Curthwaite
Green Head
Buckabank
Moor Row
Aikhead
Wreay
Waverbridge
West Curthwaite
Cumdivock
Bridge End
Unthank
Wheyrigg
Wigton
Hawksdale
Foulbridge
Blencogo
Waverton
B5302
Highmoor
Howrigg
Raughton
Gaitsgill
B5299
Parkgate
Low Hesket
High Scales
Brackenthwaite
Red Dial
Chalk Beck
Mellguards
Waterside
A595
Rosley
Raughton Head
Skiprigg
Southwaite
Low Row
Bolton Low Houses
B5305
Westward
Nether Welton
Stockdalewath
Welton
Grassgarth
Thethwaite
R Ive
Crookdake
Bolton New Houses
Ivegill
Low Braithwaite
Watchill
Fletchertown
Brocklebank
Middlesceugh
M6
Baggrow
Mealsgate
Blennerhasset
Sebergham
166
Thomas Close
343
FAULDS BROW
Ratten Row
Kirkland Guards
Boltongate
Sandale
Sowerby Row
Torpenhow
Whelpo
Caldbeck
Roe Beck
Morton
Upton
Newlands
Bothel
Whitrigg
Ireby
B5299
Hesket Newmarket
Southernby
Hutton End
Aughertree
Fell Side
High Ireby
Uldale
Nether Row
Millhouse
A591
Ruthwaite
Branthwaite
Haltcliff Bridge
Low Row
Lamonby
Unthank
447
BINSEY
Longlands
High Row
Sunderland
Bewaldeth
Ellonby
Skelton
663
CARROCK FELL
High Bewaldeth
Orthwaite
Hutton Roof
Little Blencow
Trotters World of Animals
R Derwent
710
KNOTT
Johnby
Kilnhill
B5291
Bassenthwaite
Great Blencow
North Row
Chapel
Mosedale
Bowscale
690
GREAT CALVA
River Caldew
703
BOWSCALE FELL
357
BERRIER HILL
Greystoke
High Side
Mungrisdale
Scarness
Gill
Wythop Mill
Bassenthwaite Lake
931
SKIDDAW
Berrier
Motherby
Newbiggin
Mirehouse
Tarn Moss
Penruddock
868
SADDLEBACK
Scales
A66
Little Crosthwaite
552
LORDS SEAT
Troutbeck
Dalemain
A66
Millbeck
Hutton
Applethwaite
Threlkeld
Wallthwaite
Thackthwaite
Sparket
Dacre
Thornthwaite
A591
Ormathwaite
536
GREAT MELL FELL
A5091
Soulby
Whinlatter
Great Crosthwaite
LATRIGG
367
R Greta
Quarry and Mining
Trout Beck
Bennet Head
318
Whinlatter Pass
Briery
Mosedale Beck
506
LITTLE MELL FELL
Wreay
Portinscale
Brigham
Castlerigg Stone Circle
Matterdale End
Longthwaite
Braithwaite
Keswick
Thornythwaite
Ulcat Row
Watermillock
790
GRISEDALE PIKE
770
HOBCARTON PIKE
B5322
Dale Bottom
Stair
Swinside
High Row
Dockray
30
Derwent Water
A591
A592
856
GREAT DODD
Aira Force
851
GRASMOOR
Little Town
Borrowdale
Legburthwaite
Ullswater
Sandwick
Howtown
Martindale
840
STYBARROW DODD
671
LOADPOT HILL
Lodore Falls
608
HIGH SEAT
Grange
166
657
PLACE FELL
Bowder Stone
Watendlath
Glenridding
Hassness
DALE HEAD
754
Patterdale
R Derwent
Gatesgarth
Rosthwaite
Thirlmere
950
HELVELLYN
356
B5289
Honister Pass
Wythburn
Bridgend
Stonethwaite
803
HIGH RAISE
Seatoller
Brothers Water
Hartsop
Grisdale Tarn
Hayes Water
PARK
892
PILLAR
Seathwaite
DISTRICT
873
FAIRFIELD
817
HIGH STREET
780
GLARAMARA
MOUNTAINS
Blea Water
802
KIRK FELL
899
GREAT GABLE
762
HIGH WHITE STONES
156
Wasdale Head
Kirkstone
Kentmere Reservoir

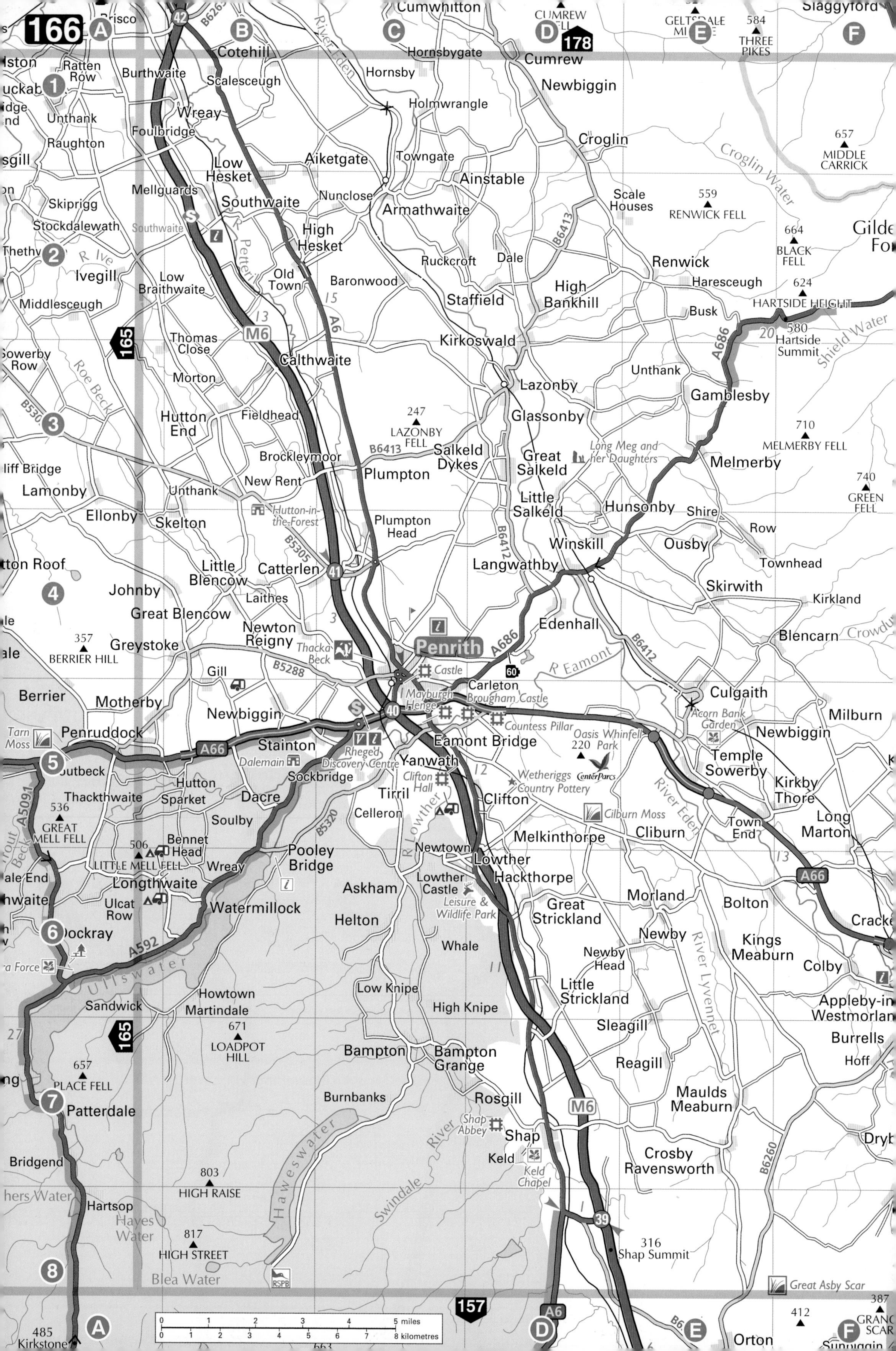

166
178
165
157
Cotehill
Cumwhitton
Cumrew
Newbiggin
Croglin
Ainstable
Armathwaite
Aiketgate
Low Hesket
High Hesket
Southwaite
Ivegill
Kirkoswald
Lazonby
Glassonby
Great Salkeld
Little Salkeld
Plumpton
Calthwaite
Hutton End
Skelton
Catterlen
Langwathby
Penrith
Edenhall
Culgaith
Temple Sowerby
Kirkby Thore
Greystoke
Penruddock
Stainton
Dacre
Pooley Bridge
Watermillock
Eamont Bridge
Yanwath
Clifton
Lowther
Askham
Helton
Bampton
Shap
Patterdale
Hartsop
Ullswater
Haweswater
Morland
Appleby-in-Westmorland
Orton
Renwick
Gamblesby
Melmerby
Ousby
Skirwith
Milburn
Long Marton
Bolton
Great Strickland
Little Strickland
Crosby Ravensworth
Maulds Meaburn
Kings Meaburn
M6
A6
A66
A686
A592
A5091
B6413
B6412
B5305
B5288
B5320
B6260
HIGH RAISE
HIGH STREET
PLACE FELL
LOADPOT HILL
GREAT MELL FELL
LITTLE MELL FELL
BERRIER HILL
LAZONBY FELL
RENWICK FELL
BLACK FELL
HARTSIDE HEIGHT
MELMERBY FELL
GREEN FELL
MIDDLE CARRICK
THREE PIKES
Shap Summit
0 1 2 3 4 5 miles
0 1 2 3 4 5 6 7 8 kilometres

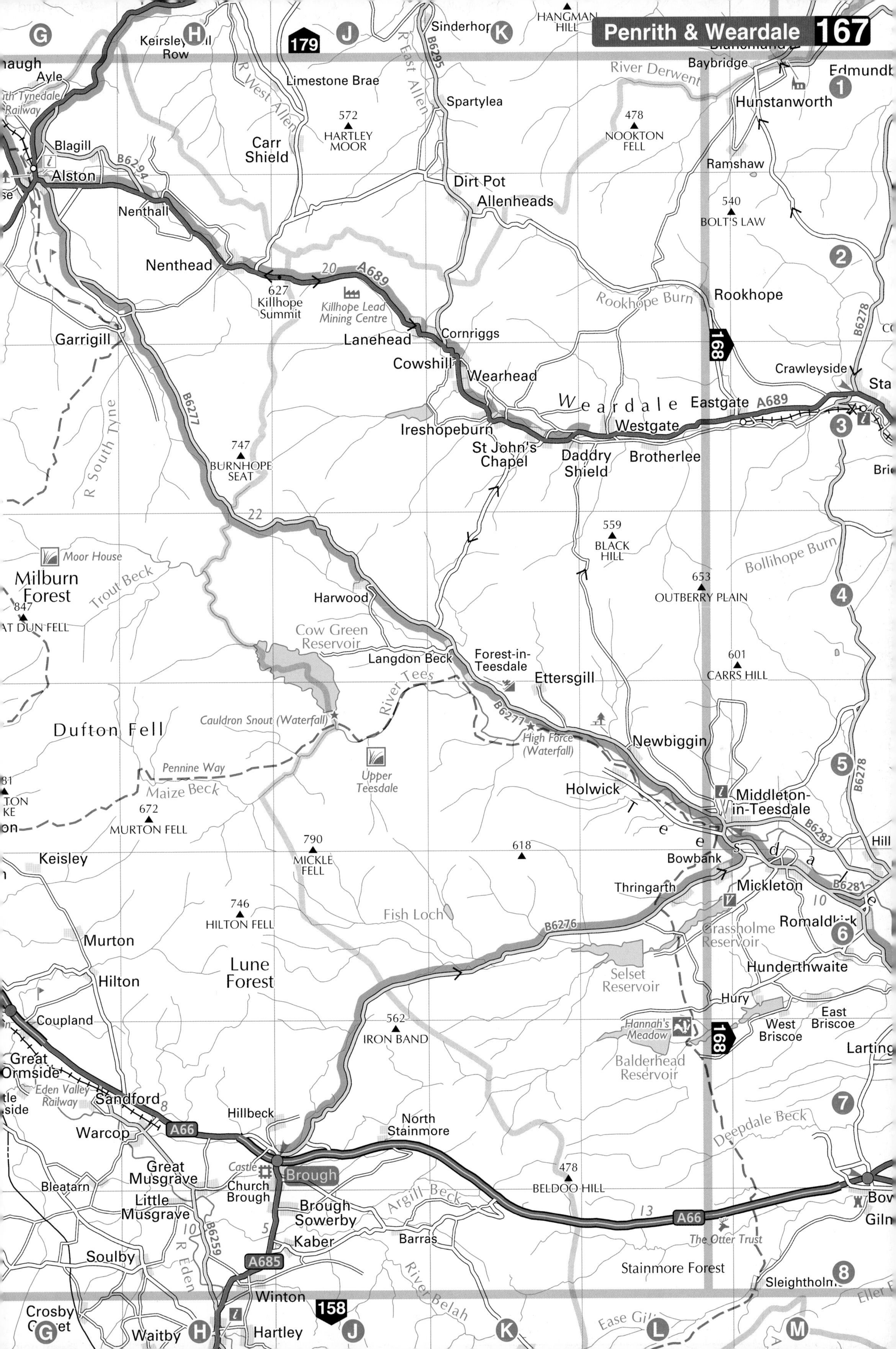

Penrith & Weardale
167
179
168
158
G
H
J
K
L
M
1
2
3
4
5
6
7
8
Keisley Hill Row
Sinderhope
HANGMAN HILL
Baybridge
Edmundbyers
River Derwent
Ayle
South Tynedale Railway
Limestone Brae
R West Allen
R East Allen
B6295
Spartylea
572
HARTLEY MOOR
478
NOOKTON FELL
Hunstanworth
Blagill
Carr Shield
Alston
B6294
Ramshaw
Dirt Pot
Allenheads
540
BOLT'S LAW
Nenthall
Nenthead
20
A689
627
Killhope Summit
Killhope Lead Mining Centre
Rookhope Burn
Rookhope
B6278
Garrigill
Lanehead
Cornriggs
Cowshill
Wearhead
Crawleyside
Weardale
Eastgate
A689
R South Tyne
B6277
Ireshopeburn
Westgate
747
BURNHOPE SEAT
St John's Chapel
Daddry Shield
Brotherlee
22
559
BLACK HILL
Moor House
Milburn Forest
Trout Beck
847
GREAT DUN FELL
Bollihope Burn
653
OUTBERRY PLAIN
Harwood
Cow Green Reservoir
Langdon Beck
Forest-in-Teesdale
601
CARRS HILL
River Tees
Ettersgill
Dufton Fell
Cauldron Snout (Waterfall)
High Force (Waterfall)
Newbiggin
Pennine Way
Upper Teesdale
Maize Beck
Holwick
Middleton-in-Teesdale
672
MURTON FELL
B6282
Teesdale
790
MICKLE FELL
618
Bowbank
Keisley
Thringarth
Mickleton
B6281
746
HILTON FELL
Fish Loch
10
Romaldkirk
B6276
Grassholme Reservoir
Murton
Lune Forest
Selset Reservoir
Hunderthwaite
Hilton
Hury
Coupland
562
IRON BAND
Hannah's Meadow
West Briscoe
East Briscoe
Great Ormside
Balderhead Reservoir
Eden Valley Railway
Sandford
8
Hillbeck
Warcop
A66
North Stainmore
Deepdale Beck
Great Musgrave
Castle
Brough
478
BELDOO HILL
Bleatarn
Church Brough
Little Musgrave
Brough Sowerby
Argill Beck
13
A66
10
R Eden
B6259
5
Kaber
Barras
The Otter Trust
Soulby
A685
River Belah
Stainmore Forest
Winton
Crosby Garret
Waitby
Hartley
Ease Gill

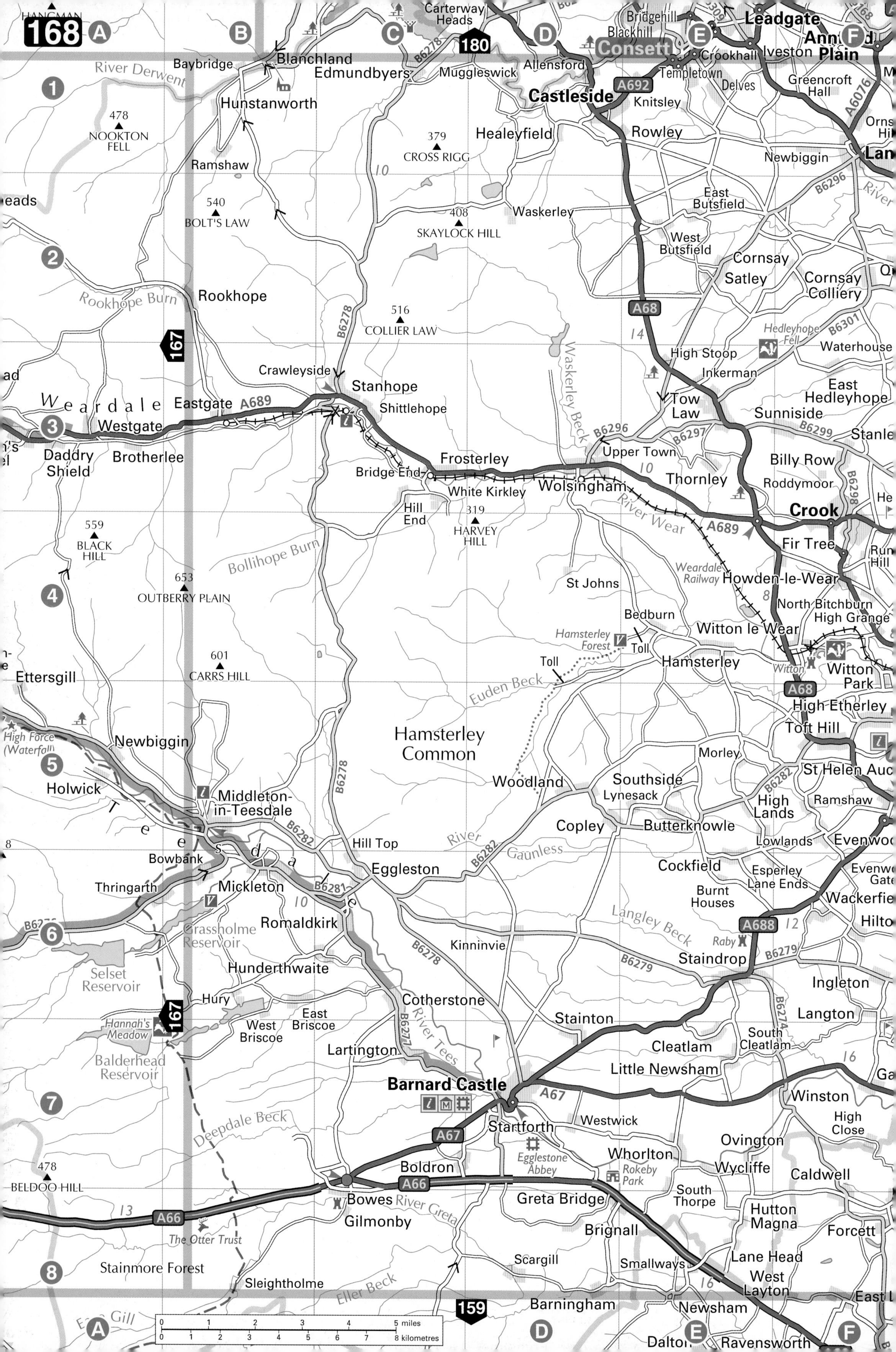
168
A
B
C
D
E
F
Carterway Heads
180
Bridgehill
Blackhill
Leadgate
Annfield Plain
Consett
Crookhall
Iveston
Baybridge
Blanchland
Edmundbyers
B6278
Muggleswick
Allensford
Templetown
A692
Delves
Greencroft Hall
A6076
River Derwent
1
478
NOOKTON FELL
Hunstanworth
Castleside
Knitsley
Healeyfield
Rowley
379
CROSS RIGG
Newbiggin
Ramshaw
10
540
BOLT'S LAW
408
SKAYLOCK HILL
Waskerley
East Butsfield
B6296
West Butsfield
2
Cornsay
Satley
Cornsay Colliery
Rookhope Burn
Rookhope
516
COLLIER LAW
A68
167
14
Hedleyhope Fell
B6301
Waterhouse
High Stoop
Crawleyside
Stanhope
Inkerman
Waskerley Beck
Tow Law
East Hedleyhope
Weardale
Eastgate
A689
Shittlehope
Sunniside
3
Westgate
B6296
B6297
B6299
Daddry Shield
Brotherlee
Frosterley
Upper Town
Billy Row
Bridge End
10
Thornley
White Kirkley
Wolsingham
Roddymoor
B6298
Hill End
319
HARVEY HILL
River Wear
Crook
A689
559
BLACK HILL
Bollihope Burn
Fir Tree
Weardale Railway
Howden-le-Wear
653
OUTBERRY PLAIN
St Johns
8
4
North Bitchburn
High Grange
Bedburn
Witton le Wear
Hamsterley Forest
Toll
Toll
601
CARRS HILL
Hamsterley
Witton
Witton Park
Ettersgill
Euden Beck
A68
High Etherley
High Force (Waterfall)
Newbiggin
Hamsterley Common
Toft Hill
5
Morley
B6278
St Helen Auckland
Holwick
Woodland
Southside
Lynesack
B6282
High Lands
Middleton-in-Teesdale
Ramshaw
Copley
Butterknowle
B6282
Hill Top
River Gaunless
Lowlands
Evenwood
8
Bowbank
Teesdale
Eggleston
Cockfield
Esperley Lane Ends
Evenwood Gate
Thringarth
Mickleton
B6281
10
Burnt Houses
Wackerfield
B6277
6
Romaldkirk
Langley Beck
A688
12
Hilton
Grassholme Reservoir
Raby
Kinninvie
B6278
Staindrop
B6279
B6279
Selset Reservoir
Hunderthwaite
Ingleton
Hury
167
B6274
Cotherstone
Langton
Hannah's Meadow
West Briscoe
East Briscoe
River Tees
B6277
Stainton
South Cleatlam
Cleatlam
Balderhead Reservoir
Lartington
16
Little Newsham
Barnard Castle
A67
Winston
7
High Close
Westwick
Startforth
A67
Deepdale Beck
Ovington
Egglestone Abbey
Whorlton
Wycliffe
Caldwell
Boldron
Rokeby Park
478
BELDOO HILL
A66
Greta Bridge
South Thorpe
Bowes
River Greta
13
A66
Hutton Magna
Gilmonby
Forcett
Brignall
The Otter Trust
Scargill
Lane Head
Smallways
8
Stainmore Forest
West Layton
Sleightholme
16
Eller Beck
159
East Layton
Barningham
Newsham
Dalton
Ravensworth
0 1 2 3 4 5 miles
0 1 2 3 4 5 6 7 8 kilometres

Durham & Teesdale
169
Chester-le-Street
Craghead
Waldridge
Waldridge Fell
Edmondsley
Nettlesworth
Sacriston
Witton Gilbert
Kimblesworth
Plawsworth
Chester Moor
Great Lumley
Finchale Priory
Leamside
Pity Me
Langley Park
Framwellgate Moor
Bearpark
Crook Hall
Gilesgate Moor
Ushaw Moor
Durham
New Brancepeth
Broompark
Langley Moor
Brandon
Meadowfield
Brancepeth
Croxdale
Sunderland Bridge
Bowburn
Shincliffe
Willington
Page Bank
Tudhoe
Mount Pleasant
Todhills
Byers Green
Spennymoor
Middlestone Moor
North Close
Binchester Blocks
Middlestone
Auckland Castle
Kirk Merrington
Leasingthorne
Coundon
Coundon Grange
Eldon
Old Eldon
Rushyford
South Church
Shildon
Middridge
Newton Aycliffe
Woodham
Royal Oak
Redworth
School Aycliffe
Heighington
Houghton le Side
Walworth Gate
Denton
Walworth
Archdeacon Newton
Carlbury
High Coniscliffe
Low Coniscliffe
Cleasby
Manfield
Lucy Cross
Stapleton
Croft-on-Tees
Newton Morrell
Houghton Gate
Philadelphia
Newbottle
Houghton-le-Spring
Fence Houses
High Dubmire
Colliery Row
West Rainton
East Rainton
Hetton-le-Hole
Seaton
Seaham
Parkside
Dalton-le-Dale
Murton
Dalton Park
Cold Hesledon
South Hetton
Hawthorn
Easington Colliery
Durham Heritage Coast
Low Moorsley
High Moorsley
Easington Lane
Pittington
Hallgarth
High Haswell
Littletown
Haswell
Haswell Plough
Easington
Little Thorpe
Peterlee
Carrville
Sherburn
Sherburn Hill
Ludworth
Shotton Colliery
Shadforth
Horden
Old Cassop
Thornley
Shotton
Blackhall Colliery
Durham Coast
Blackhall Rocks
Cassop Colliery
Wheatley Hill
Castle Eden
Blackhall
Old Quarrington
Quarrington Hill
Hesleden
Wingate
Station Town
Kelloe
Town Kelloe
Hutton Henry
Hart Station
Coxhoe
Trimdon Grange
Trimdon Colliery
Sheraton
Hart
Cornforth
South Wingate
High Throston
Thrislington
Trimdon
Elwick
Hurworth Burn
Dalton Piercy
Ferryhill
Fishburn
River Skerne
Summerhill
Mainsforth
Bishop Middleham
Brierton
Hardwick Hall
Butterwick
Owton Manor
Sedgefield
Embleton
Chilton
Bradbury
Newton Bewley
Thorpe Larches
Wynyard Village
Wynyard Park
Mordon
Shotton
Grindon
Billingham
Wolviston
Wynyard Woodland Park
Foxton
Cowpen Bewley
Stillington
Thorpe Thewles
Haverton Hill
Billingham Beck Valley
Elstob
Whitton
Great Stainton
Aycliffe
Bishopton
Carlton
Roseworth
Norton
Brafferton
Coatham Mundeville
Little Stainton
Redmarshall
Whinny Hill
Stockton-on-Tees
Beaumont Hill
Barmpton
West Newbiggin
Harrowgate Village
Great Burdon
Sadberge
East Hartburn
Thornaby-on-Tees
Teesside Park
Acklam
Nature's World
Haughton le Skerne
Darlington
Elton
Longnewton
Preston on Tees
Eaglescliffe
Ingleby Barwick
Stainton
Urlay Nook
Eastbourne
Train Sculpture
Blackwell
Middleton St George
Oak Tree
Durham Tees Valley
Egglescliffe
Thornton
Maltby
Newby
Yarm
High Leven
Middleton One Row
Aislaby
Hurworth-on-Tees
Low Dinsdale
Low Worsall
Hilton
Seamer
Neasham
Kirklevington
Middleton-on-Leven
Hurworth Place
Rockliffe Hall
A19
A690
A1(M)
A167
A181
A182
A688
A177
A179
A689
A6072
A68
A66
A66(M)
A67
A135
A1150
A1185
A1086
A1027
A1046
A139
A1044
B6313
B1284
B1404
B1285
B1287
B6532
B1432
B1283
B1280
B6302
B1320
B6300
B6291
B1281
B6287
B1278
B6282
B6443
B6444
B6275
B6279
B6280
B1274
B1275
R Wear
181
170
160
60
61
62
63
59
58
57
G
H
J
K
L
M
1
2
3
4
5
6
7
8

170
181
Seaham
Parkside
Dalton-le-Dale
Murton
Dalton Park
Cold Hesledon
South Hetton
Hawthorn
Easington Colliery
Durham Heritage Coast
Easington
Haswell
Little Thorpe
Shotton Colliery
Peterlee
Horden
Shotton
169
Blackhall Colliery
Durham Coast
Blackhall Rocks
Wheatley Hill
Castle Eden
Blackhall
Hesleden
Wingate
Station Town
Hart Station
Hutton Henry
Sheraton
Hart
Trimdon Colliery
South Wingate
High Throston
Historic Quay
The Headland
Elwick
HARTLEPOOL
Hurworth Burn
Dalton Piercy
Hartlepool Bay
River Skerne
Summerhill
Butterwick
Brierton
Seaton Carew
Owton Manor
Embleton
Greatham
Graythorpe
Tees Bay
Thorpe Larches
Wynyard Village
Newton Bewley
Hartlepool Power Station Visitor Centre
Wynyard Park
Grindon
Coatham Marsh
Coatham
Billingham
Wolviston
Wynyard Woodland Park
Warrenby
Redcar
Thorpe Thewles
Cowpen Bewley
Marske-by-the-Sea
Billingham Beck Valley
Haverton Hill
Teesport
Saltburn-by-the-Sea
Port Clarence
River Tees
Roseworth
Norton
Kirkleatham
Old Hall
Carlton
Redmarshall
Tolls
Yearby
New Marske
South Bank
Grangetown
Lazenby
North Ormesby
Lackenby
Upleatham
Brotton
STOCKTON-ON-TEES
Eston
Wilton
Skelton
MIDDLESBROUGH
Dunsdale
New Skelton
East Hartburn
Thornaby-on-Tees
Teesside Park
Normanby
Tocketts
Acklam
Nature's World
Ormesby
Boosbeck
Elton
Ormesby Hall
Margrove Park
Long Newton
Preston on Tees
Marton
Stanghow
Eaglescliffe
Guisborough
Urlay Nook
Ingleby Barwick
Stainton
Nunthorpe
Pinchinthorpe
Guisborough Forest
Hemlington
Newton under Roseberry
Hutton Lowcross
Cleveland Way
Durham Tees Valley
Egglescliffe
Thornton
Maltby
Newby
Nunthorpe Village
322
ROSEBERRY TOPPING
Yarm
High Leven
Aislaby
Langbaugh
Great Ayton
Commondale
Low Worsall
Hilton
Tanton
Captain Cook Monument
Seamer
Middleton-
161
Little Ayton
Kirklevington
5 miles
8 kilometres
A19
A182
A179
A689
A1086
A178
A1185
A1027
A139
A1046
A66
A1042
A1085
A174
A171
A172
A1032
A173
A135
A67
A1044
A177
B1287
B1432
B1283
B1280
B1281
B1277
B1274
B1275
B1269
B1268
B1380
B1365
B1292
A
B
C
D
E
F
1
2
3
4
5
6
7
8

G
H
J
1
2
3
4
5
6
7
8
Brotton
Hummersea Scar
Carlin How
Skinningrove
Upton
Boulby
Loftus
Staithes
Heritage Centre
Dalehouse
Easington
Port Mulgrave
Liverton Mines
Hinderwell
Runswick Bay
North Yorkshire and Cleveland Heritage Coast
Roxby
Newton Mulgrave
Runswick
Handale
Borrowby
Kettleness
Goldsborough
Ellerby
Overdale Wyke
B1266
B1366
Scaling
A174
Lythe
Gerrick
Mickleby
Sandsend
Sandsend Wyke
Scaling Dam
East Barnby
West Barnby
Whitby
Raithwaite
Dunsley
Saltwick Bay
Abbey
Ugthorpe
Newholm
The Moors Centre
301
162
Hutton Mulgrave
Ruswarp
K
L
M
A171

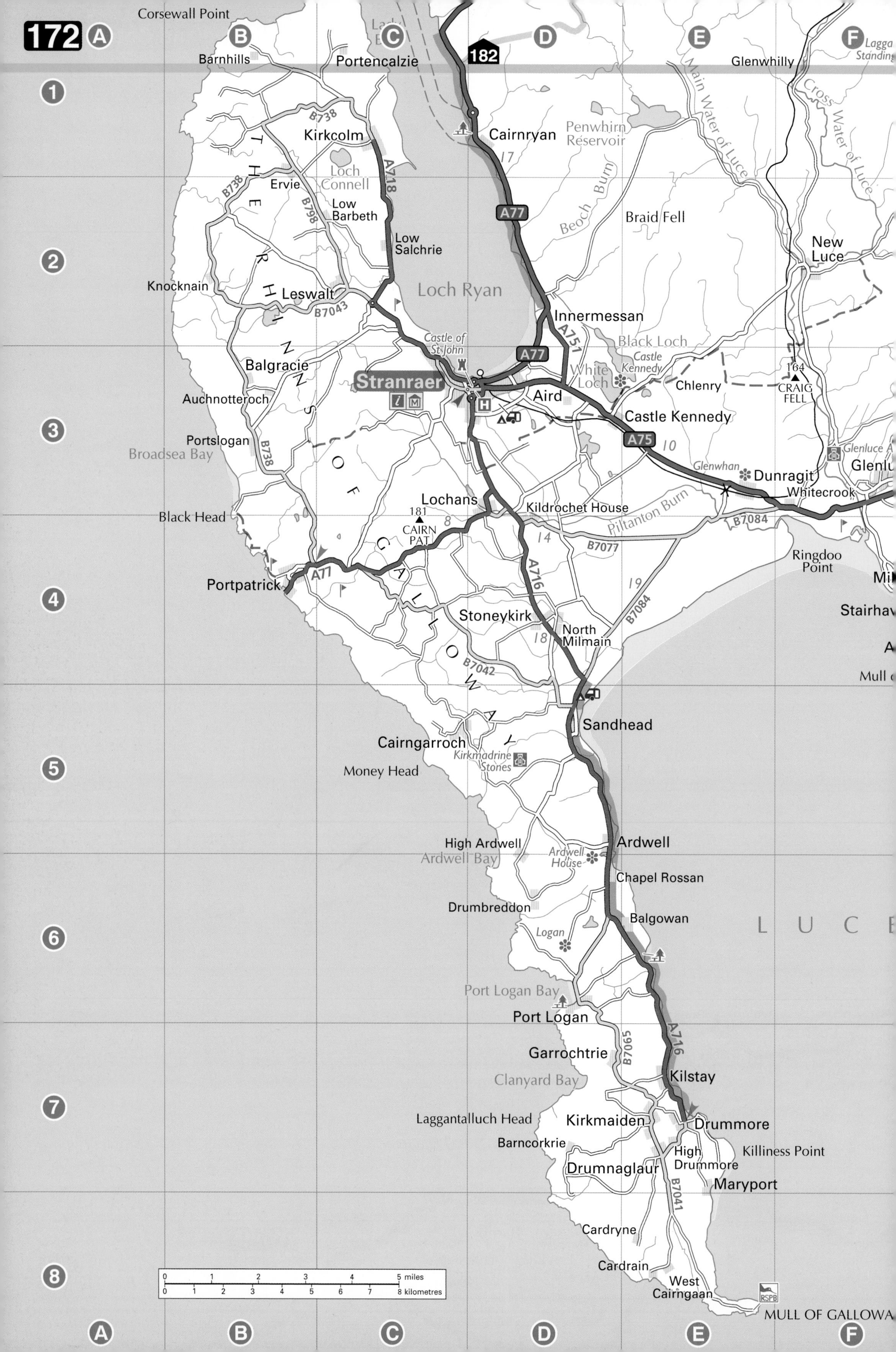

182
Corsewall Point
Barnhills
Portencalzie
Glenwhilly
Lagga Standing
Kirkcolm
B738
Cairnryan
Penwhirn Reservoir
Main Water of Luce
Cross Water of Luce
Loch Connell
Ervie
A718
B798
Low Barbeth
Low Salchrie
A77
Beoch Burn
Braid Fell
New Luce
THE RHINNS OF GALLOWAY
Knocknain
Leswalt
B7043
Loch Ryan
Innermessan
A751
Castle of St John
Stranraer
Black Loch
Castle Kennedy
White Loch
Balgracie
164 CRAIG FELL
Chlenry
Auchnotteroch
Aird
Castle Kennedy
Portslogan
Broadsea Bay
A75
Glenluce Abbey
Glenwhan
Dunragit
Glenluce
Whitecrook
Lochans
Kildrochet House
Piltanton Burn
Black Head
181 CAIRN PAT
B7084
B7077
A716
Ringdoo Point
Portpatrick
Stoneykirk
Stairhaven
North Milmain
B7042
Mull of
Sandhead
Cairngarroch
Kirkmadrine Stones
Money Head
High Ardwell
Ardwell
Ardwell Bay
Ardwell House
Chapel Rossan
Drumbreddon
Balgowan
LUCE
Logan
Port Logan Bay
Port Logan
Garrochtrie
B7065
Clanyard Bay
Kilstay
Laggantalluch Head
Kirkmaiden
Drummore
Barncorkrie
High Drummore
Killiness Point
Drumnaglaur
B7041
Maryport
Cardryne
Cardrain
West Cairngaan
RSPB
MULL OF GALLOWAY
0 1 2 3 4 5 miles
0 1 2 3 4 5 6 7 8 kilometres

G
H
J
K
Knowe
183
RSPB
River Bladnoch
Black Burn
184
URRALL
FELL
G A L L O W A Y
Penkill Burn
Carseriggan
271
FELL
710
CAIRNSMORE
OF FLEET
Challoch
R Cree
Minnigaff
Barfad
Newton
Stewart
214
CULVENNAN
FELL
Creebridge
Kirroughtree
Loch Ronald
A714
Palnure
Shennanton
Tarf Water
15
174
A75
B735
B733
Baltersan
Craighlaw
Kirkcowan
A75
Causeway
End
R Bladnoch
Gem Rock
B733
Creetown
Dernaglar Loch
Clugston
18
Torhouse
Stone Circle
Kirkmabreck
Fell
Loch
B7052
THE
B733
Wigtown
Bladnoch
Carsluith
Cairnholy
Chambered Cairn
Castle
Loch
B7005
MACHARS
Kirwaugh
Carsluith
Castle
Water of Malzie
Mochrum Loch
Braehead
Ravenshall
Point
B7052
B7085
Kirkinner
Orchardton
Bay
Auchenmalg
Bay
B7005
Culshabbin
Barrachan
Chapel
Finian
(ruin)
Whauphill
B7004
11
Little
Airies
Culscadden
A746
12
A747
13
Elrig
Druchtag
Motte
B7085
Sorbie
B7052
Garlieston
Mochrum
Pouton
Drumtrodden
Cup & Ring
Drummoddie
Broughton
Mains
Cruggleton
Bay
Drumtrodden
Standing Stones
B7004
Port William
Big Balcraig
B7063
B A Y
174
'Wren's Egg'
Standing Stones
B7021
Priory
Barsalloch Fort
Monreith
Whithorn
Story
Barsalloch Point
Whithorn
Rispain
Camp
Point of Leg
A747
10
A746
Portyerrock
St Ninian's
Cave
B7004
Isle of
Whithorn
Kidsdale
St Ninian's
Chapel
(ruin)
Cutcloy
BURROW HEAD
1
2
3
4
5
6
7
8
Wig
M
L

A
B
C
D
E
F
1
2
3
4
5
6
7
8
GARLICK HILL
Galloway Deer Range
184
402
ROUND FELL
471
FELL OF FLEET
208
AUCHENCLOY H
RSPB
G A L L O W A Y
Loch Grannoch
Loch Fleet
Carseriggan
Challoch
R Cree
Penkill Burn
Minnigaff
710
CAIRNSMORE OF FLEET
Barfad
Newton Stewart
Creebridge
Kirroughtree
Big Water of Fleet
Big Water of Fleet
Little Water of Fleet
Shennanton
A714
Palnure
335
WHITE TOP OF CULREACH
B735
173
A75
Baltersan
Upper Ruscoe
Carstramon Wood
Kirkcowan
Causeway End
Gem Rock
B796
R Bladnoch
B733
Creetown
Fleet Valley
Clugston
Torhouse Stone Circle
18
Kirkmabreck
455
CAIRNHARROW
Skyre Burn
Anwoth
Cardoness Castle
B7052
THE MACHARS
B733
Wigtown
Bladnoch
B7005
Carsluith
Carsluith Castle
Cairnholy Chambered Cairns
Kirwaugh
Water of Malzie
Girthon
Braehead
Ravenshall Point
Mossyard
Fleet Bay
Lennox Plunton
B7005
B7052
B7085
Kirkinner
Orchardton Bay
Margrie
Barrachan
Whauphill
B7004
Islands of Fleet
Culscadden
Little Airies
A746
12
Kirkandrews
Druchtag Motte
B7085
Sorbie
B7052
Wigtown Bay
Mochrum
Garlieston
Pouton
Drumtrodden Cup & Ring
Drumtrodden Standing Stones
Drummoddie
Broughton Mains
Borness
Cruggleton Bay
Ringdoo Point
Big Balcraig
B7004
B7063
'Wren's Egg' Standing Stones
B7021
173
Priory
Barsalloch Fort
Monreith
Barsalloch Point
Whithorn Story
Point of Leg
A747
10
Rispain Camp
A746
Whithorn
Portyerrock
St Ninian's Cave
B7004
Isle of Whithorn
Kidsdale
St Ninian's Chapel (ruin)
Cutcloy
BURROW HEAD
0 1 2 3 4 5 miles
0 1 2 3 4 5 6 7 8 kilometres

185
176
Crocketford
Auchenreoch Loch
Milton Loch
Lochober Loch
Mossdale
Airds of Kells
Loch Ken
RSPB
Woodhall Loch
Knockvennie Smithy
Loch Roan
Walbutt
Kirkpatrick Durham
Old Bridge of Urr
Springholm
Milton
Drumcoltran Tower
Beeswing
334 LOTUS HILL
Glensone Burn
Kinharvie
Crossmichael
Kirkgunzeon
Hardgate
Haugh of Urr
Redcastle
Clarebrand
Glenlochar
Laurieston
Townhead of Greenlaw
Hillowton
Threave Castle
Castle Douglas
Carlingwark Loch
Threave Garden
Urr Water
Glaisters Burn
430 CUIL HILL
Edingham
Longwood
Little Knox
Dalbeattie
Bridge of Dee
Rhonehouse
Gelston
Craigley
Barlochan
Palnackie
Barnbarroch
Caulkerbush
Fairgirth
Ringford
River Dee
Airieland
Fleet
343 SCREEL HILL
390 BENGAIRN
Orchardton Tower
Kippford or Scaur
Mote of Mark
Drumburn
Sandyhills
Tongland
Colvend
Rockcliffe
Portling
East Stewartry Coast
Twynholm
Compstonend
Little Sypland
Wildlife Park
Whinnie Liggate
Castlehill Point
Kirkchrist
MacLellan's Castle
Kirkcudbright
Auchencairn
Culnaightrie
Auchencairn Bay
Heston Island
Balcary
Balcary Point
Mutehill
Dundrennan
Rascarrel
Orroland
Dundrennan Abbey
Kirkcudbright Bay
Ross
Balmae
Netherlaw
Abbey Head
Little Ross
A713
A762
A75
A745
A711
A710
A755
B794
B795
B736
B727
B793
G
H
J
K
L
M
1
2
3
4
5
6
7
8

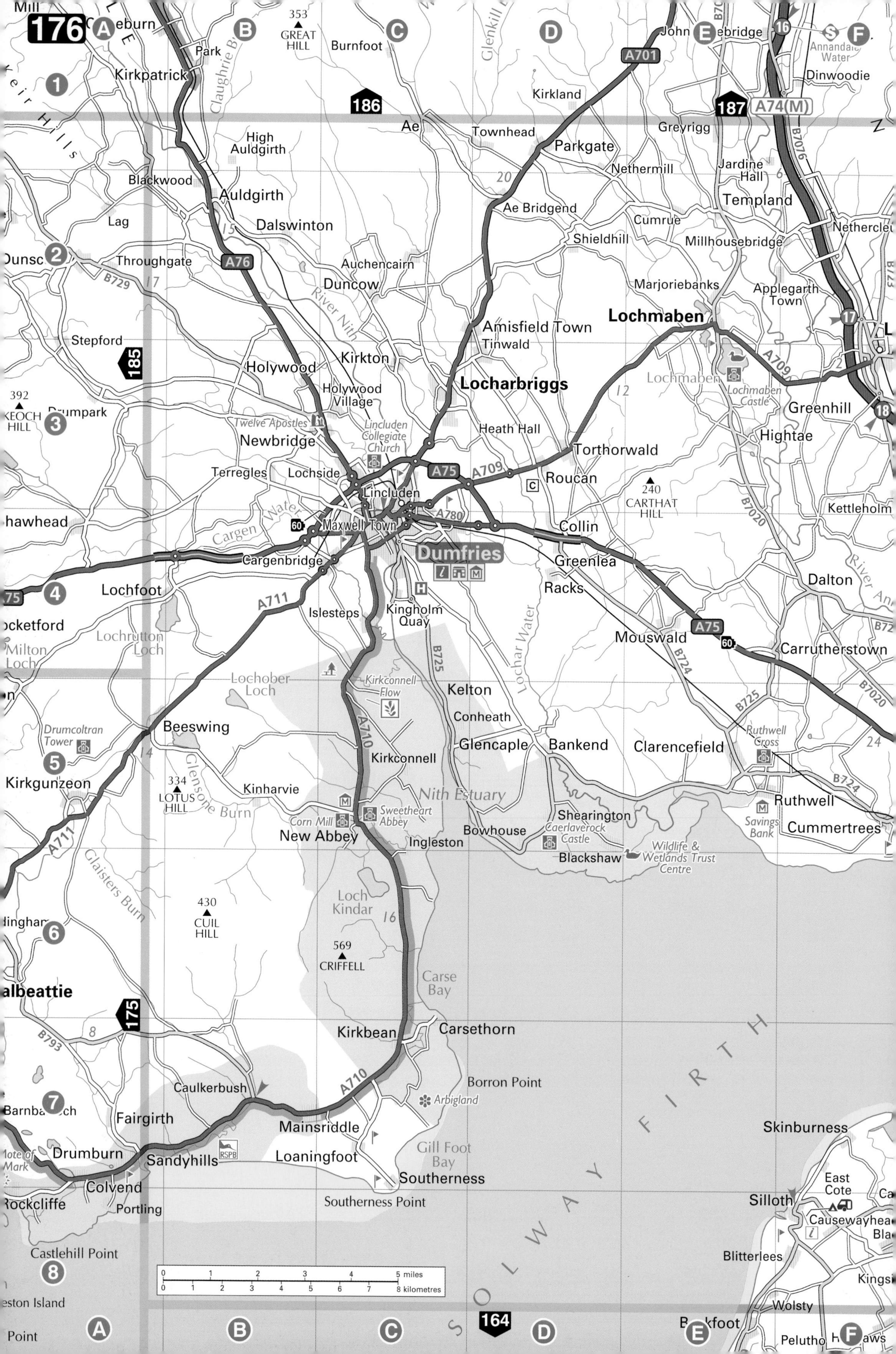

176
A
B
C
D
E
F
353
GREAT HILL
Burnfoot
Park
Kirkpatrick
Claughrie B.
186
187
A701
A74(M)
Dinwoodie
Annandale Water
Kirkland
Ae
Townhead
Greyrigg
Parkgate
Nethermill
Jardine Hall
High Auldgirth
Blackwood
Auldgirth
Dalswinton
Lag
Ae Bridgend
Templand
Cumrue
Shieldhill
Millhousebridge
A76
Throughgate
B729
Auchencairn
Duncow
River Nith
Marjoriebanks
Applegarth Town
Lochmaben
Amisfield Town
Tinwald
Stepford
185
Holywood
Kirkton
Locharbriggs
Lochmaben Castle
A709
Greenhill
Hightae
392
KEOCH HILL
Holywood Village
Twelve Apostles
Lincluden Collegiate Church
Heath Hall
Newbridge
Terregles
Lochside
A75
Torthorwald
Roucan
240
CARTHAT HILL
Lincluden
A780
Kettleholm
Cargen Water
Maxwell Town
Collin
B7020
Dumfries
Cargenbridge
Greenlea
Racks
Dalton
Lochfoot
A711
Islesteps
Kingholm Quay
Lochar Water
Mouswald
Carrutherstown
B724
B725
Lochrutton Loch
Milton Loch
Lochober Loch
Kirkconnell Flow
Kelton
Conheath
Glencaple
Bankend
Clarencefield
Ruthwell Cross
Beeswing
Drumcoltran Tower
A710
Kirkconnell
Kirkgunzeon
334
LOTUS HILL
Glensone Burn
Kinharvie
Nith Estuary
Sweetheart Abbey
Corn Mill
New Abbey
Ingleston
Bowhouse
Shearington
Caerlaverock Castle
Blackshaw
Wildlife & Wetlands Trust Centre
Ruthwell
Savings Bank
Cummertrees
Glaisters Burn
430
CUIL HILL
Loch Kindar
569
CRIFFELL
Carse Bay
Kirkbean
Carsethorn
B793
Caulkerbush
Borron Point
Arbigland
Fairgirth
Mainsriddle
Drumburn
Sandyhills
RSPB
Loaningfoot
Gill Foot Bay
Southerness
Colvend
Portling
Southerness Point
SOLWAY FIRTH
Skinburness
Silloth
East Cote
Causewayhead
Blitterlees
Castlehill Point
Wolsty
Pelutho
164
0 1 2 3 4 5 miles
0 1 2 3 4 5 6 7 8 kilometres

Dumfries & Carlisle
177
Castle O'er
Effgill
Georgefield
Arkleton
ROAN FELL
HILL
Boreland
Kirkstile
Bentpath
187
188
B709
Burnfoot
331
HART FELL
450
CAULDKINERIG
Craigcleuch
Water of Milk
Corrie
ESKDALE
404
TINNIS HILL
Langholm
New Langholm
Malcolm Memorial
Skipper's Bridge
Under Burnmouth
LIDDESDALE
B7068
319
GRANGE FELL
Bankshill
B7068
Wauchope Water
B6318
Tarras Water
178
A7
Tundergarth
Bigholms
252
COLLIN HAGS
Caulside
B6357
R Esk
Claygate
Harelaw
Warwicksland
Roman Camp
Waterbeck
B722
Solwaybank
Hollows
B725
B720
Evertown
Rowanburn
Canonbie
Pentonbridge
Middlebie
Kirtle Water
B6357
Milltown
Woodhouselees
Scuggate
Ecclefechan
B7076
B722
A74(M)
Eaglesfield
Timpanheck
B7201
Hoddom Cross
B725
Thomas Carlyle's Birthplace
Chapelknowe
Carwinley
Merkland Cross
Scotsdike
R Sark
Kirtlebridge
Bonshaw Tower
B6357
Netherby
Hoddom Mains
Robgill Tower
Brydekirk
Kirkpatrick-Fleming
B722
Creca
Hollee
B7076 Gretna
Longtown
B723
B6357
Springfield
River Lyne
Prior
Annan
Gretna Green
A6071
Kirklinton
Howes
A75
Rigg
Gretna
B721
River Esk
A7
Hetherside
Dornock
Eastriggs
Sandysike
Skitby
Newbie
Redkirk Point
Westlinton
Smithfield
A6071
M6
Todhills
Scalebyhill
Scaleby
Torduff Point
Rockcliffe Cross
Newtown
Bowness-on-Solway
Port Carlisle
R Eden
Todhills
Blackford
Longpark
Rockcliffe
Wallhead
Walby
RSPB
Glasson
Hadrian's Wall Path
Harker
Solway Aviation
Drumburgh
Boustead Hill
Burgh by Sands
North End
Beaumont
Low Crosby
Bowness Common
Easton
Cargo
Kingstown
High
Grinsdale
Houghton
Newby
Longcroft
Drumburgh Moss
Longburgh
West End
Monkhill
Kirkandrews upon Eden
Knowlefield
Linstock
Anthorn
Whitrigg
Fingland
Thurstonfield
Moorhouse
Stanwix
Angerton
Finglandrigg Woods
Whitrigglees
Stainton
Castle
CARLISLE
Kirkbride
Studholme
Kirkbampton
Bow
B5307
Belle Vue
Warwick on Eden
B5307
Laythes
Little Bampton
Oughterby
Little Orton
A689
Morton
Harraby
Scotby
Powhill
Wetheral
Newton Arlosh
Wampool
A595
Salt Coates
Great Orton
Newby West
Wedholme Flow
Aikton
Cummersdale
Upperby
M6
Biglands
Wiggonby
Brownrigg
Newby Cross
Blackwell
Carleton
Moss Side
Gamelsby
Woodhouses
Orton Rigg
A595
Raby
Drumleaning
Thornby
Baldwinholme
Brisco
Abbey Town
Whinnow
Cardewlees
Durdar
B6263
Holm Cultram
Moorhouse
Kelsick
Oulton
A596
Cotehill
Micklethwaite
Thursby
165
Dalston
Ratten Row
Dundraw
Dockray
Crofton
Burthwaite
Moor Row
Aikhead
Green Head
Buckabank
Scalesceugh

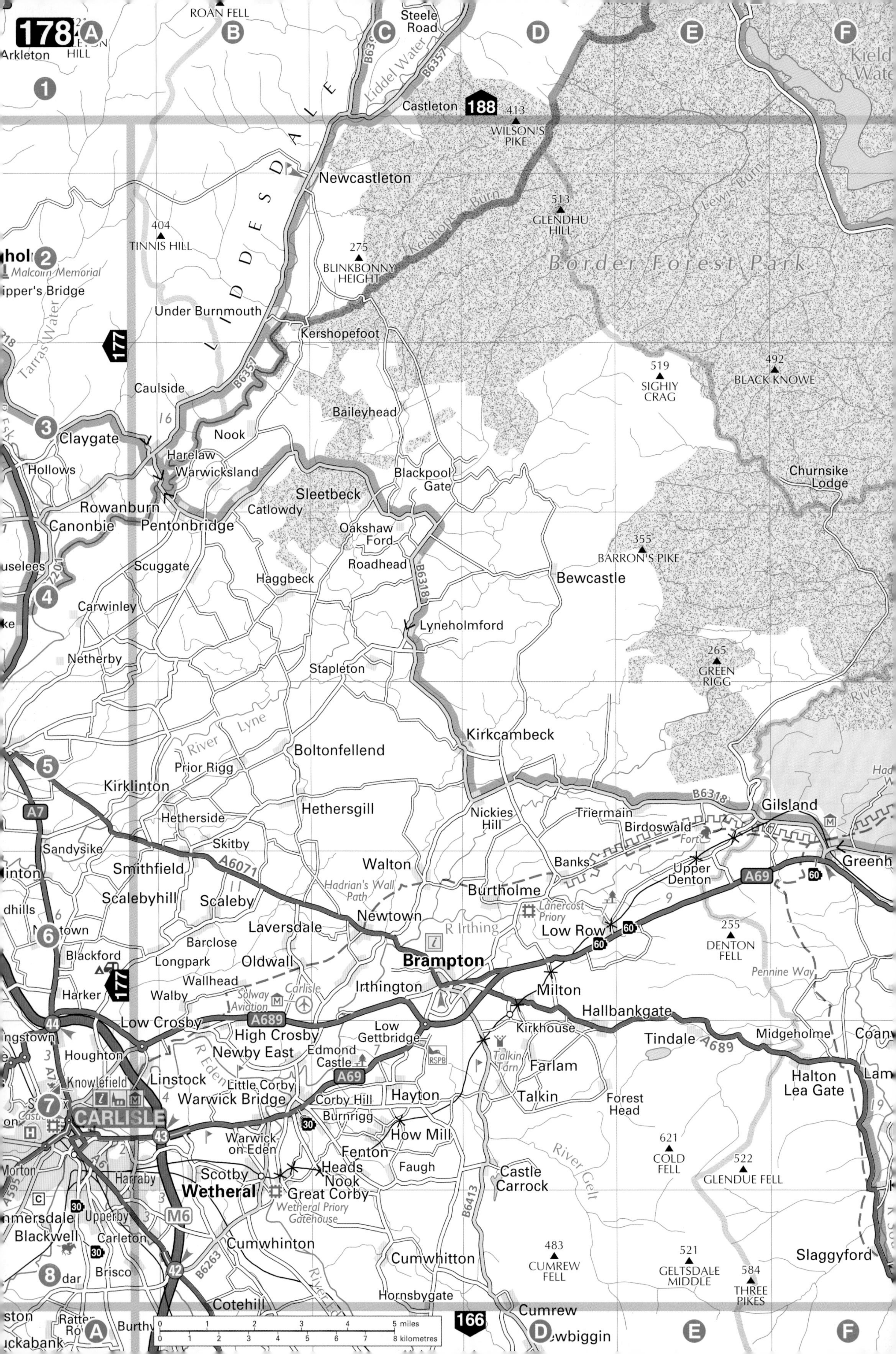

ROAN FELL
Steele Road
Arkleton
Liddel Water
B6357
Castleton
188
413
WILSON'S PIKE
Kielder Water
LIDDESDALE
Newcastleton
Kershope Burn
513
GLENDHU HILL
Lewis Burn
404
TINNIS HILL
275
BLINKBONNY HEIGHT
Border Forest Park
Malcolm Memorial
Skipper's Bridge
Tarras Water
Under Burnmouth
177
Kershopefoot
519
SIGHTY CRAG
492
BLACK KNOWE
Caulside
Baileyhead
Claygate
Nook
Harelaw
Warwicksland
Hollows
Blackpool Gate
Churnsike Lodge
Sleetbeck
Rowanburn
Catlowdy
Canonbie
Pentonbridge
Oakshaw Ford
355
BARRON'S PIKE
Scuggate
Roadhead
B6318
Haggbeck
Bewcastle
Carwinley
Lyneholmford
Netherby
265
GREEN RIGG
Stapleton
River Lyne
Kirkcambeck
Boltonfellend
Prior Rigg
Kirklinton
A7
Hethersgill
Nickies Hill
Triermain
Gilsland
Hetherside
Birdoswald Fort
Sandysike
Skitby
Walton
Banks
Upper Denton
Greenhead
Smithfield
A6071
Hadrian's Wall Path
Burtholme
A69
Scalebyhill
Scaleby
Lanercost Priory
Newtown
R Irthing
Low Row
255
DENTON FELL
Laversdale
Barclose
Blackford
Longpark
Oldwall
Brampton
Pennine Way
Wallhead
Solway Aviation
Carlisle
Irthington
Milton
Harker
Walby
Low Crosby
A689
Hallbankgate
High Crosby
Low Gettbridge
Kirkhouse
Tindale
Midgeholme
Houghton
Newby East
Edmond Castle
Talkin Tarn
Farlam
Knowlefield
Linstock
Little Corby
Halton Lea Gate
Warwick Bridge
Corby Hill
Hayton
Talkin
Forest Head
CARLISLE
Burnrigg
How Mill
Warwick-on-Eden
Fenton
621
COLD FELL
522
GLENDUE FELL
Scotby
Heads Nook
Faugh
Castle Carrock
River Gelt
Harraby
Wetheral
Great Corby
Wetheral Priory Gatehouse
M6
Upperby
B6413
Blackwell
Carleton
Cumwhinton
483
CUMREW FELL
521
GELTSDALE MIDDLE
584
THREE PIKES
Slaggyford
Brisco
Cumwhitton
B6263
River Eden
Hornsbygate
Cotehill
Cumrew
166
Newbiggin
0 1 2 3 4 5 miles
0 1 2 3 4 5 6 7 8 kilometres

Troughend
Highgreen Manor
Black Middens Bastle House
Gatehouse
WHITE HILL
Falstone
Greenhaugh
Stannersburn
Tower Knowe
Lanehead
Hott
Charlton
Hesleyside
Bellingham
West Woodburn
East Woodburn
Fort
Ray Fell
Kirkwhelpington
Ridsdale
Sweethope Loughs
NORTHUMBERLAND NATIONAL PARK
Redesmouth
Chirdon Burn
Great Bavington
Thockrington
Little Swinburne
Little Bavington
Colt Crag Reservoir
Hallington Reservoir
Hallington
Birtley
ROUND TOP
Wark
Chipchase Castle
Stonehaugh
Park End
Gunnerton
Great Swinburne
Colwell
Warks Burn
Simonburn
Nunwick
R North Tyne
Barrasford
Black Fell
Chollerton
Bingfield
Humshaugh
Chollerford
Hadrian's Wall
Little Whittington
Pennine Way
Broomlee Lough
Greenlee Lough
Hadrian's Wall Path
Carrawburgh: Temple of Mithras
Walwick
Chesters Fort
Wall
Fallowfield
Grindon Hill
Fourstones
High Warden
Halton
Housesteads Fort
Newbrough
Acomb
Sandhoe
Aydon Castle
R South Tyne
Warden
Once Brewed
Chesterholm (Vindolanda)
Birkshaw
Westend Town
Oakwood
Anick
Chesterwood
Haydon Bridge
Westwood
Thorngrafton
Haltwhistle
Henshaw
Bardon Mill
Redburn
Low Gate
Tyne Green
Corbridge
Melkridge
Beltingham
Ridley
Hexham
Elrington
Plenmeller
Langley Castle
Deanraw
West Dipton Burn
Allen Banks and Staward Gorge
Langley
Fellhouse Fell
Diptonmill
Broom
Ordley
Juniper
Steel
Wolf Hills
Slaley
Whitfield
Catton
Whitley Chapel
Whitfield Hall
Allendale
Thornley Gate
DUKESFIELD FELL
Derwent Reservoir
Ninebanks
HANGMAN HILL
Sinderhope
Keirsleywell Row
Blanchland
Baybridge
River Derwent
Limestone Brae
Edmundbyers
A68
A696
A6079
B6320
B6342
B6318
B6319
A69
B6531
A695
B6306
B6307
A686
B6305
B6304
B6295
189
190
180
167
60
30
70

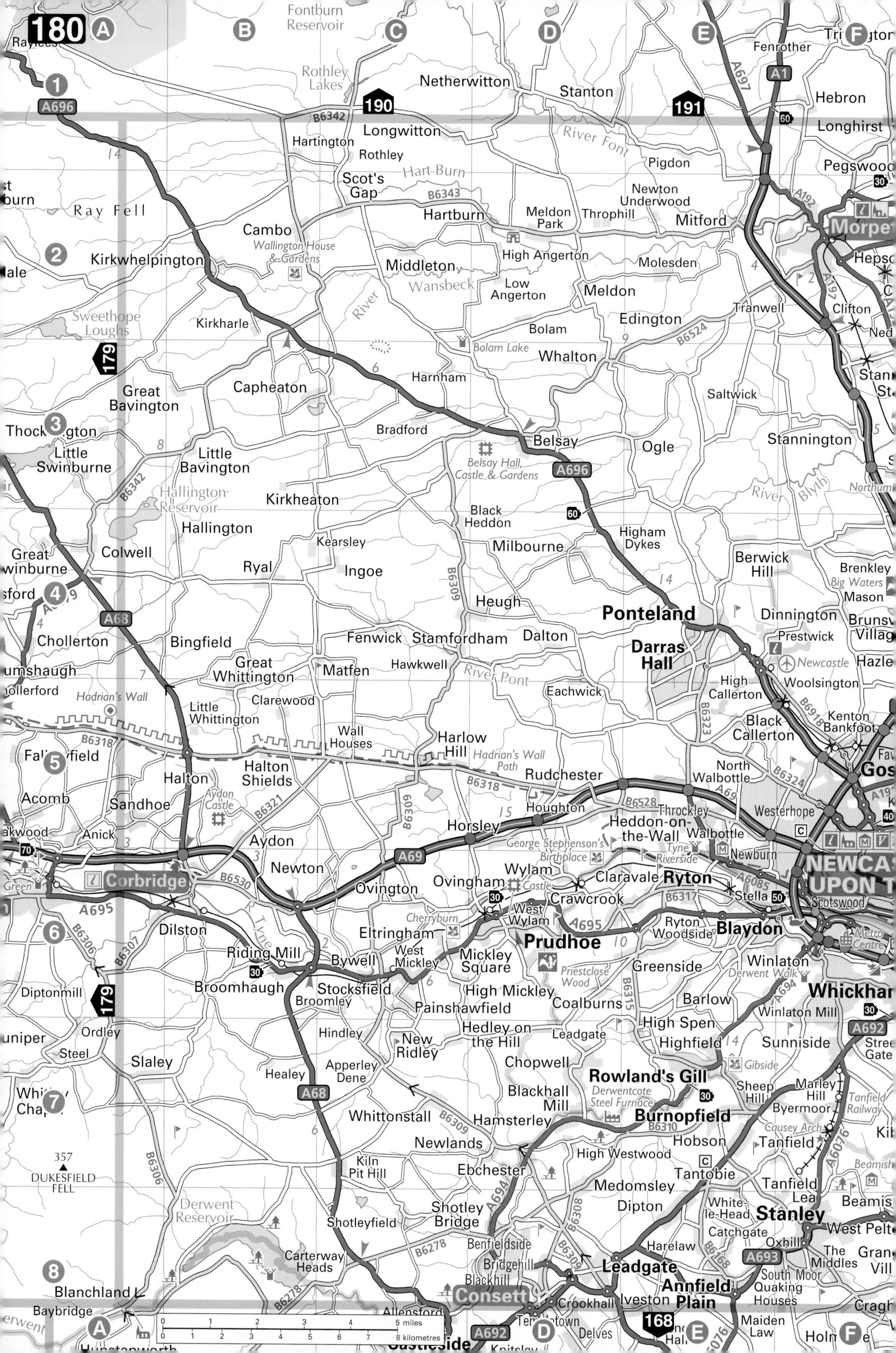

180
A
B
C
D
E
F
Fontburn Reservoir
Rothley Lakes
Netherwitton
Stanton
Fenrother
A1
A697
Hebron
Longhirst
Pegswood
190
191
B6342
Longwitton
Hartington
Rothley
Scot's Gap
Hart Burn
River Font
Pigdon
Newton Underwood
Mitford
A192
Morpeth
A696
1
2
3
4
5
6
7
8
Ray Fell
Cambo
Wallington House & Gardens
B6343
Hartburn
Meldon Park
Throphill
Kirkwhelpington
High Angerton
Molesden
Middleton
Wansbeck
Low Angerton
Meldon
Clifton
Sweethope Loughs
Kirkharle
River
Bolam
Edington
Tranwell
B6524
179
Bolam Lake
Whalton
Harnham
Capheaton
Great Bavington
Saltwick
Stannington
Bradford
Belsay
Ogle
Little Swinburne
Little Bavington
Belsay Hall, Castle & Gardens
River Blyth
Hallington Reservoir
Kirkheaton
B6342
Black Heddon
Hallington
Higham Dykes
Kearsley
Milbourne
Berwick Hill
Brenkley
Big Waters
Mason
Colwell
Ryal
Ingoe
Great Swinburne
B6309
Heugh
Ponteland
Dinnington
Prestwick
A68
Chollerton
Bingfield
Fenwick
Stamfordham
Dalton
Darras Hall
Newcastle
Great Whittington
Matfen
Hawkwell
River Pont
High Callerton
Woolsington
Hadrian's Wall
Little Whittington
Clarewood
Eachwick
B6323
B6918
Kenton Bankfoot
B6318
Wall Houses
Harlow Hill
Hadrian's Wall Path
Black Callerton
Halton
Halton Shields
Rudchester
North Walbottle
B6324
Acomb
Sandhoe
Aydon Castle
B6321
B6309
Houghton
B6528
Throckley
A69
Westerhope
Anick
Horsley
Heddon-on-the-Wall
Walbottle
Aydon
George Stephenson's Birthplace
Tyne Riverside
Newburn
Corbridge
Newton
B6530
Wylam
Claravale
Ryton
A6085
Stella
Scotswood
A695
Ovington
Ovingham
Castle
Crawcrook
Dilston
Cherryburn
West Wylam
Ryton Woodside
Blaydon
6
B6306
B6307
R. Tyne
Eltringham
Prudhoe
Metro Centre
Riding Mill
Bywell
West Mickley
Mickley Square
Greenside
Winlaton
Derwent Walk
Diptonmill
179
Broomhaugh
Stocksfield
Broomley
Priestclose Wood
High Mickley
Coalburns
B6315
Barlow
A694
Whickham
Winlaton Mill
Ordley
Hindley
Painshawfield
High Spen
Steel
New Ridley
Hedley on the Hill
Leadgate
Highfield
Sunniside
A692
Slaley
Healey
Apperley Dene
Chopwell
Gibside
Rowland's Gill
Sheep Hill
Marley Hill
Tanfield Railway
A68
Blackhall Mill
Derwentcote Steel Furnace
Byermoor
Whittonstall
B6309
Hamsterley
Burnopfield
B6310
Causey Arch
Tanfield
Newlands
Hobson
A6076
357
DUKESFIELD FELL
B6306
Kiln Pit Hill
High Westwood
Ebchester
Tantobie
Beamish
A694
Medomsley
Tanfield Lea
Beamish
Derwent Reservoir
Shotley Bridge
Dipton
White-le-Head
Stanley
West Pelton
Shotleyfield
B6308
Catchgate
Oxhill
Benfieldside
Harelaw
The Middles
B6278
Carterway Heads
Bridgehill
B6309
Leadgate
B6168
A693
South Moor
Blackhill
Annfield Plain
Quaking Houses
Blanchland
Consett
Crookhall
Baybridge
B6278
Allensford
Delves
168
Maiden Law
A692
0 1 2 3 4 5 miles
0 1 2 3 4 5 6 7 8 kilometres

Ellington
Lynemouth
191
Beacon Point
Woodhorn
Woodhorn Demesne
Newbiggin-by-the-Sea
North Seaton
Wansbeck Riverside
North Seaton Colliery
West Sleekburn
Bomarsund
Cambois
East Sleekburn
North Blyth
Blyth
Cowpen
Bebside
Newsham
New Delaval
East Hartford
Shankhouse
New Hartley
Seaton Sluice
East Cramlington
Seaton
Hartley
Seaton Delaval
St Mary's Lighthouse
Seghill
Holywell
Annitsford
Burradon
Earsdon
Camperdown
Backworth
Monkseaton
Whitley Bay
Cullercoats
Killingworth
Shiremoor
Murton
Tynemouth
Forest Hall
New York
Tynemouth Priory & Castle
Amsterdam (IJmuiden)
Rising Sun
North Shields
Longbenton
Willington Quay
SOUTH SHIELDS
Wallsend
Int. Ferry Terminal
Heaton
Jarrow
Tyne Tunnel
Westoe
Marsden Bay
Walker
Harton
Byker
Hebburn
Marsden
Souter Lighthouse
River Tyne
Monkton
Felling
Souter Point
Cleadon
Whitburn
West Boldon
Wardley
Boldon Colliery
GATESHEAD
East Boldon
Whitburn Bay
Low Fell
Wrekenton
Seaburn
Bowes Railway & Museum
Fulwell
Roker
Hylton
Southwick
Monkwearmouth
Springwell
Usworth
Castletown
Wildfowl & Wetlands Trust
Birtley
South Hylton
SUNDERLAND
Portobello
WASHINGTON
Pennywell
Hendon
Washington
Offerton
Ouston
Penshaw Monument
High Newport
Grangetown
Fatfield
Penshaw
Tunstall
Herrington
New Silksworth
Ryhope
Durham Heritage Coast
River Wear
Shiney Row
New Herrington
Pelton Fell
Philadelphia
Houghton Gate
Bournmoor
Newbottle
Houghton-le-Spring
High Dubmire
Seaton
169
Seaham
A1068
A189
A197
B1334
A193
B1331
B1505
A192
A1061
A190
B1326
B1322
B1325
A1148
B1317
A191
A19
A1058
A187
A185
A1300
B1298
A183
B1313
A184
B1296
B1288
A194
A1018
B1299
A194(M)
A1290
A195
A1231
A6127
A693
A690
B1405
B1522
B1286
B1284
B1287
B1404

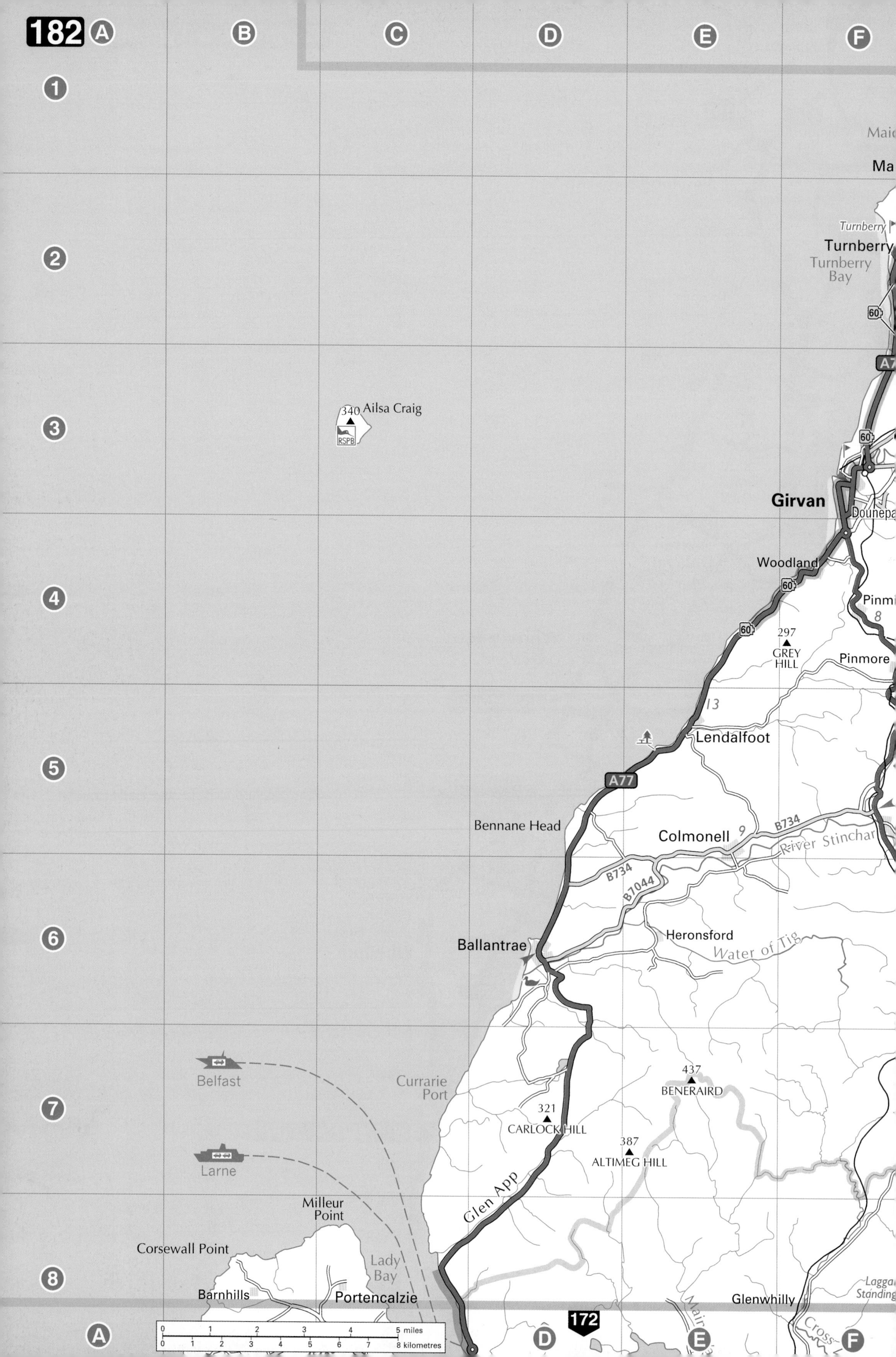

A
B
C
D
E
F
1
2
3
4
5
6
7
8
Maid
Ma
Turnberry
Turnberry
Turnberry Bay
60
A77
340
Ailsa Craig
RSPB
60
Girvan
Dounepa
Woodland
60
60
Pinm
8
297
GREY HILL
Pinmore
13
Lendalfoot
A77
Bennane Head
Colmonell
9
B734
River Stinchar
B734
B7044
Heronsford
Ballantrae
Water of Tig
Belfast
Currarie Port
437
BENERAIRD
321
CARLOCK HILL
387
ALTIMEG HILL
Larne
Glen App
Milleur Point
Corsewall Point
Lady Bay
Barnhills
Portencalzie
Glenwhilly
Lagga Standing
0 1 2 3 4 5 miles
0 1 2 3 4 5 6 7 8 kilometres
172

Knoweside
Croy Brae (Electric Brae)
Pennyglen
Whitefaulds
Maybole
Culzean Castle Country Park
Kirkoswald
Souter Johnnie's Cottage
Crossraguel Abbey
Grimmet
Guiltreehill
Kirkmichael
Patna
Waterside
Dunaskin
KILMEIN HILL
BENBEOCH
High Pennyvenie
Dalmellington
KEIRS HILL
Threave
Crosshill
Straiton
Roan of Craigoch
Wallacetown
Kilgrammie
Dailly
Water of Girvan
Ness Glen
Mossdale
MARATZ HILL
Loch Finlas
Loch Doon
Drumjohn
GARLEFFIN FELL
Linfern Loch
Tallaminnock
Loch Bradan
CRAIGLEE
Loch Doon Castle
Dalquhairn
River Stinchar
Knockeen
Balloch
Barr
C A R R I C K
Loch Recar
Loch Macaterick
MEAUL
Garryhorn
POLMADDIE HILL
SHALLOCH ON MINNOCH
Galloway Forest Park
KIRRIEREOCH HILL
MERRICK
CORSERINE
Loch Enoch
MILFIRE
Loch Dungeon
Muck Water
Loch Moan
GARWALL HILL
Loch Neldricken
Silver Flowe
Barrhill
Feoch Burn
River Cree
Water of Minnoch
Glen Trool Lodge
Bruce Memorial
Loch Dee
Loch Trool
Lochton
Glentrool Village
Glen Trool
Creebank
Bargrennan
LAMACHAN HILL
LARG HILL
MILLFORE
Clatteringshaws Loch
Drumlamford
Loch Dornal
Loch Maberry
Loch Ochiltree
GARLICK HILL
Galloway Deer Range
Knowe
River Bladnoch
RSPB
A77
A713
A714
B7023
B7045
B741
B734
B7027
196
184
173

184
A
B
C
D
E
F
196
1
2
3
4
5
6
7
8
A77
River Doon
Rankinston
Dalgig
River Nith
Connel Park
Bankglen
Craigbank
429
KILMEIN HILL
Guiltreehill
Patna
Waterside
Dunaskin
Kirkmichael
B7023
B741
464
BENBEOCH
306
KEIRS HILL
A713
Threave
B7045
High Pennyvenie
568
ENOCH HILL
Crosshill
Dalmellington
Straiton
B741
Ness Glen
Mossdale
536
Water of Girvan
183
320
MARATZ HILL
10
Loch Finlas
Loch Doon
429
GARLEFFIN FELL
Lintern Loch
Tallaminnock
Loch Bradan
Bow Burn
796
CAIRNSMORE OF CARSPHAIRN
Drumjohn
A713
River Stinchar
523
CRAIGLEE
Loch Doon Castle
Balloch
R
I
C
K
Loch Recar
622
Garryhorn Burn
Carsphairn
Loch Macaterick
Water of Deugh
B729
549
768
SHALLOCH ON MINNOCH
695
MEAUL
9
Polmaddy Burn
Galloway
781
KIRRIEREOCH HILL
813
CORSERINE
A713
Loch Moan
842
MERRICK
Loch Enoch
716
MILFIRE
346
GARWALL HILL
Forest Park
Loch Dungeon
Water of Minnoch
Loch Neldricken
Silver Flowe
Knocksheen
Garroch
12
183
Glen Trool Lodge
Bruce Memorial
Loch Dee
Loch Trool
A714
22
Glentrool Village
Glen Trool
380
BENNAN
Bargrennan
Bruce's Stone
New G
716
LAMACHAN HILL
Clatteringshaws Forest & Wildlife Centre
675
LARG HILL
Clatteringshaws Loch
654
MILLFORE
A712
Black Water of Dee
19
Loch Ochiltree
440
GARLICK HILL
Galloway Deer Range
402
ROUND FELL
Knowe
RSPB
471
FELL OF FLEET
174
0 1 2 3 4 5 miles
0 1 2 3 4 5 6 7 8 kilometres

G
H
J
197
Kirkconnel
Kelloholm
A76
Newtown
Sanquhar
594
HARE HILL
Kello Water
Ulzieside
Mennock
700
BLACKCRAIG
Euchan Water
450
CLOUD HILL
478
Polgown
475
COUNTAM
554
CAIRNKINNA HILL
Cleuch-head
598
COLT HILL
Big Carlae
Old Auchenbrack
Auchenhessnane
Shinnel Water
Scaur Water
Benbuie
337
BENNAN
532
CORNHARROW HILL
Southern Upland Way
Stenhouse
Tynron
Moniaive
Kirkland
B729
A702
Maxwelton
Glencrosh
Craigneston
Black Water
385
WETHER HILL
431
BOGRIE HILL
Skelston
Snade
Sundaywell
Loch Urr
Loch Howie
Bogue
B7075
Balmaclellan
A712
281
LARGLEAR HILL
Corsock
Ironmacannie
Eastlands
A75
Knockvennie Smithy
B794
Auchenreoch Loch
A713
175
Kirkpatrick
Springholm
Milton
Airds of Kells
K
L
M
Wanlockhead
GREEN LOWTHER
725
LOWTHER HILL
1
Lowther Hills
B797
Enterkin Burn
River Nith
Enterkinfoot
Durisdeermill
Durisdeer
2
691
Gateslack
East Morton
186
NITHSDALE
A76
Drumlanrig
Morton Castle
3
Carronbridge
Tibbers
Burnhead
Penpont
Thornhill
B731
Closeburnmill
4
Cample
Keir Mill
Closeburn
Park
Claughrie Burn
Kirkpatrick
Keir Hills
5
Blackwood
Auldgirth
Lag
Dunscore
Throughgate
B729
A76
6
Stepford
Holywood
176
392
SKEOCH HILL
Drumpark
Twelve Apostles
Newbridge
7
Shawhead
Cargen Water
Cargenbridge
Lochfoot
A711
Crocketford
Lochrutton Loch
Milton Loch
8
Lochober Loch

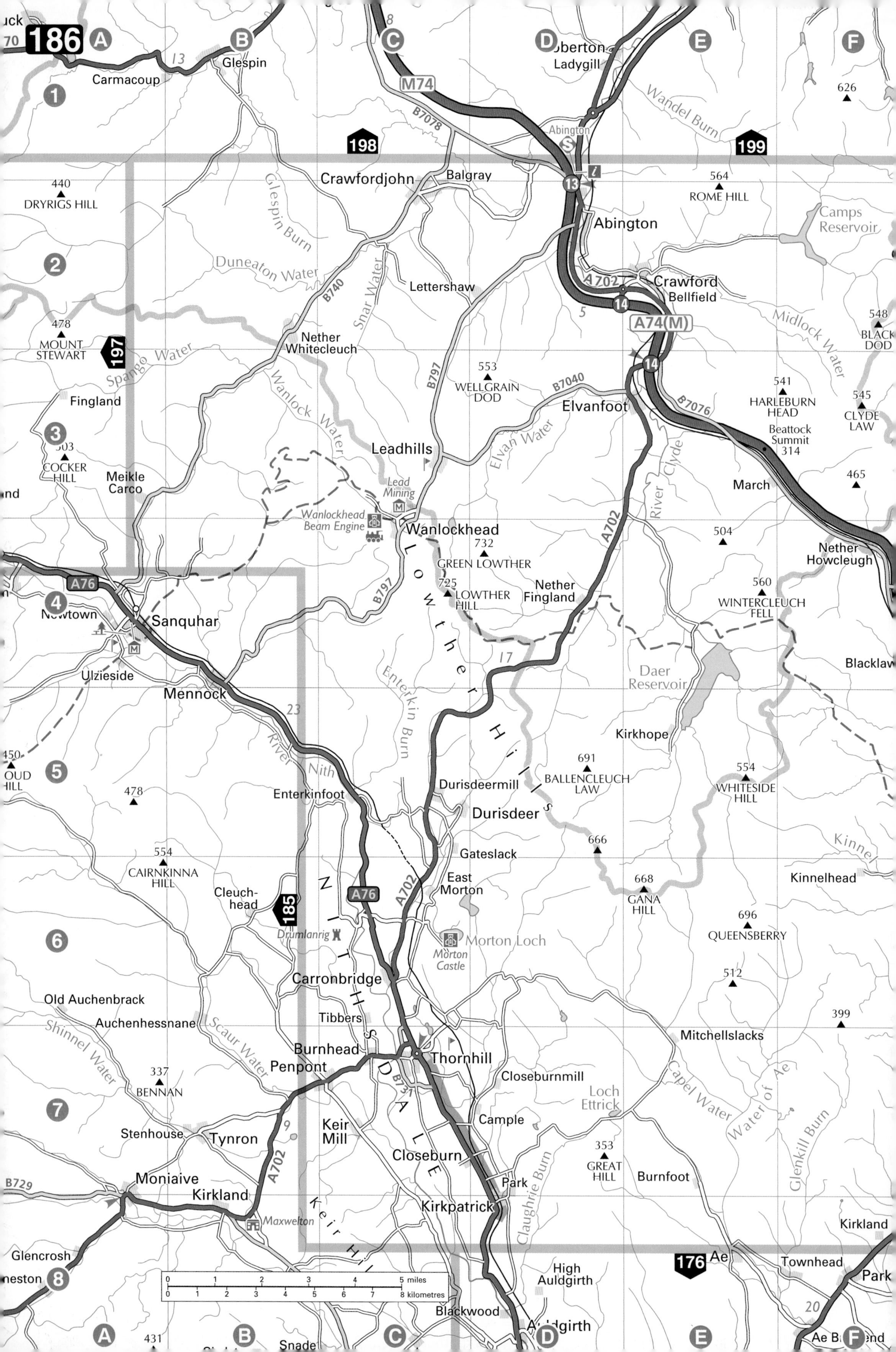
186
A
B
C
D
E
F
Glespin
Carmacoup
13
1
8
M74
Roberton
Ladygill
Wandel Burn
626
B7078
Abington
198
199
Crawfordjohn
Balgray
13
440
DRYRIGS HILL
564
ROME HILL
Camps Reservoir
Glespin Burn
Abington
2
Duneaton Water
A702
Crawford
Bellfield
B740
Snar Water
Lettershaw
14
5
A74(M)
Midlock Water
548
BLACK DOD
478
MOUNT STEWART
197
Spango Water
Nether Whitecleuch
14
553
WELLGRAIN DOD
B797
B7040
Elvanfoot
541
HARLEBURN HEAD
545
CLYDE LAW
Fingland
Wanlock Water
B7076
Beattock Summit 314
3
503
COCKER HILL
Meikle Carco
Leadhills
Elvan Water
River Clyde
465
March
Lead Mining
Wanlockhead Beam Engine
Wanlockhead
A702
504
732
GREEN LOWTHER
Nether Howcleugh
A76
725
LOWTHER HILL
Nether Fingland
560
WINTERCLEUCH FELL
4
Newtown
Sanquhar
B797
Lowther Hills
Ulzieside
17
Daer Reservoir
Blacklaw
Mennock
Enterkin Burn
23
River Nith
Kirkhope
450
5
691
BALLENCLEUCH LAW
554
WHITESIDE HILL
478
Enterkinfoot
Durisdeermill
Durisdeer
666
Kinnel
554
CAIRNKINNA HILL
Gateslack
East Morton
668
GANA HILL
Kinnelhead
Cleuch-head
185
A76
A702
Nithsdale
696
QUEENSBERRY
6
Drumlanrig
Morton Loch
Morton Castle
512
Carronbridge
Old Auchenbrack
399
Auchenhessnane
Tibbers
Shinnel Water
Scaur Water
Mitchellslacks
Burnhead
Thornhill
337
BENNAN
Penpont
B731
Closeburnmill
Loch Ettrick
Capel Water
Water of Ae
7
Keir Mill
Cample
Glenkill Burn
Stenhouse
Tynron
9
353
GREAT HILL
Closeburn
Burnfoot
B729
Moniaive
A702
Park
Claughrie Burn
Kirkland
Kirkpatrick
Kirkland
Maxwelton
Keir Hills
Glencrosh
176
Ae
Townhead
Park
High Auldgirth
8
0 1 2 3 4 5 miles
0 1 2 3 4 5 6 7 8 kilometres
Blackwood
20
Auldgirth
431
Snade
Ae Bridgend

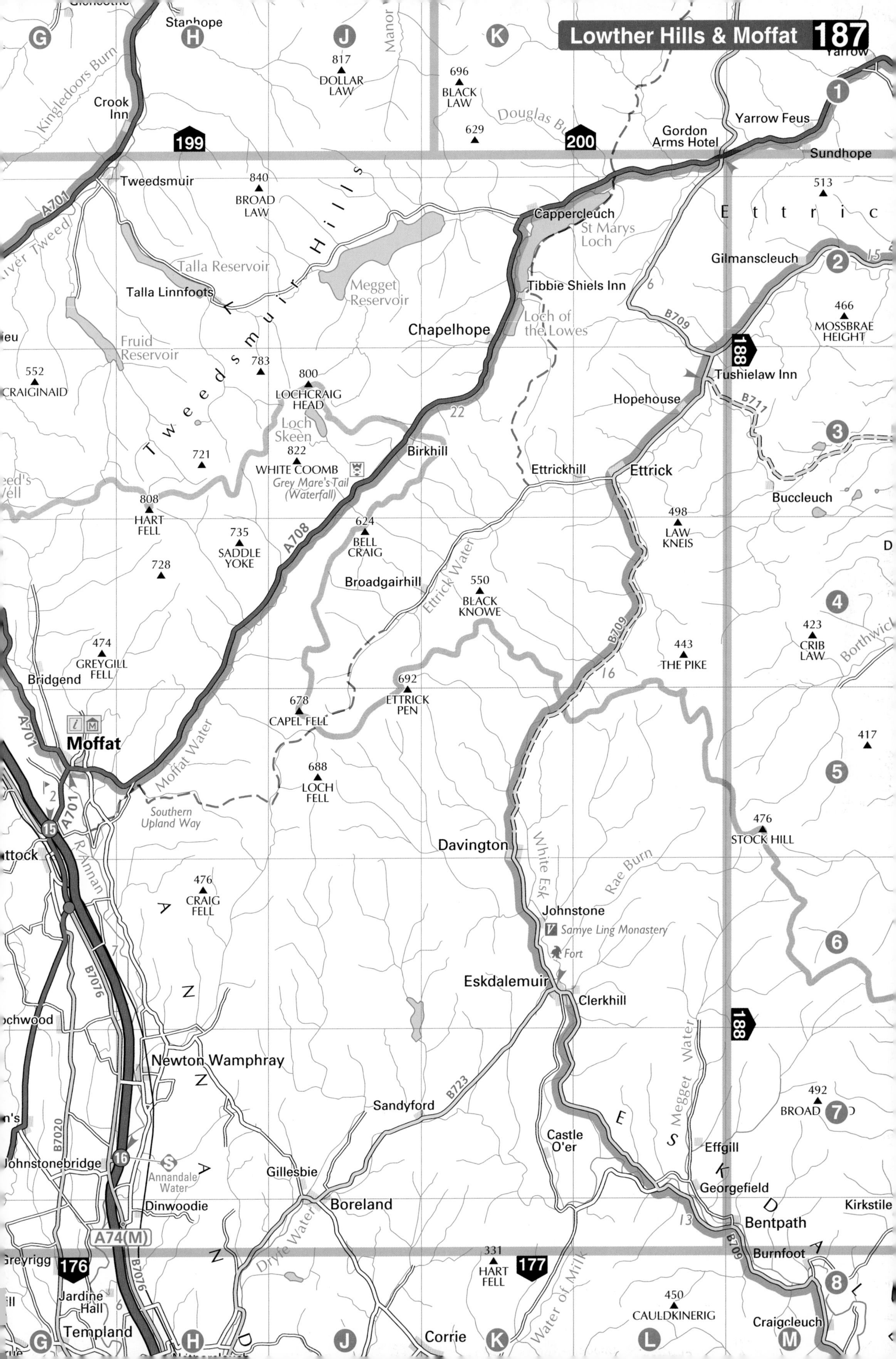
Stanhope
Crook Inn
Kingledoors Burn
817
DOLLAR LAW
Manor
696
BLACK LAW
629
Douglas Burn
199
200
Yarrow
Yarrow Feus
Gordon Arms Hotel
Sundhope
A701
Tweedsmuir
840
BROAD LAW
River Tweed
Cappercleuch
St Marys Loch
513
Ettric
Talla Reservoir
Talla Linnfoots
Megget Reservoir
Tibbie Shiels Inn
Gilmanscleuch
Tweedsmuir Hills
Loch of the Lowes
Chapelhope
B709
466
MOSSBRAE HEIGHT
Fruid Reservoir
552
CRAIGINAID
783
800
LOCHCRAIG HEAD
188
Tushielaw Inn
Hopehouse
B711
Loch Skeen
822
WHITE COOMB
721
Grey Mare's Tail (Waterfall)
Birkhill
Ettrickhill
Ettrick
Buccleuch
808
HART FELL
735
SADDLE YOKE
728
624
BELL CRAIG
498
LAW KNEIS
A708
Broadgairhill
Ettrick Water
550
BLACK KNOWE
474
GREYGILL FELL
Bridgend
443
THE PIKE
423
CRIB LAW
Borthwick
692
ETTRICK PEN
678
CAPEL FELL
Moffat
Moffat Water
688
LOCH FELL
417
Southern Upland Way
476
STOCK HILL
Davington
R. Annan
White Esk
Rae Burn
476
CRAIG FELL
Johnstone
Samye Ling Monastery
Fort
Eskdalemuir
Clerkhill
Newton Wamphray
B7076
Megget Water
B723
Sandyford
492
BROAD
Castle O'er
Effgill
Johnstonebridge
Annandale Water
Gillesbie
Georgefield
Dinwoodie
Boreland
Bentpath
Kirkstile
A74(M)
Dryfe Water
331
HART FELL
177
176
Burnfoot
Greyrigg
Jardine Hall
450
CAULDKINERIG
Water of Milk
Templand
Corrie
Craigcleuch
B7020
ANNANDALE
ESKDALE

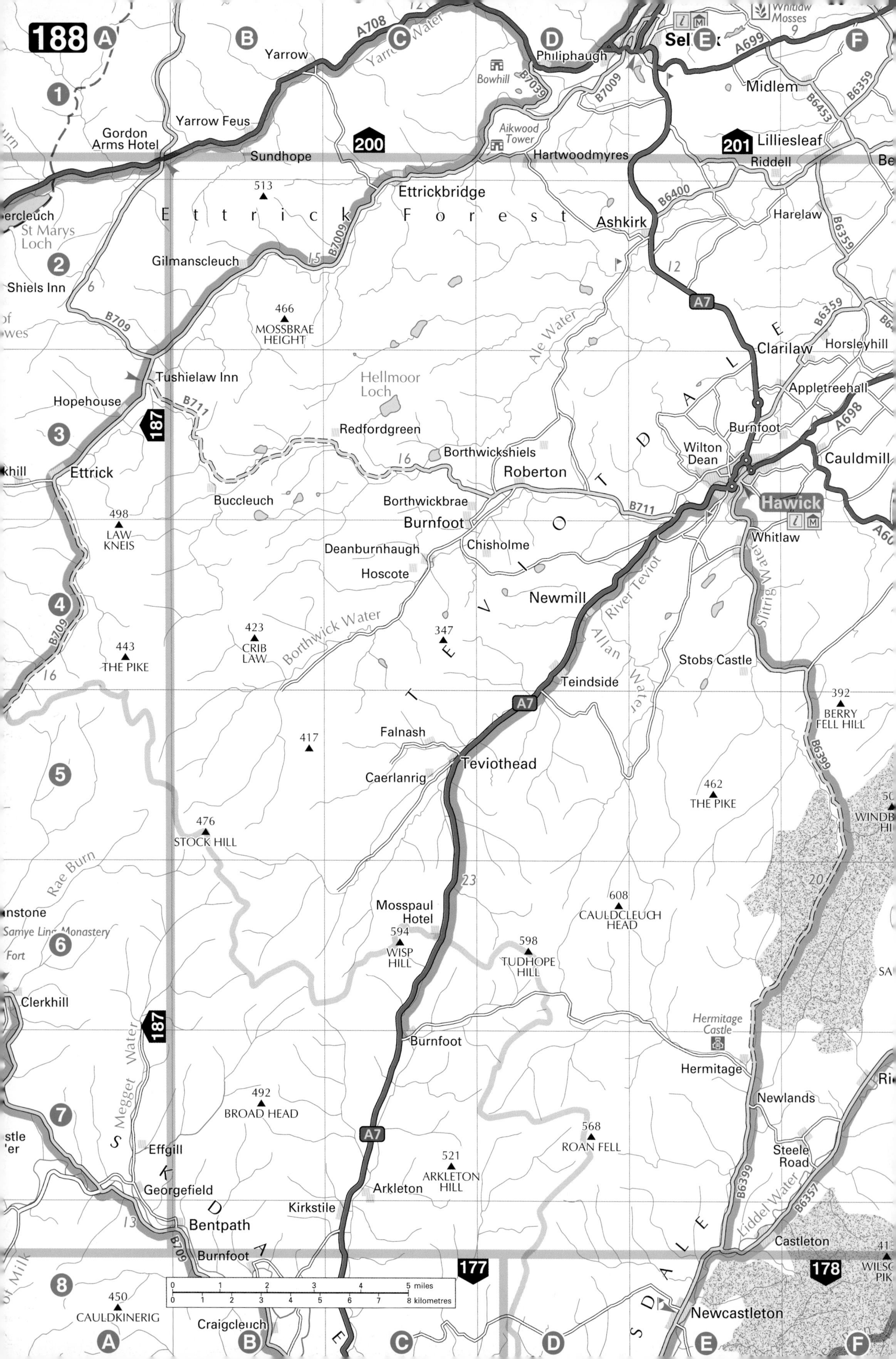

A
B
C
D
E
F
1
2
3
4
5
6
7
8
Yarrow
A708
Yarrow Water
Philiphaugh
Selkirk
Whitlaw Mosses
A699
Bowhill
B7039
B7009
Midlem
B6453
B6359
Gordon Arms Hotel
Yarrow Feus
Aikwood Tower
200
201
Lilliesleaf
Sundhope
Hartwoodmyres
Riddell
Ettrickbridge
513
B6400
St Marys Loch
Ettrick Forest
Ashkirk
Harelaw
B7009
Gilmanscleuch
15
12
Shiels Inn
466
MOSSBRAE HEIGHT
A7
B709
Ale Water
B6359
Clarilaw
Horsleyhill
Tushielaw Inn
Hellmoor Loch
Appletreehall
Hopehouse
B711
187
Redfordgreen
Burnfoot
A698
Wilton Dean
Borthwickshiels
16
Cauldmill
Ettrick
Roberton
Teviotdale
Buccleuch
Borthwickbrae
B711
Hawick
498
LAW KNEIS
Burnfoot
Whitlaw
Chisholme
Deanburnhaugh
Hoscote
Newmill
River Teviot
Slitrig Water
Borthwick Water
347
B709
423
CRIB LAW
443
THE PIKE
Allan Water
Stobs Castle
16
Teindside
392
BERRY FELL HILL
417
Falnash
Teviothead
Caerlanrig
B6399
462
THE PIKE
476
STOCK HILL
Rae Burn
23
20
608
CAULDCLEUCH HEAD
Mosspaul Hotel
594
WISP HILL
598
TUDHOPE HILL
Samye Ling Monastery
Clerkhill
187
Megget Water
Hermitage Castle
Burnfoot
Hermitage
492
BROAD HEAD
Newlands
568
ROAN FELL
Eskdale
Effgill
521
ARKLETON HILL
Steele Road
Georgefield
Arkleton
B6399
Liddel Water
B6357
Kirkstile
Bentpath
13
Liddesdale
B709
Burnfoot
Castleton
177
178
450
CAULDKINERIG
0 1 2 3 4 5 miles
0 1 2 3 4 5 6 7 8 kilometres
Craigcleuch
Newcastleton

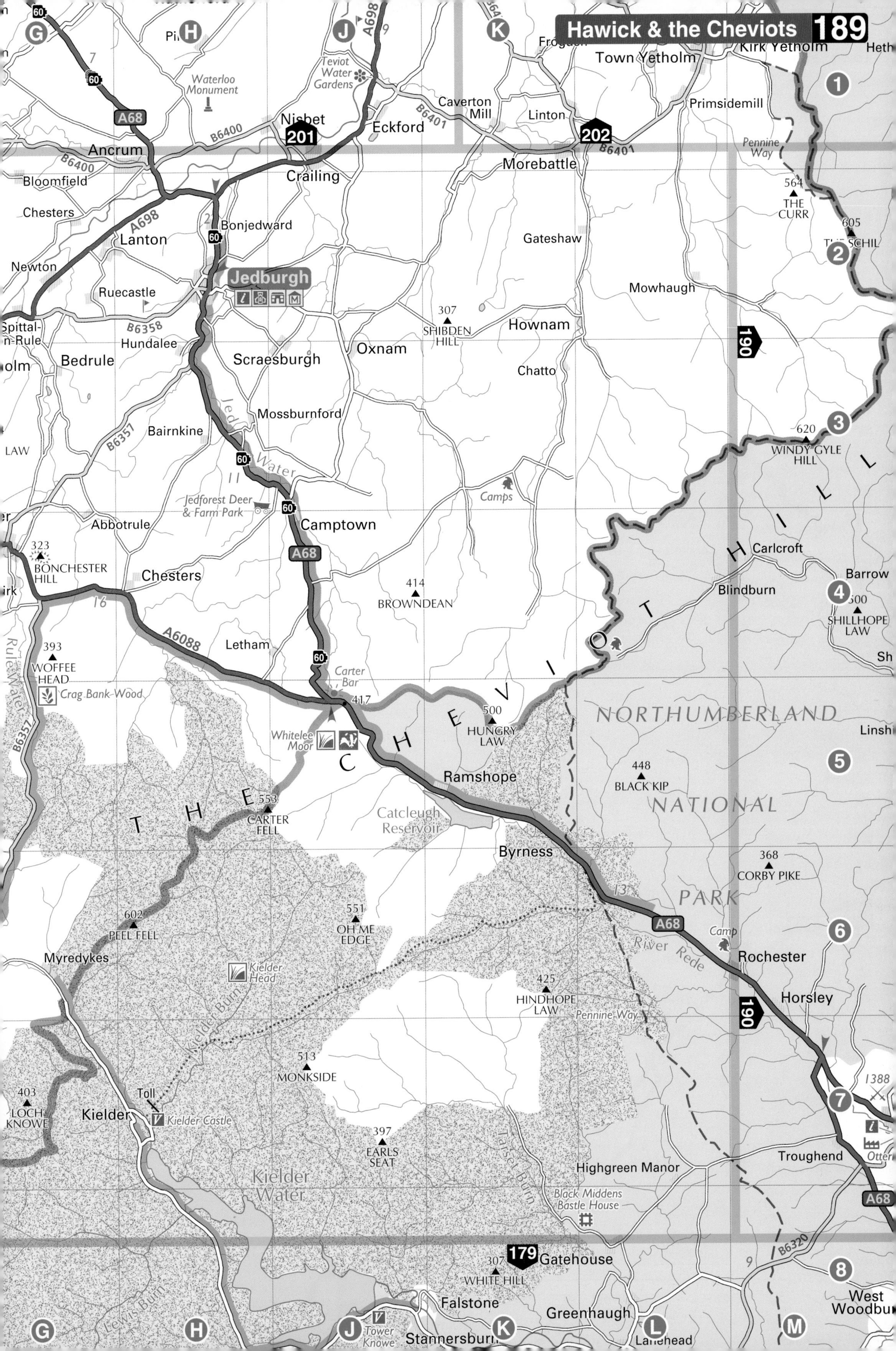
Town Yetholm
Kirk Yetholm
Teviot Water Gardens
Waterloo Monument
Caverton Mill
Linton
Primsidemill
Nisbet
201
Eckford
202
Ancrum
Crailing
Morebattle
Pennine Way
Bloomfield
Chesters
564 THE CURR
605
Bonjedward
Lanton
Gateshaw
Newton
Jedburgh
Ruecastle
Mowhaugh
307 SHIBDEN HILL
Hownam
Spittal-on-Rule
Hundalee
Bedrule
Scraesburgh
Oxnam
190
Chatto
Mossburnford
Bairnkine
Jed Water
620 WINDY GYLE HILL
Jedforest Deer & Farm Park
Camps
Abbotrule
Camptown
323 BONCHESTER HILL
Chesters
Carlcroft
Barrow
414 BROWNDEAN
Blindburn
500 SHILLHOPE LAW
Rule Water
393 WOFFEE HEAD
Letham
Carter Bar
Crag Bank Wood
417
500 HUNGRY LAW
Whitelee Moor
NORTHUMBERLAND NATIONAL PARK
THE CHEVIOT HILLS
Ramshope
448 BLACK KIP
553 CARTER FELL
Catcleugh Reservoir
Byrness
368 CORBY PIKE
602 PEEL FELL
551 OH ME EDGE
Camp
Rochester
River Rede
Myredykes
Kielder Head
425 HINDHOPE LAW
Pennine Way
Horsley
Kielder Burn
513 MONKSIDE
1388
403 LOCH KNOWE
Kielder
Toll
Kielder Castle
397 EARLS SEAT
Tarset Burn
Troughend
Highgreen Manor
Kielder Water
Black Middens Bastle House
179
Gatehouse
307 WHITE HILL
Falstone
Greenhaugh
West Woodburn
Lewis Burn
Tower Knowe
Stannersburn
Lanehead
A68
A698
A6088
B6400
B6401
B6358
B6357
B6320

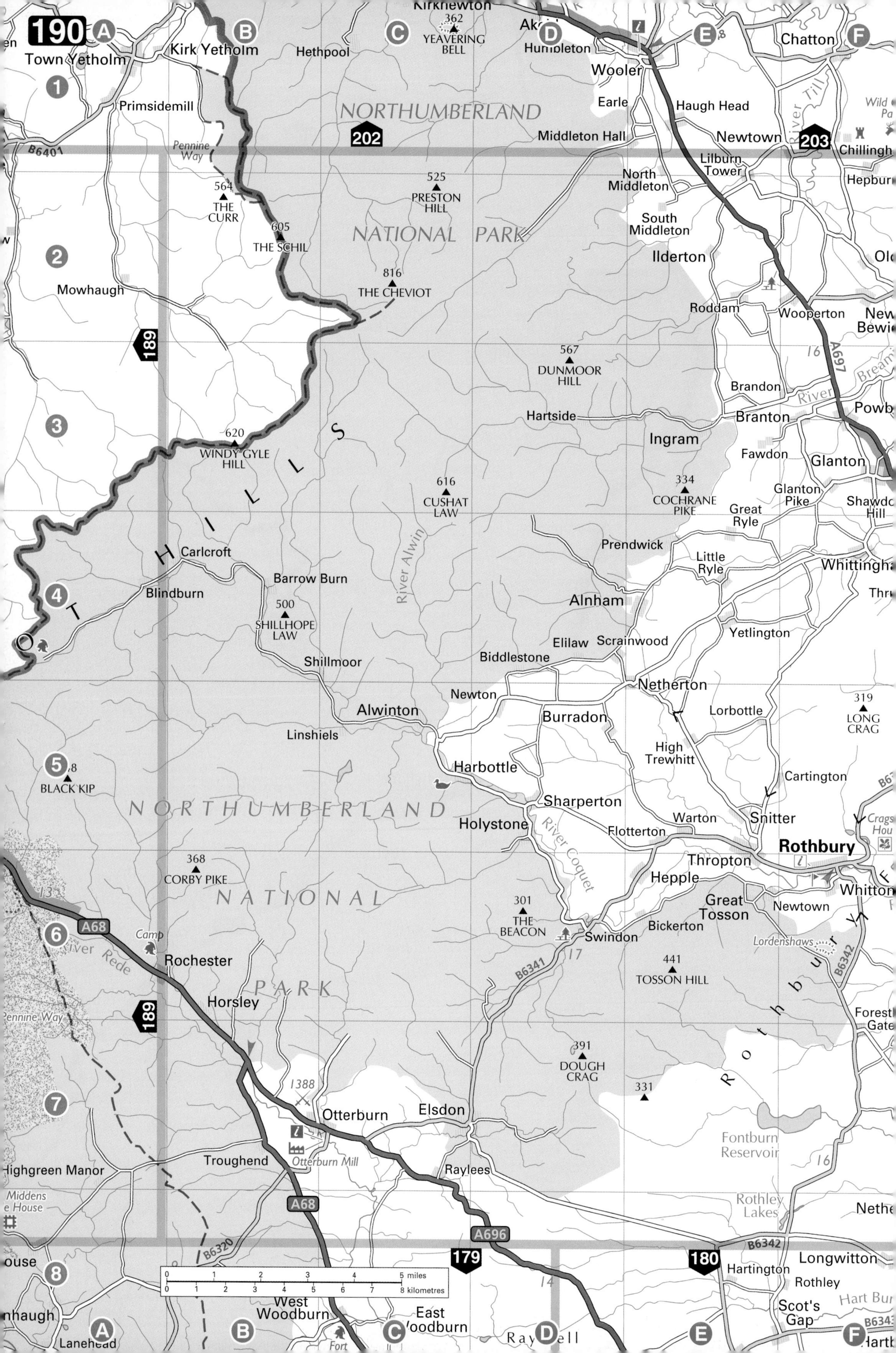

Town Yetholm
Kirk Yetholm
Hethpool
Kirknewton
362 YEAVERING BELL
Akeld
Humbleton
Wooler
Chatton
Earle
Haugh Head
Primsidemill
NORTHUMBERLAND
202
Middleton Hall
Newtown
203
Chillingham
Pennine Way
B6401
Lilburn Tower
Hepburn
North Middleton
564 THE CURR
525 PRESTON HILL
605 THE SCHIL
NATIONAL PARK
South Middleton
Ilderton
816 THE CHEVIOT
Mowhaugh
Roddam
Wooperton
New Bewick
189
567 DUNMOOR HILL
A697
Brandon
River Breamish
Powburn
Hartside
Branton
620 WINDY GYLE HILL
Ingram
Fawdon
Glanton
616 CUSHAT LAW
334 COCHRANE PIKE
Glanton Pike
Great Ryle
Shawdon Hill
Prendwick
Carlcroft
Little Ryle
Whittingham
Barrow Burn
River Alwin
Blindburn
Alnham
500 SHILLHOPE LAW
Yetlington
Elilaw
Scrainwood
Shillmoor
Biddlestone
Netherton
Newton
319 LONG CRAG
Alwinton
Burradon
Lorbottle
Linshiels
High Trewhitt
Harbottle
Cartington
BLACK KIP
NORTHUMBERLAND
Sharperton
Holystone
Warton
Snitter
River Coquet
Flotterton
Cragside House
Rothbury
368 CORBY PIKE
Thropton
Hepple
Whitton
NATIONAL
Great Tosson
Newtown
301 THE BEACON
Bickerton
A68
Camp
Swindon
Lordenshaws
River Rede
Rochester
441 TOSSON HILL
B6341
B6342
PARK
Horsley
Pennine Way
Forest Gate
391 DOUGH CRAG
Rothbury
1388
331
Otterburn
Elsdon
Fontburn Reservoir
Troughend
Otterburn Mill
Highgreen Manor
Raylees
Middens House
A68
Rothley Lakes
Netherwitton
A696
B6320
179
180
B6342
Longwitton
Hartington
Rothley
0 1 2 3 4 5 miles
0 1 2 3 4 5 6 7 8 kilometres
West Woodburn
East Woodburn
Hart Burn
Scot's Gap
B6343
Ray Dell
Lanehead
Fort
A B C D E F
1 2 3 4 5 6 7 8

Northumberland south 191
Adderstone
Warenford
Newham
Beadnell
Swinhoe
Beadnell Bay
Chathill
Newstead
Tughall
Ellingham
Preston
203
Newton-by-the-Sea
Preston Pele Tower
Brunton
Embleton & Newton Links
Christon Bank
Brownieside
Doxford
Embleton
Embleton Bay
North Charlton
Fallodon
Dunstan Steads
Dunstanburgh Castle
West Ditchburn
South Charlton
Dunstan
Craster
Eglingham
Rock
Rennington
Stamford
Howick Hall
Howick
Cullernose Point
Broxfield
Littlehoughton
East Bolton
Longhoughton
Denwick
Boulmer
River Aln
Abberwick
Alnwick
Hawkhill
Seaton Point
Broome Park
Lesbury
Bilton
Hipsburn
Alnmouth
Castle
Alnmouth Bay
Bilton Banks
High Buston
Edlingham
Shilbottle
Low Buston
Birling
260
GLANTLEES HILL
Newton-on-the-Moor
Warkworth Castle & Hermitage
Warkworth
Amble
Coquet Island
Gloster Hill
Swarland
Guyzance
North Togston
High Hauxley
Old Swarland
Acklington
Togston
Radcliffe
North End
Felton
amlington
East Thirston
Broomhill
Pauperhaugh
South Broomhill
West Thirston
Druridge Bay
Brinkburn Priory
Weldon Bridge
Red Row
Eshott
West Chevington
Helm
Druridge
Todburn
Causey Park
Stobswood
Widdrington
North Northumberland Heritage Coast
Vingates
Causey Park Bridge
Widdrington Station
Cresswell
Longhorsley
Earsdon
Tritlington
Ulgham
Ellington
Fenrother
Linton
Lynemouth
Stanton
Hebron
Beacon Point
Longhirst
Woodhorn
River Font
180
Ashington
Woodhorn Demesne
Pigdon
Pegswood
Hirst
North Seaton
Newbiggin-by-the-Sea
Newton Underwood
Wansbeck Riverside
Bothal
Meldon Park
Throphill
Mitford
Morpeth
Sheepwash
Stakeford
North Seaton Colliery
A1
A697
A1068
A189
A197
A192
B1340
B1339
B6347
B6341
B6346
B6345
B6344
B1330
B1337
B1334

205
194
Muasdale
Glenacardoch Point
Belloch
Barr Water
Glenbarr
MacAlister Clan
454
BEINN AN TUIRC
319
408
BORD MOR
Cleongart
Bellochantuy Bay
Bellochantuy
396
SGREADAN HILL
Tangy Loch
Glen Lussa
Peninver
Kilkenzie
A83
Kilmichael
B842
Machrihanish Bay
Campbeltown
Campbeltown
Machrihanish
B842
Campbeltown Loch
Island D
6
Drumlemble
B843
Kilkerran
Kildalloig
352
BEINN GHUILEAN
Earadale Point
Achinhoan
385
THE STATE
446
CNOC MOY
10
Dalsmeran
Conie Glen
Glen Kerran
Glen Breakevie
B842
Strone Glen
Cattadale
Polliwilline Bay
BEINN NA LICE
428
Macharioch
MULL OF KINTYRE
Carskey
Southend
Dunaverty
Carskey Bay
Sanda Sound
Borgadalemore Point
Sheep Island
Sanda Island
0 1 2 3 4 5 miles
0 1 2 3 4 5 6 7 8 kilometres

Imachar
Balliekine
792
BEINN NUIS
Glen Rosa
Carradale
Carradale House
Carradale Point
Carradale Bay
Iorsa Water
ARRAN
Merkland Point
Brodick Castle, Garden & Country Club
Brodick Bay
Brodick
Strathwhillan
Corriegills
Auchagallon Stone Circle
Machrie
Machrie Bay
Machrie Moor Stone Circles
Tormore
Moss Farm Road Stone Circle
B880
512
A'CHRUACH
Clauchlands Point
A841
Margnaheglish
Lamlash
Lamlash Bay
Holy Island
Cordon
Balmichael
503
BEINN BHREAC
Torbeg
Shiskine
Blackwaterfoot
Drumadoon Bay
Kilpatrick
Kilpatrick Dun
Glen Scorrodale
Carn Ban
Auchencairn
Kingscross
Knockenkelly
Whiting Bay
Glen Ashdale
Largymore
Largybeg
Dippen Head
Dippen
KILBRANNAN
194
Brown Head
Corriecravie
Torr a' Chaisteal Fort
Sliddery
Kilmory Water
Kilmory
Lagg
Torrylin Cairn
Bennan
Kildonan
Bennan Head
Pladda
195
340
Ailsa Craig
RSPB

Loch Ciàran
Loch Garasdale
Crossaig
247
CRUACH MHIC GOUGAIN
264
CNOC-AN T-SAMHLAIDH
Cour Bay
Cour
Rhunahaorine
38
Grogport
Barmollack
Pirnmill
354
CRUACH NAN GABHAR
Whitefarland
Carradale Water
39
B842
B879
Carradale
Bridgend
Carradale House
Dippen
Carradale Point
Carradale Bay
454
BEINN-AN TUIRC
Torrisdale
319
408
BORD MOR
Saddell
Saddell Bay
396
SGREADAN HILL
Ugadale
Glen Lussa
Peninver
Ardnacross Bay
Campbeltown
Campbeltown Loch
Island Davarr
Kilkerran
Kildalloig
352
Achinhoan
Ru Stafnish
Polliwilline Bay
KILBRANNAN SOUND
206
205
192
193
Cock of Arran
Castle
Lochranza
Catacol
Glen Chalmadale
A841
Glen Catacol
North Arran
834
CAISTEAL ABHAIL
Penrioch
Loch Tanna
715
BEINN BHARRAIN
Glen Iorsa
874
GOATFEL
Imachar
792
BEINN NUIS
Balliekine
Glen Rosa
Iorsa Water
ARRAN
Auchagallon Stone Circle
Machrie
Machrie Bay
B880
512
A'CHRUACH
Machrie Moor Stone Circles
Tormore
Moss Farm Road Stone Circle
Balmichael
503
BEINN BHREAC
Torbeg
Shiskine
Blackwaterfoot
Drumadoon Bay
Kilpatrick
Kilpatrick Dun
Glen Scorrodale
Carn Ban
Brown Head
Kilmory Water
Corriecravie
Torr a' Chaisteal Fort
Sliddery
Kilmory
Lagg
Torrylin Cairn
Bennan Head
0 1 2 3 4 5 miles
0 1 2 3 4 5 6 7 8 kilometres

G
H
J
K
207
Garroch Head
Little Cumbrae Island
Hunterston Power Station
Fairlie Road
Drakemyre
Dalry
Portencross
Farland Head
B7048
Blackshaw
Munnoch
B780
B781
West Kilbride
A737
Seamill
B7047
Dalgarven Mill
Dalgarven
B780
B714
A78
Kilwinning
B778
Ardrossan
Horse Isle
A78
A738
Stevenston
B780
Ardeer
B779
Saltcoats
196
Irvine
Maritime
Corrie
Merkland Point
Brodick Castle, Garden & Country Club
Brodick Bay
Strathwhillan
Corriegills
Clauchlands Point
Margnaheglish
Lamlash Bay
Holy Island
Cordon
Kingscross
Knockenkelly
Whiting Bay
Ashdale
Largymore
Largybeg
Dippen
Dippen Head
Kildonan
FIRTH OF CLYDE
Irvine Bay
Troon
(Mar-Oct)
Larne
Royal
Ayr Bay
196
Heads of Ayr
Doonfoot
Burns Cottage
Fisherton
A719
Dunure
Culroy
Drumshang
Croy Brae (Electric Brae)
Knoweside
Culzean Bay
Culzean Castle & Country Park
Pennyglen
Whitefaulds
182
G
H
J
K
L
M

196
195
208
183
184
West Kilbride
Dalry
Kilwinning
Ardrossan
Saltcoats
Stevenston
Irvine
Stewarton
Kilmaurs
KILMARNOCK
Troon
Prestwick
Ayr
Mauchline
Irvine Bay
Ayr Bay
Culzean Bay
Larne
Dunlop
Dreghorn
Crosshouse
Dundonald
Symington
Tarbolton
Monkton
Alloway
Dalrymple
Coylton
Drongan
Patna
Heads of Ayr
Dunure
Fisherton
Annbank
Mossblown
Hurlford
Galston
Fenwick
Glengarnock
Gateside
Lugt
Barrmill
Burnhouse
Drakemyre
Crosshands
Craigie
Loans
Barassie
Gailes
Whitletts
Wallacetown
Doonfoot
Belmont
Minishant
Culroy
Hollybush
Rankinston
Sinclairston
Ochiltree
Trabboch
Stair
Failford
Culzean Castle & Country Park
Robert Burns Birthplace
Burns Cottage
Wallace Monument Tower
Dean Castle
Eglinton
Royal Troon
Prestwick
Croy Brae (Electric Brae)
Martnaham Loch
Ayr Gorge Woodland
Bachelors' Club
COCK LAW
KILMEIN HILL
A77
A78
A71
A70
A719
A76
A736
A737
A735
A759
A713
0 1 2 3 4 5 miles
0 1 2 3 4 5 6 7 8 kilometres

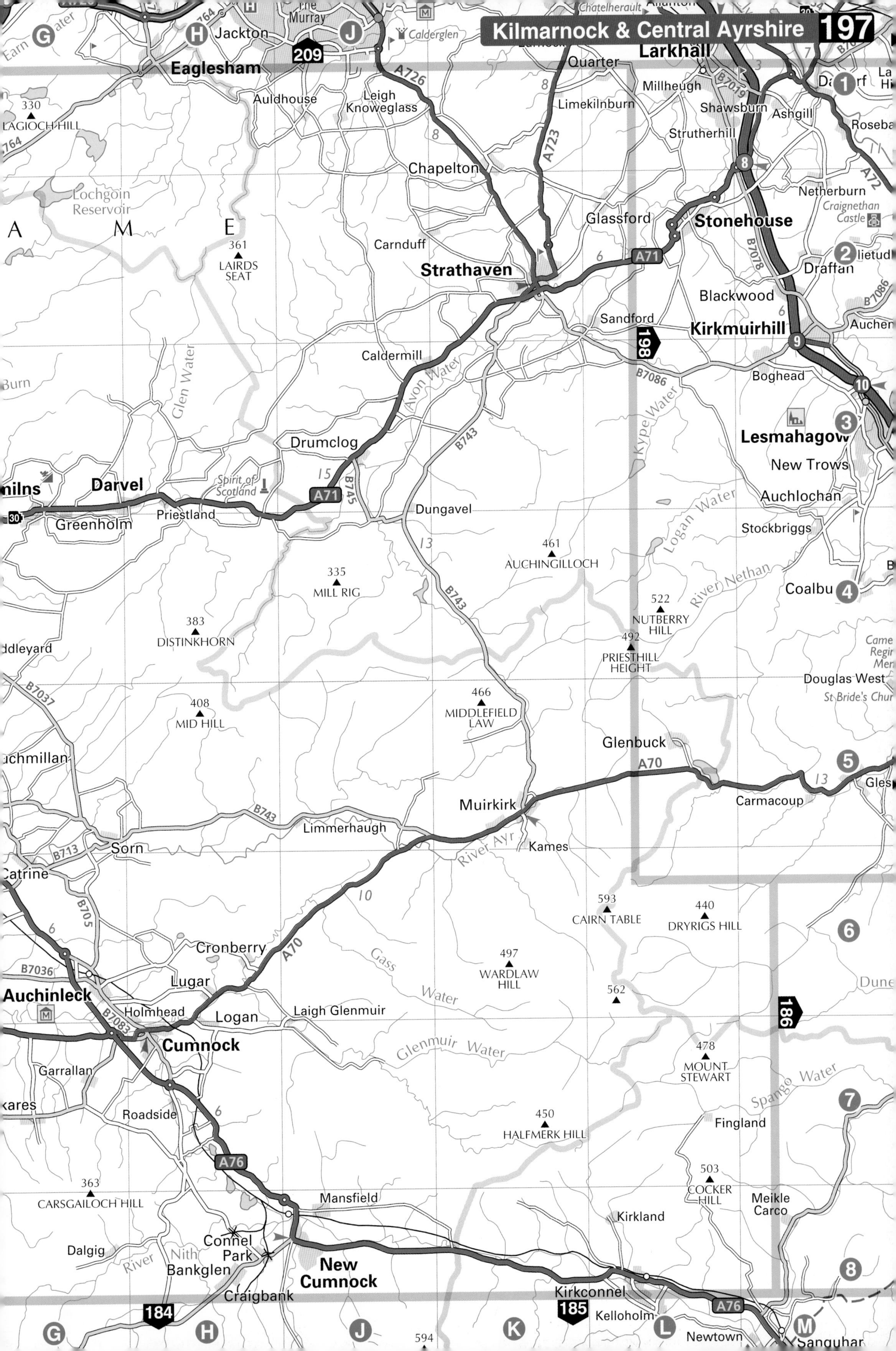

209
198
186
184
185

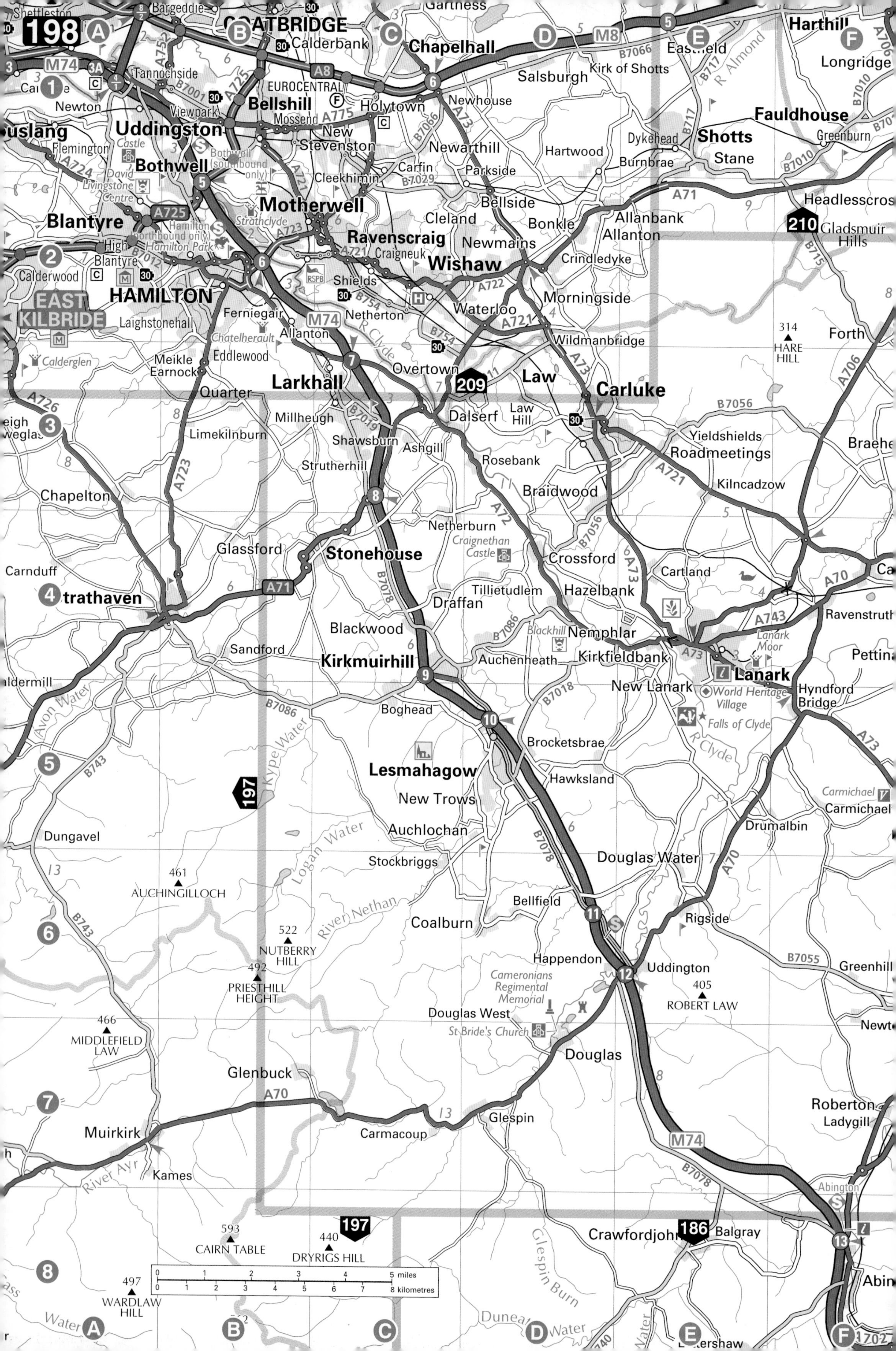
198
210
209
197
186
Coatbridge
Calderbank
Chapelhall
Salsburgh
Kirk of Shotts
Eastfield
Harthill
Longridge
Fauldhouse
Greenburn
Shotts
Stane
Dykehead
Burnbrae
Hartwood
Newhouse
Holytown
Eurocentral
Bellshill
Mossend
New Stevenston
Newarthill
Carfin
Cleekhimin
Parkside
Bellside
Tannochside
Viewpark
Uddingston
Newton
Flemington
Bothwell
David Livingstone Centre
Blantyre
High Blantyre
Calderwood
Hamilton
Hamilton Park
East Kilbride
Motherwell
Strathclyde
Ravenscraig
Craigneuk
Cleland
Bonkle
Allanbank
Allanton
Headlesscross
Gladsmuir Hills
Newmains
Wishaw
Crindledyke
Morningside
Waterloo
Shields
Netherton
Ferniegair
Laighstonehall
Chatelherault
Allanton
Calderglen
Meikle Earnock
Eddlewood
Overtown
Wildmanbridge
Law
Carluke
Forth
Hare Hill
Quarter
Larkhall
Dalserf
Law Hill
Millheugh
Limekilnburn
Shawsburn
Ashgill
Rosebank
Yieldshields
Roadmeetings
Braehead
Strutherhill
Chapelton
Braidwood
Kilncadzow
Netherburn
Craignethan Castle
Glassford
Stonehouse
Crossford
Cartland
Carnduff
Strathaven
Tillietudlem
Hazelbank
Draffan
Ravenstruther
Blackwood
Nemphlar
Blackhill
Lanark Moor
Sandford
Kirkmuirhill
Auchenheath
Kirkfieldbank
Pettinain
Lanark
New Lanark
World Heritage Village
Hyndford Bridge
Avon Water
Boghead
Falls of Clyde
Brocketsbrae
R Clyde
Lesmahagow
Hawksland
Kype Water
New Trows
Carmichael
Dungavel
Auchlochan
Drumalbin
Logan Water
Stockbriggs
Douglas Water
461 Auchingilloch
River Nethan
Bellfield
Coalburn
Rigside
522 Nutberry Hill
492 Priesthill Height
Happendon
Uddington
Greenhill
Cameronians Regimental Memorial
405 Robert Law
Douglas West
St Bride's Church
466 Middlefield Law
Douglas
Newton
Glenbuck
Roberton
Ladygill
Glespin
Carmacoup
Muirkirk
Kames
River Ayr
Abington
593 Cairn Table
440 Dryrigs Hill
Crawfordjohn
Balgray
497 Wardlaw Hill
Glespin Burn
Duneaton Water
Abington
M74
M8
A8
A71
A70
A73
A721
A723
A725
A726
B743
B7078
B7086
0 1 2 3 4 5 miles
0 1 2 3 4 5 6 7 8 kilometres

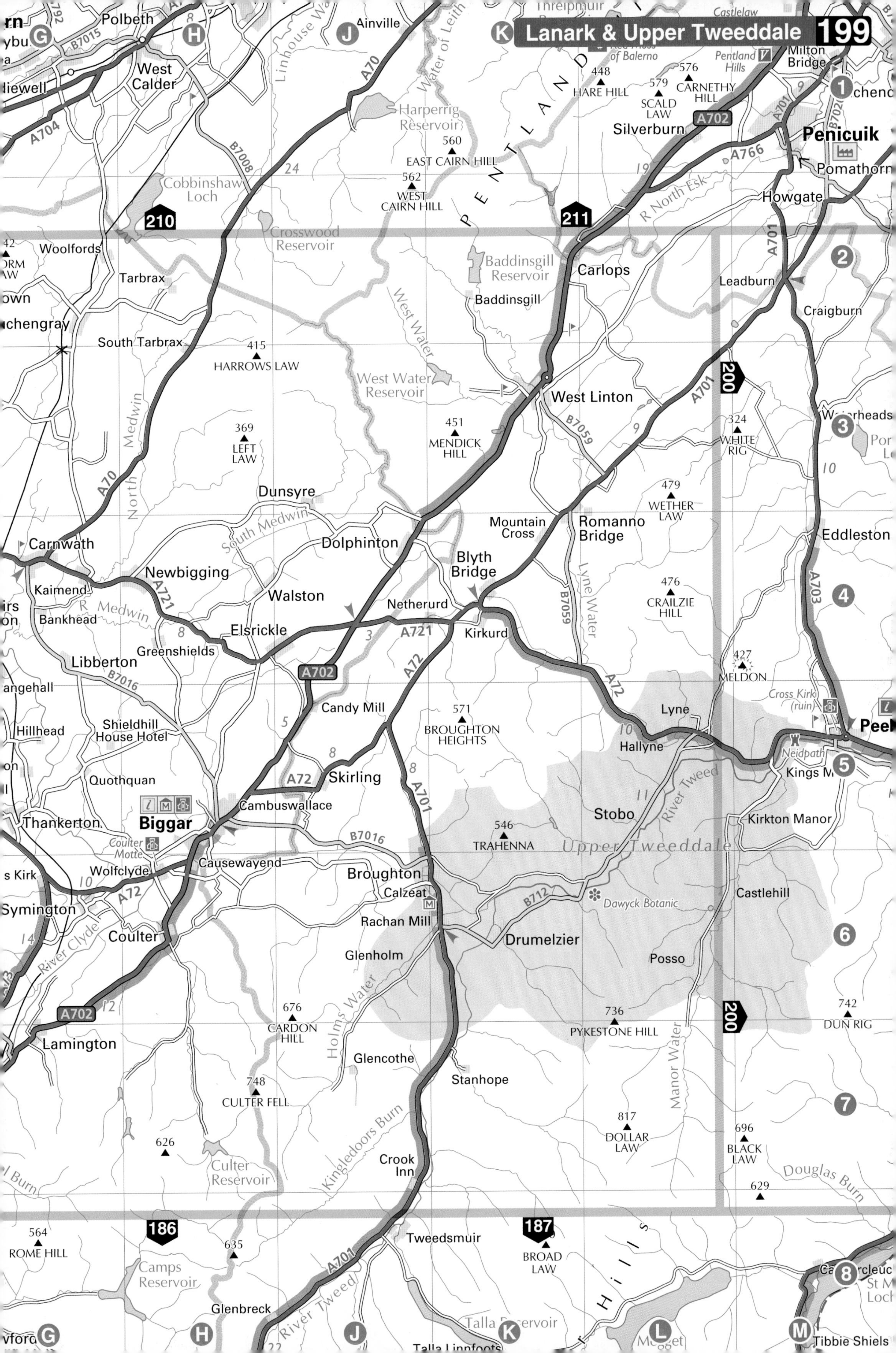
G
H
J
K
Polbeth
West Calder
Ainville
Linhouse Water
Water of Leith
Threipmuir
Castlelaw
Red Moss of Balerno
Pentland Hills
Milton Bridge
448
HARE HILL
579
SCALD LAW
576
CARNETHY HILL
Silverburn
A702
A701
B7026
Penicuik
1
A766
Pomathorn
R North Esk
Howgate
B7015
A704
A70
B7008
Harperrig Reservoir
560
EAST CAIRN HILL
562
WEST CAIRN HILL
PENTLAND
Cobbinshaw Loch
210
211
24
19
Crosswood Reservoir
Baddinsgill Reservoir
Carlops
Baddinsgill
Woolfords
Tarbrax
Auchengray
South Tarbrax
415
HARROWS LAW
West Water
West Water Reservoir
Leadburn
2
Craigburn
200
West Linton
B7059
9
324
WHITE RIG
3
10
369
LEFT LAW
451
MENDICK HILL
North Medwin
479
WETHER LAW
Dunsyre
South Medwin
Mountain Cross
Romanno Bridge
Eddleston
Carnwath
Dolphinton
Blyth Bridge
Newbigging
A721
Kaimend
R. Medwin
Walston
Netherurd
476
CRAILZIE HILL
A703
4
Bankhead
8
Elsrickle
3
Kirkurd
Lyne Water
Libberton
Greenshields
B7016
A702
A72
427
MELDON
Cross Kirk (ruin)
Candy Mill
571
BROUGHTON HEIGHTS
Lyne
Peebles
Hillhead
Shieldhill House Hotel
5
10
Hallyne
Neidpath
Kings Muir
Quothquan
Skirling
A72
8
A701
River Tweed
11
Stobo
Kirkton Manor
Thankerton
Biggar
Cambuswallace
546
TRAHENNA
Upper Tweeddale
Coulter Motte
B7016
Wolfclyde
Causewayend
Broughton
Calzeat
Castlehill
Symington
A72
B712
Dawyck Botanic
Rachan Mill
14
River Clyde
Coulter
Drumelzier
6
Glenholm
Posso
Holms Water
676
CARDON HILL
736
PYKESTONE HILL
742
DUN RIG
A702
12
Lamington
Glencothe
Manor Water
Stanhope
748
CULTER FELL
7
817
DOLLAR LAW
696
BLACK LAW
626
Kingledoors Burn
Culter Reservoir
Crook Inn
Douglas Burn
629
564
ROME HILL
186
635
Tweedsmuir
187
BROAD LAW
Camps Reservoir
A701
Hills
8
Glenbreck
River Tweed
Talla Reservoir
Megget
Tibbie Shiels
L
M

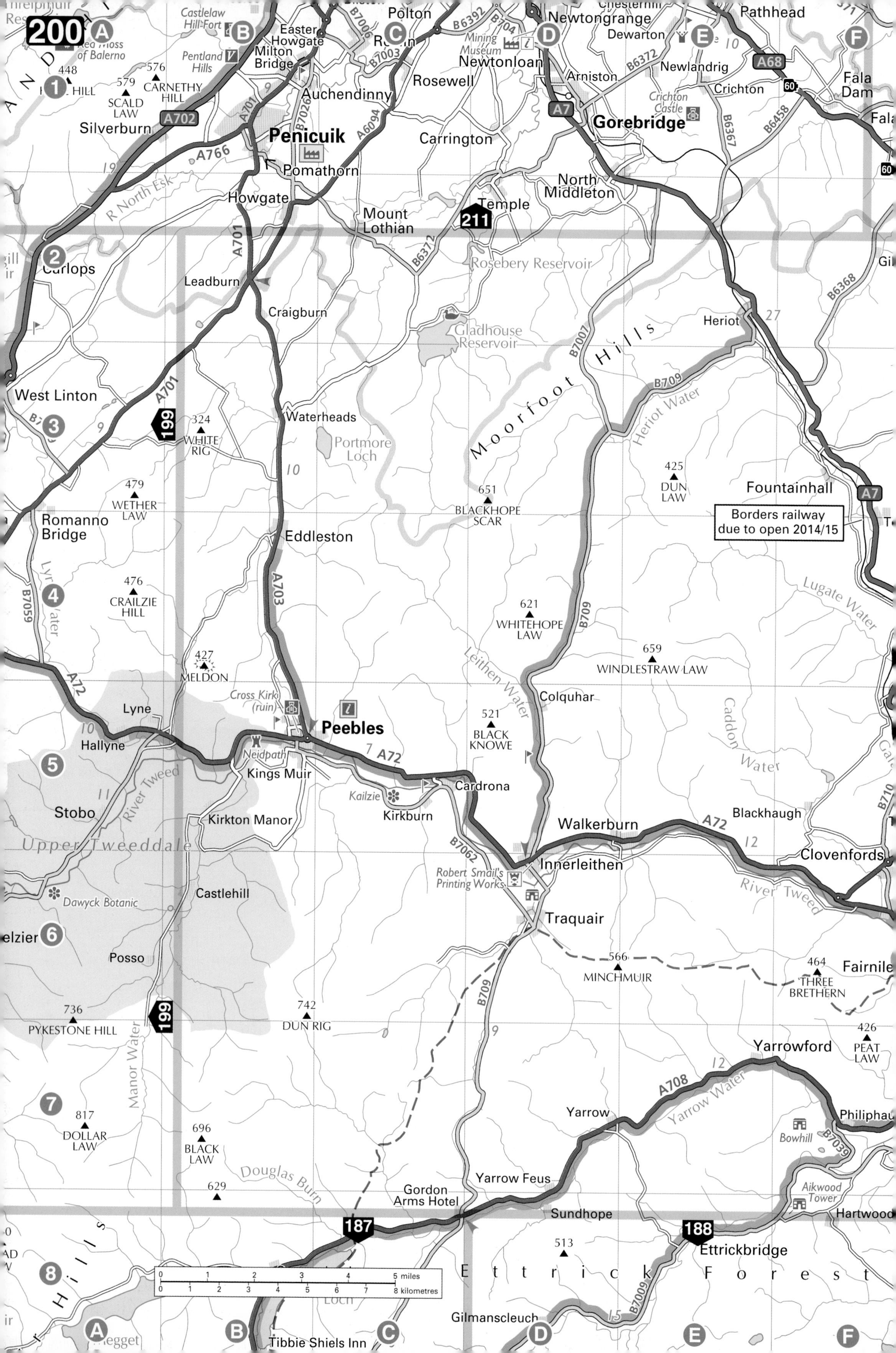

200
A
B
C
D
E
F
Castlelaw Hill Fort
Red Moss of Balerno
Pentland Hills
Easter Howgate
Milton Bridge
Polton
Roslin
Mining Museum
Newtongrange
Newtonloan
Dewarton
Pathhead
Newlandrig
Arniston
Crichton
Crichton Castle
Fala Dam
Fala
A68
60
448
576
CARNETHY HILL
579
SCALD LAW
Silverburn
A702
Auchendinny
Rosewell
Penicuik
Carrington
Gorebridge
A7
B6367
B6458
B6372
B6392
B7006
B7003
B7026
B704
A6094
A701
A766
R North Esk
Pomathorn
Howgate
North Middleton
Temple
211
Mount Lothian
B6372
Rosebery Reservoir
B6368
Carlops
Leadburn
Craigburn
Gladhouse Reservoir
Moorfoot Hills
B7007
Heriot
27
B709
Heriot Water
West Linton
A701
199
324
WHITE RIG
Waterheads
Portmore Loch
10
651
BLACKHOPE SCAR
425
DUN LAW
Fountainhall
Borders railway due to open 2014/15
479
WETHER LAW
Romanno Bridge
Eddleston
476
CRAILZIE HILL
Lyne Water
B7059
A703
621
WHITEHOPE LAW
Lugate Water
659
WINDLESTRAW LAW
427
MELDON
A72
Leithen Water
Colquhar
Cross Kirk (ruin)
Peebles
521
BLACK KNOWE
Caddon Water
Lyne
Hallyne
Neidpath
Kings Muir
Cardrona
Kailzie
Kirkburn
River Tweed
Stobo
Kirkton Manor
Walkerburn
Blackhaugh
Upper Tweeddale
B7062
Innerleithen
Clovenfords
Robert Smail's Printing Works
Dawyck Botanic
Castlehill
Traquair
River Tweed
Posso
566
MINCHMUIR
464
THREE BRETHERN
Fairnilee
736
PYKESTONE HILL
742
DUN RIG
426
PEAT LAW
Manor Water
Yarrowford
A708
Yarrow Water
Philiphaugh
Yarrow
Bowhill
B7039
817
DOLLAR LAW
696
BLACK LAW
Douglas Burn
629
Gordon Arms Hotel
Yarrow Feus
Aikwood Tower
Hartwood
Sundhope
187
188
513
Ettrickbridge
Ettrick Forest
B7009
Gilmanscleuch
Tibbie Shiels Inn
Megget
0 1 2 3 4 5 miles
0 1 2 3 4 5 6 7 8 kilometres
1
2
3
4
5
6
7
8

Whiteadder Reservoir
LAMMERMUIR
MEIKLE SAYS LAW 533
LAMMER LAW 528
Blegbie
CRIB LAW 509
SEENES LAW 513
MEIKLE LAW 467
HUNT LAW 495
Cranshaws
Abbey St Bathans
Ellemford
Whitchester
COCKBURN LAW 325
Longformacus
Southern Upland Way
Primrosehill
212
HOGS LAW 448
Soonhope Burn
DIRRINGTON GREAT LAW 399
Wedderlie Burn
Oxton
Carfraemill
202
Gavinton
COLLIE LAW 383
LAUDERDALE
A697
B6456
Polwarth
Fogo
Blythe
Spottiswoode
Westruther
Thornydykes
Thirlestane
Lauder
Houndslow
A6105
Thirlestane
A6089
B6362
Boon
Leader Water
Bassendean
Greenlaw
Blackadder Water
B6460
Nether Blainslie
Legerwood
Greenknowe Tower
Gordon
Middlethird
Lambden
Hume
B6364
Eccles
West Morriston
Fans
A68
B6397
Mellerstain
B6461
Earlston
Stichill
Nenthorn
A698
Galashiels
B6356
Harmony and Priorwood Gardens
Redpath
Eden Water
Smailholm
Ednam
Kelso
Langlee
Gattonside
Abbey
B6360
Tweedbank
B6361
Newstead
Scott's View
Smailholm Tower
B6404
Floors
Sprouston
A6091
Darnick
Melrose
Trimontium
Wallace Monument
Eildon and Leaderfoot
Manorhill
Kelso
Abbotsford
EILDON HILLS 422
Clintmains
Border Union
Newtown St Boswells
Dryburgh
Abbey
Mertoun
River Tweed
A699
Easter Softlaw
B6359
B6398
St Boswells
Maxton
Roxburgh
Heiton
Bowden
B6352
Rutherford
Whitlaw Mosses
Camieston
B6436
Selkirk
Pirnie
Frogden
Longnewton
Midlem
Ale Water
Teviot Water Gardens
Waterloo Monument
B6453
Caverton Mill
Linton
Nisbet
Eckford
B6401
Lilliesleaf
B6400
Riddell
188
Belses
Ancrum
189
Morebattle
Crailing
Greenhouse
Bloomfield
Chesters
Harelaw
Bonjedward
Lanton
Gateshaw
Minto 276
Jedburgh

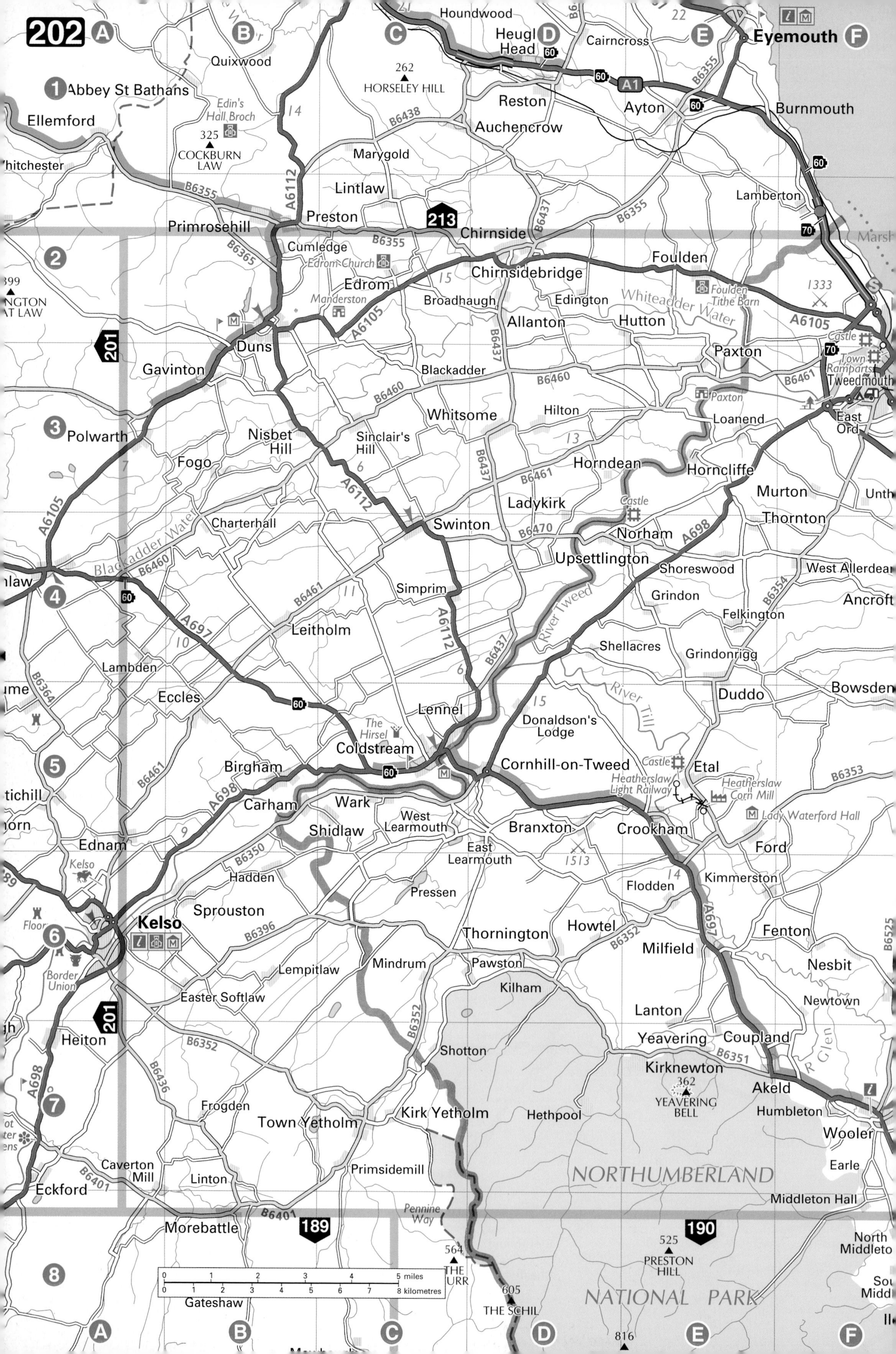
A
B
C
D
E
F
1
2
3
4
5
6
7
8
Houndwood
Heugh Head
Cairncross
Eyemouth
Quixwood
262
HORSELEY HILL
Abbey St Bathans
Edin's Hall Broch
325
COCKBURN LAW
Ellemford
Reston
Ayton
A1
Burnmouth
B6438
Auchencrow
Marygold
B6355
A6112
Lintlaw
Lamberton
Preston
213
B6437
Chirnside
Primrosehill
Cumledge
Edrom Church
B6365
Foulden
Chirnsidebridge
Edrom
Manderston
Broadhaugh
Edington
Whiteadder Water
Foulden Tithe Barn
1333
A6105
Allanton
Hutton
Castle
Paxton
Town Ramparts
201
Duns
Gavinton
Blackadder
B6460
B6461
Tweedmouth
East Ord
Loanend
Hilton
Whitsome
Polwarth
Nisbet Hill
Sinclair's Hill
Fogo
Horndean
Horncliffe
Murton
Ladykirk
Charterhall
Swinton
B6470
Norham
Thornton
A698
Upsettlington
Blackadder Water
Shoreswood
West Allerdean
Simprim
Grindon
Ancroft
A697
B6354
Felkington
Leitholm
River Tweed
Shellacres
Grindonrigg
Lambden
B6364
River Till
Bowsden
Eccles
Duddo
Donaldson's Lodge
Lennel
The Hirsel
Coldstream
Birgham
Cornhill-on-Tweed
Castle
Etal
B6353
Heatherslaw Light Railway
Heatherslaw Corn Mill
Carham
Wark
West Learmouth
Lady Waterford Hall
Branxton
Crookham
Shidlaw
Ednam
East Learmouth
1513
Ford
B6350
Hadden
Kelso
Flodden
Kimmerston
Pressen
Sprouston
Floors
Kelso
Howtel
Thornington
Fenton
B6396
B6352
Milfield
Border Union
Lempitlaw
Mindrum
Pawston
Nesbit
Kilham
Easter Softlaw
Newtown
Heiton
Lanton
Yeavering
Coupland
B6436
Shotton
Kirknewton
B6351
R Glen
362
YEAVERING BELL
Akeld
Humbleton
Frogden
Town Yetholm
Kirk Yetholm
Hethpool
Wooler
Caverton Mill
Primsidemill
NORTHUMBERLAND
Earle
Eckford
B6401
Linton
Middleton Hall
Pennine Way
189
190
Morebattle
564
THE CURR
525
PRESTON HILL
North Middleton
0 1 2 3 4 5 miles
0 1 2 3 4 5 6 7 8 kilometres
Gateshaw
605
THE SCHIL
NATIONAL PARK
816
B6525

CAUSEWAY FLOODED AT HIGH TIDE
HOLY ISLAND
Holy Island
Lindisfarne Castle
Lindisfarne Priory
Castle Point
Guile Point
Cheswick
Goswick
Haggerston
Beal
Fenham
West Kyloe
Fenwick
Buckton
Smeafield
Elwick
Ross
Detchant
Holburn
St Cuthbert's Cave
Low Middleton
Middleton
Easington
Budle Bay
Bamburgh
Inner Sound
Staple Sound
Longstone Lighthouse
FARNE ISLANDS
North Northumberland Heritage Coast
Hetton Steads
North Hazelrigg
Belford
Waren Mill
Budle
Outchester
Spindlestone
Burton
New Shoreston
Seahouses
South Hazelrigg
Bradford
North Sunderland
East Horton
Bellshill
Elford
Warenton
Lucker
Adderstone
Beadnell
Chatton
Warenford
Newham
Swinhoe
Chathill
Beadnell Bay
Tughall
Newstead
Wild Cattle Park
Ellingham
River Till
Preston
Ros Castle
Chillingham
Newton-by-the-Sea
Preston Pele Tower
Brunton
190
191
Hepburn
Embleton & Newton Links
Christon Bank
Embleton
267 CATERAN HILL
Brownieside
Doxford
North Charlton
Fallodon
Embleton Bay
Dunstan Steads
Dunstanburgh Castle
Old Bewick
West Ditchburn
South Charlton
k-upon-Tweed
A1
B1342
B1340
B6349
B1341
B6348
B1339
B6353
60
G H J K L M
1 2 3 4 5 6 7 8

214
Rudha Bholsa
Nave Island
Ardnave Point
Gortantaoid Point
Bunnahabhain
316
GUIR-BHEINN
Ton Mhòr
Kilnave
Sanaigmore
Eilean Mòr
Loch Gruinart
Loch Gòrr
Rudha Lamanais
Lecht Gruinart
RSPB
Finlaggan
Loch Finlaggan
Saligo Bay
B8018
B8017
Gruinart
Gleann Mòr
Ballygrant
Loch Gorm
Coul Point
A846
Sunderland
Kilchoman
Machir Bay
A847
Bridgend
Bruichladdich
Loch Indaal
Gartachossan
Kilchiaran Bay
Bowmore
Kilennan Burn
ISLAY
Port Charlotte
231
BEINN TART A'MHILL
RHINNS OF ISLAY
River Laggan
Lossit Bay
Nereabolls
Duich R
B8016
454
BEINN URAR
Rudha na Faing
Portnahaven
Port Wemyss
Glenegedale
Orsay
Laggan Bay
Islay
RHINNS POINT
346
BEINN SHOLUM
Rudha Mòr
Kintra
Port Ellen
165
MAOL BUIDHE
Laphroaig
Texa
THE OA
Kilnaughton Bay
Lower Killeyan
Risabus
Kinnabus
Loch Kinnabus
American Monument
MULL OF OA
Rudha nan Leacan
0 1 2 3 4 5 miles
0 1 2 3 4 5 6 7 8 kilometres

214
215
192
206
194
Jura Forest
506 SCRINADLE
398 BEINN TARSUINN
784 BEINN AN OIR
734
Loch a' Chnuic Bhric
Paps of Jura
Jura
JURA
Knockrome
Ardfernal
24
A846
560 GLASS BHEINN
Feolin Ferry
Keils
529 DUBHA BHEINN
Craighouse
Small Isles
342 BRAT BHEINN
Rudha na Gaillich
Cabrach
Am Fraoch Eilean
Brosdale Island
Rudha na Tràille
McArthur's Head
Port Askaig - Kennacraig
Port Ellen - Kennacraig
Rudha Liath
Ardtalla
Claggain Bay
Kintour
Kildalton Cross
Ardmore Point
Eilean a' Chuirn
Rudha na Gainmhich
Danna Island
Loch na
St Cormac's Chapel
Kilmory Knap Chapel
Kilmory
Kilmory Bay
Ellary
Point of Knap
Loch Caolisport
Coulaghailt
Kilberry Sculptured Stones
Kilberry
Kilberry Head
213 CRUACH AIR
Keppoch Point
Tiretigan
Loch Stornoway
Kinerarach
Tarbert
GIGHA
Ardminish
Achamore
Rhunahaorine Point
Rhunahaorine
38
Tayinloan
Sound of Gigha
Cara
A83
Muasdale
Glenacardoch Point
Belloch
Barr Water
G H J K L M
1 2 3 4 5 6 7 8

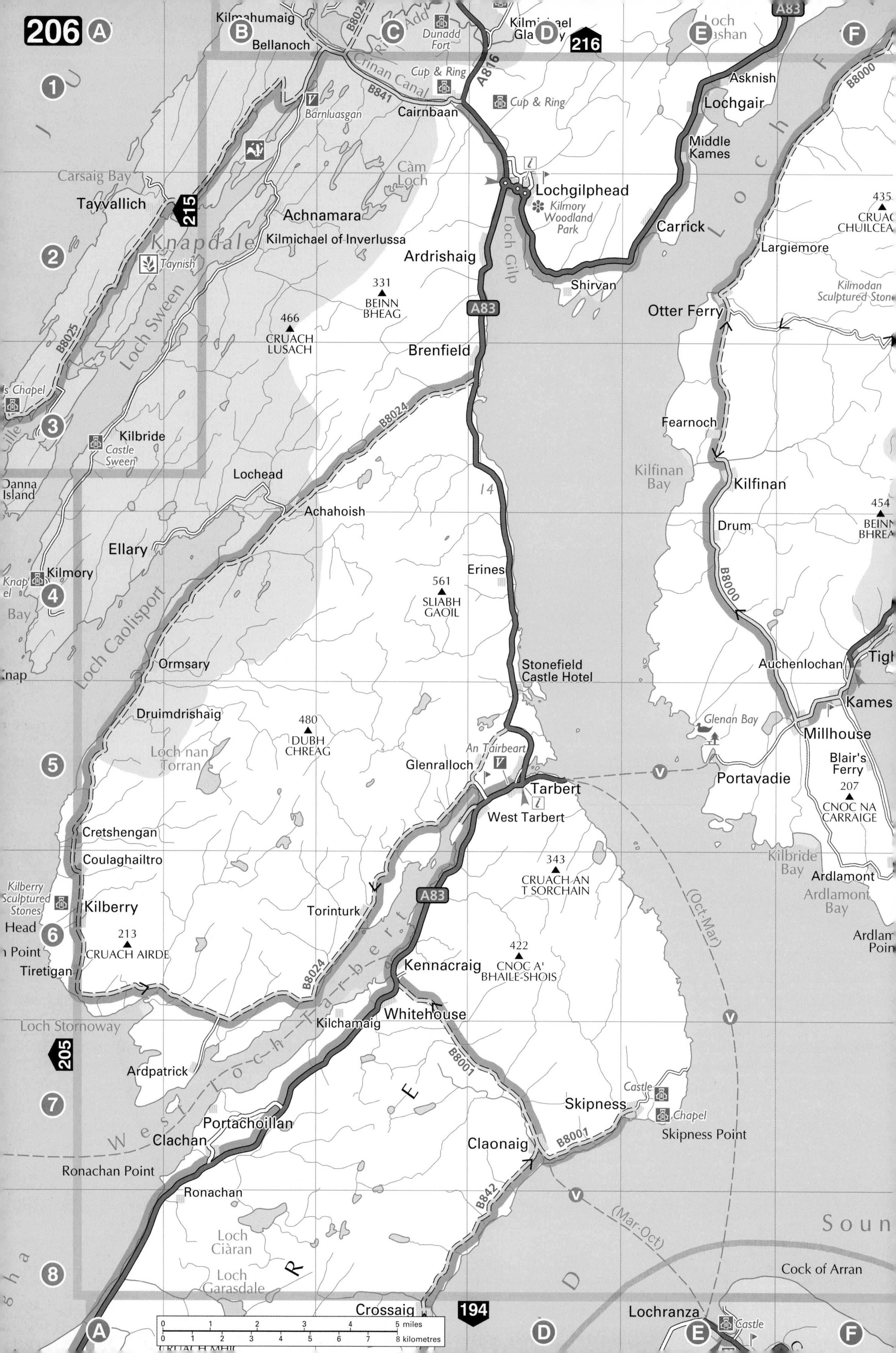

Kilmahumaig
Bellanoch
Dunadd Fort
Kilmichael Glassary
216
Loch Glashan
Crinan Canal
Cup & Ring
B841
Cairnbaan
A816
Asknish
Lochgair
Middle Kames
Barnluasgan
Carsaig Bay
Tayvallich
215
Càm Loch
Lochgilphead
Kilmory Woodland Park
Achnamara
Knapdale
Kilmichael of Inverlussa
Taynish
Ardrishaig
Loch Gilp
Carrick
Loch Fyne
435 CRUACH CHUILCEACH
Largiemore
Shirvan
331 BEINN BHEAG
466 CRUACH LUSACH
A83
Otter Ferry
Kilmodan Sculptured Stones
B8025
Loch Sween
Brenfield
Chapel
B8024
Fearnoch
Kilbride
Castle Sween
Lochead
Kilfinan Bay
Kilfinan
Danna Island
Achahoish
454 BEINN BHREAC
Drum
Ellary
Kilmory
Knap
Bay
Loch Caolisport
Erines
561 SLIABH GAOIL
B8000
Ormsary
Stonefield Castle Hotel
Auchenlochan
Tighnabruaich
Kames
Druimdrishaig
480 DUBH CHREAG
An Tairbeart
Glenan Bay
Millhouse
Loch nan Torran
Glenralloch
Tarbert
Portavadie
Blair's Ferry
207 CNOC NA CARRAIGE
West Tarbert
Cretshengan
Coulaghailtro
343 CRUACH AN T SORCHAIN
Kilbride Bay
Ardlamont
Ardlamont Bay
Kilberry Sculptured Stones
Kilberry
Head
Torinturk
(Oct-Mar)
213 CRUACH AIRDE
Point
Tiretigan
422 CNOC A' BHAILE-SHOIS
Kennacraig
Ardlamont Point
Whitehouse
Kilchamaig
Loch Stornoway
205
West Loch Tarbert
B8001
Ardpatrick
Castle
Skipness
Chapel
Skipness Point
Portachoillan
Clachan
Claonaig
Ronachan Point
Ronachan
B842
(Mar-Oct)
Sound
Loch Ciàran
Loch Garasdale
Cock of Arran
Crossaig
194
Lochranza
Castle
0 1 2 3 4 5 miles
0 1 2 3 4 5 6 7 8 kilometres

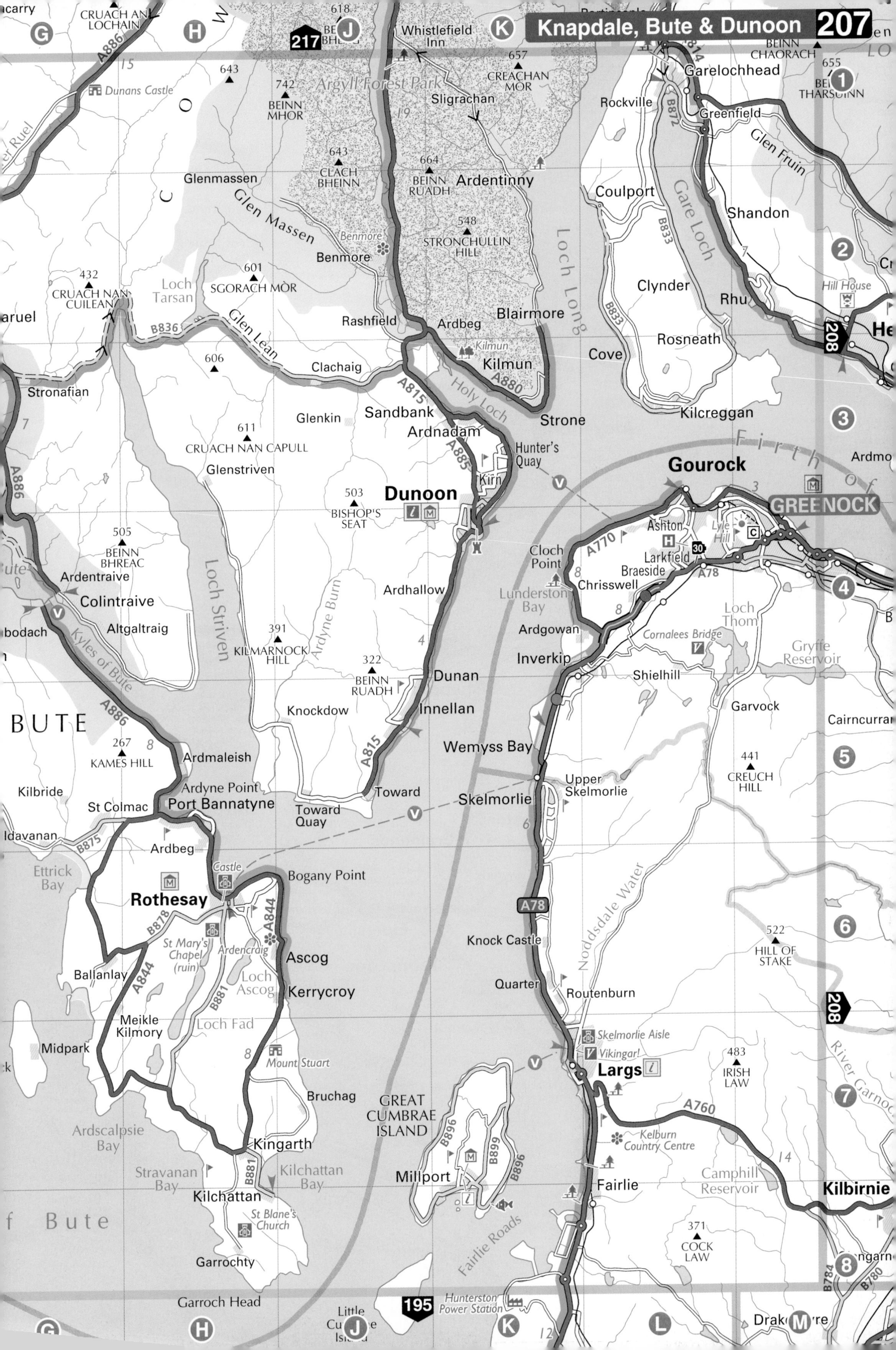
Argyll Forest Park
Whistlefield Inn
Sligrachan
Ardentinny
Garelochhead
Greenfield
Glen Fruin
Rockville
Coulport
Gare Loch
Shandon
Clynder
Rhu
Rosneath
Cove
Kilcreggan
Loch Long
Blairmore
Ardbeg
Kilmun
Strone
Holy Loch
Sandbank
Ardnadam
Hunter's Quay
Kirn
Dunoon
Glenmassen
Glen Massen
Benmore
Rashfield
Loch Tarsan
Glen Lean
Clachaig
Glenkin
Glenstriven
Loch Striven
Stronafian
Colintraive
Altgaltraig
Ardentraive
Kyles of Bute
BUTE
Ardmaleish
Ardyne Point
Port Bannatyne
St Colmac
Kilbride
Ardbeg
Ettrick Bay
Rothesay
Bogany Point
Ascog
Kerrycroy
Loch Ascog
Loch Fad
Ballanlay
Meikle Kilmory
Midpark
Mount Stuart
Bruchag
Kingarth
Kilchattan
Kilchattan Bay
Ardscalpsie Bay
Stravanan Bay
St Blane's Church
Garrochty
Garroch Head
Ardhallow
Ardyne Burn
Knockdow
Dunan
Innellan
Toward
Toward Quay
Gourock
Firth of
GREENOCK
Ashton
Lyle Hill
Larkfield
Braeside
Chrisswell
Cloch Point
Lunderston Bay
Ardgowan
Inverkip
Loch Thom
Cornalees Bridge
Gryffe Reservoir
Shielhill
Garvock
Wemyss Bay
Skelmorlie
Upper Skelmorlie
Noddsdale Water
Knock Castle
Quarter
Routenburn
Skelmorlie Aisle
Vikingar!
Largs
Kelburn Country Centre
Fairlie
Camphill Reservoir
Kilbirnie
GREAT CUMBRAE ISLAND
Millport
Fairlie Roads
Hunterston Power Station
Little Cumbrae Island
Drakemyre
River Garnock
A886
A815
A885
A880
A770
A78
A844
A760
B836
B872
B833
B875
B878
B881
B896
B899
B784
B780
BEINN MHOR 742
CLACH BHEINN 643
BEINN RUADH 664
STRONCHULLIN HILL 548
CREACHAN MOR 657
BEINN CHAORACH
BEINN THARSUINN 655
SGORACH MÒR 601
CRUACH NAN CUILEAN 432
CRUACH NAN CAPULL 611
BISHOP'S SEAT 503
BEINN BHREAC 505
KILMARNOCK HILL 391
BEINN RUADH 322
KAMES HILL 267
CREUCH HILL 441
HILL OF STAKE 522
IRISH LAW 483
COCK LAW 371
Dunans Castle
Hill House
217
208
195
1 2 3 4 5 6 7 8
G H J K L M

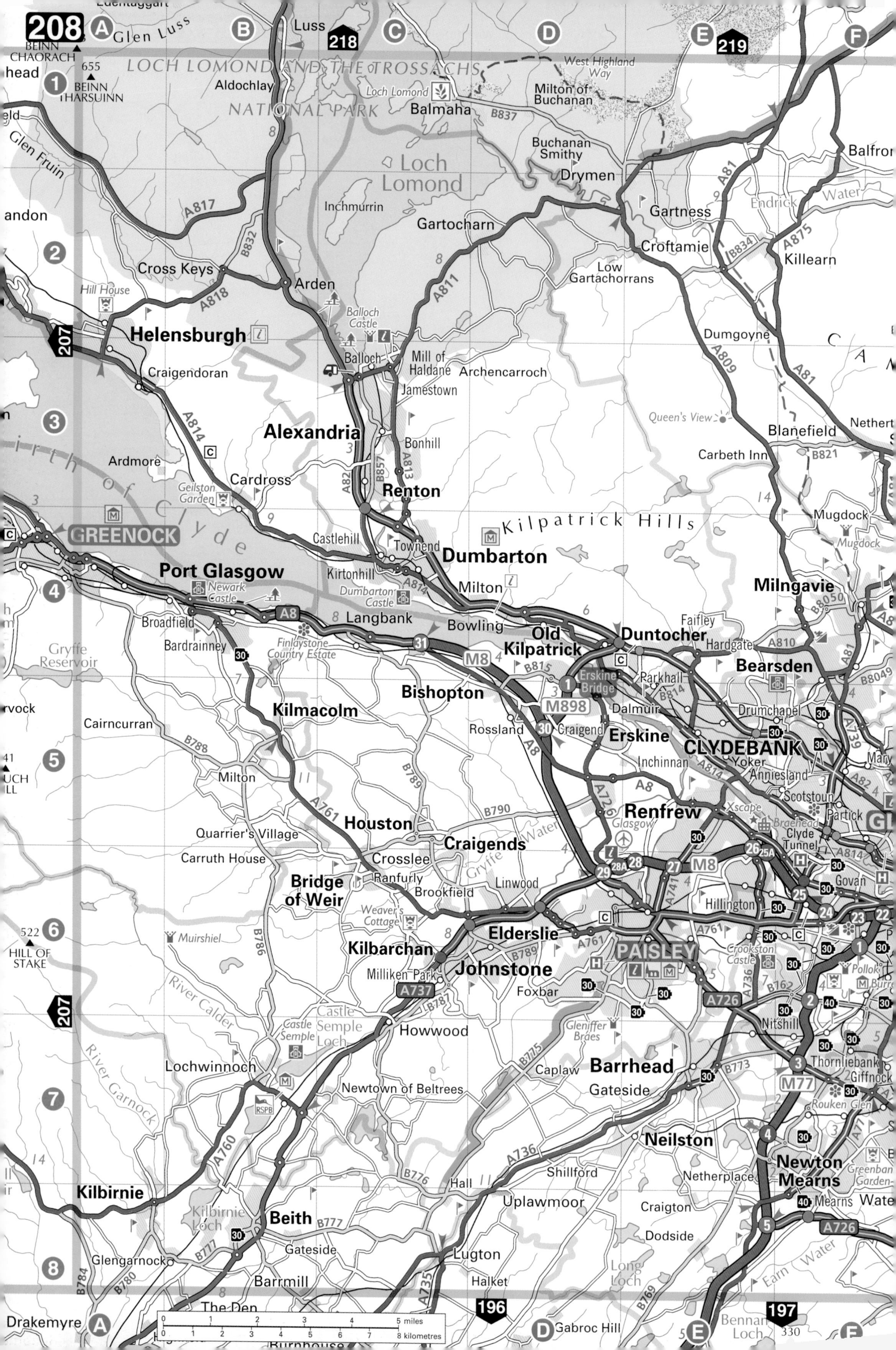

A
B
C
D
E
F
Glen Luss
Luss
218
219
BEINN CHAORACH
655
BEINN THARSUINN
LOCH LOMOND AND THE TROSSACHS NATIONAL PARK
Aldochlay
Loch Lomond
Balmaha
B837
West Highland Way
Milton of Buchanan
Buchanan Smithy
Drymen
Glen Fruin
Loch Lomond
Inchmurrin
A817
Gartocharn
Gartness
Balfron
Endrick Water
A81
A875
Croftamie
B834
Killearn
Low Gartachorrans
Cross Keys
B832
Arden
A818
Hill House
Helensburgh
Balloch Castle
A811
Balloch
Mill of Haldane
Archencarroch
Jamestown
Craigendoran
Dumgoyne
A809
A81
Queen's View
Blanefield
Carbeth Inn
B821
Alexandria
Bonhill
A814
Ardmore
Cardross
Geilston Garden
A82
B857
A813
Renton
Firth of Clyde
GREENOCK
Castlehill
Townend
Dumbarton
Kilpatrick Hills
Mugdock
Port Glasgow
Newark Castle
Kirtonhill
Dumbarton Castle
A814
Milton
Milngavie
B8050
Broadfield
A8
Langbank
Bowling
Old Kilpatrick
Duntocher
Faifley
Hardgate
A810
Bardrainney
Finlaystone Country Estate
M8
B815
Erskine Bridge
Parkhall
Bearsden
B8049
Gryffe Reservoir
Bishopton
M898
Dalmuir
B814
Drumchapel
Kilmacolm
Cairncurran
Rossland
Craigend
Erskine
CLYDEBANK
A739
B788
Milton
A8
Inchinnan
A814
Yoker
Anniesland
Scotstoun
Partick
A82
B789
A726
A8
Renfrew
Xscape
Braehead
Clyde Tunnel
A761
Houston
B790
Glasgow
Quarrier's Village
Craigends
Gryffe Water
Carruth House
Crosslee
M8
A814
Govan
Bridge of Weir
Ranfurly
Brookfield
Linwood
A741
Hillington
Weaver's Cottage
522
HILL OF STAKE
Muirshiel
B786
Elderslie
A761
A761
Kilbarchan
B789
PAISLEY
Crookston Castle
Milliken Park
Johnstone
A737
Foxbar
A736
B762
Pollok
Burrell
River Calder
B787
Castle Semple Loch
Castle Semple
Howwood
Gleniffer Braes
A726
Nitshill
207
River Garnock
Lochwinnoch
B775
Caplaw
Barrhead
Thornliebank
Giffnock
B773
M77
RSPB
Newtown of Beltrees
Gateside
Rouken Glen
A760
A77
A736
Neilston
Newton Mearns
Greenbank Garden
B776
Shillford
Netherplace
Kilbirnie
Hall
Uplawmoor
Mearns
Kilbirnie Loch
Beith
B777
Craigton
A726
Dodside
B777
Gateside
Lugton
Glengarnock
Long Loch
Earn Water
B780
B784
Barrmill
A735
Halket
B769
196
197
The Den
Drakemyre
Gabroc Hill
Bennan Loch
330
5 miles
8 kilometres

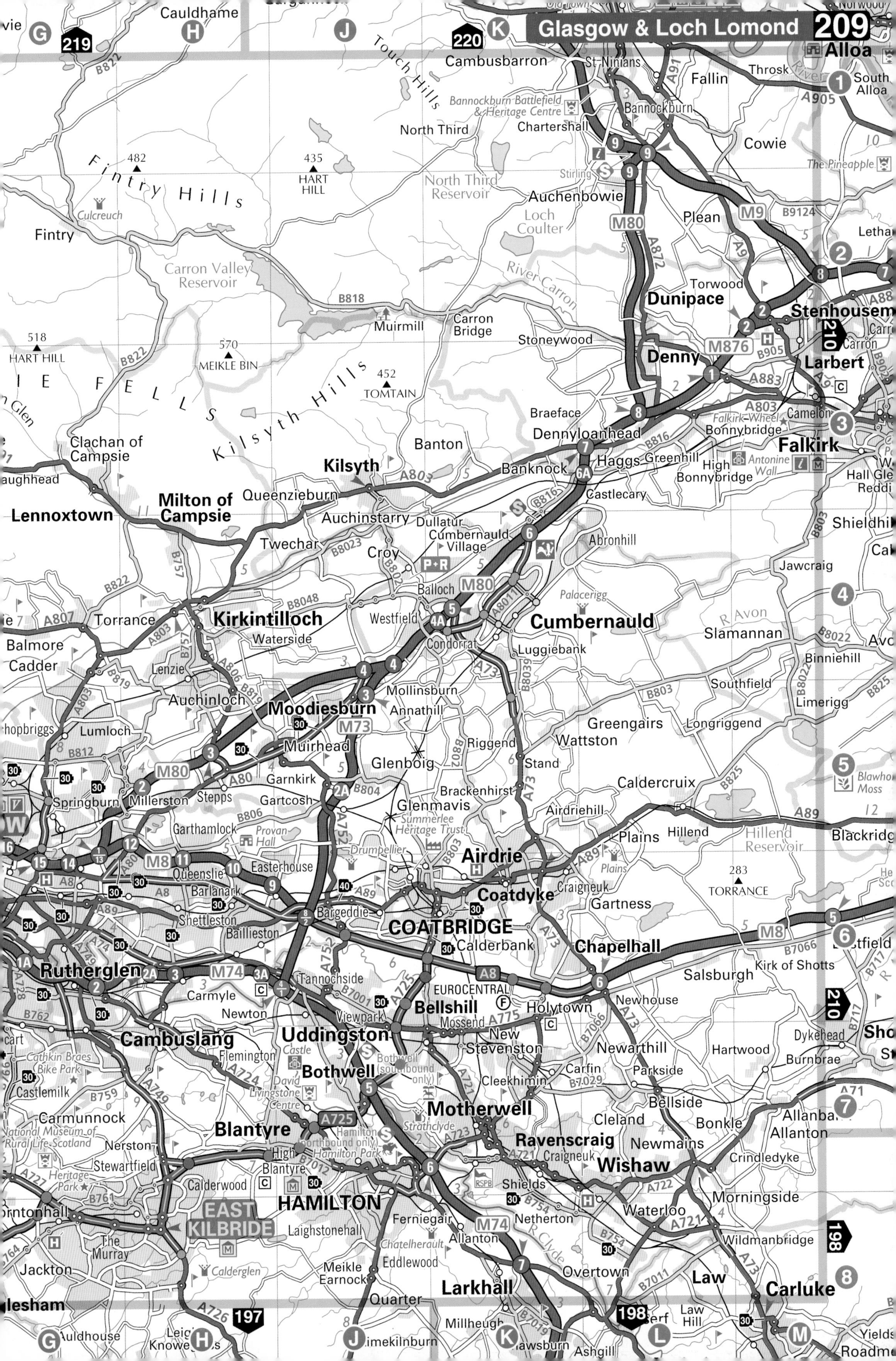
Cauldhame
Cambusbarron
Touch Hills
Bannockburn Battlefield & Heritage Centre
North Third
Chartershall
Alloa
Fallin
Throsk
South Alloa
Bannockburn
Cowie
The Pineapple
Stirling
Fintry Hills
HART HILL
North Third Reservoir
Auchenbowie
Culcreuch
Fintry
Loch Coulter
Plean
Carron Valley Reservoir
River Carron
Torwood
Dunipace
Stenhousemuir
Muirmill
Carron Bridge
Stoneywood
Denny
Larbert
HART HILL
MEIKLE BIN
TOMTAIN
Kilsyth Hills
Braeface
Falkirk Wheel
Camelon
Bonnybridge
Dennyloanhead
Falkirk
Clachan of Campsie
Banton
Haggs
Greenhill
High Bonnybridge
Antonine Wall
Kilsyth
Banknock
Lennoxtown
Milton of Campsie
Queenzieburn
Castlecary
Auchinstarry
Dullatur
Cumbernauld Village
Twechar
Croy
Abronhill
Balloch
Westfield
Palacerigg
Torrance
Kirkintilloch
Waterside
Cumbernauld
Condorrat
Luggiebank
Balmore
Cadder
Lenzie
Slamannan
Binniehill
Mollinsburn
Auchinloch
Annathill
Moodiesburn
Southfield
Limerigg
Lumloch
Muirhead
Greengairs
Longriggend
Wattston
Riggend
Glenboig
Stand
Garnkirk
Millerston
Stepps
Springburn
Gartcosh
Brackenhirst
Caldercruix
Glenmavis
Summerlee Heritage Trust
Garthamlock
Provan Hall
Airdriehill
Plains
Hillend
Hillend Reservoir
Drumpellier
Airdrie
Easterhouse
Queenslie
Barlanark
Coatdyke
Craigneuk
Gartness
TORRANCE
Shettleston
Bargeddie
Baillieston
COATBRIDGE
Calderbank
Chapelhall
Rutherglen
Tannochside
Salsburgh
Kirk of Shotts
Carmyle
EUROCENTRAL
Newton
Bellshill
Holytown
Newhouse
Mossend
Viewpark
Uddingston
New Stevenston
Cambuslang
Flemington
Cathkin Braes Bike Park
Castle
Newarthill
Hartwood
Dykehead
Burnbrae
Bothwell
Carfin
Parkside
Castlemilk
David Livingstone Centre
Cleekhimin
Bellside
Motherwell
Carmunnock
Cleland
Bonkle
Allanton
Blantyre
Strathclyde
Ravenscraig
National Museum of Rural Life Scotland
Nerston
Hamilton
High Blantyre
Hamilton Park
Craigneuk
Newmains
Wishaw
Stewartfield
Crindledyke
Heritage Park
Calderwood
Shields
Waterloo
Morningside
EAST KILBRIDE
HAMILTON
Ferniegair
Netherton
Laighstonehall
Chatelherault
Allanton
Wildmanbridge
The Murray
Jackton
Calderglen
Meikle Earnock
Eddlewood
Overtown
Law
Carluke
Larkhall
Quarter
Millheugh
Law Hill
Yieldshields
Roadmeetings
Ashgill
Limekilnburn
Auldhouse
Leigh Knowes

Alloa
Clackmannan
Forest Mill
Balgonar
Oakley
Steelend
KNOCK HILL
Bowershall
Kingseat
Townhill
Halbeath
South Alloa
Kennet
Cowie
Dunmore
Airth
Kincardine
Kincardine Bridge
Comrie
Carnock
Milesmark
Blairhall
High Valleyfield
Cairneyhill
Newmills
Culross Abbey
Culross Palace
Culross
Low Torry
Torryburn
Torry Bay
Crossford
DUNFERMLINE
Crombie
Charlestown
Rosyth
Limekilns
Letham
Stenhousemuir
Carronshore
Carron
Larbert
Skinflats
Grangemouth
Bo'ness
Bo'ness & Kinneil Railway
Grangepans
Carriden
Camelon
Falkirk
Antonine Wall
Laurieston
Callendar Park
Dovecot
Westquarter
Redding
Hall Glen
Reddingmuirhead
Polmont
Rumford
Whitecross
Kinneil House
Birkhill Claymine
Borrowstoun
Castle
Blackness
House of the Binns
Hopetoun
Forth Road Bridge
Newton
Brightons
Shieldhill
Maddiston
California
Jawcraig
Loan
Union Canal
Muiravonside
Linlithgow
Philpstoun
Burnside
Bridgend
Three Miletown
Winchburgh
Kirkliston
Standburn
Cockleroy
Beecraigs
Wester Ochiltree
Ecclesmachan
Newbridge
Avonbridge
Binniehill
Preceptory
Torphichen
Broxburn
Uphall
Limerigg
Strathloanhead
Westfield
Cairnpapple Hill
Dechmont
Ratho Viaduct
Ratho Station
Dechmont Road
Almondell & Calderwood
Ratho
Woodend
Blawhorn Moss
Bathgate
Pumpherston
Deans
Livingston
Armadale
Bathville
Boghall
Camps
Wilkieston
East Calder
Mid Calder
Kirknewton
Hillend Reservoir
Blackridge
Westrigg
Almond Valley
Polkemmet
Heart of Scotland
Livingston Village
Seafield
Oakbank
East Whitburn
Blackburn
Bellsquarry
Harthill
Whitburn
Polbeth
Eastfield
Stoneyburn
Linhouse Water
Ainville
Kirk of Shotts
Longridge
Loganlea
Water of Leith
R Almond
Addiewell
West Calder
Fauldhouse
Greenburn
Harperrig Reservoir
Dykehead
Shotts
Breich
Burnbrae
Stane
EAST CAIRN HILL
WEST CAIRN HILL
Headlesscross
Cobbinshaw Loch
Allanbank
Allanton
Gladsmuir Hills
Crosswood Reservoir
WORM LAW
Woolfords
Tarbrax
Wilsontown
Auchengray
HARE HILL
Forth
South Tarbrax
HARROWS LAW
West Water
West Water Reservoir
Baddinsgill Reservoir
Carluke
Yieldshields
Roadmeetings
Braehead
Medwin
LEFT
MENDICK
0 1 2 3 4 5 miles
0 1 2 3 4 5 6 7 8 kilometres
209
221
198
199

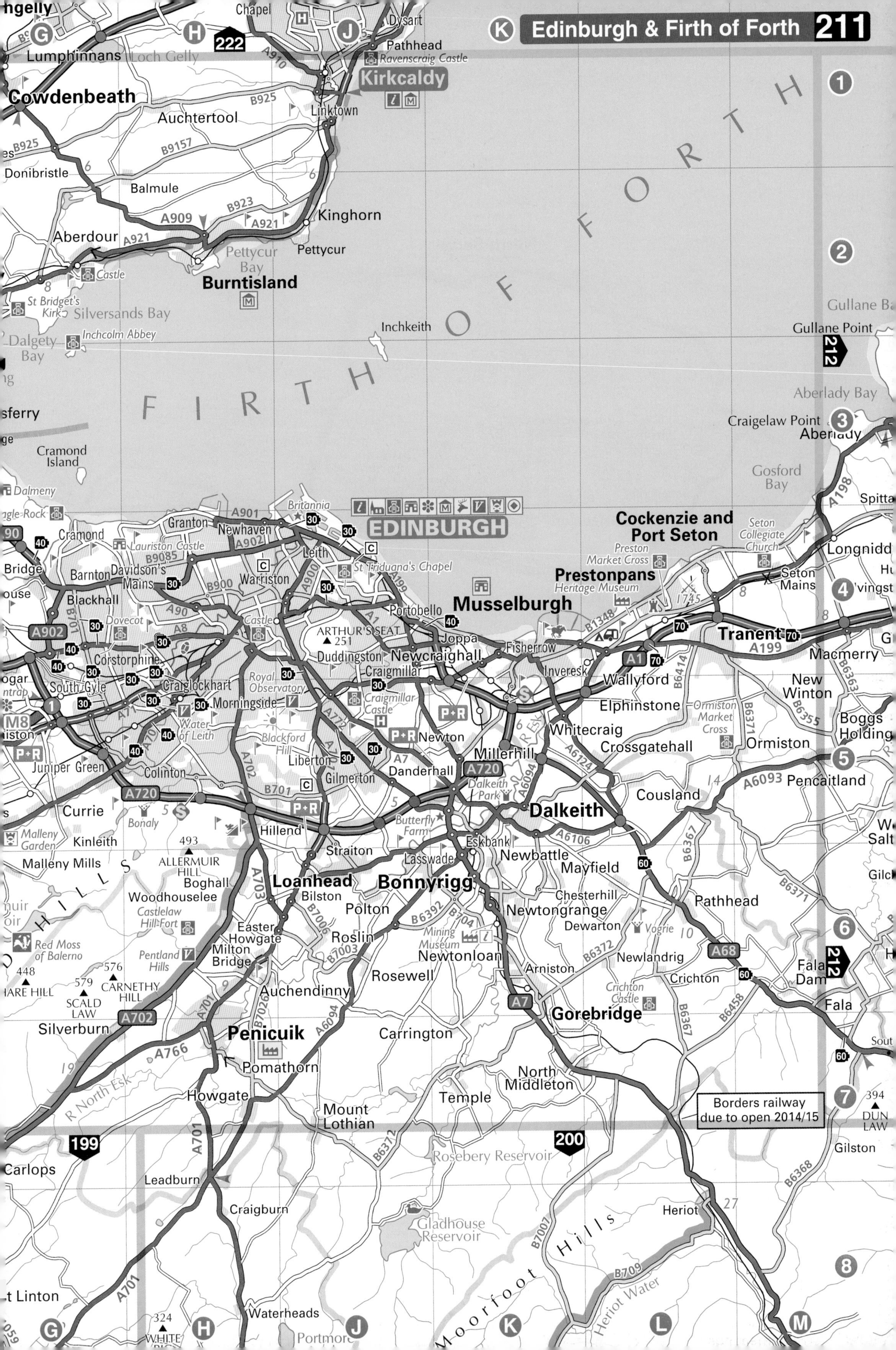
FIRTH OF FORTH
EDINBURGH
Kirkcaldy
Pathhead
Ravenscraig Castle
Dysart
Chapel
Linktown
Lumphinnans
Loch Gelly
Cowdenbeath
Auchtertool
Donibristle
Balmule
Kinghorn
Aberdour
Castle
Pettycur Bay
Pettycur
Burntisland
St Bridget's Kirk
Silversands Bay
Dalgety Bay
Inchcolm Abbey
Inchkeith
Cramond Island
Dalmeny
Eagle Rock
Britannia
Granton
Newhaven
Cramond
Lauriston Castle
Leith
Warriston
St Triduana's Chapel
Barnton
Davidson's Mains
Blackhall
Dovecot
Castle
Corstorphine
South Gyle
Craiglockhart
Morningside
Royal Observatory
ARTHUR'S SEAT 251
Duddingston
Portobello
Joppa
Newcraighall
Craigmillar
Craigmillar Castle
Water of Leith
Blackford Hill
Liberton
Gilmerton
Juniper Green
Colinton
Currie
Bonaly
Malleny Garden
Kinleith
Malleny Mills
Hillend
Straiton
Loanhead
Bilston
ALLERMUIR HILL 493
Boghall
Woodhouselee
Castlelaw Hill Fort
Red Moss of Balerno
Pentland Hills
Easter Howgate
Milton Bridge
HARE HILL 448
SCALD LAW 579
CARNETHY HILL 576
Silverburn
Auchendinny
Penicuik
Pomathorn
Howgate
R North Esk
Carlops
Leadburn
Craigburn
Linton
Waterheads
WHITE
Portmore
Newton
Danderhall
Millerhill
Dalkeith Park
Butterfly Farm
Eskbank
Lasswade
Bonnyrigg
Polton
Roslin
Rosewell
Mining Museum
Newtonloan
Carrington
Mount Lothian
Temple
Rosebery Reservoir
Gladhouse Reservoir
Moorfoot Hills
Heriot Water
Heriot
Musselburgh
Fisherrow
Inveresk
Wallyford
Whitecraig
Dalkeith
Newbattle
Mayfield
Chesterhill
Newtongrange
Dewarton
Vogrie
Newlandrig
Arniston
Gorebridge
North Middleton
Crichton
Crichton Castle
Pathhead
Elphinstone
Crossgatehall
Cousland
Ormiston Market Cross
Ormiston
Pencaitland
Prestonpans
Heritage Museum
Preston Market Cross
Cockenzie and Port Seton
Seton Collegiate Church
Seton Mains
1745
Tranent
Macmerry
New Winton
Boggs Holding
Longniddry
Gosford Bay
Aberlady Bay
Craigelaw Point
Aberlady
Gullane Point
Gullane Bay
Spittal
Fala Dam
Fala
Gilston
DUN LAW 394
Borders railway due to open 2014/15
A910
B925
B9157
A909
B923
A921
A901
A902
B9085
B900
A900
A199
A1
A90
A8
B701
A71
A70
A702
A772
A7
A720
A6094
A6124
A6106
B6414
B6371
B6363
B6355
A6093
B6367
A68
B6372
B6458
A703
B7006
B6392
B704
B7003
B7026
A6094
A701
A766
B1348
A198
B6368
B7007
B709
M8
P+R
222
212
199
200
211

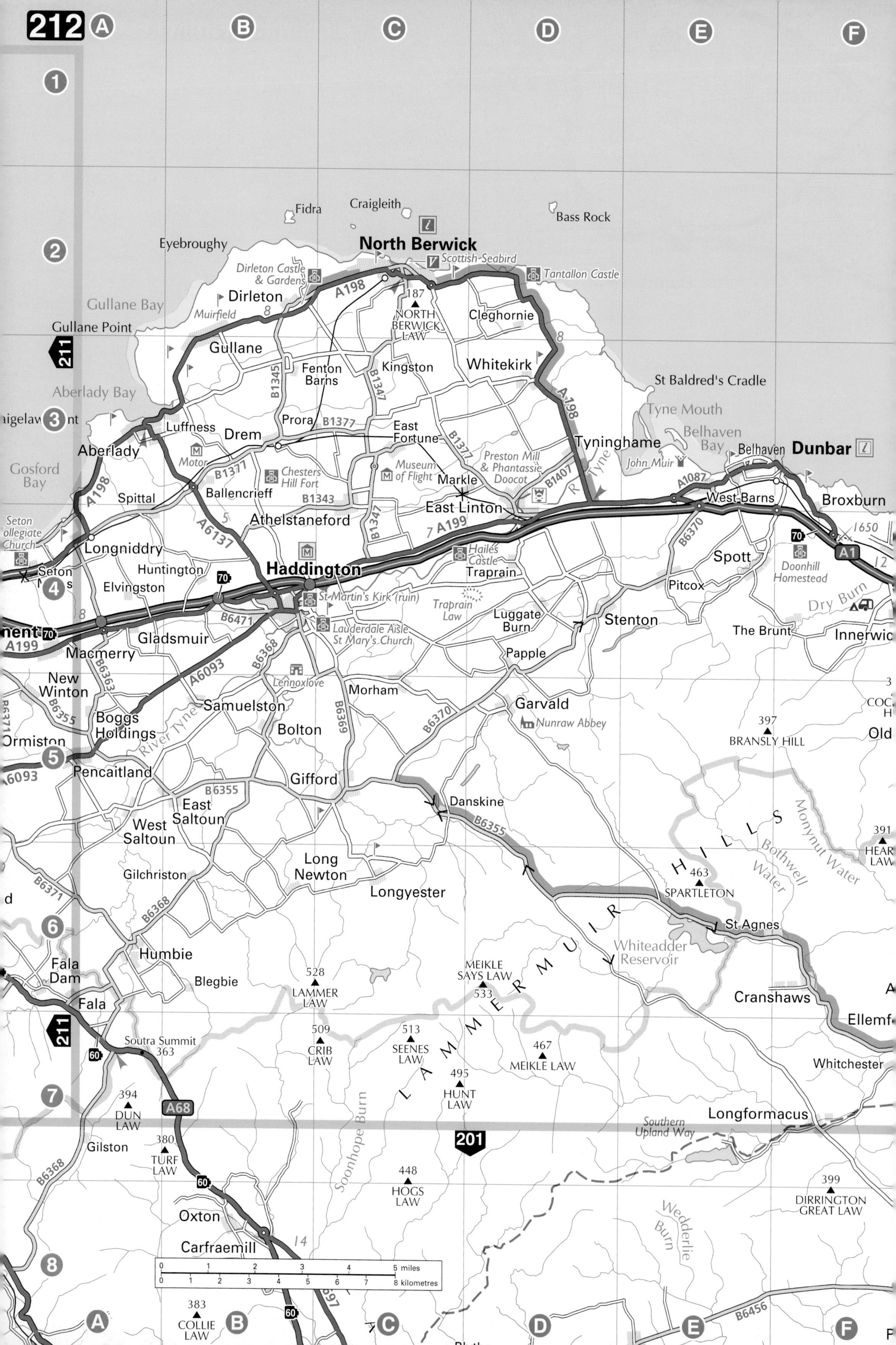
A
B
C
D
E
F
1
2
3
4
5
6
7
8
Fidra
Craigleith
Bass Rock
North Berwick
Scottish Seabird
Tantallon Castle
Eyebroughy
Dirleton Castle & Gardens
Dirleton
Muirfield
Gullane Bay
Gullane Point
211
Gullane
187
NORTH BERWICK LAW
Cleghornie
Whitekirk
Fenton Barns
Kingston
B1345
B1347
A198
Aberlady Bay
St Baldred's Cradle
Tyne Mouth
Belhaven Bay
Belhaven
Dunbar
Luffness
Drem
Prora
B1377
East Fortune
Aberlady
Motor
Chesters Hill Fort
Museum of Flight
Markle
Preston Mill & Phantassie Doocot
Tyninghame
John Muir
A1087
Gosford Bay
Spittal
Ballencrieff
B1343
East Linton
B1407
R Tyne
West Barns
Broxburn
Seton Collegiate Church
A6137
Athelstaneford
A199
B6370
1650
Longniddry
Haddington
Hailes Castle
Traprain
Spott
70
A1
Doonhill Homestead
12
Seton
Huntington
Elvingston
St Martin's Kirk (ruin)
Traprain Law
Pitcox
Dry Burn
Luggate Burn
Stenton
The Brunt
Innerwic
B6471
Gladsmuir
Lauderdale Aisle St Mary's Church
Macmerry
B6363
B6368
Papple
New Winton
A6093
Lennoxlove
Morham
B6355
Samuelston
Garvald
Nunraw Abbey
Boggs Holdings
River Tyne
B6369
Bolton
397
BRANSLY HILL
Ormiston
Old
Pencaitland
Gifford
B6355
Danskine
East Saltoun
West Saltoun
Monynut Water
391
HEAR LAW
Bothwell Water
Long Newton
Gilchriston
463
SPARTLETON
B6371
Longyester
B6368
St Agnes
LAMMERMUIR HILLS
Humbie
Whiteadder Reservoir
Fala Dam
528
LAMMER LAW
MEIKLE SAYS LAW
533
Blegbie
Cranshaws
Fala
Ellemf
509
CRIB LAW
513
SEENES LAW
467
MEIKLE LAW
Soutra Summit
363
60
495
HUNT LAW
Whitchester
394
DUN LAW
A68
Soonhope Burn
Southern Upland Way
Longformacus
201
Gilston
380
TURF LAW
448
HOGS LAW
399
DIRRINGTON GREAT LAW
Wedderlie Burn
Oxton
Carfraemill
14
0 1 2 3 4 5 miles
0 1 2 3 4 5 6 7 8 kilometres
383
COLLIE LAW
B6456

G
H
J
1
2
3
4
5
6
7
8
Thorntonloch
Reed Point
Cove
Pease Bay
Siccar Point
Dunglass Collegiate Church
Cockburnspath
Fast Castle Head
A1107
Pease Dean
196
BROWN RIG
Coldingham Loch
ST ABB'S HEAD
St Abbs
Ecclaw
Grantshouse
Coldingham
Coldingham Bay
Southern Upland Way
Butterdean
Eye Water
Houndwood
B6438
A1107
Eyemouth
Heugh Head
Cairncross
Quixwood
262
HORSELEY HILL
A1
B6355
Reston
Ayton
Burnmouth
Edin's Hall Broch
325
COCKBURN LAW
B6438
Auchencrow
Marygold
A6112
Lintlaw
B6355
Lamberton
Primrosehill
Preston
B6437
B6355
Chirnside
Marshall Meadows Bay
202
Cumledge
Edrom Church
B6365
Chirnsidebridge
Foulden
North Northumberland Heritage Coast
Edrom
1333
Manderston
A6105
Broadhaugh
Edington
Whiteadder Water
Foulden Tithe Barn
A6105
Berwick-upon
Allanton
Hutton
Castle
Barracks
Duns
B6437
Paxton
Town Ramparts
Gavinton
Blackadder
B6460
B6461
Tweedmouth
B6460
Paxton
Spittal
Whitsome
Hilton
Loanend
East Ord
Huds Head
Nisbet
Sinclair's
K
L
M

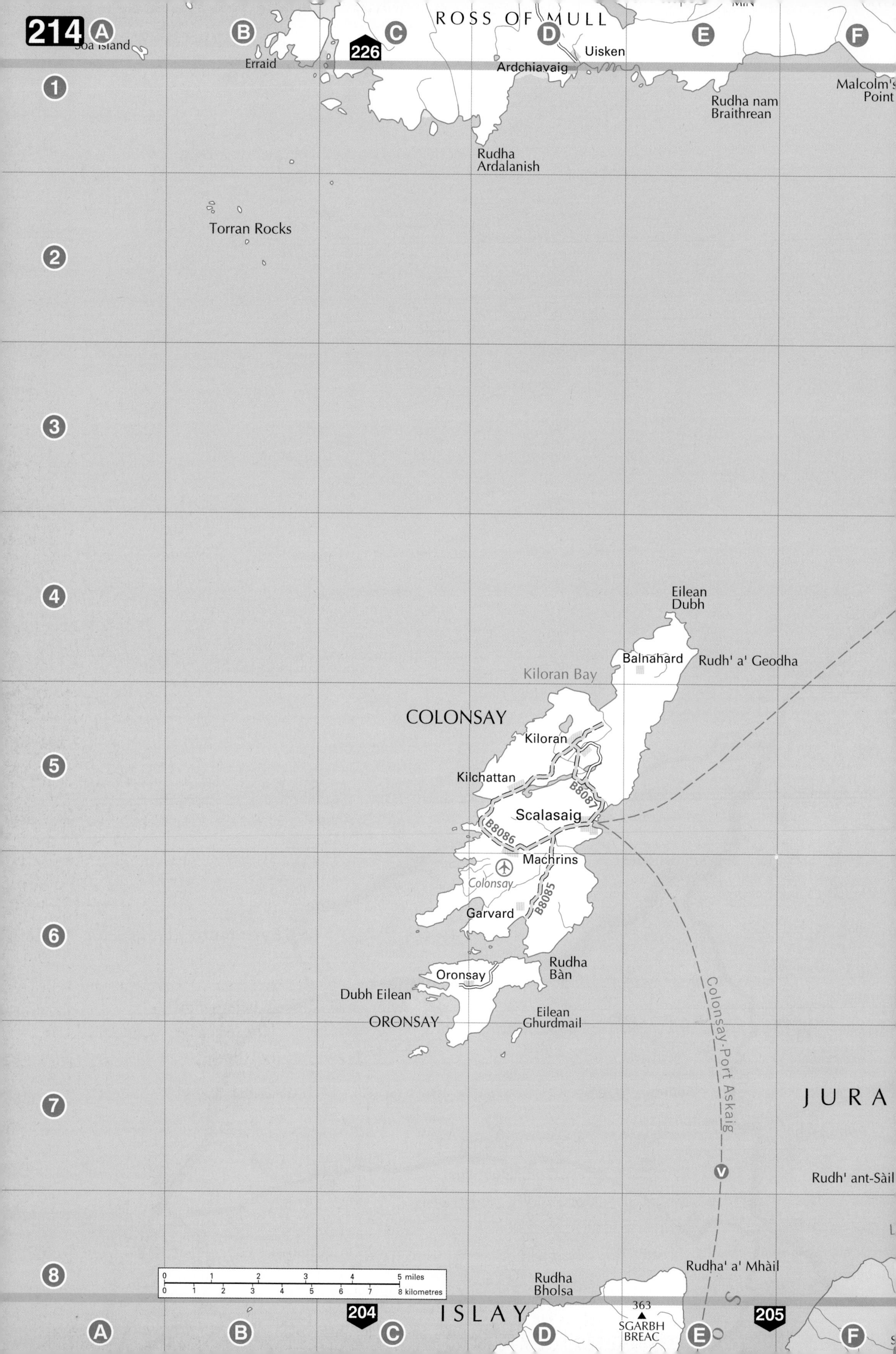

A
B
C
D
E
F
226
Soa Island
Erraid
ROSS OF MULL
Uisken
Ardchiavaig
Malcolm's Point
Rudha nam Braithrean
Rudha Ardalanish
Torran Rocks
1
2
3
4
5
6
7
8
Eilean Dubh
Balnahard
Rudh' a' Geodha
Kiloran Bay
COLONSAY
Kiloran
Kilchattan
B8087
Scalasaig
B8086
Machrins
Colonsay
B8085
Garvard
Rudha Bàn
Oronsay
Dubh Eilean
ORONSAY
Eilean Ghurdmail
Colonsay-Port Askaig
JURA
Rudh' ant-Sàil
Rudha' a' Mhàil
Rudha Bholsa
0 1 2 3 4 5 miles
0 1 2 3 4 5 6 7 8 kilometres
204
ISLAY
363
SGARBH BREAC
205

227
216
206
205
FIRTH
Colonsay - Oban
Dubh
Insh Island
Clachan-Seil
SEIL
Ellenabeich
Easdale
Balvicar
Easdale
B844
B8003
Cuan
Seil Sound
Cullipool
Torsa
Degnish
Loch Melfort
A816
Garbh Eileach
Eilean Dubh Mòr
GARVELLACHS
Monastery & Beehive Cells
Eileach an Naoimh
LUING
Arduaine
Toberonochy
Sound of Luing
Shuna Sound
SHUNA
LUNGA
Scarba, Lunga and the Garvellachs
Shuna Point
Craigdhu
SCARBA
448
CRUACH SCARBA
Ardfern
B8002
Gulf of Corryvreckan
Aird
Loch Craignish
Craignish Point
Island Macaskin
Slockavullin
Temple Wood Stone Circles
Poltalloch
295
CRUACH NA SEILCHEIG
Glengarrisdale Bay
Glendebadel Bay
364
BEN GARRISDALE
Lealt Burn
Loch Crinan
Crinan
Kilmahumaig
B8025
Bellanoch
Crinan
B841
Corpach Bay
Lussa River
466
BEINN BHREAC
Glen Grundale
Barnluc
SOUND OF JURA
Carsaig Bay
453
RAINBERG MÒR
Ardlussa
Tayvallich
Achnamara
Lussa Point
Lussagiven
Knapdale
Kilmichael of Inverluss
Taynish
A846
331
BEINN BHEAG
466
CRUACH LUSACH
Loch Sween
B8025
Keills Chapel
Loch na Cille
Kilbride
Castle Sween
Lochead
Danna Island
B8024

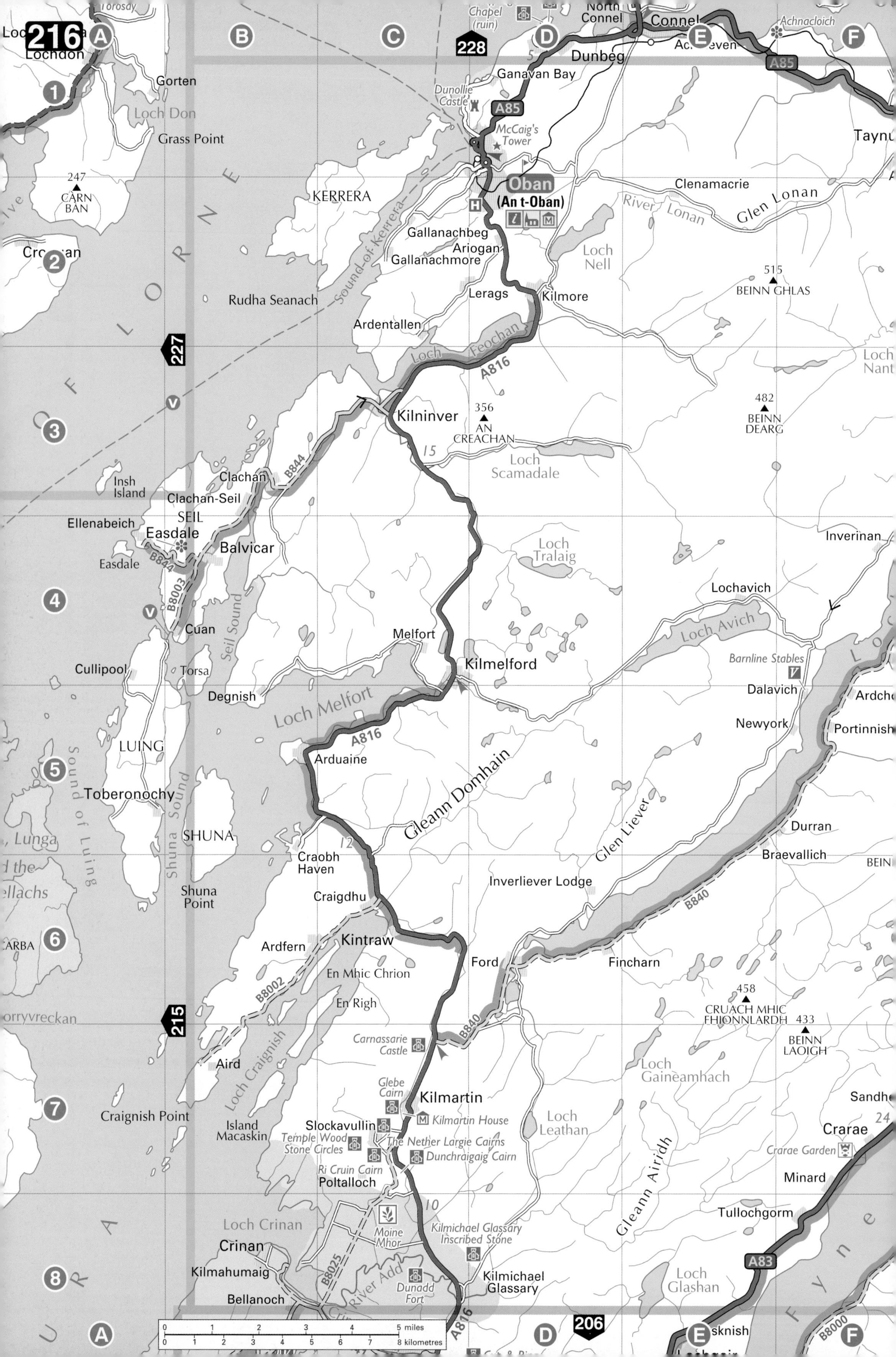

216
228
227
215
206
Lochdon
Gorten
Loch Don
Grass Point
CARN BAN
KERRERA
Sound of Kerrera
Rudha Seanach
FIRTH OF LORNE
Dunollie Castle
McCaig's Tower
Oban
(An t-Oban)
Ganavan Bay
Dunbeg
Connel
North Connel
Achnacloich
A85
Taynuilt
Clenamacrie
River Lonan
Glen Lonan
Gallanachbeg
Ariogan
Gallanachmore
Loch Nell
Lerags
Kilmore
Ardentallen
Loch Feochan
A816
BEINN GHLAS
Kilninver
AN CREACHAN
Loch Scamadale
BEINN DEARG
Insh Island
Clachan
Clachan-Seil
SEIL
B844
Ellenabeich
Easdale
Balvicar
B8003
Cuan
Seil Sound
Loch Tralaig
Inverinan
Lochavich
Loch Avich
Melfort
Kilmelford
Cullipool
Torsa
Degnish
Loch Melfort
Barnline Stables
Dalavich
Newyork
Portinnisherrich
Arduaine
LUING
Toberonochy
Sound of Luing
Shuna Sound
SHUNA
Gleann Domhain
Glen Liever
Craobh Haven
Shuna Point
Durran
Braevallich
Craigdhu
Inverliever Lodge
B840
Ardfern
Kintraw
En Mhic Chrion
En Righ
Ford
Fincharn
B8002
Loch Craignish
Carnassarie Castle
CRUACH MHIC FHIONNLARDH
BEINN LAOIGH
Aird
Glebe Cairn
Kilmartin
Kilmartin House
Loch Gaineamhach
Craignish Point
Island Macaskin
Slockavullin
Temple Wood Stone Circles
The Nether Largie Cairns
Dunchraigaig Cairn
Ri Cruin Cairn
Poltalloch
Loch Leathan
Gleann Airidh
Crarae
Crarae Garden
Minard
Tullochgorm
Loch Crinan
Crinan
Moine Mhor
Kilmichael Glassary Inscribed Stone
B8025
River Add
Kilmahumaig
Dunadd Fort
Kilmichael Glassary
Loch Glashan
A83
Loch Fyne
Bellanoch
Sound of Jura
B8000
5 miles
8 kilometres

G
H
J
K
229
River Noe
988
BEINN EUNAICH
Glen Strae
nawe Historic
n Furnace
nroy
chan
1124
BEN
CRUACHAN
20
River Awe
Pass of Brander
Cruachan
Reservoir
Kilchurn
Castle
B8077
Stronmilchan
Lochawe
Cruachan
Power Station
B845
A819
Upper
Kinchrackine
Dalmally
Inverlochy
A85
648
BEINN
DONACHAN
River Orchy
B8074
771
BEINN UDLAIDH
1
12
River Lochy
Glen Lochy
Tyndrum
Ber
1130
BEN LUI
2
1028
BEN OSS
977
BEINN
DUBHCHRA
636
218
739
LOCH LOMOND AND
THE TROSSACHS
NATIONAL PARK
3
Ardanaiseig
Ardanaiseig Hotel
Hayfield
enan
Taychreggan
Hotel
Cladich
Portsonachan
Hotel
B840
Lochan
Shira
947
BEINN
BHUIDHE
A82
17
Glenfyne
Lodge
645
MAOL BREAC
4
589
CRUACH
MHOR
ghour
9
A819
Glen Aray
Glen Shira
658
CLACHAN
HILL
Glen Fyne
942
BEN
VORLICH
Loch
Sloy
Water
Tower
11
Cairndow
Ardkinglas
Woodland
Garden
5
Inveruglas
Inveraray Castle
Inveraray
Inveraray Jail
Loch Shira
Loch Fyne
Glen Kinglas
1011
BEN IME
912
BEINN AN
LOCHAIN
Rest and be thankful
10
St Catherines
B839
Douglas Water
A83
A815
565
CRUACH
NAN CAPULL
B828
925
BEINN NARNAIN
881
THE
COBBLER
Glen Croe
Succoth
416
CRUACH
TAIRBEIRT
845
BEN
DONICH
A83
Arrochar
6
2
Ardgartan
Argyll Forest Park
River Goil
Auchindrain
Strachur
218
Lochgoilhead
661
BEN
REACH
Furnace
A886
River Cur
Corrow
Douglas Pier
Loch Long
Glen Douglas
7
Newton
Balliemore
779
BEINN
BHEULA
Invernoaden
10
Glenbranter
Loch Goil
A814
480
CRUACH
NAN CAPULL
734
DOUNE
HILL
Loch
Eck
A815
Arddarroch
702
BEINN EICH
505
CRUACH AN
LOCHAIN
Carrick Castle
Edentaggart
618
BEINN
BHEAG
Portincaple
Whistlefield
Inn
Whistlefield
8
713
BEINN
CHAORACH
Glen Lu
LOCH
A886
A814
15
207
657
Dunans Castle
742
Argyll Forest Park
arelochhead
L
M

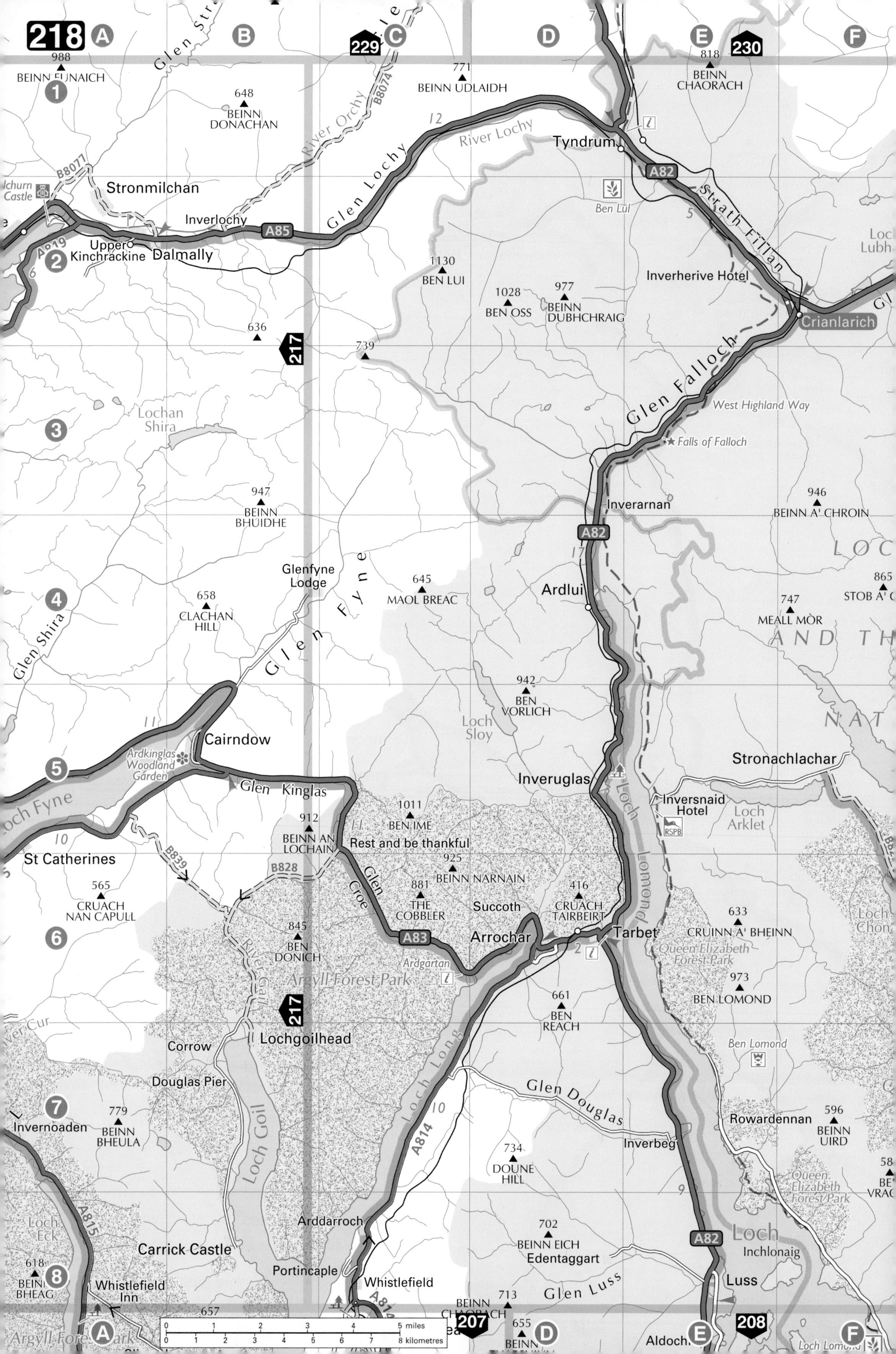

229
230
217
207
208
BEINN EUNAICH 988
BEINN DONACHAN 648
BEINN UDLAIDH 771
BEINN CHAORACH 818
Glen Strae
River Orchy
B8074
B8077
Stronmilchan
Inverlochy
Upper Kinchrackine
Dalmally
A85
A819
Glen Lochy
River Lochy
Tyndrum
A82
Strath Fillan
Ben Lui
BEN LUI 1130
BEN OSS 1028
BEINN DUBHCHRAIG 977
Inverherive Hotel
Crianlarich
Glen Falloch
West Highland Way
Falls of Falloch
636
739
Lochan Shira
BEINN BHUIDHE 947
Inverarnan
BEINN A' CHROIN 946
A82
Glenfyne Lodge
Glen Fyne
MAOL BREAC 645
CLACHAN HILL 658
Ardlui
Glen Shira
MEALL MÒR 747
STOB A' C 865
BEN VORLICH 942
Loch Sloy
Cairndow
Ardkinglas Woodland Garden
Loch Fyne
Glen Kinglas
Inveruglas
Stronachlachar
Inversnaid Hotel
RSPB
Loch Arklet
BEN IME 1011
BEINN AN LOCHAIN 912
Rest and be thankful
St Catherines
B839
B828
BEINN NARNAIN 925
Glen Croe
THE COBBLER 881
Succoth
CRUACH TAIRBEIRT 416
Loch Lomond
CRUACH NAN CAPULL 565
BEN DONICH 845
A83
Arrochar
Tarbet
CRUINN A' BHEINN 633
Queen Elizabeth Forest Park
Ardgartan
Argyll Forest Park
River Goil
BEN REACH 661
BEN LOMOND 973
Lochgoilhead
Corrow
Loch Long
Ben Lomond
Douglas Pier
Glen Douglas
Invernoaden
BEINN BHEULA 779
Rowardennan
BEINN UIRD 596
Loch Goil
A814
Inverbeg
DOUNE HILL 734
A815
Loch Eck
Arddarroch
BEINN EICH 702
Edentaggart
Loch Lomond
Inchlonaig
Carrick Castle
BEINN BHEAG 618
Portincaple
Whistlefield Inn
Whistlefield
Glen Luss
Luss
BEINN CHAORACH 713
655
657
Aldochlay
Argyll Forest Park
5 miles
8 kilometres

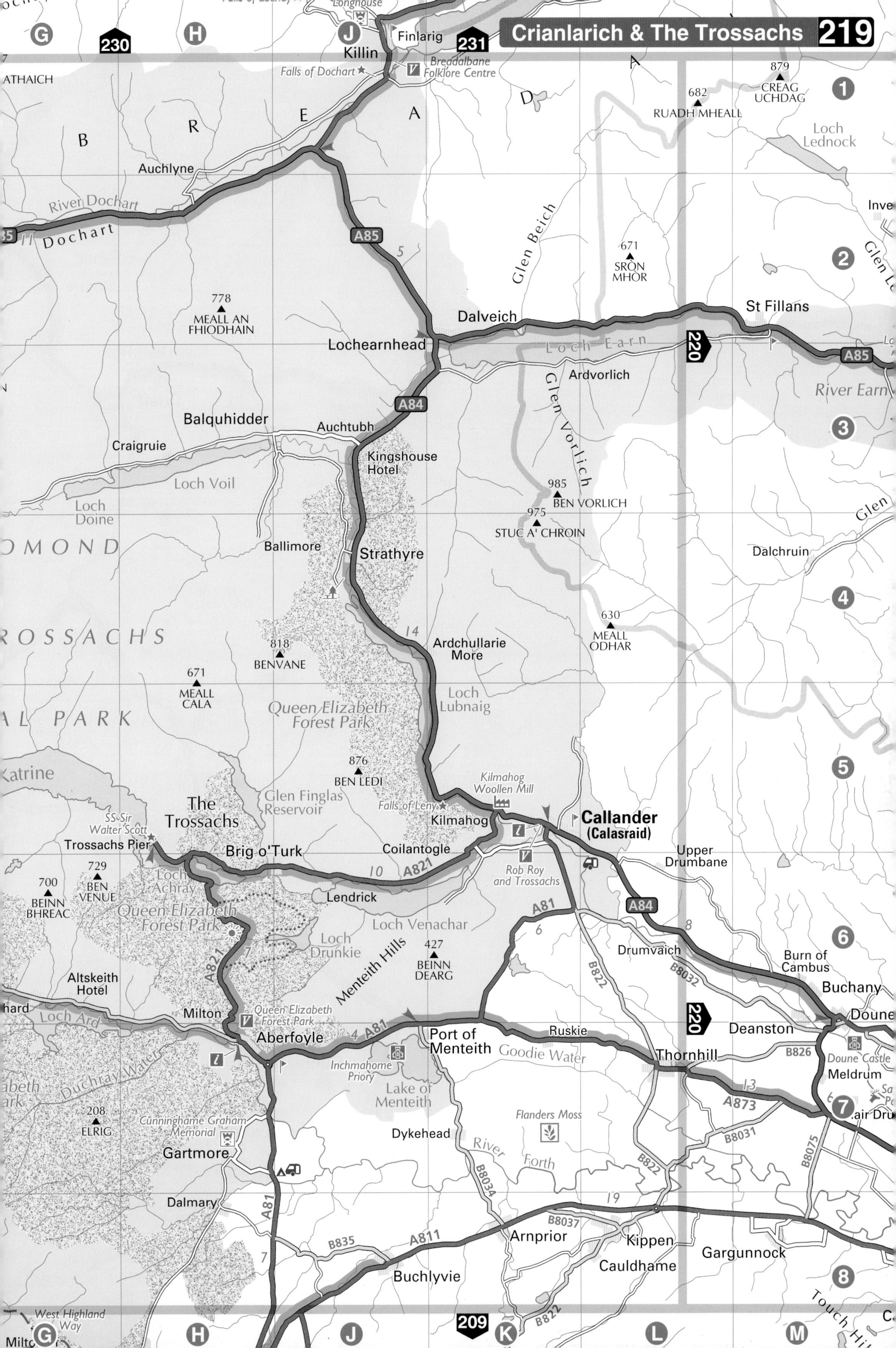
Killin
Finlarig
Falls of Dochart
Breadalbane Folklore Centre
Auchlyne
River Dochart
Glen Dochart
Loch Lednock
CREAG UCHDAG
RUADH MHEALL
Glen Beich
SRON MHOR
Dalveich
St Fillans
Lochearnhead
Loch Earn
Ardvorlich
River Earn
Glen Vorlich
MEALL AN FHIODHAIN
Balquhidder
Auchtubh
Craigruie
Kingshouse Hotel
Loch Voil
Loch Doine
BEN VORLICH
STUC A' CHROIN
Ballimore
Strathyre
Dalchruin
MEALL ODHAR
BENVANE
Ardchullarie More
MEALL CALA
Loch Lubnaig
Queen Elizabeth Forest Park
BEN LEDI
Glen Finglas Reservoir
Falls of Leny
Kilmahog Woollen Mill
Kilmahog
Callander (Calasraid)
The Trossachs
SS Sir Walter Scott
Trossachs Pier
Brig o'Turk
Coilantogle
Upper Drumbane
Rob Roy and Trossachs
Loch Achray
BEN VENUE
BEINN BHREAC
Lendrick
Loch Venachar
Loch Drunkie
Menteith Hills
BEINN DEARG
Drumvaich
Burn of Cambus
Buchany
Altskeith Hotel
Loch Ard
Milton
Aberfoyle
Port of Menteith
Ruskie
Deanston
Doune
Thornhill
Goodie Water
Doune Castle
Meldrum
Inchmahome Priory
Lake of Menteith
Duchray Water
ELRIG
Cunninghame Graham Memorial
Gartmore
Dykehead
Flanders Moss
River Forth
Dalmary
Arnprior
Kippen
Gargunnock
Cauldhame
Buchlyvie
West Highland Way
A85
A84
A821
A81
A873
A811
B822
B8032
B826
B8031
B8075
B8034
B8037
B835
230
231
220
209

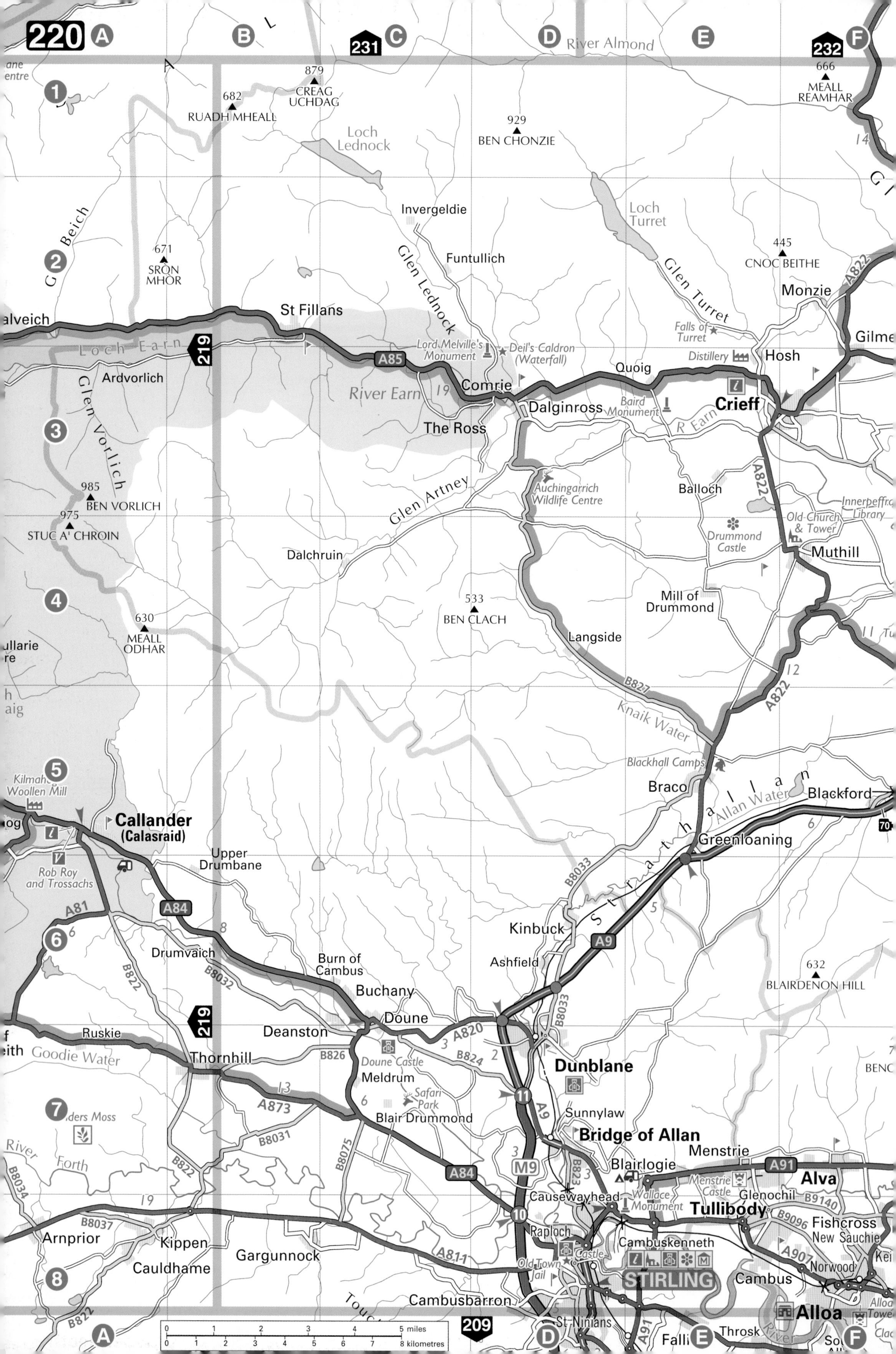
A
B
231 C
D
River Almond
E
232 F
879
CREAG
UCHDAG
682
RUADH MHEALL
666
MEALL
REAMHAR
929
BEN CHONZIE
Loch
Lednock
Invergeldie
Loch
Turret
Glen Beich
671
SRON
MHOR
Funtullich
Glen Lednock
Glen Turret
445
CNOC BEITHE
Monzie
St Fillans
Falls of
Turret
Distillery
Hosh
Loch Earn
219
Lord Melville's
Monument
Deil's Caldron
(Waterfall)
A85
Quoig
Ardvorlich
River Earn
Comrie
Baird
Monument
Crieff
Dalginross
R Earn
The Ross
Glen Vorlich
Glen Artney
Auchingarrich
Wildlife Centre
Balloch
A822
985
BEN VORLICH
975
STUC A' CHROIN
Innerpeffray
Library
Old Church
& Tower
Drummond
Castle
Muthill
Dalchruin
Mill of
Drummond
533
BEN CLACH
630
MEALL
ODHAR
Langside
B827
Knaik Water
Blackhall Camps
Kilmahog
Woollen Mill
Braco
Strathallan
Allan Water
Blackford
Callander
(Calasraid)
Greenloaning
Upper
Drumbane
Rob Roy
and Trossachs
B8033
A81
A84
Kinbuck
A9
Drumvaich
B822
B8032
Burn of
Cambus
Ashfield
632
BLAIRDENON HILL
Buchany
219
Doune
Ruskie
Deanston
A820
Goodie Water
Thornhill
B826
B824
Doune Castle
Dunblane
Meldrum
A873
Safari
Park
Sunnylaw
Blair Drummond
B8031
Bridge of Allan
Menstrie
River Forth
B8075
B822
A84
M9
B823
Blairlogie
A91
Alva
Menstrie
Castle
Glenochil
B9140
B8034
Causewayhead
Wallace
Monument
Tullibody
B8037
B9096
Fishcross
Arnprior
Raploch
New Sauchie
Kippen
Cambuskenneth
Gargunnock
A811
A907
Cauldhame
Old Town
Jail
Castle
STIRLING
Cambus
Norwood
Cambusbarron
Alloa
B822
A
0 1 2 3 4 5 miles
0 1 2 3 4 5 6 7 8 kilometres
209
St Ninians
D
Throsk
E
F

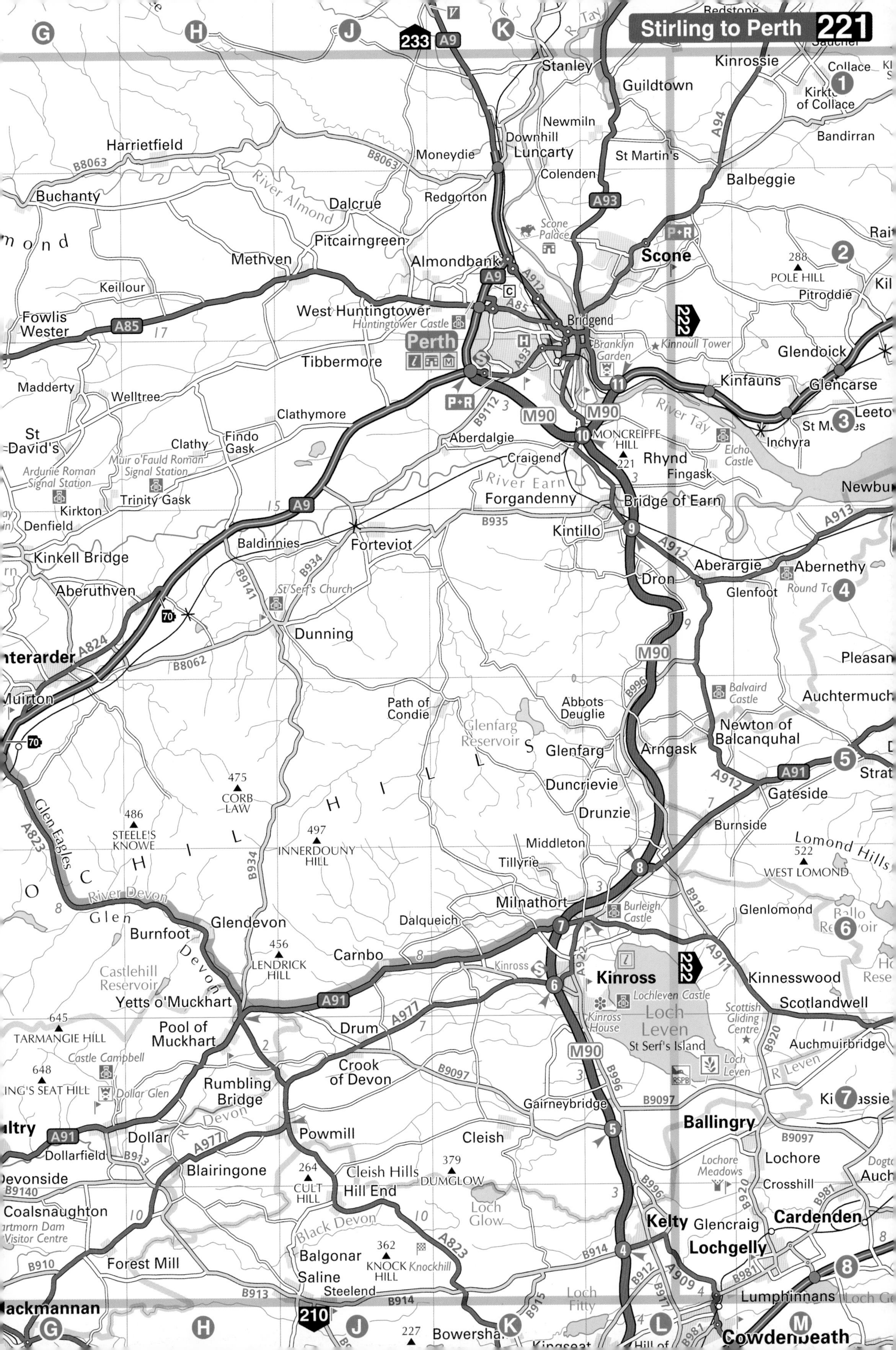
Stanley
Guildtown
Kinrossie
Collace
Kirkton of Collace
Newmiln
Downhill
Luncarty
St Martin's
Bandirran
Harrietfield
Moneydie
Colenden
Balbeggie
Buchanty
Dalcrue
Redgorton
Scone Palace
Scone
Pitcairngreen
Almondbank
Methven
Keillour
Pole Hill
Pitroddie
West Huntingtower
Huntingtower Castle
Fowlis Wester
Bridgend
Perth
Branklyn Garden
Kinnoull Tower
Glendoick
Tibbermore
Kinfauns
Glencarse
Madderty
Welltree
Clathymore
St David's
Clathy
Findo Gask
Aberdalgie
Moncreiffe Hill
Rhynd
Inchyra
Elcho Castle
Muir o'Fauld Roman Signal Station
Ardunie Roman Signal Station
Craigend
Fingask
Trinity Gask
River Earn
Kirkton
Forgandenny
Bridge of Earn
Denfield
Kintillo
Baldinnies
Forteviot
Kinkell Bridge
Aberargie
Abernethy
Dron
Glenfoot
Aberuthven
St Serf's Church
Dunning
Auchterarder
Pleasance
Balvaird Castle
Auchtermuchty
Path of Condie
Abbots Deuglie
Glenfarg Reservoir
Glenfarg
Newton of Balcanquhal
Arngask
Corb Law
Duncrievie
Gateside
Steele's Knowe
Innerdouny Hill
Drunzie
Burnside
Glen Eagles
Lomond Hills
West Lomond
Middleton
Tillyrie
Ochil Hills
River Devon
Milnathort
Burleigh Castle
Glenlomond
Glen Devon
Burnfoot
Glendevon
Dalqueich
Lendrick Hill
Carnbo
Kinross
Castlehill Reservoir
Lochleven Castle
Kinnesswood
Yetts o'Muckhart
Scotlandwell
Tarmangie Hill
Pool of Muckhart
Drum
Kinross House
Loch Leven
Scottish Gliding Centre
Castle Campbell
St Serf's Island
Auchmuirbridge
Crook of Devon
King's Seat Hill
Dollar Glen
Rumbling Bridge
Gairneybridge
Dollar
Powmill
Cleish
Ballingry
Dollarfield
Lochore
Blairingone
Cult Hill
Cleish Hills
Dumglow
Hill End
Lochore Meadows
Crosshill
Devonside
Coalsnaughton
Loch Glow
Black Devon
Kelty
Glencraig
Cardenden
Gartmorn Dam Visitor Centre
Knock Hill
Knockhill
Balgonar
Lochgelly
Forest Mill
Saline
Steelend
Lumphinnans
Clackmannan
Bowershall
Loch Fitty
Cowdenbeath
Kingseat
Hill of Beath
A9
A85
A93
A912
A94
A93
B8063
M90
A913
A824
B8062
B9141
B934
B935
B9112
B996
A91
A912
A823
A977
A911
B919
B920
B9097
B913
B914
B910
B9140
A909
B912
B981
B915
R Leven
River Tay
River Almond

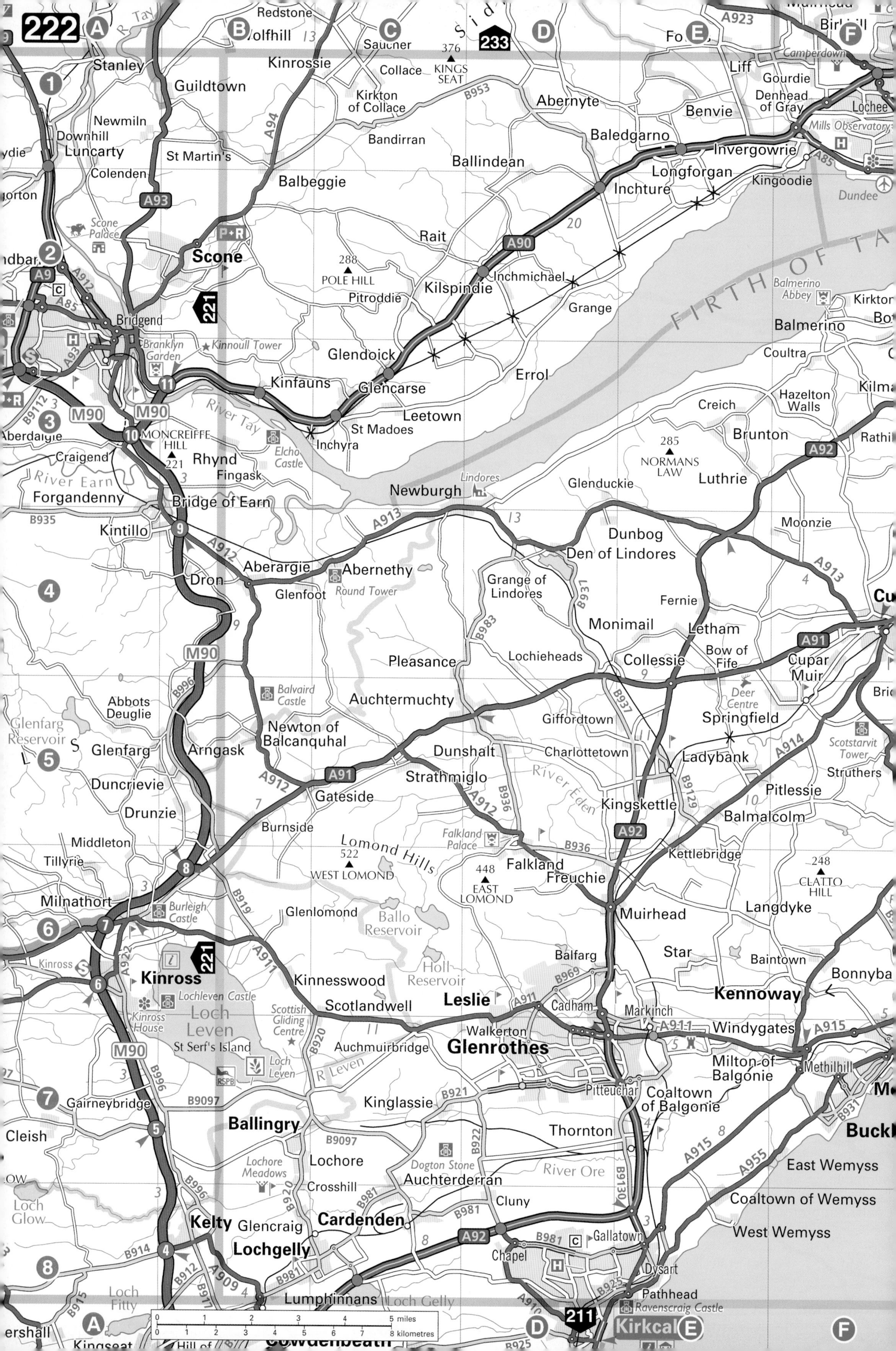
233
221
211
Redstone
Wolfhill
Saucher
Stanley
Kinrossie
Collace
376 KINGS SEAT
Guildtown
Kirkton of Collace
Newmiln
Downhill
Luncarty
Colenden
St Martin's
Bandirran
Balbeggie
Scone Palace
Scone
Bridgend
Branklyn Garden
Kinnoull Tower
288 POLE HILL
Pitroddie
Rait
Kilspindie
Inchmichael
Glendoick
Kinfauns
Glencarse
Leetown
St Madoes
Inchyra
Errol
Grange
Abernyte
Ballindean
Baledgarno
Benvie
Liff
Gourdie
Denhead of Gray
Lochee
Camperdown
Mills Observatory
Invergowrie
Longforgan
Inchture
Kingoodie
Dundee
FIRTH OF TAY
Balmerino Abbey
Balmerino
Coultra
Hazelton Walls
Creich
Brunton
285 NORMANS LAW
Luthrie
Glenduckie
Lindores
Newburgh
River Tay
Elcho Castle
MONCREIFFE HILL 221
Rhynd
Fingask
Craigend
River Earn
Forgandenny
Bridge of Earn
Kintillo
Aberdalgie
Dron
Aberargie
Abernethy Round Tower
Glenfoot
Dunbog
Den of Lindores
Grange of Lindores
Moonzie
Fernie
Monimail
Letham
Lochieheads
Collessie
Bow of Fife
Cupar Muir
Pleasance
Balvaird Castle
Auchtermuchty
Giffordtown
Deer Centre
Springfield
Abbots Deuglie
Glenfarg Reservoir
Glenfarg
Arngask
Newton of Balcanquhal
Dunshalt
Charlottetown
Ladybank
Scotstarvit Tower
Struthers
Duncrievie
Strathmiglo
River Eden
Kingskettle
Pitlessie
Drunzie
Gateside
Burnside
Balmalcolm
Middleton
Tillyrie
Lomond Hills
522 WEST LOMOND
Falkland Palace
448 EAST LOMOND
Falkland
Freuchie
Kettlebridge
248 CLATTO HILL
Milnathort
Burleigh Castle
Glenlomond
Ballo Reservoir
Muirhead
Langdyke
Kinross
Lochleven Castle
Kinross House
Loch Leven
St Serf's Island
Holl Reservoir
Kinnesswood
Scotlandwell
Balfarg
Star
Baintown
Bonnyba
Scottish Gliding Centre
Leslie
Cadham
Markinch
Kennoway
Windygates
Walkerton
Glenrothes
Auchmuirbridge
R Leven
Loch Leven
RSPB
Milton of Balgonie
Methilhill
Pitteuchar
Coaltown of Balgonie
Gairneybridge
Kinglassie
Ballingry
Thornton
Buck
Cleish
Lochore Meadows
Lochore
Dogton Stone
Auchterderran
River Ore
East Wemyss
Crosshill
Cluny
Coaltown of Wemyss
Loch Glow
Kelty
Glencraig
Cardenden
West Wemyss
Lochgelly
Chapel
Gallatown
Dysart
Pathhead
Ravenscraig Castle
Loch Fitty
Lumphinnans
Loch Gelly
Kirkcal
ershall
Kingseat
Hill of
Cowdenbeath
A9
A93
A94
A85
A912
B9112
M90
A90
B953
A913
B931
B983
B937
A91
B996
A912
B936
A92
A914
B9129
B919
A911
A922
B969
A911
A911
A915
B920
B9097
B921
B922
B9130
A955
B931
B981
B914
B912
A909
B915
B925
A910
0 1 2 3 4 5 miles
0 1 2 3 4 5 6 7 8 kilometres

Mains of Fintry
Whitfield
Murroes
Barry
West Haven
Carnoustie
234
Douglas and Angus
Baldovie
Monifieth
Claypotts Castle
Barnhill
Broughty Ferry
Broughty Castle
DUNDEE
North Carr Lightship
BUDDON NESS
A92 Tay Bridge
HM Frigate 'Unicorn'
Tayport
Tentsmuir Point
Newport-on-Tay
Wormit
Scottish National Golf Centre
Tentsmuir Point
Leuchars
RAF Leuchars
Balmullo
ST ANDREWS BAY
Guardbridge
St Andrews
Kincaple
River Eden
Castle
St Andrews
Strathkinness
Botanic Garden
B939
Blebocraigs
Brownhills
Boarhills
Craigtoun
Denhead
Pitscottie
Cameron Reservoir
Kingsbarns
Ceres
Baldinnie
Dunino
Peat Inn
Radernie
Balcomie Links
FIFE NESS
New Gilston
Kingsmuir
Lathones
Scotland's Secret Bunker
Crail
Woodside
Largoward
Lochty
Carnbee
Easter Pitkierie
Kellie Castle
Wester Pitkierie
Kilrenny
Cellardyke
Arncroach
Upper Largo
Newton of Balcormo
Colinsburgh
Fisheries
Anstruther
Lundin Mill
Drumeldrie
Pittenweem
Lower Largo
Lundin Links
Kilconquhar
St Monans
Largo Bay
Earlsferry
Elie
Isle of May
A90
A92
A930
A914
A919
A91
A915
A917
B961
B962
B959
B960
B946
B945
B940
B9131
B941
B9171
B942
G
H
J
K
L
M
1
2
3
4
5
6
7
8

A
B
C
D
E
F
1
2
3
4
5
6
7
8
Gris
Clabhac
Hogh Bay
Bally
Totron
Bagh a Chaisteil
(Castlebay)
Coll
Ac
Feall
Bay
Arileod
Uig
RSPB
(Mar-Oct)
Calgary Point
Crossapol
Bay
Loch Breachacha
Rudh
Fàsac
Gunna
Caoles
Rudha Dubh
Rudha Port
Bhiosd
Clachan
Mor
Balephetrish
Bay
B8069
Ruaig
Loch
Bhasapoll
B8068
Haugh
Bay
Ballevullin
Cornoigmore
Kenovay
Gott
Bay
Tiree
Kilkenneth
B8068
B8065
Scarinish
Moss
Heylipoll
Middleton
Crossapoll
TIREE
B8065
Barrapoll
Hynish Bay
B8067
Balemartine
Loch a'
Phuill
Mannel
Rinn
Thorbhais
Balephuil
Bay
Hynish
0 1 2 3 4 5 miles
0 1 2 3 4 5 6 7 8 kilometres

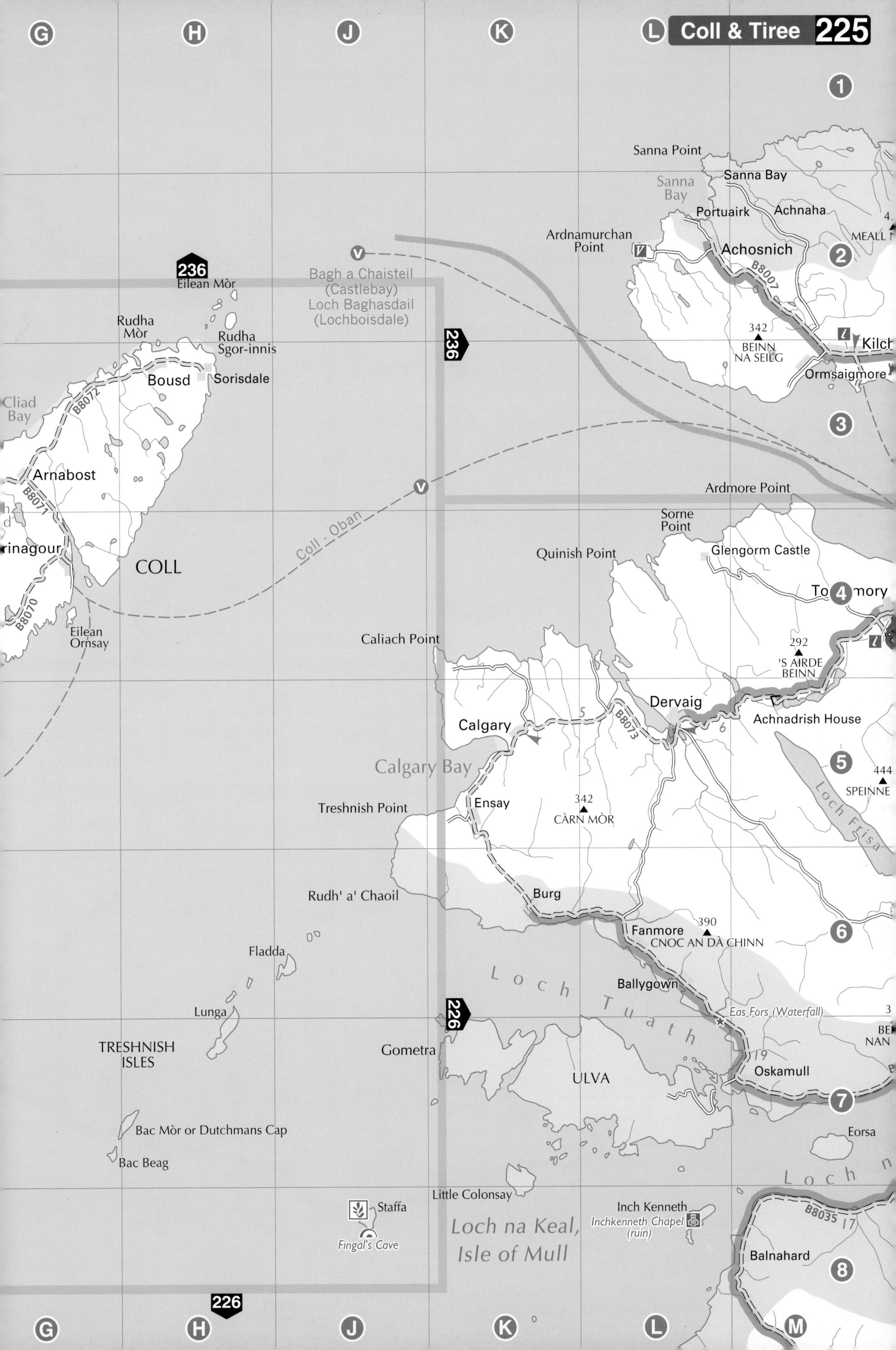
G
H
J
K
L
M
1
2
3
4
5
6
7
8
Sanna Point
Sanna Bay
Sanna Bay
Portuairk
Achnaha
Ardnamurchan Point
Achosnich
B8007
342
BEINN NA SEILG
Kilch
Ormsaigmore
MEALL
236
Eilean Mòr
Bagh a Chaisteil (Castlebay)
Loch Baghasdail (Lochboisdale)
Rudha Mòr
Rudha Sgor-innis
Bousd
Sorisdale
Cliad Bay
B8072
Arnabost
B8071
rinagour
COLL
B8070
Eilean Ornsay
Coll - Oban
Ardmore Point
Sorne Point
Quinish Point
Glengorm Castle
Tobermory
Caliach Point
292
'S AIRDE BEINN
Dervaig
Achnadrish House
Calgary
B8073
Calgary Bay
444
SPEINNE
Loch Frisa
Treshnish Point
Ensay
342
CÀRN MÒR
Rudh' a' Chaoil
Burg
Fanmore
390
CNOC AN DÀ CHINN
Fladda
Loch Tuath
Ballygown
Eas Fors (Waterfall)
Lunga
226
TRESHNISH ISLES
Gometra
ULVA
Oskamull
BE
NAN
Eorsa
Bac Mòr or Dutchmans Cap
Bac Beag
Loch
Little Colonsay
Inch Kenneth
Inchkenneth Chapel (ruin)
B8035
Staffa
Fingal's Cave
Loch na Keal, Isle of Mull
Balnahard
226

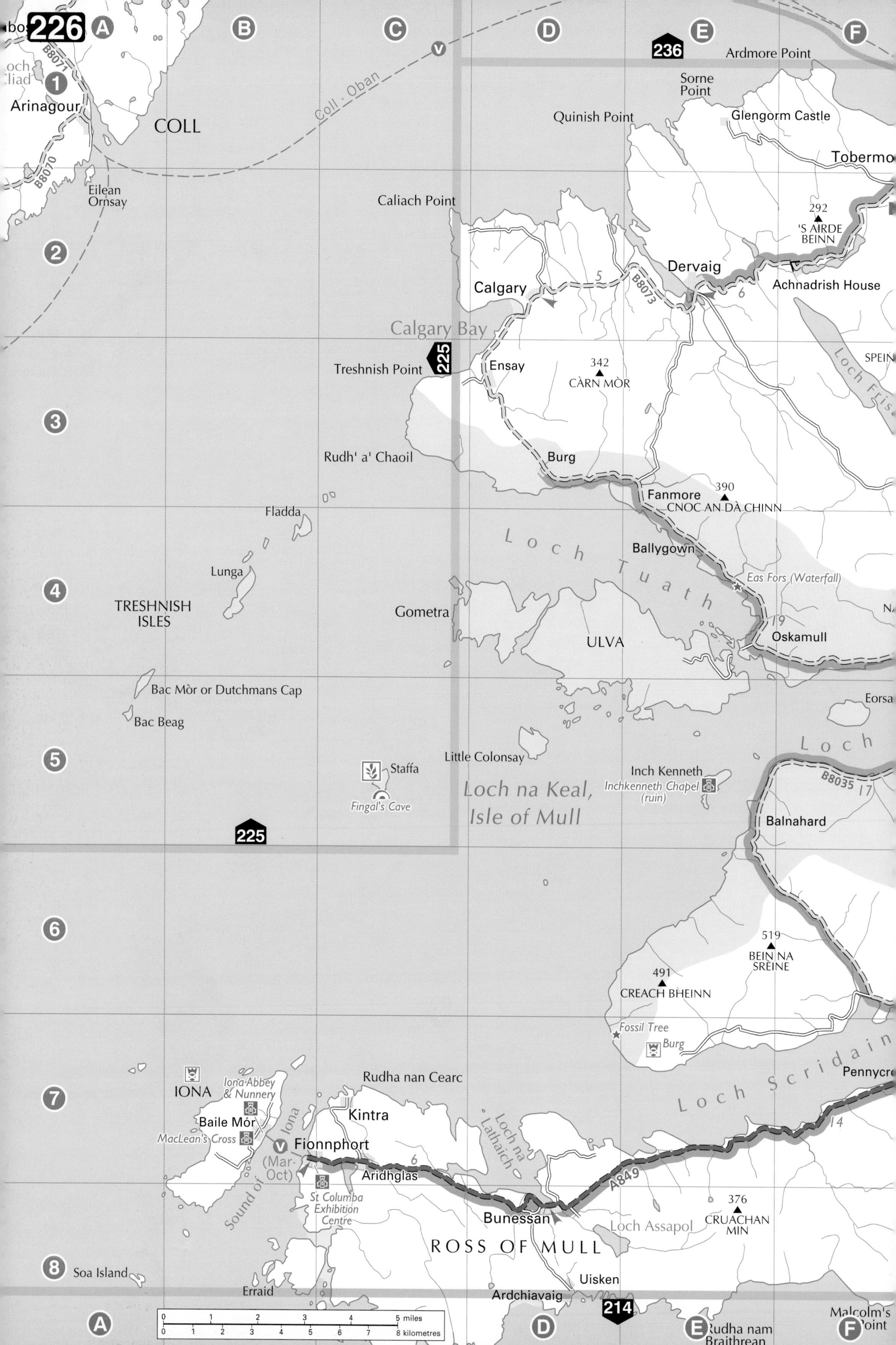
COLL
Arinagour
B8071
B8070
Eilean Ornsay
Coll - Oban
236
Ardmore Point
Sorne Point
Quinish Point
Glengorm Castle
Tobermo
Caliach Point
292 'S AIRDE BEINN
Dervaig
Achnadrish House
Calgary
B8073
Calgary Bay
225
Treshnish Point
Ensay
342 CÀRN MÒR
SPEIN
Loch Fris
Rudh' a' Chaoil
Burg
Fanmore
390 CNOC AN DÀ CHINN
Fladda
Loch Tuath
Ballygown
Lunga
Eas Fors (Waterfall)
TRESHNISH ISLES
Gometra
ULVA
Oskamull
Bac Mòr or Dutchmans Cap
Bac Beag
Eorsa
Loch
Little Colonsay
Staffa
Fingal's Cave
Inch Kenneth
Inchkenneth Chapel (ruin)
B8035
Loch na Keal, Isle of Mull
Balnahard
225
519 BEIN NA SREINE
491 CREACH BHEINN
Fossil Tree
Burg
Loch Scridain
Pennycr
Rudha nan Cearc
IONA
Iona Abbey & Nunnery
Kintra
Baile Mór
MacLean's Cross
Fionnphort
(Mar-Oct)
Sound of Iona
Loch na Lathaich
Aridhglas
A849
St Columba Exhibition Centre
Bunessan
Loch Assapol
376 CRUACHAN MIN
ROSS OF MULL
Soa Island
Erraid
Uisken
Ardchiavaig
214
Rudha nam Braithrean
Malcolm's Point
5 miles
8 kilometres

237
228
216
215

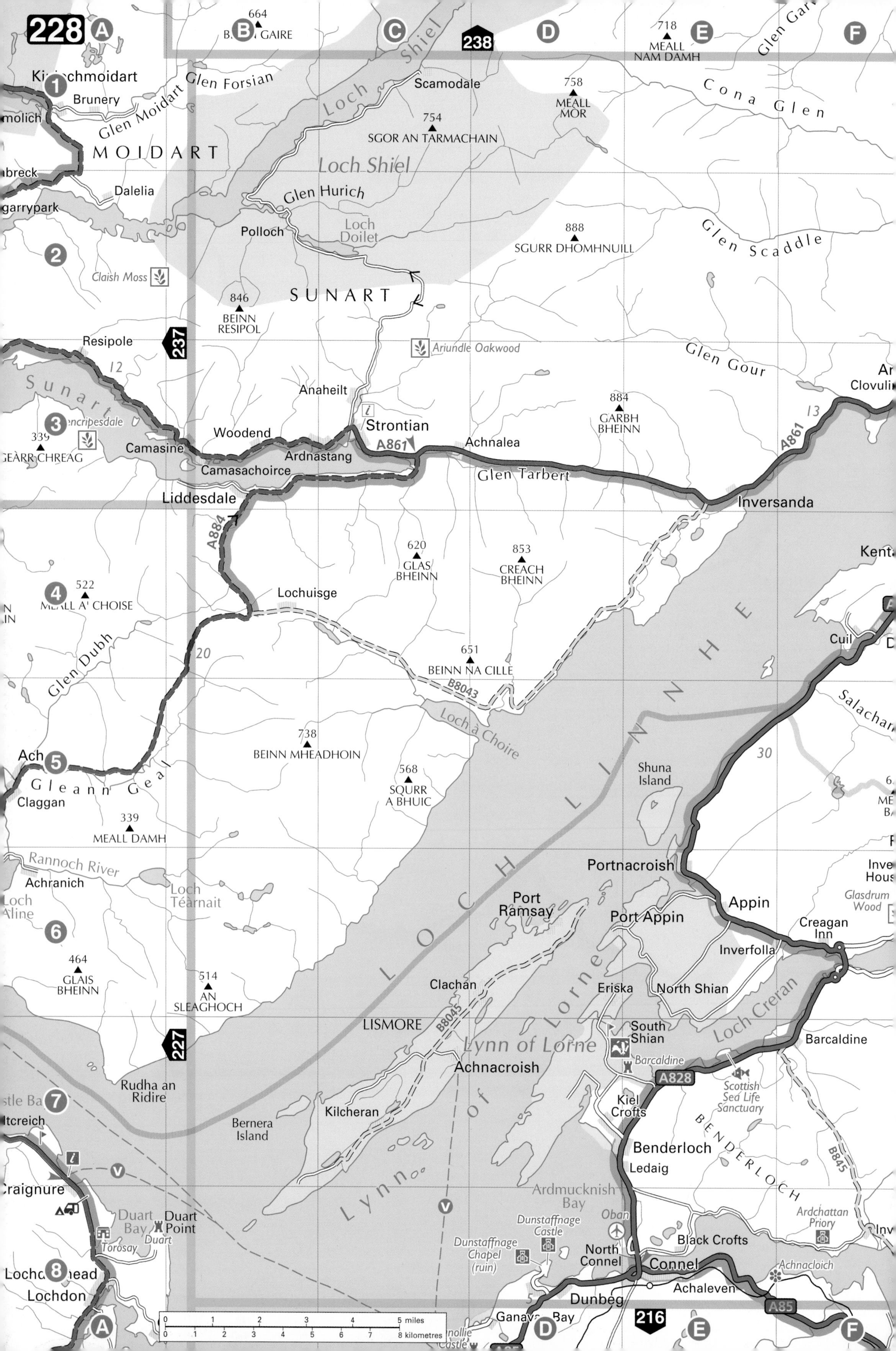228
A
B
C
D
E
F
238
664
718
MEALL NAM DAMH
Glen Forsian
Loch Shiel
Scamodale
758
MEALL MOR
Cona Glen
Brunery
Glen Moidart
754
SGOR AN TARMACHAIN
MOIDART
Dalelia
Glen Hurich
Loch Doilet
Polloch
888
SGURR DHOMHNUILL
Glen Scaddle
Claish Moss
846
BEINN RESIPOL
SUNART
Resipole
237
Ariundle Oakwood
Glen Gour
Clovulin
Anaheilt
884
GARBH BHEINN
12
13
Sunart
Strontian
Woodend
339
Camasine
Ardnastang
A861
Achnalea
Camasachoirce
Glen Tarbert
Liddesdale
Inversanda
A884
620
GLAS BHEINN
853
CREACH BHEINN
522
MEALL A' CHOISE
Lochuisge
LOCH LINNHE
Cuil
Glen Dubh
20
651
BEINN NA CILLE
B8043
Loch à Choire
738
BEINN MHEADHOIN
30
Gleann Geal
568
SGURR A BHUIC
Shuna Island
Claggan
339
MEALL DAMH
Rannoch River
Achranich
Loch Téarnait
Portnacroish
Port Ramsay
Appin
Port Appin
Glasdrum Wood
Creagan Inn
464
GLAIS BHEINN
514
AN SLEAGHOCH
Inverfolla
Clachan
Eriska
North Shian
LISMORE
B8045
South Shian
Lynn of Lorne
Loch Creran
Barcaldine
227
Achnacroish
A828
Scottish Sea Life Sanctuary
Rudha an Ridire
Kiel Crofts
BENDERLOCH
Kilcheran
Bernera Island
Benderloch
Ledaig
B845
Craignure
Ardmucknish Bay
Ardchattan Priory
Duart Bay
Duart Point
Dunstaffnage Castle
Oban
Torosay
Duart
Dunstaffnage Chapel (ruin)
North Connel
Black Crofts
Connel
Achnacloich
Lochdon
Dunbeg
Achaleven
A85
216
0 1 2 3 4 5 miles
0 1 2 3 4 5 6 7 8 kilometres

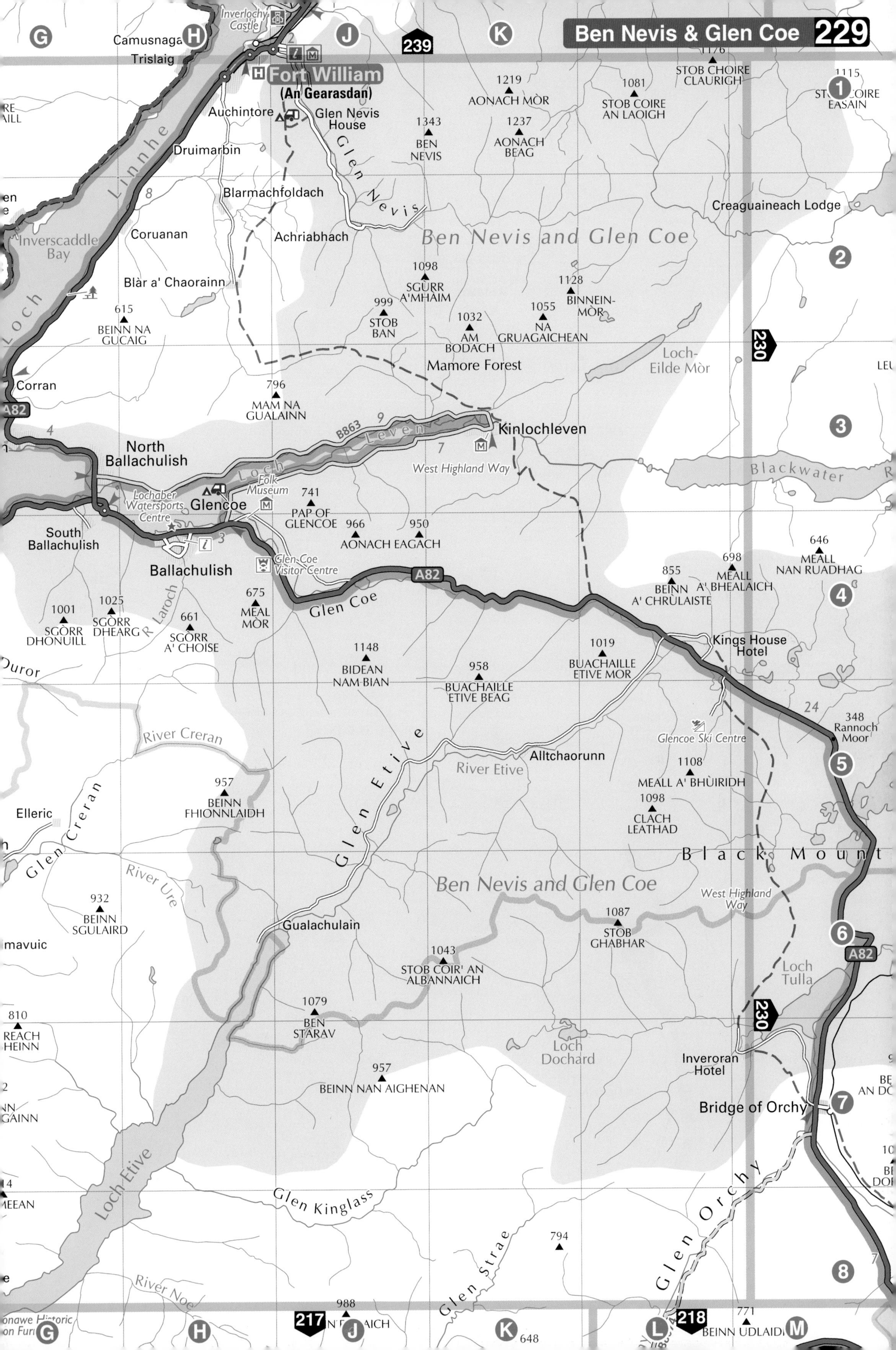

Fort William
(An Gearasdan)
Inverlochy Castle
Camusnaga
Trislaig
Auchintore
Glen Nevis House
Glen Nevis
Druimarbin
Blarmachfoldach
Loch Linnhe
Coruanan
Achriabhach
Inverscaddle Bay
Blàr a' Chaorainn
615 BEINN NA GUCAIG
Corran
A82
1219 AONACH MÒR
1343 BEN NEVIS
1237 AONACH BEAG
1081 STOB COIRE AN LAOIGH
STOB CHOIRE CLAURIGH
Creaguaineach Lodge
Ben Nevis and Glen Coe
1098 SGURR A'MHAIM
999 STOB BAN
1032 AM BODACH
1128 BINNEIN-MÒR
1055 NA GRUAGAICHEAN
Mamore Forest
Loch Eilde Mòr
796 MAM NA GUALAINN
Kinlochleven
Loch Leven
B863
West Highland Way
Blackwater
North Ballachulish
South Ballachulish
Lochaber Watersports Centre
Glencoe
Folk Museum
Ballachulish
741 PAP OF GLENCOE
966 AONACH EAGACH
950
Glen Coe Visitor Centre
Glen Coe
675 MEAL MÒR
661 SGÒRR A' CHOISE
1001 SGÒRR DHONUILL
1025 SGÒRR DHEARG
R. Laroch
Duror
855 BEINN A' CHRÙLAISTE
698 MEALL A' BHEALAICH
646 MEALL NAN RUADHAG
Kings House Hotel
1019 BUACHAILLE ETIVE MOR
1148 BIDEAN NAM BIAN
958 BUACHAILLE ETIVE BEAG
348 Rannoch Moor
Glencoe Ski Centre
River Creran
Alltchaorunn
River Etive
Glen Etive
957 BEINN FHIONNLAIDH
1108 MEALL A' BHÙIRIDH
1098 CLACH LEATHAD
Elleric
Glen Creran
Black Mount
River Ure
Ben Nevis and Glen Coe
932 BEINN SGULAIRD
West Highland Way
1087 STOB GHABHAR
Gualachulain
1043 STOB COIR' AN ALBANNAICH
Loch Tulla
1079 BEN STARAV
810
Loch Dochard
Inveroran Hotel
957 BEINN NAN AIGHENAN
Bridge of Orchy
Loch Etive
Glen Kinglass
Glen Orchy
794
Glen Strae
River Noe
988
771 BEINN UDLAIDH
648

A
B
C
D
E
F
240
1176
STOB CHOIRE CLAURIGH
1081
STOB COIRE AN LAOIGH
1115
STOB COIRE EASAIN
Loch Treig
1046
CHNO DEARG
Loch Gulbin
1101
BEINN EIBHINN
DEARG
1145
BEN ALDER
Glen Ossian
Creaguaineach Lodge
Glen Coe
Loch Ossian
844
MEALL A'BHEALAICH
952
SGOR GAIBHRE
Corrour Station
626
SRON A CHLAONAID
229
Loch-Eilde Mòr
906
LEUM UILLEIM
864
BEINN PHARIAGAIN
R Ericht
Blackwater Reservoir
Rannoch Station
Bridge of Ericht
646
MEALL NAN RUADHAG
698
MEALL A' BHEALAICH
855
738
A' CHRUACH
Dunan
B846
Loch Laidon
Loch Eigheach
Bridge of Gaur
Kings House Hotel
24
348
Rannoch Moor
Rannoch Moor
Glencoe Ski Centre
1108
MEALL A' BHÙIRIDH
1098
CLACH LEATHAD
Loch Bà
931
MEALL BUIDHE
Water of Tulla
Black Mount
West Highland Way
Loch an Daimh
1087
A82
1079
BEINN A' CHREACHAIN
Loch Tulla
229
Inveroran Hotel
996
BEINN AN DOTHAIDH
953
BEINN MHANACH
Loch Lyon
Bridge of Orchy
1038
MEALL GHAORDIE
1076
BEINN HEASGARNICH
1074
BEN DORAIN
Glen Orchy
River Lochay
Glen Lochay
7
818
771
937
BEINN CHEATHAICH
B8074
218
219
0 1 2 3 4 5 miles
0 1 2 3 4 5 6 7 8 kilometres

A' MHARCONAICH
1008
BEINN UDLAMAIN
991
SGAIRNEACH MHOR
Dalnaspidal
Loch Garry
Dalnacardoch
Glen Garry
A9
491
CRAIG BHAGAILTEACH
Bruar Water
Loch Con
Loch Errochty
841
BEINN MHOLACH
Calvine
Bruar
Struan
Pitagowan
Old Struan
Blair
Trinafour
B847
Glen Errochty
511
TORR DUBH
892
BEINN A' CHUALLAICH
Tay Forest Park
Tressait
B8019
Queen's View
Loch Tummel
B846
Kinloch Rannoch
Drumchastle
Dunalastair
R Tummel
Tummel Bridge
Dunalastair Water
Loch Rannoch
Foss
Frenich
Daloist
Inverhadden
Tempar
Carie
Camghouran
1081
SCHIEHALLION
780
FARRAGON HILL
780
MEALL TAIRNEACHAN
Loch Glassie
Glengoulandie Deer Park
Loch Rannoch and Glen Lyon
1042
CARN MAIRG
745
MEALL A' MHUIC
824
BEINN DEARG
1027
CARN GORM
Coshieville
Keltneyburn
Dull
Camserney
Menzies
Dewars
River Tay
Glen Lyon
Bridge of Balgie
River Lyon
Fortingall
Croftmoraig Stone Circle
Kenmore
A827
Fearnan
Acharn
The Crannog Centre
780
MEALL LUAIDHE
924
MEALL A' CHOIRE LEITH
1116
MEALL GARBH
1000
MEALL GREIGH
1214
BEN LAWERS
Lochan na Làirige
Loch Tay
Leckbuie
713
BEINN BHREAC
Glen Quaich
River Quaich
Lawers
Ben Lawers
A827
864
SRÒN A' CHAOINEIDH
802
MEALL NAM FUARAN
Milton Morenish
Morenish
Ardeonaig
Moirlanich Longhouse
Finlarig
Killin
Breadalbane Folklore Centre
River Almond
BREADALBANE
879
CREAG UCHDAG
682
G H J K L M
1 2 3 4 5 6 7 8
241 232 219 220

A
B
241
C
D
242
E
F
897
BEINN A' CHART
Loch
Loch
1119
CÀRN NAN CABHAR
1068
CAIRNGORMS NATIONAL PARK
Bruar Water
491
CRAIG BHAGAILTEACH
Glen Banvie
Glen Tilt
Glen Fender
CARN LIATH
973
903
BEN VUIRICH
Gleann
A9
Garry
Clan Donnachaidh
Calvine
Bruar
Blair Castle
Middlebridge
B8079
Bridge of Tilt
Struan
Pitagowan
Glen Girnaig
Old Struan
Blair Atholl
231
B847
470
TULACH HILL
60
Aldclune
River Garry
Killiecrankie
511
TORR DUBH
Errochty
840
BEN VRACKIE
12
RSPB
Killiecrankie
A924
Tay Forest Park
622
CREAG DHUBA
Tressait
B8019
Tay Forest Park
Moulin
Kinnaird
Queen's View
Loch Tummel
Tummel Bridge
Faskally Wayside Centre
Frenich
13
Queen's View
Foss
Tay Forest Park
Pitlochry
(Baile Chloichridh)
Edradour Distillery
Loch Broom
Daloist
Loch Tummel
5
Tay Forest Park
Dunfallandy Stone
R Tummel
Dalcapon
780
FARRAGON HILL
780
MEALL TAIRNEACHAN
Loch Derculich
Strathtay
A827
A9
Glengoulandie Deer Park
Loch Glassie
Derculich
Grandtully
Tulliemet
Edradynate
9
Logierait
Ballinluig
B846
Balnaguard
B898
R Tay
14
St Mary's
Kindallachan
Menzies
Weem
Camserney
Coshieville
Dull
Kincraigie
Guay
Keltneyburn
Dewars
Aberfeldy
Tay Forest Park
River Tay
Dowally
Fortingall
532
GRANDTULLY HILL
Dalguise
509
DEUCHARY HILL
Croftmoraig Stone Circle
Tay Forest Park
Loch Skiach
B898
8
A827
9
Kenmore
Loch Kennard
River Tay
Acharn
A826
Dunkeld Town
Cathedral
Dunkeld
The Crannog Centre
Ballinloan Burn
231
Inver
616
MEALL DUBH
The Hermitage
60
Glen Quaich
Trochry
River Quaich
8
A822
Strath Braan
Loch Freuchie
864
SRÒN A' CHAOINEIDH
802
MEALL NAM FUARAN
Achnafauld
Amulree
Glen Shee
Obney
Balquharn
River Almond
A
220
D
E
221
F
0 1 2 3 4 5 miles
0 1 2 3 4 5 6 7 8 kilometres

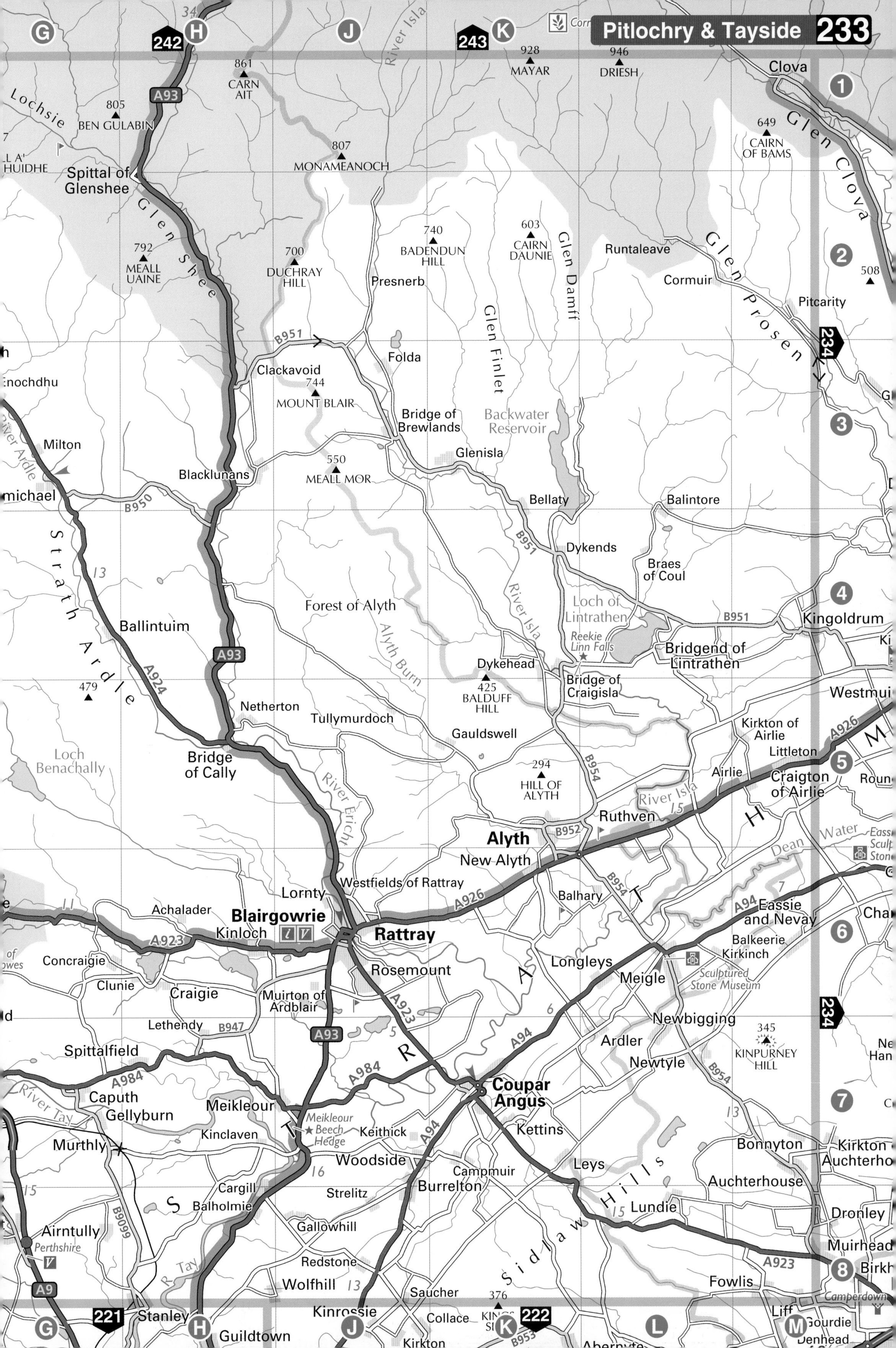

Spittal of Glenshee
Glen Shee
Clova
Glen Clova
Glen Prosen
Pitcarity
Cormuir
Runtaleave
Glen Damff
Glen Finlet
Presnerb
Folda
Clackavoid
MOUNT BLAIR
Bridge of Brewlands
Backwater Reservoir
Glenisla
Bellaty
Blacklunans
MEALL MOR
Balintore
Dykends
Braes of Coul
Loch of Lintrathen
Reekie Linn Falls
Kingoldrum
Bridgend of Lintrathen
Forest of Alyth
Alyth Burn
River Isla
Dykehead
BALDUFF HILL
Bridge of Craigisla
Westmuir
Kirkton of Airlie
Littleton
Airlie
Craigton of Airlie
Ballintuim
Strath Ardle
Milton
Netherton
Tullymurdoch
Gauldswell
HILL OF ALYTH
Ruthven
Loch Benachally
Bridge of Cally
River Ericht
Alyth
New Alyth
Westfields of Rattray
Lornty
Blairgowrie
Rattray
Kinloch
Achalader
Balhary
Eassie and Nevay
Balkeerie
Kirkinch
Meigle
Sculptured Stone Museum
Longleys
Rosemount
Concraigie
Clunie
Craigie
Muirton of Ardblair
Lethendy
Newbigging
Ardler
Newtyle
KINPURNEY HILL
Spittalfield
Coupar Angus
Caputh
Gellyburn
Meikleour
Meikleour Beech Hedge
Kinclaven
Keithick
Kettins
Murthly
Woodside
Campmuir
Burrelton
Leys
Bonnyton
Kirkton of Auchterhouse
Auchterhouse
Cargill
Balholmie
Strelitz
Lundie
Sidlaw Hills
Dronley
Airntully
Gallowhill
Muirhead
Redstone
Wolfhill
Fowlis
Saucher
Stanley
Kinrossie
Collace
Liff
Gourdie
Denhead
Guildtown
Kirkton
River Tay
BEN GULABIN
CARN AIT
MAYAR
DRIESH
CAIRN OF BAMS
MONAMEANOCH
BADENDUN HILL
CAIRN DAUNIE
DUCHRAY HILL
MEALL UAINE
STRATHMORE

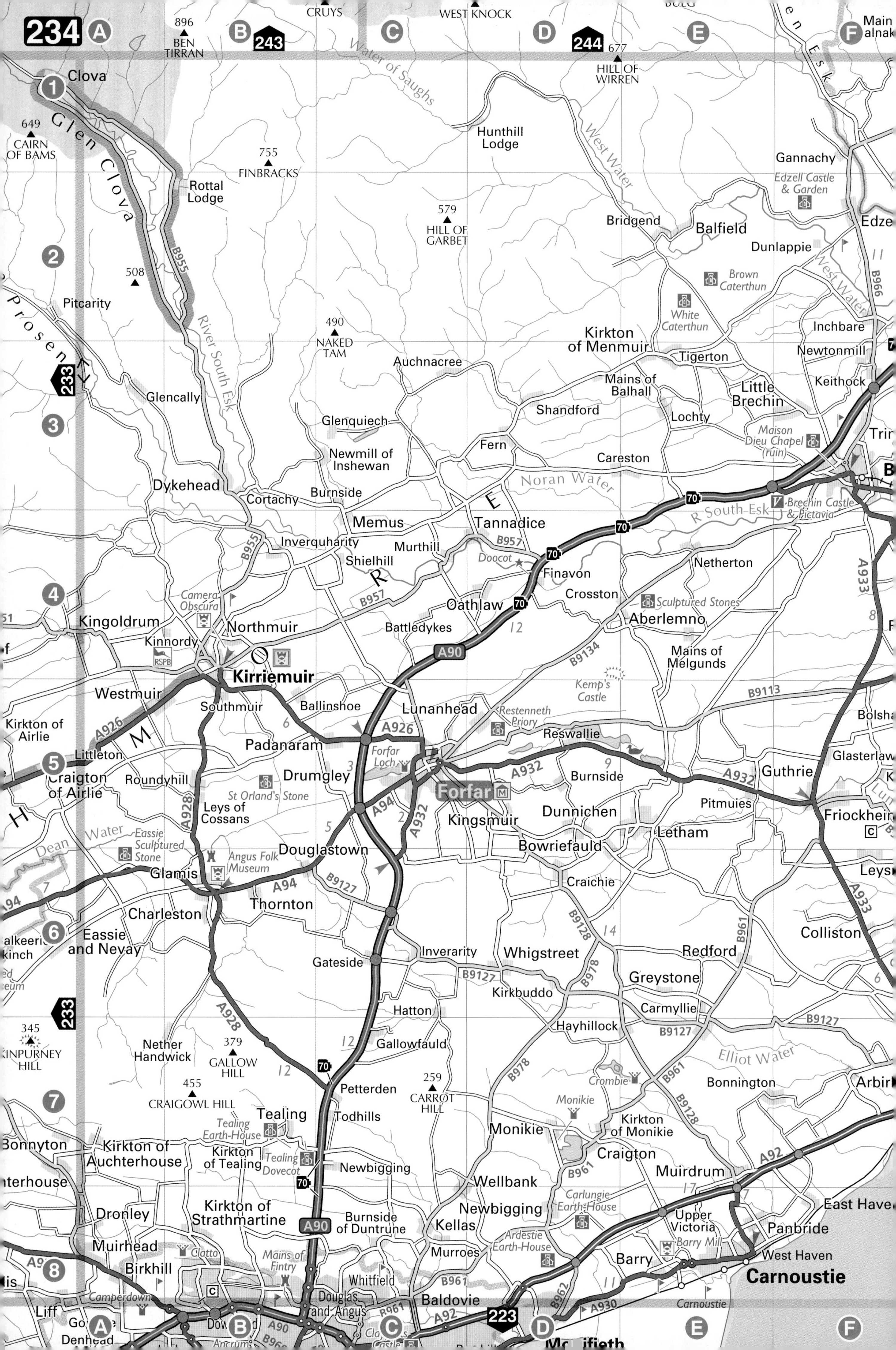
A
B
C
D
E
F
243
244
896
BEN TIRRAN
CRUYS
WEST KNOCK
677
HILL OF WIRREN
Clova
Glen Clova
649
CAIRN OF BAMS
Water of Saughs
Hunthill Lodge
West Water
755
FINBRACKS
Rottal Lodge
B955
579
HILL OF GARBET
Gannachy
Edzell Castle & Garden
Edze
Bridgend
Balfield
Dunlappie
508
Brown Caterthun
Pitcarity
River South Esk
White Caterthun
B966
490
NAKED TAM
Kirkton of Menmuir
Inchbare
Newtonmill
233
Auchnacree
Tigerton
Mains of Balhall
Little Brechin
Keithock
Glencally
Shandford
Lochty
Glenquiech
Maison Dieu Chapel (ruin)
Trir
Newmill of Inshewan
Fern
Careston
Dykehead
Noran Water
Cortachy
Burnside
70
Brechin Castle & Pictavia
Memus
Tannadice
R South Esk
B957
Inverquharity
Murthill
Shielhill
Doocot
Finavon
Netherton
B955
A933
Camera Obscura
Crosston
Sculptured Stones
B957
Oathlaw
Aberlemno
Kingoldrum
Northmuir
Battledykes
12
Kinnordy
RSPB
A90
B9134
Mains of Melgunds
Kirriemuir
Kemp's Castle
Westmuir
Southmuir
Ballinshoe
Lunanhead
Restenneth Priory
B9113
Kirkton of Airlie
A926
6
A926
Reswallie
Bolsha
Littleton
Padanaram
Forfar Loch
9
Glasterlaw
Craigton of Airlie
Roundyhill
Drumgley
A932
Burnside
A932
Guthrie
Forfar
St Orland's Stone
Leys of Cossans
A94
Dunnichen
Pitmuies
Friockhein
A928
Kingsmuir
Water
5
Letham
Eassie Sculptured Stone
Dean
Douglastown
Bowriefauld
Angus Folk Museum
Glamis
A94
B9127
Craichie
Leys
Thornton
Charleston
B9128
14
A933
Eassie and Nevay
Colliston
Inverarity
Whigstreet
Redford
B961
Gateside
B9127
B978
Greystone
Kirkbuddo
Carmyllie
Hatton
345
KINPURNEY HILL
A928
Hayhillock
B9127
B9127
Nether Handwick
379
GALLOW HILL
Gallowfauld
Elliot Water
12
455
CRAIGOWL HILL
Petterden
259
CARROT HILL
B978
Crombie
B961
Bonnington
Arbir
Tealing
Tealing Earth-House
Todhills
Monikie
B9128
Monikie
Kirkton of Monikie
Bonnyton
Kirkton of Auchterhouse
Kirkton of Tealing
Tealing Dovecot
Newbigging
Craigton
Muirdrum
A92
Wellbank
B961
Dronley
Kirkton of Strathmartine
Newbigging
Carlungie Earth-House
East Haven
Burnside of Duntrune
Kellas
Upper Victoria
Panbride
Muirhead
Ardestie Earth-House
Barry Mill
Clatto
Mains of Fintry
Murroes
Barry
West Haven
Birkhill
Carnoustie
Whitfield
B961
Camperdown
Douglas and Angus
Baldovie
B962
A930
Carnoustie
Liff
A92
223
Denhead
A90
1
2
3
4
5
6
7
8

Pittarrow
244
245
Mains of Haulkerton
B9120
Inverbervie
Bervie Bay
Laurencekirk
Gourdon
B974
Redford
Benholm
Dykelands
A90
A937
Johnshaven
North Esk
Marykirk
Bush
Craigo
Lochside
Milton Ness
Logie Pert
St Cyrus
Logie
Morphie
Hillside
A92
House of Dun
Dun
Montrose Air Station
A935
Montrose
Montrose Basin
Barnhead
Scurdie Ness
Maryton
Ferryden
Craig
A934
Usan
Westerton of Rossie
Boddin Point
Braehead
Lunan
Lunan Bay
Inverkeilor
Red Head
Marywell
Auchmithie
Carlingheugh Bay
The Deil's Head
Arbroath
5 miles
8 kilometres

A
B
C
D
E
F
1
2
3
4
5
6
7
8
246
MULLACH MÒR
Rudha na Roinne
A Bhrideanach
Kinloch
Loch Scresort
570
ORVAL
RÙM
810
ASKIVAL
763
SGÙRR NAN GILLEAN
The Small Isles
Rudha nam Meirleach
Sound of Rum
Bay of Laig
Cleadale
299
AN CRUACHAN
Rudha an Fhasaidh
Laig
EIGG
Kild
393
AN SGÙRR
Sandav
Sound of Eigg
Eilean Chathastail
Eilean nan Each
MUCK
Port Mor
Sanna Point
Sanna Bay
Sanna Bay
Portuairk
Achnaha
Ardnamurchan Point
Achosnich
MEA
B8007
342
BEINN NA SEILG
Ormsaigmo
Eilean Mòr
Bagh a Chaisteil (Castlebay)
Loch Baghasdail (Lochboisdale)
Rudha Mòr
Rudha Sgor-innis
Bousd
Sorisdale
COLL
225
Cliad Bay
B8072
Coll - Oban
0 1 2 3 4 5 miles
0 1 2 3 4 5 6 7 8 kilometres
B8071
Arinagour
Ardmore Point
Sorne
226

Aird of Sleat
Ard Thurinish
Point of Sleat
247
Inverie Bay
Rudha Raonuill
KNOYDA
Courteachan
Mallaig (Malaig)
Mallaigvaig
547
CÀRN A'GHOBHAIR
Glasnacardoch Bay
Loch an Nostaire
437
SGÙRR BHUIDHE
Loch Nevis
854
BEINN BH
Beoraidbeg
Morar
Bracorina
Bracora
Tarbet
238
Swordland
Glenancross
Loch Morar
Lettermorar
B8008
A830
503
CÀRN A' MHÀDAIDH-RUAIDH
Bunacaimb
Eilean Ighe
Meoble
River Meoble
710
MEITH BH
Back of Keppoch
Arisaig
Loch nan Ceall
Luinga Mhòr
600
SIDHEAN MÒR
Prince Charlie's Cairn
Rudh' Arisaig
103
CRUACH DOIRE
Druimindarroch
Arisaig House
Kinlochnanuagh
Loch nan Uamh
Polnish
Lochailort
Loch Eilt
Inverailort
Ardnish
Sound of Arisaig
Rudha Choalais
Loch Ailort
A861
877
ROIS-BHEINN
Smearisary
Glenuig
712
664
BEINN GAIRE
Eilean Shona
Rudha Aird Druimnich
Loch Moidart
Kinlochmoidart
Glen Forsian
Ockle Point
Tioram
Brunery
Glen Moidart
Morar, Moidart and Ardnamurchan
239
BEINN BHREAC
Ardmolich
MOIDART
Ardtoe
Shielfoot
Ockle
Dalnabreck
Loch Shiel
Glen Hurich
Branault
356
BEINN BHREAC
B8044
Kentra
Blain
Mingarrypark
Dalelia
228
Polloch
Loch Doilet
Arevegaig
ARDNAMURCHAN
Acharacle
Claish Moss
437
Loch Mudle
A861
SUNAR
846
BEINN RESIPOL
Salen
Resipole
527
BEN HIANT
Loch Sunart
Anaheilt
Glenbeg
512
BEN LAGA
B8007
Glencripesdale
Glenborrodale
RSPB
Laga
339
GEÀRR CHREAG
Woodend
Camasine
Ardnastang
Ardslignish
Camasachoirce
Oronsay
Carna
Liddesdale
227
Auliston Point
A884

238
248
247
237
228
SOUND OF SLEAT
Sandaig Island
Rudha Buidhe
Rudh' Ard Slisneach
Loch Hourn
Arnisdale
Corran
Glen Arnisdale
974 BEINN SGRITHEAL
773 BEINN NAN CAORACH
1011 THE SADDLE
945 SGURR NA SGINE
Glen Shiel
Glean Beag
614
709 DRUM FADA
Kinloch Hourn
Barrisdale Bay
Inverguseran
784 BEINN NA CAILLICH
Glen Guseran
Airor
518 DRUIM NA CLUAIN-AIRIDHE
1019 LADHAR BHEINN
Knoydart
KNOYDART
Sandaig
Sandaig Bay
Inverie
940 LUINNE BHEINN
Loch an Dubh-Lochain
Inverie Bay
Rudha Raonuill
1003 SGURR MÒR
547 CÀRN A'GHOBHAIR
854 BEINN BHUIDHE
1039 SGURR NA CICHE
Loch Nevis
Loch an Nostaire
437 SGÙRR BHUIDHE
Bracorina
Bracora
Kylesmorar
Tarbet
Swordland
859 SGURR NAH-AIDE
723 SGARR BREAC
Glen Dessarry
Loch Morar
Glen Pean
Lettermorar
503 CÀRN A' MHÀDAIDH-RUAIDH
716 AN STAC
Meoble
River Meoble
710 MEITH BHEINN
949 SGURR NAN COIREACHAN
964 SGÙRR THUILM
600 SIDHEAN MÒR
Prince Charlie's Cairn
Arisaig House
Kinlochnanuagh
Loch Beoriad
Loch nan Uamh
633
796 SGÙRR AN UTHA
Glen Finnan
Gleann Dubhlighe
Polnish
Lochailort
Inverailort
Loch Eilt
A830
Ardnish
Glenfinnan
Glenfinnan Visitor Centre
Glenfinnan Monument
Kinlochei
Drimsallie
Loch Ailort
A861
877 ROIS-BHEINN
882 BEINN ODHAR BHEAG
Garvan
712
664 BEINN GAIRE
Shiel
718 MEALL NAM DAMH
Glen Garvan
Scamodale
758
0 1 2 3 4 5 miles
0 1 2 3 4 5 6 7 8 kilometres

A87
Cluanie Inn
Cluanie Lodge
Loch Cluanie
Ceannacroc Lodge
Tomchrasky
Dalchreichart
Glen Moriston
SQÙRR A'BHEALAICH
A'CHRALAIG
SGURR NAN CONBHAIREAN
River Doe
AONACH AIR CHRITH
CREAG A'MHAIM
GLEOURAICH
SPIDEAN MIALACH
Glenquoich Forest
Loch Loyne
Glen Loyne
Glen Garry
Inchlaggan
Tomdoun
Loch Garry
Greenfield
Mandally
MEALL DUBH
CEANN A'MHAIM
Loch Quoich
River Garry
GAIRICH
Glen Kingie
River Kingie
GLAS BHEINN
BEN TEE
Glengarry Forest
Kilfinnan
MEALL BLÀIR
MEALL COIRE NAN SAOBHAIDH
SRON A'CHOIRE GHAIRBH
SGURR MHURLAGAIN
Loch Blair
Caonich
Loch Arkaig
Ardechive
Gleann Cia-aig
Letterfinlay Lodge Hotel
Loch Lochy
Corriegour Lodge Hotel
BEINNIARUIN
Clunes
Achnacarry
Clan Cameron
Bunarkaig
Invergloy
Glen Gloy
Glenfintaig Lodge
Glen Mallie
BEINN BHAN
Great Glen Way
B8005
A82
COIRE CEIRSLE
Glen Roy
Gairlochy
Stronenaba
Bohuntine
MEALL A' PHÙBUILL
Glen Loy
B8004
Spean Bridge
Brackletter
Commando Memorial
Inverroy
Killiechonate
Roy Bridge
River Spean
STOB A' GHRIANAIN
DRUIM FADA
Strone
Muirshearlich
River Lochy
The Cour
BEINN CHLIANAIG
Fassfern
A830
Treasures of the Earth
Neptune's Staircase (Locks)
Torcastle
Nevis Range
Corpach
Loch Eil
Banavie
River Lundy
SGÙRR FINNISG-AIG
Blaich
A861
Caol
B8006
Inverlochy Castle
Fort William (An Gearasdan)
Camusnagaul
Trislaig
STOB CHOIRE CLAURIGH

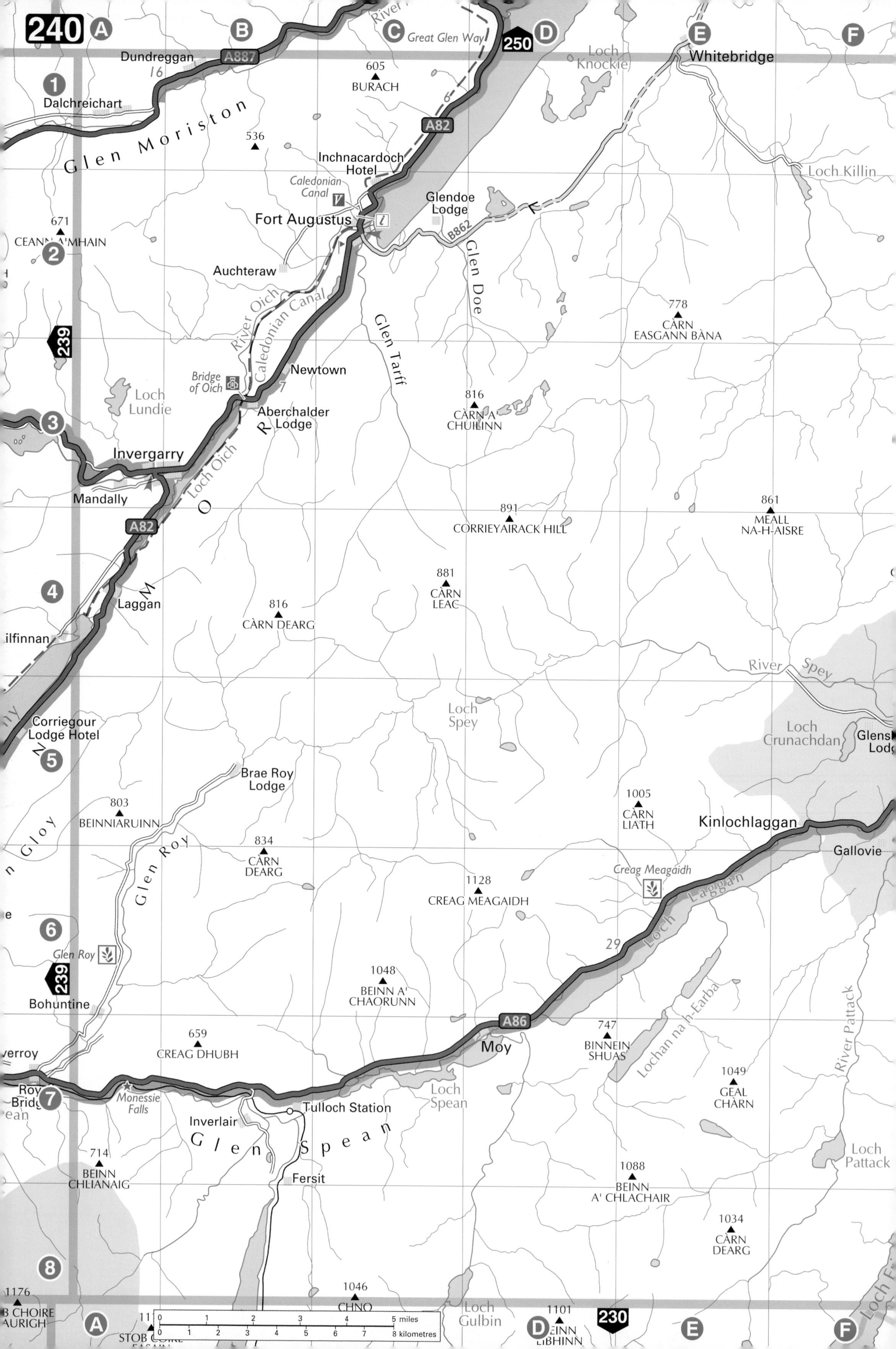

Dundreggan
A887
Dalchreichart
Glen Moriston
605
BURACH
Great Glen Way
250
Loch Knockie
Whitebridge
536
A82
Inchnacardoch Hotel
Caledonian Canal
Glendoe Lodge
Fort Augustus
671
CEANN A'MHAIN
B862
Glen Doe
Auchteraw
Loch Killin
River Oich
Caledonian Canal
Glen Tarff
778
CÀRN EASGANN BÀNA
239
Newtown
Bridge of Oich
Loch Lundie
816
CÀRN A' CHUILINN
Aberchalder Lodge
Invergarry
Loch Oich
Mandally
891
CORRIEYAIRACK HILL
861
MEALL NA-H-AISRE
A82
881
CÀRN LEAC
Laggan
816
CÀRN DEARG
River Spey
Corriegour Lodge Hotel
Loch Spey
Loch Crunachdan
Brae Roy Lodge
803
BEINNIARUINN
1005
CÀRN LIATH
Kinlochlaggan
Glen Gloy
Glen Roy
834
CÀRN DEARG
Gallovie
Creag Meagaidh
1128
CREAG MEAGAIDH
Loch Laggan
29
Glen Roy
239
1048
BEINN A' CHAORUNN
Bohuntine
A86
747
BINNEIN SHUAS
Lochan na h-Earba
River Pattack
659
CREAG DHUBH
Moy
1049
GEAL CHÀRN
Roy Bridge
Monessie Falls
Loch Spean
Tulloch Station
Inverlair
Glen Spean
714
BEINN CHLIANAIG
Loch Pattack
Fersit
1088
BEINN A' CHLACHAIR
1034
CÀRN DEARG
1176
1046
CHNO
Loch Gulbin
1101
230
0 1 2 3 4 5 miles
0 1 2 3 4 5 6 7 8 kilometres

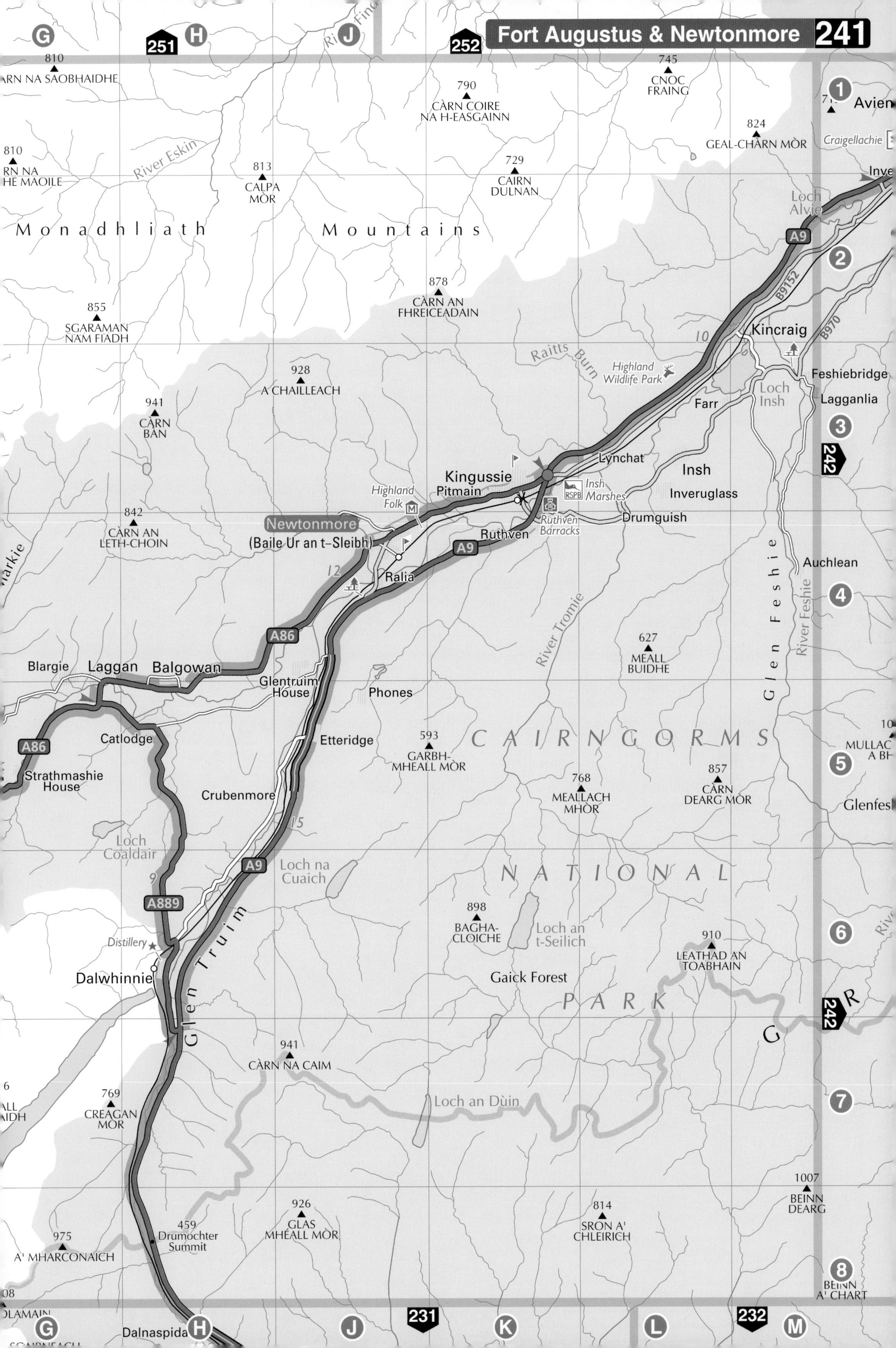

251 252 242 231 232

A
B
C
D
E
F
253
254
Straanruie
River Spey
B970
River Nethy
Aviemore
712
824
CHÀRN MÒR
Craigellachie
Rothiemurchus
Inverdruie
Coylumbridge
Glenmore Forest Park
809
MEALL A' BHUACHAILLE
Glenmore
Reindeer Centre
Glenmore Lodge
Glen More
Loch Morlich
730
MAIM SUIM
821
GEAL CHÀRN
803
CARN BHEADHAIR
606
CARN TUADHA
Loch Alvie
A9
B9152
241
Loch an Eilean
Rothiemurchus Lodge
Cairngorm Ski Area
CAIRNGORMS
Kincraig
B970
Feshiebridge
Loch Insh
Lagganlia
Glen A
713
THE BRUACH
1245
CAIRN GORM
NATIONAL
CAIRNGORM
MOUNTAINS
Lairig Ghru
Lochan Buidhe
1083
BEINN A CHAORRUINN
1196
NORTH TOP
1108
SGÒR AN DUBH MÒR
1295
BRAERIACH
1309
BEN MACDHUI
Loch Einich
Auchlean
1084
CÀRN EAS
PARK
1177
SOUTH TOP
1049
CÀRN BAN MÒR
1293
CAIRN TOUL
930
BEINN BHREAC
Glen Derry
Glen Feshie
River Feshie
1017
MULLACH CLACH A BHLÀIR
1157
BEINN BHROTAIN
River Eldart
River Dee
Glen Dee
813
SGÒR MÒR
Glen Lui
Linn of Dee
Quoich Water
Mar Lodge Estate
Allanaquoich
Glenfeshie
Forest
Inverey
859
MORR HIL
GRAMPIAN MO
River Feshie
816
CARN LIATH
999
CARN EALAR
1006
AN SGARSOCH
241
919
CARN BHAC
Glen Ey
886
SGOR MOR
Tarf Water
Baddoch Burn
Gleann Mòr
1007
BEINN DEARG
River Tilt
1050
GLAS TULAICHEAN
Loch Loch
897
BEINN A' CHART
1
2
3
4
5
6
7
8
232
233
Glen
0 1 2 3 4 5 miles
0 1 2 3 4 5 6 7 8 kilometres

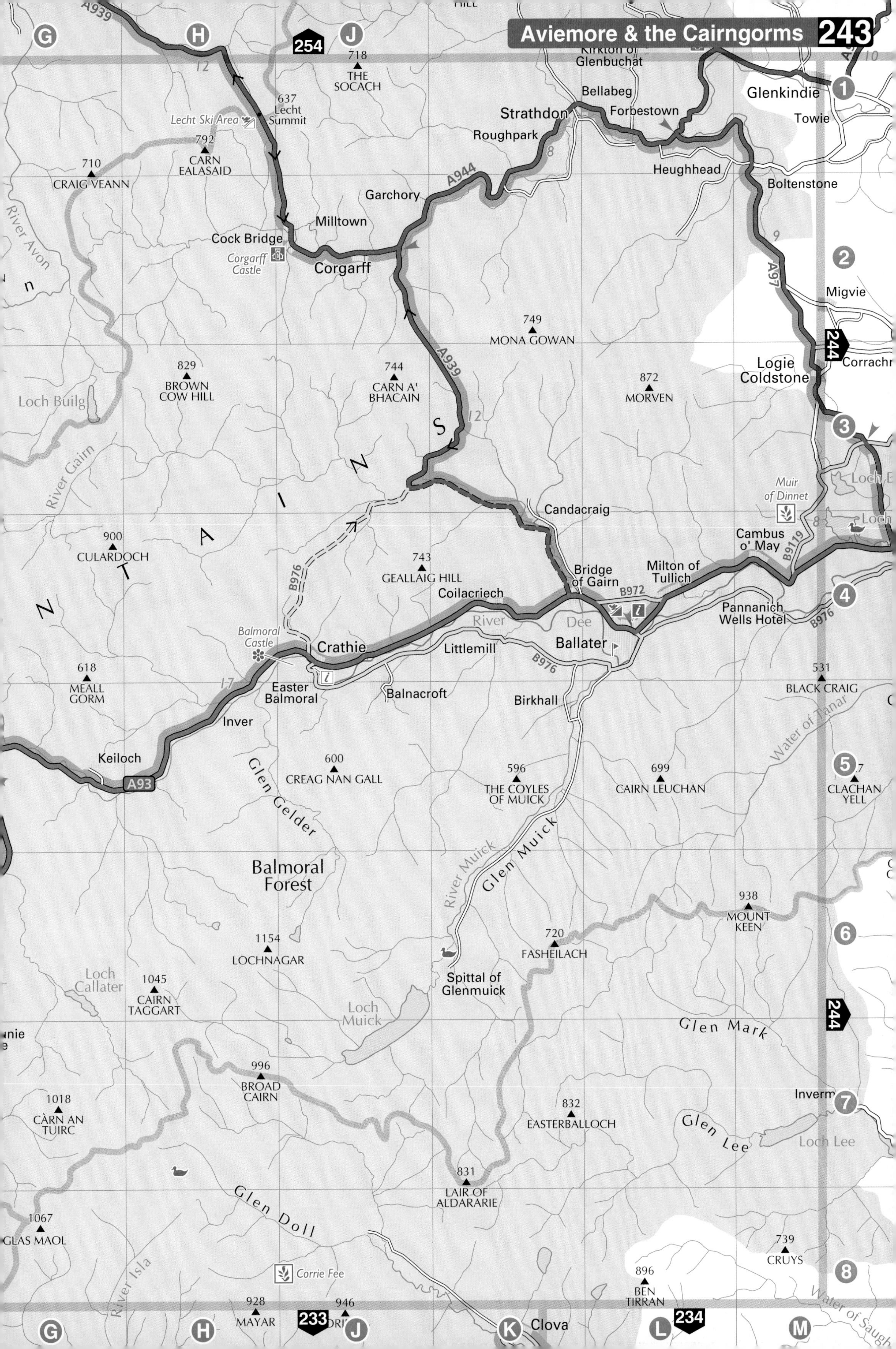
G
H
J
254
718
THE SOCACH
Kirkton of Glenbuchat
Glenkindie
Towie
Bellabeg
Strathdon
Forbestown
Roughpark
637
Lecht Summit
Lecht Ski Area
792
CARN EALASAID
710
CRAIG VEANN
A944
A939
Garchory
Heughhead
Boltenstone
Milltown
Cock Bridge
Corgarff Castle
Corgarff
River Avon
A97
Migvie
749
MONA GOWAN
244
Corrachr
Logie Coldstone
829
BROWN COW HILL
744
CARN A' BHACAIN
872
MORVEN
Loch Builg
River Gairn
C
A
I
N
G
S
R
T
N
Muir of Dinnet
Loch
Candacraig
900
CULARDOCH
Cambus o' May
B9119
743
GEALLAIG HILL
Bridge of Gairn
Milton of Tullich
B972
B976
Coilacriech
River
Dee
Pannanich Wells Hotel
Balmoral Castle
Crathie
Littlemill
Ballater
618
MEALL GORM
Easter Balmoral
Balnacroft
Birkhall
531
BLACK CRAIG
Inver
Water of Tanar
Keiloch
A93
600
CREAG NAN GALL
596
THE COYLES OF MUICK
699
CAIRN LEUCHAN
CLACHAN YELL
Glen Gelder
Glen Muick
River Muick
Balmoral Forest
938
MOUNT KEEN
1154
LOCHNAGAR
720
FASHEILACH
Spittal of Glenmuick
Loch Callater
1045
CAIRN TAGGART
Loch Muick
Glen Mark
996
BROAD CAIRN
1018
CÀRN AN TUIRC
832
EASTERBALLOCH
Inverm
Glen Lee
Loch Lee
831
LAIR OF ALDARARIE
Glen Doll
1067
GLAS MAOL
739
CRUYS
River Isla
Corrie Fee
896
BEN TIRRAN
928
MAYAR
946
233
234
Clova
Water of Saugh
K
L
M
1
2
3
4
5
6
7
8
12
8
9
17

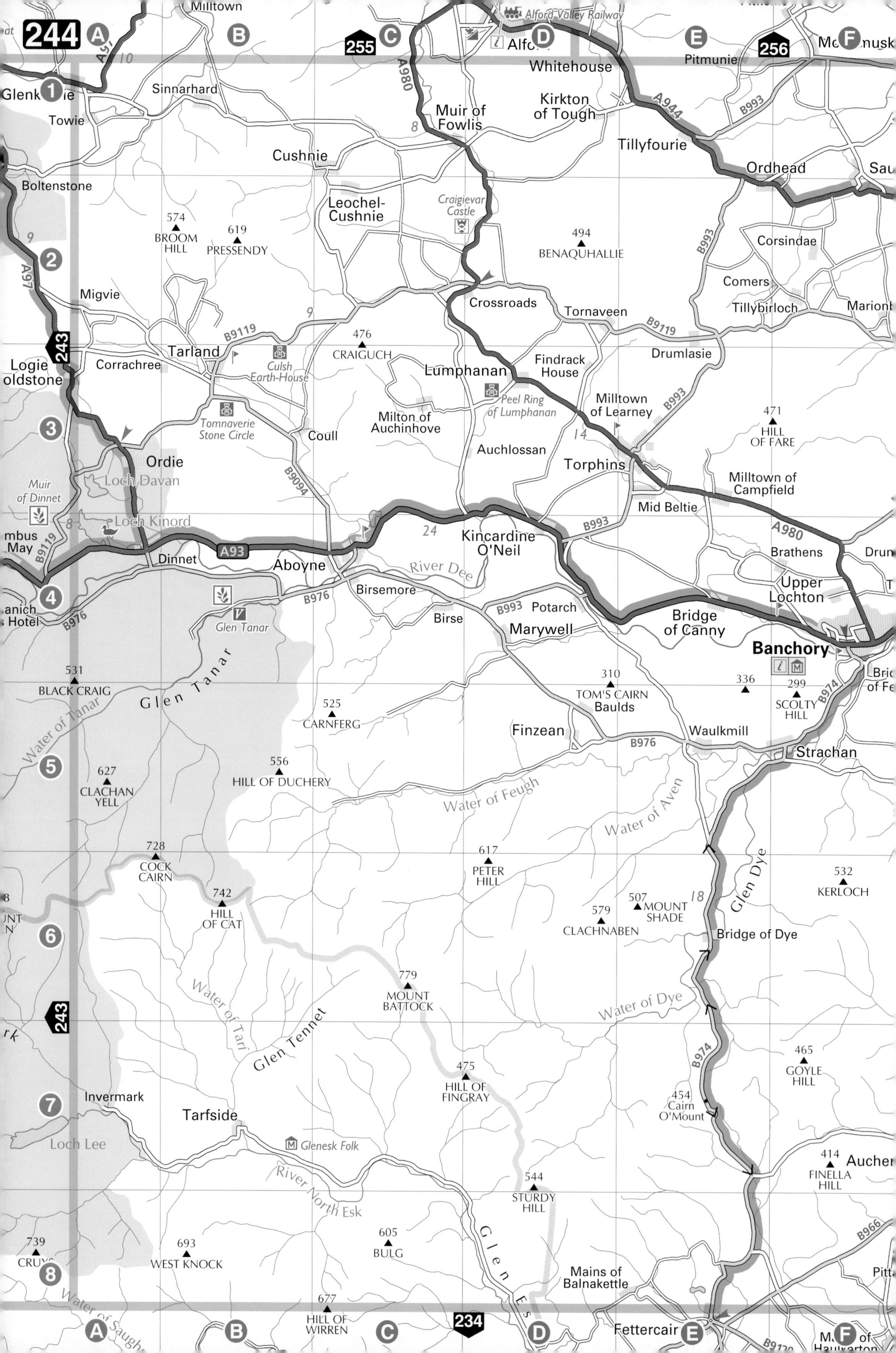

244
A
B
C
D
E
F
255
256
Milltown
Alford Valley Railway
Alford
A97
A980
Whitehouse
Pitmunie
Glenkindie
1
Sinnarhard
Towie
Muir of Fowlis
Kirkton of Tough
A944
B993
Tillyfourie
Cushnie
Ordhead
Boltenstone
Leochel-Cushnie
Craigievar Castle
574
BROOM HILL
619
PRESSENDY
494
BENAQUHALLIE
Corsindae
2
Migvie
Crossroads
Tornaveen
Comers
Tillybirloch
Marionburgh
B9119
476
CRAIGUCH
Drumlasie
243
Logie Coldstone
Corrachree
Tarland
Culsh Earth-House
Lumphanan
Findrack House
Milltown of Learney
Peel Ring of Lumphanan
471
HILL OF FARE
3
Tomnaverie Stone Circle
Milton of Auchinhove
Coull
Auchlossan
Torphins
Ordie
B9094
Milltown of Campfield
Muir of Dinnet
Loch Davan
Loch Kinord
Mid Beltie
Kincardine O'Neil
A980
Dinnet
A93
Aboyne
River Dee
Brathens
Upper Lochton
4
B976
Birsemore
B993
Potarch
Birse
Marywell
Bridge of Canny
Glen Tanar
Banchory
531
BLACK CRAIG
310
TOM'S CAIRN
336
299
SCOLTY HILL
B974
Bauld
525
CARNFERG
Finzean
Waulkmill
Strachan
Water of Tanar
5
556
HILL OF DUCHERY
627
CLACHAN YELL
Water of Feugh
Water of Aven
728
COCK CAIRN
617
PETER HILL
532
KERLOCH
742
HILL OF CAT
507
MOUNT SHADE
579
CLACHNABEN
Glen Dye
Bridge of Dye
6
779
MOUNT BATTOCK
Water of Dye
Water of Tarf
Glen Tennet
243
475
HILL OF FINGRAY
465
GOYLE HILL
454
Cairn O'Mount
7
Invermark
Tarfside
Loch Lee
Glenesk Folk
544
STURDY HILL
414
FINELLA HILL
Auchenblae
River North Esk
Glen Esk
B966
739
8
693
WEST KNOCK
605
BULG
Mains of Balnakettle
677
HILL OF WIRREN
Water of Saughs
234
Fettercairn
Mains of Haulkerton
B9120

Kintore
Cottown
Leylodge
Blackburn
Overton
Dyce Symbol Stones
Aberdeen
Dyce
Blackdog
Middleton Park
Denmore
Stoneywood
Clinterty
Lyne of Skene
Bankhead
Bucksburn
Bridge of Don
Kirkwall
Lerwick
Skene House
Millbuie
BRIMMOND HILL
Northfield
Old Aberdeen
Loch of Skene
Westhill
Kingswells
Kittybrewster
Kirkton of Skene
Kingsford
Garlogie
Carnie
Elrick
ABERDEEN
Echt
Redhill
Ruthrieston
Torry
Nigg Bay
Cullerlie Stone Circle
Easter Ord
Blacktop
Mannofield
Cullerlie
Benthoul
Cults
Bieldside
Kincorth
Milltimber
Nigg
Altens Haven
Craigton
Milton of Murtle
Banchory-Devenick
Hardgate
Cove Bay
Drum Castle
Peterculter
Kingcausie
Charlestown
West Park
River Dee
Maryculter
Marywell
Myrebird
Hillside
Crathes Castle
Auchlee
Findon
Portlethen
Durris
Denside
Cammachmore Bay
Woodlands
Downies
Deeside Railway
Cammachmore
Crossroads
Cookney
Newtonhill
Netherley
Skateraw
Muchalls
Doonie Point
MONGOUR
Garron Point
Stonehaven Bay
HILL OF TRUSTA
Kirktown of Fetteresso
Stonehaven
Elfhill
Dunnottar
Tannachie
New Mill
Drumlithie
Glenbervie
Temple of Fiddes
Crawton
Mondynes
Fowlsheugh
Trelong Bay
Catterline
Kinneff
Todhead Point
Arbuthnott
Redmyre
Inverbervie
5 miles
8 kilometres

HEALAVAL BHEAG
Harlosh
258
Loch
Os
368
BEINN NA BOINEID
Harlosh Island
Colbost Point
Tarner Island
Dun Beag
Bracadale
Loch Duagrich
Struan
Coillore
Loch Bracadale
Ullinish Lodge Hotel
Wiay
23
Idrigill Point
Oronsay
Portnalong
Fiskavaig
Loch Harport
439
ROINEVAL
Rudha nan Clach
B8009
Fernilea
Drynoch
369
ARNAVAL
Carbost
A863
Merkadale
Talisker Bay
Talisker
Glen Eynort
Glen Drynoch
369
447
BEINN BHREAC
Grula
Loch Eynort
434
AN CRUACHIN
Glenbrittle House
Bualintur
Loch Brittle
225
CEANN NA BEINNE
Rudh' an Dùnain
Soay Sound
CUILLIN
CANNA
210
CÀRN A' GHAILL
Garrisdale Point
A'Chill
Canna Harbour
Sanday
Rudha Shamhnan Insir
RÙM
Sound of Canna
302
MULLACH MÒR
Rudha na Roinne
0 1 2 3 4 5 miles
0 1 2 3 4 5 6 7 8 kilometres
A Bhrideanach
236
570
ORVAL
Kinloch
Loch Scresort
A B C D E F
1 2 3 4 5 6 7 8

259
248
238
237

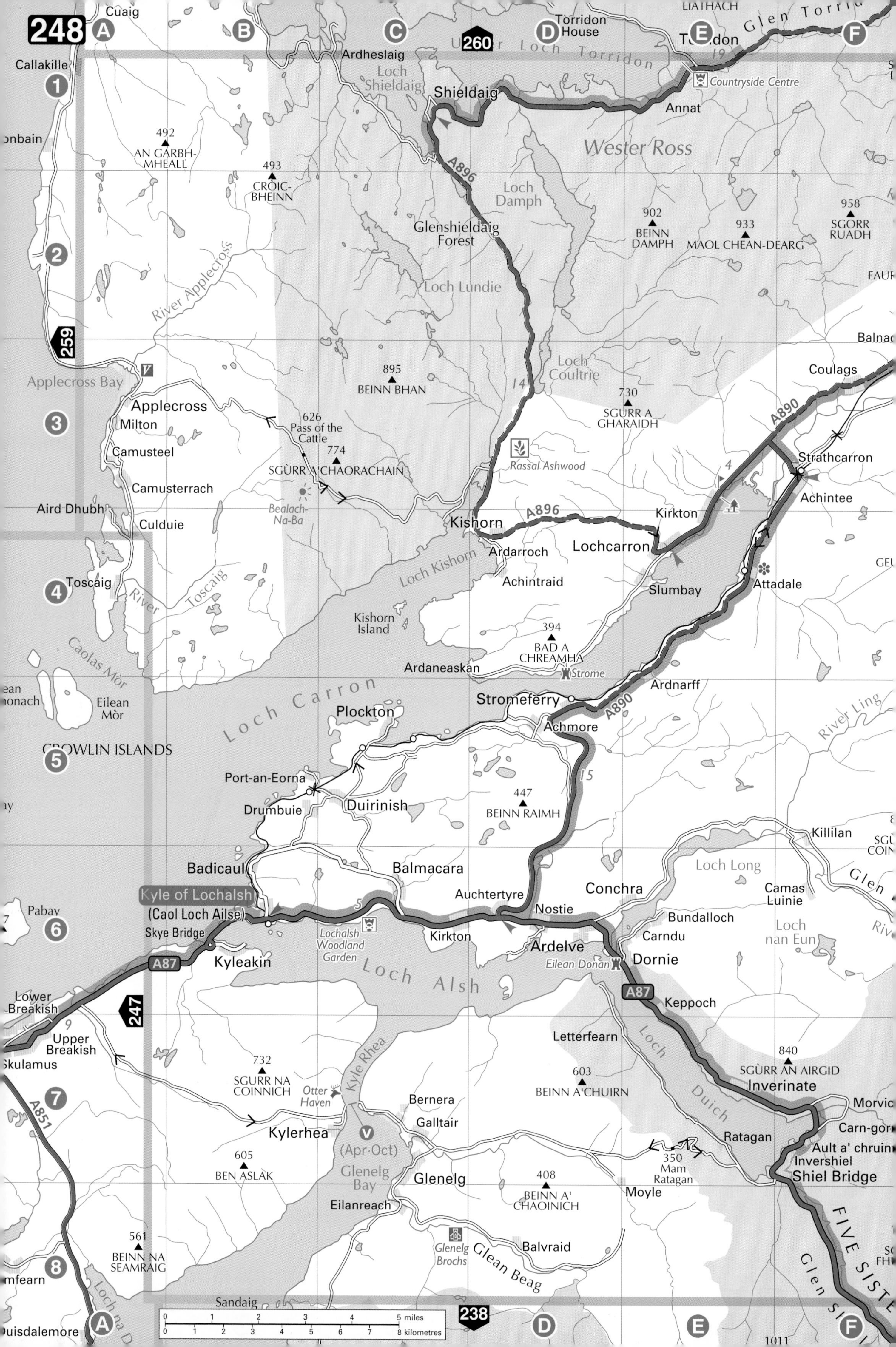
A
B
C
D
E
F
1
2
3
4
5
6
7
8
Cuaig
Callakille
Ardheslaig
Loch Shieldaig
Shieldaig
Upper Loch Torridon
260
Torridon House
LIATHACH
Torridon
Glen Torridon
Countryside Centre
Annat
Wester Ross
A896
Loch Damph
902
BEINN DAMPH
933
MAOL CHEAN-DEARG
958
SGORR RUADH
492
AN GARBH-MHEALL
493
CROIC-BHEINN
Glenshieldaig Forest
Loch Lundie
River Applecross
259
Applecross Bay
895
BEINN BHAN
Loch Coultrie
730
SGURR A GHARAIDH
Coulags
Balnac
A890
Applecross
Milton
626
Pass of the Cattle
774
SGÙRR A'CHAORACHAIN
Camusteel
Camusterrach
Bealach-Na-Ba
Rassal Ashwood
Strathcarron
Achintee
Aird Dhubh
Culduie
Kishorn
Kirkton
Lochcarron
Ardarroch
Achintraid
Slumbay
Attadale
Loch Kishorn
Toscaig
River Toscaig
Kishorn Island
394
BAD A CHREAMHA
Strome
Ardaneaskan
Ardnarff
Caolas Mòr
Eilean Mòr
Loch Carron
Plockton
Stromeferry
Achmore
River Ling
CROWLIN ISLANDS
Port-an-Eorna
Drumbuie
Duirinish
447
BEINN RAIMH
Killilan
Loch Long
Badicaul
Balmacara
Conchra
Camas Luinie
Glen
Kyle of Lochalsh
(Caol Loch Ailse)
Skye Bridge
Auchtertyre
Nostie
Bundalloch
Pabay
Lochalsh Woodland Garden
Kirkton
Carndu
Loch nan Eun
Ardelve
Dornie
Eilean Donan
Kyleakin
A87
Loch Alsh
Lower Breakish
247
Keppoch
Upper Breakish
Skulamus
Letterfearn
Loch Duich
840
SGÙRR AN AIRGID
Inverinate
732
SGURR NA COINNICH
Otter Haven
Kyle Rhea
603
BEINN A'CHUIRN
Morvich
A851
Bernera
Galltair
Kylerhea
(Apr-Oct)
Ratagan
Carn-gorm
Ault a' chruinn
Inverhiel
350
Mam Ratagan
605
BEN ASLAK
Glenelg Bay
Glenelg
408
BEINN A' CHAOINICH
Moyle
Shiel Bridge
Eilanreach
FIVE SISTERS
Glenelg Brochs
Glean Beag
Balvraid
561
BEINN NA SEAMRAIG
Loch na D
Sandaig
238
0 1 2 3 4 5 miles
0 1 2 3 4 5 6 7 8 kilometres
Glen Shiel
1011

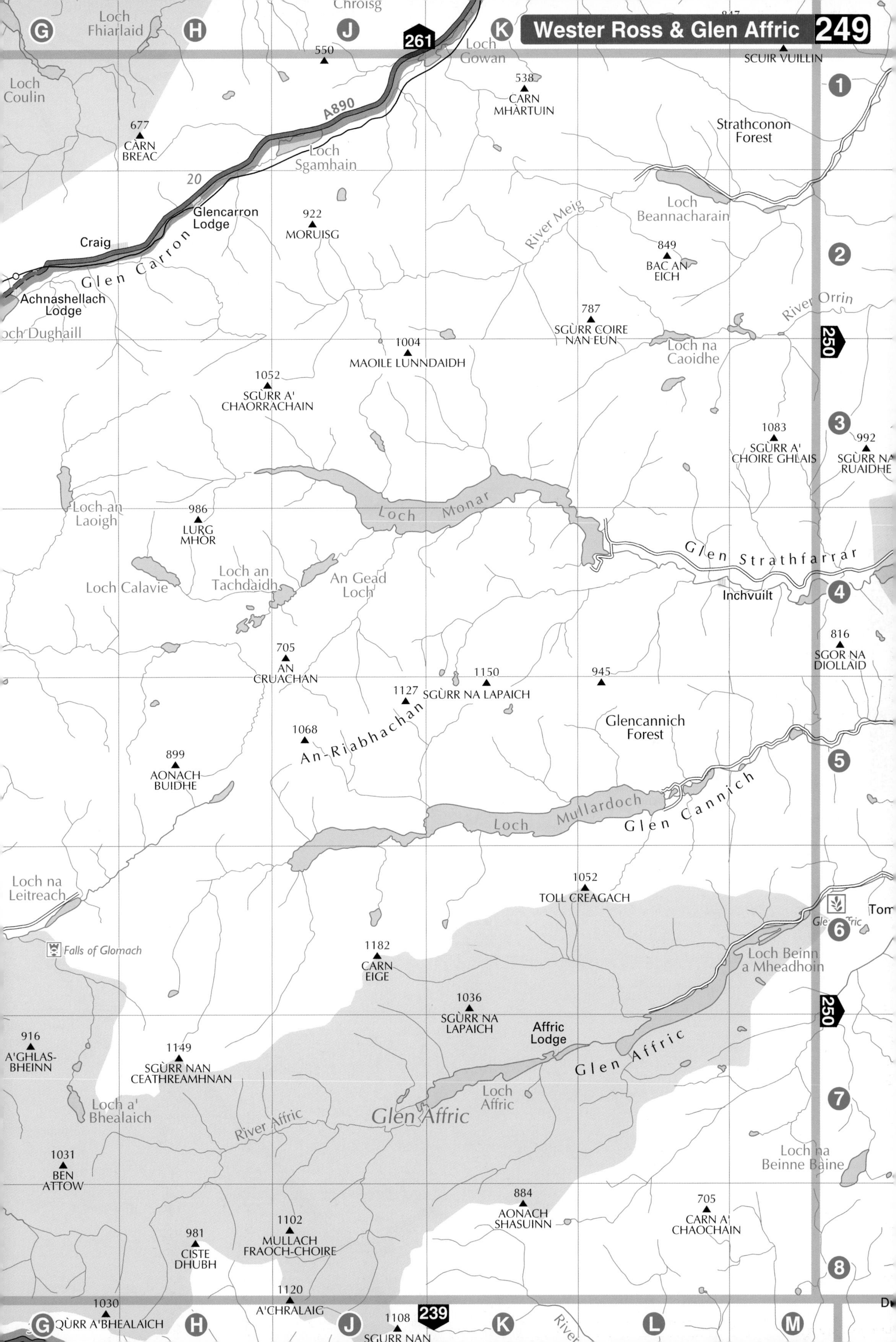

Loch Fhiarlaid
Loch Coulin
550
261
Loch Gowan
538 CARN MHÀRTUIN
SCUIR VUILLIN
677 CARN BREAC
A890
Loch Sgamhain
Strathconon Forest
20
Glencarron Lodge
922 MORUISG
Loch Beannacharain
River Meig
Craig
Glen Carron
849 BAC AN EICH
Achnashellach Lodge
Loch Dughaill
787 SGÙRR COIRE NAN EUN
River Orrin
Loch na Caoidhe
250
1004 MAOILE LUNNDAIDH
1052 SGÙRR A' CHAORRACHAIN
1083 SGÙRR A' CHOIRE GHLAIS
992 SGÙRR NA RUAIDHE
Loch an Laoigh
986 LURG MHOR
Loch Monar
Glen Strathfarrar
Loch Calavie
Loch an Tachdaidh
An Gead Loch
Inchvuilt
816 SGOR NA DIOLLAID
705 AN CRUACHAN
1150
945
1127 SGÙRR NA LAPAICH
An-Riabhachan
1068
Glencannich Forest
899 AONACH BUIDHE
Loch Mullardoch
Glen Cannich
Loch na Leitreach
1052 TOLL CREAGACH
Tom
Falls of Glomach
1182 CARN EIGE
Loch Beinn a Mheadhoin
1036 SGÙRR NA LAPAICH
Affric Lodge
916 A'GHLAS-BHEINN
1149 SGÙRR NAN CEATHREAMHNAN
Glen Affric
Loch a' Bhealaich
River Affric
Loch Affric
Glen Affric
1031 BEN ATTOW
Loch na Beinne Bàine
884 AONACH SHASUINN
705 CARN A' CHAOCHAIN
1102 MULLACH FRAOCH-CHOIRE
981 CISTE DHUBH
1120 A'CHRALAIG
1030 SGÙRR A'BHEALAICH
1108 SGURR NAN
239
River

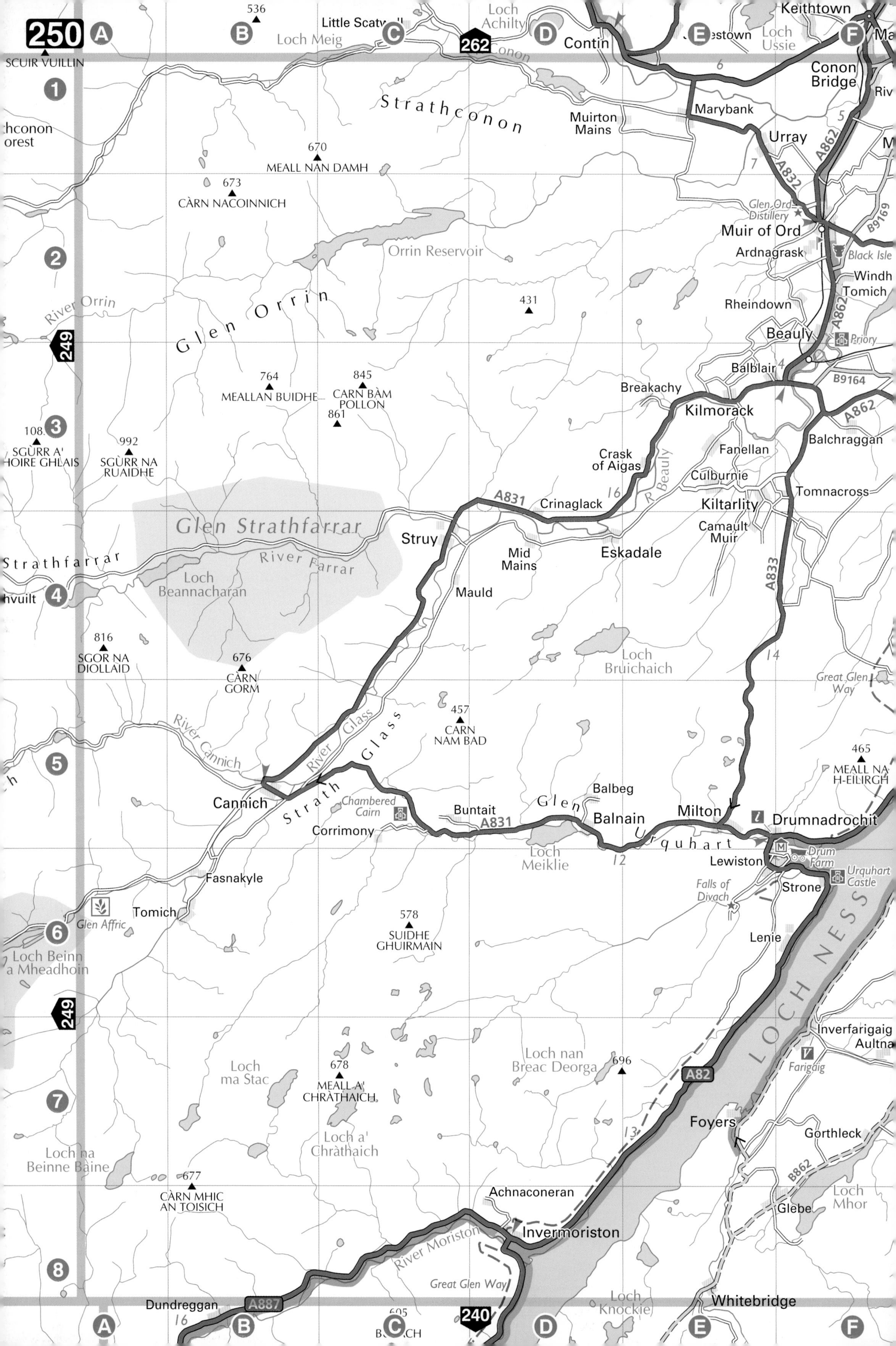

250
A
B
C
D
E
F
1
2
3
4
5
6
7
8
262
249
249
240
SCUIR VUILLIN
536
Little Scatwell
Loch Meig
Loch Achilty
Contin
Loch Ussie
Keithtown
Conon
Conon Bridge
Strathconon
Marybank
Muirton Mains
Urray
A862
A832
670
MEALL NAN DAMH
673
CÀRN NACOINNICH
Glen Ord Distillery
Muir of Ord
B9169
Ardnagrask
Black Isle
Orrin Reservoir
River Orrin
Glen Orrin
431
Rheindown
Tomich
Beauly
Priory
Balblair
B9164
Breakachy
Kilmorack
A862
764
MEALLAN BUIDHE
845
CARN BÀM POLLON
861
108
SGÙRR A' CHOIRE GHLAIS
992
SGÙRR NA RUAIDHE
Balchraggan
Fanellan
Crask of Aigas
R. Beauly
Culburnie
Tomnacross
A831
Crinaglack
Kiltarlity
Glen Strathfarrar
Strathfarrar
River Farrar
Struy
Camault Muir
Mid Mains
Eskadale
Loch Beannacharan
A833
Mauld
816
SGOR NA DIOLLAID
676
CÀRN GORM
Loch Bruichaich
Great Glen Way
457
CARN NAM BAD
River Glass
Strath Glass
River Cannich
465
MEALL NA H-EILIRGH
Cannich
Chambered Cairn
Buntait
A831
Glen Urquhart
Balbeg
Balnain
Milton
Drumnadrochit
Corrimony
Loch Meiklie
Lewiston
Drum Farm
Urquhart Castle
Fasnakyle
Falls of Divach
Strone
Tomich
Glen Affric
578
SUIDHE GHUIRMAIN
Lenie
Loch Beinn a Mheadhoin
LOCH NESS
Inverfarigaig
Aultna
Farigaig
Loch ma Stac
678
MEALL A' CHRÀTHAICH
Loch nan Breac Deorga
696
A82
Foyers
Gorthleck
Loch a' Chràthaich
Loch na Beinne Bàine
B862
677
CÀRN MHIC AN TOISICH
Achnaconeran
Loch Mhor
Glebe
Invermoriston
River Moriston
Great Glen Way
Dundreggan
A887
Loch Knockie
Whitebridge

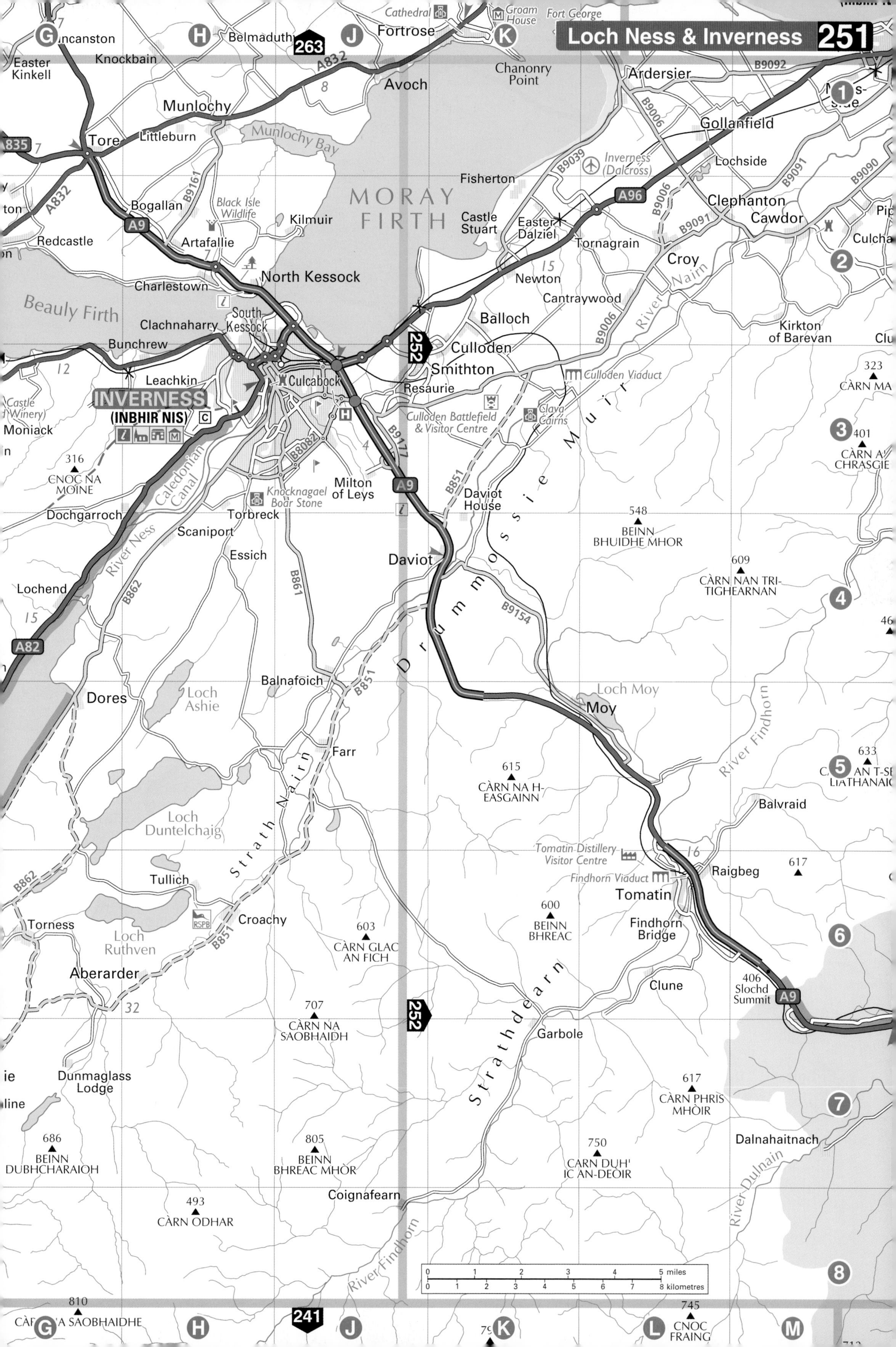

Cathedral
Groam House
Fort George
Fortrose
Belmaduthy
263
Knockbain
Easter Kinkell
A832
Avoch
Chanonry Point
Ardersier
B9092
Munlochy
Munlochy Bay
Tore
Littleburn
B9006
Gollanfield
B9039
Inverness (Dalcross)
Lochside
Fisherton
MORAY FIRTH
A96
B9091
B9090
Clephanton
Cawdor
Bogallan
B9161
Black Isle Wildlife
Kilmuir
Castle Stuart
Easter Dalziel
Tornagrain
Croy
Redcastle
Artafallie
Newton
River Nairn
Charlestown
North Kessock
Cantraywood
Beauly Firth
South Kessock
Clachnaharry
Balloch
Kirkton of Barevan
Bunchrew
252
Culloden
Smithton
Leachkin
Culcabock
Culloden Viaduct
INVERNESS
(INBHIR NIS)
Resaurie
Castle Winery
Moniack
Culloden Battlefield & Visitor Centre
Clava Cairns
B9177
B8082
Caledonian Canal
316
CNOC NA MOINE
Knocknagael Boar Stone
Milton of Leys
Daviot House
B851
Drummossie Muir
Dochgarroch
Torbreck
Scaniport
River Ness
Essich
548
BEINN BHUIDHE MHOR
Daviot
609
CÀRN NAN TRI-TIGHEARNAN
B861
Lochend
B862
B9154
A82
Balnafoich
Dores
Loch Ashie
Loch Moy
Moy
Farr
615
CÀRN NA H-EASGAINN
River Findhorn
Loch Duntelchaig
Strath Nairn
Balvraid
Tomatin Distillery Visitor Centre
Findhorn Viaduct
Raigbeg
617
Tullich
Tomatin
600
BEINN BHREAC
Torness
Croachy
RSPB
603
CÀRN GLAC AN FHICH
Findhorn Bridge
Loch Ruthven
Aberarder
Clune
406
Slochd Summit
A9
707
CÀRN NA SAOBHAIDH
Garbole
Strathdearn
Dunmaglass Lodge
617
CÀRN PHRIS MHÒIR
686
BEINN DUBHCHARAIOH
805
BEINN BHREAC MHÒR
750
CARN DUH' IC AN-DEÒIR
Dalnahaitnach
River Dulnain
493
CÀRN ODHAR
Coignafearn
River Findhorn
0 1 2 3 4 5 miles
0 1 2 3 4 5 6 7 8 kilometres
810
241
745
CNOC FRAING
323
401
633

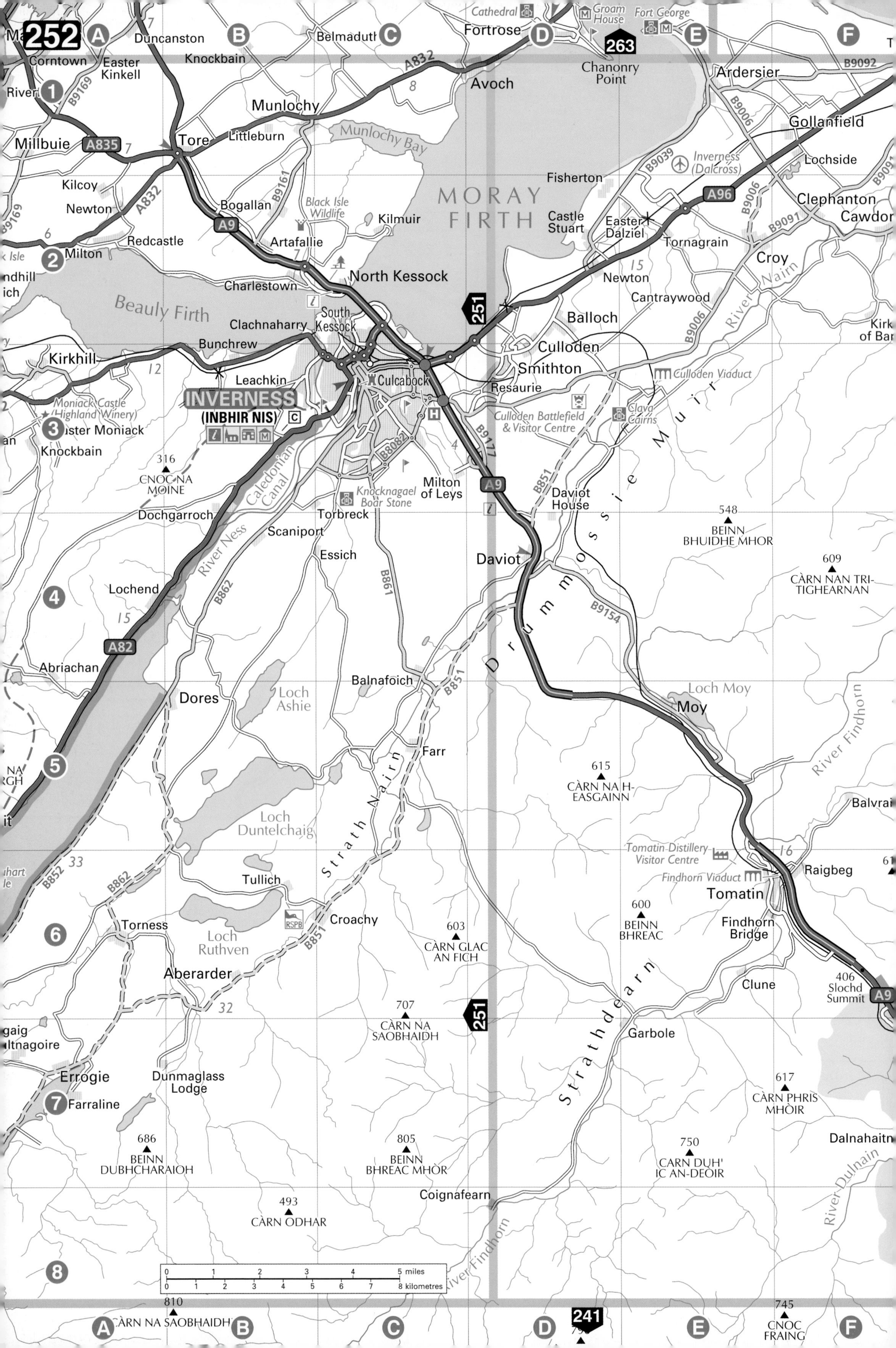

252
A
B
C
D
E
F
Duncanston
Belmaduthy
Cathedral
Fortrose
Groam House
Fort George
263
Corntown
Easter Kinkell
Knockbain
A832
Avoch
Chanonry Point
Ardersier
B9092
River
1
B9169
Munlochy
8
B9006
Gollanfield
Millbuie
A835
7
Tore
Littleburn
Munlochy Bay
B9039
Inverness (Dalcross)
Lochside
Kilcoy
B9161
Fisherton
Newton
A832
Bogallan
Black Isle Wildlife
MORAY FIRTH
Kilmuir
Castle Stuart
Easter Dalziel
A96
Clephanton
Cawdor
A9
B9091
Redcastle
Artafallie
Tornagrain
2
Milton
Croy
Charlestown
North Kessock
15
Newton
River Nairn
Beauly Firth
251
Cantraywood
Balloch
Clachnaharry
South Kessock
B9006
Bunchrew
Culloden
Kirkhill
12
Smithton
Leachkin
Culcabock
Culloden Viaduct
Resaurie
INVERNESS
(INBHIR NIS)
Moniack Castle (Highland Winery)
3
Easter Moniack
Knockbain
Culloden Battlefield & Visitor Centre
Clava Cairns
Drummossie Muir
B8082
B9177
316
CNOC NA MOINE
Caledonian Canal
4
Knocknagael Boar Stone
Milton of Leys
A9
B851
Daviot House
Dochgarroch
Torbreck
548
BEINN BHUIDHE MHOR
Scaniport
River Ness
Essich
Daviot
609
CÀRN NAN TRI-TIGHEARNAN
B862
B861
4
Lochend
15
B9154
A82
Abriachan
Balnafoich
Loch Ashie
Dores
B851
Loch Moy
Moy
River Findhorn
5
Farr
615
CÀRN NA H-EASGAINN
Strath Nairn
Loch Duntelchaig
Balvraid
Tomatin Distillery Visitor Centre
16
33
B852
B862
Tullich
Findhorn Viaduct
Raigbeg
Tomatin
6
Torness
RSPB
Croachy
600
BEINN BHREAC
Findhorn Bridge
603
CÀRN GLAC AN FICH
Loch Ruthven
B851
Aberarder
Clune
406
Slochd Summit
A9
32
707
CÀRN NA SAOBHAIDH
251
Strathdearn
Garbole
Altnagoire
Errogie
Dunmaglass Lodge
7
Farraline
617
CÀRN PHRIS MHÒIR
686
BEINN DUBHCHARAIOH
805
BEINN BHREAC MHÒR
750
CARN DUH' IC AN-DEOIR
Dalnahaitnach
River Dulnain
Coignafearn
493
CÀRN ODHAR
River Findhorn
8
0 1 2 3 4 5 miles
0 1 2 3 4 5 6 7 8 kilometres
810
CÀRN NA SAOBHAIDH
241
745
CNOC FRAING

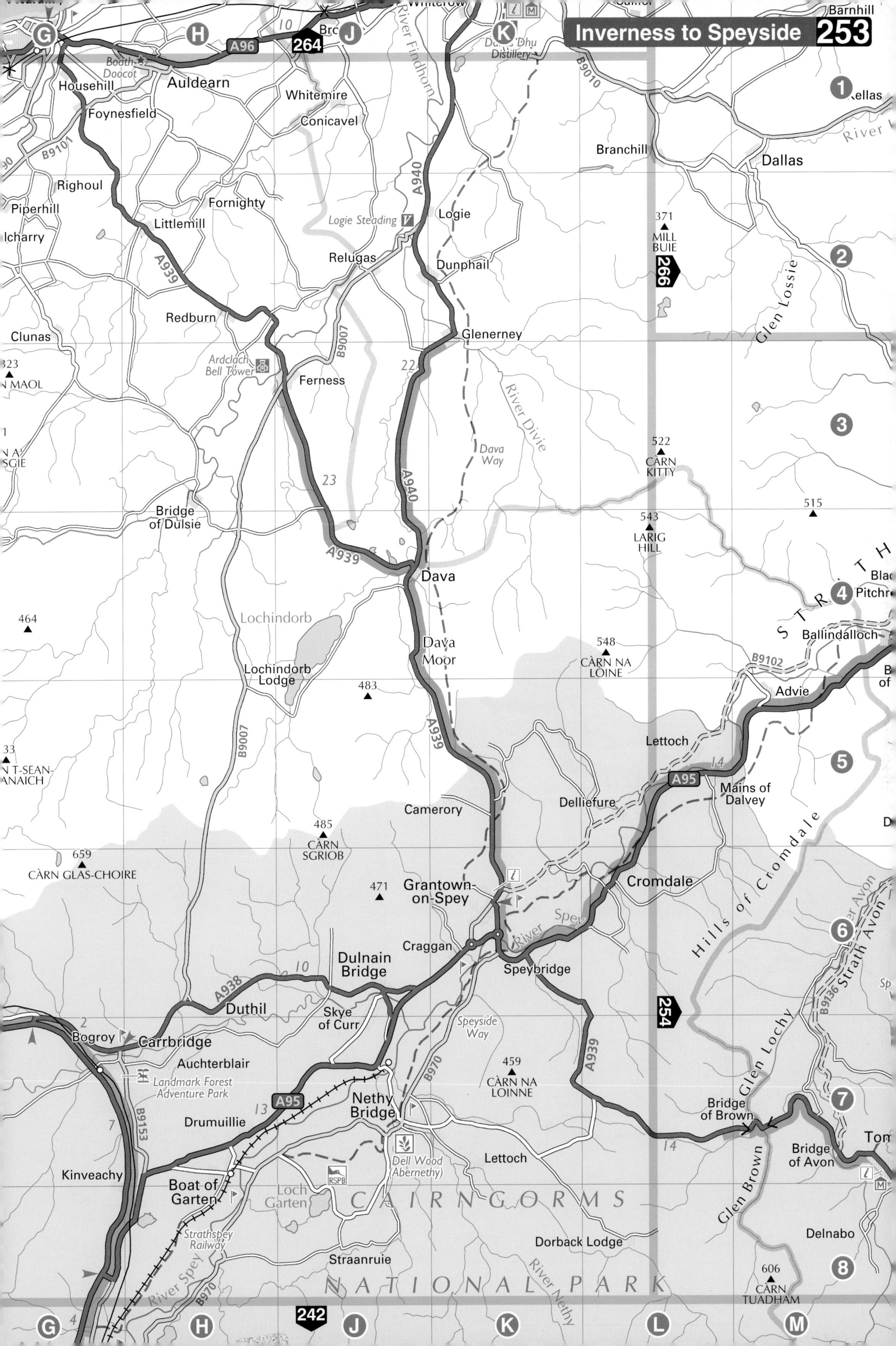
Auldearn
Househill
Foynesfield
Whitemire
Conicavel
Boath Doocot
Righoul
Piperhill
Fornighty
Littlemill
Logie Steading
Logie
Relugas
Dunphail
Redburn
Clunas
Glenerney
Ardclach Bell Tower
Ferness
River Divie
Dava Way
Bridge of Dulsie
Dava
Lochindorb
Dava Moor
Lochindorb Lodge
Camerory
Grantown-on-Spey
Craggan
Dulnain Bridge
Speybridge
Duthil
Skye of Curr
Bogroy
Carrbridge
Auchterblair
Landmark Forest Adventure Park
Drumuillie
Nethy Bridge
Kinveachy
Boat of Garten
Loch Garten
Dell Wood (Abernethy)
Lettoch
Strathspey Railway
Straanruie
River Spey
River Nethy
Dorback Lodge
CAIRNGORMS NATIONAL PARK
Speyside Way
Cromdale
Hills of Cromdale
Delliefure
Mains of Dalvey
Advie
Ballindalloch
Glen Lochy
Bridge of Brown
Glen Brown
Bridge of Avon
Delnabo
Branchill
Dallas
Glen Lossie
River Findhorn
Dallas Dhu Distillery
Barnhill
Kellas
MILL BUIE
CÀRN KITTY
LARIG HILL
CÀRN NA LOINE
CÀRN SGRIOB
CÀRN GLAS-CHOIRE
CÀRN NA LOINNE
CÀRN TUADHAM
Strath Avon
A96
A939
A940
A938
A95
B9101
B9007
B9010
B9102
B9153
B970
B9136
264
266
254
242

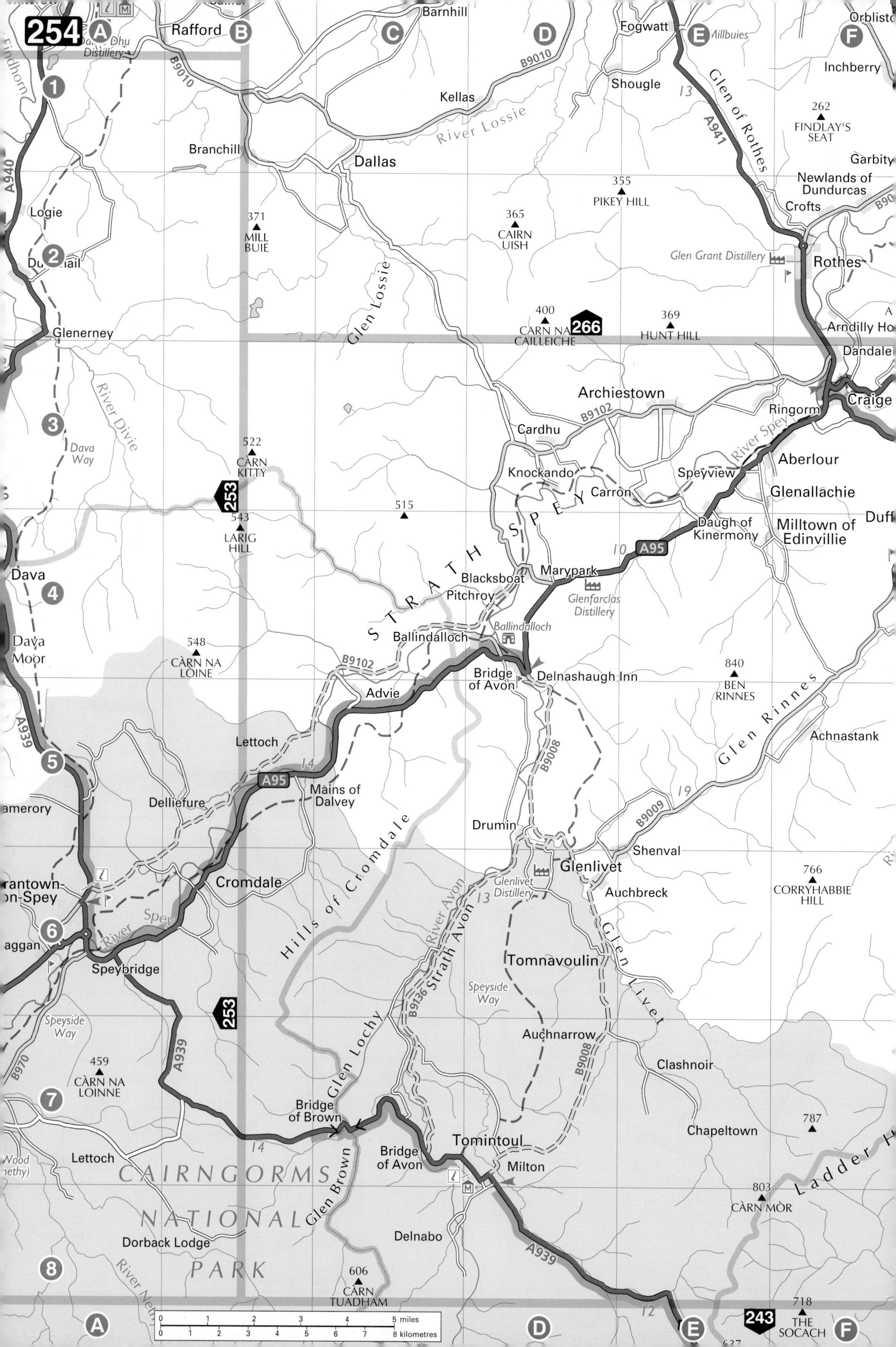

254
A
B
C
D
E
F
Rafford
Barnhill
Fogwatt
Millbuies
Orbliston
Dallas Dhu Distillery
Findhorn
B9010
Kellas
Shougle
Inchberry
Glen of Rothes
A941
262
FINDLAY'S SEAT
River Lossie
Branchill
Dallas
Garbity
Newlands of Dundurcas
Crofts
355
PIKEY HILL
365
CAIRN UISH
371
MILL BUIE
A940
Logie
Glen Grant Distillery
Rothes
Glen Lossie
400
CARN NA CAILLEICHE
266
369
HUNT HILL
Glenerney
Arndilly House
Dandale
Archiestown
B9102
Ringorm
Craigellachie
River Divie
Dava Way
Cardhu
River Spey
Aberlour
522
CÀRN KITTY
Knockando
Speyview
Carron
Glenallachie
253
515
543
LARIG HILL
STRATH SPEY
Daugh of Kinermony
Milltown of Edinvillie
Duff
A95
Dava
Marypark
Blacksboat
Pitchroy
Glenfarclas Distillery
Dava Moor
Ballindalloch
548
CÀRN NA LOINE
B9102
Bridge of Avon
Delnashaugh Inn
840
BEN RINNES
Advie
A939
Glen Rinnes
Achnastank
Lettoch
B9008
A95
Mains of Dalvey
Dellefure
Grantown-on-Spey
Cromdale
B9009
Drumin
Shenval
Glenlivet
Glenlivet Distillery
Auchbreck
766
CORRYHABBIE HILL
Hills of Cromdale
River Avon
Strath Avon
Glen Livet
Speybridge
Tomnavoulin
Speyside Way
B9136
Glen Lochy
Auchnarrow
B970
459
CÀRN NA LOINNE
A939
B9008
Clashnoir
Bridge of Brown
787
Chapeltown
Tomintoul
Bridge of Avon
Milton
Lettoch
Ladder Hills
CAIRNGORMS NATIONAL PARK
Glen Brown
803
CÀRN MÒR
Delnabo
A939
Dorback Lodge
River Nethy
606
CÀRN TUADHAM
718
THE SOCACH
243
1
2
3
4
5
6
7
8
10
12
13
14
19
0 1 2 3 4 5 miles
0 1 2 3 4 5 6 7 8 kilometres

WHITEASH HILL
301
MILLSTONE HILL
LURG HILL
quish
A96
429
KNOCK HILL
Glenbarry
250
THIEF'S HILL
Forgie
Grange Crossroads
Berryhillock
271
WETHER HILL
Lootcherbrae
Aultmore
Forgieside
Bracobrae
Knock
Sound Muir
Newmill
Davoch of Grange
Drumnagorrach
Rumbach
B9017
Strath Isla
Farmtown
Upper Mulben
A95
B9022
Bridge of Marnoch
Strathisla Distillery
Mulben
Fife Keith
Keith
River Isla
Deanshaugh
Rosarie
365
MEIKLE BALLOCH
Tauchers
B9117
Rothiemay
338
HILL OF TOWIE
B9014
Keith and Dufftown Railway
A96
267
Inverkeith
372
KNOCKAN
Ruthven
Bogniebrae
Forgue
gieknockater
Cairnie
B9022
River Deveron
A97
B9115
Drummuir
256
Nordic Ski Centre
Castle
Affleck
Balvenie Castle
A920
Drumblade
Huntly
Haugh of Glass
Brideswell
Auchindoun Castle
A96
Strath Bogie
Thomastown
Bridgend
Kirkstile
Hillhead
Bainshole
A941
Glens of Foudlan
503
Culdrain
419
WICHACH HILL
466
HILL OF FOUDLAN
525
Gartly
Kirkney
440
CRANSMILL HILL
Largie
Bridgend
A97
Leith Hall
Picardy Symbol Stone
564
TAP O' NOTH
Mains of Lesmoir
Insch
Dunnideer
Kennethmont
A941
B9002
571
ROUND HILL
Belhinnie
Cabrach
Cottown
Rhynie
Clatt
Duncanstone
Aldivalloch
Aldunie
A97
B9002
Leslie
256
B992
St Mary's Kirk (Ruin)
722
THE BUCK
484
MIRE OF MIDGATES
629
HILL OF THREE STONES
Lumsden
475
BRUX HILL
CORREEN HILLS
Lethenty
A944
Mossat
632
CREAG AN EUNAN
Tullynessle
Scotsmill
Keig
Kildrummy Castle
Kildrummy
Bridge of Alford
Montgarrie
Belnacraig
Milltown
Haughton House
Alford Valley Railway
Glenbuchat Castle
Alford
Kirkton of Glenbuchat
243
A97
244
Whitehouse
Bellabeg
Glenkindie
Sinnarhard
Kirkton

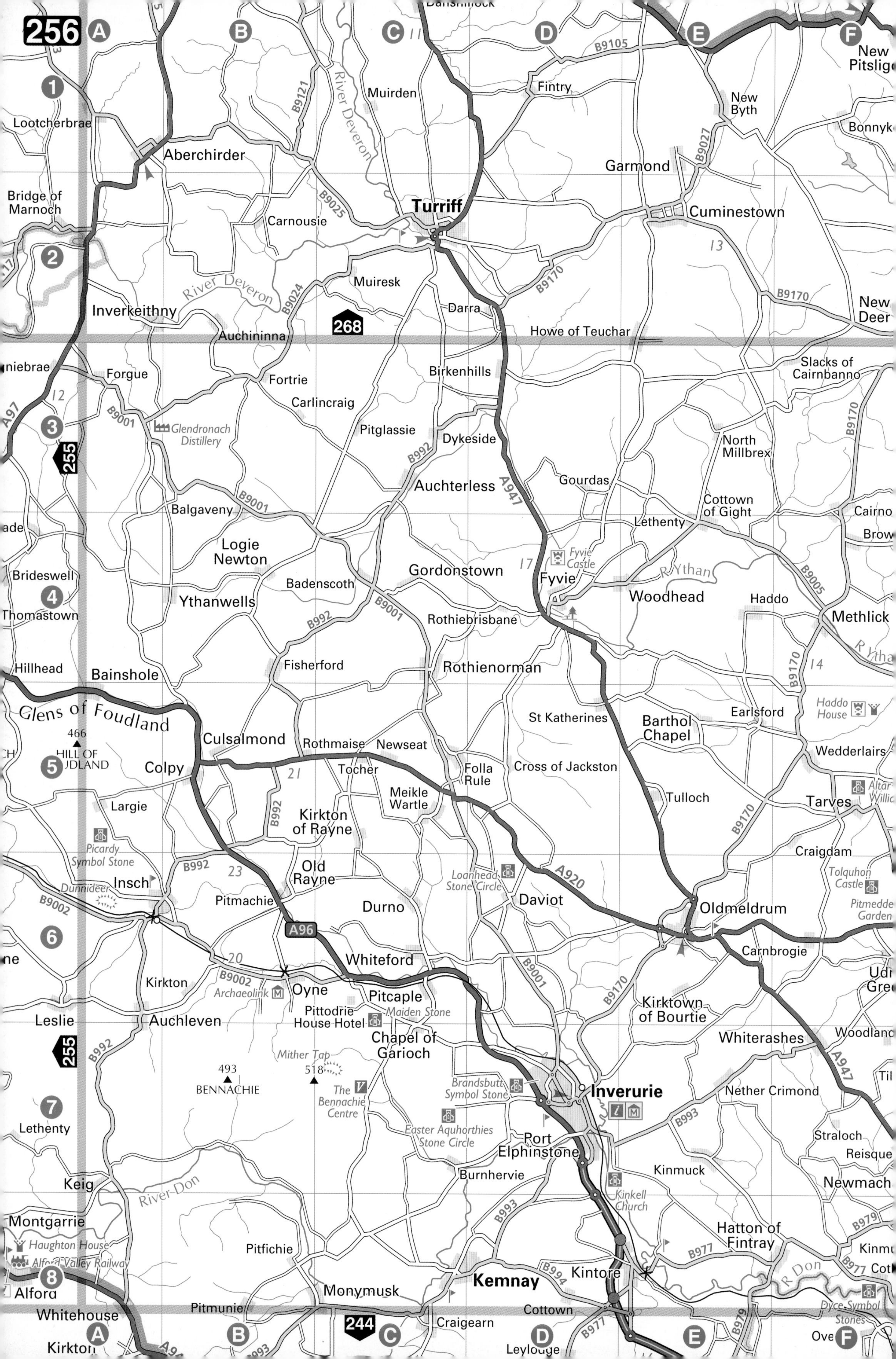

256
A
B
C
D
E
F
1
2
3
4
5
6
7
8
Lootcherbrae
Aberchirder
Bridge of Marnoch
Inverkeithny
Muirden
River Deveron
B9121
B9025
Carnousie
Turriff
Muiresk
B9024
268
Darra
Fintry
B9105
New Byth
New Pitsligo
Bonnyk
B9027
Garmond
Cuminestown
13
B9170
New Deer
Howe of Teuchar
Auchininna
Forgue
Fortrie
Carlincraig
Birkenhills
Slacks of Cairnbanno
A97
12
B9001
Glendronach Distillery
255
Pitglassie
Dykeside
B992
North Millbrex
Gourdas
Auchterless
A947
Cottown of Gight
Lethenty
Cairno
Brow
Balgaveny
Logie Newton
Gordonstown
17
Fyvie Castle
Fyvie
R Ythan
Woodhead
Haddo
B9005
Methlick
Brideswell
Badenscoth
Ythanwells
Rothiebrisbane
Thomastown
Fisherford
Rothienorman
Hillhead
Bainshole
14
Glens of Foudland
466
HILL OF FOUDLAND
St Katherines
Barthol Chapel
Earlsford
Haddo House
Culsalmond
Rothmaise
Newseat
Wedderlairs
Colpy
21
Tocher
Folla Rule
Cross of Jackston
Meikle Wartle
Tulloch
Tarves
Largie
Kirkton of Rayne
Picardy Symbol Stone
Craigdam
B992
23
Old Rayne
Loanhead Stone Circle
A920
Tolquhon Castle
Insch
Dunnideer
B9002
Pitmachie
Durno
Daviot
Oldmeldrum
Pitmedden Garden
A96
20
Whiteford
Carnbrogie
Kirkton
B9002
Oyne
Pitcaple
Archaeolink
Pittodrie House Hotel
Maiden Stone
B9001
B9170
Kirktown of Bourtie
Leslie
Auchleven
Chapel of Garioch
Whiterashes
Woodland
Mither Tap
518
493
BENNACHIE
The Bennachie Centre
Brandsbutt Symbol Stone
Inverurie
Nether Crimond
Lethenty
Easter Aquhorthies Stone Circle
B993
Port Elphinstone
Straloch
Reisque
Kinmuck
Keig
River Don
Burnhervie
Kinkell Church
Newmach
Montgarrie
Haughton House
Alford Valley Railway
Pitfichie
Hatton of Fintray
B979
B977
R Don
Kemnay
B994
Kintore
Alford
Monymusk
Dyce Symbol Stones
Whitehouse
Pitmunie
Cottown
244
Craigearn
Kirkton
Leylodge

Strichen
New Leeds
B9093
Crimond
Strathbeg
Blackhill
Leys
Denhead
Backfolds
Kirktown
St Fergus
Fetterangus
Rora
A90
A981
A950
Deer Abbey
Dunshillock
River Ugie
Maud
B9106
Aden
Mintlaw
Longside
Inverugie
B9029
Old Deer
Blackhill of Clackriach
269
Peterhead
Buchanhaven
Inverquhomery
Stuartfield
Drymuir
Bulwark
B9028
Millbreck
Nether Kinmundy
Hillhead of Cocklaw
A982
Peterhead Bay
Burnhaven
Nethermuir
Clola
B9030
Kinnadie
Blackhill
Stirling
Buchan Ness
Boddam
Lendrum Terrace
Kinknockie
Longhaven
Inkhorn
Ardallie
A952
Coldwells
Bullers of Buchan
Auchiries
A948
Hatton
North Haven
Arthrath
Muirtack
Slains
Cruden Bay
Bogbrae
Chapel Hill
Bay of Cruden
A975
Ythanbank
Birness
The Skares
Whinnyfold
Artrochie
Kinharrachie
Ellon
P+R
B9005
Esslemont
A920
Kirkton of Logie Buchan
Kirktown of Slains
Collieston
Forvie
Logierieve
B9000
Udny Station
Newburgh
Foveran
Cultercullen
Delfrigs
Causeyend
B979
Balmedie
Belhelvie
B977
B999
Potterton
245
0 1 2 3 4 5 miles
0 1 2 3 4 5 6 7 8 kilometres
G H J K L M
1 2 3 4 5 6 7 8

The Little Minch
Fladda-chùain
Rudha Hu
Tairbeart (Tarbert)
Lùb Score
Borneskitaig
Kilmuir
Balgown
Loch nam Madadh (Lochmaddy)
Waternish Point
Totscore
Ascrib Islands
Idrigill
Uig Bay
283 BEN GEARY
Geary
Trumpan
Loch Snizort
Earlish
Ardmore Point
Gillen
Hallin
A87
DUNVEGAN HEAD
Isay
Mingay
Stein
Lusta
Loch Bay
214 BEN DIUBAIG
Greshornish House Hotel
Loch Greshornish
Loch Snizort
Loch Dunvegan
Claigan
Boreraig
Bay
327 BEINN BHREAC
B886
Uig
Treaslane
Flashader
A850
Loch Pooltiel
Upperglen
Feriniquarrie
Totaig
Edinbane
Bernisdale
Oisgill Bay
Milovaig
Glendale
Colbost
Dunvegan
Lephin
B884
Waterstein
Colbost Croft
Toy
Dunvegan
Giant Angus MacAskill
ISLE OF SKYE
Skinidin
Kilmuir
A864
Caroy River
Neist Point
Lonmore
265 BEN AKETIL
271 CRUACHAN BEINN A' CHEARCAILL
Moonen Bay
Roskhill
469 HEALAVAL MORE
Roag
Ramasaig
Orbost
Hoe Rape
Vatten
Glen Ose
488 HEALAVAL BHEAG
Harlosh
A863
Loch Caroy
Hoe Point
Ose
368
Harlosh Island
Colbost Point
246
Dun Beag
Bracadale
Tarner Island
5 miles
8 kilometres

G
H
J
K
L
Trodday
North Duntulm
Kilmaluag
Flodigarry
Poldorais
Eilean Flodigarry
542
MEAL NA SUIREAMACH
Digg
Staffin Bay
Staffin Island
Brogaig
Stenscholl
Staffin
464
BIODA BUIDHE
Trotternish
Kilt Rock Waterfall
Ellishader
Maligar
Marishader
Valtos
Rudha nam Brathairean
611
BEINN EDRA
Garros
Culnaknock
River Conon
Lealt
Tote
A855
608
CREAG A' LAIN
451
BEINN A' SGÀ
River Romesdal
Old Man of Storr
719
THE STORR
Kensaleyre
River Haulton
Loch Leathan
Loch Fada
B8036
Carbost
Borve
Drumuie
Glengrasco
312
Torvaig
Portree
Seafield
417
BEINN NA GRÈINE
Penifiler
412
BEN TIANAVAIG
Glenmore
Glenvarragill
Mugeary
A87
Camastianavaig
Tianavaig
SOUND OF RAASAY
Loch a' Bhràige
RONA
Eilean Tigh
Eilean Fladday
Manish Point
Loch Arnish
Torran
Arnish
Brochel
RAASAY
INNER SOUND
444
DÙN CAAN
Oskaig
Rudha na' Leac
247
260
248
1
2
3
4
5
6
7
8
Rudha na Fearn
Òb Chuaig
Callakille
Lonbain
Applecross Bay
Milton
Aird Dhu
M
Toscaig

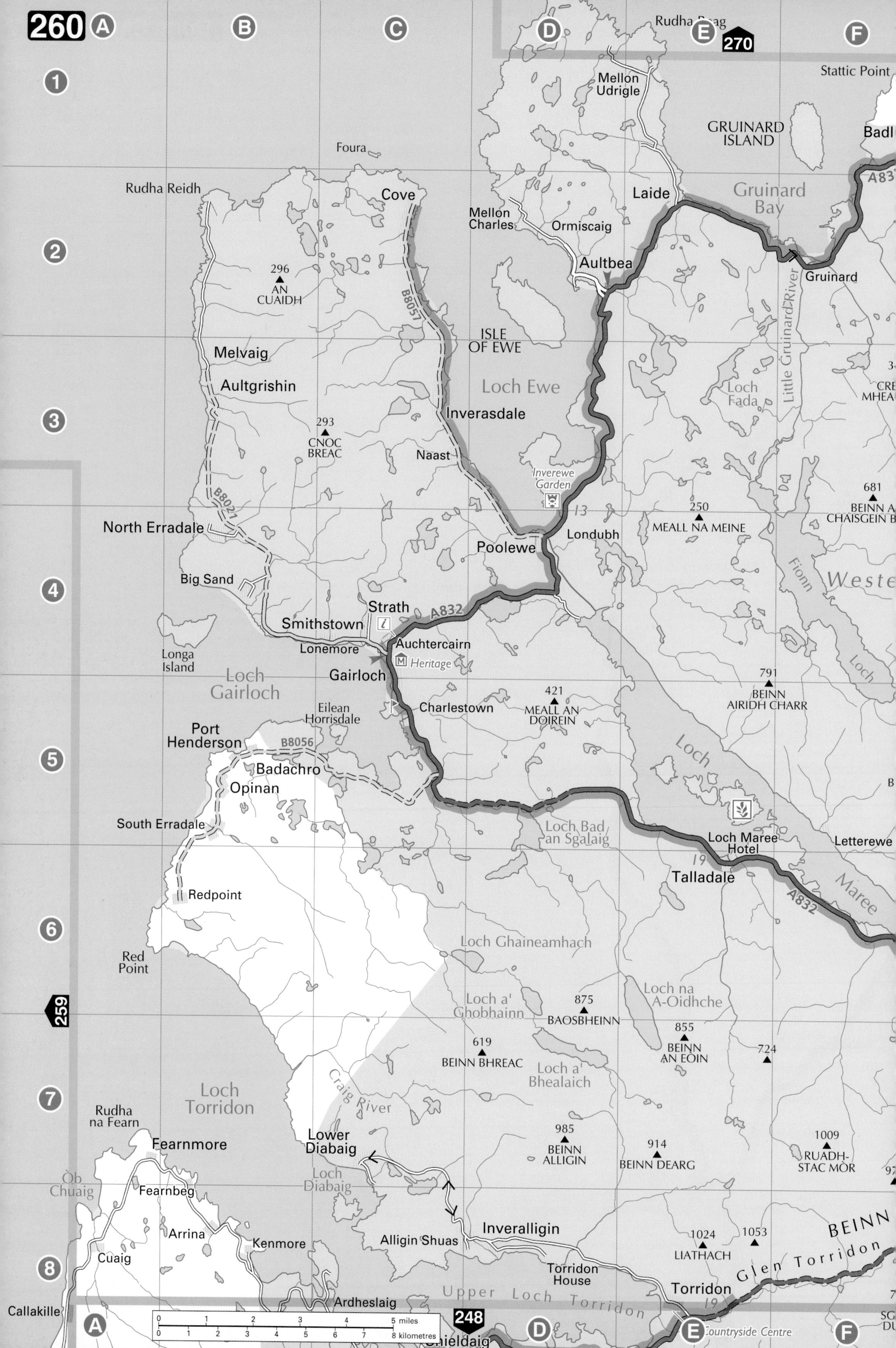

A
B
C
D
E
F
1
2
3
4
5
6
7
8
270
259
248
Rudha Reidh
Foura
Cove
Mellon Udrigle
Rudha Beag
Stattic Point
GRUINARD ISLAND
Badl
Laide
Gruinard Bay
A832
Mellon Charles
Ormiscaig
Aultbea
Gruinard
Little Gruinard River
296
AN CUAIDH
B8057
ISLE OF EWE
Melvaig
Aultgrishin
Loch Ewe
Loch Fada
Inverasdale
293
CNOC BREAC
Naast
Inverewe Garden
681
BEINN A' CHAISGEIN B
250
MEALL NA MEINE
B8021
North Erradale
Londubh
Poolewe
Fionn
Weste
Big Sand
Strath
A832
Smithstown
Longa Island
Lonemore
Auchtercairn
Heritage
Loch Gairloch
Gairloch
791
BEINN AIRIDH CHARR
Eilean Horrisdale
Charlestown
421
MEALL AN DOIREIN
Port Henderson
B8056
Badachro
Opinan
Loch
South Erradale
Loch Bad an Sgalaig
Loch Maree Hotel
Letterewe
Talladale
Maree
Redpoint
Loch Ghaineamhach
Red Point
Loch na A-Oidhche
Loch a' Ghobhainn
875
BAOSBHEINN
855
BEINN AN EOIN
619
BEINN BHREAC
724
Loch a' Bhealaich
Loch Torridon
Craig River
Rudha na Fearn
985
BEINN ALLIGIN
914
BEINN DEARG
1009
RUADH-STAC MÒR
Fearnmore
Lower Diabaig
Òb Chuaig
Loch Diabaig
Fearnbeg
Arrina
Inveralligin
Kenmore
Alligin Shuas
1024
LIATHACH
1053
BEINN
Glen Torridon
Cuaig
Torridon House
Torridon
Upper Loch Torridon
Callakille
Ardheslaig
Countryside Centre
Shieldaig
0 1 2 3 4 5 miles
0 1 2 3 4 5 6 7 8 kilometres

G
270
H
J
K
271
Ardmair
Annat Bay
Scoraig
Rhireavach
Morefield
Ullapool
(Ulapul)
Glen Achall
Loch Achall
Loch an Daimh
635
BEINN GHOBHLACH
Little Loch Broom
Badrallach
A835
558
BEINN EILIDEACH
Badcaul
Ardessie
Camusnagaul
Loch Broom
Leckmelm
642
MEALL DUBH
677
MEALL NAM BRADHAN
764
SAIL MHOR
32
Dundonnell
Ardindrean
Ardcharnich
Loch a' Choire Mhòi
Letters
647
CÀRN MÒR
262
Lochan Gaineamhaich
Inverlael
Strathnasheallag Forest
1062
AN TEALLACH
507
CARN BHIORAIN
Croftown
12
River Lael
R Broom
Loch na Sealga
1081
BEINN DEARG
Auchindrean
906
BEINN DEARG MHOR
387
CARN BREAC BEAG
Braemore
Corrieshalloch Gorge
Falls of Measach
Loch Coire Lair
618
MEALL LEACACHAIN
601
MEALL AN T-SITHE
A832
Loch a' Bhraoin
974
SGÙRRBÀN
1019
MULLACH COIRE MHIC FHEARCHAIR
Loch Droma
662
BEINN LIATH BHEAG
Lochan Fada
999
A' CHAILLEACH
1109
SGÙRR MÒR
981
SLIOCH
680
711
BEINN NAN RAMH
Fannich Lodge
Loch Fannich
680
BEINN A' MHÙINIDH
Kinlochewe Forest
558
AN CABAR
Beinn Eighe
Incheril
Kinlochewe
933
FIONN BHEINN
Strath Bran
Achanalt
A832
Loch Achanalt
Glen Docherty
A832
10
Achnasheen
Loch a' Chroisg
Loch Fhiarlaid
847
867
SCUIR VUILLIN
550
249
Loch Gowan
538
G
H
J
K
L
M
1
2
3
4
5
6
7
8

271
272
261
250
BEINN ULBHAIDH
412 CREAG LOISGTE
463 BREAC BHEINN
506 MEALL DHEIRGIDH
Loch an Daimh
Strath Mulzie
Brealangwell Lodge
701 CARN A' CHOIN DEIRG
Giasha Burn
Croick
Strathcarron
677
Loch a' Choire Mhòir
842 CARN BAN
River Carron
Glencalvie Forest
634 CÀRN BHREN
Gleann Beag
838 CÀRN CHUINNEAG
Crom Loch
710 BEINN THARSUINN
628
1081 BEINN DEARG
602 CÀRN CAS NAN GABHAR
Loch a' Chaorunn
Loch Coire Làir
771 MEALL A' GHRIANAIN
Strathkvaich Forest
Loch Morie
Loch Vaich
742 BEINN NAN EUN
742 TOM BÀN MÒR
Loch Droma
Loch Glascarnoch
737 MEALL MOR
Loch Glass
Aultguish Inn
20
A835
600
Inchbae Lodge Hotel
Glen Glass
680 BEINN DEARG
1045 BEN WYVIS
479
Ben Wyvis
Corriemoille Forest
Strath Garve
439 CÀRN NA DUBH CHOILLE
761 LITTLE WYVIS
558
Lochluichart
Corriemoille
484 CLOCH MHÒR
Gorstan
A832
16
Loch Luichart
Garve
Loch Achanalt
Loch Garve
Dingwall
(Inbhir Pheofharain)
579 SGÙRR MARCASAIDH
Rogie Falls
Auchterneed
A834
7
Strathpeffer
Gower
Highland Museum of Childhood
536
Loch Achilty
Keithtown
Little Scatwell
Jamestown
Loch Ussie
Loch Meig
Contin
R Conon
Conon Brid
6
0 1 2 3 4 5 miles
0 1 2 3 4 5 6 7 8 kilometres
A B C D E F
1 2 3 4 5 6 7 8

Sleasdairidh
349
BEINN DONUILL
Cambusavie Platform
Loch Fleet
River Evelix
Badninish
Skelbo
Skelbo Street
Fourpenny
Embo
Achvaich
Rearquhar
Birichin
Astle
Embo Street
Pitgrudy
Royal Dornoch
Evelix
Kyle of Sutherland
Lower
Bonar Bridge
Loch Migdale
Spinningdale
Clashmore
Camore
Dornoch
Historylinks
Ardgay
Kincardine
Upper Ardchronie
Whiteface
Dornoch Firth
Cuthill
Ferrytown
Ardmore
Cambuscurrie Bay
Ferry Point
Struie Hill
Innis Mhor
Edderton
477
BEINN CLACH AN FHEADAIN
Glenmorangie Distillery
Morangie
Inver
Aultnamain Inn
284
Tain
(Baile Dhubhthaich)
Toulva
Lochslin
Loch Eye
ROSS
692
BEINN THARSUINN
379
CNOC AN T-SABHAIL
Hill of Fearn
Newfield
Fearn
Tullich
Arabella
Ballchraggan
Shandwick
Kildary
Ankerville
Ardross
Rusdale
River Alness
Milton
Kilmuir
Achandunie
Delny
Rhicullen
Barbaraville
Pitcalnie
Nigg
Millcraig
Tomich
Nigg Bay
Moultavie
523
CNOC CEISLEIN
Balintraid
Achnagarron
Saltburn
Nigg Ferry
Alness
(Alanais)
Invergordon
Dalmore
(Jun-Oct)
Cromarty
Cromarty Firth
Balblair
Cromarty Bay
Hugh Miller's Cottage
Evanton
Resolis
Udale Bay
Newton
Navity
Allerton
Teanord
Jemimaville
Clanland & Seapoint
Cullicudden
Upper Eathie
Brae
Findon Mains
BLACK ISLE
Raddery
Whiteness Head
Culbokie
255
MOUNT EAGLE
Killen
Rosemarkie
Groam House
Cathedral
Fort George
Fortrose
Tradespark
Duncanston
Belmaduthy
Easter Kinkell
Knockbain
Chanonry Point
Avoch
Moss-side

A
B
C
D
E
F
273
Cambusavie Platform
Loch Fleet
Badninish
Skelbo
Skelbo Street
Achvaich
Fourpenny
Embo
Rearquhar
Birichin
Astle
Embo Street
B9168
Pitgrudy
Evelix
Royal Dornoch
A949
Clashmore
A9
Camore
Dornoch
Whiteface
Historylinks
Firth
Cuthill
263
Ferrytown
Ardmore
Cambuscurrie Bay
Ferry Point
Dornoch Firth
Innis Mhor
Tarbat Ness
Wilkhaven
Brucefield
Portmahomack
Glenmorangie Distillery
A836
Morangie
Inver
Rockfield
Arboll
B9165
284
Tain
(Baile Dhubhthaich)
Toulvaddie
Lochslin
Loch Eye
Hill of Fearn
Rhynie
Balmuchy
B9165
Newfield
Hilton of Cadboll Chapel (ruin)
Fearn
Tullich
B9166
Hilton
Arabella
Balintore
Shandwick
Shandwick Bay
Ballchraggan
Kildary
Ankerville
Milton
B9175
Kilmuir
Delny
Pitcalnie
Barbaraville
A9
Nigg
Nigg Bay
Balintraid
Saltburn
B817
Nigg Ferry
Invergordon
(Jun-Oct)
Cromarty
Cromarty Bay
Udale Bay
Hugh Miller's Cottage
Newton
B9163
Jemimaville
Allerton
263
Navity
MORAY FIRTH
Upper Eathie
A832
B9160
Culbin Forest
Kintessack
Raddery
Whiteness Head
Nairn
(Inbhir Nàrann)
Brodie Castle
Rosemarkie
Cathedral
Groam House
Fort George
Tradespark
Brodie
A96
B9092
Boath Doocot
252
253
Avoch
Household
0 1 2 3 4 5 miles
0 1 2 3 4 5 6 7 8 kilometres

G
H
J
K
L
1
2
3
4
5
6
7
8
M
Branderburgh
Stotfield
Lossiemouth
B9040
Burghead Well
Hopeman
Burnside
Burghead
B9012
Duffus
St Peter's Kirk & Parish Cross
Cummingston
B9013
B9135
Loch Spynie
Roseisle
B9012
Duffus Castle
Burghead Bay
College of Roseisle
A941
Spynie Palace
Stonewells
Lochill
B9103
Viewfield
Findhorn
Hempriggs
B9089
Quarrywood
B9011
Bishopmill
Elgin
Calcots
Innesmill
Findhorn Bay
Kinloss
Newton
A96
Coltfield
Glen Moray Distillery
Urquhart
Alves
New Elgin
Lhanbryde
The Lochs
266
Grange Hall
Kilbuiack
Linkwood
Mosstodloch
Muir of Miltonduff
Crofts of Dipple
Clackmarras
B9103
Forres
Pluscarden
Califer
Barnhill
Longmorn
Rafford
Fogwatt
Millbuies
B9015
Dallas Dhu Distillery
253
B9010
B9010
Inchberry
Shougle
Kellas
Glen

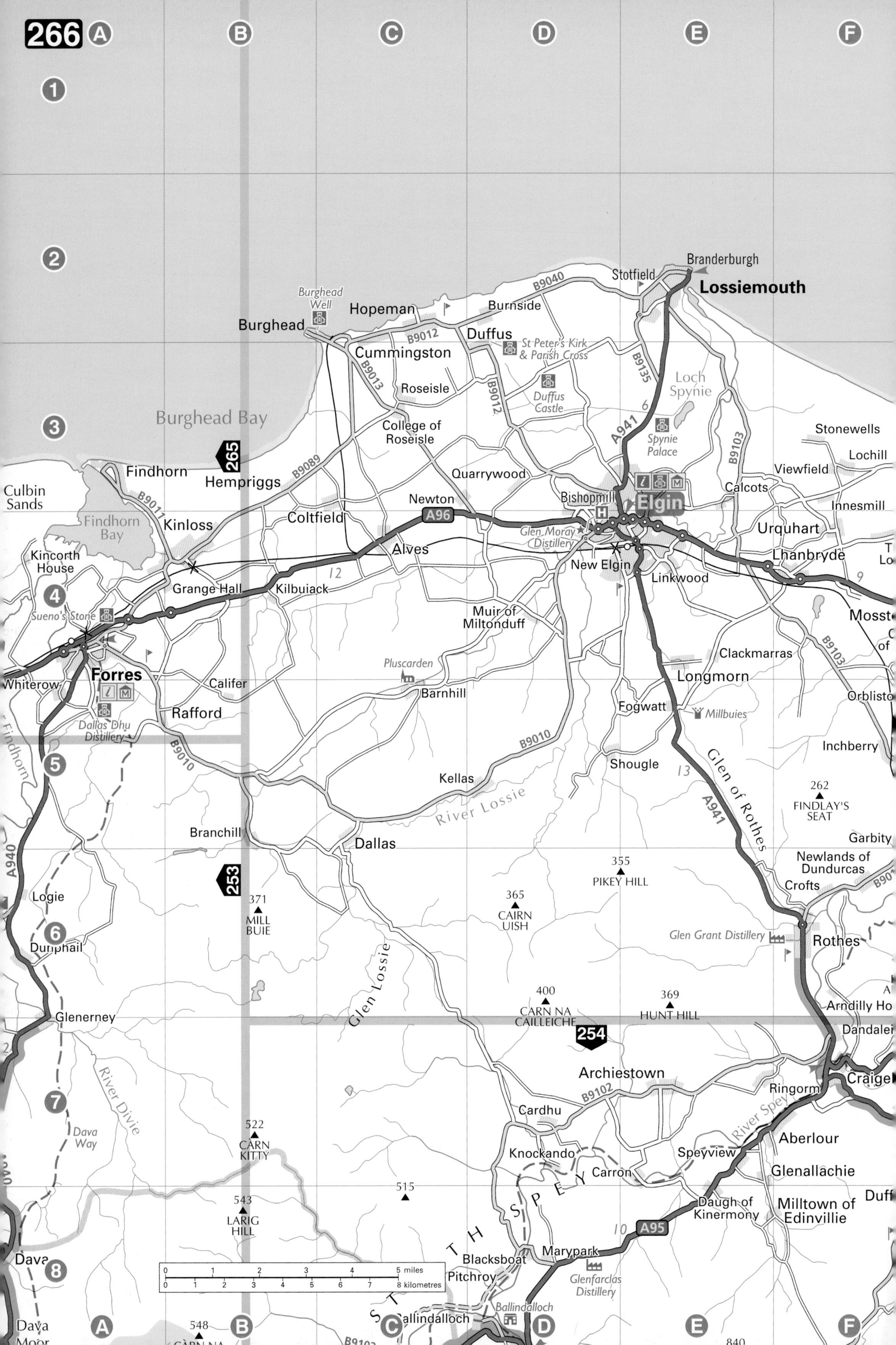

Branderburgh
Stotfield
Lossiemouth
Burghead Well
Hopeman
Burnside
Burghead
Cummingston
Duffus
St Peter's Kirk & Parish Cross
Roseisle
Loch Spynie
Duffus Castle
Burghead Bay
College of Roseisle
Spynie Palace
Stonewells
Lochill
Findhorn
Hempriggs
Quarrywood
Viewfield
Culbin Sands
Bishopmill
Calcots
Elgin
Newton
Innesmill
Findhorn Bay
Kinloss
Coltfield
Glen Moray Distillery
Urquhart
Kincorth House
Alves
New Elgin
Lhanbryde
Grange Hall
Kilbuiack
Linkwood
Sueno's Stone
Muir of Miltonduff
Clackmarras
Pluscarden
Longmorn
Forres
Whiterow
Califer
Barnhill
Fogwatt
Millbuies
Orbliston
Rafford
Dallas Dhu Distillery
Inchberry
Shougle
Glen of Rothes
Kellas
River Lossie
262 FINDLAY'S SEAT
Branchill
Dallas
Garbity
355 PIKEY HILL
Newlands of Dundurcas
Crofts
365 CAIRN UISH
371 MILL BUIE
Logie
Glen Grant Distillery
Rothes
Dunphail
Glen Lossie
400 CARN NA CAILLEICHE
369 HUNT HILL
Arndilly Ho
Glenerney
Dandaleith
Archiestown
Ringorm
Craigellachie
River Divie
Cardhu
River Spey
Aberlour
Dava Way
522 CARN KITTY
Knockando
Speyview
Carron
Glenallachie
515
STRATHSPEY
543 LARIG HILL
Daugh of Kinermony
Milltown of Edinvillie
Marypark
Blacksboat
Dava
Pitchroy
Glenfarclas Distillery
Ballindalloch
Dava Moor
548
840
A96
A941
A940
A95
B9040
B9012
B9013
B9135
B9089
B9011
B9103
B9010
B9102
265
253
254
0 1 2 3 4 5 miles
0 1 2 3 4 5 6 7 8 kilometres

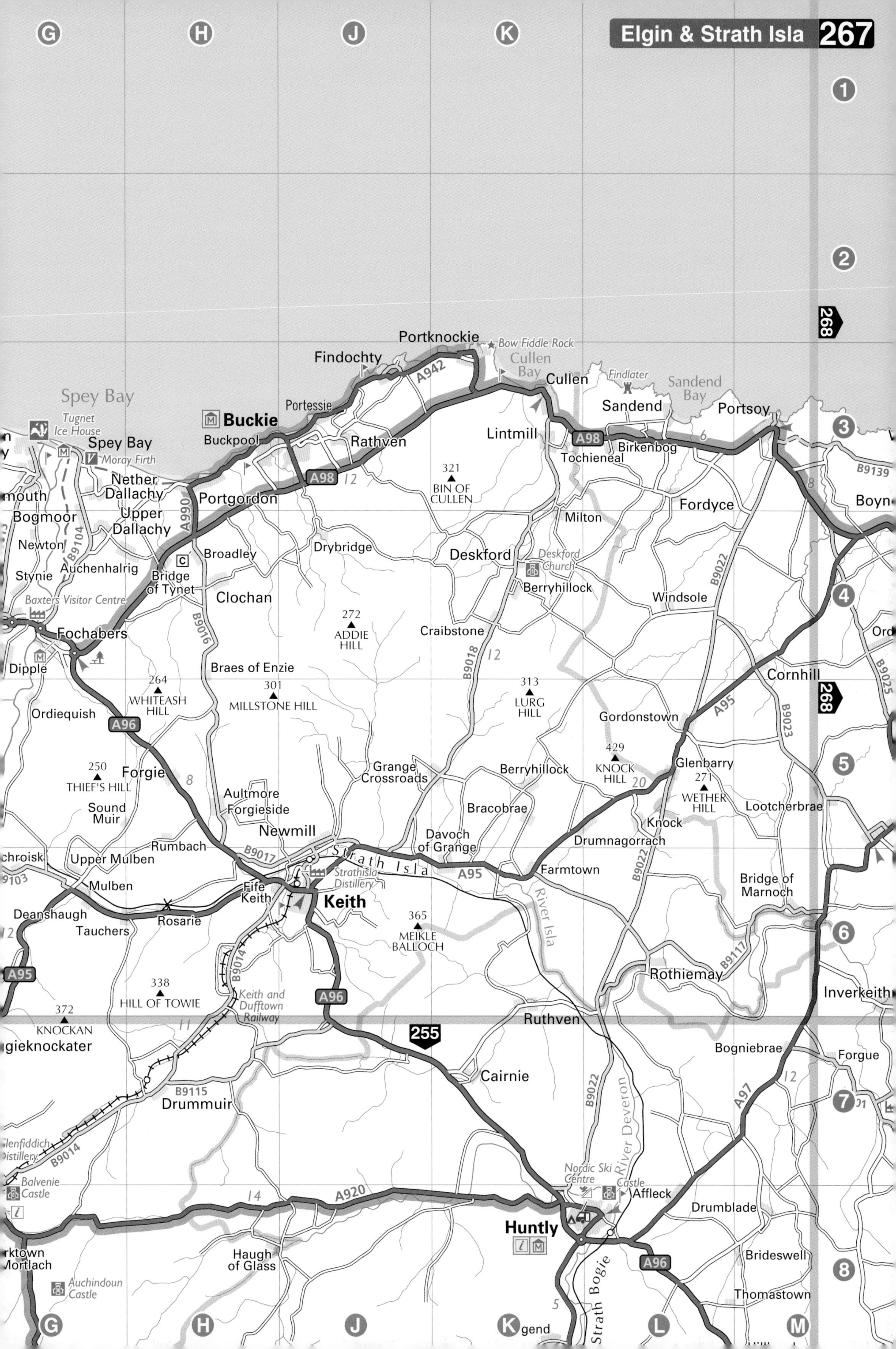
Spey Bay
Tugnet Ice House
Spey Bay
Moray Firth
Findochty
Portknockie
Bow Fiddle Rock
Cullen Bay
Cullen
Findlater
Sandend Bay
Sandend
Portsoy
Portessie
Buckie
Buckpool
Rathven
Lintmill
Tochieneal
Birkenbog
Nether Dallachy
Upper Dallachy
Portgordon
321 BIN OF CULLEN
Fordyce
Boyn
Bogmoor
Newton
Stynie
Auchenhalrig
Bridge of Tynet
Broadley
Drybridge
Deskford
Deskford Church
Milton
Berryhillock
Windsole
Baxters Visitor Centre
Clochan
Fochabers
272 ADDIE HILL
Craibstone
Dipple
Braes of Enzie
264 WHITEASH HILL
301 MILLSTONE HILL
313 LURG HILL
Cornhill
Ordiequish
Gordonstown
429 KNOCK HILL
Glenbarry
271 WETHER HILL
250 THIEF'S HILL
Forgie
Grange Crossroads
Berryhillock
Bracobrae
Lootcherbrae
Sound Muir
Aultmore
Forgieside
Newmill
Knock
Drumnagorrach
Davoch of Grange
Rumbach
Upper Mulben
Strath Isla
Farmtown
Mulben
Fife Keith
Strathisla Distillery
Keith
Bridge of Marnoch
Deanshaugh
Rosarie
Tauchers
365 MEIKLE BALLOCH
River Isla
Rothiemay
Inverkeith
338 HILL OF TOWIE
Keith and Dufftown Railway
372 KNOCKAN
Ruthven
Bogniebrae
Forgue
Cairnie
Drummuir
Glenfiddich Distillery
River Deveron
Nordic Ski Centre
Castle
Affleck
Drumblade
Balvenie Castle
Huntly
Haugh of Glass
Brideswell
Auchindoun Castle
Thomastown
Strath Bogie
A98
A942
A990
B9104
B9016
B9018
B9022
B9023
B9025
B9139
A96
A95
B9017
B9014
B9117
B9115
A920
A97

268
268
255

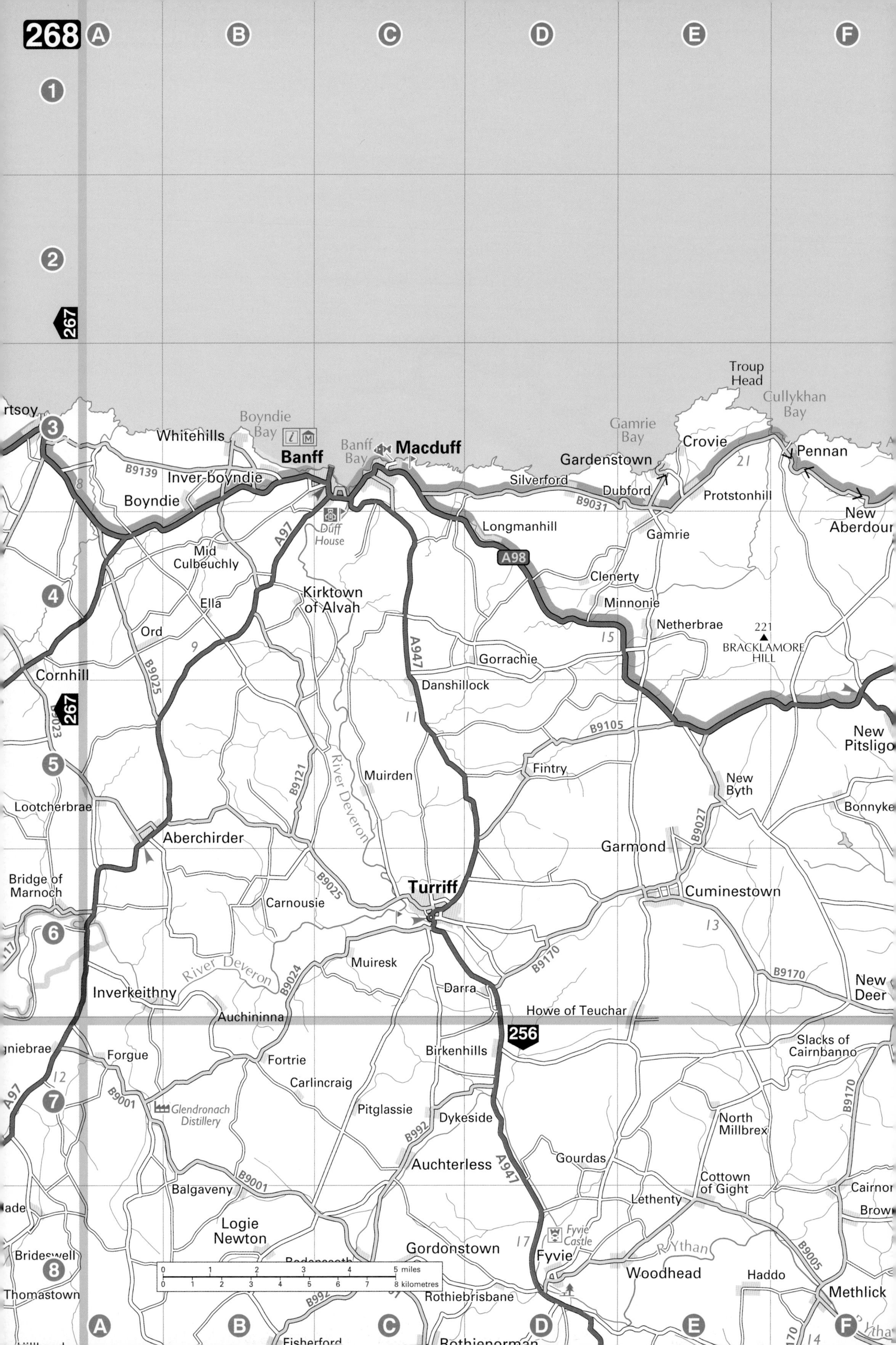

A
B
C
D
E
F
1
2
3
4
5
6
7
8
267
Troup Head
Cullykhan Bay
Gamrie Bay
Boyndie Bay
Banff Bay
rtsoy
Whitehills
Banff
Macduff
Crovie
Pennan
Gardenstown
Silverford
Dubford
Protstonhill
New Aberdour
B9139
Inver-boyndie
Boyndie
Duff House
Longmanhill
B9031
Gamrie
A98
A97
Mid Culbeuchly
Ella
Ord
Kirktown of Alvah
Clenerty
Minnonie
Netherbrae
221
BRACKLAMORE HILL
A947
Gorrachie
Danshillock
Cornhill
B9025
B9023
B9105
New Pitsligo
Fintry
Muirden
River Deveron
B9121
New Byth
Bonnyke
Lootcherbrae
Aberchirder
B9027
Garmond
Bridge of Marnoch
Turriff
Cuminestown
Carnousie
Muiresk
B9170
River Deveron
B9024
Inverkeithny
Darra
New Deer
Howe of Teuchar
Auchininna
256
Slacks of Cairnbanno
niebrae
Forgue
Fortrie
Birkenhills
Carlincraig
B9001
Glendronach Distillery
Pitglassie
B992
Dykeside
North Millbrex
Auchterless
Gourdas
Cottown of Gight
Balgaveny
Cairnor
Lethenty
Brow
ade
Logie Newton
Fyvie Castle
R. Ythan
Brideswell
Gordonstown
Fyvie
B9005
Woodhead
Haddo
Methlick
Thomastown
Rothiebrisbane
0 1 2 3 4 5 miles
0 1 2 3 4 5 6 7 8 kilometres
Fisherford
Rothienorman

G
H
J
K
1
2
3
4
5
6
7
8
Castle Lighthouse & Museum
Rosehearty
Sandhaven
Kinnaird Head
Pittulie
Fraserburgh
Peathill
Fraserburgh Bay
aigiefold
Kirktown
Cairnbulg
Percyhorner
Maggie's Hoosie
Inverallochy
B9031
Coburby
Pitblae
Whitelinks Bay
Mid Ardlaw
A90
B9033
St Combs
B9032
dlie
10
Memsie
A98
Memsie Cairn
Rathen
Crofts of Savoch
12
A981
Newburgh
Lonmay
Rattray Head
RSPB
Loch of Strathbeg
234
WAUGHTON HILL
12
Blackhill
Crimond
B9093
A952
Strichen
18
New Leeds
B9093
Leys
Kirktown
Denhead
Backfolds
St Fergus
Fetterangus
Rora
A90
A950
A981
6
Deer Abbey
River Ugie
B9106
Dunshillock
Maud
Aden
Inverugie
B9029
B9029
Mintlaw
Longside
Old Deer
Blackhill of Clackriach
Buchanhaven
A950
Peterhead
Peterhead
B9028
Stuartfield
257
Inverquhomery
9
Drymuir
Bulwark
A982
Peterhead Bay
Millbreck
Hillhead of Cocklaw
Nether Kinmundy
Nethermuir
Burnhaven
Clola
B9030
Kinnadie
Buchan Ness
Blackhill
Stirling
Boddam
uchnagatt
Lendrum Terrace
Kinknockie
12
Longhaven
Inkhorn
Ardallie
A90
Bullers of Buchan
Coldwells
A948
A952
Auchiries
Hatton
North Haven
Arthrat
Muirtack
Slains
14
17
L
M
Cruden Bay

A
B
C
D
E
F
1
2
3
4
5
6
7
8
Point of Stoer
OLDANY ISLAND
Eddrachillis Bay
Old Man of Stoer
Culkein Drumbeg
Culkein
Clashnessie Bay
Oldany
Drumbeg
Achnacarnin
Nedd
Clashmore
Clashnessie
Loch Poll
Stoer
Clachtoll
B869
Bay of Clachtoll
Loch Beannach
Rhicarn
Achmelvich Bay
Achmelvich
A837
Baddidarrach
Soyea Island
Loch Inver
Lochinver
Strathan
Inverkirkaig
River Kirkaig
Rhu Coigach
Fionn Loch
Eilean Mòr
Enard Bay
Rubha Mòr
Reiff
Achnahaird
Loch Sionasc
Altandhu
Eilean Mullagrach
Loch Osgaig
Isle Ristol
Polbain
612
STAC POLLAIDH
Glas-leac Mòr
SUMMER ISLES
769
Achiltibuie
Loch Lurgainn
Tanera Beg
Badentarbat Bay
Polglass
Steornabhagh (Stornoway)
Ben Mor Coigach
Tanera Mòr
Glas-leac Beag
Horse Island
Horse Sound
COIGACH
652
Achduart
BEN MORE COIGACH
Culnacraig
Eilean Dubh
Priest Island
Strathcanaird
Greenstone Point
Leac Dhonn
Cailleach Head
Isle Martin
A835
Rudha Beag
Ardmair
Scoraig
Annat Bay
0 1 2 3 4 5 miles
0 1 2 3 4 5 6 7 8 kilometres
Rhireavach

261

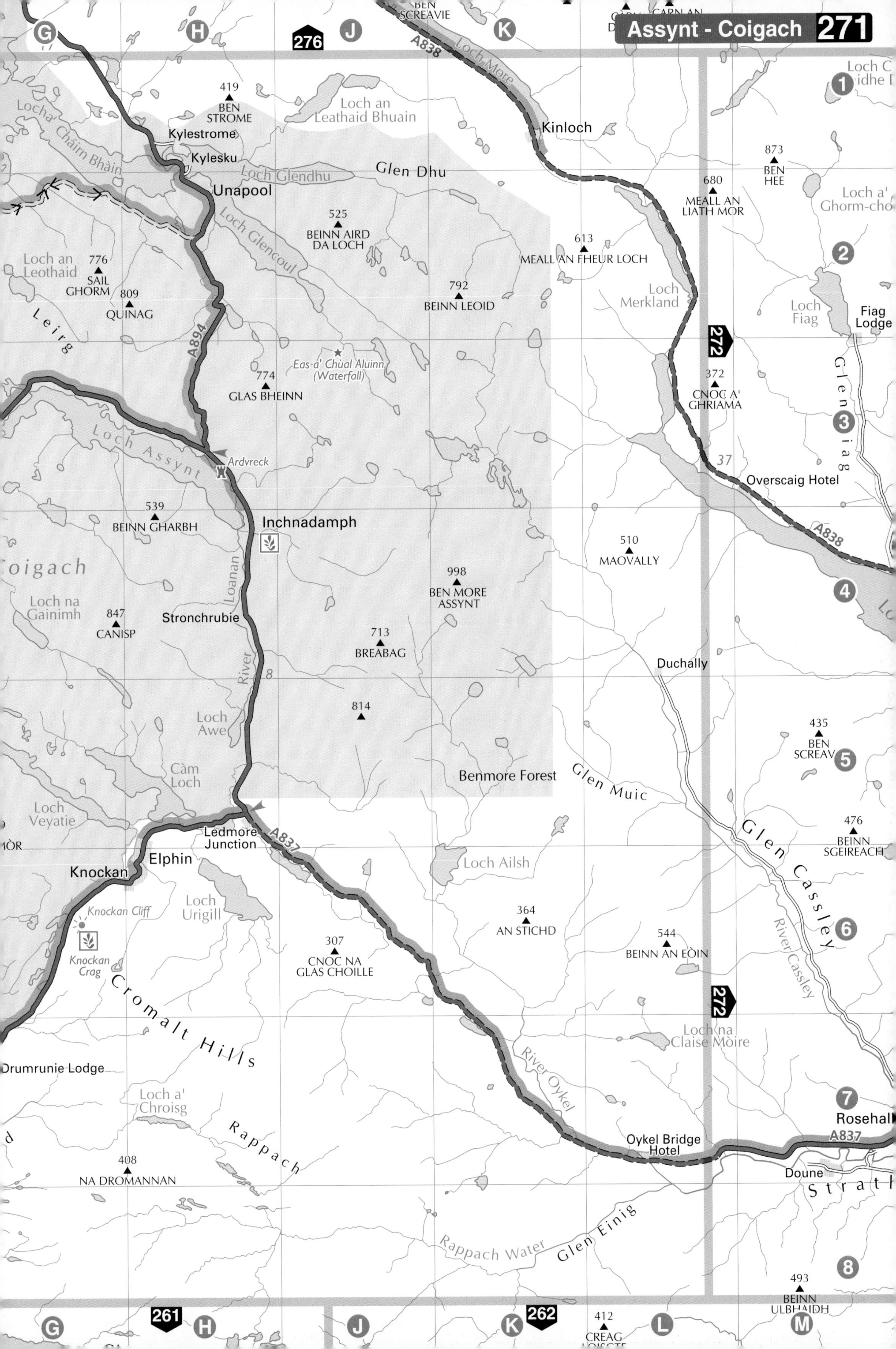
Kylestrome
Kylesku
Unapool
Loch Glendhu
Glen Dhu
Loch Glencoul
Loch an Leathaid Bhuain
419 BEN STROME
525 BEINN AIRD DA LOCH
776 SAIL GHORM
809 QUINAG
Loch an Leothaid
792 BEINN LEOID
613 MEALL AN FHEUR LOCH
Kinloch
Loch More
A838
Loch Merkland
680 MEALL AN LIATH MOR
873 BEN HEE
Loch Fiag
Fiag Lodge
Glen Fiag
Eas a' Chùal Aluinn (Waterfall)
774 GLAS BHEINN
372 CNOC A' GHRIAMA
Loch Assynt
Ardvreck
A894
Overscaig Hotel
539 BEINN GHARBH
Inchnadamph
510 MAOVALLY
998 BEN MORE ASSYNT
Coigach
Loch na Gainimh
847 CANISP
Stronchrubie
River Loanan
713 BREABAG
Duchally
814
Loch Awe
Càm Loch
Loch Veyatie
Benmore Forest
Glen Muic
435 BEN SCREAVIE
476 BEINN SGEIREACH
Ledmore Junction
A837
Elphin
Knockan
Loch Ailsh
Glen Cassley
Knockan Cliff
Knockan Crag
Loch Urigill
364 AN STICHD
307 CNOC NA GLAS CHOILLE
544 BEINN AN EÒIN
River Cassley
Cromalt Hills
Loch na Claise Mòire
Drumrunie Lodge
River Oykel
Loch a' Chroisg
Rappach
Oykel Bridge Hotel
Rosehall
Doune
408 NA DROMANNAN
Rappach Water
Glen Einig
493 BEINN ULBHAIDH
412 CREAG
276
272
261
262
G H J K L M
1 2 3 4 5 6 7 8

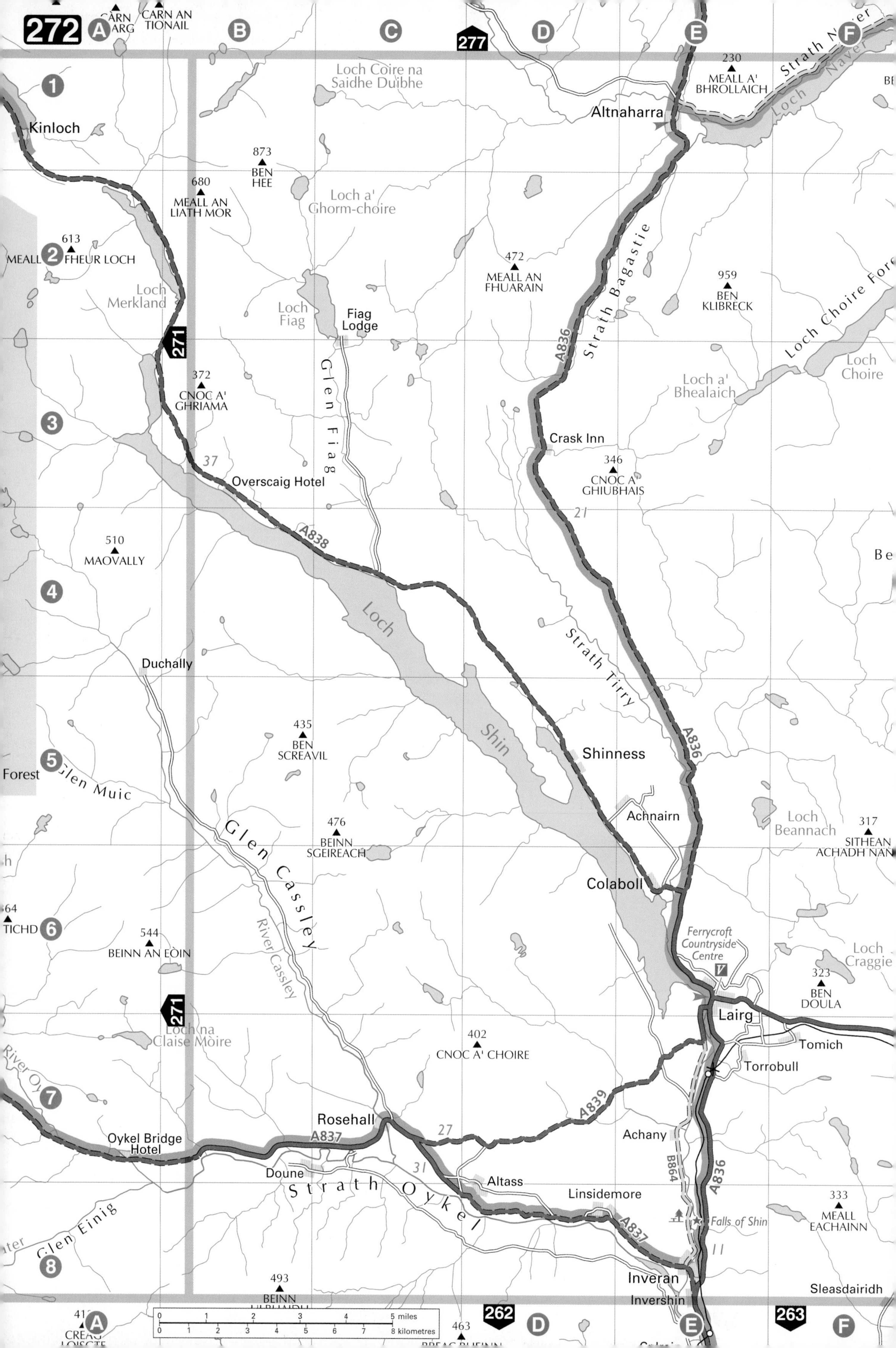

CARN ARG
CARN AN TIONAIL
277
Loch Coire na Saidhe Duibhe
Strath Naver
230
MEALL A' BHROLLAICH
Loch Naver
Kinloch
Altnaharra
873
BEN HEE
680
MEALL AN LIATH MOR
Loch a' Ghorm-choire
613
MEALL FHEUR LOCH
472
MEALL AN FHUARAIN
Strath Bagastie
959
BEN KLIBRECK
Loch Choire Forest
Loch Merkland
Loch Fiag
Fiag Lodge
271
A836
372
CNOC A' GHRIAMA
Glen Fiag
Loch Choire
Loch a' Bhealaich
Crask Inn
37
Overscaig Hotel
346
CNOC A' GHIUBHAIS
21
A838
510
MAOVALLY
Loch Shin
Strath Tirry
Duchally
435
BEN SCREAVIL
Shinness
Forest
Glen Muic
Achnairn
Glen Cassley
476
BEINN SGEIREACH
Loch Beannach
317
SITHEAN ACHADH NAN
Colaboll
River Cassley
TICHD
544
BEINN AN EÒIN
Ferrycroft Countryside Centre
Loch Craggie
323
BEN DOULA
Lairg
Loch na Claise Mòire
402
CNOC A' CHOIRE
Tomich
Torrobull
River Oykel
A839
Rosehall
27
Achany
Oykel Bridge Hotel
A837
Doune
31
Altass
Strath Oykel
Linsidemore
B864
333
MEALL EACHAINN
Falls of Shin
Glen Einig
11
493
Inveran
Invershin
Sleasdairidh
262
263
5 miles
8 kilometres
463

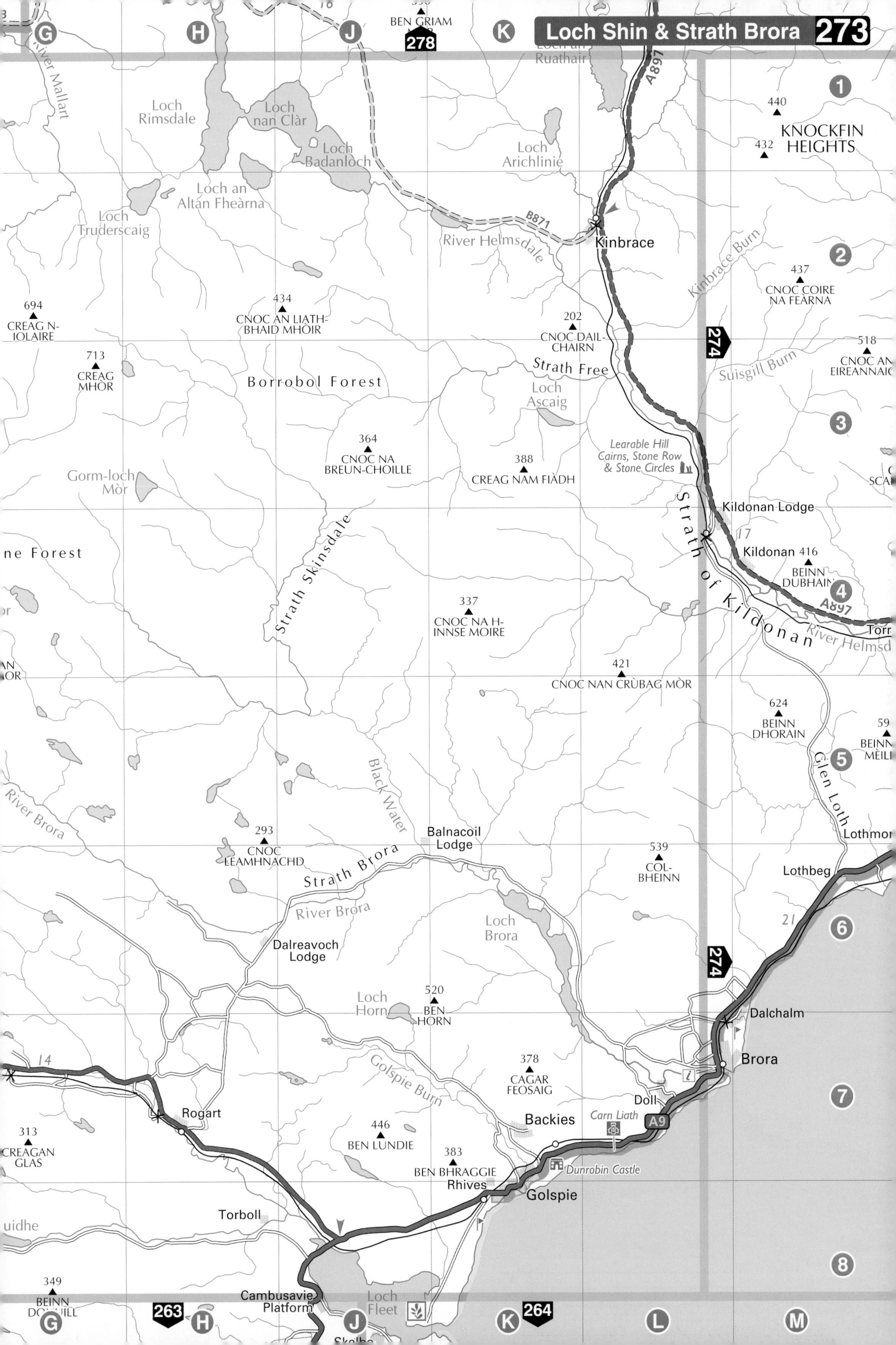

Loch Rimsdale
Loch nan Clàr
Loch Badanloch
Loch an Altan Fheàrna
Loch Truderscaig
River Mallart
Loch Arichlinie
Kinbrace
River Helmsdale
B871
A897
KNOCKFIN HEIGHTS
440
432
437
CNOC COIRE NA FEÀRNA
Kinbrace Burn
694
CREAG N-IOLAIRE
434
CNOC AN LIATH-BHAID MHÒIR
202
CNOC DAIL-CHAIRN
713
CREAG MHÒR
Borrobol Forest
Strath Free
Loch Ascaig
Suisgill Burn
518
364
CNOC NA BREUN-CHOILLE
388
CREAG NAM FIÀDH
Learable Hill Cairns, Stone Row & Stone Circles
Gorm-loch Mòr
Strath Skinsdale
Strath of Kildonan
Kildonan Lodge
Kildonan
416
BEINN DUBHAIN
337
CNOC NA H-INNSE MOIRE
421
CNOC NAN CRÙBAG MÒR
624
BEINN DHORAIN
River Brora
Black Water
Glen Loth
Lothmor
Lothbeg
293
CNOC LEAMHNACHD
Strath Brora
Balnacoil Lodge
539
COL-BHEINN
Loch Brora
Dalreavoch Lodge
520
BEN HORN
Loch Horn
Dalchalm
Brora
378
CAGAR FEOSAIG
Golspie Burn
Doll
Backies
Carn Liath
A9
Rogart
313
CREAGAN GLAS
446
BEN LUNDIE
383
BEN BHRAGGIE
Dunrobin Castle
Rhives
Golspie
Torboll
349
Cambusavie Platform
Loch Fleet
278
274
263
264

279
273
Glutt Lodge
348 BEN ALISKY
440
KNOCKFIN HEIGHTS
432
264 CNOCAN CONACHREAG
Loch Ruathair
Loch richlinie
A897
B871
Kinbrace
317 CNOC LOCH MHADADH
Dunbeath
Berriedale Water
Kinbrace Burn
437 CNOC COIRE NA FEARNA
484 MAIDEN PAP
Braemore
202 CNOC DAIL-CHAIRN
705 MORVEN
Knock
Strath Free
Suisgill Burn
518 CNOC AN EIREANNAICH
626 SCARABEN
Ramscr
Loch Ascaig
Langwell Forest
Learable Hill Cairns, Stone Row & Stone Circles
388 NAM FIÀDH
554 CREAG SCALABSDALE
Newport
Langwell House
Berried
Strath of Kildonan
Kildonan Lodge
Kildonan
416 BEINN DUBHAIN
401 CNOC NA MAOILE
A9
404 CREAG THORARAIDH
Torrish
River Helmsdale
Ord of Caithness
421 CNOC NAN CRÙBAG MÒR
Timespan
Navidale House Hotel
624 BEINN DHORAIN
591 BEINN NA MÈILICH
West Helmsdale
East Helmsdale
Helmsdale
Gartymore
Portgower
Glen Loth
Lothmore
539 COL-BHEINN
Lothbeg
Dalchalm
Brora
378 AGAR OSAIG
Doll
Backies
Carn Liath
Dunrobin Castle
Golspie
0 1 2 3 4 5 miles
0 1 2 3 4 5 6 7 8 kilometres

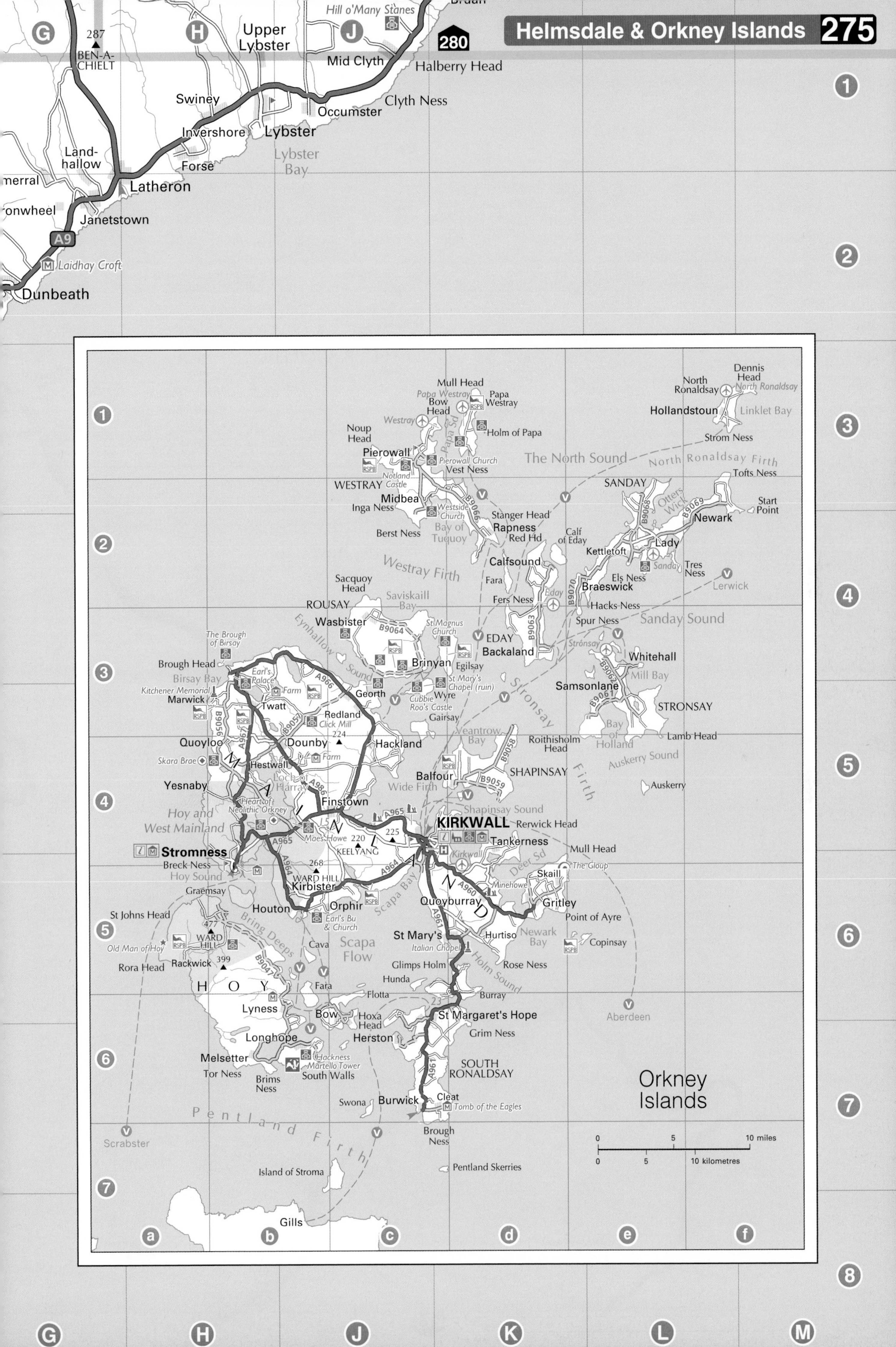
Upper Lybster
Hill o'Many Stanes
Mid Clyth
Halberry Head
280
BEN-A-CHIELT
287
Swiney
Occumster
Clyth Ness
Invers
shore
Lybster
Lybster Bay
Land-hallow
Forse
Latheron
Janetstown
A9
Laidhay Croft
Dunbeath
Orkney Islands
Mull Head
Papa Westray
Bow Head
Papa Westray
Holm of Papa
Westray
Noup Head
Pierowall
Pierowall Church
Notland Castle
Vest Ness
WESTRAY
Midbea
Inga Ness
Westside Church
Bay of Tuquoy
Berst Ness
The North Sound
North Ronaldsay
Dennis Head
Hollandstoun
Linklet Bay
Strom Ness
North Ronaldsay Firth
Tofts Ness
SANDAY
Otters Wick
Newark
Start Point
Stanger Head
Rapness
Red Hd
Calf of Eday
Lady
Kettletoft
Sanday
Tres Ness
Calfsound
Els Ness
Braeswick
Lerwick
Westray Firth
Fara
Sacquoy Head
Saviskaill Bay
Eday
Fers Ness
Hacks Ness
ROUSAY
Wasbister
Spur Ness
Sanday Sound
St Magnus Church
EDAY
Backaland
Stronsay
Whitehall
Brinyan
Egilsay
Mill Bay
Samsonlane
The Brough of Birsay
Brough Head
Birsay Bay
Earl's Palace
Kitchener Memorial
Marwick
Twatt
Farm
Georth
St Mary's Chapel (ruin)
Cubbie Roo's Castle
Wyre
Gairsay
Redland
Click Mill
224
STRONSAY
Bay of Holland
Lamb Head
Roithisholm Head
Quoyloo
Dounby
Hackland
Veantrow Bay
Skara Brae
Hestwall
Farm
Loch of Harray
Balfour
SHAPINSAY
Auskerry Sound
Auskerry
Yesnaby
Wide Firth
Finstown
Heart of Neolithic Orkney
Shapinsay Sound
Hoy and West Mainland
KIRKWALL
Rerwick Head
Maes Howe
220
KEELYANG
225
Tankerness
Stromness
Kirkwall
Mull Head
The Gloup
Breck Ness
Hoy Sound
268
WARD HILL
Kirbister
Deer Sd
Skaill
Minehowe
Graemsay
Houton
Orphir
Scapa Bay
Quoyburray
Gritley
St Johns Head
Earl's Bu & Church
Point of Ayre
477
WARD HILL
Bring Deeps
Cava
Scapa Flow
St Mary's
Italian Chapel
Hurtiso
Newark Bay
Copinsay
Old Man of Hoy
399
Rackwick
Rora Head
Glimps Holm
Holm Sound
Rose Ness
Hunda
HOY
Fara
Flotta
Burray
Lyness
Bow
Hoxa Head
St Margaret's Hope
Aberdeen
Longhope
Herston
Grim Ness
Melsetter
Hackness Martello Tower
SOUTH RONALDSAY
Tor Ness
Brims Ness
South Walls
Swona
Burwick
Cleat
Tomb of the Eagles
Pentland Firth
Scrabster
Brough Ness
Island of Stroma
Pentland Skerries
Gills
A965
A966
A967
A986
A964
A960
A961
B9056
B9057
B9064
B9066
B9068
B9069
B9063
B9070
B9058
B9059
B9062
B9061
B9047
0 5 10 miles
0 5 10 kilometres
MAINLAND
G H J K L M

A
B
C
D
E
F
1
2
3
4
5
6
7
8
CAPE WRATH
Cléit Dhubh
371 SGRIBHIS-BHEINN
Faraid Head
297 CNOC A GHIUBHAIS
300 MAOVALLY
Balnakeil Bay
Balnakeil
Durness
Sangomo
Keold
THE PARPH
457 FASHVEN
Sandwood Bay
Loch Airigh na Beinne
Kyle of Durness
Sandwood Loch
485 CREAG RIABACH
Rudh' an Fhir Leithe
468 BEINN DEARG MHÒR
464 MEALL NA MÒINE
Strath Shinary
331 GHLAS-BHEINN
A838
Sheigra
Balchreick
Blairmore
Oldshoremore
521 FARVEALL
19
489 MEALL NA CRÀ
355 AN SOCACH
Kinlochbervie
773 BEINN SPIONNAIDH
Loch Clash
Badcall
B801
801 CRANSTACKIE
Loch Inchard
Achriesgill
Strath Dionard
River Dionard
Strath Beag
Rhiconich
Loch na Claise Càrnaich
Rudha Ruadh
908 FOINAVEN
Fanagmore
Skerricha
Loch Laxford
Tarbet
A838
HANDA ISLAND
Foindle
North-west Sutherland
Loch na Tuadh
River Laxford
786 ARKLE
Scourie Bay
7
Laxford Bridge
A894
Scourie
Scourie More
Loch Stack
729 SÀBHAL BEAG
721 BEN STACK
Badcall
Strath Stack
Badcall Bay
386 BEN AUSKAIRD
Loch a' Mhuilinn
Achfary
333 BEN SCREAVIE
800
796 CÀRN DEARG
757 CARN A TIONA
Rudh' a' Mhucard
17
A838
Loch More
0 1 2 3 4 5 miles
0 1 2 3 4 5 6 7 8 kilometres

271

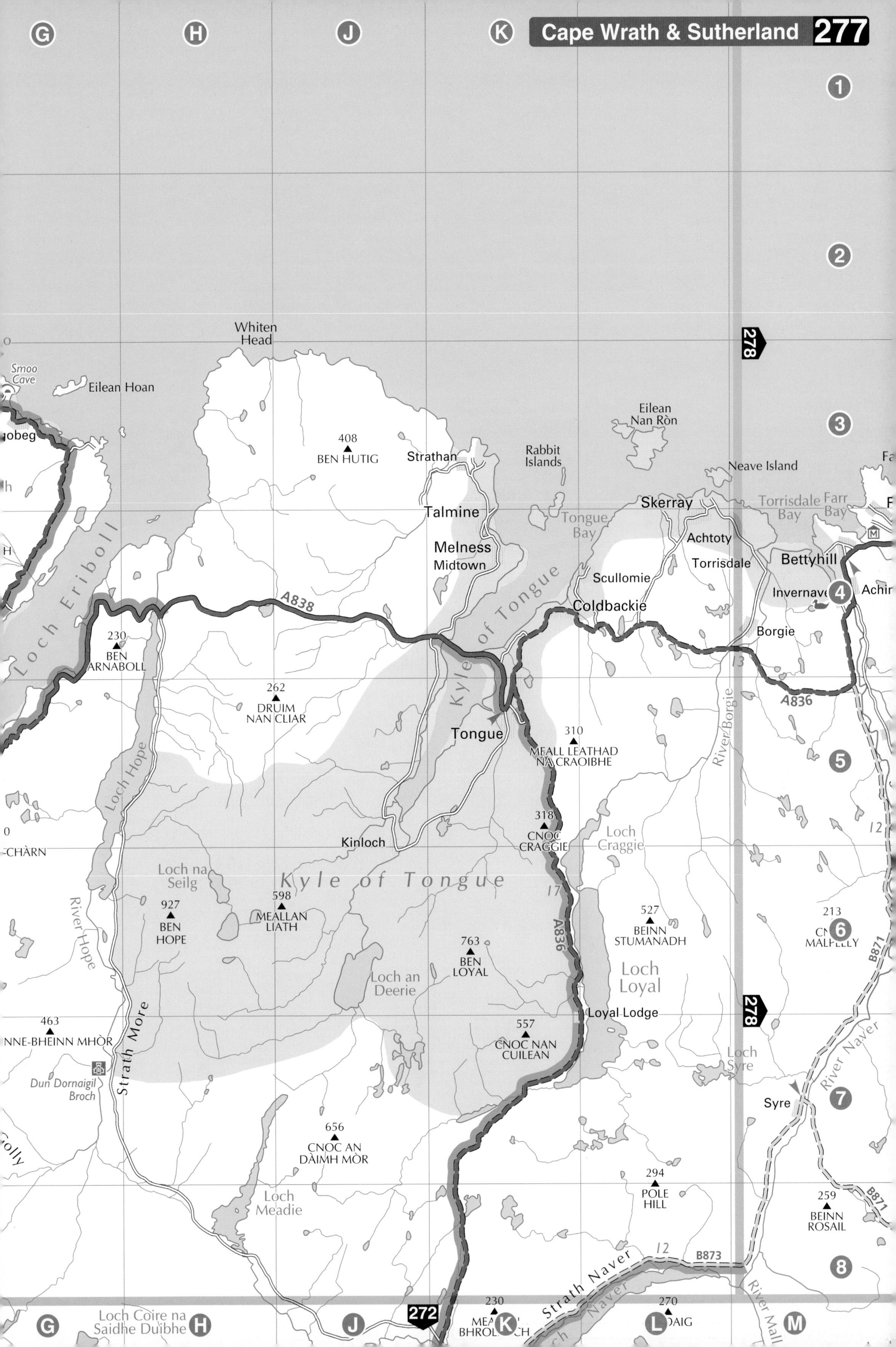

Whiten Head
Smoo Cave
Eilean Hoan
Loch Eriboll
408 BEN HUTIG
Strathan
Talmine
Melness
Midtown
Rabbit Islands
Eilean Nan Ròn
Neave Island
Skerray
Tongue Bay
Achtoty
Torrisdale
Torrisdale Bay
Farr Bay
Bettyhill
Scullomie
Coldbackie
Invernaver
Borgie
A838
A836
230 BEN ARNABOLL
262 DRUIM NAN CLIAR
Kyle of Tongue
Tongue
310 MEALL LEATHAD NA CRAOIBHE
River Borgie
Loch Hope
318 CNOC CRAGGIE
Loch Craggie
Kinloch
Loch na Seilg
598 MEALLAN LIATH
927 BEN HOPE
River Hope
763 BEN LOYAL
Loch an Deerie
527 BEINN STUMANADH
Loch Loyal
Loyal Lodge
213 MALPELLY
B871
463
557 CNOC NAN CUILEAN
Strath More
Dun Dornaigil Broch
Loch Syre
River Naver
Syre
656 CNOC AN DÀIMH MÒR
294 POLE HILL
259 BEINN ROSAIL
Loch Meadie
B873
Strath Naver
River Mall
230
270
Loch Coire na Saidhe Duibhe

278
272

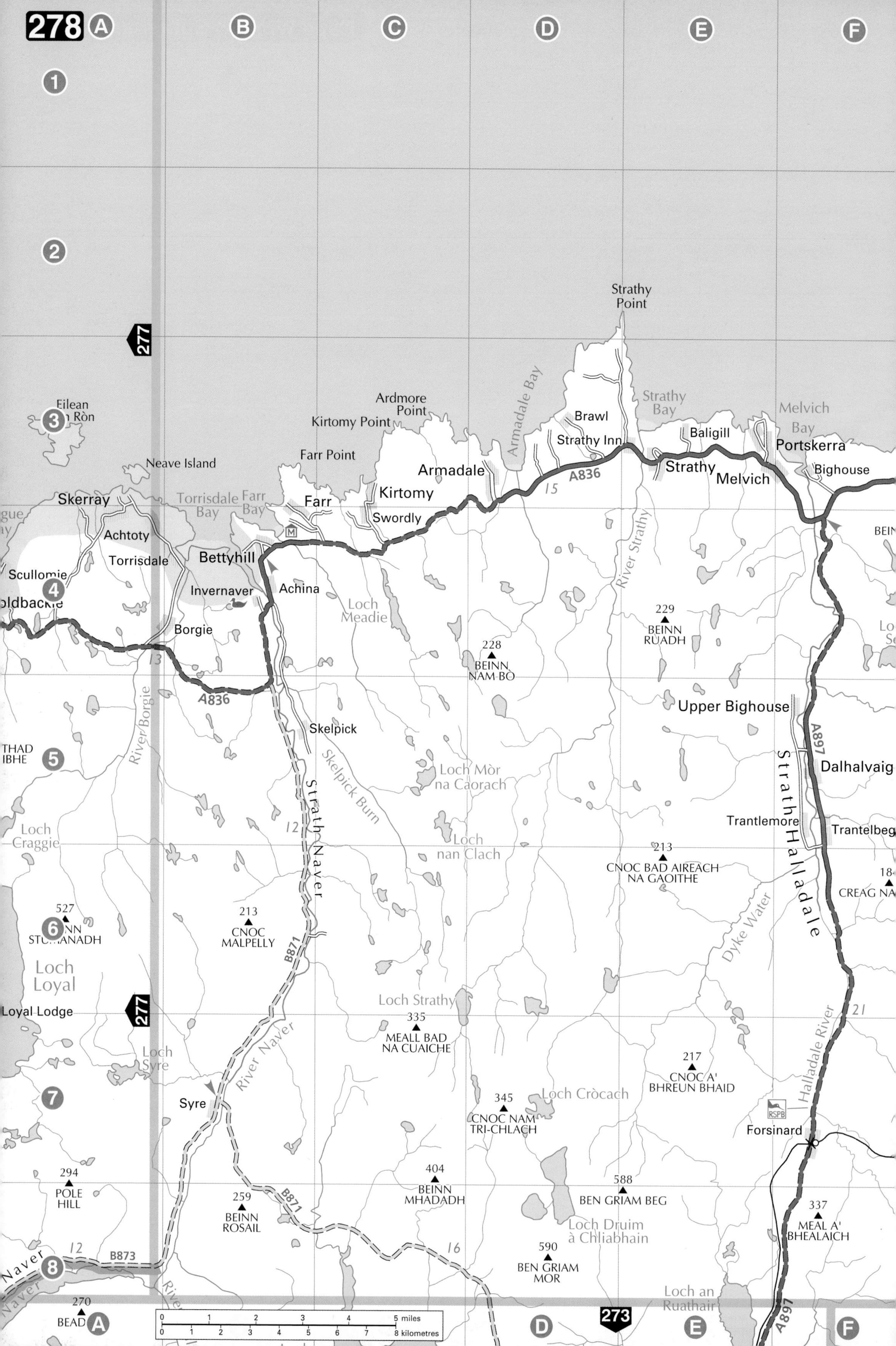

Strathy Point
Armadale Bay
Strathy Bay
Melvich Bay
Ardmore Point
Kirtomy Point
Eilean nan Ròn
Neave Island
Farr Point
Brawl
Strathy Inn
Baligill
Portskerra
Bighouse
Armadale
Strathy
Melvich
Skerray
Torrisdale Bay
Farr Bay
Farr
Kirtomy
Swordly
A836
Achtoty
Torrisdale
Bettyhill
Scullomie
Invernaver
Achina
Loch Meadie
River Strathy
229 BEINN RUADH
228 BEINN NAM BO
Borgie
A836
River Borgie
Skelpick
Upper Bighouse
A897
Dalhalvaig
Strath Halladale
Skelpick Burn
Loch Mòr na Caorach
Strath Naver
Loch nan Clach
Loch Craggie
Trantlemore
Trantelbeg
213 CNOC BAD AIREACH NA GAOITHE
527
213 CNOC MALPELLY
Dyke Water
B871
Loch Loyal
Loyal Lodge
Loch Strathy
335 MEALL BAD NA CUAICHE
Loch Syre
River Naver
217 CNOC A' BHREUN BHAID
Halladale River
Syre
345 CNOC NAM TRI-CHLACH
Loch Cròcach
RSPB
Forsinard
404 BEINN MHADADH
588 BEN GRIAM BEG
294 POLE HILL
259 BEINN ROSAIL
B871
Loch Druim à Chliabhain
337 MEAL A' BHEALAICH
B873
590 BEN GRIAM MOR
270 BEAD
Loch an Ruathair
A897
0 1 2 3 4 5 miles
0 1 2 3 4 5 6 7 8 kilometres

277
273

DUNNET HEAD
127
Briga Head
Stromness
121
DUNNET HILL
Brough
St John's Loch
B855
West Dunnet
Dunnet
Dunnet Bay
Brims Ness
Holborn Head
St Mary's Chapel (ruin)
Scrabster
Crosskirk
A836
A9
Thurso Bay
Thurso
Murkle
280
Castlehill
Castletown
Bridge of Forss
Skiall
Sandside Bay
Upper Dounreay
Achreamie
Forss Water
Lythmore
B874
Olrig House
Isauld
Cnoc Freiceadain Long Cairns
Glengolly
Weydale
B876
Reay
Achvarasdal
Shebster
Westfield
Hilliclay
Bower
Sordale
242
BEINN RATHA
Loch Calder
B874
Roadside
Knockdee
Loch Scarmclate
Halcro
Broubster
Clayock
Gillock
Halkirk
Georgemas Junction Station
B870
Shurrery
Shurrery Lodge
Scotscalder Station
Harpsdale
176
SPITTAL HILL
Loch Watten
Loch Scye
290
BEIN NAM BAD MHÒR
Loch Shurrery
Dorrery
Olgrinmore
River Thurso
Spittal
B870
Watten
243
CNOC AN DARAIN BHÀIN
160
BRAIGH FÉITH HEMIGAL
132
DRUIM A' CHRACAIRNIE
Mybster
Loch of Toftingall
Loch Tuim Ghlais
Loch Caluim
Westerdale
Strath Beg
203
CNOC PREAS A'MHADAIDH
200
CNOC BEUL NA FAIRE
136
BEINN CHÀITEAG
280
Altnabreac Station
A9
Loch More
Loch Ruard
Achavanich
Loch Stemster
BALLH HIL
Strathmore Water
Loch an Thulachan
Loch Sand
Loch Rangag
248
STEMSTER HILL
Rumsdale Water
Dalnawillan Lodge
226
COIRE NA BEINN
Glutt Water
348
BEN ALISKY
287
BEN-A-CHIELT
274
Swiney
G H J K L M
1 2 3 4 5 6 7 8

PENTLAND FIRTH
DUNNET HEAD
Briga Head
Brough
DUNNET HILL
West Dunnet
Dunnet Bay
Dunnet
Murkle
Castlehill
Castletown
A836
Olrig House
Hilliclay
Sordale
Knockdee
Clayock
Georgemas Junction Station
SPITTAL HILL
Spittal
Mybster
Loch of Toftingall
Strath Beg
A9
Achavanich
Loch Rangag
Loch Stemster
STEMSTER HILL
COIRE NA BEINN
BEN-A-CHIELT
Scarfskerry
Castle of Mey
St John's Loch
Rattar
Mey
Loch Mey
Barrock
Inkstack
Loch Heilen
Greenland
Tain
B876
Bowermadden
Bower
Lyth
Halcro
Loch Scarmclate
Gillock
B874
Loch Watten
Watten
B870
A882
Wick River
Bilbster
Badlipster
Achairn Burn
BALLHARN HILL
Grey Cairns of Camster
Roster
Hill o'Many Stanes
Upper Lybster
Mid Clyth
Halberry Head
Swiney
Langaton Point
Nethertown
ISLAND OF STROMA
Uppertown
Mell Head
St John's Point
Inner Sound
St Margaret's Hope
Gills Bay
Gills
Kirkstyle
Huna
DUNCANSBY HEAD
Muckle Stack
John o' Groats
Canisbay
Stacks of Duncansby
A99
Brabstermire
Skirza
Gill Burn
Freswick
Freswick Bay
Ness Head
Slickly
Auckengill
Kirk Burn
Broch
Nybster
Sortat
Brough Head
Howe
Burn of Lyth
Keiss
Mireland
Kirk
Loch of Wester
Sinclair Bay
Killimster
Castle Girnigoe & Sinclair
Noss Head
Reiss
Winless
Sibster
Ackergill
Wick John o' Groats
Staxigoe
Janetstown
Papigoe
Haster
Milton
Wick
Wick Bay
Newton
Old Wick
South Head
Castle of Old Wick
Whiterow
Loch Hempriggs
Tannach
Thrumster
Sarclet
Loch of Yarrows
HILL OF YARROWS
Cairn o'Get
Ulbster
Whaligoe
Whaligoe Steps
Bruan
0 1 2 3 4 5 miles
0 1 2 3 4 5 6 7 8 kilometres

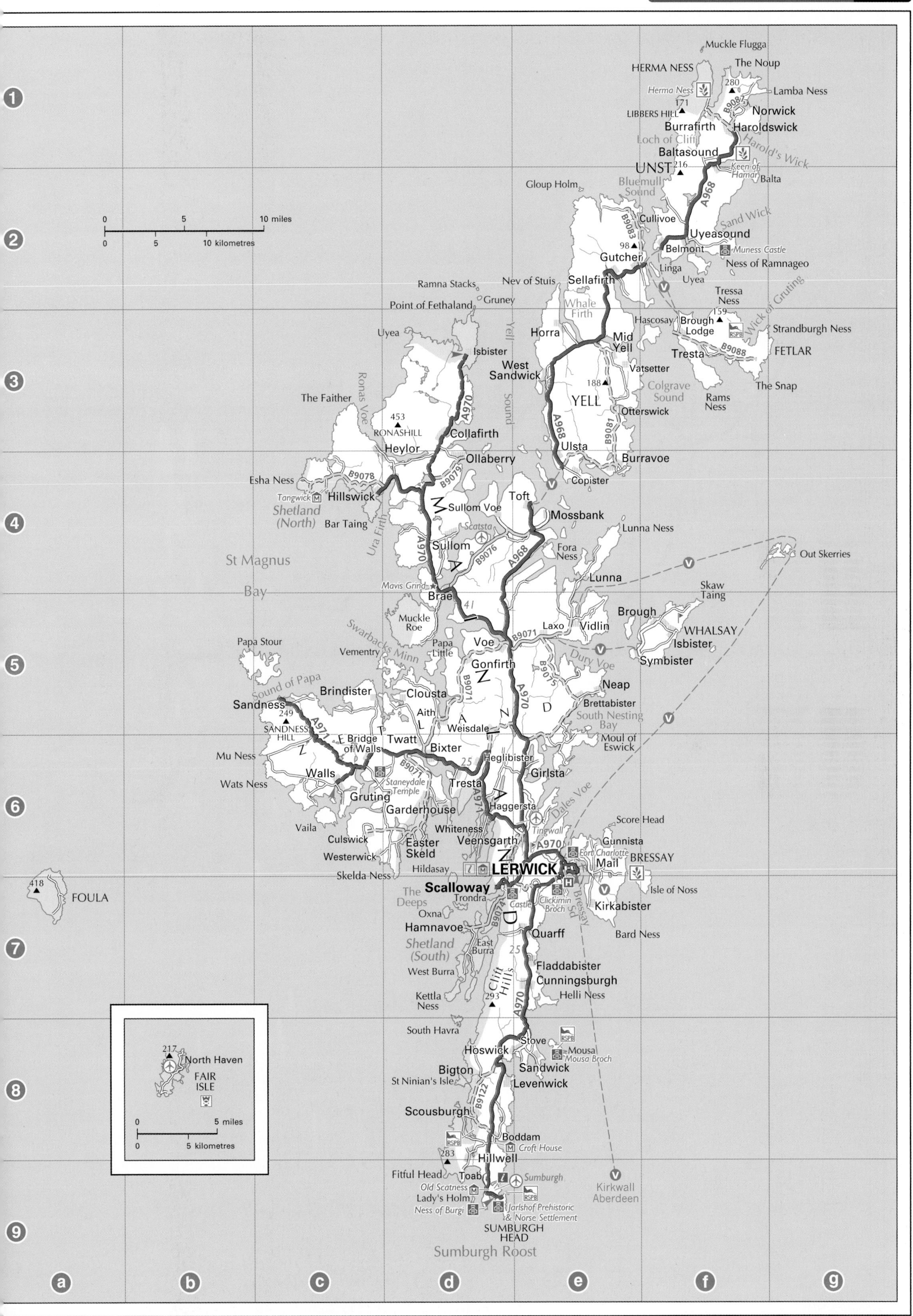

Muckle Flugga
HERMA NESS
The Noup
Lamba Ness
Herma Ness
LIBBERS HILL
Norwick
Haroldswick
Burrafirth
Loch of Cliff
Baltasound
Harold's Wick
UNST
Keen of Hamar
Balta
Gloup Holm
Bluemull Sound
Cullivoe
Sand Wick
Uyeasound
Belmont
Muness Castle
Gutcher
Ness of Ramnageo
Linga
Uyea
Ramna Stacks
Nev of Stuis
Sellafirth
Tressa Ness
Gruney
Whale Firth
Point of Fethaland
Hascosay
Brough Lodge
Wick of Gruting
Strandburgh Ness
Uyea
Isbister
Horra
Mid Yell
FETLAR
Tresta
West Sandwick
Vatsetter
The Snap
Yell Sound
Colgrave Sound
YELL
Rams Ness
The Faither
Ronas Voe
RONASHILL
Otterswick
Collafirth
Ulsta
Heylor
Ollaberry
Burravoe
Esha Ness
Copister
Tangwick
Hillswick
Toft
Shetland (North)
Sullom Voe
Mossbank
Bar Taing
Scatsta
Lunna Ness
Ura Firth
Sullom
Fora Ness
Out Skerries
St Magnus Bay
Lunna
Mavis Grind
Skaw Taing
Brae
Brough
Muckle Roe
Laxo
Vidlin
WHALSAY
Swarbacks Minn
Papa Little
Voe
Isbister
Papa Stour
Vementry
Symbister
Dury Voe
Gonfirth
Sound of Papa
Neap
Brindister
Clousta
Brettabister
Sandness
Aith
South Nesting Bay
SANDNESS HILL
Weisdale
Bridge of Walls
Twatt
Moul of Eswick
Mu Ness
Bixter
Heglibister
Girlsta
Walls
Staneydale Temple
Tresta
Wats Ness
Gruting
Dales Voe
Garderhouse
Haggersta
Score Head
Vaila
Whiteness
Tingwall
Gunnista
Culswick
Easter Skeld
Veensgarth
Fort Charlotte
BRESSAY
Westerwick
Mail
Hildasay
LERWICK
Skelda Ness
Scalloway
Isle of Noss
FOULA
The Deeps
Trondra
Clickimin Broch
Bressay Sd
Castle
Kirkabister
Oxna
Hamnavoe
Quarff
Bard Ness
Shetland (South)
East Burra
West Burra
Fladdabister
Cliff Hills
Cunningsburgh
Kettla Ness
Helli Ness
South Havra
Stove
Mousa
Mousa Broch
Hoswick
North Haven
FAIR ISLE
Sandwick
Bigton
St Ninian's Isle
Levenwick
Scousburgh
Boddam
Croft House
Hillwell
Fitful Head
Toab
Sumburgh
Old Scatness
Kirkwall
Aberdeen
Lady's Holm
Ness of Burgi
Jarlshof Prehistoric & Norse Settlement
SUMBURGH HEAD
Sumburgh Roost
A968
B9087
B9083
B9088
A970
B9081
B9078
B9079
B9076
B9071
B9075
A971
B9074
B9122
0 5 10 miles
0 5 10 kilometres
0 5 miles
0 5 kilometres

Western Isles
0 5 10 miles
0 5 10 kilometres
RUDHA RHOBHANAIS (BUTT OF LEWIS)
Port Nis (Port of Ness)
Lional
Cros
Sgiogarstaigh (Skigersta)
NESS
Borgh (Borve)
Siadar (Shader)
Cellar Head
Steinacleit Cairn & Stone Circle
158 DIAVAL
ISLE OF LEWIS
Arnol
Barabhas (Barvas)
Tolastadh (Tolsta)
Tolsta Head
Bragar
The Block House
Siabost (Shawbost)
Loch Breivat
Gress River
Carlabhagh (Carloway)
Dun Carloway Broch
Great Bernera
West Loch Roag
East Loch Roag
Col
Gallan Head
280 BEN BRAVAS
Port nan Giuran (Portnaguran)
Tiumpan Head
Aird
EYE PENINSULA
Bhaltos (Valtos)
Breascleit (Breasclete)
Broad Bay
Newmarket
Lacasdal (Laxdale)
Timsgearraidh (Timsgarry)
Miabhig (Miavaig)
Calanais (Callanish)
Standing Stones
Steornabhagh (Stornoway)
Garrabost
Aird Uig (Uig)
233 EITSHAL
Sanndabhaig (Sandwick)
Cnoc (Knock)
Pabail (Bayble)
Islibhig (Islivig)
Chicken Head
Acha Mor (Achmore)
Loch Orasaigh
Aird Brenish
Liurbost (Leurbost)
Griomaisiader (Grimshader)
Breanais (Brenish)
496 TEINNASVAL
Crosbost
Lacasaigh (Laxay)
Mealasta Island
Loch Tealasavay
Cromor
Baile Ailein (Balallan)
Loch Erisort
Gearraidh Bhaird (Garyvard)
Airidh a bhruaich (Aribruach)
Cearsiadar (Kershader)
Loch Resort
Scarp
Loch Langavat
Grabhair (Gravir)
Loch Ouirn
401 MOR MHONADH
Kebock Head
Ullapool
THE MINCH
679 TIRGA MORE
Seaforth Island
PARK
Leumrabhagh (Lemreway)
Hushinish Point
Aird a Mhulaidh (Ardvourlie)
571 BEINN MHOR
Amhuinnsuidhe
Loch Shell
South Lewis, Harris and North Uist
799 CLISHAM
Loch Seaforth
Loch Claidh
Soay More
OUTER HEBRIDES
West Loch Tarbert
Loch Brollum
Taransay
Aird Asaig (Ardhasig)
Tairbeart (Tarbert)
Sound of Shiant
Rudha Sgeirigin
Caolas Scalpaigh (Kyles Scalpay)
Shiant Islands
Sound of Taransay
East Loch Tarbert
Na Buirgh (Borve)
Toe Head
Scalpay
333 CHAIPAVAL
Greosabhagh (Grosebay)
Shillay
HARRIS
Rudha Bocaig
Taobh Tuath (Northton)
Manais (Manish)
Pabbay
Sound of Harris
An t-Ob (Leverburgh)
Fionnsbhagh (Finsbay)
Tairbeart (Tarbert) : Uig
Sound of Pabbay
Roghadal (Rodel)
St Clement's Church
Berneray
Killegray
Boreray
Renish Point
Otternish
Griminish Point
Vallay
Port nan Long (Newton Ferry)
196

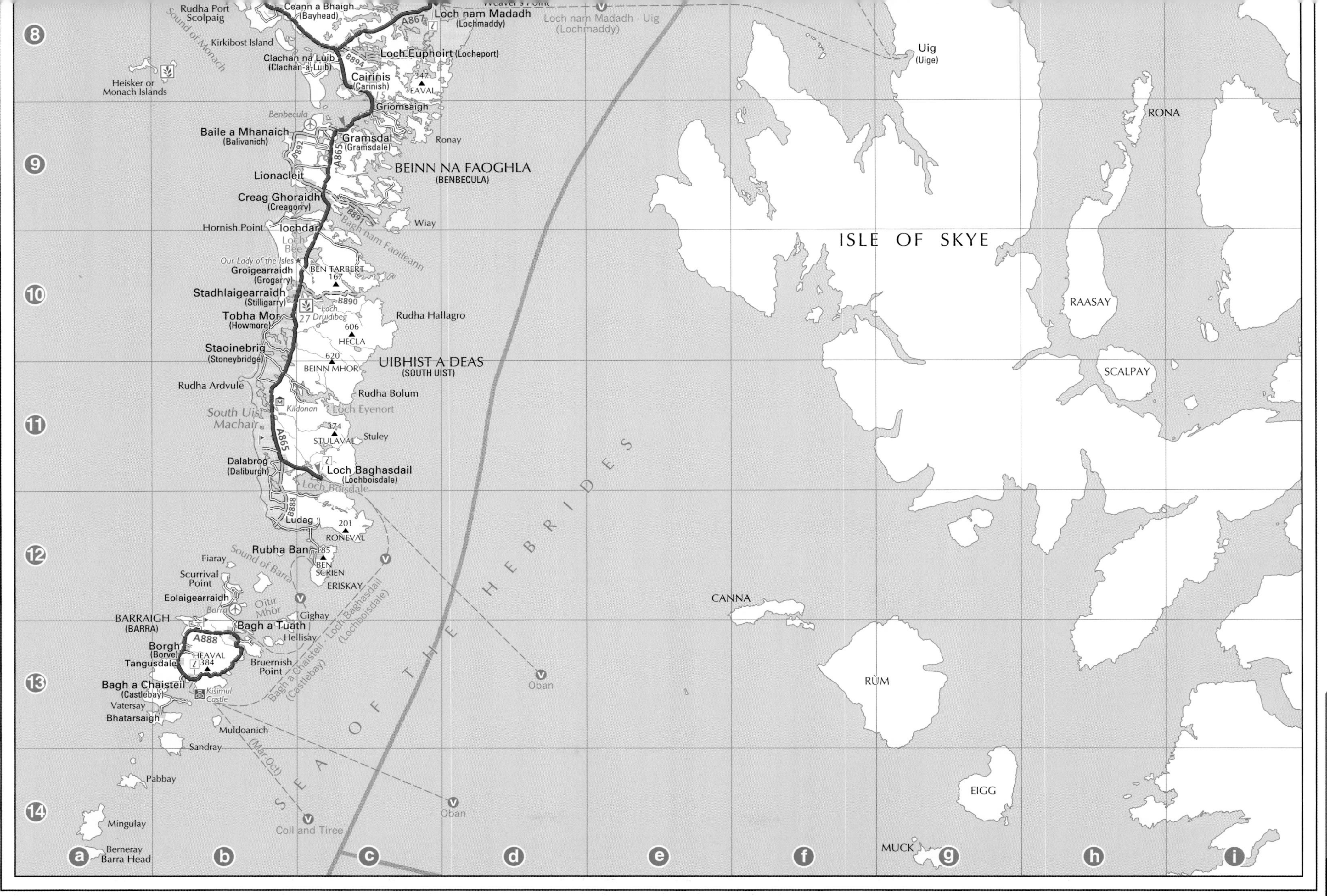

Rudha Port Scolpaig
Ceann a Bhaigh
(Bayhead)
Loch nam Madadh
(Lochmaddy)
Loch nam Madadh - Uig
(Lochmaddy)
Sound of Monach
Kirkibost Island
Heisker or
Monach Islands
Clachan na Luib
(Clachan-a-Luib)
Loch Euphoirt (Locheport)
Cairinis
(Carinish)
347
EAVAL
Uig
(Uige)
Griomsaigh
Benbecula
Baile a Mhanaich
(Balivanich)
Gramsdal
(Gramsdale)
Ronay
BEINN NA FAOGHLA
(BENBECULA)
Lionacleit
Creag Ghoraidh
(Creagorry)
Wiay
Hornish Point
Iochdar
Loch Bee
Bagh nam Faoileann
ISLE OF SKYE
RONA
Our Lady of the Isles
Groigearraidh
(Grogarry)
BEN TARBERT
167
Stadhlaigearraidh
(Stilligarry)
Loch Druidibeg
Tobha Mor
(Howmore)
Rudha Hallagro
606
HECLA
RAASAY
Staoinebrig
(Stoneybridge)
620
BEINN MHOR
UIBHIST A DEAS
(SOUTH UIST)
SCALPAY
Rudha Ardvule
Rudha Bolum
South Uist Machair
Kildonan
Loch Eynort
374
STULAVAL
Stuley
A865
Dalabrog
(Daliburgh)
Loch Baghasdail
(Lochboisdale)
Loch Boisdale
Ludag
201
RONEVAL
Rubha Ban
185
BEN SCRIEN
ERISKAY
Fiaray
Sound of Barra
Scurrival Point
Eolaigearraidh
Barra
Oitir Mhor
Gighay
CANNA
BARRAIGH
(BARRA)
Bagh a Tuath
Hellisay
A888
Borgh
(Borve)
HEAVAL
384
Tangusdale
Bruernish Point
Bagh a Chaisteil - Loch Baghasdail
(Castlebay - Lochboisdale)
Oban
RÙM
Bagh a Chaisteil
(Castlebay)
Kisimul Castle
Vatersay
Bhatarsaigh
Muldoanich
Sandray
(Mar-Oct)
SEA OF THE HEBRIDES
Pabbay
EIGG
Mingulay
Coll and Tiree
Oban
Berneray
Barra Head
MUCK
8
9
10
11
12
13
14
a
b
c
d
e
f
g
h
i

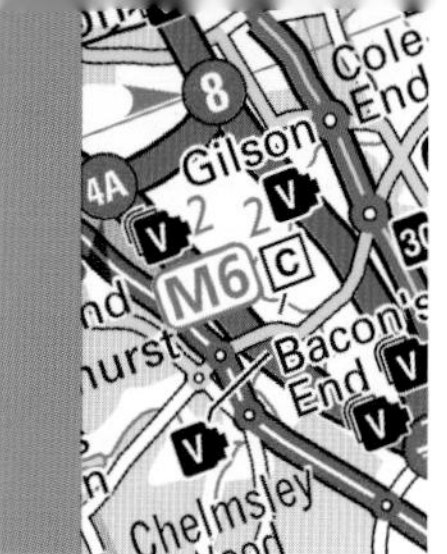

Restricted junctions

Motorway and Primary Route junctions which have access or exit restrictions are shown on the map pages thus:

M1 London - Leeds

Junction	Northbound	Southbound
2	Access only from A1 *(northbound)*	Exit only to A1 *(southbound)*
4	Access only from A41 *(northbound)*	Exit only to A41 *(southbound)*
6A	Access only from M25 (no link from A405)	Exit only to M25 (no link from A405)
7	Access only from A414	Exit only to A414
17	Exit only to M45	Access only from M45
19	Exit only to M6 *(northbound)*	Access only from M6
21A	Exit only, no access	Access only, no exit
23A	Access only from A42	No restriction
24A	Access only, no exit	Exit only, no access
35A	Exit only, no access	Access only, no exit
43	Exit only to M621	Access only from M621
48	Exit only to A1(M) *(northbound)*	Access only from A1(M) *(southbound)*

M2 Rochester - Faversham

Junction	Westbound	Eastbound
1	No exit to A2 *(eastbound)*	No access from A2 *(westbound)*

M3 Sunbury - Southampton

Junction	Northeastbound	Southwestbound
8	Access only from A303, no exit	Exit only to A303, no access
10	Exit only, no access	Access only, no exit
14	Access from M27 only, no exit	No access to M27 *(westbound)*

M4 London - South Wales

Junction	Westbound	Eastbound
1	Access only from A4 *(westbound)*	Exit only to A4 *(eastbound)*
21	Exit only to M48	Access only from M48
23	Access only from M48	Exit only to M48
25	Exit only, no access	Access only, no exit
25A	Exit only, no access	Access only, no exit
29	Exit only to A48(M)	Access only from A48(M)
38	Exit only, no access	No restriction
39	Access only, no exit	No access or exit

M5 Birmingham - Exeter

Junction	Northeastbound	Southwestbound
10	Access only, no exit	Exit only, no access
11A	Access only from A417 *(westbound)*	Exit only to A417 *(eastbound)*
18A	Exit only to M49	Access only from M49
18	Exit only, no access	Access only, no exit
29	No restriction	Access only from A30 *(westbound)*

M6 Toll Motorway

Junction	Northwestbound	Southeastbound
T1	Access only, no exit	No access or exit
T2	No access or exit	Exit only, no access
T3	Staggered junction, follow signs - access only from A38 *(northbound)*	Staggered junction, follow signs - access only from A38 *(southbound)*
T5	Access only, no exit	Exit only to A5148 *(northbound)*, no access
T7	Exit only, no access	Access only, no exit
T8	Exit only, no access	Access only, no exit

M6 Rugby - Carlisle

Junction	Northbound	Southbound
3A	Exit only to M6 Toll	Access only from M6 Toll
4A	Access only from M42 *(southbound)*	Exit only to M42
5	Exit only, no access	Access only, no exit
10A	Exit only to M54	Access only from M54
11A	Access only from M6 Toll	Exit only to M6 Toll
with M56 (jct 20A)	No restriction	Access only from M56 *(eastbound)*
20	Access only, no exit	No restriction
24	Access only, no exit	Exit only, no access
25	Exit only, no access	Access only, no exit
29	No direct access, use adjacent slip road to jct 29A	No direct exit, use adjacent slip road from jct 29A
29A	Access only, no exit	Exit only, no access
30	Access only from M61	Exit only to M61
31A	Exit only, no access	Access only, no exit
45	Exit only, no access	Access only, no exit

M8 Edinburgh - Bishopton

Junction	Westbound	Eastbound
8	No access from M73 *(southbound)* or from A8 *(eastbound)* & A89	No exit to M73 *(northbound)* or to A8 *(westbound)* & A89
9	Access only, no exit	Exit only, no access
13	Access only from M80 *(southbound)*	Exit only to M80 *(northbound)*
14	Access only, no exit	Exit only, no access
16	Exit only to A804	Access only from A879
17	Exit only to A82	No restriction
18	Access only from A82 *(eastbound)*	Exit only to A814
19	No access from A814 *(westbound)*	Exit only to A814 *(westbound)*
20	Exit only, no access	Access only, no exit
21	Access only, no exit	Exit only to A8
22	Exit only to M77 *(southbound)*	Access only from M77 *(northbound)*
23	Exit only to B768	Access only from B768
25	No access or exit from or to A8	No access or exit from or to A8
25A	Exit only, no access	Access only, no exit
28	Exit only, no access	Access only, no exit
28A	Exit only to A737	Access only from A737

M9 Edinburgh - Dunblane

Junction	Northwestbound	Southeastbound
1A	Exit only to M9 spur	Access only from M9 spur
2	Access only, no exit	Exit only, no access
3	Exit only, no access	Access only, no exit
6	Access only, no exit	Exit only to A905
8	Exit only to M876 *(southwestbound)*	Access only from M876 *(northeastbound)*

M11 London - Cambridge

Junction	Northbound	Southbound
4	Access only from A406 *(eastbound)*	Exit only to A406
5	Exit only, no access	Access only, no exit
9	Exit only to A11	Access only from A11
13	Exit only, no access	Access only, no exit
14	Exit only, no access	Access only, no exit

M20 Swanley - Folkestone

Junction	Northwestbound	Southeastbound
2	Staggered junction; follow signs - access only	Staggered junction; follow signs - exit only
3	Exit only to M26 *(westbound)*	Access only from M26 *(eastbound)*
5	Access only from A20	For access follow signs - exit only to A20
6	No restriction	For exit follow signs
11A	Access only, no exit	Exit only, no access

M23 Hooley - Crawley

Junction	Northbound	Southbound
7	Exit only to A23 *(northbound)*	Access only from A23 *(southbound)*
10A	Access only, no exit	Exit only, no access

M25 London Orbital Motorway

Junction	Clockwise	Anticlockwise
1B	No direct access, use slip road to Jct 2. Exit only	Access only, no exit
5	No exit to M26 *(eastbound)*	No access from M26
19	Exit only, no access	Access only, no exit
21	Access only from M1 *(southbound)*. Exit only to M1 *(northbound)*	Access only from M1 *(southbound)*. Exit only to M1 *(northbound)*
31	No exit (use slip road via jct 30), access only	No access (use slip road via jct 30), exit only

M26 Sevenoaks - Wrotham

Junction	Westbound	Eastbound
with M25 (jct 5)	Exit only to clockwise M25 *(westbound)*	Access only from anticlockwise M25 *(eastbound)*
with M20 (jct 3)	Access only from M20 *(northwestbound)*	Exit only to M20 *(southeastbound)*

M27 Cadnam - Portsmouth

Junction	Westbound	Eastbound
4	Staggered junction; follow signs - access only from M3 *(southbound)*. Exit only to M3 *(northbound)*	Staggered junction; follow signs - access only from M3 *(southbound)*. Exit only to M3 *(northbound)*
10	Exit only, no access	Access only, no exit
12	Staggered junction; follow signs - exit only to M275 *(southbound)*	Staggered junction; follow signs - access only from M275 *(northbound)*

M40 London - Birmingham

Junction	Northwestbound	Southeastbound
3	Exit only, no access	Access only, no exit
7	Exit only, no access	Access only, no exit
8	Exit only to M40/A40	Access only from M40/A40
13	Exit only, no access	Access only, no exit
14	Access only, no exit	Exit only, no access
16	Access only, no exit	Exit only, no access

M42 Bromsgrove - Measham

Junction	Northeastbound	Southwestbound
1	Access only, no exit	Exit only, no access
7	Exit only to M6 *(northwestbound)*	Access only from M6 *(northwestbound)*
7A	Exit only to M6 *(southeastbound)*	No access or exit
8	Access only from M6 *(southeastbound)*	Exit only to M6 *(northwestbound)*

M45 Coventry - M1

Junction	Westbound	Eastbound
Dunchurch (unnumbered)	Access only from A45	Exit only, no access
with M1 (jct 17)	Access only from M1 *(northbound)*	Exit only to M1 *(southbound)*

M53 Mersey Tunnel - Chester

Junction	Northbound	Southbound
11	Access only from M56 *(westbound)*. Exit only to M56 *(eastbound)*	Access only from M56 *(westbound)*. Exit only to M56 *(eastbound)*

M54 Telford

Junction	Westbound	Eastbound
with M6 (jct 10A)	Access only from M6 *(northbound)*	Exit only to M6 *(southbound)*

M56 North Cheshire

Junction	Westbound	Eastbound
1	Access only from M60 *(westbound)*	Exit only to M60 *(eastbound)* & A34 *(northbound)*
2	Exit only, no access	Access only, no exit
3	Access only, no exit	Exit only, no access

4	Exit only, no access	Access only, no exit
7	Exit only, no access	No restriction
8	Access only, no exit	No access or exit
15	Exit only to M53	Access only from M53
16	No access or exit	No restriction

M57 Liverpool Outer Ring Road

Junction	Northwestbound	Southeastbound
3	Access only, no exit	Exit only, no access
5	Access only from A580 *(westbound)*	Exit only, no access

M58 Liverpool - Wigan

Junction	Westbound	Eastbound
1	Exit only, no access	Access only, no exit

M60 Manchester Orbital

Junction	Clockwise	Anticlockwise
2	Access only, no exit	Exit only, no access
3	No access from M56	Access only from A34 *(northbound)*
4	Access only from A34 *(northbound)*. Exit only to M56	Access only from M56 *(eastbound)*. Exit only to A34 *(southbound)*
5	Access and exit only from and to A5103 *(northbound)*	Access and exit only from and to A5103 *(southbound)*
7	No direct access, use slip road to jct 8. Exit only to A56	Access only from A56. No exit - use jct 8
14	Access from A580 *(eastbound)*	Exit only to A580 *(westbound)*
16	Access only, no exit	Exit only, no access
20	Exit only, no access	Access only, no exit
22	No restriction	Exit only, no access
25	Exit only, no access	No restriction
26	No restriction	Exit only, no access
27	Access only, no exit	Exit only, no access

M61 Manchester - Preston

Junction	Northwestbound	Southeastbound
3	No access or exit	Exit only, no access
with M6 (jct 30)	Exit only to M6 *(northbound)*	Access only from M6 *(southbound)*

M62 Liverpool - Kingston upon Hull

Junction	Westbound	Eastbound
23	Access only, no exit	Exit only, no access
32A	No access to A1(M) *(southbound)*	No restriction

M65 Preston - Colne

Junction	Northeastbound	Southwestbound
9	Exit only, no access	Access only, no exit
11	Access only, no exit	Exit only, no access

M66 Bury

Junction	Northbound	Southbound
with A56	Exit only to A56 *(northbound)*	Access only from A56 *(southbound)*
1	Exit only, no access	Access only, no exit

M67 Hyde Bypass

Junction	Westbound	Eastbound
1	Access only, no exit	Exit only, no access
2	Exit only, no access	Access only, no exit
3	Exit only, no access	No restriction

M69 Coventry - Leicester

Junction	Northbound	Southbound
2	Access only, no exit	Exit only, no access

M73 East of Glasgow

Junction	Northbound	Southbound
2	No access from or exit to A89. No access from M8 *(eastbound)*	No access from or exit to A89. No exit to M8 *(westbound)*
3	Exit only to A80 *(northeastbound)*	Access only from A80 *(southwestbound)*

M74 and A74(M) Glasgow - Gretna

Junction	Northbound	Southbound
3	Exit only, no access	Access only, no exit
3A	Access only, no exit	Exit only, no access
7	Access only, no exit	Exit only, no access

9	No access or exit	Exit only, no access
10	No restrictions	Access only, no exit
11	Access only, no exit	Exit only, no access
12	Exit only, no access	Access only, no exit
18	Exit only, no access	Access only, no exit

M77 South of Glasgow

Junction	Northbound	Southbound
with M8 (jct 22)	No exit to M8 *(westbound)*	No access from M8 *(eastbound)*
4	Access only, no exit	Exit only, no access
6	Access only, no exit	Exit only, no access
7	Access only, no exit	No restriction

M80 Glasgow - Stirling

Junction	Northbound	Southbound
4A	Exit only, no access	Access only, no exit
6A	Access only, no exit	Exit only, no access
8	Exit only to M876 *(northeastbound)*	Access only from M876 *(southwestbound)*

M90 Forth Road Bridge - Perth

Junction	Northbound	Southbound
2A	Exit only to A92 *(eastbound)*	Access only from A92 *(westbound)*
7	Access only, no exit	Exit only, no access
8	Exit only, no access	Access only, no exit
10	No access from A912. No exit to A912 *(southbound)*	No access from A912 *(northbound)*. No exit to A912

M180 Doncaster - Grimsby

Junction	Westbound	Eastbound
1	Access only, no exit	Exit only, no access

M606 Bradford Spur

Junction	Northbound	Southbound
2	Exit only, no access	No restriction

M621 Leeds - M1

Junction	Clockwise	Anticlockwise
2A	Access only, no exit	Exit only, no access
4	No exit or access	No restriction
5	Access only, no exit	Exit only, no access
6	Exit only, no access	Access only, no exit
with M1 (jct 43)	Exit only to M1 *(southbound)*	Access only from M1 *(northbound)*

M876 Bonnybridge - Kincardine Bridge

Junction	Northeastbound	Southwestbound
with M80 (jct 5)	Access only from M80 *(northbound)*	Exit only to M80 *(southbound)*
with M9 (jct 8)	Exit only to M9 *(eastbound)*	Access only from M9 *(westbound)*

A1(M) South Mimms - Baldock

Junction	Northbound	Southbound
2	Exit only, no access	Access only, no exit
3	No restriction	Exit only, no access
5	Access only, no exit	No access or exit

A1(M) Pontefract - Bedale

Junction	Northbound	Southbound
41	No access to M62 *(eastbound)*	No restriction
43	Access only from M1 *(northbound)*	Exit only to M1 *(southbound)*

A1(M) Scotch Corner - Newcastle upon Tyne

Junction	Northbound	Southbound
57	Exit only to A66(M) *(eastbound)*	Access only from A66(M) *(westbound)*
65	No access Exit only to A194(M) & A1 *(northbound)*	No exit Access only from A194(M) & A1 *(southbound)*

A3(M) Horndean - Havant

Junction	Northbound	Southbound
1	Access only from A3	Exit only to A3
4	Exit only, no access	Access only, no exit

A48(M) Cardiff Spur

Junction	Westbound	Eastbound
29	Access only from M4 *(westbound)*	Exit only to M4 *(eastbound)*
29A	Exit only to A48 *(westbound)*	Access only from A48 *(eastbound)*

A66(M) Darlington Spur

Junction	Westbound	Eastbound
with A1(M) (jct 57)	Exit only to A1(M) *(southbound)*	Access only from A1(M) *(northbound)*

A194(M) Newcastle upon Tyne

Junction	Northbound	Southbound
with A1(M) (jct 65)	Access only from A1(M) *(northbound)*	Exit only to A1(M) *(southbound)*

A12 M25 - Ipswich

Junction	Northeastbound	Southwestbound
13	Access only, no exit	No restriction
14	Exit only, no access	Access only, no exit
20A	Exit only, no access	Access only, no exit
20B	Access only, no exit	Exit only, no access
21	No restriction	Access only, no exit
23	Exit only, no access	Access only, no exit
24	Access only, no exit	Exit only, no access
27	Exit only, no access	Access only, no exit
Dedham & Stratford St Mary (unnumbered)	Exit only	Access only

A14 M1 - Felixstowe

Junction	Westbound	Eastbound
With M1/M6 (jct19)	Exit only to M6 and M1 *(northbound)*	Access only from M6 and M1 *(southbound)*
4	Exit only, no access	Access only, no exit
31	Access only from A1307	Exit only to A1307
34	Access only, no exit	Exit only, no access
36	Exit only to A11, access only from A1303	Access only from A11
38	Access only from A11	Exit only to A11
39	Exit only, no access	Access only, no exit
61	Access only, no exit	Exit only, no access

A55 Holyhead - Chester

Junction	Westbound	Eastbound
8A	Exit only, no access	Access only, no exit
23A	Access only, no exit	Exit only, no access
24A	Exit only, no access	No access or exit
33A	Exit only, no access	No access or exit
33B	Exit only, no access	Access only, no exit
36A	Exit only to A5104	Access only from A5104

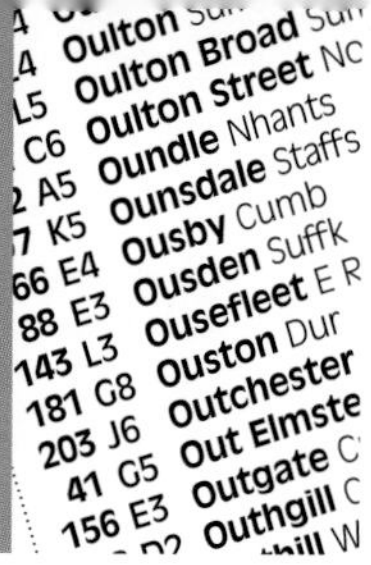

Index to place names

This index lists places appearing in the main-map section of the atlas in alphabetical order. The reference following each name gives the atlas page number and grid reference of the square in which the place appears. The map shows counties, unitary authorities and administrative areas, together with a list of the abbreviated name forms used in the index.

Scotland

Abers	**Aberdeenshire**
Ag & B	**Argyll and Bute**
Angus	**Angus**
Border	**Scottish Borders**
C Aber	**City of Aberdeen**
C Dund	**City of Dundee**
C Edin	**City of Edinburgh**
C Glas	**City of Glasgow**
Clacks	**Clackmannanshire (1)**
D & G	**Dumfries & Galloway**
E Ayrs	**East Ayrshire**
E Duns	**East Dunbartonshire (2)**
E Loth	**East Lothian**
E Rens	**East Renfrewshire (3)**
Falk	**Falkirk**
Fife	**Fife**
Highld	**Highland**
Inver	**Inverclyde (4)**
Mdloth	**Midlothian (5)**
Moray	**Moray**
N Ayrs	**North Ayrshire**
N Lans	**North Lanarkshire (6)**
Ork	**Orkney Islands**
P & K	**Perth & Kinross**
Rens	**Renfrewshire (7)**
S Ayrs	**South Ayrshire**
Shet	**Shetland Islands**
S Lans	**South Lanarkshire**
Stirlg	**Stirling**
W Duns	**West Dunbartonshire (8)**
W Isls	**Western Isles (Na h-Eileanan an Iar)**
W Loth	**West Lothian**

Wales

Blae G	**Blaenau Gwent (9)**
Brdgnd	**Bridgend (10)**
Caerph	**Caerphilly (11)**
Cardif	**Cardiff**
Carmth	**Carmarthenshire**
Cerdgn	**Ceredigion**
Conwy	**Conwy**
Denbgs	**Denbighshire**
Flints	**Flintshire**
Gwynd	**Gwynedd**
IoA	**Isle of Anglesey**
Mons	**Monmouthshire**
Myr Td	**Merthyr Tydfil (12)**
Neath	**Neath Port Talbot (13)**
Newpt	**Newport (14)**
Pembks	**Pembrokeshire**
Powys	**Powys**
Rhondd	**Rhondda Cynon Taff (15)**
Swans	**Swansea**
Torfn	**Torfaen (16)**
V Glam	**Vale of Glamorgan (17)**
Wrexhm	**Wrexham**

Channel Islands & Isle of Man

Guern	**Guernsey**
Jersey	**Jersey**
IoM	**Isle of Man**

England

BaNES	**Bath & N E Somerset (18)**
Barns	**Barnsley (19)**
Bed	**Bedford**
Birm	**Birmingham**
Bl w D	**Blackburn with Darwen (20)**
Bmouth	**Bournemouth**
Bolton	**Bolton (21)**
Bpool	**Blackpool**
Br & H	**Brighton & Hove (22)**
Br For	**Bracknell Forest (23)**
Bristl	**City of Bristol**
Bucks	**Buckinghamshire**
Bury	**Bury (24)**
C Beds	**Central Bedfordshire**
C Brad	**City of Bradford**
C Derb	**City of Derby**
C KuH	**City of Kingston upon Hull**
C Leic	**City of Leicester**
C Nott	**City of Nottingham**
C Pete	**City of Peterborough**
C Plym	**City of Plymouth**
C Port	**City of Portsmouth**
C Sotn	**City of Southampton**
C Stke	**City of Stoke-on-Trent**
C York	**City of York**
Calder	**Calderdale (25)**
Cambs	**Cambridgeshire**
Ches E	**Cheshire East**
Ches W	**Cheshire West and Chester**
Cnwll	**Cornwall**
Covtry	**Coventry**
Cumb	**Cumbria**
Darltn	**Darlington (26)**
Derbys	**Derbyshire**
Devon	**Devon**
Donc	**Doncaster (27)**
Dorset	**Dorset**
Dudley	**Dudley (28)**
Dur	**Durham**
E R Yk	**East Riding of Yorkshire**
E Susx	**East Sussex**
Essex	**Essex**
Gatesd	**Gateshead (29)**
Gloucs	**Gloucestershire**
Gt Lon	**Greater London**
Halton	**Halton (30)**
Hants	**Hampshire**
Hartpl	**Hartlepool (31)**
Herefs	**Herefordshire**
Herts	**Hertfordshire**
IoS	**Isles of Scilly**
IoW	**Isle of Wight**
Kent	**Kent**
Kirk	**Kirklees (32)**
Knows	**Knowsley (33)**
Lancs	**Lancashire**
Leeds	**Leeds**
Leics	**Leicestershire**
Lincs	**Lincolnshire**
Lpool	**Liverpool**
Luton	**Luton**
M Keyn	**Milton Keynes**
Manch	**Manchester**
Medway	**Medway**
Middsb	**Middlesbrough**
NE Lin	**North East Lincolnshire**
N Linc	**North Lincolnshire**
N Som	**North Somerset (34)**
N Tyne	**North Tyneside (35)**
N u Ty	**Newcastle upon Tyne**
N York	**North Yorkshire**
Nhants	**Northamptonshire**
Norfk	**Norfolk**
Notts	**Nottinghamshire**
Nthumb	**Northumberland**
Oldham	**Oldham (36)**
Oxon	**Oxfordshire**
Poole	**Poole**
R & Cl	**Redcar & Cleveland**
Readg	**Reading**
Rochdl	**Rochdale (37)**
Rothm	**Rotherham (38)**
Rutlnd	**Rutland**
S Glos	**South Gloucestershire (39)**
S on T	**Stockton-on-Tees (40)**
S Tyne	**South Tyneside (41)**
Salfd	**Salford (42)**
Sandw	**Sandwell (43)**
Sefton	**Sefton (44)**
Sheff	**Sheffield**
Shrops	**Shropshire**
Slough	**Slough (45)**
Solhll	**Solihull (46)**
Somset	**Somerset**
St Hel	**St Helens (47)**
Staffs	**Staffordshire**
Sthend	**Southend-on-Sea**
Stockp	**Stockport (48)**
Suffk	**Suffolk**
Sundld	**Sunderland**
Surrey	**Surrey**
Swindn	**Swindon**
Tamesd	**Tameside (49)**
Thurr	**Thurrock (50)**
Torbay	**Torbay**
Traffd	**Trafford (51)**
W & M	**Windsor and Maidenhead**
W Berk	**West Berkshire**
W Susx	**West Sussex**
Wakefd	**Wakefield (53)**
Warrtn	**Warrington (54)**
Warwks	**Warwickshire**
Wigan	**Wigan (55)**
Wilts	**Wiltshire**
Wirral	**Wirral (56)**
Wokham	**Wokingham (57)**
Wolves	**Wolverhampton (58)**
Worcs	**Worcestershire**
Wrekin	**Telford & Wrekin (59)**
Wsall	**Walsall (60)**

ORKNEY ISLANDS
SHETLAND ISLANDS
WESTERN ISLES (Na h-Eileanan an Iar)
HIGHLAND
MORAY
SCOTLAND
ABERDEENSHIRE
Aberdeen
ANGUS
PERTH & KINROSS
Dundee
ARGYLL & BUTE
STIRLING
FIFE
FALK
Edinburgh
W LOTH
E LOTH
Glasgow
NORTH AYRSHIRE
S LANS
SCOTTISH BORDERS
E AYRS
S AYRS
DUMFRIES & GALLOWAY
NORTHUMBERLAND
Newcastle upon Tyne
Sunderland
DURHAM
R & CL
Middlesbrough
CUMBRIA
IoM
NORTH YORKSHIRE
York
EAST RIDING OF YORKSHIRE
Kingston upon Hull
Bradford
Leeds
Blackpool
LANCASHIRE
N LINCS
N E LINCS
Liverpool
Manchester
Sheffield
IoA
CONWY
FLINTS
CHES W
CHES E
DERBYS
NOTTS
LINCOLNSHIRE
DENBGS
WREXHAM
Stoke-on-Trent
Nottingham
GWYNEDD
Derby
STAFFS
LEICS
RUTLAND
NORFOLK
Leicester
Peterborough
SHROPSHIRE
Birmingham
Coventry
CAMBS
POWYS
WORCS
WARWKS
NHANTS
SUFFOLK
CERDGN
Milton Keynes
BED
HEREFS
WALES
ENGLAND
PEMBKS
CARMTH
C
BEDS
Luton
HERTS
ESSEX
GLOUCS
MONS
OXON
Swansea
Cardiff
BUCKS
Southend-on-Sea
Bristol
Swindon
Reading
GREATER LONDON
W BERKS
MEDWAY
WILTSHIRE
SURREY
KENT
SOMERSET
HAMPSHIRE
W SUSX
E SUSX
DEVON
DORSET
Southampton
Bournemouth
Portsmouth
Poole
IoW
CORNWALL
Guernsey
Torbay
CHANNEL ISLANDS
Plymouth
Jersey
IoS
1 2 3 4 5 6 7 8 9 10 11 12 13 14 15 16 17 18 19 20 21 22 23 24 25 26 27 28 29 30 31 32 33 34 35 36 37 38 39 40 41 42 43 44 45 46 47 48 49 50 51 52 53 54 55 56 57 58 59 60

A

Abbas Combe Somset 32 B6
Abberley Worcs 81 H2
Abberley Common Worcs 81 G2
Abberton Essex 72 E3
Abberton Worcs 82 A4
Abberwick Nthumb 191 G3
Abbess Roding Essex 70 E5
Abbey Devon 29 L8
Abbey-Cwm-Hir Powys 78 E1
Abbeydale Sheff 132 F3
Abbey Dore Herefs 62 D1
Abbey Green Staffs 131 J8
Abbey Hill Somset 30 D7
Abbey St Bathans Border 213 G6
Abbeystead Lancs 147 L5
Abbey Town Cumb 177 G8
Abbey Village Lancs 139 J3
Abbey Wood Gt Lon 52 A3
Abbotrule Border 189 G4
Abbots Bickington Devon 27 G8
Abbots Bromley Staffs 115 H6
Abbotsbury Dorset 16 A5
Abbot's Chair Derbys 131 K2
Abbots Deuglie P & K 221 K5
Abbotsham Devon 27 G5
Abbotskerswell Devon 8 C1
Abbots Langley Herts 68 E6
Abbotsleigh Devon 8 B5
Abbots Leigh N Som 45 G4
Abbotsley Cambs 86 E4
Abbots Morton Worcs 82 B4
Abbots Ripton Cambs 102 E7
Abbot's Salford Warwks 82 C5
Abbotstone Hants 35 H4
Abbotswood Hants 34 D6
Abbots Worthy Hants 35 G4
Abbotts Ann Hants 34 D2
Abbott Street Dorset 17 J3
Abcott Shrops 95 J7
Abdon Shrops 96 D6
Abenhall Gloucs 63 K4
Aberaeron Cerdgn 76 E3
Aberaman Rhondd 60 F7
Aberangell Gwynd 93 J2
Aber-arad Carmth 76 B7
Aberarder Highld 251 H6
Aberargie P & K 222 B4
Aberarth Cerdgn 76 E3
Aberavon Neath 57 K7
Aber-banc Cerdgn 76 C7
Aberbargoed Caerph 61 J7
Aberbeeg Blae G 61 K6
Abercanaid Myr Td 61 G6
Abercarn Caerph 43 K3
Abercastle Pembks 74 D5
Abercegir Powys 93 H3
Aberchalder Lodge Highld 240 B3
Aberchirder Abers 268 A5
Aber Clydach Powys 61 H3
Abercraf Powys 59 M6
Abercregan Neath 42 C2
Abercwmboi Rhondd 60 F7
Abercych Pembks 75 M4
Abercynon Rhondd 43 G3
Aberdalgie P & K 221 K3
Aberdare Rhondd 60 F6
Aberdaron Gwynd 108 C6
Aberdeen C Aber 245 L2
Aberdeen Crematorium C Aber 245 K2
Aberdesach Gwynd 109 G1
Aberdour Fife 211 G2
Aberdulais Neath 57 L5
Aberdyfi Gwynd 92 D4
Aberedw Powys 78 F6
Abereiddy Pembks 74 C6
Abererch Gwynd 109 G4
Aberfan Myr Td 61 G7
Aberfeldy P & K 232 C5
Aberffraw IoA 124 F6
Aberffrwd Cerdgn 92 E7
Aberford Leeds 150 F8
Aberfoyle Stirlg 219 H7
Abergarw Brdgnd 42 D5
Abergarwed Neath 60 B6
Abergavenny Mons 62 C4
Abergele Conwy 127 J4
Aber-giar Carmth 76 F7
Abergorlech Carmth 59 G2
Abergwesyn Powys 78 A4
Abergwili Carmth 58 D5
Abergwydol Powys 93 G3
Abergwynfi Neath 42 D3
Abergwyngregyn Gwynd 126 C5
Abergynolwyn Gwynd 92 E2
Aberhafesp Powys 94 C5
Aberhosan Powys 93 H4
Aberkenfig Brdgnd 42 D5
Aberlady E Loth 212 A3
Aberlemno Angus 234 E4
Aberllefenni Gwynd 93 G2
Aberllynfi Powys 79 H7
Aberlour Moray 254 E3
Aber-Magwr Cerdgn 92 E8
Aber-meurig Cerdgn 77 G4
Abermorddu Flints 129 G8
Abermule Powys 94 E4
Abernant Carmth 58 C4
Aber-nant Rhondd 60 F6
Abernethy P & K 222 C4
Abernyte P & K 222 D1
Aberporth Cerdgn 76 A5
Abersoch Gwynd 108 E6
Abersychan Torfn 62 B6
Aberthin V Glam 42 F6
Abertillery Blae G 61 K6
Abertridwr Caerph 43 H4
Abertridwr Powys 111 K7
Abertysswg Caerph 61 H6
Aberuthven P & K 221 H4
Aberyscir Powys 60 F1
Aberystwyth Cerdgn 92 C7
Aberystwyth Crematorium Cerdgn 92 D6
Abingdon-on-Thames Oxon 66 C7
Abinger Common Surrey 37 H2
Abinger Hammer Surrey 37 G2
Abington Nhants 84 F3
Abington S Lans 186 D2
Abington Pigotts Cambs 86 F6
Abingworth W Susx 21 J3
Ab Kettleby Leics 117 J7
Ab Lench Worcs 82 B5
Ablington Gloucs 65 G5
Ablington Wilts 33 K2
Abney Derbys 132 D4
Above Church Staffs 115 G2
Aboyne Abers 244 C4
Abram Wigan 139 J7
Abriachan Highld 250 F4
Abridge Essex 70 C7
Abronhill N Lans 209 L4
Abson S Glos 45 L4
Abthorpe Nhants 84 C6
Aby Lincs 137 H4
Acaster Malbis C York 151 J6
Acaster Selby N York 151 J7
Accrington Lancs 139 M2
Accrington Crematorium Lancs 140 A2
Acha Ag & B 224 F4
Achahoish Ag & B 206 B3
Achalader P & K 233 H6
Achaleven Ag & B 228 E8
Acha Mor W Isls 282 f3
Achanalt Highld 261 M7
Achandunie Highld 263 H5
Achany Highld 272 E7
Acharacle Highld 237 K7
Acharn Highld 227 K2
Acharn P & K 231 L6
Achavanich Highld 279 L7
Achduart Highld 270 D7
Achfary Highld 276 D8
A'Chill Highld 246 C7
Achiltibuie Highld 270 D6
Achina Highld 278 B4
Achinhoan Ag & B 192 F5
Achintee Highld 248 F3
Achintraid Highld 248 D4
Achmelvich Highld 270 E3
Achmore Highld 248 D5
Achmore W Isls 282 f3
Achnacarnin Highld 270 D2
Achnacarry Highld 239 K6
Achnacloich Highld 247 J6
Achnaconeran Highld 250 D8
Achnacroish Ag & B 228 C7
Achnadrish House Ag & B 226 F2
Achnafauld P & K 232 C8
Achnagarron Highld 263 J6
Achnaha Highld 236 F6
Achnahaird Highld 270 D5
Achnairn Highld 272 E5
Achnalea Highld 228 C3
Achnamara Ag & B 206 B2
Achnasheen Highld 261 K8
Achnashellach Lodge Highld 249 G2
Achnastank Moray 254 F5
Achosnich Highld 236 E7
Achranich Highld 227 K3
Achreamie Highld 279 H3
Achriabhach Highld 229 J2
Achriesgill Highld 276 D5
Achtoty Highld 277 M4
Achurch Nhants 102 A6
Achvaich Highld 263 J1
Achvarasdal Highld 279 H3
Ackergill Highld 280 E5
Acklam Middsb 170 C7
Acklam N York 152 B3
Ackleton Shrops 97 H4
Acklington Nthumb 191 J6
Ackton Wakefd 142 C3
Ackworth Moor Top Wakefd 142 C4
Acle Norfk 107 H1
Acock's Green Birm 98 E6
Acol Kent 41 J2
Acomb C York 151 J5
Acomb Nthumb 179 L5
Acombe Somset 30 B8
Aconbury Herefs 80 C8
Acre Lancs 140 B3
Acrefair Wrexhm 112 D3
Acton Ches E 113 K1
Acton Dorset 17 J7
Acton Gt Lon 51 G3
Acton Shrops 95 H6
Acton Staffs 114 C3
Acton Suffk 89 H6
Acton Worcs 81 J2
Acton Beauchamp Herefs 80 F5
Acton Bridge Ches W 130 B4
Acton Burnell Shrops 96 C3
Acton Green Herefs 81 G5
Acton Park Wrexhm 112 E1
Acton Pigott Shrops 96 C3
Acton Round Shrops 96 E4
Acton Scott Shrops 95 L5
Acton Trussell Staffs 114 E7
Acton Turville S Glos 46 A3
Adbaston Staffs 114 B6
Adber Dorset 31 K6
Adbolton Notts 117 G4
Adderbury Oxon 83 L8
Adderley Shrops 113 L3
Adderstone Nthumb 203 J7
Addiewell W Loth 210 C6
Addingham C Brad 149 K6
Addington Bucks 67 H2
Addington Gt Lon 51 K6
Addington Kent 52 E7
Addiscombe Gt Lon 51 J5
Addlestone Surrey 50 D6
Addlestonemoor Surrey 50 D6
Addlethorpe Lincs 137 K6
Adeney Wrekin 113 M7
Adeyfield Herts 68 D5
Adfa Powys 94 C3
Adforton Herefs 79 M1
Adisham Kent 41 H4
Adlestrop Gloucs 65 K2
Adlingfleet E R Yk 143 L3
Adlington Ches E 131 H4
Adlington Lancs 139 J5
Admaston Staffs 115 G7
Admaston Wrekin 96 E1
Admington Warwks 82 E6
Adpar Cerdgn 76 B7
Adsborough Somset 30 D5
Adscombe Somset 30 B3
Adstock Bucks 67 H1
Adstone Nhants 84 B5
Adswood Stockp 131 H2
Adversane W Susx 37 G6
Advie Highld 254 C5
Adwalton Leeds 141 K2
Adwell Oxon 67 G7
Adwick Le Street Donc 142 E6
Adwick upon Dearne Donc 142 D7
Ae D & G 176 C1
Ae Bridgend D & G 176 D2
Affetside Bury 139 M5
Affleck Abers 255 L4
Affpuddle Dorset 16 F4
Affric Lodge Highld 249 K7
Afon-wen Flints 128 D5
Afton Devon 8 C2
Afton IoW 18 E6
Agecroft Crematorium Salfd 140 B7
Agglethorpe N York 159 K5
Aigburth Lpool 129 J2
Aike E R Yk 153 G6
Aiketgate Cumb 166 B1
Aikhead Cumb 165 H1
Aikton Cumb 177 J8
Ailby Lincs 137 H4
Ailey Herefs 79 L5
Ailsworth C Pete 102 C4
Ainderby Quernhow N York 160 E6
Ainderby Steeple N York 160 E4
Aingers Green Essex 73 G3
Ainsdale Sefton 138 C5
Ainsdale-on-Sea Sefton 138 C5
Ainstable Cumb 166 C2
Ainsworth Bury 139 M5
Ainthorpe N York 162 C1
Aintree Sefton 138 D8
Ainville W Loth 210 F6
Aird Ag & B 216 B7
Aird D & G 172 D3
Aird W Isls 282 h3
Aird a Mhulaidh W Isls 282 e5
Aird Asaig W Isls 282 e5
Aird Dhubh Highld 248 A4
Airdeny Ag & B 216 F1
Aird of Kinloch Ag & B 227 G6
Aird of Sleat Highld 247 J8
Airdrie N Lans 209 K6
Airdriehill N Lans 209 K5
Airds of Kells D & G 175 G1
Aird Uig W Isls 282 d3
Airidh a bhruaich W Isls 282 f4
Airieland D & G 175 J3
Airlie Angus 233 M5
Airmyn E R Yk 143 J3
Airntully P & K 233 G8
Airor Highld 247 M7
Airth Falk 210 B2
Airton N York 148 F4
Aisby Lincs 118 D4
Aisby Lincs 135 H1
Aisgill Cumb 158 D3
Aish Devon 7 K3
Aish Devon 8 C3
Aisholt Somset 30 B4
Aiskew N York 160 C5
Aislaby N York 162 D5
Aislaby N York 162 F1
Aislaby S on T 169 L8
Aisthorpe Lincs 135 J4
Aith Shet 281 d5
Akeld Nthumb 202 E7
Akeley Bucks 84 D7
Akenham Suffk 90 D5
Albaston Cnwll 12 A8
Alberbury Shrops 112 E8
Albourne W Susx 22 C4
Albourne Green W Susx 22 C4
Albrighton Shrops 97 H3
Albrighton Shrops 113 H7
Alburgh Norfk 106 F6
Albury Herts 70 B2
Albury Oxon 67 G6
Albury Surrey 37 G2
Albury End Herts 70 B2
Albury Heath Surrey 37 G2
Alby Hill Norfk 122 D5
Alcaig Highld 263 G8
Alcaston Shrops 95 L6
Alcester Warwks 82 C4
Alcester Lane End Birm 98 D7
Alciston E Susx 23 H6
Alcombe Somset 29 H2
Alcombe Wilts 46 A5
Alconbury Cambs 102 D8
Alconbury Weston Cambs 102 D7
Aldborough N York 150 F3
Aldborough Norfk 122 D5
Aldbourne Wilts 47 K4
Aldbrough E R Yk 153 L8
Aldbrough St John N York 169 G8
Aldbury Herts 68 B4
Aldcliffe Lancs 147 J4
Aldclune P & K 232 D3
Aldeburgh Suffk 91 K4
Aldeby Norfk 107 J5
Aldenham Herts 68 F7
Alderbury Wilts 33 L5
Aldercar Derbys 116 D2
Alderford Norfk 122 C7
Alderholt Dorset 33 K8
Alderley Gloucs 45 M1
Alderley Edge Ches E 131 G4
Aldermans Green Covtry 99 K6
Aldermaston W Berk 48 E6
Alderminster Warwks 82 F5
Alder Moor Staffs 115 L6
Aldersey Green Ches W 129 K8
Aldershot Hants 36 C1
Alderton Gloucs 82 B8
Alderton Nhants 84 E6
Alderton Shrops 113 H6
Alderton Suffk 91 H7
Alderton Wilts 46 B2
Alderwasley Derbys 116 A1
Aldfield N York 150 C2
Alford Ches W 129 K7
Aldgate Rutlnd 101 L3
Aldham Essex 72 D2
Aldham Suffk 90 B6
Aldingbourne W Susx 20 F5
Aldingham Cumb 146 E2
Aldington Kent 40 E8
Aldington Worcs 82 C6
Aldington Corner Kent 40 E7
Aldivalloch Moray 255 G6

Aldochlay Ag & B 208 B1
Aldon Shrops 95 K7
Aldoth Cumb 164 F1
Aldreth Cambs 103 J8
Aldridge Wsall 98 D3
Aldringham Suffk 91 K3
Aldro N York 152 B3
Aldsworth Gloucs 65 H5
Aldsworth W Susx 20 C5
Aldunie Moray 255 G6
Aldwark Derbys 132 E8
Aldwark N York 151 G3
Aldwick W Susx 20 E7
Aldwincle Nhants 101 M7
Aldworth W Berk 48 E3
Alexandria W Duns 208 C3
Aley Somset 30 B3
Alfardisworthy Devon 26 E8
Alfington Devon 14 D3
Alfold Surrey 36 F4
Alfold Bars W Susx 36 F4
Alfold Crossways Surrey 36 F4
Alford Abers 255 M8
Alford Lincs 137 H4
Alford Somset 31 K4
Alford Crematorium Lincs 137 H4
Alfreton Derbys 133 H8
Alfrick Worcs 81 H4
Alfrick Pound Worcs 81 G5
Alfriston E Susx 23 H6
Algarkirk Lincs 119 J4
Alhampton Somset 31 K4
Alkborough N Linc 143 M3
Alkerton Gloucs 63 M6
Alkerton Oxon 83 J6
Alkham Kent 41 H6
Alkington Shrops 113 H4
Alkmonton Derbys 115 K4
Allaleigh Devon 8 B4
Allanaquoich Abers 242 F5
Allanbank N Lans 209 M7
Allanton Border 202 D2
Allanton N Lans 209 M7
Allanton S Lans 209 K8
Allaston Gloucs 63 J6
Allbrook Hants 34 F6
All Cannings Wilts 46 F6
Allendale Nthumb 179 J7
Allen End Warwks 98 F4
Allenheads Nthumb 167 K2
Allensford Dur 168 D1
Allen's Green Herts 70 C4
Allensmore Herefs 80 B8
Allenton C Derb 116 B5
Aller Devon 28 D5
Aller Somset 30 F5
Allerby Cumb 164 E3
Allercombe Devon 14 B4
Allerford Somset 28 F2
Allerston N York 162 F6
Allerthorpe E R Yk 152 B6
Allerton C Brad 141 H1
Allerton Highld 263 K6
Allerton Lpool 129 J2
Allerton Bywater Leeds 142 C2
Allerton Mauleverer N York 150 F4
Allesley Covtry 99 J7
Allestree C Derb 116 B4
Allet Common Cnwll 4 C5
Allexton Leics 101 H3
Allgreave Ches E 131 J6
Allhallows Medway 53 H3
Allhallows-on-Sea Medway 53 H3
Alligin Shuas Highld 260 D8
Allimore Green Staffs 114 D7
Allington Dorset 15 K4
Allington Kent 53 G7
Allington Lincs 117 M3
Allington Wilts 33 L3
Allington Wilts 46 C4
Allington Wilts 46 F6
Allithwaite Cumb 156 E7
Alloa Clacks 220 F8
Allonby Cumb 164 E2
Allostock Ches W 130 E5
Alloway S Ayrs 196 C7
Allowenshay Somset 30 F8
All Saints South Elmham Suffk 107 G7
Allscott Shrops 97 G4
Allscott Wrekin 96 E1
All Stretton Shrops 95 L4
Alltami Flints 129 G6
Alltchaorunn Highld 229 K5
Alltmawr Powys 78 F6
Alltwalis Carmth 58 E3
Alltwen Neath 57 K4
Alltyblaca Cerdgn 76 F6
Allweston Dorset 31 L8
Allwood Green Suffk 90 B1
Almeley Herefs 79 L5
Almeley Wooton Herefs 79 L5
Almer Dorset 17 H3
Almholme Donc 142 F6
Almington Staffs 113 M4
Almodington W Susx 20 D7
Almondbank P & K 221 J2
Almondbury Kirk 141 J5
Almondsbury S Glos 45 J2
Alne N York 151 G3
Alness Highld 263 H6
Alnham Nthumb 190 E4
Alnmouth Nthumb 191 J4
Alnwick Nthumb 191 H3
Alperton Gt Lon 50 F2
Alphamstone Essex 89 H8
Alpheton Suffk 89 H5
Alphington Devon 13 L4
Alpington Norfk 106 F3
Alport Derbys 132 D6
Alpraham Ches E 130 B7
Alresford Essex 72 F3
Alrewas Staffs 115 K8
Alsager Ches E 130 F8
Alsagers Bank Staffs 114 C2
Alsop en le Dale Derbys 132 C8
Alston Cumb 167 G2
Alston Devon 15 G2
Alstone Gloucs 82 A8
Alstone Somset 30 D2
Alstonefield Staffs 132 C8
Alston Sutton Somset 44 E8
Alswear Devon 28 C6
Alt Oldham 140 E7
Altandhu Highld 270 C5
Altarnun Cnwll 11 J6
Altass Highld 272 D8
Altcreich Ag & B 227 K5
Altgaltraig Ag & B 207 G4
Altham Lancs 140 A1
Althorne Essex 72 D7
Althorpe N Linc 143 L6
Altnabreac Station Highld 279 H7
Altnaharra Highld 272 E1
Altofts Wakefd 142 B3
Alton Derbys 133 G6
Alton Hants 35 L3
Alton Staffs 115 H3
Alton Wilts 33 K2
Alton Barnes Wilts 47 G6
Alton Pancras Dorset 16 D2
Alton Priors Wilts 47 G6
Altrincham Traffd 130 E2
Altrincham Crematorium Traffd 130 E2
Altskeith Hotel Stirlg 219 G6
Alva Clacks 220 F7
Alvanley Ches W 129 L5
Alvaston C Derb 116 C5
Alvechurch Worcs 82 B1
Alvecote Warwks 99 H3
Alvediston Wilts 33 G6
Alveley Shrops 97 G6
Alverdiscott Devon 27 J6
Alverstoke Hants 19 K4
Alverstone IoW 19 K6
Alverthorpe Wakefd 141 M3
Alverton Notts 117 L3
Alves Moray 266 C4
Alvescot Oxon 65 K6
Alveston S Glos 45 J1
Alveston Warwks 82 F4
Alvingham Lincs 137 G2
Alvington Gloucs 63 J7
Alwalton C Pete 102 C4
Alwinton Nthumb 190 C5
Alwoodley Leeds 150 C7
Alwoodley Gates Leeds 150 D7
Alyth P & K 233 K5
Ambergate Derbys 116 B1
Amber Hill Lincs 119 H2
Amberley Gloucs 64 B6
Amberley W Susx 21 H4
Amber Row Derbys 133 G8
Amberstone E Susx 23 K5
Amble Nthumb 191 K5
Amblecote Dudley 97 K6
Ambler Thorn C Brad 141 H2
Ambleside Cumb 156 E2
Ambleston Pembks 75 G7
Ambrosden Oxon 66 F3
Amcotts N Linc 143 L5
America Cambs 103 J7
Amersham Bucks 68 B7
Amersham Common Bucks 68 B7
Amersham Old Town Bucks 68 B7
Amersham on the Hill Bucks 68 B7
Amerton Staffs 114 F6
Amesbury Wilts 33 K3
Amhuinnsuidhe W Isls 282 d5
Amington Staffs 99 G3
Amisfield Town D & G 176 D2
Amlwch IoA 125 H1
Ammanford Carmth 59 H6
Amotherby N York 162 C7
Ampfield Hants 34 E6
Ampleforth N York 161 J7
Ampney Crucis Gloucs 64 F6
Ampney St Mary Gloucs 65 G6
Ampney St Peter Gloucs 65 G6
Amport Hants 34 C2
Ampthill C Beds 85 K7
Ampton Suffk 89 H1
Amroth Pembks 55 K5
Amulree P & K 232 D8
Amwell Herts 68 F4
Anaheilt Highld 228 C3
Ancaster Lincs 118 C3
Anchor Shrops 94 E6
Ancroft Nthumb 202 F4
Ancrum Border 189 H1
Ancton W Susx 21 G6
Anderby Lincs 137 K4
Andersea Somset 30 E4
Andersfield Somset 30 C4
Anderson Dorset 17 G3
Anderton Ches W 130 C4
Anderton Cnwll 6 E4
Andover Hants 34 D2
Andoversford Gloucs 64 F3
Andreas IoM 154 f2
Anelog Gwynd 108 B6
Anerley Gt Lon 51 J5
Anfield Lpool 129 J1
Anfield Crematorium Lpool 129 J1
Angarrack Cnwll 2 F3
Angarrick Cnwll 3 K4
Angelbank Shrops 96 D8
Angersleigh Somset 30 B7
Angerton Cumb 177 H7
Angle Pembks 54 D6
Anglesey IoA 125 G3
Angmering W Susx 21 H6
Angram N York 151 H6
Angram N York 158 F3
Angrouse Cnwll 3 H7
Anick Nthumb 179 L5
Ankerville Highld 264 C5
Ankle Hill Leics 117 K7
Anlaby E R Yk 144 C2
Anmer Norfk 121 G5
Anmore Hants 19 L1
Annan D & G 177 G5
Annaside Cumb 155 K5
Annat Highld 248 E1
Annathill N Lans 209 J5
Anna Valley Hants 34 D2
Annbank S Ayrs 196 E6
Annesley Notts 116 E1
Annesley Woodhouse Notts 116 E1
Annfield Plain Dur 180 E8
Anniesland C Glas 208 F5
Annitsford N Tyne 181 G4
Annscroft Shrops 95 L2
Ansdell Lancs 138 D2
Ansford Somset 31 L4
Ansley Warwks 99 J5
Anslow Staffs 115 L6
Anslow Gate Staffs 115 K6
Anslow Lees Staffs 115 K6
Ansteadbrook Surrey 36 D4
Anstey Hants 35 L3
Anstey Herts 87 H8
Anstey Leics 100 C2
Anstruther Fife 223 K6
Ansty W Susx 37 L6
Ansty Warwks 99 L6
Ansty Wilts 33 G5
Ansty Cross Dorset 16 E2
Anthill Common Hants 19 L1
Anthonys Surrey 50 C6
Anthorn Cumb 177 G7
Antingham Norfk 122 E5
An t-Ob W Isls 282 d6
Anton's Gowt Lincs 119 J2
Antony Cnwll 6 D4
Antrobus Ches W 130 C4
Anvil Corner Devon 11 M2
Anvil Green Kent 40 E5
Anwick Lincs 118 F2
Anwoth D & G 174 F4
Aperfield Gt Lon 51 L7
Apes Dale Worcs 82 A1
Apethorpe Nhants 102 A4
Apeton Staffs 114 D7
Apley Lincs 136 B5
Apperknowle Derbys 133 H4
Apperley Gloucs 64 B2
Apperley Bridge C Brad 150 B8
Apperley Dene Nthumb 180 C7
Appersett N York 158 E4
Appin Ag & B 228 E6
Appleby N Linc 144 B5
Appleby-in-Westmorland Cumb 166 F6
Appleby Magna Leics 99 J2
Appleby Parva Leics 99 J2
Appleby Street Herts 69 J6
Applecross Highld 248 A3
Appledore Devon 27 H5
Appledore Devon 29 K7
Appledore Kent 25 H2
Appledore Heath Kent 25 H1
Appleford Oxon 66 D8
Applegarth Town D & G 176 F2
Applehaigh Wakefd 142 A5
Appleshaw Hants 34 C1
Applethwaite Cumb 165 J5
Appleton Halton 129 M2
Appleton Oxon 66 C6
Appleton Warrtn 130 B3
Appleton-le-Moors N York 162 C5
Appleton-le-Street N York 162 C7
Appleton Roebuck N York 151 J7
Appleton Thorn Warrtn 130 C3
Appleton Wiske N York 160 F2
Appletreehall Border 188 F3
Appletreewick N York 149 J4
Appley Somset 29 K6
Appley Bridge Lancs 139 G6
Apse Heath IoW 19 J7
Apsley End C Beds 86 C8
Apuldram W Susx 20 D6
Arabella Highld 264 C5
Arbirlot Angus 234 F7
Arboll Highld 264 D3
Arborfield Wokham 49 H5
Arborfield Cross Wokham 49 J5
Arbourthorne Sheff 133 G3
Arbroath Angus 235 G7
Arbuthnott Abers 245 H8
Arcadia Kent 39 L6
Archddu Carmth 56 E4
Archdeacon Newton Darltn 169 H7
Archencarroch W Duns 208 C3
Archiestown Moray 254 E3
Archirondel Jersey 9 f2
Arclid Green Ches E 130 F7
Ardallie Abers 257 J4
Ardanaiseig Hotel Ag & B 217 H2
Ardaneaskan Highld 248 D4
Ardarroch Highld 248 D4
Ardbeg Ag & B 204 F7
Ardbeg Ag & B 207 H5
Ardbeg Ag & B 207 K2
Ardcharnich Highld 261 K2
Ardchiavaig Ag & B 214 D1
Ardchonnel Ag & B 216 F5
Ardchullarie More Stirlg 219 K4
Arddarroch Ag & B 218 C8
Arddleen Powys 112 C8
Ardechive Highld 239 J5
Ardeer N Ayrs 196 B3
Ardeley Herts 69 J2
Ardelve Highld 248 D6
Arden Ag & B 208 B2
Ardens Grafton Warwks 82 D4
Ardentallen Ag & B 216 C2
Ardentinny Ag & B 207 K2
Ardentraive Ag & B 207 G4
Ardeonaig Stirlg 231 J8
Ardersier Highld 252 E1
Ardessie Highld 261 H2
Ardfern Ag & B 216 C6
Ardfernal Ag & B 205 J2
Ardgay Highld 263 G2
Ardgour Highld 229 G3
Ardgowan Inver 207 L4
Ardhallow Ag & B 207 K4
Ardhasig W Isls 282 e5
Ardheslaig Highld 260 C8
Ardindrean Highld 261 K2
Ardingly W Susx 38 A7
Ardington Oxon 48 B1
Ardington Wick Oxon 48 B1
Ardlamont Ag & B 206 F6
Ardleigh Essex 72 F1
Ardleigh Heath Essex 72 F1
Ardler P & K 233 L7
Ardley Oxon 66 D2
Ardley End Essex 70 D4
Ardlui Ag & B 218 D4
Ardlussa Ag & B 215 J6
Ardmair Highld 270 F8
Ardmaleish Ag & B 207 H5
Ardminish Ag & B 205 L6
Ardmolich Highld 237 K6
Ardmore Ag & B 208 A3
Ardmore Highld 263 J3
Ardnadam Ag & B 207 K3
Ardnagrask Highld 250 F2

Ardnarff Highld 248 E4
Ardnastang Highld 228 B3
Ardpatrick Ag & B 206 B7
Ardrishaig Ag & B 206 D2
Ardross Highld 263 H5
Ardrossan N Ayrs 195 L3
Ardsley Barns 142 B6
Ardsley East Leeds 141 M3
Ardslignish Highld 237 H8
Ardtalla Ag & B 205 G5
Ardtoe Highld 237 J6
Arduaine Ag & B 216 B5
Ardullie Highld 263 G7
Ardvasar Highld 247 K7
Ardvorlich P & K 219 K3
Ardvourlie W Isls 282 e5
Ardwell D & G 172 D5
Ardwick Manch 140 C8
Areley Kings Worcs 81 H1
Arevegaig Highld 237 J7
Arford Hants 36 B3
Argoed Caerph 61 J7
Argoed Shrops 112 E7
Argoed Mill Powys 78 D3
Argos Hill E Susx 23 J2
Aribruach W Isls 282 f4
Aridhglas Ag & B 226 C7
Arileod Ag & B 224 F4
Arinagour Ag & B 225 G4
Ariogan Ag & B 216 D2
Arisaig Highld 237 J3
Arisaig House Highld 237 K4
Arkendale N York 150 E4
Arkesden Essex 87 K8
Arkholme Lancs 147 L2
Arkleby Cumb 164 F3
Arkleton D & G 188 C7
Arkle Town N York 159 H2
Arkley Gt Lon 69 G7
Arksey Donc 142 F6
Arkwright Town Derbys 133 H5
Arle Gloucs 64 D2
Arlecdon Cumb 164 D7
Arlescote Warwks 83 J5
Arlesey C Beds 86 D7
Arleston Wrekin 96 F1
Arley Ches E 130 C3
Arley Warwks 99 H5
Arlingham Gloucs 63 L5
Arlington Devon 27 L3
Arlington E Susx 23 J5
Arlington Gloucs 65 G5
Arlington Beccott Devon 27 L3
Armadale Highld 247 K7
Armadale Highld 278 D3
Armadale W Loth 210 B5
Armaside Cumb 164 F5
Armathwaite Cumb 166 C2
Arminghall Norfk 106 E3
Armitage Staffs 115 H8
Armitage Bridge Kirk 141 H5
Armley Leeds 141 L1
Armscote Warwks 82 F6
Armshead Staffs 114 E2
Armston Nhants 102 B6
Armthorpe Donc 143 G6
Arnabost Ag & B 225 G3
Arnaby Cumb 156 A5
Arncliffe N York 149 G2
Arncliffe Cote N York 149 G2
Arncroach Fife 223 J6
Arndilly House Moray 266 F6
Arne Dorset 17 J5
Arnesby Leics 100 D5
Arngask P & K 221 L5
Arnisdale Highld 238 D2
Arnish Highld 259 K7
Arniston Mdloth 211 K6
Arnol W Isls 282 f2
Arnold E R Yk 153 H7
Arnold Notts 117 G2
Arnprior Stirlg 219 K8
Arnside Cumb 157 G7
Aros Ag & B 227 G3
Arowry Wrexhm 113 G4
Arrad Foot Cumb 156 D6
Arram E R Yk 153 G7
Arran N Ayrs 194 E4
Arrathorne N York 160 B4
Arreton IoW 19 J6
Arrina Highld 260 B8
Arrington Cambs 87 G5
Arrochar Ag & B 218 D6
Arrow Warwks 82 C4
Arrowfield Top Worcs 98 C8
Arscott Shrops 95 K2
Artafallie Highld 251 H2
Arthington Leeds 150 C6
Arthingworth Nhants 101 G7
Arthog Gwynd 110 C8
Arthrath Abers 257 H4
Arthursdale Leeds 150 E8
Artrochie Abers 257 J5
Arundel W Susx 21 G5
Asby Cumb 164 E6
Ascog Ag & B 207 J6
Ascot W & M 50 A5
Ascott Warwks 83 H8
Ascott Earl Oxon 65 L3
Ascott-under-Wychwood Oxon 65 L3
Asenby N York 160 F7
Asfordby Leics 117 J7
Asfordby Hill Leics 117 J7
Asgarby Lincs 118 F3
Asgarby Lincs 136 F6
Ash Devon 8 C5
Ash Devon 12 C1
Ash Dorset 32 E8
Ash Kent 41 J4
Ash Kent 52 D6
Ash Somset 30 D6
Ash Somset 31 G6
Ash Surrey 36 D1
Ashampstead W Berk 48 E4
Ashampstead Green W Berk 48 E3
Ashbocking Suffk 90 E4
Ashbourne Derbys 115 K2
Ashbrittle Somset 29 J6
Ashburnham Place E Susx 24 C4
Ashburton Devon 13 H8
Ashbury Devon 12 C3
Ashbury Oxon 47 K2
Ashby N Linc 143 M6
Ashby by Partney Lincs 137 H6
Ashby cum Fenby NE Lin 145 H7
Ashby de la Launde Lincs 135 L8
Ashby-de-la-Zouch Leics 116 B8
Ashby Folville Leics 100 F1
Ashby Magna Leics 100 C5
Ashby Parva Leics 100 C5
Ashby Puerorum Lincs 136 F5
Ashby St Ledgers Nhants 84 B2
Ashby St Mary Norfk 107 G3
Ashchurch Gloucs 81 L8
Ashcombe Devon 13 L6
Ashcombe N Som 44 C6
Ashcott Somset 31 G3
Ashdon Essex 88 B6
Ashe Hants 35 H1
Asheldham Essex 72 E6
Ashen Essex 88 E6
Ashendon Bucks 67 H4
Asheridge Bucks 68 B6
Ashfield Hants 34 E7
Ashfield Herefs 63 H2
Ashfield Stirlg 220 D6
Ashfield cum Thorpe Suffk 90 F3
Ashfield Green Suffk 88 F4
Ashfield Green Suffk 106 F8
Ashfold Crossways W Susx 37 K5
Ashford Devon 7 K5
Ashford Devon 27 J4
Ashford Kent 40 D6
Ashford Surrey 50 D4
Ashford Bowdler Shrops 80 C1
Ashford Carbonell Shrops 80 C1
Ashford Hill Hants 48 E6
Ashford in the Water Derbys 132 D5
Ashgill S Lans 198 C3
Ash Green Surrey 36 D1
Ash Green Warwks 99 J6
Ashill Devon 29 K8
Ashill Norfk 105 H3
Ashill Somset 30 D7
Ashingdon Essex 72 C8
Ashington Nthumb 181 G1
Ashington Poole 17 K3
Ashington Somset 31 J6
Ashington W Susx 21 K4
Ashkirk Border 188 E2
Ashlett Hants 19 G3
Ashleworth Gloucs 64 A2
Ashleworth Quay Gloucs 64 B2
Ashley Cambs 88 D3
Ashley Ches E 130 F3
Ashley Devon 28 B8
Ashley Dorset 18 A3
Ashley Gloucs 64 D8
Ashley Hants 18 C4
Ashley Hants 34 E4
Ashley Kent 41 J5
Ashley Nhants 101 H5
Ashley Staffs 114 B4
Ashley Wilts 46 B5
Ashley Green Bucks 68 B6
Ashleyhay Derbys 115 M1
Ashley Heath Dorset 17 M2
Ashley Moor Herefs 80 B2
Ash Magna Shrops 113 J4
Ashmansworth Hants 48 B7
Ashmansworthy Devon 26 F7
Ashmead Green Gloucs 63 M7
Ashmill Devon 11 M3
Ash Mill Devon 28 D6
Ashmore Dorset 32 F7
Ashmore Green W Berk 48 D5
Ashorne Warwks 83 G4
Ashover Derbys 133 G7
Ashover Hay Derbys 133 G7
Ashow Warwks 83 H1
Ash Parva Shrops 113 J4
Ashperton Herefs 80 E7
Ashprington Devon 8 B3
Ash Priors Somset 29 L5
Ashreigney Devon 27 L8
Ash Street Suffk 89 K6
Ashtead Surrey 50 F7
Ash Thomas Devon 29 H8
Ashton C Pete 102 B2
Ashton Ches W 129 L6
Ashton Cnwll 2 F5
Ashton Devon 13 K5
Ashton Hants 35 H7
Ashton Herefs 80 C2
Ashton Inver 207 L4
Ashton Nhants 84 E5
Ashton Nhants 102 B5
Ashton Somset 30 F1
Ashton Common Wilts 46 C7
Ashton Hill Wilts 46 C7
Ashton-in-Makerfield Wigan 139 H7
Ashton Keynes Wilts 64 F8
Ashton under Hill Worcs 82 A7
Ashton-under-Lyne Tamesd 140 E7
Ashton upon Mersey Traffd 130 F1
Ashurst Hants 18 E2
Ashurst Kent 38 D5
Ashurst Lancs 138 F6
Ashurst W Susx 21 L4
Ashurstwood W Susx 38 B6
Ash Vale Surrey 49 L8
Ashwater Devon 11 M4
Ashwell Herts 86 F7
Ashwell Rutlnd 101 J1
Ashwell Somset 30 E7
Ashwell End Herts 86 E7
Ashwellthorpe Norfk 106 C4
Ashwick Somset 31 K1
Ashwicken Norfk 120 F7
Ashwood Staffs 97 K5
Askam in Furness Cumb 156 B7
Askern Donc 142 F5
Askerswell Dorset 15 M4
Askett Bucks 67 K6
Askham Cumb 166 C6
Askham Notts 134 E5
Askham Bryan C York 151 H6
Askham Richard C York 151 H6
Asknish Ag & B 206 E1
Askrigg N York 159 G4
Askwith N York 149 L6
Aslackby Lincs 118 E5
Aslacton Norfk 106 D5
Aslockton Notts 117 K3
Asney Somset 31 G3
Aspall Suffk 90 E2
Aspatria Cumb 164 F2
Aspenden Herts 69 K2
Aspenshaw Derbys 131 K2
Asperton Lincs 119 J4
Aspley Staffs 114 C5
Aspley Guise C Beds 85 J8
Aspley Heath C Beds 85 H8
Aspley Heath Warwks 82 C1
Aspull Wigan 139 J6
Aspull Common Wigan 139 J8
Asselby E R Yk 143 H2
Asserby Lincs 137 J4
Asserby Turn Lincs 137 J4
Assington Suffk 89 J7
Assington Green Suffk 88 F5
Astbury Ches E 131 G7
Astcote Nhants 84 D4
Asterby Lincs 136 E4
Asterley Shrops 95 J2
Asterton Shrops 95 K5
Asthall Oxon 65 L5
Asthall Leigh Oxon 65 L4
Astle Highld 263 K2
Astley Shrops 113 H7
Astley Warwks 99 J5
Astley Wigan 139 L7
Astley Worcs 81 H2
Astley Abbots Shrops 96 F4
Astley Bridge Bolton 139 L5
Astley Cross Worcs 81 J1
Astley Green Wigan 139 L7
Aston Birm 98 D5
Aston Ches E 113 K2
Aston Ches W 130 A
Aston Derbys 132 D
Aston Flints 129 G
Aston Herefs 80 B
Aston Herts 69 H
Aston Oxon 65 M
Aston Rothm 133 J
Aston Shrops 97 H5
Aston Shrops 113 H
Aston Staffs 114 B
Aston Staffs 114 D
Aston Wokham 49 J
Aston Wrekin 96 E
Aston Abbotts Bucks 67 K
Aston Botterell Shrops 96 E
Aston-by-Stone Staffs 114 E
Aston Cantlow Warwks 82 D
Aston Clinton Bucks 67 L
Aston Crews Herefs 63 K3
Aston Cross Gloucs 81 L8
Aston End Herts 69 H2
Aston-Eyre Shrops 96 E4
Aston Fields Worcs 81 M2
Aston Flamville Leics 100 A5
Aston Heath Ches W 130 A4
Aston Ingham Herefs 63 K3
Aston juxta Mondrum Ches E 130 C8
Aston le Walls Nhants 83 L5
Aston Magna Gloucs 82 E8
Aston Munslow Shrops 96 C6
Aston on Clun Shrops 95 J
Aston Pigott Shrops 95 H2
Aston Rogers Shrops 95 H2
Aston Rowant Oxon 67 H7
Aston Sandford Bucks 67 J5
Aston Somerville Worcs 82 B7
Aston-sub-Edge Gloucs 82 D7
Aston Tirrold Oxon 48 E
Aston-upon-Trent Derbys 116 C5
Aston Upthorpe Oxon 48 E2
Astrop Nhants 83 L
Astrope Herts 67 L4
Astwick C Beds 86 E7
Astwith Derbys 133 J6
Astwood M Keyn 85 J5
Astwood Worcs 81 L
Astwood Bank Worcs 82 B3
Astwood Crematorium Worcs 81 K4
Aswarby Lincs 118 E4
Aswardby Lincs 137 G5
Atcham Shrops 96 C2
Atch Lench Worcs 82 B5
Athelhampton Dorset 16 E4
Athelington Suffk 90 F1
Athelney Somset 30 E5
Athelstaneford E Loth 212 C4
Atherfield Green IoW 19 G7
Atherington Devon 27 L6
Atherington W Susx 21 G6
Atherstone Somset 30 F7
Atherstone Warwks 99 J4
Atherstone on Stour Warwks 82 F5
Atherton Wigan 139 K7
Atley Hill N York 160 D2
Atlow Derbys 115 L2
Attadale Highld 248 E4
Attenborough Notts 116 E5
Atterby Lincs 135 K1
Attercliffe Sheff 133 G2
Atterley Shrops 96 E4
Atterton Leics 99 K4
Attleborough Norfk 105 L4
Attleborough Warwks 99 K5
Attlebridge Norfk 122 C8
Attleton Green Suffk 88 E4
Atwick E R Yk 153 K5
Atworth Wilts 46 B6
Auberrow Herefs 80 C6
Aubourn Lincs 135 J7
Auchbreck Moray 254 D6
Auchedly Abers 257 G5
Auchenblae Abers 244 F7
Auchenbowie Stirlg 209 L2
Auchencairn D & G 175 K4
Auchencairn D & G 176 C2
Auchencairn N Ayrs 195 G5
Auchencrow Border 213 J7
Auchendinny Mdloth 211 H6
Auchengray S Lans 199 G2
Auchenhalrig Moray 267 H4
Auchenheath S Lans 198 D4
Auchenhessnane D & G 185 K4
Auchenlochan Ag & B 206 F4
Auchenmade N Ayrs 196 C2
Auchenmalg D & G 173 G4
Auchentiber N Ayrs 196 D2
Auchindrain Ag & B 217 G6
Auchindrean Highld 261 K4
Auchininna Abers 268 B6
Auchinleck E Ayrs 197 G6

Auchinloch N Lans 209 H5
Auchinstarry N Lans 209 J4
Auchintore Highld 229 H1
Auchiries Abers 257 K4
Auchlean Highld 241 M4
Auchlee Abers 245 K4
Auchleven Abers 256 A6
Auchlochan S Lans 198 D5
Auchlossan Abers 244 D3
Auchlyne Stirlg 219 H1
Auchmillan E Ayrs 197 G5
Auchmithie Angus 235 G6
Auchmuirbridge Fife 222 C7
Auchnacree Angus 234 C3
Auchnagatt Abers 257 G3
Auchnarrow Moray 254 D7
Auchnotteroch D & G 172 B3
Auchroisk Moray 267 G6
Auchterarder P & K 221 G4
Auchteraw Highld 240 B2
Auchterblair Highld 253 H7
Auchtercairn Highld 260 C4
Auchterderran Fife 222 C8
Auchterhouse Angus 233 M7
Auchterless Abers 256 C3
Auchtermuchty Fife 222 D5
Auchterneed Highld 262 E7
Auchtertool Fife 211 H1
Auchtertyre Highld 248 D6
Auchtubh Stirlg 219 J3
Auckengill Highld 280 E3
Auckley Donc 143 G7
Audenshaw Tamesd 140 D8
Audlem Ches E 113 L3
Audley Staffs 114 C2
Audley End Essex 87 L7
Audley End Essex 89 G7
Audley End Suffk 89 G4
Audmore Staffs 114 C7
Audnam Dudley 97 K6
Aughertree Cumb 165 H3
Aughton E R Yk 151 L8
Aughton Lancs 138 E6
Aughton Lancs 147 L2
Aughton Rothm 133 J2
Aughton Wilts 47 K7
Aughton Park Lancs 138 E6
Auldearn Highld 253 H1
Aulden Herefs 80 B4
Auldgirth D & G 176 B2
Auldhouse S Lans 197 J1
Ault a' chruinn Highld 248 F7
Aultbea Highld 260 D2
Aultgrishin Highld 260 B3
Aultguish Inn Highld 262 B6
Ault Hucknall Derbys 133 J6
Aultmore Moray 267 H5
Aultnagoire Highld 250 F7
Aultnamain Inn Highld 263 J4
Aunby Lincs 118 D8
Aunk Devon 14 B3
Aunsby Lincs 118 D4
Aust S Glos 45 H1
Austendike Lincs 119 J7
Austerfield Donc 134 D1
Austerlands Oldham 140 E6
Austhorpe Leeds 142 B1
Austonley Kirk 141 H6
Austrey Warwks 99 J2
Austwick N York 148 D2
Authorpe Lincs 137 G3
Authorpe Row Lincs 137 K5
Avebury Wilts 47 G5
Avebury Trusloe Wilts 47 G5
Aveley Thurr 52 C3
Avening Gloucs 64 C7
Averham Notts 117 K1
Aveton Gifford Devon 7 K5
Aviemore Highld 242 B1
Avington W Berk 48 A5
Avoch Highld 251 J1
Avon Hants 18 A4
Avonbridge Falk 210 B4
Avon Dassett Warwks 83 K5
Avonmouth Bristl 45 G3
Avonwick Devon 7 K3
Awbridge Hants 34 D6
Awkley S Glos 45 H2
Awliscombe Devon 14 D2
Awre Gloucs 63 L5
Awsworth Notts 116 E3
Axborough Worcs 97 J7
Axbridge Somset 44 E8
Axford Hants 35 J2
Axford Wilts 47 K5
Axminster Devon 15 G3
Axmouth Devon 14 F4
Axton Flints 128 D4
Aycliffe Dur 169 H6
Aydon Nthumb 180 B5
Aylburton Gloucs 63 J6
Ayle Nthumb 167 G1
Aylesbeare Devon 14 B4
Aylesbury Bucks 67 K4
Aylesby NE Lin 145 G6
Aylesford Kent 52 F7
Aylesham Kent 41 H5
Aylestone C Leic 100 C3
Aylestone Park C Leic 100 D3
Aylmerton Norfk 122 D4
Aylsham Norfk 122 D6
Aylton Herefs 80 F7
Aylworth Gloucs 65 G3
Aymestrey Herefs 80 A2
Aynho Nhants 83 L8
Ayot Green Herts 69 G4
Ayot St Lawrence Herts 69 G4
Ayot St Peter Herts 69 G4
Ayr S Ayrs 196 C6
Aysgarth N York 159 H5
Ayshford Devon 29 J7
Ayside Cumb 156 F6
Ayston Rutlnd 101 J3
Aythorpe Roding Essex 70 E4
Ayton Border 213 K6
Azerley N York 160 C7

B

Babbacombe Torbay 8 D2
Babbington Notts 116 E3
Babbinswood Shrops 112 E5
Babbs Green Herts 69 K4
Babcary Somset 31 J5
Babel Carmth 59 M2
Babel Green Suffk 88 E5
Babell Flints 128 E5
Babeny Devon 12 F7
Bablock Hythe Oxon 66 B6
Babraham Cambs 87 K5
Babworth Notts 134 D3
Bachau IoA 125 H3
Bache Shrops 95 L7
Bacheldre Powys 94 F5
Bachelor's Bump E Susx 24 F5
Backaland Ork 275 d3
Backbarrow Cumb 156 E5
Backe Carmth 58 A5
Backfolds Abers 269 J5
Backford Ches W 129 J5
Backford Cross Ches W 129 J5
Backies Highld 273 K7
Back of Keppoch Highld 237 J3
Back o' th' Brook Staffs 115 H1
Back Street Suffk 88 E3
Backwell N Som 44 F5
Backworth N Tyne 181 H4
Bacon's End Solhll 98 F6
Baconsthorpe Norfk 122 C4
Bacton Herefs 62 D1
Bacton Norfk 123 G5
Bacton Suffk 90 C2
Bacton Green Suffk 90 B2
Bacup Lancs 140 C3
Badachro Highld 260 C5
Badbury Swindn 47 J3
Badby Nhants 84 A3
Badcall Highld 276 B7
Badcall Highld 276 C5
Badcaul Highld 261 G2
Baddeley Edge C Stke 114 E1
Baddeley Green C Stke 114 E1
Baddesley Clinton Warwks 82 F1
Baddesley Ensor Warwks 99 H4
Baddidarrach Highld 270 E3
Baddinsgill Border 199 K2
Badenscoth Abers 256 C4
Badenyon Abers 255 G7
Badgall Cnwll 11 J5
Badgeney Cambs 103 J4
Badger Shrops 97 H3
Badger's Cross Cnwll 2 D4
Badgers Mount Kent 52 B6
Badgeworth Gloucs 64 C3
Badgworth Somset 44 E8
Badharlick Cnwll 11 J5
Badicaul Highld 248 B6
Badingham Suffk 91 G2
Badlesmere Kent 40 D4
Badlieu Border 187 G2
Badlipster Highld 280 B6
Badluachrach Highld 261 G1
Badninish Highld 263 K1
Badrallach Highld 261 H2
Badsey Worcs 82 C6
Badshot Lea Surrey 36 C1
Badsworth Wakefd 142 D5
Badwell Ash Suffk 89 K2
Badwell Green Suffk 89 K2
Bagber Dorset 32 C8
Bagby N York 161 G6
Bag Enderby Lincs 136 F5
Bagendon Gloucs 64 E5
Bagginswood Shrops 96 F7
Baggrow Cumb 165 G2
Bagh a Chaisteil W Isls 283 b13
Bagham Kent 40 E4
Bagh a Tuath W Isls 283 b13
Bagillt Flints 128 F4
Baginton Warwks 99 K8
Baglan Neath 57 K6
Bagley Leeds 141 K1
Bagley Shrops 112 F6
Bagley Somset 31 G2
Bagmore Hants 35 K2
Bagnall Staffs 114 E1
Bagnor W Berk 48 C5
Bagot Shrops 96 D8
Bagshot Surrey 49 M6
Bagshot Wilts 47 L6
Bagstone S Glos 45 K2
Bagthorpe Notts 116 D1
Bagworth Leics 99 M2
Bagwy Llydiart Herefs 62 F2
Baildon C Brad 149 L7
Baildon Green C Brad 149 L7
Baile Ailein W Isls 282 f4
Baile a Mhanaich W Isls 283 c9
Baile Mor Ag & B 226 B7
Bailey Green Hants 35 K5
Baileyhead Cumb 178 C3
Bailiff Bridge Calder 141 J3
Baillieston C Glas 209 H6
Bailrigg Lancs 147 J4
Bainbridge N York 159 G4
Bainshole Abers 256 A5
Bainton C Pete 102 B2
Bainton E R Yk 152 E5
Bainton Oxon 66 E2
Baintown Fife 222 F6
Bairnkine Border 189 H3
Baker's End Herts 69 L4
Baker Street Thurr 52 D3
Bakewell Derbys 132 D6
Bala Gwynd 111 H4
Balallan W Isls 282 f4
Balbeg Highld 250 D5
Balbeggie P & K 222 B1
Balblair Highld 250 E3
Balblair Highld 263 J6
Balby Donc 142 E7
Balcary D & G 175 K5
Balchraggan Highld 250 F3
Balchreick Highld 276 B4
Balcombe W Susx 37 M5
Balcombe Lane W Susx 37 M4
Balcomie Links Fife 223 L5
Baldersby N York 160 E7
Baldersby St James N York 160 E7
Balderstone Lancs 139 J1
Balderstone Rochdl 140 D5
Balderton Notts 117 L1
Baldhu Cnwll 4 C6
Baldinnie Fife 223 G5
Baldinnies P & K 221 J4
Baldock Herts 86 E8
Baldovie C Dund 234 C8
Baldrine IoM 154 f5
Baldslow E Susx 24 E4
Baldwin IoM 154 e6
Baldwinholme Cumb 177 K8
Baldwin's Gate Staffs 114 B3
Baldwin's Hill W Susx 38 B5
Bale Norfk 121 M4
Baledgarno P & K 222 D1
Balemartine Ag & B 224 C7
Balerno C Edin 211 G5
Balfarg Fife 222 D6
Balfield Angus 234 E2
Balfour Ork 275 d4
Balfron Stirlg 208 F1
Balgaveny Abers 256 B4
Balgonar Fife 221 J8
Balgowan D & G 172 E6
Balgowan Highld 241 H4
Balgown Highld 258 F3
Balgracie D & G 172 B3
Balgray S Lans 186 C2
Balham Gt Lon 51 H4
Balhary P & K 233 L6
Balholmie P & K 233 H8
Baligill Highld 278 E3
Balintore Angus 233 L4
Balintore Highld 264 D5
Balintraid Highld 263 K5
Balivanich W Isls 283 c9
Balk N York 161 G6
Balkeerie Angus 233 M6
Balkholme E R Yk 143 K2
Ballabeg IoM 154 c7
Ballachulish Highld 229 H4
Ballafesson IoM 154 b7
Ballajora IoM 154 g4
Ballakilpheric IoM 154 b7
Ballamodha IoM 154 c7
Ballanlay Ag & B 207 G6
Ballantrae S Ayrs 182 D6
Ballards Gore Essex 72 C8
Ballards Green Warwks 99 H5
Ballasalla IoM 154 c7
Ballater Abers 243 L4
Ballaugh IoM 154 d3
Ballchraggan Highld 263 K5
Ballencrieff E Loth 212 B3
Ballevullin Ag & B 224 B6
Ball Green C Stke 114 D1
Ball Haye Green Staffs 131 K8
Ball Hill Hants 48 B6
Ballidon Derbys 115 K1
Balliekine N Ayrs 194 D3
Balliemore Ag & B 217 H7
Balligmorrie S Ayrs 183 G5
Ballimore Stirlg 219 H4
Ballindalloch Moray 254 D4
Ballindean P & K 222 D2
Ballingdon Suffk 89 H7
Ballinger Common Bucks 67 M6
Ballingham Herefs 63 H1
Ballingry Fife 222 B7
Ballinluig P & K 232 E5
Ballinshoe Angus 234 B5
Ballintuim P & K 233 G4
Balloch Highld 252 D2
Balloch N Lans 209 K4
Balloch P & K 220 E3
Balloch S Ayrs 183 J4
Balloch W Duns 208 C3
Balls Cross W Susx 36 E5
Balls Green E Susx 38 D6
Ball's Green Gloucs 64 B7
Ballygown Ag & B 226 E4
Ballygrant Ag & B 204 F3
Ballyhaugh Ag & B 224 F4
Balmacara Highld 248 C6
Balmaclellan D & G 185 G7
Balmae D & G 175 H6
Balmaha Stirlg 208 C1
Balmalcolm Fife 222 E5
Balmangan D & G 175 G5
Balmedie Abers 257 H8
Balmer Heath Shrops 113 G4
Balmerino Fife 222 F2
Balmerlawn Hants 18 D3
Balmichael N Ayrs 194 E5
Balmore E Duns 209 G4
Balmuchy Highld 264 D4
Balmule Fife 211 H2
Balmullo Fife 223 G3
Balnacoil Lodge Highld 273 J5
Balnacra Highld 248 F3
Balnacroft Abers 243 J5
Balnafoich Highld 251 J4
Balnaguard P & K 232 D5
Balnahard Ag & B 214 E4
Balnahard Ag & B 226 E5
Balnain Highld 250 D5
Balnakeil Highld 276 F3
Balne N York 142 F4
Balquharn P & K 232 F8
Balquhidder Stirlg 219 H3
Balsall Common Solhll 99 G8
Balsall Heath Birm 98 D6
Balsall Street Solhll 99 G8
Balscote Oxon 83 J6
Balsham Cambs 88 B5
Baltasound Shet 281 f1
Balterley Staffs 114 B2
Balterley Green Staffs 114 B2
Balterley Heath Staffs 114 B2
Baltersan D & G 174 C3
Baltonsborough Somset 31 J4
Balvicar Ag & B 216 B4
Balvraid Highld 248 D8
Balvraid Highld 252 F5
Balwest Cnwll 2 F5
Bamber Bridge Lancs 139 H3
Bamber's Green Essex 70 E3
Bamburgh Nthumb 203 K6
Bamford Derbys 132 D3
Bamford Rochdl 140 C5
Bampton Cumb 166 C7
Bampton Devon 29 G6
Bampton Oxon 65 L6
Bampton Grange Cumb 166 C7
Banavie Highld 239 J8
Banbury Oxon 83 K7
Banbury Crematorium Oxon 83 K6
Bancffosfelen Carmth 58 E6
Banchory Abers 244 F4

Banchory-Devenick Abers 245 K3
Bancycapel Carmth 58 D6
Bancyfelin Carmth 58 B5
Banc-y-ffordd Carmth 76 D7
Bandirran P & K 222 C1
Bandrake Head Cumb 156 D5
Banff Abers 268 C3
Bangor Gwynd 125 K5
Bangor Crematorium Gwynd 125 L5
Bangor-is-y-coed Wrexhm 112 F2
Bangors Cnwll 11 H3
Bangor's Green Lancs 138 D6
Bangrove Suffk 89 J1
Banham Norfk 106 B6
Bank Hants 18 D2
Bankend D & G 176 D5
Bankfoot P & K 233 G8
Bankglen E Ayrs 197 H8
Bank Ground Cumb 156 D3
Bankhead C Aber 245 K2
Bankhead S Lans 199 G4
Bank Newton N York 148 F5
Banknock Falk 209 K3
Banks Cumb 178 D6
Banks Lancs 138 E4
Banks Green Worcs 82 A2
Bankshill D & G 177 G3
Bank Street Worcs 80 E3
Bank Top Calder 141 H3
Bank Top Lancs 139 G6
Banningham Norfk 122 E5
Bannister Green Essex 71 G3
Bannockburn Stirlg 209 L1
Banstead Surrey 51 H7
Bantham Devon 7 K6
Banton N Lans 209 K3
Banwell N Som 44 E7
Bapchild Kent 40 B3
Bapton Wilts 33 G3
Barabhas W Isls 282 g2
Barassie S Ayrs 196 C4
Barbaraville Highld 263 K5
Barber Booth Derbys 132 B3
Barber Green Cumb 156 F6
Barbieston S Ayrs 196 E7
Barbon Cumb 157 K6
Barbridge Ches E 130 B8
Barbrook Devon 28 C2
Barby Nhants 84 A1
Barcaldine Ag & B 228 F7
Barcheston Warwks 83 G7
Barclose Cumb 178 B6
Barcombe E Susx 22 F4
Barcombe Cross E Susx 23 G4
Barcroft C Brad 149 J8
Barden N York 159 L4
Barden Park Kent 38 F4
Bardfield End Green Essex 70 F1
Bardfield Saling Essex 71 G2
Bardney Lincs 136 B6
Bardon Leics 99 M1
Bardon Mill Nthumb 179 H6
Bardowie E Duns 209 G4
Bardown E Susx 39 G7
Bardrainney Inver 208 B4
Bardsea Cumb 156 D7
Bardsey Leeds 150 E7
Bardsey Island Gwynd 108 A7
Bardsley Oldham 140 D7
Bardwell Suffk 105 J8
Bare Lancs 147 J3
Bareppa Cnwll 3 K5
Barfad D & G 173 J2
Barford Norfk 106 C2
Barford Warwks 83 G3
Barford St John Oxon 83 K8
Barford St Martin Wilts 33 J4
Barford St Michael Oxon 83 K8
Barfrestone Kent 41 H5
Bargate Derbys 116 B2
Bargeddie N Lans 209 J6
Bargoed Caerph 61 J7
Bargrennan D & G 183 J7
Barham Cambs 102 C8
Barham Kent 41 G5
Barham Suffk 90 D5
Barham Crematorium Kent 41 H5
Bar Hill Cambs 87 H3
Barholm Lincs 102 B1
Barkby Leics 100 E2
Barkby Thorpe Leics 100 E2
Barkers Green Shrops 113 H6
Barkestone-le-Vale Leics 117 K4
Barkham Wokham 49 J5
Barking Gt Lon 51 L2
Barking Suffk 90 C4
Barkingside Gt Lon 51 L1
Barking Tye Suffk 90 C5
Barkisland Calder 141 G4
Barkla Shop Cnwll 4 B5
Barkston Lincs 118 B3
Barkston Ash N York 151 G8
Barkway Herts 87 H8
Barlanark C Glas 209 H6
Barlaston Staffs 114 D4
Barlavington W Susx 21 G4
Barlborough Derbys 133 J4
Barlby N York 143 G1
Barlestone Leics 99 L2
Barley Herts 87 H7
Barley Lancs 148 E7
Barleycroft End Herts 70 B2
Barley Hole Rothm 142 B8
Barleythorpe Rutlnd 101 J2
Barling Essex 53 K1
Barlings Lincs 135 M5
Barlochan D & G 175 K3
Barlow Derbys 133 G5
Barlow Gatesd 180 E6
Barlow N York 143 G2
Barmby Moor E R Yk 152 B6
Barmby on the Marsh E R Yk 143 H2
Barmer Norfk 121 H5
Barming Heath Kent 39 J2
Barmollack Ag & B 194 C2
Barmouth Gwynd 109 L8
Barmpton Darltn 169 J7
Barmston E R Yk 153 J4
Barnaby Green Suffk 107 K7
Barnacarry Ag & B 216 F8
Barnack C Pete 102 B2
Barnacle Warwks 99 K6
Barnard Castle Dur 168 D7
Barnard Gate Oxon 66 B5
Barnardiston Suffk 88 E5
Barnbarroch D & G 175 L3
Barnburgh Donc 142 D7
Barnby Suffk 107 K5
Barnby Dun Donc 142 F6
Barnby in the Willows Notts 117 M1
Barnby Moor Notts 134 D3
Barncorkrie D & G 172 D7
Barnehurst Gt Lon 52 B4
Barnes Gt Lon 51 G4
Barnes Street Kent 39 G4
Barnet Gt Lon 69 H7
Barnetby le Wold N Linc 144 D6
Barnet Gate Gt Lon 69 G8
Barney Norfk 121 M5
Barnham Suffk 105 H7
Barnham W Susx 20 F6
Barnham Broom Norfk 106 B2
Barnhead Angus 235 G4
Barnhill C Dund 223 H1
Barnhill Ches W 113 H1
Barnhill Moray 266 C5
Barnhills D & G 182 B8
Barningham Dur 168 D8
Barningham Suffk 105 K8
Barnoldby le Beck NE Lin 145 G7
Barnoldswick Lancs 148 F6
Barnsdale Bar Donc 142 D5
Barns Green W Susx 37 H5
Barnsley Barns 142 A6
Barnsley Gloucs 65 G6
Barnsley Crematorium Barns 142 B6
Barnsole Kent 41 J4
Barnstaple Devon 27 K4
Barnston Essex 70 F3
Barnston Wirral 129 G3
Barnstone Notts 117 J4
Barnt Green Worcs 98 C8
Barnton C Edin 211 G4
Barnton Ches W 130 C5
Barnwell All Saints Nhants 102 A6
Barnwell St Andrew Nhants 102 A6
Barnwood Gloucs 64 B3
Baron's Cross Herefs 80 B4
Baronwood Cumb 166 C2
Barr S Ayrs 183 H4
Barra W Isls 283 b13
Barrachan D & G 173 J5
Barraigh W Isls 283 b13
Barrapoll Ag & B 224 B6
Barras Cumb 167 J8
Barrasford Nthumb 179 L4
Barregarrow IoM 154 d4
Barrets Green Ches E 130 B7
Barrhead E Rens 208 E7
Barrhill S Ayrs 183 G6
Barrington Cambs 87 H5
Barrington Somset 30 F7
Barripper Cnwll 3 G3
Barrmill N Ayrs 196 D1
Barrock Highld 280 C2
Barrow Gloucs 64 C2
Barrow Lancs 148 C8
Barrow Rutlnd 118 A8
Barrow Shrops 96 E3
Barrow Somset 32 B4
Barrow Suffk 88 F3
Barroway Drove Norfk 104 B3
Barrow Bridge Bolton 139 K5
Barrow Burn Nthumb 190 B4
Barrowby Lincs 118 A4
Barrowden Rutlnd 101 L3
Barrowford Lancs 148 E7
Barrow Gurney N Som 45 G5
Barrow Haven N Linc 144 D3
Barrow Hill Derbys 133 H4
Barrow-in-Furness Cumb 146 D2
Barrow Island Cumb 146 D2
Barrow Nook Lancs 138 F7
Barrow's Green Ches E 130 D8
Barrow Street Wilts 32 D5
Barrow-upon-Humber N Linc 144 D4
Barrow upon Soar Leics 116 F8
Barrow upon Trent Derbys 116 B6
Barrow Vale BaNES 45 J7
Barry Angus 234 E8
Barry V Glam 43 H7
Barry Island V Glam 43 H8
Barsby Leics 100 F1
Barsham Suffk 107 H5
Barston Solhll 99 G7
Bartestree Herefs 80 D7
Barthol Chapel Abers 256 E5
Bartholomew Green Essex 71 H3
Barthomley Ches E 114 B1
Bartley Hants 18 D1
Bartley Green Birm 98 C7
Bartlow Cambs 88 B6
Barton Cambs 87 H4
Barton Ches W 113 G1
Barton Gloucs 65 G2
Barton Herefs 79 K4
Barton Lancs 138 D6
Barton Lancs 147 K8
Barton N York 160 C1
Barton Oxon 66 E5
Barton Torbay 8 D2
Barton Warwks 82 D5
Barton Bendish Norfk 104 E2
Barton End Gloucs 64 B7
Barton Green Staffs 115 K7
Barton Hartshorn Bucks 66 F1
Barton Hill N York 151 L3
Barton in Fabis Notts 116 E5
Barton in the Beans Leics 99 L2
Barton-le-Clay C Beds 68 D1
Barton-le-Street N York 162 C7
Barton-le-Willows N York 151 M3
Barton Mills Suffk 104 E8
Barton-on-Sea Hants 18 C5
Barton-on-the-Heath Warwks 83 G8
Barton St David Somset 31 J4
Barton Seagrave Nhants 101 J7
Barton Stacey Hants 34 F3
Barton Town Devon 28 B3
Barton Turf Norfk 123 G7
Barton-under-Needwood Staffs 115 K7
Barton-upon-Humber N Linc 144 C3
Barton upon Irwell Salfd 140 A8
Barton Waterside N Linc 144 C3
Barugh Barns 141 M6
Barugh Green Barns 141 M6
Barvas W Isls 282 g2
Barway Cambs 103 L8
Barwell Leics 99 L4
Barwick Devon 12 E1
Barwick Herts 69 K3
Barwick Somset 31 J8
Barwick in Elmet Leeds 150 F8
Baschurch Shrops 112 F7
Bascote Warwks 83 J3
Bascote Heath Warwks 83 J3
Base Green Suffk 89 L3
Basford Green Staffs 114 F1
Bashall Eaves Lancs 148 B7
Bashall Town Lancs 148 C7
Bashley Hants 18 C4
Basildon Essex 52 F1
Basildon & District Crematorium Essex 53 G2
Basingstoke Hants 48 F8
Basingstoke Crematorium Hants 35 H2
Baslow Derbys 132 E5
Bason Bridge Somset 30 E2
Bassaleg Newpt 44 B2
Bassendean Border 201 K4
Bassenthwaite Cumb 165 H4
Bassett C Sotn 34 F7
Bassingbourn Cambs 87 G6
Bassingfield Notts 117 G4
Bassingham Lincs 135 H7
Bassingthorpe Lincs 118 C6
Bassus Green Herts 69 J2
Basted Kent 38 F2
Baston Lincs 102 C1
Bastwick Norfk 123 J8
Batch Somset 44 C7
Batchworth Herts 68 D8
Batchworth Heath Herts 68 D8
Batcombe Dorset 16 B2
Batcombe Somset 31 M3
Bate Heath Ches E 130 D4
Batford Herts 68 F4
Bath BaNES 45 L6
Bathampton BaNES 45 M5
Bathealton Somset 29 K6
Batheaston BaNES 45 M5
Bathford BaNES 46 A5
Bathgate W Loth 210 C5
Bathley Notts 134 F7
Bathpool Cnwll 11 K7
Bathpool Somset 30 C5
Bath Side Essex 73 K1
Bathville W Loth 210 B5
Bathway Somset 45 H8
Batley Kirk 141 K3
Batsford Gloucs 82 E8
Batson Devon 7 L7
Battersby N York 161 K1
Battersea Gt Lon 51 H4
Battisborough Cross Devon 7 H5
Battisford Suffk 90 C4
Battisford Tye Suffk 89 L4
Battle E Susx 24 D4
Battle Powys 60 F1
Battleborough Somset 30 E1
Battledown Gloucs 64 D3
Battledykes Angus 234 C4
Battlefield Shrops 113 H8
Battlesbridge Essex 71 J8
Battlesden C Beds 68 B2
Battleton Somset 29 G5
Battlies Green Suffk 89 H2
Battramsley Cross Hants 18 E4
Batt's Corner Hants 36 B3
Baughton Worcs 81 K6
Baughurst Hants 48 E7
Baulds Abers 244 D5
Baulking Oxon 47 L1
Baumber Lincs 136 D5
Baunton Gloucs 64 E6
Baveney Wood Shrops 96 F7
Baverstock Wilts 33 H4
Bawburgh Norfk 106 D2
Bawdeswell Norfk 122 A7
Bawdrip Somset 30 E3
Bawdsey Suffk 91 H7
Bawsey Norfk 120 E7
Bawtry Donc 134 C1
Baxenden Lancs 140 A2
Baxterley Warwks 99 H4
Baxter's Green Suffk 88 E4
Bay Highld 258 D6
Bayble W Isls 282 h3
Baybridge Hants 35 H6
Baybridge Nthumb 168 B1
Baycliff Cumb 146 F2
Baydon Wilts 47 L3
Bayford Herts 69 J5
Bayford Somset 32 B5
Bayhead W Isls 283 b8
Bay Horse Lancs 147 K5
Bayley's Hill Kent 38 D3
Baylham Suffk 90 C5
Baynard's Green Oxon 66 E1
Baysdale Abbey N York 161 K1
Baysham Herefs 63 H2
Bayston Hill Shrops 96 B2
Baythorne End Essex 88 E6
Bayton Worcs 96 F8
Bayton Common Worcs 81 G1
Bayworth Oxon 66 D6
Beach S Glos 45 L5
Beachampton Bucks 84 E7
Beachamwell Norfk 104 E2
Beachley Gloucs 45 H1
Beacon Devon 14 E2
Beacon End Essex 72 D2
Beacon Hill E Susx 38 D7
Beacon Hill Kent 39 K6
Beacon Hill Notts 117 L1
Beacon Hill Surrey 36 C3
Beacon's Bottom Bucks 67 J8
Beaconsfield Bucks 50 B1
Beadlam N York 161 L5
Beadlow C Beds 86 C7
Beadnell Nthumb 203 L7
Beaford Devon 27 K7
Beal N York 142 E3
Beal Nthumb 203 H4
Bealbury Cnwll 6 D2
Bealsmill Cnwll 11 L7
Beam Hill Staffs 115 L6
Beamhurst Staffs 115 H4

Beaminster Dorset 15 L2
Beamish Dur 180 F8
Beamsley N York 149 K5
Bean Kent 52 C4
Beanacre Wilts 46 C5
Beanley Nthumb 190 F3
Beardon Devon 12 C5
Beardwood Bl w D 139 K2
Beare Devon 14 A2
Beare Green Surrey 37 J2
Bearley Warwks 82 E3
Bearley Cross Warwks 82 E3
Bearpark Dur 169 G2
Bearsden E Duns 208 F4
Bearsted Kent 39 K2
Bearstone Shrops 114 A4
Bearwood Birm 98 C6
Bearwood Herefs 79 M4
Bearwood Poole 17 L3
Beattock D & G 187 G6
Beauchamp Roding Essex 70 E5
Beauchief Sheff 132 F3
Beaudesert Warwks 82 E2
Beaufort Blae G 61 J5
Beaulieu Hants 18 F3
Beaulieu Road Station Hants 18 E2
Beauly Highld 250 F2
Beaumaris IoA 126 B4
Beaumont Cumb 177 K7
Beaumont Essex 73 H2
Beaumont Jersey 9 c3
Beaumont Hill Darltn 169 J7
Beausale Warwks 82 F1
Beauworth Hants 35 J5
Beaworthy Devon 12 B3
Beazley End Essex 71 H1
Bebington Wirral 129 H3
Bebside Nthumb 181 G3
Beccles Suffk 107 J5
Becconsall Lancs 138 F3
Beckbury Shrops 97 H3
Beckenham Gt Lon 51 K5
Beckenham Crematorium Gt Lon 51 K5
Beckermet Cumb 155 J1
Beckett End Norfk 104 F4
Beckfoot Cumb 155 L3
Beckfoot Cumb 156 B5
Beck Foot Cumb 157 K3
Beckfoot Cumb 164 E1
Beckford Worcs 82 A8
Beckhampton Wilts 47 G5
Beck Hole N York 162 E2
Beckingham Lincs 118 A1
Beckingham Notts 134 F2
Beckington Somset 46 A8
Beckjay Shrops 95 J7
Beckley E Susx 24 F3
Beckley Hants 18 C4
Beckley Oxon 66 E5
Beck Row Suffk 104 D7
Becks C Brad 149 J6
Beck Side Cumb 156 B6
Beck Side Cumb 156 E6
Beckton Gt Lon 51 L3
Beckwithshaw N York 150 C5
Becontree Gt Lon 52 A2
Becquet Vincent Jersey 9 d2
Bedale N York 160 C5
Bedburn Dur 168 E4
Bedchester Dorset 32 E7
Beddau Rhondd 43 G4
Beddgelert Gwynd 109 L2
Beddingham E Susx 23 G5
Beddington Gt Lon 51 J6
Beddington Corner Gt Lon 51 H5
Bedfield Suffk 90 F2
Bedfield Little Green Suffk 90 F2
Bedford Bed 85 L5
Bedford Crematorium Bed 86 B5
Bedgebury Cross Kent 39 H6
Bedham W Susx 36 F6
Bedhampton Hants 20 A5
Bedingfield Suffk 90 E2
Bedingfield Green Suffk 90 E2
Bedlam N York 150 C3
Bedlington Nthumb 181 G3
Bedlinog Myr Td 61 H6
Bedminster Bristl 45 H5
Bedminster Down Bristl 45 H5
Bedmond Herts 68 E6
Bednall Staffs 114 F7
Bedrule Border 189 G3
Bedstone Shrops 95 J8
Bedwas Caerph 43 J4
Bedwellty Caerph 61 J7
Bedworth Warwks 99 K6
Bedworth Woodlands Warwks 99 K6
Beeby Leics 100 E2
Beech Hants 35 L3
Beech Staffs 114 D4
Beech Hill W Berk 49 G6
Beechingstoke Wilts 47 G7
Beedon W Berk 48 C3
Beedon Hill W Berk 48 C3
Beeford E R Yk 153 H5
Beeley Derbys 132 E6
Beelsby NE Lin 145 G7
Beenham W Berk 48 E5
Beenham's Heath W & M 49 K4
Beeny Cnwll 11 G4
Beer Devon 14 F5
Beer Somset 30 F4
Beercrocombe Somset 30 D6
Beer Hackett Dorset 31 K8
Beesands Devon 8 B6
Beesby Lincs 137 J4
Beeson Devon 8 B6
Beeston C Beds 86 D5
Beeston Ches W 129 M7
Beeston Leeds 141 L2
Beeston Norfk 121 K8
Beeston Notts 116 E4
Beeston Regis Norfk 122 D3
Beeswing D & G 176 A5
Beetham Cumb 157 H6
Beetham Somset 30 D8
Beetley Norfk 121 L8
Began Cardif 43 K5
Begbroke Oxon 66 C4
Begdale Cambs 103 J2
Begelly Pembks 55 J5
Beggarington Hill Leeds 141 L3
Beggar's Bush Powys 79 J2
Beguildy Powys 94 F7
Beighton Norfk 107 H2
Beighton Sheff 133 J3
Beinn Na Faoghla W Isls 283 c9
Beith N Ayrs 208 B8
Bekesbourne Kent 41 G4
Bekesbourne Hill Kent 41 G4
Belaugh Norfk 122 F7
Belbroughton Worcs 97 L7
Belchalwell Dorset 16 F1
Belchalwell Street Dorset 16 F1
Belchamp Otten Essex 88 F6
Belchamp St Paul Essex 88 F6
Belchamp Walter Essex 89 G7
Belchford Lincs 136 E4
Belford Nthumb 203 H6
Belgrave C Leic 100 D2
Belhaven E Loth 212 E3
Belhelvie Abers 257 H8
Belhinnie Abers 255 J6
Bellabeg Abers 243 K1
Bellamore Herefs 79 M7
Bellanoch Ag & B 216 B8
Bellasize E R Yk 143 K2
Bellaty Angus 233 K3
Bell Bar Herts 69 H6
Bell Busk N York 148 F4
Belleau Lincs 137 G4
Bell End Worcs 97 L7
Bellerby N York 159 K4
Bellever Devon 12 F7
Belle Vue Cumb 177 L7
Belle Vue Wakefd 142 A4
Bellfield S Lans 186 E2
Bellfield S Lans 198 D6
Bell Heath Worcs 97 L7
Bell Hill Hants 35 M6
Bellingdon Bucks 68 B6
Bellingham Nthumb 179 J2
Belloch Ag & B 192 D1
Bellochantuy Ag & B 192 D2
Bell o' th' Hill Ches W 113 H2
Bellows Cross Dorset 33 J8
Bells Cross Suffk 90 D5
Bellshill N Lans 209 J7
Bellshill Nthumb 203 J7
Bellside N Lans 209 L7
Bellsquarry W Loth 210 D6
Bells Yew Green E Susx 38 F6
Belluton BaNES 45 J6
Belmaduthy Highld 263 H8
Belmesthorpe Rutlnd 102 A2
Belmont Bl w D 139 K4
Belmont Gt Lon 51 H6
Belmont S Ayrs 196 C7
Belmont Shet 281 f2
Belnacraig Abers 255 H8
Belowda Cnwll 4 F3
Belper Derbys 116 B2
Belper Lane End Derbys 116 B2
Belph Derbys 133 L4
Belsay Nthumb 180 D3
Belses Border 201 J8
Belsford Devon 7 L3
Belsize Herts 68 D7
Belstead Suffk 90 D7
Belstone Devon 12 E4
Belthorn Lancs 139 L3
Beltinge Kent 41 G2
Beltingham Nthumb 179 H6
Beltoft N Linc 143 K6
Belton Leics 116 D7
Belton Lincs 118 B3
Belton N Linc 143 K6
Belton Norfk 107 K3
Belton Rutlnd 101 H3
Beltring Kent 39 H4
Belvedere Gt Lon 52 B3
Belvoir Leics 117 L5
Bembridge IoW 19 L6
Bemerton Wilts 33 K5
Bempton E R Yk 153 K2
Benacre Suffk 107 K6
Benbecula W Isls 283 c9
Benbuie D & G 185 H4
Benderloch Ag & B 228 D7
Benenden Kent 39 K6
Benfieldside Dur 180 D8
Bengates Norfk 122 F6
Bengeo Herts 69 J4
Bengeworth Worcs 82 B6
Benhall Green Suffk 91 J3
Benhall Street Suffk 91 H3
Benholm Abers 235 K2
Beningbrough N York 151 H4
Benington Herts 69 J2
Benington Lincs 119 L2
Benington Sea End Lincs 119 L2
Benllech IoA 125 J3
Benmore Ag & B 207 J2
Bennacott Cnwll 11 K4
Bennan N Ayrs 193 K4
Bennet Head Cumb 166 B6
Bennetland E R Yk 143 L2
Bennett End Bucks 67 J7
Benniworth Lincs 136 D3
Benover Kent 39 H4
Ben Rhydding C Brad 149 L6
Benslie N Ayrs 196 C2
Benson Oxon 66 F8
Bentfield Green Essex 70 D2
Benthall Shrops 96 F3
Bentham Gloucs 64 C4
Benthoul C Aber 245 H3
Bentlawn Shrops 95 H3
Bentley Donc 142 E6
Bentley E R Yk 152 F8
Bentley Hants 36 A2
Bentley Suffk 90 D7
Bentley Warwks 99 H4
Bentley Crematorium Essex 70 E7
Bentley Heath Herts 69 H7
Bentley Heath Solhll 98 F8
Benton Devon 28 B4
Bentpath D & G 188 B8
Bentwichen Devon 28 C4
Bentworth Hants 35 K3
Benvie Angus 222 E1
Benville Dorset 15 M2
Benwick Cambs 103 G5
Beoley Worcs 82 C1
Beoraidbeg Highld 237 K2
Bepton W Susx 20 D3
Berden Essex 70 C1
Berea Pembks 74 C6
Bere Alston Devon 6 E2
Bere Ferrers Devon 6 E2
Berepper Cnwll 3 G6
Bere Regis Dorset 17 G4
Bergh Apton Norfk 106 F3
Berhill Somset 31 G4
Berinsfield Oxon 66 E7
Berkeley Gloucs 63 K7
Berkeley Heath Gloucs 63 K7
Berkeley Road Gloucs 63 L7
Berkhamsted Herts 68 C5
Berkley Somset 32 D1
Berkswell Solhll 99 H7
Bermondsey Gt Lon 51 J3
Bermuda Warwks 99 K5
Bernera Highld 248 C7
Bernisdale Highld 258 F6
Berrick Prior Oxon 66 F8
Berrick Salome Oxon 66 F8
Berriedale Highld 274 F3
Berrier Cumb 165 L5
Berriew Powys 94 E3
Berrington Nthumb 202 F4
Berrington Shrops 96 C2
Berrington Worcs 80 D2
Berrington Green Worcs 80 D2
Berrow Somset 44 C8
Berrow Worcs 81 H8
Berrow Green Worcs 81 H3
Berry Brow Kirk 141 H5
Berry Cross Devon 27 H7
Berry Down Cross Devon 27 K2
Berry Hill Gloucs 63 H4
Berry Hill Pembks 75 H4
Berryhillock Moray 267 K4
Berryhillock Moray 267 K5
Berrynarbor Devon 27 K2
Berry Pomeroy Devon 8 B3
Berry's Green Gt Lon 51 L7
Bersham Wrexhm 112 D2
Berthengam Flints 128 D4
Berwick E Susx 23 H6
Berwick Bassett Wilts 47 G4
Berwick Hill Nthumb 180 E4
Berwick St James Wilts 33 J3
Berwick St John Wilts 32 F6
Berwick St Leonard Wilts 32 F4
Berwick-upon-Tweed Nthumb 202 F3
Bescaby Leics 117 L6
Bescar Lancs 138 E5
Besford Shrops 113 J6
Besford Worcs 81 L6
Bessacarr Donc 142 F7
Bessels Leigh Oxon 66 C6
Besses o' th' Barn Bury 140 B6
Bessingby E R Yk 153 J3
Bessingham Norfk 122 D4
Bestbeech Hill E Susx 38 F7
Besthorpe Norfk 106 B4
Besthorpe Notts 135 G6
Bestwood Village Notts 116 F2
Beswick E R Yk 152 F6
Betchcott Shrops 95 K4
Betchworth Surrey 37 K1
Bethania Cerdgn 77 G3
Bethania Gwynd 110 D3
Bethel Gwynd 111 J4
Bethel Gwynd 125 J6
Bethel IoA 125 G5
Bethel Powys 111 L7
Bethersden Kent 40 B7
Bethesda Gwynd 126 C6
Bethesda Pembks 55 J3
Bethlehem Carmth 59 J4
Bethnal Green Gt Lon 51 K2
Betley Staffs 114 B2
Betsham Kent 52 D4
Betteshanger Kent 41 J5
Bettiscombe Dorset 15 J3
Bettisfield Wrexhm 113 G4
Betton Shrops 113 M4
Betton Strange Shrops 96 C2
Bettws Newpt 44 C1
Bettws Bledrws Cerdgn 77 H5
Bettws Cedewain Powys 94 D4
Bettws Evan Cerdgn 76 B5
Bettws-Newydd Mons 62 D6
Bettyhill Highld 278 B4
Betws Brdgnd 42 D4
Betws Carmth 59 H6
Betws Garmon Gwynd 125 K8
Betws Gwerfil Goch Denbgs 111 K2
Betws-y-Coed Conwy 126 F8
Betws-yn-Rhos Conwy 127 H5
Beulah Cerdgn 76 B6
Beulah Powys 78 C5
Bevendean Br & H 22 E6
Bevercotes Notts 134 D5
Beverley E R Yk 153 G7
Beverston Gloucs 64 B8
Bevington Gloucs 63 K7
Bewaldeth Cumb 165 H4
Bewcastle Cumb 178 D4
Bewdley Worcs 97 H8
Bewerley N York 149 L3
Bewholme E R Yk 153 J6
Bewlbridge Kent 39 H6
Bexhill E Susx 24 D5
Bexley Gt Lon 52 B4
Bexleyheath Gt Lon 52 A4
Bexleyhill W Susx 36 D6
Bexon Kent 53 J7
Bexwell Norfk 104 C3
Beyton Suffk 89 J3
Beyton Green Suffk 89 J3
Bhaltos W Isls 282 e3
Bhatarsaigh W Isls 283 b13
Bibstone S Glos 45 K1
Bibury Gloucs 65 G5
Bicester Oxon 66 E3
Bickenhill Solhll 99 G7
Bicker Lincs 119 H4
Bicker Bar Lincs 119 H4
Bicker Gauntlet Lincs 119 H4
Bickershaw Wigan 139 J7
Bickerstaffe Lancs 138 F7
Bickerton Ches E 113 H1
Bickerton Devon 8 B7
Bickerton N York 151 G5
Bickerton Nthumb 190 E6
Bickford Staffs 114 D8

Bickington Devon 13 J8
Bickington Devon 27 J4
Bickleigh Devon 7 G2
Bickleigh Devon 13 M1
Bickleton Devon 27 J5
Bickley Ches W 113 J2
Bickley Gt Lon 51 L5
Bickley N York 163 G4
Bickley Worcs 80 E1
Bickley Moss Ches W 113 J2
Bicknacre Essex 71 J6
Bicknoller Somset 29 K3
Bicknor Kent 53 J7
Bickton Hants 33 K8
Bicton Herefs 80 B2
Bicton Shrops 95 G6
Bicton Shrops 113 G8
Bidborough Kent 38 E5
Bidden Hants 35 L1
Biddenden Kent 39 L5
Biddenden Green Kent 39 M5
Biddenham Bed 85 K5
Biddestone Wilts 46 B4
Biddisham Somset 44 D8
Biddlesden Bucks 84 C7
Biddlestone Nthumb 190 D4
Biddulph Staffs 131 H7
Biddulph Moor Staffs 131 H8
Bideford Devon 27 H5
Bidford-on-Avon Warwks 82 D5
Bidston Wirral 129 G2
Bielby E R Yk 152 B7
Bieldside C Aber 245 K3
Bierley IoW 19 H8
Bierton Bucks 67 K4
Big Balcraig D & G 173 K6
Bigbury Devon 7 K5
Bigbury-on-Sea Devon 7 J6
Bigby Lincs 144 D6
Big Carlae D & G 185 G3
Biggar Cumb 146 D3
Biggar S Lans 199 H5
Biggin Derbys 115 L2
Biggin Derbys 132 C7
Biggin N York 142 E1
Biggin Hill Gt Lon 51 L7
Biggleswade C Beds 86 D6
Bigholms D & G 177 K3
Bighouse Highld 278 F3
Bighton Hants 35 J4
Biglands Cumb 177 H8
Bignor W Susx 21 G4
Bigrigg Cumb 164 D8
Big Sand Highld 260 B4
Bigton Shet 281 d8
Bilborough C Nott 116 E3
Bilbrook Somset 29 J3
Bilbrook Staffs 97 K3
Bilbrough N York 151 H6
Bilbster Highld 280 C5
Bildershaw Dur 169 G6
Bildeston Suffk 89 K5
Billacott Cnwll 11 J4
Billericay Essex 71 G8
Billesdon Leics 100 F3
Billesley Warwks 82 D4
Billingborough Lincs 118 F5
Billinge St Hel 139 G7
Billingford Norfk 106 D7
Billingford Norfk 121 M7
Billingham S on T 170 B6
Billinghay Lincs 136 C8
Billingley Barns 142 C6
Billingshurst W Susx 37 G5
Billingsley Shrops 97 G6
Billington C Beds 68 B3
Billington Lancs 148 C8
Billington Staffs 114 D7
Billockby Norfk 107 J1
Billy Row Dur 168 F3
Bilsborrow Lancs 147 K7
Bilsby Lincs 137 J4
Bilsham W Susx 21 G6
Bilsington Kent 40 D8
Bilsthorpe Notts 134 C7
Bilsthorpe Moor Notts 134 C7
Bilston Mdloth 211 J6
Bilston Wolves 98 B4
Bilstone Leics 99 K2
Bilting Kent 40 D5
Bilton E R Yk 144 F1
Bilton N York 150 D4
Bilton N York 151 G6
Bilton Nthumb 191 J4
Bilton Warwks 100 B8
Bilton Banks Nthumb 191 J4
Binbrook Lincs 136 D1
Binchester Blocks Dur 169 G4
Bincombe Dorset 16 D5
Binegar Somset 31 K1
Bines Green W Susx 21 L3
Binfield Br For 49 K4
Binfield Heath Oxon 49 H3
Bingfield Nthumb 180 A4
Bingham Notts 117 J3
Bingham's Melcombe Dorset 16 E2
Bingley C Brad 149 K7
Bings Shrops 113 J7
Binham Norfk 121 L4
Binley Covtry 99 K7
Binley Hants 48 B8
Binley Woods Warwks 99 L7
Binnegar Dorset 17 G5
Binniehill Falk 209 M4
Binscombe Surrey 36 E2
Binsey Oxon 66 C5
Binstead IoW 19 K5
Binsted Hants 36 A3
Binsted W Susx 21 G5
Binton Warwks 82 D4
Bintree Norfk 121 M7
Binweston Shrops 95 H3
Birch Essex 72 D3
Birch Rochdl 140 C6
Bircham Newton Norfk 121 G5
Bircham Tofts Norfk 121 G5
Birchanger Essex 70 D3
Birch Cross Staffs 115 J5
Birchencliffe Kirk 141 H4
Bircher Herefs 80 B2
Birchfield Birm 98 D5
Birch Green Essex 72 D3
Birch Green Herts 69 J5
Birch Green Worcs 81 K6
Birchgrove Cardif 43 J5
Birchgrove Swans 57 K5
Birchgrove W Susx 38 B7
Birch Heath Ches W 130 A7
Birch Hill Ches W 129 M5
Birchington Kent 41 J2
Birchley Heath Warwks 99 H4
Birchmoor Warwks 99 H3
Birchmoor Green C Beds 85 J8
Birchover Derbys 132 E7
Birch Vale Derbys 131 K2
Birchwood Lincs 135 J6
Birch Wood Somset 30 C8
Birchwood Warrtn 130 C2
Bircotes Notts 134 C2
Birdbrook Essex 88 E7
Birdforth N York 161 G7
Birdham W Susx 20 D6
Birdingbury Warwks 83 K2
Birdlip Gloucs 64 D4
Birdoswald Cumb 178 E5
Birdsall N York 152 B3
Birds Edge Kirk 141 K6
Birds Green Essex 70 E5
Birdsgreen Shrops 97 H6
Birdsmoorgate Dorset 15 J3
Bird Street Suffk 89 K5
Birdwell Barns 142 A7
Birdwood Gloucs 63 L3
Birgham Border 202 B5
Birichin Highld 263 K2
Birkacre Lancs 139 H5
Birkby N York 160 D2
Birkdale Sefton 138 C5
Birkenbog Abers 267 L3
Birkenhead Wirral 129 H2
Birkenhills Abers 256 D3
Birkenshaw Kirk 141 K2
Birkhall Abers 243 K5
Birkhill Angus 234 A8
Birkhill D & G 187 J3
Birkholme Lincs 118 C6
Birkin N York 142 E2
Birks Leeds 141 L2
Birkshaw Nthumb 179 H5
Birley Herefs 80 B4
Birley Carr Sheff 133 G1
Birling Kent 52 E6
Birling Nthumb 191 K5
Birling Gap E Susx 23 J8
Birlingham Worcs 81 L6
Birmingham Birm 98 D6
Birnam P & K 232 F7
Birness Abers 257 H5
Birse Abers 244 C4
Birsemore Abers 244 C4
Birstall Kirk 141 K3
Birstall Leics 100 D2
Birstwith N York 150 B4
Birthorpe Lincs 118 E5
Birtley Gatesd 181 G7
Birtley Herefs 79 L2
Birtley Nthumb 179 K3
Birtley Crematorium Gatesd 181 G7
Birts Street Worcs 81 H7
Bisbrooke RutInd 101 J3
Biscathorpe Lincs 136 D3
Biscovey Cnwll 5 H4
Bisham W & M 49 K2
Bishampton Worcs 82 A5
Bish Mill Devon 28 C6
Bishop Auckland Dur 169 G5
Bishopbridge Lincs 135 L2
Bishopbriggs E Duns 209 G5
Bishop Burton E R Yk 152 F7
Bishop Middleham Dur 169 J4
Bishopmill Moray 266 E3
Bishop Monkton N York 150 D3
Bishop Norton Lincs 135 K1
Bishopsbourne Kent 41 G5
Bishops Cannings Wilts 46 F6
Bishop's Castle Shrops 95 H5
Bishop's Caundle Dorset 32 B8
Bishop's Cleeve Gloucs 64 D2
Bishop's Frome Herefs 80 F5
Bishops Gate Surrey 50 B5
Bishop's Green Essex 70 F3
Bishop's Green Hants 48 D6
Bishops Hull Somset 30 B6
Bishop's Itchington Warwks 83 J4
Bishops Lydeard Somset 29 M5
Bishop's Norton Gloucs 64 B2
Bishop's Nympton Devon 28 D6
Bishop's Offley Staffs 114 B5
Bishop's Stortford Herts 70 C3
Bishop's Sutton Hants 35 J4
Bishop's Tachbrook Warwks 83 H3
Bishop's Tawton Devon 27 K5
Bishopsteignton Devon 13 L7
Bishopstoke Hants 34 F7
Bishopston Swans 57 G7
Bishopstone Bucks 67 J5
Bishopstone E Susx 23 G7
Bishopstone Herefs 80 A6
Bishopstone Kent 41 G2
Bishopstone Swindn 47 K2
Bishopstone Wilts 33 J5
Bishopstrow Wilts 32 E2
Bishop Sutton BaNES 45 H7
Bishop's Waltham Hants 35 H7
Bishopswood Somset 30 C8
Bishop's Wood Staffs 97 J2
Bishopsworth Bristl 45 H5
Bishop Thornton N York 150 C3
Bishopthorpe C York 151 J6
Bishopton Darltn 169 K6
Bishopton Rens 208 D5
Bishopton Warwks 82 E4
Bishop Wilton E R Yk 152 B5
Bishton Newpt 44 D2
Bishton Staffs 115 G7
Bisley Gloucs 64 C6
Bisley Surrey 50 B7
Bisley Camp Surrey 50 B7
Bispham Bpool 146 F7
Bispham Green Lancs 138 F5
Bissoe Cnwll 3 K3
Bisterne Hants 18 A3
Bitchet Green Kent 38 E3
Bitchfield Lincs 118 C6
Bittadon Devon 27 K3
Bittaford Devon 7 K3
Bittering Norfk 121 K8
Bitterley Shrops 96 D7
Bitterne C Sotn 34 F8
Bitteswell Leics 100 C6
Bitton S Glos 45 K5
Bix Oxon 49 H2
Bixter Shet 281 d6
Blaby Leics 100 C4
Blackadder Border 202 C3
Blackawton Devon 8 B4
Blackbeck Cumb 155 J1
Blackborough Devon 14 C1
Blackborough End Norfk 120 E8
Black Bourton Oxon 65 L6
Blackboys E Susx 23 J3
Blackbrook Derbys 116 B2
Blackbrook St Hel 139 G8
Blackbrook Staffs 114 B4
Blackbrook Surrey 37 J2
Blackburn Abers 245 J1
Blackburn Bl w D 139 K2
Blackburn Rothm 133 H1
Blackburn W Loth 210 C6
Black Callerton N u Ty 180 E5
Black Car Norfk 106 B4
Black Corner W Susx 37 L3
Blackcraig E Ayrs 185 G1
Black Crofts Ag & B 228 E8
Black Cross Cnwll 4 E3
Blackden Heath Ches E 130 F5
Blackdog Abers 245 L1
Black Dog Devon 13 J1
Blackdown Devon 12 C6
Blackdown Dorset 15 J2
Blackdyke Cumb 176 F8
Blacker Barns 142 A5
Blacker Hill Barns 142 B7
Blackfen Gt Lon 51 M4
Blackfield Hants 19 G3
Blackford Cumb 177 L6
Blackford P & K 220 F5
Blackford Somset 30 F2
Blackford Somset 31 L5
Blackfordby Leics 116 B7
Blackgang IoW 19 H8
Blackhall C Edin 211 G4
Blackhall Dur 170 B3
Blackhall Colliery Dur 170 B3
Blackhall Mill Gatesd 180 D7
Blackhaugh Border 200 F5
Blackheath Essex 72 E3
Blackheath Gt Lon 51 K4
Blackheath Sandw 98 B6
Blackheath Suffk 107 J8
Blackheath Surrey 36 F2
Black Heddon Nthumb 180 C4
Blackhill Abers 257 K3
Blackhill Abers 269 K5
Blackhill Dur 180 D8
Blackhill of Clackriach Abers 269 G7
Blackhorse Devon 14 A4
Blackjack Lincs 119 H4
Blackland Wilts 46 E5
Black Lane Ends Lancs 149 G7
Blacklaw D & G 186 F4
Blackley Manch 140 C7
Blackley Crematorium Manch 140 C7
Blacklunans P & K 233 H3
Blackmarstone Herefs 80 C7
Blackmill Brdgnd 42 E4
Blackmoor Hants 36 A4
Black Moor Leeds 150 D7
Blackmoor N Som 44 F6
Blackmoorfoot Kirk 141 H5
Blackmore Essex 70 F6
Blackmore End Essex 71 H1
Blackmore End Herts 68 F4
Blackness Falk 210 E3
Blacknest Hants 36 B3
Blacknest W & M 50 B5
Black Notley Essex 71 J3
Blacko Lancs 148 E7
Black Pill Swans 57 H6
Blackpool Bpool 146 F8
Blackpool Devon 8 C5
Blackpool Devon 13 J7
Blackpool Gate Cumb 178 C3
Blackridge W Loth 210 A5
Blackrock Cnwll 3 G4
Blackrock Mons 61 K4
Blackrod Bolton 139 J5
Blacksboat Moray 254 D4
Blackshaw D & G 176 D5
Blackshaw Head Calder 140 E2
Blacksmith's Green Suffk 90 D2
Blacksnape Bl w D 139 L3
Blackstone W Susx 22 C4
Black Street Suffk 107 K6
Black Tar Pembks 55 G5
Blackthorn Oxon 66 F3
Blackthorpe Suffk 89 H3
Blacktoft E R Yk 143 L3
Blacktop C Aber 245 J3
Black Torrington Devon 12 B2
Blackwall Derbys 115 L2
Blackwater Cnwll 4 B5
Blackwater Hants 49 K7
Blackwater IoW 19 H6
Blackwater Somset 30 C7
Blackwaterfoot N Ayrs 194 D5
Blackwell Cumb 177 L8
Blackwell Darltn 169 H8
Blackwell Derbys 132 C5
Blackwell Derbys 133 J7
Blackwell Warwks 82 F6
Blackwell Worcs 82 A1
Blackwellsend Green Gloucs 63 M2
Blackwood Caerph 43 J2
Blackwood D & G 176 B2
Blackwood S Lans 198 C4
Blackwood Hill Staffs 131 H8
Blacon Ches W 129 J6
Bladbean Kent 41 G6
Bladnoch D & G 174 C4
Bladon Oxon 66 C4
Bladon Somset 30 F6
Blaenannerch Cerdgn 75 M2
Blaenau Ffestiniog Gwynd 110 D2
Blaenavon Torfn 61 L5
Blaen Dyryn Powys 78 C7
Blaenffos Pembks 75 L5
Blaengarw Brdgnd 42 D3
Blaengeuffordd Cerdgn 92 E7
Blaengwrach Neath 60 C6

Blaengwynfi Neath 42 D2
Blaenllechau Rhondd 42 F2
Blaenpennal Cerdgn 77 H2
Blaenplwyf Cerdgn 92 C8
Blaenporth Cerdgn 76 A5
Blaenrhondda Rhondd 60 D7
Blaenwaun Carmth 75 M6
Blaen-y-Coed Carmth 58 C3
Blaen-y-cwm Blae G 61 H5
Blaenycwm Cerdgn 93 H8
Blaen-y-cwm Rhondd 60 D7
Blagdon N Som 45 G7
Blagdon Somset 30 B7
Blagdon Torbay 8 C3
Blagdon Hill Somset 30 B7
Blagill Cumb 167 G1
Blaguegate Lancs 138 F6
Blaich Highld 239 G8
Blain Highld 237 K6
Blaina Blae G 61 K5
Blair Atholl P & K 232 C2
Blair Drummond Stirlg 220 C7
Blairgowrie P & K 233 J6
Blairhall Fife 210 C2
Blairingone P & K 221 H7
Blairlogie Stirlg 220 E7
Blairmore Ag & B 207 K2
Blairmore Highld 276 B4
Blair's Ferry Ag & B 206 F5
Blaisdon Gloucs 63 K4
Blakebrook Worcs 97 J8
Blakedown Worcs 97 K7
Blake End Essex 71 H3
Blakeley Lane Staffs 114 F2
Blakemere Ches W 130 A5
Blakemere Herefs 79 L7
Blakemore Devon 7 M3
Blakenall Heath Wsall 98 C3
Blakeney Gloucs 63 K5
Blakeney Norfk 122 A3
Blakenhall Ches E 114 A2
Blakenhall Wolves 97 K4
Blakeshall Worcs 97 J7
Blakesley Nhants 84 C5
Blanchland Nthumb 168 B1
Blandford Camp Dorset 17 H1
Blandford Forum Dorset 17 G1
Blandford St Mary Dorset 17 G2
Bland Hill N York 150 B5
Blanefield Stirlg 208 F3
Blankney Lincs 135 L7
Blantyre S Lans 209 J7
Blar a' Chaorainn Highld 229 H2
Blargie Highld 241 G4
Blarmachfoldach Highld 229 H2
Blashford Hants 18 A2
Blaston Leics 101 H4
Blatherwycke Nhants 101 L4
Blawith Cumb 156 C5
Blawquhairn D & G 184 F6
Blaxhall Suffk 91 J4
Blaxton Donc 143 H7
Blaydon Gatesd 180 F6
Bleadney Somset 31 H2
Bleadon N Som 44 C7
Bleak Street Somset 32 C4
Blean Kent 40 F3
Bleasby Lincs 136 B3
Bleasby Notts 117 J2
Bleasdale Lancs 147 L6
Bleatarn Cumb 167 G7
Bleathwood Herefs 80 D1
Blebocraigs Fife 223 G4
Bleddfa Powys 79 H2
Bledington Gloucs 65 K3
Bledlow Bucks 67 J6
Bledlow Ridge Bucks 67 J7
Bleet Wilts 46 C7
Blegbie E Loth 212 B6
Blencarn Cumb 166 E4
Blencogo Cumb 165 G1
Blendworth Hants 35 L8
Blennerhasset Cumb 165 G2
Bletchingdon Oxon 66 D3
Bletchingley Surrey 37 M1
Bletchley M Keyn 85 G8
Bletchley Shrops 113 K5
Bletherston Pembks 55 H3
Bletsoe Bed 85 K4
Blewbury Oxon 48 D2
Blickling Norfk 122 D6
Blidworth Notts 134 B8
Blidworth Bottoms Notts 117 G1
Blindburn Nthumb 189 L4
Blindcrake Cumb 164 F4
Blindley Heath Surrey 38 A4
Blisland Cnwll 10 F8
Blissford Hants 33 L8
Bliss Gate Worcs 81 G1
Blisworth Nhants 84 D4
Blithbury Staffs 115 H7
Blitterlees Cumb 176 F8
Blockley Gloucs 82 E8
Blofield Norfk 107 G2
Blofield Heath Norfk 107 G1
Blo Norton Norfk 105 K7
Bloomfield Border 189 G2
Blore Staffs 114 A4
Blore Staffs 115 J2
Blounce Hants 35 L2
Blounts Green Staffs 115 H5
Blowick Sefton 138 D4
Bloxham Oxon 83 K8
Bloxholm Lincs 118 E1
Bloxwich Wsall 98 C3
Bloxworth Dorset 17 G4
Blubberhouses N York 149 L5
Blue Anchor Cnwll 4 E3
Blue Anchor Somset 29 J2
Blue Bell Hill Kent 52 F6
Blundellsands Sefton 138 C7
Blundeston Suffk 107 L4
Blunham C Beds 86 C5
Blunsdon St Andrew Swindn 47 H1
Bluntington Worcs 97 K8
Bluntisham Cambs 103 H8
Blunts Cnwll 6 C2
Blunts Green Warwks 82 D2
Blurton C Stke 114 D3
Blyborough Lincs 135 J1
Blyford Suffk 107 J8
Blymhill Staffs 97 H1
Blymhill Lawn Staffs 97 J1
Blyth Notts 134 C2
Blyth Nthumb 181 H3
Blyth Bridge Border 199 K4
Blythburgh Suffk 107 J8
Blyth Crematorium Nthumb 181 H3
Blythe Border 201 J3
Blythe Bridge Staffs 114 F3
Blythe End Warwks 99 G5
Blythe Marsh Staffs 114 F3
Blyton Lincs 135 G1
Boarhills Fife 223 K4
Boarhunt Hants 19 K2
Boarley Kent 53 G7
Boarsgreave Lancs 140 C4
Boarshead E Susx 38 E6
Boar's Head Wigan 139 H6
Boars Hill Oxon 66 D6
Boarstall Bucks 66 F4
Boasley Cross Devon 12 C4
Boath Highld 263 G5
Boat of Garten Highld 253 H7
Bobbing Kent 53 J6
Bobbington Staffs 97 H5
Bobbingworth Essex 70 D6
Bocaddon Cnwll 5 L3
Bocking Essex 71 J2
Bocking Churchstreet Essex 71 J2
Bockleton Worcs 80 D3
Boconnoc Cnwll 5 K3
Boddam Abers 257 L3
Boddam Shet 281 d8
Boddington Gloucs 64 C2
Bodedern IoA 124 F4
Bodelwyddan Denbgs 127 K4
Bodenham Herefs 80 C5
Bodenham Wilts 33 L5
Bodenham Moor Herefs 80 D5
Bodewryd IoA 125 G2
Bodfari Denbgs 128 C5
Bodffordd IoA 125 G4
Bodfuan Gwynd 108 E4
Bodham Norfk 122 C3
Bodiam E Susx 24 E2
Bodicote Oxon 83 K7
Bodieve Cnwll 10 D7
Bodinnick Cnwll 5 K4
Bodle Street Green E Susx 23 L4
Bodmin Cnwll 5 H2
Bodney Norfk 105 G4
Bodorgan IoA 125 G6
Bodsham Kent 40 E6
Bodwen Cnwll 5 H3
Bodymoor Heath Warwks 99 G4
Bogallan Highld 251 H2
Bogbrae Abers 257 J4
Bogend S Ayrs 196 D4
Boggs Holdings E Loth 212 A5
Boghall Mdloth 211 H6
Boghall W Loth 210 C5
Boghead S Lans 198 C5
Bogmoor Moray 267 G4
Bogmuir Abers 235 G1
Bogniebrae Abers 255 M3
Bognor Regis W Susx 20 F7
Bogroy Highld 253 G7
Bogue D & G 185 G6
Bohetherick Cnwll 6 E1
Bohortha Cnwll 3 L4
Bohuntine Highld 240 A6
Bojewyan Cnwll 2 B4
Bokiddick Cnwll 5 H2
Bolam Dur 169 G6
Bolam Nthumb 180 D2
Bolberry Devon 7 K7
Bold Heath St Hel 129 M2
Boldmere Birm 98 E4
Boldon Colliery S Tyne 181 J6
Boldre Hants 18 E4
Boldron Dur 168 C7
Bole Notts 134 F2
Bolehill Derbys 132 F8
Bole Hill Derbys 133 G5
Bolenowe Cnwll 3 H3
Bolham Devon 29 G7
Bolham Water Devon 29 L8
Bolingey Cnwll 4 C4
Bollington Ches E 131 J4
Bollington Cross Ches E 131 H4
Bollow Gloucs 63 L4
Bolney W Susx 37 L6
Bolnhurst Bed 86 B3
Bolshan Angus 234 F5
Bolsover Derbys 133 J5
Bolster Moor Kirk 141 G5
Bolsterstone Sheff 141 L8
Boltby N York 161 H5
Boltenstone Abers 243 M2
Bolter End Bucks 67 J8
Bolton Bolton 139 L6
Bolton Cumb 166 E6
Bolton E Loth 212 B5
Bolton E R Yk 152 B5
Bolton Nthumb 191 G3
Bolton Abbey N York 149 K5
Bolton Bridge N York 149 K5
Bolton by Bowland Lancs 148 D6
Boltonfellend Cumb 178 B5
Boltongate Cumb 165 H3
Bolton le Sands Lancs 147 J2
Bolton Low Houses Cumb 165 H2
Bolton New Houses Cumb 165 H2
Bolton-on-Swale N York 160 C3
Bolton Percy N York 151 H7
Bolton Town End Lancs 147 J2
Bolton Upon Dearne Barns 142 C7
Bolventor Cnwll 11 H7
Bomarsund Nthumb 181 G2
Bomere Heath Shrops 113 G7
Bonar Bridge Highld 263 G2
Bonawe Ag & B 228 F8
Bonby N Linc 144 C5
Boncath Pembks 75 L4
Bonchester Bridge Border 189 G4
Bonchurch IoW 19 K8
Bondleigh Devon 12 F2
Bonds Lancs 147 J6
Bonehill Devon 13 G7
Bonehill Staffs 99 G3
Bo'ness Falk 210 D3
Boney Hay Staffs 98 D2
Bonhill W Duns 208 C3
Boningale Shrops 97 J3
Bonjedward Border 189 H2
Bonkle N Lans 209 M7
Bonnington Angus 234 F7
Bonnington Kent 40 D8
Bonnybank Fife 222 F6
Bonnybridge Falk 209 L3
Bonnykelly Abers 268 F5
Bonnyrigg Mdloth 211 J6
Bonnyton Angus 233 M7
Bonsall Derbys 132 E8
Bonshaw Tower D & G 177 H4
Bont Mons 62 D3
Bontddu Gwynd 110 C7
Bont-Dolgadfan Powys 93 J3
Bont-goch or Elerch Cerdgn 92 E6
Bonthorpe Lincs 137 J5
Bontnewydd Cerdgn 77 H2
Bontnewydd Gwynd 125 J7
Bontuchel Denbgs 128 C8
Bonvilston V Glam 43 G7
Bonwm Denbgs 111 L3
Bon-y-maen Swans 57 J6
Boode Devon 27 J3
Booker Bucks 49 K1
Booley Shrops 113 J6
Boon Border 201 J4
Boon Hill Staffs 114 C2
Boorley Green Hants 35 G8
Boosbeck R & Cl 170 F7
Boose's Green Essex 71 K1
Boot Cumb 155 M3
Booth Calder 141 G2
Boothby Graffoe Lincs 135 K7
Boothby Pagnell Lincs 118 C5
Boothferry E R Yk 143 J3
Booth Green Ches E 131 H3
Boothstown Salfd 139 L7
Booth Town Calder 141 G2
Boothville Nhants 84 F2
Bootle Cumb 155 K5
Bootle Sefton 138 D8
Boots Green Ches W 130 E5
Boot Street Suffk 90 F5
Booze N York 159 H2
Boraston Shrops 80 E1
Bordeaux Guern 9 k2
Borden Kent 53 J6
Borden W Susx 36 B6
Border Cumb 177 G8
Borders Crematorium Border 201 H6
Bordley N York 149 G3
Bordon Camp Hants 36 B4
Boreham Essex 71 J5
Boreham Wilts 32 E2
Boreham Street E Susx 24 B5
Borehamwood Herts 69 G7
Boreland D & G 187 J8
Boreraig Highld 258 B6
Boreton Shrops 96 C2
Borgh W Isls 282 g1
Borgh W Isls 283 b13
Borgie Highld 278 B4
Borgue D & G 175 G5
Borgue Highld 274 F3
Borley Essex 89 G6
Borley Green Essex 89 G6
Borley Green Suffk 89 K3
Borneskitaig Highld 258 F2
Borness D & G 174 F5
Boroughbridge N York 150 E3
Borough Green Kent 38 F2
Borras Head Wrexhm 112 E1
Borrowash Derbys 116 C4
Borrowby N York 160 F5
Borrowby N York 171 H7
Borrowstoun Falk 210 D3
Borstal Medway 52 F5
Borth Cerdgn 92 D5
Borthwickbrae Border 188 C3
Borthwickshiels Border 188 D3
Borth-y-Gest Gwynd 109 K4
Borve Highld 259 G7
Borve W Isls 282 d6
Borve W Isls 282 g1
Borve W Isls 283 b13
Borwick Lancs 147 K1
Borwick Lodge Cumb 156 E3
Borwick Rails Cumb 156 A6
Bosavern Cnwll 2 B5
Bosbury Herefs 80 F6
Boscarne Cnwll 5 H1
Boscastle Cnwll 10 F4
Boscombe Bmouth 17 M4
Boscombe Wilts 33 L3
Boscoppa Cnwll 5 H4
Bosham W Susx 20 C6
Bosham Hoe W Susx 20 D6
Bosherston Pembks 54 F7
Boskednan Cnwll 2 C4
Boskenna Cnwll 2 C6
Bosley Ches E 131 H6
Bosoughan Cnwll 4 E3
Bossall N York 151 M4
Bossiney Cnwll 10 F5
Bossingham Kent 40 F5
Bossington Somset 28 F1
Bostock Green Ches W 130 C6
Boston Lincs 119 K3
Boston Crematorium Lincs 119 K3
Boston Spa Leeds 150 F6
Boswarthan Cnwll 2 C4
Boswinger Cnwll 5 G6
Botallack Cnwll 2 B4
Botany Bay Gt Lon 69 J7
Botcheston Leics 100 B2
Botesdale Suffk 105 L8
Bothal Nthumb 180 F2
Bothampstead W Berk 48 D4
Bothamsall Notts 134 D5
Bothel Cumb 165 G3
Bothenhampton Dorset 15 L4
Bothwell S Lans 209 J7
Botley Bucks 68 B6
Botley Hants 35 G8
Botley Oxon 66 C6
Botolph Claydon Bucks 67 H2
Botolphs W Susx 21 L5
Botolph's Bridge Kent 40 F8
Bottesford Leics 117 L4
Bottesford N Linc 143 M6
Bottisham Cambs 87 L3
Bottomcraig Fife 222 F2
Bottom of Hutton Lancs 138 F2
Bottom o' th' Moor Bolton 139 K5
Bottoms Calder 140 D3

Bottoms Cnwll 2 B6
Botts Green Warwks 99 H5
Botusfleming Cnwll 6 E3
Botwnnog Gwynd 108 D5
Bough Beech Kent 38 D4
Boughrood Powys 79 G7
Boughspring Gloucs 63 H7
Boughton Nhants 84 E2
Boughton Norfk 104 D3
Boughton Notts 134 D6
Boughton Aluph Kent 40 D6
Boughton End C Beds 85 J7
Boughton Green Kent 39 J3
Boughton Malherbe Kent 39 M3
Boughton Monchelsea Kent 39 J3
Boughton Street Kent 40 D3
Boulby R & Cl 171 H7
Boulder Clough Calder 140 F3
Bouldnor IoW 18 F5
Bouldon Shrops 96 C6
Boulmer Nthumb 191 K3
Boulston Pembks 55 G4
Boultham Lincs 135 J6
Bourn Cambs 87 G4
Bourne Lincs 118 E7
Bournebridge Essex 70 D8
Bournebrook Birm 98 D6
Bourne End Bed 85 K3
Bourne End Bucks 49 L2
Bourne End C Beds 85 J6
Bourne End Herts 68 C6
Bournemouth Bmouth 17 L4
Bournemouth Crematorium
Bmouth 17 M4
Bournes Green Gloucs 64 C6
Bournes Green Sthend 53 K2
Bournheath Worcs 98 B8
Bournmoor Dur 181 H8
Bournstream Gloucs 63 L8
Bournville Birm 98 D7
Bourton Dorset 32 C5
Bourton N Som 44 D6
Bourton Oxon 47 K2
Bourton Shrops 96 D4
Bourton Wilts 46 F6
Bourton on Dunsmore
Warwks 83 K1
Bourton-on-the-Hill Gloucs 65 J1
Bourton-on-the-Water Gloucs 65 H3
Bousd Ag & B 225 H3
Boustead Hill Cumb 177 J7
Bouth Cumb 156 D5
Bouthwaite N York 149 L2
Bouts Worcs 82 B3
Boveney Bucks 50 B3
Boveridge Dorset 33 J7
Bovey Tracey Devon 13 J7
Bovingdon Herts 68 C6
Bovingdon Green Bucks 49 K2
Bovinger Essex 70 D6
Bovington Dorset 16 F5
Bovington Camp Dorset 16 F5
Bow Cumb 177 K7
Bow Devon 8 B3
Bow Devon 13 G2
Bow Gt Lon 51 K2
Bow Ork 275 c6
Bowbank Dur 168 B6
Bow Brickhill M Keyn 85 H8
Bowbridge Gloucs 64 B6
Bowburn Dur 169 J3
Bowcombe IoW 19 H6
Bowd Devon 14 D4
Bowden Border 201 H7
Bowden Devon 8 C5
Bowden Hill Wilts 46 D5
Bowdon Traffd 130 E2
Bower Highld 280 B4
Bower Ashton Bristl 45 H4
Bowerchalke Wilts 33 H6
Bowerhill Wilts 46 C6
Bower Hinton Somset 31 G7
Bower House Tye Suffk 89 K7
Bowermadden Highld 280 B3
Bowers Staffs 114 C4
Bowers Gifford Essex 53 G1
Bowershall Fife 210 E1
Bower's Row Leeds 142 B2
Bowes Dur 168 C7
Bowgreave Lancs 147 K7
Bowhouse D & G 176 D5
Bowithick Cnwll 11 H6
Bowker's Green Lancs 138 E6
Bowland Border 200 F5
Bowland Bridge Cumb 156 F5
Bowley Herefs 80 C5
Bowley Town Herefs 80 C5
Bowlhead Green Surrey 36 D3
Bowling C Brad 141 J2
Bowling W Duns 208 D4
Bowling Bank Wrexhm 112 F2
Bowling Green Worcs 81 J5
Bowmanstead Cumb 156 D3
Bowmore Ag & B 204 D4
Bowness-on-Solway Cumb 177 H6
Bowness-on-Windermere
Cumb 156 F3
Bow of Fife Fife 222 E4
Bowriefauld Angus 234 D6
Bowscale Cumb 165 K4
Bowsden Nthumb 202 F5
Bowston Cumb 157 H3
Bow Street Cerdgn 92 D6
Bow Street Norfk 105 L4
Bowthorpe Norfk 106 D2
Box Gloucs 64 B7
Box Wilts 46 B5
Boxbush Gloucs 63 K3
Boxbush Gloucs 63 L4
Box End Bed 85 K5
Boxford Suffk 89 K7
Boxford W Berk 48 B4
Boxgrove W Susx 20 E5
Box Hill Surrey 51 G8
Boxley Kent 53 G7
Boxmoor Herts 68 D6
Box's Shop Cnwll 11 H2
Boxted Essex 72 E1
Boxted Essex 89 K8
Boxted Suffk 89 G5
Boxted Cross Essex 72 E1
Boxwell Gloucs 64 A8
Boxworth Cambs 87 G2
Boxworth End Cambs 87 G2
Boyden End Suffk 88 E4
Boyden Gate Kent 41 H2
Boylestone Derbys 115 K4
Boyndie Abers 268 B3
Boyndlie Abers 269 G4
Boynton E R Yk 153 J2
Boysack Angus 234 F5
Boys Hill Dorset 16 C1
Boythorpe Derbys 133 G5
Boyton Cnwll 11 L4
Boyton Suffk 91 J6
Boyton Wilts 32 F3
Boyton Cross Essex 70 F5
Boyton End Suffk 88 E6
Bozeat Nhants 85 H3
Braaid IoM 154 d6
Brabling Green Suffk 91 G2
Brabourne Kent 40 E7
Brabourne Lees Kent 40 E7
Brabstermire Highld 280 D2
Bracadale Highld 246 E1
Braceborough Lincs 102 B1
Bracebridge Heath Lincs 135 K6
Bracebridge Low Fields Lincs 135 J6
Braceby Lincs 118 D4
Bracewell Lancs 148 F6
Brackenfield Derbys 133 G7
Brackenhirst N Lans 209 K5
Brackenthwaite Cumb 165 J1
Brackenthwaite N York 150 C5
Bracklesham W Susx 20 C7
Brackletter Highld 239 K7
Brackley Nhants 84 B7
Brackley Hatch Nhants 84 C7
Bracknell Br For 49 L5
Braco P & K 220 E5
Bracobrae Moray 267 K5
Bracon Ash Norfk 106 D3
Bracora Highld 237 L2
Bracorina Highld 237 L2
Bradaford Devon 11 M4
Bradbourne Derbys 115 K1
Bradbury Dur 169 J5
Bradden Nhants 84 C5
Braddock Cnwll 5 K2
Bradeley C Stke 114 D1
Bradenham Bucks 67 K7
Bradenstoke Wilts 46 E3
Bradfield Devon 14 B1
Bradfield Essex 73 H1
Bradfield Norfk 122 F5
Bradfield Sheff 132 E1
Bradfield W Berk 48 F4
Bradfield Combust Suffk 89 H4
Bradfield Green Ches E 130 D7
Bradfield Heath Essex 73 H1
Bradfield St Clare Suffk 89 H4
Bradfield St George Suffk 89 H3
Bradford C Brad 141 J1
Bradford Cnwll 11 G7
Bradford Devon 12 A1
Bradford Nthumb 180 C3
Bradford Nthumb 203 J6
Bradford Abbas Dorset 31 K8
Bradford Leigh Wilts 46 B6
Bradford-on-Avon Wilts 46 B6
Bradford-on-Tone Somset 30 B6
Bradford Peverell Dorset 16 C4
Bradiford Devon 27 K4
Brading IoW 19 K6
Bradley Derbys 115 L2
Bradley Hants 35 K3
Bradley Kirk 141 J4
Bradley N York 159 J6
Bradley NE Lin 145 G6
Bradley Staffs 114 D7
Bradley Wolves 98 B4
Bradley Worcs 82 A3
Bradley Wrexhm 112 E1
Bradley Common Ches W 113 H2
Bradley Green Somset 30 C3
Bradley Green Warwks 99 H3
Bradley Green Worcs 82 A3
Bradley in the Moors Staffs 115 H3
Bradley Stoke S Glos 45 J3
Bradmore Notts 117 G5
Bradney Somset 30 E3
Bradninch Devon 14 A2
Bradninch Devon 27 L4
Bradnop Staffs 131 K8
Bradnor Green Herefs 79 K4
Bradpole Dorset 15 L4
Bradshaw Bolton 139 L5
Bradshaw Calder 141 G2
Bradshaw Kirk 141 G5
Bradstone Devon 11 M6
Bradwall Green Ches E 130 E7
Bradwell Derbys 132 C3
Bradwell Devon 27 J2
Bradwell Essex 71 K3
Bradwell M Keyn 85 G7
Bradwell Norfk 107 K3
Bradwell Crematorium Staffs 114 D2
Bradwell-on-Sea Essex 72 E5
Bradwell Waterside Essex 72 E5
Bradworthy Devon 26 E8
Brae Highld 263 H7
Brae Shet 281 d4
Braeface Falk 209 K3
Braehead Angus 235 H5
Braehead D & G 173 K4
Braehead S Lans 198 F3
Braemar Abers 243 G5
Braemore Highld 261 L4
Braemore Highld 274 E2
Brae Roy Lodge Highld 240 B5
Braeside Inver 207 L4
Braes of Coul Angus 233 L4
Braes of Enzie Moray 267 H4
Braeswick Ork 275 e2
Braevallich Ag & B 216 E5
Brafferton Darltn 169 H6
Brafferton N York 150 F2
Brafield-on-the-Green Nhants 84 F3
Bragar W Isls 282 f2
Bragbury End Herts 69 H3
Braidwood S Lans 198 D3
Brailsford Derbys 115 L3
Brailsford Green Derbys 115 L3
Brain's Green Gloucs 63 K5
Braintree Essex 71 J2
Braiseworth Suffk 90 D1
Braishfield Hants 34 E6
Braithwaite C Brad 149 J7
Braithwaite Cumb 165 H6
Braithwell Donc 133 K1
Braken Hill Wakefd 142 C4
Bramber W Susx 21 L5
Brambridge Hants 35 G6
Bramcote Notts 116 E4
Bramcote Warwks 99 L5
Bramcote Crematorium Notts 116 E4
Bramdean Hants 35 J5
Bramerton Norfk 106 F2
Bramfield Herts 69 H4
Bramfield Suffk 107 H8
Bramford Suffk 90 D6
Bramhall Stockp 131 H3
Bramham Leeds 150 F7
Bramhope Leeds 150 C7
Bramley Hants 49 G7
Bramley Leeds 141 K1
Bramley Rothm 133 K1
Bramley Surrey 36 F2
Bramley Corner Hants 48 F7
Bramley Green Hants 49 G7
Bramley Head N York 149 L4
Bramling Kent 41 H4
Brampford Speke Devon 13 L3
Brampton Cambs 86 E1
Brampton Cumb 166 F6
Brampton Cumb 178 C6
Brampton Lincs 135 G4
Brampton Norfk 122 E6
Brampton Rothm 142 C7
Brampton Suffk 107 J7
Brampton Abbotts Herefs 63 J
Brampton Ash Nhants 101 H
Brampton Bryan Herefs 79 L
Brampton-en-le-Morthen
Rothm 133 J
Bramshall Staffs 115 H
Bramshaw Hants 34 C
Bramshill Hants 49 H
Bramshott Hants 36 C
Bramwell Somset 31 G
Branault Highld 237 G
Brancaster Norfk 121 G
Brancaster Staithe Norfk 121 H
Brancepeth Dur 169 G
Branchill Moray 266 B
Brand End Lincs 119 L
Branderburgh Moray 266 E
Brandesburton E R Yk 153 H
Brandeston Suffk 90 F
Brand Green Gloucs 63 L
Brandis Corner Devon 12 A
Brandiston Norfk 122 C
Brandon Dur 169 G
Brandon Lincs 118 B
Brandon Nthumb 190 F
Brandon Suffk 104 F
Brandon Warwks 99 L
Brandon Bank Norfk 104 C
Brandon Creek Norfk 104 C
Brandon Parva Norfk 106 B
Brandsby N York 151 J
Brandy Wharf Lincs 144 C
Brane Cnwll 2 B
Bran End Essex 71 G
Branksome Poole 17 L
Branksome Park Poole 17 L
Bransbury Hants 34 F
Bransby Lincs 135 H
Branscombe Devon 14 E
Bransford Worcs 81 H
Bransgore Hants 18 B
Bransholme C KuH 144 E
Bransley Shrops 96 E
Branson's Cross Worcs 82 C
Branston Leics 117 L
Branston Lincs 135 K
Branston Staffs 115 L
Branston Booths Lincs 135 L
Branstone IoW 19 J
Brant Broughton Lincs 118 B
Brantham Suffk 90 D
Branthwaite Cumb 164 E
Branthwaite Cumb 165 J
Brantingham E R Yk 144 B
Branton Donc 143 G
Branton Nthumb 190 F
Branton Green N York 150 F
Branxton Nthumb 202 D
Brassey Green Ches W 129 M
Brassington Derbys 115 L
Brasted Kent 38 D
Brasted Chart Kent 51 M
Brathens Abers 244 F
Bratoft Lincs 137 J
Brattleby Lincs 135 J
Bratton Somset 29 G
Bratton Wilts 46 C
Bratton Wrekin 96 E
Bratton Clovelly Devon 12 B
Bratton Fleming Devon 27 M
Bratton Seymour Somset 31 L5
Braughing Herts 69 K
Braughing Friars Herts 70 B
Braunston Nhants 84 A
Braunston Rutlnd 101 H
Braunstone Leics 100 C
Braunton Devon 27 J
Brawby N York 162 C
Brawl Highld 278 D
Braworth N York 161 H
Bray W & M 49 L
Braybrooke Nhants 101 G
Braydon Wilts 46 F
Braydon Brook Wilts 64 E
Braydon Side Wilts 46 E
Brayford Devon 28 B4
Bray's Hill E Susx 24 B4
Bray Shop Cnwll 11 L7
Braystones Cumb 155 H
Braythorn N York 150 C
Brayton N York 142 F
Braywick W & M 49 L
Braywoodside W & M 49 L
Brazacott Cnwll 11 K
Breach Kent 41 G
Breach Kent 53 H
Breachwood Green Herts 68 F3
Breaden Heath Shrops 113 G
Breadsall Derbys 116 B
Breadstone Gloucs 63 L7

Breadward Herefs 79 K4
Breage Cnwll 3 G5
Breakachy Highld 250 E3
Breakspear Crematorium Gt Lon 50 D1
Brealangwell Lodge Highld 262 F1
Bream Gloucs 63 J6
Breamore Hants 33 L7
Brean Somset 44 C7
Breanais W Isls 282 d4
Brearley Calder 140 F3
Brearton N York 150 D4
Breascleit W Isls 282 f3
Breasclete W Isls 282 f3
Breaston Derbys 116 D5
Brechfa Carmth 58 F3
Brechin Angus 234 F3
Breckles Norfk 105 J4
Brecon Powys 61 G2
Bredbury Stockp 131 H2
Brede E Susx 24 E4
Bredenbury Herefs 80 E4
Bredfield Suffk 91 G4
Bredgar Kent 53 J7
Bredhurst Kent 53 G6
Bredon Worcs 81 L7
Bredon's Hardwick Worcs 81 L8
Bredon's Norton Worcs 81 L7
Bredwardine Herefs 79 L6
Breedon on the Hill Leics 116 C7
Breich W Loth 210 C7
Breightmet Bolton 139 L6
Breighton E R Yk 143 H1
Breinton Herefs 80 B7
Bremhill Wilts 46 E4
Bremridge Devon 28 B5
Brenchley Kent 39 H5
Brendon Devon 11 L1
Brendon Devon 28 D1
Brendon Hill Somset 29 J4
Brenfield Ag & B 206 D3
Brenish W Isls 282 d4
Brenkley N u Ty 180 F4
Brent Eleigh Suffk 89 J5
Brentford Gt Lon 50 F3
Brentingby Leics 117 K7
Brent Knoll Somset 30 E1
Brent Mill Devon 7 K3
Brent Pelham Herts 70 B1
Brentwood Essex 70 E8
Brenzett Kent 25 J2
Brenzett Green Kent 25 J2
Brereton Staffs 115 G8
Brereton Green Ches E 130 F6
Brereton Heath Ches E 130 F6
Brereton Hill Staffs 115 G8
Bressay Shet 281 e6
Bressingham Norfk 106 B7
Bressingham Common Norfk 106 B7
Bretby Derbys 116 A7
Bretby Crematorium Derbys 115 M7
Bretford Warwks 99 L7
Bretforton Worcs 82 C6
Bretherton Lancs 138 F4
Brettabister Shet 281 e5
Brettenham Norfk 105 J6
Brettenham Suffk 89 K4
Bretton Derbys 132 D4
Bretton Flints 129 H7
Brewers End Essex 70 E3
Brewer Street Surrey 51 J8
Brewood Staffs 97 K2
Briantspuddle Dorset 16 F4
Brick End Essex 70 E2
Brickendon Herts 69 J5
Bricket Wood Herts 68 E6
Brick Houses Sheff 132 F3
Brickkiln Green Essex 71 H1
Bricklehampton Worcs 82 A6
Bride IoM 154 f2
Bridekirk Cumb 164 F4
Bridell Pembks 75 L4
Bridestowe Devon 12 C5
Brideswell Abers 255 M4
Bridford Devon 13 J5
Bridge Kent 41 G4
Bridge End Cumb 156 A6
Bridge End Cumb 165 L1
Bridge End Devon 7 K5
Bridge End Dur 168 C3
Bridge End Essex 71 G1
Bridge End Lincs 118 F4
Bridgefoot Cumb 164 E5
Bridge Green Essex 87 K7
Bridgehampton Somset 31 J6
Bridge Hewick N York 150 D2
Bridgehill Dur 180 D8
Bridgehouse Gate N York 149 L3
Bridgemary Hants 19 K3
Bridgemere Ches E 113 M2
Bridgend Abers 255 K4
Bridgend Ag & B 194 B3
Bridgend Ag & B 204 E4
Bridgend Angus 234 E2
Bridgend Brdgnd 42 D5
Bridgend Cerdgn 75 L3
Bridgend Cumb 165 L7
Bridgend D & G 187 G4
Bridgend Devon 7 G5
Bridgend Fife 223 G5
Bridgend Moray 255 H5
Bridgend P & K 221 L2
Bridgend W Loth 210 D4
Bridgend of Lintrathen Angus 233 L4
Bridge of Alford Abers 255 L8
Bridge of Allan Stirlg 220 D7
Bridge of Avon Moray 254 C7
Bridge of Avon Moray 254 D4
Bridge of Balgie P & K 231 G6
Bridge of Brewlands Angus 233 J3
Bridge of Brown Highld 254 C7
Bridge of Cally P & K 233 H5
Bridge of Canny Abers 244 E4
Bridge of Craigisla Angus 233 K4
Bridge of Dee D & G 175 J3
Bridge of Don C Aber 245 L2
Bridge of Dulsie Highld 253 H3
Bridge of Dye Abers 244 E6
Bridge of Earn P & K 221 L3
Bridge of Ericht P & K 230 F4
Bridge of Feugh Abers 244 F4
Bridge of Forss Highld 279 J3
Bridge of Gairn Abers 243 K4
Bridge of Gaur P & K 230 F4
Bridge of Marnoch Abers 267 M6
Bridge of Orchy Ag & B 230 B7
Bridge of Tilt P & K 232 C2
Bridge of Tynet Moray 267 H4
Bridge of Walls Shet 281 c6
Bridge of Weir Rens 208 C6
Bridge Reeve Devon 28 B8
Bridgerule Devon 11 K2
Bridges Shrops 95 J4
Bridge Sollers Herefs 80 A6
Bridge Street Suffk 89 H5
Bridgetown Cnwll 11 L5
Bridgetown Somset 29 G4
Bridge Trafford Ches W 129 K5
Bridge Yate S Glos 45 K4
Bridgham Norfk 105 J6
Bridgnorth Shrops 97 G5
Bridgwater Somset 30 D3
Bridlington E R Yk 153 K3
Bridport Dorset 15 K4
Bridstow Herefs 63 H2
Brierfield Lancs 148 E8
Brierley Barns 142 B5
Brierley Gloucs 63 J4
Brierley Herefs 80 C4
Brierley Hill Dudley 97 L6
Brierton Hartpl 170 B5
Briery Cumb 165 J6
Brigg N Linc 144 C6
Briggate Norfk 123 G6
Briggswath N York 162 F1
Brigham Cumb 164 E4
Brigham Cumb 165 J6
Brigham E R Yk 153 H5
Brighouse Calder 141 J3
Brighstone IoW 19 G7
Brightgate Derbys 132 E7
Brighthampton Oxon 66 A6
Brightholmlee Sheff 132 F1
Brightley Devon 12 E3
Brightling E Susx 24 C3
Brightlingsea Essex 73 G4
Brighton Br & H 22 D6
Brighton Cnwll 4 E4
Brighton le Sands Sefton 138 C7
Brightons Falk 210 B3
Brightwalton W Berk 48 B3
Brightwalton Green W Berk 48 B3
Brightwalton Holt W Berk 48 B3
Brightwell Suffk 90 F6
Brightwell Baldwin Oxon 67 G8
Brightwell-cum-Sotwell Oxon 48 E1
Brightwell Upperton Oxon 67 G8
Brignall Dur 168 D8
Brig o'Turk Stirlg 219 J6
Brigsley NE Lin 145 H7
Brigsteer Cumb 157 G5
Brigstock Nhants 101 L6
Brill Bucks 67 G4
Brill Cnwll 3 J5
Brilley Herefs 79 J5
Brimfield Herefs 80 C2
Brimfield Cross Herefs 80 C2
Brimington Derbys 133 H5
Brimley Devon 13 J7
Brimpsfield Gloucs 64 D4
Brimpton W Berk 48 E6
Brimpton Common W Berk 48 E6
Brimscombe Gloucs 64 C6
Brimstage Wirral 129 G3
Brincliffe Sheff 132 F3
Brind E R Yk 143 J2
Brindham Somset 31 H3
Brindister Shet 281 c5
Brindle Lancs 139 J3
Brineton Staffs 97 H1
Bringhurst Leics 101 J5
Bringsty Common Herefs 81 G4
Brington Cambs 102 B8
Briningham Norfk 122 A5
Brinkely Notts 117 J1
Brinkhill Lincs 137 G5
Brinkley Cambs 88 C4
Brinklow Warwks 99 L7
Brinkworth Wilts 46 E2
Brinscall Lancs 139 J3
Brinscombe Somset 44 E8
Brinsea N Som 44 F6
Brinsley Notts 116 D2
Brinsop Herefs 80 B6
Brinsworth Rothm 133 H2
Brinton Norfk 122 A4
Brinyan Ork 275 c3
Brisco Cumb 178 A8
Brisley Norfk 121 L7
Brislington Bristl 45 J5
Brissenden Green Kent 40 B7
Bristol Bristl 45 H4
Briston Norfk 122 B5
Brisworthy Devon 7 G2
Britannia Lancs 140 C3
Britford Wilts 33 L5
Brithdir Caerph 61 J6
Brithdir Gwynd 110 E7
British Legion Village Kent 52 F7
Briton Ferry Neath 57 K6
Britwell Salome Oxon 67 G8
Brixham Torbay 8 D4
Brixton Devon 7 G4
Brixton Gt Lon 51 J4
Brixton Deverill Wilts 32 E3
Brixworth Nhants 84 E1
Brize Norton Oxon 65 L5
Broad Alley Worcs 81 K2
Broad Blunsdon Swindn 47 H1
Broadbottom Tamesd 131 K1
Broadbridge W Susx 20 D6
Broadbridge Heath W Susx 37 H4
Broad Campden Gloucs 82 E7
Broad Carr Calder 141 H4
Broad Chalke Wilts 33 H5
Broad Clough Lancs 140 C3
Broadclyst Devon 14 A3
Broadfield Inver 208 B4
Broadfield Pembks 55 K6
Broadford Highld 247 K4
Broad Ford Kent 39 H5
Broadford Bridge W Susx 37 G6
Broadgairhill Border 187 K4
Broadgrass Green Suffk 89 K3
Broad Green Cambs 88 D3
Broad Green Essex 72 C2
Broad Green Worcs 81 H4
Broad Green Worcs 82 A1
Broadhaugh Border 202 D2
Broad Haven Pembks 54 D4
Broadheath Traffd 130 E2
Broadheath Worcs 80 F2
Broadhembury Devon 14 C2
Broadhempston Devon 8 B2
Broad Hill Cambs 104 B8
Broad Hinton Wilts 47 G4
Broadholme Lincs 135 H5
Broadland Row E Susx 24 F3
Broadlay Carmth 56 C3
Broad Layings Hants 48 B6
Broadley Essex 70 B5
Broadley Lancs 140 C4
Broadley Moray 267 H4
Broadley Common Essex 70 B5
Broad Marston Worcs 82 D6
Broadmayne Dorset 16 D5
Broad Meadow Staffs 114 C2
Broadmere Hants 35 J2
Broadmoor Gloucs 63 J4
Broadmoor Pembks 55 J5
Broadnymett Devon 13 G2
Broad Oak Cumb 155 K4
Broadoak Dorset 15 K3
Broad Oak E Susx 23 K3
Broad Oak E Susx 24 E3
Broadoak Gloucs 63 K4
Broad Oak Hants 49 H8
Broad Oak Herefs 62 F3
Broad Oak Kent 41 G3
Broad Oak St Hel 139 G8
Broadoak Wrexhm 129 J7
Broad Road Suffk 106 F8
Broad's Green Essex 71 G4
Broadstairs Kent 41 L2
Broadstone Mons 63 G6
Broadstone Poole 17 K3
Broadstone Shrops 96 C5
Broad Street E Susx 24 F4
Broad Street Essex 70 E4
Broad Street Kent 39 L2
Broad Street Kent 40 F7
Broad Street Medway 53 G4
Broad Street Wilts 47 G7
Broad Street Green Essex 71 L5
Broad Town Wilts 47 G3
Broadwas Worcs 81 H4
Broadwater Herts 69 H3
Broadwater W Susx 21 K6
Broadwaters Worcs 97 J7
Broadway Carmth 56 B3
Broadway Carmth 56 C3
Broadway Pembks 54 E4
Broadway Somset 30 D7
Broadway Suffk 107 H7
Broadway Worcs 82 C7
Broadwell Gloucs 63 H5
Broadwell Gloucs 65 J2
Broadwell Oxon 65 K6
Broadwell Warwks 83 K2
Broadwey Dorset 16 C6
Broadwindsor Dorset 15 K2
Broadwood Kelly Devon 12 E2
Broadwoodwidger Devon 12 A5
Brobury Herefs 79 L6
Brochel Highld 259 K7
Brochroy Ag & B 216 F1
Brock Lancs 147 K7
Brockamin Worcs 81 H4
Brockbridge Hants 35 J7
Brockdish Norfk 106 E7
Brockencote Worcs 97 K8
Brockenhurst Hants 18 D3
Brocketsbrae S Lans 198 D5
Brockford Green Suffk 90 D2
Brockford Street Suffk 90 D2
Brockhall Nhants 84 C3
Brockham Surrey 37 J1
Brockhampton Gloucs 64 D2
Brockhampton Gloucs 64 F3
Brockhampton Hants 20 B5
Brockhampton Herefs 63 H1
Brockhampton Green Dorset 16 D2
Brockholes Kirk 141 J5
Brockhurst Derbys 133 G6
Brockhurst Warwks 100 A6
Brocklebank Cumb 165 J2
Brocklesby Lincs 144 E5
Brockley N Som 44 F5
Brockley Suffk 89 G1
Brockley Green Suffk 88 E6
Brockley Green Suffk 89 G4
Brockleymoor Cumb 166 C3
Brockmoor Dudley 97 K5
Brockscombe Devon 12 B4
Brock's Green Hants 48 D6
Brockton Shrops 95 H3
Brockton Shrops 95 H6
Brockton Shrops 96 D4
Brockton Shrops 97 G3
Brockton Staffs 114 C5
Brockweir Gloucs 63 G6
Brockwood Park Hants 35 K5
Brockworth Gloucs 64 C4
Brocton Cnwll 5 G1
Brocton Staffs 114 F7
Brodick N Ayrs 195 G4
Brodie Moray 264 F8
Brodsworth Donc 142 D6
Brogaig Highld 259 H3
Brogborough C Beds 85 J7
Brokenborough Wilts 46 D1
Broken Cross Ches E 131 H5
Broken Cross Ches W 130 D5
Brokerswood Wilts 46 B8
Bromborough Wirral 129 H3
Brome Suffk 106 C8
Brome Street Suffk 106 C8
Bromeswell Suffk 91 G5
Bromfield Cumb 165 G1
Bromfield Shrops 96 B8
Bromham Bed 85 K5
Bromham Wilts 46 D6
Bromley Barns 141 M7
Bromley Dudley 97 K5
Bromley Gt Lon 51 L5
Bromley Shrops 97 G4
Bromley Common Gt Lon 51 L5
Bromley Cross Essex 72 F2
Bromley Green Kent 40 C8
Bromlow Shrops 95 H3

Brompton Medway 53 G5
Brompton N York 160 E3
Brompton-by-Sawdon N York 163 G6
Brompton-on-Swale N York 160 B3
Brompton Ralph Somset 29 K4
Brompton Regis Somset 29 G4
Bromsash Herefs 63 J2
Bromsberrow Gloucs 81 G8
Bromsberrow Heath Gloucs 81 G8
Bromsgrove Worcs 81 M1
Bromstead Heath Staffs 114 B8
Bromyard Herefs 80 F4
Bromyard Downs Herefs 80 F4
Bronaber Gwynd 110 D5
Bronant Cerdgn 77 H2
Broncroft Shrops 96 C6
Brongest Cerdgn 76 B6
Bronington Wrexhm 113 H3
Bronllys Powys 79 G8
Bronwydd Carmth 58 D4
Bronydd Powys 79 J6
Bronygarth Shrops 112 C4
Bron-y-Nant Crematorium Conwy 127 G4
Brook Carmth 56 A3
Brook Hants 34 C8
Brook Hants 34 D5
Brook IoW 18 F6
Brook Kent 40 E6
Brook Surrey 36 D3
Brook Surrey 37 G2
Brooke Norfk 106 F3
Brooke Rutlnd 101 J2
Brookenby Lincs 145 G8
Brook End Bed 86 B3
Brook End C Beds 86 D5
Brook End Cambs 86 B1
Brook End M Keyn 85 H6
Brookfield Rens 208 C6
Brookhampton Oxon 66 F7
Brookhampton Somset 31 K5
Brook Hill Hants 34 C7
Brook House Denbgs 128 C6
Brookhouse Lancs 147 K3
Brookhouse Rothm 133 K2
Brookhouse Green Ches E 130 F7
Brookhouses Derbys 131 K2
Brookland Kent 25 J2
Brooklands Traffd 130 F2
Brookmans Park Herts 69 H6
Brooks Powys 94 E3
Brooksby Leics 117 H8
Brooks End Kent 41 J2
Brooks Green W Susx 37 H6
Brook Street Essex 70 E8
Brook Street Kent 40 B8
Brook Street Suffk 89 G5
Brook Street W Susx 22 D2
Brookthorpe Gloucs 64 B4
Brookville Norfk 104 E4
Brookwood Surrey 50 B7
Broom C Beds 86 D6
Broom Rothm 133 J1
Broom Warwks 82 C4
Broome Norfk 107 G5
Broome Shrops 95 K7
Broome Worcs 97 K7
Broomedge Warrtn 130 D3
Broome Park Nthumb 191 G4
Broomer's Corner W Susx 21 K3
Broomershill W Susx 21 H3
Broomfield Essex 71 H5
Broomfield Kent 39 L3
Broomfield Kent 41 G2
Broomfield Somset 30 B4
Broomfields Shrops 112 F7
Broomfleet E R Yk 143 M2
Broom Green Norfk 121 L6
Broomhall W & M 50 B5
Broomhaugh Nthumb 180 B6
Broom Hill Barns 142 C7
Broom Hill Dorset 17 K2
Broom Hill Notts 116 F2
Broomhill Nthumb 191 K6
Broom Hill Worcs 97 L8
Broomhill Green Ches E 113 K2
Broomley Nthumb 180 C6
Broompark Dur 169 H2
Broom's Green Gloucs 81 G8
Broomsthorpe Norfk 121 J6
Broom Street Kent 40 D3
Brora Highld 274 B7
Broseley Shrops 96 F3
Brotherhouse Bar Lincs 119 J8
Brotherlee Dur 167 L3
Brothertoft Lincs 119 J2
Brotherton N York 142 D3
Brotton R & Cl 170 F6
Broubster Highld 279 J4
Brough Cumb 167 J7
Brough Derbys 132 D3
Brough E R Yk 144 B2
Brough Highld 280 B2
Brough Notts 135 G7
Brough Shet 281 f5
Broughall Shrops 113 J3
Brough Lodge Shet 281 f3
Brough Sowerby Cumb 167 J8
Broughton Border 199 K6
Broughton Bucks 67 K4
Broughton Cambs 102 F7
Broughton Flints 129 H7
Broughton Hants 34 C4
Broughton Lancs 139 G1
Broughton M Keyn 85 H7
Broughton N Linc 144 B6
Broughton N York 149 G5
Broughton N York 162 D8
Broughton Nhants 101 H8
Broughton Oxon 83 K7
Broughton Salfd 140 B7
Broughton Staffs 114 B5
Broughton V Glam 42 D7
Broughton Astley Leics 100 C5
Broughton Beck Cumb 156 C6
Broughton Gifford Wilts 46 C6
Broughton Green Worcs 81 M3
Broughton Hackett Worcs 81 L4
Broughton-in-Furness Cumb 156 B5
Broughton Mains D & G 174 C6
Broughton Mills Cumb 156 B4
Broughton Moor Cumb 164 E4
Broughton Poggs Oxon 65 K6
Broughton Tower Cumb 156 B5
Broughty Ferry C Dund 223 H1
Brow End Cumb 156 C7
Brownber Cumb 158 B2
Brown Candover Hants 35 J3
Brown Edge Lancs 138 D5
Brown Edge Staffs 114 E1
Brown Heath Ches W 129 K6
Brownheath Shrops 113 G5
Brownhill Abers 256 F4
Brownhills Fife 223 J4
Brownhills Wsall 98 D2
Brownieside Nthumb 191 H2
Browninghill Green Hants 48 E7
Brown Lees Staffs 131 G8
Brownlow Heath Ches E 131 G7
Brownrigg Cumb 164 D6
Brownrigg Cumb 177 G8
Brownsea Island Dorset 17 K5
Brown's Green Birm 98 D5
Brownsham Devon 26 E5
Browns Hill Gloucs 64 C6
Brownsover Warwks 100 B7
Brownston Devon 7 K4
Brown Street Suffk 90 C3
Brow-of-the-Hill Norfk 120 E7
Browston Green Norfk 107 K3
Broxa N York 163 G4
Broxbourne Herts 69 K5
Broxburn E Loth 212 F3
Broxburn W Loth 210 E4
Broxfield Nthumb 191 J3
Broxted Essex 70 E2
Broxton Ches W 113 H1
Broyle Side E Susx 23 G4
Bruan Highld 280 D8
Bruar P & K 232 B2
Brucefield Highld 264 E3
Bruchag Ag & B 207 J7
Bruera Ches W 129 K7
Bruern Abbey Oxon 65 K3
Bruichladdich Ag & B 204 C4
Bruisyard Suffk 91 H2
Bruisyard Street Suffk 91 H2
Brumby N Linc 143 M6
Brund Staffs 132 B7
Brundall Norfk 107 G2
Brundish Suffk 91 G1
Brundish Street Suffk 91 G1
Brunery Highld 237 L6
Brunnion Cnwll 2 D4
Brunslow Shrops 95 J6
Brunswick Village N u Ty 180 F4
Bruntcliffe Leeds 141 L2
Brunthwaite C Brad 149 J6
Bruntingthorpe Leics 100 D5
Brunton Fife 222 E3
Brunton Nthumb 191 J1
Brunton Wilts 47 K7
Brushford Devon 12 F1
Brushford Somset 29 G5
Bruton Somset 31 L4
Bryan's Green Worcs 81 K2
Bryanston Dorset 17 G1
Bryant's Bottom Bucks 67 L7
Brydekirk D & G 177 G5
Bryher IoS 10 b2
Brymbo Wrexhm 112 D1
Brympton Somset 31 H7
Bryn Carmth 57 G5
Bryn Ches W 130 B5
Bryn Neath 42 B3
Bryn Shrops 95 H6
Bryn Wigan 139 H7
Brynamman Carmth 59 K6
Brynberian Pembks 75 J5
Brynbryddan Neath 57 L6
Bryn-bwbach Gwynd 110 B4
Bryncae Rhondd 42 F5
Bryncethin Brdgnd 42 D5
Bryncir Gwynd 109 H3
Bryn-coch Neath 57 K5
Bryncroes Gwynd 108 C5
Bryncrug Gwynd 92 D3
Bryn Du IoA 124 F5
Bryn-Eden Gwynd 110 D5
Bryneglwys Denbgs 112 A2
Brynfields Wrexhm 112 D3
Brynford Flints 128 E5
Bryn Gates Wigan 139 J7
Bryn Golau Rhondd 42 F4
Bryngwran IoA 124 F4
Bryngwyn Mons 62 D5
Bryngwyn Powys 79 H5
Bryn-Henllan Pembks 75 G4
Brynhoffnant Cerdgn 76 B5
Bryning Lancs 138 E2
Brynithel Blae G 61 K6
Brynmawr Blae G 61 J5
Bryn-mawr Gwynd 108 D5
Brynmenyn Brdgnd 42 D5
Brynmill Swans 57 H6
Brynna Rhondd 42 F5
Bryn-penarth Powys 94 D3
Brynrefail Gwynd 125 K7
Brynrefail IoA 125 H2
Brynsadler Rhondd 42 F5
Bryn Saith Marchog Denbgs 111 L2
Brynsiencyn IoA 125 H6
Brynteg IoA 125 J3
Bryn-y-bal Flints 128 F6
Bryn-y-Maen Conwy 127 G4
Bryn-yr-Eos Wrexhm 112 D3
Bualintur Highld 246 F4
Buarth-draw Flints 128 E4
Bubbenhall Warwks 83 J1
Bubwith E R Yk 151 M8
Buccleuch Border 188 B3
Buchanan Smithy Stirlg 208 D1
Buchanhaven Abers 269 L6
Buchanty P & K 221 G2
Buchany Stirlg 220 C6
Buchlyvie Stirlg 219 J8
Buckabank Cumb 165 L1
Buckden Cambs 86 D2
Buckden N York 159 G7
Buckenham Norfk 107 G2
Buckerell Devon 14 D3
Buckfast Devon 7 L2
Buckfastleigh Devon 7 L2
Buckhaven Fife 222 F7
Buckholt Mons 63 G4
Buckhorn Devon 11 M3
Buckhorn Weston Dorset 32 C6
Buckhurst Hill Essex 69 L8
Buckie Moray 267 J3
Buckingham Bucks 84 D8
Buckland Bucks 67 L4
Buckland Devon 7 K6
Buckland Gloucs 82 C8
Buckland Hants 18 E4
Buckland Herts 87 G8
Buckland Kent 41 J6
Buckland Oxon 65 M7
Buckland Surrey 37 K1
Buckland Brewer Devon 27 G6
Buckland Common Bucks 68 A5
Buckland Dinham Somset 32 C1
Buckland Filleigh Devon 12 B1
Buckland in the Moor Devon 13 G7
Buckland Monachorum Devon 6 F1
Buckland Newton Dorset 16 D2
Buckland Ripers Dorset 16 C6
Buckland St Mary Somset 30 C8
Buckland-Tout-Saints Devon 7 L5
Bucklebury W Berk 48 E5
Bucklers Hard Hants 18 F4
Bucklesham Suffk 90 F6
Buckley Flints 129 G7
Buckley Green Warwks 82 E2
Bucklow Hill Ches E 130 E3
Buckminster Leics 118 A7
Bucknall C Stke 114 E2
Bucknall Lincs 136 C6
Bucknell Oxon 66 E2
Bucknell Shrops 95 J8
Buckpool Moray 267 H3
Bucksburn C Aber 245 K
Buck's Cross Devon 26 F6
Bucks Green W Susx 37 G
Buckshaw Village Lancs 139 H4
Bucks Hill Herts 68 D7
Bucks Horn Oak Hants 36 B
Buck's Mills Devon 26 F6
Buckton E R Yk 153 K1
Buckton Herefs 95 J8
Buckton Nthumb 203 H5
Buckworth Cambs 102 C8
Budby Notts 134 C5
Buddileigh Staffs 114 B2
Bude Cnwll 11 H2
Budge's Shop Cnwll 6 C3
Budlake Devon 14 A3
Budle Nthumb 203 J6
Budleigh Salterton Devon 14 C6
Budlett's Common E Susx 23 H3
Budock Water Cnwll 3 K5
Buerton Ches E 113 L3
Bugbrooke Nhants 84 D4
Bugford Devon 8 B5
Buglawton Ches E 131 G7
Bugle Cnwll 5 G3
Bugley Dorset 32 C6
Bugthorpe E R Yk 152 B4
Buildwas Shrops 96 E2
Builth Road Powys 78 E4
Builth Wells Powys 78 E5
Bulbourne Herts 68 B4
Bulbridge Wilts 33 J5
Bulby Lincs 118 D6
Bulford Wilts 33 L2
Bulford Camp Wilts 33 L2
Bulkeley Ches E 113 J1
Bulkington Warwks 99 K6
Bulkington Wilts 46 D7
Bulkworthy Devon 27 G8
Bullamoor N York 160 F4
Bull Bay IoA 125 G1
Bullbridge Derbys 116 B1
Bullbrook Br For 49 L5
Bullen's Green Herts 69 G6
Bulley Gloucs 63 M3
Bullgill Cumb 164 E3
Bullinghope Herefs 80 C7
Bullington Hants 34 F3
Bullington Lincs 136 A4
Bullockstone Kent 41 G2
Bull's Green Herts 69 H4
Bull's Green Norfk 107 J4
Bulmer Essex 89 G7
Bulmer N York 151 L2
Bulmer Tye Essex 89 G7
Bulphan Thurr 52 D2
Bulstone Devon 14 E4
Bulstrode Herts 68 C6
Bulverhythe E Susx 24 D5
Bulwark Abers 257 G3
Bulwell C Nott 116 F3
Bulwick Nhants 101 L4
Bumble's Green Essex 69 L6
Bunacaimb Highld 237 J3
Bunarkaig Highld 239 K6
Bunbury Ches E 130 A8
Bunbury Heath Ches E 130 A8
Bunchrew Highld 251 H3
Buncton W Susx 21 K4
Bundalloch Highld 248 E6
Bunessan Ag & B 226 D8
Bungay Suffk 107 G5
Bunker's Hill Lincs 119 J1
Bunnahabhain Ag & B 204 F2
Bunny Notts 117 G5
Buntait Highld 250 C5
Buntingford Herts 69 K1
Bunwell Norfk 106 C4
Bunwell Hill Norfk 106 C5
Bupton Derbys 115 L4
Burbage Derbys 131 L5
Burbage Leics 99 L5
Burbage Wilts 47 K6
Burcher Herefs 79 L3
Burchett's Green E Susx 39 G7
Burchett's Green W & M 49 K3
Burcombe Wilts 33 J5
Burcot Oxon 66 E7
Burcot Worcs 82 A1
Burcote Shrops 97 G4
Burcott Bucks 67 K4
Burcott Bucks 67 L2
Burdale N York 152 D3
Bures Essex 89 H8
Burford Oxon 65 K5
Burford Shrops 80 D2
Burg Ag & B 226 D3
Burgate Suffk 106 B8
Burgates Hants 36 A5
Burge End Herts 68 F1

Burgess Hill W Susx 22 E3
Burgh Suffk 90 F5
Burgh by Sands Cumb 177 K7
Burgh Castle Norfk 107 K2
Burghclere Hants 48 C6
Burghead Moray 266 C2
Burghfield W Berk 49 G5
Burghfield Common W Berk 49 G5
Burgh Heath Surrey 51 H7
Burgh Hill E Susx 24 C2
Burghill Herefs 80 B6
Burgh Island Devon 7 J6
Burgh le Marsh Lincs 137 J6
Burgh next Aylsham Norfk 122 E6
Burgh on Bain Lincs 136 D2
Burgh St Margaret Norfk 123 J8
Burgh St Peter Norfk 107 K5
Burghwallis Donc 142 E5
Burham Kent 52 F6
Buriton Hants 20 B3
Burland Ches E 113 K1
Burlawn Cnwll 10 D8
Burleigh Gloucs 64 C6
Burlescombe Devon 29 K7
Burleston Dorset 16 E4
Burlestone Devon 8 B5
Burley Hants 18 C3
Burley Rutlnd 101 J1
Burley Shrops 96 B7
Burleydam Ches E 113 K3
Burley Gate Herefs 80 E6
Burley in Wharfedale C Brad 149 L6
Burley Lawn Hants 18 C3
Burley Street Hants 18 B3
Burley Wood Head C Brad 149 L7
Burlingham Green Norfk 107 H1
Burlingjobb Powys 79 J4
Burlington Shrops 97 H1
Burlton Shrops 113 G6
Burmarsh Kent 25 L1
Burmington Warwks 83 G7
Burn N York 142 F2
Burnage Manch 131 G1
Burnaston Derbys 115 M5
Burnbanks Cumb 166 C7
Burnbrae N Lans 210 A7
Burnby E R Yk 152 C6
Burn Cross Sheff 142 A8
Burndell W Susx 21 G6
Burnden Bolton 139 L6
Burnedge Rochdl 140 D5
Burneside Cumb 157 H3
Burneston N York 160 D5
Burnett BaNES 45 K6
Burnfoot Border 188 C4
Burnfoot Border 188 F3
Burnfoot D & G 177 K1
Burnfoot D & G 186 E7
Burnfoot D & G 188 C6
Burnfoot P & K 221 H6
Burnham Bucks 50 A3
Burnham N Linc 144 D4
Burnham Deepdale Norfk 121 H3
Burnham Green Herts 69 H4
Burnham Market Norfk 121 H3
Burnham Norton Norfk 121 H3
Burnham-on-Crouch Essex 72 D7
Burnham-on-Sea Somset 30 D1
Burnham Overy Norfk 121 J3
Burnham Overy Staithe Norfk 121 J3
Burnham Thorpe Norfk 121 J3
Burnhaven Abers 257 L3
Burnhead D & G 186 C7
Burnhervie Abers 256 C7
Burnhill Green Staffs 97 H3
Burnhope Dur 169 G1
Burnhouse N Ayrs 196 D1
Burniston N York 163 H4
Burnley Lancs 140 C1
Burnley Crematorium Lancs 140 B2
Burnmouth Border 213 L6
Burn Naze Lancs 147 G7
Burn of Cambus Stirlg 220 C6
Burnopfield Dur 180 E7
Burnrigg Cumb 178 C7
Burnsall N York 149 J3
Burnside Angus 234 C3
Burnside Angus 234 D5
Burnside Fife 222 B5
Burnside Moray 266 D2
Burnside W Loth 210 E4
Burnside of Duntrune Angus 234 C8
Burntcommon Surrey 50 D8
Burntheath Derbys 115 L5
Burnt Heath Essex 72 F2
Burnt Hill W Berk 48 E4
Burnthouse Cnwll 3 K4
Burnt Houses Dur 168 E6
Burntisland Fife 211 H2
Burnt Oak E Susx 23 H2
Burntwood Staffs 98 D2
Burntwood Green Staffs 98 D2
Burnt Yates N York 150 C4
Burnworthy Somset 30 B7
Burpham Surrey 50 C8
Burpham W Susx 21 H5
Burradon N Tyne 181 G4
Burradon Nthumb 190 D5
Burrafirth Shet 281 f1
Burras Cnwll 3 H4
Burraton Cnwll 6 E2
Burravoe Shet 281 e4
Burrells Cumb 166 F7
Burrelton P & K 233 J7
Burridge Devon 15 H2
Burridge Devon 27 K4
Burridge Hants 19 J2
Burrill N York 160 C5
Burringham N Linc 143 L6
Burrington Devon 27 L7
Burrington Herefs 80 B1
Burrington N Som 44 F7
Burrough End Cambs 88 C4
Burrough Green Cambs 88 C4
Burrough on the Hill Leics 101 G1
Burrow Lancs 157 K7
Burrow Somset 29 G2
Burrow Bridge Somset 30 E5
Burrowhill Surrey 50 B6
Burrows Cross Surrey 37 G2
Burry Swans 56 E6
Burry Green Swans 56 E6
Burry Port Carmth 56 E5
Burscough Lancs 138 E5
Burscough Bridge Lancs 138 F5
Bursea E R Yk 143 K1
Burshill E R Yk 153 H6
Bursledon Hants 19 H2
Burslem C Stke 114 D2
Burstall Suffk 90 C6
Burstock Dorset 15 K2
Burston Norfk 106 C6
Burston Staffs 114 E5
Burstow Surrey 37 M3
Burstwick E R Yk 145 G2
Burtersett N York 158 F5
Burtholme Cumb 178 D6
Burthorpe Green Suffk 88 F2
Burthwaite Cumb 165 M1
Burthy Cnwll 4 E4
Burtle Hill Somset 30 F2
Burtoft Lincs 119 J4
Burton Ches W 129 H5
Burton Ches W 129 L7
Burton Dorset 16 D4
Burton Dorset 18 B5
Burton Lincs 135 J5
Burton Nthumb 203 K6
Burton Pembks 55 G5
Burton Somset 30 B2
Burton Somset 31 H8
Burton Wilts 32 D4
Burton Wilts 46 B3
Burton Agnes E R Yk 153 H3
Burton Bradstock Dorset 15 L5
Burton Coggles Lincs 118 C6
Burton Dassett Warwks 83 J5
Burton End Essex 70 D2
Burton End Suffk 88 D6
Burton Fleming E R Yk 153 H2
Burton Green Warwks 99 H8
Burton Green Wrexhm 129 H7
Burton Hastings Warwks 99 L5
Burton-in-Kendal Cumb 157 H7
Burton in Lonsdale N York 148 A2
Burton Joyce Notts 117 H3
Burton Latimer Nhants 101 K8
Burton Lazars Leics 117 K8
Burton Leonard N York 150 D3
Burton on the Wolds Leics 117 G7
Burton Overy Leics 100 E4
Burton Pedwardine Lincs 118 F3
Burton Pidsea E R Yk 145 H2
Burton Salmon N York 142 D2
Burton's Green Essex 71 K2
Burton upon Stather N Linc 143 L4
Burton upon Trent Staffs 115 L6
Burton Waters Lincs 135 J5
Burtonwood Warrtn 130 A1
Burwardsley Ches W 129 L8
Burwarton Shrops 96 E6
Burwash E Susx 24 B2
Burwash Common E Susx 23 L3
Burwash Weald E Susx 23 L3
Burwell Cambs 88 B2
Burwell Lincs 137 G4
Burwen IoA 125 G1
Burwick Ork 275 c6
Bury Bury 140 B5
Bury Cambs 102 F6
Bury Somset 29 G5
Bury W Susx 21 G4
Bury End C Beds 86 C8
Bury Green Herts 70 C3
Bury St Edmunds Suffk 89 G2
Burythorpe N York 152 B3
Busby E Rens 208 F7
Busby Stoop N York 160 E6
Buscot Oxon 65 J7
Bush Abers 235 J2
Bush Cnwll 11 J1
Bush Bank Herefs 80 B5
Bushbury Wolves 97 L3
Bushbury Crematorium Wolves 97 L3
Bushby Leics 100 E3
Bushey Herts 68 E8
Bushey Heath Herts 68 F8
Bush Green Norfk 106 E6
Bush Green Suffk 89 H4
Bush Hill Park Gt Lon 69 J7
Bushley Worcs 81 K8
Bushley Green Worcs 81 K8
Bushmead Bed 86 C3
Bushmoor Shrops 95 K6
Bushton Wilts 46 F3
Busk Cumb 166 E2
Buslingthorpe Lincs 135 M3
Bussage Gloucs 64 C6
Bussex Somset 30 E4
Butcher's Cross E Susx 23 J2
Butcombe N Som 45 G6
Bute Ag & B 207 G5
Butleigh Somset 31 H4
Butleigh Wootton Somset 31 H4
Butler's Cross Bucks 67 K5
Butler's Hill Notts 116 F2
Butlers Marston Warwks 83 H5
Butley Suffk 91 J5
Butley High Corner Suffk 91 J5
Buttercrambe N York 151 M4
Butterdean Border 213 H6
Butterknowle Dur 168 E5
Butterleigh Devon 14 A1
Butterley Derbys 116 C1
Buttermere Cumb 165 G7
Buttermere Wilts 47 M6
Butters Green Staffs 114 C2
Buttershaw C Brad 141 H2
Butterstone P & K 233 G6
Butterton Staffs 114 C3
Butterton Staffs 131 L8
Butterwick Dur 169 K5
Butterwick Lincs 119 L3
Butterwick N York 152 F2
Butterwick N York 162 C7
Butt Green Ches E 113 L1
Buttington Powys 95 G2
Buttonbridge Shrops 97 G7
Buttonoak Shrops 97 G7
Buttsash Hants 19 G2
Buttsbear Cross Cnwll 11 K2
Butt's Green Essex 71 J6
Buxhall Suffk 89 K4
Buxhall Fen Street Suffk 89 K3
Buxted E Susx 23 H3
Buxton Derbys 131 L5
Buxton Norfk 122 E7
Buxton Heath Norfk 122 D7
Bwlch Powys 61 J3
Bwlchgwyn Wrexhm 112 C1
Bwlchllan Cerdgn 77 G3
Bwlchnewydd Carmth 58 C4
Bwlchtocyn Gwynd 108 E6
Bwlch-y-cibau Powys 112 B8
Bwlch-y-Ddar Powys 112 B7
Bwlchyfadfa Cerdgn 76 D5
Bwlch-y-ffridd Powys 94 C4
Bwlch-y-groes Pembks 75 M5
Bwlchymyrdd Swans 57 G5
Bwlch-y-sarnau Powys 94 B8
Byermoor Gatesd 180 F7
Byers Green Dur 169 G4
Byfield Nhants 83 M4
Byfleet Surrey 50 D6
Byford Herefs 79 M6
Bygrave Herts 86 F7
Byker N u Ty 181 G6
Byland Abbey N York 161 J6
Bylchau Conwy 127 K7
Byley Ches W 130 E6
Bynea Carmth 57 G5
Byrness Nthumb 189 K5
Bystock Devon 14 B6
Bythorn Cambs 102 B8
Byton Herefs 79 L2
Bywell Nthumb 180 C6
Byworth W Susx 36 E6

C

Cabbacott Devon 27 G6
Cabourne Lincs 144 E7
Cabrach Ag & B 205 H3
Cabrach Moray 255 H6
Cabus Lancs 147 J6
Cackle Street E Susx 23 G2
Cackle Street E Susx 24 C3
Cackle Street E Susx 24 E3
Cadbury Devon 13 L2
Cadbury Barton Devon 28 B7
Cadder E Duns 209 G4
Caddington C Beds 68 D3
Caddonfoot Border 200 F6
Cadeby Donc 142 E7
Cadeby Leics 99 L3
Cadeleigh Devon 13 L1
Cade Street E Susx 23 K3
Cadgwith Cnwll 3 J8
Cadham Fife 222 D6
Cadishead Salfd 130 D1
Cadle Swans 57 H5
Cadley Lancs 139 G2
Cadley Wilts 47 J5
Cadley Wilts 47 K8
Cadmore End Bucks 67 J8
Cadnam Hants 34 C8
Cadney N Linc 144 C7
Cadole Flints 128 E7
Cadoxton V Glam 43 H7
Cadoxton Juxta-Neath Neath 57 L5
Cadwst Denbgs 111 K4
Caeathro Gwynd 125 J7
Caehopkin Powys 59 M6
Caenby Lincs 135 K2
Caeo Carmth 77 J7
Caerau Brdgnd 42 C3
Caerau Cardif 43 H6
Cae'r-bont Powys 59 M6
Cae'r bryn Carmth 59 H6
Caerdeon Gwynd 110 C7
Caer Farchell Pembks 74 C6
Caergeiliog IoA 124 E4
Caergwrle Flints 129 G8
Caerhun Conwy 126 F5
Caerlanrig Border 188 C5
Caerleon Newpt 44 D1
Caernarfon Gwynd 125 H7
Caerphilly Caerph 43 J4
Caersws Powys 94 B5
Caerwedros Cerdgn 76 C4
Caerwent Mons 44 F1
Caerwys Flints 128 D5
Caerynwch Gwynd 110 E8
Caggle Street Mons 62 D4
Caim IoA 126 C3
Cairinis W Isls 283 c8
Cairnbaan Ag & B 206 C1
Cairnbulg Abers 269 J3
Cairncross Border 213 K6
Cairncurran Inver 208 A5
Cairndow Ag & B 217 K5
Cairneyhill Fife 210 D2
Cairngarroch D & G 172 C5
Cairnie Abers 255 K3
Cairnorrie Abers 256 F3
Cairnryan D & G 172 D1
Cairnty Moray 267 G5
Caister-on-Sea Norfk 107 L1
Caistor Lincs 144 E7
Caistor St Edmund Norfk 106 E3
Cakebole Worcs 81 K1
Cake Street Norfk 106 B5
Calais Street Suffk 89 K7
Calanais W Isls 282 f3
Calbourne IoW 19 G6
Calceby Lincs 137 G4
Calcot Flints 128 E5
Calcot Gloucs 65 G5
Calcot W Berk 49 G4
Calcot Row W Berk 49 G4
Calcots Moray 266 E3
Calcott Kent 95 K1
Calcott Shrops 95 K1
Calcutt N York 150 E4
Calcutt Wilts 65 G8
Caldbeck Cumb 165 K3
Caldbergh N York 159 K5
Caldecote Cambs 87 G4
Caldecote Cambs 102 C5
Caldecote Herts 86 E7
Caldecote Nhants 84 D5
Caldecote Highfields Cambs 87 G3
Caldecott Nhants 85 K2
Caldecott Oxon 66 D7
Caldecott Rutlnd 101 J4
Caldecotte M Keyn 85 H8
Calder Cumb 155 J2

Calderbank N Lans 209 K6
Calder Bridge Cumb 155 J2
Calderbrook Rochdl 140 E4
Caldercruix N Lans 209 L5
Calder Grove Wakefd 141 M4
Caldermill S Lans 197 J3
Caldermore Rochdl 140 D4
Calder Vale Lancs 147 K6
Calderwood S Lans 209 H7
Caldey Island Pembks 55 K7
Caldicot Mons 44 F1
Caldmore Wsall 98 C4
Caldwell N York 168 F8
Caldy Wirral 128 F3
Caledfwlch Carmth 59 J4
Calenick Cnwll 4 D6
Calf of Man IoM 154 a8
Calford Green Suffk 88 D6
Calfsound Ork 275 d2
Calgary Ag & B 226 D2
Califer Moray 265 H8
California Falk 210 B4
California Norfk 123 K8
California Cross Devon 7 K4
Calke Derbys 116 B7
Callakille Highld 259 M5
Callander Stirlg 219 K5
Callanish W Isls 282 f3
Callaughton Shrops 96 E4
Callestick Cnwll 4 C5
Calligarry Highld 247 K7
Callington Cnwll 6 D1
Callingwood Staffs 115 K6
Callow Herefs 80 C8
Callow End Worcs 81 J5
Callow Hill Wilts 46 F2
Callow Hill Worcs 82 B2
Callow Hill Worcs 97 G8
Callows Grave Worcs 80 D2
Calmore Hants 34 D7
Calmsden Gloucs 64 F5
Calne Wilts 46 E5
Calow Derbys 133 H5
Calshot Hants 19 H3
Calstock Cnwll 6 E1
Calstone Wellington Wilts 46 F5
Calthorpe Norfk 122 D5
Calthorpe Street Norfk 123 H6
Calthwaite Cumb 166 B3
Calton N York 148 F4
Calton Staffs 115 H2
Calveley Ches E 130 B7
Calver Derbys 132 E5
Calverhall Shrops 113 K4
Calver Hill Herefs 79 L5
Calverleigh Devon 29 G8
Calverley Leeds 150 B8
Calver Sough Derbys 132 E5
Calvert Bucks 67 G2
Calverton M Keyn 84 F7
Calverton Notts 117 G2
Calvine P & K 232 B2
Calvo Cumb 176 F8
Calzeat Border 199 K6
Cam Gloucs 63 M7
Camasachoirce Highld 228 B3
Camasine Highld 237 L8
Camas Luinie Highld 248 F6
Camastianavaig Highld 247 G1
Camault Muir Highld 250 E4
Camber E Susx 25 H3
Camberley Surrey 49 L6
Camberwell Gt Lon 51 J4
Camblesforth N York 143 G3
Cambo Nthumb 180 B2
Cambois Nthumb 181 H2
Camborne Cnwll 3 G3
Cambourne Cambs 87 G3
Cambridge Cambs 87 J3
Cambridge Gloucs 63 L6
Cambridge City Crematorium Cambs 87 H3
Cambrose Cnwll 4 A5
Cambus Clacks 220 E8
Cambusavie Platform Highld 263 L1
Cambusbarron Stirlg 220 D8
Cambuskenneth Stirlg 220 D8
Cambuslang S Lans 209 H7
Cambus o' May Abers 243 M4
Cambuswallace S Lans 199 H5
Camden Town Gt Lon 51 H2
Cameley BaNES 45 J7
Camelford Cnwll 10 F6
Camelon Falk 209 M3
Camerory Highld 253 K5
Camer's Green Worcs 81 H8
Camerton BaNES 45 K7
Camerton Cumb 164 D4
Camghouran P & K 231 G4
Camieston Border 201 J7
Cammachmore Abers 245 K4
Cammeringham Lincs 135 J3
Camore Highld 263 L2
Campbeltown Ag & B 192 E4
Camperdown N Tyne 181 G4
Cample D & G 186 D7
Campmuir P & K 233 K7
Camps W Loth 210 E5
Campsall Donc 142 E5
Campsea Ash Suffk 91 H4
Camps End Cambs 88 C6
Campton C Beds 86 C7
Camptown Border 189 J4
Camrose Pembks 54 F3
Camserney P & K 232 B5
Camusnagaul Highld 239 H8
Camusnagaul Highld 261 H2
Camusteel Highld 248 A3
Camusterrach Highld 248 A3
Canada Hants 34 C7
Canal Foot Cumb 156 D7
Canaston Bridge Pembks 55 H4
Candacraig Abers 243 K4
Candlesby Lincs 137 H6
Candle Street Suffk 105 L8
Candover Green Shrops 96 C2
Candy Mill Border 199 J5
Cane End Oxon 49 G3
Canewdon Essex 72 C8
Canford Bottom Dorset 17 K3
Canford Cliffs Poole 17 L5
Canford Crematorium Bristl 45 H3
Canford Heath Poole 17 K4
Canford Magna Poole 17 K3
Canhams Green Suffk 90 C2
Canisbay Highld 280 D2
Canklow Rothm 133 H2
Canley Covtry 99 J7
Canley Crematorium Covtry 99 J8
Cann Dorset 32 E6
Canna Highld 246 B7
Cannich Highld 250 B5
Cannington Somset 30 C3
Canning Town Gt Lon 51 L3
Cannock Staffs 98 B2
Cannock Wood Staffs 98 D1
Cannon Bridge Herefs 80 A7
Canonbie D & G 177 L4
Canon Frome Herefs 80 F6
Canon Pyon Herefs 80 B5
Canons Ashby Nhants 84 B5
Canonstown Cnwll 2 E4
Canterbury Kent 40 F4
Cantley Norfk 107 H3
Cantlop Shrops 96 C2
Canton Cardif 43 J6
Cantraywood Highld 252 E2
Cantsfield Lancs 147 M1
Canvey Island Essex 53 G2
Canwick Lincs 135 K6
Canworthy Water Cnwll 11 J4
Caol Highld 239 J8
Caolas Scalpaigh W Isls 282 f6
Caoles Ag & B 224 D5
Caonich Highld 239 H5
Capel Kent 39 G4
Capel Surrey 37 J3
Capel Bangor Cerdgn 92 E7
Capel Betws Lleucu Cerdgn 77 H4
Capel Coch IoA 125 H3
Capel Curig Conwy 126 E8
Capel Cynon Cerdgn 76 C5
Capel Dewi Carmth 58 E5
Capel Dewi Cerdgn 76 E6
Capel-Dewi Cerdgn 92 D7
Capel Garmon Conwy 127 G8
Capel Green Suffk 91 J5
Capel Gwyn Carmth 58 E4
Capel Gwyn IoA 124 F4
Capel Gwynfe Carmth 59 K4
Capel Hendre Carmth 59 G6
Capel Isaac Carmth 59 G3
Capel Iwan Carmth 58 B2
Capel le Ferne Kent 41 H7
Capelles Guern 9 j2
Capel Llanilltern Cardif 43 H5
Capel Mawr IoA 125 G5
Capel Parc IoA 125 H2
Capel St Andrew Suffk 91 J5
Capel St Mary Suffk 90 C7
Capel Seion Cerdgn 92 D7
Capel Trisant Cerdgn 92 F8
Capeluchaf Gwynd 109 H2
Capelulo Conwy 126 E4
Capel-y-ffin Powys 61 L1
Capel-y-graig Gwynd 125 K6
Capenhurst Ches W 129 J5
Capernwray Lancs 147 K2
Capheaton Nthumb 180 C3
Caplaw E Rens 208 D7
Capon's Green Suffk 91 G2
Cappercleuch Border 187 K2
Capstone Medway 53 G6
Capton Devon 8 C4
Capton Somset 29 K3
Caputh P & K 233 G7
Caradon Town Cnwll 11 K8
Carbeth Inn Stirlg 208 E3
Carbis Cnwll 5 G3
Carbis Bay Cnwll 2 E3
Carbost Highld 246 E2
Carbost Highld 259 G7
Carbrook Sheff 133 G2
Carbrooke Norfk 105 J3
Carburton Notts 134 C5
Carclaze Cnwll 5 H4
Car Colston Notts 117 J3
Carcroft Donc 142 E6
Cardenden Fife 222 C8
Cardeston Shrops 95 J1
Cardewlees Cumb 177 K8
Cardhu Moray 254 D3
Cardiff Cardif 43 J6
Cardigan Cerdgn 75 L3
Cardinal's Green Cambs 88 C6
Cardington Bed 86 B5
Cardington Shrops 96 C4
Cardinham Cnwll 5 J1
Cardrain D & G 172 E8
Cardrona Border 200 C5
Cardross Ag & B 208 B3
Cardross Crematorium Ag & B 208 B3
Cardryne D & G 172 E8
Cardurnock Cumb 177 G7
Careby Lincs 118 D8
Careston Angus 234 E3
Carew Pembks 55 H6
Carew Cheriton Pembks 55 H6
Carew Newton Pembks 55 H6
Carey Herefs 63 H1
Carfin N Lans 209 K7
Carfraemill Border 201 G2
Cargate Green Norfk 107 H1
Cargenbridge D & G 176 C4
Cargill P & K 233 H8
Cargo Cumb 177 L7
Cargreen Cnwll 6 E2
Cargurrel Cnwll 3 M4
Carham Nthumb 202 B5
Carhampton Somset 29 H2
Carharrack Cnwll 3 J3
Carie P & K 231 H4
Carinish W Isls 283 c8
Carisbrooke IoW 19 H6
Cark Cumb 156 E7
Carkeel Cnwll 6 E3
Carlabhagh W Isls 282 e2
Carland Cross Cnwll 4 D4
Carlbury Darltn 169 G7
Carlby Lincs 102 A1
Carlcroft Nthumb 190 B4
Carlecotes Barns 141 J7
Carleen Cnwll 3 G5
Carlesmoor N York 160 B7
Carleton Cumb 155 J1
Carleton Cumb 166 C5
Carleton Cumb 178 A8
Carleton Lancs 146 F7
Carleton N York 149 H6
Carleton Wakefd 142 D4
Carleton Crematorium Bpool 146 F7
Carleton Forehoe Norfk 106 B2
Carleton Rode Norfk 106 C5
Carleton St Peter Norfk 107 G3
Carlidnack Cnwll 3 K5
Carlincraig Abers 256 B3
Carlingcott BaNES 45 K7
Carlin How R & Cl 171 G6
Carlisle Cumb 177 L7
Carlisle Crematorium Cumb 177 L8
Carloggas Cnwll 4 E2
Carlops Border 199 K2
Carloway W Isls 282 e2
Carlton Barns 142 B5
Carlton Bed 85 J4
Carlton Cambs 88 C4
Carlton Leeds 142 A2
Carlton Leics 99 L2
Carlton N York 143 G3
Carlton N York 159 J5
Carlton N York 161 K5
Carlton Notts 117 G3
Carlton S on T 169 K6
Carlton Suffk 91 J2
Carlton Colville Suffk 107 K5
Carlton Curlieu Leics 100 F4
Carlton Green Cambs 88 C5
Carlton Husthwaite N York 161 H7
Carlton-in-Cleveland N York 161 H2
Carlton in Lindrick Notts 134 B3
Carlton-le-Moorland Lincs 135 H8
Carlton Miniott N York 160 F6
Carlton-on-Trent Notts 134 F7
Carlton Scroop Lincs 118 B3
Carluke S Lans 198 D3
Carlyon Bay Cnwll 5 H4
Carmacoup S Lans 198 C7
Carmarthen Carmth 58 D5
Carmel Carmth 59 G5
Carmel Flints 128 E4
Carmel Gwynd 125 J8
Carmichael S Lans 198 F5
Carmountside Crematorium C Stke 114 E2
Carmunnock C Glas 209 G7
Carmyle C Glas 209 H6
Carmyllie Angus 234 E6
Carnaby E R Yk 153 J3
Carnbee Fife 223 J6
Carnbo P & K 221 J6
Carn Brea Cnwll 3 H3
Carnbrogie Abers 256 F6
Carndu Highld 248 E6
Carnduff S Lans 197 J2
Carne Cnwll 3 K6
Carne Cnwll 4 E7
Carne Cnwll 4 F3
Carnell E Ayrs 196 F4
Carnewas Cnwll 4 D1
Carnforth Lancs 147 K2
Carn-gorm Highld 248 F7
Carnhedryn Pembks 74 C6
Carnhell Green Cnwll 3 G4
Carnie Abers 245 H2
Carnkie Cnwll 3 H3
Carnkie Cnwll 3 H4
Carnkiet Cnwll 4 C4
Carno Powys 93 L4
Carnock Fife 210 D1
Carnon Downs Cnwll 3 K3
Carnousie Abers 268 B6
Carnoustie Angus 234 E8
Carnsmerry Cnwll 5 G3
Carnwath S Lans 199 G4
Carnyorth Cnwll 2 B4
Carol Green Solhll 99 H7
Carpalla Cnwll 4 F4
Carperby N York 159 H5
Carr Rothm 133 K2
Carradale Ag & B 194 C3
Carrbridge Highld 253 G7
Carrbrook Tamesd 140 E7
Carrefour Jersey 9 c2
Carreglefn IoA 125 G2
Carr Gate Wakefd 141 M3
Carrhouse N Linc 143 K6
Carrick Ag & B 206 E2
Carrick Castle Ag & B 217 K8
Carriden Falk 210 D3
Carrington Lincs 136 F8
Carrington Mdloth 211 K7
Carrington Traffd 130 E1
Carrog Conwy 110 E2
Carrog Denbgs 111 L3
Carron Falk 210 A3
Carron Moray 254 E3
Carronbridge D & G 186 C6
Carron Bridge Stirlg 209 K2
Carronshore Falk 210 A2
Carrow Hill Mons 44 E1
Carr Shield Nthumb 167 J1
Carrutherstown D & G 176 E4
Carruth House Inver 208 B6
Carr Vale Derbys 133 J5
Carrville Dur 169 J2
Carsaig Ag & B 227 G8
Carseriggan D & G 173 H1
Carsethorn D & G 176 C7
Carshalton Gt Lon 51 H6
Carsington Derbys 115 L1
Carskey Ag & B 192 D6
Carsluith D & G 174 D4
Carsphairn D & G 184 E4
Carstairs S Lans 198 F4
Carstairs Junction S Lans 198 F4
Carswell Marsh Oxon 65 L7
Carter's Clay Hants 34 C6
Carters Green Essex 70 D5
Carterton Oxon 65 L5
Carterway Heads Nthumb 180 C8
Carthew Cnwll 5 G4
Carthorpe N York 160 D6
Cartington Nthumb 190 E5
Cartland S Lans 198 E4
Cartledge Derbys 132 F4
Cartmel Cumb 156 E7
Cartmel Fell Cumb 156 F5
Carway Carmth 56 E3
Carwinley Cumb 177 L4
Cashe's Green Gloucs 64 B6

Cashmoor Dorset 33 G8
Cassington Oxon 66 C5
Cassop Colliery Dur 169 K3
Castallack Cnwll 2 C6
Castel Guern 9 j3
Castell Conwy 126 F6
Castell-y-bwch Torfn 62 B8
Casterton Cumb 157 K6
Castle Cnwll 5 J3
Castle Acre Norfk 121 H8
Castle Ashby Nhants 85 G3
Castlebay W Isls 283 b13
Castle Bolton N York 159 J4
Castle Bromwich Solhll 98 F5
Castle Bytham Lincs 118 C7
Castlebythe Pembks 75 H6
Castle Caereinion Powys 94 E2
Castle Camps Cambs 88 C6
Castle Carrock Cumb 178 D7
Castlecary Falk 209 L3
Castle Cary Somset 31 L4
Castle Combe Wilts 46 B3
Castle Donington Leics 116 D6
Castle Douglas D & G 175 J2
Castle Eaton Swindn 65 H7
Castle Eden Dur 169 L3
Castle End C Pete 102 C2
Castleford Wakefd 142 C3
Castle Frome Herefs 80 F6
Castle Gate Cnwll 2 D4
Castle Green Cumb 157 H4
Castle Green Surrey 50 B6
Castle Gresley Derbys 115 M7
Castle Hedingham Essex 88 F8
Castlehill Border 200 B6
Castlehill Highld 280 B3
Castle Hill Kent 39 H5
Castle Hill Suffk 90 D6
Castlehill W Duns 208 C4
Castle Kennedy D & G 172 D3
Castle Lachlan Ag & B 217 G8
Castlemartin Pembks 54 E7
Castlemilk C Glas 209 G7
Castle Morris Pembks 74 E6
Castlemorton Worcs 81 H7
Castlemorton Common Worcs 81 H7
Castle O'er D & G 187 K7
Castle Pulverbatch Shrops 95 K3
Castle Rising Norfk 120 E6
Castleside Dur 168 D1
Castle Stuart Highld 252 D2
Castlethorpe M Keyn 84 F6
Castlethorpe N Linc 144 B6
Castleton Border 188 E8
Castleton Derbys 132 C3
Castleton N York 162 B1
Castleton Newpt 43 L5
Castleton Rochdl 140 C5
Castletown Dorset 16 D7
Castletown Highld 280 A3
Castletown IoM 154 c8
Castletown Sundld 181 J7
Castley N York 150 C6
Caston Norfk 105 J4
Castor C Pete 102 C4
Caswell Bay Swans 57 G7
Catacol N Ayrs 194 E1
Cat and Fiddle Derbys 131 K5
Catbrain S Glos 45 H3
Catbrook Mons 63 G6
Catch Flints 128 F5
Catchall Cnwll 2 C5
Catchem's Corner Solhll 99 H8
Catchgate Dur 180 E8
Catcliffe Rothm 133 H2
Catcomb Wilts 46 E4
Catcott Somset 30 F3
Catcott Burtle Somset 30 F2
Caterham Surrey 51 J7
Catfield Norfk 123 H7
Catfield Common Norfk 123 H7
Catford Gt Lon 51 K4
Catforth Lancs 138 F1
Cathcart C Glas 209 G7
Cathedine Powys 61 J2
Catherine-de-Barnes Solhll 98 F7
Catherine Slack C Brad 141 G2
Catherington Hants 35 L8
Catherston Leweston Dorset 15 J4
Catherton Shrops 96 E7
Catisfield Hants 19 J2
Catley Herefs 80 F6
Catley Lane Head Rochdl 140 C4
Catlodge Highld 241 H5
Catlow Lancs 148 F8
Catlowdy Cumb 178 B3
Catmere End Essex 87 K7
Catmore W Berk 48 C3
Caton Devon 13 H8
Caton Lancs 147 K3
Caton Green Lancs 147 L3
Cator Court Devon 13 G7
Catrine E Ayrs 197 G6
Cat's Ash Newpt 44 D1
Catsfield E Susx 24 C4
Catsfield Stream E Susx 24 C4
Catsgore Somset 31 H5
Catsham Somset 31 J4
Catshill Worcs 98 B8
Catstree Shrops 97 G4
Cattadale Ag & B 192 D6
Cattal N York 150 F5
Cattawade Suffk 90 C8
Catterall Lancs 147 K7
Catteralslane Shrops 113 J3
Catterick N York 160 C3
Catterick Bridge N York 160 B3
Catterick Garrison N York 160 B3
Catterlen Cumb 166 B4
Catterline Abers 245 J7
Catterton N York 151 H6
Catteshall Surrey 36 E2
Catthorpe Leics 100 C7
Cattishall Suffk 89 H2
Cattistock Dorset 16 B3
Catton N York 160 E7
Catton Nthumb 179 J7
Catwick E R Yk 153 J6
Catworth Cambs 86 B1
Caudle Green Gloucs 64 D5
Caulcott C Beds 85 K6
Caulcott Oxon 66 D2
Cauldcots Angus 235 G6
Cauldhame Stirlg 219 L8
Cauldmill Border 188 F3
Cauldon Staffs 115 H2
Cauldon Lowe Staffs 115 H2
Cauldwell Derbys 115 L8
Caulkerbush D & G 176 B7
Caulside D & G 178 B3
Caundle Marsh Dorset 31 L8
Caunsall Worcs 97 J7
Caunton Notts 134 E7
Causeway Hants 35 M6
Causeway End Cumb 157 G5
Causeway End D & G 173 K3
Causeway End Essex 71 G3
Causewayend S Lans 199 H6
Causewayhead Cumb 176 F8
Causewayhead Stirlg 220 D8
Causeyend Abers 257 H7
Causey Park Nthumb 191 H7
Causey Park Bridge Nthumb 191 H7
Cavendish Suffk 88 F6
Cavenham Suffk 88 F1
Caversfield Oxon 66 E2
Caversham Readg 49 H4
Caverswall Staffs 114 F3
Caverton Mill Border 202 A7
Cavil E R Yk 143 J2
Cawdor Highld 252 F2
Cawkwell Lincs 136 E4
Cawood N York 151 J8
Cawsand Cnwll 6 E5
Cawston Norfk 122 C6
Cawston Warwks 100 A8
Cawthorn N York 162 D5
Cawthorne Barns 141 L6
Cawton N York 161 K7
Caxton Cambs 86 F3
Caxton End Cambs 87 G4
Caxton Gibbet Cambs 86 F3
Caynham Shrops 80 D1
Caythorpe Lincs 118 B2
Caythorpe Notts 117 J2
Cayton N York 163 J6
Ceann a Bhaigh W Isls 283 b8
Ceannacroc Lodge Highld 239 L1
Cearsiadar W Isls 282 f4
Ceciliford Mons 63 G6
Cefn Newpt 44 B1
Cefn Berain Conwy 127 K6
Cefn-brith Conwy 111 H2
Cefn-bryn-brain Carmth 59 K6
Cefn Byrle Powys 60 C5
Cefn Canel Powys 112 C5
Cefn Coch Powys 111 L6
Cefn-coed-y-cymmer Myr Td 60 F5
Cefn Cribwr Brdgnd 42 C5
Cefn Cross Brdgnd 42 C5
Cefn-ddwysarn Gwynd 111 J4
Cefn-Einion Shrops 95 G6
Cefneithin Carmth 59 G6
Cefngorwydd Powys 78 B6
Cefn-mawr Wrexhm 112 D3
Cefnpennar Rhondd 61 G7
Cefn-y-bedd Flints 129 H8
Cefn-y-pant Carmth 75 L7
Ceint IoA 125 J4
Cellan Cerdgn 77 H5
Cellardyke Fife 223 K6
Cellarhead Staffs 114 F2
Celleron Cumb 166 C5
Celynen Caerph 43 K3
Cemaes IoA 124 F1
Cemmaes Powys 93 H2
Cemmaes Road Powys 93 H3
Cenarth Cerdgn 76 A7
Cerbyd Pembks 74 D6
Ceres Fife 223 G5
Cerne Abbas Dorset 16 C2
Cerney Wick Gloucs 65 G7
Cerrigceinwen IoA 125 G5
Cerrigydrudion Conwy 111 J2
Cess Norfk 123 J7
Ceunant Gwynd 125 J7
Chaceley Gloucs 64 B1
Chacewater Cnwll 4 B6
Chackmore Bucks 84 D8
Chacombe Nhants 83 L6
Chadbury Worcs 82 B6
Chadderton Oldham 140 D6
Chadderton Fold Oldham 140 D6
Chaddesden C Derb 116 C4
Chaddesley Corbett Worcs 97 K8
Chaddlehanger Devon 12 B7
Chaddleworth W Berk 48 B3
Chadlington Oxon 65 M3
Chadshunt Warwks 83 H4
Chadwell Leics 117 K6
Chadwell Shrops 114 B8
Chadwell End Bed 86 B2
Chadwell Heath Gt Lon 52 A1
Chadwell St Mary Thurr 52 E3
Chadwick Worcs 81 J2
Chadwick End Solhll 82 F1
Chadwick Green St Hel 139 G7
Chaffcombe Somset 15 H1
Chafford Hundred Thurr 52 D3
Chagford Devon 13 G5
Chailey E Susx 22 F3
Chainbridge Cambs 103 J3
Chainhurst Kent 39 J4
Chalbury Dorset 17 K1
Chalbury Common Dorset 17 K2
Chaldon Surrey 51 J7
Chale IoW 19 H8
Chale Green IoW 19 H7
Chalfont Common Bucks 68 C8
Chalfont St Giles Bucks 68 C8
Chalfont St Peter Bucks 50 C1
Chalford Gloucs 64 C6
Chalford Oxon 67 H7
Chalford Wilts 32 E1
Chalgrave C Beds 68 C2
Chalgrove Oxon 66 F7
Chalk Kent 52 E4
Chalk End Essex 70 F5
Chalkhouse Green Oxon 49 H3
Chalkway Somset 15 J1
Chalkwell Kent 53 J6
Challaborough Devon 7 J6
Challacombe Devon 28 B3
Challoch D & G 173 K2
Challock Kent 40 C5
Chalmington Dorset 16 B2
Chalton C Beds 68 C2
Chalton C Beds 86 C5
Chalton Hants 20 B4
Chalvey Slough 50 B3
Chalvington E Susx 23 H5
Chambers Green Kent 40 B6
Chandler's Cross Herts 68 D7
Chandlers Cross Worcs 81 H7
Chandler's Ford Hants 34 F7
Channel's End Bed 86 C4
Chanterlands Crematorium C KuH 144 D2
Chantry Somset 32 B2
Chantry Suffk 90 D6
Chapel Cumb 165 H4
Chapel Fife 222 D8
Chapel Allerton Leeds 150 D8
Chapel Allerton Somset 30 F1
Chapel Amble Cnwll 10 D7
Chapel Brampton Nhants 84 E2
Chapelbridge Cambs 102 F4
Chapel Chorlton Staffs 114 C4
Chapel Cross E Susx 23 K3
Chapel End Bed 86 B4
Chapel End C Beds 85 L6
Chapel End Cambs 102 C6
Chapel End Warwks 99 J5
Chapelend Way Essex 88 E7
Chapel-en-le-Frith Derbys 131 L3
Chapel Field Bury 140 B6
Chapelgate Lincs 119 L6
Chapel Green Warwks 83 L3
Chapel Green Warwks 99 H6
Chapel Haddlesey N York 142 F3
Chapelhall N Lans 209 K6
Chapel Hill Abers 257 K4
Chapel Hill Lincs 119 G1
Chapel Hill Mons 63 G7
Chapel Hill N York 150 D6
Chapelhope Border 187 K2
Chapelknowe D & G 177 K4
Chapel Lawn Shrops 95 H8
Chapel le Dale N York 158 C7
Chapel Leigh Somset 29 L5
Chapel Milton Derbys 131 L3
Chapel of Garioch Abers 256 C7
Chapel Rossan D & G 172 D6
Chapel Row E Susx 23 L5
Chapel Row Essex 71 J7
Chapel Row W Berk 48 E5
Chapels Cumb 156 B6
Chapel St Leonards Lincs 137 K5
Chapel Stile Cumb 156 D2
Chapelton Angus 234 F6
Chapelton Devon 27 K5
Chapelton S Lans 197 K1
Chapeltown Bl w D 139 L4
Chapel Town Cnwll 4 E4
Chapeltown Moray 254 E7
Chapeltown Sheff 142 A8
Chapmanslade Wilts 32 D1
Chapmans Well Devon 11 L4
Chapmore End Herts 69 J4
Chappel Essex 72 C2
Charaton Cnwll 6 B1
Chard Somset 15 H1
Chard Junction Somset 15 H2
Chardleigh Green Somset 30 D8
Chardstock Devon 15 G2
Charfield S Glos 63 L8
Chargrove Gloucs 64 D3
Charing Kent 40 B5
Charing Crematorium Kent 40 B5
Charing Heath Kent 40 B5
Charing Hill Kent 40 B5
Charingworth Gloucs 82 E7
Charlbury Oxon 66 A3
Charlcombe BaNES 45 L5
Charlcutt Wilts 46 E4
Charlecote Warwks 83 G4
Charlemont Sandw 98 C4
Charles Devon 28 B4
Charleshill Surrey 36 D2
Charleston Angus 234 B6
Charlestown C Aber 245 L3
Charlestown C Brad 149 L8
Charlestown Calder 140 E2
Charlestown Cnwll 5 H4
Charlestown Derbys 131 L1
Charlestown Dorset 16 C6
Charlestown Fife 210 E2
Charlestown Highld 251 H2
Charlestown Highld 260 C5
Charlestown Salfd 140 B7
Charles Tye Suffk 89 L5
Charlesworth Derbys 131 K1
Charlinch Somset 30 C3
Charlottetown Fife 222 E5
Charlton Gt Lon 51 L3
Charlton Hants 34 D2
Charlton Herts 68 F2
Charlton Nhants 83 M8
Charlton Nthumb 179 J2
Charlton Oxon 48 B1
Charlton Somset 30 D5
Charlton Somset 31 K2
Charlton Somset 45 K8
Charlton Surrey 50 D5
Charlton W Susx 20 E4
Charlton Wilts 32 F6
Charlton Wilts 46 D1
Charlton Worcs 81 J1
Charlton Worcs 82 B6
Charlton Wrekin 96 D1
Charlton Abbots Gloucs 64 F2
Charlton Adam Somset 31 J5
Charlton All Saints Wilts 33 L6
Charlton Down Dorset 16 C4
Charlton Hill Shrops 96 D2
Charlton Horethorne Somset 31 L6
Charlton Kings Gloucs 64 D3
Charlton Mackrell Somset 31 H5
Charlton Marshall Dorset 17 H2
Charlton Musgrove Somset 32 B5
Charlton-on-Otmoor Oxon 66 E4
Charlton on the Hill Dorset 17 H2
Charlton St Peter Wilts 47 G7
Charlwood Hants 35 K4
Charlwood Surrey 37 K3
Charminster Dorset 16 C4
Charmouth Dorset 15 H4
Charndon Bucks 67 G2
Charney Bassett Oxon 66 A8
Charnock Green Lancs 139 H4

Charnock Richard Lancs 139 H4
Charnock Richard Crematorium Lancs 139 H4
Charsfield Suffk 90 F4
Chart Corner Kent 39 K3
Charter Alley Hants 48 E7
Charterhall Border 202 B4
Charterhouse Somset 45 G7
Chartershall Stirlg 209 L1
Charterville Allotments Oxon 65 L5
Chartham Kent 40 E4
Chartham Hatch Kent 40 E4
Chart Hill Kent 39 K3
Chartridge Bucks 68 B6
Chart Sutton Kent 39 K3
Chartway Street Kent 39 L3
Charvil Wokham 49 J4
Charwelton Nhants 83 M4
Chase Terrace Staffs 98 D2
Chasetown Staffs 98 D2
Chastleton Oxon 65 K1
Chasty Devon 11 L2
Chatburn Lancs 148 D7
Chatcull Staffs 114 B4
Chatham Caerph 43 K4
Chatham Medway 53 G5
Chatham Green Essex 71 H4
Chathill Nthumb 203 K7
Chatley Worcs 81 J3
Chattenden Medway 53 G4
Chatter End Essex 70 C2
Chatteris Cambs 103 H6
Chatterton Lancs 140 B4
Chattisham Suffk 90 C6
Chatto Border 189 K3
Chatton Nthumb 203 G7
Chaul End C Beds 68 D3
Chawleigh Devon 28 C8
Chawley Oxon 66 C6
Chawston Bed 86 C4
Chawton Hants 35 L3
Chaxhill Gloucs 63 L4
Chazey Heath Oxon 49 G3
Cheadle Staffs 115 G3
Cheadle Stockp 131 G2
Cheadle Heath Stockp 131 G2
Cheadle Hulme Stockp 131 G2
Cheam Gt Lon 51 H6
Cheapside W & M 50 B5
Chearsley Bucks 67 H5
Chebsey Staffs 114 D6
Checkendon Oxon 49 G2
Checkley Ches E 114 A2
Checkley Herefs 80 E7
Checkley Staffs 115 G4
Checkley Green Ches E 114 A2
Chedburgh Suffk 88 F4
Cheddar Somset 44 F8
Cheddington Bucks 68 A4
Cheddleton Staffs 114 F1
Cheddleton Heath Staffs 114 F1
Cheddon Fitzpaine Somset 30 C5
Chedglow Wilts 64 D8
Chedgrave Norfk 107 H3
Chedington Dorset 15 L2
Chediston Suffk 107 G7
Chediston Green Suffk 107 G7
Chedworth Gloucs 64 F5
Chedzoy Somset 30 E3
Cheeseman's Green Kent 40 D7
Cheetham Hill Manch 140 C7
Cheldon Devon 28 C8
Chelford Ches E 130 F5
Chellaston C Derb 116 C5
Chellington Bed 85 J4
Chelmarsh Shrops 97 G5
Chelmick Shrops 95 L5
Chelmondiston Suffk 90 E7
Chelmorton Derbys 132 B5
Chelmsford Essex 71 H5
Chelmsford Crematorium Essex 71 G6
Chelmsley Wood Solhll 98 F6
Chelsea Gt Lon 51 H3
Chelsfield Gt Lon 52 A6
Chelsham Surrey 51 K7
Chelston Somset 29 L6
Chelsworth Suffk 89 K5
Cheltenham Gloucs 64 D3
Cheltenham Crematorium Gloucs 64 E3
Chelveston Nhants 85 K1
Chelvey N Som 44 F5
Chelwood BaNES 45 J6
Chelwood Common E Susx 38 B7
Chelwood Gate E Susx 38 B7
Chelworth Wilts 64 E8
Chelworth Lower Green Wilts 65 G8
Chelworth Upper Green Wilts 65 G8
Cheney Longville Shrops 95 K6
Chenies Bucks 68 C7
Chepstow Mons 63 G8
Chequerbent Bolton 139 K6
Chequers Corner Norfk 103 K2
Cherhill Wilts 46 F5
Cherington Gloucs 64 C7
Cherington Warwks 83 G7
Cheriton Devon 28 C2
Cheriton Hants 35 J5
Cheriton Kent 41 G7
Cheriton Swans 56 E6
Cheriton Bishop Devon 13 H4
Cheriton Fitzpaine Devon 13 K2
Cheriton or Stackpole Elidor Pembks 55 G7
Cherrington Wrekin 113 L7
Cherry Burton E R Yk 152 F7
Cherry Hinton Cambs 87 K4
Cherry Orchard Worcs 81 K4
Cherry Willingham Lincs 135 L5
Chertsey Surrey 50 D5
Cheselbourne Dorset 16 E3
Chesham Bucks 68 B6
Chesham Bury 140 B5
Chesham Bois Bucks 68 B7
Cheshunt Herts 69 K6
Chesley Kent 53 J6
Cheslyn Hay Staffs 98 B2
Chessetts Wood Warwks 99 G8
Chessington Gt Lon 50 F6
Chester Ches W 129 J6
Chesterblade Somset 31 L3
Chester Crematorium Ches W 129 J6
Chesterfield Derbys 133 G5
Chesterfield Staffs 98 E2
Chesterfield Crematorium Derbys 133 H5
Chesterhill Mdloth 211 L6
Chester-le-Street Dur 181 G8
Chester Moor Dur 169 H1
Chesters Border 189 G2
Chesters Border 189 H4
Chesterton Cambs 87 K3
Chesterton Cambs 102 C4
Chesterton Gloucs 64 E7
Chesterton Oxon 66 E3
Chesterton Shrops 97 H4
Chesterton Staffs 114 C2
Chesterton Green Warwks 83 H4
Chesterwood Nthumb 179 J6
Chestfield Kent 40 F2
Chestnut Street Kent 53 J6
Cheston Devon 7 K3
Cheswardine Shrops 114 A5
Cheswick Nthumb 203 G4
Cheswick Green Solhll 98 E8
Chetnole Dorset 16 B1
Chettiscombe Devon 29 H7
Chettisham Cambs 103 L6
Chettle Dorset 32 F8
Chetton Shrops 96 F5
Chetwode Bucks 66 F1
Chetwynd Wrekin 114 A7
Chetwynd Aston Wrekin 114 B8
Cheveley Cambs 88 D3
Chevening Kent 52 A7
Cheverton IoW 19 G6
Chevington Suffk 88 F3
Chevithorne Devon 29 H7
Chew Magna BaNES 45 H6
Chew Moor Bolton 139 K6
Chew Stoke BaNES 45 H6
Chewton Keynsham BaNES 45 K5
Chewton Mendip Somset 45 H8
Chichacott Devon 12 E3
Chicheley M Keyn 85 H6
Chichester W Susx 20 E6
Chichester Crematorium W Susx 20 E5
Chickerell Dorset 16 C6
Chickering Suffk 106 E8
Chicklade Wilts 32 F4
Chickward Herefs 79 K4
Chidden Hants 35 K7
Chiddingfold Surrey 36 E4
Chiddingly E Susx 23 J4
Chiddingstone Kent 38 D4
Chiddingstone Causeway Kent 38 E4
Chideock Dorset 15 K4
Chidham W Susx 20 C6
Chidswell Kirk 141 L3
Chieveley W Berk 48 C4
Chignall St James Essex 71 G5
Chignall Smealy Essex 71 G5
Chigwell Essex 70 B8
Chigwell Row Essex 70 C8
Chilbolton Hants 34 E3
Chilcomb Hants 35 G5
Chilcombe Dorset 15 M4
Chilcompton Somset 45 J8
Chilcote Leics 99 H1
Childer Thornton Ches W 129 J4
Child Okeford Dorset 32 D8
Childrey Oxon 48 A2
Child's Ercall Shrops 113 L6
Childswickham Worcs 82 C7
Childwall Lpool 129 K2
Childwick Bury Herts 68 F5
Childwick Green Herts 68 F5
Chilfrome Dorset 16 B3
Chilgrove W Susx 20 D4
Chilham Kent 40 E4
Chilla Devon 12 B2
Chillaton Devon 12 B6
Chillenden Kent 41 J4
Chillerton IoW 19 H6
Chillesford Suffk 91 J5
Chillingham Nthumb 203 G8
Chillington Devon 8 B6
Chillington Somset 30 F8
Chilmark Wilts 33 G4
Chilmington Green Kent 40 C7
Chilson Oxon 65 L3
Chilsworthy Cnwll 12 A8
Chilsworthy Devon 11 L1
Chiltern Green C Beds 68 E3
Chilterns Crematorium Bucks 68 B7
Chilthorne Domer Somset 31 H7
Chilton Bucks 67 G5
Chilton Devon 13 K2
Chilton Dur 169 H5
Chilton Kent 41 J6
Chilton Oxon 48 C2
Chilton Suffk 89 H6
Chilton Candover Hants 35 J3
Chilton Cantelo Somset 31 J6
Chilton Foliat Wilts 47 L5
Chilton Polden Somset 30 E3
Chilton Street Suffk 88 E6
Chilton Trinity Somset 30 D3
Chilwell Notts 116 E4
Chilworth Hants 34 E7
Chilworth Surrey 36 F2
Chimney Oxon 65 M7
Chineham Hants 49 G7
Chingford Gt Lon 69 K8
Chinley Derbys 131 L3
Chinnor Oxon 67 J6
Chipchase Castle Nthumb 179 K4
Chipnall Shrops 114 A5
Chippenham Cambs 88 D1
Chippenham Wilts 46 D4
Chipperfield Herts 68 D6
Chipping Herts 69 K1
Chipping Lancs 147 M7
Chipping Campden Gloucs 82 E7
Chipping Hill Essex 71 K4
Chipping Norton Oxon 65 L2
Chipping Ongar Essex 70 E6
Chipping Sodbury S Glos 45 L3
Chipping Warden Nhants 83 L5
Chipstable Somset 29 J5
Chipstead Kent 38 D2
Chipstead Surrey 51 H7
Chirbury Shrops 95 G4
Chirk Wrexhm 112 D4
Chirnside Border 202 D2
Chirnsidebridge Border 202 C2
Chirton Wilts 47 G7
Chisbury Wilts 47 K5
Chiselborough Somset 31 G7
Chiseldon Swindn 47 J3
Chiselhampton Oxon 66 E7
Chisholme Border 188 D4
Chislehurst Gt Lon 51 L5
Chislet Kent 41 H2
Chisley Calder 140 F2
Chiswell Green Herts 68 E6
Chiswick Gt Lon 51 G3
Chiswick End Cambs 87 H6
Chisworth Derbys 131 K2
Chitcombe E Susx 24 E3
Chithurst W Susx 36 C6
Chittering Cambs 87 K1
Chitterne Wilts 33 G2
Chittlehamholt Devon 28 B6
Chittlehampton Devon 27 L5
Chittoe Wilts 46 D5
Chivelstone Devon 8 A7
Chivenor Devon 27 J4
Chlenry D & G 172 E3
Chobham Surrey 50 B6
Cholderton Wilts 34 B2
Cholesbury Bucks 68 B5
Chollerford Nthumb 179 L5
Chollerton Nthumb 179 L4
Cholmondeston Ches E 130 C7
Cholsey Oxon 48 E2
Cholstrey Herefs 80 B3
Chop Gate N York 161 J
Choppington Nthumb 181 G
Chopwell Gatesd 180 D
Chorley Ches E 113 J
Chorley Lancs 139 H
Chorley Shrops 96 F
Chorley Staffs 98 D
Chorleywood Herts 68 D
Chorleywood West Herts 68 C
Chorlton Ches E 114 A
Chorlton-cum-Hardy Manch 130 F
Chorlton Lane Ches W 113 G
Choulton Shrops 95 J
Chowley Ches W 129 L
Chrishall Essex 87 J
Chrisswell Inver 207 L4
Christchurch Cambs 103 K4
Christchurch Dorset 18 B5
Christchurch Gloucs 63 H4
Christchurch Newpt 44 D1
Christian Malford Wilts 46 D3
Christleton Ches W 129 K6
Christmas Common Oxon 67 H8
Christon N Som 44 D7
Christon Bank Nthumb 191 J2
Christow Devon 13 J5
Christ's Hospital W Susx 37 H5
Chuck Hatch E Susx 38 D6
Chudleigh Devon 13 K6
Chudleigh Knighton Devon 13 K7
Chulmleigh Devon 28 B8
Chunal Derbys 131 L2
Church Lancs 139 L2
Churcham Gloucs 63 M3
Church Aston Wrekin 114 A8
Church Brampton Nhants 84 D2
Church Brough Cumb 167 J7
Church Broughton Derbys 115 K5
Church Cove Cnwll 3 H8
Church Crookham Hants 49 K8
Churchdown Gloucs 64 C3
Church Eaton Staffs 114 C8
Church End Bed 85 L3
Church End Bed 86 C3
Church End Bucks 67 H5
Church End C Beds 68 C3
Church End C Beds 68 C3
Church End C Beds 85 J8
Church End C Beds 85 K8
Church End C Beds 86 D4
Church End C Beds 86 D7
Church End Cambs 87 K4
Church End Cambs 102 B8
Church End Cambs 102 E6
Church End Cambs 103 G7
Church End Essex 70 F3
Church End Essex 71 H2
Church End Essex 71 H4
Churchend Essex 72 E8
Church End Gloucs 81 K8
Church End Gt Lon 51 H1
Church End Herts 68 E5
Church End Herts 69 H1
Church End Herts 70 C3
Church End Lincs 119 H5
Church End Lincs 145 L8
Church End Warwks 99 H5
Church End Warwks 99 H5
Church Enstone Oxon 66 A2
Church Fenton N York 151 H8
Churchfield Sandw 98 C5
Churchgate Herts 69 K6
Churchgate Street Essex 70 C5
Church Green Devon 14 E3
Church Gresley Derbys 115 M7
Church Hanborough Oxon 66 B4
Church Hill Staffs 98 C1
Church Houses N York 161 L3
Churchill Devon 15 G2
Churchill Devon 27 L3
Churchill N Som 44 E7
Churchill Oxon 65 L2
Churchill Worcs 81 L4
Churchill Worcs 97 K7
Churchinford Somset 30 B8
Church Knowle Dorset 17 H6
Church Laneham Notts 135 G4
Church Langton Leics 100 F5
Church Lawford Warwks 99 M8
Church Lawton Ches E 130 F8
Church Leigh Staffs 115 G4
Church Lench Worcs 82 B5
Church Mayfield Staffs 115 J3
Church Minshull Ches E 130 C7
Church Norton W Susx 20 E7
Churchover Warwks 100 B7
Church Preen Shrops 96 C4
Church Pulverbatch Shrops 95 K3
Churchstanton Somset 30 B7
Churchstoke Powys 95 G4

Churchstow Devon 7 K5
Church Stowe Nhants 84 C4
Church Street Essex 88 F6
Church Street Kent 52 F4
Church Street Suffk 107 K6
Church Stretton Shrops 95 L4
Churchthorpe Lincs 145 J8
Churchtown Bpool 146 F7
Churchtown Cnwll 10 F7
Churchtown Derbys 132 E7
Churchtown Devon 28 B2
Churchtown IoM 154 f3
Churchtown Lancs 147 J7
Church Town N Linc 143 K6
Churchtown Sefton 138 D4
Church Village Rhondd 43 G4
Church Warsop Notts 133 L6
Church Wilne Derbys 116 D5
Churnsike Lodge Nthumb 178 F3
Churston Ferrers Torbay 8 D4
Churt Surrey 36 C3
Churton Ches W 129 K8
Churwell Leeds 141 L2
Chwilog Gwynd 109 H4
Chyandour Cnwll 2 D5
Chyanvounder Cnwll 3 G6
Chyeowling Cnwll 3 K3
Chyvarloe Cnwll 3 G6
Cil Powys 94 E3
Cilcain Flints 128 E6
Cilcennin Cerdgn 76 F3
Cilcewydd Powys 94 F3
Cilfrew Neath 57 L5
Cilfynydd Rhondd 43 H3
Cilgerran Pembks 75 L4
Cilgwyn Carmth 59 K3
Cilgwyn Gwynd 109 J1
Ciliau-Aeron Cerdgn 76 F4
Cilmaengwyn Neath 57 K4
Cilmery Powys 78 D5
Cilrhedyn Pembks 58 A2
Cilsan Carmth 59 H4
Ciltalgarth Gwynd 111 G3
Cilycwm Carmth 77 L7
Cimla Neath 57 L5
Cinderford Gloucs 63 K4
Cinder Hill Wolves 97 L4
Cippenham Slough 50 B3
Cirencester Gloucs 64 F6
Citadilla N York 160 B3
City Gt Lon 51 J3
City V Glam 42 F6
City Dulas IoA 125 H2
City of London Crematorium Gt Lon 51 L2
Clabhach Ag & B 224 F3
Clachaig Ag & B 207 J3
Clachan Ag & B 206 B7
Clachan Ag & B 216 B3
Clachan Ag & B 228 D6
Clachan Highld 247 H1
Clachan-a-Luib W Isls 283 c8
Clachan Mor Ag & B 224 C5
Clachan na Luib W Isls 283 c8
Clachan of Campsie E Duns 209 G3
Clachan-Seil Ag & B 216 B3
Clachnaharry Highld 251 H2
Clachtoll Highld 270 D3
Clackavoid P & K 233 H3
Clackmannan Clacks 210 B1
Clackmarras Moray 266 E4
Clacton-on-Sea Essex 73 J4
Cladich Ag & B 217 H3
Cladswell Worcs 82 C3
Claggan Highld 227 K3
Claigan Highld 258 C6
Clandown BaNES 45 K7
Clanfield Hants 35 L7
Clanfield Oxon 65 L6
Clannaborough Devon 13 H2
Clanville Hants 34 D1
Clanville Somset 31 K4
Claonaig Ag & B 206 D7
Clapgate Dorset 17 K2
Clapgate Herts 70 C2
Clapham Bed 85 K5
Clapham Devon 13 L5
Clapham Gt Lon 51 H4
Clapham N York 148 C2
Clapham W Susx 21 J5
Clapham Green Bed 85 K4
Clap Hill Kent 40 D7
Clappersgate Cumb 156 E2
Clapton Somset 15 J1
Clapton Somset 45 J8
Clapton-in-Gordano N Som 44 F4
Clapton-on-the-Hill Gloucs 65 H3
Clapworthy Devon 28 B6
Clarach Cerdgn 92 D6
Claravale Gatesd 180 E6
Clarbeston Pembks 55 H3
Clarbeston Road Pembks 55 G3
Clarborough Notts 134 E3
Clare Suffk 88 F6
Clarebrand D & G 175 J2
Clarencefield D & G 176 E5
Clarewood Nthumb 180 B5
Clarilaw Border 188 F3
Clark's Green Surrey 37 J3
Clarkston E Rens 208 F7
Clashmore Highld 263 K2
Clashmore Highld 270 D2
Clashnessie Highld 270 E2
Clashnoir Moray 254 E7
Clathy P & K 221 H3
Clathymore P & K 221 H3
Clatt Abers 255 L6
Clatter Powys 94 B4
Clatterford End Essex 70 F4
Clatworthy Somset 29 J4
Claughton Lancs 147 K7
Claughton Lancs 147 L3
Claughton Wirral 129 G2
Clavelshay Somset 30 C4
Claverdon Warwks 82 E2
Claverham N Som 44 F5
Clavering Essex 70 C1
Claverley Shrops 97 H5
Claverton BaNES 46 A6
Claverton Down BaNES 45 M6
Clawdd-coch V Glam 43 G6
Clawdd-newydd Denbgs 111 L1
Clawthorpe Cumb 157 H7
Clawton Devon 11 L3
Claxby Lincs 136 B1
Claxby Lincs 137 H5
Claxton N York 151 L4
Claxton Norfk 107 G3
Claybrooke Magna Leics 100 B5
Clay Common Suffk 107 K7
Clay Coton Nhants 100 D8
Clay Cross Derbys 133 H7
Claydon Oxon 83 K5
Claydon Suffk 90 D5
Clay End Herts 69 J2
Claygate D & G 177 L3
Claygate Kent 39 H4
Claygate Surrey 50 F6
Claygate Cross Kent 38 F2
Clayhall Gt Lon 51 L1
Clayhanger Devon 29 J6
Clayhanger Wsall 98 D3
Clayhidon Devon 29 L7
Clayhill E Susx 24 F3
Clayhill Hants 18 D2
Clayhithe Cambs 87 K2
Clayock Highld 279 L4
Claypit Hill Cambs 87 G4
Claypits Gloucs 63 M6
Claypole Lincs 117 M2
Claythorpe Lincs 137 H4
Clayton C Brad 141 H2
Clayton Donc 142 C6
Clayton W Susx 22 D4
Clayton Green Lancs 139 H3
Clayton-le-Moors Lancs 139 M2
Clayton-le-Woods Lancs 139 H3
Clayton West Kirk 141 L5
Clayworth Notts 134 E2
Cleadale Highld 236 F3
Cleadon S Tyne 181 J6
Clearbrook Devon 7 G2
Clearwell Gloucs 63 H5
Clearwell Meend Gloucs 63 H5
Cleasby N York 169 H8
Cleat Ork 275 c6
Cleatlam Dur 168 E7
Cleator Cumb 164 D7
Cleator Moor Cumb 164 D7
Cleckheaton Kirk 141 J3
Cleedownton Shrops 96 D7
Cleehill Shrops 96 D8
Cleekhimin N Lans 209 K7
Clee St Margaret Shrops 96 D6
Cleestanton Shrops 96 D7
Cleethorpes NE Lin 145 J6
Cleeton St Mary Shrops 96 E7
Cleeve N Som 44 F5
Cleeve Oxon 48 F3
Cleeve Hill Gloucs 64 E2
Cleeve Prior Worcs 82 C5
Cleghornie E Loth 212 D2
Clehonger Herefs 80 B7
Cleish P & K 221 K7
Cleland N Lans 209 L7
Clement's End C Beds 68 C4
Clement Street Kent 52 B5
Clenamacrie Ag & B 216 E2
Clench Common Wilts 47 H6
Clenchwarton Norfk 120 D7
Clenerty Abers 268 D4
Clent Worcs 97 L7
Cleobury Mortimer Shrops 96 F8
Cleobury North Shrops 96 E6
Cleongart Ag & B 192 D2
Clephanton Highld 252 F2
Clerkhill D & G 187 L6
Cleuch-head D & G 185 K3
Clevancy Wilts 46 F4
Clevedon N Som 44 E5
Cleveley Oxon 66 B2
Cleveleys Lancs 146 F7
Cleverton Wilts 46 E2
Clewer Somset 31 G1
Cley next the Sea Norfk 122 A3
Cliburn Cumb 166 E5
Cliddesden Hants 35 K1
Cliff Warwks 99 G4
Cliffe Lancs 139 L1
Cliffe Medway 52 F4
Cliffe N York 143 G2
Cliffe N York 169 G7
Cliff End E Susx 25 G4
Cliffe Woods Medway 52 F4
Clifford Herefs 79 J6
Clifford Leeds 150 F7
Clifford Chambers Warwks 82 E5
Clifford's Mesne Gloucs 63 K2
Cliffsend Kent 41 K2
Clifton Bristl 45 H4
Clifton C Beds 86 D7
Clifton C Nott 116 F4
Clifton C York 151 J5
Clifton Calder 141 J3
Clifton Cumb 166 C5
Clifton Derbys 115 K3
Clifton Devon 27 L3
Clifton Donc 142 E8
Clifton Lancs 138 F2
Clifton N York 150 B6
Clifton Nthumb 180 F2
Clifton Oxon 66 C1
Clifton Salfd 140 A7
Clifton Worcs 81 J6
Clifton Campville Staffs 99 H1
Clifton Hampden Oxon 66 D7
Clifton Reynes M Keyn 85 H5
Clifton upon Dunsmore Warwks 100 C8
Clifton upon Teme Worcs 81 G3
Cliftonville Kent 41 L1
Climping W Susx 21 G6
Clink Somset 32 C1
Clint N York 150 C4
Clinterty C Aber 245 J1
Clint Green Norfk 105 L1
Clintmains Border 201 J6
Clipiau Gwynd 93 H1
Clippesby Norfk 123 J8
Clipsham Rutlnd 118 C8
Clipston Nhants 100 F7
Clipston Notts 117 H5
Clipstone C Beds 68 B2
Clipstone Notts 134 B7
Clitheroe Lancs 148 C7
Clive Shrops 113 H6
Clixby Lincs 144 E7
Cloatley Wilts 46 E1
Clocaenog Denbgs 111 L1
Clochan Moray 267 H4
Clock Face St Hel 129 M2
Cloddiau Powys 94 F2
Clodock Herefs 62 C2
Cloford Somset 32 B2
Clola Abers 257 J3
Clophill C Beds 86 B7
Clopton Nhants 102 B7
Clopton Suffk 90 F4
Clopton Corner Suffk 90 F4
Clopton Green Suffk 88 F4
Clopton Green Suffk 89 K3
Clos du Valle Guern 9 k1
Closeburn D & G 186 D7
Closeburnmill D & G 186 D7
Closeclark IoM 154 c7
Closworth Somset 16 A1
Clothall Herts 69 H1
Clotton Ches W 129 M6
Cloudesley Bush Warwks 100 A6
Clouds Herefs 80 D7
Clough Oldham 140 E6
Clough Foot Calder 140 D3
Clough Head Calder 141 H4
Cloughton N York 163 H4
Cloughton Newlands N York 163 H3
Clousta Shet 281 d5
Clova Angus 233 M1
Clovelly Devon 26 E6
Clovenfords Border 200 F6
Clovulin Highld 228 F3
Clow Bridge Lancs 140 B2
Clowne Derbys 133 K4
Clows Top Worcs 81 G1
Cloy Wrexhm 112 F3
Cluanie Inn Highld 239 H1
Cluanie Lodge Highld 239 H2
Clubworthy Cnwll 11 K4
Clugston D & G 173 J3
Clun Shrops 95 H7
Clunas Highld 253 G2
Clunbury Shrops 95 J7
Clunderwen Carmth 55 J3
Clune Highld 252 E6
Clunes Highld 239 K6
Clungunford Shrops 95 K7
Clunie P & K 233 H6
Clunton Shrops 95 H7
Cluny Fife 222 D8
Clutton BaNES 45 J7
Clutton Ches W 113 G1
Clutton Hill BaNES 45 J7
Clwt-y-bont Gwynd 125 K7
Clydach Mons 61 K4
Clydach Swans 57 J4
Clydach Vale Rhondd 42 E3
Clydebank W Duns 208 E5
Clydebank Crematorium W Duns 208 E4
Clydey Pembks 75 M5
Clyffe Pypard Wilts 47 G3
Clynder Ag & B 207 L2
Clyne Neath 60 B7
Clynnog-fawr Gwynd 109 G2
Clyro Powys 79 H6
Clyst Honiton Devon 14 A4
Clyst Hydon Devon 14 B2
Clyst St George Devon 14 A5
Clyst St Lawrence Devon 14 B3
Clyst St Mary Devon 14 A4
Cnoc W Isls 282 g3
Cnwch Coch Cerdgn 92 E8
Coad's Green Cnwll 11 K7
Coal Aston Derbys 133 G4
Coalbrookvale Blae G 61 K5
Coalburn S Lans 198 D6
Coalburns Gatesd 180 D6
Coaley Gloucs 63 M6
Coalhill Essex 71 J7
Coalmoor Wrekin 96 F2
Coalpit Heath S Glos 45 K3
Coal Pool Wsall 98 C3
Coalport Wrekin 96 F3
Coalsnaughton Clacks 221 G8
Coal Street Suffk 90 F1
Coaltown of Balgonie Fife 222 E7
Coaltown of Wemyss Fife 222 E8
Coalville Leics 99 L1
Coanwood Nthumb 178 F7
Coat Somset 31 G6
Coatbridge N Lans 209 J6
Coatdyke N Lans 209 K6
Coate Swindn 47 J2
Coate Wilts 46 F6
Coates Cambs 102 F4
Coates Gloucs 64 E7
Coates Lincs 135 H3
Coates Notts 135 G3
Coates W Susx 21 G3
Coatham R & Cl 170 E5
Coatham Mundeville Darltn 169 H6
Cobbaton Devon 27 L5
Coberley Gloucs 64 D4
Cobhall Common Herefs 80 B8
Cobham Kent 52 E5
Cobham Surrey 50 E7
Coblers Green Essex 71 G3
Cobley Dorset 33 H6
Cobnash Herefs 80 B3
Cobo Guern 9 j2
Cobridge C Stke 114 D2
Coburby Abers 269 G3
Cock Alley Derbys 133 H5
Cockayne N York 161 K3
Cockayne Hatley C Beds 86 F5
Cock Bank Wrexhm 112 E2
Cock Bevington Warwks 82 C5
Cock Bridge Abers 243 J2
Cockburnspath Border 213 G5
Cock Clarks Essex 71 K6
Cock & End Suffk 88 E4
Cockenzie and Port Seton E Loth 211 L4
Cocker Bar Lancs 139 G3
Cocker Brook Lancs 139 L3
Cockerham Lancs 147 J5
Cockermouth Cumb 164 F4
Cockernhoe Herts 68 E2
Cockersdale Leeds 141 K2
Cockett Swans 57 H6
Cockfield Dur 168 E6

Cockfield Suffk 89 H4
Cockfosters Gt Lon 69 H7
Cock Green Essex 71 G3
Cocking W Susx 20 E3
Cocking Causeway W Susx 20 E3
Cockington Torbay 8 D2
Cocklake Somset 31 G1
Cockley Beck Cumb 156 C2
Cockley Cley Norfk 104 F3
Cock Marling E Susx 24 F3
Cockpole Green Wokham 49 J3
Cocks Cnwll 4 C4
Cockshutford Shrops 96 D6
Cockshutt Shrops 113 G5
Cock Street Kent 39 K3
Cockthorpe Norfk 121 L3
Cockwells Cnwll 2 E4
Cockwood Devon 14 A6
Cockwood Somset 30 B2
Cockyard Derbys 131 L4
Cockyard Herefs 80 A8
Coddenham Suffk 90 D4
Coddington Ches W 129 K8
Coddington Herefs 81 G6
Coddington Notts 117 L1
Codford St Mary Wilts 33 G3
Codford St Peter Wilts 33 G3
Codicote Herts 69 G3
Codmore Hill W Susx 21 H3
Codnor Derbys 116 C2
Codrington S Glos 45 L3
Codsall Staffs 97 K3
Codsall Wood Staffs 97 J2
Coedely Rhondd 42 F4
Coedkernew Newpt 44 B2
Coed Morgan Mons 62 D5
Coedpoeth Wrexhm 112 D1
Coed Talon Flints 129 G7
Coedway Powys 112 E8
Coed-y-Bryn Cerdgn 76 C6
Coed-y-caerau Newpt 44 D1
Coed-y-paen Mons 62 C7
Coed-yr-ynys Powys 61 J3
Coed Ystumgwern Gwynd 109 K6
Coelbren Powys 60 C5
Coffinswell Devon 8 D1
Coffle End Bed 85 K3
Cofton Devon 13 M6
Cofton Hackett Worcs 98 C8
Cogan V Glam 43 J7
Cogenhoe Nhants 84 F3
Cogges Oxon 65 M5
Coggeshall Essex 71 K3
Coggin's Mill E Susx 23 K2
Coignafearn Highld 251 J8
Coilacriech Abers 243 K4
Coilantogle Stirlg 219 K5
Coillore Highld 246 E1
Coity Brdgnd 42 D5
Col W Isls 282 g3
Colaboll Highld 272 E6
Colan Cnwll 4 E3
Colaton Raleigh Devon 14 C5
Colbost Highld 258 C7
Colburn N York 160 B3
Colby Cumb 166 F6
Colby IoM 154 b7
Colby Norfk 122 E5
Colchester Essex 72 E2
Colchester Crematorium Essex 72 E3
Cold Ash W Berk 48 D5
Cold Ashby Nhants 100 E8
Cold Ashton S Glos 45 L4
Cold Aston Gloucs 65 H3
Coldbackie Highld 277 K4
Coldbeck Cumb 158 C2
Cold Blow Pembks 55 J4
Cold Brayfield M Keyn 85 H5
Cold Cotes N York 148 C2
Coldean Br & H 22 E5
Coldeast Devon 13 J7
Colden Calder 140 E2
Colden Common Hants 35 G6
Coldfair Green Suffk 91 K3
Coldham Cambs 103 J3
Cold Hanworth Lincs 135 L3
Coldharbour Cnwll 4 B5
Coldharbour Devon 29 J8
Coldharbour Gloucs 63 H6
Cold Harbour Herts 68 F4
Cold Harbour Oxon 48 F3
Coldharbour Surrey 37 H2
Cold Harbour Wilts 32 E2
Cold Hatton Wrekin 113 K7
Cold Hatton Heath Wrekin 113 K7
Cold Hesledon Dur 169 L2
Cold Hiendley Wakefd 142 B5
Cold Higham Nhants 84 C4
Coldingham Border 213 K6
Cold Kirby N York 161 H6
Coldmeece Staffs 114 D5
Cold Newton Leics 100 F2
Cold Northcott Cnwll 11 H5
Cold Norton Essex 71 K7
Cold Overton Leics 101 H2
Coldred Kent 41 J6
Coldridge Devon 13 G1
Coldstream Border 202 C5
Coldwaltham W Susx 21 H3
Coldwell Herefs 80 A8
Coldwells Abers 257 H4
Cold Weston Shrops 96 C6
Cole Somset 31 L4
Colebatch Shrops 95 H6
Colebrook C Plym 7 G3
Colebrook Devon 14 B2
Colebrooke Devon 13 H3
Coleby Lincs 135 K7
Coleby N Linc 143 M4
Cole End Warwks 99 G5
Coleford Devon 13 H2
Coleford Gloucs 63 H5
Coleford Somset 31 L1
Coleford Water Somset 29 L4
Colegate End Norfk 106 D6
Cole Green Herts 69 H5
Cole Green Herts 70 B1
Cole Henley Hants 34 F1
Colehill Dorset 17 K2
Coleman Green Herts 69 G4
Coleman's Hatch E Susx 38 C6
Colemere Shrops 113 G5
Colemore Hants 35 L5
Colemore Green Shrops 97 G4
Colenden P & K 221 K1
Coleorton Leics 116 C8
Colerne Wilts 46 B5
Colesbourne Gloucs 64 E4
Cole's Cross Devon 8 A5
Coles Cross Dorset 15 J2
Colesden Bed 86 C4
Coles Green Suffk 90 C7
Coleshill Bucks 68 B8
Coleshill Oxon 65 K8
Coleshill Warwks 99 G5
Colestocks Devon 14 C3
Coley BaNES 45 H7
Colgate W Susx 37 K4
Colinsburgh Fife 223 H6
Colinton C Edin 211 H5
Colintraive Ag & B 207 G4
Colkirk Norfk 121 K6
Coll Ag & B 225 G4
Collace P & K 222 C1
Collafirth Shet 281 d3
Collaton Devon 7 L7
Collaton St Mary Torbay 8 C3
College of Roseisle Moray 266 C3
College Town Br For 49 K6
Collessie Fife 222 D4
Colleton Mills Devon 28 B7
Collier Row Gt Lon 52 B1
Collier's End Herts 69 K3
Collier's Green E Susx 24 E3
Colliers Green Kent 39 J5
Collier Street Kent 39 H4
Colliery Row Sundld 169 J1
Collieston Abers 257 J6
Collin D & G 176 D4
Collingbourne Ducis Wilts 47 K8
Collingbourne Kingston Wilts 47 K7
Collingham Leeds 150 E6
Collingham Notts 135 G7
Collington Herefs 80 F3
Collingtree Nhants 84 E4
Collins Green Warrtn 130 A1
Collins Green Worcs 81 G4
Colliston Angus 234 F6
Colliton Devon 14 C2
Collyweston Nhants 101 M3
Colmonell S Ayrs 182 E5
Colmworth Bed 86 C4
Colnbrook Slough 50 C3
Colne Cambs 103 H8
Colne Lancs 148 F7
Colne Bridge Kirk 141 J4
Colne Edge Lancs 148 F7
Colne Engaine Essex 71 K1
Colney Norfk 106 D2
Colney Heath Herts 69 G6
Colney Street Herts 68 F6
Coln Rogers Gloucs 65 G5
Coln St Aldwyns Gloucs 65 H6
Coln St Dennis Gloucs 65 G5
Colonsay Ag & B 214 D5
Colpy Abers 256 B5
Colquhar Border 200 D5
Colquite Cnwll 10 E8
Colscott Devon 26 F7
Colsterdale N York 159 L6
Colsterworth Lincs 118 B6
Colston Bassett Notts 117 J5
Coltfield Moray 266 C3
Colt Hill Hants 49 H8
Coltishall Norfk 122 F7
Colton Cumb 156 D5
Colton Leeds 142 B1
Colton N York 151 H6
Colton Norfk 106 C2
Colton Staffs 115 G7
Colt's Hill Kent 39 G4
Columbjohn Devon 13 M3
Colva Powys 79 H4
Colvend D & G 175 L4
Colwall Herefs 81 H6
Colwell Nthumb 179 M4
Colwich Staffs 115 G7
Colwick Notts 117 G3
Colwinston V Glam 42 E6
Colworth W Susx 20 F6
Colwyn Bay Conwy 127 G4
Colyford Devon 14 F4
Colyton Devon 14 F4
Combe Devon 7 L7
Combe Herefs 79 L3
Combe Oxon 66 B4
Combe W Berk 48 A6
Combe Almer Dorset 17 J3
Combe Common Surrey 36 E4
Combe Down BaNES 45 M6
Combe Fishacre Devon 8 C2
Combe Florey Somset 29 L4
Combe Hay BaNES 45 L7
Combeinteignhead Devon 13 L8
Combe Martin Devon 27 K2
Combe Raleigh Devon 14 E2
Comberbach Ches W 130 C4
Comberford Staffs 99 G2
Comberton Cambs 87 H4
Comberton Herefs 80 C2
Combe St Nicholas Somset 30 D8
Combpyne Devon 15 G4
Combridge Staffs 115 H4
Combrook Warwks 83 H5
Combs Derbys 131 L4
Combs Suffk 90 B4
Combs Ford Suffk 90 B4
Combwich Somset 30 C2
Comers Abers 244 F2
Comhampton Worcs 81 J2
Commercial End Cambs 87 L3
Commins Coch Powys 93 H3
Commondale N York 170 F8
Common Edge Bpool 138 C1
Common End Cumb 164 D6
Common Moor Cnwll 6 A1
Common Platt Wilts 47 G2
Commonside Ches W 130 A5
Commonside Derbys 115 L3
Common Side Derbys 133 G4
Commonwood Shrops 113 H6
Commonwood Wrexhm 112 F1
Compass Somset 30 D4
Compstall Stockp 131 J2
Compstonend D & G 175 G4
Compton Devon 8 C2
Compton Hants 34 D5
Compton Hants 34 F5
Compton Staffs 97 J6
Compton Surrey 36 E2
Compton W Berk 48 D3
Compton W Susx 20 C4
Compton Wilts 47 H8
Compton Abbas Dorset 32 E7
Compton Abdale Gloucs 64 F4
Compton Bassett Wilts 46 F4
Compton Beauchamp Oxon 47 K2
Compton Bishop Somset 44 E7
Compton Chamberlayne Wilts 33 H5
Compton Dando BaNES 45 J6
Compton Dundon Somset 31 H4
Compton Durville Somset 30 F7
Compton Greenfield S Glos 45 H3
Compton Martin BaNES 45 G7
Compton Pauncefoot Somset 31 L5
Compton Valence Dorset 16 B4
Compton Verney Warwks 83 H5
Comrie Fife 210 D1
Comrie P & K 220 D3
Conaglen House Highld 229 G2
Conchra Highld 248 E6
Concraigie P & K 233 G6
Conder Green Lancs 147 J4
Conderton Worcs 81 M7
Condicote Gloucs 65 H2
Condorrat N Lans 209 K4
Condover Shrops 96 B2
Coney Hill Gloucs 64 B3
Coneyhurst Common W Susx 37 H6
Coneysthorpe N York 151 M2
Coneythorpe N York 150 E4
Coney Weston Suffk 105 J7
Conford Hants 36 B4
Congdon's Shop Cnwll 11 K7
Congerstone Leics 99 K2
Congham Norfk 120 F6
Congleton Ches E 131 G7
Congl-y-wal Gwynd 110 D3
Congresbury N Som 44 E6
Congreve Staffs 97 K1
Conheath D & G 176 C5
Conicavel Moray 253 J1
Coningsby Lincs 136 D8
Conington Cambs 87 G2
Conington Cambs 102 D6
Conisbrough Donc 142 D8
Conisholme Lincs 145 K8
Coniston Cumb 156 D3
Coniston E R Yk 144 F1
Coniston Cold N York 148 F5
Conistone N York 149 H2
Connah's Quay Flints 129 G6
Connel Ag & B 228 E8
Connel Park E Ayrs 197 H8
Connor Downs Cnwll 2 F3
Conon Bridge Highld 250 F1
Cononley N York 149 H6
Consall Staffs 114 F2
Consett Dur 180 D8
Constable Burton N York 159 L4
Constable Lee Lancs 140 B3
Constantine Cnwll 3 J5
Constantine Bay Cnwll 10 B7
Contin Highld 262 D8
Conwy Conwy 126 F4
Conyer Kent 40 C2
Conyer's Green Suffk 89 H2
Cooden E Susx 24 C6
Cookbury Devon 12 A2
Cookbury Wick Devon 11 M2
Cookham W & M 49 L2
Cookham Dean W & M 49 L2
Cookham Rise W & M 49 L2
Cookhill Worcs 82 C3
Cookley Suffk 107 G8
Cookley Worcs 97 J7
Cookley Green Oxon 49 G1
Cookney Abers 245 J5
Cooksbridge E Susx 22 F4
Cooksey Green Worcs 81 L1
Cook's Green Essex 73 J3
Cooks Green Suffk 89 K4
Cookshill Staffs 114 E3
Cooksland Cnwll 5 J1
Cooksmill Green Essex 70 F6
Cookson Green Ches W 130 B5
Coolham W Susx 37 H6
Cooling Medway 53 G4
Cooling Street Medway 52 F4
Coombe Cnwll 3 G3
Coombe Cnwll 3 L3
Coombe Cnwll 4 F4
Coombe Devon 13 J6
Coombe Devon 13 L7
Coombe Devon 14 C4
Coombe Gloucs 63 M8
Coombe Hants 35 K6
Coombe Wilts 33 K1
Coombe Bissett Wilts 33 K5
Coombe Cellars Devon 13 L8
Coombe Cross Hants 35 K6
Coombe Hill Gloucs 64 C2
Coombe Keynes Dorset 17 G6
Coombe Pafford Torbay 8 D2
Coombes W Susx 21 L5
Coombes-Moor Herefs 79 L3
Coombe Street Somset 32 C4
Coombeswood Dudley 98 B6
Coopersale Common Essex 70 C6
Coopersale Street Essex 70 C6
Cooper's Corner Kent 38 D3
Coopers Green E Susx 23 H3
Coopers Green Herts 69 G5
Cooper Street Kent 41 J3
Cooper Turning Bolton 139 J6
Cootham W Susx 21 J4
Copdock Suffk 90 D6
Copford Green Essex 72 D3
Copgrove N York 150 D3
Copister Shet 281 e4
Cople Bed 86 C5
Copley Calder 141 G3
Copley Dur 168 D5
Copley Tamesd 140 E8
Coplow Dale Derbys 132 C4
Copmanthorpe C York 151 J6
Copmere End Staffs 114 C5
Copp Lancs 147 H7
Coppathorne Cnwll 11 H3

Coppenhall Staffs 114 E7
Coppenhall Moss Ches E 130 D8
Copperhouse Cnwll 2 F3
Coppicegate Shrops 97 G7
Coppingford Cambs 102 D7
Coppins Corner Kent 40 B5
Copplestone Devon 13 H2
Coppull Lancs 139 H5
Coppull Moor Lancs 139 H5
Copsale W Susx 37 J6
Copster Green Lancs 139 K1
Copston Magna Warwks 99 M5
Cop Street Kent 41 J3
Copthall Green Essex 70 B7
Copt Heath Solhll 98 F7
Copt Hewick N York 150 D2
Copthorne Cnwll 11 K4
Copthorne W Susx 37 M3
Copt Oak Leics 100 B1
Copy's Green Norfk 121 L4
Copythorne Hants 34 C8
Coram Street Suffk 89 K6
Corbets Tey Gt Lon 52 C2
Corbiere Jersey 9 a3
Corbridge Nthumb 180 B6
Corby Nhants 101 K5
Corby Glen Lincs 118 C6
Corby Hill Cumb 178 B7
Cordon N Ayrs 195 G5
Cordwell Derbys 132 F4
Coreley Shrops 96 E8
Cores End Bucks 49 L2
Corfe Somset 30 C7
Corfe Castle Dorset 17 J6
Corfe Mullen Dorset 17 J3
Corfton Shrops 96 B6
Corgarff Abers 243 J2
Corhampton Hants 35 J6
Corks Pond Kent 39 G5
Corley Warwks 99 J6
Corley Ash Warwks 99 J6
Corley Moor Warwks 99 H6
Cormuir Angus 233 L2
Cornard Tye Suffk 89 H7
Corndon Devon 13 G5
Corner Row Lancs 138 E1
Corney Cumb 155 K4
Cornforth Dur 169 J4
Cornhill Abers 267 M4
Cornhill-on-Tweed Nthumb 202 D5
Cornholme Calder 140 D3
Cornish Hall End Essex 88 D7
Cornoigmore Ag & B 224 C6
Cornriggs Dur 167 K2
Cornsay Dur 168 F2
Cornsay Colliery Dur 168 F2
Corntown Highld 262 F8
Corntown V Glam 42 D6
Cornwell Oxon 65 K2
Cornwood Devon 7 H3
Cornworthy Devon 8 B4
Corpach Highld 239 H8
Corpusty Norfk 122 C5
Corrachree Abers 244 B3
Corran Highld 229 G3
Corran Highld 238 D2
Corrany IoM 154 f4
Corrie D & G 177 G2
Corrie N Ayrs 195 G2
Corriecravie N Ayrs 193 J4
Corriegills N Ayrs 195 G4
Corriegour Lodge Hotel Highld 239 M5
Corriemoille Highld 262 C7
Corrimony Highld 250 C5
Corringham Lincs 135 H2
Corringham Thurr 52 F2
Corris Gwynd 93 G2
Corris Uchaf Gwynd 92 F2
Corrow Ag & B 217 K7
Corry Highld 247 K4
Corscombe Devon 12 E3
Corscombe Dorset 15 L2
Corse Gloucs 64 A2
Corse Lawn Gloucs 64 B1
Corsham Wilts 46 C5
Corsindae Abers 244 F2
Corsley Wilts 32 D2
Corsley Heath Wilts 32 D2
Corsock D & G 185 J7
Corston BaNES 45 K6
Corston Wilts 46 D2
Corstorphine C Edin 211 G4
Cors-y-Gedol Gwynd 109 L7
Cortachy Angus 234 B3
Corton Suffk 107 L4
Corton Wilts 32 F3
Corton Denham Somset 31 K6
Coruanan Highld 229 H2
Corwen Denbgs 111 L3
Coryates Dorset 16 B5
Coryton Devon 12 B6
Coryton Thurr 52 F2
Cosby Leics 100 C4
Coseley Dudley 97 L4
Cosford Shrops 97 H2
Cosgrove Nhants 84 F6
Cosham C Port 19 L3
Cosheston Pembks 55 G6
Coshieville P & K 231 L5
Cossall Notts 116 E3
Cossall Marsh Notts 116 E3
Cossington Leics 100 D1
Cossington Somset 30 E3
Costessey Norfk 106 D1
Costock Notts 116 F6
Coston Leics 117 M7
Coston Norfk 106 B2
Cote Oxon 65 M6
Cote Somset 30 E2
Cotebrook Ches W 130 B6
Cotehill Cumb 166 B1
Cotes Cumb 157 G5
Cotes Leics 116 F7
Cotes Staffs 114 C4
Cotesbach Leics 100 C7
Cotes Heath Staffs 114 C4
Cotford St Luke Somset 30 A5
Cotgrave Notts 117 H4
Cothal Abers 256 F8
Cotham Notts 117 L2
Cothelstone Somset 30 B4
Cotherstone Dur 168 C6
Cothill Oxon 66 C7
Cotleigh Devon 14 E2
Cotmanhay Derbys 116 D3
Coton Cambs 87 H3
Coton Nhants 84 D1
Coton Shrops 113 J4
Coton Staffs 98 F2
Coton Staffs 114 C7
Coton Staffs 114 F5
Coton Clanford Staffs 114 D7
Coton Hayes Staffs 114 F5
Coton Hill Shrops 96 B1
Coton in the Clay Staffs 115 K5
Coton in the Elms Derbys 115 L8
Coton Park Derbys 115 M7
Cott Devon 8 B3
Cottage End Hants 34 E2
Cottam Lancs 139 G1
Cottam Notts 135 G4
Cottenham Cambs 87 J2
Cotterdale N York 158 E4
Cottered Herts 69 J1
Cotteridge Birm 98 D7
Cotterstock Nhants 102 A5
Cottesbrooke Nhants 100 F8
Cottesmore Rutlnd 101 K1
Cottingham E R Yk 144 D1
Cottingham Nhants 101 J5
Cottingley C Brad 149 K8
Cottingley Hall Crematorium Leeds 141 L2
Cottisford Oxon 66 E1
Cotton Suffk 90 C2
Cotton End Bed 86 B6
Cotton Tree Lancs 148 F7
Cottown Abers 255 K6
Cottown Abers 256 D8
Cottown of Gight Abers 256 E4
Cotts Devon 6 E2
Cotwall Wrekin 113 K8
Cotwalton Staffs 114 E4
Couch's Mill Cnwll 5 K3
Coughton Herefs 63 H3
Coughton Warwks 82 C3
Coulaghailtro Ag & B 206 A6
Coulags Highld 248 F3
Coulderton Cumb 155 H1
Coull Abers 244 B3
Coulport Ag & B 207 L2
Coulsdon Gt Lon 51 J7
Coulston Wilts 46 D8
Coulter S Lans 199 H6
Coultershaw Bridge W Susx 21 G3
Coultings Somset 30 C3
Coulton N York 161 K7
Coultra Fife 222 F3
Cound Shrops 96 D2
Coundlane Shrops 96 D2
Coundon Dur 169 G5
Coundon Grange Dur 169 G5
Countersett N York 159 G5
Countess Wilts 33 K2
Countess Cross Essex 72 C1
Countess Wear Devon 13 M5
Countesthorpe Leics 100 D4
Countisbury Devon 28 C1
Coupar Angus P & K 233 K7
Coup Green Lancs 139 H2
Coupland Cumb 167 G7
Coupland Nthumb 202 E7
Cour Ag & B 194 C2
Court-at-Street Kent 40 E8
Courteachan Highld 237 K1
Courteenhall Nhants 84 E4
Court Henry Carmth 59 G4
Courtsend Essex 72 F8
Courtway Somset 30 B4
Cousland Mdloth 211 L5
Cousley Wood E Susx 39 G6
Cove Ag & B 207 L3
Cove Border 213 G4
Cove Devon 29 G7
Cove Hants 49 L7
Cove Highld 260 C2
Cove Bay C Aber 245 L3
Cove Bottom Suffk 107 K7
Covehithe Suffk 107 L7
Coven Staffs 97 K2
Coveney Cambs 103 K7
Covenham St Bartholomew Lincs 136 F1
Covenham St Mary Lincs 136 F1
Coven Heath Staffs 97 K2
Coventry Covtry 99 J7
Coverack Cnwll 3 K7
Coverack Bridges Cnwll 3 H5
Coverham N York 159 K5
Covington Cambs 85 L1
Covington S Lans 199 G5
Cowan Bridge Lancs 157 K7
Cowbeech E Susx 23 K4
Cowbit Lincs 119 H7
Cowbridge V Glam 42 F6
Cowdale Derbys 132 B5
Cowden Kent 38 C5
Cowdenbeath Fife 211 G1
Cowden Pound Kent 38 C5
Cowden Station Kent 38 D5
Cowers Lane Derbys 116 A2
Cowes IoW 19 H4
Cowesby N York 161 G5
Cowesfield Green Wilts 34 B6
Cowfold W Susx 37 K6
Cowgill Cumb 158 C5
Cow Green Suffk 90 C2
Cowhill S Glos 45 J1
Cowie Stirlg 209 M1
Cowlam E R Yk 152 E3
Cowley Devon 13 L3
Cowley Gloucs 64 D4
Cowley Gt Lon 50 D3
Cowley Oxon 66 D6
Cowling Lancs 139 J4
Cowling N York 149 H7
Cowling N York 160 C5
Cowlinge Suffk 88 E4
Cowmes Kirk 141 J4
Cowpe Lancs 140 C4
Cowpen Nthumb 181 H3
Cowpen Bewley S on T 170 B5
Cowplain Hants 19 M2
Cowshill Dur 167 K3
Cowslip Green N Som 44 F6
Cowthorpe N York 150 F5
Coxall Herefs 95 J8
Coxbank Ches E 113 L3
Coxbench Derbys 116 C3
Coxbridge Somset 31 J3
Cox Common Suffk 107 H7
Coxford Cnwll 11 H3
Coxford Norfk 121 J5
Coxgreen Staffs 97 H6
Coxheath Kent 39 J3
Coxhoe Dur 169 J3
Coxley Somset 31 H2
Coxley Wakefd 141 L4
Coxley Wick Somset 31 H2
Coxpark Cnwll 12 A8
Coxtie Green Essex 70 E7
Coxwold N York 161 H7
Coychurch Brdgnd 42 E6
Coychurch Crematorium Brdgnd 42 D5
Coylton S Ayrs 196 E7
Coylumbridge Highld 242 B1
Coytrahen Brdgnd 42 D4
Crabbs Cross Worcs 82 B2
Crab Orchard Dorset 17 L1
Crabtree W Susx 37 K6
Crabtree Green Wrexhm 112 E3
Crackenthorpe Cumb 166 F6
Crackington Haven Cnwll 11 G3
Crackley Staffs 114 C2
Crackley Warwks 99 J8
Crackleybank Shrops 97 G1
Crackpot N York 159 H3
Cracoe N York 149 H4
Craddock Devon 29 K8
Cradle End Herts 70 C3
Cradley Dudley 97 L6
Cradley Herefs 81 G6
Cradley Heath Sandw 97 L6
Cradoc Powys 60 F1
Crafthole Cnwll 6 D4
Crafton Bucks 67 L3
Crag Foot Lancs 157 G7
Craggan Highld 253 K6
Cragg Hill Leeds 150 B8
Craghead Dur 180 F8
Crai Powys 60 D2
Craibstone Moray 267 K4
Craichie Angus 234 D6
Craig Angus 235 H4
Craig Highld 249 H2
Craigbank E Ayrs 197 H8
Craigburn Border 200 B2
Craigcefnparc Swans 57 J4
Craigcleuch D & G 177 K2
Craigdam Abers 256 F5
Craigdhu Ag & B 216 C6
Craigearn Abers 245 G1
Craigellachie Moray 254 F3
Craigend P & K 221 K3
Craigend Rens 208 D5
Craigendoran Ag & B 208 A3
Craigends Rens 208 C6
Craighlaw D & G 173 H3
Craighouse Ag & B 205 H3
Craigie P & K 233 H6
Craigie S Ayrs 196 E4
Craigiefold Abers 269 G3
Craigley D & G 175 J3
Craig Llangiwg Neath 57 K4
Craiglockhart C Edin 211 H5
Craigmillar C Edin 211 J4
Craignant Shrops 112 C4
Craigneston D & G 185 J5
Craigneuk N Lans 209 K6
Craigneuk N Lans 209 K7
Craignure Ag & B 227 L5
Craigo Angus 235 H3
Craig Penllyn V Glam 42 E6
Craigrothie Fife 222 F5
Craigruie Stirlg 219 H3
Craig's End Essex 88 E7
Craigton Angus 234 D7
Craigton C Aber 245 J3
Craigton E Rens 208 E8
Craigton Crematorium C Glas 208 F6
Craigton of Airlie Angus 233 M5
Craig-y-Duke Neath 57 K4
Craig-y-nos Powys 60 C4
Crail Fife 223 L5
Crailing Border 189 J1
Craiselound N Linc 143 J8
Crakehall N York 160 C5
Crakehill N York 160 F7
Crakemarsh Staffs 115 H4
Crambe N York 151 M3
Cramlington Nthumb 181 G3
Cramond C Edin 211 G4
Cramond Bridge C Edin 211 G4
Crampmoor Hants 34 E6
Cranage Ches E 130 E6
Cranberry Staffs 114 C4
Cranborne Dorset 33 H8
Cranbourne Br For 50 A4
Cranbrook Kent 39 J6
Cranbrook Common Kent 39 K5
Crane Moor Barns 141 M7
Crane's Corner Norfk 105 J1
Cranfield C Beds 85 J6
Cranford Devon 26 F6
Cranford Gt Lon 50 E4
Cranford St Andrew Nhants 101 K7
Cranford St John Nhants 101 K8
Cranham Gloucs 64 C4
Cranham Gt Lon 52 C2
Cranhill Warwks 82 D4
Crank St Hel 139 G7
Cranleigh Surrey 37 G3
Cranmer Green Suffk 89 L1
Cranmore IoW 18 F5
Cranmore Somset 31 L2
Cranoe Leics 101 G4
Cransford Suffk 91 H2
Cranshaws Border 212 F6
Cranstal IoM 154 f2
Cranswick E R Yk 152 F5
Crantock Cnwll 4 C3
Cranwell Lincs 118 D2
Cranwich Norfk 104 F4
Cranworth Norfk 105 K3
Craobh Haven Ag & B 216 B5
Crapstone Devon 6 F1
Crarae Ag & B 216 F7
Crask Inn Highld 272 D3

Crask of Aigas Highld 250 E3
Craster Nthumb 191 K2
Craswall Herefs 79 K8
Crateford Staffs 97 K2
Cratfield Suffk 107 G8
Crathes Abers 245 G4
Crathie Abers 243 J4
Crathie Highld 241 G5
Crathorne N York 161 G1
Craven Arms Shrops 95 K6
Crawcrook Gatesd 180 D6
Crawford Lancs 139 G7
Crawford S Lans 186 E2
Crawfordjohn S Lans 186 C2
Crawley Hants 34 F4
Crawley Oxon 65 M4
Crawley W Susx 37 L4
Crawley Down W Susx 38 A6
Crawleyside Dur 168 C3
Crawshawbooth Lancs 140 B3
Crawton Abers 245 J7
Craxe's Green Essex 72 D3
Cray N York 159 G6
Crayford Gt Lon 52 B4
Crayke N York 151 J2
Craymere Beck Norfk 122 B5
Crays Hill Essex 71 H8
Cray's Pond Oxon 48 F3
Craythorne Staffs 115 L6
Craze Lowman Devon 29 H8
Crazies Hill Wokham 49 J3
Creacombe Devon 28 E7
Creagan Inn Ag & B 228 F6
Creag Ghoraidh W Isls 283 c9
Creagorry W Isls 283 c9
Creaguaineach Lodge Highld 230 B2
Creamore Bank Shrops 113 H5
Creaton Nhants 84 D1
Creca D & G 177 H5
Credenhill Herefs 80 B6
Crediton Devon 13 J3
Creebank D & G 183 J7
Creebridge D & G 173 K2
Creech Dorset 17 H6
Creech Heathfield Somset 30 D5
Creech St Michael Somset 30 C6
Creed Cnwll 4 F5
Creekmouth Gt Lon 51 M3
Creeksea Essex 72 D7
Creeting St Mary Suffk 90 C4
Creeton Lincs 118 D7
Creetown D & G 174 D3
Cregneash IoM 154 b8
Cregny Baa IoM 154 e5
Cregrina Powys 79 G5
Creich Fife 222 E3
Creigiau Cardif 43 G5
Cremyll Cnwll 6 E4
Cressage Shrops 96 D3
Cressbrook Derbys 132 C5
Cresselly Pembks 55 H5
Cressex Bucks 67 K8
Cressing Essex 71 J3
Cresswell Nthumb 191 K7
Cresswell Pembks 55 H5
Cresswell Staffs 114 F4
Creswell Derbys 133 K5
Creswell Green Staffs 98 D1
Cretingham Suffk 90 F3
Cretshengan Ag & B 206 A5
Crewe Ches E 130 D8
Crewe Ches W 112 F1
Crewe Crematorium Ches E 130 D8
Crewe Green Ches E 130 E8
Crew Green Powys 112 D8
Crewkerne Somset 15 K1
Crews Hill Station Gt Lon 69 J7
Crewton C Derb 116 C5
Crianlarich Stirlg 218 F2
Cribyn Cerdgn 76 F5
Criccieth Gwynd 109 J4
Crich Derbys 116 B1
Crich Carr Derbys 116 B1
Crichton Mdloth 211 L6
Crick Mons 44 F1
Crick Nhants 84 B1
Crickadarn Powys 78 F6
Cricket St Thomas Somset 15 J1
Crickheath Shrops 112 D7
Crickhowell Powys 61 K3
Cricklade Wilts 65 G8
Cricklewood Gt Lon 51 G2
Cridling Stubbs N York 142 E3
Crieff P & K 220 F3
Criggan Cnwll 5 G3
Criggion Powys 112 D8
Crigglestone Wakefd 141 M4
Crimble Rochdl 140 C5
Crimond Abers 269 K5
Crimplesham Norfk 104 C3
Crimscote Warwks 82 F5
Crinaglack Highld 250 D4
Crinan Ag & B 216 B8
Crindledyke N Lans 209 L7
Cringleford Norfk 106 D2
Cringles C Brad 149 J6
Crinow Pembks 55 K4
Cripplesease Cnwll 2 D4
Cripplestyle Dorset 33 J8
Cripp's Corner E Susx 24 D3
Croachy Highld 251 H6
Croanford Cnwll 10 E8
Crockenhill Kent 52 B5
Crocker End Oxon 49 H2
Crockerhill W Susx 20 F5
Crockernwell Devon 13 H4
Crocker's Ash Herefs 63 G4
Crockerton Wilts 32 E2
Crocketford D & G 185 K8
Crockey Hill C York 151 K6
Crockham Hill Kent 38 C3
Crockhurst Street Kent 39 G4
Crockleford Heath Essex 72 F2
Crock Street Somset 30 D8
Croeserw Neath 42 C3
Croes-goch Pembks 74 D6
Croes-lan Cerdgn 76 C6
Croesor Gwynd 110 B3
Croesyceiliog Carmth 58 D5
Croesyceiliog Torfn 62 C7
Croes-y-mwyalch Torfn 62 C8
Croes-y-pant Mons 62 C6
Croft Leics 100 B4
Croft Lincs 137 J7
Croft Warrtn 130 C1
Croftamie Stirlg 208 E2
Croft Mitchell Cnwll 3 H4
Crofton Cumb 165 J1
Crofton Wakefd 142 B4
Crofton Wilts 47 K6
Croft-on-Tees N York 160 D1
Croftown Highld 261 K3
Crofts Moray 266 F6
Crofts Bank Traffd 139 M8
Crofts of Dipple Moray 267 G4
Crofts of Savoch Abers 269 J4
Crofty Swans 56 F6
Crogen Gwynd 111 K4
Croggan Ag & B 227 K7
Croglin Cumb 166 D1
Croick Highld 262 D2
Cromarty Highld 264 B6
Crombie Fife 210 E2
Cromdale Highld 253 L6
Cromer Herts 69 J2
Cromer Norfk 122 E3
Cromford Derbys 132 F8
Cromhall S Glos 45 K1
Cromhall Common S Glos 45 K1
Cromor W Isls 282 g4
Crompton Fold Oldham 140 E6
Cromwell Notts 134 F7
Cronberry E Ayrs 197 H6
Crondall Hants 36 B1
Cronkbourne IoM 154 e6
Cronk-y-Voddy IoM 154 d5
Cronton Knows 129 L2
Crook Cumb 157 G4
Crook Dur 168 F4
Crookdake Cumb 165 G2
Crooke Wigan 139 H6
Crooked End Gloucs 63 J3
Crookedholm E Ayrs 196 E3
Crooked Soley Wilts 47 L4
Crookes Sheff 132 F2
Crookhall Dur 180 D8
Crookham Nthumb 202 E5
Crookham W Berk 48 D6
Crookham Village Hants 49 J8
Crook Inn Border 199 J7
Crooklands Cumb 157 H6
Crook of Devon P & K 221 J7
Cropper Derbys 115 L4
Cropredy Oxon 83 L6
Cropston Leics 100 C1
Cropthorne Worcs 82 B6
Cropton N York 162 D5
Cropwell Bishop Notts 117 H4
Cropwell Butler Notts 117 J4
Cros W Isls 282 h1
Crosbost W Isls 282 g4
Crosby Cumb 164 E3
Crosby IoM 154 d6
Crosby N Linc 143 M5
Crosby Sefton 138 C8
Crosby Garret Cumb 158 C1
Crosby Ravensworth Cumb 166 E7
Crosby Villa Cumb 164 E3
Croscombe Somset 31 K2
Crosemere Shrops 113 G5
Crosland Edge Kirk 141 H5
Crosland Hill Kirk 141 H5
Cross Somset 44 E8
Crossaig Ag & B 194 C1
Crossapoll Ag & B 224 C6
Cross Ash Mons 62 E3
Cross-at-Hand Kent 39 K4
Crossbush W Susx 21 H5
Crosscanonby Cumb 164 E3
Cross Coombe Cnwll 4 B4
Crossdale Street Norfk 122 E4
Cross End Bed 85 L4
Cross End Essex 89 G8
Crossens Sefton 138 D4
Cross Flatts C Brad 149 K7
Crossford Fife 210 E2
Crossford S Lans 198 D4
Crossgate Cnwll 11 L5
Crossgate Lincs 119 H6
Crossgate Staffs 114 E4
Crossgatehall E Loth 211 L5
Crossgates E Ayrs 196 D2
Crossgates Fife 210 F1
Cross Gates Leeds 142 B1
Crossgates N York 163 J6
Crossgates Powys 78 F2
Crossgill Lancs 147 L3
Cross Green Devon 11 M5
Cross Green Leeds 141 M2
Cross Green Staffs 97 K2
Cross Green Suffk 89 G4
Cross Green Suffk 89 H4
Cross Green Suffk 89 K4
Crosshands Carmth 55 L2
Cross Hands Carmth 59 G6
Crosshands E Ayrs 196 F5
Cross Hands Pembks 55 H4
Cross Hill Derbys 116 C2
Crosshill Fife 222 B7
Crosshill S Ayrs 183 J2
Cross Hills N York 149 H6
Crosshouse E Ayrs 196 D3
Cross Houses Shrops 96 C2
Cross Houses Shrops 96 F5
Cross in Hand E Susx 23 J3
Cross Inn Cerdgn 76 D4
Cross Inn Cerdgn 77 G2
Cross Inn Pembks 55 J5
Cross Inn Rhondd 43 G5
Cross Keys Ag & B 208 B2
Crosskeys Caerph 43 K3
Cross Keys Wilts 46 C5
Crosskirk Highld 279 H2
Crosslands Cumb 156 E5
Cross Lane IoW 19 H5
Cross Lane Head Shrops 97 G4
Cross Lanes Cnwll 3 H6
Cross Lanes Cnwll 4 C6
Cross Lanes N York 151 H3
Crosslanes Shrops 112 E7
Cross Lanes Wrexhm 112 E2
Crosslee Rens 208 C6
Crossley Kirk 141 K3
Crossmichael D & G 175 J2
Cross Oak Powys 61 H2
Cross of Jackston Abers 256 D5
Cross o' th' hands Derbys 115 M2
Crosspost W Susx 37 L6
Crossroads Abers 244 D2
Crossroads Abers 245 G5
Cross Street Suffk 106 D8
Crosston Angus 234 E4
Cross Town Ches E 130 E4
Crossway Mons 62 F3
Crossway Powys 78 E4
Crossway Green Mons 63 G8
Crossway Green Worcs 81 J2
Crossways Dorset 16 E5
Crosswell Pembks 75 J5
Crosthwaite Cumb 156 F4
Croston Lancs 138 F4
Crostwick Norfk 122 E8
Crostwight Norfk 123 G5
Crouch Kent 38 F2
Crouch Kent 40 D4
Crouch End Gt Lon 51 J1
Croucheston Wilts 33 J6
Crouch Hill Dorset 32 B8
Crough House Green Kent 38 C4
Croughton Nhants 84 A8
Crovie Abers 268 E3
Crow Hants 18 B3
Crowan Cnwll 3 G4
Crowborough E Susx 38 D7
Crowborough Town E Susx 38 D7
Crowcombe Somset 29 L3
Crowdecote Derbys 132 B6
Crowden Derbys 141 G7
Crowden Devon 12 C3
Crowdhill Hants 35 G6
Crowdleham Kent 52 C7
Crow Edge Barns 141 J6
Crowell Oxon 67 H7
Crow End Cambs 87 G4
Crowfield Nhants 84 B7
Crowfield Suffk 90 D4
Crowfield Green Suffk 90 D4
Crowgate Street Norfk 123 G7
Crow Green Essex 70 E7
Crowhill E Loth 213 G4
Crow Hill Herefs 63 J2
Crowhole Derbys 133 G4
Crowhurst E Susx 24 D5
Crowhurst Surrey 38 B4
Crowhurst Lane End Surrey 38 B4
Crowland Lincs 102 E2
Crowland Suffk 89 K1
Crowlas Cnwll 2 E4
Crowle N Linc 143 K5
Crowle Worcs 81 L4
Crowle Green Worcs 81 L4
Crowmarsh Gifford Oxon 48 F1
Crown Corner Suffk 90 F1
Crownhill C Plym 6 F3
Crownhill Crematorium M Keyn 84 F7
Crownpits Surrey 36 E2
Crownthorpe Norfk 106 B3
Crowntown Cnwll 3 G5
Crows-an-Wra Cnwll 2 B5
Crow's Green Essex 71 G2
Crowshill Norfk 105 J2
Crow's Nest Cnwll 6 B1
Crowsnest Shrops 95 J3
Crowthorne Wokham 49 K6
Crowton Ches W 130 B5
Croxall Staffs 99 G1
Croxby Lincs 144 F8
Croxdale Dur 169 H3
Croxden Staffs 115 H4
Croxley Green Herts 68 D7
Croxteth Lpool 138 E8
Croxton Cambs 86 E3
Croxton N Linc 144 E5
Croxton Norfk 105 H6
Croxton Norfk 121 L5
Croxton Staffs 114 B5
Croxtonbank Staffs 114 B5
Croxton Green Ches E 113 J1
Croxton Kerrial Leics 117 L5
Croy Highld 252 E2
Croy N Lans 209 J4
Croyde Devon 27 H3
Croyde Bay Devon 27 G3
Croydon Cambs 87 G5
Croydon Gt Lon 51 J6
Croydon Crematorium Gt Lon 51 J5
Crubenmore Highld 241 J5
Cruckmeole Shrops 95 K2
Cruckton Shrops 95 K1
Cruden Bay Abers 257 K4
Crudgington Wrekin 113 K7
Crudwell Wilts 64 D8
Cruft Devon 12 C3
Crug Powys 79 H1
Crugmeer Cnwll 10 C7
Crugybar Carmth 77 J7
Crug-y-byddar Powys 94 E7
Crumlin Caerph 43 K2
Crumplehorn Cnwll 5 L4
Crumpsall Manch 140 C7
Crundale Kent 40 E5
Crundale Pembks 54 F3
Crunwear Pembks 55 L5
Cruwys Morchard Devon 28 F8
Crux Easton Hants 48 B7
Cruxton Dorset 16 B3
Crwbin Carmth 58 E6
Cryers Hill Bucks 67 L7
Crymmych Pembks 75 L5
Crynant Neath 60 B6
Crystal Palace Gt Lon 51 J5
Cuaig Highld 260 A8
Cuan Ag & B 215 L2
Cubbington Warwks 83 H2
Cubert Cnwll 4 C3
Cubley Barns 141 K7
Cublington Bucks 67 K3
Cublington Herefs 79 M7
Cuckfield W Susx 22 D2
Cucklington Somset 32 C5
Cuckney Notts 133 L5
Cuckoo Bridge Lincs 119 G7
Cuckoo's Corner Hants 35 M3
Cuckoo's Nest Ches W 129 J7
Cuddesdon Oxon 66 F6
Cuddington Bucks 67 H5
Cuddington Ches W 130 B5
Cuddington Heath Ches W 113 G2
Cuddy Hill Lancs 147 J8

Cudham Gt Lon 51 L7
Cudliptown Devon 12 C6
Cudnell Bmouth 17 L3
Cudworth Barns 142 B6
Cudworth Somset 30 F8
Cuerdley Cross Warrtn 130 A2
Cufaude Hants 49 G7
Cuffley Herts 69 J6
Cuil Highld 228 F4
Culbokie Highld 263 G7
Culbone Somset 28 E1
Culburnie Highld 250 E3
Culcabock Highld 251 J3
Culcharry Highld 253 G2
Culcheth Warrtn 130 C1
Culdrain Abers 255 K5
Culduie Highld 248 A4
Culford Suffk 89 G1
Culgaith Cumb 166 E5
Culham Oxon 66 D8
Culkein Highld 270 D2
Culkein Drumbeg Highld 270 F1
Culkerton Gloucs 64 D7
Cullen Moray 267 K3
Cullercoats N Tyne 181 J4
Cullerlie Abers 245 G3
Cullicudden Highld 263 H7
Cullingworth C Brad 149 J8
Cullipool Ag & B 215 L2
Cullivoe Shet 281 e2
Culloden Highld 252 D3
Cullompton Devon 14 B1
Culm Davy Devon 29 L7
Culmington Shrops 96 B7
Culmstock Devon 29 K8
Culnacraig Highld 270 E7
Culnaightrie D & G 175 J5
Culnaknock Highld 259 J4
Culpho Suffk 90 F5
Culrain Highld 263 G1
Culross Fife 210 C2
Culroy S Ayrs 196 C8
Culsalmond Abers 256 B5
Culscadden D & G 174 D5
Culshabbin D & G 173 H4
Culswick Shet 281 c6
Cultercullen Abers 257 G7
Cults C Aber 245 K3
Culverstone Green Kent 52 D6
Culverthorpe Lincs 118 D3
Culworth Nhants 84 A6
Cumbernauld N Lans 209 K4
Cumbernauld Village N Lans 209 K4
Cumberworth Lincs 137 J5
Cumdivock Cumb 165 K1
Cuminestown Abers 268 E6
Cumledge Border 202 B2
Cummersdale Cumb 177 L8
Cummertrees D & G 176 F5
Cummingston Moray 266 C2
Cumnock E Ayrs 197 H7
Cumnor Oxon 66 C6
Cumrew Cumb 178 D8
Cumrue D & G 176 E2
Cumwhinton Cumb 178 B8
Cumwhitton Cumb 178 C8
Cundall N York 150 F1
Cunninghamhead N Ayrs 196 D3
Cunningsburgh Shet 281 e7
Cupar Fife 222 F4
Cupar Muir Fife 222 F4
Curbar Derbys 132 E5
Curbridge Hants 19 J1
Curbridge Oxon 65 M5
Curdridge Hants 35 H8
Curdworth Warwks 98 F5
Curland Somset 30 C7
Curridge W Berk 48 C4
Currie C Edin 211 G5
Curry Mallet Somset 30 E6
Curry Rivel Somset 30 F6
Curteis Corner Kent 39 L5
Curtisden Green Kent 39 J5
Curtisknowle Devon 7 L4
Cury Cnwll 3 H6
Cushnie Abers 244 C1
Cushuish Somset 30 B5
Cusop Herefs 79 J7
Cutcloy D & G 174 C7
Cutcombe Somset 29 G3
Cutgate Rochdl 140 C5
Cuthill Highld 263 K2
Cutiau Gwynd 110 B8
Cutler's Green Essex 70 E1
Cutmadoc Cnwll 5 J2
Cutmere Cnwll 6 C3
Cutnall Green Worcs 81 K2
Cutsdean Gloucs 65 G1
Cutsyke Wakefd 142 C3
Cutthorpe Derbys 133 G5
Cuttivett Cnwll 6 D2
Cuxham Oxon 67 G8
Cuxton Medway 52 F5
Cuxwold Lincs 144 F7
Cwm Blae G 61 J6
Cwm Denbgs 128 C4
Cwmafan Neath 57 L6
Cwmaman Rhondd 60 F7
Cwmann Carmth 77 G6
Cwmavon Torfn 62 B6
Cwm-bach Carmth 56 E4
Cwmbach Carmth 75 M7
Cwmbach Powys 79 G7
Cwmbach Rhondd 60 F6
Cwmbach Llechrhyd Powys 78 E4
Cwmbelan Powys 93 K7
Cwmbran Torfn 62 C8
Cwmbrwyno Cerdgn 92 F7
Cwm Capel Carmth 56 E4
Cwmcarn Caerph 43 K3
Cwmcarvan Mons 62 F5
Cwm-celyn Blae G 61 K5
Cwm-Cewydd Gwynd 93 J1
Cwm-cou Cerdgn 76 B6
Cwm Crawnon Powys 61 J3
Cwmdare Rhondd 60 F6
Cwmdu Carmth 59 H3
Cwmdu Powys 61 J2
Cwmdu Swans 57 H6
Cwmduad Carmth 58 C3
Cwm Dulais Swans 57 H4
Cwmdwr Carmth 59 K2
Cwmfelin Brdgnd 42 C4
Cwmfelin Myr Td 61 H6
Cwmfelin Boeth Carmth 55 L3
Cwmfelinfach Caerph 43 J3
Cwmfelin Mynach Carmth 75 L7
Cwmffrwd Carmth 58 D5
Cwmgiedd Powys 59 L6
Cwmgorse Carmth 57 K3
Cwmgwili Carmth 57 G3
Cwmgwrach Neath 60 C6
Cwmhiraeth Carmth 76 C7
Cwm-Ifor Carmth 59 J4
Cwm Irfon Powys 78 A5
Cwmisfael Carmth 58 F5
Cwm Llinau Powys 93 J2
Cwmllynfell Neath 59 K6
Cwmmawr Carmth 58 F6
Cwm Morgan Carmth 58 B2
Cwmparc Rhondd 42 E3
Cwmpengraig Carmth 58 C2
Cwm Penmachno Conwy 110 E2
Cwmpennar Rhondd 61 G7
Cwmrhos Powys 61 J2
Cwmrhydyceirw Swans 57 J5
Cwmsychbant Cerdgn 76 E6
Cwmtillery Blae G 61 K6
Cwm-twrch Isaf Powys 57 L3
Cwm-twrch Uchaf Powys 59 L6
Cwm-y-glo Carmth 59 G6
Cwm-y-glo Gwynd 125 K7
Cwmyoy Mons 62 C3
Cwmystwyth Cerdgn 93 G8
Cwrt Gwynd 92 E3
Cwrt-newydd Cerdgn 76 E5
Cwrt-y-gollen Powys 61 K4
Cyfronydd Powys 94 E2
Cylibebyll Neath 57 K4
Cymau Flints 129 G8
Cymer Neath 42 C3
Cymmer Rhondd 42 F3
Cynghordy Carmth 77 M7
Cynheidre Carmth 56 E3
Cynonville Neath 42 C3
Cynwyd Denbgs 111 K3
Cynwyl Elfed Carmth 58 C3

D

Daccombe Devon 8 D1
Dacre Cumb 166 B5
Dacre N York 150 B4
Dacre Banks N York 150 B3
Daddry Shield Dur 167 K3
Dadford Bucks 84 C7
Dadlington Leics 99 L4
Dafen Carmth 56 F4
Daffy Green Norfk 105 J2
Dagenham Gt Lon 52 B2
Daglingworth Gloucs 64 E6
Dagnall Bucks 68 C4
Dagworth Suffk 89 L3
Dailly S Ayrs 183 H3
Dainton Devon 8 C2
Dairsie Fife 223 G4
Daisy Hill Bolton 139 K6
Daisy Hill Leeds 141 L2
Dalabrog W Isls 283 b11
Dalavich Ag & B 216 F5
Dalbeattie D & G 175 L3
Dalbury Derbys 115 M5
Dalby IoM 154 b6
Dalby Lincs 137 H5
Dalby N York 151 K2
Dalcapon P & K 232 E4
Dalchalm Highld 274 B6
Dalchreichart Highld 240 A1
Dalchruin P & K 220 C4
Dalcrue P & K 221 J2
Dalderby Lincs 136 E6
Dalditch Devon 14 B6
Daldowie Crematorium C Glas 209 H6
Dale Cumb 166 D2
Dale Derbys 116 D4
Dale Pembks 54 C5
Dale Bottom Cumb 165 J6
Dale End Derbys 132 D7
Dale End N York 149 G6
Dale Hill E Susx 39 H7
Dalehouse N York 171 H7
Dalelia Highld 237 L6
Dalgarven N Ayrs 196 B2
Dalgety Bay Fife 211 G2
Dalgig E Ayrs 197 G8
Dalginross P & K 220 D3
Dalguise P & K 232 E6
Dalhalvaig Highld 278 F5
Dalham Suffk 88 E3
Daliburgh W Isls 283 b11
Dalkeith Mdloth 211 K5
Dallas Moray 266 C5
Dallinghoo Suffk 91 G4
Dallington E Susx 24 B3
Dallington Nhants 84 E3
Dallow N York 150 B2
Dalmally Ag & B 217 K2
Dalmary Stirlg 219 H8
Dalmellington E Ayrs 184 D2
Dalmeny C Edin 210 F3
Dalmore Highld 263 H6
Dalmuir W Duns 208 E5
Dalnabreck Highld 237 K6
Dalnacardoch P & K 231 K1
Dalnahaitnach Highld 252 F7
Dalnaspidal P & K 231 J1
Dalnawillan Lodge Highld 279 H8
Daloist P & K 231 L4
Dalqueich P & K 221 K6
Dalquhairn S Ayrs 183 J4
Dalreavoch Lodge Highld 273 H6
Dalry N Ayrs 196 B1
Dalrymple E Ayrs 196 D8
Dalserf S Lans 198 C3
Dalsmeran Ag & B 192 D5
Dalston Cumb 165 L1
Dalston Gt Lon 51 J2
Dalswinton D & G 176 B2
Dalton Cumb 157 H7
Dalton D & G 176 F4
Dalton Lancs 139 G6
Dalton N York 159 K1
Dalton N York 160 F7
Dalton Nthumb 180 D4
Dalton Rothm 133 J1
Dalton-in-Furness Cumb 156 B7
Dalton-le-Dale Dur 169 L1
Dalton Magna Rothm 133 J1
Dalton-on-Tees N York 160 D1
Dalton Parva Rothm 133 J1
Dalton Piercy Hartpl 170 B4
Dalveich Stirlg 219 K2
Dalwhinnie Highld 241 H6
Dalwood Devon 14 F3
Damask Green Herts 69 H1
Damerham Hants 33 J7
Damgate Norfk 107 H2
Dam Green Norfk 105 L6
Danaway Kent 53 J6
Danbury Essex 71 J6
Danby N York 162 C1
Danby Bottom N York 162 B2
Danby Wiske N York 160 E3
Dandaleith Moray 254 F3
Danderhall Mdloth 211 J5
Danebridge Ches E 131 J6
Dane End Herts 69 J3
Danegate E Susx 38 E6
Danehill E Susx 22 F2
Dane Hills C Leic 100 C3
Danemoor Green Norfk 105 L2
Danesford Shrops 97 G5
Danesmoor Derbys 133 H7
Dane Street Kent 40 D5
Daniel's Water Kent 40 C7
Danshillock Abers 268 C5
Danskine E Loth 212 C5
Danthorpe E R Yk 145 H1
Danzey Green Warwks 82 D2
Dapple Heath Staffs 115 G6
Darby Green Hants 49 K7
Darcy Lever Bolton 139 L6
Dardy Powys 61 K3
Daren-felen Mons 61 K4
Darenth Kent 52 C5
Daresbury Halton 130 B3
Darfield Barns 142 C6
Darfoulds Notts 133 L4
Dargate Kent 40 E3
Darite Cnwll 6 B1
Darland Medway 53 G6
Darland Wrexhm 129 J8
Darlaston Wsall 98 B4
Darlaston Green Wsall 98 B4
Darley N York 150 B4
Darley Abbey C Derb 116 B4
Darley Bridge Derbys 132 E7
Darley Dale Derbys 132 E7
Darley Green Solhll 98 F8
Darleyhall Herts 68 F3
Darley Head N York 150 B4
Darlingscott Warwks 82 F6
Darlington Darltn 169 H7
Darlington Crematorium Darltn 169 H7
Darliston Shrops 113 J5
Darlton Notts 134 F5
Darnford Staffs 98 E2
Darnick Border 201 H6
Darowen Powys 93 H3
Darra Abers 268 D6
Darracott Devon 26 D7
Darracott Devon 27 H3
Darras Hall Nthumb 180 E5
Darrington Wakefd 142 D4
Darsham Suffk 91 K1
Darshill Somset 31 K2
Dartford Kent 52 B4
Dartington Devon 8 B2
Dartmeet Devon 12 F7
Dartmouth Devon 8 C4
Darton Barns 141 M5
Darvel E Ayrs 197 H3
Darwell Hole E Susx 24 C3
Darwen Bl w D 139 K3
Datchet W & M 50 C3
Datchworth Herts 69 H3
Datchworth Green Herts 69 H3
Daubhill Bolton 139 L6
Daugh of Kinermony Moray 254 E3
Dauntsey Wilts 46 E3
Dava Highld 253 J4
Davenham Ches W 130 C5
Davenport Stockp 131 H2
Davenport Green Ches E 131 G4
Davenport Green Traffd 130 F2
Daventry Nhants 84 B3
Davidson's Mains C Edin 211 H4
Davidstow Cnwll 11 G5
David Street Kent 52 E6
Davington D & G 187 K5
Davington Hill Kent 40 D3
Daviot Abers 256 D6
Daviot Highld 252 D4
Daviot House Highld 252 D4
Davis's Town E Susx 23 J4
Davoch of Grange Moray 267 K6
Davyhulme Traffd 139 M8
Daw End Wsall 98 C3
Dawesgreen Surrey 37 K2
Dawley Wrekin 96 F2
Dawlish Devon 13 M7
Dawlish Warren Devon 14 A7
Dawn Conwy 127 G5
Daws Green Somset 30 B6
Daws Heath Essex 53 H1
Daw's House Cnwll 11 K6
Dawsmere Lincs 120 A5
Daybrook Notts 116 F3
Day Green Ches E 130 F8
Dayhills Staffs 114 F5
Dayhouse Bank Worcs 98 B7
Daylesford Gloucs 65 K2
Ddol Flints 128 D5
Ddol-Cownwy Powys 111 K8
Deal Kent 41 L5
Dean Cumb 164 E5
Dean Devon 7 L2
Dean Devon 27 L2
Dean Devon 28 C1
Dean Dorset 33 G7
Dean Hants 34 F4
Dean Hants 35 H7
Dean Lancs 140 C3
Dean Oxon 65 M3
Dean Somset 31 L2
Dean Bottom Kent 52 C5
Deanburnhaugh Border 188 C4
Deancombe Devon 7 L2

Dean Court Oxon 66 C6
Deane Bolton 139 K6
Deane Hants 35 H1
Dean End Dorset 33 G7
Dean Head Barns 141 L7
Deanhead Kirk 141 G4
Deanland Dorset 33 G7
Deanlane End W Susx 20 B4
Dean Prior Devon 7 L2
Deanraw Nthumb 179 J6
Dean Row Ches E 131 G3
Deans W Loth 210 D5
Deanscales Cumb 164 E5
Deanshanger Nhants 84 E7
Deanshaugh Moray 267 G6
Deanston Stirlg 220 C6
Dean Street Kent 39 J3
Dearham Cumb 164 E3
Dearnley Rochdl 140 D4
Debach Suffk 90 F4
Debden Essex 70 C7
Debden Essex 87 L8
Debden Green Essex 70 E1
Debenham Suffk 90 E3
Deblin's Green Worcs 81 J5
Dechmont W Loth 210 D5
Dechmont Road W Loth 210 D5
Deddington Oxon 66 C1
Dedham Essex 90 C8
Dedham Heath Essex 72 F1
Dedworth W & M 50 B4
Deene Nhants 101 L5
Deenethorpe Nhants 101 L5
Deepcar Sheff 141 L8
Deepcut Surrey 49 L7
Deepdale Cumb 158 C5
Deepdale N York 158 F6
Deeping Gate C Pete 102 C2
Deeping St James Lincs 102 D2
Deeping St Nicholas Lincs 119 H8
Deerhurst Gloucs 64 C1
Deerhurst Walton Gloucs 64 C2
Deerton Street Kent 40 C3
Defford Worcs 81 L6
Defynnog Powys 60 D2
Deganwy Conwy 126 F4
Degnish Ag & B 216 B5
Deighton C York 151 K7
Deighton N York 160 E2
Deiniolen Gwynd 125 K7
Delabole Cnwll 10 F6
Delamere Ches W 130 A6
Delfrigs Abers 257 H7
Delley Devon 27 K6
Delliefure Highld 253 L5
Dell Quay W Susx 20 D6
Delly End Oxon 65 M4
Delnabo Moray 254 C8
Delnashaugh Inn Moray 254 D4
Delny Highld 263 K5
Delph Oldham 140 E6
Delves Dur 168 E1
Delvin End Essex 88 F8
Dembleby Lincs 118 D4
Demelza Cnwll 5 G2
Denaby Donc 142 D7
Denaby Main Donc 142 D7
Denbies Surrey 37 H1
Denbigh Denbgs 128 C6
Denbrae Fife 222 F3
Denbury Devon 8 B1
Denby Derbys 116 C2
Denby Bottles Derbys 116 C2
Denby Dale Kirk 141 K6
Denchworth Oxon 48 A1
Dendron Cumb 146 E2
Denel End C Beds 85 K8
Denfield P & K 221 G4
Denford Nhants 101 L8
Dengie Essex 72 E6
Denham Bucks 50 D2
Denham Suffk 88 E3
Denham Suffk 106 D8
Denham End Suffk 88 F3
Denham Green Bucks 50 D1
Denham Green Suffk 106 D8
Denhead Abers 269 J5
Denhead Fife 223 H4
Denhead of Gray C Dund 222 F1
Denholm Border 189 G3
Denholme C Brad 141 G1
Denholme Clough C Brad 141 G1
Denio Gwynd 108 F4
Denmead Hants 19 L1
Denmore C Aber 245 L1
Denne Park W Susx 37 J5
Dennington Suffk 91 G2
Denny Falk 209 L3
Dennyloanhead Falk 209 L3
Den of Lindores Fife 222 D4
Denshaw Oldham 140 E5
Denside Abers 245 H4
Densole Kent 41 G7
Denston Suffk 88 F5
Denstone Staffs 115 H3
Denstroude Kent 40 E3
Dent Cumb 158 B5
Denton Cambs 102 C6
Denton Darltn 169 G7
Denton E Susx 23 G6
Denton Kent 41 G6
Denton Kent 52 E4
Denton Lincs 117 M5
Denton N York 149 L6
Denton Nhants 85 G4
Denton Norfk 106 F5
Denton Oxon 66 E6
Denton Tamesd 131 H1
Denver Norfk 104 C3
Denwick Nthumb 191 J3
Deopham Norfk 105 L3
Deopham Green Norfk 105 L4
Depden Suffk 88 F4
Depden Green Suffk 88 F4
Deptford Gt Lon 51 K3
Deptford Wilts 33 H3
Derby C Derb 116 B4
Derby Devon 27 K4
Derbyhaven IoM 154 c8
Derculich P & K 232 C5
Dereham Norfk 105 K1
Deri Caerph 61 H6
Derril Devon 11 K2
Derringstone Kent 41 G5
Derrington Staffs 114 D7
Derriton Devon 11 L2
Derry Hill Wilts 46 D5
Derrythorpe N Linc 143 L6
Dersingham Norfk 120 F5
Dervaig Ag & B 226 E2
Derwen Denbgs 111 L2
Derwen Fawr Carmth 59 G4
Derwenlas Powys 92 F4
Derwydd Carmth 59 H5
Desborough Nhants 101 H6
Desford Leics 100 B3
Deskford Moray 267 K4
Detchant Nthumb 203 H6
Detling Kent 53 G7
Deuxhill Shrops 96 F6
Devauden Mons 62 F7
Devil's Bridge Cerdgn 92 F8
Devitts Green Warwks 99 H5
Devizes Wilts 46 E6
Devonport C Plym 6 E4
Devonside Clacks 221 G7
Devoran Cnwll 3 K3
Dewarton Mdloth 211 L6
Dewlish Dorset 16 E3
Dewsbury Kirk 141 K3
Dewsbury Moor Kirk 141 K3
Dewsbury Moor Crematorium Kirk 141 K3
Deytheur Powys 112 C8
Dial N Som 45 G5
Dial Green W Susx 36 D5
Dial Post W Susx 21 K3
Dibberford Dorset 15 K2
Dibden Hants 18 F2
Dibden Purlieu Hants 18 F2
Dickens Heath Solhll 98 E8
Dickleburgh Norfk 106 D7
Didbrook Gloucs 64 F1
Didcot Oxon 48 D1
Diddington Cambs 86 D2
Diddlebury Shrops 96 C6
Didley Herefs 62 F1
Didling W Susx 20 D3
Didmarton Gloucs 46 B2
Didsbury Manch 131 G1
Didworthy Devon 7 K2
Digby Lincs 135 M8
Digg Highld 259 H3
Diggle Oldham 140 F6
Digmoor Lancs 139 G6
Digswell Herts 69 H4
Digswell Water Herts 69 H4
Dihewyd Cerdgn 76 E4
Dilham Norfk 123 G6
Dilhorne Staffs 114 F3
Dill Hall Lancs 139 M2
Dillington Cambs 86 C2
Dilston Nthumb 180 A6
Dilton Wilts 32 E1
Dilton Marsh Wilts 32 D1
Dilwyn Herefs 80 A4
Dimple Bolton 139 L4
Dimple Derbys 132 F7
Dinas Carmth 58 A3
Dinas Cnwll 10 C7
Dinas Gwynd 108 D4
Dinas Pembks 75 G4
Dinas Rhondd 42 F3
Dinas Dinlle Gwynd 125 H8
Dinas-Mawddwy Gwynd 111 G8
Dinas Powys V Glam 43 J7
Dinder Somset 31 J2
Dinedor Herefs 80 C7
Dingestow Mons 62 F5
Dingle Lpool 129 J2
Dingleden Kent 39 K7
Dingley Nhants 101 G6
Dingwall Highld 262 F8
Dinmael Conwy 111 J3
Dinnet Abers 244 A4
Dinnington N u Ty 180 F4
Dinnington Rothm 133 K3
Dinnington Somset 30 F8
Dinorwic Gwynd 125 L7
Dinton Bucks 67 J5
Dinton Wilts 33 H4
Dinwoodie D & G 187 H8
Dinworthy Devon 26 E7
Dipford Somset 30 B6
Dipley Hants 49 H7
Dippen Ag & B 194 B3
Dippen N Ayrs 195 G6
Dippenhall Surrey 36 B2
Dippermill Devon 12 B1
Dippertown Devon 12 B5
Dipple Moray 267 G4
Dipple S Ayrs 182 F2
Diptford Devon 7 L3
Dipton Dur 180 E8
Diptonmill Nthumb 179 L6
Dirleton E Loth 212 B2
Dirt Pot Nthumb 167 K2
Discoed Powys 79 K2
Diseworth Leics 116 D6
Dishforth N York 160 E8
Disley Ches E 131 J3
Diss Norfk 106 C7
Disserth Powys 78 E4
Distington Cumb 164 D6
Distington Hall Crematorium Cumb 164 D6
Ditchampton Wilts 33 J4
Ditcheat Somset 31 K4
Ditchingham Norfk 107 G5
Ditchling E Susx 22 E4
Ditherington Shrops 113 H8
Ditteridge Wilts 46 B5
Dittisham Devon 8 C4
Ditton Kent 52 F7
Ditton Green Cambs 88 D4
Ditton Priors Shrops 96 E5
Dixton Gloucs 64 E1
Dixton Mons 63 G4
Dizzard Cnwll 11 H3
Dobcross Oldham 140 F6
Dobwalls Cnwll 5 L2
Doccombe Devon 13 H5
Dochgarroch Highld 251 H3
Dockenfield Surrey 36 B3
Docker Lancs 157 J7
Docking Norfk 121 G4
Docklow Herefs 80 D4
Dockray Cumb 165 J1
Dockray Cumb 165 L6
Dodbrooke Devon 7 L6
Doddinghurst Essex 70 E7
Doddington Cambs 103 H5
Doddington Kent 40 B4
Doddington Lincs 135 H5
Doddington Nthumb 202 F6
Doddington Shrops 96 E8
Doddiscombsleigh Devon 13 K5
Dodd's Green Ches E 113 K3
Doddshill Norfk 120 F5
Doddy Cross Cnwll 6 C2
Dodford Nhants 84 B3
Dodford Worcs 97 L8
Dodington S Glos 45 L3
Dodington Somset 30 A3
Dodleston Ches W 129 J7
Dodscott Devon 27 K7
Dodside E Rens 208 E8
Dod's Leigh Staffs 115 G4
Dodworth Barns 141 M6
Dodworth Bottom Barns 141 M7
Dodworth Green Barns 141 M6
Doe Bank Birm 98 E4
Doe Lea Derbys 133 J6
Dogdyke Lincs 136 D8
Dogley Lane Kirk 141 J5
Dogmersfield Hants 49 J8
Dogridge Wilts 47 G2
Dogsthorpe C Pete 102 D3
Dog Village Devon 14 A3
Dolanog Powys 94 C1
Dolau Powys 79 G2
Dolaucothi Carmth 77 J7
Dolbenmaen Gwynd 109 J3
Doley Staffs 114 A5
Dolfach Powys 93 K3
Dol-for Powys 93 H2
Dolfor Powys 94 D6
Dolgarrog Conwy 126 F6
Dolgellau Gwynd 110 D7
Dolgoch Gwynd 92 E3
Dol-gran Carmth 58 D2
Doll Highld 273 L7
Dollar Clacks 221 G7
Dollarfield Clacks 221 G7
Dolley Green Powys 79 K2
Dollwen Cerdgn 92 E7
Dolphin Flints 128 E5
Dolphinholme Lancs 147 K5
Dolphinton S Lans 199 J4
Dolton Devon 27 K8
Dolwen Conwy 127 H5
Dolwyddelan Conwy 110 D1
Dolybont Cerdgn 92 D5
Dolyhir Powys 79 J4
Domgay Powys 112 D7
Donaldson's Lodge Nthumb 202 D5
Doncaster Donc 142 F7
Doncaster Carr Donc 142 F7
Donhead St Andrew Wilts 32 F6
Donhead St Mary Wilts 32 F6
Donibristle Fife 211 G1
Doniford Somset 29 K2
Donington Lincs 119 H4
Donington on Bain Lincs 136 D3
Donington Southing Lincs 119 G5
Donisthorpe Leics 99 J1
Donkey Street Kent 25 L1
Donkey Town Surrey 50 B6
Donnington Gloucs 65 J2
Donnington Herefs 81 G8
Donnington Shrops 96 D2
Donnington W Berk 48 C5
Donnington W Susx 20 D6
Donnington Wrekin 113 M8
Donnington Wood Wrekin 97 G1
Donyatt Somset 30 E8
Doomsday Green W Susx 37 J5
Doonfoot S Ayrs 196 C7
Dorback Lodge Highld 253 L8
Dorchester Dorset 16 D4
Dorchester Oxon 66 E8
Dordon Warwks 99 H3
Dore Sheff 132 F3
Dores Highld 251 G5
Dorking Surrey 37 J1
Dorking Tye Suffk 89 J7
Dormans Land Surrey 38 B5
Dormans Park Surrey 38 B5
Dormington Herefs 80 D7
Dormston Worcs 82 A4
Dorn Gloucs 82 F8
Dorney Bucks 50 B3
Dornie Highld 248 D6
Dornoch Highld 264 B2
Dornock D & G 177 H5
Dorrery Highld 279 J5
Dorridge Solhll 98 F8
Dorrington Lincs 118 E1
Dorrington Shrops 96 B3
Dorrington Shrops 114 A3
Dorsington Warwks 82 D5
Dorstone Herefs 79 K7
Dorton Bucks 67 G4
Dosthill Staffs 99 G3
Dothan IoA 124 F5
Dottery Dorset 15 K4
Doublebois Cnwll 5 L2
Doughton Gloucs 46 C1
Douglas IoM 154 e6
Douglas S Lans 198 D7
Douglas and Angus C Dund 234 C8
Douglas Borough Crematorium IoM 154 e6
Douglas Pier Ag & B 217 K7
Douglastown Angus 234 B6
Douglas Water S Lans 198 E6
Douglas West S Lans 198 D7
Doulting Somset 31 L2
Dounby Ork 275 b4
Doune Highld 272 B7
Doune Stirlg 220 C6
Dounepark S Ayrs 182 F3
Dounie Highld 263 G2
Dousland Devon 7 G1
Dovaston Shrops 112 E7
Dove Green Notts 116 D1
Dove Holes Derbys 131 L4
Dovenby Cumb 164 E4
Dover Kent 41 K7
Dover Wigan 139 J7

Dovercourt Essex 73 K1
Doverdale Worcs 81 K2
Doveridge Derbys 115 J5
Doversgreen Surrey 37 L1
Dowally P & K 232 F5
Dowbridge Lancs 138 E2
Dowdeswell Gloucs 64 E3
Dowlais Myr Td 61 G5
Dowland Devon 12 D1
Dowlish Ford Somset 30 E8
Dowlish Wake Somset 30 E8
Down Ampney Gloucs 65 G7
Downderry Cnwll 6 C4
Downe Gt Lon 51 L6
Downend Gloucs 64 B7
Downend IoW 19 J6
Downend S Glos 45 K3
Downend W Berk 48 C4
Downfield C Dund 223 G1
Downgate Cnwll 11 K8
Downgate Cnwll 11 L8
Downham Essex 71 H7
Downham Gt Lon 51 K4
Downham Lancs 148 D7
Downham Market Norfk 104 C3
Down Hatherley Gloucs 64 C3
Downhead Somset 31 J6
Downhead Somset 32 A2
Downhill Cnwll 4 D1
Downhill P & K 221 K1
Downholland Cross Lancs 138 D6
Downholme N York 159 K3
Downicarey Devon 11 M4
Downies Abers 245 K4
Downing Flints 128 D4
Downley Bucks 67 K8
Down St Mary Devon 13 H2
Downs Crematorium Br & H 22 E6
Downside Somset 31 K2
Downside Somset 31 L1
Downside Surrey 50 E7
Down Thomas Devon 6 F5
Downton Hants 18 D5
Downton Wilts 33 L6
Dowsby Lincs 118 F5
Dowsdale Lincs 102 F2
Doxey Staffs 114 D6
Doxford Nthumb 191 H2
Doynton S Glos 45 L4
Draethen Caerph 43 K4
Draffan S Lans 198 C4
Dragonby N Linc 143 M5
Dragons Green W Susx 37 H6
Drakeholes Notts 134 E2
Drakelow Worcs 97 J7
Drakemyre N Ayrs 196 B1
Drakes Broughton Worcs 81 L5
Drakewalls Cnwll 12 B8
Draughton N York 149 J5
Draughton Nhants 101 G8
Drax N York 143 H3
Drax Hales N York 143 H3
Draycote Warwks 83 K1
Draycot Foliat Swindn 47 J3
Draycott Derbys 116 D5
Draycott Gloucs 82 E8
Draycott Shrops 97 H5
Draycott Somset 31 G1
Draycott Somset 31 J6
Draycott Worcs 81 K5
Draycott in the Clay Staffs 115 J6
Draycott in the Moors Staffs 114 F3
Drayford Devon 28 D8
Drayton C Port 19 L3
Drayton Leics 101 H5
Drayton Lincs 119 H4
Drayton Norfk 106 D1
Drayton Oxon 66 C8
Drayton Oxon 83 K7
Drayton Somset 30 F6
Drayton Worcs 97 K8
Drayton Bassett Staffs 99 G3
Drayton Beauchamp Bucks 67 L5
Drayton Parslow Bucks 67 K2
Drayton St Leonard Oxon 66 E7
Drebley N York 149 J4
Dreemskerry IoM 154 g4
Dreen Hill Pembks 54 F4
Drefach Carmth 58 F6
Drefach Carmth 76 C7
Drefach Cerdgn 76 F6
Drefelin Carmth 76 C7
Dreghorn N Ayrs 196 C3
Drellingore Kent 41 H7
Drem E Loth 212 B3
Dresden C Stke 114 E3
Drewsteignton Devon 13 H4
Driby Lincs 137 G5
Driffield E R Yk 152 F4
Driffield Gloucs 65 G7
Driffield Cross Roads Gloucs 64 F7
Drift Cnwll 2 C5
Drigg Cumb 155 K3
Drighlington Leeds 141 K2
Drimnin Highld 227 G2
Drimpton Dorset 15 K2
Drimsallie Highld 238 F7
Dringhouses C York 151 J6
Drinkstone Suffk 89 J3
Drinkstone Green Suffk 89 J3
Drive End Dorset 16 B1
Driver's End Herts 69 G3
Drointon Staffs 115 G6
Droitwich Worcs 81 K3
Dron P & K 221 L4
Dronfield Derbys 133 G4
Dronfield Woodhouse Derbys 133 G4
Drongan E Ayrs 196 E7
Dronley Angus 234 A8
Droop Dorset 16 E1
Dropping Well Rothm 133 H1
Droxford Hants 35 J7
Droylsden Tamesd 140 D8
Druid Denbgs 111 K3
Druidston Pembks 54 E3
Druimarbin Highld 229 H1
Druimavuic Ag & B 229 G6
Druimdrishaig Ag & B 206 A5
Druimindarroch Highld 237 K4
Drum Ag & B 206 E4
Drum P & K 221 J7
Drumalbin S Lans 198 F5
Drumbeg Highld 270 F2
Drumblade Abers 255 M4
Drumbreddon D & G 172 D6
Drumbuie Highld 248 B5
Drumburgh Cumb 177 J7
Drumburn D & G 175 L4
Drumchapel C Glas 208 E5
Drumchastle P & K 231 J4
Drumclog S Lans 197 J3
Drumeldrie Fife 223 G6
Drumelzier Border 199 K6
Drumfearn Highld 247 L5
Drumfrennie Abers 244 F4
Drumgley Angus 234 C5
Drumguish Highld 241 L3
Drumin Moray 254 D5
Drumjohn D & G 184 E3
Drumlamford S Ayrs 183 H7
Drumlasie Abers 244 E2
Drumleaning Cumb 177 J8
Drumlemble Ag & B 192 D4
Drumlithie Abers 245 H7
Drummoddie D & G 173 K6
Drummore D & G 172 E7
Drummuir Moray 255 H3
Drumnadrochit Highld 250 E5
Drumnaglaur D & G 172 E7
Drumnagorrach Moray 267 L5
Drumpark D & G 185 L7
Drumrunie Lodge Highld 271 G7
Drumshang S Ayrs 195 L8
Drumuie Highld 259 G7
Drumuillie Highld 253 H7
Drumvaich Stirlg 220 B6
Drunzie P & K 221 L5
Druridge Nthumb 191 K7
Drury Flints 129 G6
Drybeck Cumb 166 F7
Drybridge Moray 267 J4
Drybridge N Ayrs 196 D4
Drybrook Gloucs 63 J4
Dryburgh Border 201 J6
Dry Doddington Lincs 117 M2
Dry Drayton Cambs 87 H3
Drymen Stirlg 208 E1
Drymuir Abers 257 G3
Drynoch Highld 246 F2
Dry Sandford Oxon 66 C7
Dryslwyn Carmth 59 G5
Dry Street Essex 52 E2
Dryton Shrops 96 D2
Dubford Abers 268 E3
Dublin Suffk 90 E1
Duchally Highld 271 L4
Duck End Bed 85 L6
Duck End Cambs 86 E2
Duck End Essex 71 G2
Duck End Essex 88 D8
Duckend Green Essex 71 H3
Duckington Ches W 113 H1
Ducklington Oxon 65 M5
Duck's Cross Bed 86 C4
Duddenhoe End Essex 87 J7
Duddingston C Edin 211 J4
Duddington Nhants 101 L3
Duddlestone Somset 30 C6
Duddleswell E Susx 38 C7
Duddlewick Shrops 96 F6
Duddo Nthumb 202 E4
Duddon Ches W 129 L6
Duddon Bridge Cumb 156 B5
Duddon Common Ches W 129 M6
Dudleston Shrops 112 E4
Dudleston Heath Shrops 112 E4
Dudley Dudley 97 L5
Dudley N Tyne 181 G4
Dudley Hill C Brad 141 J2
Dudley Port Sandw 98 B5
Dudnill Shrops 96 E8
Dudsbury Dorset 17 L3
Dudswell Herts 68 B5
Duffield Derbys 116 B3
Duffryn Neath 42 C3
Dufftown Moray 255 G4
Duffus Moray 266 D3
Dufton Cumb 166 F5
Duggleby N York 152 D2
Duirinish Highld 248 C5
Duisdalemore Highld 247 L6
Duisky Highld 239 G8
Dukestown Blae G 61 J5
Duke Street Suffk 90 C6
Dukinfield Tamesd 140 E8
Dukinfield Crematorium Tamesd 140 E8
Dulas IoA 125 H2
Dulcote Somset 31 J2
Dulford Devon 14 C2
Dull P & K 232 B5
Dullatur N Lans 209 K4
Dullingham Cambs 88 C4
Dullingham Ley Cambs 88 C4
Dulnain Bridge Highld 253 J6
Duloe Bed 86 D3
Duloe Cnwll 5 M3
Dulverton Somset 29 G5
Dulwich Gt Lon 51 J4
Dumbarton W Duns 208 C4
Dumbleton Gloucs 82 B8
Dumfries D & G 176 C4
Dumgoyne Stirlg 208 E2
Dummer Hants 35 J2
Dumpton Kent 41 L2
Dun Angus 235 G3
Dunalastair P & K 231 K4
Dunan Ag & B 207 J5
Dunan Highld 247 J3
Dunan P & K 230 E4
Dunaverty Ag & B 192 E6
Dunball Somset 30 D3
Dunbar E Loth 212 E3
Dunbeath Highld 275 G2
Dunbeg Ag & B 228 D8
Dunblane Stirlg 220 D7
Dunbog Fife 222 D4
Dunbridge Hants 34 D5
Duncanston Highld 263 G8
Duncanstone Abers 255 L6
Dunchideock Devon 13 K5
Dunchurch Warwks 83 L1
Duncote Nhants 84 C5
Duncow D & G 176 C2
Duncrievie P & K 221 L5
Duncton W Susx 20 F3
Dundee C Dund 223 G1
Dundee Crematorium C Dund 222 F1
Dundon Somset 31 G4
Dundonald S Ayrs 196 D4
Dundonnell Highld 261 J2
Dundraw Cumb 165 H1
Dundreggan Highld 240 B1
Dundrennan D & G 175 J5
Dundry N Som 45 H5
Dunecht Abers 245 G2
Dunfermline Fife 210 E2
Dunfermline Crematorium Fife 210 F2
Dunfield Gloucs 65 H7
Dunford Bridge Barns 141 J7
Dungate Kent 40 B3
Dungavel S Lans 197 J3
Dunge Wilts 46 C8
Dungworth Sheff 132 E2
Dunham Notts 135 G5
Dunham-on-the-Hill Ches W 129 L5
Dunhampstead Worcs 81 L3
Dunhampton Worcs 81 J2
Dunham Town Traffd 130 E2
Dunham Woodhouses Traffd 130 E2
Dunholme Lincs 135 L4
Dunino Fife 223 J5
Dunipace Falk 209 L2
Dunkeld P & K 232 F6
Dunkerton BaNES 45 L7
Dunkeswell Devon 14 D1
Dunkeswick N York 150 D6
Dunkirk Ches W 129 J5
Dunkirk Kent 40 E3
Dunkirk S Glos 46 A2
Dunkirk Wilts 46 E6
Dunk's Green Kent 38 F3
Dunlappie Angus 234 F2
Dunley Hants 48 C8
Dunley Worcs 81 H2
Dunlop E Ayrs 196 E1
Dunmaglass Highld 251 G7
Dunmere Cnwll 5 H1
Dunmore Falk 210 A1
Dunnet Highld 280 B2
Dunnichen Angus 234 D5
Dunning P & K 221 J4
Dunnington C York 151 L5
Dunnington E R Yk 153 J5
Dunnington Warwks 82 C4
Dunnockshaw Lancs 140 B2
Dunn Street Kent 53 G6
Dunoon Ag & B 207 K4
Dunphail Moray 253 J2
Dunragit D & G 172 E3
Duns Border 202 B2
Dunsa Derbys 132 E5
Dunsby Lincs 118 E6
Dunscar Bolton 139 L5
Dunscore D & G 185 L6
Dunscroft Donc 143 G6
Dunsdale R & Cl 170 E6
Dunsden Green Oxon 49 H3
Dunsdon Devon 11 K1
Dunsfold Surrey 36 F4
Dunsford Devon 13 J5
Dunshalt Fife 222 D5
Dunshillock Abers 269 H6
Dunsill Notts 133 J7
Dunsley N York 171 K8
Dunsley Staffs 97 J6
Dunsmore Bucks 67 L6
Dunsop Bridge Lancs 148 B6
Dunstable C Beds 68 C3
Dunstall Staffs 115 K7
Dunstall Common Worcs 81 K6
Dunstall Green Suffk 88 E3
Dunstan Nthumb 191 K2
Dunstan Steads Nthumb 191 J2
Dunster Somset 29 H2
Duns Tew Oxon 66 C2
Dunston Gatesd 180 F6
Dunston Lincs 135 L7
Dunston Norfk 106 E3
Dunston Staffs 114 E8
Dunstone Devon 7 H4
Dunstone Devon 13 G7
Dunston Heath Staffs 114 E8
Dunsville Donc 143 G6
Dunswell E R Yk 144 D1
Dunsyre S Lans 199 J3
Dunterton Devon 11 M6
Dunthrop Oxon 65 M2
Duntisbourne Abbots Gloucs 64 E5
Duntisbourne Leer Gloucs 64 E5
Duntisbourne Rouse Gloucs 64 E6
Duntish Dorset 16 D2
Duntocher W Duns 208 E4
Dunton Bucks 67 K2
Dunton C Beds 86 E6
Dunton Norfk 121 J5
Dunton Bassett Leics 100 C5
Dunton Green Kent 38 D2
Dunton Wayletts Essex 52 E1
Duntulm Highld 259 G2
Dunure S Ayrs 195 L7
Dunvant Swans 57 G6
Dunvegan Highld 258 C7
Dunwich Suffk 91 L1
Dunwood Staffs 131 J8
Durdar Cumb 177 L8
Durgan Cnwll 3 K5
Durham Dur 169 H2
Durham Crematorium Dur 169 H3
Durisdeer D & G 186 C5
Durisdeermill D & G 186 C5
Durkar Wakefd 141 M4
Durleigh Somset 30 C4
Durley Hants 35 G7
Durley Wilts 47 K6
Durley Street Hants 35 H7
Durlock Kent 41 J2
Durlock Kent 41 J4
Durlow Common Herefs 80 E7
Durn Rochdl 140 E4
Durness Highld 276 F3
Durno Abers 256 C6
Duror Highld 228 F4
Durran Ag & B 216 F5
Durrington W Susx 21 J6
Durrington Wilts 33 K2
Durris Abers 245 G4
Dursley Gloucs 63 M7
Dursley Cross Gloucs 63 K3

Durston Somset 30 D5
Durweston Dorset 17 G1
Duston Nhants 84 D8
Duthil Highld 253 H6
Dutlas Powys 94 F7
Duton Hill Essex 70 F2
Dutson Cnwll 11 L5
Dutton Ches W 130 B4
Duxford Cambs 87 K6
Duxford Oxon 66 A7
Dwygyfylchi Conwy 126 E4
Dwyran IoA 125 H6
Dyce C Aber 245 K1
Dyer's End Essex 88 E7
Dyfatty Carmth 56 E5
Dyffrydan Gwynd 110 D8
Dyffryn Brdgnd 42 C3
Dyffryn Myr Td 61 G6
Dyffryn V Glam 43 H7
Dyffryn Ardudwy Gwynd 109 K7
Dyffryn Castell Cerdgn 93 G7
Dyffryn Cellwen Neath 60 C5
Dyke Lincs 118 E7
Dyke Moray 264 F8
Dykehead Angus 233 K4
Dykehead Angus 234 B3
Dykehead N Lans 210 A7
Dykehead Stirlg 219 K7
Dykelands Abers 235 H2
Dykends Angus 233 K4
Dykeside Abers 256 C3
Dylife Powys 93 J4
Dymchurch Kent 25 L1
Dymock Gloucs 63 K1
Dyrham S Glos 45 L4
Dysart Fife 222 E8
Dyserth Denbgs 128 C4

E

Eachway Worcs 98 C8
Eachwick Nthumb 180 D4
Eagland Hill Lancs 147 H6
Eagle Lincs 135 H6
Eagle Barnsdale Lincs 135 H6
Eagle Moor Lincs 135 H6
Eaglescliffe S on T 169 L7
Eaglesfield Cumb 164 E5
Eaglesfield D & G 177 H4
Eaglesham E Rens 208 F8
Eagley Bolton 139 L5
Eairy IoM 154 d6
Eakring Notts 134 D7
Ealand N Linc 143 K5
Ealing Gt Lon 50 F3
Eals Nthumb 178 F7
Eamont Bridge Cumb 166 C5
Earby Lancs 148 F6
Earcroft Bl w D 139 K3
Eardington Shrops 97 G5
Eardisland Herefs 80 A4
Eardisley Herefs 79 K5
Eardiston Shrops 112 E6
Eardiston Worcs 80 F2
Earith Cambs 103 H8
Earle Nthumb 202 F7
Earlestown St Hel 130 B1
Earley Wokham 49 H4
Earlham Norfk 106 D2
Earlham Crematorium Norfk 106 E2
Earlish Highld 258 F4
Earls Barton Nhants 85 G3
Earls Colne Essex 71 L1
Earls Common Worcs 81 M3
Earl's Croome Worcs 81 K6
Earlsditton Shrops 96 E8
Earlsdon Covtry 99 J7
Earl's Down E Susx 23 L3
Earlsferry Fife 223 H7
Earlsfield Gt Lon 51 H4
Earlsford Abers 256 E5
Earl's Green Suffk 90 B2
Earlsheaton Kirk 141 L3
Earl Shilton Leics 100 A4
Earl Soham Suffk 90 F3
Earl Sterndale Derbys 132 B6
Earlston Border 201 J5
Earlston E Ayrs 196 D4
Earl Stonham Suffk 90 D3
Earlswood Surrey 37 L1
Earlswood Warwks 98 E8
Earlswood Common Mons 62 F8
Earnley W Susx 20 D7
Earnshaw Bridge Lancs 139 G3
Earsdon N Tyne 181 H4
Earsdon Nthumb 191 J7
Earsham Norfk 107 G5
Earswick C York 151 K4
Eartham W Susx 20 F5
Earthcott S Glos 45 K2
Easby N York 161 J1
Easdale Ag & B 215 L1
Easebourne W Susx 36 D6
Easenhall Warwks 100 A7
Eashing Surrey 36 E2
Easington Bucks 67 G5
Easington Dur 169 L2
Easington E R Yk 145 K4
Easington Nthumb 203 J6
Easington Oxon 67 G7
Easington R & Cl 171 H7
Easington Colliery Dur 169 L2
Easington Lane Sundld 169 K2
Easingwold N York 151 H2
Easole Street Kent 41 H5
Eassie and Nevay Angus 233 M6
East Aberthaw V Glam 42 F8
East Allington Devon 7 M5
East Anstey Devon 28 F5
East Anton Hants 34 E1
East Appleton N York 160 C3
East Ashey IoW 19 K6
East Ashling W Susx 20 D5
East Aston Hants 34 F2
East Ayton N York 163 H5
East Balsdon Cnwll 11 K3
East Bank Blae G 61 K6
East Barkwith Lincs 136 C3
East Barming Kent 39 H3
East Barnby N York 171 J8
East Barnet Gt Lon 69 H8
East Barns E Loth 212 F4
East Barsham Norfk 121 K5
East Beckham Norfk 122 D4
East Bedfont Gt Lon 50 D4
East Bergholt Suffk 90 C8
East Bierley Kirk 141 J2
East Bilney Norfk 121 L7
East Blatchington E Susx 23 H7
East Bloxworth Dorset 17 H4
East Boldon S Tyne 181 J6
East Boldre Hants 18 F4
East Bolton Nthumb 191 G3
Eastbourne Darltn 169 J7
Eastbourne E Susx 23 K7
Eastbourne Crematorium E Susx 23 L6
East Bower Somset 30 D3
East Bradenham Norfk 105 J2
East Brent Somset 44 D8
Eastbridge Suffk 91 K2
East Bridgford Notts 117 J3
East Briscoe Dur 168 B6
Eastbrook V Glam 43 J7
East Buckland Devon 28 B4
East Budleigh Devon 14 C5
Eastburn C Brad 149 J7
Eastburn E R Yk 152 F4
East Burnham Bucks 50 B2
East Burton Dorset 16 F5
Eastbury Herts 68 E8
Eastbury W Berk 47 M3
East Butsfield Dur 168 E2
East Butterwick N Linc 143 L6
Eastby N York 149 J5
East Calder W Loth 210 E5
East Carleton Norfk 106 D3
East Carlton Leeds 150 B7
East Carlton Nhants 101 H5
East Chaldon (Chaldon Herring) Dorset 16 F6
East Challow Oxon 48 A1
East Charleton Devon 7 L6
East Chelborough Dorset 16 A2
East Chiltington E Susx 22 F4
East Chinnock Somset 31 H8
East Chisenbury Wilts 47 H8
East Cholderton Hants 34 C2
Eastchurch Kent 53 L5
East Clandon Surrey 50 D8
East Claydon Bucks 67 H2
East Clevedon N Som 44 E5
East Coker Somset 31 J8
Eastcombe Gloucs 64 C6
Eastcombe Somset 29 L4
East Compton Somset 31 K3
East Cornworthy Devon 8 C4
East Cote Cumb 176 F7
Eastcote Gt Lon 50 E1
Eastcote Nhants 84 D4
Eastcote Solhll 99 G7
Eastcott Cnwll 26 D7
Eastcott Wilts 46 F7
East Cottingwith E R Yk 151 L7
Eastcourt Wilts 47 K6
Eastcourt Wilts 64 E8
East Cowes IoW 19 H4
East Cowick E R Yk 143 G4
East Cowton N York 160 D2
East Cramlington Nthumb 181 G4
East Cranmore Somset 31 L2
East Creech Dorset 17 H6
East Curthwaite Cumb 165 K1
East Dean E Susx 23 J7
East Dean Gloucs 63 K3
East Dean Hants 34 C5
East Dean W Susx 20 E4
East Devon Crematorium Devon 14 B3
Eastdown Devon 8 B5
East Down Devon 27 L3
East Drayton Notts 134 F4
East Dulwich Gt Lon 51 J4
East Dundry N Som 45 H5
East Ella C KuH 144 D2
East End Bed 86 C4
East End C Beds 85 J6
East End E R Yk 145 G2
East End E R Yk 145 H2
East End Essex 70 B5
Eastend Essex 72 D8
East End Hants 18 E4
East End Hants 48 B6
East End Herts 70 C2
East End Kent 39 L6
East End Kent 53 L4
East End M Keyn 85 J6
East End N Som 44 F5
East End Oxon 66 B4
East End Somset 31 L2
East End Suffk 90 C8
Easter Balmoral Abers 243 J5
Easter Compton S Glos 45 H2
Easter Dalziel Highld 252 E2
Eastergate W Susx 20 F6
Easterhouse C Glas 209 J6
Easter Howgate Mdloth 211 H6
Easter Kinkell Highld 263 G8
Easter Moniack Highld 250 F3
Eastern Green Covtry 99 H7
Easter Ord Abers 245 J3
Easter Pitkierie Fife 223 K6
Easter Skeld Shet 281 d6
Easter Softlaw Border 202 B6
Easterton Wilts 46 F8
Eastertown Somset 44 D8
East Everleigh Wilts 47 J8
East Farleigh Kent 39 J3
East Farndon Nhants 100 F6
East Ferry Lincs 143 K7
Eastfield N Lans 210 A6
Eastfield N York 163 J6
East Firsby Lincs 135 K3
East Fortune E Loth 212 C3
East Garforth Leeds 142 C1
East Garston W Berk 47 M4
Eastgate Dur 168 B3
Eastgate Lincs 118 F7
Eastgate Norfk 122 C7
East Ginge Oxon 48 C2
East Goscote Leics 100 E1
East Grafton Wilts 47 K6
East Green Suffk 91 J2
East Grimstead Wilts 34 B5
East Grinstead W Susx 38 B5
East Guldeford E Susx 25 H3
East Haddon Nhants 84 C2
East Hagbourne Oxon 48 D1
East Halton N Linc 144 E4
East Ham Gt Lon 51 L2
Eastham Wirral 129 H4
Eastham Ferry Wirral 129 J3
Easthampstead Park Crematorium Br For 49 K5
Easthampton Herefs 80 A3
East Hanney Oxon 66 B8
East Hanningfield Essex 71 J6
East Hardwick Wakefd 142 D4
East Harling Norfk 105 K6
East Harlsey N York 160 F3
East Harnham Wilts 33 K5
East Harptree BaNES 45 H7
East Hartburn S on T 169 L7
East Hartford Nthumb 181 G3
East Harting W Susx 20 C3
East Hatch Wilts 32 F5
East Hatley Cambs 86 F5
East Hauxwell N York 159 L4
East Haven Angus 234 F8
Eastheath Wokham 49 J5
East Heckington Lincs 119 G3
East Hedleyhope Dur 168 F3
East Helmsdale Highld 274 D5
East Hendred Oxon 48 C1
East Heslerton N York 163 G7
East Hewish N Som 44 E6
East Hoathly E Susx 23 H4
East Holme Dorset 17 H5
Easthope Shrops 96 D4
Easthorpe Essex 72 C3
Easthorpe Notts 117 J1
East Horrington Somset 31 J2
East Horsley Surrey 50 E8
East Horton Nthumb 203 G7
East Howe Bmouth 17 L3
East Huntington C York 151 K5
East Huntspill Somset 30 E2
East Hyde C Beds 68 E4
East Ilkerton Devon 28 C2
East Ilsley W Berk 48 D3
Eastington Devon 13 H1
Eastington Gloucs 63 M6
Eastington Gloucs 65 H4
East Keal Lincs 137 G7
East Kennett Wilts 47 G5
East Keswick Leeds 150 E7
East Kilbride S Lans 209 H8
East Kimber Devon 12 C3
East Kirkby Lincs 136 F7
East Knighton Dorset 16 F5
East Knowstone Devon 28 E6
East Knoyle Wilts 32 E5
East Lambrook Somset 31 G7
East Lancashire Crematorium Bury 140 A6
Eastlands D & G 185 K8
East Langdon Kent 41 K6
East Langton Leics 100 F5
East Lavant W Susx 20 D5
East Lavington W Susx 20 F4
East Layton N York 159 L1
Eastleach Martin Gloucs 65 J6
Eastleach Turville Gloucs 65 J6
East Leake Notts 116 F6
East Learmouth Nthumb 202 D5
East Leigh Devon 7 K4
East Leigh Devon 7 L3
East Leigh Devon 13 G2
Eastleigh Devon 27 J5
Eastleigh Hants 34 F7
East Lexham Norfk 121 J8
Eastling Kent 40 C4
East Linton E Loth 212 D3
East Liss Hants 36 A5
East Lockinge Oxon 48 B2
East London Crematorium Gt Lon 51 L2
East Lound N Linc 143 K7
East Lulworth Dorset 17 G6
East Lutton N York 152 E2
East Lydeard Somset 30 B5
East Lydford Somset 31 J4
East Malling Kent 39 H2
East Malling Heath Kent 39 H2
East Marden W Susx 20 C4
East Markham Notts 134 E5
East Martin Hants 33 J7
East Marton N York 148 F5
East Meon Hants 35 L6
East Mere Devon 29 H7
East Mersea Essex 72 F4
East Molesey Surrey 50 F5
Eastmoor Norfk 104 E3
East Morden Dorset 17 H4
East Morton C Brad 149 K7
East Morton D & G 186 C6
East Ness N York 162 B7
East Newton E R Yk 153 L8
Eastney C Port 19 L4
Eastnor Herefs 81 G7
East Norton Leics 101 G3
Eastoft N Linc 143 K4
East Ogwell Devon 13 J8
Easton Cambs 86 C1
Easton Cumb 177 J7
Easton Devon 13 G5
Easton Dorset 16 D8
Easton Hants 35 G4
Easton Lincs 118 B6
Easton Norfk 106 C1
Easton Somset 31 H2
Easton Suffk 91 G3
Easton W Berk 48 B4
Easton Wilts 46 C5
Easton Grey Wilts 46 C2
Easton-in-Gordano N Som 45 G4
Easton Maudit Nhants 85 H3
Easton-on-the-Hill Nhants 101 M3
Easton Royal Wilts 47 J7
East Orchard Dorset 32 D7
East Ord Nthumb 202 F3
East Panson Devon 11 L4
East Parley Dorset 17 M3
East Peckham Kent 39 G4
East Pennar Pembks 54 F6
East Pennard Somset 31 K3
East Perry Cambs 86 C2
East Portlemouth Devon 7 L7
East Prawle Devon 8 A7

East Preston W Susx 21 J6
East Pulham Dorset 16 D1
East Putford Devon 26 F7
East Quantoxhead Somset 29 L2
East Rainham Medway 53 H5
East Rainton Sundld 169 J1
East Ravendale NE Lin 145 G7
East Raynham Norfk 121 J6
Eastrea Cambs 102 F4
East Riding Crematorium E R Yk 152 F2
Eastriggs D & G 177 H5
East Rigton Leeds 150 E7
Eastrington E R Yk 143 K2
East Rolstone N Som 44 E6
Eastrop Swindn 65 J8
East Rounton N York 160 F2
East Rudham Norfk 121 H6
East Runton Norfk 122 D3
East Ruston Norfk 123 G6
Eastry Kent 41 J4
East Saltoun E Loth 212 B5
Eastshaw W Susx 36 C6
East Sheen Gt Lon 51 G4
East Shefford W Berk 48 A4
East Sleekburn Nthumb 181 G2
East Somerton Norfk 123 K7
East Stockwith Lincs 134 F1
East Stoke Dorset 17 G5
East Stoke Notts 117 K2
East Stour Dorset 32 D6
East Stourmouth Kent 41 H3
East Stowford Devon 27 L5
East Stratton Hants 35 H3
East Studdal Kent 41 J5
East Sutton Kent 39 L3
East Taphouse Cnwll 5 L2
East-the-Water Devon 27 H5
East Thirston Nthumb 191 J6
East Tilbury Thurr 52 E3
East Tisted Hants 35 L4
East Torrington Lincs 136 B3
East Tuddenham Norfk 106 B1
East Tytherley Hants 34 C5
East Tytherton Wilts 46 D4
East Village Devon 13 K2
Eastville Bristl 45 J4
Eastville Lincs 137 H8
East Wall Shrops 96 C4
East Walton Norfk 121 G8
East Water Somset 31 J1
East Week Devon 12 F4
Eastwell Leics 117 K6
East Wellow Hants 34 C6
East Wemyss Fife 222 F7
East Whitburn W Loth 210 C6
Eastwick Herts 70 B5
East Wickham Gt Lon 51 M3
East Williamston Pembks 55 J6
East Winch Norfk 120 F8
East Winterslow Wilts 34 B4
East Wittering W Susx 20 C7
East Witton N York 159 L5
Eastwood Notts 116 D2
Eastwood Sthend 53 H2
East Woodburn Nthumb 179 L2
Eastwood End Cambs 103 J5
East Woodhay Hants 48 B6
East Woodlands Somset 32 C2
East Worldham Hants 35 M3
East Wretham Norfk 105 J5
East Youlstone Devon 26 D7
Eathorpe Warwks 83 J2
Eaton Ches E 131 G6
Eaton Ches W 130 B7
Eaton Leics 117 L5
Eaton Norfk 106 E2
Eaton Notts 134 E4
Eaton Oxon 66 C6
Eaton Shrops 95 J5
Eaton Shrops 96 B5
Eaton Bishop Herefs 80 B7
Eaton Bray C Beds 68 B3
Eaton Constantine Shrops 96 D2
Eaton Ford Cambs 86 D3
Eaton Green C Beds 68 B3
Eaton Hastings Oxon 65 K7
Eaton Mascott Shrops 96 C2
Eaton Socon Cambs 86 D3
Eaton upon Tern Shrops 113 L7
Eaves Brow Warrtn 130 C1
Eaves Green Solhll 99 H6
Ebberston N York 162 F6
Ebbesborne Wake Wilts 33 G6
Ebbw Vale Blae G 61 J5
Ebchester Dur 180 D7
Ebdon N Som 44 D6
Ebford Devon 14 A5
Ebley Gloucs 64 B6
Ebnal Ches W 113 H2
Ebnall Herefs 80 B3
Ebrington Gloucs 82 E7
Ebsworthy Devon 12 C4
Ecchinswell Hants 48 D7
Ecclaw Border 213 G5
Ecclefechan D & G 177 G4
Eccles Border 202 B5
Eccles Kent 52 F6
Eccles Salfd 140 A8
Ecclesall Sheff 132 F3
Eccles Crematorium Salfd 139 M8
Ecclesfield Sheff 133 G1
Eccles Green Herefs 79 L5
Eccleshall Staffs 114 C5
Eccleshill C Brad 149 M8
Ecclesmachan W Loth 210 E4
Eccles on Sea Norfk 123 H5
Eccles Road Norfk 105 L5
Eccleston Ches W 129 J7
Eccleston Lancs 139 G4
Eccleston St Hel 138 F8
Eccleston Green Lancs 139 G4
Echt Abers 245 G2
Eckford Border 201 L7
Eckington Derbys 133 H4
Eckington Worcs 81 L7
Ecton Nhants 84 F3
Ecton Staffs 132 B8
Edale Derbys 132 B3
Eday Ork 275 d3
Edburton W Susx 22 C5
Edderside Cumb 164 E2
Edderton Highld 263 J3
Eddington Kent 41 G2
Eddleston Border 200 B4
Eddlewood S Lans 209 J8
Edenbridge Kent 38 C4
Edenfield Lancs 140 B4
Edenhall Cumb 166 D4
Edenham Lincs 118 E7
Eden Mount Cumb 156 F7
Eden Park Gt Lon 51 K5
Edensor Derbys 132 E5
Edentaggart Ag & B 218 D8
Edenthorpe Donc 143 G6
Edern Gwynd 108 E4
Edgarley Somset 31 H3
Edgbaston Birm 98 D6
Edgcombe Cnwll 3 J4
Edgcott Bucks 67 G3
Edgcott Somset 28 E3
Edge Gloucs 64 B5
Edge Shrops 95 K2
Edgebolton Shrops 113 J7
Edge End Gloucs 63 H4
Edgefield Norfk 122 B5
Edgefield Green Norfk 122 B4
Edgefold Bolton 139 L6
Edge Green Ches W 113 H1
Edgehill Warwks 83 J5
Edgerley Shrops 112 E7
Edgerton Kirk 141 H4
Edgeside Lancs 140 C3
Edgeworth Gloucs 64 D6
Edgeworthy Devon 28 E8
Edginswell Torbay 8 C2
Edgiock Worcs 82 B3
Edgmond Wrekin 114 A7
Edgmond Marsh Wrekin 114 A7
Edgton Shrops 95 J6
Edgware Gt Lon 51 G1
Edgworth Bl w D 139 L4
Edinbane Highld 258 E6
Edinburgh C Edin 211 J4
Edingale Staffs 99 G1
Edingham D & G 175 L2
Edingley Notts 134 D8
Edingthorpe Norfk 123 G5
Edingthorpe Green Norfk 122 F5
Edington Border 202 D2
Edington Nthumb 180 E2
Edington Somset 30 F3
Edington Wilts 46 D8
Edington Burtle Somset 30 F2
Edingworth Somset 44 D8
Edistone Devon 26 D6
Edithmead Somset 30 E1
Edith Weston RutInd 101 K2
Edlesborough Bucks 68 B3
Edlingham Nthumb 191 G4
Edlington Lincs 136 D5
Edmond Castle Cumb 178 C7
Edmondsham Dorset 33 J8
Edmondsley Dur 169 G1
Edmondthorpe Leics 117 M8
Edmonton Cnwll 10 D8
Edmonton Gt Lon 69 J8
Edmundbyers Dur 168 C1
Ednam Border 202 A5
Ednaston Derbys 115 L3
Edradynate P & K 232 C5
Edrom Border 202 C2
Edstaston Shrops 113 H5
Edstone Warwks 82 E3
Edvin Loach Herefs 80 F3
Edwalton Notts 117 G4
Edwardstone Suffk 89 J6
Edwardsville Myr Td 43 G2
Edwinsford Carmth 59 H2
Edwinstowe Notts 134 C6
Edworth C Beds 86 E7
Edwyn Ralph Herefs 80 F4
Edzell Angus 234 F2
Edzell Woods Abers 234 F2
Efail-fach Neath 57 L6
Efail Isaf Rhondd 43 H5
Efailnewydd Gwynd 108 F4
Efail-Rhyd Powys 112 A6
Efailwen Carmth 75 K7
Efenechtyd Denbgs 128 D8
Effgill D & G 187 L7
Effingham Surrey 50 E8
Efflinch Staffs 115 K8
Efford Devon 13 K2
Efford Crematorium C Plym 6 F3
Egbury Hants 48 B8
Egdean W Susx 21 G3
Egerton Bolton 139 L5
Egerton Kent 40 B6
Egerton Forstal Kent 40 A6
Eggborough N York 142 E3
Eggbuckland C Plym 6 F3
Eggesford Devon 28 B8
Eggington C Beds 68 B2
Egginton Derbys 115 M6
Egglescliffe S on T 169 L7
Eggleston Dur 168 C6
Egham Surrey 50 C5
Egham Wick Surrey 50 B5
Egleton Rutlnd 101 J2
Eglingham Nthumb 191 G2
Egloshayle Cnwll 10 D8
Egloskerry Cnwll 11 K5
Eglwysbach Conwy 126 F5
Eglwys-Brewis V Glam 42 F7
Eglwys Cross Wrexhm 113 G3
Eglwys Fach Cerdgn 92 F4
Eglwyswrw Pembks 75 K4
Egmanton Notts 134 E6
Egremont Cumb 164 D8
Egremont Wirral 129 H1
Egton N York 162 E2
Egton Bridge N York 162 D2
Egypt Bucks 50 B2
Egypt Hants 34 F3
Eigg Highld 236 F3
Eight Ash Green Essex 72 D2
Eilanreach Highld 248 C8
Eisteddfa Gurig Cerdgn 93 H6
Elan Village Powys 78 C2
Elberton S Glos 45 J1
Elbridge W Susx 20 F6
Elburton C Plym 7 G4
Elcombe Swindn 47 H3
Elcot W Berk 48 B5
Eldernell Cambs 103 G4
Eldersfield Worcs 64 A1
Elderslie Rens 208 D6
Elder Street Essex 88 B8
Eldon Dur 169 G5
Eldwick C Brad 149 L7
Elfhill Abers 245 H6
Elford Nthumb 203 K7
Elford Staffs 98 F1
Elgin Moray 266 E4
Elgol Highld 247 H6
Elham Kent 41 G6
Elie Fife 223 J7
Elilaw Nthumb 190 D4
Elim IoA 124 F3
Eling Hants 18 F1
Elkesley Notts 134 D4
Elkstone Gloucs 64 D4
Ella Abers 268 B4
Ellacombe Torbay 8 D2
Elland Calder 141 H4
Elland Lower Edge Calder 141 H3
Ellary Ag & B 206 A4
Ellastone Staffs 115 J3
Ellel Lancs 147 J4
Ellemford Border 212 F7
Ellenabeich Ag & B 215 L1
Ellenborough Cumb 164 D3
Ellenbrook Salfd 139 L7
Ellenhall Staffs 114 C6
Ellen's Green Surrey 37 G4
Ellerbeck N York 160 F3
Ellerby N York 171 J7
Ellerdine Heath Wrekin 113 K7
Ellerhayes Devon 14 A2
Elleric Ag & B 229 G5
Ellerker E R Yk 144 A2
Ellers N York 149 H7
Ellerton E R Yk 151 L7
Ellerton N York 160 C3
Ellerton Shrops 113 M6
Ellesborough Bucks 67 K6
Ellesmere Shrops 112 F4
Ellesmere Port Ches W 129 J4
Ellingham Hants 18 A2
Ellingham Norfk 107 H5
Ellingham Nthumb 203 K8
Ellingstring N York 159 M6
Ellington Cambs 86 D1
Ellington Nthumb 191 K7
Ellington Thorpe Cambs 86 D1
Elliots Green Somset 32 D2
Ellisfield Hants 35 K2
Ellishader Highld 259 H3
Ellistown Leics 99 L1
Ellon Abers 257 H5
Ellonby Cumb 166 A4
Ellough Suffk 107 J6
Elloughton E R Yk 144 B2
Ellwood Gloucs 63 H5
Elm Cambs 103 K2
Elmbridge Worcs 81 K2
Elmdon Essex 87 J7
Elmdon Solhll 98 F6
Elmdon Heath Solhll 98 F7
Elmer W Susx 21 G6
Elmers End Gt Lon 51 K5
Elmer's Green Lancs 139 G6
Elmesthorpe Leics 100 A4
Elm Green Essex 71 J6
Elmhurst Staffs 98 E1
Elmley Castle Worcs 82 A7
Elmley Lovett Worcs 81 K1
Elmore Gloucs 64 A4
Elmore Back Gloucs 63 M4
Elm Park Gt Lon 52 B2
Elmscott Devon 26 D6
Elmsett Suffk 90 C6
Elms Green Worcs 81 G2
Elmstead Heath Essex 72 F3
Elmstead Market Essex 72 F2
Elmstead Row Essex 72 F3
Elmsted Kent 40 F6
Elmstone Kent 41 H3
Elmstone Hardwicke Gloucs 64 D2
Elmswell E R Yk 152 F4
Elmswell Suffk 89 K2
Elmton Derbys 133 K5
Elphin Highld 271 H6
Elphinstone E Loth 211 L5
Elrick Abers 245 H2
Elrig D & G 173 J5
Elrington Nthumb 179 K6
Elsdon Nthumb 190 C7
Elsecar Barns 142 B7
Elsenham Essex 70 D2
Elsfield Oxon 66 D5
Elsham N Linc 144 C5
Elsing Norfk 122 B8
Elslack N York 149 G6
Elson Hants 19 K3
Elson Shrops 112 F4
Elsrickle S Lans 199 J4
Elstead Surrey 36 D2
Elsted W Susx 20 D3
Elsthorpe Lincs 118 E6
Elstob Dur 169 J6
Elston Lancs 139 J1
Elston Notts 117 K2
Elston Wilts 33 J2
Elstone Devon 28 B7
Elstow Bed 85 L6
Elstree Herts 68 F8
Elstronwick E R Yk 145 G1
Elswick Lancs 147 H8
Elswick N u Ty 180 F6
Elsworth Cambs 87 G3
Elterwater Cumb 156 D2
Eltham Gt Lon 51 L4
Eltham Crematorium Gt Lon 51 L4
Eltisley Cambs 86 F3
Elton Bury 140 B5
Elton Cambs 102 B4
Elton Ches W 129 K4
Elton Derbys 132 D7
Elton Gloucs 63 K4
Elton Herefs 80 B1
Elton Notts 117 K4
Elton S on T 169 L7
Elton Green Ches W 129 K5
Eltringham Nthumb 180 C6
Elvanfoot S Lans 186 E3
Elvaston Derbys 116 C5
Elveden Suffk 105 G7
Elvetham Heath Hants 49 K7

Elvingston E Loth 212 A4
Elvington C York 151 L6
Elvington Kent 41 J5
Elwell Devon 28 B4
Elwick Hartpl 170 B4
Elwick Nthumb 203 J5
Elworth Ches E 130 E7
Elworthy Somset 29 K4
Ely Cambs 103 L7
Ely Cardif 43 J6
Emberton M Keyn 85 H5
Embleton Cumb 165 G4
Embleton Dur 169 L5
Embleton Nthumb 191 J2
Embo Highld 264 C1
Emborough Somset 31 K1
Embo Street Highld 264 C2
Embsay N York 149 H5
Emery Down Hants 18 D2
Emley Kirk 141 K5
Emley Moor Kirk 141 K5
Emmbrook Wokham 49 J5
Emmer Green Readg 49 H4
Emmett Carr Derbys 133 J4
Emmington Oxon 67 H6
Emneth Norfk 103 K2
Emneth Hungate Norfk 103 K2
Empingham Rutlnd 101 L2
Empshott Hants 35 M4
Empshott Green Hants 35 M5
Emstrey Crematorium Shrops 96 C1
Emsworth Hants 20 B5
Enborne W Berk 48 B6
Enborne Row W Berk 48 C6
Enchmarsh Shrops 96 B4
Enderby Leics 100 C3
Endmoor Cumb 157 H5
Endon Staffs 114 E1
Endon Bank Staffs 114 E1
Enfield Gt Lon 69 K7
Enfield Crematorium Gt Lon 69 K7
Enfield Lock Gt Lon 69 K7
Enfield Wash Gt Lon 69 K7
Enford Wilts 47 H8
Engine Common S Glos 45 K2
England's Gate Herefs 80 D5
Englefield W Berk 48 F4
Englefield Green Surrey 50 C4
Engleseabrook Ches E 114 B1
English Bicknor Gloucs 63 H4
Englishcombe BaNES 45 L6
English Frankton Shrops 113 G5
Engollan Cnwll 10 B8
Enham-Alamein Hants 34 D1
Enmore Somset 30 C4
Enmore Green Dorset 32 E6
Ennerdale Bridge Cumb 164 E7
Enniscaven Cnwll 4 F3
Enochdhu P & K 233 G3
Ensay Ag & B 226 D3
Ensbury Bmouth 17 L3
Ensdon Shrops 112 F8
Ensis Devon 27 K5
Enson Staffs 114 E6
Enstone Oxon 66 A2
Enterkinfoot D & G 186 C5
Enterpen N York 161 G2
Enville Staffs 97 J6
Eolaigearraidh W Isls 283 b12
Epney Gloucs 63 M5
Epperstone Notts 117 H2
Epping Essex 70 C6
Epping Green Essex 70 B6
Epping Green Herts 69 J5
Epping Upland Essex 70 C6
Eppleby N York 168 F8
Eppleworth E R Yk 144 C2
Epsom Surrey 51 G6
Epwell Oxon 83 H7
Epworth N Linc 143 K7
Epworth Turbary N Linc 143 J7
Erbistock Wrexhm 112 E3
Erdington Birm 98 E5
Eridge Green E Susx 38 E6
Eridge Station E Susx 38 E6
Erines Ag & B 206 D4
Eriska Ag & B 228 D6
Eriswell Suffk 104 E7
Erith Gt Lon 52 B3
Erlestoke Wilts 46 D8
Ermington Devon 7 J4
Erpingham Norfk 122 D5
Erriottwood Kent 40 B3
Errogie Highld 250 F7
Errol P & K 222 D3
Erskine Rens 208 D5
Ervie D & G 172 B1
Erwarton Suffk 90 F8
Erwood Powys 78 F6
Eryholme N York 160 D1
Eryrys Denbgs 128 E8
Escalls Cnwll 2 B5
Escomb Dur 168 F4
Escott Somset 29 K3
Escrick N York 151 K7
Esgair Carmth 58 C3
Esgair Cerdgn 77 G2
Esgairgeiliog Powys 93 G2
Esgerdawe Carmth 77 H7
Esgyryn Conwy 126 F4
Esh Dur 169 G2
Esher Surrey 50 E6
Esholt C Brad 150 A7
Eshott Nthumb 191 J6
Eshton N York 149 G4
Esh Winning Dur 169 G2
Eskadale Highld 250 D4
Eskbank Mdloth 211 K5
Eskdale Green Cumb 155 L3
Eskdalemuir D & G 187 K6
Eskham Lincs 145 K8
Eskholme Donc 143 G4
Esperley Lane Ends Dur 168 E6
Esprick Lancs 147 H8
Essendine Rutlnd 102 A1
Essendon Herts 69 H5
Essich Highld 251 H4
Essington Staffs 98 B3
Esslemont Abers 257 G6
Eston R & Cl 170 D7
Etal Nthumb 202 E5
Etchilhampton Wilts 46 F7
Etchingham E Susx 24 C2
Etchinghill Kent 41 G7
Etchinghill Staffs 115 G7
Etchingwood E Susx 23 H3
Etling Green Norfk 105 K1
Etloe Gloucs 63 K6
Eton W & M 50 B3
Eton Wick W & M 50 B3
Etruria C Stke 114 D2
Etteridge Highld 241 J5
Ettersgill Dur 167 K5
Ettiley Heath Ches E 130 E7
Ettingshall Wolves 97 L4
Ettington Warwks 83 G5
Etton C Pete 102 C2
Etton E R Yk 152 F7
Ettrick Border 187 L3
Ettrickbridge Border 188 C1
Ettrickhill Border 187 L3
Etwall Derbys 115 M5
Eudon George Shrops 96 F5
Euston Suffk 105 H7
Euximoor Drove Cambs 103 K4
Euxton Lancs 139 H4
Evancoyd Powys 79 J3
Evanton Highld 263 G6
Evedon Lincs 118 E2
Evelith Shrops 97 G2
Evelix Highld 263 L2
Evenjobb Powys 79 J3
Evenley Nhants 84 B8
Evenlode Gloucs 65 J1
Evenwood Dur 168 F5
Evenwood Gate Dur 168 F6
Evercreech Somset 31 L3
Everingham E R Yk 152 B7
Everleigh Wilts 47 J8
Everley N York 163 H5
Eversholt C Beds 85 K8
Evershot Dorset 16 A2
Eversley Hants 49 J6
Eversley Cross Hants 49 J6
Everthorpe E R Yk 144 A2
Everton C Beds 86 D5
Everton Hants 18 D5
Everton Lpool 129 H1
Everton Notts 134 D2
Evertown D & G 177 K4
Evesbatch Herefs 80 F5
Evesham Worcs 82 B6
Evington C Leic 100 D3
Ewden Village Sheff 141 L8
Ewell Surrey 51 G6
Ewell Minnis Kent 41 H6
Ewelme Oxon 48 F1
Ewen Gloucs 64 E7
Ewenny V Glam 42 D6
Ewerby Lincs 118 F2
Ewerby Thorpe Lincs 118 F2
Ewhurst Surrey 37 G3
Ewhurst Green E Susx 24 E2
Ewhurst Green Surrey 37 G3
Ewloe Flints 129 G6
Ewloe Green Flints 129 G6
Ewood Bl w D 139 K3
Ewood Bridge Lancs 140 B4
Eworthy Devon 12 B4
Ewshot Hants 36 B1
Ewyas Harold Herefs 62 D2
Exbourne Devon 12 E2
Exbridge Somset 29 G6
Exbury Hants 19 G4
Exceat E Susx 23 H7
Exelby N York 160 D5
Exeter Devon 13 L4
Exeter & Devon Crematorium Devon 13 L4
Exford Somset 28 E3
Exfordsgreen Shrops 95 L2
Exhall Warwks 82 D4
Exhall Warwks 99 K6
Exlade Street Oxon 49 G3
Exley Head C Brad 149 J7
Exminster Devon 13 M5
Exmouth Devon 14 A6
Exning Suffk 88 C2
Exted Kent 41 G6
Exton Devon 14 A5
Exton Hants 35 J6
Exton Rutlnd 101 K1
Exton Somset 29 G4
Exwick Devon 13 L4
Eyam Derbys 132 D4
Eydon Nhants 83 M5
Eye C Pete 102 E3
Eye Herefs 80 C2
Eye Suffk 106 C8
Eye Green C Pete 102 E3
Eye Kettleby Leics 117 K8
Eyemouth Border 213 L6
Eyeworth C Beds 86 E6
Eyhorne Street Kent 39 L2
Eyke Suffk 91 H5
Eynesbury Cambs 86 D3
Eynsford Kent 52 C6
Eynsham Oxon 66 B5
Eype Dorset 15 K4
Eyre Highld 259 G6
Eythorne Kent 41 J5
Eyton Herefs 80 B3
Eyton Shrops 95 J6
Eyton Shrops 112 F8
Eyton Shrops 113 G7
Eyton Wrexhm 112 E3
Eyton on Severn Shrops 96 D2
Eyton upon the Weald Moors Wrekin 113 L8

F

Faccombe Hants 48 A7
Faceby N York 161 H2
Fachwen Powys 111 K8
Facit Lancs 140 D4
Fackley Notts 133 J7
Faddiley Ches E 113 K1
Fadmoor N York 161 L5
Faerdre Swans 57 J4
Fagwyr Swans 57 J4
Faifley W Duns 208 E4
Failand N Som 45 G4
Failford S Ayrs 196 F5
Failsworth Oldham 140 D7
Fairbourne Gwynd 92 D1
Fairburn N York 142 D2
Fairfield Derbys 131 L5
Fairfield Kent 25 H2
Fairfield Worcs 97 L8
Fairford Gloucs 65 H6
Fairford Park Gloucs 65 H6
Fairgirth D & G 175 L3
Fair Green Norfk 120 E8
Fairhaven Lancs 138 C2
Fairlands Surrey 50 B8
Fairlie N Ayrs 207 L8
Fairlight E Susx 24 F5
Fairmile Devon 14 C3
Fairmile Surrey 50 E6
Fairnilee Border 200 F6
Fair Oak Hants 35 G7
Fairoak Staffs 114 B5
Fair Oak Green Hants 49 G6
Fairseat Kent 52 D6
Fairstead Essex 71 J4
Fairstead Norfk 120 E7
Fairstead Norfk 122 F6
Fairwarp E Susx 23 G2
Fairwater Cardif 43 J6
Fairy Cross Devon 27 G6
Fakenham Norfk 121 K5
Fakenham Magna Suffk 105 H8
Fala Mdloth 211 M6
Fala Dam Mdloth 211 M6
Falcut Nhants 84 B6
Faldingworth Lincs 135 L3
Faldouet Jersey 9 f2
Falfield S Glos 63 K8
Falkenham Suffk 91 G7
Falkirk Falk 210 A3
Falkirk Crematorium Falk 210 A3
Falkland Fife 222 D5
Fallburn S Lans 199 G5
Fallgate Derbys 133 G7
Fallin Stirlg 209 L1
Fallodon Nthumb 191 H2
Fallowfield Manch 131 G1
Fallowfield Nthumb 179 L5
Falls of Blarghour Ag & B 216 F4
Falmer E Susx 22 E5
Falmouth Cnwll 3 K4
Falnash Border 188 C5
Falsgrave N York 163 J5
Falstone Nthumb 179 G2
Fanagmore Highld 276 B6
Fancott C Beds 68 C2
Fanellan Highld 250 E3
Fangdale Beck N York 161 J4
Fangfoss E R Yk 152 A5
Fanmore Ag & B 226 E3
Fannich Lodge Highld 261 L6
Fans Border 201 J5
Far Bletchley M Keyn 85 G8
Farcet Cambs 102 D4
Far Cotton Nhants 84 E3
Farden Shrops 96 D8
Fareham Hants 19 K2
Far End Cumb 156 D3
Farewell Staffs 98 D1
Far Forest Worcs 97 G8
Farforth Lincs 136 F4
Far Green Gloucs 63 M7
Faringdon Oxon 65 L8
Farington Lancs 139 G3
Farlam Cumb 178 D7
Farleigh N Som 45 G5
Farleigh Surrey 51 K7
Farleigh Hungerford Somset 46 A7
Farleigh Wallop Hants 35 J2
Farlesthorpe Lincs 137 J5
Farleton Cumb 157 H6
Farleton Lancs 147 L2
Farley Derbys 132 F7
Farley Staffs 115 H3
Farley Wilts 34 B5
Farley Green Suffk 88 E4
Farley Green Surrey 37 G2
Farley Hill Wokham 49 H6
Farleys End Gloucs 63 M4
Farlington C Port 19 M3
Farlington N York 151 K2
Farlow Shrops 96 E7
Farmborough BaNES 45 K7
Farmbridge End Essex 70 F5
Farmcote Gloucs 64 F1
Farmcote Shrops 97 H5
Farmers Carmth 77 J6
Farmington Gloucs 65 H4
Farmoor Oxon 66 C5
Far Moor Wigan 139 G7
Farms Common Cnwll 3 H4
Farm Town Leics 116 C8
Farmtown Moray 267 K6
Farnah Green Derbys 116 B2
Farnborough Gt Lon 51 L6
Farnborough Hants 49 L8
Farnborough W Berk 48 B3
Farnborough Warwks 83 K5
Farnborough Park Hants 49 L7
Farnborough Street Hants 49 L7
Farncombe Surrey 36 E2
Farndish Bed 85 H3
Farndon Ches W 112 F1
Farndon Notts 117 K1
Farnell Angus 235 G4
Farnham Dorset 33 G7
Farnham Essex 70 C2
Farnham N York 150 E4
Farnham Suffk 91 H3
Farnham Surrey 36 B2
Farnham Common Bucks 50 B2
Farnham Green Essex 70 C2
Farnham Royal Bucks 50 B2
Farningham Kent 52 C5
Farnley Leeds 141 L1
Farnley N York 150 B6
Farnley Tyas Kirk 141 J5
Farnsfield Notts 134 C8
Farnworth Bolton 139 L6
Farnworth Halton 129 L2
Far Oakridge Gloucs 64 D6
Farr Highld 241 L3
Farr Highld 251 J5
Farr Highld 278 B4
Farraline Highld 251 G7
Farringdon Devon 14 B4
Farrington Gurney BaNES 45 J7
Far Sawrey Cumb 156 E4

Farsley Leeds 141 K1
Farther Howegreen Essex 71 K6
Farthing Green Kent 39 K4
Farthinghoe Nhants 83 M7
Farthingloe Kent 41 J7
Farthingstone Nhants 84 B4
Farthing Street Gt Lon 51 L6
Fartown Kirk 141 J4
Fartown Leeds 141 K1
Farway Devon 14 E3
Fasnacloich Ag & B 229 G6
Fasnakyle Highld 250 B6
Fassfern Highld 239 G7
Fatfield Sundld 181 H8
Faugh Cumb 178 C7
Fauld Staffs 115 K6
Fauldhouse W Loth 210 B6
Faulkbourne Essex 71 J4
Faulkland Somset 45 L8
Fauls Shrops 113 K5
Faversham Kent 40 D3
Fawdington N York 150 F1
Fawdon N u Ty 180 F5
Fawdon Nthumb 190 E3
Fawfieldhead Staffs 131 L7
Fawkham Green Kent 52 C6
Fawler Oxon 66 A4
Fawley Bucks 49 J2
Fawley Hants 19 G3
Fawley W Berk 48 B3
Fawley Chapel Herefs 63 H1
Fawnog Flints 128 F6
Fawsley Nhants 84 A4
Faxfleet E R Yk 143 L3
Faygate W Susx 37 K4
Fazakerley Lpool 138 D8
Fazeley Staffs 99 G3
Fearby N York 160 B6
Fearn Highld 264 C4
Fearnan P & K 231 K6
Fearnbeg Highld 260 B7
Fearnhead Warrtn 130 C2
Fearnmore Highld 260 A7
Fearnoch Ag & B 206 E3
Featherstone Staffs 97 L2
Featherstone Wakefd 142 C3
Feckenham Worcs 82 B3
Feering Essex 72 C3
Feetham N York 159 H3
Feizor N York 148 D2
Felbridge Surrey 38 B5
Felbrigg Norfk 122 E4
Felcourt Surrey 38 B5
Felden Herts 68 D6
Felindre Carmth 59 G4
Felindre Carmth 59 K3
Felindre Carmth 76 C7
Felindre Cerdgn 77 G4
Felindre Powys 61 J2
Felindre Powys 94 E7
Felindre Swans 57 H4
Felindre Farchog Pembks 75 J4
Felin Fach Cerdgn 76 F4
Felinfach Powys 78 F8
Felinfoel Carmth 56 F4
Felingwm Isaf Carmth 58 F4
Felingwm Uchaf Carmth 58 F4
Felin-newydd Powys 78 F8
Felixkirk N York 161 G5
Felixstowe Suffk 91 G8
Felixstowe Ferry Suffk 91 H7
Felkington Nthumb 202 E4
Felkirk Wakefd 142 B5
Felling Gatesd 181 G6
Fell Lane C Brad 149 J7
Fell Side Cumb 165 J3
Felmersham Bed 85 K4
Felmingham Norfk 122 E5
Felpham W Susx 20 F7
Felsham Suffk 89 J4
Felsted Essex 71 G3
Feltham Gt Lon 50 E4
Felthamhill Surrey 50 E5
Felthorpe Norfk 122 D7
Felton Herefs 80 D5
Felton N Som 45 G6
Felton Nthumb 191 H6
Felton Butler Shrops 112 F8
Feltwell Norfk 104 E5
Fenay Bridge Kirk 141 J4
Fence Lancs 148 E8
Fence Rothm 133 J3
Fence Houses Sundld 169 J1
Fencott Oxon 66 E4
Fendike Corner Lincs 137 H7
Fen Ditton Cambs 87 K3
Fen Drayton Cambs 87 G2
Fen End Lincs 119 H7
Fen End Solhll 99 G8
Fenham Nthumb 203 H5
Feniscliffe Bl w D 139 K2
Feniscowles Bl w D 139 K3
Feniton Devon 14 D3
Fenland Crematorium Cambs 103 H4
Fenn Green Shrops 97 H6
Fenn Street Medway 53 G4
Fenny Bentley Derbys 115 K2
Fenny Bridges Devon 14 D3
Fenny Compton Warwks 83 K5
Fenny Drayton Leics 99 K4
Fenny Stratford M Keyn 85 G8
Fenrother Nthumb 191 H7
Fenstanton Cambs 87 G2
Fenstead End Suffk 88 F5
Fen Street Norfk 105 K4
Fen Street Suffk 90 E3
Fenton C Stke 114 D3
Fenton Cambs 103 G7
Fenton Cumb 178 C7
Fenton Lincs 118 A1
Fenton Lincs 135 G4
Fenton Notts 134 F3
Fenton Nthumb 202 F6
Fenton Barns E Loth 212 B3
Fenwick Donc 142 F4
Fenwick E Ayrs 196 F2
Fenwick Nthumb 180 C4
Fenwick Nthumb 203 H5
Feock Cnwll 3 L3
Feolin Ferry Ag & B 205 G3
Fergushill N Ayrs 196 C2
Feriniquarrie Highld 258 B6
Fermain Bay Guern 9 k3
Fern Angus 234 D3
Ferndale Rhondd 42 F2
Ferndown Dorset 17 L3
Ferness Highld 253 J3
Fernham Oxon 65 L8
Fernhill Heath Worcs 81 K3
Fernhurst W Susx 36 D5
Fernie Fife 222 E4
Ferniegair S Lans 209 K8
Fernilea Highld 246 E2
Fernilee Derbys 131 K4
Fernwood Notts 117 L2
Ferrensby N York 150 E4
Ferriby Sluice N Linc 144 B4
Ferrindonald Highld 247 L7
Ferring W Susx 21 J6
Ferrybridge Wakefd 142 D3
Ferryden Angus 235 H4
Ferryhill Dur 169 H4
Ferry Point Highld 263 K3
Ferryside Carmth 56 C3
Ferrytown Highld 263 K2
Fersfield Norfk 106 B6
Fersit Highld 240 B7
Feshiebridge Highld 241 M3
Fetcham Surrey 50 F7
Fetlar Shet 281 f3
Fetterangus Abers 269 H6
Fettercairn Abers 235 G1
Fewcott Oxon 66 D2
Fewston N York 150 B5
Ffairfach Carmth 59 H4
Ffair Rhos Cerdgn 77 K2
Ffald-y-Brenin Carmth 77 H6
Ffawyddog Powys 61 K3
Ffestiniog Gwynd 110 D3
Ffordd-las Denbgs 128 D6
Fforest Carmth 57 G4
Fforest Mons 62 B3
Fforest Fach Swans 57 H5
Fforest Goch Neath 57 K4
Ffostrasol Cerdgn 76 C5
Ffrith Flints 129 G8
Ffynnonddewi Cerdgn 76 C4
Ffynnongroyw Flints 128 D3
Ffynnon-Oer Cerdgn 76 F4
Fiag Lodge Highld 272 C2
Fickleshole Surrey 51 K6
Fiddington Gloucs 64 D1
Fiddington Somset 30 B3
Fiddleford Dorset 32 D8
Fiddlers Green Cnwll 4 D4
Fiddlers Hamlet Essex 70 C6
Field Staffs 115 G5
Field Broughton Cumb 156 E6
Field Dalling Norfk 121 M4
Fieldhead Cumb 166 B3
Field Head Leics 100 B2
Fifehead Magdalen Dorset 32 C6
Fifehead Neville Dorset 32 C8
Fifehead St Quintin Dorset 16 E1
Fife Keith Moray 267 H6
Fifield Oxon 65 K3
Fifield W & M 49 L4
Fifield Wilts 33 K1
Figheldean Wilts 33 K2
Filands Wilts 46 D1
Filby Norfk 107 K1
Filey N York 163 L6
Filgrave M Keyn 85 G5
Filkins Oxon 65 K6
Filleigh Devon 28 B5
Filleigh Devon 28 C8
Fillingham Lincs 135 J3
Fillongley Warwks 99 H6
Filmore Hill Hants 35 K5
Filton S Glos 45 J3
Fimber E R Yk 152 D4
Finavon Angus 234 D4
Fincham Norfk 104 D2
Finchampstead Wokham 49 J6
Fincharn Ag & B 216 D6
Finchdean Hants 20 B4
Finchingfield Essex 88 D8
Finchley Gt Lon 51 H1
Findern Derbys 116 A5
Findhorn Moray 265 G7
Findhorn Bridge Highld 252 E6
Findochty Moray 267 J3
Findo Gask P & K 221 H3
Findon Abers 245 L4
Findon W Susx 21 J5
Findon Mains Highld 263 G7
Findrack House Abers 244 D3
Finedon Nhants 85 H1
Fineshade Nhants 101 L4
Fingal Street Suffk 90 F1
Fingask P & K 222 B3
Fingest Bucks 49 J1
Finghall N York 160 B5
Fingland Cumb 177 H7
Fingland D & G 197 L7
Finglesham Kent 41 K4
Fingringhoe Essex 72 F3
Finkle Green Essex 88 D7
Finkle Street Barns 141 M7
Finlarig Stirlg 231 G8
Finmere Oxon 84 C8
Finnart P & K 230 F4
Finningham Suffk 90 C2
Finningley Donc 143 H7
Finsbay W Isls 282 e6
Finstall Worcs 82 A1
Finsthwaite Cumb 156 E5
Finstock Oxon 66 A4
Finstown Ork 275 c4
Fintry Abers 268 D5
Fintry Stirlg 209 G2
Finzean Abers 244 D5
Fionnphort Ag & B 226 B7
Fionnsbhagh W Isls 282 e6
Firbank Cumb 157 K4
Firbeck Rothm 133 L2
Firby N York 152 A3
Firby N York 160 C5
Firgrove Rochdl 140 D5
Firle E Susx 23 G6
Firsby Lincs 137 H7
Firsdown Wilts 34 B4
Fir Tree Dur 168 F4
Fishbourne IoW 19 J5
Fishbourne W Susx 20 D6
Fishburn Dur 169 K4
Fishcross Clacks 220 F8
Fisher W Susx 20 E6
Fisherford Abers 256 B4
Fisherrow E Loth 211 K4
Fisher's Pond Hants 35 G6
Fisher's Row Lancs 147 H6
Fisherstreet W Susx 36 E4
Fisherton Highld 252 D2
Fisherton S Ayrs 196 B7
Fisherton de la Mere Wilts 33 G3
Fisherwick Staffs 98 F2
Fishery Estate W & M 49 L3
Fishguard Pembks 74 F5
Fishlake Donc 143 G5
Fishleigh Devon 12 D2
Fishmere End Lincs 119 J4
Fishnish Pier Ag & B 227 J4
Fishpond Bottom Dorset 15 J3
Fishponds Bristl 45 J4
Fishtoft Lincs 119 K3
Fishtoft Drove Lincs 119 K2
Fishwick Lancs 139 H2
Fiskavaig Highld 246 D2
Fiskerton Lincs 135 L5
Fiskerton Notts 117 K1
Fitling E R Yk 145 H1
Fittleton Wilts 33 K1
Fittleworth W Susx 21 G3
Fitton End Cambs 103 J1
Fitz Shrops 113 G7
Fitzhead Somset 29 L5
Fitzroy Somset 30 B5
Fitzwilliam Wakefd 142 C5
Five Ash Down E Susx 23 H3
Five Ashes E Susx 23 J2
Five Bells Somset 29 K2
Five Bridges Herefs 80 F6
Fivecrosses Ches W 129 M4
Fivehead Somset 30 E6
Fivelanes Cnwll 11 J6
Five Lanes Mons 44 F1
Five Oak Green Kent 39 G4
Five Oaks Jersey 9 e3
Five Oaks W Susx 37 G5
Five Roads Carmth 56 E4
Five Wents Kent 39 K3
Flack's Green Essex 71 J4
Flackwell Heath Bucks 49 L1
Fladbury Worcs 82 A6
Fladdabister Shet 281 e7
Flagg Derbys 132 C6
Flamborough E R Yk 153 K2
Flamstead Herts 68 D4
Flansham W Susx 20 F6
Flanshaw Wakefd 141 M4
Flappit Spring C Brad 149 J8
Flasby N York 149 G4
Flash Staffs 131 K6
Flashader Highld 258 E6
Flaunden Herts 68 C7
Flawborough Notts 117 K3
Flawith N York 151 G3
Flax Bourton N Som 45 G5
Flaxby N York 150 E4
Flaxley Gloucs 63 K4
Flaxmere Ches W 130 A5
Flaxpool Somset 29 L4
Flaxton N York 151 L3
Fleckney Leics 100 E5
Flecknoe Warwks 83 M3
Fledborough Notts 134 F5
Fleet Dorset 16 C6
Fleet Hants 20 B6
Fleet Hants 49 K8
Fleet Lincs 119 L6
Fleetend Hants 19 H3
Fleet Hargate Lincs 119 L6
Fleetwood Lancs 146 F6
Flemingston V Glam 42 F7
Flemington S Lans 209 H7
Flempton Suffk 89 G1
Fletcher Green Kent 38 E3
Fletchersbridge Cnwll 5 J2
Fletchertown Cumb 165 G2
Fletching E Susx 23 G3
Fleur-de-lis Caerph 43 J3
Flexbury Cnwll 11 J1
Flexford Surrey 36 D1
Flimby Cumb 164 D4
Flimwell E Susx 39 H7
Flint Flints 128 F5
Flintham Notts 117 K2
Flint Mountain Flints 128 F5
Flinton E R Yk 153 K8
Flint's Green Solhll 99 H7
Flishinghurst Kent 39 J6
Flitcham Norfk 120 F6
Flitton C Beds 85 L8
Flitwick C Beds 85 K8
Flixborough N Linc 143 L5
Flixborough Stather N Linc 143 L5
Flixton N York 163 J6
Flixton Suffk 107 G6
Flixton Traffd 130 E1
Flockton Kirk 141 K5
Flockton Green Kirk 141 L5
Flodden Nthumb 202 E6
Flodigarry Highld 259 H2
Flookburgh Cumb 156 E7
Flordon Norfk 106 D4
Flore Nhants 84 C3
Flotterton Nthumb 190 E5
Flowers Green E Susx 23 L5
Flowton Suffk 90 C6
Flushdyke Wakefd 141 L3
Flushing Cnwll 3 K4
Fluxton Devon 14 C4
Flyford Flavell Worcs 82 A4
Fobbing Thurr 52 F2
Fochabers Moray 267 G4
Fochriw Caerph 61 H6
Fockerby N Linc 143 L4
Foddington Somset 31 J5
Foel Powys 94 B1
Foelgastell Carmth 59 G6
Foel y Dyffryn Brdgnd 42 C3
Foggathorpe E R Yk 152 A8
Fogo Border 202 B3
Fogwatt Moray 266 E5
Foindle Highld 276 B6
Folda Angus 233 J3
Fole Staffs 115 G4
Foleshill Covtry 99 K7
Folke Dorset 31 L8

Folkestone Kent 41 H8
Folkingham Lincs 118 E5
Folkington E Susx 23 J6
Folksworth Cambs 102 C5
Folkton N York 163 J6
Folla Rule Abers 256 C5
Follifoot N York 150 D5
Folly Gate Devon 12 D3
Folly Hill Surrey 36 B1
Fonmon V Glam 43 G8
Fonthill Bishop Wilts 32 F4
Fonthill Gifford Wilts 32 F4
Fontmell Magna Dorset 32 E7
Fontmell Parva Dorset 32 D7
Fontwell W Susx 20 F5
Font-y-gary V Glam 43 G8
Foolow Derbys 132 D4
Foots Cray Gt Lon 52 A5
Forbestown Abers 243 L1
Forcett N York 168 F8
Ford Ag & B 216 D6
Ford Bucks 67 J5
Ford Derbys 133 H4
Ford Devon 7 J5
Ford Devon 8 B6
Ford Devon 27 G6
Ford Gloucs 65 G1
Ford Nthumb 202 E5
Ford Shrops 95 K1
Ford Somset 29 K5
Ford Somset 45 H8
Ford Staffs 115 H1
Ford W Susx 21 G6
Ford Wilts 33 L4
Ford Wilts 46 B4
Forda Devon 12 D4
Fordcombe Kent 38 E5
Fordell Fife 211 G1
Forden Powys 94 F3
Ford End Essex 71 G4
Forder Green Devon 8 B2
Ford Green Lancs 147 J6
Fordham Cambs 88 C1
Fordham Essex 72 D2
Fordham Norfk 104 C3
Fordham Heath Essex 72 D2
Ford Heath Shrops 95 K1
Fordingbridge Hants 33 K8
Fordon E R Yk 163 J7
Fordoun Abers 245 G8
Ford's Green Suffk 90 C2
Fordstreet Essex 72 D2
Ford Street Somset 29 L7
Fordton Devon 13 J3
Fordwells Oxon 65 L4
Fordwich Kent 41 G3
Fordyce Abers 267 L3
Forebridge Staffs 114 E7
Foremark Derbys 116 B6
Forest Guern 9 j4
Forest N York 160 C3
Forest Becks Lancs 148 D5
Forestburn Gate Nthumb 190 F7
Forest Chapel Ches E 131 J5
Forest Gate Gt Lon 51 L2
Forest Green Surrey 37 H3
Forest Hall N Tyne 181 G5
Forest Head Cumb 178 D7
Forest Hill Gt Lon 51 K4
Forest Hill Oxon 66 E5
Forest-in-Teesdale Dur 167 K4
Forest Lane Head N York 150 D4
Forest Mill Clacks 221 G8
Forest Park Crematorium Gt Lon 70 C8
Forest Row E Susx 38 C6
Forest Side IoW 19 H5
Forestside W Susx 20 C4
Forest Town Notts 133 L7
Forfar Angus 234 C5
Forgandenny P & K 221 K3
Forge Powys 93 G3
Forge Hammer Torfn 62 B7
Forge Side Torfn 61 L5
Forgie Moray 267 H5
Forgieside Moray 267 H5
Forgue Abers 256 A3
Forhill Worcs 98 D8
Formby Sefton 138 C6
Forncett End Norfk 106 C4
Forncett St Mary Norfk 106 D4
Forncett St Peter Norfk 106 D5
Fornham All Saints Suffk 89 G2
Fornham St Martin Suffk 89 G2
Fornighty Highld 253 H2
Forres Moray 265 G8
Forsbrook Staffs 114 F3
Forse Highld 275 H1
Forshaw Heath Warwks 98 E8
Forsinard Highld 278 F7
Forston Dorset 16 C3
Fort Augustus Highld 240 C2
Forteviot P & K 221 J4
Forth S Lans 198 F2
Forthampton Gloucs 64 B1
Fort Hommet Guern 9 i2
Fortingall P & K 231 K6
Fort le Marchant Guern 9 k1
Forton Hants 34 F2
Forton Lancs 147 J5
Forton Shrops 113 G8
Forton Somset 15 H1
Forton Staffs 114 B7
Fortrie Abers 256 B3
Fortrose Highld 263 K8
Fortuneswell Dorset 16 D7
Fort William Highld 239 J8
Forty Green Bucks 50 A1
Forty Hill Gt Lon 69 J7
Forward Green Suffk 90 C3
Fosbury Wilts 47 L7
Foscot Oxon 65 K3
Foscote Nhants 84 C6
Fosdyke Lincs 119 K5
Fosdyke Bridge Lincs 119 K5
Foss P & K 231 L4
Fossebridge Gloucs 65 G5
Foss-y-ffin Cerdgn 76 E3
Fosterhouses Donc 143 G5
Foster Street Essex 70 C5
Foston Derbys 115 K5
Foston Leics 100 D4
Foston Lincs 117 M3
Foston N York 151 L3
Foston on the Wolds E R Yk 153 H4
Fotherby Lincs 136 F2
Fothergill Cumb 164 D4
Fotheringhay Nhants 102 B5
Foula Shet 281 a7
Foulbridge Cumb 165 M1
Foulby Wakefd 142 B4
Foulden Border 202 E2
Foulden Norfk 104 F4
Foul End Warwks 99 H4
Foul Mile E Susx 23 K4
Foulness Island Essex 53 L1
Foulon Vale Crematorium Guern 9 j3
Foulridge Lancs 148 F7
Foulsham Norfk 122 A6
Fountainhall Border 200 F3
Four Ashes Solhll 98 F8
Four Ashes Staffs 97 H6
Four Ashes Staffs 97 L2
Four Ashes Suffk 89 K1
Four Cabots Guern 9 j3
Four Crosses Powys 112 C7
Four Crosses Staffs 98 B2
Four Elms Kent 38 C4
Four Foot Somset 31 J4
Four Forks Somset 30 C3
Four Gates Bolton 139 J6
Four Gotes Cambs 120 A8
Four Lane End Barns 141 L7
Four Lane Ends Ches W 130 A7
Four Lanes Cnwll 3 H3
Fourlanes End Ches E 130 F7
Four Marks Hants 35 K4
Four Mile Bridge IoA 124 E4
Four Oaks Birm 98 E4
Four Oaks E Susx 24 F2
Four Oaks Gloucs 63 K2
Four Oaks Solhll 99 H7
Fourpenny Highld 264 C1
Four Points W Berk 48 E3
Four Roads Carmth 56 E3
Four Shire Stone Warwks 65 K1
Fourstones Nthumb 179 K5
Four Throws Kent 39 J7
Four Wents Kent 38 F3
Fovant Wilts 33 H5
Foveran Abers 257 H7
Fowey Cnwll 5 K4
Fowley Common Warrtn 139 K8
Fowlhall Kent 39 H4
Fowlis Angus 233 M8
Fowlis Wester P & K 221 G2
Fowlmere Cambs 87 J6
Fownhope Herefs 80 D8
Foxbar Rens 208 D6
Foxcombe Devon 12 C5
Fox Corner Surrey 50 B7
Foxcote Gloucs 64 E3
Foxcote Somset 45 L7
Foxdale IoM 154 c6
Foxearth Essex 89 G6
Foxendown Kent 52 E5
Foxfield Cumb 156 B5
Foxham Wilts 46 E3
Fox Hatch Essex 70 E7
Foxhills Hants 18 E1
Foxhole Cnwll 4 F4
Foxholes N York 163 H8
Foxhunt Green E Susx 23 J4
Foxley Nhants 84 C5
Foxley Norfk 122 A7
Foxley Wilts 46 C2
Foxlydiate Worcs 82 B2
Fox Street Essex 72 F2
Foxt Staffs 115 G2
Foxton Cambs 87 H5
Foxton Dur 169 K5
Foxton Leics 100 F5
Foxton N York 160 F3
Foxup N York 158 F7
Foxwist Green Ches W 130 C6
Foxwood Shrops 96 E8
Foy Herefs 63 H2
Foyers Highld 250 E7
Foynesfield Highld 253 G1
Fraddam Cnwll 2 F4
Fraddon Cnwll 4 E3
Fradley Staffs 98 F1
Fradswell Staffs 114 F5
Fraisthorpe E R Yk 153 J3
Framfield E Susx 23 H3
Framingham Earl Norfk 106 F3
Framingham Pigot Norfk 106 F3
Framlingham Suffk 91 G3
Frampton Dorset 16 B4
Frampton Lincs 119 K4
Frampton Cotterell S Glos 45 K3
Frampton Mansell Gloucs 64 D6
Frampton on Severn Gloucs 63 L5
Frampton West End Lincs 119 J3
Framsden Suffk 90 E3
Framwellgate Moor Dur 169 H2
Franche Worcs 97 J7
Frandley Ches W 130 C4
Frankaborough Devon 11 M4
Frankby Wirral 128 F2
Frankfort Norfk 122 F6
Franklands Gate Herefs 80 C6
Frankley Worcs 98 C7
Franksbridge Powys 78 F4
Frankton Warwks 83 K1
Frant E Susx 38 F6
Fraserburgh Abers 269 J3
Frating Essex 73 G3
Frating Green Essex 73 G2
Fratton C Port 19 L4
Freathy Cnwll 6 D4
Freckenham Suffk 88 D1
Freckleton Lancs 138 E2
Freebirch Derbys 132 F5
Freeby Leics 117 L7
Freefolk Hants 35 G1
Freehay Staffs 115 G3
Freeland Oxon 66 B4
Freethorpe Norfk 107 H2
Freethorpe Common Norfk 107 H2
Freiston Lincs 119 L3
Fremington Devon 27 J4
Fremington N York 159 J3
Frenchay S Glos 45 J3
Frenchbeer Devon 12 F5
French Street Kent 51 M8
Frenich P & K 232 B4
Frensham Surrey 36 C3
Freshfield Sefton 138 C6
Freshford Wilts 46 A7
Freshwater IoW 18 E6
Freshwater Bay IoW 18 E6
Freshwater East Pembks 55 G7
Fressingfield Suffk 106 F7
Freston Suffk 90 E7
Freswick Highld 280 E3
Fretherne Gloucs 63 L5
Frettenham Norfk 122 E8
Freuchie Fife 222 D6
Freystrop Pembks 54 F4
Friar Park Sandw 98 C4
Friar's Gate E Susx 38 D6
Friars' Hill N York 162 C5
Friar Waddon Dorset 16 C5
Friday Bridge Cambs 103 K2
Friday Street Suffk 90 F3
Friday Street Suffk 91 H5
Friday Street Suffk 91 J3
Friday Street Surrey 37 H2
Fridaythorpe E R Yk 152 D4
Friden Derbys 132 C7
Friendly Calder 141 G3
Friern Barnet Gt Lon 69 H8
Friesthorpe Lincs 135 M3
Frieston Lincs 118 B2
Frieth Bucks 49 J1
Friezeland Notts 116 D2
Frilford Oxon 66 B7
Frilsham W Berk 48 E4
Frimley Surrey 49 L7
Frimley Green Surrey 49 L7
Frindsbury Medway 52 F5
Fring Norfk 121 G4
Fringford Oxon 66 F1
Frinsted Kent 40 A4
Frinton-on-Sea Essex 73 K3
Friockheim Angus 234 F5
Friog Gwynd 92 D1
Frisby on the Wreake Leics 117 J8
Friskney Lincs 137 J8
Friskney Eaudike Lincs 137 J8
Friston E Susx 23 J7
Friston Suffk 91 J3
Fritchley Derbys 116 B1
Fritham Hants 34 B8
Frith Bank Lincs 119 K2
Frith Common Worcs 80 F1
Frithelstock Devon 27 H7
Frithelstock Stone Devon 27 H7
Frithend Hants 36 B3
Frithsden Herts 68 C5
Frithville Lincs 119 K2
Frittenden Kent 39 K5
Frittiscombe Devon 8 B6
Fritton Norfk 106 E5
Fritton Norfk 107 K3
Fritwell Oxon 66 D1
Frizinghall C Brad 149 L8
Frizington Cumb 164 D7
Frocester Gloucs 63 M6
Frodesley Shrops 96 C3
Frodsham Ches W 129 M4
Frogden Border 202 B7
Frog End Cambs 87 H6
Frog End Cambs 87 L3
Froggatt Derbys 132 E4
Froghall Staffs 115 G2
Frogham Hants 33 L8
Frogham Kent 41 H5
Frogmore Devon 7 M6
Frognall Lincs 102 D2
Frogpool Cnwll 3 J3
Frog Pool Worcs 81 J2
Frogwell Cnwll 6 C1
Frolesworth Leics 100 B5
Frome Somset 32 C1
Frome St Quintin Dorset 16 B2
Fromes Hill Herefs 80 F6
Fron Denbgs 128 C6
Fron Gwynd 108 F4
Fron Gwynd 109 J1
Fron Powys 94 E4
Fron Powys 94 F3
Froncysyllte Denbgs 112 C3
Fron-goch Gwynd 111 H4
Fron Isaf Wrexhm 112 C3
Frostenden Suffk 107 K7
Frosterley Dur 168 C3
Froxfield C Beds 85 J8
Froxfield Wilts 47 L5
Froxfield Green Hants 35 L5
Fryern Hill Hants 34 F6
Fryerning Essex 70 F7
Fryton N York 162 B7
Fuinary Highld 227 J3
Fulbeck Lincs 118 B2
Fulbourn Cambs 87 L4
Fulbrook Oxon 65 K4
Fulflood Hants 35 G5
Fulford C York 151 K6
Fulford Somset 30 B5
Fulford Staffs 114 F4
Fulham Gt Lon 51 H4
Fulking W Susx 22 C5
Fullaford Devon 28 B3
Fullarton N Ayrs 196 C3
Fuller's End Essex 70 D2
Fuller's Moor Ches W 113 H1
Fuller Street Essex 71 H4
Fuller Street Kent 38 E2
Fullerton Hants 34 E3
Fulletby Lincs 136 E5
Fullready Warwks 83 G6
Full Sutton E R Yk 152 A5
Fullwood E Ayrs 196 E1
Fulmer Bucks 50 C2
Fulmodeston Norfk 121 M5
Fulnetby Lincs 136 B4
Fulney Lincs 119 J6
Fulstone Kirk 141 J6
Fulstow Lincs 145 J8
Fulwell Oxon 66 A3
Fulwell Sundld 181 J7
Fulwood Lancs 139 H2
Fulwood Notts 133 J8
Fulwood Sheff 132 F3
Fulwood Somset 30 B6
Fundenhall Norfk 106 C4
Funtington W Susx 20 C5

Funtley Hants 19 J2
Funtullich P & K 220 C2
Furley Devon 15 G2
Furnace Ag & B 217 G7
Furnace Carmth 56 F4
Furnace Cerdgn 92 E4
Furnace End Warwks 99 H5
Furner's Green E Susx 22 F2
Furness Vale Derbys 131 K3
Furneux Pelham Herts 70 B2
Further Quarter Kent 39 M5
Furtho Nhants 84 E6
Furzehill Devon 28 C2
Furzehill Dorset 17 K2
Furzehills Lincs 136 E5
Furzeley Corner Hants 19 L2
Furze Platt W & M 49 L3
Furzley Hants 34 C7
Fyfett Somset 30 C7
Fyfield Essex 70 E5
Fyfield Hants 34 C2
Fyfield Oxon 66 B7
Fyfield Wilts 47 H5
Fyfield Wilts 47 H6
Fyfield Bavant Wilts 33 H6
Fylingthorpe N York 163 G2
Fyning W Susx 36 B6
Fyvie Abers 256 D4

G

Gabroc Hill E Ayrs 196 E1
Gaddesby Leics 100 F1
Gaddesden Row Herts 68 D4
Gadfa IoA 125 H2
Gadgirth S Ayrs 196 E6
Gadlas Shrops 112 E4
Gaer Powys 61 J3
Gaer-llwyd Mons 62 F7
Gaerwen IoA 125 H5
Gagingwell Oxon 66 B2
Gailes N Ayrs 196 C4
Gailey Staffs 97 K1
Gainford Dur 168 F7
Gainsborough Lincs 135 G2
Gainsford End Essex 88 E8
Gairloch Highld 260 C4
Gairlochy Highld 239 K6
Gairneybridge P & K 221 L7
Gaisgill Cumb 157 K2
Gaitsgill Cumb 165 L1
Galashiels Border 201 G6
Galgate Lancs 147 J5
Galhampton Somset 31 K5
Gallanachbeg Ag & B 216 C2
Gallanachmore Ag & B 216 C2
Gallantry Bank Ches E 113 H1
Gallatown Fife 222 E8
Galley Common Warwks 99 J5
Galleywood Essex 71 H6
Gallovie Highld 240 F5
Gallowfauld Angus 234 C7
Gallowhill P & K 233 J8
Gallows Green Essex 72 D2
Gallows Green Worcs 81 L3
Gallowstree Common Oxon 49 G3
Galltair Highld 248 C7
Gallt-y-foel Gwynd 125 K7
Gally Hill Hants 49 K8
Gallypot Street E Susx 38 D6
Galmpton Devon 7 K6
Galmpton Torbay 8 D4
Galphay N York 150 C1
Galston E Ayrs 196 F4
Gamballs Green Staffs 131 L6
Gamblesby Cumb 166 E3
Gambles Green Essex 71 J4
Gamelsby Cumb 177 H8
Gamesley Derbys 131 K1
Gamlingay Cambs 86 E5
Gamlingay Cinques Cambs 86 E4
Gamlingay Great Heath Cambs 86 E5
Gammersgill N York 159 J6
Gamrie Abers 268 E4
Gamston Notts 117 G4
Gamston Notts 134 E4
Ganarew Herefs 63 G4
Ganavan Bay Ag & B 216 D1
Gang Cnwll 6 C1
Ganllwyd Gwynd 110 D6
Gannachy Angus 234 F1
Ganstead E R Yk 144 F1
Ganthorpe N York 151 L2
Ganton N York 163 H7
Ganwick Corner Herts 69 H7
Gappah Devon 13 K7
Garbity Moray 266 F5
Garboldisham Norfk 105 K7
Garbole Highld 252 E7
Garchory Abers 243 J2
Garden City Flints 129 H6
Gardeners Green Wokham 49 K5
Gardenstown Abers 268 E3
Garden Village Sheff 141 L8
Garderhouse Shet 281 d6
Gardham E R Yk 152 E7
Gare Hill Somset 32 C3
Garelochhead Ag & B 207 L1
Garford Oxon 66 B7
Garforth Leeds 142 B1
Gargrave N York 149 G5
Gargunnock Stirlg 220 B8
Garizim Conwy 126 D4
Garlic Street Norfk 106 E6
Garlieston D & G 174 D5
Garlinge Kent 41 K2
Garlinge Green Kent 40 F5
Garlogie Abers 245 H2
Garmond Abers 268 E5
Garmouth Moray 267 G3
Garmston Shrops 96 E2
Garnant Carmth 59 J6
Garn-Dolbenmaen Gwynd 109 J3
Garnett Bridge Cumb 157 H3
Garnfadryn Gwynd 108 E5
Garnkirk N Lans 209 H5
Garnswllt Swans 57 H3
Garn-yr-erw Torfn 61 K5
Garrabost W Isls 282 h3
Garrallan E Ayrs 197 G7
Garras Cnwll 3 H6
Garreg Gwynd 109 L3
Garrigill Cumb 167 H2
Garriston N York 159 L4
Garroch D & G 184 F6
Garrochtrie D & G 172 D7
Garrochty Ag & B 207 H8
Garros Highld 259 H4
Garsdale Cumb 158 C5
Garsdale Head Cumb 158 D4
Garsdon Wilts 46 D2
Garshall Green Staffs 114 F5
Garsington Oxon 66 E6
Garstang Lancs 147 J6
Garston Herts 68 E7
Garston Lpool 129 J3
Gartachossan Ag & B 204 E4
Gartcosh N Lans 209 J5
Garth Brdgnd 42 C4
Garth Mons 62 D8
Garth Powys 78 C5
Garth Powys 79 J1
Garth Wrexhm 112 C3
Garthamlock C Glas 209 H5
Garthbrengy Powys 78 E8
Gartheli Cerdgn 77 G4
Garthmyl Powys 94 F3
Garthorpe Leics 117 L7
Garthorpe N Linc 143 L4
Garth Penrhyncoch Cerdgn 92 E6
Garth Row Cumb 157 H3
Garths Cumb 157 H5
Gartly Abers 255 K5
Gartmore Stirlg 219 H7
Gartness N Lans 209 K6
Gartness Stirlg 208 E2
Gartocharn W Duns 208 D2
Garton E R Yk 145 H1
Garton-on-the-Wolds E R Yk 152 F4
Gartymore Highld 274 D5
Garvald E Loth 212 D5
Garvan Highld 238 F8
Garvard Ag & B 214 D6
Garve Highld 262 C7
Garvellachs Ag & B 215 J2
Garvestone Norfk 105 L2
Garvock Inver 207 L5
Garway Herefs 62 F3
Garway Common Herefs 62 F3
Garway Hill Herefs 62 F2
Garyvard W Isls 282 g4
Gasper Wilts 32 C4
Gastard Wilts 46 C5
Gasthorpe Norfk 105 K7
Gaston Green Essex 70 D4
Gatcombe IoW 19 H6
Gatebeck Cumb 157 J5
Gate Burton Lincs 135 G3
Gateford Notts 134 B3
Gateforth N York 142 E2
Gatehead E Ayrs 196 D4
Gate Helmsley N York 151 L5
Gatehouse Nthumb 179 H1
Gatehouse of Fleet D & G 174 F4
Gateley Norfk 121 L6
Gatenby N York 160 D5
Gatesgarth Cumb 165 G7
Gateshaw Border 189 L2
Gateshead Gatesd 181 G6
Gates Heath Ches W 129 L7
Gateside Angus 234 C6
Gateside E Rens 208 E7
Gateside Fife 222 B5
Gateside N Ayrs 208 B8
Gateslack D & G 186 C5
Gathurst Wigan 139 G6
Gatley Stockp 131 G2
Gatton Surrey 51 H8
Gattonside Border 201 H6
Gaufron Powys 78 D2
Gaulby Leics 100 F3
Gauldry Fife 222 F2
Gauldswell P & K 233 K5
Gaulkthorn Lancs 139 M3
Gaultree Norfk 103 K2
Gaunton's Bank Ches E 113 J2
Gaunt's Common Dorset 17 K2
Gaunt's End Essex 70 E2
Gautby Lincs 136 C5
Gavinton Border 202 B3
Gawber Barns 141 M6
Gawcott Bucks 67 G1
Gawsworth Ches E 131 H5
Gawthorpe Wakefd 141 L3
Gawthrop Cumb 158 B5
Gawthwaite Cumb 156 C5
Gay Bowers Essex 71 J6
Gaydon Warwks 83 J4
Gayhurst M Keyn 85 G6
Gayle N York 158 F5
Gayles N York 159 L1
Gay Street W Susx 21 J3
Gayton Nhants 84 D4
Gayton Norfk 120 F7
Gayton Staffs 114 F6
Gayton Wirral 129 G4
Gayton le Marsh Lincs 137 H3
Gayton Thorpe Norfk 121 G7
Gaywood Norfk 120 E7
Gazeley Suffk 88 E2
Gear Cnwll 3 J6
Gearraidh Bhaird W Isls 282 g4
Geary Highld 258 D4
Gedding Suffk 89 J4
Geddington Nhants 101 K6
Gedling Notts 117 G3
Gedney Lincs 119 L6
Gedney Broadgate Lincs 119 L7
Gedney Drove End Lincs 120 A5
Gedney Dyke Lincs 119 L6
Gedney Hill Lincs 103 G1
Gee Cross Tamesd 131 J1
Geeston RutInd 101 L3
Geldeston Norfk 107 H5
Gelli Rhondd 42 E3
Gelli Torfn 62 B8
Gellifor Denbgs 128 D7
Gelligaer Caerph 43 H2
Gelligroes Caerph 43 J3
Gelligron Neath 57 K4
Gellilydan Gwynd 110 C4
Gellinudd Neath 57 K4
Gelly Pembks 55 J3
Gellyburn P & K 233 G7
Gellywen Carmth 58 A4
Gelston D & G 175 J3
Gelston Lincs 118 B3
Gembling E R Yk 153 H4
Gentleshaw Staffs 98 D1
Georgefield D & G 187 L7
George Green Bucks 50 C3
Georgeham Devon 27 H3
Georgemas Junction Station Highld 279 L4
George Nympton Devon 28 B6
Georgetown Blae G 61 J5
Georgia Cnwll 2 D4
Georth Ork 275 c3
Gerlan Gwynd 126 C6
Germansweek Devon 12 B4
Germoe Cnwll 2 F5
Gerrans Cnwll 3 M4
Gerrards Cross Bucks 50 C1
Gerrick R & Cl 171 G8
Gestingthorpe Essex 89 G7
Geuffordd Powys 112 B8
Gib Hill Ches W 130 C4
Gibraltar Lincs 137 K7
Gibsmere Notts 117 J2
Giddeahall Wilts 46 B4
Giddy Green Dorset 16 F5
Gidea Park Gt Lon 52 B1
Gidleigh Devon 12 F5
Giffnock E Rens 208 F7
Gifford E Loth 212 C5
Giffordtown Fife 222 E5
Giggleswick N York 148 D3
Gigha Ag & B 205 L6
Gilberdyke E R Yk 143 L2
Gilbert's End Worcs 81 J6
Gilbert Street Hants 35 K4
Gilchriston E Loth 212 B6
Gilcrux Cumb 164 F3
Gildersome Leeds 141 K2
Gildingwells Rothm 133 L3
Gilesgate Moor Dur 169 J2
Gileston V Glam 42 F8
Gilfach Caerph 43 J2
Gilfach Goch Brdgnd 42 E4
Gilfachrheda Cerdgn 76 D3
Gilgarran Cumb 164 D6
Gill Cumb 166 B5
Gillamoor N York 162 B4
Gillan Cnwll 3 K6
Gillen Highld 258 D5
Gillesbie D & G 187 J7
Gilling East N York 161 K7
Gillingham Dorset 32 D5
Gillingham Medway 53 G5
Gillingham Norfk 107 H5
Gilling West N York 160 B2
Gillock Highld 280 B4
Gillow Heath Staffs 131 H7
Gills Highld 280 D2
Gill's Green Kent 39 J7
Gilmanscleuch Border 188 B2
Gilmerton C Edin 211 J5
Gilmerton P & K 220 F2
Gilmonby Dur 168 C8
Gilmorton Leics 100 C6
Gilroes Crematorium C Leic 100 C2
Gilsland Nthumb 178 E5
Gilson Warwks 99 G5
Gilstead C Brad 149 L7
Gilston Border 200 F2
Gilston Herts 70 C4
Gilston Park Herts 70 B4
Giltbrook Notts 116 E2
Gilwern Mons 61 L4
Gimingham Norfk 122 F4
Ginclough Ches E 131 J4
Gingers Green E Susx 23 K5
Gipping Suffk 90 C3
Gipsey Bridge Lincs 119 J2
Girdle Toll N Ayrs 196 C3
Girlington C Brad 141 H1
Girlsta Shet 281 e6
Girsby N York 160 E1
Girtford C Beds 86 D5
Girthon D & G 174 F4
Girton Cambs 87 J3
Girton Notts 135 G6
Girvan S Ayrs 182 F3
Gisburn Lancs 148 E6
Gisleham Suffk 107 K5
Gislingham Suffk 90 C1
Gissing Norfk 106 C6
Gittisham Devon 14 D3
Gladestry Powys 79 J4
Gladsmuir E Loth 212 A4
Glais Swans 57 K5
Glaisdale N York 162 D2
Glamis Angus 234 B6
Glanaber Gwynd 110 B1
Glanafon Pembks 54 F3
Glanaman Carmth 59 J6
Glandford Norfk 122 A3
Glan-Duar Carmth 76 F6
Glandwr Pembks 75 L6
Glan-Dwyfach Gwynd 109 J3
Glandyfi Cerdgn 92 F4
Glangrwyney Powys 61 K4
Glanllynfi Brdgnd 42 C3
Glanmule Powys 94 E5
Glanrhyd Pembks 75 K4
Glan-rhyd Powys 57 L3
Glanton Nthumb 190 F3
Glanton Pike Nthumb 190 F3
Glanvilles Wootton Dorset 16 C1
Glan-y-don Flints 128 E4
Glan-y-llyn Rhondd 43 H5
Glan-y-nant Powys 93 K6
Glan-yr-afon Gwynd 111 H3
Glan-yr-afon Gwynd 111 K3
Glan-yr-afon IoA 126 B4
Glan-yr-afon Swans 57 H4
Glapthorn Nhants 101 M5
Glapwell Derbys 133 J6
Glasbury Powys 79 H7
Glascoed Denbgs 127 K5
Glascoed Mons 62 C6
Glascote Staffs 99 G3
Glascwm Powys 79 G5
Glasfryn Conwy 111 H2
Glasgow C Glas 209 G6
Glasinfryn Gwynd 125 K6
Glasnacardoch Bay Highld 237 K2
Glasnakille Highld 247 H6

Glaspwll Powys 92 F4
Glassenbury Kent 39 J6
Glassford S Lans 197 L2
Glass Houghton Wakefd 142 C3
Glasshouse Gloucs 63 L3
Glasshouse Hill Gloucs 63 L3
Glasshouses N York 149 L3
Glasson Cumb 177 H6
Glasson Lancs 147 J4
Glassonby Cumb 166 D3
Glasterlaw Angus 234 F5
Glaston Rutlnd 101 K3
Glastonbury Somset 31 H3
Glatton Cambs 102 C6
Glazebrook Warrtn 130 D1
Glazebury Warrtn 139 K8
Glazeley Shrops 96 F5
Gleadless Sheff 133 G3
Gleadsmoss Ches E 130 F6
Gleaston Cumb 146 E2
Glebe Highld 250 F8
Gledhow Leeds 150 D8
Gledpark D & G 175 G5
Gledrid Shrops 112 D4
Glemsford Suffk 89 G5
Glenallachie Moray 254 E3
Glenancross Highld 237 K2
Glenaros House Ag & B 227 G4
Glen Auldyn IoM 154 f4
Glenbarr Ag & B 192 D1
Glenbarry Abers 267 L5
Glenbeg Highld 237 H8
Glenbervie Abers 245 G7
Glenboig N Lans 209 J5
Glenborrodale Highld 237 H8
Glenbranter Ag & B 217 J7
Glenbreck Border 187 G2
Glenbrittle House Highld 246 F4
Glenbuck E Ayrs 198 B7
Glencally Angus 234 A3
Glencaple D & G 176 C5
Glencarron Lodge Highld 249 H2
Glencarse P & K 222 C3
Glen Clunie Lodge Abers 242 F7
Glencoe Highld 229 H4
Glencothe Border 199 J7
Glencraig Fife 222 B8
Glencrosh D & G 185 J5
Glendale Highld 258 B6
Glendaruel Ag & B 206 F2
Glendevon P & K 221 H6
Glendoe Lodge Highld 240 C2
Glendoick P & K 222 C3
Glenduckie Fife 222 D3
Glenegedale Ag & B 204 E6
Glenelg Highld 248 C7
Glenerney Moray 253 K2
Glenfarg P & K 221 L5
Glenfield Leics 100 C2
Glenfinnan Highld 238 E7
Glenfintaig Lodge Highld 239 L6
Glenfoot P & K 222 B4
Glenfyne Lodge Ag & B 218 B4
Glengarnock N Ayrs 208 B8
Glengolly Highld 279 K3
Glengorm Castle Ag & B 226 E1
Glengrasco Highld 259 G7
Glenholm Border 199 J6
Glenhoul D & G 184 F5
Glenisla Angus 233 K3
Glenkin Ag & B 207 J3
Glenkindie Abers 243 M1
Glenlivet Moray 254 D6
Glenlochar D & G 175 J2
Glenlomond P & K 222 B6
Glenluce D & G 172 F3
Glenmassen Ag & B 207 H2
Glenmavis N Lans 209 K5
Glen Maye IoM 154 b6
Glen Mona IoM 154 f4
Glenmore Highld 259 G8
Glenmore Lodge Highld 242 C2
Glen Nevis House Highld 229 J1
Glenochil Clacks 220 F8
Glen Parva Leics 100 C4
Glenquiech Angus 234 C3
Glenralloch Ag & B 206 D5
Glenridding Cumb 165 L7
Glenrothes Fife 222 D7
Glenshero Lodge Highld 240 F5
Glenstriven Ag & B 207 H3
Glentham Lincs 135 K2
Glen Trool Lodge D & G 183 K7
Glentrool Village D & G 183 J7
Glentruim House Highld 241 J4
Glentworth Lincs 135 J2
Glenuig Highld 237 K5
Glenvarragill Highld 259 H8
Glen Vine IoM 154 d6
Glenwhilly D & G 182 F8
Glespin S Lans 198 D7
Glewstone Herefs 63 H3
Glinton C Pete 102 C2
Glooston Leics 101 G4
Glossop Derbys 131 L1
Gloster Hill Nthumb 191 K5
Gloucester Gloucs 64 B3
Gloucester Crematorium Gloucs 64 B4
Glusburn N York 149 H6
Glutt Lodge Highld 274 D1
Gluvian Cnwll 4 F2
Glympton Oxon 66 B3
Glynarthen Cerdgn 76 B5
Glyn Ceiriog Wrexhm 112 B4
Glyncorrwg Neath 60 C7
Glynde E Susx 23 G5
Glyndebourne E Susx 23 G5
Glyndyfrdwy Denbgs 112 A3
Glynneath Neath 60 D5
Glynn Valley Crematorium Cnwll 5 J2
Glyntaff Rhondd 43 H4
Glyntaff Crematorium Rhondd 43 H4
Glyntawe Powys 60 C4
Glynteg Carmth 76 C7
Gnosall Staffs 114 C7
Gnosall Heath Staffs 114 C7
Goadby Leics 101 G4
Goadby Marwood Leics 117 K6
Goatacre Wilts 46 F4
Goatham Green E Susx 24 E3
Goathill Dorset 31 L7
Goathland N York 162 E2
Goathurst Somset 30 C4
Goathurst Common Kent 38 D3
Goat Lees Kent 40 D6
Gobowen Shrops 112 D5
Godalming Surrey 36 E2
Goddard's Corner Suffk 91 G2
Goddard's Green Kent 39 K6
Godford Cross Devon 14 D2
Godington Oxon 66 F2
Godley Tamesd 140 E8
Godmanchester Cambs 86 E1
Godmanstone Dorset 16 C3
Godmersham Kent 40 D5
Godney Somset 31 H2
Godolphin Cross Cnwll 2 F5
Godre'r-graig Neath 57 L3
Godshill Hants 33 L7
Godshill IoW 19 J7
Godstone Staffs 115 G5
Godstone Surrey 51 K8
Godsworthy Devon 12 C7
Godwinscroft Hants 18 B4
Goetre Mons 62 C6
Goff's Oak Herts 69 J6
Gofilon Mons 61 L4
Gogar C Edin 211 G4
Goginan Cerdgn 92 E7
Golan Gwynd 109 J3
Golant Cnwll 5 K4
Golberdon Cnwll 11 L8
Golborne Wigan 139 J8
Golcar Kirk 141 H4
Goldcliff Newpt 44 D2
Golden Cross E Susx 23 J5
Golden Green Kent 39 G4
Golden Grove Carmth 59 G5
Goldenhill C Stke 114 D1
Golden Hill Pembks 55 G6
Golden Pot Hants 35 L2
Golden Valley Derbys 116 C1
Golders Green Gt Lon 51 H2
Golders Green Crematorium Gt Lon 51 H1
Goldfinch Bottom W Berk 48 D6
Goldhanger Essex 72 C5
Gold Hill Cambs 103 L5
Gold Hill Dorset 32 D8
Golding Shrops 96 C3
Goldington Bed 86 B5
Goldsborough N York 150 E4
Goldsborough N York 171 J7
Golds Green Sandw 98 C5
Goldsithney Cnwll 2 E5
Goldstone Kent 41 J3
Goldstone Shrops 113 M6
Goldsworth Park Surrey 50 C7
Goldthorpe Barns 142 C7
Goldworthy Devon 27 G6
Golford Kent 39 K6
Golford Green Kent 39 K6
Gollanfield Highld 252 F1
Gollinglith Foot N York 159 L6
Golly Wrexhm 129 H7
Golsoncott Somset 29 J3
Golspie Highld 273 K8
Gomeldon Wilts 33 L4
Gomersal Kirk 141 K3
Gomshall Surrey 37 G1
Gonalston Notts 117 H2
Gonerby Hill Foot Lincs 118 B4
Gonfirth Shet 281 d5
Goodameavy Devon 7 G2
Good Easter Essex 70 F5
Gooderstone Norfk 104 F3
Goodleigh Devon 27 L4
Goodmanham E R Yk 152 D7
Goodmayes Gt Lon 51 M2
Goodnestone Kent 40 D3
Goodnestone Kent 41 H4
Goodrich Herefs 63 H3
Goodrington Torbay 8 D3
Goodshaw Lancs 140 B3
Goodshaw Fold Lancs 140 B2
Goodstone Devon 13 H8
Goodwick Pembks 74 F4
Goodworth Clatford Hants 34 D2
Goodyers End Warwks 99 J6
Goole E R Yk 143 J3
Goole Fields E R Yk 143 J4
Goom's Hill Worcs 82 B4
Goonbell Cnwll 4 B5
Goonhavern Cnwll 4 C4
Goonvrea Cnwll 4 B5
Goosecruives Abers 245 G7
Gooseford Devon 12 F4
Goose Green Essex 73 H2
Goose Green Kent 39 G3
Goose Green Kent 39 L6
Goose Green S Glos 45 K4
Goose Green W Susx 21 J3
Goose Green Wigan 139 H7
Gooseham Cnwll 26 D7
Gooseham Mill Cnwll 26 D7
Goosehill Green Worcs 81 L3
Goose Pool Herefs 80 B7
Goosey Oxon 47 M1
Goosnargh Lancs 147 L8
Goostrey Ches E 130 F5
Gorddinog Conwy 126 D5
Gordon Border 201 K4
Gordon Arms Hotel Border 200 C8
Gordonstoun Abers 256 C4
Gordonstown Abers 267 L5
Gore Powys 79 J3
Gorebridge Mdloth 211 K6
Gorefield Cambs 103 J1
Gore Pit Essex 72 C3
Gores Wilts 47 G7
Gore Street Kent 41 J2
Gorey Jersey 9 f3
Goring Oxon 48 F3
Goring-by-Sea W Susx 21 J6
Goring Heath Oxon 49 G3
Gorleston on Sea Norfk 107 L3
Gornal Wood Crematorium Dudley 97 K5
Gorrachie Abers 268 D4
Gorran Churchtown Cnwll 5 G6
Gorran Haven Cnwll 5 G6
Gorran High Lanes Cnwll 5 G6
Gorrig Cerdgn 76 D6
Gors Cerdgn 92 D7
Gorsedd Flints 128 E4
Gorse Hill Swindn 47 H2
Gorseinon Swans 57 G5
Gorseybank Derbys 115 M1
Gorsgoch Cerdgn 76 E5
Gorslas Carmth 59 G6
Gorsley Gloucs 63 K2
Gorsley Common Herefs 63 K2
Gorstage Ches W 130 B5
Gorstan Highld 262 C7
Gorstella Ches W 129 H7
Gorst Hill Worcs 97 G8
Gorsty Hill Staffs 115 H6
Gorten Ag & B 227 L6
Gorthleck Highld 250 F7
Gorton Manch 140 C8
Gosbeck Suffk 90 D4
Gosberton Lincs 119 H5
Gosberton Clough Lincs 119 G5
Gosfield Essex 71 J1
Gosford Devon 14 C3
Gosforth Cumb 155 J2
Gosforth N u Ty 180 F5
Gosling Street Somset 31 J4
Gosmore Herts 68 F2
Gospel End Staffs 97 K4
Gospel Green W Susx 36 D4
Gosport Hants 19 K4
Gossard's Green C Beds 85 J6
Gossington Gloucs 63 L6
Goswick Nthumb 203 G4
Gotham Notts 116 F5
Gotherington Gloucs 64 D1
Gotton Somset 30 C5
Goudhurst Kent 39 H6
Goulceby Lincs 136 E4
Gourdas Abers 256 D3
Gourdie C Dund 222 F1
Gourdon Abers 235 K1
Gourock Inver 207 L3
Govan C Glas 208 F6
Goveton Devon 7 L5
Gowdall E R Yk 143 G3
Gower Highld 262 E8
Gowerton Swans 57 G5
Gowkhall Fife 210 E1
Gowthorpe E R Yk 152 A5
Goxhill E R Yk 153 K6
Goxhill N Linc 144 E3
Grabhair W Isls 282 g4
Graby Lincs 118 E5
Grade Cnwll 3 H8
Gradeley Green Ches E 113 K1
Graffham W Susx 20 F3
Grafham Cambs 86 D2
Grafham Surrey 36 F3
Grafton Herefs 80 C7
Grafton N York 150 F3
Grafton Oxon 65 K7
Grafton Shrops 113 G7
Grafton Worcs 80 D3
Grafton Worcs 82 A7
Grafton Flyford Worcs 81 M4
Grafton Regis Nhants 84 E6
Grafton Underwood Nhants 101 K7
Grafty Green Kent 39 L4
Graianrhyd Denbgs 128 F8
Graig Conwy 126 F5
Graig Denbgs 128 C5
Graig-fechan Denbgs 112 A1
Grain Medway 53 J4
Grains Bar Oldham 140 E6
Grainsby Lincs 145 H7
Grainthorpe Lincs 145 K8
Grampound Cnwll 4 F5
Grampound Road Cnwll 4 E5
Gramsdal W Isls 283 c9
Gramsdale W Isls 283 c9
Granborough Bucks 67 J2
Granby Notts 117 K4
Grandborough Warwks 83 L2
Grand Chemins Jersey 9 e3
Grandes Rocques Guern 9 j2
Grandtully P & K 232 D5
Grange Cumb 165 H7
Grange Medway 53 G5
Grange P & K 222 D2
Grange Wirral 128 F2
Grange Crossroads Moray 267 K5
Grange Hall Moray 265 H7
Grangehall S Lans 199 G4
Grange Hill Essex 70 C8
Grangemill Derbys 132 E8
Grange Moor Kirk 141 K4
Grangemouth Falk 210 B3
Grange of Lindores Fife 222 D4
Grange-over-Sands Cumb 156 F7
Grangepans Falk 210 D3
Grangetown R & Cl 170 D6
Grangetown Sundld 181 K8
Grange Villa Dur 180 F8
Gransmoor E R Yk 153 H4
Gransmore Green Essex 71 G3
Granston Pembks 74 E5
Grantchester Cambs 87 J4
Grantham Lincs 118 B4
Grantham Crematorium Lincs 118 B4
Granton C Edin 211 H4
Grantown-on-Spey Highld 253 K6
Grantsfield Herefs 80 C3
Grantshouse Border 213 H6
Grappenhall Warrtn 130 C2
Grasby Lincs 144 D6
Grasmere Cumb 156 D1
Grasscroft Oldham 140 E6
Grassendale Lpool 129 J3
Grassgarth Cumb 165 K2
Grass Green Essex 88 E7
Grassington N York 149 H3
Grassmoor Derbys 133 H6
Grassthorpe Notts 134 F6
Grateley Hants 34 C3
Gratwich Staffs 115 G5
Graveley Cambs 86 E3
Graveley Herts 69 G2
Gravelly Hill Birm 98 E5
Gravelsbank Shrops 95 H3
Graveney Kent 40 D3
Gravesend Kent 52 E4
Gravir W Isls 282 g4
Grayingham Lincs 144 A8
Grayrigg Cumb 157 J3
Grays Thurr 52 D3

Grayshott Hants 36 C4
Grayson Green Cumb 164 C5
Grayswood Surrey 36 D4
Graythorpe Hartpl 170 C5
Grazeley Wokham 49 G5
Greasbrough Rothm 142 C8
Greasby Wirral 128 F2
Greasley Notts 116 E2
Great Abington Cambs 87 L5
Great Addington Nhants 101 L8
Great Alne Warwks 82 D3
Great Altcar Lancs 138 C6
Great Amwell Herts 69 K4
Great Asby Cumb 166 F8
Great Ashfield Suffk 89 K2
Great Ayton N York 170 D8
Great Baddow Essex 71 H6
Great Badminton S Glos 46 A2
Great Bardfield Essex 71 G1
Great Barford Bed 86 C5
Great Barr Sandw 98 D4
Great Barrington Gloucs 65 J4
Great Barrow Ches W 129 L6
Great Barton Suffk 89 H2
Great Barugh N York 162 C6
Great Bavington Nthumb 180 B3
Great Bealings Suffk 90 F5
Great Bedwyn Wilts 47 K6
Great Bentley Essex 73 G3
Great Billing Nhants 84 F3
Great Bircham Norfk 121 G5
Great Blakenham Suffk 90 D5
Great Blencow Cumb 166 B4
Great Bolas Wrekin 113 L7
Great Bookham Surrey 50 E8
Great Bosullow Cnwll 2 C4
Great Bourton Oxon 83 K6
Great Bowden Leics 101 G5
Great Bradley Suffk 88 D4
Great Braxted Essex 72 B4
Great Bricett Suffk 90 B5
Great Brickhill Bucks 67 L1
Great Bridgeford Staffs 114 D6
Great Brington Nhants 84 C2
Great Bromley Essex 73 G2
Great Broughton Cumb 164 E4
Great Broughton N York 161 J2
Great Budworth Ches W 130 C4
Great Burdon Darltn 169 J7
Great Burstead Essex 71 G8
Great Busby N York 161 H2
Great Canfield Essex 70 E3
Great Carlton Lincs 137 H3
Great Casterton Rutlnd 101 M2
Great Chalfield Wilts 46 B6
Great Chart Kent 40 C7
Great Chatwell Staffs 114 B8
Great Chell C Stke 114 D1
Great Chesterford Essex 87 K6
Great Cheverell Wilts 46 E8
Great Chishill Cambs 87 J7
Great Clacton Essex 73 J4
Great Cliffe Wakefd 141 M4
Great Clifton Cumb 164 D5
Great Coates NE Lin 145 G6
Great Comberton Worcs 81 L6
Great Comp Kent 39 G2
Great Corby Cumb 178 B7
Great Cornard Suffk 89 H7
Great Cowden E R Yk 153 L7
Great Coxwell Oxon 65 K8
Great Cransley Nhants 101 H8
Great Cressingham Norfk 105 G3
Great Crosthwaite Cumb 165 J6
Great Cubley Derbys 115 K4
Great Cumbrae Island N Ayrs 207 K7
Great Dalby Leics 117 K8
Great Doddington Nhants 85 H2
Great Doward Herefs 63 G4
Great Dunham Norfk 121 J8
Great Dunmow Essex 70 F3
Great Durnford Wilts 33 K3
Great Easton Essex 70 F2
Great Easton Leics 101 J5
Great Eccleston Lancs 147 H7
Great Edstone N York 162 C6
Great Ellingham Norfk 105 L4
Great Elm Somset 32 C1
Great Everdon Nhants 84 B4
Great Eversden Cambs 87 H4
Great Fencote N York 160 D4
Greatfield Wilts 47 G2
Great Finborough Suffk 89 K4
Greatford Lincs 102 B1
Great Fransham Norfk 105 H1
Great Gaddesden Herts 68 C5
Greatgate Staffs 115 G3
Great Gidding Cambs 102 C6
Great Givendale E R Yk 152 B5
Great Glemham Suffk 91 H3
Great Glen Leics 100 E4
Great Gonerby Lincs 118 B4
Great Gransden Cambs 86 F4
Great Green Cambs 86 F6
Great Green Norfk 106 F6
Great Green Suffk 89 J2
Great Green Suffk 89 J4
Great Habton N York 162 D7
Great Hale Lincs 118 F3
Great Hallingbury Essex 70 D3
Greatham Hants 36 A5
Greatham Hartpl 170 C5
Greatham W Susx 21 H4
Great Hampden Bucks 67 K6
Great Harrowden Nhants 85 G1
Great Harwood Lancs 139 L1
Great Haseley Oxon 66 F6
Great Hatfield E R Yk 153 K7
Great Haywood Staffs 114 F7
Great Heck N York 142 F3
Great Henny Essex 89 H7
Great Hinton Wilts 46 C7
Great Hockham Norfk 105 J5
Great Holland Essex 73 J3
Great Hollands Br For 49 L5
Great Horkesley Essex 72 E1
Great Hormead Herts 69 L1
Great Horton C Brad 141 J2
Great Horwood Bucks 67 J1
Great Houghton Barns 142 C6
Great Houghton Nhants 84 F3
Great Hucklow Derbys 132 D4
Great Kelk E R Yk 153 H4
Great Kimble Bucks 67 K6
Great Kingshill Bucks 67 L7
Great Langdale Cumb 156 D2
Great Langton N York 160 D3
Great Leighs Essex 71 H4
Great Limber Lincs 144 E6
Great Linford M Keyn 85 G6
Great Livermere Suffk 89 H1
Great Longstone Derbys 132 D5
Great Lumley Dur 169 J1
Great Lyth Shrops 95 L2
Great Malvern Worcs 81 H6
Great Maplestead Essex 89 G8
Great Marton Bpool 138 C1
Great Massingham Norfk 121 H7
Great Melton Norfk 106 C2
Great Meols Wirral 128 F2
Great Milton Oxon 66 F6
Great Missenden Bucks 67 L6
Great Mitton Lancs 148 C8
Great Mongeham Kent 41 K5
Great Moulton Norfk 106 D5
Great Munden Herts 69 K2
Great Musgrave Cumb 167 H7
Great Ness Shrops 112 F7
Great Notley Essex 71 H3
Great Oak Mons 62 D5
Great Oakley Essex 73 J2
Great Oakley Nhants 101 J6
Great Offley Herts 68 F2
Great Ormside Cumb 167 G7
Great Orton Cumb 177 K7
Great Ouseburn N York 150 F3
Great Oxendon Nhants 100 F6
Great Oxney Green Essex 71 G6
Great Palgrave Norfk 105 G1
Great Pattenden Kent 39 J4
Great Paxton Cambs 86 E2
Great Plumpton Lancs 138 D1
Great Plumstead Norfk 106 F2
Great Ponton Lincs 118 B5
Great Potheridge Devon 27 J7
Great Preston Leeds 142 B2
Great Purston Nhants 83 M7
Great Raveley Cambs 102 E7
Great Rissington Gloucs 65 J4
Great Rollright Oxon 65 L1
Great Rudbaxton Pembks 54 F3
Great Ryburgh Norfk 121 L6
Great Ryle Nthumb 190 E4
Great Ryton Shrops 96 B3
Great Saling Essex 71 G2
Great Salkeld Cumb 166 D3
Great Sampford Essex 88 C8
Great Saredon Staffs 98 B2
Great Saughall Ches W 129 H5
Great Saxham Suffk 88 F3
Great Shefford W Berk 48 A4
Great Shelford Cambs 87 J5
Great Smeaton N York 160 E2
Great Snoring Norfk 121 L4
Great Somerford Wilts 46 D2
Great Soudley Shrops 114 A5
Great Stainton Darltn 169 J6
Great Stambridge Essex 53 J1
Great Staughton Cambs 86 C2
Great Steeping Lincs 137 H6
Great Stoke S Glos 45 J3
Great Stonar Kent 41 K3
Greatstone-on-Sea Kent 25 K3
Great Strickland Cumb 166 D6
Great Stukeley Cambs 102 E8
Great Sturton Lincs 136 D4
Great Sutton Ches W 129 J4
Great Sutton Shrops 96 C6
Great Swinburne Nthumb 179 L4
Great Tew Oxon 66 B1
Great Tey Essex 72 C2
Great Thurlow Suffk 88 D5
Great Torrington Devon 27 J7
Great Tosson Nthumb 190 E6
Great Totham Essex 72 B5
Great Totham Essex 72 C4
Great Tows Lincs 136 D2
Great Urswick Cumb 156 C7
Great Wakering Essex 53 K2
Great Waldingfield Suffk 89 J6
Great Walsingham Norfk 121 L4
Great Waltham Essex 71 G4
Great Warford Ches E 130 F4
Great Warley Essex 52 C1
Great Washbourne Gloucs 82 A8
Great Weeke Devon 13 G5
Great Weldon Nhants 101 K5
Great Welnetham Suffk 89 H3
Great Wenham Suffk 90 C7
Great Whittington Nthumb 180 B5
Great Wigborough Essex 72 D4
Great Wilbraham Cambs 87 L4
Great Wishford Wilts 33 J4
Great Witchingham Norfk 122 C7
Great Witcombe Gloucs 64 D4
Great Witley Worcs 81 H2
Great Wolford Warwks 82 F8
Greatworth Nhants 84 A6
Great Wratting Suffk 88 D5
Great Wymondley Herts 69 G2
Great Wyrley Staffs 98 C2
Great Wytheford Shrops 113 J7
Great Yarmouth Norfk 107 L2
Great Yarmouth Crematorium Norfk 107 K3
Great Yeldham Essex 88 F7
Grebby Lincs 137 H6
Greeba IoM 154 d6
Green Denbgs 128 C6
Green Bank Cumb 156 E6
Greenburn W Loth 210 B7
Greencroft Hall Dur 168 F1
Green Cross Surrey 36 C3
Green Down Somset 45 H8
Green End Bed 85 K5
Green End Bed 86 B2
Green End Bed 86 B3
Green End Bed 86 C5
Green End Cambs 87 H4
Green End Cambs 87 K2
Green End Cambs 87 K3
Green End Cambs 102 D6
Green End Cambs 102 E8
Green End Herts 69 H1
Green End Herts 69 J3
Green End Herts 87 G8
Greenend Oxon 65 L3
Green End Warwks 99 H6
Greenfield Ag & B 207 L1
Greenfield C Beds 85 L8
Greenfield Flints 128 E4
Greenfield Highld 239 L3
Greenfield Oldham 140 F7
Greenfield Oxon 49 H1
Greenford Gt Lon 50 F3
Greengairs N Lans 209 L5
Greengates C Brad 150 B8
Greengill Cumb 164 F3
Greenhalgh Lancs 147 H8
Greenham Somset 29 K6
Greenham W Berk 48 C6
Green Hammerton N York 151 G4
Greenhaugh Nthumb 179 J2
Green Head Cumb 165 L1
Greenhead Nthumb 178 F6
Green Heath Staffs 98 C1
Greenheys Salfd 139 L7
Greenhill D & G 176 F3
Greenhill Falk 209 L3
Greenhill Herefs 81 G5
Greenhill Kent 40 F2
Greenhill S Lans 198 F6
Green Hill Wilts 46 F2
Greenhillocks Derbys 116 C2
Greenhithe Kent 52 C4
Greenholm E Ayrs 197 G3
Greenholme Cumb 157 J2
Greenhouse Border 188 F2
Greenhow Hill N York 149 K3
Greenland Highld 280 B3
Greenland Sheff 133 H2
Greenlands Bucks 49 J2
Green Lane Devon 13 H7
Green Lane Worcs 82 C2
Greenlaw Border 201 L4
Greenlea D & G 176 D4
Greenloaning P & K 220 E5
Green Moor Barns 141 L7
Greenmount Bury 140 A5
Green Oak E R Yk 143 K2
Greenock Inver 207 M4
Greenock Crematorium Inver 207 M4
Greenodd Cumb 156 D6
Green Ore Somset 31 J1
Green Quarter Cumb 157 G2
Greensgate Norfk 122 B8
Greenshields S Lans 199 H4
Greenside Gatesd 180 E6
Greenside Kirk 141 J4
Greens Norton Nhants 84 C5
Greenstead Essex 72 E2
Greenstead Green Essex 71 K2
Greensted Essex 70 D6
Green Street E Susx 24 D5
Green Street Gloucs 64 C4
Green Street Herts 69 G7
Green Street Herts 70 C3
Green Street Worcs 81 K5
Green Street Green Gt Lon 51 M6
Green Street Green Kent 52 C5
Greenstreet Green Suffk 90 B5
Green Tye Herts 70 C3
Greenway Gloucs 81 G8
Greenway Somset 30 D6
Greenway V Glam 43 G7
Greenway Worcs 81 G1
Greenwich Gt Lon 51 K3
Greet Gloucs 64 F1
Greete Shrops 80 D1
Greetham Lincs 136 F5
Greetham Rutlnd 118 B8
Greetland Calder 141 G3
Gregson Lane Lancs 139 J2
Greinton Somset 30 F4
Grenaby IoM 154 c7
Grendon Nhants 85 G3
Grendon Warwks 99 H3
Grendon Green Herefs 80 E4
Grendon Underwood Bucks 67 G3
Grenofen Devon 12 C8
Grenoside Sheff 133 G1
Grenoside Crematorium Sheff 132 F1
Greosabhagh W Isls 282 e6
Gresford Wrexhm 112 E1
Gresham Norfk 122 D4
Greshornish House Hotel Highld 258 E6
Gressenhall Norfk 121 L8
Gressenhall Green Norfk 121 L8
Gressingham Lancs 147 L2
Gresty Green Ches E 113 M1
Greta Bridge Dur 168 D8
Gretna D & G 177 K5
Gretna Green D & G 177 K5
Gretton Gloucs 64 E1
Gretton Nhants 101 K4
Gretton Shrops 96 C4
Grewelthorpe N York 160 C7
Grey Friars Suffk 91 L1
Greygarth N York 150 A1
Grey Green N Linc 143 K6
Greylake Somset 30 F4
Greyrigg D & G 176 E1
Greys Green Oxon 49 H2
Greysouthen Cumb 164 E5
Greystoke Cumb 166 B4
Greystone Angus 234 E6
Greywell Hants 35 L1
Gribb Dorset 15 J2
Gribthorpe E R Yk 143 J1
Griff Warwks 99 K5
Griffithstown Torfn 62 C7
Griffydam Leics 116 C7
Griggs Green Hants 36 B4
Grimeford Village Lancs 139 J5
Grimesthorpe Sheff 133 G2
Grimethorpe Barns 142 C6
Grimley Worcs 81 J3
Grimmet S Ayrs 183 J1
Grimoldby Lincs 137 G2
Grimpo Shrops 112 E6
Grimsargh Lancs 139 H1
Grimsby NE Lin 145 H5
Grimsby Crematorium NE Lin 145 H6
Grimscote Nhants 84 C4
Grimscott Cnwll 11 J1
Grimshader W Isls 282 g4
Grimshaw Bl w D 139 L3
Grimshaw Green Lancs 139 G5
Grimsthorpe Lincs 118 D7

Grimston E R Yk 145 H1
Grimston Leics 117 J7
Grimston Norfk 120 F7
Grimstone Dorset 16 C4
Grimstone End Suffk 89 J2
Grinacombe Moor Devon 12 A4
Grindale E R Yk 153 J2
Grindle Shrops 97 G3
Grindleford Derbys 132 E4
Grindleton Lancs 148 D6
Grindley Brook Shrops 113 H3
Grindlow Derbys 132 D4
Grindon Nthumb 202 E4
Grindon S on T 169 K5
Grindon Staffs 115 H1
Grindon Hill Nthumb 179 J5
Grindonrigg Nthumb 202 E4
Gringley on the Hill Notts 134 E2
Grinsdale Cumb 177 L7
Grinshill Shrops 113 H6
Grinton N York 159 J3
Griomaisiader W Isls 282 g4
Griomsaigh W Isls 283 c9
Grishipoll Ag & B 224 F3
Grisling Common E Susx 23 G3
Gristhorpe N York 163 K6
Griston Norfk 105 J4
Gritley Ork 275 d5
Grittenham Wilts 46 F2
Grittleton Wilts 46 B3
Grizebeck Cumb 156 C5
Grizedale Cumb 156 D4
Groby Leics 100 B2
Groes Conwy 127 K6
Groes-faen Rhondd 43 G5
Groesffordd Gwynd 108 D4
Groesffordd Marli Denbgs 127 K5
Groesllwyd Powys 94 F1
Groeslon Gwynd 125 H8
Groeslon Gwynd 125 J7
Groes-Wen Caerph 43 H4
Grogarry W Isls 283 c10
Grogport Ag & B 194 C2
Groigearraidh W Isls 283 c10
Gromford Suffk 91 J3
Gronant Flints 128 C3
Groombridge E Susx 38 E6
Grosebay W Isls 282 e6
Grosmont Mons 62 E2
Grosmont N York 162 E2
Groton Suffk 89 J7
Grotton Oldham 140 E6
Grouville Jersey 9 e3
Grove Bucks 67 M3
Grove Dorset 16 D8
Grove Kent 41 H3
Grove Notts 134 E4
Grove Oxon 48 B1
Grove Pembks 55 G6
Grove Green Kent 39 K2
Grovenhurst Kent 39 H5
Grove Park Gt Lon 51 L4
Grovesend S Glos 45 K1
Grovesend Swans 57 G5
Grubb Street Kent 52 C5
Gruinard Highld 260 F2
Gruinart Ag & B 204 D3
Grula Highld 246 E3
Gruline Ag & B 227 G4
Grumbla Cnwll 2 C5
Grundisburgh Suffk 90 F5
Gruting Shet 281 c6
Gualachulain Highld 229 J6
Guanockgate Lincs 103 H2
Guardbridge Fife 223 H3
Guarlford Worcs 81 J6
Guay P & K 232 F5
Guernsey Guern 9 j3
Guestling Green E Susx 24 F4
Guestling Thorn E Susx 24 F4
Guestwick Norfk 122 B6
Guide Bridge Tamesd 140 D8
Guide Post Nthumb 181 G2
Guilden Morden Cambs 86 F6
Guilden Sutton Ches W 129 K6
Guildford Surrey 36 F1
Guildford Crematorium Surrey 36 E2
Guildstead Kent 53 H6
Guildtown P & K 221 L1
Guilsborough Nhants 84 D1
Guilsfield Powys 94 F1
Guilton Kent 41 J4
Guiltreehill S Ayrs 183 J1
Guineaford Devon 27 K3
Guisborough R & Cl 170 E7
Guiseley Leeds 150 B7
Guist Norfk 121 M6
Guiting Power Gloucs 65 G2
Gullane E Loth 212 B2
Gulling Green Suffk 89 G4
Gulval Cnwll 2 D5
Gulworthy Devon 12 B8
Gumfreston Pembks 55 J6
Gumley Leics 100 F5
Gummow's Shop Cnwll 4 E3
Gunby E R Yk 143 H1
Gunby Lincs 118 B7
Gunby Lincs 137 J6
Gundleton Hants 35 J4
Gun Green Kent 39 J7
Gun Hill E Susx 23 J4
Gun Hill Warwks 99 H5
Gunn Devon 27 L4
Gunnerside N York 159 G3
Gunnerton Nthumb 179 L4
Gunness N Linc 143 L5
Gunnislake Cnwll 12 B8
Gunnista Shet 281 e6
Gunthorpe C Pete 102 D3
Gunthorpe N Linc 143 K8
Gunthorpe Norfk 121 M4
Gunthorpe Notts 117 H3
Gunton Suffk 107 L4
Gunwalloe Cnwll 3 G6
Gupworthy Somset 29 H4
Gurnard IoW 19 H4
Gurnett Ches E 131 H5
Gurney Slade Somset 31 K1
Gurnos Powys 57 L3
Gushmere Kent 40 D4
Gussage All Saints Dorset 33 G8
Gussage St Andrew Dorset 33 G8
Gussage St Michael Dorset 33 G8
Guston Kent 41 K6
Gutcher Shet 281 f2
Guthrie Angus 234 E5
Guyhirn Cambs 103 H3
Guyhirn Gull Cambs 103 H3
Guy's Marsh Dorset 32 D6
Guyzance Nthumb 191 J5
Gwaenysgor Flints 128 C3
Gwalchmai IoA 125 G4
Gwastadnant Gwynd 126 C8
Gwaun-Cae-Gurwen Carmth 59 J6
Gwbert on Sea Cerdgn 75 K2
Gwealavellan Cnwll 2 F3
Gweek Cnwll 3 H5
Gwehelog Mons 62 D6
Gwenddwr Powys 78 E6
Gwennap Cnwll 3 J3
Gwent Crematorium Mons 62 C7
Gwenter Cnwll 3 J7
Gwernaffield Flints 128 F6
Gwernesney Mons 62 E6
Gwernogle Carmth 58 F2
Gwernymynydd Flints 128 F7
Gwersyllt Wrexhm 112 D1
Gwespyr Flints 128 D3
Gwindra Cnwll 4 F4
Gwinear Cnwll 2 F4
Gwithian Cnwll 2 F3
Gwredog IoA 125 G3
Gwrhay Caerph 61 J7
Gwyddelwern Denbgs 111 L2
Gwyddgrug Carmth 58 E2
Gwynfryn Wrexhm 112 C1
Gwystre Powys 78 E2
Gwytherin Conwy 127 H7
Gyfelia Wrexhm 112 E3
Gyrn-goch Gwynd 109 G2

H

Habberley Shrops 95 K3
Habberley Worcs 97 H7
Habergham Lancs 140 B1
Habertoft Lincs 137 J6
Habin W Susx 36 B6
Habrough NE Lin 144 F5
Hacconby Lincs 118 E6
Haceby Lincs 118 D4
Hacheston Suffk 91 G3
Hackbridge Gt Lon 51 H5
Hackenthorpe Sheff 133 H3
Hackford Norfk 106 B3
Hackforth N York 160 C4
Hack Green Ches E 113 L2
Hackland Ork 275 c4
Hackleton Nhants 84 F4
Hacklinge Kent 41 K4
Hackman's Gate Worcs 97 K7
Hackness N York 163 H4
Hackness Somset 30 E2
Hackney Gt Lon 51 K2
Hackthorn Lincs 135 K3
Hackthorpe Cumb 166 D6
Hacton Gt Lon 52 C2
Hadden Border 202 B6
Haddenham Bucks 67 H5
Haddenham Cambs 103 J8
Haddington E Loth 212 B4
Haddington Lincs 135 H7
Haddiscoe Norfk 107 J4
Haddo Abers 256 E4
Haddon Cambs 102 C5
Hade Edge Kirk 141 J6
Hadfield Derbys 140 F8
Hadham Cross Herts 70 B3
Hadham Ford Herts 70 B3
Hadleigh Essex 53 H2
Hadleigh Suffk 89 L6
Hadleigh Heath Suffk 89 K7
Hadley Worcs 81 K2
Hadley Wrekin 96 F1
Hadley End Staffs 115 J7
Hadley Wood Gt Lon 69 H7
Hadlow Kent 39 G3
Hadlow Down E Susx 23 J2
Hadnall Shrops 113 H7
Hadstock Essex 88 B6
Hadzor Worcs 81 L3
Haffenden Quarter Kent 39 M5
Hafodunos Conwy 127 H6
Hafod-y-bwch Wrexhm 112 D2
Hafod-y-coed Blae G 61 K7
Hafodyrynys Caerph 61 K7
Haggate Lancs 140 C1
Haggbeck Cumb 178 B4
Haggersta Shet 281 d6
Haggerston Nthumb 203 G4
Haggington Hill Devon 27 K2
Haggs Falk 209 L3
Hagley Herefs 80 D7
Hagley Worcs 97 K7
Hagmore Green Suffk 89 J7
Hagnaby Lincs 136 F7
Hagnaby Lincs 137 J4
Hagworthingham Lincs 136 F6
Haigh Wigan 139 J6
Haighton Green Lancs 139 H1
Haile Cumb 155 J1
Hailes Gloucs 64 F1
Hailey Herts 69 K5
Hailey Oxon 48 F2
Hailey Oxon 65 M4
Hailsham E Susx 23 K5
Hail Weston Cambs 86 D3
Hainault Gt Lon 70 C8
Haine Kent 41 K2
Hainford Norfk 122 E7
Hainton Lincs 136 C3
Hainworth C Brad 149 J8
Haisthorpe E R Yk 153 H3
Hakin Pembks 54 E5
Halam Notts 117 H1
Halbeath Fife 210 F1
Halberton Devon 29 H8
Halcro Highld 280 B4
Hale Cumb 157 H7
Hale Halton 129 L3
Hale Hants 33 L7
Hale Somset 32 C5
Hale Surrey 36 C1
Hale Traffd 130 F2
Hale Bank Halton 129 L3
Halebarns Traffd 130 F3
Hale Green E Susx 23 J4
Hale Nook Lancs 147 G7
Hales Norfk 107 H4
Hales Staffs 113 M5
Halesgate Lincs 119 K6
Hales Green Derbys 115 K3
Halesowen Dudley 98 B6
Hales Place Kent 40 F3
Hale Street Kent 39 G3
Halesville Essex 72 C8
Halesworth Suffk 107 H7
Halewood Knows 129 K3
Halford Devon 13 J7
Halford Shrops 95 K6
Halford Warwks 83 G6
Halfpenny Cumb 157 H5
Halfpenny Green Staffs 97 J5
Halfpenny Houses N York 160 B5
Halfway Carmth 59 J3
Halfway Carmth 59 M2
Halfway Sheff 133 J3
Halfway W Berk 48 B5
Halfway Bridge W Susx 36 D6
Halfway House Shrops 95 H1
Halfway Houses Kent 53 K4
Halifax Calder 141 H3
Halket E Ayrs 208 D8
Halkirk Highld 279 K4
Halkyn Flints 128 F5
Hall E Rens 208 C8
Hallam Fields Derbys 116 D4
Halland E Susx 23 H4
Hallaton Leics 101 H4
Hallatrow BaNES 45 J7
Hallbankgate Cumb 178 D7
Hallbeck Cumb 157 K5
Hall Cliffe Wakefd 141 L4
Hall Cross Lancs 138 E2
Hall Dunnerdale Cumb 156 B3
Hallen S Glos 45 H3
Hall End Bed 85 K6
Hall End C Beds 86 B7
Hallfield Gate Derbys 133 H8
Hallgarth Dur 169 J2
Hall Glen Falk 210 A3
Hall Green Birm 98 E7
Hallin Highld 258 C5
Halling Medway 52 F6
Hallington Lincs 136 F3
Hallington Nthumb 180 B4
Halliwell Bolton 139 L5
Halloughton Notts 117 J1
Hallow Worcs 81 J3
Hallow Heath Worcs 81 J3
Hallsands Devon 8 B7
Hall's Green Essex 69 L5
Hall's Green Herts 69 H2
Hallthwaites Cumb 156 A5
Hallworthy Cnwll 11 H5
Hallyne Border 199 L5
Halmer End Staffs 114 B2
Halmond's Frome Herefs 80 F5
Halmore Gloucs 63 K6
Halnaker W Susx 20 E5
Halsall Lancs 138 D5
Halse Nhants 84 A7
Halse Somset 29 L5
Halsetown Cnwll 2 D3
Halsham E R Yk 145 H2
Halsinger Devon 27 J3
Halstead Essex 71 K1
Halstead Kent 52 A6
Halstead Leics 101 G2
Halstock Dorset 15 M1
Halsway Somset 29 L3
Haltcliff Bridge Cumb 165 L3
Haltemprice Crematorium E R Yk 144 C2
Haltham Lincs 136 D7
Haltoft End Lincs 119 L3
Halton Bucks 67 L5
Halton Halton 129 M3
Halton Lancs 147 K3
Halton Leeds 142 A1
Halton Nthumb 180 B5
Halton Wrexhm 112 D3
Halton East N York 149 J5
Halton Fenside Lincs 137 H7
Halton Gill N York 158 F7
Halton Green Lancs 147 K3
Halton Holegate Lincs 137 H6
Halton Lea Gate Nthumb 178 F7
Halton Quay Cnwll 6 E2
Halton Shields Nthumb 180 B5
Halton West N York 148 E5
Haltwhistle Nthumb 179 G6
Halvergate Norfk 107 J2
Halwell Devon 8 A4
Halwill Devon 12 B3
Halwill Junction Devon 12 B3
Ham Devon 14 F2
Ham Gloucs 63 K7
Ham Gloucs 64 E3
Ham Gt Lon 50 F4
Ham Kent 41 K4
Ham Somset 30 D6
Ham Somset 31 L1
Ham Wilts 47 L6
Hambleden Bucks 49 J2
Hambledon Hants 35 K7
Hambledon Surrey 36 E3
Hamble-le-Rice Hants 19 H2
Hambleton Lancs 147 G7
Hambleton N York 142 E2
Hambleton Moss Side Lancs 147 G7
Hambridge Somset 30 F6
Hambrook S Glos 45 J3
Hambrook W Susx 20 C5
Ham Common Dorset 32 D5
Hameringham Lincs 136 F6
Hamerton Cambs 102 C7
Ham Green Herefs 81 H6
Ham Green Kent 25 G2
Ham Green Kent 53 H5
Ham Green N Som 45 G4
Ham Green Worcs 82 B3
Ham Hill Kent 52 F6
Hamilton S Lans 209 J7
Hamlet Dorset 16 B1
Hamlins E Susx 23 K5
Hammerpot W Susx 21 H5
Hammersmith Gt Lon 51 G3
Hammerwich Staffs 98 D2

Hammerwood E Susx 38 C5
Hammond Street Herts 69 J6
Hammoon Dorset 32 D7
Hamnavoe Shet 281 d7
Hampden Park E Susx 23 K6
Hamperden End Essex 70 E1
Hampnett Gloucs 65 G4
Hampole Donc 142 D5
Hampreston Dorset 17 L3
Hampsfield Cumb 156 F6
Hampson Green Lancs 147 J5
Hampstead Gt Lon 51 H2
Hampstead Norreys W Berk 48 D4
Hampsthwaite N York 150 C4
Hampton C Pete 102 D4
Hampton Devon 15 G3
Hampton Gt Lon 50 F5
Hampton Kent 40 F2
Hampton Shrops 97 G6
Hampton Swindn 65 J8
Hampton Worcs 82 B6
Hampton Bishop Herefs 80 D7
Hampton Fields Gloucs 64 C7
Hampton Green Ches W 113 H2
Hampton Heath Ches W 113 H2
Hampton in Arden Solhll 99 G7
Hampton Loade Shrops 97 G6
Hampton Lovett Worcs 81 K2
Hampton Lucy Warwks 83 G4
Hampton Magna Warwks 83 G2
Hampton on the Hill Warwks 82 F2
Hampton Poyle Oxon 66 D4
Hampton Wick Gt Lon 50 F5
Hamptworth Wilts 34 B7
Hamrow Norfk 121 K6
Hamsey E Susx 22 F5
Hamsey Green Surrey 51 K7
Hamstall Ridware Staffs 115 H7
Hamstead Birm 98 D5
Hamstead IoW 18 F5
Hamstead Marshall W Berk 48 B6
Hamsterley Dur 168 E4
Hamsterley Dur 180 D7
Hamstreet Kent 40 C8
Ham Street Somset 31 J4
Hamwood N Som 44 D7
Hamworthy Poole 17 K4
Hanbury Staffs 115 K6
Hanbury Worcs 81 M2
Hanby Lincs 118 D5
Hanchet End Suffk 88 C6
Hanchurch Staffs 114 C3
Handa Island Highld 276 A6
Handale R & Cl 171 G7
Hand and Pen Devon 14 B3
Handbridge Ches W 129 J6
Handcross W Susx 37 L5
Handforth Ches E 131 G3
Hand Green Ches W 130 A7
Handley Ches W 129 L8
Handley Derbys 133 G7
Handley Green Essex 71 G6
Handsacre Staffs 115 H8
Handsworth Birm 98 D5
Handsworth Sheff 133 H2
Handy Cross Bucks 49 K1
Hanford C Stke 114 D3
Hanford Dorset 32 D8
Hanging Heaton Kirk 141 L3
Hanging Houghton Nhants 101 G8
Hanging Langford Wilts 33 H3
Hangleton Br & H 22 D6
Hangleton W Susx 21 J6
Hanham S Glos 45 J4
Hankelow Ches E 113 L2
Hankerton Wilts 46 E1
Hankham E Susx 23 K6
Hanley C Stke 114 D2
Hanley Castle Worcs 81 J6
Hanley Child Worcs 80 F2
Hanley Swan Worcs 81 J6
Hanley William Worcs 80 F2
Hanlith N York 148 F3
Hanmer Wrexhm 113 G3
Hannaford Devon 27 L5
Hannah Lincs 137 J4
Hannington Hants 48 D7
Hannington Nhants 84 F1
Hannington Swindn 65 H8
Hannington Wick Swindn 65 H8
Hanscombe End C Beds 86 C8
Hanslope M Keyn 84 F6
Hanthorpe Lincs 118 E6
Hanwell Gt Lon 50 F3
Hanwell Oxon 83 K6
Hanwood Shrops 95 K2
Hanworth Gt Lon 50 E5
Hanworth Norfk 122 D4
Happendon S Lans 198 E6
Happisburgh Norfk 123 H5
Happisburgh Common Norfk 123 H5
Hapsford Ches W 129 L5
Hapton Lancs 140 B2
Hapton Norfk 106 D4
Harberton Devon 8 A3
Harbertonford Devon 8 A4
Harbledown Kent 40 F4
Harborne Birm 98 C6
Harborough Magna Warwks 100 B7
Harbottle Nthumb 190 C5
Harbourneford Devon 7 K2
Harbours Hill Worcs 81 M2
Harbridge Hants 18 A2
Harbridge Green Hants 33 K8
Harbury Warwks 83 J3
Harby Leics 117 K5
Harby Notts 135 H5
Harcombe Devon 13 K6
Harcombe Devon 14 D4
Harcombe Bottom Devon 15 H3
Harden C Brad 149 K8
Harden Wsall 98 C3
Hardenhuish Wilts 46 C4
Hardgate Abers 245 H3
Hardgate D & G 175 K2
Hardgate N York 150 C3
Hardgate W Duns 208 E4
Hardham W Susx 21 H3
Hardhorn Lancs 147 G8
Hardingham Norfk 105 L3
Hardingstone Nhants 84 E4
Hardington Somset 45 L8
Hardington Mandeville Somset 31 H8
Hardington Marsh Somset 15 L1
Hardington Moor Somset 31 H8
Hardisworthy Devon 26 D6
Hardley Hants 19 G3
Hardley Street Norfk 107 H3
Hardmead M Keyn 85 H5
Hardraw N York 158 F4
Hardsough Lancs 140 B4
Hardstoft Derbys 133 J7
Hardway Hants 19 K3
Hardway Somset 32 B4
Hardwick Bucks 67 K3
Hardwick Cambs 87 H3
Hardwick Nhants 85 G1
Hardwick Norfk 106 E5
Hardwick Oxon 66 A6
Hardwick Oxon 66 E1
Hardwick Rothm 133 K3
Hardwick Wsall 98 D4
Hardwicke Gloucs 64 A4
Hardwicke Gloucs 64 C2
Hardy's Green Essex 72 D3
Harebeating E Susx 23 K5
Hareby Lincs 136 F6
Hare Croft C Brad 149 K8
Harefield Gt Lon 50 D1
Hare Green Essex 73 G2
Hare Hatch Wokham 49 J3
Harehill Derbys 115 K4
Harehills Leeds 141 M1
Harehope Nthumb 191 G2
Harelaw Border 188 F2
Harelaw D & G 178 B3
Harelaw Dur 180 E8
Hareplain Kent 39 L5
Haresceugh Cumb 166 E2
Harescombe Gloucs 64 B5
Haresfield Gloucs 64 A5
Harestock Hants 34 F4
Hare Street Essex 70 B5
Hare Street Essex 70 D7
Hare Street Herts 69 K1
Harewood Leeds 150 D6
Harewood End Herefs 63 G2
Harford Devon 7 J3
Hargate Norfk 106 C5
Hargatewall Derbys 132 B4
Hargrave Ches W 129 L7
Hargrave Nhants 85 K1
Hargrave Suffk 88 F3
Harker Cumb 177 L6
Harkstead Suffk 90 E8
Harlaston Staffs 99 G1
Harlaxton Lincs 118 A5
Harlech Gwynd 109 K5
Harlescott Shrops 113 H8
Harlesden Gt Lon 51 G2
Harlesthorpe Derbys 133 K4
Harleston Devon 8 B6
Harleston Norfk 106 E6
Harleston Suffk 89 L3
Harlestone Nhants 84 D2
Harle Syke Lancs 140 C1
Harley Rothm 142 B8
Harley Shrops 96 D3
Harlington C Beds 68 D1
Harlington Donc 142 D7
Harlington Gt Lon 50 E3
Harlosh Highld 258 D8
Harlow Essex 70 C5
Harlow Hill Nthumb 180 C5
Harlthorpe E R Yk 152 A8
Harlton Cambs 87 H5
Harlyn Cnwll 10 B7
Harman's Cross Dorset 17 J6
Harmby N York 159 L5
Harmer Green Herts 69 H4
Harmer Hill Shrops 113 H7
Harmondsworth Gt Lon 50 D3
Harmston Lincs 135 K7
Harnage Shrops 96 D3
Harnham Nthumb 180 C3
Harnhill Gloucs 64 F7
Harold Hill Gt Lon 70 D8
Haroldston West Pembks 54 D4
Haroldswick Shet 281 f1
Harold Wood Gt Lon 52 C1
Harome N York 161 L6
Harpenden Herts 68 E4
Harpford Devon 14 C4
Harpham E R Yk 153 H3
Harpley Norfk 121 H6
Harpley Worcs 80 F3
Harpole Nhants 84 D3
Harpsdale Highld 279 K5
Harpsden Oxon 49 J3
Harpswell Lincs 135 J2
Harpurhey Manch 140 C7
Harpur Hill Derbys 131 L5
Harraby Cumb 177 M7
Harracott Devon 27 K5
Harrapool Highld 247 K4
Harrietfield P & K 221 H1
Harrietsham Kent 39 L3
Harringay Gt Lon 51 J1
Harrington Cumb 164 C5
Harrington Lincs 137 G5
Harrington Nhants 101 G7
Harringworth Nhants 101 K4
Harris W Isls 282 e6
Harriseahead Staffs 131 G8
Harriston Cumb 165 G2
Harrogate N York 150 D5
Harrogate Crematorium N York 150 D5
Harrold Bed 85 J4
Harrop Dale Oldham 140 F6
Harrow Gt Lon 50 F1
Harrowbarrow Cnwll 12 A8
Harrowden Bed 85 L6
Harrowgate Village Darltn 169 H7
Harrow Green Suffk 89 H4
Harrow on the Hill Gt Lon 50 F2
Harrow Weald Gt Lon 50 F1
Harston Cambs 87 J5
Harston Leics 117 L5
Harswell E R Yk 152 C7
Hart Hartpl 170 B4
Hartburn Nthumb 180 D2
Hartest Suffk 89 G5
Hartfield E Susx 38 D6
Hartford Cambs 86 E1
Hartford Ches W 130 C5
Hartford Somset 29 G5
Hartfordbridge Hants 49 J7
Hartford End Essex 71 G3
Hartforth N York 159 L2
Hartgrove Dorset 32 D7
Harthill Ches W 129 L8
Harthill N Lans 210 B6
Harthill Rothm 133 K3
Hartington Derbys 132 C7
Hartington Nthumb 180 B1
Hartland Devon 26 D6
Hartland Quay Devon 26 C6
Hartlebury Worcs 81 J1
Hartlepool Hartpl 170 C4
Hartlepool Crematorium Hartpl 170 C4
Hartley Cumb 158 D1
Hartley Kent 39 J6
Hartley Kent 52 D5
Hartley Nthumb 181 H4
Hartley Green Kent 52 D5
Hartley Green Staffs 114 F5
Hartley Wespall Hants 49 G7
Hartley Wintney Hants 49 J7
Hartlip Kent 53 H6
Hartoft End N York 162 C4
Harton N York 151 L3
Harton S Tyne 181 J6
Harton Shrops 96 B5
Hartpury Gloucs 64 A2
Hartshead Kirk 141 J3
Hartshill C Stke 114 D2
Hartshill Warwks 99 J4
Hartshorne Derbys 116 B7
Hartside Nthumb 190 D3
Hartsop Cumb 165 L8
Hart Station Hartpl 170 B3
Hartswell Somset 29 K5
Hartwell Nhants 84 F5
Hartwith N York 150 B3
Hartwood N Lans 209 M7
Hartwoodmyres Border 188 D1
Harvel Kent 52 E6
Harvington Worcs 82 C5
Harvington Worcs 97 K8
Harwell Notts 134 D2
Harwell Oxon 48 C1
Harwich Essex 73 K1
Harwood Bolton 139 L5
Harwood Dur 167 J4
Harwood Dale N York 163 H3
Harwood Lee Bolton 139 L5
Harwood Park Crematorium Herts 69 H3
Harworth Notts 134 C2
Hasbury Dudley 98 B6
Hascombe Surrey 36 F3
Haselbech Nhants 100 F7
Haselbury Plucknett Somset 31 G8
Haseley Warwks 82 F2
Haseley Green Warwks 82 F1
Haseley Knob Warwks 82 F1
Haselor Warwks 82 D4
Hasfield Gloucs 64 B2
Hasguard Pembks 54 D5
Haskayne Lancs 138 D6
Hasketon Suffk 90 F5
Hasland Derbys 133 H5
Haslemere Surrey 36 D4
Haslingden Lancs 140 B3
Haslingfield Cambs 87 H5
Haslington Ches E 130 E8
Hassall Ches E 130 E8
Hassall Green Ches E 130 F7
Hassell Street Kent 40 E6
Hassingham Norfk 107 H2
Hassness Cumb 165 G7
Hassocks W Susx 22 D4
Hassop Derbys 132 D5
Haste Hill Surrey 36 D4
Haster Highld 280 D6
Hasthorpe Lincs 137 J5
Hastingleigh Kent 40 E6
Hastings E Susx 24 E5
Hastings Somset 30 D7
Hastings Borough Crematorium E Susx 24 E5
Hastingwood Essex 70 C5
Hastoe Herts 68 A5
Haswell Dur 169 K2
Haswell Plough Dur 169 K2
Hatch C Beds 86 D5
Hatch Beauchamp Somset 30 D6
Hatch End Bed 86 B3
Hatch End Gt Lon 50 E1
Hatchet Gate Hants 18 F3
Hatching Green Herts 68 E4
Hatchmere Ches W 130 A5
Hatcliffe NE Lin 145 G7
Hatfield Donc 143 G6
Hatfield Herefs 80 E3
Hatfield Herts 69 G5
Hatfield Worcs 81 K5
Hatfield Broad Oak Essex 70 E4
Hatfield Heath Essex 70 D4
Hatfield Peverel Essex 71 J5
Hatfield Woodhouse Donc 143 H6
Hatford Oxon 65 M8
Hatherden Hants 34 D1
Hatherleigh Devon 12 D2
Hathern Leics 116 E7
Hatherop Gloucs 65 H6
Hathersage Derbys 132 E3
Hathersage Booths Derbys 132 E3
Hatherton Ches E 113 L2
Hatherton Staffs 98 B1
Hatley St George Cambs 86 F5
Hatt Cnwll 6 D2
Hattersley Tamesd 131 K1
Hattingley Hants 35 K3
Hatton Abers 257 K4
Hatton Angus 234 C6
Hatton Derbys 115 L5
Hatton Gt Lon 50 E4
Hatton Lincs 136 C4
Hatton Shrops 95 L5
Hatton Warrtn 130 B3
Hatton Warwks 82 F2
Hatton Heath Ches W 129 K7
Hatton of Fintray Abers 256 F8
Haugh E Ayrs 196 F6
Haugh Lincs 137 H4
Haugh Rochdl 140 D5

Haugham Lincs 136 F3
Haughhead E Duns 209 G3
Haugh Head Nthumb 202 F7
Haughley Suffk 89 L3
Haughley Green Suffk 89 L2
Haugh of Glass Moray 255 H4
Haugh of Urr D & G 175 K2
Haughs of Kinnaird Angus 235 G4
Haughton Notts 134 D5
Haughton Powys 112 D7
Haughton Shrops 96 F4
Haughton Shrops 97 G2
Haughton Shrops 112 F6
Haughton Shrops 113 J8
Haughton Staffs 114 D7
Haughton Green Tamesd 131 J1
Haughton le Skerne Darltn 169 J7
Haughton Moss Ches E 130 B8
Haultwick Herts 69 J3
Haunton Staffs 99 G1
Hautes Croix Jersey 9 d1
Hauxton Cambs 87 J5
Havannah Ches E 131 G6
Havant Hants 20 B5
Haven Herefs 79 M4
Haven Bank Lincs 119 H1
Haven Side E R Yk 144 F2
Havenstreet IoW 19 J5
Havercroft Wakefd 142 B5
Haverfordwest Pembks 54 F4
Haverhill Suffk 88 D6
Haverigg Cumb 155 L7
Havering-atte-Bower Gt Lon 70 D8
Haversham M Keyn 84 F6
Haverthwaite Cumb 156 E6
Haverton Hill S on T 170 C6
Havyat N Som 44 F6
Havyatt Somset 31 H3
Hawarden Flints 129 H6
Hawbridge Worcs 81 L5
Hawbush Green Essex 71 J3
Hawcoat Cumb 146 D2
Hawen Cerdgn 76 C6
Hawes N York 158 F5
Hawe's Green Norfk 106 E4
Hawford Worcs 81 J3
Hawick Border 188 E3
Hawkchurch Devon 15 H3
Hawkedon Suffk 88 F4
Hawkenbury Kent 39 K4
Hawkeridge Wilts 46 B8
Hawkerland Devon 14 C5
Hawkesbury S Glos 45 M2
Hawkesbury Warwks 99 K6
Hawkesbury Upton S Glos 45 M2
Hawkes End Covtry 99 J6
Hawk Green Stockp 131 J2
Hawkhill Nthumb 191 J4
Hawkhurst Kent 39 J7
Hawkhurst Common E Susx 23 J4
Hawkinge Kent 41 H7
Hawkinge Crematorium Kent 41 G7
Hawkley Hants 35 M5
Hawkley Wigan 139 H7
Hawkridge Somset 28 F5
Hawksdale Cumb 165 L1
Hawkshaw Bury 139 M5
Hawkshead Cumb 156 E3
Hawkshead Hill Cumb 156 D3
Hawksland S Lans 198 D5
Hawkspur Green Essex 71 G1
Hawkstone Shrops 113 J5
Hawkswick N York 149 G2
Hawksworth Leeds 149 L7
Hawksworth Notts 117 K3
Hawkwell Essex 53 J1
Hawkwell Nthumb 180 C4
Hawley Hants 49 L7
Hawley Kent 52 C4
Hawling Gloucs 64 F3
Hawnby N York 161 J5
Haworth C Brad 149 J8
Hawridge Bucks 68 B6
Hawstead Suffk 89 G3
Hawstead Green Suffk 89 H3
Hawthorn Dur 169 L2
Hawthorn Hants 35 K4
Hawthorn Rhondd 43 H4
Hawthorn Hill Br For 49 L4
Hawthorn Hill Lincs 136 D8
Hawthorpe Lincs 118 D6
Hawton Notts 117 L1
Haxby C York 151 K4
Haxby Gates C York 151 K4
Haxey N Linc 143 J7
Haxey Carr N Linc 143 J7
Haxted Surrey 38 C4
Haxton Wilts 33 K1
Hay Cnwll 4 F4
Hay Cnwll 10 D8
Haycombe Crematorium BaNES 45 L6
Haydock St Hel 139 H8
Haydon BaNES 45 K8
Haydon Dorset 31 L7
Haydon Somset 30 C6
Haydon Bridge Nthumb 179 J6
Haydon Wick Swindn 47 H2
Haye Cnwll 11 L8
Hayes Gt Lon 50 E3
Hayes Gt Lon 51 L5
Hayes End Gt Lon 50 D3
Hayfield Ag & B 217 H2
Hayfield Derbys 131 L2
Haygate Wrekin 96 E1
Hay Green Norfk 120 C7
Hayhillock Angus 234 E7
Hayle Cnwll 2 F4
Hayley Green Dudley 98 B6
Hayling Island Hants 20 B6
Haymoor Green Ches E 113 L2
Hayne Devon 13 H5
Hayne Devon 29 G7
Haynes (Church End) C Beds 86 B7
Haynes (Northwood End) C Beds 86 B6
Haynes (Silver End) C Beds 86 B6
Haynes (West End) C Beds 85 L7
Hay-on-Wye Powys 79 J6
Hayscastle Pembks 74 E7
Hayscastle Cross Pembks 74 E7
Haysden Kent 38 F4
Hay Street Herts 69 K2
Hayton Cumb 164 F2
Hayton Cumb 178 C7
Hayton E R Yk 152 C6
Hayton Notts 134 E3
Hayton's Bent Shrops 96 C7
Haytor Vale Devon 13 H7
Haytown Devon 26 F7
Haywards Heath W Susx 22 E2
Haywood Donc 142 F5
Haywood Herefs 80 B8
Haywood Oaks Notts 134 C8
Hazards Green E Susx 24 C5
Hazelbank S Lans 198 D4
Hazelbury Bryan Dorset 16 E1
Hazeleigh Essex 71 K6
Hazeley Hants 49 H7
Hazelford Notts 117 J2
Hazel Grove Stockp 131 H2
Hazelhurst Tamesd 140 E7
Hazelslade Staffs 98 C1
Hazel Street Kent 39 H5
Hazel Stub Suffk 88 D6
Hazelton Walls Fife 222 E3
Hazelwood Derbys 116 B2
Hazlemere Bucks 67 L8
Hazlerigg N u Ty 180 F4
Hazles Staffs 114 F2
Hazleton Gloucs 65 G3
Heacham Norfk 120 E4
Headbourne Worthy Hants 35 G4
Headbrook Herefs 79 K4
Headcorn Kent 39 L4
Headingley Leeds 150 C8
Headington Oxon 66 D5
Headlam Dur 168 F7
Headlesscross N Lans 210 B7
Headless Cross Worcs 82 B2
Headley Hants 36 B4
Headley Hants 48 D6
Headley Surrey 51 G8
Headley Down Hants 36 B4
Headley Heath Worcs 98 D8
Headon Devon 11 M2
Headon Notts 134 E4
Heads Nook Cumb 178 C7
Heage Derbys 116 B2
Healaugh N York 151 G6
Healaugh N York 159 H3
Heald Green Stockp 131 G3
Heale Devon 28 A2
Heale Somset 30 C6
Heale Somset 30 F5
Healey N York 160 B6
Healey Nthumb 180 B7
Healey Rochdl 140 D4
Healey Wakefd 141 L4
Healeyfield Dur 168 D1
Healing NE Lin 145 G5
Heamoor Cnwll 2 D5
Heanor Derbys 116 D2
Heanton Punchardon Devon 27 J4
Heapham Lincs 135 H2
Hearn Hants 36 B3
Heart of England Crematorium Warwks 99 K5
Hearts Delight Kent 53 J6
Heasley Mill Devon 28 C4
Heast Highld 247 K5
Heath Derbys 133 J6
Heath Wakefd 142 A4
Heath and Reach C Beds 68 A2
Heath Common W Susx 21 J4
Heathcote Derbys 132 C7
Heathcote Shrops 113 L6
Heath End Bucks 67 L7
Heath End Hants 48 B6
Heath End Leics 116 B7
Heath End Warwks 82 F3
Heather Leics 99 K1
Heathfield Devon 13 J7
Heathfield E Susx 23 K3
Heathfield N York 149 L2
Heathfield Somset 29 L5
Heathfield Village Oxon 66 D4
Heath Green Worcs 82 C1
Heath Hall D & G 176 C3
Heath Hayes & Wimblebury Staffs 98 C2
Heath Hill Shrops 97 H1
Heath House Somset 30 F2
Heathstock Devon 14 F2
Heathton Shrops 97 H5
Heath Town Wolves 97 L3
Heathwaite N York 161 G2
Heatley Staffs 115 H6
Heatley Warrtn 130 D2
Heaton Bolton 139 L6
Heaton C Brad 149 L8
Heaton Lancs 147 J4
Heaton N u Ty 181 G5
Heaton Staffs 131 J7
Heaton Chapel Stockp 131 H1
Heaton Mersey Stockp 131 G2
Heaton Norris Stockp 131 H2
Heaton's Bridge Lancs 138 E5
Heaverham Kent 52 C7
Heaviley Stockp 131 H2
Heavitree Devon 13 L4
Hebburn S Tyne 181 H6
Hebden N York 149 J3
Hebden Bridge Calder 140 F2
Hebden Green Ches W 130 C6
Hebing End Herts 69 J3
Hebron Carmth 75 L6
Hebron IoA 125 H3
Hebron Nthumb 191 J8
Heckfield Hants 49 H6
Heckfield Green Suffk 106 D8
Heckfordbridge Essex 72 D3
Heckington Lincs 118 F3
Heckmondwike Kirk 141 K3
Heddington Wilts 46 E5
Heddon-on-the-Wall Nthumb 180 D5
Hedenham Norfk 107 G5
Hedge End Hants 19 H1
Hedgerley Bucks 50 B2
Hedgerley Green Bucks 50 B2
Hedging Somset 30 D5
Hedley on the Hill Nthumb 180 C7
Hednesford Staffs 98 C1
Hedon E R Yk 145 F2
Hedsor Bucks 49 L2
Hegdon Hill Herefs 80 D4
Heglibister Shet 281 d6
Heighington Darltn 169 H6
Heighington Lincs 135 L6
Heightington Worcs 81 H1
Heiton Border 201 L7
Hele Devon 13 H8
Hele Devon 14 A2
Hele Devon 27 J2
Hele Somset 30 B6
Helebridge Cnwll 11 J2
Hele Lane Devon 28 D8
Helensburgh Ag & B 208 A3
Helenton S Ayrs 196 D5
Helford Cnwll 3 J6
Helford Passage Cnwll 3 J5
Helhoughton Norfk 121 J6
Helions Bumpstead Essex 88 C7
Hellaby Rothm 133 K1
Helland Cnwll 10 F8
Hellandbridge Cnwll 10 F8
Hell Corner W Berk 48 A6
Hellescott Cnwll 11 K5
Hellesdon Norfk 106 E1
Hellesveor Cnwll 2 D3
Hellidon Nhants 83 M4
Hellifield N York 148 E4
Hellingly E Susx 23 K5
Hellington Norfk 107 G3
Helm Nthumb 191 H7
Helmdon Nhants 84 B6
Helme Kirk 141 H5
Helmingham Suffk 90 E4
Helmington Row Dur 168 F4
Helmsdale Highld 274 D5
Helmshore Lancs 140 B3
Helmsley N York 161 K6
Helperby N York 150 F2
Helperthorpe N York 152 E2
Helpringham Lincs 118 F3
Helpston C Pete 102 C2
Helsby Ches W 129 L4
Helsey Lincs 137 K5
Helston Cnwll 3 G5
Helstone Cnwll 10 F6
Helton Cumb 166 C6
Helwith N York 159 K2
Helwith Bridge N York 148 D2
Hemblington Norfk 107 G1
Hembridge Somset 31 K3
Hemel Hempstead Herts 68 D5
Hemerdon Devon 7 H3
Hemingbrough N York 143 H2
Hemingby Lincs 136 D5
Hemingfield Barns 142 B7
Hemingford Abbots Cambs 86 F1
Hemingford Grey Cambs 86 F1
Hemingstone Suffk 90 D4
Hemington Leics 116 D6
Hemington Nhants 102 B6
Hemington Somset 45 L8
Hemley Suffk 91 G6
Hemlington Middsb 170 C7
Hempholme E R Yk 153 H5
Hempnall Norfk 106 E4
Hempnall Green Norfk 106 E5
Hempriggs Moray 266 B3
Hempstead Essex 88 C7
Hempstead Medway 53 G6
Hempstead Norfk 122 C4
Hempstead Norfk 123 H6
Hempsted Gloucs 64 B4
Hempton Norfk 121 K5
Hempton Oxon 66 C1
Hemsby Norfk 123 K8
Hemswell Lincs 135 J2
Hemswell Cliff Lincs 135 J2
Hemsworth Wakefd 142 C5
Hemyock Devon 29 L8
Henbury Bristl 45 H3
Henbury Ches E 131 H5
Hendham Devon 7 L5
Hendomen Powys 94 F4
Hendon Gt Lon 51 G1
Hendon Sundld 181 K7
Hendon Crematorium Gt Lon 51 G1
Hendra Cnwll 3 J4
Hendra Cnwll 10 E7
Hendre Brdgnd 42 E5
Hendre Flints 128 E6
Hendre Mons 62 F4
Hendy Carmth 57 G4
Heneglwys IoA 125 G4
Henfield W Susx 22 C4
Henford Devon 11 M4
Henghurst Kent 40 B8
Hengoed Caerph 43 J3
Hengoed Powys 79 J4
Hengoed Shrops 112 D5
Hengrave Suffk 89 G2
Henham Essex 70 E2
Heniarth Powys 94 D2
Henlade Somset 30 C6
Henley Dorset 16 D2
Henley Gloucs 64 C4
Henley Shrops 95 L5
Henley Shrops 96 C8
Henley Somset 30 F4
Henley Suffk 90 E5
Henley W Susx 36 D5
Henley Green Covtry 99 K7
Henley-in-Arden Warwks 82 E2
Henley-on-Thames Oxon 49 J2
Henley Park Surrey 50 B8
Henley's Down E Susx 24 D5
Henley Street Kent 52 E5
Henllan Cerdgn 76 C7
Henllan Denbgs 127 L6
Henllan Amgoed Carmth 55 L3
Henllys Torfn 44 B1
Henlow C Beds 86 D7
Hennock Devon 13 J6
Henny Street Essex 89 H7
Henryd Conwy 126 F5
Henry's Moat (Castell Hendre) Pembks 75 H6
Hensall N York 142 F3
Henshaw Nthumb 179 H6
Hensingham Cumb 164 C7
Henstead Suffk 107 K6
Hensting Hants 35 G6
Henstridge Somset 32 B7
Henstridge Ash Somset 32 B6
Henstridge Marsh Somset 32 B6
Henton Oxon 67 J6

Henton Somset 31 H2
Henwick Worcs 81 J4
Henwood Cnwll 11 K7
Henwood Oxon 66 C6
Heol-las Swans 57 J5
Heol Senni Powys 60 D2
Heol-y-Cyw Brdgnd 42 E5
Hepburn Nthumb 190 F1
Hepple Nthumb 190 E6
Hepscott Nthumb 180 F2
Heptonstall Calder 140 E2
Hepworth Kirk 141 J6
Hepworth Suffk 105 K8
Herbrandston Pembks 54 E5
Hereford Herefs 80 C7
Hereford Crematorium Herefs 80 C7
Hereson Kent 41 L2
Heribusta Highld 258 F3
Heriot Border 200 E2
Hermiston C Edin 211 G5
Hermitage Border 188 E7
Hermitage Dorset 16 C1
Hermitage W Berk 48 D4
Hermitage W Susx 20 B5
Hermit Hill Barns 141 M7
Hermon Carmth 58 C3
Hermon IoA 125 G6
Hermon Pembks 75 L6
Herne Kent 41 G2
Herne Bay Kent 41 G2
Herne Common Kent 41 G2
Herne Hill Gt Lon 51 J4
Herne Pound Kent 39 G3
Herner Devon 27 K5
Hernhill Kent 40 E3
Herodsfoot Cnwll 5 L3
Heronden Kent 41 J4
Herongate Essex 52 D1
Heronsford S Ayrs 182 E6
Heronsgate Herts 68 C8
Herriard Hants 35 K2
Herringfleet Suffk 107 K4
Herring's Green Bed 86 B6
Herringswell Suffk 88 E1
Herringthorpe Rothm 133 J1
Herrington Sundld 181 J8
Hersden Kent 41 G3
Hersham Cnwll 11 J1
Hersham Surrey 50 E6
Herstmonceux E Susx 23 L5
Herston Dorset 17 K6
Herston Ork 275 c6
Hertford Herts 69 J4
Hertford Heath Herts 69 K5
Hertingfordbury Herts 69 J5
Hesketh Bank Lancs 138 F3
Hesketh Lane Lancs 147 M7
Hesket Newmarket Cumb 165 K3
Heskin Green Lancs 139 G4
Hesleden Dur 170 B3
Hesleden N York 158 F7
Hesley Donc 134 C1
Hesleyside Nthumb 179 J2
Heslington C York 151 K5
Hessay C York 151 H5
Hessenford Cnwll 6 C3
Hessett Suffk 89 J3
Hessle E R Yk 144 C3
Hessle Wakefd 142 C4
Hest Bank Lancs 147 J3
Hestley Green Suffk 90 D2
Heston Gt Lon 50 E3
Hestwall Ork 275 b4
Heswall Wirral 129 G3
Hethe Oxon 66 E1
Hethersett Norfk 106 C2
Hethersgill Cumb 178 B5
Hetherside Cumb 178 B5
Hetherson Green Ches W 113 H2
Hethpool Nthumb 202 D7
Hett Dur 169 H3
Hetton N York 149 G4
Hetton-le-Hole Sundld 169 K1
Hetton Steads Nthumb 203 G6
Heugh Nthumb 180 D4
Heughhead Abers 243 L1
Heugh Head Border 213 J6
Heveningham Suffk 91 H1
Hever Kent 38 D4
Heversham Cumb 157 H6
Hevingham Norfk 122 D7
Hewas Water Cnwll 4 F5
Hewelsfield Gloucs 63 H6
Hewenden C Brad 149 K8
Hewish N Som 44 E6
Hewish Somset 15 K1
Hewood Dorset 15 H2
Hexham Nthumb 179 L6
Hextable Kent 52 B5
Hexthorpe Donc 142 F7
Hexton Herts 68 E1
Hexworthy Cnwll 11 L6
Hexworthy Devon 12 F8
Hey Lancs 148 F7
Heybridge Essex 70 F7
Heybridge Essex 71 L5
Heybridge Basin Essex 72 C5
Heybrook Bay Devon 6 F5
Heydon Cambs 87 J7
Heydon Norfk 122 C6
Heydour Lincs 118 D4
Heyhead Manch 131 G3
Hey Houses Lancs 138 D2
Heylipoll Ag & B 224 B6
Heylor Shet 281 d4
Heyrod Tamesd 140 E7
Heysham Lancs 147 H4
Heyshaw N York 149 L3
Heyshott W Susx 20 E3
Heyside Oldham 140 D6
Heytesbury Wilts 32 F2
Heythrop Oxon 65 M2
Heywood Rochdl 140 C5
Heywood Wilts 46 C8
Hibaldstow N Linc 144 B7
Hickleton Donc 142 D6
Hickling Norfk 123 J6
Hickling Notts 117 J6
Hickling Green Norfk 123 H6
Hickling Heath Norfk 123 H7
Hickmans Green Kent 40 E4
Hicks Forstal Kent 41 G3
Hickstead W Susx 22 D3
Hidcote Bartrim Gloucs 82 E6
Hidcote Boyce Gloucs 82 E6
High Ackworth Wakefd 142 C4
Higham Barns 141 M6
Higham Derbys 133 H7
Higham Kent 38 F4
Higham Kent 52 F5
Higham Lancs 148 E8
Higham Suffk 88 E2
Higham Suffk 89 L8
Higham Dykes Nthumb 180 D4
Higham Ferrers Nhants 85 J2
Higham Gobion C Beds 86 C8
Higham Hill Gt Lon 51 K1
Higham on the Hill Leics 99 K4
Highampton Devon 12 C2
Highams Park Gt Lon 69 K8
High Angerton Nthumb 180 D2
High Ardwell D & G 172 D5
High Auldgirth D & G 176 B1
High Bankhill Cumb 166 D2
High Beach Essex 69 L7
High Bentham N York 148 B2
High Bewaldeth Cumb 165 H4
High Bickington Devon 27 L6
High Bickwith N York 158 D7
High Biggins Cumb 157 K7
High Blantyre S Lans 209 H7
High Bonnybridge Falk 209 L3
High Borrans Cumb 156 F3
High Bradley N York 149 H6
High Bray Devon 28 B4
Highbridge Hants 34 F6
Highbridge Somset 30 D2
Highbrook W Susx 38 A7
High Brooms Kent 38 F5
High Bullen Devon 27 J6
Highburton Kirk 141 J5
Highbury Gt Lon 51 J2
Highbury Somset 31 M1
High Buston Nthumb 191 J4
High Callerton Nthumb 180 E5
High Casterton Cumb 157 K7
High Catton E R Yk 151 M5
Highclere Hants 48 B7
Highcliffe Dorset 18 C5
High Close Dur 168 F7
High Cogges Oxon 66 A5
High Common Norfk 105 K2
High Coniscliffe Darltn 169 G7
High Crosby Cumb 178 B6
High Cross Cnwll 3 J5
High Cross E Ayrs 196 D2
High Cross Hants 35 L5
High Cross Herts 69 K3
Highcross Lancs 147 G8
High Cross W Susx 22 C4
High Cross Warwks 82 E2
High Drummore D & G 172 E7
High Dubmire Sundld 169 J1
High Easter Essex 70 F4
High Eggborough N York 142 F3
High Ellington N York 160 B6
Higher Alham Somset 31 L3
Higher Ansty Dorset 16 E2
Higher Ballam Lancs 138 D2
Higher Bartle Lancs 139 G1
Higher Berry End C Beds 85 J8
Higher Bockhampton Dorset 16 D4
Higher Brixham Torbay 8 D4
Higher Burrowton Devon 14 B3
Higher Burwardsley Ches W 129 M8
High Ercall Wrekin 113 K8
Higher Chillington Somset 15 J1
Higher Clovelly Devon 26 E6
Highercombe Somset 28 F5
Higher Coombe Dorset 15 M4
Higher Disley Ches E 131 J3
Higher Folds Wigan 139 K7
Higherford Lancs 148 F7
Higher Gabwell Devon 8 D1
Higher Halstock Leigh Dorset 15 L1
Higher Harpers Lancs 148 E8
Higher Heysham Lancs 147 H4
Higher Hurdsfield Ches E 131 J5
Higher Irlam Salfd 130 E1
Higher Kingcombe Dorset 15 M3
Higher Kinnerton Flints 129 H7
Higher Marston Ches W 130 C4
Higher Muddiford Devon 27 K3
Higher Nyland Dorset 32 B6
Higher Ogden Rochdl 140 E5
Higher Pentire Cnwll 3 G6
Higher Penwortham Lancs 139 G2
Higher Prestacott Devon 11 M3
Higher Studfold N York 148 E2
Higher Town Cnwll 4 C6
Higher Town Cnwll 5 G3
Higher Town IoS 10 c2
Higher Tregantle Cnwll 6 D4
Higher Walton Lancs 139 H2
Higher Walton Warrtn 130 B3
Higher Wambrook Somset 15 G1
Higher Waterston Dorset 16 D3
Higher Whatcombe Dorset 17 G2
Higher Wheelton Lancs 139 J3
Higher Whitley Ches W 130 B4
Higher Wincham Ches W 130 D4
Higher Wraxhall Dorset 16 A2
Higher Wych Ches W 113 H3
High Etherley Dur 168 F5
High Ferry Lincs 119 K2
Highfield E R Yk 151 M8
Highfield Gatesd 180 E7
Highfield N Ayrs 196 C1
Highfields Donc 142 E6
High Flats Kirk 141 K6
High Garrett Essex 71 J2
Highgate E Susx 38 C6
Highgate Gt Lon 51 H2
Highgate Kent 39 J7
High Grange Dur 168 F4
High Grantley N York 150 B2
High Green Cumb 156 F2
High Green Kirk 141 K5
High Green Norfk 106 C2
High Green Norfk 106 D5
High Green Sheff 142 A8
High Green Shrops 96 F6
High Green Suffk 89 G3
High Green Worcs 81 K6
Highgreen Manor Nthumb 189 L7
High Halden Kent 40 A7
High Halstow Medway 53 G4
High Ham Somset 30 F4
High Harrington Cumb 164 D5
High Harrogate N York 150 D5
High Haswell Dur 169 K2
High Hatton Shrops 113 K6
High Hauxley Nthumb 191 K5
High Hawsker N York 163 G1
High Hesket Cumb 166 B2
High Hoyland Barns 141 L5
High Hunsley E R Yk 144 B1
High Hurstwood E Susx 23 H2
High Hutton N York 152 A2
High Ireby Cumb 165 H3
High Kelling Norfk 122 C3
High Kilburn N York 161 H6
High Killerby N York 163 J6
High Knipe Cumb 166 C6
High Lands Dur 168 E5
Highlane Ches E 131 H6
Highlane Derbys 133 H3
High Lane Stockp 131 J3
High Lanes Cnwll 2 F4
High Laver Essex 70 D5
Highlaws Cumb 164 F1
Highleadon Gloucs 63 M2
High Legh Ches E 130 D3
Highleigh W Susx 20 D7
High Leven S on T 170 B8
Highley Shrops 97 G6
High Littleton BaNES 45 J7
High Lorton Cumb 165 G5
High Marishes N York 162 E7
High Marnham Notts 134 F5
High Melton Donc 142 D7
High Mickley Nthumb 180 C6
Highmoor Cumb 165 J1
Highmoor Oxon 49 H2
Highmoor Cross Oxon 49 H2
Highmoor Hill Mons 44 F1
High Moorsley Sundld 169 J2
Highnam Gloucs 64 A3
Highnam Green Gloucs 64 A3
High Newport Sundld 181 J8
High Newton Cumb 156 F6
High Nibthwaite Cumb 156 D5
High Offley Staffs 114 B6
High Ongar Essex 70 E6
High Onn Staffs 114 C8
High Park Corner Essex 72 F3
High Pennyvenie E Ayrs 184 D2
High Post Wilts 33 K4
Highridge N Som 45 H5
High Roding Essex 70 F4
High Row Cumb 165 K3
High Row Cumb 165 L6
High Salter Lancs 147 M3
High Salvington W Susx 21 K5
High Scales Cumb 165 G2
High Seaton Cumb 164 D4
High Shaw N York 158 F4
High Side Cumb 165 H4
High Spen Gatesd 180 E7
Highstead Kent 41 G2
Highsted Kent 40 B3
High Stoop Dur 168 E3
High Street Cnwll 5 G4
High Street Kent 39 J7
Highstreet Kent 40 E3
High Street Suffk 91 J1
High Street Suffk 91 K4
Highstreet Green Essex 88 F8
Highstreet Green Surrey 36 E4
Hightae D & G 176 E3
Highter's Heath Birm 98 E7
High Throston Hartpl 170 C4
Hightown Ches E 131 G7
Hightown Hants 18 B3
Hightown Sefton 138 C7
High Town Staffs 98 C1
Hightown Green Suffk 89 K4
High Toynton Lincs 136 E5
High Trewhitt Nthumb 190 E5
High Urpeth Dur 181 G8
High Valleyfield Fife 210 D2
High Warden Nthumb 179 L5
Highway Herefs 80 B5
Highway Wilts 46 F4
Highweek Devon 13 K8
High Westwood Dur 180 D7
Highwood Staffs 115 H5
Highwood Hill Gt Lon 69 G8
High Woolaston Gloucs 63 H7
High Worsall N York 160 F1
Highworth Swindn 65 J8
High Wray Cumb 156 E3
High Wych Herts 70 C4
High Wycombe Bucks 67 L8
Hilborough Norfk 105 G3
Hilcote Derbys 133 J8
Hilcott Wilts 47 G7
Hildenborough Kent 38 E4
Hilden Park Kent 38 F4
Hildersham Cambs 87 L5
Hilderstone Staffs 114 E4
Hilderthorpe E R Yk 153 J3
Hilfield Dorset 16 C2
Hilgay Norfk 104 C4
Hill S Glos 63 J8
Hill Warwks 83 K2
Hillam N York 142 D2
Hillbeck Cumb 167 H7
Hillborough Kent 41 G2
Hill Brow Hants 36 B5
Hillbutts Dorset 17 K2
Hill Chorlton Staffs 114 B4
Hillclifflane Derbys 115 M2
Hill Common Norfk 123 H7
Hill Common Somset 29 L5
Hill Deverill Wilts 32 E3
Hilldyke Lincs 119 K2
Hill End Dur 168 C3
Hillend Fife 210 F2
Hill End Fife 221 J8
Hill End Gloucs 81 K7
Hillend Mdloth 211 H5
Hillend N Lans 209 L5
Hillend Swans 56 D6
Hillersland Gloucs 63 H4
Hillerton Devon 13 G3
Hillesden Bucks 67 G1
Hillesley Gloucs 45 M1
Hillfarrance Somset 29 L6
Hill Green Kent 53 H6

Hillgrove W Susx 36 D5
Hillhampton Herefs 80 D6
Hillhead Abers 255 M4
Hillhead Devon 8 D4
Hill Head Hants 19 J3
Hillhead S Lans 199 G5
Hillhead of Cocklaw Abers 257 K3
Hilliard's Cross Staffs 98 F1
Hilliclay Highld 279 L3
Hillingdon Gt Lon 50 D2
Hillington C Glas 208 E6
Hillington Norfk 120 F6
Hillis Corner IoW 19 H5
Hillmorton Warwks 100 C8
Hillock Vale Lancs 140 A2
Hill of Beath Fife 210 F1
Hill of Fearn Highld 264 C4
Hillowton D & G 175 J2
Hillpool Worcs 97 K8
Hillpound Hants 35 J7
Hill Ridware Staffs 115 H8
Hillside Abers 245 K4
Hillside Angus 235 H3
Hillside Devon 7 K3
Hill Side Kirk 141 J4
Hill Side Worcs 81 H3
Hills Town Derbys 133 J5
Hillstreet Hants 34 D7
Hillswick Shet 281 c4
Hill Top Dur 168 C6
Hill Top Hants 18 F3
Hill Top Kirk 141 G5
Hill Top Rothm 133 H1
Hill Top Sandw 98 C5
Hill Top Wakefd 142 A4
Hillwell Shet 281 d8
Hilmarton Wilts 46 E4
Hilperton Wilts 46 C7
Hilperton Marsh Wilts 46 C7
Hilsea C Port 19 L3
Hilston E R Yk 145 H1
Hiltingbury Hants 34 F6
Hilton Border 202 D3
Hilton Cambs 86 F2
Hilton Cumb 167 G6
Hilton Derbys 115 L5
Hilton Dorset 16 E2
Hilton Dur 168 F6
Hilton Highld 264 D4
Hilton S on T 170 B8
Hilton Shrops 97 H4
Himbleton Worcs 81 L3
Himley Staffs 97 K5
Hincaster Cumb 157 H5
Hinchley Wood Surrey 50 F6
Hinckley Leics 99 L4
Hinderclay Suffk 105 L8
Hinderwell N York 171 J7
Hindford Shrops 112 E5
Hindhead Surrey 36 C4
Hindle Fold Lancs 139 L1
Hindley Nthumb 180 C7
Hindley Wigan 139 J6
Hindley Green Wigan 139 J7
Hindlip Worcs 81 K3
Hindolveston Norfk 122 A5
Hindon Wilts 32 F4
Hindringham Norfk 121 L4
Hingham Norfk 105 L3
Hinksford Staffs 97 J5
Hinstock Shrops 113 M6
Hintlesham Suffk 90 C6
Hinton Gloucs 63 K6
Hinton Hants 18 C4
Hinton Herefs 79 L7
Hinton S Glos 45 L4
Hinton Shrops 95 K2
Hinton Shrops 96 E7
Hinton Admiral Hants 18 C4
Hinton Ampner Hants 35 J5
Hinton Blewett BaNES 45 H7
Hinton Charterhouse BaNES 45 M7
Hinton Green Worcs 82 B7
Hinton-in-the-Hedges Nhants 84 A7
Hinton Marsh Hants 35 J5
Hinton Martell Dorset 17 K2
Hinton on the Green Worcs 82 B7
Hinton Parva Swindn 47 K2
Hinton St George Somset 30 F8
Hinton St Mary Dorset 32 C7
Hinton Waldrist Oxon 66 A7
Hints Shrops 96 E8
Hints Staffs 98 F3
Hinwick Bed 85 J3
Hinxhill Kent 40 D6
Hinxton Cambs 87 K6
Hinxworth Herts 86 E7
Hipperholme Calder 141 H3
Hipsburn Nthumb 191 J4
Hipswell N York 160 B3
Hirn Abers 245 G3
Hirnant Powys 111 K7
Hirst Nthumb 181 G2
Hirst Courtney N York 142 F3
Hirwaen Denbgs 128 D7
Hirwaun Rhondd 60 E6
Hiscott Devon 27 K5
Histon Cambs 87 J3
Hitcham Suffk 89 K5
Hitcham Causeway Suffk 89 K5
Hitcham Street Suffk 89 K5
Hitchin Herts 68 F1
Hither Green Gt Lon 51 K4
Hittisleigh Devon 13 G3
Hive E R Yk 143 K2
Hixon Staffs 114 F6
Hoaden Kent 41 J3
Hoar Cross Staffs 115 J7
Hoarwithy Herefs 63 G1
Hoath Kent 41 G2
Hoathly Kent 39 G6
Hobarris Shrops 95 H7
Hobbles Green Suffk 88 D4
Hobbs Cross Essex 70 C7
Hobbs Cross Essex 70 D5
Hobkirk Border 189 G4
Hobland Hall Norfk 107 K3
Hobsick Notts 116 D2
Hobson Dur 180 E7
Hoby Leics 117 H8
Hoccombe Somset 29 K5
Hockering Norfk 106 B1
Hockerton Notts 134 E8
Hockley Ches E 131 J3
Hockley Covtry 99 H7
Hockley Essex 71 K8
Hockley Staffs 99 G3
Hockley Heath Solhll 82 E1
Hockliffe C Beds 68 B2
Hockwold cum Wilton Norfk 104 E6
Hockworthy Devon 29 J7
Hoddesdon Herts 69 K5
Hoddlesden Bl w D 139 L3
Hoddom Cross D & G 177 G4
Hoddom Mains D & G 177 G4
Hodgehill Ches E 131 G5
Hodgeston Pembks 55 H7
Hodnet Shrops 113 K6
Hodsock Notts 134 C3
Hodsoll Street Kent 52 D6
Hodson Swindn 47 H3
Hodthorpe Derbys 133 L4
Hoe Hants 35 H7
Hoe Norfk 121 M8
Hoe Gate Hants 35 K8
Hoff Cumb 166 F7
Hogben's Hill Kent 40 D4
Hoggards Green Suffk 89 H4
Hoggeston Bucks 67 K2
Hoggrill's End Warwks 99 G5
Hog Hill E Susx 25 G4
Hoghton Lancs 139 J2
Hoghton Bottoms Lancs 139 J2
Hognaston Derbys 115 L2
Hogsthorpe Lincs 137 K5
Holbeach Lincs 119 K6
Holbeach Bank Lincs 119 K6
Holbeach Clough Lincs 119 K6
Holbeach Drove Lincs 103 G1
Holbeach Hurn Lincs 119 L6
Holbeach St Johns Lincs 119 K7
Holbeach St Mark's Lincs 119 L5
Holbeach St Matthew Lincs 119 L5
Holbeck Notts 133 L5
Holbeck Woodhouse Notts 133 L5
Holberrow Green Worcs 82 B3
Holbeton Devon 7 J5
Holborn Gt Lon 51 J3
Holborough Kent 52 F6
Holbrook Derbys 116 B3
Holbrook Sheff 133 J3
Holbrook Suffk 90 E7
Holbrook Moor Derbys 116 B3
Holbrooks Covtry 99 J6
Holburn Nthumb 203 G6
Holbury Hants 19 G3
Holcombe Devon 13 M7
Holcombe Somset 31 L1
Holcombe Rogus Devon 29 J7
Holcot Nhants 84 F1
Holden Lancs 148 D6
Holdenby Nhants 84 D2
Holden Gate Calder 140 D3
Holder's Green Essex 70 F1
Holdgate Shrops 96 D5
Holdingham Lincs 118 E2
Holditch Dorset 15 H2
Holdsworth Calder 141 G2
Holehouse Derbys 131 K1
Hole-in-the-Wall Herefs 63 J2
Holemoor Devon 12 A2
Hole Street W Susx 21 K4
Holford Somset 29 L3
Holgate C York 151 J5
Holker Cumb 156 E7
Holkham Norfk 121 K3
Hollacombe Devon 11 M2
Holland Fen Lincs 119 H2
Holland Lees Lancs 139 G6
Holland-on-Sea Essex 73 J4
Hollandstoun Ork 275 f1
Hollee D & G 177 J5
Hollesley Suffk 91 H6
Hollicombe Torbay 8 D2
Hollingbourne Kent 39 L2
Hollingbury Br & H 22 D5
Hollingdon Bucks 67 L2
Hollingthorpe Leeds 142 B2
Hollington Derbys 115 L4
Hollington Staffs 115 G4
Hollingworth Tamesd 140 F8
Hollinlane Ches E 131 G3
Hollins Bury 140 B6
Hollins Derbys 132 F5
Hollins Staffs 114 F2
Hollinsclough Staffs 131 L6
Hollins End Sheff 133 H3
Hollins Green Warrtn 130 D2
Hollins Lane Lancs 147 K5
Hollinswood Wrekin 96 F2
Hollinwood Shrops 113 H4
Hollinwood Crematorium Oldham 140 D7
Hollingrove E Susx 24 C3
Hollocombe Devon 27 L8
Holloway Derbys 132 F8
Holloway Gt Lon 51 J2
Holloway Wilts 32 E5
Hollowell Nhants 84 D1
Hollowmoor Heath Ches W 129 L6
Hollows D & G 177 L3
Hollybush Caerph 61 J6
Hollybush E Ayrs 196 D7
Hollybush Herefs 81 H7
Holly End Norfk 103 K2
Holly Green Worcs 81 K7
Hollyhurst Ches E 113 J3
Hollym E R Yk 145 J3
Hollywood Worcs 98 D7
Holmbridge Kirk 141 H6
Holmbury St Mary Surrey 37 H2
Holmbush Cnwll 5 H4
Holmcroft Staffs 114 E6
Holme Cambs 102 D6
Holme Cumb 157 H7
Holme Kirk 141 H6
Holme N Linc 144 A6
Holme N York 160 E6
Holme Notts 134 F7
Holme Chapel Lancs 140 C2
Holme Green N York 151 J7
Holme Hale Norfk 105 H2
Holme Lacy Herefs 80 D8
Holme Marsh Herefs 79 L4
Holme next the Sea Norfk 120 F3
Holme on the Wolds E R Yk 152 E6
Holme Pierrepont Notts 117 G4
Holmer Herefs 80 C6
Holmer Green Bucks 67 L7
Holme St Cuthbert Cumb 164 F1
Holmes Chapel Ches E 130 E6
Holmesfield Derbys 132 F4
Holmes Hill E Susx 23 J4
Holmeswood Lancs 138 E4
Holmethorpe Surrey 51 H8
Holme upon Spalding Moor E R Yk 152 B8
Holmewood Derbys 133 H6
Holmfield Calder 141 G2
Holmfirth Kirk 141 H6
Holmhead E Ayrs 197 H7
Holmpton E R Yk 145 K3
Holmrook Cumb 155 K3
Holmsford Bridge Crematorium N Ayrs 196 D3
Holmshurst E Susx 23 L2
Holmside Dur 169 G1
Holmwrangle Cumb 166 C1
Holne Devon 7 K1
Holnest Dorset 16 C1
Holnicote Somset 29 G2
Holsworthy Devon 11 L2
Holsworthy Beacon Devon 11 L1
Holt Dorset 17 K2
Holt Norfk 122 B4
Holt Wilts 46 B6
Holt Worcs 81 J3
Holt Wrexhm 112 F1
Holtby C York 151 L5
Holt End Worcs 82 C1
Holt Fleet Worcs 81 J3
Holt Green Lancs 138 E6
Holt Heath Dorset 17 L2
Holt Heath Worcs 81 J3
Holton Oxon 66 F5
Holton Somset 31 L5
Holton Suffk 107 H7
Holton cum Beckering Lincs 136 B3
Holton Heath Dorset 17 J4
Holton Hill E Susx 24 B2
Holton le Clay Lincs 145 H7
Holton le Moor Lincs 144 D8
Holton St Mary Suffk 90 C7
Holt Street Kent 41 H5
Holtye E Susx 38 C5
Holway Flints 128 E4
Holwell Dorset 32 B8
Holwell Herts 86 D8
Holwell Leics 117 J6
Holwell Oxon 65 K5
Holwick Dur 167 L5
Holworth Dorset 16 E6
Holybourne Hants 35 M3
Holy Cross Worcs 97 L7
Holyfield Essex 69 K6
Holyhead IoA 124 D3
Holy Island IoA 124 D3
Holy Island Nthumb 203 J5
Holymoorside Derbys 133 G6
Holyport W & M 49 L3
Holystone Nthumb 190 D5
Holytown N Lans 209 K6
Holytown Crematorium N Lans 209 K6
Holywell C Beds 68 C4
Holywell Cambs 87 G1
Holywell Cnwll 4 C3
Holywell Dorset 16 B2
Holywell Flints 128 E4
Holywell Nthumb 181 H4
Holywell Warwks 82 E2
Holywell Green Calder 141 G4
Holywell Lake Somset 29 K6
Holywell Row Suffk 104 E7
Holywood D & G 176 B3
Holywood Village D & G 176 C3
Homer Shrops 96 E3
Homer Green Sefton 138 D7
Homersfield Suffk 106 F6
Homescales Cumb 157 J5
Hom Green Herefs 63 H3
Homington Wilts 33 K5
Honeyborough Pembks 54 F5
Honeybourne Worcs 82 D6
Honeychurch Devon 12 E2
Honey Hill Kent 40 F3
Honeystreet Wilts 47 G6
Honey Tye Suffk 89 J8
Honiley Warwks 82 F1
Honing Norfk 123 G6
Honingham Norfk 106 C1
Honington Lincs 118 B3
Honington Suffk 105 H8
Honington Warwks 83 G6
Honiton Devon 14 E3
Honley Kirk 141 H5
Honnington Wrekin 114 A8
Honor Oak Crematorium Gt Lon 51 K4
Hoo Kent 41 J2
Hoobrook Worcs 97 J8
Hood Green Barns 141 M7
Hood Hill Rothm 142 B8
Hooe C Plym 6 F4
Hooe E Susx 24 C5
Hoo End Herts 68 F3
Hoo Green Ches E 130 D3
Hoohill Bpool 146 F8
Hook Cambs 103 J5
Hook Devon 15 G2
Hook E R Yk 143 J3
Hook Gt Lon 50 F6
Hook Hants 19 H3
Hook Hants 49 H8
Hook Pembks 55 G4
Hook Wilts 47 G2
Hookagate Shrops 95 L2
Hook Bank Worcs 81 J7
Hooke Dorset 15 M3
Hook End Essex 70 E7
Hookgate Staffs 114 A4
Hook Green Kent 39 G6
Hook Green Kent 52 D5
Hook Norton Oxon 83 H8
Hook Street Gloucs 63 K7
Hook Street Wilts 47 G2
Hookway Devon 13 K3
Hookwood Surrey 37 L2
Hooley Surrey 51 H7
Hooley Bridge Rochdl 140 C5

Hoo Meavy Devon 7 G2
Hoo St Werburgh Medway 53 G4
Hooton Ches W 129 J4
Hooton Levitt Rothm 133 K2
Hooton Pagnell Donc 142 D6
Hooton Roberts Rothm 142 D8
Hopcrofts Holt Oxon 66 C2
Hope Derbys 132 C3
Hope Devon 7 K6
Hope Flints 129 G7
Hope Powys 95 G2
Hope Shrops 95 H3
Hope Shrops 96 D8
Hope Staffs 132 B8
Hope Bowdler Shrops 95 L5
Hope End Green Essex 70 E3
Hopehouse Border 187 L3
Hopeman Moray 266 C2
Hope Mansell Herefs 63 J3
Hopesay Shrops 95 J6
Hopetown Wakefd 142 B3
Hope under Dinmore Herefs 80 C5
Hopgrove C York 151 K5
Hopperton N York 150 F4
Hop Pole Lincs 102 D1
Hopsford Warwks 99 L6
Hopstone Shrops 97 H4
Hopton Derbys 115 L1
Hopton Shrops 112 F7
Hopton Staffs 114 E6
Hopton Suffk 105 K7
Hopton Cangeford Shrops 96 C7
Hopton Castle Shrops 95 J7
Hoptonheath Shrops 95 J7
Hopton on Sea Norfk 107 L3
Hopton Wafers Shrops 96 E8
Hopwas Staffs 98 F3
Hopwood Rochdl 140 C6
Hopwood Worcs 98 C8
Horam E Susx 23 K4
Horbling Lincs 118 F4
Horbury Wakefd 141 L4
Horcott Gloucs 65 H7
Horden Dur 170 B3
Horderley Shrops 95 K6
Hordle Hants 18 D4
Hordley Shrops 112 F5
Horeb Carmth 56 F4
Horeb Cerdgn 76 D6
Horfield Bristl 45 H4
Horham Suffk 90 F1
Horkesley Heath Essex 72 E1
Horkstow N Linc 144 B4
Horley Oxon 83 K6
Horley Surrey 37 L2
Hornblotton Green Somset 31 K4
Hornby Lancs 147 L2
Hornby N York 160 B4
Hornby N York 160 E2
Horncastle Lincs 136 E6
Hornchurch Gt Lon 52 B2
Horncliffe Nthumb 202 E3
Horndean Border 202 D3
Horndean Hants 35 L8
Horndon Devon 12 C6
Horndon on the Hill Thurr 52 E2
Horne Surrey 38 A4
Horner Somset 28 F2
Horne Row Essex 71 J6
Horners Green Suffk 89 K7
Horney Common E Susx 23 G2
Horn Hill Bucks 68 C8
Horning Norfk 123 G8
Horninghold Leics 101 H4
Horninglow Staffs 115 L6
Horningsea Cambs 87 K3
Horningsham Wilts 32 D3
Horningtoft Norfk 121 K6
Horningtops Cnwll 6 B3
Hornsbury Somset 30 E8
Hornsby Cumb 166 C1
Hornsbygate Cumb 166 C1
Horns Cross Devon 27 G6
Horns Cross E Susx 24 E3
Hornsea E R Yk 153 K6
Hornsey Gt Lon 51 J1
Horn's Green Gt Lon 51 M7
Horn Street Kent 41 G8
Hornton Oxon 83 J6
Horpit Swindn 47 J2
Horra Shet 281 e3
Horrabridge Devon 7 G1
Horringer Suffk 89 G3
Horringford IoW 19 J6
Horrocks Fold Bolton 139 L5
Horrocksford Lancs 148 C7
Horsacott Devon 27 J4
Horsebridge Devon 12 A7
Horsebridge E Susx 23 K5
Horsebridge Hants 34 D5
Horsebridge Shrops 95 J2
Horsebridge Staffs 114 F1
Horsebrook Staffs 97 K1
Horsecastle N Som 44 E5
Horsedown Cnwll 3 G4
Horsegate Lincs 102 C2
Horsehay Wrekin 96 F2
Horseheath Cambs 88 C5
Horsehouse N York 159 J6
Horsell Surrey 50 C7
Horseman's Green Wrexhm 113 G3
Horsenden Bucks 67 J6
Horsey Norfk 123 J7
Horsey Somset 30 D3
Horsey Corner Norfk 123 J6
Horsford Norfk 122 D8
Horsforth Leeds 150 B8
Horsham W Susx 37 J5
Horsham Worcs 81 G4
Horsham St Faith Norfk 122 E8
Horsington Lincs 136 C6
Horsington Somset 32 B6
Horsley Derbys 116 C3
Horsley Gloucs 64 B7
Horsley Nthumb 180 D5
Horsley Nthumb 190 B6
Horsley Cross Essex 73 H2
Horsleycross Street Essex 73 G1
Horsley-Gate Derbys 132 F4
Horsleyhill Border 188 F2
Horsley's Green Bucks 67 J8
Horsley Woodhouse Derbys 116 C3
Horsmonden Kent 39 H5
Horspath Oxon 66 E6
Horstead Norfk 122 F7
Horsted Keynes W Susx 22 F2
Horton Bucks 68 A3
Horton Dorset 17 K1
Horton Lancs 148 E6
Horton Nhants 84 F4
Horton S Glos 45 M2
Horton Shrops 113 H5
Horton Somset 30 D7
Horton Staffs 131 J8
Horton Surrey 51 G6
Horton Swans 56 E7
Horton W & M 50 C4
Horton Wilts 46 F6
Horton Wrekin 113 L8
Horton Cross Somset 30 E7
Horton-cum-Studley Oxon 66 F4
Horton Green Ches W 113 G2
Horton Heath Hants 35 G7
Horton in Ribblesdale N York 148 D2
Horton Kirby Kent 52 C5
Horwich Bolton 139 J5
Horwich End Derbys 131 K3
Horwood Devon 27 J5
Hoscar Lancs 138 F5
Hoscote Border 188 C4
Hose Leics 117 J5
Hosey Hill Kent 51 M8
Hosh P & K 220 E3
Hoswick Shet 281 e8
Hotham E R Yk 143 M1
Hothfield Kent 40 C6
Hoton Leics 116 F7
Hott Nthumb 179 H2
Hough Ches E 113 M1
Hough Ches E 131 G4
Hougham Lincs 118 A3
Hough End Leeds 141 K1
Hough Green Halton 129 L2
Hough-on-the-Hill Lincs 118 B2
Houghton Cambs 86 F1
Houghton Cumb 177 L7
Houghton Hants 34 D4
Houghton Nthumb 180 D5
Houghton Pembks 55 G5
Houghton W Susx 21 H4
Houghton Conquest C Beds 85 L7
Houghton Gate Dur 181 H8
Houghton Green E Susx 25 G3
Houghton Green Warrtn 130 C1
Houghton le Side Darltn 169 G6
Houghton-le-Spring Sundld 169 J1
Houghton on the Hill Leics 100 E3
Houghton Regis C Beds 68 C2
Houghton St Giles Norfk 121 K4
Hound Green Hants 49 H7
Houndslow Border 201 K4
Houndsmoor Somset 29 L5
Houndwood Border 213 J6
Hounslow Gt Lon 50 F4
Househill Highld 253 G1
Houses Hill Kirk 141 K4
Housieside Abers 257 G6
Houston Rens 208 C5
Houstry Highld 275 G1
Houton Ork 275 b5
Hove Br & H 22 D6
Hove Edge Calder 141 H3
Hoveringham Notts 117 J2
Hoveton Norfk 122 F7
Hovingham N York 161 L7
Howbrook Barns 141 M8
How Caple Herefs 63 J1
Howden E R Yk 143 J2
Howden-le-Wear Dur 168 F4
Howe Highld 280 D4
Howe IoM 154 b8
Howe N York 160 E6
Howe Norfk 106 F3
Howe Bridge Wigan 139 K7
Howe Bridge Crematorium Wigan 139 K7
Howe Green Essex 71 H6
Howegreen Essex 71 K6
Howell Lincs 118 F2
How End C Beds 85 K7
Howe of Teuchar Abers 268 E6
Howes D & G 177 G5
Howe Street Essex 71 G4
Howe Street Essex 88 D8
Howey Powys 78 E3
Howgate Cumb 164 C6
Howgate Mdloth 211 H7
Howgill Lancs 148 E6
Howick Nthumb 191 K3
Howle Wrekin 113 M6
Howle Hill Herefs 63 J3
Howlett End Essex 88 B8
Howley Somset 15 G1
How Mill Cumb 178 C7
Howmore W Isls 283 b10
Hownam Border 189 L2
Howrigg Cumb 165 K1
Howsham N Linc 144 D6
Howsham N York 151 M3
Howtel Nthumb 202 D6
Howt Green Kent 53 J6
Howton Herefs 62 E1
Howtown Cumb 166 B6
Howwood Rens 208 C7
Hoxne Suffk 106 D7
Hoy Ork 275 b5
Hoylake Wirral 128 F2
Hoyland Common Barns 142 B7
Hoyland Nether Barns 142 B7
Hoyland Swaine Barns 141 L6
Hoyle W Susx 20 E3
Hoyle Mill Barns 142 A6
Hubberholme N York 159 G7
Hubberston Pembks 54 E5
Hubbert's Bridge Lincs 119 J3
Huby N York 150 C6
Huby N York 151 J3
Huccaby Devon 12 F8
Hucclecote Gloucs 64 C4
Hucking Kent 53 H7
Hucknall Notts 116 F2
Huddersfield Kirk 141 H4
Huddersfield Crematorium Kirk 141 J4
Huddington Worcs 81 L4
Hudnall Herts 68 C4
Hudswell N York 159 L3
Huggate E R Yk 152 D5
Hugglescote Leics 99 L1
Hughenden Valley Bucks 67 L7
Hughley Shrops 96 D4
Hugh Town IoS 10 c3
Huish Devon 27 J8
Huish Wilts 47 H6
Huish Champflower Somset 29 J5
Huish Episcopi Somset 31 G5
Hulcote C Beds 85 J7
Hulcott Bucks 67 K4
Hulham Devon 14 B6
Hulland Derbys 115 L2
Hulland Ward Derbys 115 L2
Hullavington Wilts 46 C3
Hullbridge Essex 71 K8
Hull, Kingston upon C KuH 144 D2
Hulme Manch 140 C8
Hulme Staffs 114 E2
Hulme Warrtn 130 B2
Hulme End Staffs 132 B7
Hulme Walfield Ches E 131 G6
Hulse Heath Ches E 130 E3
Hulton Lane Ends Bolton 139 K6
Hulverstone IoW 18 F6
Hulver Street Norfk 105 J1
Hulver Street Suffk 107 K6
Humber Devon 13 L7
Humber Herefs 80 C4
Humberston NE Lin 145 J6
Humberstone C Leic 100 E2
Humberton N York 150 F2
Humbie E Loth 212 A6
Humbleton E R Yk 145 G1
Humbleton Nthumb 202 F7
Humby Lincs 118 D5
Hume Border 201 L5
Humshaugh Nthumb 179 L4
Huna Highld 280 E2
Huncoat Lancs 140 A2
Huncote Leics 100 B4
Hundalee Border 189 H3
Hundall Derbys 133 H4
Hunderthwaite Dur 168 C6
Hundleby Lincs 137 G6
Hundle Houses Lincs 119 H1
Hundleton Pembks 54 F6
Hundon Suffk 88 E5
Hundred End Lancs 138 E3
Hundred House Powys 78 F4
Hungarton Leics 100 F2
Hungerford Hants 33 L8
Hungerford Somset 29 J3
Hungerford W Berk 47 M5
Hungerford Newtown W Berk 47 M4
Hunger Hill Bolton 139 K6
Hunger Hill Lancs 139 G5
Hungerstone Herefs 80 B8
Hungerton Lincs 118 A5
Hungryhatton Shrops 113 L6
Hunmanby N York 163 K7
Hunningham Warwks 83 J2
Hunnington Worcs 98 B7
Hunsbury Hill Nhants 84 E4
Hunsdon Herts 69 L4
Hunsingore N York 150 F5
Hunslet Leeds 141 M2
Hunsonby Cumb 166 D4
Hunstanton Norfk 120 E3
Hunstanworth Dur 168 B1
Hunsterson Ches E 113 M2
Hunston Suffk 89 K2
Hunston W Susx 20 D6
Hunston Green Suffk 89 K2
Hunstrete BaNES 45 J6
Hunsworth Kirk 141 J2
Hunt End Worcs 82 B2
Hunter's Inn Devon 28 B1
Hunter's Quay Ag & B 207 K3
Huntham Somset 30 E5
Hunthill Lodge Angus 234 D1
Huntingdon Cambs 86 E1
Huntingfield Suffk 107 G8
Huntingford Dorset 32 D5
Huntington C York 151 K4
Huntington Ches W 129 K6
Huntington E Loth 212 B4
Huntington Herefs 79 J4
Huntington Herefs 80 B6
Huntington Staffs 98 B1
Huntley Gloucs 63 L3
Huntly Abers 255 L4
Hunton Hants 35 G3
Hunton Kent 39 H3
Hunton N York 160 B4
Hunton Bridge Herts 68 D7
Hunt's Corner Norfk 105 L5
Huntscott Somset 29 G2
Hunt's Cross Lpool 129 K3
Hunts Green Bucks 67 L6
Hunts Green Warwks 98 F4
Huntsham Devon 29 H6
Huntshaw Devon 27 J6
Huntshaw Cross Devon 27 J6
Huntspill Somset 30 D2
Huntstile Somset 30 C4
Huntworth Somset 30 D4
Hunwick Dur 168 F4
Hunworth Norfk 122 B4
Hurcott Somset 30 F7
Hurdcott Wilts 33 L4
Hurdsfield Ches E 131 H5
Hurley W & M 49 K2
Hurley Warwks 99 H4
Hurley Bottom W & M 49 K2
Hurley Common Warwks 99 H4
Hurlford E Ayrs 196 E4
Hurlston Green Lancs 138 E5
Hurn Dorset 18 A4
Hurn's End Lincs 119 M2
Hursley Hants 34 F6
Hurst Dorset 16 F4
Hurst N York 159 J2
Hurst Somset 31 G7
Hurst Wokham 49 J4
Hurstbourne Priors Hants 34 F2
Hurstbourne Tarrant Hants 48 A8
Hurst Green E Susx 24 D2
Hurst Green Essex 73 G4
Hurst Green Lancs 148 B8
Hurst Green Surrey 51 K8
Hurst Hill Dudley 97 L4
Hurstley Herefs 79 L5

Hurstpierpoint W Susx 22 D4
Hurst Wickham W Susx 22 D4
Hurstwood Lancs 140 C2
Hurtiso Ork 275 d5
Hurtmore Surrey 36 E2
Hurworth Burn Dur 169 L4
Hurworth-on-Tees Darltn 169 J8
Hurworth Place Darltn 160 D1
Hury Dur 168 B6
Husbands Bosworth Leics 100 E6
Husborne Crawley C Beds 85 J8
Husthwaite N York 161 H7
Hutcherleigh Devon 8 A5
Hutcliffe Wood Crematorium Sheff 133 G3
Hut Green N York 142 F3
Huthwaite Notts 133 J7
Huttoft Lincs 137 K4
Hutton Border 202 E2
Hutton Cumb 166 B5
Hutton E R Yk 152 F5
Hutton Essex 70 F8
Hutton Lancs 139 G2
Hutton N Som 44 D7
Hutton Bonville N York 160 E3
Hutton Buscel N York 163 H6
Hutton Conyers N York 160 D7
Hutton Cranswick E R Yk 153 G5
Hutton End Cumb 166 B3
Hutton Hang N York 159 L5
Hutton Henry Dur 169 L3
Hutton-le-Hole N York 162 B4
Hutton Lowcross R & Cl 170 E7
Hutton Magna Dur 168 E8
Hutton Mulgrave N York 162 E1
Hutton Roof Cumb 157 J7
Hutton Roof Cumb 165 L4
Hutton Rudby N York 161 G2
Hutton Sessay N York 161 G7
Hutton Wandesley N York 151 H5
Huxham Devon 13 M3
Huxham Green Somset 31 K4
Huxley Ches W 129 L7
Huyton Knows 129 K2
Hycemoor Cumb 155 K5
Hyde Gloucs 64 C6
Hyde Hants 33 L8
Hyde Tamesd 131 J1
Hyde End Wokham 49 H5
Hyde Heath Bucks 68 B7
Hyde Lea Staffs 114 E7
Hydestile Surrey 36 E3
Hykeham Moor Lincs 135 J6
Hyndford Bridge S Lans 198 F5
Hynish Ag & B 224 C7
Hyssington Powys 95 H4
Hystfield Gloucs 63 K7
Hythe Hants 19 G2
Hythe Kent 41 G8
Hythe Somset 44 F8
Hythe End W & M 50 C4
Hyton Cumb 155 K5

I

Ibberton Dorset 16 F1
Ible Derbys 132 E8
Ibsley Hants 18 A2
Ibstock Leics 99 L2
Ibstone Bucks 67 J8
Ibthorpe Hants 48 A8
Iburndale N York 162 F1
Ibworth Hants 48 E7
Icelton N Som 44 D6
Ichrachan Ag & B 217 G1
Ickburgh Norfk 105 G4
Ickenham Gt Lon 50 D2
Ickford Bucks 66 F5
Ickham Kent 41 H4
Ickleford Herts 68 F1
Icklesham E Susx 24 F4
Ickleton Cambs 87 K6
Icklingham Suffk 88 F1
Ickornshaw N York 149 G7
Ickwell Green C Beds 86 C6
Icomb Gloucs 65 J3
Idbury Oxon 65 K3
Iddesleigh Devon 12 D1
Ide Devon 13 L4
Ideford Devon 13 K7
Ide Hill Kent 38 D3
Iden E Susx 25 G3
Iden Green Kent 39 J6
Iden Green Kent 39 K7
Idle C Brad 149 M8
Idless Cnwll 4 D5
Idlicote Warwks 83 G6
Idmiston Wilts 33 L3
Idole Carmth 58 D5
Idridgehay Derbys 115 M2
Idrigill Highld 258 F4
Idstone Oxon 47 K2
Iffley Oxon 66 D6
Ifield W Susx 37 K3
Ifold W Susx 36 F4
Iford Bmouth 18 A5
Iford E Susx 22 F5
Ifton Mons 44 F1
Ifton Heath Shrops 112 E4
Ightfield Shrops 113 K4
Ightham Kent 38 F2
Iken Suffk 91 J4
Ilam Staffs 115 J2
Ilchester Somset 31 H6
Ilderton Nthumb 190 E2
Ilford Gt Lon 51 L2
Ilford Somset 30 E7
Ilfracombe Devon 27 J2
Ilkeston Derbys 116 D3
Ilketshall St Andrew Suffk 107 H6
Ilketshall St John Suffk 107 H6
Ilketshall St Lawrence Suffk 107 H6
Ilketshall St Margaret Suffk 107 G6
Ilkley C Brad 149 K6
Illand Cnwll 11 K7
Illey Dudley 98 B7
Illidge Green Ches E 130 F7
Illingworth Calder 141 G2
Illogan Cnwll 3 H2
Illston on the Hill Leics 100 F3
Ilmer Bucks 67 J6
Ilmington Warwks 82 F6
Ilminster Somset 30 E7
Ilsington Devon 13 H7
Ilsington Dorset 16 E4
Ilston Swans 57 G6
Ilton N York 160 B7
Ilton Somset 30 E7
Imachar N Ayrs 194 D3
Immingham NE Lin 144 F5
Immingham Dock NE Lin 145 G4
Impington Cambs 87 J3
Ince Ches W 129 K4
Ince Blundell Sefton 138 C7
Ince-in-Makerfield Wigan 139 J6
Inchbae Lodge Hotel Highld 262 C6
Inchbare Angus 234 F2
Inchberry Moray 266 F5
Incheril Highld 261 G7
Inchinnan Rens 208 E5
Inchlaggan Highld 239 K3
Inchmichael P & K 222 D2
Inchnacardoch Hotel Highld 240 C2
Inchnadamph Highld 271 H4
Inchture P & K 222 D2
Inchvuilt Highld 249 L4
Inchyra P & K 222 C3
Indian Queens Cnwll 4 E3
Ingate Place Suffk 107 J5
Ingatestone Essex 70 F7
Ingbirchworth Barns 141 K6
Ingerthorpe N York 150 C3
Ingestre Staffs 114 F6
Ingham Lincs 135 J3
Ingham Norfk 123 H6
Ingham Suffk 89 G1
Ingham Corner Norfk 123 H6
Ingleborough Norfk 120 B8
Ingleby Derbys 116 B6
Ingleby Arncliffe N York 161 G3
Ingleby Barwick S on T 170 B7
Ingleby Cross N York 161 G3
Ingleby Greenhow N York 161 J2
Ingleigh Green Devon 12 E1
Inglesbatch BaNES 45 L6
Inglesham Swindn 65 J7
Ingleston D & G 176 C6
Ingleton Dur 168 F6
Ingleton N York 158 B8
Inglewhite Lancs 147 L7
Ingoe Nthumb 180 C4
Ingol Lancs 139 G1
Ingoldisthorpe Norfk 120 F5
Ingoldmells Lincs 137 K6
Ingoldsby Lincs 118 D5
Ingram Nthumb 190 E3
Ingrave Essex 52 D1
Ingrow C Brad 149 J7
Ings Cumb 157 G3
Ingst S Glos 45 H2
Ingthorpe Rutlnd 101 M2
Ingworth Norfk 122 D5
Inkberrow Worcs 82 B4
Inkerman Dur 168 E3
Inkhorn Abers 257 G4
Inkpen W Berk 48 A6
Inkstack Highld 280 C2
Inmarsh Wilts 46 D6
Innellan Ag & B 207 J5
Innerleithen Border 200 D6
Innerleven Fife 222 F7
Innermessan D & G 172 D2
Innerwick E Loth 212 F4
Innesmill Moray 266 F3
Insch Abers 256 A6
Insh Highld 241 L3
Inskip Lancs 147 J8
Inskip Moss Side Lancs 147 J8
Instow Devon 27 H5
Insworke Cnwll 6 E4
Intake Sheff 133 H3
Inver Abers 243 H5
Inver Highld 264 D3
Inver P & K 232 F7
Inverailort Highld 238 B7
Inveralligin Highld 260 D8
Inverallochy Abers 269 J3
Inveran Highld 272 E8
Inveraray Ag & B 217 H5
Inverarish Highld 247 H2
Inverarity Angus 234 C6
Inverarnan Stirlg 218 D3
Inverasdale Highld 260 C3
Inverbeg Ag & B 218 E7
Inverbervie Abers 235 K1
Inver-boyndie Abers 268 B3
Invercreran House Hotel Ag & B 229 G6
Inverdruie Highld 242 B1
Inveresk E Loth 211 K5
Inveresragan Ag & B 228 F8
Inverey Abers 242 E5
Inverfarigaig Highld 250 F7
Inverfolla Ag & B 228 E6
Invergarry Highld 240 A3
Invergeldie P & K 220 C2
Invergloy Highld 239 L6
Invergordon Highld 263 J6
Invergowrie P & K 222 F1
Inverguseran Highld 238 B2
Inverhadden P & K 231 J4
Inverherive Hotel Stirlg 218 E2
Inverie Highld 238 B3
Inverinan Ag & B 216 F4
Inverinate Highld 248 E7
Inverkeilor Angus 235 G5
Inverkeithing Fife 210 F2
Inverkeithny Abers 268 A6
Inverkip Inver 207 K4
Inverkirkaig Highld 270 E4
Inverlael Highld 261 K3
Inverlair Highld 240 B7
Inverliever Lodge Ag & B 216 D6
Inverlochy Ag & B 217 K2
Invermark Angus 244 A7
Invermoriston Highld 250 D8
Invernaver Highld 278 B4
Inverness Highld 251 H3
Inverness Crematorium Highld 251 H3
Invernoaden Ag & B 217 J7
Inveroran Hotel Ag & B 229 M7
Inverquharity Angus 234 B4
Inverquhomery Abers 257 J2
Inverroy Highld 239 M7
Inversanda Highld 228 E3
Invershiel Highld 248 F7
Invershin Highld 272 E8
Invershore Highld 275 H1
Inversnaid Hotel Stirlg 218 E5
Inverugie Abers 269 L6
Inveruglas Ag & B 218 D5
Inveruglass Highld 241 L3
Inverurie Abers 256 D7
Inwardleigh Devon 12 D3
Inworth Essex 72 C3
Iochdar W Isls 283 b9
Iona Ag & B 226 B7
Iping W Susx 36 C6
Ipplepen Devon 8 B2
Ipsden Oxon 48 F2
Ipstones Staffs 115 G2
Ipswich Suffk 90 E6
Ipswich Crematorium Suffk 90 E6
Irby Wirral 128 F3
Irby in the Marsh Lincs 137 J7
Irby upon Humber NE Lin 145 G6
Irchester Nhants 85 H2
Ireby Cumb 165 H3
Ireby Lancs 157 L7
Ireland C Beds 86 C7
Ireleth Cumb 156 B7
Ireshopeburn Dur 167 K3
Ireton Wood Derbys 115 M2
Irlam Salfd 130 E1
Irnham Lincs 118 D6
Iron Acton S Glos 45 K2
Iron Bridge Cambs 103 K4
Ironbridge Wrekin 96 F3
Iron Cross Warwks 82 C5
Ironmacannie D & G 185 G7
Irons Bottom Surrey 37 K2
Ironville Derbys 116 D1
Irstead Norfk 123 H7
Irthington Cumb 178 C6
Irthlingborough Nhants 85 J1
Irton N York 163 H6
Irvine N Ayrs 196 C3
Isauld Highld 279 G3
Isbister Shet 281 d3
Isbister Shet 281 f5
Isfield E Susx 23 G4
Isham Nhants 101 J8
Isington Hants 36 A2
Islandpool Worcs 97 K7
Islay Ag & B 204 E1
Isle Abbotts Somset 30 E6
Isle Brewers Somset 30 E6
Isleham Cambs 104 C8
Isle of Dogs Gt Lon 51 K3
Isle of Lewis W Isls 282 f3
Isle of Man IoM 154 e5
Isle of Mull Ag & B 227 H5
Isle of Sheppey Kent 40 C2
Isle of Skye Highld 246 F1
Isle of Walney Cumb 146 D3
Isle of Whithorn D & G 174 D7
Isle of Wight IoW 19 J6
Isle of Wight Crematorium IoW 19 J5
Isleornsay Highld 247 L6
Islesteps D & G 176 C4
Islet Village Guern 9 k2
Isleworth Gt Lon 50 F4
Isley Walton Leics 116 C6
Islibhig W Isls 282 d3
Islington Gt Lon 51 J2
Islington Crematorium Gt Lon 51 H1
Islip Nhants 101 L7
Islip Oxon 66 D4
Islivig W Isls 282 d3
Isombridge Wrekin 96 E1
Istead Rise Kent 52 D5
Itchen Abbas Hants 35 H4
Itchen Stoke Hants 35 H4
Itchingfield W Susx 37 H5
Itchington S Glos 45 K2
Itteringham Norfk 122 C5
Itton Devon 12 F3
Itton Mons 62 F8
Itton Common Mons 62 F7
Ivegill Cumb 165 M2
Ivelet N York 159 G3
Iver Bucks 50 D3
Iver Heath Bucks 50 C2
Iveston Dur 168 E1
Ivinghoe Bucks 68 B4
Ivinghoe Aston Bucks 68 B3
Ivington Herefs 80 B4
Ivington Green Herefs 80 B4
Ivybridge Devon 7 J4
Ivychurch Kent 25 J2
Ivy Cross Dorset 32 E6
Ivy Hatch Kent 38 F3
Ivy Todd Norfk 105 H2
Iwade Kent 40 A2
Iwerne Courtney or Shroton Dorset 32 E8
Iwerne Minster Dorset 32 E8
Ixworth Suffk 89 J1
Ixworth Thorpe Suffk 89 J1

J

Jack Green Lancs 139 J3
Jack Hill N York 150 B5
Jack-in-the-Green Devon 14 B3
Jack's Bush Hants 34 C3
Jacksdale Notts 116 D1
Jackson Bridge Kirk 141 J6
Jackton S Lans 209 G8
Jacobstow Cnwll 11 H3
Jacobstowe Devon 12 E2
Jacobs Well Surrey 50 C8
Jameston Pembks 55 H7
Jamestown Highld 262 E8
Jamestown W Duns 208 C3
Janetstown Highld 275 G2
Janets-town Highld 280 D6
Jardine Hall D & G 176 E1
Jarrow S Tyne 181 H6
Jarvis Brook E Susx 38 E7
Jasper's Green Essex 71 H2
Jawcraig Falk 209 M4
Jaywick Essex 73 H4
Jealott's Hill Br For 49 L4
Jeater Houses N York 160 F4
Jedburgh Border 189 H2

Jeffreyston Pembks 55 J5
Jemimaville Highld 263 K7
Jerbourg Guern 9 k4
Jersey Jersey 9 d2
Jersey Crematorium Jersey 9 d3
Jersey Marine Neath 57 K6
Jerusalem Lincs 135 J5
Jesmond N u Ty 181 G5
Jevington E Susx 23 J7
Jingle Street Mons 62 F5
Jockey End Herts 68 D4
Jodrell Bank Ches E 130 F5
Johnby Cumb 166 B4
John o' Groats Highld 280 E2
John's Cross E Susx 24 D3
Johnshaven Abers 235 K2
Johnson's Street Norfk 123 H8
Johnston Pembks 54 F5
Johnstone D & G 187 K6
Johnstone Rens 208 D6
Johnstonebridge D & G 187 G7
Johnstown Carmth 58 D5
Johnstown Wrexhm 112 D2
Joppa C Edin 211 K4
Joppa Cerdgn 77 G2
Joppa S Ayrs 196 E7
Jordans Bucks 50 B1
Jordanston Pembks 74 F5
Jordanthorpe Sheff 133 G3
Joyden's Wood Kent 52 B4
Jubilee Corner Kent 39 L4
Jump Barns 142 B7
Jumper's Town E Susx 38 C6
Juniper Nthumb 179 L7
Juniper Green C Edin 211 G5
Jura Ag & B 215 G7
Jurby IoM 154 e3
Jurston Devon 13 G5

K

Kaber Cumb 167 J8
Kaimend S Lans 199 G4
Kames Ag & B 206 F5
Kames E Ayrs 197 K5
Kea Cnwll 4 C6
Keadby N Linc 143 L5
Keal Cotes Lincs 137 G7
Kearby Town End N York 150 E6
Kearsley Bolton 139 M6
Kearsley Nthumb 180 B4
Kearsney Kent 41 J6
Kearstwick Cumb 157 K6
Kearton N York 159 H3
Keasden N York 148 C3
Keaton Devon 7 J4
Keckwick Halton 130 B3
Keddington Lincs 136 F2
Keddington Corner Lincs 137 G2
Kedington Suffk 88 E6
Kedleston Derbys 116 A3
Keelby Lincs 144 F5
Keele Staffs 114 C3
Keele University Staffs 114 C3
Keeley Green Bed 85 K6
Keelham C Brad 141 G1
Keeston Pembks 54 E3
Keevil Wilts 46 D7
Kegworth Leics 116 E6
Kehelland Cnwll 3 G3
Keig Abers 256 A7
Keighley C Brad 149 J7
Keighley Crematorium C Brad 149 J8
Keilarsbrae Clacks 220 F8
Keillour P & K 221 H2
Keiloch Abers 243 G5
Keils Ag & B 205 H3
Keinton Mandeville Somset 31 J5
Keir Mill D & G 186 C7
Keirsleywell Row Nthumb 179 H8
Keisby Lincs 118 D6
Keisley Cumb 167 G6
Keiss Highld 280 D4
Keith Moray 267 J6
Keithick P & K 233 J7
Keithock Angus 234 F3
Keithtown Highld 262 F8
Kelbrook Lancs 148 F7
Kelby Lincs 118 D3
Keld Cumb 166 D7
Keld N York 158 F3
Keld Head N York 162 D5
Keldholme N York 162 C5
Kelfield N Linc 143 L7
Kelfield N York 151 J8
Kelham Notts 134 F8
Kelhead D & G 176 F5
Kellacott Devon 12 A5
Kellamergh Lancs 138 E2
Kellas Angus 234 C8
Kellas Moray 266 D5
Kellaton Devon 8 B7
Kelleth Cumb 157 L2
Kelling Norfk 122 B3
Kellington N York 142 E3
Kelloe Dur 169 K3
Kelloholm D & G 185 J1
Kells Cumb 164 C7
Kelly Devon 11 M6
Kelly Bray Cnwll 11 L8
Kelmarsh Nhants 101 G7
Kelmscott Oxon 65 K7
Kelsale Suffk 91 J2
Kelsall Ches W 129 M6
Kelshall Herts 87 G7
Kelsick Cumb 165 G1
Kelso Border 201 M6
Kelstedge Derbys 133 G7
Kelstern Lincs 136 D2
Kelsterton Flints 129 G5
Kelston BaNES 45 K5
Keltneyburn P & K 231 L5
Kelton D & G 176 C5
Kelty Fife 221 L8
Kelvedon Essex 72 C3
Kelvedon Hatch Essex 70 E7
Kelynack Cnwll 2 B5
Kemacott Devon 28 B2
Kemback Fife 223 G4
Kemberton Shrops 97 G3
Kemble Gloucs 64 E7
Kemble Wick Gloucs 64 E7
Kemerton Worcs 81 L7
Kemeys Commander Mons 62 D6
Kemnay Abers 256 D8
Kempe's Corner Kent 40 D6
Kempley Gloucs 63 K1
Kempley Green Gloucs 63 K1
Kempsey Worcs 81 J5
Kempsford Gloucs 65 H7
Kemps Green Warwks 82 D1
Kempshott Hants 35 J1
Kempston Bed 85 K5
Kempston Hardwick Bed 85 K6
Kempton Shrops 95 J6
Kemp Town Br & H 22 E6
Kemsing Kent 52 C7
Kemsley Kent 40 B2
Kemsley Street Kent 53 H6
Kenardington Kent 25 H1
Kenchester Herefs 80 B6
Kencot Oxon 65 K6
Kendal Cumb 157 H4
Kenderchurch Herefs 62 E2
Kendleshire S Glos 45 K3
Kenfig Brdgnd 42 B5
Kenfig Hill Brdgnd 42 C5
Kenilworth Warwks 83 G1
Kenley Gt Lon 51 J7
Kenley Shrops 96 D3
Kenmore Highld 260 B8
Kenmore P & K 231 L6
Kenn Devon 13 L5
Kenn N Som 44 E5
Kennacraig Ag & B 206 C6
Kennards House Cnwll 11 K6
Kenneggy Cnwll 2 F5
Kennerleigh Devon 13 J1
Kennessee Green Sefton 138 D7
Kennet Clacks 210 B1
Kennethmont Abers 255 L6
Kennett Cambs 88 D2
Kennford Devon 13 L5
Kenninghall Norfk 105 L6
Kennington Kent 40 D6
Kennington Oxon 66 D6
Kennoway Fife 222 F6
Kenny Somset 30 D7
Kennyhill Suffk 104 D7
Kennythorpe N York 152 B3
Kenovay Ag & B 224 C6
Kensaleyre Highld 259 G6
Kensington Gt Lon 51 H3
Kensworth Common C Beds 68 C3
Kentallen Highld 228 F4
Kent and Sussex Crematorium Kent 38 F6
Kentchurch Herefs 62 E2
Kentford Suffk 88 E2
Kent Green Ches E 131 G8
Kentisbeare Devon 14 C1
Kentisbury Devon 27 L2
Kentisbury Ford Devon 27 L2
Kentish Town Gt Lon 51 H2
Kentmere Cumb 157 G2
Kenton Devon 13 M6
Kenton Gt Lon 50 F1
Kenton N u Ty 180 F5
Kenton Suffk 90 E2
Kenton Bankfoot N u Ty 180 F5
Kentra Highld 237 J6
Kents Bank Cumb 156 F7
Kent's Green Gloucs 63 L2
Kent's Oak Hants 34 D6
Kent Street E Susx 24 E4
Kent Street Kent 39 G2
Kenwick Shrops 112 F5
Kenwyn Cnwll 4 D5
Kenyon Warrtn 139 J8
Keoldale Highld 276 F3
Keppoch Highld 248 E6
Kepwick N York 161 G4
Keresley Covtry 99 J6
Kermincham Ches E 130 F6
Kernborough Devon 8 B6
Kerne Bridge Herefs 63 H3
Kerrera Ag & B 216 C2
Kerridge Ches E 131 J4
Kerridge-end Ches E 131 J4
Kerris Cnwll 2 C5
Kerry Powys 94 E5
Kerrycroy Ag & B 207 J6
Kersall Notts 134 E7
Kersbrook Devon 14 C6
Kerscott Devon 27 L5
Kersey Suffk 89 K6
Kersey Tye Suffk 89 K6
Kersey Upland Suffk 89 K6
Kershader W Isls 282 f4
Kershopefoot Cumb 178 B2
Kersoe Worcs 82 A7
Kerswell Devon 14 C2
Kerswell Green Worcs 81 K6
Kerthen Wood Cnwll 2 F4
Kesgrave Suffk 90 F6
Kessingland Suffk 107 L6
Kessingland Beach Suffk 107 L6
Kestle Cnwll 5 G5
Kestle Mill Cnwll 4 D3
Keston Gt Lon 51 L6
Keswick Cumb 165 J6
Keswick Norfk 106 E2
Ketsby Lincs 137 G4
Kettering Nhants 101 J7
Kettering Crematorium Nhants 101 J7
Ketteringham Norfk 106 D3
Kettins P & K 233 K7
Kettlebaston Suffk 89 K5
Kettlebridge Fife 222 E5
Kettlebrook Staffs 99 G3
Kettleburgh Suffk 91 G3
Kettle Green Herts 69 L3
Kettleholm D & G 176 F3
Kettleness N York 171 J7
Kettleshulme Ches E 131 K4
Kettlesing N York 150 B4
Kettlesing Bottom N York 150 B4
Kettlestone Norfk 121 L5
Kettlethorpe Lincs 135 G4
Kettletoft Ork 275 e2
Kettlewell N York 149 H2
Ketton Rutlnd 101 L3
Kew Gt Lon 50 F4
Kewstoke N Som 44 C6
Kexbrough Barns 141 M6
Kexby C York 151 L5
Kexby Lincs 135 H3
Key Green Ches E 131 H7
Key Green N York 162 D2
Keyham Leics 100 E2
Keyhaven Hants 18 D5
Keyingham E R Yk 145 H3
Keymer W Susx 22 D4
Keynsham BaNES 45 K5
Keysoe Bed 86 B3
Keysoe Row Bed 86 B3
Keyston Cambs 102 A8
Key Street Kent 53 J6
Keyworth Notts 117 G5
Kibbear Somset 30 B6
Kibblesworth Gatesd 181 G7
Kibworth Beauchamp Leics 100 F4
Kibworth Harcourt Leics 100 F4
Kidbrooke Gt Lon 51 L4
Kidburngill Cumb 164 E6
Kiddemore Green Staffs 97 J2
Kidderminster Worcs 97 J8
Kiddington Oxon 66 B3
Kidd's Moor Norfk 106 C3
Kidlington Oxon 66 D4
Kidmore End Oxon 49 G3
Kidsdale D & G 174 C7
Kidsgrove Staffs 131 G8
Kidstones N York 159 G6
Kidwelly Carmth 56 D3
Kiel Crofts Ag & B 228 D7
Kielder Nthumb 189 H7
Kiells Ag & B 204 F3
Kilbarchan Rens 208 C6
Kilbeg Highld 247 K7
Kilberry Ag & B 206 A6
Kilbirnie N Ayrs 208 A8
Kilbride Ag & B 207 G5
Kilbride Ag & B 215 L8
Kilbuiack Moray 266 B4
Kilburn Derbys 116 C2
Kilburn Gt Lon 51 H2
Kilburn N York 161 H6
Kilby Leics 100 D4
Kilchamaig Ag & B 206 C6
Kilchattan Ag & B 207 H8
Kilchattan Ag & B 214 D5
Kilcheran Ag & B 228 C7
Kilchoan Highld 236 F7
Kilchoman Ag & B 204 B4
Kilchrenan Ag & B 217 G3
Kilconquhar Fife 223 H6
Kilcot Gloucs 63 K2
Kilcoy Highld 251 G2
Kilcreggan Ag & B 207 L3
Kildale N York 161 K1
Kildalloig Ag & B 192 F4
Kildary Highld 263 K5
Kildavaig Ag & B 206 F6
Kildavanan Ag & B 207 G5
Kildonan Highld 274 B4
Kildonan N Ayrs 195 G6
Kildonan Lodge Highld 274 B4
Kildonnan Highld 236 F3
Kildrochet House D & G 172 D4
Kildrummy Abers 255 J8
Kildwick N York 149 H6
Kilfinan Ag & B 206 E3
Kilfinnan Highld 239 M4
Kilford Denbgs 128 C6
Kilgetty Pembks 55 K5
Kilgrammie S Ayrs 183 G3
Kilgwrrwg Common Mons 62 F7
Kilham E R Yk 153 G3
Kilham Nthumb 202 D6
Kilkenneth Ag & B 224 B6
Kilkenzie Ag & B 192 D3
Kilkerran Ag & B 192 E4
Kilkhampton Cnwll 26 D8
Killamarsh Derbys 133 J3
Killay Swans 57 H6
Killearn Stirlg 208 E2
Killen Highld 263 J8
Killerby Darltn 169 G6
Killerton Devon 14 A3
Killichonan P & K 231 G4
Killiechonate Highld 239 L7
Killiechronan Ag & B 227 G4
Killiecrankie P & K 232 D3
Killilan Highld 248 F5
Killimster Highld 280 D5
Killin Stirlg 231 G8
Killinghall N York 150 C4
Killington Cumb 157 K5
Killington Devon 28 B2
Killingworth N Tyne 181 G5
Killiow Cnwll 4 C6
Killochyett Border 200 F4
Kilmacolm Inver 208 B5
Kilmahog Stirlg 219 K5
Kilmahumaig Ag & B 216 B8
Kilmaluag Highld 259 G2
Kilmany Fife 222 F3
Kilmarnock E Ayrs 196 E3
Kilmartin Ag & B 216 C7
Kilmaurs E Ayrs 196 E3
Kilmelford Ag & B 216 C4
Kilmersdon Somset 45 K8
Kilmeston Hants 35 J5
Kilmichael Ag & B 192 E4
Kilmichael Glassary Ag & B 216 D8
Kilmichael of Inverlussa Ag & B 206 B2
Kilmington Devon 15 G3
Kilmington Wilts 32 C3
Kilmington Common Wilts 32 C4
Kilmington Street Wilts 32 C4
Kilmorack Highld 250 E3
Kilmore Ag & B 216 D2
Kilmore Highld 247 K7
Kilmory Ag & B 205 M2
Kilmory Highld 237 G6
Kilmory N Ayrs 193 K4
Kilmuir Highld 251 J2
Kilmuir Highld 258 D7
Kilmuir Highld 258 F3
Kilmuir Highld 263 K5
Kilmun Ag & B 207 K3
Kilnave Ag & B 204 D2
Kilncadzow S Lans 198 E3
Kilndown Kent 39 H6
Kiln Green Wokham 49 K3
Kilnhill Cumb 165 H4

Kilnhouses Ches W 130 C6
Kilnhurst Rothm 142 C8
Kilninver Ag & B 216 C3
Kiln Pit Hill Nthumb 180 C7
Kilnsea E R Yk 145 L4
Kilnsey N York 149 H2
Kilnwick E R Yk 152 F6
Kilnwick Percy E R Yk 152 C6
Kiloran Ag & B 214 D5
Kilpatrick N Ayrs 194 D5
Kilpeck Herefs 62 F1
Kilpin E R Yk 143 K2
Kilpin Pike E R Yk 143 J2
Kilrenny Fife 223 K6
Kilsby Nhants 84 A1
Kilspindie P & K 222 C2
Kilstay D & G 172 E7
Kilsyth N Lans 209 J3
Kiltarlity Highld 250 E3
Kilton R & Cl 171 G7
Kilton Thorpe R & Cl 171 G7
Kilvaxter Highld 258 F3
Kilve Somset 29 L2
Kilvington Notts 117 L3
Kilwinning N Ayrs 196 B2
Kimberley Norfk 106 B3
Kimberley Notts 116 E3
Kimberworth Rothm 133 H1
Kimblesworth Dur 169 H1
Kimble Wick Bucks 67 J5
Kimbolton Cambs 86 B2
Kimbolton Herefs 80 C3
Kimcote Leics 100 D6
Kimmeridge Dorset 17 H6
Kimmerston Nthumb 202 E6
Kimpton Hants 34 C2
Kimpton Herts 68 F3
Kimworthy Devon 26 E8
Kinbrace Highld 273 L2
Kinbuck Stirlg 220 D6
Kincaple Fife 223 H3
Kincardine Fife 210 B2
Kincardine Highld 263 G2
Kincardine O'Neil Abers 244 D4
Kinclaven P & K 233 H7
Kincorth C Aber 245 L3
Kincorth House Moray 265 G7
Kincraig Highld 241 M2
Kincraigie P & K 232 E5
Kindallachan P & K 232 E5
Kinerarach Ag & B 205 L5
Kineton Gloucs 65 G2
Kineton Warwks 83 H5
Kinfauns P & K 222 B3
Kingarth Ag & B 207 H7
Kingcausie Abers 245 J3
Kingcoed Mons 62 E6
Kingerby Lincs 135 L1
Kingford Devon 11 K2
Kingham Oxon 65 K2
Kingholm Quay D & G 176 C4
Kinghorn Fife 211 J2
Kinglassie Fife 222 C7
Kingoldrum Angus 233 M4
Kingoodie P & K 222 F1
King's Acre Herefs 80 B7
Kingsand Cnwll 6 E5
Kingsash Bucks 67 L6
Kingsbarns Fife 223 K5
Kingsbridge Devon 7 L6
Kingsbridge Somset 29 H3
Kings Bridge Swans 57 G5
King's Bromley Staffs 115 J8
Kingsburgh Highld 258 F5
Kingsbury Gt Lon 51 G1
Kingsbury Warwks 99 G4
Kingsbury Episcopi Somset 31 G6
King's Caple Herefs 63 H2
Kingsclere Hants 48 D7
King's Cliffe Nhants 101 M4
Kingscote Gloucs 64 B7
Kingscott Devon 27 K7
King's Coughton Warwks 82 C3
Kingscross N Ayrs 195 G5
Kingsdon Somset 31 H5
Kingsdown Kent 41 L5
Kingsdown Swindn 47 H1
Kingsdown Wilts 46 A5
Kingsdown Crematorium Swindn 47 H1
Kingseat Fife 210 F1
Kingsey Bucks 67 H6
Kingsfold W Susx 37 J4
Kingsford C Aber 245 J2
Kingsford E Ayrs 196 E2
Kingsford Worcs 97 J7
Kingsgate Kent 41 L1
Kings Green Gloucs 81 H8
Kingshall Street Suffk 89 J3
Kingsheanton Devon 27 K3
King's Heath Birm 98 D7
Kings Hill Kent 39 H2
King's Hill Wsall 98 C4
Kings House Hotel Highld 229 L4
Kingshouse Hotel Stirlg 219 J3
Kingshurst Solhll 98 F5
Kingside Hill Cumb 177 G8
Kingskerswell Devon 8 C1
Kingskettle Fife 222 E5
Kingsland Dorset 15 K3
Kingsland Herefs 80 B3
Kingsland IoA 124 D3
Kings Langley Herts 68 D6
Kingsley Ches W 130 A5
Kingsley Hants 36 B3
Kingsley Staffs 115 G2
Kingsley Green W Susx 36 D5
Kingsley Park Nhants 84 E3
Kingslow Shrops 97 H4
King's Lynn Norfk 120 D7
Kings Meaburn Cumb 166 E6
Kingsmead Hants 35 J8
King's Mills Guern 9 i3
King's Moss St Hel 139 G7
Kingsmuir Angus 234 D5
Kings Muir Border 200 B5
Kingsmuir Fife 223 J5
Kings Newnham Warwks 99 M7
King's Newton Derbys 116 C6
Kingsnorth Kent 40 C7
King's Norton Birm 98 D7
King's Norton Leics 100 F3
Kings Nympton Devon 28 B7
King's Pyon Herefs 80 B5
Kings Ripton Cambs 102 F8
King's Somborne Hants 34 D4
King's Stag Dorset 32 B8
King's Stanley Gloucs 64 A6
King's Sutton Nhants 83 L8
Kingstanding Birm 98 D4
Kingsteignton Devon 13 K8
King Sterndale Derbys 132 B5
Kingsthorne Herefs 63 G1
Kingsthorpe Nhants 84 E3
Kingston Cambs 87 G4
Kingston Cnwll 11 L7
Kingston Devon 7 J5
Kingston Devon 14 C5
Kingston Dorset 16 E1
Kingston Dorset 17 J6
Kingston E Loth 212 C3
Kingston Hants 18 A3
Kingston IoW 19 H7
Kingston Kent 41 G5
Kingston W Susx 21 J6
Kingston Bagpuize Oxon 66 B7
Kingston Blount Oxon 67 H7
Kingston Deverill Wilts 32 D3
Kingstone Herefs 80 A8
Kingstone Somset 30 E8
Kingstone Staffs 115 H5
Kingstone Winslow Oxon 47 K2
Kingston Lisle Oxon 47 L2
Kingston near Lewes E Susx 22 F5
Kingston on Soar Notts 116 E6
Kingston on Spey Moray 267 G3
Kingston Russell Dorset 16 A4
Kingston St Mary Somset 30 B5
Kingston Seymour N Som 44 E5
Kingston Stert Oxon 67 H7
Kingston upon Hull C KuH 144 D2
Kingston upon Thames Gt Lon 50 F5
Kingston upon Thames Crematorium Gt Lon 51 G5
Kingstown Cumb 177 L7
King's Walden Herts 68 F2
Kingswear Devon 8 C4
Kingswells C Aber 245 J2
Kings Weston Bristl 45 G3
Kingswinford Dudley 97 K5
Kingswood Bucks 67 G3
Kingswood Gloucs 63 L8
Kingswood Kent 39 L3
Kingswood Powys 94 F3
Kingswood S Glos 45 J4
Kingswood Somset 29 K3
Kingswood Surrey 51 H7
Kingswood Warwks 82 E1
Kingswood Brook Warwks 82 E1
Kingswood Common Herefs 79 K4
Kingswood Common Staffs 97 J3
Kings Worthy Hants 35 G4
Kingthorpe Lincs 136 B4
Kington Herefs 79 K4
Kington S Glos 45 J1
Kington Worcs 82 A4
Kington Langley Wilts 46 D3
Kington Magna Dorset 32 C6
Kington St Michael Wilts 46 C3
Kingussie Highld 241 K3
Kingweston Somset 31 H5
Kinharrachie Abers 257 G5
Kinharvie D & G 176 B5
Kinkell Bridge P & K 221 G4
Kinknockie Abers 257 J3
Kinleith C Edin 211 G5
Kinlet Shrops 97 G7
Kinloch Highld 246 E8
Kinloch Highld 271 K1
Kinloch Highld 277 J5
Kinloch P & K 233 H6
Kinlochard Stirlg 219 G6
Kinlochbervie Highld 276 C5
Kinlocheil Highld 238 F7
Kinlochewe Highld 261 G7
Kinloch Hourn Highld 238 F2
Kinlochlaggan Highld 240 F5
Kinlochleven Highld 229 K3
Kinlochmoidart Highld 237 K6
Kinlochnanuagh Highld 237 L4
Kinloch Rannoch P & K 231 J4
Kinloss Moray 265 H7
Kinmel Bay Conwy 127 K4
Kinmuck Abers 256 E7
Kinmundy Abers 256 F8
Kinnabus Ag & B 204 D7
Kinnadie Abers 257 H3
Kinnaird P & K 232 E4
Kinneff Abers 245 J8
Kinnelhead D & G 186 F6
Kinnell Angus 234 F5
Kinnerley Shrops 112 E7
Kinnersley Herefs 79 L5
Kinnersley Worcs 81 K6
Kinnerton Powys 79 J3
Kinnerton Shrops 95 J4
Kinnerton Green Flints 129 H7
Kinnesswood P & K 222 B6
Kinninvie Dur 168 D6
Kinnordy Angus 234 B4
Kinoulton Notts 117 H5
Kinross P & K 221 K6
Kinrossie P & K 222 C1
Kinsbourne Green Herts 68 E4
Kinsey Heath Ches E 113 L3
Kinsham Herefs 79 L2
Kinsham Worcs 81 L8
Kinsley Wakefd 142 C5
Kinson Bmouth 17 L3
Kintbury W Berk 48 A5
Kintessack Moray 264 F7
Kintillo P & K 221 L4
Kinton Herefs 95 K8
Kinton Shrops 112 E7
Kintore Abers 256 E8
Kintour Ag & B 205 G6
Kintra Ag & B 204 D6
Kintra Ag & B 226 C7
Kintraw Ag & B 216 C6
Kinveachy Highld 253 G7
Kinver Staffs 97 J6
Kiplin N York 160 C3
Kippax Leeds 142 C2
Kippen Stirlg 219 L8
Kippford or Scaur D & G 175 L4
Kipping's Cross Kent 39 G5
Kirbister Ork 275 c5
Kirby Bedon Norfk 106 F2
Kirby Bellars Leics 117 J7
Kirby Cane Norfk 107 H5
Kirby Corner Covtry 99 J8
Kirby Cross Essex 73 J3
Kirby Fields Leics 100 B3
Kirby Grindalythe N York 152 D2
Kirby Hill N York 150 E2
Kirby Hill N York 159 L2
Kirby Knowle N York 161 G5
Kirby le Soken Essex 73 J3
Kirby Misperton N York 162 D6
Kirby Muxloe Leics 100 B3
Kirby Sigston N York 160 F4
Kirby Underdale E R Yk 152 B4
Kirby Wiske N York 160 E5
Kirdford W Susx 36 F5
Kirk Highld 280 C4
Kirkabister Shet 281 e7
Kirkandrews D & G 174 F5
Kirkandrews upon Eden Cumb 177 K7
Kirkbampton Cumb 177 J7
Kirkbean D & G 176 C7
Kirk Bramwith Donc 143 G5
Kirkbride Cumb 177 H7
Kirkbridge N York 160 C4
Kirkbuddo Angus 234 D6
Kirkburn Border 200 C5
Kirkburn E R Yk 152 F5
Kirkburton Kirk 141 K5
Kirkby Knows 138 E7
Kirkby Lincs 135 L1
Kirkby N York 161 H2
Kirkby Fleetham N York 160 D4
Kirkby Green Lincs 136 A8
Kirkby in Ashfield Notts 133 K8
Kirkby-in-Furness Cumb 156 B6
Kirkby la Thorpe Lincs 118 E2
Kirkby Lonsdale Cumb 157 K7
Kirkby Malham N York 148 F4
Kirkby Mallory Leics 99 M3
Kirkby Malzeard N York 160 C7
Kirkby Mills N York 162 C5
Kirkbymoorside N York 162 B5
Kirkby on Bain Lincs 136 D7
Kirkby Overblow N York 150 D6
Kirkby Stephen Cumb 158 D1
Kirkby Thore Cumb 166 E5
Kirkby Underwood Lincs 118 E6
Kirkby Wharf N York 151 H7
Kirkby Woodhouse Notts 116 E1
Kirkcaldy Fife 211 J1
Kirkcaldy Crematorium Fife 222 D8
Kirkcambeck Cumb 178 C5
Kirkchrist D & G 175 G4
Kirkcolm D & G 172 C1
Kirkconnel D & G 197 L8
Kirkconnell D & G 176 C5
Kirkcowan D & G 173 J3
Kirkcudbright D & G 175 H5
Kirkdale Lpool 129 H1
Kirk Deighton N York 150 F5
Kirk Ella E R Yk 144 C2
Kirkfieldbank S Lans 198 E4
Kirkgunzeon D & G 175 L2
Kirk Hallam Derbys 116 D3
Kirkham Lancs 138 E1
Kirkham N York 151 M3
Kirkhamgate Wakefd 141 L3
Kirk Hammerton N York 151 G5
Kirkharle Nthumb 180 B2
Kirkhaugh Nthumb 167 G1
Kirkheaton Kirk 141 J4
Kirkheaton Nthumb 180 B3
Kirkhill Highld 250 F3
Kirkhope S Lans 186 E5
Kirkhouse Cumb 178 D7
Kirkhouse Green Donc 143 G5
Kirkibost Highld 247 H5
Kirkinch P & K 233 L6
Kirkinner D & G 174 C4
Kirkintilloch E Duns 209 H4
Kirk Ireton Derbys 115 M2
Kirkland Cumb 164 E7
Kirkland Cumb 166 F4
Kirkland D & G 185 K5
Kirkland D & G 186 F8
Kirkland D & G 197 L8
Kirkland Guards Cumb 165 G3
Kirk Langley Derbys 115 M4
Kirkleatham R & Cl 170 E6
Kirklevington S on T 160 F1
Kirkley Suffk 107 L5
Kirklington N York 160 D6
Kirklington Notts 134 D8
Kirklinton Cumb 178 B5
Kirkliston C Edin 210 F4
Kirkmabreck D & G 174 D4
Kirkmaiden D & G 172 E7
Kirk Merrington Dur 169 H4
Kirk Michael IoM 154 d4
Kirkmichael P & K 233 G3
Kirkmichael S Ayrs 183 J1
Kirkmuirhill S Lans 198 C4
Kirknewton Nthumb 202 E7
Kirknewton W Loth 210 F5
Kirkney Abers 255 K5
Kirk of Shotts N Lans 209 M6
Kirkoswald Cumb 166 D3
Kirkoswald S Ayrs 183 G2
Kirkpatrick D & G 186 D8
Kirkpatrick Durham D & G 175 K1
Kirkpatrick-Fleming D & G 177 J5
Kirk Sandall Donc 142 F6
Kirksanton Cumb 155 L6
Kirk Smeaton N York 142 E4
Kirkstall Leeds 150 C8
Kirkstead Lincs 136 C7
Kirkstile Abers 255 L5
Kirkstile D & G 188 C8
Kirkstone Pass Inn Cumb 156 F1
Kirkstyle Highld 280 D2
Kirkthorpe Wakefd 142 B3
Kirkton Abers 256 B6
Kirkton D & G 176 C3
Kirkton Fife 222 F2
Kirkton Highld 248 C6
Kirkton Highld 248 E3
Kirkton P & K 221 G3
Kirkton Manor Border 200 B5
Kirkton of Airlie Angus 233 M5

Kirkton of Auchterhouse Angus 234 A7
Kirkton of Barevan Highld 252 F2
Kirkton of Collace P & K 222 C1
Kirkton of Glenbuchat Abers 255 H8
Kirkton of Logie Buchan Abers 257 H6
Kirkton of Menmuir Angus 234 E3
Kirkton of Monikie Angus 234 D7
Kirkton of Rayne Abers 256 C5
Kirkton of Skene Abers 245 H2
Kirkton of Strathmartine Angus 234 B8
Kirkton of Tealing Angus 234 B7
Kirkton of Tough Abers 244 D1
Kirktown Abers 269 J3
Kirktown Abers 269 K6
Kirktown of Alvah Abers 268 B4
Kirktown of Bourtie Abers 256 E6
Kirktown of Fetteresso Abers 245 J6
Kirktown of Mortlach Moray 255 G4
Kirktown of Slains Abers 257 J6
Kirkurd Border 199 K4
Kirkwall Ork 275 c4
Kirkwhelpington Nthumb 180 B2
Kirk Yetholm Border 202 C7
Kirmington N Linc 144 E5
Kirmond le Mire Lincs 136 C1
Kirn Ag & B 207 K3
Kirriemuir Angus 234 B4
Kirstead Green Norfk 106 F4
Kirtlebridge D & G 177 H4
Kirtling Cambs 88 D4
Kirtling Green Cambs 88 D4
Kirtlington Oxon 66 D3
Kirtomy Highld 278 C3
Kirton Lincs 119 J4
Kirton Notts 134 D6
Kirton Suffk 91 G7
Kirton End Lincs 119 J3
Kirtonhill W Duns 208 C4
Kirton Holme Lincs 119 J3
Kirton in Lindsey N Linc 144 A8
Kirwaugh D & G 173 K4
Kishorn Highld 248 D4
Kislingbury Nhants 84 D3
Kitebrook Warwks 65 K1
Kite Green Warwks 82 E2
Kites Hardwick Warwks 83 L2
Kitleigh Cnwll 11 J3
Kitt Green Wigan 139 H6
Kittisford Somset 29 K6
Kittle Swans 57 G7
Kitt's Green Birm 98 F6
Kittybrewster C Aber 245 K2
Kitwood Hants 35 K4
Kivernoll Herefs 62 F1
Kiveton Park Rothm 133 K3
Knaith Lincs 135 G3
Knaith Park Lincs 135 G3
Knap Corner Dorset 32 D6
Knaphill Surrey 50 B7
Knapp Somset 30 D5
Knapp Hill Hants 34 E6
Knapthorpe Notts 134 E7
Knapton C York 151 J5
Knapton N York 162 F7
Knapton Norfk 122 F5
Knapton Green Herefs 80 B5
Knapwell Cambs 87 G3
Knaresborough N York 150 E4
Knarsdale Nthumb 178 F8
Knaven Abers 257 G3
Knayton N York 160 F5
Knebworth Herts 69 H3
Knedlington E R Yk 143 J2
Kneesall Notts 134 D6
Kneesworth Cambs 87 G6
Kneeton Notts 117 J2
Knelston Swans 56 E7
Knenhall Staffs 114 E4
Knettishall Suffk 105 K7
Knightacott Devon 28 B3
Knightcote Warwks 83 J4
Knightley Staffs 114 C6
Knightley Dale Staffs 114 C6
Knighton C Leic 100 D3
Knighton Devon 7 G5
Knighton Dorset 31 K8
Knighton Poole 17 L3
Knighton Powys 79 K1
Knighton Somset 30 B2
Knighton Staffs 114 A3
Knighton Staffs 114 B6
Knighton Wilts 47 L4
Knighton on Teme Worcs 80 E1
Knightsbridge Gloucs 64 C2
Knightsmill Cnwll 10 F6
Knightwick Worcs 81 G4
Knill Herefs 79 K3
Knipton Leics 117 L5
Knitsley Dur 168 E1
Kniveton Derbys 115 K2
Knock Cumb 166 F5
Knock Highld 247 L6
Knock Moray 267 L5
Knock W Isls 282 g3
Knockally Highld 274 F2
Knockan Highld 271 H6
Knockando Moray 254 D3
Knockbain Highld 250 F3
Knockbain Highld 263 H8
Knock Castle N Ayrs 207 K6
Knockdee Highld 279 L4
Knockdow Ag & B 207 J5
Knockdown Wilts 46 B1
Knockeen S Ayrs 183 H4
Knockenkelly N Ayrs 195 G5
Knockentiber E Ayrs 196 D3
Knockhall Kent 52 C4
Knockholt Kent 51 M7
Knockholt Pound Kent 52 A7
Knockin Shrops 112 E7
Knockinlaw E Ayrs 196 E3
Knockmill Kent 52 C6
Knocknain D & G 172 B2
Knockrome Ag & B 205 J2
Knocksharry IoM 154 c5
Knocksheen D & G 184 F6
Knockvennie Smithy D & G 175 J1
Knodishall Suffk 91 K3
Knodishall Common Suffk 91 K3
Knole Somset 31 G6
Knole Park S Glos 45 H2
Knolls Green Ches E 130 F4
Knolton Wrexhm 112 F4
Knook Wilts 32 F3
Knossington Leics 101 H2
Knott End-on-Sea Lancs 147 G6
Knotting Bed 85 K3
Knotting Green Bed 85 K3
Knottingley Wakefd 142 D3
Knotty Ash Lpool 129 J1
Knotty Green Bucks 68 B8
Knowbury Shrops 96 D8
Knowe D & G 183 H8
Knowehead D & G 184 F5
Knoweside S Ayrs 195 L8
Knowle Bristl 45 J5
Knowle Devon 13 H2
Knowle Devon 14 B1
Knowle Devon 14 B6
Knowle Devon 27 J3
Knowle Shrops 96 D8
Knowle Solhll 98 F8
Knowle Somset 29 H2
Knowle Cross Devon 14 B3
Knowlefield Cumb 177 L7
Knowle Green Lancs 148 A8
Knowle Hill Surrey 50 C5
Knowle St Giles Somset 30 E8
Knowle Village Hants 19 J2
Knowle Wood Calder 140 D3
Knowl Green Essex 88 F7
Knowl Hill W & M 49 K3
Knowlton Dorset 17 K1
Knowlton Kent 41 J4
Knowsley Knows 138 E8
Knowstone Devon 28 E6
Knox N York 150 C4
Knox Bridge Kent 39 K5
Knucklas Powys 95 G8
Knuston Nhants 85 H2
Knutsford Ches E 130 E4
Knutton Staffs 114 C2
Krumlin Calder 141 G4
Kuggar Cnwll 3 J7
Kyleakin Highld 248 B6
Kyle of Lochalsh Highld 248 B6
Kylerhea Highld 248 C7
Kylesku Highld 271 H1
Kylesmorar Highld 238 C5
Kyles Scalpay W Isls 282 f6
Kylestrome Highld 271 H1
Kynaston Herefs 80 E8
Kynaston Shrops 112 E7
Kynnersley Wrekin 113 L8
Kyre Green Worcs 80 E3
Kyre Park Worcs 80 E3
Kyrewood Worcs 80 E2
Kyrle Somset 29 J6

L

La Bellieuse Guern 9 j3
Lacasaigh W Isls 282 f4
Lacasdal W Isls 282 g3
Laceby NE Lin 145 G6
Lacey Green Bucks 67 K7
Lach Dennis Ches W 130 D5
Lackenby R & Cl 170 D6
Lackford Suffk 88 F1
Lackford Green Suffk 88 F1
Lacock Wilts 46 C5
Ladbroke Warwks 83 K3
Ladderedge Staffs 114 F1
Laddingford Kent 39 H4
Lade Bank Lincs 119 L1
Ladock Cnwll 4 E5
Lady Ork 275 e2
Ladybank Fife 222 E5
Ladycross Cnwll 11 L5
Ladygill S Lans 198 F7
Lady Hall Cumb 156 B5
Ladykirk Border 202 D3
Ladyridge Herefs 63 H1
Lady's Green Suffk 88 E3
Ladywood Birm 98 D6
Ladywood Worcs 81 K3
La Fontenelle Guern 9 k1
La Fosse Guern 9 j4
Lag D & G 185 L5
Laga Highld 237 J8
Lagavulin Ag & B 204 F7
Lagg N Ayrs 193 K4
Laggan Highld 240 A4
Laggan Highld 241 G5
Lagganlia Highld 241 M3
La Greve Guern 9 k2
La Greve de Lecq Jersey 9 b1
La Hougue Bie Jersey 9 e3
La Houguette Guern 9 h3
Laid Highld 277 G4
Laide Highld 260 E2
Laig Highld 236 F3
Laigh Clunch E Ayrs 196 F2
Laigh Fenwick E Ayrs 196 F3
Laigh Glenmuir E Ayrs 197 J7
Laighstonehall S Lans 209 J8
Laindon Essex 52 E1
Lairg Highld 272 E6
Laisterdyke C Brad 141 J1
Laithes Cumb 166 B4
Lake Devon 12 C5
Lake Devon 27 K4
Lake IoW 19 K7
Lake Poole 17 J4
Lake Wilts 33 K3
Lakenheath Suffk 104 E6
Laker's Green Surrey 36 F4
Lakesend Norfk 103 L4
Lakeside Cumb 156 E5
Laleham Surrey 50 D5
Laleston Brdgnd 42 C5
Lamanva Cnwll 3 J5
Lamarsh Essex 89 H8
Lamas Norfk 122 E7
Lambden Border 202 A4
Lamberhurst Kent 39 H6
Lamberhurst Down Kent 39 G6
Lamberton Border 213 L7
Lambeth Gt Lon 51 J3
Lambeth Crematorium Gt Lon 51 H4
Lambfair Green Suffk 88 E4
Lambley Notts 117 H2
Lambley Nthumb 178 F7
Lambourn W Berk 47 L3
Lambourne End Essex 70 C8
Lambourn Woodlands W Berk 47 L4
Lamb Roe Lancs 148 C8
Lambs Green W Susx 37 K3
Lambston Pembks 54 E3
Lamellion Cnwll 6 A2
Lamerton Devon 12 B7
Lamesley Gatesd 181 G7
Lamington S Lans 199 G7
Lamlash N Ayrs 195 G5
Lamonby Cumb 165 L3
Lamorick Cnwll 5 H2
Lamorna Cnwll 2 C6
Lamorran Cnwll 4 E6
Lampen Cnwll 5 L2
Lampeter Cerdgn 77 G5
Lampeter Velfrey Pembks 55 K4
Lamphey Pembks 55 G6
Lamplugh Cumb 164 E6
Lamport Nhants 101 G8
Lamyatt Somset 31 L4
Lana Devon 11 K1
Lana Devon 11 L3
Lanark S Lans 198 E4
Lancaster Lancs 147 J3
Lancaster & Morecambe Crematorium Lancs 147 J3
Lancaut Gloucs 63 G7
Lanchester Dur 168 F1
Lancing W Susx 21 L6
L'Ancresse Guern 9 k1
Landbeach Cambs 87 K2
Landcross Devon 27 H6
Landerberry Abers 245 G3
Landford Wilts 34 B7
Land-hallow Highld 275 G2
Landican Crematorium Wirral 129 G3
Landimore Swans 56 E6
Landkey Devon 27 L4
Landore Swans 57 J5
Landrake Cnwll 6 D3
Landscove Devon 7 M2
Land's End Cnwll 2 A6
Landshipping Pembks 55 G4
Landue Cnwll 11 L6
Landulph Cnwll 6 E3
Landwade Suffk 88 C2
Lane Cnwll 4 D3
Laneast Cnwll 11 J6
Lane Bottom Lancs 140 C1
Lane End Bucks 49 K1
Lane End Cnwll 5 H1
Lane End Hants 35 H5
Lane End Kent 52 C4
Lane End Lancs 148 F6
Lane End Warrtn 130 D2
Lane End Wilts 32 D2
Lane Ends Derbys 115 L4
Lane Ends Lancs 140 B2
Lane Ends N York 149 H7
Lane Green Staffs 97 K3
Laneham Notts 134 F4
Lanehead Dur 167 J2
Lane Head Dur 168 E8
Lanehead Nthumb 179 H2
Lane Head Wigan 139 J8
Lane Head Wsall 98 B3
Lane Heads Lancs 147 H7
Laneshaw Bridge Lancs 149 G7
Lane Side Lancs 140 B3
Langaford Devon 12 A3
Langaller Somset 30 C5
Langar Notts 117 J4
Langbank Rens 208 C4
Langbar N York 149 K5
Langbaurgh N York 170 D8
Langcliffe N York 148 E3
Langdale End N York 163 G4
Langdon Cnwll 11 K5
Langdon Beck Dur 167 K4
Langdown Hants 19 G2
Langdyke Fife 222 E6
Langenhoe Essex 72 E3
Langford C Beds 86 D7
Langford Devon 14 B2
Langford Essex 71 K5
Langford N Som 44 F6
Langford Notts 135 G7
Langford Oxon 65 K6
Langford Budville Somset 29 K6
Langham Dorset 32 C5
Langham Essex 72 F1
Langham Norfk 121 M3
Langham Rutlnd 101 J1
Langham Suffk 89 K1
Langho Lancs 139 L1
Langholm D & G 177 L2
Langland Swans 57 H7
Langlee Border 201 G6
Langley Ches E 131 J5
Langley Derbys 116 D2
Langley Gloucs 64 E2
Langley Hants 19 G3
Langley Herts 69 G3
Langley Kent 39 K3
Langley Nthumb 179 J6
Langley Oxon 65 L4
Langley Rochdl 140 C6
Langley Slough 50 C3
Langley Somset 29 K5
Langley W Susx 36 B5
Langley Warwks 82 E3
Langley Burrell Wilts 46 D4
Langley Castle Nthumb 179 J6
Langley Common Derbys 115 M4
Langley Green Derbys 115 M4
Langley Green Essex 72 C3
Langley Green Warwks 82 E3
Langley Lower Green Essex 87 J8
Langley Marsh Somset 29 K5
Langley Mill Derbys 116 D2
Langley Moor Dur 169 H3
Langley Park Dur 169 G2
Langley Street Norfk 107 H3
Langley Upper Green Essex 87 J8
Langney E Susx 23 L6
Langold Notts 134 B2
Langore Cnwll 11 K5
Langport Somset 30 F5
Langrick Lincs 119 J2
Langridge BaNES 45 L5
Langridgeford Devon 27 K6

Langrigg Cumb 165 G2
Langrish Hants 35 L6
Langsett Barns 141 K7
Langside P & K 220 D4
Langstone Hants 20 B6
Langstone Newpt 44 D1
Langthorne N York 160 C4
Langthorpe N York 150 E2
Langthwaite N York 159 H2
Langtoft E R Yk 152 F3
Langtoft Lincs 102 C1
Langton Dur 168 F6
Langton Lincs 136 D6
Langton Lincs 137 G5
Langton N York 152 B2
Langton by Wragby Lincs 136 C4
Langton Green Kent 38 E5
Langton Green Suffk 106 C8
Langton Herring Dorset 16 B6
Langton Long Blandford Dorset 17 H2
Langton Matravers Dorset 17 K6
Langtree Devon 27 H7
Langtree Week Devon 27 H7
Langwathby Cumb 166 D4
Langwell House Highld 274 F3
Langwith Derbys 133 K5
Langwith Junction Derbys 133 K6
Langworth Lincs 135 L4
Lanivet Cnwll 5 H2
Lanjeth Cnwll 5 G4
Lank Cnwll 10 F7
Lanlivery Cnwll 5 J3
Lanner Cnwll 3 J3
Lanoy Cnwll 11 K7
Lanreath Cnwll 5 L3
Lansallos Cnwll 5 K4
Lanteglos Cnwll 10 F6
Lanteglos Highway Cnwll 5 K4
Lanton Border 189 G2
Lanton Nthumb 202 E6
La Passee Guern 9 j2
Lapford Devon 13 G1
Laphroaig Ag & B 204 F7
Lapley Staffs 97 K1
La Pulente Jersey 9 a3
Lapworth Warwks 82 E1
Larachbeg Highld 227 K3
Larbert Falk 209 M3
Larbreck Lancs 147 H7
Largie Abers 256 A5
Largiemore Ag & B 206 E2
Largoward Fife 223 H5
Largs N Ayrs 207 K7
Largybeg N Ayrs 195 G6
Largymore N Ayrs 195 G6
Larkbeare Devon 14 C3
Larkfield Inver 207 L4
Larkfield Kent 52 F7
Larkhall S Lans 198 C3
Larkhill Wilts 33 K2
Larling Norfk 105 K5
La Rocque Jersey 9 f4
La Rousaillerie Guern 9 j2
Lartington Dur 168 C7
Lasborough Gloucs 64 B8
Lasham Hants 35 K2
Lashbrook Devon 12 A1
Lashbrook Devon 12 B2
Lashenden Kent 39 L5
Lask Edge Staffs 131 H8
Lasswade Mdloth 211 J6
Lastingham N York 162 C4
Latcham Somset 31 G2
Latchford Herts 69 K3
Latchford Oxon 67 G6
Latchingdon Essex 72 C7
Latchley Cnwll 12 A7
Lately Common Warrtn 139 K8
Lathbury M Keyn 85 G6
Latheron Highld 275 G2
Latheronwheel Highld 275 G2
Lathones Fife 223 H5
Latimer Bucks 68 C7
Latteridge S Glos 45 K2
Lattiford Somset 32 B5
Latton Wilts 65 G7
Lauder Border 201 H4
Laugharne Carmth 56 B3
Laughterton Lincs 135 G4
Laughton E Susx 23 H4
Laughton Leics 100 E5
Laughton Lincs 118 E5
Laughton Lincs 143 L8
Laughton-en-le-Morthen Rothm 133 K2
Launcells Cnwll 11 J2
Launcells Cross Cnwll 11 K2
Launceston Cnwll 11 L5
Launton Oxon 66 F3
Laurencekirk Abers 235 H1
Laurieston D & G 175 H2
Laurieston Falk 210 B3
Lavendon M Keyn 85 H4
Lavenham Suffk 89 J5
Lavernock V Glam 43 J8
Laversdale Cumb 178 B6
Laverstock Wilts 33 L5
Laverstoke Hants 35 G1
Laverton Gloucs 82 C8
Laverton N York 160 B7
Laverton Somset 45 M8
La Villette Guern 9 j3
Lavister Wrexhm 129 J8
Law S Lans 209 L8
Lawers P & K 231 J7
Lawford Essex 73 G1
Lawford Somset 29 L4
Law Hill S Lans 209 L8
Lawhitton Cnwll 11 L6
Lawkland N York 148 D3
Lawkland Green N York 148 D3
Lawley Wrekin 96 F2
Lawnhead Staffs 114 C6
Lawns Wood Crematorium Leeds 150 C8
Lawrenny Pembks 55 G5
Lawshall Suffk 89 H4
Lawshall Green Suffk 89 H4
Lawton Herefs 80 B3
Laxay W Isls 282 f4
Laxdale W Isls 282 g3
Laxey IoM 154 f5
Laxfield Suffk 91 G1
Laxford Bridge Highld 276 C7
Laxo Shet 281 e5
Laxton E R Yk 143 K3
Laxton Nhants 101 L4
Laxton Notts 134 E6
Laycock C Brad 149 J7
Layer Breton Essex 72 D3
Layer-de-la-Haye Essex 72 D3
Layer Marney Essex 72 D4
Layham Suffk 89 L7
Layland's Green W Berk 48 A5
Laymore Dorset 15 J2
Layter's Green Bucks 50 C1
Laytham E R Yk 152 A7
Laythes Cumb 177 H7
Lazenby R & Cl 170 D6
Lazonby Cumb 166 D3
Lea Derbys 132 F8
Lea Herefs 63 K3
Lea Lincs 135 G2
Lea Shrops 95 J5
Lea Shrops 95 K2
Lea Wilts 46 D2
Leachkin Highld 251 H3
Leadburn Border 200 B2
Leadenham Lincs 118 B1
Leaden Roding Essex 70 E4
Leadgate Dur 180 D8
Leadgate Nthumb 180 D7
Leadhills S Lans 186 C3
Leadingcross Green Kent 39 M3
Leadmill Derbys 132 E4
Leafield Oxon 65 L4
Leagrave Luton 68 D2
Leahead Ches W 130 D6
Lea Heath Staffs 115 G6
Leake N York 160 F4
Leake Common Side Lincs 119 L1
Lealholm N York 162 D1
Lealholm Side N York 162 D1
Lealt Highld 259 H4
Leam Derbys 132 E4
Lea Marston Warwks 99 G5
Leamington Hastings Warwks 83 K2
Leamington Spa Warwks 83 H2
Leamside Dur 169 J1
Leap Cross E Susx 23 K5
Leasgill Cumb 157 H6
Leasingham Lincs 118 E2
Leasingthorne Dur 169 H4
Leatherhead Surrey 50 F7
Leathley N York 150 B6
Leaton Shrops 113 G7
Leaton Wrekin 96 E1
Lea Town Lancs 138 F2
Leaveland Kent 40 C4
Leavenheath Suffk 89 J7
Leavening N York 152 B3
Leaves Green Gt Lon 51 L6
Lea Yeat Cumb 158 D5
Lebberston N York 163 K6
Le Bigard Guern 9 i4
Le Bourg Guern 9 j4
Le Bourg Jersey 9 f4
Lechlade on Thames Gloucs 65 J7
Lecht Gruinart Ag & B 204 D3
Leck Lancs 157 K7
Leckbuie P & K 231 K7
Leckford Hants 34 E3
Leckhampstead Bucks 84 D7
Leckhampstead W Berk 48 B4
Leckhampstead Thicket W Berk 48 B4
Leckhampton Gloucs 64 D3
Leckmelm Highld 261 K2
Leckwith V Glam 43 J6
Leconfield E R Yk 152 F7
Ledaig Ag & B 228 E7
Ledburn Bucks 67 L3
Ledbury Herefs 81 G7
Leddington Gloucs 80 F8
Ledgemoor Herefs 80 A5
Ledicot Herefs 80 A3
Ledmore Junction Highld 271 H5
Ledsham Ches W 129 H5
Ledsham Leeds 142 C2
Ledston Leeds 142 C2
Ledstone Devon 7 L5
Ledston Luck Leeds 142 C2
Ledwell Oxon 66 B2
Lee Devon 27 H2
Lee Gt Lon 51 K4
Lee Hants 34 D7
Lee Shrops 112 F5
Leebotwood Shrops 96 B4
Lee Brockhurst Shrops 113 J6
Leece Cumb 146 E2
Lee Chapel Essex 52 E2
Lee Clump Bucks 67 M6
Lee Common Bucks 67 M6
Leeds Kent 39 K3
Leeds Leeds 141 L1
Leedstown Cnwll 2 F4
Lee Green Ches E 130 C7
Leek Staffs 131 K8
Leek Wootton Warwks 83 G2
Lee Mill Devon 7 H4
Leeming C Brad 141 G1
Leeming N York 160 D5
Leeming Bar N York 160 D4
Lee Moor Devon 7 H3
Lee-on-the-Solent Hants 19 J3
Lees C Brad 149 J8
Lees Derbys 115 L4
Lees Oldham 140 E6
Lees Green Derbys 115 L4
Leesthorpe Leics 101 H1
Lee Street Surrey 37 L2
Leeswood Flints 129 G7
Leetown P & K 222 C3
Leftwich Ches W 130 C5
Legar Powys 61 K4
Legbourne Lincs 137 G3
Legburthwaite Cumb 165 K6
Legerwood Border 201 J4
Le Gron Guern 9 i3
Legsby Lincs 136 B3
Le Haguais Jersey 9 e4
Le Hocq Jersey 9 e4
Leicester C Leic 100 D3
Leicester Forest East Leics 100 B3
Leigh Devon 28 C8
Leigh Dorset 16 B1
Leigh Gloucs 64 C2
Leigh Kent 38 E4
Leigh Shrops 95 H3
Leigh Surrey 37 K2
Leigh Wigan 139 K7
Leigh Wilts 64 F8
Leigh Worcs 81 H4
Leigh Beck Essex 53 H2
Leigh Delamere Wilts 46 C3
Leigh Green Kent 40 A8
Leigh Knoweglass S Lans 197 J1
Leighland Chapel Somset 29 J4
Leigh-on-Sea Sthend 53 H2
Leigh Park Dorset 17 K3
Leigh Sinton Worcs 81 H5
Leighswood Wsall 98 D3
Leighterton Gloucs 46 B1
Leighton N York 159 L6
Leighton Powys 94 F2
Leighton Shrops 96 E2
Leighton Somset 32 B2
Leighton Bromswold Cambs 102 C8
Leighton Buzzard C Beds 68 A2
Leigh upon Mendip Somset 31 M2
Leigh Woods N Som 45 H4
Leinthall Earls Herefs 80 B2
Leinthall Starkes Herefs 80 A1
Leintwardine Herefs 95 K8
Leire Leics 100 B5
Leiston Suffk 91 K3
Leith C Edin 211 J4
Leitholm Border 202 B4
Lelant Cnwll 2 E4
Lelley E R Yk 145 G1
Lem Hill Worcs 97 G8
Lempitlaw Border 202 B6
Lemreway W Isls 282 g5
Lemsford Herts 69 G4
Lenchwick Worcs 82 B6
Lendalfoot S Ayrs 182 E5
Lendrick Stirlg 219 J6
Lendrum Terrace Abers 257 L3
Lenham Kent 40 A5
Lenham Heath Kent 40 B5
Lenie Highld 250 F6
Lennel Border 202 C5
Lennox Plunton D & G 174 F4
Lennoxtown E Duns 209 G3
Lent Bucks 50 A3
Lenton C Nott 116 F4
Lenton Lincs 118 D5
Lenwade Norfk 122 B7
Lenzie E Duns 209 H4
Leochel-Cushnie Abers 244 C2
Leomansley Staffs 98 E2
Leominster Herefs 80 C3
Leonard Stanley Gloucs 64 A6
Leoville Jersey 9 b2
Lepe Hants 19 G4
Lephin Highld 258 B6
Leppington N York 152 A4
Lepton Kirk 141 K5
Lerags Ag & B 216 C2
L'Eree Guern 9 h3
Lerryn Cnwll 5 K3
Lerwick Shet 281 e6
Les Arquets Guern 9 h3
Lesbury Nthumb 191 J4
Les Hubits Guern 9 k3
Leslie Abers 255 M6
Leslie Fife 222 D6
Les Lohiers Guern 9 i3
Lesmahagow S Lans 198 D5
Les Murchez Guern 9 i4
Lesnewth Cnwll 11 G4
Les Nicolles Guern 9 j4
Les Quartiers Guern 9 j2
Les Quennevais Jersey 9 b3
Les Sages Guern 9 i3
Lessingham Norfk 123 H6
Lessonhall Cumb 165 H1
Lestowder Cnwll 3 K6
Les Villets Guern 9 i4
Leswalt D & G 172 C2
L'Etacq Jersey 9 a2
Letchmore Heath Herts 68 F7
Letchworth Garden City Herts 86 E8
Letcombe Bassett Oxon 48 A2
Letcombe Regis Oxon 48 A2
Letham Angus 234 E5
Letham Border 189 J4
Letham Falk 210 B2
Letham Fife 222 E4
Letham Grange Angus 235 G6
Lethendy P & K 233 H7
Lethenty Abers 255 M7
Lethenty Abers 256 E4
Letheringham Suffk 91 G4
Letheringsett Norfk 122 B4
Lettaford Devon 13 G6
Letterewe Highld 260 F5
Letterfearn Highld 248 D7
Letterfinlay Lodge Hotel Highld 239 L5
Lettermorar Highld 237 L3
Letters Highld 261 K2
Lettershaw S Lans 186 D2
Letterston Pembks 74 F6
Lettoch Highld 253 K7
Lettoch Highld 254 B5
Letton Herefs 79 L1
Letton Herefs 79 L6
Lett's Green Kent 51 M7
Letty Green Herts 69 H5
Letwell Rothm 133 L2
Leuchars Fife 223 H3
Leumrabhagh W Isls 282 g5
Leurbost W Isls 282 g4
Levalsa Meor Cnwll 5 G5
Levedale Staffs 114 D8
Level's Green Essex 70 C2
Leven E R Yk 153 H6
Leven Fife 222 F7
Levens Cumb 157 G5
Levens Green Herts 69 K3
Levenshulme Manch 131 G1
Levenwick Shet 281 d8
Leverburgh W Isls 282 d6
Leverington Cambs 103 J1
Leverstock Green Herts 68 D5
Leverton Lincs 119 L2
Le Villocq Guern 9 j2
Levington Suffk 90 F7

Levisham N York 162 E4
Lew Oxon 65 L6
Lewannick Cnwll 11 K6
Lewdown Devon 12 B5
Lewes E Susx 22 F5
Leweston Pembks 54 F2
Lewisham Gt Lon 51 K4
Lewisham Crematorium Gt Lon 51 L4
Lewiston Highld 250 F6
Lewistown Brdgnd 42 E4
Lewis Wych Herefs 79 L4
Lewknor Oxon 67 H7
Leworthy Devon 11 L2
Leworthy Devon 28 B3
Lewson Street Kent 40 C3
Lewth Lancs 147 J8
Lewtrenchard Devon 12 B5
Lexden Essex 72 D2
Lexworthy Somset 30 C4
Ley Cnwll 5 K2
Leybourne Kent 52 E7
Leyburn N York 159 K4
Leycett Staffs 114 B2
Leygreen Herts 68 F2
Ley Hill Bucks 68 C6
Leyland Lancs 139 H3
Leyland Green St Hel 139 H7
Leylodge Abers 245 G1
Leys Abers 269 J5
Leys P & K 233 K7
Leysdown-on-Sea Kent 53 M5
Leysmill Angus 234 F6
Leys of Cossans Angus 234 B5
Leysters Herefs 80 D2
Leyton Gt Lon 51 K2
Leytonstone Gt Lon 51 K2
Lezant Cnwll 11 L6
Lezerea Cnwll 3 H4
Lhanbryde Moray 266 F4
Libanus Powys 60 F2
Libberton S Lans 199 G4
Liberton C Edin 211 J5
Lichfield Staffs 98 E2
Lickey Worcs 98 C8
Lickey End Worcs 81 M1
Lickey Rock Worcs 98 B8
Lickfold W Susx 36 D5
Liddaton Green Devon 12 B6
Liddesdale Highld 228 B3
Liddington Swindn 47 J3
Lidgate Derbys 132 F4
Lidgate Suffk 88 E4
Lidget Donc 143 G7
Lidgett Notts 134 C6
Lidham Hill E Susx 24 F4
Lidlington C Beds 85 K7
Lidsing Kent 53 G6
Liff Angus 222 E1
Lifford Birm 98 D7
Lifton Devon 11 M5
Liftondown Devon 11 M5
Lighthorne Warwks 83 H4
Lighthorne Heath Warwks 83 H4
Lightwater Surrey 50 B6
Lightwood C Stke 114 E3
Lightwood Green Ches E 113 L3
Lightwood Green Wrexhm 112 F3
Lilbourne Nhants 100 C8
Lilburn Tower Nthumb 190 E1
Lilleshall Wrekin 114 A8
Lilley Herts 68 E2
Lilley W Berk 48 C3
Lilliesleaf Border 201 H8
Lillingstone Dayrell Bucks 84 D7
Lillingstone Lovell Bucks 84 D7
Lillington Dorset 31 K8
Lilliput Poole 17 K5
Lilstock Somset 29 L2
Lilyhurst Shrops 97 G1
Limbrick Lancs 139 J4
Limbury Luton 68 D2
Limebrook Herefs 79 L2
Limefield Bury 140 B5
Limekilnburn S Lans 197 K1
Limekilns Fife 210 E2
Limerigg Falk 209 M5
Limerstone IoW 19 G7
Limestone Brae Nthumb 167 J1
Lime Street Worcs 64 A1
Limington Somset 31 J6
Limmerhaugh E Ayrs 197 J5
Limpenhoe Norfk 107 H3
Limpley Stoke Wilts 45 M6
Limpsfield Surrey 51 L8
Limpsfield Chart Surrey 51 L8
Linby Notts 116 F1
Linchmere W Susx 36 C5
Lincluden D & G 176 C3
Lincoln Lincs 135 K5
Lincoln Crematorium Lincs 135 K5
Lincomb Worcs 81 J2
Lincombe Devon 7 L6
Lincombe Devon 27 J2
Lindale Cumb 156 F6
Lindal in Furness Cumb 156 C7
Lindfield W Susx 22 E2
Lindford Hants 36 B4
Lindley Kirk 141 H4
Lindley N York 150 B6
Lindow End Ches E 130 F4
Lindridge Worcs 80 F2
Lindsell Essex 70 F2
Lindsey Suffk 89 K6
Lindsey Tye Suffk 89 K6
Liney Somset 30 E4
Linford Hants 18 B2
Linford Thurr 52 E3
Lingbob C Brad 149 K8
Lingdale R & Cl 170 F7
Lingen Herefs 79 L2
Lingfield Surrey 38 B4
Lingwood Norfk 107 G2
Linicro Highld 258 F3
Linkend Worcs 64 B1
Linkenholt Hants 48 A7
Linkhill Kent 24 E2
Linkinhorne Cnwll 11 L7
Linktown Fife 211 J1
Linkwood Moray 266 E4
Linley Shrops 95 J5
Linley Green Herefs 80 F4
Linleygreen Shrops 96 F4
Linlithgow W Loth 210 C4
Linshiels Nthumb 190 C5
Linsidemore Highld 272 D8
Linslade C Beds 67 M2
Linstead Parva Suffk 107 G7
Linstock Cumb 178 A7
Linthurst Worcs 82 B1
Linthwaite Kirk 141 H5
Lintlaw Border 213 H7
Lintmill Moray 267 K3
Linton Border 202 B7
Linton Cambs 88 B6
Linton Derbys 115 M8
Linton Herefs 63 K2
Linton Kent 39 J3
Linton Leeds 150 E6
Linton N York 149 H3
Linton Nthumb 191 K7
Linton Heath Derbys 115 M8
Linton Hill Herefs 63 K2
Linton-on-Ouse N York 151 G4
Linwood Hants 18 B2
Linwood Lincs 136 B2
Linwood Rens 208 D6
Lionacleit W Isls 283 c9
Lional W Isls 282 h1
Lions Green E Susx 23 J4
Liphook Hants 36 C4
Lipley Shrops 114 A5
Liscard Wirral 129 G1
Liscombe Somset 28 F4
Liskeard Cnwll 6 B2
Lismore Ag & B 228 C7
Liss Hants 36 A5
Lissett E R Yk 153 J4
Liss Forest Hants 36 A5
Lissington Lincs 136 B3
Liston Essex 89 G6
Lisvane Cardif 43 J5
Liswerry Newpt 44 D2
Litcham Norfk 121 J8
Litchard Brdgnd 42 D5
Litchborough Nhants 84 C4
Litchfield Hants 48 C8
Litherland Sefton 138 D8
Litlington Cambs 87 G6
Litlington E Susx 23 J7
Little Abington Cambs 87 L5
Little Addington Nhants 101 L8
Little Airies D & G 173 K5
Little Almshoe Herts 69 G2
Little Alne Warwks 82 D3
Little Altcar Sefton 138 C6
Little Amwell Herts 69 K5
Little Asby Cumb 158 B1
Little Aston Staffs 98 E3
Little Atherfield IoW 19 G7
Little Ayton N York 170 D8
Little Baddow Essex 71 J5
Little Badminton S Glos 46 A2
Little Bampton Cumb 177 J7
Little Bardfield Essex 71 G1
Little Barford Bed 86 D4
Little Barningham Norfk 122 C5
Little Barrington Gloucs 65 J4
Little Barrow Ches W 129 L5
Little Barugh N York 162 D6
Little Bavington Nthumb 180 B3
Little Bealings Suffk 90 F5
Littlebeck N York 162 F2
Little Bedwyn Wilts 47 L5
Little Bentley Essex 73 G2
Little Berkhamsted Herts 69 H5
Little Billing Nhants 84 F3
Little Billington C Beds 68 B3
Little Birch Herefs 63 G1
Little Bispham Bpool 146 F7
Little Blakenham Suffk 90 C5
Little Blencow Cumb 166 B4
Little Bloxwich Wsall 98 C3
Little Bognor W Susx 21 G3
Little Bolehill Derbys 116 A1
Little Bollington Ches E 130 E2
Little Bookham Surrey 50 E8
Littleborough Devon 28 E8
Littleborough Notts 135 G3
Littleborough Rochdl 140 E4
Littlebourne Kent 41 G4
Little Bourton Oxon 83 K6
Little Bowden Leics 101 G6
Little Bradley Suffk 88 D5
Little Brampton Herefs 79 K3
Little Brampton Shrops 95 J7
Little Braxted Essex 71 K4
Little Brechin Angus 234 F3
Littlebredy Dorset 16 B5
Little Brickhill M Keyn 67 L1
Little Bridgeford Staffs 114 D6
Little Brington Nhants 84 C3
Little Bromley Essex 73 G2
Little Broughton Cumb 164 E4
Little Budworth Ches W 130 B6
Littleburn Highld 251 H1
Little Burstead Essex 71 G8
Littlebury Essex 87 L7
Littlebury Green Essex 87 K7
Little Bytham Lincs 118 D7
Little Canfield Essex 70 E3
Little Carlton Lincs 137 G3
Little Carlton Notts 134 F8
Little Casterton RutInd 101 M2
Little Catwick E R Yk 153 H6
Little Catworth Cambs 86 B1
Little Cawthorpe Lincs 137 G3
Little Chalfont Bucks 68 C7
Little Chart Kent 40 B6
Little Chesterford Essex 87 L7
Little Cheverey Kent 39 H4
Little Cheverell Wilts 46 E8
Little Chishill Cambs 87 J7
Little Clacton Essex 73 H3
Little Clanfield Oxon 65 K6
Little Clifton Cumb 164 E5
Little Coates NE Lin 145 H6
Little Comberton Worcs 81 M6
Little Common E Susx 24 C5
Little Comp Kent 39 G2
Little Compton Warwks 65 K1
Little Corby Cumb 178 B7
Little Cornard Suffk 89 H7
Littlecott Wilts 47 H8
Little Cowarne Herefs 80 E5
Little Coxwell Oxon 65 L8
Little Crakehall N York 160 C4
Little Cransley Nhants 101 H8
Little Cressingham Norfk 105 H3
Little Crosby Sefton 138 C7
Little Crosthwaite Cumb 165 H5
Little Cubley Derbys 115 J4
Little Dalby Leics 117 K8
Littledean Gloucs 63 K4
Little Dewchurch Herefs 63 G1
Little Ditton Cambs 88 D3
Little Doward Herefs 63 G4
Littledown Hants 47 M7
Little Downham Cambs 103 L6
Little Driffield E R Yk 152 F4
Little Dunham Norfk 105 H1
Little Dunkeld P & K 232 F7
Little Dunmow Essex 71 G3
Little Durnford Wilts 33 K4
Little Easton Essex 70 F2
Little Eaton Derbys 116 B3
Little Ellingham Norfk 105 K3
Little Elm Somset 32 B2
Little Everdon Nhants 84 B4
Little Eversden Cambs 87 H4
Little Faringdon Oxon 65 J6
Little Fencote N York 160 D4
Little Fenton N York 142 E1
Little Fransham Norfk 105 H1
Little Gaddesden Herts 68 C4
Little Garway Herefs 62 F2
Little Gidding Cambs 102 C7
Little Glemham Suffk 91 H4
Little Gorsley Herefs 63 K2
Little Gransden Cambs 86 F4
Little Green Notts 117 J3
Little Green Somset 32 B1
Little Grimsby Lincs 136 F2
Little Gringley Notts 134 E3
Little Habton N York 162 C7
Little Hadham Herts 70 B3
Little Hale Lincs 118 F3
Little Hallam Derbys 116 D3
Little Hallingbury Essex 70 D4
Littleham Devon 14 B6
Littleham Devon 27 H6
Little Hampden Bucks 67 L6
Littlehampton W Susx 21 H6
Little Hanford Dorset 32 D8
Little Harrowden Nhants 85 G1
Little Haseley Oxon 66 F7
Little Hatfield E R Yk 153 J7
Little Hautbois Norfk 122 E7
Little Haven Pembks 54 D4
Littlehaven W Susx 37 J4
Little Hay Staffs 98 E3
Little Hayfield Derbys 131 K2
Little Haywood Staffs 115 G7
Little Heath Staffs 114 D8
Little Heath W Berk 49 G4
Littlehempston Devon 8 B2
Little Hereford Herefs 80 D2
Little Horkesley Essex 72 D1
Little Hormead Herts 69 L2
Little Horsted E Susx 23 G4
Little Horton C Brad 141 J2
Little Horton Wilts 46 F6
Little Horwood Bucks 67 J1
Little Houghton Barns 142 C6
Little Houghton Nhants 84 F3
Littlehoughton Nthumb 191 J3
Little Hucklow Derbys 132 C4
Little Hulton Salfd 139 L7
Little Hungerford W Berk 48 D4
Little Hutton N York 161 G7
Little Irchester Nhants 85 H2
Little Kelk E R Yk 153 H4
Little Keyford Somset 32 C2
Little Kimble Bucks 67 K5
Little Kineton Warwks 83 H5
Little Kingshill Bucks 67 L7
Little Knox D & G 175 K3
Little Langdale Cumb 156 D2
Little Langford Wilts 33 H4
Little Laver Essex 70 E5
Little Leigh Ches W 130 B4
Little Leighs Essex 71 H4
Little Lever Bolton 139 M6
Little Linford M Keyn 85 G6
Little Load Somset 31 G6
Little London Bucks 66 F4
Little London Cambs 103 J4
Little London E Susx 23 J3
Little London Essex 70 C1
Little London Essex 88 D8
Little London Gloucs 63 L3
Little London Hants 34 E1
Little London Hants 48 F7
Little London Leeds 150 B7
Little London Lincs 119 H7
Little London Lincs 119 M6
Little London Lincs 136 F5
Little London Norfk 120 C7
Little London Powys 94 C5
Little Longstone Derbys 132 D5
Little Madeley Staffs 114 B3
Little Malvern Worcs 81 H7
Little Mancot Flints 129 H6
Little Maplestead Essex 89 G8
Little Marcle Herefs 80 F7
Little Marland Devon 27 J8
Little Marlow Bucks 49 L2
Little Massingham Norfk 121 H6
Little Melton Norfk 106 D2
Littlemill Abers 243 K4
Littlemill Highld 253 H2
Little Mill Mons 62 C6
Little Milton Oxon 66 F7
Little Missenden Bucks 68 A7
Little Mongeham Kent 41 K5
Littlemoor Derbys 133 G7
Little Moor Somset 30 D4
Littlemore Oxon 66 D6
Little Musgrave Cumb 167 H8
Little Ness Shrops 112 F7
Little Neston Ches W 129 G4
Little Newcastle Pembks 75 G6
Little Newsham Dur 168 E7
Little Norton Somset 31 G7
Little Oakley Essex 73 J1
Little Oakley Nhants 101 K6
Little Odell Bed 85 J4
Little Offley Herts 68 E2
Little Ormside Cumb 167 G7
Little Orton Cumb 177 K7

Little Ouse Cambs 104 C5
Little Ouseburn N York 150 F4
Littleover C Derb 116 B5
Little Oxendon Nhants 100 F6
Little Packington Warwks 99 G6
Little Pattenden Kent 39 J4
Little Paxton Cambs 86 D3
Little Petherick Cnwll 10 C8
Little Plumpton Lancs 138 D1
Little Plumstead Norfk 107 G1
Little Ponton Lincs 118 B5
Littleport Cambs 104 B6
Littleport Bridge Cambs 104 B6
Little Posbrook Hants 19 J3
Little Potheridge Devon 27 J8
Little Preston Leeds 142 B2
Little Preston Nhants 84 B4
Littler Ches W 130 C6
Little Raveley Cambs 102 E7
Little Reedness E R Yk 143 K3
Little Ribston N York 150 E5
Little Rissington Gloucs 65 J3
Little Rollright Oxon 65 L1
Little Rowsley Derbys 132 E6
Little Ryburgh Norfk 121 L6
Little Ryle Nthumb 190 E4
Little Ryton Shrops 96 B3
Little Salkeld Cumb 166 D3
Little Sampford Essex 88 C8
Little Sandhurst Br For 49 K6
Little Saredon Staffs 97 L2
Little Saughall Ches W 129 J6
Little Saxham Suffk 88 F3
Little Scatwell Highld 262 C8
Little Shelford Cambs 87 J5
Little Shrewley Warwks 82 F2
Little Silver Devon 13 L1
Little Singleton Lancs 147 G7
Little Skipwith N York 151 K8
Little Smeaton N York 142 E4
Little Snoring Norfk 121 L5
Little Sodbury S Glos 45 M2
Little Sodbury End S Glos 45 L2
Little Somborne Hants 34 E4
Little Somerford Wilts 46 D2
Little Soudley Shrops 114 A6
Little Stainforth N York 148 E2
Little Stainton Darltn 169 K6
Little Stanney Ches W 129 J5
Little Staughton Bed 86 B3
Little Steeping Lincs 137 H7
Little Stoke Staffs 114 E5
Littlestone-on-Sea Kent 25 K2
Little Stonham Suffk 90 D3
Little Stretton Leics 100 E3
Little Stretton Shrops 95 K5
Little Strickland Cumb 166 D6
Little Stukeley Cambs 102 E8
Little Sugnall Staffs 114 C5
Little Sutton Ches W 129 J4
Little Sutton Shrops 96 C6
Little Swinburne Nthumb 179 M3
Little Sypland D & G 175 H4
Little Tew Oxon 66 A2
Little Tey Essex 72 C2
Little Thetford Cambs 103 L8
Little Thirkleby N York 161 G7
Little Thornage Norfk 122 B4
Little Thornton Lancs 147 G7
Little Thorpe Dur 169 L2
Littlethorpe Leics 100 C4
Littlethorpe N York 150 D2
Little Thurlow Suffk 88 D5
Little Thurlow Green Suffk 88 D5
Little Thurrock Thurr 52 D3
Littleton Angus 233 M5
Littleton BaNES 45 H6
Littleton Ches W 129 K6
Littleton D & G 175 G4
Littleton Dorset 17 H2
Littleton Hants 34 F4
Littleton Somset 31 H5
Littleton Surrey 36 E2
Littleton Surrey 50 D5
Littleton Drew Wilts 46 B3
Littleton-on-Severn S Glos 45 H1
Littleton Pannell Wilts 46 E8
Little Torrington Devon 27 J7
Little Totham Essex 72 C5
Little Town Cumb 165 H6
Littletown Dur 169 J2
Little Town Lancs 148 B8
Little Town Warrtn 130 C1
Little Twycross Leics 99 J2
Little Urswick Cumb 156 C7
Little Wakering Essex 53 K1
Little Walden Essex 87 L7
Little Waldingfield Suffk 89 J6
Little Walsingham Norfk 121 K4
Little Waltham Essex 71 H4
Little Warley Essex 52 D1
Little Washbourne Gloucs 82 A8
Little Weighton E R Yk 144 B1
Little Weldon Nhants 101 K5
Little Welnetham Suffk 89 H3
Little Welton Lincs 136 F2
Little Wenham Suffk 90 C7
Little Wenlock Wrekin 96 E2
Little Weston Somset 31 K5
Little Whitefield IoW 19 K5
Little Whittingham Green Suffk 106 F8
Little Whittington Nthumb 180 B5
Littlewick Green W & M 49 K3
Little Wilbraham Cambs 87 L3
Littlewindsor Dorset 15 K2
Little Witcombe Gloucs 64 C4
Little Witley Worcs 81 H3
Little Wittenham Oxon 66 E8
Little Wolford Warwks 83 G8
Littlewood Staffs 98 C2
Little Woodcote Gt Lon 51 H6
Littleworth Bucks 67 L3
Littleworth Oxon 65 L7
Littleworth Staffs 98 C1
Littleworth Staffs 114 E7
Littleworth W Susx 21 L3
Littleworth Worcs 81 K5
Littleworth Worcs 82 B3
Littleworth Common Bucks 50 B2
Little Wratting Suffk 88 D5
Little Wymington Bed 85 J2
Little Wymondley Herts 69 G2
Little Wyrley Staffs 98 C2
Little Wytheford Shrops 113 J7
Little Yeldham Essex 88 F7
Littley Green Essex 71 G4
Litton Derbys 132 C4
Litton N York 158 F7
Litton Somset 45 H8
Litton Cheney Dorset 15 M4
Liurbost W Isls 282 g4
Liverpool Lpool 129 H2
Liversedge Kirk 141 J3
Liverton Devon 13 J7
Liverton R & Cl 171 G7
Liverton Mines R & Cl 171 G7
Liverton Street Kent 39 L3
Livingston W Loth 210 E5
Livingston Village W Loth 210 D5
Lixwm Flints 128 E5
Lizard Cnwll 3 H8
Llaingoch IoA 124 D3
Llaithddu Powys 94 C7
Llan Powys 93 J3
Llanaber Gwynd 109 L7
Llanaelhaearn Gwynd 109 G3
Llanafan Cerdgn 77 J1
Llanafan-Fawr Powys 78 D4
Llanafan-fechan Powys 78 D5
Llanallgo IoA 125 J3
Llanarmon Gwynd 109 G4
Llanarmon Dyffryn Ceiriog Wrexhm 112 A5
Llanarmon-yn-Ial Denbgs 128 E8
Llanarth Cerdgn 76 D4
Llanarth Mons 62 D5
Llanarthne Carmth 58 F5
Llanasa Flints 128 D3
Llanbabo IoA 124 F2
Llanbadarn Fawr Cerdgn 92 D7
Llanbadarn Fynydd Powys 94 D7
Llanbadarn-y-garreg Powys 78 F5
Llanbadoc Mons 62 D7
Llanbadrig IoA 124 F1
Llanbeder Newpt 44 D1
Llanbedr Gwynd 109 K6
Llanbedr Powys 61 K3
Llanbedr Powys 79 G6
Llanbedr-Dyffryn-Clwyd Denbgs 128 D7
Llanbedrgoch IoA 125 J4
Llanbedrog Gwynd 108 F5
Llanbedr-y-Cennin Conwy 126 E6
Llanberis Gwynd 125 K7
Llanbethery V Glam 43 G7
Llanbister Powys 94 D8
Llanblethian V Glam 42 F7
Llanboidy Carmth 55 L2
Llanbradach Caerph 43 J4
Llanbrynmair Powys 93 K3
Llancadle V Glam 42 F8
Llancarfan V Glam 43 G7
Llancayo Mons 62 D6
Llancloudy Herefs 63 G3
Llancynfelyn Cerdgn 92 E5
Llandaff Cardif 43 J6
Llandanwg Gwynd 109 K6
Llandarcy Neath 57 K6
Llandawke Carmth 58 A6
Llanddaniel Fab IoA 125 J5
Llanddarog Carmth 58 F5
Llanddeiniol Cerdgn 77 G1
Llanddeiniolen Gwynd 125 K6
Llandderfel Gwynd 111 J4
Llanddeusant Carmth 59 L4
Llanddeusant IoA 124 F3
Llanddew Powys 61 G1
Llanddewi Swans 56 E7
Llanddewi Brefi Cerdgn 77 J4
Llanddewi'r Cwm Powys 78 E5
Llanddewi Rhydderch Mons 62 D4
Llanddewi Velfrey Pembks 55 K3
Llanddewi Ystradenni Powys 78 F2
Llanddoget Conwy 126 F7
Llanddona IoA 125 K4
Llanddowror Carmth 55 M4
Llanddulas Conwy 127 H4
Llanddwywe Gwynd 109 K7
Llanddyfnan IoA 125 J4
Llandecwyn Gwynd 110 B4
Llandefaelog Powys 60 F1
Llandefaelog-Tre'r-Graig Powys 61 H1
Llandefalle Powys 78 F8
Llandegfan IoA 125 K5
Llandegla Denbgs 112 B1
Llandegley Powys 79 G3
Llandegveth Mons 62 C8
Llandegwning Gwynd 108 D5
Llandeilo Carmth 59 H4
Llandeilo Graban Powys 78 F6
Llandeilo'r Fan Powys 78 B8
Llandeloy Pembks 74 D6
Llandenny Mons 62 E6
Llandevaud Newpt 44 E1
Llandevenny Mons 44 E2
Llandinabo Herefs 63 G2
Llandinam Powys 94 B5
Llandissilio Pembks 55 J3
Llandogo Mons 63 G6
Llandough V Glam 42 F7
Llandough V Glam 43 J7
Llandovery Carmth 59 L2
Llandow V Glam 42 E7
Llandre Carmth 77 J6
Llandre Cerdgn 92 D6
Llandre Isaf Pembks 75 K6
Llandrillo Denbgs 111 K4
Llandrillo-yn-Rhos Conwy 127 G4
Llandrindod Wells Powys 78 E3
Llandrinio Powys 112 D8
Llandudno Conwy 126 F3
Llandudno Junction Conwy 126 F4
Llandulas Powys 78 B7
Llandwrog Gwynd 125 H8
Llandybie Carmth 59 H6
Llandyfaelog Carmth 58 D6
Llandyfan Carmth 59 H5
Llandyfriog Cerdgn 76 B7
Llandyfrydog IoA 125 H3
Llandygai Gwynd 126 B5
Llandygwydd Cerdgn 75 M3
Llandynan Denbgs 112 B3
Llandyrnog Denbgs 128 D6
Llandyssil Powys 94 F4
Llandysul Cerdgn 76 D7
Llanedeyrn Cardif 43 K5
Llanedi Carmth 57 G3
Llaneglwys Powys 78 E7
Llanegryn Gwynd 92 D2
Llanegwad Carmth 58 F4
Llaneilian IoA 125 H1
Llanelian-yn-Rhôs Conwy 127 G4
Llanelidan Denbgs 111 L2
Llanelieu Powys 79 H8
Llanellen Mons 62 C5
Llanelli Carmth 56 F5
Llanelli Crematorium Carmth 56 F4
Llanelltyd Gwynd 110 D7
Llanelly Mons 61 K4
Llanelwedd Powys 78 E5
Llanenddwyn Gwynd 109 L6
Llanengan Gwynd 108 E6
Llanerch Gwynd 111 G8
Llanerch Powys 95 H4
Llanerchymedd IoA 125 G3
Llanerfyl Powys 94 B2
Llanfachraeth IoA 124 E3
Llanfachreth Gwynd 110 E7
Llanfaelog IoA 124 F5
Llanfaelrhys Gwynd 108 C6
Llanfaenor Mons 62 E4
Llanfaes IoA 126 B4
Llanfaes Powys 61 G2
Llanfaethlu IoA 124 E2
Llanfair Gwynd 109 K5
Llanfair Caereinion Powys 94 D2
Llanfair Clydogau Cerdgn 77 H5
Llanfair Dyffryn Clwyd Denbgs 128 D8
Llanfairfechan Conwy 126 D5
Llanfair Kilgeddin Mons 62 D5
Llanfair-Nant-Gwyn Pembks 75 K5
Llanfair P G IoA 125 J5
Llanfair Talhaiarn Conwy 127 J5
Llanfair Waterdine Shrops 94 F8
Llanfairynghornwy IoA 124 E2
Llanfair-yn-Neubwll IoA 124 E4
Llanfallteg Carmth 55 K3
Llanfallteg West Carmth 55 K3
Llanfarian Cerdgn 92 D7
Llanfechain Powys 112 B7
Llanfechell IoA 124 F2
Llanferres Denbgs 128 E7
Llanfflewyn IoA 124 F2
Llanfigael IoA 124 F3
Llanfihangel-ar-arth Carmth 76 E7
Llanfihangel Glyn Myfyr Conwy 111 J2
Llanfihangel Nant Bran Powys 78 C8
Llanfihangel-nant-Melan Powys 79 H4
Llanfihangel Rhydithon Powys 79 G2
Llanfihangel Rogiet Mons 44 F2
Llanfihangel Tal-y-llyn Powys 61 H2
Llanfihangel-uwch-Gwili Carmth 58 E4
Llanfihangel-y-Creuddyn Cerdgn 92 E8
Llanfihangel-yng-Ngwynfa Powys 111 L8
Llanfihangel yn Nhowyn IoA 124 E4
Llanfihangel-y-pennant Gwynd 92 E2
Llanfihangel-y-pennant Gwynd 109 J3
Llanfihangel-y-traethau Gwynd 109 L4
Llanfilo Powys 78 F8
Llanfoist Mons 62 B4
Llanfor Gwynd 111 H4
Llanfrechfa Torfn 62 C8
Llanfrothen Gwynd 110 B3
Llanfrynach Powys 61 G2
Llanfwrog Denbgs 128 D8
Llanfwrog IoA 124 E3
Llanfyllin Powys 112 A7
Llanfynydd Carmth 59 G3
Llanfynydd Flints 129 G8
Llanfyrnach Pembks 75 L6
Llangadfan Powys 94 B1
Llangadog Carmth 56 D3
Llangadog Carmth 59 K3
Llangadwaladr IoA 125 G6
Llangadwaladr Powys 112 B5
Llangaffo IoA 125 H6
Llangain Carmth 58 C5
Llangammarch Wells Powys 78 C6
Llangan V Glam 42 E6
Llangarron Herefs 63 G3
Llangasty-Talyllyn Powys 61 H2
Llangathen Carmth 59 G4
Llangattock Powys 61 K3
Llangattock Lingoed Mons 62 D3
Llangattock-Vibon-Avel Mons 62 F4
Llangedwyn Powys 112 B6
Llangefni IoA 125 H4
Llangeinor Brdgnd 42 D4
Llangeitho Cerdgn 77 H3
Llangeler Carmth 76 C7
Llangelynin Gwynd 92 C2
Llangendeirne Carmth 58 E6
Llangennech Carmth 57 G4
Llangennith Swans 56 D6
Llangenny Powys 61 K3
Llangernyw Conwy 127 H6
Llangian Gwynd 108 E5
Llangiwg Neath 57 K4
Llangloffan Pembks 74 E5
Llanglydwen Carmth 75 L6
Llangoed IoA 126 C4
Llangoedmor Cerdgn 75 L3
Llangollen Denbgs 112 B3
Llangolman Pembks 75 J6
Llangors Powys 61 H2
Llangovan Mons 62 F6
Llangower Gwynd 111 G5
Llangrannog Cerdgn 76 B4
Llangristiolus IoA 125 H5
Llangrove Herefs 63 G3
Llangua Mons 62 E2
Llangunllo Powys 79 H1
Llangunnor Carmth 58 D5
Llangurig Powys 93 K7
Llangwm Conwy 111 J3
Llangwm Mons 62 E7
Llangwm Pembks 55 G5

Llangwnnadl Gwynd 108 C5
Llangwyfan Denbgs 128 D6
Llangwyllog IoA 125 H4
Llangwyryfon Cerdgn 77 H1
Llangybi Cerdgn 77 H4
Llangybi Gwynd 109 G3
Llangybi Mons 62 D7
Llangyfelach Swans 57 H5
Llangynhafal Denbgs 128 D7
Llangynidr Powys 61 J3
Llangynin Carmth 55 M3
Llangynllo Cerdgn 76 C6
Llangynog Carmth 58 C6
Llangynog Powys 111 K6
Llangynwyd Brdgnd 42 C4
Llanhamlach Powys 61 H2
Llanharan Rhondd 42 F5
Llanharry Rhondd 42 F5
Llanhennock Mons 62 D8
Llanhilleth Blae G 61 K7
Llanidan IoA 125 J6
Llanidloes Powys 93 L6
Llaniestyn Gwynd 108 D5
Llanigon Powys 79 H7
Llanilar Cerdgn 92 D8
Llanilid Rhondd 42 E5
Llanina Cerdgn 76 D3
Llanio Cerdgn 77 H4
Llanishen Cardif 43 J5
Llanishen Mons 62 F6
Llanllechid Gwynd 126 C6
Llanlleonfel Powys 78 C5
Llanllowell Mons 62 D7
Llanllugan Powys 94 C3
Llanllwch Carmth 58 C5
Llanllwchaiarn Powys 94 D5
Llanllwni Carmth 76 E7
Llanllyfni Gwynd 109 H1
Llanmadoc Swans 56 D6
Llanmaes V Glam 42 E7
Llanmartin Newpt 44 E1
Llanmerewig Powys 94 E5
Llanmihangel V Glam 42 E7
Llanmiloe Carmth 55 M5
Llanmorlais Swans 56 F6
Llannefydd Conwy 127 K5
Llannon Carmth 56 F3
Llannor Gwynd 108 F4
Llanon Cerdgn 76 F2
Llanover Mons 62 C5
Llanpumsaint Carmth 58 D3
Llanrhaeadr-ym-Mochnant Powys 111 M6
Llanrhian Pembks 74 D6
Llanrhidian Swans 56 F6
Llanrhos Conwy 126 F4
Llanrhychwyn Conwy 126 F7
Llanrhyddlad IoA 124 F2
Llanrhystud Cerdgn 76 F1
Llanrothal Herefs 62 F3
Llanrug Gwynd 125 J7
Llanrumney Cardif 43 K5
Llanrwst Conwy 126 F7
Llansadurnen Carmth 56 A3
Llansadwrn Carmth 59 J3
Llansadwrn IoA 125 K4
Llansaint Carmth 56 C3
Llansamlet Swans 57 J5
Llansanffraid Glan Conwy Conwy 126 F4
Llansannan Conwy 127 J6
Llansannor V Glam 42 F6
Llansantffraed Powys 61 H2
Llansantffraed-Cwmdeuddwr Powys 78 D2
Llansantffraed-in-Elvel Powys 78 F4
Llansantffraid Cerdgn 76 F2
Llansantffraid-ym-Mechain Powys 112 C7
Llansawel Carmth 59 H2
Llansilin Powys 112 B6
Llansoy Mons 62 E6
Llanspyddid Powys 60 F2
Llanstadwell Pembks 54 F6
Llansteffan Carmth 56 C3
Llanstephan Powys 78 F6
Llantarnam Torfn 62 C8
Llanteg Pembks 55 L5
Llanthewy Skirrid Mons 62 D4
Llanthony Mons 62 B2
Llantilio-Crossenny Mons 62 E4
Llantilio Pertholey Mons 62 C4
Llantrisant IoA 124 F3
Llantrisant Mons 62 D7
Llantrisant Rhondd 43 G5
Llantrithyd V Glam 43 G7
Llantwit Fardre Rhondd 43 G4
Llantwit Major V Glam 42 E7
Llantysilio Denbgs 112 B3
Llanuwchllyn Gwynd 111 G5
Llanvaches Newpt 44 E1
Llanvair Discoed Mons 62 F8
Llanvapley Mons 62 D4
Llanvetherine Mons 62 D4
Llanveynoe Herefs 62 C1
Llanvihangel Crucorney Mons 62 C3
Llanvihangel Gobion Mons 62 D5
Llanvihangel-Ystern-Llewern Mons 62 E4
Llanwarne Herefs 63 G2
Llanwddyn Powys 111 K7
Llanwenarth Mons 62 B4
Llanwenog Cerdgn 76 F6
Llanwern Newpt 44 D2
Llanwinio Carmth 58 A4
Llanwnda Gwynd 125 H8
Llanwnda Pembks 74 F4
Llanwnnen Cerdgn 76 F6
Llanwnog Powys 94 B4
Llanwonno Rhondd 42 F3
Llanwrda Carmth 59 K3
Llanwrin Powys 93 G3
Llanwrthwl Powys 78 D3
Llanwrtyd Powys 78 B5
Llanwrtyd Wells Powys 78 B6
Llanwyddelan Powys 94 C3
Llanyblodwel Shrops 112 C7
Llanybri Carmth 58 B6
Llanybydder Carmth 76 F6
Llanycefn Pembks 55 J2
Llanychaer Bridge Pembks 75 G5
Llanycrwys Carmth 77 H6
Llanymawddwy Gwynd 111 G7
Llanymynech Powys 112 C7
Llanynghenedl IoA 124 E3
Llanynys Denbgs 128 C7
Llan-y-pwll Wrexhm 112 F1
Llanyre Powys 78 E3
Llanystumdwy Gwynd 109 H4
Llanywern Powys 61 H2
Llawhaden Pembks 55 H3
Llawnt Shrops 112 C5
Llawryglyn Powys 93 K5
Llay Wrexhm 129 H8
Llechcynfarwy IoA 125 G3
Llechfaen Powys 61 G2
Llechrhyd Caerph 61 H5
Llechryd Cerdgn 75 L3
Llechylched IoA 124 F4
Lledrod Cerdgn 77 H1
Llidiardau Gwynd 111 G4
Llidiartnenog Carmth 77 G7
Llidiart-y-parc Denbgs 111 M3
Llithfaen Gwynd 108 F3
Lloc Flints 128 D4
Llowes Powys 79 H7
Llwydcoed Rhondd 60 F6
Llwydcoed Crematorium Rhondd 60 F6
Llwydiarth Powys 111 K8
Llwyn Denbgs 128 C6
Llwyncelyn Cerdgn 76 E3
Llwyndafydd Cerdgn 76 C4
Llwynderw Powys 94 F3
Llwyn-drain Pembks 58 A2
Llwyn-du Mons 62 C4
Llwyndyrys Gwynd 108 F3
Llwyngwril Gwynd 92 D2
Llwynhendy Carmth 56 F5
Llwynmawr Wrexhm 112 C4
Llwyn-on Myr Td 60 F5
Llwyn-y-brain Carmth 55 L4
Llwyn-y-groes Cerdgn 77 G4
Llwynypia Rhondd 42 F3
Llynclys Shrops 112 D6
Llynfaes IoA 125 G4
Llyn-y-pandy Flints 128 E6
Llysfaen Conwy 127 H4
Llyswen Cerdgn 76 E3
Llyswen Powys 79 G7
Llysworney V Glam 42 E6
Llys-y-frân Pembks 55 H2
Llywel Powys 60 C1
Load Brook Sheff 132 E2
Loan Falk 210 C4
Loanend Nthumb 202 E3
Loanhead Mdloth 211 J6
Loaningfoot D & G 176 C7
Loans S Ayrs 196 C4
Lobb Devon 27 H3
Lobhillcross Devon 12 B5
Lochailort Highld 238 B7
Lochaline Highld 227 K3
Lochans D & G 172 D3
Locharbriggs D & G 176 C3
Lochavich Ag & B 216 E4
Lochawe Ag & B 217 J2
Loch Baghasdail W Isls 283 c11
Lochboisdale W Isls 283 c11
Lochbuie Ag & B 227 H7
Lochcarron Highld 248 E4
Lochdon Ag & B 227 L6
Lochdonhead Ag & B 227 L5
Lochead Ag & B 206 B3
Lochearnhead Stirlg 219 K2
Lochee C Dund 222 F1
Locheilside Station Highld 239 G7
Lochend Highld 251 G4
Locheport W Isls 283 c8
Loch Euphoirt W Isls 283 c8
Lochfoot D & G 176 B4
Lochgair Ag & B 206 E1
Lochgelly Fife 222 C8
Lochgilphead Ag & B 206 D2
Lochgoilhead Ag & B 217 K7
Lochieheads Fife 222 D4
Lochill Moray 266 F3
Lochindorb Lodge Highld 253 J4
Lochinver Highld 270 E4
Lochluichart Highld 262 B7
Lochmaben D & G 176 E2
Lochmaddy W Isls 283 d8
Loch Maree Hotel Highld 260 E6
Loch nam Madadh W Isls 283 d8
Lochore Fife 222 B7
Lochranza N Ayrs 194 E1
Lochside Abers 235 J3
Lochside D & G 176 C3
Lochside Highld 252 F1
Lochslin Highld 264 C4
Lochton S Ayrs 183 G7
Lochty Angus 234 E3
Lochty Fife 223 J5
Lochuisge Highld 228 B4
Lochwinnoch Rens 208 B7
Lochwood D & G 187 G6
Lockengate Cnwll 5 H3
Lockerbie D & G 176 F3
Lockeridge Wilts 47 H5
Lockerley Hants 34 C5
Locking N Som 44 D7
Locking Stumps Warrtn 130 C1
Lockington E R Yk 152 F6
Lockington Leics 116 D6
Lockleywood Shrops 113 M6
Locksbottom Gt Lon 51 L6
Locksgreen IoW 19 G5
Locks Heath Hants 19 H2
Lockton N York 162 E5
Loddington Leics 101 H3
Loddington Nhants 101 H7
Loddiswell Devon 7 L5
Loddon Norfk 107 G4
Lode Cambs 87 L3
Lode Heath Solhll 98 F7
Loders Dorset 15 L4
Lodge Hill Crematorium Birm 98 C7
Lodsworth W Susx 36 D6
Lofthouse Leeds 142 A3
Lofthouse N York 159 K8
Lofthouse Gate Wakefd 142 A3
Loftus R & Cl 171 G7
Logan E Ayrs 197 H6
Loganbeck Cumb 156 A4
Loganlea W Loth 210 C6
Loggerheads Staffs 114 A4
Logie Angus 235 H3
Logie Fife 223 G3
Logie Moray 253 K2
Logie Coldstone Abers 243 M3
Logie Newton Abers 256 B4
Logie Pert Angus 235 G3
Logierait P & K 232 E5
Logierieve Abers 257 G6
Login Carmth 55 K2
Lolworth Cambs 87 H2
Lonbain Highld 259 M6
Londesborough E R Yk 152 C6
London Gt Lon 51 H3
London Apprentice Cnwll 5 G5
London Beach Kent 39 M6
London Colney Herts 68 F6
Londonderry N York 160 D5
London End Nhants 85 H2
Londonthorpe Lincs 118 C4
Londubh Highld 260 D4
Lonemore Highld 260 C4
Long Ashton N Som 45 H5
Long Bank Worcs 97 H8
Long Bennington Lincs 117 L3
Longbenton N Tyne 181 G5
Longborough Gloucs 65 J1
Long Bredy Dorset 16 A4
Longbridge Birm 98 C7
Longbridge Warwks 83 G3
Longbridge Deverill Wilts 32 E3
Long Buckby Nhants 84 C2
Longburgh Cumb 177 J7
Longburton Dorset 31 L8
Long Cause Devon 8 B3
Long Clawson Leics 117 J6
Longcliffe Derbys 132 D8
Longcombe Devon 8 C3
Long Common Hants 35 G7
Long Compton Staffs 114 D7
Long Compton Warwks 83 G8
Longcot Oxon 47 K1
Long Crendon Bucks 67 G5
Long Crichel Dorset 17 J1
Longcroft Cumb 177 H7
Longcross Surrey 50 C6
Longden Shrops 95 K2
Longden Common Shrops 95 K2
Long Ditton Surrey 50 F5
Longdon Staffs 115 H8
Longdon Worcs 81 J7
Longdon Green Staffs 98 D1
Longdon Heath Worcs 81 J7
Longdon upon Tern Wrekin 113 K8
Longdown Devon 13 K4
Longdowns Cnwll 3 J4
Long Drax N York 143 H2
Long Duckmanton Derbys 133 J5
Long Eaton Derbys 116 E5
Longfield Kent 52 D5
Longford Covtry 99 K6
Longford Derbys 115 L4
Longford Gloucs 64 B3
Longford Gt Lon 50 D4
Longford Kent 38 D2
Longford Shrops 113 L5
Longford Wrekin 114 A7
Longforgan P & K 222 E1
Longformacus Border 212 F7
Longframlington Nthumb 191 G6
Long Green Ches W 129 L5
Long Green Worcs 81 J8
Longham Dorset 17 L3
Longham Norfk 121 L8
Long Hanborough Oxon 66 B4
Longhaven Abers 257 L4
Long Hedges Lincs 119 K2
Longhirst Nthumb 191 J8
Longhope Gloucs 63 K3
Longhope Ork 275 b6
Longhorsley Nthumb 191 H7
Longhoughton Nthumb 191 J3
Long Itchington Warwks 83 K2
Longlands Cumb 165 J3
Longlane Derbys 115 L4
Long Lawford Warwks 100 A8
Longlevens Gloucs 64 B3
Longley Calder 141 G3
Longley Kirk 141 J6
Longley Green Worcs 81 G5
Longleys P & K 233 L6
Long Load Somset 31 G6
Longmanhill Abers 268 D4
Long Marston Herts 67 L4
Long Marston N York 151 H5
Long Marston Warwks 82 E5
Long Marton Cumb 166 F5
Long Meadowend Shrops 95 K7
Long Melford Suffk 89 H6
Longmoor Camp Hants 36 B4
Longmorn Moray 266 E4
Longmoss Ches E 131 H5
Long Newnton Gloucs 64 C8
Longnewton Border 201 J7
Long Newton E Loth 212 B6
Longnewton S on T 169 K7
Longney Gloucs 63 M4
Longniddry E Loth 212 A4
Longnor Shrops 96 B3
Longnor Staffs 132 B6
Longparish Hants 34 F2
Longpark Cumb 178 A6
Long Preston N York 148 E4
Longridge Lancs 147 M8
Longridge Staffs 114 E8
Longridge W Loth 210 C6
Longriggend N Lans 209 L5
Long Riston E R Yk 153 H7
Longrock Cnwll 2 D5
Longsdon Staffs 114 F1
Longshaw Wigan 139 G7
Longside Abers 269 J6
Long Sight Oldham 140 D6
Longslow Shrops 113 L4
Longstanton Cambs 87 H2
Longstock Hants 34 D3
Longstone Pembks 55 K5
Longstowe Cambs 86 F4
Long Stratton Norfk 106 D5
Long Street M Keyn 84 F5
Longstreet Wilts 47 H8
Long Sutton Hants 35 M2
Long Sutton Lincs 119 M7
Long Sutton Somset 31 G6
Longthorpe C Pete 102 D4

Long Thurlow Suffk 89 K2
Longthwaite Cumb 166 B6
Longton C Stke 114 E3
Longton Lancs 138 F3
Longtown Cumb 177 L5
Longtown Herefs 62 C1
Longueville Jersey 9 e3
Longville in the Dale Shrops 96 C4
Long Waste Wrekin 113 K8
Long Whatton Leics 116 D6
Longwick Bucks 67 J6
Long Wittenham Oxon 66 E8
Longwitton Nthumb 180 C1
Longwood D & G 175 H3
Longwood Shrops 96 D2
Longworth Oxon 66 A7
Longyester E Loth 212 C6
Lon-las Swans 57 K5
Lonmay Abers 269 J4
Lonmore Highld 258 D7
Looe Cnwll 6 B4
Loose Kent 39 J3
Loosebeare Devon 13 G2
Loosegate Lincs 119 K6
Loosley Row Bucks 67 K7
Lootcherbrae Abers 268 A5
Lopcombe Corner Wilts 34 B4
Lopen Somset 30 F8
Loppington Shrops 113 G5
Lorbottle Nthumb 190 E5
Lordington W Susx 20 C5
Lordsbridge Norfk 104 B1
Lords Wood Medway 53 G6
Lornty P & K 233 J6
Loscoe Derbys 116 C2
Loscombe Dorset 15 L3
Lossiemouth Moray 266 E2
Lostford Shrops 113 K5
Lostock Gralam Ches W 130 D5
Lostock Green Ches W 130 D5
Lostock Hall Lancs 139 H3
Lostock Hall Fold Bolton 139 K6
Lostock Junction Bolton 139 K6
Lostwithiel Cnwll 5 J3
Lothbeg Highld 274 C6
Lothersdale N York 149 G6
Lothmore Highld 274 C6
Loudwater Bucks 49 L1
Loughborough Leics 116 F7
Loughborough Crematorium Leics 116 F7
Loughor Swans 57 G5
Loughton Essex 70 B7
Loughton M Keyn 85 G7
Loughton Shrops 96 E6
Lound Lincs 118 E7
Lound Notts 134 D2
Lound Suffk 107 K4
Lounston Devon 13 J7
Lount Leics 116 C7
Louth Lincs 136 F2
Love Clough Lancs 140 B2
Lovedean Hants 19 M1
Lover Wilts 34 B6
Loversall Donc 142 F8
Loves Green Essex 70 F6
Lovesome Hill N York 160 E3
Loveston Pembks 55 J5
Lovington Somset 31 K5
Low Ackworth Wakefd 142 C4
Low Angerton Nthumb 180 D2
Lowbands Gloucs 63 M1
Low Barbeth D & G 172 C2
Low Barlings Lincs 136 A5
Low Bell End N York 162 C3
Low Bentham N York 148 A2
Low Biggins Cumb 157 K7
Low Borrowbridge Cumb 157 K2
Low Bradfield Sheff 132 E2
Low Bradley N York 149 H6
Low Braithwaite Cumb 166 A2
Low Burnham N Linc 143 K7
Low Buston Nthumb 191 J5
Lowca Cumb 164 C6
Low Catton E R Yk 151 L5
Low Coniscliffe Darltn 169 H7
Low Crosby Cumb 178 B7
Lowdham Notts 117 H2
Low Dinsdale Darltn 169 K8
Lowe Shrops 113 H5
Lowe Hill Staffs 131 K8
Low Ellington N York 160 B6
Lower Aisholt Somset 30 B4
Lower Ansty Dorset 16 E2
Lower Apperley Gloucs 64 B2
Lower Arncott Oxon 66 F3
Lower Ashton Devon 13 K6
Lower Assendon Oxon 49 H2
Lower Ballam Lancs 138 D2
Lower Bartle Lancs 139 G1
Lower Basildon W Berk 48 F3
Lower Bearwood Herefs 79 M4
Lower Beeding W Susx 37 K5
Lower Benefield Nhants 101 L5
Lower Bentley Worcs 82 A2
Lower Beobridge Shrops 97 H5
Lower Birchwood Derbys 116 D1
Lower Boddington Nhants 83 L5
Lower Boscaswell Cnwll 2 B4
Lower Bourne Surrey 36 C2
Lower Brailes Warwks 83 H7
Lower Breakish Highld 247 L4
Lower Bredbury Stockp 131 H2
Lower Broadheath Worcs 81 J4
Lower Broxwood Herefs 79 L4
Lower Buckenhill Herefs 80 E8
Lower Bullingham Herefs 80 C7
Lower Burgate Hants 33 K7
Lower Burrowton Devon 14 B3
Lower Burton Herefs 80 A4
Lower Caldecote C Beds 86 D6
Lower Cam Gloucs 63 L7
Lower Canada N Som 44 D7
Lower Catesby Nhants 83 M3
Lower Chapel Powys 78 E8
Lower Chicksgrove Wilts 33 G5
Lower Chute Wilts 47 L8
Lower Clapton Gt Lon 51 K2
Lower Clent Worcs 97 L7
Lower Creedy Devon 13 K2
Lower Crossings Derbys 131 L4
Lower Cumberworth Kirk 141 K6
Lower Darwen Bl w D 139 K3
Lower Dean Bed 85 L2
Lower Denby Kirk 141 K6
Lower Diabaig Highld 260 C7
Lower Dicker E Susx 23 J5
Lower Dinchope Shrops 95 L6
Lower Down Shrops 95 H6
Lower Dunsforth N York 150 F3
Lower Egleton Herefs 80 E6
Lower Elkstone Staffs 131 L8
Lower Ellastone Staffs 115 J3
Lower End Bucks 67 G5
Lower End M Keyn 85 H7
Lower End Nhants 84 F3
Lower End Nhants 85 H3
Lower Everleigh Wilts 47 J8
Lower Exbury Hants 19 G4
Lower Eythorne Kent 41 J5
Lower Failand N Som 45 G4
Lower Farringdon Hants 35 L4
Lower Feltham Gt Lon 50 E4
Lower Fittleworth W Susx 21 G3
Lower Foxdale IoM 154 c6
Lower Frankton Shrops 112 E5
Lower Freystrop Pembks 54 F4
Lower Froyle Hants 36 A2
Lower Gabwell Devon 8 D1
Lower Gledfield Highld 263 G2
Lower Godney Somset 31 G2
Lower Gornal Dudley 97 L5
Lower Gravenhurst C Beds 86 C8
Lower Green Herts 86 D8
Lower Green Herts 87 J8
Lower Green Kent 38 E5
Lower Green Kent 39 G5
Lower Green Norfk 121 L4
Lower Green Staffs 97 K2
Lower Green Suffk 88 E2
Lower Hacheston Suffk 91 H4
Lower Halliford Surrey 50 E5
Lower Halstock Leigh Dorset 15 M1
Lower Halstow Kent 53 J5
Lower Hamworthy Poole 17 K4
Lower Hardres Kent 40 F5
Lower Harpton Herefs 79 K3
Lower Hartlip Kent 53 H6
Lower Hartshay Derbys 116 C1
Lower Hartwell Bucks 67 J4
Lower Hatton Staffs 114 C4
Lower Hawthwaite Cumb 156 B5
Lower Hergest Herefs 79 K4
Lower Heyford Oxon 66 C2
Lower Heysham Lancs 147 H4
Lower Higham Kent 52 F4
Lower Holbrook Suffk 90 E8
Lower Hordley Shrops 112 F5
Lower Horncroft W Susx 21 G3
Lowerhouse Lancs 140 B1
Lower Houses Kirk 141 J5
Lower Howsell Worcs 81 H5
Lower Irlam Salfd 130 D1
Lower Kilburn Derbys 116 C3
Lower Kilcott Gloucs 46 A1
Lower Killeyan Ag & B 204 D7
Lower Kingcombe Dorset 16 A3
Lower Kingswood Surrey 51 H8
Lower Kinnerton Ches W 129 H7
Lower Langford N Som 44 F6
Lower Largo Fife 223 G6
Lower Leigh Staffs 115 G4
Lower Lemington Gloucs 82 F8
Lower Llanfadog Powys 78 C2
Lower Lovacott Devon 27 J5
Lower Loxhore Devon 27 L3
Lower Lydbrook Gloucs 63 H4
Lower Lye Herefs 79 M2
Lower Machen Newpt 43 K4
Lower Maes-coed Herefs 62 D1
Lower Mannington Dorset 17 L2
Lower Marston Somset 32 C2
Lower Meend Gloucs 63 H6
Lower Merridge Somset 30 B4
Lower Middleton Cheney Nhants 83 L7
Lower Milton Somset 31 J2
Lower Moor Worcs 82 A6
Lower Morton S Glos 63 J8
Lower Nazeing Essex 69 K6
Lower Norton Warwks 82 F3
Lower Nyland Dorset 32 C6
Lower Penarth V Glam 43 J7
Lower Penn Staffs 97 K4
Lower Pennington Hants 18 E5
Lower Penwortham Lancs 139 G2
Lower Peover Ches E 130 E5
Lower Place Rochdl 140 D5
Lower Pollicott Bucks 67 H4
Lower Quinton Warwks 82 E6
Lower Rainham Medway 53 H5
Lower Raydon Suffk 90 B7
Lower Roadwater Somset 29 J3
Lower Salter Lancs 147 M3
Lower Seagry Wilts 46 D3
Lower Sheering Essex 70 C4
Lower Shelton C Beds 85 K6
Lower Shiplake Oxon 49 J3
Lower Shuckburgh Warwks 83 L3
Lower Slaughter Gloucs 65 H3
Lower Soothill Kirk 141 L3
Lower Soudley Gloucs 63 K5
Lower Standen Kent 41 H7
Lower Stanton St Quintin Wilts 46 D3
Lower Stoke Medway 53 H4
Lower Stone Gloucs 63 K8
Lower Stonnall Staffs 98 D3
Lower Stow Bedon Norfk 105 K4
Lower Street Dorset 17 G3
Lower Street E Susx 24 C5
Lower Street Norfk 122 F4
Lower Street Suffk 88 F5
Lower Street Suffk 90 D5
Lower Stretton Warrtn 130 C3
Lower Stroud Dorset 15 K3
Lower Sundon C Beds 68 D2
Lower Swanwick Hants 19 H2
Lower Swell Gloucs 65 H2
Lower Tadmarton Oxon 83 J7
Lower Tale Devon 14 C2
Lower Tean Staffs 115 G4
Lower Thurlton Norfk 107 J3
Lower Town Cnwll 3 G5
Lower Town Devon 13 G8
Lower Town Herefs 80 E6
Lower Town Pembks 74 F5
Lower Trebullett Cnwll 11 L7
Lower Treluswell Cnwll 3 K4
Lower Tysoe Warwks 83 H6
Lower Ufford Suffk 91 G5
Lower Upcott Devon 13 K6
Lower Upham Hants 35 H7
Lower Upnor Medway 53 G5
Lower Vexford Somset 29 L4
Lower Walton Warrtn 130 B3
Lower Waterston Dorset 16 E4
Lower Weare Somset 44 E8
Lower Weedon Nhants 84 C3
Lower Welson Herefs 79 K5
Lower Westmancote Worcs 81 L7
Lower Whatcombe Dorset 17 G2
Lower Whatley Somset 32 B2
Lower Whitley Ches W 130 B4
Lower Wick Gloucs 63 L7
Lower Wick Worcs 81 J5
Lower Wield Hants 35 K3
Lower Willingdon E Susx 23 K6
Lower Withington Ches E 130 F5
Lower Woodend Bucks 49 K2
Lower Woodford Wilts 33 K4
Lower Wraxhall Dorset 16 A2
Lower Wyche Worcs 81 H6
Lower Wyke C Brad 141 J3
Lowesby Leics 100 F2
Lowestoft Suffk 107 L5
Loweswater Cumb 164 F6
Low Fell Gatesd 181 G7
Lowfield Heath W Susx 37 L3
Low Gartachorrans Stirlg 208 D2
Low Gate Nthumb 179 L6
Low Gettbridge Cumb 178 C7
Lowgill Cumb 157 K3
Lowgill Lancs 148 A3
Low Grantley N York 150 B2
Low Green N York 150 B4
Low Habberley Worcs 97 H7
Low Ham Somset 30 F5
Low Harrogate N York 150 C5
Low Hawsker N York 163 G1
Low Hesket Cumb 166 B2
Low Hutton N York 152 A2
Lowick Cumb 156 D5
Lowick Nhants 101 L7
Lowick Nthumb 203 G5
Lowick Bridge Cumb 156 D5
Lowick Green Cumb 156 D5
Low Knipe Cumb 166 C6
Low Laithe N York 150 B3
Lowlands Dur 168 E5
Lowlands Torfn 62 C7
Low Langton Lincs 136 C4
Low Leighton Derbys 131 K3
Low Lorton Cumb 164 F5
Low Marishes N York 162 E7
Low Marnham Notts 134 F6
Low Middleton Nthumb 203 H6
Low Mill N York 161 L4
Low Moor C Brad 141 J2
Low Moorsley Sundld 169 J2
Low Moresby Cumb 164 C6
Low Newton Cumb 156 F6
Low Row Cumb 165 G2
Low Row Cumb 165 K3
Low Row Cumb 178 D6
Low Row N York 159 H3
Low Salchrie D & G 172 C2
Low Santon N Linc 144 B5
Lowsonford Warwks 82 E2
Low Street Norfk 123 G6
Low Street Thurr 52 E3
Low Tharston Norfk 106 D4
Lowther Cumb 166 D6
Lowther Castle Cumb 166 C6
Lowthorpe E R Yk 153 H4
Lowton Devon 12 F2
Lowton Somset 30 B7
Lowton Wigan 139 J8
Lowton Common Wigan 139 J8
Lowton St Mary's Wigan 139 J8
Low Torry Fife 210 D2
Low Toynton Lincs 136 E5
Low Valley Barns 142 B7
Low Wood Cumb 156 E6
Low Worsall N York 160 F1
Low Wray Cumb 156 E2
Loxbeare Devon 29 G7
Loxhill Surrey 36 F3
Loxhore Devon 27 L3
Loxhore Cott Devon 27 L3
Loxley Warwks 83 G4
Loxley Green Staffs 115 H5
Loxter Herefs 81 G7
Loxton N Som 44 D7
Loxwood W Susx 36 F4
Loyal Lodge Highld 277 L7
Lubenham Leics 100 F6
Lucasgate Lincs 119 M2
Lucas Green Surrey 50 B7
Luccombe Somset 29 G2
Luccombe Village IoW 19 K7
Lucker Nthumb 203 J7
Luckett Cnwll 11 M7
Lucking Street Essex 89 G8
Luckington Wilts 46 B2
Lucklawhill Fife 223 G3
Lucknam Wilts 46 B4
Luckwell Bridge Somset 28 F3
Lucton Herefs 80 B2
Lucy Cross N York 169 G8
Ludag W Isls 283 c12
Ludborough Lincs 145 H8
Ludbrook Devon 7 J4
Ludchurch Pembks 55 K4
Luddenden Calder 141 G3
Luddenden Foot Calder 140 F3
Luddenham Court Kent 40 C3
Luddesdown Kent 52 E5
Luddington N Linc 143 L4
Luddington Warwks 82 E5
Luddington in the Brook Nhants 102 C6
Ludford Lincs 136 D2
Ludford Shrops 96 C8
Ludgershall Bucks 67 G4
Ludgershall Wilts 34 B1
Ludgvan Cnwll 2 D4
Ludham Norfk 123 H7
Ludlow Shrops 96 C8
Ludney Somset 30 F8

Ludwell Wilts 32 F6
Ludworth Dur 169 K2
Luffenhall Herts 69 J1
Luffincott Devon 11 L4
Luffness E Loth 212 B3
Lugar E Ayrs 197 H6
Luggate Burn E Loth 212 D4
Lugg Green Herefs 80 B3
Luggiebank N Lans 209 K4
Lugton E Ayrs 208 C8
Lugwardine Herefs 80 D7
Luib Highld 247 J3
Luing Ag & B 215 L2
Lulham Herefs 80 A7
Lullington Derbys 99 H1
Lullington E Susx 23 J6
Lullington Somset 45 M8
Lulsgate Bottom N Som 45 G6
Lulsley Worcs 81 G4
Lulworth Camp Dorset 16 F6
Lumb Calder 140 F3
Lumb Lancs 140 C3
Lumbutts Calder 140 E3
Lumby N York 142 D2
Lumloch E Duns 209 H5
Lumphanan Abers 244 D3
Lumphinnans Fife 222 B8
Lumsden Abers 255 K7
Lunan Angus 235 H5
Lunanhead Angus 234 D5
Luncarty P & K 221 K1
Lund E R Yk 152 E6
Lund N York 143 G1
Lundie Angus 233 L8
Lundin Links Fife 223 G6
Lundin Mill Fife 223 G6
Lundy Devon 26 B2
Lundy Green Norfk 106 E5
Lunga Ag & B 215 K3
Lunna Shet 281 e4
Lunsford Kent 52 F7
Lunsford's Cross E Susx 24 C5
Lunt Sefton 138 D7
Luntley Herefs 79 M4
Luppitt Devon 14 E1
Lupridge Devon 7 L4
Lupset Wakefd 141 M4
Lupton Cumb 157 J6
Lurgashall W Susx 36 D5
Lurley Devon 29 G7
Lusby Lincs 136 F6
Luscombe Devon 8 B3
Luson Devon 7 H5
Luss Ag & B 218 E8
Lussagiven Ag & B 215 J7
Lusta Highld 258 D5
Lustleigh Devon 13 H6
Luston Herefs 80 B3
Luthermuir Abers 235 G2
Luthrie Fife 222 E3
Lutley Dudley 97 L6
Luton Devon 13 L7
Luton Devon 14 C2
Luton Luton 68 E3
Luton Medway 53 G5
Lutterworth Leics 100 C6
Lutton Devon 7 H3
Lutton Devon 7 K3
Lutton Lincs 119 M6
Lutton Nhants 102 C6
Luxborough Somset 29 H3
Luxulyan Cnwll 5 H3
Luzley Tamesd 140 E7
Lybster Highld 275 H1
Lydbury North Shrops 95 J6
Lydcott Devon 28 B4
Lydd Kent 25 K3
Lydden Kent 41 H6
Lydden Kent 41 K2
Lyddington Rutlnd 101 J4
Lydeard St Lawrence Somset 29 L4
Lyde Green Hants 49 H7
Lydford Devon 12 C5
Lydford on Fosse Somset 31 J5
Lydgate Calder 140 D3
Lydgate Rochdl 140 E4
Lydham Shrops 95 H5
Lydiard Green Wilts 47 G2
Lydiard Millicent Wilts 47 G2
Lydiard Tregoze Swindn 47 G2
Lydiate Sefton 138 D7
Lydiate Ash Worcs 98 B8
Lydlinch Dorset 32 B8
Lydney Gloucs 63 J6
Lydstep Pembks 55 J7
Lye Dudley 97 L6
Lye Cross N Som 44 F6
Lye Green Bucks 68 B6
Lye Green E Susx 38 D6
Lye Green Warwks 82 E2
Lye Head Worcs 97 G8
Lye's Green Wilts 32 D2
Lyford Oxon 66 B8
Lymbridge Green Kent 40 F6
Lyme Regis Dorset 15 H4
Lyminge Kent 40 F7
Lymington Hants 18 E4
Lyminster W Susx 21 H6
Lymm Warrtn 130 D2
Lympne Kent 40 F8
Lympsham Somset 44 C8
Lympstone Devon 14 A6
Lynbridge Devon 28 C1
Lynchat Highld 241 L3
Lynch Green Norfk 106 C2
Lyndhurst Hants 18 D2
Lyndon Rutlnd 101 K3
Lyndon Green Birm 98 F6
Lyne Border 199 L5
Lyne Surrey 50 C5
Lyneal Shrops 113 G5
Lyne Down Herefs 63 J1
Lyneham Devon 13 K6
Lyneham Oxon 65 K3
Lyneham Wilts 46 F3
Lyneholmford Cumb 178 C4
Lynemouth Nthumb 191 K7
Lyne of Skene Abers 245 G2
Lynesack Dur 168 E5
Lyness Ork 275 b6
Lyng Norfk 122 B7
Lyng Somset 30 E5
Lynmouth Devon 28 C1
Lynn Staffs 98 D3
Lynn Wrekin 114 B8
Lynsted Kent 40 B3
Lynstone Cnwll 11 H2
Lynton Devon 28 C1
Lyon's Gate Dorset 16 C2
Lyonshall Herefs 79 L4
Lytchett Matravers Dorset 17 J3
Lytchett Minster Dorset 17 J4
Lyth Highld 280 C4
Lytham Lancs 138 D2
Lytham St Anne's Lancs 138 D2
Lythbank Shrops 95 L2
Lythe N York 171 K8
Lythmore Highld 279 J3

M

Mabe Burnthouse Cnwll 3 J4
Mablethorpe Lincs 137 J3
Macclesfield Ches E 131 H5
Macclesfield Crematorium Ches E 131 H5
Macduff Abers 268 C3
Macharioch Ag & B 192 E6
Machen Caerph 43 K4
Machrie N Ayrs 194 D4
Machrihanish Ag & B 192 D4
Machrins Ag & B 214 D5
Machynlleth Powys 93 G3
Machynys Carmth 56 F5
Mackworth Derbys 116 A4
Macmerry E Loth 211 M4
Maddaford Devon 12 D4
Madderty P & K 221 G3
Maddington Wilts 33 J2
Maddiston Falk 210 B4
Madehurst W Susx 21 G5
Madeley Staffs 114 B3
Madeley Wrekin 96 F3
Madeley Heath Staffs 114 B2
Madford Devon 29 L8
Madingley Cambs 87 H3
Madley Herefs 80 A7
Madresfield Worcs 81 J5
Madron Cnwll 2 C5
Maenaddwyn IoA 125 H3
Maenan Conwy 126 F6
Maenclochog Pembks 75 J6
Maendy V Glam 42 F6
Maenporth Cnwll 3 K5
Maentwrog Gwynd 110 C3
Maen-y-groes Cerdgn 76 C3
Maer Cnwll 11 H1
Maer Staffs 114 B4
Maerdy Carmth 59 J3
Maerdy Rhondd 42 E2
Maesbrook Shrops 112 D7
Maesbury Shrops 112 D6
Maesbury Marsh Shrops 112 D6
Maes-glas Newpt 44 C2
Maesgwynne Carmth 55 L2
Maeshafn Denbgs 128 E7
Maesllyn Cerdgn 76 C6
Maesmynis Powys 78 D6
Maesmynis Powys 78 E5
Maesteg Brdgnd 42 C3
Maesybont Carmth 59 G5
Maesycwmmer Caerph 43 J3
Magdalen Laver Essex 70 D5
Maggieknockater Moray 254 F3
Maggots End Essex 70 C2
Magham Down E Susx 23 K5
Maghull Sefton 138 D7
Magna Park Leics 100 B6
Magor Mons 44 E2
Maidenbower W Susx 37 L4
Maiden Bradley Wilts 32 D3
Maidencombe Torbay 8 D1
Maidenhayne Devon 15 G3
Maiden Head N Som 45 H5
Maidenhead W & M 49 L3
Maiden Law Dur 168 F1
Maiden Newton Dorset 16 B3
Maidens S Ayrs 182 F1
Maiden's Green Br For 49 L4
Maidenwell Lincs 136 F4
Maiden Wells Pembks 55 G7
Maidford Nhants 84 B5
Maids Moreton Bucks 84 D8
Maidstone Kent 39 J2
Maidwell Nhants 101 G8
Mail Shet 281 e6
Maindee Newpt 44 C1
Mainland Ork 275 c4
Mainland Shet 281 d6
Mainsforth Dur 169 J4
Mains of Balhall Angus 234 D3
Mains of Balnakettle Abers 244 E8
Mains of Dalvey Highld 254 B5
Mains of Haulkerton Abers 235 H1
Mains of Lesmoir Abers 255 J6
Mains of Melgunds Angus 234 E4
Mainsriddle D & G 176 B7
Mainstone Shrops 95 G6
Maisemore Gloucs 64 A3
Major's Green Worcs 98 E7
Makeney Derbys 116 B3
Malborough Devon 7 K7
Malcoff Derbys 131 L3
Malden Rushett Gt Lon 50 F6
Maldon Essex 71 K5
Malham N York 148 F3
Maligar Highld 259 H4
Mallaig Highld 237 K1
Mallaigvaig Highld 237 K1
Malleny Mills C Edin 211 G6
Mallows Green Essex 70 C2
Malltraeth IoA 125 G6
Mallwyd Gwynd 93 J1
Malmesbury Wilts 46 D2
Malmsmead Devon 28 D1
Malpas Ches W 113 H2
Malpas Cnwll 4 D6
Malpas Newpt 44 C1
Malswick Gloucs 63 L2
Maltby Lincs 136 F3
Maltby Rothm 133 K1
Maltby S on T 170 B8
Maltby le Marsh Lincs 137 J3
Malting Green Essex 72 E3
Maltman's Hill Kent 40 A6
Malton N York 152 B2
Malvern Link Worcs 81 H5
Malvern Wells Worcs 81 H6
Mamble Worcs 80 F1
Mamhilad Mons 62 C6
Manaccan Cnwll 3 J6
Manafon Powys 94 D3
Manais W Isls 282 e6
Manaton Devon 13 H6
Manby Lincs 137 G2
Mancetter Warwks 99 J4
Manchester Manch 140 C8
Mancot Flints 129 H6
Mandally Highld 240 A3
Manea Cambs 103 K5
Maney Birm 98 E4
Manfield N York 169 G8
Mangerton Dorset 15 L3
Mangotsfield S Glos 45 K4
Mangrove Green Herts 68 E2
Manhay Cnwll 3 H5
Manish W Isls 282 e6
Mankinholes Calder 140 E3
Manley Ches W 129 L5
Manmoel Caerph 61 J6
Mannel Ag & B 224 C7
Manningford Bohune Wilts 47 H7
Manningford Bruce Wilts 47 H7
Manningham C Brad 141 J1
Manning's Heath W Susx 37 K5
Mannington Dorset 17 L2
Manningtree Essex 73 G1
Mannofield C Aber 245 K3
Manorbier Pembks 55 H7
Manorbier Newton Pembks 55 H6
Manordeilo Carmth 59 J4
Manorhill Border 201 K6
Manorowen Pembks 74 F5
Manor Park Gt Lon 51 L2
Manor Park Crematorium Gt Lon 51 L2
Mansell Gamage Herefs 79 M6
Mansell Lacy Herefs 80 A6
Mansergh Cumb 157 K6
Mansfield E Ayrs 197 J8
Mansfield Notts 133 K7
Mansfield & District Crematorium Notts 133 K7
Mansfield Woodhouse Notts 133 K7
Mansriggs Cumb 156 D6
Manston Dorset 32 D7
Manston Kent 41 K2
Manston Leeds 142 B1
Manswood Dorset 17 J1
Manthorpe Lincs 118 B4
Manthorpe Lincs 118 E8
Manton N Linc 144 A7
Manton Notts 134 C4
Manton Rutlnd 101 J3
Manton Wilts 47 H5
Manuden Essex 70 C2
Manwood Green Essex 70 E4
Maperton Somset 31 L5
Maplebeck Notts 134 E7
Maple Cross Herts 68 C8
Mapledurham Oxon 49 G4
Mapledurwell Hants 49 G8
Maplehurst W Susx 37 J6
Maplescombe Kent 52 C6
Mapleton Derbys 115 K2
Mapleton Kent 38 C3
Mapperley Derbys 116 D3
Mapperley Park C Nott 117 G3
Mapperton Dorset 15 L3
Mappleborough Green Warwks 82 C2
Mappleton E R Yk 153 K7
Mapplewell Barns 141 M5
Mappowder Dorset 16 E2
Marazanvose Cnwll 4 C5
Marazion Cnwll 2 E5
Marbury Ches E 113 J2
March Cambs 103 J4
March S Lans 186 E3
Marcham Oxon 66 C7
Marchamley Shrops 113 K5
Marchamley Wood Shrops 113 K5
Marchington Staffs 115 J5
Marchington Woodlands Staffs 115 J6
Marchros Gwynd 108 E6
Marchwiel Wrexhm 112 E2
Marchwood Hants 18 F2
Marcross V Glam 42 D7
Marden Herefs 80 C6
Marden Kent 39 J4
Marden Wilts 47 G7
Marden Ash Essex 70 E6
Marden Beech Kent 39 J5
Mardens Hill E Susx 38 D7
Marden Thorn Kent 39 J5
Mardlebury Herts 69 H3
Mardy Mons 62 C4
Marefield Leics 101 G2
Mareham le Fen Lincs 136 E7
Mareham on the Hill Lincs 136 E6
Marehay Derbys 116 C2
Marehill W Susx 21 H3
Maresfield E Susx 23 G2
Marfleet C KuH 144 E2
Marford Wrexhm 129 H8
Margam Neath 57 L7
Margam Crematorium Neath 42 B4
Margaret Marsh Dorset 32 D7
Margaret Roding Essex 70 F5
Margaretting Essex 71 G6
Margaretting Tye Essex 71 G7
Margate Kent 41 K1
Margnaheglish N Ayrs 195 G4
Margrie D & G 174 F5
Margrove Park R & Cl 170 F7
Marham Norfk 104 E2
Marhamchurch Cnwll 11 J2
Marholm C Pete 102 C3
Marian-glas IoA 125 J3
Mariansleigh Devon 28 C6
Marine Town Kent 53 K4
Marionburgh Abers 244 F2
Marishader Highld 259 H4
Maristow Devon 6 F2
Marjoriebanks D & G 176 E2
Mark Somset 30 F1
Markbeech Kent 38 D5
Markby Lincs 137 J4

Mark Causeway Somset 30 E2
Mark Cross E Susx 38 F7
Markeaton C Derb 116 B4
Markeaton Crematorium C Derb 116 B4
Market Bosworth Leics 99 L3
Market Deeping Lincs 102 C2
Market Drayton Shrops 113 L5
Market Harborough Leics 100 F6
Market Lavington Wilts 46 E8
Market Overton Rutlnd 118 A8
Market Rasen Lincs 136 B2
Market Stainton Lincs 136 D4
Market Warsop Notts 133 L6
Market Weighton E R Yk 152 D7
Market Weston Suffk 105 K7
Markfield Leics 100 B2
Markham Caerph 61 J6
Markham Moor Notts 134 E5
Markinch Fife 222 E6
Markington N York 150 C3
Markle E Loth 212 C3
Marksbury BaNES 45 K6
Mark's Corner IoW 19 H5
Marks Tey Essex 72 C2
Markwell Cnwll 6 D3
Markyate Herts 68 D4
Marlborough Wilts 47 J5
Marlbrook Herefs 80 C4
Marlbrook Worcs 98 B8
Marlcliff Warwks 82 C5
Marldon Devon 8 C2
Marle Green E Susx 23 K4
Marlesford Suffk 91 H3
Marley Kent 41 G5
Marley Kent 41 K4
Marley Green Ches E 113 J2
Marley Hill Gatesd 180 F7
Marlingford Norfk 106 C2
Marloes Pembks 54 C5
Marlow Bucks 49 K2
Marlow Herefs 95 K8
Marlow Bottom Bucks 49 K1
Marlpit Hill Kent 38 C4
Marlpits E Susx 24 C4
Marlpits E Susx 38 C7
Marlpool Derbys 116 D3
Marnhull Dorset 32 C7
Marple Stockp 131 J2
Marple Bridge Stockp 131 J2
Marr Donc 142 E6
Marrick N York 159 K3
Marros Carmth 55 L5
Marsden Kirk 141 G5
Marsden S Tyne 181 K6
Marsden Height Lancs 148 F8
Marsett N York 158 F5
Marsh Bucks 67 K5
Marsh C Brad 149 J8
Marsh Devon 30 C8
Marshall's Heath Herts 68 F4
Marshalswick Herts 68 F5
Marsham Norfk 122 D6
Marsh Baldon Oxon 66 E7
Marsh Benham W Berk 48 B5
Marshborough Kent 41 J4
Marshbrook Shrops 95 K5
Marshchapel Lincs 145 K7
Marsh Farm Luton 68 D2
Marshfield Newpt 43 L5
Marshfield S Glos 45 M4
Marshgate Cnwll 11 G4
Marsh Gibbon Bucks 66 F3
Marsh Green Devon 14 B4
Marsh Green Kent 38 C4
Marsh Green Wrekin 113 K8
Marshland St James Norfk 103 L2
Marsh Lane Derbys 133 H4
Marsh Lane Gloucs 63 H5
Marshside Sefton 138 D4
Marsh Street Somset 29 H2
Marshwood Dorset 15 J3
Marske N York 159 K3
Marske-by-the-Sea R & Cl 170 E6
Marsland Green Wigan 139 K7
Marston Ches W 130 D5
Marston Herefs 79 L4
Marston Lincs 118 A3
Marston Oxon 66 D5
Marston Staffs 97 J1
Marston Staffs 114 E6
Marston Warwks 99 G4
Marston Wilts 46 D7
Marston Green Solhll 98 F6
Marston Jabbet Warwks 99 K5
Marston Magna Somset 31 K6
Marston Meysey Wilts 65 H7
Marston Montgomery Derbys 115 J4
Marston Moretaine C Beds 85 K7
Marston on Dove Derbys 115 L5
Marston St Lawrence Nhants 83 M6
Marston Stannett Herefs 80 D4
Marston Trussell Nhants 100 F6
Marstow Herefs 63 H3
Marsworth Bucks 68 A4
Marten Wilts 47 L7
Marthall Ches E 130 F4
Martham Norfk 123 J7
Martin Hants 33 J7
Martin Kent 41 K6
Martin Lincs 136 B7
Martin Lincs 136 D6
Martindale Cumb 166 B6
Martin Dales Lincs 136 C7
Martin Drove End Hants 33 H6
Martinhoe Devon 28 B1
Martin Hussingtree Worcs 81 K3
Martinscroft Warrtn 130 C2
Martinstown Dorset 16 C5
Martlesham Suffk 90 F6
Martlesham Heath Suffk 90 F6
Martletwy Pembks 55 H5
Martley Worcs 81 H3
Martock Somset 31 G7
Marton Ches E 131 G6
Marton Ches W 130 C6
Marton Cumb 156 C7
Marton E R Yk 153 J7
Marton E R Yk 153 K2
Marton Lincs 135 G3
Marton Middsb 170 C7
Marton N York 150 F3
Marton N York 162 C6
Marton Shrops 95 G3
Marton Warwks 83 J2
Marton-le-Moor N York 150 E2
Martyr's Green Surrey 50 E7
Martyr Worthy Hants 35 G4
Marwick Ork 275 b3
Marwood Devon 27 K3
Marybank Highld 250 E1
Maryburgh Highld 262 F8
Maryculter Abers 245 J4
Marygold Border 213 H7
Maryhill C Glas 208 F5
Maryhill Crematorium C Glas 208 F5
Marykirk Abers 235 H2
Maryland Mons 63 G6
Marylebone Gt Lon 51 H3
Marylebone Wigan 139 H6
Marypark Moray 254 D4
Maryport Cumb 164 D3
Maryport D & G 172 E7
Marystow Devon 12 B6
Mary Tavy Devon 12 C6
Maryton Angus 235 H4
Marywell Abers 244 D4
Marywell Abers 245 L4
Marywell Angus 235 G6
Masham N York 160 B6
Mashbury Essex 71 G5
Mason N u Ty 180 F4
Masongill N York 157 L7
Masonhill Crematorium S Ayrs 196 D7
Mastin Moor Derbys 133 J4
Matching Essex 70 D5
Matching Green Essex 70 D5
Matching Tye Essex 70 D5
Matfen Nthumb 180 C4
Matfield Kent 39 G5
Mathern Mons 45 G1
Mathon Herefs 81 G6
Mathry Pembks 74 E6
Matlask Norfk 122 C4
Matlock Derbys 132 F7
Matlock Bank Derbys 132 F7
Matlock Bath Derbys 132 F8
Matlock Dale Derbys 132 F7
Matson Gloucs 64 B4
Matterdale End Cumb 165 L6
Mattersey Notts 134 D2
Mattersey Thorpe Notts 134 D2
Mattingley Hants 49 H7
Mattishall Norfk 105 L1
Mattishall Burgh Norfk 105 L1
Mauchline E Ayrs 196 F5
Maud Abers 269 G6
Maufant Jersey 9 e2
Maugersbury Gloucs 65 J2
Maughold IoM 154 g4
Mauld Highld 250 C4
Maulden C Beds 85 L7
Maulds Meaburn Cumb 166 E7
Maunby N York 160 E5
Maund Bryan Herefs 80 D5
Maundown Somset 29 J5
Mautby Norfk 107 K1
Mavesyn Ridware Staffs 115 H8
Mavis Enderby Lincs 137 G6
Mawbray Cumb 164 E1
Mawdesley Lancs 139 G5
Mawdlam Brdgnd 42 B5
Mawgan Cnwll 3 H6
Mawgan Porth Cnwll 4 D2
Maw Green Ches E 130 D8
Mawla Cnwll 4 A5
Mawnan Cnwll 3 K5
Mawnan Smith Cnwll 3 K5
Mawsley Nhants 101 H8
Mawthorpe Lincs 137 J5
Maxey C Pete 102 C2
Maxstoke Warwks 99 G6
Maxted Street Kent 40 F6
Maxton Border 201 J7
Maxton Kent 41 J7
Maxwell Town D & G 176 C4
Maxworthy Cnwll 11 J4
Mayals Swans 57 H6
May Bank Staffs 114 D2
Maybole S Ayrs 183 H1
Maybury Surrey 50 C7
Mayes Green Surrey 37 H3
Mayfield E Susx 23 K2
Mayfield Mdloth 211 K6
Mayfield Staffs 115 J2
Mayford Surrey 50 C7
May Hill Gloucs 63 L3
Mayland Essex 72 D6
Maylandsea Essex 72 C6
Maynard's Green E Susx 23 K3
Maypole Birm 98 D7
Maypole Kent 41 G2
Maypole Mons 62 F4
Maypole Green Norfk 107 J4
Maypole Green Suffk 89 J3
Maypole Green Suffk 91 G2
May's Green Oxon 49 H3
May's Green Surrey 50 E7
Mead Devon 26 C7
Meadgate BaNES 45 K7
Meadle Bucks 67 K6
Meadowfield Dur 169 H3
Meadowtown Shrops 95 H3
Meadwell Devon 12 A6
Meaford Staffs 114 D4
Meal Bank Cumb 157 H4
Mealrigg Cumb 164 F2
Mealsgate Cumb 165 H2
Meanwood Leeds 150 C8
Mearbeck N York 148 E4
Meare Somset 31 G3
Meare Green Somset 30 D6
Meare Green Somset 30 E5
Mearns E Rens 208 F7
Mears Ashby Nhants 85 G2
Measham Leics 99 J1
Meathop Cumb 156 F6
Meaux E R Yk 153 H7
Meavy Devon 7 G2
Medbourne Leics 101 H5
Meddon Devon 26 D7
Meden Vale Notts 134 B5
Medlam Lincs 136 F8
Medlar Lancs 147 H8
Medmenham Bucks 49 K2
Medomsley Dur 180 D7
Medstead Hants 35 K3
Medway Crematorium Kent 53 G6
Meerbrook Staffs 131 K7
Meer Common Herefs 79 L5
Meesden Herts 70 B1
Meeson Wrekin 113 L7
Meeth Devon 12 D1
Meeting Green Suffk 88 E4
Meeting House Hill Norfk 122 F6
Meidrim Carmth 58 B5
Meifod Powys 94 E1
Meigle P & K 233 L6
Meikle Carco D & G 186 A3
Meikle Earnock S Lans 209 J8
Meikle Kilmory Ag & B 207 G6
Meikle Obney P & K 232 F7
Meikleour P & K 233 J7
Meikle Wartle Abers 256 C5
Meinciau Carmth 56 E3
Meir C Stke 114 E3
Meir Heath Staffs 114 E3
Melbourn Cambs 87 H6
Melbourne Derbys 116 C6
Melbourne E R Yk 152 A7
Melbur Cnwll 4 F4
Melbury Devon 26 F7
Melbury Abbas Dorset 32 E6
Melbury Bubb Dorset 16 B2
Melbury Osmond Dorset 16 A1
Melbury Sampford Dorset 16 A2
Melchbourne Bed 85 K2
Melcombe Bingham Dorset 16 E2
Meldon Devon 12 D4
Meldon Nthumb 180 D2
Meldon Park Nthumb 180 D2
Meldreth Cambs 87 H6
Meldrum Stirlg 220 C7
Melfort Ag & B 216 C4
Meliden Denbgs 128 C3
Melinau Pembks 55 K4
Melin-byrhedyn Powys 93 H4
Melincourt Neath 60 B6
Melin-y-coed Conwy 127 G7
Melin-y-ddol Powys 94 D2
Melin-y-wig Denbgs 111 K2
Melkinthorpe Cumb 166 D5
Melkridge Nthumb 179 G6
Melksham Wilts 46 C6
Mellangoose Cnwll 3 H5
Mell Green W Berk 48 C3
Mellguards Cumb 166 B2
Melling Lancs 147 M2
Melling Sefton 138 E7
Melling Mount Sefton 138 E7
Mellis Suffk 106 B8
Mellon Charles Highld 260 D2
Mellon Udrigle Highld 260 E1
Mellor Lancs 139 K2
Mellor Stockp 131 K2
Mellor Brook Lancs 139 J2
Mells Somset 32 B1
Mells Suffk 107 H8
Melmerby Cumb 166 E3
Melmerby N York 159 K5
Melmerby N York 160 E7
Melness Highld 277 K4
Melon Green Suffk 89 G4
Melplash Dorset 15 L3
Melrose Border 201 H6
Melsetter Ork 275 b6
Melsonby N York 160 B1
Meltham Kirk 141 H5
Meltham Mills Kirk 141 H5
Melton E R Yk 144 B2
Melton Suffk 91 G5
Meltonby E R Yk 152 B5
Melton Constable Norfk 122 A5
Melton Mowbray Leics 117 K7
Melton Ross N Linc 144 D5
Melvaig Highld 260 B3
Melverley Shrops 112 E8
Melverley Green Shrops 112 E7
Melvich Highld 278 E3
Membury Devon 15 G2
Memsie Abers 269 H4
Memus Angus 234 C4
Menabilly Cnwll 5 J4
Menagissey Cnwll 4 B5
Menai Bridge IoA 125 K5
Mendham Suffk 106 F6
Mendip Crematorium Somset 31 K2
Mendlesham Suffk 90 D2
Mendlesham Green Suffk 90 C3
Menheniot Cnwll 6 B2
Menithwood Worcs 81 G2
Mennock D & G 185 K2
Menston C Brad 149 L7
Menstrie Clacks 220 E7
Menthorpe N York 143 H1
Mentmore Bucks 67 M3
Meoble Highld 238 C6
Meole Brace Shrops 96 B1
Meonstoke Hants 35 J7
Meopham Kent 52 D5
Meopham Green Kent 52 D6
Meopham Station Kent 52 D5
Mepal Cambs 103 J7
Meppershall C Beds 86 C8
Merbach Herefs 79 K6
Mere Ches E 130 E3
Mere Wilts 32 D4
Mere Brow Lancs 138 E4
Mereclough Lancs 140 C2
Mere Green Birm 98 E4
Mere Green Worcs 81 L3
Mere Heath Ches W 130 C5
Meresborough Medway 53 H6
Mereworth Kent 39 G3
Meriden Solhll 99 G7
Merkadale Highld 246 E2
Merley Poole 17 K3
Merlin's Bridge Pembks 54 F4
Merrington Shrops 113 G7
Merrion Pembks 54 F7
Merriott Somset 31 G8
Merrivale Devon 12 D7
Merrow Surrey 36 F1
Merry Field Hill Dorset 17 K2
Merry Hill Herts 68 E8
Merryhill Wolves 97 K4
Merry Lees Leics 100 A2
Merrymeet Cnwll 6 B2
Mersea Island Essex 72 F4
Mersham Kent 40 D7

Merstham Surrey 51 H8
Merston W Susx 20 E6
Merstone IoW 19 J6
Merther Cnwll 4 D6
Merthyr Carmth 58 C5
Merthyr Cynog Powys 78 D7
Merthyr Dyfan V Glam 43 H7
Merthyr Mawr Brdgnd 42 D6
Merthyr Tydfil Myr Td 61 G6
Merthyr Vale Myr Td 61 G7
Merton Devon 27 J8
Merton Gt Lon 51 H5
Merton Norfk 105 H4
Merton Oxon 66 E3
Meshaw Devon 28 D7
Messing Essex 72 C3
Messingham N Linc 143 M6
Metfield Suffk 106 F7
Metherell Cnwll 6 E1
Metheringham Lincs 135 L7
Methil Fife 222 F7
Methilhill Fife 222 F7
Methley Leeds 142 B2
Methley Junction Leeds 142 B3
Methlick Abers 256 F4
Methven P & K 221 J2
Methwold Norfk 104 E4
Methwold Hythe Norfk 104 E4
Mettingham Suffk 107 H5
Metton Norfk 122 D4
Mevagissey Cnwll 5 G6
Mexborough Donc 142 D7
Mey Highld 280 C2
Meyllteyrn Gwynd 108 D5
Meysey Hampton Gloucs 65 G7
Miabhig W Isls 282 e3
Miavaig W Isls 282 e3
Michaelchurch Herefs 63 G2
Michaelchurch Escley Herefs 79 K8
Michaelchurch-on-Arrow Powys 79 J5
Michaelstone-y-Fedw Newpt 43 K5
Michaelston-le-Pit V Glam 43 J7
Michaelstow Cnwll 10 F6
Michelcombe Devon 7 K1
Micheldever Hants 35 G3
Micheldever Station Hants 35 G2
Michelmersh Hants 34 D5
Mickfield Suffk 90 D3
Micklebring Donc 133 K1
Mickleby N York 171 J8
Micklefield Leeds 142 C1
Micklefield Green Herts 68 D7
Mickleham Surrey 50 F8
Mickleover C Derb 116 A5
Micklethwaite C Brad 149 K7
Micklethwaite Cumb 165 J1
Mickleton Dur 168 B6
Mickleton Gloucs 82 E6
Mickletown Leeds 142 B2
Mickle Trafford Ches W 129 K5
Mickley Derbys 132 F4
Mickley N York 160 C7
Mickley Green Suffk 89 G4
Mickley Square Nthumb 180 C6
Mid Ardlaw Abers 269 H3
Midbea Ork 275 c2
Mid Beltie Abers 244 E3
Mid Bockhampton Dorset 18 B4
Mid Calder W Loth 210 E5
Mid Clyth Highld 280 C8
Mid Culbeuchly Abers 268 B4
Middle Assendon Oxon 49 H2
Middle Aston Oxon 66 C2
Middle Barton Oxon 66 B2
Middlebie D & G 177 H4
Middlebridge P & K 232 C2
Middle Chinnock Somset 31 G8
Middle Claydon Bucks 67 H2
Middlecliffe Barns 142 C6
Middlecott Devon 13 G5
Middle Duntisbourne Gloucs 64 E6
Middleham N York 159 L5
Middle Handley Derbys 133 H4
Middle Harling Norfk 105 K6
Middlehill Cnwll 6 B1
Middlehill Wilts 46 B5
Middlehope Shrops 96 B5
Middle Kames Ag & B 206 E1
Middle Littleton Worcs 82 C6
Middle Madeley Staffs 114 B3
Middle Maes-coed Herefs 79 L8
Middlemarsh Dorset 16 C1
Middle Mayfield Staffs 115 J3
Middle Mill Pembks 74 C7
Middlemore Devon 12 C8
Middle Quarter Kent 40 A7
Middle Rasen Lincs 136 A2
Middle Rocombe Devon 8 D1
Middle Salter Lancs 147 M3
Middlesbrough Middsb 170 C6
Middlesceugh Cumb 165 L2
Middleshaw Cumb 157 J5
Middlesmoor N York 159 K7
Middle Stoford Somset 30 B6
Middle Stoke Medway 53 H4
Middlestone Dur 169 H4
Middlestone Moor Dur 169 H4
Middle Stoughton Somset 30 F1
Middlestown Wakefd 141 L4
Middle Street Gloucs 63 M6
Middle Taphouse Cnwll 5 K2
Middlethird Border 201 L4
Middleton Ag & B 224 B6
Middleton Cumb 157 K5
Middleton Derbys 132 D7
Middleton Derbys 132 E8
Middleton Essex 89 H7
Middleton Hants 34 F2
Middleton Herefs 80 D1
Middleton Lancs 147 H4
Middleton Leeds 141 M2
Middleton N York 149 L6
Middleton N York 162 D5
Middleton Nhants 101 J5
Middleton Norfk 120 E8
Middleton Nthumb 180 C2
Middleton Nthumb 203 H6
Middleton P & K 221 L6
Middleton Rochdl 140 C6
Middleton Shrops 96 C7
Middleton Shrops 112 D5
Middleton Suffk 91 K2
Middleton Swans 56 D7
Middleton Warwks 98 F4
Middleton Cheney Nhants 83 L7
Middleton Crematorium Rochdl 140 C6
Middleton Green Staffs 114 F4
Middleton Hall Nthumb 202 F8
Middleton-in-Teesdale Dur 168 B5
Middleton Moor Suffk 91 J2
Middleton One Row Darltn 169 K8
Middleton-on-Leven N York 161 G1
Middleton-on-Sea W Susx 20 F6
Middleton on the Hill Herefs 80 C2
Middleton on the Wolds E R Yk 152 E6
Middleton Park C Aber 245 K1
Middleton Priors Shrops 96 E5
Middleton Quernhow N York 160 E7
Middleton St George Darltn 169 K8
Middleton Scriven Shrops 96 F6
Middleton Stoney Oxon 66 D2
Middleton Tyas N York 160 B2
Middletown Cumb 155 H1
Middle Town IoS 10 b3
Middletown N Som 44 F4
Middletown Powys 95 H1
Middle Tysoe Warwks 83 H6
Middle Wallop Hants 34 C3
Middlewich Ches E 130 D6
Middle Winterslow Wilts 34 B4
Middlewood Cnwll 11 K7
Middlewood Herefs 79 K6
Middle Woodford Wilts 33 K4
Middlewood Green Suffk 90 C3
Middleyard E Ayrs 197 G4
Middle Yard Gloucs 64 B6
Middlezoy Somset 30 E4
Middridge Dur 169 H5
Midford BaNES 45 M6
Midge Hall Lancs 139 G3
Midgeholme Cumb 178 E7
Midgham W Berk 48 E5
Midgley Calder 140 F3
Midgley Wakefd 141 L5
Mid Holmwood Surrey 37 J2
Midhopestones Sheff 141 K7
Midhurst W Susx 36 C6
Mid Lavant W Susx 20 D5
Midlem Border 201 H7
Mid Mains Highld 250 D4
Midney Somset 31 H5
Midpark Ag & B 207 G7
Midsomer Norton BaNES 45 K8
Midtown Highld 277 K4
Midville Lincs 137 G8
Mid Warwickshire Crematorium Warwks 83 G3
Midway Ches E 131 H3
Mid Yell Shet 281 e3
Migvie Abers 244 A2
Milborne Port Somset 31 L7
Milborne St Andrew Dorset 16 F3
Milborne Wick Somset 31 L6
Milbourne Nthumb 180 D4
Milbourne Wilts 46 D2
Milburn Cumb 166 F5
Milbury Heath S Glos 45 K1
Milby N York 150 F2
Milcombe Oxon 83 K8
Milden Suffk 89 J6
Mildenhall Suffk 104 E8
Mildenhall Wilts 47 J5
Milebrook Powys 79 K1
Milebush Kent 39 J4
Mile Elm Wilts 46 E5
Mile End Essex 72 E2
Mile End Gloucs 63 H5
Mile End Suffk 107 G5
Mileham Norfk 121 K7
Mile Oak Br & H 22 C5
Mile Oak Kent 39 H4
Mile Oak Staffs 98 F3
Miles Hope Herefs 80 D2
Milesmark Fife 210 E1
Miles Platting Manch 140 C7
Mile Town Kent 53 K4
Milfield Nthumb 202 E6
Milford Derbys 116 B3
Milford Devon 26 D6
Milford Powys 94 D5
Milford Staffs 114 F7
Milford Surrey 36 E2
Milford Haven Pembks 54 E5
Milford on Sea Hants 18 D5
Milkwall Gloucs 63 H5
Millais Jersey 9 a1
Milland W Susx 36 B5
Milland Marsh W Susx 36 C5
Mill Bank Calder 140 F3
Millbeck Cumb 165 H5
Millbreck Abers 257 J3
Millbridge Surrey 36 C2
Millbrook C Beds 85 K7
Millbrook C Sotn 34 E8
Millbrook Cnwll 6 E4
Millbrook Jersey 9 c3
Millbrook Tamesd 140 E7
Mill Brow Stockp 131 J2
Millbuie Abers 245 H2
Millbuie Highld 250 F1
Millcombe Devon 8 B5
Mill Common Norfk 107 G3
Mill Common Suffk 107 H7
Millcorner E Susx 24 E3
Millcraig Highld 263 H5
Mill Cross Devon 7 L3
Milldale Staffs 115 J1
Mill End Bucks 49 J2
Mill End Cambs 103 G7
Millend Gloucs 63 L7
Mill End Herts 87 G8
Millerhill Mdloth 211 K5
Miller's Dale Derbys 132 C5
Millers Green Derbys 115 M1
Miller's Green Essex 70 E5
Millerston C Glas 209 H5
Millgate Lancs 140 D4
Mill Green Cambs 88 C6
Mill Green Essex 70 F6
Mill Green Herts 69 G5
Mill Green Lincs 119 H6
Mill Green Norfk 106 C6
Millgreen Shrops 113 L6
Mill Green Staffs 98 D3
Mill Green Staffs 115 H7
Mill Green Suffk 89 J6
Mill Green Suffk 89 K4
Mill Green Suffk 90 D3
Mill Green Suffk 91 H3
Millhalf Herefs 79 K5
Millhayes Devon 14 F2
Millhead Lancs 147 K2
Millheugh S Lans 198 B3
Mill Hill E Susx 23 L6
Mill Hill Gt Lon 69 G8
Millhouse Ag & B 206 F5
Millhouse Cumb 165 K3
Millhousebridge D & G 176 F2
Millhouse Green Barns 141 K7
Millhouses Barns 142 C6
Millhouses Sheff 133 G3
Milliken Park Rens 208 C6
Millin Cross Pembks 55 G4
Millington E R Yk 152 C5
Millmeece Staffs 114 C5
Millness Cumb 157 H6
Mill of Drummond P & K 220 E4
Mill of Haldane W Duns 208 C3
Millom Cumb 155 M6
Millook Cnwll 11 H3
Millpool Cnwll 2 F5
Millpool Cnwll 11 G8
Millport N Ayrs 207 K8
Mill Side Cumb 157 G6
Mill Street Kent 39 H2
Mill Street Norfk 122 B7
Mill Street Suffk 90 C1
Millthorpe Derbys 132 F4
Millthrop Cumb 157 L4
Milltimber C Aber 245 J3
Milltown Abers 243 J2
Milltown Abers 255 J8
Milltown Cnwll 5 J3
Milltown D & G 177 K4
Milltown Derbys 133 G7
Milltown Devon 27 K3
Milltown of Campfield Abers 244 E3
Milltown of Edinvillie Moray 254 F4
Milltown of Learney Abers 244 E3
Milnathort P & K 221 L6
Milngavie E Duns 208 F4
Milnrow Rochdl 140 D5
Milnthorpe Cumb 157 H6
Milnthorpe Wakefd 142 A4
Milovaig Highld 258 B6
Milson Shrops 80 E1
Milstead Kent 40 A3
Milston Wilts 33 L2
Milthorpe Lincs 118 F5
Milthorpe Nhants 84 B6
Milton C Stke 114 E2
Milton Cambs 87 K3
Milton Cumb 178 D6
Milton D & G 172 F4
Milton D & G 175 L1
Milton Derbys 116 A6
Milton Highld 248 A3
Milton Highld 250 E5
Milton Highld 251 G2
Milton Highld 263 K5
Milton Highld 280 D6
Milton Inver 208 B5
Milton Kent 52 E4
Milton Moray 254 D7
Milton Moray 267 K4
Milton N Som 44 D6
Milton Newpt 44 D1
Milton Notts 134 E5
Milton Oxon 66 C8
Milton Oxon 83 K8
Milton P & K 233 G3
Milton Pembks 55 H6
Milton Somset 31 G6
Milton Stirlg 219 H7
Milton W Duns 208 D4
Milton Abbas Dorset 16 F2
Milton Abbot Devon 12 A6
Milton Bridge Mdloth 211 H6
Milton Bryan C Beds 68 B1
Milton Clevedon Somset 31 L3
Milton Combe Devon 6 F2
Milton Common Oxon 67 G6
Milton Damerel Devon 27 G8
Milton End Gloucs 63 L5
Milton End Gloucs 65 H7
Milton Ernest Bed 85 K4
Milton Green Ches W 129 K7
Milton Hill Oxon 48 C1
Milton Keynes M Keyn 85 G7
Milton Lilbourne Wilts 47 J7
Milton Malsor Nhants 84 E4
Milton Morenish P & K 231 H8
Milton of Auchinhove Abers 244 C3
Milton of Balgonie Fife 222 E7
Milton of Buchanan Stirlg 208 D1
Milton of Campsie E Duns 209 H4
Milton of Leys Highld 251 J3
Milton of Murtle C Aber 245 J3
Milton of Tullich Abers 243 L4
Milton on Stour Dorset 32 D5
Milton Regis Kent 40 A2
Milton Street E Susx 23 J6
Milton-under-Wychwood Oxon 65 K3
Milverton Somset 29 L5
Milverton Warwks 83 H2
Milwich Staffs 114 F5
Milwr Flints 128 E5
Minard Ag & B 216 F7
Minchington Dorset 33 G7
Minchinhampton Gloucs 64 C7
Mindrum Nthumb 202 C6
Minehead Somset 29 H2
Minera Wrexhm 112 C1
Minety Wilts 46 F1
Minffordd Gwynd 109 L4
Mingarrypark Highld 237 K6
Miningsby Lincs 136 F6
Minions Cnwll 11 J8
Minishant S Ayrs 196 C8
Minllyn Gwynd 111 G8
Minnigaff D & G 173 K2
Minnis Bay Kent 41 J2
Minnonie Abers 268 D4
Minshull Vernon Ches E 130 D7
Minskip N York 150 E3
Minstead Hants 18 D2

Minsted W Susx 20 D3
Minster Kent 41 J2
Minster Kent 53 L4
Minsterley Shrops 95 J2
Minster Lovell Oxon 65 L5
Minsterworth Gloucs 63 M4
Minterne Magna Dorset 16 C2
Minterne Parva Dorset 16 C2
Minting Lincs 136 C5
Mintlaw Abers 269 J6
Mintlyn Crematorium Norfk 120 E7
Minto Border 188 F2
Minton Shrops 95 K5
Minwear Pembks 55 H4
Minworth Birm 98 F5
Mirehouse Cumb 164 C7
Mireland Highld 280 D4
Mirfield Kirk 141 K4
Miserden Gloucs 64 D5
Miskin Rhondd 43 G2
Miskin Rhondd 43 G5
Misson Notts 134 D1
Misterton Leics 100 C6
Misterton Notts 134 F1
Misterton Somset 15 K1
Mistley Essex 73 G1
Mistley Heath Essex 73 H1
Mitcham Gt Lon 51 H5
Mitcheldean Gloucs 63 K3
Mitchell Cnwll 4 D4
Mitchellslacks D & G 186 E7
Mitchel Troy Mons 62 F5
Mitford Nthumb 180 E2
Mithian Cnwll 4 B5
Mitton Staffs 114 D8
Mixbury Oxon 84 B8
Mixenden Calder 141 G2
Moats Tye Suffk 90 B4
Mobberley Ches E 130 F4
Mobberley Staffs 115 G3
Moccas Herefs 79 L6
Mochdre Conwy 127 G4
Mochdre Powys 94 C5
Mochrum D & G 173 J5
Mockbeggar Hants 18 B2
Mockbeggar Kent 39 H4
Mockerkin Cumb 164 E6
Modbury Devon 7 J4
Moddershall Staffs 114 E4
Moelfre IoA 125 J2
Moelfre Powys 112 B6
Moel Tryfan Gwynd 125 J8
Moffat D & G 187 G5
Moggerhanger C Beds 86 C5
Moira Leics 116 A8
Molash Kent 40 D5
Mol-chlach Highld 246 F6
Mold Flints 128 F7
Moldgreen Kirk 141 J4
Molehill Green Essex 70 E2
Molehill Green Essex 71 H3
Molescroft E R Yk 152 F7
Molesden Nthumb 180 E2
Molesworth Cambs 102 B8
Molland Devon 28 E5
Mollington Ches W 129 J5
Mollington Oxon 83 K5
Mollinsburn N Lans 209 J5
Monachty Cerdgn 76 F3
Mondynes Abers 245 G7
Monewden Suffk 90 F3
Moneydie P & K 221 J1
Moneyrow Green W & M 49 L3
Moniaive D & G 185 J5
Monifieth Angus 223 J1
Monikie Angus 234 D7
Monimail Fife 222 E4
Monington Pembks 75 K3
Monk Bretton Barns 142 B6
Monken Hadley Gt Lon 69 H7
Monk Fryston N York 142 D2
Monkhide Herefs 80 E6
Monkhill Cumb 177 K7
Monkhopton Shrops 96 E5
Monkland Herefs 80 B4
Monkleigh Devon 27 H6
Monknash V Glam 42 D7
Monkokehampton Devon 12 E2
Monkseaton N Tyne 181 J4
Monks Eleigh Suffk 89 K5
Monk's Gate W Susx 37 K5
Monks Heath Ches E 131 G5
Monk Sherborne Hants 48 F7
Monks Horton Kent 40 E7
Monksilver Somset 29 K3
Monks Kirby Warwks 100 A6
Monk Soham Suffk 90 F2
Monkspath Solhll 98 E8
Monks Risborough Bucks 67 K6
Monksthorpe Lincs 137 H6
Monk Street Essex 70 F2
Monkswood Mons 62 D6
Monkton Devon 14 E2
Monkton Kent 41 J2
Monkton S Ayrs 196 D5
Monkton S Tyne 181 H6
Monkton V Glam 42 D7
Monkton Combe BaNES 45 M6
Monkton Deverill Wilts 32 E3
Monkton Farleigh Wilts 46 A6
Monkton Heathfield Somset 30 C5
Monkton Up Wimborne Dorset 33 H8
Monkton Wyld Dorset 15 H3
Monkwearmouth Sundld 181 K7
Monkwood Hants 35 K5
Monmore Green Wolves 97 L4
Monmouth Mons 63 G4
Monnington on Wye Herefs 79 L6
Monreith D & G 173 J6
Montacute Somset 31 H7
Montcliffe Bolton 139 K5
Montford Shrops 112 F8
Montford Bridge Shrops 113 G8
Montgarrie Abers 255 L8
Montgomery Powys 94 F4
Monton Salfd 140 A7
Montrose Angus 235 H4
Mont Saint Guern 9 i3
Monxton Hants 34 C2
Monyash Derbys 132 C6
Monymusk Abers 256 C8
Monzie P & K 220 F2
Moodiesburn N Lans 209 J5
Moonzie Fife 222 F4
Moor Allerton Leeds 150 D8
Moorbath Dorset 15 K4
Moorby Lincs 136 E6
Moorcot Herefs 79 L4
Moor Crichel Dorset 17 K1
Moordown Bmouth 17 L4
Moore Halton 130 B3
Moor End C Beds 68 B3
Moor End Calder 141 G2
Moor End Devon 12 F1
Moorend Gloucs 63 L6
Moor End Lancs 147 G6
Moor End N York 151 J8
Moorends Donc 143 H4
Moorgreen Hants 35 G7
Moor Green Herts 69 J2
Moorgreen Notts 116 E2
Moorhall Derbys 132 F5
Moorhampton Herefs 79 M6
Moorhead C Brad 149 L8
Moor Head Leeds 141 K2
Moorhouse Cumb 177 H8
Moorhouse Cumb 177 K7
Moorhouse Donc 142 D5
Moorhouse Notts 134 E6
Moorhouse Bank Surrey 51 L8
Moorland Somset 30 E4
Moorlinch Somset 30 F3
Moor Monkton N York 151 H4
Moor Row Cumb 164 D7
Moor Row Cumb 165 H1
Moorsholm R & Cl 170 F7
Moorside Dorset 32 D7
Moor Side Lancs 138 E1
Moor Side Lancs 147 K8
Moorside Leeds 150 C8
Moor Side Lincs 136 E8
Moorside Oldham 140 E6
Moorstock Kent 40 E7
Moor Street Birm 98 C6
Moor Street Medway 53 H6
Moorswater Cnwll 5 M2
Moorthorpe Wakefd 142 C5
Moortown Devon 12 C7
Moortown Hants 18 A3
Moortown IoW 19 G7
Moortown Leeds 150 D7
Moortown Lincs 144 D7
Moortown Wrekin 113 K7
Morangie Highld 263 K3
Morar Highld 237 K2
Moray Crematorium Moray 267 H4
Morborne Cambs 102 C5
Morchard Bishop Devon 13 H1
Morcombelake Dorset 15 J4
Morcott Rutlnd 101 K3
Morda Shrops 112 D6
Morden Dorset 17 H3
Morden Gt Lon 51 H5
Mordiford Herefs 80 D7
Mordon Dur 169 J5
More Shrops 95 H5
Morebath Devon 29 G6
Morebattle Border 189 K1
Morecambe Lancs 147 H3
Moredon Swindn 47 H2
Morefield Highld 261 J1
Morehall Kent 41 G7
Moreleigh Devon 7 L4
Morenish P & K 231 H8
Moresby Parks Cumb 164 C6
Morestead Hants 35 G6
Moreton Dorset 16 F5
Moreton Essex 70 D5
Moreton Herefs 80 C2
Moreton Oxon 67 G6
Moreton Staffs 114 B8
Moreton Staffs 115 J5
Moreton Wirral 129 G2
Moreton Corbet Shrops 113 J6
Moretonhampstead Devon 13 H5
Moreton-in-Marsh Gloucs 65 J1
Moreton Jeffries Herefs 80 E5
Moretonmill Shrops 113 J7
Moreton Morrell Warwks 83 H4
Moreton on Lugg Herefs 80 C6
Moreton Paddox Warwks 83 H4
Moreton Pinkney Nhants 84 B5
Moreton Say Shrops 113 K4
Moreton Valence Gloucs 63 M5
Morfa Cerdgn 76 B4
Morfa Bychan Gwynd 109 K4
Morfa Dinlle Gwynd 125 H8
Morfa Glas Neath 60 C6
Morfa Nefyn Gwynd 108 E3
Morganstown Cardif 43 H5
Morgan's Vale Wilts 33 L6
Morham E Loth 212 C5
Moriah Cerdgn 92 D7
Morland Cumb 166 E6
Morley Ches E 130 F3
Morley Derbys 116 C3
Morley Dur 168 E5
Morley Leeds 141 L2
Morley Green Ches E 130 F3
Morley St Botolph Norfk 106 B3
Mornick Cnwll 11 L8
Morningside C Edin 211 H5
Morningside N Lans 209 L7
Morningthorpe Norfk 106 E5
Morpeth Nthumb 180 F2
Morphie Abers 235 H3
Morrey Staffs 115 J7
Morridge Side Staffs 115 G1
Morriston Swans 57 J5
Morston Norfk 121 M3
Mortehoe Devon 27 H2
Morthen Rothm 133 J2
Mortimer W Berk 49 G6
Mortimer Common W Berk 49 G6
Mortimer's Cross Herefs 80 A3
Mortimer West End Hants 48 F6
Mortlake Gt Lon 51 G4
Mortlake Crematorium Gt Lon 51 G4
Morton Cumb 166 B3
Morton Cumb 177 L7
Morton Derbys 133 H7
Morton IoW 19 K6
Morton Lincs 118 E6
Morton Lincs 134 F1
Morton Notts 117 J1
Morton Shrops 112 D6
Morton Hall Lincs 135 H7
Mortonhall Crematorium C Edin 211 J5
Morton-on-Swale N York 160 D4
Morton on the Hill Norfk 122 C8
Morton Tinmouth Dur 168 F6
Morvah Cnwll 2 B4
Morval Cnwll 6 B3
Morvich Highld 248 F7
Morville Shrops 96 F4
Morville Heath Shrops 96 F4
Morwenstow Cnwll 26 C7
Mosborough Sheff 133 H3
Moscow E Ayrs 196 F3
Mose Shrops 97 G5
Mosedale Cumb 165 K4
Moseley Birm 98 D6
Moseley Wolves 97 L4
Moseley Worcs 81 J3
Moses Gate Bolton 139 L6
Moss Ag & B 224 B6
Moss Donc 142 F5
Moss Wrexhm 112 D1
Mossat Abers 255 K7
Mossbank Shet 281 e4
Moss Bank St Hel 139 G8
Mossbay Cumb 164 C5
Mossblown S Ayrs 196 D6
Mossbrow Traffd 130 D2
Mossburnford Border 189 H3
Mossdale D & G 175 G1
Mossdale E Ayrs 184 D2
Moss Edge Lancs 147 H7
Moss End Ches E 130 D4
Mossend N Lans 209 K7
Mosser Mains Cumb 164 F5
Mossley Ches E 131 H7
Mossley Tamesd 140 E7
Mosspaul Hotel Border 188 C6
Moss Side Cumb 177 G8
Moss-side Highld 253 G1
Moss Side Lancs 138 D2
Moss Side Sefton 138 D7
Mosstodloch Moray 267 G4
Mossyard D & G 174 E4
Mossy Lea Lancs 139 G5
Mosterton Dorset 15 K2
Moston Manch 140 C7
Moston Shrops 113 J6
Moston Green Ches E 130 E7
Mostyn Flints 128 E4
Motcombe Dorset 32 E6
Mothecombe Devon 7 H5
Motherby Cumb 166 A5
Motherwell N Lans 209 K7
Motspur Park Gt Lon 51 G5
Mottingham Gt Lon 51 L4
Mottisfont Hants 34 D5
Mottistone IoW 18 F7
Mottram in Longdendale Tamesd 140 F8
Mottram St Andrew Ches E 131 G4
Mouilpied Guern 9 j3
Mouldsworth Ches W 129 L5
Moulin P & K 232 D3
Moulsecoomb Br & H 22 E6
Moulsford Oxon 48 E2
Moulsoe M Keyn 85 H7
Moultavie Highld 263 H5
Moulton Ches W 130 C5
Moulton Lincs 119 J6
Moulton N York 160 C2
Moulton Nhants 84 F2
Moulton Suffk 88 D2
Moulton V Glam 43 G7
Moulton Chapel Lincs 119 J7
Moulton St Mary Norfk 107 H2
Moulton Seas End Lincs 119 K6
Mount Cnwll 4 C4
Mount Cnwll 5 K1
Mount Kirk 141 H4
Mountain C Brad 141 G2
Mountain Ash Rhondd 61 G7
Mountain Cross Border 199 K4
Mountain Street Kent 40 E5
Mount Ambrose Cnwll 4 B6
Mount Bures Essex 89 H8
Mountfield E Susx 24 D3
Mountgerald House Highld 263 G7
Mount Hawke Cnwll 4 B5
Mount Hermon Cnwll 3 H7
Mountjoy Cnwll 4 E3
Mount Lothian Mdloth 200 C2
Mountnessing Essex 70 F7
Mounton Mons 63 G8
Mount Pleasant Ches E 131 G8
Mount Pleasant Derbys 115 M8
Mount Pleasant Derbys 116 B2
Mount Pleasant Dur 169 H4
Mount Pleasant E R Yk 153 L7
Mount Pleasant E Susx 23 G4
Mount Pleasant Norfk 105 K4
Mount Pleasant Suffk 88 E5
Mount Pleasant Worcs 82 B2
Mountsett Crematorium Dur 180 E7
Mountsorrel Leics 116 F8
Mount Sorrel Wilts 33 H6
Mount Tabor Calder 141 G2
Mousehill Surrey 36 E3
Mousehole Cnwll 2 D5
Mouswald D & G 176 E4
Mow Cop Ches E 131 G8
Mowhaugh Border 189 L2
Mowmacre Hill C Leic 100 D2
Mowsley Leics 100 E5
Moy Highld 240 D7
Moy Highld 252 E5
Moyle Highld 248 D7
Moylegrove Pembks 75 J3
Muasdale Ag & B 205 L8
Muchalls Abers 245 K5
Much Birch Herefs 63 G1
Much Cowarne Herefs 80 E6
Much Dewchurch Herefs 62 F1
Muchelney Somset 30 F6
Muchelney Ham Somset 31 G6
Much Hadham Herts 70 B3
Much Hoole Lancs 138 F3
Much Hoole Town Lancs 138 F3
Muchlarnick Cnwll 5 L3
Much Marcle Herefs 80 F8
Much Wenlock Shrops 96 E3
Muck Highld 236 E4

Mucking Thurr 52 E3
Muckingford Thurr 52 E3
Muckleford Dorset 16 C4
Mucklestone Staffs 114 A4
Muckley Shrops 96 E4
Muckton Lincs 137 G3
Muddiford Devon 27 K3
Muddles Green E Susx 23 J4
Mudeford Dorset 18 B5
Mudford Somset 31 J7
Mudford Sock Somset 31 J7
Mudgley Somset 31 G2
Mud Row Kent 53 M4
Mugdock Stirlg 208 F4
Mugeary Highld 246 F1
Mugginton Derbys 115 M3
Muggintonlane End Derbys 115 M3
Muggleswick Dur 168 D1
Muirden Abers 268 C5
Muirdrum Angus 234 E7
Muiresk Abers 268 C6
Muirhead Angus 233 M8
Muirhead Fife 222 D6
Muirhead N Lans 209 J5
Muirkirk E Ayrs 197 K5
Muirmill Stirlg 209 J2
Muir of Fowlis Abers 244 C1
Muir of Miltonduff Moray 266 D4
Muir of Ord Highld 250 F2
Muirshearlich Highld 239 J7
Muirtack Abers 257 J4
Muirton P & K 221 G5
Muirton Mains Highld 250 E1
Muirton of Ardblair P & K 233 J6
Muker N York 158 F3
Mulbarton Norfk 106 D3
Mulben Moray 267 G6
Mulfra Cnwll 2 C4
Mull Ag & B 227 H5
Mullacott Cross Devon 27 J2
Mullion Cnwll 3 H7
Mullion Cove Cnwll 3 H7
Mumby Lincs 137 K5
Munderfield Row Herefs 80 F5
Munderfield Stocks Herefs 80 F5
Mundesley Norfk 123 G4
Mundford Norfk 104 F4
Mundham Norfk 107 G4
Mundon Hill Essex 72 C6
Mundy Bois Kent 40 B6
Mungrisdale Cumb 165 L4
Munlochy Highld 251 H1
Munnoch N Ayrs 195 L1
Munsley Herefs 80 F7
Munslow Shrops 96 C6
Murchington Devon 13 G5
Murcot Worcs 82 C7
Murcott Oxon 66 E4
Murcott Wilts 46 D1
Murkle Highld 279 L3
Murlaggan Highld 239 G5
Murrell Green Hants 49 H7
Murroes Angus 234 C8
Murrow Cambs 103 H2
Mursley Bucks 67 K2
Murston Kent 40 B2
Murthill Angus 234 C4
Murthly P & K 233 G7
Murton C York 151 K5
Murton Cumb 167 G6
Murton Dur 169 K1
Murton N Tyne 181 H5
Murton Nthumb 202 F3
Musbury Devon 15 G4
Muscoates N York 162 B6
Musselburgh E Loth 211 K4
Muston Leics 117 L4
Muston N York 163 K6
Mustow Green Worcs 97 K8
Muswell Hill Gt Lon 51 H1
Mutehill D & G 175 H5
Mutford Suffk 107 K5
Muthill P & K 220 F4
Mutterton Devon 14 B2
Muxton Wrekin 114 A8
Mybster Highld 279 L5
Myddfai Carmth 59 L3
Myddle Shrops 113 G6
Mydroilyn Cerdgn 76 E4
Myerscough Lancs 147 K7
Mylor Cnwll 3 L4
Mylor Bridge Cnwll 3 K4
Mynachlog ddu Pembks 75 K6
Myndd-llan Flints 128 D5
Myndtown Shrops 95 J5
Mynydd-bach Mons 62 F8
Mynydd-Bach Swans 57 J5
Mynydd Buch Cerdgn 92 F8
Mynyddgarreg Carmth 56 D3
Mynydd Isa Flints 128 F7
Mynydd Llandygai Gwynd 126 B6
Mynytho Gwynd 108 E5
Myrebird Abers 245 G4
Myredykes Border 189 G6
Mytchett Surrey 49 L7
Mytholm Calder 140 E2
Mytholmroyd Calder 140 F3
Mythop Lancs 138 D1
Myton-on-Swale N York 150 F3

N

Naast Highld 260 C3
Nab's Head Lancs 139 J2
Na Buirgh W Isls 282 d6
Naburn C York 151 J6
Nab Wood Crematorium C Brad 149 L8
Naccolt Kent 40 D6
Nackington Kent 40 F4
Nacton Suffk 90 F7
Nafferton E R Yk 153 G4
Nag's Head Gloucs 64 C7
Nailbridge Gloucs 63 J4
Nailsbourne Somset 30 B5
Nailsea N Som 44 F5
Nailstone Leics 99 L2
Nailsworth Gloucs 64 B7
Nairn Highld 264 D8
Nalderswood Surrey 37 K2
Nancegollan Cnwll 3 G4
Nancledra Cnwll 2 D4
Nanhoron Gwynd 108 E5
Nannerch Flints 128 E5
Nanpantan Leics 116 E8
Nanpean Cnwll 4 F4
Nanquidno Cnwll 2 B5
Nanstallon Cnwll 5 H2
Nant-ddu Powys 60 F4
Nanternis Cerdgn 76 C4
Nantgaredig Carmth 58 F4
Nantgarw Rhondd 43 H4
Nant-glas Powys 78 D2
Nantglyn Denbgs 127 K7
Nantgwyn Powys 93 L8
Nant Gwynant Gwynd 110 B2
Nantlle Gwynd 109 J1
Nantmawr Shrops 112 C6
Nantmel Powys 78 E2
Nantmor Gwynd 109 L2
Nant Peris Gwynd 126 B7
Nantwich Ches E 113 L1
Nant-y-Bwch Blae G 61 H5
Nant-y-caws Carmth 58 E5
Nant-y-derry Mons 62 C6
Nantyffyllon Brdgnd 42 C3
Nantyglo Blae G 61 K5
Nant-y-gollen Shrops 112 C5
Nant-y-moel Brdgnd 42 D3
Nant-y-pandy Conwy 126 D5
Naphill Bucks 67 K7
Napleton Worcs 81 K5
Nappa N York 148 E5
Napton on the Hill Warwks 83 L3
Narberth Pembks 55 J4
Narborough Leics 100 C4
Narborough Norfk 104 E1
Narkurs Cnwll 6 C4
Nasareth Gwynd 109 H2
Naseby Nhants 100 F7
Nash Bucks 84 F8
Nash Gt Lon 51 L6
Nash Herefs 79 K3
Nash Newpt 44 D2
Nash Shrops 80 E1
Nash End Worcs 97 H7
Nash Lee Bucks 67 K5
Nash's Green Hants 35 K2
Nash Street Kent 52 D5
Nassington Nhants 102 B4
Nastend Gloucs 64 A6
Nasty Herts 69 K2
Nateby Cumb 158 D1
Nateby Lancs 147 J7
Natland Cumb 157 H5
Naughton Suffk 89 L5
Naunton Gloucs 65 G2
Naunton Worcs 81 K7
Naunton Beauchamp Worcs 81 M5
Navenby Lincs 135 K8
Navestock Essex 70 D7
Navestock Side Essex 70 E7
Navidale House Hotel Highld 274 D5
Navity Highld 264 B7
Nawton N York 161 L5
Nayland Suffk 89 K8
Nazeing Essex 69 L6
Nazeing Gate Essex 69 L6
Neacroft Hants 18 B4
Neal's Green Warwks 99 J6
Neap Shet 281 e5
Near Cotton Staffs 115 H2
Near Sawrey Cumb 156 E3
Neasden Gt Lon 51 G2
Neasham Darltn 169 J8
Neath Neath 57 L5
Neatham Hants 35 M3
Neatishead Norfk 123 G7
Nebo Cerdgn 77 G2
Nebo Conwy 127 G8
Nebo Gwynd 109 H2
Nebo IoA 125 H2
Necton Norfk 105 H2
Nedd Highld 270 F2
Nedderton Nthumb 180 F2
Nedging Suffk 89 K5
Nedging Tye Suffk 89 L5
Needham Norfk 106 E7
Needham Market Suffk 90 C4
Needham Street Suffk 88 E2
Needingworth Cambs 87 G1
Neen Savage Shrops 96 F7
Neen Sollars Shrops 80 F1
Neenton Shrops 96 E6
Nefyn Gwynd 108 E3
Neilston E Rens 208 E7
Nelson Caerph 43 H3
Nelson Lancs 148 F8
Nemphlar S Lans 198 E4
Nempnett Thrubwell BaNES 45 G7
Nenthall Cumb 167 H2
Nenthead Cumb 167 H2
Nenthorn Border 201 L5
Neopardy Devon 13 J3
Nep Town W Susx 22 B4
Nercwys Flints 128 F7
Nereabolls Ag & B 204 C5
Nerston S Lans 209 H7
Nesbit Nthumb 202 F6
Nesfield N York 149 K6
Ness Ches W 129 G4
Nesscliffe Shrops 112 F7
Neston Ches W 129 G4
Neston Wilts 46 B5
Netchwood Shrops 96 E5
Nether Alderley Ches E 131 G4
Netheravon Wilts 33 K1
Nether Blainslie Border 201 H4
Netherbrae Abers 268 E4
Nether Broughton Leics 117 J6
Netherburn S Lans 198 C4
Netherbury Dorset 15 L3
Netherby Cumb 177 L4
Netherby N York 150 D6
Nether Cerne Dorset 16 C3
Nethercleuch D & G 176 F2
Nether Compton Dorset 31 K7
Nethercote Warwks 83 M2
Nethercott Devon 11 L3
Nethercott Devon 27 H3
Nether Crimond Abers 256 E7
Nether Dallachy Moray 267 G3
Netherend Gloucs 63 H7
Nether Exe Devon 13 L3
Netherfield E Susx 24 C3
Netherfield Leics 117 G8
Netherfield Notts 117 G3
Nether Fingland S Lans 186 D4
Nethergate N Linc 143 J7
Nethergate Norfk 122 B5
Netherhampton Wilts 33 K5
Nether Handley Derbys 133 H4
Nether Handwick Angus 234 B7
Nether Haugh Rothm 142 C8
Netherhay Dorset 15 J2
Nether Headon Notts 134 E4
Nether Heage Derbys 116 B2
Nether Heyford Nhants 84 C3
Nether Howcleugh S Lans 186 F4
Nether Kellet Lancs 147 K2
Nether Kinmundy Abers 257 K3
Netherland Green Staffs 115 H5
Nether Langwith Notts 133 K5
Netherlaw D & G 175 J6
Netherley Abers 245 J5
Nethermill D & G 176 D1
Nethermuir Abers 257 G3
Netherne-on-the-Hill Surrey 51 J7
Netheroyd Hill Kirk 141 H4
Nether Padley Derbys 132 E4
Netherplace E Rens 208 E7
Nether Poppleton C York 151 J5
Nether Row Cumb 165 K3
Netherseal Derbys 99 H1
Nether Silton N York 161 G4
Nether Skyborry Shrops 95 G8
Nether Stowey Somset 30 B3
Nether Street Essex 70 E5
Netherstreet Wilts 46 E6
Netherthong Kirk 141 H6
Netherthorpe Derbys 133 J5
Netherton Angus 234 E4
Netherton Devon 13 L8
Netherton Dudley 97 L5
Netherton Hants 48 A7
Netherton Herefs 63 G2
Netherton Kirk 141 H5
Netherton N Lans 209 K8
Netherton Nthumb 190 E4
Netherton Oxon 66 B7
Netherton P & K 233 H5
Netherton Shrops 97 G6
Netherton Stirlg 208 F3
Netherton Wakefd 141 L4
Netherton Worcs 82 A7
Nethertown Cumb 155 H1
Nethertown Highld 280 E1
Nethertown Lancs 148 C8
Nethertown Staffs 115 J8
Netherurd Border 199 J4
Nether Wallop Hants 34 C4
Nether Wasdale Cumb 155 L2
Nether Welton Cumb 165 K2
Nether Westcote Gloucs 65 J3
Nether Whitacre Warwks 99 G5
Nether Whitecleuch S Lans 186 B2
Nether Winchendon Bucks 67 H4
Netherwitton Nthumb 191 G8
Nethy Bridge Highld 253 J7
Netley Hants 19 G2
Netley Marsh Hants 34 D8
Nettlebed Oxon 49 G2
Nettlebridge Somset 31 L1
Nettlecombe Dorset 15 L3
Nettlecombe IoW 19 J8
Nettleden Herts 68 C5
Nettleham Lincs 135 K4
Nettlestead Kent 39 H3
Nettlestead Green Kent 39 H3
Nettlestone IoW 19 L5
Nettlesworth Dur 169 H1
Nettleton Lincs 144 E7
Nettleton Wilts 46 B3
Nettleton Shrub Wilts 46 B3
Netton Devon 7 G5
Netton Wilts 33 K3
Neuadd Carmth 59 K4
Neuadd-ddu Powys 93 K8
Nevendon Essex 53 G1
Nevern Pembks 75 J4
Nevill Holt Leics 101 H4
New Abbey D & G 176 C5
New Aberdour Abers 268 F3
New Addington Gt Lon 51 K6
Newall Leeds 150 B6
New Alresford Hants 35 J4
New Alyth P & K 233 K6
Newark C Pete 102 E3
Newark Ork 275 f2
Newark-on-Trent Notts 117 L1
New Arram E R Yk 153 G7
Newarthill N Lans 209 L7
New Ash Green Kent 52 D6
New Balderton Notts 117 L1
Newbarn Kent 40 F7
New Barn Kent 52 D5
New Barnet Gt Lon 69 H7
New Barton Nhants 85 G2
Newbattle Mdloth 211 K6
New Bewick Nthumb 190 F2
Newbie D & G 177 G6
Newbiggin Cumb 146 E2
Newbiggin Cumb 155 K4
Newbiggin Cumb 166 B5
Newbiggin Cumb 166 D1
Newbiggin Cumb 166 E5
Newbiggin Dur 167 L5
Newbiggin Dur 168 F1
Newbiggin N York 159 G4
Newbiggin N York 159 H5
Newbiggin-by-the-Sea Nthumb 181 H1
Newbigging Angus 233 L7
Newbigging Angus 234 C7
Newbigging Angus 234 D8
Newbigging S Lans 199 H4
Newbiggin-on-Lune Cumb 158 C2
New Bilton Warwks 100 B8
Newbold Derbys 133 G5
Newbold Leics 116 C7
Newbold on Avon Warwks 100 B7
Newbold on Stour Warwks 82 F6
Newbold Pacey Warwks 83 G4
Newbold Revel Warwks 99 M7
Newbold Verdon Leics 99 L3
New Bolingbroke Lincs 136 F8
Newborough C Pete 102 D2
Newborough IoA 125 G6
Newborough Staffs 115 J6

Newbottle Nhants 83 M7
Newbottle Sundld 181 H8
New Boultham Lincs 135 K5
Newbourne Suffk 91 G6
New Bradwell M Keyn 84 F7
New Brampton Derbys 133 G5
New Brancepeth Dur 169 G2
Newbridge C Edin 210 F4
Newbridge Caerph 43 K2
Newbridge Cerdgn 76 F3
Newbridge Cnwll 2 C5
Newbridge Cnwll 4 C6
Newbridge D & G 176 C3
Newbridge Hants 34 C7
Newbridge IoW 18 F6
New Bridge N York 162 D5
Newbridge Oxon 66 B6
Newbridge Wrexhm 112 D3
Newbridge Green Worcs 81 J7
Newbridge-on-Usk Mons 62 D8
Newbridge on Wye Powys 78 E4
New Brighton Flints 128 F6
New Brighton Wirral 129 G1
New Brinsley Notts 116 D2
New Brotton R & Cl 171 G6
Newbrough Nthumb 179 K5
New Broughton Wrexhm 112 D1
New Buckenham Norfk 106 B5
Newbuildings Devon 13 J2
Newburgh Abers 257 J6
Newburgh Abers 269 H4
Newburgh Fife 222 C3
Newburgh Lancs 138 F5
Newburgh Priory N York 161 J7
Newburn N u Ty 180 E6
New Bury Bolton 139 L6
Newbury Somset 32 B1
Newbury W Berk 48 C5
Newbury Wilts 32 D3
Newbury Park Gt Lon 51 L1
Newby Cumb 166 E6
Newby Lancs 148 E6
Newby N York 148 C2
Newby N York 163 J4
Newby N York 170 C8
Newby Bridge Cumb 156 E5
Newby Cross Cumb 177 L8
Newby East Cumb 178 B7
Newby Head Cumb 166 E6
New Byth Abers 268 E5
Newby West Cumb 177 L8
Newby Wiske N York 160 E5
Newcastle Mons 62 F4
Newcastle Shrops 95 G7
Newcastle Emlyn Carmth 76 B7
Newcastleton Border 178 C2
Newcastle-under-Lyme Staffs 114 D2
Newcastle upon Tyne N u Ty 181 G6
Newchapel Pembks 75 L4
Newchapel Staffs 131 G8
Newchapel Surrey 38 A5
Newchurch Blae G 61 J5
Newchurch Herefs 79 L5
Newchurch IoW 19 J6
Newchurch Kent 25 K1
Newchurch Mons 62 F7
Newchurch Powys 79 H5
Newchurch Staffs 115 J7
Newchurch in Pendle Lancs 148 E7
New Costessey Norfk 106 D2
New Cowper Cumb 164 F2
Newcraighall C Edin 211 K4
New Crofton Wakefd 142 B4
New Cross Cerdgn 92 D8
New Cross Gt Lon 51 K4
New Cross Somset 30 F7
New Cumnock E Ayrs 197 J8
New Cut E Susx 24 E4
New Deer Abers 268 F6
New Delaval Nthumb 181 H3
New Delph Oldham 140 F6
New Denham Bucks 50 D2
Newdigate Surrey 37 J3
New Duston Nhants 84 D3
New Earswick C York 151 K5
New Eastwood Notts 116 D2
New Edlington Donc 142 E7
New Elgin Moray 266 E4
New Ellerby E R Yk 153 J7
Newell Green Br For 49 L5
New Eltham Gt Lon 51 L4
New End Worcs 82 C3
Newenden Kent 24 F2
New England C Pete 102 D3
New England Essex 88 E6
Newent Gloucs 63 L2
New Farnley Leeds 141 L2
New Ferry Wirral 129 H3
Newfield Dur 169 G4
Newfield Dur 181 G8
Newfield Highld 264 B4
New Fletton C Pete 102 D4
Newfound Hants 48 E8
New Fryston Wakefd 142 C2
Newgale Pembks 54 D2
New Galloway D & G 185 G7
Newgate Norfk 122 A3
Newgate Street Herts 69 J6
New Gilston Fife 223 G5
New Grimsby IoS 10 b2
Newhall Ches E 113 K2
Newhall Derbys 115 M7
Newham Nthumb 203 K7
New Hartley Nthumb 181 H3
Newhaven C Edin 211 H4
Newhaven Derbys 132 C7
Newhaven E Susx 23 G7
New Haw Surrey 50 D6
New Hedges Pembks 55 K6
New Herrington Sundld 181 H8
Newhey Rochdl 140 E5
New Holkham Norfk 121 J4
New Holland N Linc 144 D3
Newholm N York 171 K8
New Houghton Derbys 133 K6
New Houghton Norfk 121 H6
Newhouse N Lans 209 L6
New Houses N York 158 D7
New Houses Wigan 139 H7
New Hutton Cumb 157 J4
New Hythe Kent 52 F7
Newick E Susx 22 F3
Newingreen Kent 40 F8
Newington Kent 41 G7
Newington Kent 53 J6
Newington Oxon 66 F7
Newington Shrops 95 K6
Newington Bagpath Gloucs 64 B8
New Inn Carmth 58 E2
New Inn Torfn 62 C7
New Invention Shrops 95 H8
New Lakenham Norfk 106 E2
New Lanark S Lans 198 E4
Newland C KuH 144 D2
Newland Cumb 156 D6
Newland E R Yk 143 K2
Newland Gloucs 63 H5
Newland N York 143 H3
Newland Oxon 66 A5
Newland Somset 28 E3
Newland Worcs 81 H5
Newlandrig Mdloth 211 L6
Newlands Border 188 E7
Newlands Cumb 165 K3
Newlands Nthumb 180 D7
Newlands of Dundurcas Moray 266 F6
New Lane Lancs 138 E5
New Lane End Warrtn 130 C1
New Langholm D & G 177 K2
New Leake Lincs 137 G8
New Leeds Abers 269 H5
New Lodge Barns 142 A6
New Longton Lancs 139 G3
New Luce D & G 172 F2
Newlyn Cnwll 2 D5
Newlyn East Cnwll 4 D3
Newmachar Abers 256 F7
Newmains N Lans 209 L7
New Malden Gt Lon 51 G5
Newman's End Essex 70 D4
Newman's Green Suffk 89 H6
Newmarket Suffk 88 C3
Newmarket W Isls 282 g3
New Marske R & Cl 170 E6
New Marston Oxon 66 D5
New Marton Shrops 112 E4
New Mill Abers 245 H7
Newmill Border 188 D4
New Mill Cnwll 2 D4
New Mill Herts 68 A4
New Mill Kirk 141 J6
Newmill Moray 267 J5
Newmillerdam Wakefd 141 M4
Newmill of Inshewan Angus 234 C3
Newmills C Edin 211 G5
New Mills Cnwll 4 E4
New Mills Derbys 131 K3
Newmills Fife 210 D2
Newmills Mons 63 G5
New Mills Powys 94 D3
Newmiln P & K 221 L1
Newmilns E Ayrs 197 G3
New Milton Hants 18 C4
New Mistley Essex 73 H1
New Moat Pembks 75 H7
Newnes Shrops 112 F5
Newney Green Essex 71 G5
Newnham Gloucs 63 K5
Newnham Hants 49 H8
Newnham Herts 86 E7
Newnham Kent 40 B4
Newnham Nhants 84 B3
Newnham Worcs 80 E2
New Ollerton Notts 134 D6
New Oscott Birm 98 E4
New Pitsligo Abers 268 F5
New Polzeath Cnwll 10 C6
Newport Cnwll 11 L5
Newport Dorset 17 G4
Newport E R Yk 143 L2
Newport Essex 87 L8
Newport Gloucs 63 K7
Newport Highld 274 F3
Newport IoW 19 H6
Newport Newpt 44 C1
Newport Norfk 123 K8
Newport Pembks 75 H4
Newport Wrekin 114 A7
Newport-on-Tay Fife 223 G2
Newport Pagnell M Keyn 85 G6
Newpound Common W Susx 37 G5
New Prestwick S Ayrs 196 C6
New Quay Cerdgn 76 D3
Newquay Cnwll 4 D3
New Quay Essex 72 F2
New Rackheath Norfk 106 F1
New Radnor Powys 79 H3
New Rent Cumb 166 B3
New Ridley Nthumb 180 C7
New Road Side N York 149 H7
New Romney Kent 25 K2
New Rossington Donc 143 G8
New Row Cerdgn 92 F8
New Row Lancs 148 A8
New Sauchie Clacks 220 F8
Newsbank Ches E 131 G6
Newseat Abers 256 C5
Newsham Lancs 147 K8
Newsham N York 160 E5
Newsham N York 168 E8
Newsham Nthumb 181 H3
New Sharlston Wakefd 142 B4
Newsholme E R Yk 143 H2
Newsholme Lancs 148 E5
New Shoreston Nthumb 203 K6
New Silksworth Sundld 181 J8
New Skelton R & Cl 170 F7
Newsome Kirk 141 J5
New Somerby Lincs 118 B4
New Southgate Crematorium Gt Lon 69 H8
New Springs Wigan 139 J6
Newstead Border 201 H6
Newstead Notts 116 E1
Newstead Nthumb 203 J7
New Stevenston N Lans 209 K7
New Street Herefs 79 L4
New Swannington Leics 116 D8
Newthorpe N York 142 D1
Newthorpe Notts 116 E2
New Thundersley Essex 53 G1
Newtimber W Susx 22 D4
Newtoft Lincs 135 L2
Newton Ag & B 217 G7
Newton Border 189 G2
Newton Brdgnd 42 C6
Newton C Beds 86 E6
Newton Cambs 87 J5
Newton Cambs 119 M8
Newton Cardif 43 K6
Newton Ches W 129 J6
Newton Ches W 129 L7
Newton Ches W 129 M4
Newton Cumb 146 D2
Newton Derbys 133 J7
Newton Herefs 79 L1
Newton Herefs 79 L8
Newton Herefs 80 C4
Newton Highld 251 G2
Newton Highld 252 D2
Newton Highld 263 L6
Newton Highld 280 D6
Newton Lancs 147 G8
Newton Lancs 157 J7
Newton Lincs 118 D4
Newton Mdloth 211 K5
Newton Moray 266 C3
Newton Moray 267 G4
Newton N York 152 D1
Newton Nhants 101 J6
Newton Norfk 121 H8
Newton Notts 117 J3
Newton Nthumb 180 C6
Newton Nthumb 190 D5
Newton S Lans 198 F6
Newton S Lans 209 H6
Newton Sandw 98 C4
Newton Shrops 112 F4
Newton Somset 29 K3
Newton Staffs 115 G6
Newton Suffk 89 J7
Newton W Loth 210 E3
Newton Warwks 100 C7
Newton Wilts 34 B6
Newton Abbot Devon 13 K8
Newton Arlosh Cumb 177 G7
Newton Aycliffe Dur 169 H5
Newton Bewley Hartpl 170 B5
Newton Blossomville M Keyn 85 H5
Newton Bromswold Nhants 85 K2
Newton Burgoland Leics 99 K2
Newton-by-the-Sea Nthumb 203 L8
Newton by Toft Lincs 135 L2
Newton Ferrers Cnwll 6 C2
Newton Ferrers Devon 7 G5
Newton Ferry W Isls 282 c7
Newton Flotman Norfk 106 E4
Newtongrange Mdloth 211 K6
Newton Green Mons 45 G1
Newton Harcourt Leics 100 E4
Newton Heath Manch 140 C7
Newtonhill Abers 245 K5
Newton Hill Wakefd 141 M3
Newton-in-Bowland Lancs 148 B5
Newton Kyme N York 151 G6
Newton-le-Willows N York 160 B5
Newton-le-Willows St Hel 139 H8
Newtonloan Mdloth 211 K6
Newton Longville Bucks 67 K1
Newton Mearns E Rens 208 F7
Newtonmill Angus 234 F3
Newtonmore Highld 241 J4
Newton Morrell N York 160 C1
Newton Mountain Pembks 55 G5
Newton Mulgrave N York 171 H7
Newton of Balcanquhal P & K 222 B5
Newton of Balcormo Fife 223 J6
Newton on Ouse N York 151 H4
Newton-on-Rawcliffe N York 162 E4
Newton on the Hill Shrops 113 H7
Newton-on-the-Moor Nthumb 191 H5
Newton on Trent Lincs 135 G5
Newton Poppleford Devon 14 C5
Newton Purcell Oxon 66 F1
Newton Regis Warwks 99 H2
Newton Reigny Cumb 166 B4
Newton St Cyres Devon 13 K3
Newton St Faith Norfk 122 E8
Newton St Loe BaNES 45 L6
Newton St Petrock Devon 27 G8
Newton Solney Derbys 115 M6
Newton Stacey Hants 34 E3
Newton Stewart D & G 173 K2
Newton Tony Wilts 34 B3
Newton Tracey Devon 27 J5
Newton under Roseberry R & Cl 170 D8
Newton Underwood Nthumb 180 E2
Newton upon Derwent E R Yk 151 M6
Newton Valence Hants 35 L4
Newton Wamphray D & G 187 H7
Newton with Scales Lancs 138 F2
Newtown Blae G 61 J5
Newtown Ches W 129 M4
Newtown Cnwll 2 F5
Newtown Cnwll 11 K7
Newtown Cumb 164 E1
Newtown Cumb 166 C6
Newtown Cumb 177 L6
Newtown Cumb 178 C6
Newtown D & G 185 J1
Newtown Derbys 131 K3
Newtown Devon 14 C3
Newtown Devon 28 D6
Newtown Dorset 15 L2
New Town Dorset 17 K1
New Town Dorset 32 F7
New Town Dorset 33 G7
New Town E Susx 23 H3
Newtown Gloucs 63 K6
Newtown Hants 18 D2
Newtown Hants 35 J8
Newtown Hants 48 C6
Newtown Herefs 80 B4
Newtown Herefs 80 C8
Newtown Herefs 80 E6
Newtown Herefs 81 G7
Newtown Highld 240 B3
Newtown IoW 19 G5
Newtown Lancs 139 G4
New Town Nhants 101 L7
Newtown Nthumb 190 E6
Newtown Nthumb 202 F6
Newtown Nthumb 203 G8
Newtown Poole 17 K4
Newtown Powys 94 D5
Newtown Rhondd 61 G7

Newtown Shrops 112 F7
Newtown Shrops 113 H5
Newtown Somset 30 C8
Newtown Staffs 98 C3
Newtown Staffs 131 H7
Newtown Wigan 139 H6
Newtown Wilts 32 F5
New Town Wilts 47 L4
Newtown Wilts 47 L6
Newtown Worcs 81 K4
Newtown Worcs 98 B7
Newtown-in-St Martin Cnwll 3 J6
Newtown Linford Leics 100 B2
Newtown of Beltrees Rens 208 C7
Newtown St Boswells Border 201 J6
Newtown Unthank Leics 100 B3
New Tredegar Caerph 61 J6
New Trows S Lans 198 D5
New Tupton Derbys 133 H6
Newtyle Angus 233 L7
New Walsoken Cambs 103 K2
New Waltham NE Lin 145 H6
New Whittington Derbys 133 H4
New Winton E Loth 211 M5
New Yatt Oxon 66 A4
Newyears Green Gt Lon 50 D1
Newyork Ag & B 216 F5
New York Lincs 136 D8
New York N Tyne 181 H5
New York N York 150 B3
Nextend Herefs 79 L4
Neyland Pembks 54 F6
Niarbyl IoM 154 b6
Nibley Gloucs 63 K5
Nibley S Glos 45 K3
Nibley Green Gloucs 63 L7
Nicholashayne Devon 29 K7
Nicholaston Swans 56 F7
Nickies Hill Cumb 178 D5
Nidd N York 150 D4
Nigg C Aber 245 L3
Nigg Highld 264 C5
Nigg Ferry Highld 264 B6
Nimlet BaNES 45 L5
Ninebanks Nthumb 179 H8
Nine Elms Swindn 47 G2
Nine Wells Pembks 74 C7
Ninfield E Susx 24 C5
Ningwood IoW 18 F6
Nisbet Border 201 L8
Nisbet Hill Border 202 B3
Niton IoW 19 H8
Nitshill C Glas 208 E7
Noah's Ark Kent 52 C7
Noak Bridge Essex 52 E1
Noak Hill Gt Lon 70 D8
Noblethorpe Barns 141 L6
Nobold Shrops 95 L2
Nobottle Nhants 84 C3
Nocton Lincs 135 L6
Nogdam End Norfk 107 H3
Noke Oxon 66 E4
Nolton Pembks 54 E3
Nolton Haven Pembks 54 D3
No Man's Heath Ches W 113 H2
No Man's Heath Warwks 99 H2
No Man's Land Cnwll 6 B3
Nomansland Devon 28 E8
Nomansland Wilts 34 B7
Noneley Shrops 113 H6
Nonington Kent 41 H5
Nook Cumb 157 H6
Nook Cumb 178 B3
Norbiton Gt Lon 51 G5
Norbreck Bpool 146 F7
Norbridge Herefs 81 G6
Norbury Ches E 113 J2
Norbury Derbys 115 J3
Norbury Gt Lon 51 J5
Norbury Shrops 95 J5
Norbury Staffs 114 B6
Norbury Common Ches E 113 J2
Norbury Junction Staffs 114 B7
Norchard Worcs 81 J2
Norcott Brook Ches W 130 B4
Norcross Lancs 146 F7
Nordelph Norfk 103 L3
Norden Rochdl 140 C5
Nordley Shrops 96 F4
Norham Nthumb 202 D4
Norland Town Calder 141 G3
Norley Ches W 130 B5
Norleywood Hants 18 E4
Norlington E Susx 23 G4
Normanby Lincs 135 K2
Normanby N Linc 143 M4
Normanby N York 162 C6
Normanby R & Cl 170 D7
Normanby le Wold Lincs 136 B1
Norman Cross Cambs 102 D5
Normandy Surrey 50 B8
Norman's Bay E Susx 24 C6
Norman's Green Devon 14 C2
Normanton C Derb 116 B5
Normanton Leics 117 L3
Normanton Lincs 118 B2
Normanton Notts 134 E8
Normanton Rutlnd 101 K2
Normanton Wakefd 142 B3
Normanton Wilts 33 K3
Normanton le Heath Leics 99 K1
Normanton on Soar Notts 116 E7
Normanton on the Wolds Notts 117 G5
Normanton on Trent Notts 134 F6
Normoss Lancs 147 G8
Norney Surrey 36 D2
Norrington Common Wilts 46 C6
Norris Green Cnwll 6 E1
Norris Green Lpool 129 J1
Norris Hill Leics 116 B8
Norristhorpe Kirk 141 K3
Northacre Norfk 105 J4
Northall Bucks 68 B3
Northallerton N York 160 E4
Northall Green Norfk 121 M8
Northam C Sotn 19 G1
Northam Devon 27 H5
Northampton Nhants 84 E3
Northampton Worcs 81 J2
North Anston Rothm 133 K3
North Ascot Br For 49 M5
North Aston Oxon 66 C1
Northaw Herts 69 H6
Northay Somset 30 D8
North Baddesley Hants 34 E6
North Ballachulish Highld 229 G3
North Barrow Somset 31 K5
North Barsham Norfk 121 K4
North Benfleet Essex 53 G1
North Bersted W Susx 20 F6
North Berwick E Loth 212 C2
North Bitchburn Dur 168 F4
North Blyth Nthumb 181 H2
North Boarhunt Hants 19 K2
North Bockhampton Dorset 18 B4
Northborough C Pete 102 C2
Northbourne Kent 41 K5
North Bovey Devon 13 H6
North Bradley Wilts 46 B7
North Brentor Devon 12 C6
North Brewham Somset 32 B3
North Bridge Surrey 36 E3
Northbridge Street E Susx 24 D2
Northbrook Hants 35 G3
Northbrook Oxon 66 D3
North Brook End Cambs 86 F6
North Buckland Devon 27 H3
North Burlingham Norfk 107 H2
North Cadbury Somset 31 K5
North Carlton Lincs 135 J4
North Carlton Notts 134 B3
North Cave E R Yk 143 M1
North Cerney Gloucs 64 E5
North Chailey E Susx 22 F3
Northchapel W Susx 36 E5
North Charford Hants 33 L7
North Charlton Nthumb 191 H2
North Cheam Gt Lon 51 G6
North Cheriton Somset 31 M5
North Chideock Dorset 15 K4
Northchurch Herts 68 B5
North Cliffe E R Yk 152 D8
North Clifton Notts 135 G5
North Close Dur 169 H4
North Cockerington Lincs 137 G2
North Connel Ag & B 228 E8
North Cornelly Brdgnd 42 B5
North Corner Cnwll 3 K7
North Cotes Lincs 145 J7
Northcott Devon 11 L4
Northcott Devon 14 D1
Northcott Devon 29 K8
North Country Cnwll 4 A6
Northcourt Oxon 66 D7
North Cove Suffk 107 K5
North Cowton N York 160 D2
North Crawley M Keyn 85 H6
North Cray Gt Lon 52 A4
North Creake Norfk 121 J4
North Curry Somset 30 D6
North Dalton E R Yk 152 E5
North Deighton N York 150 E5
North Devon Crematorium Devon 27 K4
Northdown Kent 41 L1
North Duffield N York 151 L8
North Duntulm Highld 259 G2
North East Surrey Crematorium Gt Lon 51 G5
Northedge Derbys 133 G6
North Elham Kent 41 G6
North Elkington Lincs 136 E2
North Elmham Norfk 121 L7
North Elmsall Wakefd 142 D5
Northend Bucks 67 H8
North End C Port 19 L3
North End Cumb 177 K7
North End Dorset 32 D5
North End E R Yk 145 H2
North End E R Yk 153 K7
North End Essex 71 G3
North End Hants 33 J7
North End Hants 35 J5
North End Leics 116 F8
North End Lincs 119 H3
North End Lincs 137 H2
North End Lincs 144 D7
North End Lincs 145 J7
North End N Linc 144 E3
North End N Som 44 E5
North End Nhants 85 J2
North End Norfk 105 K5
North End Nthumb 191 G6
North End Sefton 138 C6
North End W Susx 21 G6
North End W Susx 21 J5
Northend Warwks 83 J5
Northenden Manch 131 G2
Northend Woods Bucks 49 L1
North Erradale Highld 260 B4
North Evington C Leic 100 D3
North Fambridge Essex 71 K7
North Ferriby E R Yk 144 B3
Northfield Birm 98 C7
Northfield C Aber 245 K2
Northfield E R Yk 144 C2
Northfields Lincs 102 A2
Northfleet Kent 52 D4
North Frodingham E R Yk 153 H5
North Gorley Hants 33 L8
North Green Norfk 106 E5
North Green Suffk 91 G3
North Green Suffk 91 J2
North Greetwell Lincs 135 K5
North Grimston N York 152 C2
North Halling Medway 52 F6
North Hayling Hants 20 B6
North Hazelrigg Nthumb 203 G6
North Heasley Devon 28 C4
North Heath W Susx 37 G6
North Hele Devon 29 J6
North Hill Cnwll 11 K7
North Hillingdon Gt Lon 50 D2
North Hinksey Village Oxon 66 D6
North Holmwood Surrey 37 J2
North Huish Devon 7 K3
North Hykeham Lincs 135 J6
Northiam E Susx 24 E2
Northill C Beds 86 C6
Northington Gloucs 63 L5
Northington Hants 35 H3
North Kelsey Lincs 144 D7
North Kessock Highld 251 H2
North Killingholme N Linc 144 F4
North Kilvington N York 160 F5
North Kilworth Leics 100 D6
North Kingston Hants 18 B3
North Kyme Lincs 118 F1
North Landing E R Yk 153 L2
Northlands Lincs 119 K1
Northleach Gloucs 65 G4
North Lee Bucks 67 K5
North Lees N York 160 D7
Northleigh Devon 14 E3
Northleigh Devon 27 L4
North Leigh Kent 40 F6
North Leigh Oxon 66 A4
North Leverton with Habblesthorpe Notts 134 F3
Northlew Devon 12 C3
North Littleton Worcs 82 C5
Northload Bridge Somset 31 H3
North Lopham Norfk 105 L6
North Luffenham Rutlnd 101 K3
North Marden W Susx 20 C4
North Marston Bucks 67 J3
North Middleton Mdloth 211 K7
North Middleton Nthumb 190 E1
North Millbrex Abers 256 E3
North Milmain D & G 172 D4
North Molton Devon 28 C5
Northmoor Oxon 66 B6
North Moreton Oxon 48 E1
Northmuir Angus 234 B4
North Mundham W Susx 20 E6
North Muskham Notts 134 F7
North Newbald E R Yk 152 D8
North Newington Oxon 83 K7
North Newnton Wilts 47 H7
North Newton Somset 30 D4
Northney Hants 20 B6
North Nibley Gloucs 63 L7
North Oakley Hants 48 D8
North Ockendon Gt Lon 52 C2
Northolt Gt Lon 50 E2
Northop Flints 128 F6
Northop Hall Flints 129 G6
North Ormesby Middsb 170 C6
North Ormsby Lincs 136 E1
Northorpe Kirk 141 K3
Northorpe Lincs 118 E8
Northorpe Lincs 119 G4
Northorpe Lincs 143 M8
North Otterington N York 160 E5
Northover Somset 31 H3
Northover Somset 31 H6
North Owersby Lincs 135 L1
Northowram Calder 141 H2
North Perrott Somset 15 L1
North Petherton Somset 30 D4
North Petherwin Cnwll 11 K5
North Pickenham Norfk 105 H2
North Piddle Worcs 81 M4
North Poorton Dorset 15 M3
Northport Dorset 17 H5
North Poulner Hants 18 B2
North Queensferry Fife 210 F3
North Radworthy Devon 28 C4
North Rauceby Lincs 118 D2
Northrepps Norfk 122 E4
North Reston Lincs 137 G3
North Rigton N York 150 C6
North Ripley Hants 18 B4
North Rode Ches E 131 H6
North Ronaldsay Ork 275 f1
North Row Cumb 165 H4
North Runcton Norfk 120 E8
North Scale Cumb 146 C2
North Scarle Lincs 135 G6
North Seaton Nthumb 181 H2
North Seaton Colliery Nthumb 181 H2
North Shian Ag & B 228 E6
North Shields N Tyne 181 J5
North Shoebury Sthend 53 K2
North Shore Bpool 146 F8
North Side C Pete 102 F3
North Side Cumb 164 C5
North Skelton R & Cl 170 F7
North Somercotes Lincs 145 L8
North Stainley N York 160 D7
North Stainmore Cumb 167 J7
North Stifford Thurr 52 D3
North Stoke BaNES 45 L5
North Stoke Oxon 48 F2
North Stoke W Susx 21 H5
North Street Cambs 88 B2
North Street Hants 33 K7
North Street Hants 35 K4
North Street Kent 40 D4
North Street Medway 53 H4
North Street W Berk 48 F4
North Sunderland Nthumb 203 K6
North Tamerton Cnwll 11 K3
North Tawton Devon 12 F2
North Third Stirlg 209 K1
North Thoresby Lincs 145 H8
North Togston Nthumb 191 K5
Northton W Isls 282 d6
North Town Devon 12 C1
North Town Somset 31 J2
North Town W & M 49 L3
North Tuddenham Norfk 122 A8
North Uist W Isls 283 b8
North Walbottle N u Ty 180 E5
North Walsham Norfk 122 F5
North Waltham Hants 35 H2
North Warnborough Hants 35 M1
Northway Somset 29 L5
Northway Swans 57 G7
North Weald Bassett Essex 70 D6
North Wheatley Notts 134 F3
North Whilborough Devon 8 C2
Northwich Ches W 130 C5
North Wick BaNES 45 H6
Northwick S Glos 45 H2
Northwick Somset 30 E1
Northwick Worcs 81 J4
North Widcombe BaNES 45 H7
North Willingham Lincs 136 C2
North Wingfield Derbys 133 H6
North Witham Lincs 118 B7
Northwold Norfk 104 E4
Northwood C Stke 114 D2
Northwood Derbys 132 E6
Northwood Gt Lon 50 E1
Northwood IoW 19 H5
Northwood Shrops 113 G5
Northwood Green Gloucs 63 L4
North Wootton Dorset 31 L7

North Wootton Norfk 120 E6
North Wootton Somset 31 J3
North Wraxall Wilts 46 B4
North Wroughton Swindn 47 H3
Norton Donc 142 E5
Norton E Susx 23 G7
Norton Gloucs 64 B2
Norton Halton 130 A3
Norton Herts 86 E8
Norton IoW 18 E6
Norton Mons 62 F3
Norton N Som 44 D6
Norton N York 152 B2
Norton Nhants 84 B3
Norton Notts 133 L5
Norton Powys 79 K2
Norton S on T 170 B6
Norton Sheff 133 G3
Norton Shrops 95 L7
Norton Shrops 96 D2
Norton Shrops 96 E6
Norton Shrops 97 G3
Norton Suffk 89 J2
Norton Swans 57 H7
Norton W Susx 20 F5
Norton Wilts 46 C2
Norton Worcs 81 K5
Norton Worcs 82 B5
Norton Bavant Wilts 32 F2
Norton Bridge Staffs 114 D5
Norton Canes Staffs 98 C2
Norton Canon Herefs 79 M6
Norton Corner Norfk 122 B6
Norton Disney Lincs 135 H7
Norton Ferris Wilts 32 C4
Norton Fitzwarren Somset 30 B5
Norton Green IoW 18 E6
Norton Hawkfield BaNES 45 H6
Norton Heath Essex 70 F6
Norton in Hales Shrops 113 M4
Norton in the Moors C Stke 114 D1
Norton-Juxta-Twycross Leics 99 J2
Norton-le-Clay N York 150 F2
Norton Lindsey Warwks 82 F3
Norton Little Green Suffk 89 K2
Norton Malreward BaNES 45 J6
Norton Mandeville Essex 70 E6
Norton St Philip Somset 45 M7
Norton Subcourse Norfk 107 H4
Norton sub Hamdon Somset 31 G7
Norton Wood Herefs 79 L5
Norwell Notts 134 F7
Norwell Woodhouse Notts 134 E7
Norwich Norfk 106 E2
Norwich (St Faith) Crematorium Norfk 122 E8
Norwick Shet 281 f1
Norwood Clacks 220 F8
Norwood Derbys 133 J3
Norwood Kent 25 K1
Norwood End Essex 70 E5
Norwood Green Calder 141 H2
Norwood Green Gt Lon 50 E3
Norwood Hill Surrey 37 K2
Norwoodside Cambs 103 H4
Noseley Leics 101 G4
Noss Mayo Devon 7 G5
Nosterfield N York 160 C6
Nosterfield End Cambs 88 C6
Nostie Highld 248 D6
Notgrove Gloucs 65 G3
Nottage Brdgnd 42 B6
Notter Cnwll 6 D3
Nottingham C Nott 116 F4
Nottington Dorset 16 C6
Notton Wakefd 142 A5
Notton Wilts 46 C5
Nounsley Essex 71 J5
Noutard's Green Worcs 81 J2
Nowton Suffk 89 H3
Nox Shrops 95 K1
Nuffield Oxon 49 G2
Nunburnholme E R Yk 152 C6
Nuncargate Notts 116 E1
Nunclose Cumb 166 C2
Nuneaton Warwks 99 K5
Nuneham Courtenay Oxon 66 E7
Nunhead Gt Lon 51 K4
Nunkeeling E R Yk 153 J6
Nun Monkton N York 151 H4
Nunney Somset 32 B2
Nunney Catch Somset 32 B2
Nunnington Herefs 80 D6
Nunnington N York 161 L6
Nunsthorpe NE Lin 145 H6
Nunthorpe C York 151 J6
Nunthorpe Middsb 170 C7
Nunthorpe Village Middsb 170 D8
Nunton Wilts 33 K5
Nunwick N York 160 D7
Nunwick Nthumb 179 K4
Nupdown S Glos 63 J7
Nup End Bucks 67 L3
Nupend Gloucs 64 A5
Nuptown Br For 49 L4
Nursling Hants 34 E7
Nursted Hants 36 A6
Nursteed Wilts 46 F6
Nurton Staffs 97 J3
Nutbourne W Susx 20 C6
Nutbourne W Susx 21 J3
Nutfield Surrey 37 M1
Nuthall Notts 116 E3
Nuthampstead Herts 87 H8
Nuthurst W Susx 37 J5
Nutley E Susx 23 G2
Nutley Hants 35 J2
Nuttall Bury 140 B4
Nutwell Donc 143 G7
Nybster Highld 280 E3
Nyetimber W Susx 20 E7
Nyewood W Susx 36 B6
Nymet Rowland Devon 13 G1
Nymet Tracey Devon 13 G3
Nympsfield Gloucs 64 A7
Nynehead Somset 29 L6
Nythe Somset 30 F4
Nyton W Susx 20 F5

O

Oadby Leics 100 D3
Oad Street Kent 53 J6
Oakall Green Worcs 81 J3
Oakamoor Staffs 115 G3
Oakbank W Loth 210 E5
Oak Cross Devon 12 D3
Oakdale Caerph 43 J2
Oake Somset 29 L6
Oaken Staffs 97 J3
Oakenclough Lancs 147 K6
Oakengates Wrekin 96 F1
Oakenholt Flints 129 G5
Oakenshaw Dur 169 G3
Oakenshaw Kirk 141 J2
Oakerthorpe Derbys 133 H8
Oakford Cerdgn 76 E4
Oakford Devon 29 G6
Oakfordbridge Devon 29 G6
Oakgrove Ches E 131 H6
Oakham Rutlnd 101 J2
Oakhanger Ches E 114 B1
Oakhanger Hants 36 A4
Oakhill Somset 31 K2
Oakhurst Kent 38 E3
Oakington Cambs 87 H2
Oaklands Powys 78 E5
Oakle Street Gloucs 63 M4
Oakley Bed 85 K4
Oakley Bucks 66 F4
Oakley Fife 210 D1
Oakley Hants 35 H1
Oakley Oxon 67 H7
Oakley Poole 17 K3
Oakley Suffk 106 D7
Oakley Green W & M 50 A4
Oakley Park Powys 93 L6
Oakridge Gloucs 64 C6
Oaks Lancs 139 K1
Oaks Shrops 95 K2
Oaksey Wilts 64 E8
Oaks Green Derbys 115 J5
Oakshaw Ford Cumb 178 C4
Oakshott Hants 35 M5
Oakthorpe Leics 99 J1
Oak Tree Darltn 169 K8
Oakwood C Derb 116 C4
Oakwood Nthumb 179 L5
Oakworth C Brad 149 J8
Oare Kent 40 C3
Oare Somset 28 D2
Oare Wilts 47 H6
Oasby Lincs 118 D4
Oath Somset 30 F5
Oathlaw Angus 234 D4
Oatlands Park Surrey 50 E6
Oban Ag & B 216 D1
Obley Shrops 95 H7
Obney P & K 232 F8
Oborne Dorset 31 L7
Obthorpe Lincs 118 E8
Occold Suffk 90 D1
Occumster Highld 275 J1
Ochiltree E Ayrs 196 F6
Ockbrook Derbys 116 C4
Ocker Hill Sandw 98 B4
Ockeridge Worcs 81 H3
Ockham Surrey 50 D7
Ockle Highld 237 G6
Ockley Surrey 37 H3
Ocle Pychard Herefs 80 E6
Octon E R Yk 153 G2
Odcombe Somset 31 H7
Odd Down BaNES 45 L6
Oddingley Worcs 81 L3
Oddington Gloucs 65 J2
Oddington Oxon 66 E4
Odell Bed 85 J4
Odham Devon 12 C2
Odiham Hants 49 H8
Odsal C Brad 141 J2
Odsey Cambs 86 F7
Odstock Wilts 33 K5
Odstone Leics 99 K2
Offchurch Warwks 83 J2
Offenham Worcs 82 C6
Offerton Stockp 131 H2
Offerton Sundld 181 J7
Offham E Susx 22 F5
Offham Kent 39 G2
Offham W Susx 21 H5
Offleymarsh Staffs 114 B5
Offord Cluny Cambs 86 E2
Offord D'Arcy Cambs 86 E2
Offton Suffk 90 C5
Offwell Devon 14 E3
Ogbourne Maizey Wilts 47 J4
Ogbourne St Andrew Wilts 47 J4
Ogbourne St George Wilts 47 J4
Ogden Calder 141 G2
Ogle Nthumb 180 E3
Oglet Lpool 129 K3
Ogmore V Glam 42 D6
Ogmore-by-Sea V Glam 42 C6
Ogmore Vale Brdgnd 42 E4
Ogwen Bank Gwynd 126 C6
Okeford Fitzpaine Dorset 32 D8
Okehampton Devon 12 E4
Oker Side Derbys 132 E7
Okewood Hill Surrey 37 H3
Olchard Devon 13 K7
Old Nhants 84 F1
Old Aberdeen C Aber 245 L2
Old Alresford Hants 35 J4
Oldany Highld 270 E2
Old Auchenbrack D & G 185 J3
Old Basford C Nott 116 F3
Old Basing Hants 49 G8
Old Beetley Norfk 121 L7
Oldberrow Warwks 82 D2
Old Bewick Nthumb 190 F2
Old Bolingbroke Lincs 136 F6
Old Bramhope Leeds 150 B7
Old Brampton Derbys 133 G5
Old Bridge of Urr D & G 175 J1
Old Buckenham Norfk 106 B5
Old Burghclere Hants 48 C7
Oldbury Kent 38 F2
Oldbury Sandw 98 C5
Oldbury Shrops 97 G5
Oldbury Warwks 99 J4
Oldbury Naite S Glos 63 J8
Oldbury-on-Severn S Glos 63 J8
Oldbury on the Hill Gloucs 46 B1
Old Byland N York 161 J5
Old Cantley Donc 143 G7
Old Cassop Dur 169 J3
Old Castle Brdgnd 42 D6
Oldcastle Mons 62 C2
Oldcastle Heath Ches W 113 G2
Old Catton Norfk 106 E1
Old Churchstoke Powys 95 G4
Old Clee NE Lin 145 H6
Old Cleeve Somset 29 J3
Old Clipstone Notts 134 C6
Old Colwyn Conwy 127 H4
Oldcotes Notts 134 B2
Old Dailly S Ayrs 183 G3
Old Dalby Leics 117 H6
Old Dam Derbys 132 B4
Old Deer Abers 269 H6
Old Ditch Somset 31 H1
Old Edlington Donc 142 E8
Old Eldon Dur 169 H5
Old Ellerby E R Yk 153 J8
Old Felixstowe Suffk 91 H8
Oldfield C Brad 149 H8
Oldfield Worcs 81 J2
Old Fletton C Pete 102 D4
Oldford Somset 32 C1
Old Forge Herefs 63 H3
Old Furnace Herefs 62 F2
Old Glossop Derbys 131 L1
Old Goole E R Yk 143 J3
Old Grimsby IoS 10 b2
Old Hall Green Herts 69 K3
Oldhall Green Suffk 89 H4
Old Hall Street Norfk 122 F5
Oldham Oldham 140 D6
Oldhamstocks E Loth 213 G5
Old Harlow Essex 70 C5
Old Heath Essex 72 E3
Old Hunstanton Norfk 120 F3
Old Hurst Cambs 102 F7
Old Hutton Cumb 157 J5
Old Kea Cnwll 4 D6
Old Kilpatrick W Duns 208 D4
Old Knebworth Herts 69 G3
Old Lakenham Norfk 106 E2
Oldland S Glos 45 K4
Old Langho Lancs 148 B8
Old Laxey IoM 154 f5
Old Leake Lincs 119 L2
Old Malton N York 152 B1
Oldmeldrum Abers 256 E6
Oldmill Cnwll 11 M7
Old Milverton Warwks 83 G2
Oldmixon N Som 44 C7
Old Newton Suffk 90 B3
Old Quarrington Dur 169 J3
Old Radford C Nott 116 F3
Old Radnor Powys 79 J3
Old Rayne Abers 256 B6
Old Romney Kent 25 J2
Old Shoreham W Susx 22 B6
Oldshoremore Highld 276 C4
Old Soar Kent 38 F3
Old Sodbury S Glos 45 L3
Old Somerby Lincs 118 C5
Oldstead N York 161 H6
Old Stratford Nhants 84 E7
Old Struan P & K 232 B2
Old Swarland Nthumb 191 H6
Old Swinford Dudley 97 K6
Old Tebay Cumb 157 K2
Old Thirsk N York 160 F6
Old Town Calder 140 F2
Old Town Cumb 157 J6
Old Town Cumb 166 B2
Old Town E Susx 23 K7
Old Town IoS 10 c3
Old Trafford Traffd 140 B8
Old Tupton Derbys 133 H6
Oldwall Cumb 178 B6
Oldwalls Swans 56 E6
Old Warden C Beds 86 C6
Oldways End Somset 28 F6
Old Weston Cambs 102 B7
Old Wick Highld 280 E6
Old Windsor W & M 50 C4
Old Wives Lees Kent 40 E4
Old Woking Surrey 50 C7
Old Wolverton M Keyn 84 F7
Old Woodhall Lincs 136 D6
Old Woods Shrops 113 G7
Olgrinmore Highld 279 K5
Olive Green Staffs 115 J7
Oliver's Battery Hants 34 F5
Ollaberry Shet 281 d4
Ollach Highld 247 H1
Ollerton Ches E 130 F4
Ollerton Notts 134 D6
Ollerton Shrops 113 L6
Olmarch Cerdgn 77 H4
Olmstead Green Cambs 88 C7
Olney M Keyn 85 H5
Olrig House Highld 279 L3
Olton Solhll 98 E7
Olveston S Glos 45 J2
Ombersley Worcs 81 J3
Ompton Notts 134 D6
Once Brewed Nthumb 179 H5
Onchan IoM 154 e6
Onecote Staffs 131 L8
Onehouse Suffk 89 K3
Onen Mons 62 E4
Ongar Street Herefs 79 M2
Onibury Shrops 95 L7
Onich Highld 229 G3
Onllwyn Neath 60 C5
Onneley Staffs 114 B3
Onslow Green Essex 71 G3
Onslow Village Surrey 36 E1
Onston Ches W 130 B5
Openwoodgate Derbys 116 B2
Opinan Highld 260 B5
Orbliston Moray 266 F5
Orbost Highld 258 D7
Orby Lincs 137 J6
Orchard Portman Somset 30 C6
Orcheston Wilts 33 J2
Orcop Herefs 62 F2
Orcop Hill Herefs 62 F2
Ord Abers 268 A4
Ordhead Abers 244 E2
Ordie Abers 244 A3
Ordiequish Moray 267 G5
Ordley Nthumb 179 L7
Ordsall Notts 134 D4

Ore E Susx 24 F5
Oreleton Common Herefs 80 B2
Oreton Shrops 96 E7
Orford Suffk 91 K5
Orford Warrtn 130 B2
Organford Dorset 17 H4
Orgreave Staffs 115 J8
Orkney Islands Ork 275 c4
Orlestone Kent 40 C8
Orleton Herefs 80 C2
Orleton Worcs 81 G2
Orlingbury Nhants 85 G1
Ormathwaite Cumb 165 J5
Ormesby R & Cl 170 C7
Ormesby St Margaret Norfk 123 K8
Ormesby St Michael Norfk 123 K8
Ormiscaig Highld 260 D2
Ormiston E Loth 211 M5
Ormsaigmore Highld 236 F7
Ormsary Ag & B 206 A4
Ormskirk Lancs 138 E6
Ornsby Hill Dur 168 F1
Oronsay Ag & B 214 C6
Orphir Ork 275 b5
Orpington Gt Lon 51 M5
Orrell Sefton 138 D8
Orrell Wigan 139 G7
Orrell Post Wigan 139 G6
Orrisdale IoM 154 d4
Orroland D & G 175 J5
Orsett Thurr 52 D3
Orslow Staffs 114 C8
Orston Notts 117 K3
Orthwaite Cumb 165 H4
Ortner Lancs 147 K5
Orton Cumb 157 K1
Orton Nhants 101 H7
Orton Staffs 97 K4
Orton Longueville C Pete 102 D4
Orton-on-the-Hill Leics 99 J3
Orton Rigg Cumb 177 K8
Orton Waterville C Pete 102 C4
Orwell Cambs 87 H5
Osbaldeston Lancs 139 K2
Osbaldeston Green Lancs 139 K1
Osbaldwick C York 151 K5
Osbaston Leics 99 L3
Osbaston Shrops 112 D7
Osborne IoW 19 H5
Osbournby Lincs 118 E4
Oscroft Ches W 129 L6
Ose Highld 258 E8
Osgathorpe Leics 116 D7
Osgodby Lincs 135 M1
Osgodby N York 143 G1
Osgodby N York 163 J5
Oskaig Highld 247 H1
Oskamull Ag & B 226 E4
Osmaston Derbys 115 K3
Osmington Dorset 16 D6
Osmington Mills Dorset 16 D6
Osmondthorpe Leeds 142 A1
Osmotherley N York 161 G3
Osney Oxon 66 D6
Ospringe Kent 40 C3
Ossett Wakefd 141 L4
Ossington Notts 134 E6
Ostend Essex 72 D7
Osterley Gt Lon 50 F3
Oswaldkirk N York 161 K6
Oswaldtwistle Lancs 139 L2
Oswestry Shrops 112 D5
Otford Kent 52 B7
Otham Kent 39 K3
Otham Hole Kent 39 K3
Othery Somset 30 F4
Otley Leeds 150 B6
Otley Suffk 90 E4
Otley Green Suffk 90 F4
Otterbourne Hants 34 F6
Otterburn N York 148 F4
Otterburn Nthumb 190 C7
Otter Ferry Ag & B 206 E2
Otterham Cnwll 11 H4
Otterhampton Somset 30 C2
Otterham Quay Kent 53 H5
Otterham Station Cnwll 11 G5
Otternish W Isls 282 c7
Ottershaw Surrey 50 C6
Otterswick Shet 281 e3
Otterton Devon 14 C5
Otterwood Hants 18 F3
Ottery St Mary Devon 14 C3
Ottinge Kent 41 G6
Ottringham E R Yk 145 H3
Oughterby Cumb 177 J7
Oughtershaw N York 158 F6
Oughterside Cumb 164 F3
Oughtibridge Sheff 132 F1
Oughtrington Warrtn 130 D2
Oulston N York 161 J7
Oulton Cumb 177 H8
Oulton Leeds 142 B2
Oulton Norfk 122 C6
Oulton Staffs 114 B7
Oulton Staffs 114 E4
Oulton Suffk 107 L4
Oulton Broad Suffk 107 L5
Oulton Street Norfk 122 C6
Oundle Nhants 102 A5
Ounsdale Staffs 97 K5
Ousby Cumb 166 E4
Ousden Suffk 88 E3
Ousefleet E R Yk 143 L3
Ouston Dur 181 G8
Outchester Nthumb 203 J6
Out Elmstead Kent 41 G5
Outgate Cumb 156 E3
Outhgill Cumb 158 D2
Outhill Warwks 82 D2
Outlands Staffs 114 B5
Outlane Kirk 141 G4
Out Newton E R Yk 145 K3
Out Rawcliffe Lancs 147 H7
Outwell Norfk 103 K3
Outwick Hants 33 K7
Outwood Surrey 37 M2
Outwood Wakefd 142 A3
Outwood Gate Bury 140 B6
Outwoods Leics 116 C7
Outwoods Staffs 114 B7
Ouzlewell Green Leeds 142 A3
Ovenden Calder 141 G2
Over Cambs 87 H1
Over Ches W 130 C6
Over Gloucs 64 A3
Over S Glos 45 H2
Over Burrows Derbys 115 L4
Overbury Worcs 81 M7
Overcombe Dorset 16 D6
Over Compton Dorset 31 K7
Overdale Crematorium Bolton 139 K6
Over End Cambs 102 B5
Overgreen Derbys 132 F5
Over Green Warwks 98 F4
Over Haddon Derbys 132 D6
Over Kellet Lancs 147 K2
Over Kiddington Oxon 66 B3
Overleigh Somset 31 G4
Overley Staffs 115 J8
Over Monnow Mons 63 G4
Over Norton Oxon 65 L2
Over Peover Ches E 130 F5
Overpool Ches W 129 J4
Overscaig Hotel Highld 272 B3
Overseal Derbys 115 M8
Over Silton N York 161 G4
Oversland Kent 40 D4
Oversley Green Warwks 82 C4
Overstone Nhants 84 F2
Over Stowey Somset 30 B3
Overstrand Norfk 122 E3
Over Stratton Somset 31 G7
Overstreet Wilts 33 J3
Over Tabley Ches E 130 E4
Overthorpe Nhants 83 L7
Overton C Aber 245 J1
Overton Ches W 129 M4
Overton Hants 35 G1
Overton Lancs 147 H4
Overton N York 151 J5
Overton Shrops 80 C1
Overton Swans 56 E7
Overton Wakefd 141 L4
Overton Wrexhm 112 E3
Overton Bridge Wrexhm 112 E3
Overton Green Ches E 130 F7
Overtown Lancs 157 K7
Overtown N Lans 209 L8
Overtown Swindn 47 H3
Overtown Wakefd 142 A4
Over Wallop Hants 34 C3
Over Whitacre Warwks 99 H5
Over Woodhouse Derbys 133 J5
Over Worton Oxon 66 B1
Overy Oxon 66 E8
Oving Bucks 67 J3
Oving W Susx 20 E6
Ovingdean Br & H 22 E6
Ovingham Nthumb 180 D6
Ovington Dur 168 E7
Ovington Essex 88 F6
Ovington Hants 35 H4
Ovington Norfk 105 J3
Ovington Nthumb 180 C6
Ower Hants 19 H3
Ower Hants 34 D7
Owermoigne Dorset 16 E5
Owlbury Shrops 95 H5
Owlerton Sheff 133 G2
Owlpen Gloucs 64 A7
Owl's Green Suffk 91 G1
Owlsmoor Br For 49 K6
Owlswick Bucks 67 J6
Owmby Lincs 135 K2
Owmby Lincs 144 D6
Owslebury Hants 35 G6
Owston Donc 142 E5
Owston Leics 101 G2
Owston Ferry N Linc 143 K7
Owstwick E R Yk 145 H1
Owthorne E R Yk 145 J2
Owthorpe Notts 117 H5
Owton Manor Hartpl 170 C5
Oxborough Norfk 104 E3
Oxbridge Dorset 15 L3
Oxcombe Lincs 136 F4
Oxcroft Derbys 133 J5
Oxen End Essex 71 G1
Oxenholme Cumb 157 H5
Oxenhope C Brad 140 F1
Oxen Park Cumb 156 D5
Oxenpill Somset 31 G3
Oxenton Gloucs 64 D1
Oxenwood Wilts 47 L7
Oxford Oxon 66 D6
Oxford Crematorium Oxon 66 E5
Oxhey Herts 68 E8
Oxhill Dur 180 F8
Oxhill Warwks 83 H6
Oxley Wolves 97 K3
Oxley Green Essex 72 C4
Oxley's Green E Susx 24 C3
Oxlode Cambs 103 K6
Oxnam Border 189 J3
Oxnead Norfk 122 E6
Oxshott Surrey 50 F6
Oxshott Heath Surrey 50 E6
Oxspring Barns 141 L7
Oxted Surrey 51 K8
Oxton Border 201 G2
Oxton N York 151 H7
Oxton Notts 117 G1
Oxwich Swans 56 F7
Oxwich Green Swans 56 F7
Oxwick Norfk 121 K6
Oykel Bridge Hotel Highld 271 L7
Oyne Abers 256 B6
Oystermouth Swans 57 H7
Ozleworth Gloucs 64 A8

P

Pabail W Isls 282 h3
Packers Hill Dorset 16 D1
Packington Leics 116 B8
Packmoor C Stke 114 D1
Packmores Warwks 83 G2
Padanaram Angus 234 C5
Padbury Bucks 67 H1
Paddington Gt Lon 51 H3
Paddington Warrtn 130 C2
Paddlesworth Kent 41 G7
Paddlesworth Kent 52 E6
Paddock Wood Kent 39 G4
Paddolgreen Shrops 113 H5
Padfield Derbys 140 F8
Padgate Warrtn 130 C2
Padhams Green Essex 70 F7
Padiham Lancs 140 B1
Padside N York 149 L4
Padstow Cnwll 10 C7
Padworth W Berk 48 F5
Page Bank Dur 169 G4
Pagham W Susx 20 E7
Paglesham Essex 72 D8
Paignton Torbay 8 C3
Pailton Warwks 100 A7
Paine's Cross E Susx 23 K3
Painleyhill Staffs 115 G5
Painscastle Powys 79 G6
Painshawfield Nthumb 180 C6
Painsthorpe E R Yk 152 B4
Painswick Gloucs 64 C5
Painter's Forstal Kent 40 C3
Paisley Rens 208 E6
Paisley Woodside Crematorium Rens 208 D6
Pakefield Suffk 107 L5
Pakenham Suffk 89 J2
Pale Gwynd 111 J4
Pale Green Essex 88 D6
Palestine Hants 34 B3
Paley Street W & M 49 L4
Palfrey Wsall 98 C4
Palgrave Suffk 106 C7
Pallington Dorset 16 F4
Palmersbridge Cnwll 11 H7
Palmers Green Gt Lon 69 J8
Palmerston E Ayrs 196 F7
Palmerstown V Glam 43 H7
Palnackie D & G 175 K3
Palnure D & G 174 C2
Palterton Derbys 133 J6
Pamber End Hants 48 F7
Pamber Green Hants 48 F7
Pamber Heath Hants 48 F6
Pamington Gloucs 81 L8
Pamphill Dorset 17 K3
Pampisford Cambs 87 K5
Panborough Somset 31 G2
Panbride Angus 234 E8
Pancrasweek Devon 11 K2
Pancross V Glam 43 G7
Pandy Caerph 43 J4
Pandy Gwynd 92 D3
Pandy Gwynd 111 G5
Pandy Mons 62 C3
Pandy Powys 93 K3
Pandy Wrexhm 112 B4
Pandy'r Capel Denbgs 111 L2
Pandy Tudur Conwy 127 G6
Panfield Essex 71 H2
Pangbourne W Berk 48 F4
Pangdean W Susx 22 D5
Panks Bridge Herefs 80 E5
Pannal N York 150 D5
Pannal Ash N York 150 C5
Pannanich Wells Hotel Abers 243 L4
Pant Shrops 112 D7
Pantasaph Flints 128 E4
Panteg Pembks 74 F5
Pantersbridge Cnwll 5 K1
Pant-ffrwyth Brdgnd 42 E5
Pant Glas Gwynd 109 H2
Pantglas Powys 93 G4
Pant-Gwyn Carmth 59 G4
Pant-lasau Swans 57 J5
Pant Mawr Powys 93 J7
Panton Lincs 136 C4
Pant-pastynog Denbgs 128 B7
Pantperthog Gwynd 93 G3
Pant-y-dwr Powys 93 L8
Pant-y-ffridd Powys 94 E3
Pantyffynnon Carmth 57 H3
Pantygaseg Torfn 61 L7
Pant-y-gog Brdgnd 42 D3
Pantymenyn Carmth 75 K7
Pant-y-mwyn Flints 128 E6
Panxworth Norfk 107 G1
Papcastle Cumb 164 F4
Papigoe Highld 280 E6
Papple E Loth 212 D4
Papplewick Notts 116 F1
Papworth Everard Cambs 86 F3
Papworth St Agnes Cambs 86 F2
Par Cnwll 5 H4
Paramour Street Kent 41 J3
Parbold Lancs 139 G5
Parbrook Somset 31 J4
Parbrook W Susx 37 G6
Parc Gwynd 111 G5
Parc Gwyn Crematorium Pembks 55 K4
Parcllyn Cerdgn 75 M2
Parc Seymour Newpt 44 E1
Pardshaw Cumb 164 E5
Parham Suffk 91 G3
Park D & G 186 D7
Park Nthumb 178 F6
Park Bottom Cnwll 3 H3
Park Bridge Tamesd 140 E7
Park Corner E Susx 38 E6
Park Corner Oxon 49 G1
Park Corner W & M 49 K2
Park Crematorium Lancs 138 D2
Park End Bed 85 K4
Parkend Gloucs 63 J5
Park End Nthumb 179 K4
Parkers Green Kent 38 F4
Parkeston Essex 73 K1
Parkeston Quay Essex 90 F8
Park Farm Kent 40 D7
Parkgate Ches W 129 G4
Parkgate Cumb 165 H1
Parkgate D & G 176 D1
Parkgate E Susx 24 C4
Parkgate Essex 71 G1
Park Gate Hants 19 J2
Parkgate Kent 39 L6
Parkgate Kent 52 B6
Park Gate Leeds 150 A7
Parkgate Surrey 37 K2
Park Gate Worcs 81 L1
Park Green Essex 70 C2
Park Green Suffk 90 D2
Parkgrove Crematorium Angus 234 F5

Parkhall W Duns 208 E4
Parkham Devon 27 G6
Parkham Ash Devon 26 F6
Park Head Derbys 116 B1
Park Hill Gloucs 63 H7
Parkhouse Mons 63 G6
Parkmill Swans 57 G7
Park Royal Gt Lon 51 G3
Parkside Dur 169 L1
Parkside N Lans 209 L7
Parkside Wrexhm 129 J8
Parkstone Poole 17 K4
Park Street Herts 68 F6
Park Street W Susx 37 H4
Park Wood Crematorium Calder 141 H3
Parley Green Dorset 17 M3
Parmoor Bucks 49 J1
Parndon Essex 70 B5
Parndon Wood Crematorium Essex 70 C5
Parracombe Devon 28 B2
Parrog Pembks 75 H4
Parsonby Cumb 164 F3
Parson Cross Sheff 133 G1
Parson Drove Cambs 103 H2
Parson's Heath Essex 72 F2
Parson's Hill Derbys 116 A6
Partick C Glas 208 F5
Partington Traffd 130 D2
Partney Lincs 137 H6
Parton Cumb 164 C6
Partridge Green W Susx 22 B3
Partrishow Powys 62 B3
Parwich Derbys 115 K1
Paslow Wood Common Essex 70 E6
Passenham Nhants 84 F7
Passfield Hants 36 B4
Passingford Bridge Essex 70 D7
Paston C Pete 102 D3
Paston Norfk 123 G4
Pasturefields Staffs 114 F6
Patchacott Devon 12 B3
Patcham Br & H 22 D5
Patchetts Green Herts 68 F7
Patching W Susx 21 J5
Patchole Devon 27 L2
Patchway S Glos 45 J3
Pateley Bridge N York 149 L3
Paternoster Heath Essex 72 D4
Pathe Somset 30 F5
Pathhead Fife 222 E8
Pathhead Mdloth 211 L6
Pathlow Warwks 82 E3
Path of Condie P & K 221 K5
Patmore Heath Herts 70 B2
Patna E Ayrs 183 K1
Patney Wilts 47 G7
Patrick IoM 154 c5
Patrick Brompton N York 160 B4
Patricroft Salfd 139 M8
Patrington E R Yk 145 J3
Patrington Haven E R Yk 145 J3
Patrixbourne Kent 41 G4
Patterdale Cumb 165 L7
Pattingham Staffs 97 J4
Pattishall Nhants 84 C4
Pattiswick Green Essex 71 K2
Patton Shrops 96 D4
Paul Cnwll 2 D5
Paulerspury Nhants 84 D6
Paull E R Yk 144 F3
Paul's Dene Wilts 33 K4
Paulton BaNES 45 K7
Paunton Herefs 80 F5
Pauperhaugh Nthumb 191 G6
Pave Lane Wrekin 114 B8
Pavenham Bed 85 K4
Pawlett Somset 30 D2
Pawston Nthumb 202 C6
Paxford Gloucs 82 E7
Paxton Border 202 E3
Payden Street Kent 40 B4
Payhembury Devon 14 C2
Paynter's Lane End Cnwll 3 H2
Paythorne Lancs 148 E5
Paytoe Herefs 80 A1
Peacehaven E Susx 22 F7
Peak Dale Derbys 132 B4
Peak Forest Derbys 132 B4
Peak Hill Lincs 119 J8
Peakirk C Pete 102 D2
Pearson's Green Kent 39 H4
Peartree Green Herefs 80 E8
Peasedown St John BaNES 45 K7
Peasehill Derbys 116 C2
Peaseland Green Norfk 122 B8
Peasemore W Berk 48 C3
Peasenhall Suffk 91 H2
Pease Pottage W Susx 37 L4
Peaslake Surrey 37 G2
Peasley Cross St Hel 129 M1
Peasmarsh E Susx 25 G3
Peasmarsh Somset 30 E8
Peasmarsh Surrey 36 E2
Peathill Abers 269 G3
Peat Inn Fife 223 H5
Peatling Magna Leics 100 D5
Peatling Parva Leics 100 D5
Peaton Shrops 96 C6
Pebmarsh Essex 89 G8
Pebworth Worcs 82 D6
Pecket Well Calder 140 F2
Peckforton Ches E 129 M8
Peckham Gt Lon 51 J4
Peckleton Leics 100 A3
Pedairffordd Powys 111 M6
Pedlinge Kent 40 F8
Pedmore Dudley 97 K7
Pedwell Somset 30 F4
Peebles Border 200 B5
Peel IoM 154 c5
Peel Lancs 138 D2
Peel Common Hants 19 K3
Peene Kent 41 G7
Peening Quarter Kent 39 M7
Peggs Green Leics 116 C7
Pegsdon C Beds 68 E1
Pegswood Nthumb 180 F2
Pegwell Kent 41 K3
Peinchorran Highld 247 H2
Peinlich Highld 259 G5
Pelcomb Pembks 54 F3
Pelcomb Bridge Pembks 54 F3
Pelcomb Cross Pembks 54 F3
Peldon Essex 72 E4
Pell Green E Susx 39 G6
Pelsall Wsall 98 C3
Pelsall Wood Wsall 98 C3
Pelton Dur 181 G8
Pelton Fell Dur 181 G8
Pelutho Cumb 164 F1
Pelynt Cnwll 5 L4
Pemberton Carmth 56 F5
Pemberton Wigan 139 H7
Pembles Cross Kent 39 M4
Pembrey Carmth 56 D4
Pembridge Herefs 79 M4
Pembroke Pembks 55 G6
Pembroke Dock Pembks 54 F6
Pembury Kent 39 G5
Pen-allt Herefs 63 H1
Penallt Mons 63 G5
Penally Pembks 55 J7
Penare Cnwll 5 G6
Penarth V Glam 43 J7
Penblewin Pembks 55 J4
Pen-bont Rhydybeddau Cerdgn 92 E6
Penbryn Cerdgn 76 B5
Pencader Carmth 58 E2
Pencaenewydd Gwynd 109 G3
Pencaitland E Loth 212 A5
Pencarnisiog IoA 124 F5
Pencarreg Carmth 76 F6
Pencarrow Cnwll 10 F6
Pencelli Powys 61 H2
Penclawdd Swans 57 G5
Pencoed Brdgnd 42 E5
Pencombe Herefs 80 E5
Pencoyd Herefs 63 G2
Pencraig Herefs 63 H3
Pencraig Powys 111 K6
Pendeen Cnwll 2 B4
Penderyn Rhondd 60 E5
Pendine Carmth 55 L5
Pendlebury Salfd 140 B7
Pendleton Lancs 148 D7
Pendock Worcs 81 H8
Pendoggett Cnwll 10 E6
Pendomer Somset 31 H8
Pendoylan V Glam 43 G6
Pendre Brdgnd 42 D5
Penegoes Powys 93 G3
Penelewey Cnwll 3 K3
Pen-ffordd Pembks 55 J2
Pengam Caerph 43 J2
Pengam Cardif 43 K6
Penge Gt Lon 51 K5
Pengelly Cnwll 10 F6
Pengorffwysfa IoA 125 H1
Pengover Green Cnwll 6 B2
Pen-groes-oped Mons 62 C5
Pengwern Denbgs 127 K4
Penhale Cnwll 3 H7
Penhale Cnwll 4 E3
Penhale Cnwll 5 J3
Penhale Cnwll 6 E4
Penhallow Cnwll 4 C4
Penhalurick Cnwll 3 H3
Penhalvean Cnwll 3 H3
Penhill Swindn 47 H1
Penhow Newpt 44 E1
Penhurst E Susx 24 C4
Peniarth Gwynd 92 D2
Penicuik Mdloth 211 H7
Peniel Carmth 58 D4
Peniel Denbgs 127 L7
Penifiler Highld 259 H8
Peninver Ag & B 192 F3
Penisarwaun Gwynd 125 K7
Penistone Barns 141 K7
Penjerrick Cnwll 3 K5
Penketh Warrtn 130 A2
Penkill S Ayrs 183 G3
Penkridge Staffs 97 L1
Penlean Cnwll 11 H3
Penleigh Wilts 32 E1
Penley Wrexhm 112 F3
Penllergaer Swans 57 H5
Pen-llyn IoA 124 F3
Penllyn V Glam 42 E6
Pen-lon IoA 125 G6
Penmachno Conwy 110 E2
Penmaen Caerph 43 J2
Penmaen Swans 56 F7
Penmaenan Conwy 126 E4
Penmaenmawr Conwy 126 E4
Penmaenpool Gwynd 110 C7
Penmark V Glam 43 G7
Penmon IoA 126 C3
Penmorfa Gwynd 109 K3
Penmount Crematorium Cnwll 4 D5
Penmynydd IoA 125 J5
Penn Bucks 67 M8
Penn Wolves 97 K4
Pennal Gwynd 92 F3
Pennan Abers 268 F3
Pennant Cerdgn 76 F3
Pennant Denbgs 111 K5
Pennant Powys 93 J4
Pennant-Melangell Powys 111 K6
Pennard Swans 57 G7
Pennerley Shrops 95 J3
Pennicott Devon 13 K2
Pennington Cumb 156 C7
Pennington Hants 18 D4
Pennington Green Wigan 139 J6
Pennorth Powys 61 H2
Penn Street Bucks 68 A7
Pennsylvania S Glos 45 L4
Penny Bridge Cumb 156 D6
Pennycross Ag & B 226 F7
Pennygate Norfk 123 G7
Pennyghael Ag & B 227 G7
Pennyglen S Ayrs 183 H1
Penny Green Derbys 133 L4
Penny Hill Lincs 119 K6
Pennymoor Devon 28 F8
Pennywell Sundld 181 J7
Penparc Cerdgn 75 L3
Penparcau Cerdgn 92 D7
Penpedairheol Caerph 43 J2
Penpedairheol Mons 62 C6
Penperlleni Mons 62 C6
Penpethy Cnwll 10 F5
Penpillick Cnwll 5 J4
Penpol Cnwll 3 K3
Penpoll Cnwll 5 K4
Penponds Cnwll 3 G3
Penpont Cnwll 10 F7
Penpont D & G 186 C7
Penpont Powys 60 E2
Penquit Devon 7 J4
Penrest Cnwll 11 L7
Penrherber Carmth 76 B7
Pen-rhiw Pembks 75 M4
Penrhiwceiber Rhondd 43 G2
Pen Rhiwfawr Neath 57 K3
Penrhiw-llan Cerdgn 76 C6
Penrhiw-pal Cerdgn 76 C6
Penrhos Gwynd 108 F5
Penrhos IoA 124 D3
Penrhos Mons 62 E5
Penrhos Powys 59 L6
Penrhos garnedd Gwynd 125 K5
Penrhyn Bay Conwy 127 G3
Penrhyncoch Cerdgn 92 D6
Penrhyndeudraeth Gwynd 109 L4
Penrhyn-side Conwy 126 F3
Penrice Swans 56 F7
Penrioch N Ayrs 194 D2
Penrith Cumb 166 C4
Penrose Cnwll 10 B8
Penruddock Cumb 166 A5
Penryn Cnwll 3 K4
Pensarn Conwy 127 J4
Pensax Worcs 81 G2
Pensby Wirral 129 G3
Penselwood Somset 32 C4
Pensford BaNES 45 J6
Pensham Worcs 81 L6
Penshaw Sundld 181 H8
Penshurst Kent 38 E4
Penshurst Station Kent 38 E4
Pensilva Cnwll 11 K8
Pensnett Dudley 97 K5
Penstone Devon 13 H3
Penstrowed Powys 94 C5
Pentewan Cnwll 5 G5
Pentir Gwynd 125 K6
Pentire Cnwll 4 C3
Pentlepoir Pembks 55 J5
Pentlow Essex 89 G6
Pentlow Street Essex 89 G6
Pentney Norfk 120 F8
Pentonbridge Cumb 178 B3
Penton Grafton Hants 34 D2
Penton Mewsey Hants 34 D2
Pentraeth IoA 125 J4
Pentre Denbgs 128 C7
Pentre Flints 129 H6
Pentre Mons 62 C6
Pentre Mons 62 E7
Pentre Powys 94 C6
Pentre Powys 94 E5
Pentre Powys 95 G5
Pentre Rhondd 42 E2
Pentre Shrops 112 E7
Pentre Wrexhm 112 D3
Pentre bach Cerdgn 77 G6
Pentre Bach Flints 128 F4
Pentrebach Myr Td 61 G6
Pentre-bach Powys 78 B8
Pentrebeirdd Powys 94 E1
Pentre Berw IoA 125 H5
Pentre-bont Conwy 110 D1
Pentrebychan Crematorium Wrexhm 112 D2
Pentre-cagel Carmth 76 C7
Pentre-celyn Denbgs 112 A1
Pentre-celyn Powys 93 J2
Pentre-chwyth Swans 57 J6
Pentre-clawdd Shrops 112 D5
Pentre-cwrt Carmth 76 D7
Pentredwr Denbgs 112 B2
Pentrefelin Gwynd 109 J4
Pentrefelin IoA 125 H1
Pentre Ffwrndan Flints 128 F5
Pentrefoelas Conwy 111 G1
Pentregalar Pembks 75 L6
Pentregat Cerdgn 76 C5
Pentre-Gwenlais Carmth 59 H5
Pentre Gwynfryn Gwynd 109 L6
Pentre Halkyn Flints 128 E5
Pentre Hodrey Shrops 95 H7
Pentre Isaf Conwy 127 K5
Pentre Llanrhaeadr Denbgs 128 C7
Pentre Llifior Powys 94 E4
Pentre-llwyn-llwyd Powys 78 C4
Pentre-llyn Cerdgn 92 D8
Pentre-llyn-cymmer Conwy 111 J1
Pentre-Maw Powys 93 J3
Pentre Meyrick V Glam 42 E6
Pentre-piod Torfn 62 B6
Pentre-poeth Newpt 44 B2
Pentre'rbryn Cerdgn 76 D4
Pentre'r-felin Cerdgn 77 H5
Pentre'r Felin Conwy 126 F6
Pentre'r-felin Powys 60 D1
Pentre Saron Denbgs 127 L7
Pentre-tafarn-y-fedw Conwy 126 F7
Pentre ty gwyn Carmth 59 M2
Pentrich Derbys 116 C1
Pentridge Dorset 33 H7
Pen-twyn Caerph 61 K7
Pen-twyn Mons 63 G5
Pen-twyn Torfn 61 L6
Pentwynmaur Caerph 43 K2
Pentyrch Cardif 43 H5
Penwithick Cnwll 5 H4
Penwood Hants 48 C6
Penwyllt Powys 60 C4
Penybanc Carmth 59 H4
Penybont Powys 78 F2
Pen-y-bont Powys 112 B6
Pen-y-bont-fawr Powys 111 L6
Pen-y-bryn Pembks 75 L4
Pen-y-cae Powys 60 C4
Penycae Wrexhm 112 D3
Pen-y-cae-mawr Mons 62 E8
Penycaerau Gwynd 108 C6
Pen-y-cefn Flints 128 D4
Pen-y-clawdd Mons 62 F5
Pen-y-coedcae Rhondd 43 G4
Pen-y-cwn Pembks 54 D2
Pen-y-fai Brdgnd 42 D5

Pen-y-felin Flints 128 D5
Penyffordd Flints 129 G7
Penyffridd Gwynd 125 J8
Pen-y-garn Cerdgn 92 D6
Pen-y-Garnedd Powys 111 L6
Pen-y-genffordd Powys 61 J1
Pen-y-graig Gwynd 108 C5
Penygraig Rhondd 42 F3
Penygroes Carmth 59 G6
Penygroes Gwynd 109 H1
Pen-y-Gwryd Gwynd 126 D8
Pen-y-lan V Glam 42 F6
Pen-y-Mynydd Carmth 56 E4
Penymynydd Flints 129 G7
Pen-y-pass Gwynd 126 C8
Pen-yr-Heol Mons 62 E5
Pen-yr-Heolgerrig Myr Td 60 F6
Penysarn IoA 125 H2
Pen-y-stryt Denbgs 112 B1
Penywaun Rhondd 60 E6
Penzance Cnwll 2 D5
Peopleton Worcs 81 L5
Peover Heath Ches E 130 F5
Peper Harow Surrey 36 D2
Peplow Shrops 113 K6
Pepper's Green Essex 70 F5
Pepperstock C Beds 68 D3
Perceton N Ayrs 196 C3
Percyhorner Abers 269 H3
Perelle Guern 9 i3
Perham Down Wilts 34 B1
Periton Somset 29 G2
Perivale Gt Lon 50 F2
Perkins Village Devon 14 B4
Perkinsville Dur 181 G8
Perlethorpe Notts 134 C5
Perranarworthal Cnwll 3 K3
Perranporth Cnwll 4 B4
Perranuthnoe Cnwll 2 E5
Perranwell Cnwll 3 K3
Perranwell Cnwll 4 C4
Perran Wharf Cnwll 3 K3
Perranzabuloe Cnwll 4 C4
Perrott's Brook Gloucs 64 E6
Perry Birm 98 D5
Perry Barr Birm 98 D5
Perry Barr Crematorium Birm 98 D5
Perry Green Essex 71 K3
Perry Green Herts 70 B4
Perry Green Wilts 46 E1
Perrystone Hill Herefs 63 J1
Perry Street Somset 15 H2
Pershall Staffs 114 C5
Pershore Worcs 81 L6
Pertenhall Bed 86 B2
Perth P & K 221 K3
Perth Crematorium P & K 221 K2
Perthy Shrops 112 E5
Perton Herefs 80 E7
Perton Staffs 97 J3
Pertwood Wilts 32 E4
Peterborough C Pete 102 D4
Peterborough Crematorium C Pete 102 D3
Peterchurch Herefs 79 L7
Peterculter C Aber 245 J3
Peterhead Abers 257 L2
Peterlee Dur 169 L2
Petersfield Hants 35 M6
Peter's Green Herts 68 F3
Petersham Gt Lon 50 F4
Peters Marland Devon 27 H8
Peterstone Wentlooge Newpt 43 L5
Peterston-super-Ely V Glam 43 G6
Peterstow Herefs 63 H2
Peter Tavy Devon 12 C7
Petham Kent 40 F5
Petherwin Gate Cnwll 11 K5
Petrockstow Devon 12 C1
Petsoe End M Keyn 85 H5
Pet Street Kent 40 E6
Pett E Susx 24 F4
Pettaugh Suffk 90 E3
Pett Bottom Kent 40 F5
Petterden Angus 234 C7
Pettinain S Lans 198 F4
Pettistree Suffk 91 G4
Petton Devon 29 H6
Petton Shrops 113 G6
Petts Wood Gt Lon 51 M5
Pettycur Fife 211 J2
Petty France S Glos 46 A2
Pettymuk Abers 257 G7
Petworth W Susx 36 E6
Pevensey E Susx 23 L6
Pevensey Bay E Susx 24 B6
Pewsey Wilts 47 H7
Pheasant's Hill Bucks 49 J2
Phepson Worcs 81 L3
Philadelphia Sundld 181 H8
Philham Devon 26 D6
Philiphaugh Border 200 F7
Phillack Cnwll 2 F3
Philleigh Cnwll 3 L3
Philpot End Essex 70 F3
Philpstoun W Loth 210 E4
Phocle Green Herefs 63 J2
Phoenix Green Hants 49 J7
Phones Highld 241 J5
Pibsbury Somset 31 G5
Pica Cumb 164 D6
Piccadilly Warwks 99 G4
Piccotts End Herts 68 D5
Pickburn Donc 142 E6
Pickering N York 162 D6
Picket Piece Hants 34 E2
Picket Post Hants 18 B2
Pickford Covtry 99 H7
Pickford Green Covtry 99 H7
Pickhill N York 160 E6
Picklescott Shrops 95 K3
Pickmere Ches E 130 D4
Pickney Somset 30 B5
Pickstock Wrekin 114 A6
Pickup Bank Bl w D 139 L3
Pickwell Devon 27 H3
Pickwell Leics 101 G1
Pickwick Wilts 46 B5
Pickworth Lincs 118 D5
Pickworth Rutlnd 101 L1
Picton Ches W 129 K5
Picton Flints 128 D3
Picton N York 160 F1
Piddinghoe E Susx 23 G6
Piddington Bucks 67 K8
Piddington Nhants 84 F4
Piddington Oxon 66 F4
Piddlehinton Dorset 16 D3
Piddletrenthide Dorset 16 D3
Pidley Cambs 103 G7
Piercebridge Darltn 169 G7
Pierowall Ork 275 c1
Piff's Elm Gloucs 64 C2
Pigdon Nthumb 180 E1
Pigeon Green Warwks 82 F3
Pig Oak Dorset 17 K2
Pig Street Herefs 79 L5
Pikehall Derbys 132 D7
Pilford Dorset 17 K2
Pilgrims Hatch Essex 70 E7
Pilham Lincs 135 H1
Pill N Som 45 G4
Pillaton Cnwll 6 D2
Pillatonmill Cnwll 6 D2
Pillerton Hersey Warwks 83 G5
Pillerton Priors Warwks 83 G5
Pilleth Powys 79 J2
Pilley Barns 142 A7
Pilley Hants 18 E4
Pilley Bailey Hants 18 E4
Pillgwenlly Newpt 44 C2
Pillhead Devon 27 H5
Pilling Lancs 147 H6
Pilling Lane Lancs 147 G6
Pilning S Glos 45 H2
Pilot Inn Kent 25 K4
Pilsbury Derbys 132 B7
Pilsdon Dorset 15 J3
Pilsgate C Pete 102 B2
Pilsley Derbys 132 E5
Pilsley Derbys 133 H7
Pilson Green Norfk 107 H1
Piltdown E Susx 23 G3
Pilton Devon 27 K4
Pilton Nhants 101 M6
Pilton Rutlnd 101 K3
Pilton Somset 31 K3
Pilton Green Swans 56 E7
Pimlico Lancs 148 C7
Pimlico Nhants 84 B7
Pimperne Dorset 17 H1
Pinchbeck Lincs 119 H6
Pinchbeck Bars Lincs 119 G6
Pinchbeck West Lincs 119 G6
Pincheon Green Donc 143 G4
Pinchinthorpe R & Cl 170 D7
Pincock Lancs 139 H4
Pinfold Lancs 138 E5
Pinford End Suffk 89 G3
Pinged Carmth 56 D4
Pingewood W Berk 49 G5
Pin Green Herts 69 H2
Pinhoe Devon 13 M4
Pinkett's Booth Covtry 99 H7
Pinkney Wilts 46 B2
Pinley Covtry 99 K7
Pinley Green Warwks 82 F2
Pin Mill Suffk 90 E7
Pinminnoch S Ayrs 182 F4
Pinmore S Ayrs 182 F4
Pinn Devon 14 C5
Pinner Gt Lon 50 E1
Pinner Green Gt Lon 50 E1
Pinsley Green Ches E 113 K2
Pinvin Worcs 81 M5
Pinwherry S Ayrs 182 F5
Pinxton Derbys 133 J8
Pipe and Lyde Herefs 80 C6
Pipe Aston Herefs 80 B1
Pipe Gate Shrops 114 A3
Pipehill Staffs 98 E2
Piperhill Highld 253 G2
Pipers Pool Cnwll 11 J6
Pipewell Nhants 101 J6
Pippacott Devon 27 J3
Pippin Street Lancs 139 H3
Pipton Powys 79 G7
Pirbright Surrey 50 B7
Pirbright Camp Surrey 50 B7
Pirnie Border 201 K7
Pirnmill N Ayrs 194 D2
Pirton Herts 68 F1
Pirton Worcs 81 K5
Pisgah Cerdgn 92 E7
Pishill Oxon 49 H1
Pistyll Gwynd 108 E3
Pitagowan P & K 232 B2
Pitblae Abers 269 H3
Pitcairngreen P & K 221 J2
Pitcalnie Highld 264 C5
Pitcaple Abers 256 C6
Pitcarity Angus 233 M2
Pitchcombe Gloucs 64 B5
Pitchcott Bucks 67 J3
Pitcher Row Lincs 119 J5
Pitchford Shrops 96 C3
Pitch Green Bucks 67 J6
Pitch Place Surrey 36 C3
Pitch Place Surrey 50 B8
Pitchroy Moray 254 D4
Pitcombe Somset 31 L4
Pitcot V Glam 42 D6
Pitcox E Loth 212 E4
Pitfichie Abers 256 B8
Pitglassie Abers 256 C3
Pitgrudy Highld 264 B2
Pitlessie Fife 222 E5
Pitlochry P & K 232 D4
Pitmachie Abers 256 B6
Pitmain Highld 241 K3
Pitmedden Abers 256 F6
Pitminster Somset 30 B7
Pitmuies Angus 234 E5
Pitmunie Abers 256 B8
Pitney Somset 31 G5
Pitroddie P & K 222 C2
Pitscottie Fife 223 G4
Pitsea Essex 52 F1
Pitses Oldham 140 E7
Pitsford Nhants 84 E2
Pitstone Bucks 68 B4
Pitt Devon 29 J7
Pitt Hants 34 F5
Pittarrow Abers 245 G8
Pitt Court Gloucs 63 L7
Pittenweem Fife 223 K6
Pitteuchar Fife 222 D7
Pittington Dur 169 J2
Pittodrie House Hotel Abers 256 C6
Pitton Wilts 34 B4
Pitt's Wood Kent 38 F3
Pittulie Abers 269 H3
Pityme Cnwll 10 C7
Pity Me Dur 169 H2
Pivington Kent 40 B6
Pixey Green Suffk 106 E8
Pixham Surrey 37 J1
Plains N Lans 209 L5
Plain Street Cnwll 10 D6
Plaish Shrops 96 C4
Plaistow Gt Lon 51 L2
Plaistow W Susx 36 F5
Plaitford Hants 34 C7
Plank Lane Wigan 139 J7
Plas Cymyran IoA 124 E4
Plastow Green Hants 48 D6
Platt Kent 39 G2
Platt Bridge Wigan 139 J7
Platt Lane Shrops 113 H4
Platts Heath Kent 39 L3
Plawsworth Dur 169 H1
Plaxtol Kent 38 F3
Playden E Susx 25 G3
Playford Suffk 90 F5
Play Hatch Oxon 49 H4
Playing Place Cnwll 4 C6
Playley Green Gloucs 63 M1
Plealey Shrops 95 K2
Plean Stirlg 209 M2
Pleasance Fife 222 C4
Pleasington Bl w D 139 J2
Pleasington Crematorium Bl w D 139 K2
Pleasley Derbys 133 K6
Pleasleyhill Notts 133 K6
Pleck Dorset 32 B8
Pledgdon Green Essex 70 E2
Pledwick Wakefd 142 A4
Pleinheaume Guern 9 j2
Plemont Jersey 9 a1
Plemstall Ches W 129 K5
Plenmeller Nthumb 179 G6
Pleshey Essex 71 G4
Plockton Highld 248 C5
Plowden Shrops 95 J6
Plox Green Shrops 95 J3
Pluckley Kent 40 B6
Pluckley Station Kent 40 B6
Pluckley Thorne Kent 40 B6
Plucks Gutter Kent 41 J3
Plumbland Cumb 164 F3
Plumgarths Cumb 157 G4
Plumley Ches E 130 E5
Plumpton Cumb 156 D7
Plumpton Cumb 166 C3
Plumpton E Susx 22 E4
Plumpton Nhants 84 B5
Plumpton End Nhants 84 D6
Plumpton Green E Susx 22 E4
Plumpton Head Cumb 166 C4
Plumstead Gt Lon 51 L3
Plumstead Norfk 122 C4
Plumstead Green Norfk 122 C4
Plumtree Notts 117 G5
Plumtree Green Kent 39 K4
Plungar Leics 117 K5
Plurenden Kent 40 B7
Plush Dorset 16 D2
Plusha Cnwll 11 J6
Plushabridge Cnwll 11 K8
Plwmp Cerdgn 76 C5
Plymouth C Plym 6 F4
Plympton C Plym 7 G4
Plymstock C Plym 7 G4
Plymtree Devon 14 B2
Pockley N York 161 K5
Pocklington E R Yk 152 B6
Pode Hole Lincs 119 H7
Podimore Somset 31 J6
Podington Bed 85 J3
Podmore Staffs 114 B4
Point Clear Essex 73 G4
Pointon Lincs 118 F5
Pokesdown Bmouth 18 A5
Polbain Highld 270 C6
Polbathic Cnwll 6 C3
Polbeth W Loth 210 D6
Polbrock Cnwll 5 G1
Polebrook Nhants 102 B6
Pole Elm Worcs 81 J5
Polegate E Susx 23 K6
Pole Moor Kirk 141 G4
Polesworth Warwks 99 H3
Polgigga Cnwll 2 B6
Polglass Highld 270 D6
Polgooth Cnwll 5 G5
Polgown D & G 185 H2
Poling W Susx 21 H6
Poling Corner W Susx 21 H5
Polkerris Cnwll 5 J4
Pollard Street Norfk 123 G5
Pollington E R Yk 142 F4
Polloch Highld 228 B2
Pollokshaws C Glas 208 F6
Pollokshields C Glas 208 F6
Polmassick Cnwll 5 G5
Polmear Cnwll 5 J4
Polmont Falk 210 B3
Polnish Highld 237 L4
Polperro Cnwll 5 L4
Polruan Cnwll 5 K5
Polsham Somset 31 H2
Polstead Suffk 89 K7
Polstead Heath Suffk 89 K7
Poltalloch Ag & B 216 C7
Poltescoe Cnwll 3 J7
Poltimore Devon 13 M3
Polton Mdloth 211 J6
Polwarth Border 202 A3
Polyphant Cnwll 11 J6
Polzeath Cnwll 10 C6
Pomathorn Mdloth 211 H7
Pomeroy Derbys 132 B6
Ponde Powys 78 F7
Pondersbridge Cambs 102 F5
Ponders End Gt Lon 69 K7
Ponsanooth Cnwll 3 J3
Ponsonby Cumb 155 J2
Ponsongath Cnwll 3 J7

Ponsworthy Devon 13 G7
Pontac Jersey 9 e4
Pontamman Carmth 59 H6
Pontantwn Carmth 58 E6
Pontardawe Neath 57 K4
Pontarddulais Swans 57 G4
Pont-ar-gothi Carmth 58 F4
Pont-ar-Hydfer Powys 60 C2
Pont-ar-llechau Carmth 59 K4
Pontarsais Carmth 58 E3
Pontblyddyn Flints 129 G7
Pont Cyfyng Conwy 126 E8
Pont Dolgarrog Conwy 126 F6
Pontdolgoch Powys 94 B5
Pont-Ebbw Newpt 44 C2
Pontefract Wakefd 142 C3
Pontefract Crematorium Wakefd 142 C4
Ponteland Nthumb 180 E4
Ponterwyd Cerdgn 93 G7
Pontesbury Shrops 95 K2
Pontesbury Hill Shrops 95 K2
Pontesford Shrops 95 K2
Pontfadog Wrexhm 112 C4
Pontfaen Pembks 75 H5
Pont-faen Powys 78 D8
Pontgarreg Cerdgn 76 B4
Pontgarreg Pembks 75 K4
Ponthenry Carmth 56 E3
Ponthir Torfn 62 C8
Ponthirwaun Cerdgn 76 A6
Pontllanfraith Caerph 43 J3
Pontlliw Swans 57 H5
Pontlottyn Caerph 61 H6
Pontlyfni Gwynd 109 H1
Pont Morlais Carmth 56 F3
Pontneddfechan Neath 60 D5
Pontnewydd Torfn 62 B7
Pontnewynydd Torfn 62 B6
Pont Pen-y-benglog Gwynd 126 C7
Pontrhydfendigaid Cerdgn 77 K2
Pont Rhyd-sarn Gwynd 111 G6
Pont Rhyd-y-cyff Brdgnd 42 C4
Pont-rhyd-y-fen Neath 42 B3
Pontrhydygroes Cerdgn 77 K1
Pontrhydyrun Torfn 62 C7
Pontrilas Herefs 62 E2
Pont Robert Powys 94 D1
Pont-rug Gwynd 125 J7
Ponts Green E Susx 24 B4
Pontshaen Cerdgn 76 D6
Pontshill Herefs 63 J3
Pontsticill Myr Td 61 G5
Pont Walby Neath 60 D6
Pontwelly Carmth 76 D7
Pontyates Carmth 56 E3
Pontyberem Carmth 58 F6
Pont-y-blew Wrexhm 112 D4
Pontybodkin Flints 129 G7
Pontyclun Rhondd 42 F5
Pontycymer Brdgnd 42 D3
Pontyglasier Pembks 75 K5
Pontygwaith Rhondd 42 F3
Pontygynon Pembks 75 K5
Pont-y-pant Conwy 110 E1
Pontypool Torfn 62 B7
Pontypool Road Torfn 62 C7
Pontypridd Rhondd 43 G4
Pont-yr-hafod Pembks 74 E7
Pont-yr-Rhyl Brdgnd 42 D4
Pontywaun Caerph 43 K3
Pool Cnwll 3 H3
Pool IoS 10 b2
Pool Leeds 150 C6
Poole Poole 17 K4
Poole Crematorium Poole 17 K3
Poole Keynes Gloucs 64 E8
Poolewe Highld 260 D4
Pooley Bridge Cumb 166 B6
Pooley Street Norfk 105 L7
Poolfold Staffs 131 H7
Pool Head Herefs 80 D5
Poolhill Gloucs 63 L1
Pool of Muckhart Clacks 221 H7
Pool Quay Powys 95 G1
Pool Street Essex 88 F7
Pooting's Kent 38 C3
Popham Hants 35 H2
Poplar Gt Lon 51 K3
Poplar Street Suffk 91 K2
Porchfield IoW 19 G5
Poringland Norfk 106 F3
Porkellis Cnwll 3 H4
Porlock Somset 28 F2
Porlock Weir Somset 28 F1
Portachoillan Ag & B 206 B7
Port-an-Eorna Highld 248 B5
Port Appin Ag & B 228 D6
Port Askaig Ag & B 205 G3
Portavadie Ag & B 206 E5
Port Bannatyne Ag & B 207 H5
Portbury N Som 45 G4
Port Carlisle Cumb 177 H6
Port Charlotte Ag & B 204 C4
Portchester Hants 19 K3
Portchester Crematorium Hants 19 K2
Port Clarence S on T 170 C6
Port Driseach Ag & B 206 F4
Port Ellen Ag & B 204 E7
Port Elphinstone Abers 256 D7
Portencalzie D & G 182 C8
Portencross N Ayrs 195 K1
Port Erin IoM 154 b8
Portesham Dorset 16 B5
Portessie Moray 267 J3
Port e Vullen IoM 154 g4
Port Eynon Swans 56 E7
Portfield Gate Pembks 54 F4
Portgate Devon 12 A5
Port Gaverne Cnwll 10 D6
Port Glasgow Inver 208 B4
Portgordon Moray 267 H3
Portgower Highld 274 D5
Porth Cnwll 4 D2
Porth Rhondd 42 F3
Porthallow Cnwll 3 K6
Porthallow Cnwll 5 L4
Porthcawl Brdgnd 42 B6
Porthcothan Cnwll 10 B8
Porthcurno Cnwll 2 B6
Porth Dinllaen Gwynd 108 D3
Port Henderson Highld 260 B5
Porthgain Pembks 74 D5
Porthgwarra Cnwll 2 B6
Porthill Staffs 114 D2
Porthkea Cnwll 4 D6
Porthkerry V Glam 43 G8
Porthleven Cnwll 3 G6
Porthmadog Gwynd 109 K4
Porthmeor Cnwll 2 C4
Porth Navas Cnwll 3 J5
Portholland Cnwll 4 F6
Porthoustock Cnwll 3 K6
Porthpean Cnwll 5 H5
Porthtowan Cnwll 4 A5
Porthwgan Wrexhm 112 F2
Porthyrhyd Carmth 58 F5
Porth-y-Waen Shrops 112 C6
Portincaple Ag & B 218 C8
Portinfer Jersey 9 a1
Portington E R Yk 143 K2
Portinnisherrich Ag & B 216 F5
Portinscale Cumb 165 H6
Port Isaac Cnwll 10 D6
Portishead N Som 44 F4
Portknockie Moray 267 K3
Portlethen Abers 245 K4
Portling D & G 175 L4
Portloe Cnwll 4 F7
Port Logan D & G 172 D6
Portlooe Cnwll 6 A4
Portmahomack Highld 264 E3
Portmellon Cnwll 5 G6
Port Mor Highld 236 E4
Portmore Hants 18 E4
Port Mulgrave N York 171 J7
Portnacroish Ag & B 228 E6
Portnaguran W Isls 282 h3
Portnahaven Ag & B 204 B6
Portnalong Highld 246 D2
Port nan Giuran W Isls 282 h3
Port nan Long W Isls 282 c7
Port Nis W Isls 282 h1
Portobello C Edin 211 J4
Portobello Gatesd 181 G7
Portobello Wolves 98 B4
Port of Menteith Stirlg 219 J7
Port of Ness W Isls 282 h1
Porton Wilts 33 L4
Portontown Devon 12 A7
Portpatrick D & G 172 B4
Port Quin Cnwll 10 D6
Port Ramsay Ag & B 228 D6
Portreath Cnwll 3 G2
Portree Highld 259 H7
Port St Mary IoM 154 b8
Portscatho Cnwll 3 M4
Portsea C Port 19 L4
Portskerra Highld 278 E3
Portskewett Mons 45 G1
Portslade Br & H 22 C6
Portslade-by-Sea Br & H 22 C6
Portslogan D & G 172 B3
Portsmouth C Port 19 L4
Portsmouth Calder 140 D3
Port Soderick IoM 154 d7
Port Solent C Port 19 L3
Portsonachan Hotel Ag & B 217 G3
Portsoy Abers 267 M3
Port Sunlight Wirral 129 H3
Portswood C Sotn 34 F8
Port Talbot Neath 57 L7
Port Tennant Swans 57 J6
Portuairk Highld 236 E7
Portway Herefs 80 B6
Portway Herefs 80 C8
Portway Sandw 98 B6
Portway Worcs 82 C1
Port Wemyss Ag & B 204 B6
Port William D & G 173 J6
Portwrinkle Cnwll 6 D4
Portyerrock D & G 174 D7
Posbury Devon 13 J3
Posenhall Shrops 96 E3
Poslingford Suffk 88 F5
Posso Border 199 L6
Postbridge Devon 12 F6
Postcombe Oxon 67 H7
Post Green Dorset 17 J4
Postling Kent 40 F7
Postwick Norfk 106 F2
Potarch Abers 244 D4
Potsgrove C Beds 68 B1
Potten End Herts 68 C5
Potten Street Kent 41 H2
Potter Brompton N York 163 H7
Pottergate Street Norfk 106 D5
Potterhanworth Lincs 135 L6
Potterhanworth Booths Lincs 135 M6
Potter Heigham Norfk 123 J7
Potterne Wilts 46 E7
Potterne Wick Wilts 46 E7
Potter Row Bucks 67 L6
Potters Bar Herts 69 H6
Potters Brook Lancs 147 J5
Potter's Cross Staffs 97 J6
Potters Crouch Herts 68 E6
Potter's Forstal Kent 39 M4
Potters Green Covtry 99 K7
Potter's Green E Susx 23 H3
Potter's Green Herts 69 K3
Pottersheath Herts 69 G3
Potters Marston Leics 100 B4
Potter Somersal Derbys 115 J4
Potterspury Nhants 84 E6
Potterton Abers 257 H8
Potterton Leeds 150 F8
Potthorpe Norfk 121 L7
Pottle Street Wilts 32 D3
Potto N York 161 G2
Potton C Beds 86 E5
Pott Row Norfk 120 F7
Pott's Green Essex 72 C3
Pott Shrigley Ches E 131 J4
Poughill Cnwll 11 J1
Poughill Devon 13 K1
Poulner Hants 18 B2
Poulshot Wilts 46 E7
Poulton Gloucs 65 G7
Poulton Wirral 129 G2
Poulton-le-Fylde Lancs 147 G7
Poulton Priory Gloucs 65 G7
Pound Bank Worcs 97 G8
Poundbury Dorset 16 C4
Poundffald Swans 57 G6
Poundgate E Susx 38 D7
Pound Green E Susx 23 H3
Pound Green Suffk 88 E4
Pound Green Worcs 97 G7
Pound Hill W Susx 37 L3
Poundon Bucks 66 F2
Poundsbridge Kent 38 E5
Poundsgate Devon 13 G8
Poundstock Cnwll 11 H3
Pound Street Hants 48 C6
Pounsley E Susx 23 J3
Pouton D & G 174 C5
Pouy Street Suffk 91 H1
Povey Cross Surrey 37 L3
Powburn Nthumb 190 F3
Powderham Devon 13 M5
Powerstock Dorset 15 L3
Powfoot D & G 176 F5
Pow Green Herefs 81 G6
Powhill Cumb 177 H7
Powick Worcs 81 J5
Powmill P & K 221 J7
Poxwell Dorset 16 E6
Poyle Slough 50 C4
Poynings W Susx 22 C5
Poyntington Dorset 31 L6
Poynton Ches E 131 H3
Poynton Wrekin 113 J8
Poynton Green Wrekin 113 J7
Poyston Cross Pembks 55 G3
Poystreet Green Suffk 89 K4
Praa Sands Cnwll 2 F5
Pratt's Bottom Gt Lon 52 A6
Praze-an-Beeble Cnwll 3 G4
Predannack Wollas Cnwll 3 H7
Prees Shrops 113 J5
Preesall Lancs 147 G6
Prees Green Shrops 113 J5
Preesgweene Shrops 112 D4
Prees Heath Shrops 113 J4
Prees Higher Heath Shrops 113 J4
Prees Lower Heath Shrops 113 J5
Prendwick Nthumb 190 E4
Pren-gwyn Cerdgn 76 D6
Prenteg Gwynd 109 K3
Prenton Wirral 129 G2
Prescot Knows 129 L1
Prescott Devon 29 K8
Prescott Shrops 96 F7
Prescott Shrops 112 F7
Presnerb Angus 233 J2
Pressen Nthumb 202 C6
Prestatyn Denbgs 128 C3
Prestbury Ches E 131 H4
Prestbury Gloucs 64 E2
Presteigne Powys 79 K2
Prestleigh Somset 31 K3
Prestolee Bolton 139 M6
Preston Border 213 H7
Preston Br & H 22 D6
Preston Devon 13 K7
Preston Dorset 16 D6
Preston E R Yk 144 F2
Preston Gloucs 64 F7
Preston Herts 68 F2
Preston Kent 40 D3
Preston Kent 41 H3
Preston Lancs 139 G2
Preston Nthumb 203 K8
Preston Rutlnd 101 J3
Preston Shrops 96 C1
Preston Somset 29 K4
Preston Suffk 89 J5
Preston Torbay 8 D3
Preston Wilts 46 F3
Preston Wilts 47 K4
Preston Bagot Warwks 82 E2
Preston Bissett Bucks 67 G1
Preston Bowyer Somset 29 L5
Preston Brockhurst Shrops 113 J6
Preston Brook Halton 130 B4
Preston Candover Hants 35 J3
Preston Capes Nhants 84 B4
Preston Crematorium Lancs 139 H1
Preston Crowmarsh Oxon 48 F1
Preston Deanery Nhants 84 F4
Preston Green Warwks 82 E2
Preston Gubbals Shrops 113 H7
Preston Montford Shrops 113 G8
Preston on Stour Warwks 82 F5
Preston on Tees S on T 169 L7
Preston on the Hill Halton 130 B3
Preston on Wye Herefs 79 M7
Prestonpans E Loth 211 L4
Preston Patrick Cumb 157 H6
Preston Plucknett Somset 31 H7
Preston Street Kent 41 H3
Preston-under-Scar N York 159 K4
Preston upon the Weald Moors Wrekin 113 L8
Preston Wynne Herefs 80 D6
Prestwich Bury 140 B6
Prestwick Nthumb 180 E4
Prestwick S Ayrs 196 C6
Prestwood Bucks 67 L7
Prestwood Staffs 97 K6
Price Town Brdgnd 42 E3
Prickwillow Cambs 104 B7
Priddy Somset 31 H1
Priestacott Devon 12 B1
Priestcliffe Derbys 132 C5
Priestcliffe Ditch Derbys 132 C5
Priest Hutton Lancs 157 H7
Priestland E Ayrs 197 H3
Priestley Green Calder 141 H3
Priest Weston Shrops 95 H4
Priestwood Green Kent 52 E6
Primethorpe Leics 100 B5
Primrose Green Norfk 122 B8
Primrosehill Border 213 H7
Primrose Hill Cambs 103 H5
Primrose Hill Derbys 133 J8
Primrose Hill Dudley 97 L6
Primrose Hill Lancs 138 E6
Primsidemill Border 202 C7
Princes Gate Pembks 55 K4
Princes Risborough Bucks 67 K6
Princethorpe Warwks 83 J1
Princetown Devon 12 E7
Prinsted W Susx 20 C5
Prion Denbgs 128 C7
Prior Rigg Cumb 178 B5
Priors Halton Shrops 96 B8

Priors Hardwick Warwks 83 L4
Priorslee Wrekin 97 G1
Priors Marston Warwks 83 L4
Priors Norton Gloucs 64 C2
Priory Vale Swindn 47 H1
Priory Wood Herefs 79 J6
Prisk V Glam 42 F6
Priston BaNES 45 K7
Pristow Green Norfk 106 C5
Prittlewell Sthend 53 J2
Privett Hants 35 L5
Prixford Devon 27 K3
Probus Cnwll 4 E5
Prora E Loth 212 B3
Prospect Cumb 164 F3
Prospidnick Cnwll 3 G5
Protstonhill Abers 268 E3
Prudhoe Nthumb 180 D6
Prussia Cove Cnwll 2 E5
Publow BaNES 45 J6
Puckeridge Herts 69 K2
Puckington Somset 30 E7
Pucklechurch S Glos 45 K4
Puckrup Gloucs 81 K7
Puddinglake Ches W 130 E5
Puddington Ches W 129 H5
Puddington Devon 28 E8
Puddledock Norfk 105 L5
Puddletown Dorset 16 E4
Pudleston Herefs 80 D3
Pudsey Leeds 141 K1
Pulborough W Susx 21 H3
Puleston Wrekin 114 A7
Pulford Ches W 129 J7
Pulham Dorset 16 D1
Pulham Market Norfk 106 D6
Pulham St Mary Norfk 106 E6
Pullens Green S Glos 63 J8
Pulloxhill C Beds 85 L8
Pumpherston W Loth 210 E5
Pumsaint Carmth 77 J7
Puncheston Pembks 75 G6
Puncknowle Dorset 15 M5
Punnett's Town E Susx 23 K3
Purbrook Hants 19 M2
Purfleet Thurr 52 C3
Puriton Somset 30 D3
Purleigh Essex 71 K6
Purley Gt Lon 51 J6
Purley W Berk 49 G4
Purlogue Shrops 95 G7
Purlpit Wilts 46 C5
Purls Bridge Cambs 103 K6
Purse Caundle Dorset 32 B7
Purshull Green Worcs 81 K1
Purslow Shrops 95 J7
Purston Jaglin Wakefd 142 C4
Purtington Somset 15 J1
Purton Gloucs 63 K6
Purton Gloucs 63 K6
Purton Wilts 47 G2
Purton Stoke Wilts 47 G1
Pury End Nhants 84 D6
Pusey Oxon 65 M7
Putley Herefs 80 E7
Putley Green Herefs 80 F7
Putloe Gloucs 64 A5
Putney Gt Lon 51 G4
Putney Vale Crematorium Gt Lon 51 G4
Putsborough Devon 27 H3
Puttenham Herts 67 L4
Puttenham Surrey 36 D2
Puttock End Essex 89 G7
Putton Dorset 16 C6
Puxley Nhants 84 E6
Puxton N Som 44 E6
Pwll Carmth 56 E4
Pwllcrochan Pembks 54 F6
Pwll-du Mons 61 L5
Pwll-glâs Denbgs 111 M1
Pwllgloyw Powys 78 E8
Pwllheli Gwynd 108 F4
Pwllmeyric Mons 63 G8
Pwll Trap Carmth 58 A5
Pwll-y-glaw Neath 42 B3
Pydew Conwy 126 F4
Pye Bridge Derbys 116 D1
Pyecombe W Susx 22 D4
Pye Corner Newpt 44 D2
Pye Green Staffs 114 F8
Pyle Brdgnd 42 B5
Pyleigh Somset 29 L5
Pylle Somset 31 K3
Pymoor Cambs 103 K6
Pymore Dorset 15 L4
Pyrford Surrey 50 D7
Pyrton Oxon 67 G7
Pytchley Nhants 101 J8
Pyworthy Devon 11 K2

Q

Quabbs Shrops 94 F7
Quadring Lincs 119 H5
Quadring Eaudike Lincs 119 H5
Quainton Bucks 67 H3
Quaker's Yard Myr Td 43 H3
Quaking Houses Dur 180 F8
Quarff Shet 281 e7
Quarley Hants 34 C2
Quarndon Derbys 116 B3
Quarr Hill IoW 19 K5
Quarrier's Village Inver 208 B5
Quarrington Lincs 118 E3
Quarrington Hill Dur 169 J3
Quarrybank Ches W 130 A6
Quarry Bank Dudley 97 L6
Quarrywood Moray 266 D3
Quarter N Ayrs 207 K6
Quarter S Lans 197 L1
Quatford Shrops 97 G5
Quatt Shrops 97 G5
Quebec Dur 168 F2
Quedgeley Gloucs 64 A4
Queen Adelaide Cambs 104 B7
Queenborough Kent 53 K4
Queen Camel Somset 31 K6
Queen Charlton BaNES 45 J5
Queen Dart Devon 28 E7
Queenhill Worcs 81 K7
Queen Oak Dorset 32 C4
Queen's Bower IoW 19 J6
Queensbury C Brad 141 H2
Queensferry Flints 129 H6
Queen's Head Shrops 112 E6
Queenslie C Glas 209 H6
Queen's Park Bed 85 L5
Queen's Park Nhants 84 E3
Queen Street Kent 39 H4
Queen Street Wilts 46 F2
Queenzieburn N Lans 209 J3
Quendon Essex 70 D1
Queniborough Leics 100 E1
Quenington Gloucs 65 H6
Quernmore Lancs 147 K4
Queslett Birm 98 D4
Quethiock Cnwll 6 C2
Quick's Green W Berk 48 E4
Quidenham Norfk 105 L6
Quidhampton Hants 35 G1
Quidhampton Wilts 33 K5
Quina Brook Shrops 113 H5
Quinbury End Nhants 84 B5
Quinton Dudley 98 C6
Quinton Nhants 84 E4
Quinton Green Nhants 84 F4
Quintrell Downs Cnwll 4 D3
Quixhall Staffs 115 H3
Quixwood Border 213 H6
Quoditch Devon 12 A3
Quoig P & K 220 E3
Quorn Leics 116 F8
Quothquan S Lans 199 G5
Quoyburray Ork 275 d5
Quoyloo Ork 275 b4

R

Raasay Highld 259 K8
Rabbit's Cross Kent 39 K4
Rableyheath Herts 69 G3
Raby Cumb 177 G8
Raby Wirral 129 H4
Rachan Mill Border 199 K6
Rachub Gwynd 126 C6
Rackenford Devon 28 E7
Rackham W Susx 21 H4
Rackheath Norfk 122 F8
Racks D & G 176 D4
Rackwick Ork 275 a5
Radbourne Derbys 115 M4
Radcliffe Bury 140 B6
Radcliffe Nthumb 191 K5
Radcliffe on Trent Notts 117 H4
Radclive Bucks 84 D8
Radcot Oxon 65 L7
Raddery Highld 263 J7
Raddington Somset 29 J5
Radernie Fife 223 H5
Radford Covtry 99 J7
Radford Semele Warwks 83 H2
Radlet Somset 30 B3
Radlett Herts 68 F7
Radley Devon 28 C6
Radley Oxon 66 D7
Radley Green Essex 70 F6
Radmore Green Ches E 130 B8
Radnage Bucks 67 J7
Radstock BaNES 45 K8
Radstone Nhants 84 B7
Radway Warwks 83 J5
Radwell Bed 85 K4
Radwell Herts 86 E8
Radwinter Essex 88 C7
Radwinter End Essex 88 C7
Radyr Cardif 43 H5
RAF College (Cranwell) Lincs 118 D2
Rafford Moray 265 H8
Ragdale Leics 117 H7
Ragdon Shrops 95 L5
Raginnis Cnwll 2 D6
Raglan Mons 62 E5
Ragnall Notts 134 F5
Raigbeg Highld 252 F6
Rainbow Hill Worcs 81 K4
Rainford St Hel 138 F7
Rainham Gt Lon 52 B3
Rainham Medway 53 H6
Rainhill St Hel 129 L2
Rainhill Stoops St Hel 129 L2
Rainow Ches E 131 J4
Rainsough Bury 140 B7
Rainton N York 160 E7
Rainworth Notts 134 B8
Raisbeck Cumb 157 K1
Raise Cumb 167 G2
Raisthorpe N York 152 C3
Rait P & K 222 C2
Raithby Lincs 136 F3
Raithby Lincs 137 G6
Raithwaite N York 171 K8
Rake Hants 36 B5
Rakewood Rochdl 140 E5
Ralia Highld 241 J4
Ram Carmth 77 G6
Ramasaig Highld 258 B7
Rame Cnwll 3 J4
Rame Cnwll 6 E5
Ram Hill S Glos 45 K3
Ram Lane Kent 40 C6
Rampisham Dorset 16 A2
Rampside Cumb 146 E3
Rampton Cambs 87 J2
Rampton Notts 134 F4
Ramsbottom Bury 140 B4
Ramsbury Wilts 47 K4
Ramscraigs Highld 274 F3
Ramsdean Hants 35 L6
Ramsdell Hants 48 E7
Ramsden Oxon 65 M4
Ramsden Worcs 81 L6
Ramsden Bellhouse Essex 71 H8
Ramsden Heath Essex 71 H7
Ramsey Cambs 102 F6
Ramsey Essex 73 J1
Ramsey IoM 154 f3
Ramsey Forty Foot Cambs 102 F6
Ramsey Heights Cambs 102 E6
Ramsey Island Essex 72 D6
Ramsey Island Pembks 74 A7
Ramsey Mereside Cambs 102 F5
Ramsey St Mary's Cambs 102 E6
Ramsgate Kent 41 L2
Ramsgill N York 149 K2
Ramshaw Dur 168 B1
Ramshaw Dur 168 F5
Ramsholt Suffk 91 H7
Ramshope Nthumb 189 K5
Ramshorn Staffs 115 H3
Ramsley Devon 12 F4
Ramsnest Common Surrey 36 E4
Ranby Lincs 136 D4
Ranby Notts 134 C3
Rand Lincs 136 B4
Randalls Park Crematorium Surrey 50 F7
Randwick Gloucs 64 B5
Ranfurly Rens 208 C6
Rangemore Staffs 115 K7
Rangeworthy S Glos 45 K2
Rankinston E Ayrs 196 E8
Ranksborough Rutlnd 101 H1
Rank's Green Essex 71 H3
Rannoch Station P & K 230 D4
Ranscombe Somset 29 G2
Ranskill Notts 134 C2
Ranton Staffs 114 D6
Ranton Green Staffs 114 D7
Ranworth Norfk 123 G8
Raploch Stirlg 220 D8
Rapness Ork 275 d2
Rapps Somset 30 E7
Rascarrel D & G 175 K5
Rashfield Ag & B 207 J2
Rashwood Worcs 81 L2
Raskelf N York 151 G2
Rassau Blae G 61 J5
Rastrick Calder 141 H3
Ratagan Highld 248 E7
Ratby Leics 100 B2
Ratcliffe Culey Leics 99 J3
Ratcliffe on Soar Notts 116 E6
Ratcliffe on the Wreake Leics 117 G8
Ratfyn Wilts 33 L2
Rathen Abers 269 J4
Rathillet Fife 222 F3
Rathmell N York 148 D4
Ratho C Edin 210 F5
Ratho Station C Edin 210 F4
Rathven Moray 267 J3
Ratlake Hants 34 E6
Ratley Warwks 83 J5
Ratling Kent 41 H4
Ratlinghope Shrops 95 K4
Rattan Row Norfk 120 B8
Rattar Highld 280 C2
Ratten Row Cumb 165 K3
Ratten Row Cumb 165 L1
Ratten Row Lancs 147 H7
Rattery Devon 7 L3
Rattlesden Suffk 89 K3
Ratton Village E Susx 23 K7
Rattray P & K 233 J6
Raughton Cumb 165 L1
Raughton Head Cumb 165 L2
Raunds Nhants 85 K1
Ravenfield Rothm 133 J1
Ravenglass Cumb 155 K3
Ravenhills Green Worcs 81 G4
Raveningham Norfk 107 H4
Ravenscar N York 163 H2
Ravenscraig N Lans 209 K7
Ravensdale IoM 154 e4
Ravensden Bed 86 B4
Ravenseat N York 158 E2
Ravenshead Notts 133 L8
Ravensmoor Ches E 113 K2
Ravensthorpe Kirk 141 K4
Ravensthorpe Nhants 84 C1
Ravenstone Leics 99 L1
Ravenstone M Keyn 85 G5
Ravenstonedale Cumb 158 C2
Ravenstruther S Lans 198 F4
Ravensworth N York 159 L1
Raw N York 163 G2
Rawcliffe C York 151 J5
Rawcliffe E R Yk 143 H3
Rawcliffe Bridge E R Yk 143 H3
Rawdon Leeds 150 B7
Rawdon Crematorium Leeds 150 B8
Rawling Street Kent 40 B3
Rawmarsh Rothm 142 C8
Rawnsley Staffs 98 C1
Rawreth Essex 71 J8
Rawridge Devon 14 E2
Rawtenstall Lancs 140 B3
Raydon Suffk 90 B7
Raylees Nthumb 190 C7
Rayleigh Essex 53 H1
Raymond's Hill Devon 15 H3
Rayne Essex 71 H3
Raynes Park Gt Lon 51 G5
Reach Cambs 88 B2
Read Lancs 140 A1
Reading Readg 49 H4
Reading Crematorium Readg 49 H4
Reading Street Kent 25 G1
Reading Street Kent 41 L2
Reagill Cumb 166 E7
Realwa Cnwll 2 F4
Rearquhar Highld 263 K1
Rearsby Leics 117 H8
Rease Heath Ches E 113 L1
Reay Highld 279 G3
Reculver Kent 41 H2
Red Ball Devon 29 K7
Redberth Pembks 55 J6
Redbourn Herts 68 E4
Redbourne N Linc 144 B7
Redbrook Gloucs 63 G5
Redbrook Wrexhm 113 H3
Redbrook Street Kent 40 B8
Redburn Highld 253 H2
Redburn Nthumb 179 H6
Redcar R & Cl 170 E6
Redcastle D & G 175 K2
Redcastle Highld 251 G2
Red Dial Cumb 165 H2
Redding Falk 210 B3
Reddingmuirhead Falk 210 B3
Reddish Stockp 131 H1
Redditch Worcs 82 B2
Redditch Crematorium Worcs 82 B2
Rede Suffk 88 F4
Redenhall Norfk 106 F6
Redenham Hants 34 C1
Redesmouth Nthumb 179 K3
Redford Abers 235 J2

Redford Angus 234 E6
Redford W Susx 36 C5
Redfordgreen Border 188 C3
Redgate Rhondd 42 F4
Redgorton P & K 221 K2
Redgrave Suffk 105 L7
Redhill Abers 245 H3
Red Hill Bmouth 17 L3
Redhill Herts 86 F8
Redhill N Som 45 G6
Redhill Surrey 37 L1
Red Hill Warwks 82 D4
Redisham Suffk 107 H6
Redland Bristl 45 H4
Redland Ork 275 c3
Redlingfield Suffk 90 E1
Redlingfield Green Suffk 90 E1
Red Lodge Suffk 88 D1
Red Lumb Rochdl 140 C4
Redlynch Somset 32 B4
Redlynch Wilts 33 L6
Redmain Cumb 164 F4
Redmarley Worcs 81 H2
Redmarley D'Abitot Gloucs 63 L1
Redmarshall S on T 169 K6
Redmile Leics 117 L4
Redmire N York 159 J4
Redmyre Abers 245 G8
Rednal Birm 98 C8
Rednal Shrops 112 E6
Redpath Border 201 J6
Redpoint Highld 260 B6
Red Post Cnwll 11 K2
Red Rock Wigan 139 H6
Red Roses Carmth 55 L4
Red Row Nthumb 191 K6
Redruth Cnwll 4 A6
Redstocks Wilts 46 D6
Redstone P & K 233 J8
Redstone Cross Pembks 55 J4
Red Street Staffs 114 C1
Redvales Bury 140 B6
Red Wharf Bay IoA 125 J3
Redwick Newpt 44 E2
Redwick S Glos 45 H2
Redworth Darltn 169 G6
Reed Herts 87 H8
Reedham Norfk 107 J3
Reedness E R Yk 143 K3
Reeds Beck Lincs 136 D6
Reeds Holme Lancs 140 B3
Reepham Lincs 135 L5
Reepham Norfk 122 B7
Reeth N York 159 J3
Reeves Green Solhll 99 H7
Regaby IoM 154 f3
Regil N Som 45 G6
Reiff Highld 270 C5
Reigate Surrey 37 L1
Reighton N York 163 L7
Reisque Abers 256 F7
Reiss Highld 280 D5
Rejerrah Cnwll 4 C4
Releath Cnwll 3 G4
Relubbus Cnwll 2 F4
Relugas Moray 253 J2
Remenham Wokham 49 J2
Remenham Hill Wokham 49 J2
Rempstone Notts 116 F6
Rendcomb Gloucs 64 E5
Rendham Suffk 91 H2
Rendlesham Suffk 91 H4
Renfrew Rens 208 E5
Renhold Bed 86 B5
Renishaw Derbys 133 J4
Rennington Nthumb 191 J3
Renton W Duns 208 C3
Renwick Cumb 166 E2
Repps Norfk 123 J8
Repton Derbys 116 A6
Resaurie Highld 251 J3
Rescassa Cnwll 5 G6
Rescorla Cnwll 5 G5
Resipole Highld 237 L7
Reskadinnick Cnwll 3 G3
Resolis Highld 263 J6
Resolven Neath 60 C6
Rest and be thankful Ag & B 218 C5
Reston Border 213 J6
Restronguet Cnwll 3 K4
Reswallie Angus 234 D5
Reterth Cnwll 4 F2
Retford Notts 134 D3
Retire Cnwll 5 G2
Rettendon Essex 71 J7
Retyn Cnwll 4 E3
Revesby Lincs 136 E7
Rew Devon 7 K7
Rew Devon 13 H8
Rewe Devon 13 M3
Rew Street IoW 19 H5
Rexon Devon 12 A5
Reydon Suffk 107 K7
Reymerston Norfk 105 L2
Reynalton Pembks 55 J5
Reynoldston Swans 56 E6
Rezare Cnwll 11 L7
Rhadyr Mons 62 D6
Rhandirmwyn Carmth 77 L6
Rhayader Powys 78 D2
Rheindown Highld 250 F2
Rhes-y-cae Flints 128 E5
Rhewl Denbgs 112 B3
Rhewl Denbgs 128 D7
Rhewl-fawr Flints 128 D3
Rhewl Mostyn Flints 128 D4
Rhicarn Highld 270 E3
Rhiconich Highld 276 D5
Rhicullen Highld 263 J5
Rhigos Rhondd 60 D6
Rhireavach Highld 261 G1
Rhives Highld 273 K7
Rhiwbina Cardif 43 J5
Rhiwbryfdir Gwynd 110 D2
Rhiwderyn Newpt 43 L4
Rhiwen Gwynd 125 K7
Rhiwinder Rhondd 42 F4
Rhiwlas Gwynd 111 H4
Rhiwlas Gwynd 125 K6
Rhiwlas Powys 112 B5
Rhiwsaeson Rhondd 43 G5
Rhode Somset 30 C4
Rhoden Green Kent 39 H4
Rhodesia Notts 133 L4
Rhodes Minnis Kent 40 F6
Rhodiad-y-brenin Pembks 74 C6
Rhonehouse D & G 175 J3
Rhoose V Glam 43 G8
Rhos Carmth 58 C2
Rhos Denbgs 128 D7
Rhos Neath 57 K4
Rhosbeirio IoA 125 G2
Rhoscefnhir IoA 125 J4
Rhoscolyn IoA 124 D4
Rhoscrowther Pembks 54 E6
Rhosesmor Flints 128 F6
Rhos-fawr Gwynd 109 G4
Rhosgadfan Gwynd 125 J8
Rhosgoch IoA 125 G2
Rhosgoch Powys 79 H5
Rhos Haminiog Cerdgn 76 F2
Rhoshill Pembks 75 L4
Rhoshirwaun Gwynd 108 C5
Rhoslan Gwynd 109 H3
Rhoslefain Gwynd 92 C2
Rhosllanerchrugog Wrexhm 112 D2
Rhôs Lligwy IoA 125 J2
Rhosmaen Carmth 59 H4
Rhosmeirch IoA 125 H4
Rhosneigr IoA 124 E5
Rhosnesni Wrexhm 112 E2
Rhôs-on-Sea Conwy 127 G4
Rhosrobin Wrexhm 112 E1
Rhossili Swans 56 D7
Rhostryfan Gwynd 125 J8
Rhostyllen Wrexhm 112 D2
Rhosybol IoA 125 G2
Rhos y-brithdir Powys 111 M7
Rhosygadfa Shrops 112 D4
Rhos-y-garth Cerdgn 77 H1
Rhos-y-gwaliau Gwynd 111 H4
Rhos-y-llan Gwynd 108 D4
Rhosymedre Wrexhm 112 D3
Rhos-y-meirch Powys 79 K1
Rhu Ag & B 207 M2
Rhuallt Denbgs 128 C5
Rhubodach Ag & B 207 G4
Rhuddall Heath Ches W 130 A7
Rhuddlan Cerdgn 76 F6
Rhuddlan Denbgs 127 L4
Rhulen Powys 79 G5
Rhunahaorine Ag & B 205 M6
Rhyd Gwynd 110 B3
Rhydargaeau Carmth 58 D4
Rhydcymerau Carmth 77 G7
Rhydd Worcs 81 J6
Rhyd-Ddu Gwynd 109 K1
Rhydding Neath 57 K5
Rhydgaled Conwy 127 K6
Rhydlanfair Conwy 110 F1
Rhydlewis Cerdgn 76 C5
Rhydlios Gwynd 108 C5
Rhyd-lydan Conwy 111 G2
Rhydowen Cerdgn 76 E6
Rhydrosser Cerdgn 77 G2
Rhydspence Herefs 79 J5
Rhydtalog Flints 128 F8
Rhyd-uchaf Gwynd 111 G4
Rhyd-y-clafdy Gwynd 108 E4
Rhydycroesau Shrops 112 C5
Rhydyfelin Cerdgn 92 D7
Rhydyfelin Rhondd 43 H4
Rhyd-y-foel Conwy 127 H4
Rhydyfro Neath 57 K4
Rhyd-y-groes Gwynd 125 K6
Rhydymain Gwynd 110 F7
Rhyd-y-meirch Mons 62 C5
Rhydymwyn Flints 128 E6
Rhyd-y pennau Cerdgn 92 D6
Rhyd-yr-onnen Gwynd 92 D3
Rhyd-y-sarn Gwynd 110 C3
Rhyl Denbgs 127 K3
Rhymney Caerph 61 H5
Rhynd P & K 222 B3
Rhynie Abers 255 K6
Rhynie Highld 264 C4
Ribbesford Worcs 97 H8
Ribbleton Lancs 139 H2
Ribby Lancs 138 E2
Ribchester Lancs 139 K1
Riber Derbys 132 F7
Riby Lincs 144 F6
Riccall N York 151 K8
Riccarton Border 188 F7
Riccarton E Ayrs 196 E4
Richards Castle Herefs 80 C1
Richings Park Bucks 50 C3
Richmond Gt Lon 50 F4
Richmond N York 159 M2
Richmond Sheff 133 H3
Richmond Fort Guern 9 i2
Rich's Holford Somset 29 L4
Rickerscote Staffs 114 E7
Rickford N Som 44 F7
Rickham Devon 7 L7
Rickinghall Suffk 105 L8
Rickling Essex 70 D1
Rickling Green Essex 70 D1
Rickmansworth Herts 68 D8
Riddell Border 188 E1
Riddings Derbys 116 C1
Riddlecombe Devon 27 L8
Riddlesden C Brad 149 K7
Ridge BaNES 45 H7
Ridge Dorset 17 H5
Ridge Herts 69 G7
Ridge Wilts 33 G4
Ridgebourne Powys 78 E3
Ridge Green Surrey 37 L1
Ridge Lane Warwks 99 J4
Ridge Row Kent 41 G6
Ridgeway Derbys 133 H3
Ridgeway Worcs 82 B3
Ridgeway Cross Herefs 81 G5
Ridgewell Essex 88 E7
Ridgewood E Susx 23 H3
Ridgmont C Beds 85 J8
Riding Mill Nthumb 180 B6
Ridley Kent 52 D6
Ridley Nthumb 179 H6
Ridley Green Ches E 113 J1
Ridlington Norfk 123 G5
Ridlington Rutlnd 101 J3
Ridlington Street Norfk 123 G5
Ridsdale Nthumb 179 L2
Rievaulx N York 161 J5
Rigg D & G 177 J5
Riggend N Lans 209 K5
Righoul Highld 253 G2
Rigmadon Park Cumb 157 K5
Rigsby Lincs 137 H4
Rigside S Lans 198 E6
Riley Green Lancs 139 J3
Rileyhill Staffs 115 J8
Rilla Mill Cnwll 11 K7
Rillaton Cnwll 11 K7
Rillington N York 162 E7
Rimington Lancs 148 D6
Rimpton Somset 31 K6
Rimswell E R Yk 145 J2
Rinaston Pembks 75 G7
Rindleford Shrops 97 G4
Ringford D & G 175 H3
Ringinglow Sheff 132 F3
Ringland Norfk 106 C1
Ringles Cross E Susx 23 H3
Ringlestone Kent 39 L2
Ringley Bolton 139 M6
Ringmer E Susx 23 G5
Ringmore Devon 7 J5
Ringmore Devon 13 L8
Ring o'Bells Lancs 138 F5
Ringorm Moray 254 E3
Ring's End Cambs 103 H3
Ringsfield Suffk 107 H5
Ringsfield Corner Suffk 107 H6
Ringshall Herts 68 C4
Ringshall Suffk 90 B4
Ringshall Stocks Suffk 90 B5
Ringstead Nhants 101 L8
Ringstead Norfk 120 F3
Ringwood Hants 18 A3
Ringwould Kent 41 K5
Rinsey Cnwll 2 F5
Rinsey Croft Cnwll 2 F5
Ripe E Susx 23 H5
Ripley Derbys 116 C2
Ripley Hants 18 B4
Ripley N York 150 C4
Ripley Surrey 50 D7
Riplingham E R Yk 144 B2
Riplington Hants 35 K6
Ripon N York 150 D2
Rippingale Lincs 118 E6
Ripple Kent 41 K5
Ripple Worcs 81 K7
Ripponden Calder 140 F4
Risabus Ag & B 204 D7
Risbury Herefs 80 D4
Risby N Linc 144 A5
Risby Suffk 88 F2
Risca Caerph 43 K3
Rise E R Yk 153 J7
Riseden E Susx 38 F7
Riseden Kent 39 H6
Risegate Lincs 119 H5
Riseholme Lincs 135 K5
Risehow Cumb 164 D4
Riseley Bed 85 L3
Riseley Wokham 49 H6
Rishangles Suffk 90 E2
Rishton Lancs 139 L2
Rishworth Calder 140 F4
Rising Bridge Lancs 140 A3
Risley Derbys 116 D4
Risley Warrtn 130 C1
Risplith N York 150 B2
Rivar Wilts 47 L6
Rivenhall End Essex 71 K4
River Kent 41 J6
River W Susx 36 D6
River Bank Cambs 87 L2
Riverford Highld 250 F1
Riverhead Kent 38 D2
Rivers Corner Dorset 32 C8
Rivington Lancs 139 J5
Roachill Devon 28 E6
Roade Nhants 84 E5
Road Green Norfk 106 F4
Roadhead Cumb 178 C4
Roadmeetings S Lans 198 E3
Roadside E Ayrs 197 H7
Roadside Highld 279 L4
Roadwater Somset 29 J3
Roag Highld 258 D7
Roa Island Cumb 146 D3
Roan of Craigoch S Ayrs 183 H2
Roast Green Essex 87 J8
Roath Cardif 43 K6
Roberton Border 188 D3
Roberton S Lans 198 F7
Robertsbridge E Susx 24 D3
Roberttown Kirk 141 J3
Robeston Wathen Pembks 55 J4
Robgill Tower D & G 177 H4
Robin Hill Staffs 131 H8
Robin Hood Lancs 139 G5
Robin Hood Leeds 141 M2
Robin Hood Crematorium Solhll 98 E7
Robinhood End Essex 88 E7
Robin Hood's Bay N York 163 G2
Roborough Devon 6 F2
Roborough Devon 27 K7
Roby Knows 129 K2
Roby Mill Lancs 139 G6
Rocester Staffs 115 J4
Roch Pembks 54 E3
Rochdale Rochdl 140 D5
Rochdale Crematorium Rochdl 140 C5
Roche Cnwll 5 G3
Rochester Medway 52 F5
Rochester Nthumb 189 M6
Rochford Essex 53 J1
Rochford Worcs 80 E2
Roch Gate Pembks 54 E3
Rock Cnwll 10 C7
Rock Neath 57 L6
Rock Nthumb 191 J2
Rock W Susx 21 K4
Rock Worcs 81 G1
Rockbeare Devon 14 B4
Rockbourne Hants 33 K7
Rockcliffe Cumb 177 K6
Rockcliffe D & G 175 L4
Rockcliffe Cross Cumb 177 K6
Rock End Staffs 131 H8
Rockend Torbay 8 D2
Rock Ferry Wirral 129 H2

Rockfield Highld 264 E3
Rockfield Mons 62 F4
Rockford Devon 28 D1
Rockford Hants 18 B2
Rockgreen Shrops 96 C8
Rockhampton S Glos 63 K8
Rockhead Cnwll 10 F5
Rockhill Shrops 95 G7
Rock Hill Worcs 81 L1
Rockingham Nhants 101 J5
Rockland All Saints Norfk 105 K4
Rockland St Mary Norfk 107 G3
Rockland St Peter Norfk 105 K4
Rockley Notts 134 E5
Rockley Wilts 47 H4
Rockliffe Lancs 140 C3
Rockville Ag & B 207 L1
Rockwell End Bucks 49 J1
Rockwell Green Somset 29 L6
Rodborough Gloucs 64 B6
Rodbourne Swindn 47 H2
Rodbourne Wilts 46 D2
Rodd Herefs 79 K3
Roddam Nthumb 190 E2
Rodden Dorset 16 B5
Roddymoor Dur 168 F3
Rode Somset 46 A8
Rode Heath Ches E 130 F8
Rode Heath Ches E 131 G6
Rodel W Isls 282 d7
Roden Wrekin 113 J8
Rodhuish Somset 29 J3
Rodington Wrekin 113 K8
Rodington Heath Wrekin 113 K8
Rodley Gloucs 63 L5
Rodley Leeds 150 B8
Rodmarton Gloucs 64 D7
Rodmell E Susx 22 F6
Rodmersham Kent 40 B3
Rodmersham Green Kent 40 B3
Rodney Stoke Somset 31 H1
Rodsley Derbys 115 K3
Rodway Somset 30 C3
Roecliffe N York 150 E3
Roe Cross Tamesd 140 E8
Roe Green Herts 69 G5
Roe Green Herts 87 G8
Roe Green Salfd 139 M7
Roehampton Gt Lon 51 G4
Roffey W Susx 37 J4
Rogart Highld 273 H7
Rogate W Susx 36 B6
Roger Ground Cumb 156 E3
Rogerstone Newpt 44 B2
Roghadal W Isls 282 d7
Rogiet Mons 44 F2
Roke Oxon 66 F8
Roker Sundld 181 K7
Rollesby Norfk 123 J8
Rolleston Leics 100 F3
Rolleston Notts 117 K1
Rolleston on Dove Staffs 115 L6
Rolston E R Yk 153 K6
Rolstone N Som 44 D6
Rolvenden Kent 39 L7
Rolvenden Layne Kent 39 L7
Romaldkirk Dur 168 C6
Romanby N York 160 E4
Romanno Bridge Border 199 K3
Romansleigh Devon 28 C6
Romden Castle Kent 40 A7
Romesdal Highld 258 F6
Romford Dorset 17 L1
Romford Gt Lon 52 B1
Romiley Stockp 131 J2
Romney Street Kent 52 C6
Romsey Hants 34 D6
Romsley Shrops 97 H6
Romsley Worcs 98 B7
Rona Highld 259 L5
Ronachan Ag & B 206 B8
Rood Ashton Wilts 46 C7
Rookhope Dur 167 L2
Rookley IoW 19 H6
Rookley Green IoW 19 H7
Rooks Bridge Somset 44 D8
Rooks Nest Somset 29 K4
Rookwith N York 160 B5
Roos E R Yk 145 H2
Roose Cumb 146 D2
Roosebeck Cumb 146 E2
Roothams Green Bed 86 B4
Ropley Hants 35 K4
Ropley Dean Hants 35 K4
Ropley Soke Hants 35 K4
Ropsley Lincs 118 C5
Rora Abers 269 K6
Rorrington Shrops 95 H3
Rosarie Moray 267 H6
Rose Cnwll 4 C4
Roseacre Lancs 147 H8
Rose Ash Devon 28 D6
Rosebank S Lans 198 D3
Rosebush Pembks 75 J6
Rosecare Cnwll 11 H3
Rosecliston Cnwll 4 D3
Rosedale Abbey N York 162 C3
Rose Green Essex 72 C2
Rose Green Suffk 89 J7
Rose Green Suffk 89 K6
Rose Green W Susx 20 E7
Rosehall Highld 272 C7
Rosehearty Abers 269 G3
Rose Hill E Susx 23 G4
Rose Hill Lancs 140 B2
Rosehill Shrops 113 G8
Roseisle Moray 266 C3
Roselands E Susx 23 K7
Rosemarket Pembks 54 F5
Rosemarkie Highld 263 K8
Rosemary Lane Devon 29 L7
Rosemount P & K 233 J6
Rosenannon Cnwll 4 F2
Rosenithon Cnwll 3 K6
Roser's Cross E Susx 23 J3
Rosevean Cnwll 5 H3
Rosevine Cnwll 3 M4
Rosewarne Cnwll 2 F4
Rosewell Mdloth 211 J6
Roseworth S on T 169 L6
Roseworthy Cnwll 3 G3
Rosgill Cumb 166 D7
Roskestal Cnwll 2 B6
Roskhill Highld 258 D7
Roskorwell Cnwll 3 K6
Rosley Cumb 165 K2
Roslin Mdloth 211 J6
Rosliston Derbys 115 L8
Rosneath Ag & B 207 L2
Ross D & G 175 G6
Ross Nthumb 203 J5
Rossett Wrexhm 129 J8
Rossett Green N York 150 D5
Rossington Donc 143 G8
Rossland Rens 208 D5
Ross-on-Wye Herefs 63 J2
Roster Highld 280 C8
Rostherne Ches E 130 E3
Rosthwaite Cumb 165 H7
Roston Derbys 115 J3
Rosudgeon Cnwll 2 E5
Rosyth Fife 210 F2
Rothbury Nthumb 190 F6
Rotherby Leics 117 H8
Rotherfield E Susx 38 E7
Rotherfield Greys Oxon 49 H3
Rotherfield Peppard Oxon 49 H3
Rotherham Rothm 133 H1
Rotherham Crematorium Rothm 133 J1
Rothersthorpe Nhants 84 D4
Rotherwick Hants 49 H7
Rothes Moray 266 F6
Rothesay Ag & B 207 H6
Rothiebrisbane Abers 256 D4
Rothiemay Moray 267 L6
Rothiemurchus Lodge Highld 242 C2
Rothienorman Abers 256 C4
Rothley Leics 100 D1
Rothley Nthumb 180 C1
Rothmaise Abers 256 B5
Rothwell Leeds 142 A2
Rothwell Lincs 144 F7
Rothwell Nhants 101 H7
Rotsea E R Yk 153 G5
Rottal Lodge Angus 234 B2
Rottingdean Br & H 22 F6
Rottington Cumb 164 C8
Roucan D & G 176 D3
Roucan Loch Crematorium D & G 176 D3
Roud IoW 19 H7
Rougham Norfk 121 H7
Rougham Green Suffk 89 H3
Rough Close Staffs 114 E4
Rough Common Kent 40 F3
Roughlee Lancs 148 E7
Roughpark Abers 243 K1
Roughton Lincs 136 D6
Roughton Norfk 122 E4
Roughton Shrops 97 G4
Roughway Kent 38 F3
Roundbush Essex 72 B6
Round Bush Herts 68 F7
Roundbush Green Essex 70 E4
Round Green Luton 68 E3
Roundham Somset 15 K1
Roundhay Leeds 150 F8
Rounds Green Sandw 98 C5
Round Street Kent 52 E5
Roundstreet Common W Susx 37 G5
Roundway Wilts 46 E6
Roundyhill Angus 234 B5
Rousay Ork 275 c3
Rousdon Devon 15 G4
Rousham Oxon 66 C2
Rous Lench Worcs 82 B4
Routenburn N Ayrs 207 K6
Routh E R Yk 153 H7
Rout's Green Bucks 67 J7
Row Cnwll 10 F7
Row Cumb 157 G5
Row Cumb 166 E4
Rowanburn D & G 177 L3
Rowardennan Stirlg 218 E7
Rowarth Derbys 131 K2
Row Ash Hants 35 H8
Rowberrow Somset 44 F7
Rowborough IoW 19 G6
Rowde Wilts 46 E6
Rowden Devon 12 F3
Rowen Conwy 126 E5
Rowfield Derbys 115 K2
Rowfoot Nthumb 178 F6
Rowford Somset 30 C5
Row Green Essex 71 H3
Rowhedge Essex 72 F3
Rowhook W Susx 37 H4
Rowington Warwks 82 F2
Rowland Derbys 132 D5
Rowland's Castle Hants 20 B5
Rowland's Gill Gatesd 180 E7
Rowledge Surrey 36 B2
Rowley Dur 168 E1
Rowley E R Yk 144 B1
Rowley Shrops 95 H2
Rowley Hill Kirk 141 J5
Rowley Regis Sandw 98 B6
Rowley Regis Crematorium Sandw 98 B6
Rowlstone Herefs 62 D2
Rowly Surrey 37 G3
Rowner Hants 19 K3
Rowney Green Worcs 82 B1
Rownhams Hants 34 E7
Rowrah Cumb 164 E7
Rowsham Bucks 67 K3
Rowsley Derbys 132 E6
Rows of Trees Ches E 131 G4
Rowstock Oxon 48 C1
Rowston Lincs 136 A8
Rowthorne Derbys 133 J6
Rowton Ches W 129 K6
Rowton Shrops 95 J1
Rowton Shrops 95 K7
Rowton Wrekin 113 K7
Row Town Surrey 50 D6
Roxburgh Border 201 L7
Roxby N Linc 144 A4
Roxby N York 171 H7
Roxton Bed 86 C4
Roxwell Essex 70 F5
Royal Leamington Spa Warwks 83 H2
Royal Oak Darltn 169 G6
Royal Oak Lancs 138 E7
Royal's Green Ches E 113 K3
Royal Tunbridge Wells Kent 38 F5
Royal Wootton Bassett Wilts 46 F3
Roy Bridge Highld 239 M7
Roydhouse Kirk 141 K5
Roydon Essex 69 L5
Roydon Norfk 106 C7
Roydon Norfk 120 F7
Roydon Hamlet Essex 69 L5
Royston Barns 142 B5
Royston Herts 87 G7
Royton Oldham 140 D6
Rozel Jersey 9 e2
Ruabon Wrexhm 112 D3
Ruaig Ag & B 224 D5
Ruan High Lanes Cnwll 4 E6
Ruan Lanihorne Cnwll 4 E6
Ruan Major Cnwll 3 H7
Ruan Minor Cnwll 3 J8
Ruardean Gloucs 63 J3
Ruardean Hill Gloucs 63 J4
Ruardean Woodside Gloucs 63 J4
Rubery Birm 98 C7
Rubha Ban W Isls 283 c12
Ruckcroft Cumb 166 C2
Ruckhall Herefs 80 B7
Ruckinge Kent 40 D8
Ruckland Lincs 136 F4
Ruckley Shrops 96 C3
Rudby N York 161 G1
Rudchester Nthumb 180 D5
Ruddington Notts 116 F5
Ruddle Gloucs 63 K5
Ruddlemoor Cnwll 5 G4
Rudford Gloucs 63 M3
Rudge Somset 46 B8
Rudgeway S Glos 45 J2
Rudgwick W Susx 37 G4
Rudhall Herefs 63 J2
Rudheath Ches W 130 D5
Rudheath Woods Ches E 130 E5
Rudley Green Essex 71 K6
Rudloe Wilts 46 B5
Rudry Caerph 43 K4
Rudston E R Yk 153 H2
Rudyard Staffs 131 J8
Ruecastle Border 189 G2
Rufford Lancs 138 F4
Rufforth C York 151 H5
Rug Denbgs 111 K3
Rugby Warwks 100 B8
Rugeley Staffs 115 G7
Ruishton Somset 30 C6
Ruislip Gt Lon 50 E2
Rùm Highld 236 D1
Rumbach Moray 267 H5
Rumbling Bridge P & K 221 J7
Rumburgh Suffk 107 G7
Rumby Hill Dur 168 F4
Rumford Cnwll 10 B8
Rumford Falk 210 B4
Rumney Cardif 43 K6
Rumwell Somset 30 B6
Runcorn Halton 129 L3
Runcton W Susx 20 E6
Runcton Holme Norfk 104 C2
Runfold Surrey 36 C2
Runhall Norfk 105 L2
Runham Norfk 107 J1
Runham Norfk 107 L2
Runnington Somset 29 L6
Runsell Green Essex 71 J6
Runshaw Moor Lancs 139 G4
Runswick N York 171 J7
Runtaleave Angus 233 L2
Runwell Essex 71 J8
Ruscombe Wokham 49 J4
Rushall Herefs 80 E8
Rushall Norfk 106 D6
Rushall Wilts 47 H7
Rushall Wsall 98 C3
Rushbrooke Suffk 89 H3
Rushbury Shrops 96 C5
Rushden Herts 69 J1
Rushden Nhants 85 J2
Rushenden Kent 53 K5
Rusher's Cross E Susx 38 F7
Rushford Devon 12 B7
Rushford Norfk 105 J7
Rush Green Essex 73 H4
Rush Green Gt Lon 52 B2
Rush Green Herts 69 G2
Rush Green Warrtn 130 D2
Rushlake Green E Susx 23 L3
Rushmere Suffk 107 K6
Rushmere St Andrew Suffk 90 E6
Rushmoor Surrey 36 C3
Rushock Herefs 79 K3
Rushock Worcs 81 K1
Rusholme Manch 131 G1
Rushton Ches W 130 B7
Rushton Nhants 101 J6
Rushton Shrops 96 D2
Rushton Spencer Staffs 131 J7
Rushwick Worcs 81 J4
Rushyford Dur 169 H5
Ruskie Stirlg 219 K7
Ruskington Lincs 118 E1
Rusland Cross Cumb 156 E5
Rusper W Susx 37 K3
Ruspidge Gloucs 63 K5
Russell Green Essex 71 H4
Russell's Water Oxon 49 H1
Russel's Green Suffk 90 F1
Russ Hill Surrey 37 K3
Rusthall Kent 38 E5
Rustington W Susx 21 H6
Ruston N York 163 G6
Ruston Parva E R Yk 153 G3
Ruswarp N York 162 F1
Ruthall Shrops 96 D5
Rutherford Border 201 K7
Rutherglen S Lans 209 G6
Ruthernbridge Cnwll 5 G2
Ruthin Denbgs 128 D8
Ruthrieston C Aber 245 K3
Ruthven Abers 267 K6
Ruthven Angus 233 L5
Ruthven Highld 241 K4
Ruthvoes Cnwll 4 F3
Ruthwaite Cumb 165 H3
Ruthwell D & G 176 E5
Ruxley Corner Gt Lon 52 A5
Ruxton Green Herefs 63 G3

Ruyton-XI-Towns Shrops 112 F7
Ryal Nthumb 180 B4
Ryall Dorset 15 J4
Ryall Worcs 81 K7
Ryarsh Kent 52 E7
Rycote Oxon 67 G6
Rydal Cumb 156 E2
Ryde IoW 19 K5
Rye E Susx 25 G3
Ryebank Shrops 113 H5
Ryeford Herefs 63 J3
Rye Foreign E Susx 25 G3
Rye Harbour E Susx 25 H3
Ryehill E R Yk 145 G3
Ryeish Green Wokham 49 H5
Rye Street Worcs 81 H8
Ryhall Rutlnd 102 A1
Ryhill Wakefd 142 B5
Ryhope Sundld 181 K8
Rylah Derbys 133 J6
Ryland Lincs 135 K4
Rylands Notts 116 F4
Rylstone N York 149 H4
Ryme Intrinseca Dorset 31 J8
Ryther N York 151 J7
Ryton Gatesd 180 E6
Ryton N York 162 D7
Ryton Shrops 97 G3
Ryton Warwks 99 L6
Ryton-on-Dunsmore Warwks 99 K8
Ryton Woodside Gatesd 180 E6

S

Sabden Lancs 148 D8
Sabine's Green Essex 70 E7
Sacombe Herts 69 J3
Sacombe Green Herts 69 J3
Sacriston Dur 169 G1
Sadberge Darltn 169 J7
Saddell Ag & B 194 B4
Saddington Leics 100 E5
Saddle Bow Norfk 120 D8
Saddlescombe W Susx 22 D5
Sadgill Cumb 157 G2
Saffron Walden Essex 87 L7
Sageston Pembks 55 H6
Saham Hills Norfk 105 H3
Saham Toney Norfk 105 H3
Saighton Ches W 129 K7
St Abbs Border 213 K5
St Agnes Border 212 F6
St Agnes Cnwll 4 B5
St Agnes IoS 10 b3
St Albans Herts 68 F5
St Allen Cnwll 4 D5
St Andrew Guern 9 j3
St Andrews Fife 223 J4
St Andrew's Major V Glam 43 H7
St Andrews Well Dorset 15 L4
St Anne's Lancs 138 C2
St Ann's D & G 187 G7
St Ann's Chapel Cnwll 12 A8
St Ann's Chapel Devon 7 J5
St Anthony Cnwll 3 K6
St Anthony's Hill E Susx 23 L7
St Arvans Mons 63 G7
St Asaph Denbgs 128 B5
St Athan V Glam 42 F8
St Aubin Jersey 9 c3
St Austell Cnwll 5 G4
St Bees Cumb 164 C8
St Blazey Cnwll 5 H4
St Blazey Gate Cnwll 5 H4
St Boswells Border 201 J7
St Brelade Jersey 9 b3
St Brelade's Bay Jersey 9 b3
St Breock Cnwll 10 D8
St Breward Cnwll 10 F7
St Briavels Gloucs 63 H6
St Brides Pembks 54 C5
St Bride's Major V Glam 42 D6
St Brides Netherwent Mons 44 E1
St Brides super-Ely V Glam 43 H6
St Brides Wentlooge Newpt 44 C3
St Budeaux C Plym 6 E3
Saintbury Gloucs 82 D7
St Buryan Cnwll 2 C6
St Catherine BaNES 45 M5
St Catherines Ag & B 217 J5
St Chloe Gloucs 64 B6
St Clears Carmth 58 A5
St Cleer Cnwll 6 A1
St Clement Cnwll 4 D6
St Clement Jersey 9 e4
St Clether Cnwll 11 H5
St Colmac Ag & B 207 G5
St Columb Major Cnwll 4 E2
St Columb Minor Cnwll 4 D2
St Columb Road Cnwll 4 E3
St Combs Abers 269 K4
St Cross South Elmham Suffk 106 F6
St Cyrus Abers 235 J2
St David's P & K 221 G3
St David's Pembks 74 B7
St Day Cnwll 4 B6
St Decumans Somset 29 K2
St Dennis Cnwll 4 F3
St Devereux Herefs 62 E1
St Dogmaels Pembks 75 K3
St Dogwells Pembks 75 G6
St Dominick Cnwll 6 D1
St Donats V Glam 42 E8
St Edith's Marsh Wilts 46 E6
St Endellion Cnwll 10 D6
St Enoder Cnwll 4 E3
St Erme Cnwll 4 D5
St Erney Cnwll 6 D3
St Erth Cnwll 2 E4
St Erth Praze Cnwll 2 F4
St Ervan Cnwll 10 B8
St Eval Cnwll 4 E1
St Ewe Cnwll 5 G5
St Fagans Cardif 43 H6
St Fergus Abers 269 K6
St Fillans P & K 220 B2
St Florence Pembks 55 J6
St Gennys Cnwll 11 G3
St George Conwy 127 K4
St Georges N Som 44 D6
St George's V Glam 43 H6
St George's Hill Surrey 50 D6
St Germans Cnwll 6 D3
St Giles in the Wood Devon 27 J7
St Giles-on-the-Heath Devon 11 L4
St Gluvia's Cnwll 3 K4
St Harmon Powys 78 D1
St Helen Auckland Dur 168 F5
St Helens Cumb 164 D4
St Helens E Susx 24 E5
St Helens IoW 19 L6
St Helens St Hel 139 G8
St Helens Crematorium St Hel 139 G8
St Helier Gt Lon 51 H5
St Helier Jersey 9 d3
St Hilary Cnwll 2 E5
St Hilary V Glam 42 F7
Saint Hill Devon 14 C1
Saint Hill W Susx 38 B6
St Illtyd Blae G 61 K6
St Ippollitts Herts 69 G2
St Ishmael's Pembks 54 D5
St Issey Cnwll 10 C8
St Ive Cnwll 6 C2
St Ive Cross Cnwll 6 C2
St Ives Cambs 87 G1
St Ives Cnwll 2 E3
St Ives Dorset 17 M2
St James Norfk 122 F7
St James's End Nhants 84 E3
St James South Elmham Suffk 107 G7
St Jidgey Cnwll 4 F1
St John Cnwll 6 E4
St John Jersey 9 c1
St Johns Dur 168 D4
St John's IoM 154 c5
St Johns Kent 38 E2
St Johns Surrey 50 C7
St Johns Worcs 81 J4
St John's Chapel Devon 27 J5
St John's Chapel Dur 167 K3
St John's Fen End Norfk 103 L1
St John's Highway Norfk 120 C8
St John's Kirk S Lans 199 G6
St John's Town of Dalry D & G 184 F6
St John's Wood Gt Lon 51 H2
St Jude's IoM 154 e3
St Just Cnwll 2 B5
St Just-in-Roseland Cnwll 3 L4
St Katherines Abers 256 D5
St Keverne Cnwll 3 K6
St Kew Cnwll 10 E7
St Kew Highway Cnwll 10 E7
St Keyne Cnwll 6 A3
St Lawrence Cnwll 5 H2
St Lawrence Essex 72 D6
St Lawrence IoW 19 J8
St Lawrence Jersey 9 c2
St Lawrence Kent 41 K2
St Leonards Bucks 67 M5
St Leonards Dorset 17 M2
St Leonards E Susx 24 E5
St Leonard's Street Kent 39 H2
St Levan Cnwll 2 B6
St Lythans V Glam 43 H7
St Mabyn Cnwll 10 E7
St Madoes P & K 222 C3
St Margarets Herefs 79 L8
St Margarets Herts 69 K5
St Margaret's at Cliffe Kent 41 K6
St Margaret's Hope Ork 275 c6
St Margaret South Elmham Suffk 107 G6
St Marks IoM 154 d7
St Martin Cnwll 3 J6
St Martin Cnwll 6 B4
St Martin Guern 9 j3
St Martin Jersey 9 e2
St Martin's IoS 10 c1
St Martin's P & K 221 L1
St Martins Shrops 112 D4
St Martin's Moor Shrops 112 D4
St Mary Jersey 9 c2
St Mary Bourne Hants 34 F1
St Marychurch Torbay 8 D2
St Mary Church V Glam 42 F7
St Mary Cray Gt Lon 52 A5
St Mary Hill V Glam 42 E6
St Mary in the Marsh Kent 25 K2
St Marylebone Crematorium Gt Lon 51 H1
St Mary's IoS 10 c3
St Mary's Ork 275 d5
St Mary's Bay Kent 25 K2
St Mary's Grove N Som 44 F5
St Mary's Hoo Medway 53 H4
St Maughans Mons 62 F4
St Maughans Green Mons 62 F4
St Mawes Cnwll 3 L4
St Mawgan Cnwll 4 E2
St Mellion Cnwll 6 D2
St Mellons Cardif 43 K5
St Merryn Cnwll 10 B7
St Mewan Cnwll 5 G4
St Michael Caerhays Cnwll 4 F6
St Michael Church Somset 30 D5
St Michael Penkevil Cnwll 4 D6
St Michaels Kent 39 M6
St Michaels Worcs 80 D2
St Michael's on Wyre Lancs 147 J7
St Michael South Elmham Suffk 107 G6
St Minver Cnwll 10 D7
St Monans Fife 223 J6
St Neot Cnwll 5 L1
St Neots Cambs 86 D3
St Nicholas Pembks 74 E5
St Nicholas V Glam 43 H6
St Nicholas at Wade Kent 41 J2
St Ninians Stirlg 209 L1
St Olaves Norfk 107 J3
St Osyth Essex 73 H4
St Ouen Jersey 9 b2
St Owens Cross Herefs 63 G2
St Pauls Cray Gt Lon 52 A5
St Paul's Walden Herts 69 G3
St Peter Jersey 9 b2
St Peter Port Guern 9 k3
St Peter's Guern 9 i3
St Peter's Kent 41 L2
St Peter's Hill Cambs 86 E1
St Petrox Pembks 55 G7
St Pinnock Cnwll 5 L2
St Quivox S Ayrs 196 D6
St Ruan Cnwll 3 J8
St Sampson Guern 9 k2
St Saviour Guern 9 i3
St Saviour Jersey 9 d3
St Stephen Cnwll 4 F4
St Stephens Cnwll 6 E3
St Stephens Cnwll 11 L5
St Teath Cnwll 10 F6
St Tudy Cnwll 10 F7
St Twynnells Pembks 54 F7
St Veep Cnwll 5 K4
St Vigeans Angus 235 G6
St Wenn Cnwll 5 G2
St Weonards Herefs 63 G2
St y-Nyll V Glam 43 H6
Salcombe Devon 7 L7
Salcombe Regis Devon 14 D5
Salcott-cum-Virley Essex 72 D4
Sale Traffd 130 F2
Saleby Lincs 137 J4
Sale Green Worcs 81 L4
Salehurst E Susx 24 D2
Salem Carmth 59 H4
Salem Cerdgn 92 E6
Salen Ag & B 227 H4
Salen Highld 237 K7
Salesbury Lancs 139 K1
Salford C Beds 85 H7
Salford Oxon 65 L2
Salford Salfd 140 B8
Salford Priors Warwks 82 C5
Salfords Surrey 37 L2
Salhouse Norfk 123 G8
Saline Fife 221 J8
Salisbury Wilts 33 K5
Salisbury Crematorium Wilts 33 K4
Salkeld Dykes Cumb 166 D3
Salle Norfk 122 C6
Salmonby Lincs 136 F5
Salperton Gloucs 65 G3
Salph End Bed 86 B5
Salsburgh N Lans 209 L6
Salt Staffs 114 F6
Salta Cumb 164 E2
Saltaire C Brad 149 L8
Saltash Cnwll 6 E3
Saltburn Highld 263 K6
Saltburn-by-the-Sea R & Cl 170 F6
Saltby Leics 117 M6
Salt Coates Cumb 177 G8
Saltcoats Cumb 155 K3
Saltcoats N Ayrs 195 L3
Saltcotes Lancs 138 D2
Saltdean Br & H 22 F6
Salterbeck Cumb 164 C5
Salterforth Lancs 148 F6
Salterswall Ches W 130 C6
Salterton Wilts 33 K4
Saltfleet Lincs 137 H1
Saltfleetby All Saints Lincs 137 H2
Saltfleetby St Clement Lincs 137 J1
Saltfleetby St Peter Lincs 137 H2
Saltford BaNES 45 K5
Salthouse Norfk 122 B3
Saltley Birm 98 E5
Saltmarsh Newpt 44 D2
Saltmarshe E R Yk 143 K3
Saltney Flints 129 J6
Salton N York 162 C6
Saltrens Devon 27 H6
Saltwell Crematorium Gatesd 181 G6
Saltwick Nthumb 180 E3
Saltwood Kent 40 F8
Salvington W Susx 21 K6
Salwarpe Worcs 81 K3
Salway Ash Dorset 15 K3
Sambourne Warwks 82 C3
Sambrook Wrekin 113 M6
Samlesbury Lancs 139 H2
Samlesbury Bottoms Lancs 139 J2
Sampford Arundel Somset 29 K7
Sampford Brett Somset 29 K3
Sampford Courtenay Devon 12 F2
Sampford Moor Somset 29 K7
Sampford Peverell Devon 29 J8
Sampford Spiney Devon 12 D8
Samsonlane Ork 275 e3
Samson's Corner Essex 73 G3
Samuelston E Loth 212 B5
Sanaigmore Ag & B 204 C2
Sancreed Cnwll 2 C5
Sancton E R Yk 152 D7
Sand Somset 31 G2
Sandaig Highld 247 M8
Sandale Cumb 165 H3
Sandal Magna Wakefd 142 A4
Sandavore Highld 236 F4
Sanday Ork 275 e2
Sandbach Ches E 130 E7
Sandbank Ag & B 207 K3
Sandbanks Poole 17 K5
Sandend Abers 267 L3
Sanderstead Gt Lon 51 J6
Sandford Cumb 167 G7
Sandford Devon 13 J2
Sandford Dorset 17 H5
Sandford Hants 18 B3
Sandford IoW 19 J7
Sandford N Som 44 E7
Sandford S Lans 197 L2
Sandford Shrops 112 E6
Sandford Shrops 113 J5
Sandford-on-Thames Oxon 66 D6
Sandford Orcas Dorset 31 K6
Sandford St Martin Oxon 66 B2
Sandgate Kent 41 G8
Sandhaven Abers 269 H3
Sandhead D & G 172 D5
Sandhill Rothm 142 C8
Sandhills Dorset 16 B3
Sandhills Dorset 31 L8
Sand Hills Leeds 150 E7
Sandhills Oxon 66 E5
Sandhills Surrey 36 D3
Sandhoe Nthumb 180 A5
Sandhole Ag & B 216 F7
Sand Hole E R Yk 152 B8
Sandholme E R Yk 143 L2
Sandholme Lincs 119 K4
Sandhurst Br For 49 K6
Sandhurst Gloucs 64 B2
Sandhurst Kent 39 K7
Sandhurst Cross Kent 24 E2
Sand Hutton N York 151 L4
Sandhutton N York 160 E6

Sandiacre Derbys 116 E4
Sandilands Lincs 137 K3
Sandiway Ches W 130 B5
Sandleheath Hants 33 K7
Sandleigh Oxon 66 C6
Sandley Dorset 32 C6
Sandling Kent 53 G7
Sandlow Green Ches E 130 F6
Sandness Shet 281 c5
Sandon Essex 71 H6
Sandon Herts 87 G8
Sandon Staffs 114 E5
Sandon Bank Staffs 114 E6
Sandown IoW 19 K6
Sandplace Cnwll 6 A3
Sandridge Herts 68 F5
Sandridge Wilts 46 D6
Sandringham Norfk 120 F5
Sands Bucks 67 K8
Sandsend N York 171 K8
Sand Side Cumb 156 B6
Sandside Cumb 157 G6
Sandtoft N Linc 143 J6
Sandway Kent 39 M3
Sandwich Kent 41 K4
Sandwick Cumb 166 A6
Sandwick Shet 281 e8
Sandwick W Isls 282 g3
Sandwith Cumb 164 C7
Sandwith Newtown Cumb 164 C7
Sandy C Beds 86 D5
Sandy Bank Lincs 136 E8
Sandycroft Flints 129 H6
Sandy Cross E Susx 23 K3
Sandy Cross Herefs 80 F4
Sandyford D & G 187 J7
Sandygate Devon 13 K7
Sandygate IoM 154 e3
Sandy Haven Pembks 54 D5
Sandyhills D & G 175 M4
Sandylands Lancs 147 H3
Sandy Lane C Brad 149 K8
Sandylane Staffs 113 M4
Sandylane Swans 57 G7
Sandy Lane Wilts 46 D5
Sandy Lane Wrexhm 112 F3
Sandy Park Devon 13 G5
Sandysike Cumb 177 L5
Sandyway Herefs 63 G2
Sangobeg Highld 277 G3
Sangomore Highld 276 F3
Sankey Bridges Warrtn 130 B2
Sankyn's Green Worcs 81 H2
Sanna Bay Highld 236 E6
Sanndabhaig W Isls 282 g3
Sannox N Ayrs 195 G2
Sanquhar D & G 185 K1
Santon Cumb 155 K2
Santon IoM 154 d7
Santon Bridge Cumb 155 K2
Santon Downham Suffk 105 G6
Sapcote Leics 100 B5
Sapey Common Herefs 81 G2
Sapiston Suffk 105 J8
Sapley Cambs 102 E8
Sapperton Derbys 115 K4
Sapperton Gloucs 64 D6
Sapperton Lincs 118 D5
Saracen's Head Lincs 119 K6
Sarclet Highld 280 D7
Sarisbury Hants 19 H2
Sarn Brdgnd 42 D5
Sarn Gwynd 108 D5
Sarn Powys 93 L4
Sarn Powys 94 F5
Sarnau Carmth 58 B5
Sarnau Cerdgn 76 B5
Sarnau Gwynd 111 J4
Sarnau Powys 78 E8
Sarnau Powys 112 C8
Sarn Bach Gwynd 108 E6
Sarnesfield Herefs 79 L5
Sarn-wen Powys 112 D7
Saron Carmth 59 H6
Saron Carmth 76 C7
Saron Gwynd 125 H7
Saron Gwynd 125 J6
Sarratt Herts 68 D7
Sarre Kent 41 H2
Sarsden Oxon 65 L3
Sarson Hants 34 C2
Satley Dur 168 E2
Satmar Kent 41 H7
Satron N York 159 G3
Satterleigh Devon 28 B6
Satterthwaite Cumb 156 D4
Satwell Oxon 49 H2
Sauchen Abers 244 F1
Saucher P & K 233 J8
Sauchieburn Abers 235 G2
Saul Gloucs 63 L5
Saundby Notts 134 F2
Saundersfoot Pembks 55 K6
Saunderton Bucks 67 J6
Saunton Devon 27 H3
Sausthorpe Lincs 137 G6
Saveock Cnwll 4 C6
Saverley Green Staffs 114 F4
Savile Town Kirk 141 K4
Sawbridge Warwks 83 L2
Sawbridgeworth Herts 70 C4
Sawdon N York 163 G5
Sawley Derbys 116 D5
Sawley Lancs 148 D6
Sawley N York 150 C2
Sawston Cambs 87 K5
Sawtry Cambs 102 D6
Saxby Leics 117 L7
Saxby Lincs 135 K3
Saxby All Saints N Linc 144 C4
Saxelbye Leics 117 J7
Saxham Street Suffk 90 C3
Saxilby Lincs 135 H4
Saxlingham Norfk 122 A4
Saxlingham Green Norfk 106 E4
Saxlingham Nethergate Norfk 106 E4
Saxlingham Thorpe Norfk 106 E4
Saxmundham Suffk 91 J3
Saxondale Notts 117 H3
Saxon Street Cambs 88 D3
Saxtead Suffk 91 G2
Saxtead Green Suffk 90 F2
Saxtead Little Green Suffk 90 F2
Saxthorpe Norfk 122 C5
Saxton N York 151 G8
Sayers Common W Susx 22 D4
Scackleton N York 161 L8
Scaftworth Notts 134 D2
Scagglethorpe N York 152 C1
Scalasaig Ag & B 214 D5
Scalby E R Yk 143 L2
Scalby N York 163 H4
Scald End Bed 85 L4
Scaldwell Nhants 84 E1
Scaleby Cumb 178 B6
Scalebyhill Cumb 178 B6
Scale Houses Cumb 166 E2
Scales Cumb 146 E2
Scales Cumb 165 K5
Scalesceugh Cumb 166 B1
Scalford Leics 117 K6
Scaling N York 171 H7
Scaling Dam R & Cl 171 H8
Scalloway Shet 281 d7
Scalpay Highld 247 J2
Scamblesby Lincs 136 E4
Scammonden Kirk 141 G4
Scamodale Highld 228 C1
Scampston N York 162 F7
Scampton Lincs 135 J4
Scaniport Highld 251 H4
Scapegoat Hill Kirk 141 G4
Scarba Ag & B 215 K3
Scarborough N York 163 J5
Scarcewater Cnwll 4 F4
Scarcliffe Derbys 133 K6
Scarcroft Leeds 150 E7
Scarfskerry Highld 280 C2
Scargill Dur 168 D8
Scarinish Ag & B 224 D6
Scarisbrick Lancs 138 D5
Scarness Cumb 165 H4
Scarning Norfk 105 J1
Scarrington Notts 117 J3
Scarth Hill Lancs 138 E6
Scarthingwell N York 151 G8
Scartho NE Lin 145 H6
Scawby N Linc 144 B6
Scawsby Donc 142 E6
Scawthorpe Donc 142 E6
Scawton N York 161 J6
Scayne's Hill W Susx 22 F3
Scethrog Powys 61 H2
Scholar Green Ches E 131 G8
Scholemoor Crematorium C Brad 141 H1
Scholes Kirk 141 J3
Scholes Kirk 141 J6
Scholes Leeds 150 E8
Scholes Rothm 142 B8
Scholes Wigan 139 J6
School Aycliffe Dur 169 H6
School Green C Brad 141 H1
School Green Ches W 130 C6
Schoolgreen Wokham 49 H5
School House Dorset 15 J2
Scissett Kirk 141 L5
Scleddau Pembks 74 F5
Scofton Notts 134 C4
Scole Norfk 106 C7
Scone P & K 221 L2
Sconser Highld 247 H2
Scoonie Fife 222 F6
Scopwick Lincs 135 M8
Scoraig Highld 261 G1
Scorborough E R Yk 152 F6
Scorrier Cnwll 4 B6
Scorriton Devon 7 K1
Scorton Lancs 147 K6
Scorton N York 160 C3
Sco Ruston Norfk 122 F7
Scotby Cumb 178 B7
Scotch Corner N York 160 B2
Scotforth Lancs 147 J4
Scot Hay Staffs 114 C2
Scothern Lincs 135 L4
Scotland Lincs 118 C5
Scotland Gate Nthumb 181 G2
Scotlandwell P & K 222 C7
Scot Lane End Bolton 139 J6
Scotscalder Station Highld 279 K5
Scotsdike Cumb 177 L4
Scot's Gap Nthumb 180 C2
Scotsmill Abers 255 L7
Scotstoun C Glas 208 F5
Scotswood N u Ty 180 F6
Scotter Lincs 143 M7
Scotterthorpe Lincs 143 L7
Scottlethorpe Lincs 118 D7
Scotton Lincs 143 M7
Scotton N York 150 D4
Scotton N York 160 B3
Scottow Norfk 122 F6
Scott Willoughby Lincs 118 D4
Scoulton Norfk 105 K3
Scounslow Green Staffs 115 H5
Scourie Highld 276 B7
Scourie More Highld 276 A7
Scousburgh Shet 281 d8
Scouthead Oldham 140 E6
Scrabster Highld 279 K2
Scraesburgh Border 189 J3
Scrafield Lincs 136 F6
Scrainwood Nthumb 190 D4
Scrane End Lincs 119 L3
Scraptoft Leics 100 E2
Scratby Norfk 123 K8
Scrayingham N York 151 M4
Scrays E Susx 24 D3
Scredington Lincs 118 E3
Scremby Lincs 137 H6
Scremerston Nthumb 202 F3
Screveton Notts 117 J3
Scrivelsby Lincs 136 E6
Scriven N York 150 E4
Scrooby Notts 134 C2
Scropton Derbys 115 K5
Scrub Hill Lincs 136 D8
Scruton N York 160 D4
Scuggate Cumb 178 B4
Scullomie Highld 277 L4
Sculthorpe Norfk 121 K5
Scunthorpe N Linc 143 M5
Scurlage Swans 56 E7
Sea Somset 30 E8
Seaborough Dorset 15 K2
Seabridge Staffs 114 C3
Seabrook Kent 41 G8
Seaburn Sundld 181 K6
Seacombe Wirral 129 H2
Seacroft Leeds 150 E8
Seacroft Lincs 137 L7
Seadyke Lincs 119 K4
Seafield Highld 259 H8
Seafield W Loth 210 D6
Seafield Crematorium C Edin 211 J4
Seaford E Susx 23 H7
Seaforth Sefton 138 C8
Seagrave Leics 117 G8
Seagry Heath Wilts 46 D3
Seaham Dur 169 L1
Seahouses Nthumb 203 L6
Seal Kent 38 E2
Seale Surrey 36 D1
Seamer N York 163 J6
Seamer N York 170 C8
Seamill N Ayrs 195 K2
Sea Palling Norfk 123 J6
Searby Lincs 144 D6
Seasalter Kent 40 E2
Seascale Cumb 155 J2
Seathwaite Cumb 156 B3
Seathwaite Cumb 165 H8
Seatle Cumb 156 E6
Seatoller Cumb 165 H7
Seaton Cnwll 6 C4
Seaton Cumb 164 D4
Seaton Devon 14 F4
Seaton Dur 169 L1
Seaton E R Yk 153 J6
Seaton Kent 41 H4
Seaton Nthumb 181 H3
Seaton Rutlnd 101 K4
Seaton Burn N Tyne 181 G4
Seaton Carew Hartpl 170 C5
Seaton Delaval Nthumb 181 H4
Seaton Ross E R Yk 152 B7
Seaton Sluice Nthumb 181 H3
Seatown Dorset 15 K4
Seave Green N York 161 J3
Seaview IoW 19 L5
Seaville Cumb 177 G8
Seavington St Mary Somset 30 F7
Seavington St Michael Somset 30 F7
Sebastopol Torfn 62 C7
Sebergham Cumb 165 K2
Seckington Warwks 99 H2
Sedbergh Cumb 157 L4
Sedbury Gloucs 63 H8
Sedbusk N York 158 F4
Sedgeberrow Worcs 82 B7
Sedgebrook Lincs 117 M4
Sedge Fen Suffk 104 D6
Sedgefield Dur 169 K5
Sedgeford Norfk 120 F4
Sedgehill Wilts 32 E5
Sedgley Dudley 97 L4
Sedgley Park Bury 140 B7
Sedgwick Cumb 157 H5
Sedlescombe E Susx 24 E4
Sedrup Bucks 67 J5
Seed Kent 40 B4
Seend Wilts 46 D6
Seend Cleeve Wilts 46 D6
Seer Green Bucks 68 B8
Seething Norfk 107 G4
Sefton Sefton 138 D7
Sefton Town Sefton 138 D7
Seghill Nthumb 181 G4
Seighford Staffs 114 D6
Seion Gwynd 125 K6
Seisdon Staffs 97 J4
Selattyn Shrops 112 C5
Selborne Hants 35 M4
Selby N York 142 F1
Selham W Susx 20 F3
Selhurst Gt Lon 51 J5
Selkirk Border 201 G7
Sellack Herefs 63 H2
Sellafirth Shet 281 e2
Sellan Cnwll 2 C5
Sellick's Green Somset 30 B7
Sellindge Kent 40 E7
Selling Kent 40 D4
Sells Green Wilts 46 D6
Selly Oak Birm 98 D7
Selmeston E Susx 23 H6
Selsdon Gt Lon 51 K6
Selsey Gloucs 64 B6
Selsey W Susx 20 D8
Selsfield Common W Susx 38 A6
Selside Cumb 157 H3
Selside N York 158 D7
Selsted Kent 41 H6
Selston Notts 116 D1
Selworthy Somset 29 G2
Semer Suffk 89 K6
Semington Wilts 46 C6
Semley Wilts 32 E5
Sempringham Lincs 118 F5
Send Surrey 50 C7
Send Marsh Surrey 50 D7
Senghenydd Caerph 43 H3
Sennen Cnwll 2 B6
Sennen Cove Cnwll 2 B6
Sennybridge Powys 60 D2
Serlby Notts 134 C2
Sessay N York 161 G7
Setchey Norfk 104 C1
Setley Hants 18 D3
Seton Mains E Loth 211 M4
Settle N York 148 E3
Settrington N York 152 C2
Seven Ash Somset 29 L4
Sevenhampton Gloucs 64 F3
Sevenhampton Swindn 47 J1
Seven Hills Crematorium Suffk 90 F7
Seven Kings Gt Lon 51 M2
Sevenoaks Kent 38 E2
Sevenoaks Weald Kent 38 E3
Seven Sisters Neath 60 B5
Seven Springs Gloucs 64 D4
Seven Star Green Essex 72 D2
Severn Beach S Glos 45 G2
Severn Stoke Worcs 81 K6
Sevick End Bed 86 B4
Sevington Kent 40 D7
Sewards End Essex 88 B7
Sewardstonebury Essex 69 K7
Sewell C Beds 68 C3

Sewerby E R Yk 153 K2
Seworgan Cnwll 3 H5
Sewstern Leics 118 A7
Sexhow N York 161 G2
Sezincote Gloucs 65 H1
Sgiogarstaigh W Isls 282 h1
Shabbington Bucks 67 G5
Shackerley Shrops 97 J2
Shackerstone Leics 99 K2
Shacklecross Derbys 116 C5
Shackleford Surrey 36 D2
Shade Calder 140 D3
Shader W Isls 282 g1
Shadforth Dur 169 J3
Shadingfield Suffk 107 J6
Shadoxhurst Kent 40 C7
Shadwell Leeds 150 D7
Shadwell Norfk 105 J6
Shaftenhoe End Herts 87 H7
Shaftesbury Dorset 32 E6
Shaftholme Donc 142 F6
Shafton Barns 142 B5
Shafton Two Gates Barns 142 B5
Shakerley Wigan 139 K7
Shalbourne Wilts 47 L6
Shalcombe IoW 18 F6
Shalden Hants 35 L3
Shalden Green Hants 35 L2
Shaldon Devon 13 L8
Shalfleet IoW 18 F6
Shalford Essex 71 H1
Shalford Surrey 36 F2
Shalford Green Essex 71 H2
Shallowford Staffs 114 D5
Shalmsford Street Kent 40 E4
Shalstone Bucks 84 C7
Shamley Green Surrey 36 F2
Shandford Angus 234 D3
Shandon Ag & B 207 L2
Shandwick Highld 264 D5
Shangton Leics 100 F4
Shankhouse Nthumb 181 G3
Shanklin IoW 19 K7
Shap Cumb 166 D7
Shapinsay Ork 275 d4
Shapwick Dorset 17 H2
Shapwick Somset 30 F3
Shard End Birm 98 F5
Shardlow Derbys 116 D5
Shareshill Staffs 97 L2
Sharlston Wakefd 142 B4
Sharlston Common Wakefd 142 B4
Sharman's Cross Solhll 98 E7
Sharnal Street Medway 53 G4
Sharnbrook Bed 85 K3
Sharneyford Lancs 140 C3
Sharnford Leics 100 B5
Sharnhill Green Dorset 16 D2
Sharoe Green Lancs 139 G1
Sharow N York 150 D2
Sharpenhoe C Beds 68 D1
Sharperton Nthumb 190 D5
Sharp Green Norfk 123 H7
Sharpness Gloucs 63 K6
Sharpthorne W Susx 38 B6
Sharptor Cnwll 11 J8
Sharpway Gate Worcs 81 L2
Sharrington Norfk 122 A4
Shatterford Worcs 97 H7
Shatterling Kent 41 J4
Shatton Derbys 132 D3
Shaugh Prior Devon 7 G2
Shave Cross Dorset 15 J3
Shavington Ches E 113 M1
Shaw C Brad 140 F1
Shaw Oldham 140 D6
Shaw Swindn 47 G2
Shaw W Berk 48 C5
Shaw Wilts 46 C6
Shawbirch Wrekin 113 L8
Shawbost W Isls 282 f2
Shawbury Shrops 113 J7
Shawclough Rochdl 140 D5
Shaw Common Gloucs 63 K2
Shawdon Hill Nthumb 190 F3
Shawell Leics 100 C7
Shawford Hants 34 F6
Shawforth Lancs 140 D4
Shaw Green Herts 69 J1
Shaw Green Lancs 139 G4
Shaw Green N York 150 C5
Shawhead D & G 185 L7
Shaw Mills N York 150 C3
Shawsburn S Lans 198 C3
Shear Cross Wilts 32 E3
Shearington D & G 176 D5
Shearsby Leics 100 D5
Shearston Somset 30 D5
Shebbear Devon 12 B1
Shebdon Staffs 114 B6
Shebster Highld 279 H3
Sheddens E Rens 208 F7
Shedfield Hants 35 H8
Sheen Staffs 132 B7
Sheepbridge Derbys 133 G5
Sheep Hill Dur 180 E7
Sheepridge Kirk 141 J4
Sheepscar Leeds 141 M1
Sheepscombe Gloucs 64 C5
Sheepstor Devon 7 G1
Sheepwash Devon 12 C2
Sheepwash Nthumb 181 G2
Sheepway N Som 45 G4
Sheepy Magna Leics 99 J3
Sheepy Parva Leics 99 J3
Sheering Essex 70 D4
Sheerness Kent 53 K4
Sheerwater Surrey 50 D6
Sheet Hants 36 A6
Sheffield Cnwll 2 D5
Sheffield Sheff 133 G2
Sheffield Bottom W Berk 49 G5
Sheffield City Road
Crematorium Sheff 133 G3
Sheffield Green E Susx 22 F2
Shefford C Beds 86 C7
Sheigra Highld 276 B4
Sheinton Shrops 96 E3
Shelderton Shrops 95 K7
Sheldon Birm 98 F6
Sheldon Derbys 132 C6
Sheldon Devon 14 D1
Sheldwich Kent 40 D4
Sheldwich Lees Kent 40 D4
Shelf Calder 141 H2
Shelfanger Norfk 106 C6
Shelfield Warwks 82 D3
Shelfield Wsall 98 C3
Shelfield Green Warwks 82 D3
Shelford Notts 117 H3
Shelford Warwks 99 L5
Shellacres Nthumb 202 D4
Shelley Essex 70 E6
Shelley Kirk 141 K5
Shelley Suffk 89 L7
Shelley Far Bank Kirk 141 K5
Shellingford Oxon 65 L8
Shellow Bowells Essex 70 F5
Shelsley Beauchamp Worcs 81 G3
Shelsley Walsh Worcs 81 G3
Shelton Bed 85 K2
Shelton Norfk 106 E5
Shelton Notts 117 K3
Shelton Shrops 95 L1
Shelton Green Norfk 106 E5
Shelton Lock C Derb 116 C5
Shelton Under Harley Staffs 114 C4
Shelve Shrops 95 H4
Shelwick Herefs 80 C6
Shenfield Essex 70 F8
Shenington Oxon 83 J6
Shenley Herts 68 F7
Shenley Brook End M Keyn 85 G8
Shenleybury Herts 68 F6
Shenley Church End M Keyn 85 G7
Shenmore Herefs 79 M7
Shennanton D & G 173 J2
Shenstone Staffs 98 E3
Shenstone Worcs 97 J8
Shenstone Woodend Staffs 98 E3
Shenton Leics 99 K3
Shenval Moray 254 E6
Shepeau Stow Lincs 102 F1
Shephall Herts 69 H2
Shepherd's Bush Gt Lon 51 G3
Shepherd's Green Oxon 49 H2
Shepherds Patch Gloucs 63 L6
Shepherdswell Kent 41 H5
Shepley Kirk 141 J6
Shepperdine S Glos 63 J8
Shepperton Surrey 50 D5
Shepperton Green Surrey 50 D5
Shepreth Cambs 87 H5
Shepshed Leics 116 E7
Shepton Beauchamp Somset 30 F7
Shepton Mallet Somset 31 K2
Shepton Montague Somset 31 L4
Shepway Kent 39 J3
Sheraton Dur 170 B4
Sherborne Dorset 31 L7
Sherborne Gloucs 65 H4
Sherborne Somset 45 H7
Sherborne St John Hants 48 F7
Sherbourne Warwks 83 G3
Sherburn Dur 169 J2
Sherburn N York 163 G7
Sherburn Hill Dur 169 J2
Sherburn in Elmet N York 142 D1
Shere Surrey 37 G1
Shereford Norfk 121 K5
Sherfield English Hants 34 C6
Sherfield on Loddon Hants 49 G7
Sherfin Lancs 140 B3
Sherford Devon 8 A6
Sherford Dorset 17 H4
Sheriffhales Shrops 97 G1
Sheriff Hutton N York 151 K3
Sheringham Norfk 122 D3
Sherington M Keyn 85 H6
Shermanbury W Susx 22 B3
Shernborne Norfk 120 F5
Sherrington Wilts 33 G3
Sherston Wilts 46 B2
Sherwood C Nott 116 F3
Sherwood Forest
Crematorium Notts 134 D6
Shetland Islands Shet 281 d6
Shettleston C Glas 209 H6
Shevington Wigan 139 H6
Shevington Moor Wigan 139 H5
Shevington Vale Wigan 139 G6
Sheviock Cnwll 6 D4
Shibden Head C Brad 141 H2
Shide IoW 19 H6
Shidlaw Nthumb 202 C5
Shiel Bridge Highld 248 F7
Shieldaig Highld 248 C1
Shieldhill D & G 176 D2
Shieldhill Falk 210 B4
Shieldhill House Hotel S Lans 199 G5
Shields N Lans 209 K7
Shielfoot Highld 237 J6
Shielhill Angus 234 C4
Shielhill Inver 207 L4
Shifford Oxon 66 A6
Shifnal Shrops 97 G2
Shilbottle Nthumb 191 J4
Shildon Dur 169 G5
Shillford E Rens 208 D7
Shillingford Devon 29 H6
Shillingford Oxon 66 E8
Shillingford Abbot Devon 13 L5
Shillingford St George Devon 13 L5
Shillingstone Dorset 32 D8
Shillington C Beds 86 C8
Shillmoor Nthumb 190 B4
Shilton Oxon 65 K5
Shilton Warwks 99 L6
Shimpling Norfk 106 D6
Shimpling Suffk 89 H5
Shimpling Street Suffk 89 H4
Shincliffe Dur 169 H3
Shiney Row Sundld 181 H8
Shinfield Wokham 49 H5
Shingay Cambs 86 F6
Shingle Street Suffk 91 J6
Shinnersbridge Devon 8 B2
Shinness Highld 272 D5
Shipbourne Kent 38 F3
Shipdham Norfk 105 J2
Shipham Somset 44 E7
Shiphay Torbay 8 D2
Shiplake Oxon 49 J3
Shiplake Row Oxon 49 H3
Shiplate N Som 44 D7
Shipley C Brad 149 L8
Shipley Derbys 116 D3
Shipley Shrops 97 H4
Shipley W Susx 37 H6
Shipley Bridge Surrey 37 M3
Shipley Hatch Kent 40 C7
Shipmeadow Suffk 107 H5
Shippea Hill Station Cambs 104 C6
Shippon Oxon 66 C7
Shipston on Stour Warwks 83 G7
Shipton Bucks 67 J2
Shipton Gloucs 64 F3
Shipton N York 151 H4
Shipton Shrops 96 D5
Shipton Bellinger Hants 34 B2
Shipton Gorge Dorset 15 L4
Shipton Green W Susx 20 C7
Shipton Moyne Gloucs 46 C1
Shipton-on-Cherwell Oxon 66 C4
Shiptonthorpe E R Yk 152 C7
Shipton-under-Wychwood
Oxon 65 L3
Shirburn Oxon 67 G7
Shirdley Hill Lancs 138 D5
Shire Cumb 166 E4
Shirebrook Derbys 133 K6
Shiregreen Sheff 133 G1
Shirehampton Bristl 45 G4
Shiremoor N Tyne 181 H4
Shirenewton Mons 62 F8
Shire Oak Wsall 98 D3
Shireoaks Notts 133 L3
Shirkoak Kent 40 B8
Shirland Derbys 133 H8
Shirlett Shrops 96 E4
Shirley C Sotn 34 E8
Shirley Derbys 115 L3
Shirley Gt Lon 51 K6
Shirley Solhll 98 E7
Shirl Heath Herefs 80 A3
Shirrell Heath Hants 35 H8
Shirvan Ag & B 206 D2
Shirwell Devon 27 L3
Shiskine N Ayrs 194 E5
Shittlehope Dur 168 C3
Shobdon Herefs 79 M3
Shobley Hants 18 B2
Shobrooke Devon 13 K2
Shoby Leics 117 H7
Shocklach Ches W 113 G2
Shocklach Green Ches W 113 G2
Shoeburyness Sthend 53 K2
Sholden Kent 41 K5
Sholing C Sotn 19 G2
Shoot Hill Shrops 95 K1
Shop Cnwll 10 B7
Shop Cnwll 26 D7
Shopwyke W Susx 20 E6
Shore Rochdl 140 D4
Shoreditch Gt Lon 51 J2
Shoreditch Somset 30 C6
Shoreham Kent 52 B6
Shoreham-by-Sea W Susx 22 C6
Shoreswood Nthumb 202 E4
Shorley Hants 35 J5
Shorncote Gloucs 64 F7
Shorne Kent 52 E5
Shorta Cross Cnwll 6 B3
Shortbridge E Susx 23 G3
Shortfield Common Surrey 36 C2
Shortgate E Susx 23 H4
Short Heath Birm 98 E5
Shortheath Hants 36 A4
Short Heath Wsall 98 B3
Shortlanesend Cnwll 4 C5
Shortlees E Ayrs 196 E4
Shortstown Bed 86 B6
Shorwell IoW 19 G7
Shoscombe BaNES 45 L7
Shotesham Norfk 106 E4
Shotgate Essex 71 J8
Shotley Suffk 90 F8
Shotley Bridge Dur 180 D8
Shotleyfield Nthumb 180 C8
Shotley Gate Suffk 90 F8
Shotley Street Suffk 90 F8
Shottenden Kent 40 D4
Shottermill Surrey 36 C4
Shottery Warwks 82 E4
Shotteswell Warwks 83 K6
Shottisham Suffk 91 H6
Shottle Derbys 116 A2
Shottlegate Derbys 116 A2
Shotton Dur 169 K5
Shotton Dur 169 L3
Shotton Flints 129 H6
Shotton Nthumb 180 F3
Shotton Nthumb 202 C7
Shotton Colliery Dur 169 K3
Shotts N Lans 210 A7
Shotwick Ches W 129 H5
Shougle Moray 266 D5
Shouldham Norfk 104 D2
Shouldham Thorpe Norfk 104 D2
Shoulton Worcs 81 J3
Shover's Green E Susx 39 G7
Shraleybrook Staffs 114 B2
Shrawardine Shrops 112 F8
Shrawley Worcs 81 J2
Shreding Green Bucks 50 C3
Shrewley Warwks 82 F2
Shrewsbury Shrops 96 B1
Shrewton Wilts 33 J2
Shripney W Susx 20 F6
Shrivenham Oxon 47 K1
Shropham Norfk 105 K5
Shrub End Essex 72 E2
Shucknall Herefs 80 D6
Shudy Camps Cambs 88 C6
Shuna Ag & B 216 B5
Shurdington Gloucs 64 D3
Shurlock Row W & M 49 K4
Shurnock Worcs 82 B3
Shurrery Highld 279 J4
Shurrery Lodge Highld 279 J5
Shurton Somset 30 B2
Shustoke Warwks 99 G5
Shute Devon 13 L3
Shute Devon 14 F3
Shutford Oxon 83 J7
Shut Heath Staffs 114 D7
Shuthonger Gloucs 81 K8
Shutlanger Nhants 84 E5
Shutterton Devon 13 M6
Shutt Green Staffs 97 K2

Shuttington Warwks 99 H2
Shuttlewood Derbys 133 J5
Shuttleworth Bury 140 B4
Siabost W Isls 282 f2
Siadar W Isls 282 g1
Sibbertoft Nhants 100 E6
Sibdon Carwood Shrops 95 K6
Sibford Ferris Oxon 83 H7
Sibford Gower Oxon 83 H7
Sible Hedingham Essex 88 F8
Sibley's Green Essex 70 F2
Siblyback Cnwll 11 J8
Sibsey Lincs 119 K2
Sibsey Fenside Lincs 119 K1
Sibson Cambs 102 B4
Sibson Leics 99 K3
Sibster Highld 280 D5
Sibthorpe Notts 117 K2
Sibthorpe Notts 134 E5
Sibton Suffk 91 J2
Sicklesmere Suffk 89 H3
Sicklinghall N York 150 E6
Sidbrook Somset 30 C5
Sidbury Devon 14 D4
Sidbury Shrops 96 F6
Sid Cop Barns 142 B6
Sidcot N Som 44 E7
Sidcup Gt Lon 51 M4
Siddick Cumb 164 D4
Siddington Ches E 131 G5
Siddington Gloucs 64 F7
Sidemoor Worcs 81 L1
Sidestrand Norfk 122 F3
Sidford Devon 14 D4
Sidlesham W Susx 20 D7
Sidlesham Common W Susx 20 D6
Sidley E Susx 24 D5
Sidmouth Devon 14 D5
Siefton Shrops 96 B6
Sigford Devon 13 H7
Sigglesthorne E R Yk 153 J6
Sigingstone V Glam 42 E7
Signet Oxon 65 K5
Silchester Hants 48 F6
Sileby Leics 117 G8
Silecroft Cumb 155 L6
Silfield Norfk 106 C3
Silian Cerdgn 77 G5
Silkstead Hants 34 F6
Silkstone Barns 141 L6
Silkstone Common Barns 141 L6
Silk Willoughby Lincs 118 E3
Silloth Cumb 176 F8
Silpho N York 163 H4
Silsden C Brad 149 J6
Silsoe C Beds 86 B8
Silton Dorset 32 C5
Silverburn Mdloth 211 G7
Silverdale Lancs 157 G7
Silverdale Staffs 114 C2
Silver End Essex 71 K3
Silverford Abers 268 D3
Silvergate Norfk 122 D6
Silverlace Green Suffk 91 H3
Silverley's Green Suffk 106 F8
Silverstone Nhants 84 C6
Silver Street Kent 53 J7
Silver Street Somset 31 J4
Silverton Devon 13 M2
Silverwell Cnwll 4 B5
Silvington Shrops 96 E7
Simister Bury 140 C6
Simmondley Derbys 131 K1
Simonburn Nthumb 179 K4
Simonsbath Somset 28 D3
Simonsburrow Devon 29 L7
Simonstone Lancs 140 A1
Simonstone N York 158 F4
Simprim Border 202 C4
Simpson M Keyn 85 H8
Simpson Cross Pembks 54 E3
Sinclair's Hill Border 202 C3
Sinclairston E Ayrs 196 F7
Sinderby N York 160 E6
Sinderhope Nthumb 179 K8
Sinderland Green Traffd 130 E2
Sindlesham Wokham 49 J5
Sinfin C Derb 116 B5
Singleborough Bucks 67 J1
Single Street Gt Lon 51 L7
Singleton Kent 40 C7
Singleton Lancs 147 G8
Singleton W Susx 20 E4
Singlewell Kent 52 E5
Sinkhurst Green Kent 39 K5
Sinnarhard Abers 244 B1
Sinnington N York 162 C5
Sinton Worcs 81 J3
Sinton Worcs 81 J3
Sinton Green Worcs 81 J3
Sipson Gt Lon 50 D3
Sirhowy Blae G 61 J5
Sissinghurst Kent 39 K6
Siston S Glos 45 K4
Sitcott Devon 11 L4
Sithney Cnwll 3 G5
Sithney Common Cnwll 3 G5
Sithney Green Cnwll 3 G5
Sittingbourne Kent 40 B3
Six Ashes Shrops 97 H5
Six Bells Blae G 61 K6
Sixhills Lincs 136 C2
Six Mile Bottom Cambs 88 B4
Sixmile Cottages Kent 40 F6
Sixpenny Handley Dorset 33 G7
Six Rues Jersey 9 c2
Sizewell Suffk 91 L3
Skaill Ork 275 d5
Skares E Ayrs 197 G7
Skateraw Abers 245 K5
Skateraw E Loth 213 G4
Skeabost Highld 259 G7
Skeeby N York 160 B2
Skeffington Leics 101 G3
Skeffling E R Yk 145 K4
Skegby Notts 133 K7
Skegby Notts 134 F5
Skegness Lincs 137 L7
Skelbo Highld 264 B1
Skelbo Street Highld 264 B1
Skelbrooke Donc 142 D5
Skeldyke Lincs 119 K4
Skellingthorpe Lincs 135 J5
Skellorn Green Ches E 131 H3
Skellow Donc 142 E5
Skelmanthorpe Kirk 141 K5
Skelmersdale Lancs 138 F6
Skelmorlie N Ayrs 207 K5
Skelpick Highld 278 B5
Skelston D & G 185 K6
Skelton C York 151 J4
Skelton Cumb 166 B4
Skelton E R Yk 143 J3
Skelton N York 150 E2
Skelton N York 159 K3
Skelton R & Cl 170 F7
Skelwith Bridge Cumb 156 E2
Skendleby Lincs 137 H5
Skene House Abers 245 G2
Skenfrith Mons 62 F3
Skerne E R Yk 153 G5
Skerray Highld 277 L4
Skerricha Highld 276 C6
Skerton Lancs 147 J3
Sketchley Leics 99 L5
Sketty Swans 57 H6
Skewen Neath 57 K5
Skewsby N York 151 K2
Skeyton Norfk 122 E6
Skeyton Corner Norfk 122 E6
Skiall Highld 279 H3
Skidbrooke Lincs 137 H1
Skidbrooke North End Lincs 137 H1
Skidby E R Yk 144 C1
Skigersta W Isls 282 h1
Skilgate Somset 29 H5
Skillington Lincs 118 A6
Skinburness Cumb 176 F7
Skinflats Falk 210 B2
Skinidin Highld 258 C7
Skinners Green W Berk 48 C6
Skinningrove R & Cl 171 G6
Skipness Ag & B 206 E7
Skipper's Bridge D & G 177 L2
Skiprigg Cumb 165 L2
Skipsea E R Yk 153 J5
Skipsea Brough E R Yk 153 J5
Skipton N York 149 H5
Skipton-on-Swale N York 160 E6
Skipwith N York 151 L8
Skirlaugh E R Yk 153 J7
Skirling Border 199 J5
Skirmett Bucks 49 J1
Skirpenbeck E R Yk 152 A4
Skirwith Cumb 166 E4
Skirwith N York 158 C7
Skirza Highld 280 E3
Skitby Cumb 178 B5
Skittle Green Bucks 67 J6
Skokholm Island Pembks 54 B6
Skomer Island Pembks 54 B5
Skulamus Highld 247 L4
Skyborry Green Shrops 95 G8
Skye Green Essex 72 C3
Skye of Curr Highld 253 J6
Skyreholme N York 149 J4
Slack Calder 140 E2
Slackcote Oldham 140 E6
Slack Head Cumb 157 G6
Slackholme End Lincs 137 K5
Slacks of Cairnbanno Abers 256 F3
Slad Gloucs 64 C5
Slade Devon 14 D1
Slade Devon 27 J2
Slade Devon 28 E5
Slade End Oxon 48 E1
Slade Green Gt Lon 52 B4
Slade Heath Staffs 97 L2
Slade Hooton Rothm 133 K2
Sladesbridge Cnwll 10 E8
Slades Green Worcs 81 J8
Slaggyford Nthumb 178 F8
Slaidburn Lancs 148 C5
Slaithwaite Kirk 141 G5
Slaley Derbys 132 E8
Slaley Nthumb 180 A7
Slamannan Falk 209 M4
Slapton Bucks 68 B3
Slapton Devon 8 B6
Slapton Nhants 84 C6
Slattocks Rochdl 140 D6
Slaugham W Susx 37 L5
Slaughterford Wilts 46 B4
Slawston Leics 101 G4
Sleaford Hants 36 B3
Sleaford Lincs 118 E2
Sleagill Cumb 166 E6
Sleap Shrops 113 H6
Sleapford Wrekin 113 L8
Sleapshyde Herts 69 G5
Sleasdairidh Highld 272 F8
Slebech Pembks 55 H4
Sledge Green Worcs 81 J8
Sledmere E R Yk 152 E3
Sleetbeck Cumb 178 C3
Sleight Dorset 17 J3
Sleightholme Dur 168 B8
Sleights N York 162 F1
Slepe Dorset 17 H4
Slickly Highld 280 C3
Sliddery N Ayrs 193 J4
Sligachan Highld 247 G3
Sligrachan Ag & B 207 K1
Slimbridge Gloucs 63 L6
Slindon Staffs 114 C5
Slindon W Susx 20 F5
Slinfold W Susx 37 H4
Sling Gwynd 126 B6
Slingsby N York 162 B7
Slip End C Beds 68 D3
Slip End Herts 86 F7
Slipton Nhants 101 L7
Slitting Mill Staffs 115 G8
Slockavullin Ag & B 216 C7
Sloley Norfk 122 F6
Sloncombe Devon 13 H5
Sloothby Lincs 137 J5
Slough Slough 50 C3
Slough Crematorium Bucks 50 B3
Slough Green Somset 30 C7
Slough Green W Susx 37 L5
Slumbay Highld 248 E4
Slyfield Green Surrey 50 C8
Slyne Lancs 147 J3
Smailholm Border 201 K6
Smallbridge Rochdl 140 D5
Smallbrook Devon 13 K3
Smallbrook Gloucs 63 H7
Smallburgh Norfk 123 G6
Smalldale Derbys 132 B4
Smalldale Derbys 132 C3
Small Dole W Susx 22 C5
Smalley Derbys 116 C3
Smalley Common Derbys 116 C3
Smalley Green Derbys 116 C3
Smallfield Surrey 37 M2
Small Heath Birm 98 E6
Small Hythe Kent 25 G1
Smallridge Devon 15 G2
Smallthorne C Stke 114 D2
Smallways N York 168 E8
Smallwood Ches E 130 F7
Small Wood Hey Lancs 147 H6
Smallworth Norfk 105 K7
Smannell Hants 34 E1
Smardale Cumb 158 C1
Smarden Kent 39 L5
Smarden Bell Kent 39 L5
Smart's Hill Kent 38 E5
Smeafield Nthumb 203 H5
Smearisary Highld 237 J5
Smeatharpe Devon 30 B8
Smeeth Kent 40 E7
Smeeton Westerby Leics 100 E5
Smelthouses N York 150 B3
Smerral Highld 275 G2
Smestow Staffs 97 J5
Smethwick Sandw 98 C6
Smethwick Green Ches E 130 F7
Smisby Derbys 116 B7
Smitheclose IoW 19 J5
Smith End Green Worcs 81 H5
Smithfield Cumb 178 B6
Smith Green Lancs 147 J5
Smithies Barns 142 A6
Smithincott Devon 29 J8
Smith's End Herts 87 H7
Smith's Green Essex 70 E3
Smith's Green Essex 88 D7
Smithstown Highld 260 C4
Smithton Highld 252 D3
Smithy Bridge Rochdl 140 D5
Smithy Green Ches E 130 E5
Smithy Green Stockp 131 G3
Smithy Houses Derbys 116 C2
Smockington Leics 99 M5
Smoo Highld 277 G3
Smythe's Green Essex 72 D3
Snade D & G 185 L5
Snailbeach Shrops 95 J3
Snailwell Cambs 88 C2
Snainton N York 163 G6
Snaith E R Yk 143 G3
Snake Pass Inn Derbys 132 B2
Snape N York 160 C6
Snape Suffk 91 J3
Snape Green Lancs 138 D5
Snape Street Suffk 91 J4
Snaresbrook Gt Lon 51 L1
Snarestone Leics 99 K2
Snarford Lincs 135 L3
Snargate Kent 25 J2
Snave Kent 25 J1
Sneachill Worcs 81 L4
Snead Powys 95 H5
Sneath Common Norfk 106 D5
Sneaton N York 162 F1
Sneatonthorpe N York 162 F2
Snelland Lincs 135 M4
Snelson Ches E 130 F5
Snelston Derbys 115 J3
Snetterton Norfk 105 K5
Snettisham Norfk 120 F4
Snibston Leics 116 C8
Snig's End Gloucs 64 A1
Snitter Nthumb 190 E5
Snitterby Lincs 135 K1
Snitterfield Warwks 82 F3
Snitterton Derbys 132 E7
Snitton Shrops 96 D8
Snoadhill Kent 40 B6
Snodhill Herefs 79 K7
Snodland Kent 52 F6
Snoll Hatch Kent 39 G4
Snowden Hill Barns 141 L7
Snow End Herts 69 L1
Snowshill Gloucs 82 C8
Snow Street Norfk 106 B7
Soake Hants 19 L2
Soar Cardif 43 H5
Soar Devon 7 K7
Soar Powys 60 E1
Soay Highld 246 F6
Soberton Hants 35 J7
Soberton Heath Hants 35 J8
Sockbridge Cumb 166 C5
Sockburn Darltn 160 E1
Sodom Denbgs 128 C5
Sodylt Bank Shrops 112 E3
Soham Cambs 104 B8
Soham Cotes Cambs 104 B8
Solas W Isls 282 c7
Solbury Pembks 54 E4
Soldon Devon 26 E8
Soldon Cross Devon 26 E8
Soldridge Hants 35 K4
Sole Street Kent 40 E5
Sole Street Kent 52 E5
Solihull Solhll 98 F7
Sollers Dilwyn Herefs 80 A4
Sollers Hope Herefs 80 E8
Sollom Lancs 138 F4
Solva Pembks 74 C7
Solwaybank D & G 177 J3
Somerby Leics 101 G1
Somerby Lincs 144 D6
Somercotes Derbys 116 C1
Somerford Dorset 18 B5
Somerford Keynes Gloucs 64 E8
Somerley W Susx 20 D7
Somerleyton Suffk 107 K4
Somersal Herbert Derbys 115 J4
Somersby Lincs 136 F5
Somersham Cambs 103 G7
Somersham Suffk 90 C5
Somerton Oxon 66 D2
Somerton Somset 31 H5
Somerton Suffk 89 G4
Somerwood Shrops 113 J8
Sompting W Susx 21 K6

Sonning Wokham 49 J4
Sonning Common Oxon 49 H3
Sonning Eye Oxon 49 H4
Sontley Wrexhm 112 E2
Sopley Hants 18 B4
Sopworth Wilts 46 B2
Sorbie D & G 174 C5
Sordale Highld 279 L4
Sorisdale Ag & B 225 H3
Sorn E Ayrs 197 G5
Sortat Highld 280 C4
Sotby Lincs 136 D4
Sots Hole Lincs 136 B6
Sotterley Suffk 107 J6
Soughton Flints 128 F6
Soulbury Bucks 67 L2
Soulby Cumb 166 B5
Soulby Cumb 167 H8
Souldern Oxon 66 D1
Souldrop Bed 85 J3
Sound Ches E 113 K2
Sound Muir Moray 267 G5
Soundwell S Glos 45 J4
Sourton Devon 12 D4
Soutergate Cumb 156 B6
South Acre Norfk 121 H8
South Alkham Kent 41 H7
Southall Gt Lon 50 E3
South Allington Devon 8 B7
South Alloa Falk 210 A1
Southam Gloucs 64 E2
Southam Warwks 83 K3
South Ambersham W Susx 20 F3
Southampton C Sotn 19 G1
Southampton Crematorium Hants 34 F7
South Anston Rothm 133 K3
South Ascot W & M 50 A5
South Ashford Kent 40 C7
South Baddesley Hants 18 E4
South Ballachulish Highld 229 G4
South Bank C York 151 J5
South Bank R & Cl 170 C6
South Barrow Somset 31 K5
South Beddington Gt Lon 51 H6
South Beer Cnwll 11 K4
South Benfleet Essex 53 G2
South Bersted W Susx 20 F6
South Bockhampton Dorset 18 B4
Southborough Gt Lon 51 L5
Southborough Kent 38 F5
Southbourne Bmouth 18 A5
Southbourne W Susx 20 C5
South Bowood Dorset 15 K3
South Bramwith Donc 143 G5
South Brent Devon 7 K3
South Brewham Somset 32 B4
South Bristol Crematorium Bristl 45 H5
South Broomhill Nthumb 191 K6
Southburgh Norfk 105 K2
South Burlingham Norfk 107 H2
Southburn E R Yk 152 F5
South Cadbury Somset 31 K5
South Carlton Lincs 135 J4
South Carlton Notts 134 B3
South Cave E R Yk 144 A2
South Cerney Gloucs 64 F7
South Chailey E Susx 22 F4
South Chard Somset 15 H2
South Charlton Nthumb 191 H2
South Cheriton Somset 32 B6
South Church Dur 169 G5
Southchurch Sthend 53 J2
South Cleatlam Dur 168 E7
South Cliffe E R Yk 152 D8
South Clifton Notts 135 G5
South Cockerington Lincs 137 G2
South Cornelly Brdgnd 42 B5
Southcott Cnwll 11 H3
Southcott Devon 12 D4
Southcott Devon 13 H6
Southcott Devon 27 H7
Southcott Wilts 47 H7
Southcourt Bucks 67 K5
South Cove Suffk 107 K7
South Creake Norfk 121 J4
South Crosland Kirk 141 H5
South Croxton Leics 100 F2
South Dalton E R Yk 152 E6
South Darenth Kent 52 C5
South Duffield N York 143 H1
Southease E Susx 23 G6
South Elkington Lincs 136 E2
South Elmsall Wakefd 142 D5
Southend Ag & B 192 E6
South End E R Yk 145 K4
South End Hants 33 J7
South End Herefs 81 G6
South End N Linc 144 E4
South End Norfk 105 K5
Southend Wilts 47 J4
Southend Crematorium Sthend 53 J2
Southend-on-Sea Sthend 53 J2
Southernby Cumb 165 L3
Southernden Kent 39 L4
Southerndown V Glam 42 D7
Southerness D & G 176 C7
South Erradale Highld 260 B5
Southerton Devon 14 C4
Southery Norfk 104 C4
South Essex Crematorium Gt Lon 52 C2
South Fambridge Essex 72 B8
South Fawley W Berk 48 A3
South Ferriby N Linc 144 B4
South Field E R Yk 144 C3
Southfield Falk 209 M4
Southfleet Kent 52 D5
Southford IoW 19 J7
Southgate Gt Lon 69 J8
Southgate Norfk 120 E5
Southgate Norfk 121 J4
Southgate Norfk 122 C6
Southgate Swans 57 G7
South Godstone Surrey 38 A4
South Gorley Hants 18 B2
South Gosforth N u Ty 181 G5
South Green Essex 71 G8
South Green Essex 72 F3
South Green Kent 53 J7
South Green Norfk 105 L1
South Green Suffk 106 D8
South Gyle C Edin 211 G4
South Hanningfield Essex 71 H7
South Harting W Susx 20 C3
South Hayling Hants 20 B6
South Hazelrigg Nthumb 203 G6
South Heath Bucks 67 M6
South Heighton E Susx 23 G6
South Hetton Dur 169 K2
South Hiendley Wakefd 142 B5
South Hill Cnwll 11 L8
South Hill Somset 31 G5
South Hinksey Oxon 66 D6
South Hole Devon 26 C6
South Holmwood Surrey 37 J2
South Hornchurch Gt Lon 52 B2
South Horrington Somset 31 J2
South Huish Devon 7 K6
South Hykeham Lincs 135 J6
South Hylton Sundld 181 J7
Southill C Beds 86 C6
Southington Hants 35 G1
South Kelsey Lincs 144 D8
South Kessock Highld 251 H2
South Killingholme N Linc 144 F4
South Kilvington N York 160 F6
South Kilworth Leics 100 D7
South Kirkby Wakefd 142 C5
South Knighton Devon 13 J8
South Kyme Lincs 119 G2
South Lanarkshire Crematorium S Lans 209 H7
Southleigh Devon 14 E4
South Leigh Oxon 66 B5
South Leverton Notts 134 F3
South Littleton Worcs 82 C6
South London Crematorium Gt Lon 51 H5
South Lopham Norfk 105 L7
South Luffenham Rutlnd 101 K3
South Malling E Susx 23 G5
South Marston Swindn 47 J2
South Merstham Surrey 51 H8
South Middleton Nthumb 190 E2
South Milford N York 142 D2
South Milton Devon 7 K6
South Mimms Herts 69 G6
Southminster Essex 72 D7
South Molton Devon 28 C5
South Moor Dur 180 F8
Southmoor Oxon 66 B7
South Moreton Oxon 48 E1
Southmuir Angus 234 B5
South Mundham W Susx 20 E6
South Muskham Notts 134 F8
South Newbald E R Yk 152 D8
South Newington Oxon 83 J8
South Newton Wilts 33 J4
South Normanton Derbys 133 J8
South Norwood Gt Lon 51 J5
South Nutfield Surrey 37 M1
South Ockendon Thurr 52 D2
Southoe Cambs 86 D2
Southolt Suffk 90 E2
South Ormsby Lincs 137 G4
Southorpe C Pete 102 B3
South Ossett Wakefd 141 L4
South Otterington N York 160 E5
Southover Dorset 16 B4
Southover E Susx 24 B2
South Owersby Lincs 135 L1
Southowram Calder 141 H3
South Park Surrey 37 K1
South Perrott Dorset 15 L1
South Petherton Somset 31 G7
South Petherwin Cnwll 11 K6
South Pickenham Norfk 105 G3
South Pill Cnwll 6 E3
South Pool Devon 7 M6
South Poorton Dorset 15 M3
Southport Sefton 138 D4
Southport Crematorium Lancs 138 D5
South Queensferry C Edin 210 F3
South Radworthy Devon 28 C4
South Rauceby Lincs 118 D2
South Raynham Norfk 121 J6
South Reddish Stockp 131 H1
Southrepps Norfk 122 E4
South Reston Lincs 137 G3
Southrey Lincs 136 B6
South Ronaldsay Ork 275 c6
Southrop Gloucs 65 J6
Southrope Hants 35 K2
South Runcton Norfk 104 C2
South Scarle Notts 135 G7
Southsea C Port 19 L4
Southsea Wrexhm 112 D1
South Shian Ag & B 228 E7
South Shields S Tyne 181 J5
South Shields Crematorium S Tyne 181 J6
South Shore Bpool 138 C1
Southside Dur 168 E5
South Somercotes Lincs 137 H1
South Stainley N York 150 D3
South Stifford Thurr 52 D3
South Stoke BaNES 45 L6
South Stoke Oxon 48 F2
South Stoke W Susx 21 H5
South Stour Kent 40 D7
South Street Kent 40 D4
South Street Kent 40 F2
South Street Kent 52 D6
South Tarbrax S Lans 199 H3
South Tawton Devon 12 F4
South Tehidy Cnwll 3 G3
South Thoresby Lincs 137 G4
South Thorpe Dur 168 E7
South Town Hants 35 K4
Southtown Norfk 107 L2
Southtown Somset 30 D7
South Uist W Isls 283 c10
Southwaite Cumb 166 B2
South Walsham Norfk 107 H1
Southwark Gt Lon 51 J3
South Warnborough Hants 35 L2
Southwater W Susx 37 J5
Southwater Street W Susx 37 H5
Southway Somset 31 H2
South Weald Essex 70 E8
Southwell Dorset 16 D8
Southwell Notts 117 J1
South West Middlesex Crematorium Gt Lon 50 E4
South Weston Oxon 67 H7
South Wheatley Cnwll 11 J4
Southwick Hants 19 L2
Southwick Nhants 101 M5
Southwick Somset 30 E2
Southwick Sundld 181 J7
Southwick W Susx 22 C6
Southwick Wilts 46 B7
South Widcombe BaNES 45 H7
South Wigston Leics 100 D4
South Willesborough Kent 40 D7
South Willingham Lincs 136 C3
South Wingate Dur 169 L4
South Wingfield Derbys 133 G8
South Witham Lincs 118 B7
Southwold Suffk 107 K8
South Wonston Hants 34 F4
Southwood Norfk 107 H2
Southwood Somset 31 J4
South Woodham Ferrers Essex 71 K7
South Wootton Norfk 120 E7
South Wraxall Wilts 46 B6
South Zeal Devon 12 F4
Sowerby Calder 141 G3
Sowerby N York 160 F6
Sowerby Bridge Calder 141 G3
Sowerby Row Cumb 165 L3
Sower Carr Lancs 147 G7
Sowerhill Somset 28 F6
Sowhill Torfn 62 B7
Sowley Green Suffk 88 D5
Sowood Calder 141 G4
Sowton Devon 6 F2
Sowton Devon 14 A4
Soyland Town Calder 140 F4
Spa Common Norfk 122 F5
Spain's End Essex 88 D7
Spalding Lincs 119 H7
Spaldington E R Yk 143 J1
Spaldwick Cambs 86 C1
Spalford Notts 135 G6
Spanby Lincs 118 E4
Spanish Green Hants 49 G7
Sparham Norfk 122 B7
Sparhamill Norfk 122 B7
Spark Bridge Cumb 156 D5
Sparket Cumb 166 B5
Sparkford Somset 31 K5
Sparkhill Birm 98 E6
Sparkwell Devon 7 H3
Sparrow Green Norfk 121 L8
Sparrowpit Derbys 132 B4
Sparrows Green E Susx 39 G6
Sparsholt Hants 34 F4
Sparsholt Oxon 47 M2
Spartylea Nthumb 167 K1
Spath Staffs 115 H4
Spaunton N York 162 C5
Spaxton Somset 30 C3
Spean Bridge Highld 239 L7
Spear Hill W Susx 21 K3
Spearywell Hants 34 D5
Speen Bucks 67 K7
Speen W Berk 48 C5
Speeton N York 163 L7
Speke Lpool 129 K3
Speldhurst Kent 38 E5
Spellbrook Herts 70 C4
Spelmonden Kent 39 H6
Spelsbury Oxon 65 M3
Spen Kirk 141 K3
Spencers Wood Wokham 49 H5
Spen Green Ches E 130 F7
Spennithorne N York 159 L5
Spennymoor Dur 169 H4
Spernall Warwks 82 C3
Spetchley Worcs 81 K4
Spetisbury Dorset 17 H2
Spexhall Suffk 107 H7
Spey Bay Moray 267 G3
Speybridge Highld 253 K6
Speyview Moray 254 E3
Spilsby Lincs 137 G6
Spindlestone Nthumb 203 J6
Spinkhill Derbys 133 J4
Spinningdale Highld 263 J2
Spion Kop Notts 133 L6
Spirthill Wilts 46 E4
Spital Wirral 129 H3
Spital Hill Donc 134 C1
Spital in the Street Lincs 135 K2
Spithurst E Susx 23 G4
Spittal E Loth 212 A4
Spittal E R Yk 152 B5
Spittal Highld 279 L5
Spittal Nthumb 202 F3
Spittal Pembks 55 G2
Spittalfield P & K 233 H7
Spittal of Glenmuick Abers 243 K6
Spittal of Glenshee P & K 233 H2
Spittal-on-Rule Border 189 G2
Spixworth Norfk 122 E8
Splatt Cnwll 10 C7
Splatt Cnwll 11 J5
Splatt Devon 12 E2
Splayne's Green E Susx 23 G2
Splottlands Cardif 43 K6
Spofforth N York 150 E5
Spondon C Derb 116 C4
Spon Green Flints 129 G7
Spooner Row Norfk 106 B4
Sporle Norfk 105 G1
Spott E Loth 212 E4
Spottiswoode Border 201 J3
Spratton Nhants 84 D1
Spreakley Surrey 36 B3
Spreyton Devon 13 G3
Spriddlestone Devon 7 G4
Spridlington Lincs 135 K3
Springburn C Glas 209 G5
Springfield D & G 177 K5
Springfield Essex 71 H5
Springfield Fife 222 F5
Springhill Staffs 98 B3
Springhill Staffs 98 D2
Springholm D & G 175 K1
Springside N Ayrs 196 D3
Springthorpe Lincs 135 H2
Spring Vale Barns 141 L7
Springwell Sundld 181 G7
Springwood Crematorium Lpool 129 K3

Sproatley E R Yk 145 F1
Sproston Green Ches W 130 E6
Sprotbrough Donc 142 E7
Sproughton Suffk 90 D6
Sprouston Border 202 B6
Sprowston Norfk 106 E1
Sproxton Leics 117 M6
Sproxton N York 161 K6
Spunhill Shrops 112 F5
Spurstow Ches E 130 A8
Spyway Dorset 15 M4
Square & Compass Pembks 74 D6
Stableford Shrops 97 G4
Stableford Staffs 114 C4
Stacey Bank Sheff 132 F2
Stackhouse N York 148 E3
Stackpole Pembks 55 G7
Stacksford Norfk 105 L5
Stacksteads Lancs 140 C3
Staddiscombe C Plym 7 G4
Staddlethorpe E R Yk 143 L2
Staden Derbys 131 L5
Stadhampton Oxon 66 F7
Stadhlaigearraidh W Isls 283 b10
Staffield Cumb 166 D2
Staffin Highld 259 H3
Stafford Staffs 114 E7
Stafford Crematorium Staffs 114 E6
Stagsden Bed 85 J5
Stainborough Barns 141 M7
Stainburn Cumb 164 D5
Stainburn N York 150 C6
Stainby Lincs 118 B7
Staincross Barns 141 M5
Staindrop Dur 168 E6
Staines-upon-Thames Surrey 50 D5
Stainfield Lincs 118 E6
Stainfield Lincs 136 B5
Stainforth Donc 143 G5
Stainforth N York 148 E2
Staining Lancs 147 G8
Stainland Calder 141 G4
Stainsacre N York 163 G1
Stainsby Derbys 133 J6
Stainton Cumb 157 H5
Stainton Cumb 166 C5
Stainton Cumb 177 L7
Stainton Donc 133 L1
Stainton Dur 168 D7
Stainton Middsb 170 B7
Stainton N York 159 K3
Stainton by Langworth Lincs 135 L4
Staintondale N York 163 H3
Stainton le Vale Lincs 136 C1
Stainton with Adgarley Cumb 146 E1
Stair Cumb 165 H6
Stair E Ayrs 196 E6
Stairfoot Barns 142 B6
Stairhaven D & G 172 F4
Staithes N York 171 H7
Stakeford Nthumb 181 G2
Stake Pool Lancs 147 H6
Stakes Hants 19 M2
Stalbridge Dorset 32 B7
Stalbridge Weston Dorset 32 B7
Stalham Norfk 123 H6
Stalham Green Norfk 123 H6
Stalisfield Green Kent 40 B5
Stalland Common Norfk 105 L4
Stallen Dorset 31 K7
Stallingborough NE Lin 145 G5
Stalling Busk N York 159 G5
Stallington Staffs 114 E4
Stalmine Lancs 147 G6
Stalmine Moss Side Lancs 147 G6
Stalybridge Tamesd 140 E8
Stambourne Essex 88 E7
Stambourne Green Essex 88 D7
Stamford Lincs 102 A2
Stamford Nthumb 191 J2
Stamford Bridge Ches W 129 L6
Stamford Bridge E R Yk 151 M5
Stamfordham Nthumb 180 C4
Stamford Hill Gt Lon 51 J2
Stanah Lancs 147 G7
Stanborough Herts 69 G5
Stanbridge C Beds 68 B2
Stanbridge Dorset 17 K2
Stanbury C Brad 149 H8
Stand Bury 140 B6
Stand N Lans 209 K5
Standburn Falk 210 B4
Standeford Staffs 97 K2
Standen Kent 39 L5
Standen Street Kent 39 K7
Standerwick Somset 32 D1
Standford Hants 36 B4
Standingstone Cumb 164 D4
Standish Gloucs 64 A5
Standish Wigan 139 H5
Standish Lower Ground Wigan 139 H6
Standlake Oxon 66 B6
Standon Hants 34 F5
Standon Herts 69 K3
Standon Staffs 114 C4
Standon Green End Herts 69 K3
Standwell Green Suffk 90 D1
Stane N Lans 210 A7
Stanfield Norfk 121 K7
Stanford C Beds 86 D7
Stanford Kent 40 F7
Stanford Shrops 95 H1
Stanford Bishop Herefs 80 F5
Stanford Bridge Worcs 81 G2
Stanford Bridge Wrekin 113 M6
Stanford Dingley W Berk 48 E4
Stanford in the Vale Oxon 65 M8
Stanford le Hope Thurr 52 E3
Stanford on Avon Nhants 100 D7
Stanford on Soar Notts 116 F7
Stanford on Teme Worcs 81 G2
Stanford Rivers Essex 70 D7
Stanfree Derbys 133 J5
Stanghow R & Cl 170 F7
Stanground C Pete 102 D4
Stanhill Lancs 139 L2
Stanhoe Norfk 121 H4
Stanhope Border 199 K7
Stanhope Dur 168 C3
Stanhope Kent 40 C7
Stanhope Bretby Derbys 115 M7
Stanion Nhants 101 K6
Stanklin Worcs 97 J8
Stanley Derbys 116 C3
Stanley Dur 180 F8
Stanley Notts 133 J7
Stanley P & K 221 K1
Stanley Shrops 97 G6
Stanley Staffs 114 E1
Stanley Wakefd 142 A3
Stanley Common Derbys 116 C3
Stanley Crook Dur 168 F3
Stanley Ferry Wakefd 142 A3
Stanley Gate Lancs 138 F6
Stanley Moor Staffs 114 E1
Stanley Pontlarge Gloucs 64 E1
Stanmer Br & H 22 E5
Stanmore Gt Lon 68 F8
Stanmore Hants 34 F5
Stanmore W Berk 48 C3
Stannersburn Nthumb 179 G2
Stanningfield Suffk 89 H4
Stanningley Leeds 141 K1
Stannington Nthumb 180 F3
Stannington Sheff 132 F2
Stannington Station Nthumb 180 F3
Stansbatch Herefs 79 L3
Stansfield Suffk 88 F5
Stanshope Staffs 115 J1
Stanstead Suffk 89 G5
Stanstead Abbotts Herts 69 K5
Stansted Kent 52 D6
Stansted Mountfitchet Essex 70 D2
Stanton Derbys 115 M7
Stanton Gloucs 82 C8
Stanton Mons 62 C3
Stanton Nthumb 191 G8
Stanton Staffs 115 J2
Stanton Suffk 105 K8
Stanton by Bridge Derbys 116 B6
Stanton by Dale Derbys 116 D4
Stanton Drew BaNES 45 H6
Stanton Fitzwarren Swindn 47 J1
Stanton Harcourt Oxon 66 B6
Stanton Hill Notts 133 J7
Stanton in Peak Derbys 132 E6
Stanton Lacy Shrops 96 B7
Stanton Lees Derbys 132 E7
Stanton Long Shrops 96 D5
Stanton on the Wolds Notts 117 G5
Stanton Prior BaNES 45 K6
Stanton St Bernard Wilts 47 G6
Stanton St John Oxon 66 E5
Stanton St Quintin Wilts 46 C3
Stanton Street Suffk 89 J2
Stanton under Bardon Leics 100 A1
Stanton upon Hine Heath Shrops 113 J6
Stanton Wick BaNES 45 J6
Stantway Gloucs 63 L4
Stanwardine in the Field Shrops 112 F6
Stanwardine in the Wood Shrops 113 G6
Stanway Essex 72 D2
Stanway Gloucs 64 F1
Stanway Green Essex 72 D2
Stanway Green Suffk 90 F1
Stanwell Surrey 50 D4
Stanwell Moor Surrey 50 D4
Stanwick Nhants 85 J1
Stanwix Cumb 177 L7
Staoinebrig W Isls 283 b10
Stape N York 162 D4
Stapehill Dorset 17 L3
Stapeley Ches E 113 L2
Stapenhill Staffs 115 L7
Staple Kent 41 J4
Staple Cross Devon 29 J6
Staple Cross E Susx 24 E3
Staplefield W Susx 37 L5
Staple Fitzpaine Somset 30 C7
Stapleford Cambs 87 K5
Stapleford Herts 69 J4
Stapleford Leics 117 L7
Stapleford Lincs 135 H8
Stapleford Notts 116 E4
Stapleford Wilts 33 J3
Stapleford Abbotts Essex 70 D8
Stapleford Tawney Essex 70 D7
Staplegrove Somset 30 B5
Staplehay Somset 30 B6
Staple Hill Worcs 98 B8
Staplehurst Kent 39 K5
Staplers IoW 19 H6
Staplestreet Kent 40 D3
Stapleton Cumb 178 C4
Stapleton Herefs 79 L2
Stapleton Leics 99 L4
Stapleton N York 169 H8
Stapleton Shrops 95 L3
Stapleton Somset 31 G6
Stapley Somset 30 B8
Staploe Bed 86 C3
Staplow Herefs 80 F7
Star Fife 222 E6
Star Pembks 75 M5
Star Somset 44 E7
Starbeck N York 150 D4
Starbotton N York 159 G7
Starcross Devon 14 A6
Stareton Warwks 83 H1
Starkholmes Derbys 132 F7
Starlings Green Essex 70 C1
Starr's Green E Susx 24 D4
Starston Norfk 106 E6
Start Devon 8 B6
Startforth Dur 168 D7
Startley Wilts 46 D3
Statenborough Kent 41 J4
Statham Warrtn 130 D2
Stathe Somset 30 E5
Stathern Leics 117 K5
Station Town Dur 169 L3
Staughton Green Cambs 86 C2
Staughton Highway Cambs 86 C2
Staunton Gloucs 63 H4
Staunton Gloucs 64 A1
Staunton in the Vale Notts 117 L3
Staunton on Arrow Herefs 79 L3
Staunton on Wye Herefs 79 L6
Staveley Cumb 156 E5
Staveley Cumb 157 G3
Staveley Derbys 133 H5
Staveley N York 150 E3
Staverton Devon 8 B2
Staverton Gloucs 64 C2
Staverton Nhants 83 M3
Staverton Wilts 46 B6
Staverton Bridge Gloucs 64 C3
Stawell Somset 30 E3
Stawley Somset 29 J6
Staxigoe Highld 280 E5
Staxton N York 163 J6
Staylittle Cerdgn 92 E5
Staylittle Powys 93 J5
Staynall Lancs 147 G7
Staythorpe Notts 117 K1
Stead C Brad 149 L6
Stean N York 159 K8
Stearsby N York 151 K2
Steart Somset 30 C2
Stebbing Essex 71 G2
Stebbing Green Essex 71 G2
Stechford Birm 98 E6
Stede Quarter Kent 39 L5
Stedham W Susx 36 C6
Steel Nthumb 179 L7
Steel Cross E Susx 38 E7
Steelend Fife 210 D1
Steele Road Border 188 F7
Steel Green Cumb 155 L6
Steel Heath Shrops 113 J4
Steen's Bridge Herefs 80 C4
Steep Hants 35 M6
Steephill IoW 19 J8
Steep Lane Calder 140 F3
Steeple Dorset 17 H6
Steeple Essex 72 D6
Steeple Ashton Wilts 46 C7
Steeple Aston Oxon 66 C2
Steeple Barton Oxon 66 C2
Steeple Bumpstead Essex 88 D7
Steeple Claydon Bucks 67 H2
Steeple Gidding Cambs 102 C7
Steeple Langford Wilts 33 H3
Steeple Morden Cambs 86 F6
Steeton C Brad 149 J7
Stein Highld 258 D5
Stella Gatesd 180 E6
Stelling Minnis Kent 40 F6
Stembridge Somset 30 F6
Stenalees Cnwll 5 G3
Stenhouse D & G 185 K4
Stenhousemuir Falk 210 A2
Stenigot Lincs 136 D3
Stenscholl Highld 259 H3
Stenson Fields Derbys 116 B5
Stenton E Loth 212 D4
Steornabhagh W Isls 282 g3
Stepaside Pembks 55 K5
Stepford D & G 185 L6
Stepney Gt Lon 51 K3
Stepping Hill Stockp 131 H2
Steppingley C Beds 85 K8
Stepps N Lans 209 H5
Sternfield Suffk 91 J3
Stert Wilts 46 F7
Stetchworth Cambs 88 C3
Stevenage Herts 69 G2
Steven's Crouch E Susx 24 C4
Stevenston N Ayrs 196 B3
Steventon Hants 35 H1
Steventon Oxon 48 C1
Steventon End Essex 88 B6
Stevington Bed 85 K4
Stewartby Bed 85 K6
Stewartfield S Lans 209 G7
Stewarton E Ayrs 196 E2
Stewkley Bucks 67 K2
Stewley Somset 30 D7
Stewton Lincs 137 G2
Steyne Cross IoW 19 L6
Steyning W Susx 21 L4
Steynton Pembks 54 E5
Stibb Cnwll 26 C8
Stibbard Norfk 121 L6
Stibb Cross Devon 27 G7
Stibb Green Wilts 47 J6
Stibbington Cambs 102 B4
Stichill Border 201 L5
Sticker Cnwll 5 G5
Stickford Lincs 136 F7
Sticklepath Devon 12 F4
Sticklepath Somset 29 J4
Stickling Green Essex 87 K8
Stickney Lincs 136 F8
Stiffkey Norfk 121 L3
Stifford's Bridge Herefs 81 G5
Stiff Street Kent 53 J6
Stile Bridge Kent 39 J4
Stileway Somset 31 G3
Stilligarry W Isls 283 b10
Stillingfleet N York 151 J7
Stillington N York 151 J2
Stillington S on T 169 K6
Stilton Cambs 102 D5
Stinchcombe Gloucs 63 L7
Stinsford Dorset 16 D4
Stiperstones Shrops 95 J3
Stirchley Birm 98 D7
Stirchley Wrekin 96 F2
Stirling Abers 257 L3
Stirling Stirlg 220 D8
Stirtloe Cambs 86 D2
Stirton N York 149 H5
Stisted Essex 71 J2
Stitchcombe Wilts 47 K5
Stithians Cnwll 3 J4
Stivichall Covtry 99 J8
Stixwould Lincs 136 C6
St Margaret's Bay Kent 41 K6
Stoak Ches W 129 K5
Stobo Border 199 L5
Stoborough Dorset 17 H5
Stoborough Green Dorset 17 H5
Stobs Castle Border 188 E4
Stobswood Nthumb 191 J7
Stock Essex 71 G7
Stock N Som 44 F6
Stockbridge Hants 34 D4
Stockbriggs S Lans 198 C6
Stockbury Kent 53 H6
Stockcross W Berk 48 B5
Stockdalewath Cumb 165 L2
Stocker's Hill Kent 40 C5
Stockerston Leics 101 H4
Stock Green Worcs 82 A3
Stocking Herefs 63 J1
Stockingford Warwks 99 J5

Stocking Pelham Herts 70 C1
Stockland Devon 14 F2
Stockland Bristol Somset 30 C2
Stockland Green Kent 38 E5
Stockleigh English Devon 13 K2
Stockleigh Pomeroy Devon 13 K2
Stockley Wilts 46 E5
Stockley Hill Herefs 79 L7
Stocklinch Somset 30 F7
Stockmoor Herefs 79 M4
Stockport Stockp 131 H2
Stockport Crematorium Stockp 131 H2
Stocksbridge Sheff 141 L8
Stocksfield Nthumb 180 C6
Stockton Herefs 80 C3
Stockton Norfk 107 H4
Stockton Shrops 95 G3
Stockton Shrops 97 G3
Stockton Warwks 83 K3
Stockton Wilts 33 G3
Stockton Wrekin 114 B8
Stockton Brook Staffs 114 E1
Stockton Heath Warrtn 130 B3
Stockton-on-Tees S on T 170 B6
Stockton on Teme Worcs 81 G2
Stockton on the Forest C York 151 L4
Stockwell Gloucs 64 D4
Stockwell End Wolves 97 K3
Stockwell Heath Staffs 115 G7
Stockwood Bristl 45 J5
Stockwood Dorset 16 B1
Stock Wood Worcs 82 B3
Stodday Lancs 147 J4
Stodmarsh Kent 41 H3
Stody Norfk 122 B4
Stoer Highld 270 D2
Stoford Somset 31 J8
Stoford Wilts 33 J4
Stogumber Somset 29 K3
Stogursey Somset 30 B2
Stoke Covtry 99 K7
Stoke Devon 26 D6
Stoke Hants 20 B6
Stoke Hants 48 B8
Stoke Medway 53 H4
Stoke Abbott Dorset 15 K3
Stoke Albany Nhants 101 H5
Stoke Ash Suffk 90 D1
Stoke Bardolph Notts 117 H3
Stoke Bliss Worcs 80 F3
Stoke Bruerne Nhants 84 E5
Stoke by Clare Suffk 88 E6
Stoke-by-Nayland Suffk 89 K7
Stoke Canon Devon 13 L3
Stoke Charity Hants 35 G3
Stoke Climsland Cnwll 11 L7
Stoke Cross Herefs 80 E5
Stoke D'Abernon Surrey 50 E7
Stoke Doyle Nhants 102 A6
Stoke Dry Rutlnd 101 J4
Stoke Edith Herefs 80 E7
Stoke End Warwks 98 F4
Stoke Farthing Wilts 33 H5
Stoke Ferry Norfk 104 D3
Stoke Fleming Devon 8 C5
Stokeford Dorset 17 G5
Stoke Gabriel Devon 8 C3
Stoke Gifford S Glos 45 J3
Stoke Golding Leics 99 L4
Stoke Goldington M Keyn 85 G5
Stoke Green Bucks 50 B3
Stokeham Notts 134 F4
Stoke Hammond Bucks 67 L1
Stoke Heath Shrops 113 L5
Stoke Heath Worcs 81 L2
Stoke Holy Cross Norfk 106 E3
Stokeinteignhead Devon 13 L8
Stoke Lacy Herefs 80 E5
Stoke Lyne Oxon 66 E2
Stoke Mandeville Bucks 67 K5
Stokenchurch Bucks 67 J7
Stoke Newington Gt Lon 51 J2
Stokenham Devon 8 B6
Stoke-on-Trent C Stke 114 D2
Stoke Orchard Gloucs 64 D2
Stoke Poges Bucks 50 B2
Stoke Pound Worcs 81 M2
Stoke Prior Herefs 80 C4
Stoke Prior Worcs 81 L2
Stoke Rivers Devon 27 L4
Stoke Rochford Lincs 118 B6
Stoke Row Oxon 49 G2
Stoke St Gregory Somset 30 E5
Stoke St Mary Somset 30 C6
Stoke St Michael Somset 31 L2
Stoke St Milborough Shrops 96 D7
Stokesay Shrops 95 K7
Stokesby Norfk 107 J1
Stokesley N York 161 H1
Stoke sub Hamdon Somset 31 G7
Stoke Talmage Oxon 67 G7
Stoke Trister Somset 32 B5
Stoke upon Tern Shrops 113 L6
Stoke-upon-Trent C Stke 114 D3
Stoke Wake Dorset 16 E1
Stoke Wharf Worcs 81 L2
Stolford Somset 30 C2
Stondon Massey Essex 70 E7
Stone Bucks 67 J4
Stone Gloucs 63 K8
Stone Kent 52 C4
Stone Rothm 133 L2
Stone Somset 31 J4
Stone Staffs 114 E5
Stone Worcs 97 J8
Stonea Cambs 103 J5
Stone Allerton Somset 30 F1
Ston Easton Somset 45 J8
Stonebridge N Som 44 D7
Stonebridge Norfk 105 J5
Stonebridge Warwks 99 G6
Stone Bridge Corner C Pete 102 F3
Stonebroom Derbys 133 H7
Stone Chair Calder 141 H2
Stone Cross E Susx 23 K6
Stone Cross E Susx 38 D7
Stone Cross E Susx 39 G7
Stone Cross Kent 38 E5
Stone Cross Kent 40 D7
Stone Cross Kent 41 K4
Stonecross Green Suffk 89 G4
Stonecrouch Kent 39 H6
Stone-edge-Batch N Som 44 F4
Stoneferry C KuH 144 E2
Stonefield Castle Hotel Ag & B 206 D5
Stonegate E Susx 39 G7
Stonegate N York 162 D1
Stonegrave N York 161 L7
Stonehall Worcs 81 K5
Stonehaugh Nthumb 179 J4
Stonehaven Abers 245 J6
Stone Hill Donc 143 H6
Stonehouse C Plym 6 F4
Stone House Cumb 158 D5
Stonehouse Gloucs 64 A6
Stonehouse Nthumb 179 G7
Stonehouse S Lans 198 C4
Stone in Oxney Kent 25 H2
Stoneleigh Warwks 83 H1
Stoneley Green Ches E 113 K1
Stonely Cambs 86 C2
Stoner Hill Hants 35 M5
Stonesby Leics 117 L6
Stonesfield Oxon 66 B4
Stones Green Essex 73 H2
Stone Street Kent 38 F2
Stone Street Suffk 89 K6
Stone Street Suffk 89 K7
Stone Street Suffk 107 H7
Stonestreet Green Kent 40 E7
Stonethwaite Cumb 165 J7
Stonewells Moray 266 F3
Stonewood Kent 52 D4
Stoneybridge W Isls 283 b10
Stoneybridge Worcs 97 L8
Stoneyburn W Loth 210 C6
Stoney Cross Hants 18 D1
Stoneygate C Leic 100 D3
Stoneyhills Essex 72 D7
Stoneykirk D & G 172 D4
Stoney Middleton Derbys 132 E4
Stoney Stanton Leics 100 B4
Stoney Stoke Somset 32 B4
Stoney Stratton Somset 31 L3
Stoney Stretton Shrops 95 J2
Stoneywood C Aber 245 K1
Stoneywood Falk 209 L2
Stonham Aspal Suffk 90 D3
Stonnall Staffs 98 D3
Stonor Oxon 49 H1
Stonton Wyville Leics 101 G4
Stony Cross Herefs 80 D2
Stony Cross Herefs 81 G5
Stonyford Hants 34 D7
Stony Houghton Derbys 133 K6
Stony Stratford M Keyn 84 F7
Stonywell Staffs 98 D1
Stoodleigh Devon 28 B4
Stoodleigh Devon 29 G7
Stopham W Susx 21 H3
Stopsley Luton 68 E2
Stoptide Cnwll 10 C7
Storeton Wirral 129 G3
Storeyard Green Herefs 81 G6
Stornoway W Isls 282 g3
Storridge Herefs 81 H5
Storrington W Susx 21 J4
Storth Cumb 157 G6
Storwood E R Yk 151 M7
Stotfield Moray 266 E2
Stotfold C Beds 86 E7
Stottesdon Shrops 96 F6
Stoughton Leics 100 E3
Stoughton Surrey 50 C8
Stoughton W Susx 20 C4
Stoulton Worcs 81 L5
Stourbridge Dudley 97 K6
Stourbridge Crematorium Dudley 97 K6
Stourpaine Dorset 17 G1
Stourport-on-Severn Worcs 81 J1
Stour Provost Dorset 32 C6
Stour Row Dorset 32 D6
Stourton Leeds 141 M2
Stourton Staffs 97 K6
Stourton Warwks 83 G7
Stourton Wilts 32 C4
Stourton Caundle Dorset 32 B7
Stout Somset 31 G4
Stove Shet 281 e8
Stoven Suffk 107 J7
Stow Border 200 F4
Stow Lincs 135 H3
Stow Bardolph Norfk 104 C2
Stow Bedon Norfk 105 J4
Stowbridge Norfk 104 B2
Stow-cum-Quy Cambs 87 L3
Stowe Gloucs 63 H5
Stowe Shrops 95 H8
Stowe by Chartley Staffs 114 F6
Stowehill Nhants 84 C3
Stowell Somset 31 L6
Stowey BaNES 45 H7
Stowford Devon 12 B3
Stowford Devon 12 B5
Stowford Devon 14 D5
Stowford Devon 28 B3
Stowlangtoft Suffk 89 J2
Stow Longa Cambs 86 C1
Stow Maries Essex 71 K7
Stowmarket Suffk 90 B3
Stow-on-the-Wold Gloucs 65 J2
Stowting Kent 40 F7
Stowting Common Kent 40 F6
Stowupland Suffk 90 C3
Straanruie Highld 253 J8
Strachan Abers 244 F5
Strachur Ag & B 217 H6
Stradbroke Suffk 106 E8
Stradbrook Wilts 46 D8
Stradishall Suffk 88 E5
Stradsett Norfk 104 D2
Stragglethorpe Lincs 118 B1
Stragglethorpe Notts 117 H4
Straight Soley Wilts 47 L4
Straiton Mdloth 211 J5
Straiton S Ayrs 183 K2
Straloch Abers 256 F7
Straloch P & K 232 F3
Stramshall Staffs 115 H4
Strang IoM 154 e6
Strangeways Salfd 140 B7
Strangford Herefs 63 H2
Stranraer D & G 172 C3
Strata Florida Cerdgn 77 K2
Stratfield Mortimer W Berk 49 G6
Stratfield Saye Hants 49 G6
Stratfield Turgis Hants 49 G7
Stratford C Beds 86 D5
Stratford Gt Lon 51 K2
Stratford St Andrew Suffk 91 H3
Stratford St Mary Suffk 90 B8
Stratford sub Castle Wilts 33 K4
Stratford Tony Wilts 33 J5
Stratford-upon-Avon Warwks 82 F4
Strath Highld 260 C4
Strathan Highld 270 E4
Strathan Highld 277 K3
Strathaven S Lans 197 K2
Strathblane Stirlg 208 F3
Strathcanaird Highld 270 F7
Strathcarron Highld 248 F3
Strathcoil Ag & B 227 K6
Strathdon Abers 243 K1
Strathkinness Fife 223 H4
Strathloanhead W Loth 210 B4
Strathmashie House Highld 241 G5
Strathmiglo Fife 222 C5
Strathpeffer Highld 262 E8
Strathtay P & K 232 D4
Strathwhillan N Ayrs 195 G4
Strathy Highld 278 E3
Strathy Inn Highld 278 E3
Strathyre Stirlg 219 J4
Stratton Cnwll 11 J1
Stratton Dorset 16 C4
Stratton Gloucs 64 E6
Stratton Audley Oxon 66 F2
Stratton-on-the-Fosse Somset 31 L1
Stratton St Margaret Swindn 47 H2
Stratton St Michael Norfk 106 D4
Stratton Strawless Norfk 122 E7
Stream Somset 29 K3
Streat E Susx 22 E4
Streatham Gt Lon 51 J4
Streatley C Beds 68 D2
Streatley W Berk 48 E3
Street Devon 14 E5
Street Lancs 147 K5
Street N York 162 C2
Street Somset 31 H3
Street Ashton Warwks 99 M7
Street Dinas Shrops 112 E4
Street End E Susx 23 K3
Street End Kent 40 F4
Street End W Susx 20 D7
Street Gate Gatesd 180 F7
Streethay Staffs 98 F1
Street Houses N York 151 H6
Streetlam N York 160 D3
Street Lane Derbys 116 C2
Streetly Wsall 98 D4
Streetly Crematorium Wsall 98 D4
Streetly End Cambs 88 C5
Street on the Fosse Somset 31 K3
Strefford Shrops 95 K6
Strelitz P & K 233 J8
Strelley Notts 116 E3
Strensall C York 151 K4
Strensham Worcs 81 L7
Stretcholt Somset 30 D2
Strete Devon 8 C5
Stretford Herefs 80 B4
Stretford Herefs 80 C4
Stretford Traffd 130 F1
Strethall Essex 87 K7
Stretham Cambs 103 K8
Strettington W Susx 20 E5
Stretton Ches W 113 G1
Stretton Derbys 133 H7
Stretton Rutlnd 118 B8
Stretton Staffs 97 K1
Stretton Staffs 115 L6
Stretton Warrtn 130 C3
Stretton en le Field Leics 99 J1
Stretton Grandison Herefs 80 E6
Stretton-on-Dunsmore Warwks 83 J1
Stretton on Fosse Warwks 82 F7
Stretton Sugwas Herefs 80 B6
Stretton under Fosse Warwks 99 M7
Stretton Westwood Shrops 96 D4
Strichen Abers 269 H5
Strines Stockp 131 J2
Stringston Somset 30 B2
Strixton Nhants 85 H3
Stroat Gloucs 63 H7
Stroma Highld 280 E1
Stromeferry Highld 248 D5
Stromness Ork 275 b4
Stronachlachar Stirlg 218 F5
Stronafian Ag & B 207 G3
Stronchrubie Highld 271 H4
Strone Ag & B 207 K3
Strone Highld 239 J7
Strone Highld 250 F6
Stronenaba Highld 239 L6
Stronmilchan Ag & B 217 J2
Stronsay Ork 275 e3
Strontian Highld 228 C3
Strood Kent 39 L7
Strood Medway 52 F5
Strood Green Surrey 37 J1
Strood Green W Susx 36 F6
Stroud Gloucs 64 B6
Stroud Hants 35 L6
Stroude Surrey 50 C5
Stroud Green Essex 53 J1
Stroud Green Gloucs 64 A5
Stroxton Lincs 118 B5
Struan Highld 246 D1
Struan P & K 232 B2
Strubby Lincs 137 H3
Strumpshaw Norfk 107 G2
Strutherhill S Lans 198 C3
Struthers Fife 222 F5
Struy Highld 250 C4
Stryd-y-Facsen IoA 124 F3
Stryt-issa Wrexhm 112 D2
Stuartfield Abers 257 H3
Stubbers Green Wsall 98 D3
Stubbington Hants 19 J3
Stubbins Lancs 140 B4
Stubbs Green Norfk 106 E4
Stubhampton Dorset 32 F8
Stubley Derbys 133 G4
Stubshaw Cross Wigan 139 H7

Stubton Lincs 118 A2
Stuckton Hants 33 L8
Studfold N York 148 E2
Stud Green W & M 49 L3
Studham C Beds 68 C4
Studholme Cumb 177 H7
Studland Dorset 17 K6
Studley Warwks 82 C2
Studley Wilts 46 D4
Studley Common Warwks 82 C2
Studley Roger N York 150 C2
Studley Royal N York 150 C2
Stuntney Cambs 103 L7
Stunts Green E Susx 23 K4
Sturbridge Staffs 114 C5
Sturgate Lincs 135 H2
Sturmer Essex 88 D6
Sturminster Common Dorset 32 C8
Sturminster Marshall Dorset 17 J3
Sturminster Newton Dorset 32 C8
Sturry Kent 41 G3
Sturton N Linc 144 B7
Sturton by Stow Lincs 135 H4
Sturton le Steeple Notts 134 F3
Stuston Suffk 106 C7
Stutton N York 151 G7
Stutton Suffk 90 D8
Styal Ches E 131 G3
Stydd Lancs 148 A8
Stynie Moray 267 G4
Styrrup Notts 134 C2
Succoth Ag & B 218 D6
Suckley Worcs 81 G5
Suckley Green Worcs 81 G4
Sudborough Nhants 101 L7
Sudbourne Suffk 91 J4
Sudbrook Lincs 118 C3
Sudbrook Mons 45 G2
Sudbrooke Lincs 135 L4
Sudbury Derbys 115 K5
Sudbury Gt Lon 50 F2
Sudbury Suffk 89 H7
Sudden Rochdl 140 C5
Sudgrove Gloucs 64 D5
Suffield N York 163 H4
Suffield Norfk 122 E5
Sugdon Wrekin 113 K8
Sugnall Staffs 114 B5
Sugwas Pool Herefs 80 B6
Suisnish Highld 247 J5
Sulby IoM 154 e3
Sulgrave Nhants 84 A6
Sulham W Berk 48 F4
Sulhamstead W Berk 48 F5
Sulhamstead Abbots W Berk 48 F5
Sulhamstead Bannister W Berk 48 F5
Sullington W Susx 21 J4
Sullom Shet 281 d4
Sullom Voe Shet 281 d4
Sully V Glam 43 J8
Summerbridge N York 150 B3
Summercourt Cnwll 4 E4
Summerfield Norfk 121 G4
Summerfield Worcs 97 J8
Summer Heath Bucks 49 H1
Summerhill Pembks 55 K5
Summerhill Staffs 98 D2
Summer Hill Wrexhm 112 D1
Summerhouse Darltn 169 G6
Summerlands Cumb 157 H5
Summerley Derbys 133 G4
Summersdale W Susx 20 D5
Summerseat Bury 140 B5
Summertown Oxon 66 D5
Summit Oldham 140 D6
Summit Rochdl 140 E4
Sunbiggin Cumb 157 L1
Sunbury Surrey 50 E5
Sundaywell D & G 185 K6
Sunderland Ag & B 204 C3
Sunderland Cumb 165 G4
Sunderland Lancs 147 H4
Sunderland Sundld 181 K7
Sunderland Bridge Dur 169 H3
Sunderland Crematorium Sundld 181 J7
Sundhope Border 200 D8
Sundon Park Luton 68 D2
Sundridge Kent 38 D2
Sunk Island E R Yk 145 H4
Sunningdale W & M 50 B5
Sunninghill W & M 50 B5
Sunningwell Oxon 66 D7
Sunniside Dur 168 F3
Sunniside Gatesd 180 F7
Sunny Brow Dur 169 G4
Sunnyhill C Derb 116 B5
Sunnyhurst Bl w D 139 K3
Sunnylaw Stirlg 220 D7
Sunnymead Oxon 66 D5
Sunton Wilts 47 K8
Surbiton Gt Lon 50 F5
Surfleet Lincs 119 H6
Surfleet Seas End Lincs 119 J6
Surlingham Norfk 107 G2
Surrex Essex 72 C3
Surrey & Sussex Crematorium W Susx 37 L3
Sustead Norfk 122 D4
Susworth Lincs 143 L7
Sutcombe Devon 26 F8
Sutcombemill Devon 26 F8
Suton Norfk 106 B4
Sutterby Lincs 137 G5
Sutterton Lincs 119 J4
Sutton C Beds 86 E5
Sutton C Pete 102 B4
Sutton Cambs 103 J7
Sutton Devon 7 K6
Sutton Devon 13 G2
Sutton Donc 142 E5
Sutton E Susx 23 H7
Sutton Gt Lon 51 H6
Sutton Kent 41 K5
Sutton N York 142 D3
Sutton Norfk 123 H6
Sutton Notts 117 K4
Sutton Oxon 66 B6
Sutton Pembks 54 E4
Sutton Shrops 96 C1
Sutton Shrops 97 G6
Sutton Shrops 112 E6
Sutton Shrops 113 L5
Sutton St Hel 129 M1
Sutton Staffs 114 B7
Sutton Suffk 91 G6
Sutton W Susx 21 G4
Sutton Abinger Surrey 37 H2
Sutton at Hone Kent 52 C5
Sutton Bassett Nhants 101 G5
Sutton Benger Wilts 46 D3
Sutton Bingham Somset 31 J8
Sutton Bonington Notts 116 E6
Sutton Bridge Lincs 120 B7
Sutton Cheney Leics 99 L3
Sutton Coldfield Birm 98 E4
Sutton Coldfield Crematorium Birm 98 F4
Sutton Courtenay Oxon 66 D8
Sutton Crosses Lincs 119 M7
Sutton cum Lound Notts 134 D3
Sutton Fields Notts 116 E6
Sutton Green Surrey 50 C8
Sutton Green Wrexhm 112 F2
Sutton Howgrave N York 160 D6
Sutton in Ashfield Notts 133 K7
Sutton-in-Craven N York 149 H7
Sutton in the Elms Leics 100 B4
Sutton Lane Ends Ches E 131 H5
Sutton Maddock Shrops 97 G3
Sutton Mallet Somset 30 E3
Sutton Mandeville Wilts 33 G5
Sutton Manor St Hel 129 L2
Sutton Marsh Herefs 80 D6
Sutton Montis Somset 31 K6
Sutton-on-Hull C KuH 144 E1
Sutton on Sea Lincs 137 K3
Sutton-on-the-Forest N York 151 J3
Sutton on the Hill Derbys 115 L5
Sutton on Trent Notts 134 F6
Sutton Poyntz Dorset 16 D6
Sutton St Edmund Lincs 103 H1
Sutton St James Lincs 119 L7
Sutton St Nicholas Herefs 80 C6
Sutton Scotney Hants 34 F3
Sutton Street Kent 39 K2
Sutton-under-Brailes Warwks 83 G7
Sutton-under-Whitestonecliffe N York 161 G6
Sutton upon Derwent E R Yk 151 L6
Sutton Valence Kent 39 K3
Sutton Veny Wilts 32 E3
Sutton Waldron Dorset 32 E7
Sutton Weaver Ches W 130 A4
Sutton Wick BaNES 45 H7
Sutton Wick Oxon 66 C8
Swaby Lincs 137 G4
Swadlincote Derbys 116 A7
Swaffham Norfk 105 G2
Swaffham Bulbeck Cambs 87 L3
Swaffham Prior Cambs 88 B2
Swafield Norfk 122 F5
Swainby N York 161 G2
Swainshill Herefs 80 B7
Swainsthorpe Norfk 106 E3
Swainswick BaNES 45 M5
Swalcliffe Oxon 83 J7
Swalecliffe Kent 40 F2
Swallow Lincs 144 F7
Swallow Beck Lincs 135 J6
Swallowcliffe Wilts 33 G5
Swallowfield Wokham 49 H6
Swallow Nest Rothm 133 J3
Swallows Cross Essex 70 F7
Swampton Hants 34 E1
Swanage Dorset 17 K6
Swanbourne Bucks 67 K2
Swanbridge V Glam 43 J8
Swancote Shrops 97 G4
Swan Green Ches W 130 E5
Swanland E R Yk 144 C2
Swanley Kent 52 B5
Swanley Village Kent 52 B5
Swanmore Hants 35 J7
Swannington Leics 116 C8
Swannington Norfk 122 C7
Swanpool Garden Suburb Lincs 135 J6
Swanscombe Kent 52 D4
Swansea Swans 57 J6
Swansea Crematorium Swans 57 J5
Swan Street Essex 72 C2
Swanton Abbot Norfk 122 F6
Swanton Morley Norfk 121 M8
Swanton Novers Norfk 121 M5
Swanton Street Kent 53 J7
Swan Village Sandw 98 C5
Swanwick Derbys 116 C1
Swanwick Hants 19 H2
Swarby Lincs 118 D3
Swardeston Norfk 106 D3
Swarkestone Derbys 116 B6
Swarland Nthumb 191 H5
Swarraton Hants 35 H3
Swartha C Brad 149 J6
Swarthmoor Cumb 156 C7
Swaton Lincs 118 F4
Swavesey Cambs 87 G2
Sway Hants 18 D4
Swayfield Lincs 118 C7
Swaythling C Sotn 34 F7
Sweet Green Worcs 80 F3
Sweetham Devon 13 K3
Sweethaws E Susx 38 D7
Sweetlands Corner Kent 39 K4
Sweets Cnwll 11 G3
Sweetshouse Cnwll 5 J3
Swefling Suffk 91 H3
Swepstone Leics 99 K1
Swerford Oxon 66 A1
Swettenham Ches E 130 F6
Swffryd Blae G 61 K7
Swift's Green Kent 39 L4
Swilland Suffk 90 E4
Swillbrook Lancs 138 F1
Swillington Leeds 142 B2
Swimbridge Devon 27 L5
Swimbridge Newland Devon 27 L5
Swinbrook Oxon 65 L4
Swincliffe Kirk 141 K2
Swincliffe N York 150 C4
Swincombe Devon 28 B3
Swinden N York 148 E5
Swinderby Lincs 135 H7
Swindon Gloucs 64 D2
Swindon Nthumb 190 D6
Swindon Staffs 97 J5
Swindon Swindn 47 H2
Swine E R Yk 153 J8
Swinefleet E R Yk 143 J3
Swineford S Glos 45 K5
Swineshead Bed 85 L2
Swineshead Lincs 119 H3
Swineshead Bridge Lincs 119 H3
Swiney Highld 275 H1
Swinford Leics 100 C7
Swinford Oxon 66 C5
Swingfield Minnis Kent 41 G6
Swingfield Street Kent 41 H6
Swingleton Green Suffk 89 K6
Swinhoe Nthumb 203 K7
Swinhope Lincs 145 G8
Swinithwaite N York 159 J5
Swinmore Common Herefs 80 F7
Swinscoe Staffs 115 J2
Swinside Cumb 165 H6
Swinstead Lincs 118 D7
Swinthorpe Lincs 135 L4
Swinton Border 202 C4
Swinton N York 160 B6
Swinton N York 162 D8
Swinton Rothm 142 C7
Swinton Salfd 140 A7
Swithland Leics 100 C1
Swordale Highld 263 G6
Swordland Highld 238 B5
Swordly Highld 278 C4
Sworton Heath Ches E 130 D3
Swyddffynnon Cerdgn 77 J2
Swyncombe Oxon 49 G1
Swynnerton Staffs 114 D4
Swyre Dorset 15 M5
Sycharth Powys 112 B6
Sychnant Powys 93 L7
Sychtyn Powys 94 B2
Sydallt Wrexhm 129 H8
Syde Gloucs 64 D5
Sydenham Gt Lon 51 K4
Sydenham Oxon 67 H6
Sydenham Damerel Devon 12 A7
Sydenhurst Surrey 36 E4
Syderstone Norfk 121 H5
Sydling St Nicholas Dorset 16 C3
Sydmonton Hants 48 C7
Sydnal Lane Shrops 97 H2
Syerston Notts 117 K2
Syke Rochdl 140 D4
Sykehouse Donc 143 G4
Syleham Suffk 106 E7
Sylen Carmth 56 F3
Symbister Shet 281 e5
Symington S Ayrs 196 D5
Symington S Lans 199 G6
Symondsbury Dorset 15 K4
Symonds Yat Herefs 63 H4
Sympson Green C Brad 150 A8
Synderford Dorset 15 J2
Synod Inn Cerdgn 76 D4
Syre Highld 278 B7
Syreford Gloucs 64 F3
Syresham Nhants 84 C7
Syston Leics 100 D1
Syston Lincs 118 B3
Sytchampton Worcs 81 J2
Sywell Nhants 84 F2

T

Tabley Hill Ches E 130 E4
Tackley Oxon 66 C3
Tacolneston Norfk 106 C4
Tadcaster N York 151 G7
Taddington Derbys 132 C5
Taddington Gloucs 65 G1
Taddiport Devon 27 H7
Tadley Hants 48 F6
Tadlow Cambs 86 F5
Tadmarton Oxon 83 J7
Tadwick BaNES 45 L5
Tadworth Surrey 51 G7
Tafarnaubach Blae G 61 H5
Tafarn-y-bwlch Pembks 75 J5
Tafarn-y-Gelyn Denbgs 128 E7
Taff's Well Rhondd 43 H5
Tafolwern Powys 93 J3
Taibach Neath 57 L7
Tain Highld 263 L3
Tain Highld 280 B3
Tai'n Lôn Gwynd 109 H2
Tairbeart W Isls 282 e5
Tai'r Bull Powys 60 F2
Takeley Essex 70 E3
Takeley Street Essex 70 E3
Talachddu Powys 78 F8
Talacre Flints 128 D3
Talaton Devon 14 C3
Talbenny Pembks 54 D4
Talbot Green Rhondd 43 G5
Talbot Village Bmouth 17 L4
Taleford Devon 14 C3
Talerddig Powys 93 K3
Talgarreg Cerdgn 76 D5
Talgarth Powys 79 G8
Talisker Highld 246 D3
Talke Staffs 114 C1
Talke Pits Staffs 114 C1
Talkin Cumb 178 D7
Talladale Highld 260 E6
Talla Linnfoots Border 187 H2
Tallaminnock S Ayrs 183 K3
Tallarn Green Wrexhm 113 G3
Tallentire Cumb 164 F4
Talley Carmth 59 H2
Tallington Lincs 102 B2
Tallwrn Wrexhm 112 D2
Talmine Highld 277 K4
Talog Carmth 58 B4
Talsarn Cerdgn 77 G4
Talsarnau Gwynd 109 L4
Talskiddy Cnwll 4 E2
Talwrn IoA 125 J4
Talwrn Wrexhm 112 F2
Tal-y-bont Cerdgn 92 E5
Tal-y-Bont Conwy 126 F6
Tal-y-bont Gwynd 109 L7
Tal-y-bont Gwynd 126 C5
Talybont-on-Usk Powys 61 H3
Tal-y-Cafn Conwy 126 F5

Tal-y-coed Mons 62 E4
Tal-y-garn Rhondd 42 F5
Tal-y-llyn Gwynd 92 F2
Talysarn Gwynd 109 J1
Tal-y-Waun Torfn 61 L6
Talywern Powys 93 H3
Tamer Lane End Wigan 139 J7
Tamerton Foliot C Plym 6 F3
Tamworth Staffs 99 G3
Tamworth Green Lincs 119 L3
Tancred N York 151 G4
Tancredston Pembks 74 E7
Tandridge Surrey 38 B3
Tanfield Dur 180 F7
Tanfield Lea Dur 180 F8
Tangiers Pembks 54 F3
Tangley Hants 47 L8
Tangmere W Susx 20 E5
Tangusdale W Isls 283 b13
Tan Hill N York 158 F1
Tankerness Ork 275 d4
Tankersley Barns 142 A7
Tankerton Kent 40 F2
Tannach Highld 280 D6
Tannachie Abers 245 H6
Tannadice Angus 234 D4
Tanner's Green Worcs 98 D8
Tannington Suffk 90 F2
Tannochside N Lans 209 J6
Tansley Derbys 132 F7
Tansor Nhants 102 B5
Tantobie Dur 180 E7
Tanton N York 170 C8
Tanwood Worcs 97 K8
Tanworth in Arden Warwks 82 D1
Tan-y-Bwlch Gwynd 110 C3
Tan-y-fron Conwy 127 J6
Tan-y-fron Wrexhm 112 D1
Tan-y-grisiau Gwynd 110 C3
Tan-y-groes Cerdgn 76 B5
Taobh Tuath W Isls 282 d6
Taplow Bucks 49 M3
Tarbert Ag & B 205 L6
Tarbert Ag & B 206 D5
Tarbert W Isls 282 e5
Tarbet Ag & B 218 D6
Tarbet Highld 238 C5
Tarbet Highld 276 B6
Tarbock Green Knows 129 K2
Tarbolton S Ayrs 196 E5
Tarbrax S Lans 199 H2
Tardebigge Worcs 82 B2
Tarfside Angus 244 B7
Tarland Abers 244 B3
Tarleton Lancs 138 F4
Tarlscough Lancs 138 E5
Tarlton Gloucs 64 D7
Tarnock Somset 44 D8
Tarns Cumb 164 F1
Tarnside Cumb 156 F4
Tarporley Ches W 130 A7
Tarr Somset 28 F4
Tarrant Crawford Dorset 17 H2
Tarrant Gunville Dorset 32 F8
Tarrant Hinton Dorset 32 F8
Tarrant Keyneston Dorset 17 H2
Tarrant Launceston Dorset 17 J1
Tarrant Monkton Dorset 17 J1
Tarrant Rawston Dorset 17 H1
Tarrant Rushton Dorset 17 H2
Tarring Neville E Susx 23 G6
Tarrington Herefs 80 E7
Tarskavaig Highld 247 J6
Tarves Abers 256 F5
Tarvin Ches W 129 L6
Tarvin Sands Ches W 129 L6
Tasburgh Norfk 106 D4
Tasley Shrops 96 F4
Taston Oxon 65 M3
Tatenhill Staffs 115 K7
Tathall End M Keyn 84 F6
Tatham Lancs 147 M2
Tathwell Lincs 136 F3
Tatsfield Surrey 51 L7
Tattenhall Ches W 129 L7
Tatterford Norfk 121 J6
Tattersett Norfk 121 J5
Tattershall Lincs 136 D8
Tattershall Bridge Lincs 136 C8
Tattershall Thorpe Lincs 136 D7
Tattingstone Suffk 90 D7
Tattingstone White Horse Suffk 90 D7
Tatworth Somset 15 H2
Tauchers Moray 267 H6
Taunton Somset 30 C6
Taunton Deane Crematorium Somset 30 B6
Taverham Norfk 122 D8
Taverners Green Essex 70 E3
Tavernspite Pembks 55 L4
Tavistock Devon 12 C7
Taw Green Devon 12 F3
Tawstock Devon 27 K5
Taxal Derbys 131 K4
Taychreggan Hotel Ag & B 217 G3
Tayinloan Ag & B 205 M7
Taynton Gloucs 63 L3
Taynton Oxon 65 K4
Taynuilt Ag & B 216 F1
Tayport Fife 223 H2
Tayvallich Ag & B 215 L7
Tealby Lincs 136 C2
Tealing Angus 234 B7
Team Valley Gatesd 181 G7
Teangue Highld 247 K6
Teanord Highld 263 G7
Tebay Cumb 157 K2
Tebworth C Beds 68 C2
Tedburn St Mary Devon 13 J4
Teddington Gloucs 81 M8
Teddington Gt Lon 50 F5
Tedstone Delamere Herefs 80 F3
Tedstone Wafer Herefs 80 F3
Teesport R & Cl 170 D6
Teesside Crematorium Middsb 170 C7
Teesside Park S on T 170 B7
Teeton Nhants 84 D1
Teffont Evias Wilts 33 G4
Teffont Magna Wilts 33 G4
Tegryn Pembks 75 L5
Teigh Rutlnd 117 M8
Teigncombe Devon 12 F5
Teigngrace Devon 13 K7
Teignmouth Devon 13 L8
Teindside Border 188 D4
Telford Wrekin 96 F2
Telford Crematorium Wrekin 97 G1
Tellisford Somset 46 A7
Telscombe E Susx 22 F6
Telscombe Cliffs E Susx 22 F7
Tempar P & K 231 J4
Templand D & G 176 E2
Temple Cnwll 11 G7
Temple Mdloth 211 K7
Temple Balsall Solhll 99 G8
Temple Bar Cerdgn 76 F4
Temple Cloud BaNES 45 J7
Templecombe Somset 32 B6
Temple End Suffk 88 D5
Temple Ewell Kent 41 J6
Temple Grafton Warwks 82 D4
Temple Guiting Gloucs 65 G2
Temple Hirst N York 142 F3
Temple Normanton Derbys 133 H6
Temple of Fiddes Abers 245 H7
Temple Sowerby Cumb 166 E5
Templeton Devon 28 F8
Templeton Pembks 55 J4
Templetown Dur 168 E1
Tempsford C Beds 86 D4
Tenbury Wells Worcs 80 E2
Tenby Pembks 55 K6
Tendring Essex 73 H2
Tendring Green Essex 73 H2
Tendring Heath Essex 73 H2
Ten Mile Bank Norfk 104 B4
Tenpenny Heath Essex 73 G3
Tenterden Kent 39 M6
Terling Essex 71 J4
Tern Wrekin 113 K8
Ternhill Shrops 113 L5
Terregles D & G 176 B3
Terrington N York 151 L2
Terrington St Clement Norfk 120 C7
Terrington St John Norfk 104 A1
Terry's Green Warwks 98 E8
Teston Kent 39 H3
Testwood Hants 34 D7
Tetbury Gloucs 64 C8
Tetbury Upton Gloucs 64 C8
Tetchill Shrops 112 F5
Tetcott Devon 11 L3
Tetford Lincs 136 F5
Tetney Lincs 145 J7
Tetney Lock Lincs 145 J7
Tetsworth Oxon 67 G6
Tettenhall Wolves 97 K3
Tettenhall Wood Wolves 97 K3
Teversal Notts 133 J7
Teversham Cambs 87 K3
Teviothead Border 188 C5
Tewin Herts 69 H4
Tewin Wood Herts 69 H4
Tewkesbury Gloucs 81 K8
Teynham Kent 40 B3
Thackley C Brad 149 M8
Thackthwaite Cumb 164 F6
Thackthwaite Cumb 166 A5
Thakeham W Susx 21 J3
Thame Oxon 67 H6
Thames Ditton Surrey 50 F5
Thamesmead Gt Lon 52 A3
Thanet Crematorium Kent 41 K2
Thanington Kent 40 F4
Thankerton S Lans 199 G5
Tharston Norfk 106 D4
Thatcham W Berk 48 D5
Thatto Heath St Hel 129 L1
Thaxted Essex 70 F1
Theakston N York 160 D5
Thealby N Linc 143 M4
Theale Somset 31 G2
Theale W Berk 48 F5
Thearne E R Yk 153 G8
The Bank Ches E 131 G8
The Bank Shrops 96 E3
The Beeches Gloucs 64 F6
Theberton Suffk 91 K2
The Blythe Staffs 115 G6
The Bog Shrops 95 J4
The Bourne Worcs 82 A4
The Braes Highld 247 H2
The Bratch Staffs 97 K4
The Broad Herefs 80 C3
The Brunt E Loth 212 F4
The Bungalow IoM 154 e5
The Burf Worcs 81 J2
The Butts Gloucs 64 C4
The Camp Gloucs 64 C5
The Chequer Wrexhm 113 H3
The City Bed 86 C3
The City Bucks 67 J7
The Common Oxon 65 L2
The Common Wilts 34 B4
The Common Wilts 46 F2
The Corner Kent 39 H5
The Counties Crematorium Nhants 84 E4
The Cronk IoM 154 d3
Theddingworth Leics 100 E6
Theddlethorpe All Saints Lincs 137 J2
Theddlethorpe St Helen Lincs 137 J2
The Den N Ayrs 196 C1
The Forest of Dean Crematorium Gloucs 63 J4
The Forge Herefs 79 L3
The Forstal Kent 40 D7
The Fouralls Shrops 113 L5
The Garden of England Crematorium Kent 53 J5
The Green Cumb 156 A5
The Green Essex 71 J3
The Green N York 162 D2
The Green Wilts 32 E4
The Grove Worcs 81 K7
The Haven W Susx 37 G5
The Haw Gloucs 64 B2
The Headland Hartpl 170 C4
The Hill Cumb 156 A6
The Holt Wokham 49 K3
The Hundred Herefs 80 C2
Thelbridge Cross Devon 28 D8
The Leacon Kent 40 C8
The Lee Bucks 67 L6
The Lhen IoM 154 e2
The Linn Crematorium E Rens 209 G7
Thelnetham Suffk 105 L7
The Lochs Moray 266 F4
Thelveton Norfk 106 D7
Thelwall Warrtn 130 C2
The Manchester Crematorium Manch 130 F1
The Marsh Powys 95 H4
Themelthorpe Norfk 122 B6
The Middles Dur 180 F8
The Moor Kent 39 J7
The Mumbles Swans 57 H7
The Murray S Lans 209 H8
The Mythe Gloucs 81 K8
The Narth Mons 63 G6
The Neuk Abers 245 G4
Thenford Nhants 83 M7
Theobald's Green Wilts 46 F5
The Park Crematorium Hants 36 C1
The Quarry Gloucs 63 L7
The Quarter Kent 39 M4
The Reddings Gloucs 64 C3
Therfield Herts 87 G7
The Rhôs Powys 61 J1
The Rose Hill Crematorium Donc 142 F7
The Ross P & K 220 D3
The Sands Surrey 36 C2
The Shoe Wilts 46 A4
The Smithies Shrops 96 F4
The Spike Cambs 87 K5
The Spring Warwks 83 G1
The Square Torfn 62 B7
The Stair Kent 38 F4
The Stocks Kent 25 G2
The Straits Hants 36 A3
The Strand Wilts 46 D7
Thetford Norfk 105 H6
Thethwaite Cumb 165 L2
The Towans Cnwll 2 E3
The Vale Crematorium Luton 68 E2
The Vauld Herefs 80 C5
The Wyke Shrops 97 G2
Theydon Bois Essex 70 C7
Thicket Priory N York 151 L7
Thickwood Wilts 46 B4
Thimbleby Lincs 136 D5
Thimbleby N York 161 G3
Thingwall Wirral 129 G3
Thirkleby N York 161 G6
Thirlby N York 161 G6
Thirlestane Border 201 H4
Thirn N York 160 B5
Thirsk N York 160 F6
Thirtleby E R Yk 144 F1
Thistleton Lancs 147 H8
Thistleton Rutlnd 118 B7
Thistley Green Suffk 104 D8
Thixendale N York 152 C4
Thockrington Nthumb 179 M3
Tholomas Drove Cambs 103 H2
Tholthorpe N York 151 G2
Thomas Chapel Pembks 55 J5
Thomas Close Cumb 166 B3
Thomastown Abers 255 L4
Thomas Town Warwks 82 C3
Thompson Norfk 105 J4
Thong Kent 52 E5
Thoralby N York 159 H5
Thoresby Notts 134 C5
Thoresthorpe Lincs 137 J4
Thoresway Lincs 144 F8
Thorganby Lincs 145 G8
Thorganby N York 151 L7
Thorgill N York 162 C3
Thorington Suffk 107 J8
Thorington Street Suffk 89 K8
Thorlby N York 149 H5
Thorley Herts 70 C3
Thorley IoW 18 F6
Thorley Houses Herts 70 C3
Thorley Street IoW 18 F6
Thormanby N York 161 H7
Thornaby-on-Tees S on T 170 B7
Thornage Norfk 122 B4
Thornborough Bucks 84 E8
Thornborough N York 160 D6
Thornbury C Brad 141 J1
Thornbury Devon 12 A1
Thornbury Herefs 80 E3
Thornbury S Glos 45 J1
Thornby Cumb 177 J8
Thornby Nhants 100 E8
Thorncliff Staffs 131 K7
Thorncliffe Crematorium Cumb 146 D2
Thorncombe Dorset 15 J2
Thorncombe Street Surrey 36 F3
Thorncott Green C Beds 86 C5
Thorncross IoW 19 G7
Thorndon Suffk 90 D1
Thorndon Cross Devon 12 D4
Thorne Donc 143 H5
Thorne Coffin Somset 31 H7
Thornecroft Devon 7 M2
Thornehillhead Devon 27 G7
Thorner Leeds 150 E7
Thornes Staffs 98 D3
Thornes Wakefd 141 M4
Thorne St Margaret Somset 29 K6
Thorney Bucks 50 D3
Thorney C Pete 102 F3
Thorney Notts 135 G5
Thorney Somset 30 F6
Thorney Hill Hants 18 B4
Thorney Island W Susx 20 C6
Thorney Toll Cambs 103 G3
Thornfalcon Somset 30 D6
Thornford Dorset 31 K8
Thorngrafton Nthumb 179 H6
Thorngrove Somset 30 E4
Thorngumbald E R Yk 145 G3
Thornham Norfk 121 G3
Thornham Magna Suffk 90 C1
Thornham Parva Suffk 90 D1
Thornhaugh C Pete 102 B3
Thornhill C Sotn 19 G1
Thornhill Caerph 43 J5
Thornhill Cumb 155 H1
Thornhill D & G 186 C7
Thornhill Derbys 132 D3
Thornhill Kirk 141 L4
Thornhill Stirlg 219 L7
Thornhill Crematorium Cardif 43 J5

Thornhill Lees Kirk 141 K4
Thornhills Calder 141 J3
Thornholme E R Yk 153 H3
Thornicombe Dorset 17 G2
Thornington Nthumb 202 D6
Thornley Dur 168 E3
Thornley Dur 169 K3
Thornley Gate Nthumb 179 J7
Thornliebank E Rens 208 F7
Thorns Suffk 88 E4
Thornsett Derbys 131 K2
Thorns Green Ches E 130 F3
Thornthwaite Cumb 165 H5
Thornthwaite N York 149 L4
Thornton Angus 234 B6
Thornton Bucks 84 E8
Thornton C Brad 141 H1
Thornton E R Yk 152 A6
Thornton Fife 222 E7
Thornton Lancs 146 F7
Thornton Leics 100 A2
Thornton Lincs 136 D6
Thornton Middsb 170 B7
Thornton Nthumb 202 E4
Thornton Pembks 54 E5
Thornton Sefton 138 D7
Thornton Curtis N Linc 144 D4
Thornton Garden of Rest Crematorium Sefton 138 D7
Thorntonhall S Lans 209 G8
Thornton Heath Gt Lon 51 J5
Thornton Hough Wirral 129 G3
Thornton-in-Craven N York 148 F6
Thornton in Lonsdale N York 158 B8
Thornton-le-Beans N York 160 F4
Thornton-le-Clay N York 151 L3
Thornton le Dale N York 162 E6
Thornton le Moor Lincs 144 D8
Thornton-le-Moor N York 160 F5
Thornton-le-Moors Ches W 129 K5
Thornton-le-Street N York 160 F5
Thorntonloch E Loth 213 G4
Thornton Rust N York 159 G5
Thornton Steward N York 160 A5
Thornton Watlass N York 160 C5
Thornwood Common Essex 70 C6
Thornydykes Border 201 J3
Thornythwaite Cumb 165 L6
Thoroton Notts 117 K3
Thorp Arch Leeds 150 F6
Thorpe Derbys 115 J2
Thorpe E R Yk 152 F6
Thorpe Lincs 137 J3
Thorpe N York 149 H3
Thorpe Norfk 107 J4
Thorpe Notts 117 K2
Thorpe Surrey 50 C5
Thorpe Abbotts Norfk 106 D7
Thorpe Acre Leics 116 E7
Thorpe Arnold Leics 117 K7
Thorpe Audlin Wakefd 142 D4
Thorpe Bassett N York 162 F8
Thorpe Bay Sthend 53 K2
Thorpe by Water Rutlnd 101 K4
Thorpe Common Rothm 133 G1
Thorpe Constantine Staffs 99 H2
Thorpe End Norfk 106 F1
Thorpe Green Essex 73 H3
Thorpe Green Lancs 139 H3
Thorpe Green Suffk 89 J4
Thorpe Hesley Rothm 142 B8
Thorpe in Balne Donc 142 F5
Thorpe Langton Leics 101 G5
Thorpe Larches Dur 169 K5
Thorpe Lea Surrey 50 C5
Thorpe le Fallows Lincs 135 H4
Thorpe-le-Soken Essex 73 J3
Thorpe le Street E R Yk 152 C7
Thorpe Malsor Nhants 101 H7
Thorpe Mandeville Nhants 83 M6
Thorpe Market Norfk 122 E4
Thorpe Marriot Norfk 122 D8
Thorpe Morieux Suffk 89 J4
Thorpeness Suffk 91 L3
Thorpe on the Hill Leeds 141 M2
Thorpe on the Hill Lincs 135 H6
Thorpe St Andrew Norfk 106 F2
Thorpe St Peter Lincs 137 J7
Thorpe Salvin Rothm 133 K3
Thorpe Satchville Leics 100 F1
Thorpe Thewles S on T 169 L6
Thorpe Tilney Lincs 136 B8
Thorpe Underwood N York 151 G4
Thorpe Underwood Nhants 101 H7
Thorpe Waterville Nhants 102 A7
Thorpe Willoughby N York 142 F2
Thorpland Norfk 104 C2
Thorrington Essex 73 G3
Thorverton Devon 13 L2
Thrales End C Beds 68 E4
Thrandeston Suffk 106 C8
Thrapston Nhants 101 M7
Threapland Cumb 165 G3
Threapland N York 149 H4
Threapwood Ches W 113 G3
Threapwood Staffs 115 G3
Threapwood Head Staffs 115 G3
Threave S Ayrs 183 J2
Three Ashes Herefs 63 G3
Three Bridges W Susx 37 L3
Three Burrows Cnwll 4 B5
Three Chimneys Kent 39 K5
Three Cocks Powys 79 G7
Three Counties Crematorium Essex 71 J2
Three Crosses Swans 57 G6
Three Cups Corner E Susx 23 L3
Three Gates Worcs 80 F3
Threehammer Common Norfk 123 G7
Three Hammers Cnwll 11 J5
Three Holes Norfk 103 K3
Threekingham Lincs 118 E4
Three Leg Cross E Susx 39 H7
Three Legged Cross Dorset 17 L2
Three Mile Cross Wokham 49 H5
Threemilestone Cnwll 4 C6
Three Miletown W Loth 210 E4
Three Oaks E Susx 24 F4
Threlkeld Cumb 165 K5
Threshers Bush Essex 70 D5
Threshfield N York 149 H3
Thrigby Norfk 107 J1
Thringarth Dur 167 L6
Thringstone Leics 116 D8
Thrintoft N York 160 D4
Thriplow Cambs 87 J6
Throapham Rothm 133 K2
Throckenhalt Lincs 103 G2
Throcking Herts 69 J1
Throckley N u Ty 180 E5
Throckmorton Worcs 82 A5
Throop Bmouth 17 M3
Throop Dorset 16 F4
Throphill Nthumb 180 D2
Thropton Nthumb 190 E5
Throsk Stirlg 209 M1
Througham Gloucs 64 D5
Throughgate D & G 185 L6
Throwleigh Devon 12 F4
Throwley Kent 40 C4
Throwley Forstal Kent 40 C4
Thrumpton Notts 116 E5
Thrumpton Notts 134 D4
Thrumster Highld 280 D7
Thrunscoe NE Lin 145 J6
Thrunton Nthumb 190 F4
Thrup Oxon 65 L7
Thrupp Gloucs 64 B6
Thrupp Oxon 66 C4
Thrushelton Devon 12 B5
Thrussington Leics 117 H8
Thruxton Hants 34 C2
Thruxton Herefs 80 B8
Thrybergh Rothm 142 D8
Thulston Derbys 116 C5
Thundersley Essex 53 G1
Thurcaston Leics 100 C1
Thurcroft Rothm 133 K2
Thurdon Cnwll 26 E8
Thurgarton Norfk 122 D4
Thurgarton Notts 117 J2
Thurgoland Barns 141 L7
Thurlaston Leics 100 B4
Thurlaston Warwks 83 L1
Thurlbear Somset 30 C6
Thurlby Lincs 118 E8
Thurlby Lincs 135 H7
Thurlby Lincs 137 J4
Thurleigh Bed 85 L3
Thurlestone Devon 7 K6
Thurloxton Somset 30 C5
Thurlstone Barns 141 K7
Thurlton Norfk 107 J4
Thurlwood Ches E 130 F8
Thurmaston Leics 100 D2
Thurnby Leics 100 E3
Thurne Norfk 123 H8
Thurnham Kent 53 H7
Thurning Nhants 102 B6
Thurning Norfk 122 B5
Thurnscoe Barns 142 C6
Thursby Cumb 165 K1
Thursden Lancs 140 D1
Thursford Norfk 121 L5
Thursley Surrey 36 D3
Thurso Highld 279 K3
Thurstaston Wirral 128 F3
Thurston Suffk 89 J2
Thurston Clough Oldham 140 E6
Thurstonfield Cumb 177 K7
Thurstonland Kirk 141 J5
Thurston Planch Suffk 89 J2
Thurton Norfk 107 G3
Thurvaston Derbys 115 L4
Thuxton Norfk 105 L2
Thwaite N York 158 F3
Thwaite Suffk 90 D2
Thwaite Head Cumb 156 E4
Thwaites C Brad 149 K7
Thwaite St Mary Norfk 107 G4
Thwaites Brow C Brad 149 K7
Thwing E R Yk 153 G2
Tibbermore P & K 221 J3
Tibbers D & G 186 C6
Tibberton Gloucs 63 M3
Tibberton Worcs 81 L4
Tibberton Wrekin 113 L7
Tibbie Shiels Inn Border 187 K2
Tibenham Norfk 106 C5
Tibshelf Derbys 133 J7
Tibthorpe E R Yk 152 E5
Ticehurst E Susx 39 H7
Tichborne Hants 35 H5
Tickencote Rutlnd 101 L2
Tickenham N Som 44 F4
Tickford End M Keyn 85 H6
Tickhill Donc 134 B1
Ticklerton Shrops 96 B5
Ticknall Derbys 116 B6
Tickton E R Yk 153 G7
Tidbury Green Solhll 98 E8
Tidcombe Wilts 47 L7
Tiddington Oxon 67 G6
Tiddington Warwks 82 F4
Tiddleywink Wilts 46 C4
Tidebrook E Susx 38 F7
Tideford Cnwll 6 C3
Tideford Cross Cnwll 6 C3
Tidenham Gloucs 63 H7
Tideswell Derbys 132 C4
Tidmarsh W Berk 48 F4
Tidmington Warwks 83 G7
Tidpit Hants 33 J7
Tidworth Wilts 34 B1
Tiers Cross Pembks 54 E5
Tiffield Nhants 84 D5
Tigerton Angus 234 E3
Tigh a Ghearraidh W Isls 282 b7
Tigharry W Isls 282 b7
Tighnabruaich Ag & B 206 F4
Tigley Devon 7 L3
Tilbrook Cambs 86 B2
Tilbury Thurr 52 D4
Tilbury Green Essex 88 E7
Tilbury Juxta Clare Essex 88 F7
Tile Cross Birm 98 F6
Tile Hill Covtry 99 H7
Tilehouse Green Solhll 98 F8
Tilehurst Readg 49 G4
Tilford Surrey 36 C2
Tilgate W Susx 37 L4
Tilgate Forest Row W Susx 37 L4
Tilham Street Somset 31 J4
Tillers Green Gloucs 80 F8
Tillicoultry Clacks 221 G7
Tillietudlem S Lans 198 D4
Tillingham Essex 72 E6
Tillington Herefs 80 B6
Tillington W Susx 36 E6
Tillington Common Herefs 80 B6
Tillybirloch Abers 244 F2
Tillyfourie Abers 244 E1
Tillygreig Abers 256 F7
Tillyrie P & K 221 K6
Tilmanstone Kent 41 J5
Tilney All Saints Norfk 120 C7
Tilney High End Norfk 120 C8
Tilney St Lawrence Norfk 120 C8
Tilshead Wilts 33 H1
Tilstock Shrops 113 J4
Tilston Ches W 113 G1
Tilstone Bank Ches W 130 A7
Tilstone Fearnall Ches W 130 A7
Tilsworth C Beds 68 B2
Tilton on the Hill Leics 101 G2
Tiltups End Gloucs 64 B7
Tilty Essex 70 E2
Timberland Lincs 136 B7
Timbersbrook Ches E 131 H7
Timberscombe Somset 29 G2
Timble N York 149 M5
Timewell Devon 29 H5
Timpanheck D & G 177 K4
Timperley Traffd 130 F2
Timsbury BaNES 45 K7
Timsbury Hants 34 D6
Timsgarry W Isls 282 d3
Timsgearraidh W Isls 282 d3
Timworth Suffk 89 H2
Timworth Green Suffk 89 H2
Tincleton Dorset 16 E4
Tindale Cumb 178 E7
Tindale Crescent Dur 169 G5
Tingewick Bucks 84 C8
Tingley Leeds 141 L3
Tingrith C Beds 68 C1
Tinhay Devon 12 A5
Tinker's Hill Hants 34 E2
Tinkersley Derbys 132 E6
Tinsley Sheff 133 H2
Tinsley Green W Susx 37 L3
Tintagel Cnwll 10 F5
Tintern Parva Mons 63 G7
Tintinhull Somset 31 H7
Tintwistle Derbys 140 F8
Tinwald D & G 176 D3
Tinwell Rutlnd 101 M2
Tippacott Devon 28 D2
Tipp's End Norfk 103 K4
Tiptoe Hants 18 C4
Tipton Sandw 98 B5
Tipton Green Sandw 98 B5
Tipton St John Devon 14 C4
Tiptree Essex 72 C4
Tiptree Heath Essex 72 C4
Tirabad Powys 78 B7
Tiree Ag & B 224 C6
Tiretigan Ag & B 206 A6
Tirley Gloucs 64 B2
Tirphil Caerph 61 H6
Tirril Cumb 166 C5
Tir-y-fron Flints 129 G7
Tisbury Wilts 32 F5
Tisman's Common W Susx 37 G4
Tissington Derbys 115 K1
Titchberry Devon 26 D5
Titchfield Hants 19 J3
Titchfield Common Hants 19 J2
Titchmarsh Nhants 102 A7
Titchwell Norfk 121 G3
Tithby Notts 117 J4
Titley Herefs 79 L3
Titmore Green Herts 69 G2
Titsey Surrey 51 L7
Titson Cnwll 11 J2
Tittensor Staffs 114 D4
Tittleshall Norfk 121 K7
Titton Worcs 81 J1
Tiverton Ches W 130 A7
Tiverton Devon 29 G8
Tivetshall St Margaret Norfk 106 D6
Tivetshall St Mary Norfk 106 D6
Tivington Somset 29 G2
Tivy Dale Barns 141 L6
Tixall Staffs 114 F7
Tixover Rutlnd 101 L3
Toab Shet 281 d9
Toadhole Derbys 133 H8
Toadmoor Derbys 116 B1
Tobermory Ag & B 226 F1
Toberonochy Ag & B 215 L3
Tobha Mor W Isls 283 b10
Tocher Abers 256 C5
Tochieneal Moray 267 K3
Tockenham Wilts 46 F3
Tockenham Wick Wilts 46 F3
Tocketts R & Cl 170 E7
Tockholes Bl w D 139 K3
Tockington S Glos 45 J2
Tockwith N York 151 G5
Todber Dorset 32 D7
Todburn Nthumb 191 G7
Toddington C Beds 68 C2
Toddington Gloucs 82 B8
Todds Green Herts 69 G2
Todenham Gloucs 82 F8
Todhills Angus 234 C7
Todhills Cumb 177 L6
Todhills Dur 169 G4
Todmorden Calder 140 E3
Todwick Rothm 133 K3
Toft Cambs 87 G4
Toft Ches E 130 E4
Toft Lincs 118 E8
Toft Shet 281 e4
Toft Warwks 83 L1
Toft Hill Dur 168 F5
Toft Hill Lincs 136 D7
Toft Monks Norfk 107 J4
Toft next Newton Lincs 135 L2
Toftrees Norfk 121 K6
Toftwood Norfk 105 K1
Togston Nthumb 191 J6
Tokavaig Highld 247 J6
Tokers Green Oxon 49 H3
Tolastadh W Isls 282 h2
Toldish Cnwll 4 F3
Tolland Somset 29 K4
Tollard Farnham Dorset 32 F7
Tollard Royal Wilts 32 F7

Toll Bar Donc 142 E6
Tollbar End Covtry 99 K8
Toller Fratrum Dorset 16 B3
Toller Porcorum Dorset 16 A3
Tollerton N York 151 H3
Tollerton Notts 117 G4
Toller Whelme Dorset 15 L2
Tollesbury Essex 72 D5
Tolleshunt D'Arcy Essex 72 D5
Tolleshunt Knights Essex 72 D4
Tolleshunt Major Essex 72 C5
Tolpuddle Dorset 16 F4
Tolsta W Isls 282 h2
Tolworth Gt Lon 51 G5
Tomatin Highld 252 E6
Tomchrasky Highld 239 M1
Tomdoun Highld 239 K3
Tomich Highld 250 B6
Tomich Highld 250 F2
Tomich Highld 263 J5
Tomich Highld 272 F7
Tomintoul Moray 254 D7
Tomlow Warwks 83 K3
Tomnacross Highld 250 F3
Tomnavoulin Moray 254 D6
Tompkin Staffs 114 E1
Ton Mons 62 C6
Ton Mons 62 D7
Tonbridge Kent 38 F4
Tondu Brdgnd 42 D5
Tonedale Somset 29 L6
Ton fanau Gwynd 92 C3
Tong C Brad 141 K2
Tong Kent 40 C4
Tong Shrops 97 H2
Tonge Leics 116 C7
Tong Green Kent 40 C4
Tongham Surrey 36 C1
Tongland D & G 175 H4
Tong Norton Shrops 97 H2
Tongue Highld 277 K5
Tongue End Lincs 118 F7
Tongwynlais Cardif 43 H5
Tonmawr Neath 42 B2
Tonna Neath 57 L5
Ton-teg Rhondd 43 H4
Tonwell Herts 69 J4
Tonypandy Rhondd 42 F3
Tonyrefail Rhondd 42 F4
Toot Baldon Oxon 66 E7
Toot Hill Essex 70 D6
Toothill Hants 34 E7
Toothill Swindn 47 G2
Tooting Gt Lon 51 H5
Tooting Bec Gt Lon 51 H4
Topcliffe N York 160 F7
Topcroft Norfk 106 F5
Topcroft Street Norfk 106 F5
Top End Bed 85 L3
Topham Donc 143 G4
Top of Hebers Rochdl 140 C6
Toppesfield Essex 88 E7
Toppings Bolton 139 L5
Toprow Norfk 106 D4
Topsham Devon 13 M5
Top-y-rhos Flints 128 F7
Torbeg N Ayrs 194 D5
Torboll Highld 273 H8
Torbreck Highld 251 H3
Torbryan Devon 8 B2
Torcastle Highld 239 J7
Torcross Devon 8 B6
Tore Highld 251 G1
Torfrey Cnwll 5 J4
Torinturk Ag & B 206 C6
Torksey Lincs 135 G4
Tormarton S Glos 45 M3
Tormore N Ayrs 194 D4
Tornagrain Highld 252 E2
Tornaveen Abers 244 D2
Torness Highld 251 G6
Toronto Dur 169 G4
Torpenhow Cumb 165 G3
Torphichen W Loth 210 C4
Torphins Abers 244 E3
Torpoint Cnwll 6 E4
Torquay Torbay 8 D2
Torquay Crematorium Torbay 8 D2
Torquhan Border 200 F3
Torr Devon 7 H4
Torran Highld 259 K6
Torrance E Duns 209 G4
Torranyard N Ayrs 196 D2
Torre Somset 29 J3
Torridon Highld 260 E8
Torridon House Highld 260 D8
Torrin Highld 247 J4
Torrisdale Ag & B 194 B4
Torrisdale Highld 278 B4
Torrish Highld 274 C4
Torrisholme Lancs 147 J3
Torrobull Highld 272 E7
Torry C Aber 245 L3
Torryburn Fife 210 D2
Torteval Guern 9 h4
Torthorwald D & G 176 D3
Tortington W Susx 21 G6
Torton Worcs 81 J1
Tortworth S Glos 63 L8
Torvaig Highld 259 H7
Torver Cumb 156 C4
Torwood Falk 209 M2
Torwoodlee Border 201 G5
Torworth Notts 134 D2
Tosberry Devon 26 D6
Toscaig Highld 247 L1
Toseland Cambs 86 E3
Tosside Lancs 148 D4
Tostock Suffk 89 J3
Totaig Highld 258 B6
Tote Highld 259 G6
Tote Highld 259 J4
Tote Hill W Susx 36 C6
Totford Hants 35 H3
Tothill Lincs 137 H3
Totland IoW 18 E6
Totley Sheff 132 F4
Totley Brook Sheff 132 F4
Totnes Devon 8 B3
Toton Notts 116 E4
Totronald Ag & B 224 F4
Totscore Highld 258 F3
Tottenham Gt Lon 51 J1
Tottenhill Norfk 104 C1
Totteridge Gt Lon 69 H8
Totternhoe C Beds 68 C3
Tottington Bury 140 A5
Tottleworth Lancs 139 L2
Totton Hants 34 D8
Touchen End W & M 49 L4
Toulston N York 151 G7
Toulton Somset 30 B4
Toulvaddie Highld 264 D4
Tovil Kent 39 J3
Towan Cnwll 5 G5
Towan Cnwll 10 B7
Toward Ag & B 207 J5
Toward Quay Ag & B 207 J5
Towcester Nhants 84 D5
Towednack Cnwll 2 D3
Towersey Oxon 67 H6
Towie Abers 244 A1
Tow Law Dur 168 E3
Town End Cambs 103 J4
Town End Cumb 156 E1
Town End Cumb 156 F6
Town End Cumb 166 E5
Townend W Duns 208 C4
Towngate Cumb 166 C1
Towngate Lincs 102 C1
Town Green Lancs 138 E6
Town Green Norfk 107 G1
Townhead Barns 141 J7
Town Head Cumb 156 F2
Townhead Cumb 164 E3
Townhead Cumb 166 E4
Townhead D & G 176 D1
Town Head N York 148 E4
Townhead of Greenlaw D & G 175 J2
Townhill Fife 210 F1
Town Kelloe Dur 169 K3
Townlake Devon 12 A7
Town Lane Wigan 139 K7
Town Littleworth E Susx 22 F4
Town of Lowton Wigan 139 J8
Town Row E Susx 38 E7
Towns End Hants 48 E7
Townsend Somset 30 E7
Townshend Cnwll 2 F4
Town Street Suffk 104 F6
Townwell S Glos 45 K1
Town Yetholm Border 202 C7
Towthorpe C York 151 K4
Towthorpe E R Yk 152 D3
Towton N York 151 G7
Towyn Conwy 127 K4
Toxteth Lpool 129 H2
Toynton All Saints Lincs 137 G7
Toynton Fen Side Lincs 137 G7
Toynton St Peter Lincs 137 G7
Toy's Hill Kent 38 D3
Trabboch E Ayrs 196 E6
Trabbochburn E Ayrs 196 F6
Traboe Cnwll 3 J6
Tracebridge Somset 29 K6
Tradespark Highld 264 D8
Trallong Powys 60 E1
Tranent E Loth 211 L4
Tranmere Wirral 129 H2
Trantelbeg Highld 278 F5
Trantlemore Highld 278 F5
Tranwell Nthumb 180 F2
Trapp Carmth 59 J5
Traprain E Loth 212 D4
Trap's Green Warwks 82 D1
Trapshill W Berk 48 A6
Traquair Border 200 D6
Trash Green W Berk 49 G5
Trawden Lancs 148 F8
Trawscoed Cerdgn 77 J1
Trawsfynydd Gwynd 110 D4
Trealaw Rhondd 42 F3
Treales Lancs 138 F1
Trearddur Bay IoA 124 D4
Treaslane Highld 258 F6
Treator Cnwll 10 C7
Tre Aubrey V Glam 43 G7
Trebanog Rhondd 42 F4
Trebanos Neath 57 K4
Trebartha Cnwll 11 K7
Trebarwith Cnwll 10 E5
Trebeath Cnwll 11 J5
Trebetherick Cnwll 10 C7
Treborough Somset 29 H4
Trebudannon Cnwll 4 E3
Trebullett Cnwll 11 L7
Treburgett Cnwll 10 E6
Treburley Cnwll 11 L7
Treburrick Cnwll 10 B8
Trebyan Cnwll 5 J2
Trecastle Powys 60 C1
Trecogo Cnwll 11 K6
Trecott Devon 12 F3
Trecwn Pembks 74 F5
Trecynon Rhondd 60 F6
Tredaule Cnwll 11 J6
Tredavoe Cnwll 2 C5
Tredegar Blae G 61 J5
Tredethy Cnwll 10 F8
Tredington Gloucs 64 C1
Tredington Warwks 83 G6
Tredinnick Cnwll 5 H3
Tredinnick Cnwll 5 K2
Tredinnick Cnwll 5 M3
Tredinnick Cnwll 6 B3
Tredinnick Cnwll 10 C8
Tredomen Powys 61 H1
Tredrissi Pembks 75 J4
Tredrizzick Cnwll 10 D7
Tredunnock Mons 62 D8
Tredustan Powys 61 H1
Treen Cnwll 2 B6
Treen Cnwll 2 C3
Treesmill Cnwll 5 J4
Treeton Rothm 133 J2
Trefasser Pembks 74 E4
Trefdraeth IoA 125 G5
Trefecca Powys 61 J1
Trefeglwys Powys 93 L5
Trefenter Cerdgn 77 H2
Treffgarne Pembks 54 F2
Treffgarne Owen Pembks 74 E7
Trefforest Rhondd 43 G4
Treffynnon Pembks 74 D6
Trefil Blae G 61 H4
Trefilan Cerdgn 77 G4
Trefin Pembks 74 D5
Treflach Wood Shrops 112 C6
Trefnannau Powys 112 C8
Trefnant Denbgs 128 C5
Trefonen Shrops 112 C6
Trefor Gwynd 108 F2
Trefor IoA 124 F4
Trefrew Cnwll 10 F5
Trefriw Conwy 126 F7
Tregadillett Cnwll 11 K6
Tre-gagle Mons 63 G5
Tregaian IoA 125 H4
Tregare Mons 62 E5
Tregarne Cnwll 3 K6
Tregaron Cerdgn 77 J3
Tregarth Gwynd 126 B6
Tregaswith Cnwll 4 E2
Tregatta Cnwll 10 F5
Tregawne Cnwll 5 G2
Tregeare Cnwll 11 J5
Tregeiriog Wrexhm 112 B5
Tregele IoA 124 F1
Tregellist Cnwll 10 E7
Tregenna Cnwll 4 E6
Tregeseal Cnwll 2 B5
Tregew Cnwll 3 K4
Tre-Gibbon Rhondd 60 F6
Tregidden Cnwll 3 J6
Tregiskey Cnwll 5 G5
Treglemais Pembks 74 D6
Tregole Cnwll 11 H3
Tregolls Cnwll 3 J4
Tregonce Cnwll 10 C7
Tregonetha Cnwll 4 F2
Tregony Cnwll 4 F6
Tregoodwell Cnwll 11 G6
Tregorrick Cnwll 5 G4
Tregoss Cnwll 4 F3
Tregoyd Powys 79 H7
Tregrehan Mills Cnwll 5 H4
Tre-groes Cerdgn 76 D6
Tregullon Cnwll 5 H2
Tregunna Cnwll 10 D7
Tregunnon Cnwll 11 J6
Tregurrian Cnwll 4 D2
Tregynon Powys 94 D4
Tre-gynwr Carmth 58 D5
Trehafod Rhondd 43 G3
Trehan Cnwll 6 D4
Treharris Myr Td 43 H2
Treharrock Cnwll 10 E6
Trehemborne Cnwll 10 B7
Treherbert Carmth 77 G6
Treherbert Rhondd 42 E2
Trehunist Cnwll 6 C2
Trekenner Cnwll 11 L7
Treknow Cnwll 10 E5
Trelan Cnwll 3 J7
Trelash Cnwll 11 H4
Trelassick Cnwll 4 E4
Trelawne Cnwll 5 L4
Trelawnyd Flints 128 C4
Treleague Cnwll 3 K6
Treleaver Cnwll 3 K7
Trelech Carmth 58 A3
Trelech a'r Betws Carmth 58 B3
Treleddyd-fawr Pembks 74 B6
Trelew Cnwll 3 K4
Trelewis Myr Td 43 H2
Treligga Cnwll 10 E5
Trelights Cnwll 10 D6
Trelill Cnwll 10 E7
Trelinnoe Cnwll 11 K6
Trelion Cnwll 4 F4
Trelissick Cnwll 3 L3
Trellech Mons 63 G6
Trelleck Grange Mons 62 F6
Trelogan Flints 128 D4
Trelow Cnwll 4 F1
Trelowarren Cnwll 3 J6
Trelowia Cnwll 6 B3
Treluggan Cnwll 3 M3
Trelystan Powys 95 G3
Tremadog Gwynd 109 K3
Tremail Cnwll 11 H5
Tremain Cerdgn 75 M3
Tremaine Cnwll 11 J5
Tremar Cnwll 6 B1
Trematon Cnwll 6 D3
Trembraze Cnwll 6 B2
Tremeirchion Denbgs 128 C5
Tremethick Cross Cnwll 2 C5
Tremore Cnwll 5 G2
Tre-Mostyn Flints 128 D4
Trenance Cnwll 3 K6
Trenance Cnwll 4 D1
Trenance Cnwll 10 C8
Trenarren Cnwll 5 H5
Trench Wrekin 96 F1
Trench Green Oxon 49 G3
Trendeal Cnwll 4 E4
Trendrine Cnwll 2 D3
Treneague Cnwll 10 D8
Trenear Cnwll 3 H5
Treneglos Cnwll 11 H5
Trenerth Cnwll 2 F4
Trenewan Cnwll 5 K4
Trenewth Cnwll 10 F7
Trengune Cnwll 11 H4
Treninnick Cnwll 4 D3
Trenowah Cnwll 4 C3
Trenoweth Cnwll 3 J4
Trent Dorset 31 K7
Trentham C Stke 114 D3
Trentishoe Devon 28 A1
Trentlock Derbys 116 E5
Trent Port Lincs 135 G3
Trent Vale C Stke 114 D3
Trenwheal Cnwll 3 G4
Treoes V Glam 42 E6
Treorchy Rhondd 42 E2
Trequite Cnwll 10 E7
Tre'r-ddol Cerdgn 92 E5
Trerhyngyll V Glam 42 F6
Trerulefoot Cnwll 6 C3
Tresaith Cerdgn 76 A5
Tresawle Cnwll 4 E5
Tresco IoS 10 b2
Trescott Staffs 97 J4
Trescowe Cnwll 2 F5
Tresean Cnwll 4 C3
Tresham Gloucs 46 A1

Treshnish Isles Ag & B 225 H7
Tresillian Cnwll 4 E5
Tresinney Cnwll 10 F6
Treskinnick Cross Cnwll 11 H3
Tresmeer Cnwll 11 J5
Tresparrett Cnwll 11 G4
Tressait P & K 232 B3
Tresta Shet 281 d6
Tresta Shet 281 f3
Treswell Notts 134 F4
Treswithian Cnwll 3 G3
Treswithian Downs Crematorium Cnwll 3 G3
Tre Taliesin Cerdgn 92 E5
Trethevey Cnwll 10 F5
Trethewey Cnwll 2 B6
Trethomas Caerph 43 J4
Trethosa Cnwll 4 F4
Trethurgy Cnwll 5 H4
Tretio Pembks 74 C6
Tretire Herefs 63 G2
Tretower Powys 61 J3
Treuddyn Flints 128 F8
Trevadlock Cnwll 11 K6
Trevalga Cnwll 10 F4
Trevalyn Wrexhm 129 J8
Trevanger Cnwll 10 D7
Trevanson Cnwll 10 D8
Trevarrack Cnwll 2 D5
Trevarren Cnwll 4 E3
Trevarrian Cnwll 4 D2
Trevarrick Cnwll 5 G6
Trevarth Cnwll 3 J3
Trevaughan Carmth 55 L4
Tre-Vaughan Carmth 58 D4
Treveal Cnwll 2 D3
Treveal Cnwll 4 C3
Treveighan Cnwll 10 F6
Trevellas Downs Cnwll 4 B4
Trevelmond Cnwll 5 L2
Trevemper Cnwll 4 D3
Treveor Cnwll 5 G6
Treverbyn Cnwll 4 E5
Treverbyn Cnwll 5 G3
Treverva Cnwll 3 J5
Trevescan Cnwll 2 B6
Trevethin Torfn 62 B6
Trevia Cnwll 10 F6
Trevigro Cnwll 6 C1
Trevilla Cnwll 3 L3
Trevilson Cnwll 4 D4
Treviscoe Cnwll 4 F4
Treviskey Cnwll 4 F6
Trevithick Cnwll 4 E2
Trevithick Cnwll 4 F6
Trevoll Cnwll 4 D3
Trevone Cnwll 10 B7
Trevor Wrexhm 112 C3
Trevorgans Cnwll 2 B6
Trevorrick Cnwll 10 C7
Trevose Cnwll 10 B7
Trew Cnwll 3 G5
Trewalder Cnwll 10 F6
Trewalkin Powys 61 J1
Trewarmett Cnwll 10 F5
Trewassa Cnwll 11 G5
Trewavas Cnwll 2 F5
Treween Cnwll 11 J6
Trewellard Cnwll 2 B4
Trewen Cnwll 11 J6
Trewennack Cnwll 3 H5
Trewent Pembks 55 J7
Trewern Powys 95 G1
Trewetha Cnwll 10 E6
Trewethern Cnwll 10 E7
Trewidland Cnwll 6 B3
Trewillis Cnwll 3 K7
Trewint Cnwll 6 B2
Trewint Cnwll 11 J6
Trewithian Cnwll 3 M4
Trewoodloe Cnwll 11 L8
Trewoon Cnwll 3 H7
Trewoon Cnwll 5 G4
Treworga Cnwll 4 E6
Treworgan Cnwll 4 D5
Treworlas Cnwll 4 E7
Treworld Cnwll 11 G4
Treworthal Cnwll 3 M3
Tre-wyn Mons 62 C3
Treyarnon Cnwll 10 B7
Treyford W Susx 20 D3
Trickett's Cross Dorset 17 L2
Triermain Cumb 178 E5
Triffleton Pembks 75 G7
Trillacott Cnwll 11 K4
Trimdon Dur 169 K4
Trimdon Colliery Dur 169 K4
Trimdon Grange Dur 169 K3
Trimingham Norfk 122 F4
Trimley Lower Street Suffk 91 G7
Trimley St Martin Suffk 91 G7
Trimley St Mary Suffk 91 G7
Trimpley Worcs 97 H7
Trimsaran Carmth 56 E4
Trims Green Herts 70 C4
Trimstone Devon 27 J2
Trinafour P & K 231 K3
Trinant Caerph 61 K7
Tring Herts 68 A5
Tringford Herts 67 M4
Tring Wharf Herts 68 A4
Trinity Angus 234 F3
Trinity Jersey 9 d2
Trinity Gask P & K 221 G3
Triscombe Somset 29 L4
Trislaig Highld 239 H8
Trispen Cnwll 4 D5
Tritlington Nthumb 191 J7
Troan Cnwll 4 E3
Trochry P & K 232 E7
Troedrhiwfuwch Caerph 61 H6
Troedyraur Cerdgn 76 B6
Troedyrhiw Myr Td 61 G6
Trofarth Conwy 127 G5
Trois Bois Jersey 9 c2
Troon Cnwll 3 G3
Troon S Ayrs 196 C5
Trossachs Pier Stirlg 219 H5
Troston Suffk 89 H1
Troswell Cnwll 11 J4
Trotshill Worcs 81 K4
Trottiscliffe Kent 52 D7
Trotton W Susx 36 B6
Troughend Nthumb 190 B7
Trough Gate Lancs 140 D3
Troutbeck Cumb 156 F2
Troutbeck Cumb 165 L5
Troutbeck Bridge Cumb 156 F3
Troway Derbys 133 H4
Trowbridge Wilts 46 B7
Trowell Notts 116 E3
Trowle Common Wilts 46 B7
Trowley Bottom Herts 68 D4
Trowse Newton Norfk 106 E2
Troy Leeds 150 C8
Trudoxhill Somset 32 C2
Trull Somset 30 B6
Trumfleet Donc 142 F5
Trumpan Highld 258 C4
Trumpet Herefs 80 F7
Trumpington Cambs 87 J4
Trumpsgreen Surrey 50 C5
Trunch Norfk 122 F4
Trunnah Lancs 147 G7
Truro Cnwll 4 D6
Truscott Cnwll 11 K5
Trusham Devon 13 K6
Trusley Derbys 115 L4
Trusthorpe Lincs 137 K3
Trysull Staffs 97 J4
Tubney Oxon 66 B7
Tuckenhay Devon 8 B4
Tuckhill Shrops 97 H5
Tuckingmill Cnwll 3 G3
Tuckingmill Wilts 32 F5
Tuckton Bmouth 18 A5
Tucoyse Cnwll 4 F5
Tuddenham Suffk 88 E1
Tuddenham Suffk 90 E5
Tudeley Kent 38 F4
Tudhoe Dur 169 H3
Tudorville Herefs 63 H3
Tudweiliog Gwynd 108 D4
Tuesley Surrey 36 E3
Tuffley Gloucs 64 B4
Tufton Hants 34 F2
Tufton Pembks 75 H6
Tugby Leics 101 G3
Tugford Shrops 96 D6
Tughall Nthumb 203 K7
Tullibody Clacks 220 E8
Tullich Highld 251 H6
Tullich Highld 264 D4
Tulliemet P & K 232 F5
Tulloch Abers 256 E5
Tullochgorm Ag & B 216 F8
Tulloch Station Highld 240 B7
Tullymurdoch P & K 233 J5
Tullynessle Abers 255 L7
Tulse Hill Gt Lon 51 J4
Tumble Carmth 58 F6
Tumbler's Green Essex 71 K2
Tumby Lincs 136 D7
Tumby Woodside Lincs 136 E8
Tummel Bridge P & K 231 L4
Tunbridge Wells Kent 38 F5
Tundergarth D & G 177 G3
Tungate Norfk 122 F5
Tunley BaNES 45 K7
Tunstall C Stke 114 D1
Tunstall E R Yk 145 J2
Tunstall Kent 40 A3
Tunstall Lancs 157 K8
Tunstall N York 160 B3
Tunstall Norfk 107 J2
Tunstall Staffs 114 B6
Tunstall Suffk 91 H4
Tunstall Sundld 181 J8
Tunstead Derbys 132 B5
Tunstead Norfk 122 F7
Tunstead Milton Derbys 131 K4
Tunworth Hants 35 K1
Tupsley Herefs 80 C7
Turgis Green Hants 49 G7
Turkdean Gloucs 65 G4
Tur Langton Leics 100 F4
Turleigh Wilts 46 A6
Turleygreen Shrops 97 H6
Turn Lancs 140 B4
Turnastone Herefs 79 L7
Turnberry S Ayrs 182 F2
Turnchapel C Plym 6 F4
Turnditch Derbys 116 A2
Turner Green Lancs 139 J2
Turner's Green E Susx 23 L3
Turner's Green Warwks 82 E2
Turner's Hill W Susx 38 A6
Turners Puddle Dorset 16 F4
Turnford Herts 69 K6
Turnhouse C Edin 211 G4
Turnworth Dorset 16 F1
Turriff Abers 268 C6
Turton Bottoms Bl w D 139 L4
Turves Cambs 103 G4
Turvey Bed 85 J5
Turville Bucks 49 J1
Turville Heath Bucks 49 H1
Turweston Bucks 84 B7
Tushielaw Inn Border 187 L3
Tutbury Staffs 115 L6
Tutnall Worcs 82 A1
Tutshill Gloucs 63 G8
Tuttington Norfk 122 E6
Tutwell Cnwll 11 M7
Tuxford Notts 134 E5
Twatt Ork 275 b3
Twatt Shet 281 d6
Twechar E Duns 209 J4
Tweedbank Border 201 H6
Tweedmouth Nthumb 202 F3
Tweedsmuir Border 187 G1
Twelveheads Cnwll 4 B6
Twelve Oaks E Susx 24 C3
Twemlow Green Ches E 130 F6
Twenty Lincs 118 F7
Twerton BaNES 45 L6
Twickenham Gt Lon 50 F4
Twigworth Gloucs 64 B3
Twineham W Susx 22 C3
Twineham Green W Susx 22 C3
Twinhoe BaNES 45 L7
Twinstead Essex 89 H7
Twitchen Devon 28 D5
Twitchen Shrops 95 J7
Twitham Kent 41 H4
Two Bridges Devon 12 E7
Two Dales Derbys 132 E7
Two Gates Staffs 99 G3
Two Mile Oak Cross Devon 8 C1
Two Pots Devon 27 J2
Two Waters Herts 68 D6
Twycross Leics 99 J2
Twyford Bucks 67 G2
Twyford Hants 35 G6
Twyford Leics 100 F2
Twyford Lincs 118 B6
Twyford Norfk 121 M6
Twyford Wokham 49 J4
Twyford Common Herefs 80 C8
Twyn-carno Caerph 61 H5
Twynholm D & G 175 G4
Twyning Green Gloucs 81 L7
Twynllanan Carmth 59 L4
Twyn-yr-Odyn V Glam 43 H7
Twyn-y-Sheriff Mons 62 E6
Twywell Nhants 101 L7
Tyberton Herefs 79 M7
Tyburn Birm 98 E5
Tycroes Carmth 57 H3
Ty Croes IoA 124 F5
Tycrwyn Powys 111 L7
Tydd Gote Lincs 120 A7
Tydd St Giles Cambs 119 M8
Tydd St Mary Lincs 119 M7
Tye Hants 20 B6
Tye Green Essex 70 D2
Tye Green Essex 71 J3
Tye Green Essex 88 B8
Tyersal C Brad 141 J1
Tyldesley Wigan 139 K7
Tyler Hill Kent 40 F3
Tylers Green Bucks 67 L8
Tyler's Green Essex 70 D6
Tylers Green Surrey 51 K8
Tylorstown Rhondd 42 F3
Tylwch Powys 93 L7
Ty-nant Conwy 111 J3
Ty-nant Gwynd 111 H6
Tyndrum Stirlg 218 E1
Ty'n-dwr Denbgs 112 C3
Tynemouth N Tyne 181 J5
Tynemouth Crematorium N Tyne 181 J5
Tynewydd Rhondd 60 E7
Tyninghame E Loth 212 D3
Tynron D & G 185 K4
Ty'n-y-bryn Rhondd 42 F4
Ty'n-y-coedcae Caerph 43 K4
Tynygongl IoA 125 J3
Tynygraig Cerdgn 77 J1
Ty'n-y-Groes Conwy 126 F5
Tyn-y-nant Rhondd 43 G4
Tyringham M Keyn 85 G6
Tyseley Birm 98 E6
Tythegston Brdgnd 42 C6
Tytherington Ches E 131 H4
Tytherington S Glos 45 K1
Tytherington Somset 32 C2
Tytherington Wilts 32 F3
Tytherleigh Devon 15 H2
Tytherton Lucas Wilts 46 D4
Tyttenhanger Herts 68 F6
Tywardreath Cnwll 5 J4
Tywardreath Highway Cnwll 5 J4
Tywyn Conwy 126 F4
Tywyn Gwynd 92 C3

U

Ubbeston Green Suffk 91 H1
Ubley BaNES 45 G7
Uckerby N York 160 C2
Uckfield E Susx 23 H3
Uckinghall Worcs 81 K7
Uckington Gloucs 64 C2
Uckington Shrops 96 D2
Uddingston S Lans 209 J6
Uddington S Lans 198 E6
Udimore E Susx 24 F3
Udny Green Abers 256 F6
Udny Station Abers 257 G6
Uffcott Wilts 47 H3
Uffculme Devon 29 K8
Uffington Lincs 102 B2
Uffington Oxon 47 L1
Uffington Shrops 96 C1
Ufford C Pete 102 B3
Ufford Suffk 91 G5
Ufton Warwks 83 J3
Ufton Nervet W Berk 48 F5
Ugadale Ag & B 194 B5
Ugborough Devon 7 K4
Uggeshall Suffk 107 J7
Ugglebarnby N York 162 F1
Ughill Sheff 132 E2
Ugley Essex 70 D2
Ugley Green Essex 70 D2
Ugthorpe N York 171 J8
Uibhist A Deas W Isls 283 c10
Uibhist A Tuath W Isls 283 b8
Uig Ag & B 224 F4
Uig Highld 258 B6
Uig Highld 258 F4
Uig W Isls 282 d3
Uigshader Highld 259 G7
Uisken Ag & B 226 D8
Ulbster Highld 280 D7
Ulcat Row Cumb 165 L6
Ulceby Lincs 137 H5
Ulceby N Linc 144 E5
Ulceby Skitter N Linc 144 E5
Ulcombe Kent 39 L4
Uldale Cumb 165 H3
Uley Gloucs 63 M7
Ulgham Nthumb 191 J7
Ullapool Highld 261 J1
Ullenhall Warwks 82 D2
Ullenwood Gloucs 64 D4
Ulleskelf N York 151 H7
Ullesthorpe Leics 100 B6
Ulley Rothm 133 J2
Ullingswick Herefs 80 E5
Ullinish Lodge Hotel Highld 246 D1
Ullock Cumb 164 E6
Ulpha Cumb 156 B4
Ulpha Cumb 157 G6
Ulrome E R Yk 153 J4
Ulsta Shet 281 e4
Ulting Wick Essex 71 K5

Ulva Ag & B 226 D4
Ulverley Green Solhll 98 E7
Ulverston Cumb 156 C7
Ulwell Dorset 17 K6
Ulzieside D & G 185 J1
Umberleigh Devon 27 L6
Unapool Highld 271 H2
Underbarrow Cumb 157 G4
Under Burnmouth Border 178 B2
Undercliffe C Brad 141 J1
Underdale Shrops 96 B1
Underling Green Kent 39 J4
Under River Kent 38 E3
Underwood Notts 116 D2
Undley Suffk 104 D7
Undy Mons 44 E2
Union Mills IoM 154 e6
Union Street E Susx 39 H7
Unst Shet 281 f2
Unstone Derbys 133 G4
Unstone Green Derbys 133 G4
Unthank Cumb 165 L1
Unthank Cumb 166 B3
Unthank Cumb 166 E3
Unthank Derbys 132 F4
Unthank Nthumb 202 F3
Upavon Wilts 47 H7
Up Cerne Dorset 16 C2
Upchurch Kent 53 H5
Upcott Devon 28 D5
Upcott Herefs 79 K5
Upend Cambs 88 D3
Up Exe Devon 13 L2
Upgate Norfk 122 C7
Upgate Street Norfk 106 B5
Upgate Street Norfk 106 F5
Uphall Dorset 16 A2
Uphall W Loth 210 E5
Upham Devon 13 K1
Upham Hants 35 H6
Uphampton Herefs 79 M3
Uphampton Worcs 81 J2
Uphill N Som 44 C7
Up Holland Lancs 139 G6
Uplawmoor E Rens 208 D8
Upleadon Gloucs 63 L2
Upleatham R & Cl 170 E6
Uplees Kent 40 C2
Uploders Dorset 15 L4
Uplowman Devon 29 J7
Uplyme Devon 15 H4
Up Marden W Susx 20 C4
Upminster Gt Lon 52 C2
Up Mudford Somset 31 J7
Up Nately Hants 49 G8
Upottery Devon 14 E1
Upper Affcot Shrops 95 K6
Upper Ardchronie Highld 263 G2
Upper Arley Worcs 97 H7
Upper Arncott Oxon 66 F4
Upper Astrop Nhants 83 L7
Upper Basildon W Berk 48 F4
Upper Batley Kirk 141 K3
Upper Beeding W Susx 22 B5
Upper Benefield Nhants 101 L5
Upper Bentley Worcs 82 B2
Upper Bighouse Highld 278 F5
Upper Birchwood Derbys 133 J8
Upper Boat Rhondd 43 H4
Upper Boddington Nhants 83 L5
Upper Borth Cerdgn 92 D5
Upper Brailes Warwks 83 G7
Upper Breakish Highld 247 L4
Upper Breinton Herefs 80 B7
Upper Broadheath Worcs 81 J4
Upper Broughton Notts 117 J6
Upper Bucklebury W Berk 48 D5
Upper Burgate Hants 33 K7
Upper Bush Medway 52 E5
Upperby Cumb 177 L8
Upper Caldecote C Beds 86 D6
Upper Canada N Som 44 D7
Upper Canterton Hants 18 D1
Upper Catesby Nhants 83 M3
Upper Catshill Worcs 98 B8
Upper Chapel Powys 78 D7
Upper Cheddon Somset 30 C5
Upper Chicksgrove Wilts 33 G5
Upper Chute Wilts 47 L8
Upper Clapton Gt Lon 51 K2
Upper Clatford Hants 34 D2
Upper Coberley Gloucs 64 E4
Upper Cokeham W Susx 21 K6
Upper Cotton Staffs 115 G2
Upper Cound Shrops 96 C2
Upper Cudworth Barns 142 B6
Upper Cumberworth Kirk 141 K6
Upper Dallachy Moray 267 G4
Upper Deal Kent 41 K5
Upper Dean Bed 85 L2
Upper Denby Kirk 141 K6
Upper Denton Cumb 178 E5
Upper Dicker E Susx 23 J5
Upper Dinchope Shrops 95 L6
Upper Dounreay Highld 279 H3
Upper Dovercourt Essex 73 K1
Upper Drumbane Stirlg 219 L6
Upper Dunsforth N York 150 F3
Upper Eashing Surrey 36 E2
Upper Eathie Highld 263 K7
Upper Egleton Herefs 80 E6
Upper Elkstone Staffs 131 L7
Upper Ellastone Staffs 115 J3
Upper End Derbys 132 B4
Upper Enham Hants 34 E1
Upper Farmcote Shrops 97 H5
Upper Farringdon Hants 35 L4
Upper Framilode Gloucs 63 L5
Upper Froyle Hants 35 M2
Upperglen Highld 258 E6
Upper Godney Somset 31 H2
Upper Gravenhurst C Beds 86 C8
Upper Green Mons 62 D3
Upper Green Suffk 88 E2
Upper Green W Berk 48 A6
Upper Grove Common Herefs 63 H2
Upper Hackney Derbys 132 F7
Upper Hale Surrey 36 B1
Upper Halliford Surrey 50 E5
Upper Halling Medway 52 E6
Upper Hambleton Rutlnd 101 K2
Upper Harbledown Kent 40 F4
Upper Hardres Court Kent 40 F5
Upper Hardwick Herefs 79 M4
Upper Hartfield E Susx 38 C6
Upper Hartshay Derbys 116 C2
Upper Hatherley Gloucs 64 D3
Upper Hatton Staffs 114 C4
Upper Haugh Rothm 142 C8
Upper Hayton Shrops 96 C7
Upper Heaton Kirk 141 J4
Upper Helmsley N York 151 L4
Upper Hergest Herefs 79 J4
Upper Heyford Nhants 84 C3
Upper Heyford Oxon 66 D2
Upper Hill Herefs 80 B4
Upper Hockenden Kent 52 B5
Upper Hopton Kirk 141 K4
Upper Howsell Worcs 81 H5
Upper Hulme Staffs 131 K7
Upper Ifold Surrey 36 F4
Upper Inglesham Swindn 65 J7
Upper Kilcott Gloucs 46 A1
Upper Killay Swans 57 G6
Upper Kinchrackine Ag & B 217 J2
Upper Lambourn W Berk 47 L3
Upper Landywood Staffs 98 C2
Upper Langford N Som 44 F7
Upper Langwith Derbys 133 K5
Upper Largo Fife 223 G6
Upper Leigh Staffs 115 G4
Upper Littleton N Som 45 H6
Upper Lochton Abers 244 F4
Upper Longdon Staffs 115 H8
Upper & Lower Stondon C Beds 86 D8
Upper Ludstone Shrops 97 H4
Upper Lybster Highld 275 H1
Upper Lydbrook Gloucs 63 J4
Upper Lyde Herefs 80 C6
Upper Lye Herefs 79 M2
Upper Maes-coed Herefs 79 L8
Upper Midhope Sheff 141 K7
Uppermill Oldham 140 F6
Upper Milton Worcs 81 J1
Upper Minety Wilts 46 E1
Upper Moor Worcs 82 A5
Upper Moor Side Leeds 141 K2
Upper Mulben Moray 267 G6
Upper Netchwood Shrops 96 E5
Upper Nobut Staffs 115 G4
Upper Norwood W Susx 20 F3
Upper Padley Derbys 132 E4
Upper Pennington Hants 18 D4
Upper Pollicott Bucks 67 H4
Upper Poppleton C York 151 J5
Upper Quinton Warwks 82 E6
Upper Ratley Hants 34 D6
Upper Rissington Gloucs 65 J3
Upper Rochford Worcs 80 E2
Upper Ruscoe D & G 174 E3
Upper Sapey Herefs 80 F3
Upper Seagry Wilts 46 D3
Upper Shelton C Beds 85 K6
Upper Sheringham Norfk 122 C3
Upper Skelmorlie N Ayrs 207 K5
Upper Slaughter Gloucs 65 H3
Upper Soudley Gloucs 63 K5
Upper Spond Herefs 79 K4
Upper Standen Kent 41 H7
Upper Staploe Bed 86 C3
Upper Stoke Norfk 106 E3
Upper Stowe Nhants 84 C4
Upper Street Hants 33 K7
Upper Street Norfk 106 D7
Upper Street Norfk 123 G7
Upper Street Norfk 123 G8
Upper Street Suffk 88 F5
Upper Street Suffk 90 C5
Upper Street Suffk 90 D8
Upper Strensham Worcs 81 K7
Upper Sundon C Beds 68 D2
Upper Swell Gloucs 65 H2
Upper Tankersley Barns 142 A7
Upper Tasburgh Norfk 106 E4
Upper Tean Staffs 115 G4
Upperthong Kirk 141 H6
Upperthorpe Derbys 133 J4
Upperthorpe N Linc 143 J7
Upper Threapwood Ches W 113 G3
Upperton W Susx 36 E6
Upper Town Derbys 115 L1
Uppertown Derbys 132 F6
Upper Town Dur 168 D3
Upper Town Herefs 80 D5
Uppertown Highld 280 D1
Upper Town N Som 45 G6
Upper Town Suffk 89 J2
Upper Tumble Carmth 59 G6
Upper Tysoe Warwks 83 H6
Upper Ufford Suffk 91 G4
Upperup Gloucs 64 F7
Upper Upham Wilts 47 J3
Upper Upnor Medway 53 G5
Upper Victoria Angus 234 E8
Upper Vobster Somset 32 B1
Upper Wardington Oxon 83 L6
Upper Weald M Keyn 84 F7
Upper Weedon Nhants 84 B3
Upper Welland Worcs 81 H7
Upper Wellingham E Susx 23 G4
Upper Weston BaNES 45 L5
Upper Weybread Suffk 106 E7
Upper Wick Worcs 81 J5
Upper Wield Hants 35 K3
Upper Winchendon Bucks 67 H4
Upperwood Derbys 132 F8
Upper Woodford Wilts 33 K3
Upper Wootton Hants 48 E7
Upper Wraxall Wilts 46 A4
Upper Wyche Worcs 81 H6
Uppincott Devon 13 L2
Uppingham Rutlnd 101 J3
Uppington Dorset 17 K2
Uppington Shrops 96 D2
Upsall N York 161 G5
Upsettlington Border 202 D4
Upshire Essex 69 L7
Up Somborne Hants 34 E4
Upstreet Kent 41 H3
Up Sydling Dorset 16 B2
Upthorpe Suffk 89 K1
Upton Bucks 67 J5
Upton C Pete 102 C3
Upton Cambs 102 D7
Upton Ches W 129 J6
Upton Cnwll 11 H2
Upton Cnwll 11 K8
Upton Cumb 165 K3
Upton Devon 7 K6
Upton Devon 14 C2
Upton Dorset 16 E6
Upton Dorset 17 J4
Upton E R Yk 153 J5
Upton Halton 129 L2
Upton Hants 34 E7
Upton Hants 47 M7
Upton Leics 99 K3
Upton Lincs 135 H2
Upton Nhants 84 D3
Upton Norfk 107 H1
Upton Notts 117 J1
Upton Notts 134 E4
Upton Oxon 48 D2
Upton Oxon 65 K4
Upton Pembks 55 G6
Upton R & Cl 171 G6
Upton Slough 50 B3
Upton Somset 29 H5
Upton Somset 31 G5
Upton Wakefd 142 D5
Upton Warwks 82 D4
Upton Wilts 32 E4
Upton Wirral 129 G2
Upton Bishop Herefs 63 K2
Upton Cheyney S Glos 45 K5
Upton Cressett Shrops 96 E5
Upton Crews Herefs 63 J2
Upton Cross Cnwll 11 K8
Upton End C Beds 86 C8
Upton Grey Hants 35 L1
Upton Heath Ches W 129 J5
Upton Hellions Devon 13 K2
Upton Lovell Wilts 32 F3
Upton Magna Shrops 96 C1
Upton Noble Somset 32 B3
Upton Pyne Devon 13 L3
Upton St Leonards Gloucs 64 B4
Upton Scudamore Wilts 32 E1
Upton Snodsbury Worcs 81 L4
Upton Towans Cnwll 2 F3
Upton upon Severn Worcs 81 K7
Upton Warren Worcs 81 L2
Upwaltham W Susx 20 F4
Upware Cambs 87 L1
Upwell Norfk 103 K3
Upwey Dorset 16 C5
Upwick Green Herts 70 C2
Upwood Cambs 102 E6
Urchfont Wilts 46 F7
Urdimarsh Herefs 80 C5
Ure Bank N York 150 D1
Urlay Nook S on T 169 L7
Urmston Traffd 130 E1
Urquhart Moray 266 F4
Urra N York 161 J2
Urray Highld 250 E1
Usan Angus 235 H4
Ushaw Moor Dur 169 G2
Usk Mons 62 D7
Usselby Lincs 136 A1
Usworth Sundld 181 H7
Utkinton Ches W 130 A6
Utley C Brad 149 J7
Uton Devon 13 J3
Utterby Lincs 136 F1
Uttoxeter Staffs 115 H5
Uwchmynydd Gwynd 108 B6
Uxbridge Gt Lon 50 D2
Uyeasound Shet 281 f2
Uzmaston Pembks 54 F4

V

Vale Guern 9 k2
Vale of Glamorgan Crematorium V Glam 43 H7
Valley IoA 124 E4
Valley End Surrey 50 B6
Valley Truckle Cnwll 10 F6
Valtos Highld 259 J4
Valtos W Isls 282 e3
Vange Essex 52 F2
Varteg Torfn 61 L6
Vatsetter Shet 281 e3
Vatten Highld 258 D7
Vaynor Myr Td 61 G5
Vazon Bay Guern 9 i2
Veensgarth Shet 281 e6
Velindre Powys 79 H7
Vellow Somset 29 K3
Velly Devon 26 E6
Venngreen Devon 26 F8
Vennington Shrops 95 H2
Venn Ottery Devon 14 C4
Venny Tedburn Devon 13 J3
Venterdon Cnwll 11 L7
Ventnor IoW 19 J8
Venton Devon 7 H3
Vernham Dean Hants 47 M7
Vernham Street Hants 47 M7
Vernolds Common Shrops 95 L7
Verwood Dorset 17 L1
Veryan Cnwll 4 E7
Veryan Green Cnwll 4 F6
Vicarage Devon 14 E5
Vickerstown Cumb 146 C2
Victoria Barns 141 J6
Victoria Blae G 61 J5
Victoria Cnwll 5 G3
Vidlin Shet 281 e5
Viewfield Moray 266 F3
Viewpark N Lans 209 J6
Vigo Kent 52 D6
Village de Putron Guern 9 k3
Ville la Bas Jersey 9 a1
Villiaze Guern 9 i3
Vinehall Street E Susx 24 D3
Vines Cross E Susx 23 K4
Vinters Park Crematorium Kent 39 K2
Virginia Water Surrey 50 C5
Virginstow Devon 11 M4
Vobster Somset 32 B1
Voe Shet 281 d5
Vowchurch Herefs 79 L7
Vulcan Village St Hel 130 B1

W

Waberthwaite Cumb 155 K4
Wackerfield Dur 168 F6
Wacton Norfk 106 D5
Wadborough Worcs 81 K5
Waddesdon Bucks 67 H4
Waddeton Devon 8 C3
Waddicar Sefton 138 E7
Waddingham Lincs 144 B8
Waddington Lancs 148 C7
Waddington Lincs 135 K6
Waddon Devon 13 K6
Waddon Dorset 16 B5
Wadebridge Cnwll 10 D8
Wadeford Somset 30 D8
Wadenhoe Nhants 101 M6
Wadesmill Herts 69 K4
Wadhurst E Susx 39 G7
Wadshelf Derbys 132 F5
Wadswick Wilts 46 B5
Wadworth Donc 142 F8
Waen Denbgs 127 K7
Waen Denbgs 128 D6
Waen Powys 112 C7
Waen Fach Powys 112 B8
Waen-pentir Gwynd 125 K6
Waen-wen Gwynd 125 K6
Wagbeach Shrops 95 J3
Wainfelin Torfn 62 B6
Wainfleet All Saints Lincs 137 J7
Wainfleet Bank Lincs 137 J7
Wainfleet St Mary Lincs 137 J8
Wainford Norfk 107 G5
Wainhouse Corner Cnwll 11 H3
Wainscott Medway 52 F5
Wain's Hill N Som 44 E5
Wainstalls Calder 141 G2
Waitby Cumb 158 C1
Waithe Lincs 145 H7
Wakefield Wakefd 142 A4
Wakefield Crematorium Wakefd 141 M4
Wake Green Birm 98 E6
Wakerley Nhants 101 L3
Wakes Colne Essex 72 C2
Walberswick Suffk 107 K8
Walberton W Susx 21 G5
Walbottle N u Ty 180 E5
Walbutt D & G 175 J1
Walby Cumb 178 B6
Walcombe Somset 31 J2
Walcot Lincs 118 E4
Walcot N Linc 143 M3
Walcot Shrops 95 J6
Walcot Shrops 96 D1
Walcot Swindn 47 H2
Walcot Warwks 82 D4
Walcote Leics 100 C6
Walcot Green Norfk 106 C7
Walcott Lincs 136 B8
Walcott Norfk 123 G5
Walden N York 159 H6
Walden Head N York 159 H6
Walden Stubbs N York 142 E4
Walderslade Medway 53 G6
Walderton W Susx 20 C5
Walditch Dorset 15 L4
Waldley Derbys 115 J4
Waldridge Dur 169 H1
Waldringfield Suffk 91 G6
Waldron E Susx 23 J3
Wales Rothm 133 J3
Wales Somset 31 K6
Walesby Lincs 136 B1
Walesby Notts 134 D5
Walford Herefs 63 H3
Walford Herefs 79 M1
Walford Shrops 113 G7
Walford Staffs 114 C5
Walford Heath Shrops 113 G7
Walgherton Ches E 113 M2
Walgrave Nhants 84 F1
Walhampton Hants 18 E4
Walkden Salfd 139 L7
Walker N u Ty 181 H6
Walkerburn Border 200 D5
Walker Fold Lancs 148 B7
Walkeringham Notts 134 F1
Walkerith Lincs 134 F1
Walkern Herts 69 H2
Walker's Green Herefs 80 C5
Walker's Heath Birm 98 D7
Walkerton Fife 222 C7
Walkford Dorset 18 C5
Walkhampton Devon 7 G1
Walkington E R Yk 152 F8
Walkley Sheff 133 G2
Walk Mill Lancs 140 C2
Walkwood Worcs 82 B2
Wall Nthumb 179 L5
Wall Staffs 98 E2
Wallacetown S Ayrs 183 H2
Wallacetown S Ayrs 196 C6
Wallands Park E Susx 22 F5
Wallasey Wirral 129 G1
Wall End Cumb 156 B6
Wall End Herefs 80 B4
Wallend Medway 53 J4
Waller's Green Herefs 80 F7
Wallhead Cumb 178 B6
Wall Heath Dudley 97 K5
Wall Houses Nthumb 180 C5
Wallingford Oxon 48 F1
Wallington Gt Lon 51 H6
Wallington Hants 19 K2
Wallington Herts 86 F8
Wallington Heath Wsall 98 C3
Wallis Pembks 75 G7
Wallisdown Poole 17 L4
Walliswood Surrey 37 H3
Walls Shet 281 c6
Wallsend N Tyne 181 H5
Wallthwaite Cumb 165 K5
Wall under Haywood Shrops 96 C5
Wallyford E Loth 211 L4
Walmer Kent 41 L5
Walmer Bridge Lancs 138 F3
Walmersley Bury 140 B5
Walmestone Kent 41 H3
Walmley Birm 98 F5
Walmley Ash Birm 98 F5
Walmsgate Lincs 137 G4
Walpole Somset 30 D3
Walpole Suffk 107 H8
Walpole Cross Keys Norfk 120 B7
Walpole Highway Norfk 120 B8
Walpole St Andrew Norfk 120 B8
Walpole St Peter Norfk 120 B8
Walrow Somset 30 E2
Walsall Wsall 98 C4
Walsall Wood Wsall 98 D3
Walsden Calder 140 D3
Walsgrave on Sowe Covtry 99 K7
Walsham le Willows Suffk 89 K1
Walshaw Bury 140 A5
Walshford N York 150 F5
Walsoken Norfk 103 K1
Walston S Lans 199 H4
Walsworth Herts 69 G1
Walter's Ash Bucks 67 K7
Walters Green Kent 38 D5
Walterston V Glam 43 G7
Walterstone Herefs 62 D2
Waltham Kent 40 E5
Waltham NE Lin 145 H7
Waltham Abbey Essex 69 K7
Waltham Chase Hants 35 H7
Waltham Cross Herts 69 K7
Waltham on the Wolds Leics 117 L6
Waltham St Lawrence W & M 49 K4
Waltham's Cross Essex 71 G1
Walthamstow Gt Lon 51 K1
Walton C Pete 102 D3
Walton Cumb 178 C6
Walton Derbys 133 G6
Walton Leeds 150 F6
Walton Leics 100 D6
Walton M Keyn 85 H7
Walton Powys 79 J3
Walton Shrops 95 L7
Walton Somset 31 G4
Walton Staffs 114 D5
Walton Staffs 114 D6
Walton Suffk 91 G8
Walton W Susx 20 D6
Walton Wakefd 142 A4
Walton Warwks 83 G4
Walton Wrekin 113 K7
Walton Cardiff Gloucs 64 C1
Walton East Pembks 55 H2
Walton Elm Dorset 32 C7
Walton Grounds Nhants 83 L8
Walton-in-Gordano N Som 44 E4
Walton Lea Crematorium Warrtn 130 B3
Walton-le-Dale Lancs 139 H2
Walton-on-Thames Surrey 50 E5
Walton-on-the-Hill Staffs 114 F7
Walton on the Hill Surrey 51 G7
Walton on the Naze Essex 73 K3
Walton on the Wolds Leics 117 G7
Walton-on-Trent Derbys 115 L7
Walton Park N Som 44 E4
Walton West Pembks 54 D4
Waltonwrays Crematorium N York 149 H5
Walwen Flints 128 D4
Walwen Flints 128 E4
Walwen Flints 128 E5
Walwick Nthumb 179 L5
Walworth Darltn 169 G7
Walworth Gt Lon 51 J3
Walworth Gate Darltn 169 G6
Walwyn's Castle Pembks 54 E4
Wambrook Somset 15 G1
Wampool Cumb 177 H7
Wanborough Surrey 36 D1
Wanborough Swindn 47 J2
Wandon End Herts 68 E3
Wandsworth Gt Lon 51 H4
Wangford Suffk 107 J7
Wanlip Leics 100 D1
Wanlockhead D & G 186 C4
Wannock E Susx 23 K6
Wansford C Pete 102 B3
Wansford E R Yk 153 G4
Wanshurst Green Kent 39 J4
Wanstead Gt Lon 51 L1
Wanstrow Somset 32 B3
Wanswell Gloucs 63 K6
Wantage Oxon 48 B1
Wants Green Worcs 81 H4
Wapley S Glos 45 L3
Wappenbury Warwks 83 J2
Wappenham Nhants 84 C6
Warbleton E Susx 23 K4
Warborough Oxon 66 F8
Warboys Cambs 102 F7
Warbreck Bpool 146 F8
Warbstow Cnwll 11 H4
Warburton Traffd 130 D2
Warcop Cumb 167 H7
Warden Kent 53 M5
Warden Nthumb 179 L5
Ward End Birm 98 E5
Warden Street C Beds 86 C6
Ward Green Suffk 90 B2
Ward Green Cross Lancs 148 A8
Wardhedges C Beds 85 L8
Wardington Oxon 83 L6
Wardle Ches E 130 B8
Wardle Rochdl 140 D4
Wardley Gatesd 181 H6
Wardley Rutlnd 101 H3
Wardley Salfd 140 A7
Wardlow Derbys 132 D5
Wardsend Ches E 131 J3
Wardy Hill Cambs 103 K7
Ware Herts 69 K4
Wareham Dorset 17 H5
Warehorne Kent 25 J1
Warenford Nthumb 203 J7
Waren Mill Nthumb 203 J6
Warenton Nthumb 203 H7
Wareside Herts 69 K4
Waresley Cambs 86 E4
Waresley Worcs 81 J1
Ware Street Kent 39 K2
Warfield Br For 49 L4
Warfleet Devon 8 C5
Wargate Lincs 119 H5
Wargrave Wokham 49 J3
Warham Herefs 80 B7
Warham All Saints Norfk 121 L3
Warham St Mary Norfk 121 L3
Wark Nthumb 179 K3
Wark Nthumb 202 C5
Warkleigh Devon 27 M6
Warkton Nhants 101 K7
Warkworth Nhants 83 L7
Warkworth Nthumb 191 K5
Warlaby N York 160 E4
Warland Calder 140 E4
Warleggan Cnwll 5 K1
Warleigh BaNES 46 A6
Warley Town Calder 141 G3
Warlingham Surrey 51 K7
Warmbrook Derbys 115 M1
Warmfield Wakefd 142 B4
Warmingham Ches E 130 D7
Warmington Nhants 102 B5
Warmington Warwks 83 K5
Warminster Wilts 32 E2
Warmley S Glos 45 K4
Warmsworth Donc 142 E7
Warmwell Dorset 16 E5
Warndon Worcs 81 K4
Warnford Hants 35 J6
Warnham W Susx 37 J4
Warnham Court W Susx 37 J4
Warningcamp W Susx 21 H5
Warninglid W Susx 37 K5
Warren Ches E 131 H5
Warren Pembks 54 F7
Warrenby R & Cl 170 D5
Warrenhill S Lans 198 F5
Warren Row W & M 49 K3
Warren's Green Herts 69 H2
Warren Street Kent 40 B5
Warrington M Keyn 85 H4
Warrington Warrtn 130 B2
Warriston C Edin 211 H4
Warriston Crematorium C Edin 211 H4
Warsash Hants 19 H2
Warslow Staffs 132 B7
Warsop Vale Notts 133 L6
Warter E R Yk 152 D5
Warthermaske N York 160 B6
Warthill N York 151 L5
Wartling E Susx 24 B5
Wartnaby Leics 117 J7
Warton Lancs 138 E2
Warton Lancs 147 K2
Warton Nthumb 190 E5
Warton Warwks 99 H3
Warwick Warwks 83 G2
Warwick Bridge Cumb 178 B7
Warwick-on-Eden Cumb 178 B7
Warwicksland Cumb 178 B3
Wasbister Ork 275 c3
Wasdale Head Cumb 156 B1
Wash Derbys 131 L3
Washall Green Herts 70 C1
Washaway Cnwll 5 H1
Washbourne Devon 8 B4
Washbrook Somset 30 F1
Washbrook Suffk 90 D6
Washfield Devon 29 G7
Washfold N York 159 J2
Washford Somset 29 J3
Washford Pyne Devon 28 E8
Washingborough Lincs 135 L5
Washington Sundld 181 H7
Washington W Susx 21 J4
Washwood Heath Birm 98 E5
Wasing W Berk 48 E6
Waskerley Dur 168 D2
Wasperton Warwks 83 G3
Wasps Nest Lincs 135 M6
Wass N York 161 J6
Watchet Somset 29 K2
Watchfield Oxon 47 K1
Watchfield Somset 30 E2
Watchgate Cumb 157 H3
Watchill Cumb 165 G2
Watcombe Torbay 8 D2
Watendlath Cumb 165 J7
Water Devon 13 H6
Water Lancs 140 C3
Waterbeach Cambs 87 K2
Waterbeach W Susx 20 E5
Waterbeck D & G 177 H3
Waterden Norfk 121 J4
Water Eaton Oxon 66 D5
Water Eaton Staffs 97 K1
Water End Bed 86 C5
Water End Bed 86 C5
Water End C Beds 85 L7
Waterend Cumb 164 F6
Water End E R Yk 152 B8
Water End Essex 88 B7
Water End Herts 68 D5
Water End Herts 69 G6
Waterfall Staffs 115 H1
Waterfoot E Rens 208 F7
Waterford Herts 69 J4
Water Fryston Wakefd 142 D2
Watergate Cnwll 11 G6
Waterhead Cumb 156 E2
Waterheads Border 200 B3
Waterhouses Dur 168 F3
Waterhouses Staffs 115 H2
Wateringbury Kent 39 H3
Waterlane Gloucs 64 D6
Waterloo Cnwll 10 F8
Waterloo Derbys 133 H7
Waterloo Herefs 79 L5
Waterloo Highld 247 K4
Waterloo N Lans 209 L8
Waterloo Norfk 122 E7
Waterloo P & K 233 G7
Waterloo Pembks 55 G6
Waterloo Poole 17 K4
Waterloo Sefton 138 C8
Waterloo Cross Devon 29 J8
Waterloo Port Gwynd 125 J6
Waterlooville Hants 19 M2
Watermillock Cumb 166 B6
Water Newton Cambs 102 C4
Water Orton Warwks 98 F5
Waterperry Oxon 66 F6
Waterrow Somset 29 J6
Watersfield W Susx 21 G4
Waterside Bl w D 139 L3
Waterside Bucks 68 B7
Waterside Cumb 165 H2
Waterside Donc 143 H5

Waterside E Ayrs 184 C1
Waterside E Ayrs 196 F2
Waterside E Duns 209 H4
Water's Nook Bolton 139 K6
Waterstein Highld 258 A7
Waterstock Oxon 66 F6
Waterston Pembks 54 F5
Water Stratford Bucks 84 C8
Water Street Neath 42 B5
Waters Upton Wrekin 113 K7
Water Yeat Cumb 156 D5
Watford Herts 68 E7
Watford Nhants 84 B2
Wath N York 149 L2
Wath N York 160 D7
Wath upon Dearne Rothm 142 C7
Watlington Norfk 104 C1
Watlington Oxon 67 G8
Watnall Notts 116 E2
Watten Highld 280 B5
Wattisfield Suffk 105 K8
Wattisham Suffk 89 K5
Watton Dorset 15 K4
Watton E R Yk 152 F6
Watton Norfk 105 J3
Watton-at-Stone Herts 69 J3
Watton Green Norfk 105 J3
Wattons Green Essex 70 D8
Wattston N Lans 209 K5
Wattstown Rhondd 42 F3
Wattsville Caerph 43 K3
Wauldby E R Yk 144 B2
Waulkmill Abers 244 E5
Waunarlwydd Swans 57 H6
Waunfawr Cerdgn 92 D7
Waunfawr Gwynd 125 J7
Waungron Swans 57 G4
Waunlwyd Blae G 61 J5
Wavendon M Keyn 85 H7
Waverbridge Cumb 165 H1
Waverton Ches W 129 K7
Waverton Cumb 165 H1
Wawne E R Yk 153 H8
Waxham Norfk 123 J6
Waxholme E R Yk 145 J2
Way Kent 41 K2
Waye Devon 13 H8
Wayford Somset 15 J1
Waytown Dorset 15 L3
Way Village Devon 28 F8
Way Wick N Som 44 D6
Weacombe Somset 29 K3
Weald Oxon 65 L6
Wealdstone Gt Lon 50 F1
Weardley Leeds 150 D7
Weare Somset 44 E8
Weare Giffard Devon 27 H6
Wearhead Dur 167 K3
Wearne Somset 30 F5
Wear Valley Crematorium Dur 169 H4
Weasdale Cumb 158 B2
Weasenham All Saints Norfk 121 J7
Weasenham St Peter Norfk 121 J7
Weaste Salfd 140 B8
Weatheroak Hill Worcs 98 D8
Weaverham Ches W 130 B5
Weaverslake Staffs 115 J7
Weaverthorpe N York 152 E2
Webbington Somset 44 D7
Webb's Heath S Glos 45 K4
Webheath Worcs 82 B2
Webton Herefs 80 A7
Wedderlairs Abers 256 F5
Wedding Hall Fold N York 149 G6
Weddington Kent 41 J3
Weddington Warwks 99 K5
Wedhampton Wilts 46 F7
Wedmore Somset 31 G1
Wednesbury Sandw 98 C4
Wednesfield Wolves 97 L3
Weecar Notts 135 G6
Weedon Bucks 67 K3
Weedon Nhants 84 C3
Weedon Lois Nhants 84 B6
Weeford Staffs 98 F3
Week Devon 8 A2
Week Devon 27 K5
Week Devon 28 C7
Weeke Devon 13 H2
Weeke Hants 34 F5
Weekley Nhants 101 J7
Week St Mary Cnwll 11 J3
Weel E R Yk 153 G7
Weeley Essex 73 H3
Weeley Crematorium Essex 73 H3
Weeley Heath Essex 73 H3
Weem P & K 232 B5
Weeping Cross Staffs 114 E7
Weethley Warwks 82 C4
Weeting Norfk 104 F5
Weeton E R Yk 145 K4
Weeton Lancs 138 D1
Weeton N York 150 C6
Weetwood Leeds 150 C8
Weir Lancs 140 C3
Weirbrook Shrops 112 E6
Weir Quay Devon 6 E2
Weisdale Shet 281 d5
Welborne Norfk 106 B2
Welbourn Lincs 118 C1
Welburn N York 151 M2
Welbury N York 160 F2
Welby Lincs 118 C4
Welches Dam Cambs 103 K6
Welcombe Devon 26 D7
Weldon Bridge Nthumb 191 G6
Welford Nhants 100 E7
Welford W Berk 48 B4
Welford-on-Avon Warwks 82 D5
Welham Leics 101 G5
Welham Notts 134 E3
Welham Green Herts 69 G6
Well Hants 36 A2
Well Lincs 137 H5
Well N York 160 C6
Welland Worcs 81 H7
Wellbank Angus 234 D7
Well End Bucks 49 L1
Well End Herts 69 G7
Wellesbourne Warwks 83 G4
Wellesbourne Mountford Warwks 83 G4
Well Head Herts 68 F2
Well Hill Kent 52 B6
Wellhouse W Berk 48 D4
Welling Gt Lon 51 M4
Wellingborough Nhants 85 H2
Wellingham Norfk 121 J7
Wellingore Lincs 135 K8
Wellington Cumb 155 K2
Wellington Herefs 80 C5
Wellington Somset 29 L6
Wellington Wrekin 96 E1
Wellington Heath Herefs 81 G7
Wellington Marsh Herefs 80 C6
Wellow BaNES 45 L7
Wellow IoW 18 F6
Wellow Notts 134 D6
Wellpond Green Herts 69 L3
Wells Somset 31 J2
Wellsborough Leics 99 K3
Wells Green Ches E 113 M1
Wells Head C Brad 141 G1
Wells-next-the-sea Norfk 121 K3
Wellstye Green Essex 70 F3
Well Town Devon 13 L1
Welltree P & K 221 G3
Wellwood Fife 210 E1
Welney Norfk 103 L4
Welshampton Shrops 113 G4
Welsh Bicknor Herefs 63 H4
Welsh End Shrops 113 H4
Welsh Frankton Shrops 112 E5
Welsh Hook Pembks 74 F6
Welsh Newton Herefs 63 G3
Welshpool Powys 94 F2
Welsh St Donats V Glam 42 F6
Welton Cumb 165 K2
Welton E R Yk 144 B2
Welton Lincs 135 K4
Welton Nhants 84 B2
Welton le Marsh Lincs 137 J6
Welton le Wold Lincs 136 E2
Welwick E R Yk 145 J3
Welwyn Herts 69 G4
Welwyn Garden City Herts 69 G4
Wem Shrops 113 H5
Wembdon Somset 30 D3
Wembley Gt Lon 50 F2
Wembury Devon 7 G5
Wembworthy Devon 12 F1
Wemyss Bay Inver 207 K5
Wenallt Cerdgn 77 J1
Wendens Ambo Essex 87 K8
Wendlebury Oxon 66 E3
Wendling Norfk 105 J1
Wendover Bucks 67 L5
Wendron Cnwll 3 H5
Wendy Cambs 87 G5
Wenfordbridge Cnwll 10 F7
Wenhaston Suffk 107 J8
Wennington Cambs 102 E7
Wennington Gt Lon 52 B3
Wennington Lancs 147 M2
Wensley Derbys 132 E7
Wensley N York 159 K5
Wentbridge Wakefd 142 D4
Wentnor Shrops 95 J5
Wentworth Cambs 103 K7
Wentworth Rothm 142 B8
Wentworth Castle Barns 141 M7
Wenvoe V Glam 43 H7
Weobley Herefs 79 M5
Weobley Marsh Herefs 80 A5
Wepham W Susx 21 H5
Wereham Norfk 104 D3
Wergs Wolves 97 K3
Wern Gwynd 109 K4
Wern Powys 61 H3
Wern Powys 95 G1
Wern Shrops 112 D4
Werneth Low Tamesd 131 J1
Wernffrwd Swans 56 F6
Wern-y-gaer Flints 128 F6
Werrington C Pete 102 D3
Werrington Cnwll 11 L5
Werrington Staffs 114 E2
Wervin Ches W 129 K5
Wesham Lancs 138 E1
Wessex Vale Crematorium Hants 35 G7
Wessington Derbys 133 G8
West Aberthaw V Glam 42 F8
West Acre Norfk 121 G8
West Allerdean Nthumb 202 F4
West Alvington Devon 7 L6
West Amesbury Wilts 33 K3
West Anstey Devon 28 E5
West Appleton N York 160 B4
West Ashby Lincs 136 E5
West Ashling W Susx 20 D5
West Ashton Wilts 46 C7
West Auckland Dur 168 F5
West Ayton N York 163 H5
West Bagborough Somset 30 A4
West Bank Blae G 61 K6
West Bank Halton 129 L3
West Barkwith Lincs 136 C4
West Barnby N York 171 J8
West Barns E Loth 212 E3
West Barsham Norfk 121 K5
West Bay Dorset 15 K4
West Beckham Norfk 122 C4
West Bedfont Surrey 50 D4
Westbere Kent 41 G3
West Bergholt Essex 72 D2
West Berkshire Crematorium W Berk 48 D5
West Bexington Dorset 15 M5
West Bilney Norfk 120 F8
West Blatchington Br & H 22 D6
West Boldon S Tyne 181 J6
Westborough Lincs 117 M3
Westbourne Bmouth 17 L4
Westbourne W Susx 20 B5
West Bourton Dorset 32 C5
West Bowling C Brad 141 J2
West Brabourne Kent 40 E6
West Bradenham Norfk 105 J2
West Bradford Lancs 148 C7
West Bradley Somset 31 J3
West Bretton Wakefd 141 L5
West Bridgford Notts 117 G4
West Briscoe Dur 168 B6
West Bromwich Sandw 98 C5
West Bromwich Crematorium Sandw 98 C5
Westbrook Kent 41 K1
Westbrook W Berk 48 B4
Westbrook Wilts 46 D5
West Buckland Devon 28 B4
West Buckland Somset 30 B6
West Burton N York 159 H5
West Burton W Susx 21 G4
Westbury Bucks 84 B8
Westbury Shrops 95 J2
Westbury Wilts 46 C8
Westbury Leigh Wilts 32 E1
Westbury on Severn Gloucs 63 L4
Westbury-on-Trym Bristl 45 H3
Westbury-sub-Mendip Somset 31 H1
West Butsfield Dur 168 E2
West Butterwick N Linc 143 L6
Westby Lancs 138 D2
West Byfleet Surrey 50 D6
West Cairngaan D & G 172 E8
West Caister Norfk 107 K1
West Calder W Loth 210 D6
West Camel Somset 31 J6
West Chaldon Dorset 16 E6
West Challow Oxon 48 A1
West Charleton Devon 7 L6
West Chelborough Dorset 15 M2
West Chevington Nthumb 191 J6
West Chiltington W Susx 21 J3
West Chinnock Somset 31 G8
West Chisenbury Wilts 47 H8
West Clandon Surrey 50 D8
West Cliffe Kent 41 K6
Westcliff-on-Sea Sthend 53 J2
West Coker Somset 31 H8
West Combe Devon 7 L2
Westcombe Somset 31 L3
West Compton Somset 31 K2
West Compton Abbas Dorset 16 A4
Westcote Gloucs 65 J3
Westcote Barton Oxon 66 B2
Westcott Bucks 67 H4
Westcott Devon 14 B2
Westcott Surrey 37 H1
West Cottingwith N York 151 L7
Westcourt Wilts 47 J6
West Cowick E R Yk 143 G3
West Cross Swans 57 H7
West Curry Cnwll 11 K4
West Curthwaite Cumb 165 K1
Westdean E Susx 23 J7
West Dean W Susx 20 E4
West Dean Wilts 34 B5
West Deeping Lincs 102 C2
West Derby Lpool 129 J1
West Dereham Norfk 104 D3
West Ditchburn Nthumb 191 G2
West Down Devon 27 J3
Westdown Camp Wilts 33 H2
Westdowns Cnwll 10 F6
West Drayton Gt Lon 50 D3
West Drayton Notts 134 D5
West Dunnet Highld 280 B2
Wested Kent 52 B5
West Ella E R Yk 144 C2
West End Bed 85 J4
West End Br For 49 L5
West End Caerph 43 K3
West End Cambs 87 G2
West End Cumb 177 K7
West End E R Yk 144 A2
West End E R Yk 144 F2
West End E R Yk 145 H2
Westend Gloucs 64 A5
West End Hants 34 F7
West End Hants 35 K4
West End Herts 69 H5
West End Herts 69 J6
West End Lancs 139 L2
West End Leeds 150 B8
West End Lincs 145 K8
West End N Som 44 F5
West End N York 151 H7
West End Norfk 105 H2
West End Norfk 107 K1
West End Oxon 48 E2
West End S Glos 45 L1
West End Somset 31 L4
West End Surrey 50 B6
West End Surrey 50 E6
West End W & M 49 K4
West End W Susx 22 B4
West End Wilts 32 F6
West End Wilts 33 G6
West End Wilts 46 E3
West End Green Hants 49 G6
Westend Town Nthumb 179 H6
Westenhanger Kent 40 F7
Westerdale Highld 279 K6
Westerdale N York 161 L2
Westerfield Suffk 90 E5
Westergate W Susx 20 F6
Westerham Kent 51 L8
Westerhope N u Ty 180 F5
Westerland Devon 8 C2
Westerleigh S Glos 45 K3
Westerleigh Crematorium S Glos 45 L3
Western Isles W Isls 282 e6
Wester Ochiltree W Loth 210 D4
Wester Pitkierie Fife 223 K6
Westerton W Susx 20 E5
Westerton of Rossie Angus 235 G4
Westerwick Shet 281 c6
West Ewell Surrey 51 G6
West Farleigh Kent 39 H3
West Farndon Nhants 83 M5
West Felton Shrops 112 E6
Westfield BaNES 45 K8
Westfield Cumb 164 C5
Westfield E Susx 24 E4
Westfield Highld 279 J3
Westfield N Lans 209 J4
Westfield Norfk 105 K2
Westfield W Loth 210 B4
Westfields Dorset 16 D2
Westfields Herefs 80 C7
Westfields of Rattray P & K 233 J6
Westfield Sole Kent 53 G6
West Flotmanby N York 163 K6
Westford Somset 29 L6
Westgate Dur 167 L3
Westgate N Linc 143 K6
Westgate Norfk 121 L3

Westgate Hill C Brad 141 K2
Westgate on Sea Kent 41 K1
Westgate Street Norfk 122 D7
West Ginge Oxon 48 C2
West Grafton Wilts 47 K7
West Green Hants 49 H7
West Grimstead Wilts 33 L5
West Grinstead W Susx 37 J6
West Haddlesey N York 142 E2
West Haddon Nhants 84 C1
West Hagbourne Oxon 48 D2
West Hagley Worcs 97 K7
Westhall Suffk 107 J7
West Hallam Derbys 116 D3
West Hallam Common Derbys 116 C3
West Halton N Linc 144 A4
Westham Dorset 16 C6
Westham E Susx 23 L6
West Ham Gt Lon 51 K2
Westham Somset 30 F2
Westhampnett W Susx 20 E5
West Handley Derbys 133 H4
West Hanney Oxon 66 B8
West Hanningfield Essex 71 H7
West Harnham Wilts 33 K5
West Harptree BaNES 45 H7
West Harting W Susx 20 C3
West Hatch Somset 30 D6
West Hatch Wilts 32 F5
West Haven Angus 234 E8
Westhay Somset 31 G2
Westhead Lancs 138 F6
West Head Norfk 104 B2
West Heath Birm 98 C7
West Heath Hants 48 E7
West Helmsdale Highld 274 D5
West Hendred Oxon 48 C1
West Hertfordshire Crematorium Herts 68 E6
West Heslerton N York 163 G7
West Hewish N Som 44 D6
Westhide Herefs 80 D6
Westhill Abers 245 J2
West Hill Devon 14 C4
West Hoathly W Susx 38 A6
West Holme Dorset 17 G5
Westholme Somset 31 J3
Westhope Herefs 80 B5
Westhope Shrops 95 L6
West Horndon Essex 52 D1
Westhorp Nhants 83 L5
Westhorpe Lincs 119 H5
Westhorpe Suffk 90 B2
West Horrington Somset 31 J2
West Horsley Surrey 50 D8
West Horton Nthumb 203 G7
West Hougham Kent 41 H7
Westhoughton Bolton 139 K6
Westhouse N York 157 L7
Westhouses Derbys 133 H8
West Howe Bmouth 17 L3
West Howetown Somset 29 G4
Westhumble Surrey 50 F8
West Huntingtower P & K 221 K2
West Huntspill Somset 30 D2
West Hyde C Beds 68 E4
West Hyde Herts 50 C1
West Hythe Kent 40 F8
West Ilkerton Devon 28 C2
West Ilsley W Berk 48 C3
West Itchenor W Susx 20 C6
West Keal Lincs 137 G7
West Kennett Wilts 47 G5
West Kilbride N Ayrs 195 K1
West Kingsdown Kent 52 C6
West Kington Wilts 46 A3
West Kirby Wirral 128 F2
West Knapton N York 162 F7
West Knighton Dorset 16 D5
West Knoyle Wilts 32 E4
West Kyloe Nthumb 203 G5
Westlake Devon 7 J4
West Lambrook Somset 30 F7
Westland Green Herts 70 B3
West Langdon Kent 41 K6
West Lavington W Susx 20 E3
West Lavington Wilts 46 E8
West Layton N York 168 F8
West Leake Notts 116 E6
West Learmouth Nthumb 202 C5
West Lees N York 161 G2
West Leigh Devon 13 G2
Westleigh Devon 27 H5
Westleigh Devon 29 J7
West Leigh Somset 29 L5
Westleton Suffk 91 K2
West Lexham Norfk 121 J8
Westley Shrops 95 J2
Westley Suffk 89 G2
Westley Waterless Cambs 88 C4
West Lilling N York 151 K3
Westlington Bucks 67 J5
West Linton Border 199 K3
Westlinton Cumb 177 L6
West Littleton S Glos 45 M4
West Lockinge Oxon 48 B2
West London Crematorium Gt Lon 51 G3
West Lulworth Dorset 16 F6
West Lutton N York 152 E2
West Lydford Somset 31 J4
West Lyn Devon 28 C1
West Lyng Somset 30 D5
West Lynn Norfk 120 D7
West Malling Kent 52 E7
West Malvern Worcs 81 H6
West Marden W Susx 20 C4
West Markham Notts 134 E5
Westmarsh Kent 41 J3
West Marsh NE Lin 145 H5
West Marton N York 148 F5
West Melbury Dorset 32 E6
West Melton Rothm 142 C7
West Meon Hants 35 K6
West Meon Hut Hants 35 K5
West Meon Woodlands Hants 35 K5
West Mersea Essex 72 E4
Westmeston E Susx 22 E4
West Mickley Nthumb 180 C6
Westmill Herts 69 J4
Westmill Herts 69 K2
West Milton Dorset 15 L3
Westminster Gt Lon 51 J3
West Minster Kent 53 K4
West Molesey Surrey 50 E5
West Monkton Somset 30 C5
West Moors Dorset 17 L2
West Morden Dorset 17 H3
West Morriston Border 201 J5
West Morton C Brad 149 K7
West Mudford Somset 31 J6
Westmuir Angus 234 A5
West Ness N York 162 B6
West Newbiggin Darltn 169 K7
Westnewton Cumb 164 F2
West Newton E R Yk 153 K8
West Newton Norfk 120 F6
West Newton Somset 30 D5
West Norwood Gt Lon 51 J4
West Norwood Crematorium Gt Lon 51 J4
Westoe S Tyne 181 J5
West Ogwell Devon 13 J8
Weston BaNES 45 L5
Weston Ches E 114 A1
Weston Devon 14 D3
Weston Devon 14 E5
Weston Dorset 16 D8
Weston Halton 129 L3
Weston Hants 35 M6
Weston Herefs 79 L4
Weston Herts 69 H1
Weston Lincs 119 J6
Weston N York 149 M6
Weston Nhants 84 B6
Weston Notts 134 F6
Weston Shrops 95 H8
Weston Shrops 96 D5
Weston Shrops 112 D6
Weston Staffs 114 F6
Weston W Berk 48 B4
Weston Beggard Herefs 80 D7
Westonbirt Gloucs 46 B1
Weston by Welland Nhants 101 G5
Weston Colley Hants 35 G3
Weston Colville Cambs 88 C4
Weston Corbett Hants 35 L2
Weston Coyney C Stke 114 E3
Weston Favell Nhants 84 F3
Weston Green Cambs 88 C5
Weston Heath Shrops 97 H1
Weston Hills Lincs 119 J7
Weston in Arden Warwks 99 K6
Westoning C Beds 85 K8
Weston-in-Gordano N Som 44 F4
Westoning Woodend C Beds 68 C1
Weston Jones Staffs 114 B6
Weston Longville Norfk 122 C8
Weston Lullingfields Shrops 112 F6
Weston Mill Crematorium C Plym 6 F3
Weston-on-Avon Warwks 82 E5
Weston-on-the-Green Oxon 66 D3
Weston Patrick Hants 35 L2
Weston Rhyn Shrops 112 D4
Weston-sub-Edge Gloucs 82 D7
Weston-super-Mare N Som 44 C6
Weston-super-Mare Crematorium N Som 44 D6
Weston Turville Bucks 67 K5
Weston-under-Lizard Staffs 97 H1
Weston under Penyard Herefs 63 J3
Weston-under-Redcastle Shrops 113 J5
Weston under Wetherley Warwks 83 J1
Weston Underwood Derbys 115 M3
Weston Underwood M Keyn 85 G5
Weston-upon-Trent Derbys 116 C6
Westonzoyland Somset 30 E4
West Orchard Dorset 32 D7
West Overton Wilts 47 H5
Westow N York 152 A3
West Panson Devon 11 L4
West Park Abers 245 H4
West Parley Dorset 17 L3
West Peckham Kent 39 G3
West Peeke Devon 11 L4
West Pelton Dur 180 F8
West Pennard Somset 31 J3
West Pentire Cnwll 4 C3
West Perry Cambs 86 C2
West Porlock Somset 28 F2
Westport Somset 30 F6
West Pulham Dorset 16 D1
West Putford Devon 26 F7
West Quantoxhead Somset 29 K3
Westquarter Falk 210 B3
Westra V Glam 43 J7
West Raddon Devon 13 L2
West Rainton Dur 169 J1
West Rasen Lincs 135 L2
West Ravendale NE Lin 145 G7
Westray Ork 275 c2
West Raynham Norfk 121 J6
West Retford Notts 134 D3
Westridge Green W Berk 48 E3
Westrigg W Loth 210 B5
West Road Crematorium N u Ty 180 F6
Westrop Swindn 65 J8
West Rounton N York 160 F2
West Row Suffk 104 D8
West Rudham Norfk 121 H6
West Runton Norfk 122 D3
Westruther Border 201 K3
Westry Cambs 103 H4
West Saltoun E Loth 212 A5
West Sandford Devon 13 J2
West Sandwick Shet 281 e3
West Scrafton N York 159 K6
West Sleekburn Nthumb 181 G2
West Somerton Norfk 123 K7
West Stafford Dorset 16 D5
West Stockwith Notts 134 F1
West Stoke W Susx 20 D5
West Stonesdale N York 158 F2
West Stoughton Somset 30 F1
West Stour Dorset 32 C6
West Stourmouth Kent 41 H3
West Stow Suffk 89 G1
West Stowell Wilts 47 H6
West Stratton Hants 35 H3
West Street Kent 40 A4
West Street Kent 41 K4
West Street Medway 52 F4
West Street Suffk 89 K1
West Suffolk Crematorium Suffk 89 G2
West Tanfield N York 160 C7
West Taphouse Cnwll 5 K2
West Tarbert Ag & B 206 D5
West Tarring W Susx 21 J6
West Thirston Nthumb 191 H6
West Thorney W Susx 20 C6
Westthorpe Derbys 133 J4
West Thorpe Notts 117 G6
West Thurrock Thurr 52 C3
West Tilbury Thurr 52 E3
West Tisted Hants 35 K5
West Torrington Lincs 136 B3
West Town BaNES 45 G6
West Town Hants 20 B7
West Town Herefs 80 B3
West Town N Som 44 F5
West Town Somset 31 J4
West Town Somset 32 B3
West Tytherley Hants 34 C5
West Walton Norfk 103 K1
West Walton Highway Norfk 103 K1
Westward Cumb 165 J2
Westward Ho! Devon 27 G5
Westwell Kent 40 C6
Westwell Oxon 65 J5
Westwell Leacon Kent 40 C5
West Wellow Hants 34 C7
West Wembury Devon 7 G5
West Wemyss Fife 222 E8
Westwick Cambs 87 J2
Westwick Dur 168 D7
West Wick N Som 44 D6
Westwick Norfk 122 F6
West Wickham Cambs 88 C5
West Wickham Gt Lon 51 K5
West Williamston Pembks 55 H5
West Wiltshire Crematorium Wilts 46 C7
West Winch Norfk 120 E8
West Winterslow Wilts 34 B4
West Wittering W Susx 20 C7
West Witton N York 159 J5
Westwood Devon 14 B3
Westwood Kent 41 K2
Westwood Kent 52 D5
Westwood Notts 116 D1
Westwood Nthumb 179 H6
Westwood Wilts 46 A7
West Woodburn Nthumb 179 K2
West Woodhay W Berk 48 B6
Westwood Heath Covtry 99 H8
West Woodlands Somset 32 C2
Westwoodside N Linc 143 J7
West Worldham Hants 35 M3
West Worthing W Susx 21 K6
West Wratting Cambs 88 C5
West Wycombe Bucks 67 K8
West Wylam Nthumb 180 D6
West Yatton Wilts 46 B4
West Yoke Kent 52 D5
West Youlstone Cnwll 26 D7
Wetham Green Kent 53 H5
Wetheral Cumb 178 B7
Wetherby Leeds 150 F6
Wetherden Suffk 89 K3
Wetheringsett Suffk 90 D2
Wethersfield Essex 71 H1
Wetherup Street Suffk 90 D2
Wetley Rocks Staffs 114 F2
Wettenhall Ches E 130 C7
Wetton Staffs 132 B8
Wetwang E R Yk 152 E4
Wetwood Staffs 114 B5
Wexcombe Wilts 47 K7
Wexham Slough 50 C3
Wexham Street Bucks 50 C2
Weybourne Norfk 122 C3
Weybourne Surrey 36 C1
Weybread Suffk 106 E7
Weybread Street Suffk 106 E7
Weybridge Surrey 50 D6
Weycroft Devon 15 G3
Weydale Highld 279 L3
Weyhill Hants 34 D2
Weymouth Dorset 16 C6
Weymouth Crematorium Dorset 16 C6
Whaddon Bucks 84 F8
Whaddon Cambs 87 G6
Whaddon Gloucs 64 B4
Whaddon Wilts 33 L5
Whaddon Wilts 46 C6
Whale Cumb 166 C6
Whaley Derbys 133 K5
Whaley Bridge Derbys 131 K3
Whaley Thorns Derbys 133 K5
Whaligoe Highld 280 D8
Whalley Lancs 148 C8
Whalley Banks Lancs 139 L1
Whalsay Shet 281 f5
Whalton Nthumb 180 D3
Whaplode Lincs 119 K6
Whaplode Drove Lincs 103 G1
Wharf Warwks 83 K5
Wharfe N York 148 D2
Wharles Lancs 147 J8
Wharley End C Beds 85 J6
Wharncliffe Side Sheff 132 F1
Wharram-le-Street N York 152 C3
Wharton Ches W 130 C6
Wharton Herefs 80 C4
Whashton N York 159 L2
Whasset Cumb 157 H6
Whatcote Warwks 83 G6
Whateley Warwks 99 G3
Whatfield Suffk 89 L6
Whatley Somset 15 H1
Whatley Somset 32 B2
Whatley's End S Glos 45 K3
Whatlington E Susx 24 D4
Whatsole Street Kent 40 F6
Whatstandwell Derbys 116 B1
Whatton Notts 117 K4
Whauphill D & G 173 K5
Whaw N York 159 H2
Wheal Rose Cnwll 4 B6
Wheatacre Norfk 107 J4
Wheatfield Oxon 67 G7
Wheathampstead Herts 68 F4
Wheathill Shrops 96 E7
Wheathill Somset 31 J5

Wheatley Calder 141 G3
Wheatley Hants 36 A3
Wheatley Oxon 66 E6
Wheatley Hill Dur 169 K3
Wheatley Hills Donc 142 F6
Wheatley Lane Lancs 148 E8
Wheaton Aston Staffs 97 J1
Wheatsheaf Wrexhm 112 D1
Wheddon Cross Somset 29 G3
Wheelbarrow Town Kent 40 F6
Wheeler End Bucks 67 K8
Wheeler's Green Wokham 49 J4
Wheeler's Street Kent 39 L4
Wheelerstreet Surrey 36 E3
Wheelock Ches E 130 E7
Wheelock Heath Ches E 130 E8
Wheelton Lancs 139 J3
Wheldale Wakefd 142 C3
Wheldrake C York 151 L6
Whelford Gloucs 65 H7
Whelpley Hill Bucks 68 C6
Whelpo Cumb 165 J3
Whelston Flints 128 F4
Whempstead Herts 69 J3
Whenby N York 151 K2
Whepstead Suffk 89 G4
Wherstead Suffk 90 E7
Wherwell Hants 34 E3
Wheston Derbys 132 C4
Whetsted Kent 39 G4
Whetstone Gt Lon 69 H8
Whetstone Leics 100 C4
Wheyrigg Cumb 165 G1
Whicham Cumb 155 L6
Whichford Warwks 83 H8
Whickham Gatesd 180 F6
Whiddon Devon 12 B3
Whiddon Down Devon 13 G4
Whight's Corner Suffk 90 D6
Whigstreet Angus 234 D6
Whilton Nhants 84 C2
Whimble Devon 11 L2
Whimple Devon 14 B3
Whimpwell Green Norfk 123 H5
Whinburgh Norfk 105 K2
Whin Lane End Lancs 147 H7
Whinnie Liggate D & G 175 H4
Whinnow Cumb 177 J8
Whinnyfold Abers 257 K5
Whinny Hill S on T 169 K7
Whippingham IoW 19 H5
Whipsnade C Beds 68 C3
Whipton Devon 13 M4
Whirlow Sheff 132 F3
Whisby Lincs 135 H6
Whissendine Rutlnd 117 L8
Whissonsett Norfk 121 K7
Whistlefield Ag & B 218 C8
Whistlefield Inn Ag & B 217 J8
Whistley Green Wokham 49 J4
Whiston Knows 129 L2
Whiston Nhants 85 G3
Whiston Rothm 133 J2
Whiston Staffs 114 D8
Whiston Staffs 115 G2
Whiston Cross Shrops 97 H3
Whiston Eaves Staffs 115 G2
Whitacre Fields Warwks 99 H5
Whitbeck Cumb 155 K5
Whitbourne Herefs 81 G4
Whitburn S Tyne 181 K6
Whitburn W Loth 210 C6
Whitby Ches W 129 J4
Whitby N York 171 K8
Whitbyheath Ches W 129 J5
Whitchester Border 212 F7
Whitchurch BaNES 45 J5
Whitchurch Bucks 67 J3
Whitchurch Cardif 43 J5
Whitchurch Devon 12 C8
Whitchurch Hants 34 F1
Whitchurch Herefs 63 H4
Whitchurch Oxon 48 F3
Whitchurch Pembks 74 C7
Whitchurch Shrops 113 J3
Whitchurch Canonicorum
Dorset 15 J3
Whitchurch Hill Oxon 48 F3
Whitcombe Dorset 16 D5
Whitcot Shrops 95 J5
Whitcott Keysett Shrops 95 G6
Whiteacre Kent 40 E5
Whiteacre Heath Warwks 99 G5
Whiteash Green Essex 71 J1
White Ball Somset 29 K7
Whitebridge Highld 250 E8
Whitebrook Mons 63 G6
Whitecairns Abers 257 G8
Whitechapel Gt Lon 51 J3
White Chapel Lancs 147 L7
Whitechurch Pembks 75 K5
Whitecliffe Gloucs 63 H5
White Colne Essex 72 C1
White Coppice Lancs 139 J4
Whitecraig E Loth 211 K5
Whitecroft Gloucs 63 J6
Whitecrook D & G 172 F3
Whitecross Cnwll 2 E4
White Cross Cnwll 3 H6
Whitecross Cnwll 10 D8
Whitecross Falk 210 C4
White End Worcs 81 H8
Whiteface Highld 263 J2
Whitefarland N Ayrs 194 D3
Whitefaulds S Ayrs 183 H1
Whitefield Bury 140 B6
Whitefield Devon 28 C4
Whitefield Somset 29 K5
Whitefield Lane End Knows 129 K2
Whiteford Abers 256 C6
Whitegate Ches W 130 C6
Whitehall Hants 49 H8
Whitehall Ork 275 e3
Whitehall W Susx 37 H6
Whitehaven Cumb 164 C7
Whitehill Kent 40 C3
Whitehill Leics 99 L1
Whitehill and Bordon Hants 36 A4
Whitehills Abers 268 B3
Whitehouse Abers 256 A8
Whitehouse Ag & B 206 C6
Whitehouse Common Birm 98 E4
Whitekirk E Loth 212 D3
White Kirkley Dur 168 C3
White Lackington Dorset 16 D3
Whitelackington Somset 30 F7
White Ladies Aston Worcs 81 L4
Whiteleaf Bucks 67 K6
White-le-Head Dur 180 E7
Whiteley Hants 19 J2
Whiteley Bank IoW 19 J7
Whiteley Green Ches E 131 H4
Whiteley Village Surrey 50 E6
Whitemans Green W Susx 22 D2
White Mill Carmth 58 E4
Whitemire Moray 253 J1
Whitemoor C Nott 116 F3
Whitemoor Cnwll 5 G3
Whitemoor Derbys 116 B2
Whitemoor Staffs 131 H7
Whiteness Shet 281 d6
White Notley Essex 71 J3
Whiteoak Green Oxon 65 M4
White Ox Mead BaNES 45 L7
Whiteparish Wilts 34 B6
White Pit Lincs 137 G4
Whiterashes Abers 256 F7
White Roding Essex 70 E4
Whiterow Highld 280 E6
Whiterow Moray 265 G8
Whiteshill Gloucs 64 B5
Whitesmith E Susx 23 J4
White Stake Lancs 139 G3
Whitestaunton Somset 30 D8
Whitestone Devon 13 K4
White Stone Herefs 80 D6
Whitestone Cross Devon 13 L4
Whitestreet Green Suffk 89 K7
Whitewall Corner N York 152 B2
White Waltham W & M 49 K3
Whiteway BaNES 45 L6
Whiteway Gloucs 64 C5
Whitewell Lancs 148 B6
Whiteworks Devon 12 E8
Whitfield C Dund 234 C8
Whitfield Kent 41 J6
Whitfield Nhants 84 B7
Whitfield Nthumb 179 H7
Whitfield S Glos 63 K8
Whitfield Hall Nthumb 179 H7
Whitford Devon 14 F3
Whitford Flints 128 D4
Whitgift E R Yk 143 K3
Whitgreave Staffs 114 D6
Whithorn D & G 174 C6
Whiting Bay N Ayrs 195 G6
Whitkirk Leeds 142 B1
Whitland Carmth 55 L3
Whitlaw Border 188 E4
Whitletts S Ayrs 196 D6
Whitley N York 142 E4
Whitley Readg 49 H5
Whitley Sheff 133 G1
Whitley Wilts 46 C5
Whitley Bay N Tyne 181 J4
Whitley Bay Crematorium
N Tyne 181 J4
Whitley Chapel Nthumb 179 L7
Whitley Heath Staffs 114 C6
Whitley Lower Kirk 141 K4
Whitley Row Kent 38 D3
Whitlock's End Solhll 98 E8
Whitminster Gloucs 63 M5
Whitmore Dorset 17 L1
Whitmore Staffs 114 C3
Whitnage Devon 29 J7
Whitnash Warwks 83 H3
Whitney-on-Wye Herefs 79 J5
Whitrigg Cumb 165 G3
Whitrigg Cumb 177 H7
Whitrigglees Cumb 177 H7
Whitsbury Hants 33 K7
Whitsome Border 202 D3
Whitson Newpt 44 D2
Whitstable Kent 40 E2
Whitstone Cnwll 11 K3
Whittingham Nthumb 190 F4
Whittingslow Shrops 95 K5
Whittington Derbys 133 H4
Whittington Gloucs 64 E3
Whittington Lancs 157 K7
Whittington Norfk 104 E3
Whittington Shrops 112 E5
Whittington Staffs 97 J6
Whittington Staffs 98 F2
Whittington Warwks 99 J4
Whittington Worcs 81 K4
Whittington Moor Derbys 133 G5
Whittlebury Nhants 84 D6
Whittle-le-Woods Lancs 139 H3
Whittlesey Cambs 102 F4
Whittlesford Cambs 87 K5
Whittlestone Head Bl w D 139 L4
Whitton N Linc 143 M3
Whitton Nthumb 190 F6
Whitton Powys 79 J2
Whitton S on T 169 K6
Whitton Shrops 80 D1
Whitton Suffk 90 D5
Whittonditch Wilts 47 L4
Whittonstall Nthumb 180 C7
Whitway Hants 48 C7
Whitwell Derbys 133 K4
Whitwell Herts 68 F3
Whitwell IoW 19 J8
Whitwell N York 160 D3
Whitwell Rutlnd 101 K2
Whitwell-on-the-Hill N York 151 M3
Whitwell Street Norfk 122 B7
Whitwick Leics 116 D8
Whitwood Wakefd 142 B3
Whitworth Lancs 140 D4
Whixall Shrops 113 H4
Whixley N York 150 F4
Whorlton Dur 168 E7
Whorlton N York 161 G2
Whyle Herefs 80 D3
Whyteleafe Surrey 51 J7
Wibdon Gloucs 63 H7
Wibsey C Brad 141 J2
Wibtoft Warwks 100 B6
Wichenford Worcs 81 H3
Wichling Kent 40 B4
Wick Bmouth 18 B5
Wick Devon 14 E2
Wick Highld 280 E6
Wick S Glos 45 K4
Wick Somset 30 B2
Wick Somset 30 F5
Wick V Glam 42 D7
Wick W Susx 21 H6
Wick Wilts 33 L6
Wick Worcs 81 M6
Wicken Cambs 88 B1
Wicken Nhants 84 E7
Wicken Bonhunt Essex 87 K8
Wickenby Lincs 136 A3
Wick End Bed 85 K5
Wicken Green Village Norfk 121 J5
Wickersley Rothm 133 J2
Wicker Street Green Suffk 89 K6
Wickford Essex 71 H8
Wickham Hants 19 K2
Wickham W Berk 48 B5
Wickham Bishops Essex 71 K5
Wickhambreaux Kent 41 H3
Wickhambrook Suffk 88 E4
Wickhamford Worcs 82 C7
Wickham Green Suffk 90 C2
Wickham Green W Berk 48 B4
Wickham Heath W Berk 48 B5
Wickham Market Suffk 91 G4
Wickhampton Norfk 107 J2
Wickham St Paul Essex 89 G7
Wickham Skeith Suffk 90 C2
Wickham Street Suffk 88 F4
Wickham Street Suffk 90 C1
Wicklewood Norfk 106 B3
Wickmere Norfk 122 D5
Wick St Lawrence N Som 44 D6
Wickstreet E Susx 23 J5
Wickwar S Glos 45 L1
Widdington Essex 70 D1
Widdop Calder 140 D1
Widdrington Nthumb 191 K7
Widdrington Station Nthumb 191 J7
Widecombe in the Moor
Devon 13 G7
Widegates Cnwll 6 B3
Widemouth Bay Cnwll 11 H2
Wide Open N Tyne 181 G4
Widford Essex 71 G6
Widford Herts 70 B4
Widham Wilts 47 G1
Widley Hants 19 M2
Widmer End Bucks 67 L7
Widmerpool Notts 117 G6
Widmore Gt Lon 51 L5
Widnes Halton 129 L3
Widnes Crematorium Halton 129 L2
Widworthy Devon 14 F3
Wigan Wigan 139 H6
Wigan Crematorium Wigan 139 H7
Wigborough Somset 31 G7
Wiggaton Devon 14 C4
Wiggenhall St Germans Norfk 120 D8
Wiggenhall St Mary Magdalen
Norfk 104 B1
Wiggenhall St Mary the
Virgin Norfk 104 B1
Wiggens Green Essex 88 D6
Wiggenstall Staffs 132 B7
Wiggington Shrops 112 E4
Wigginton C York 151 J4
Wigginton Herts 68 B5
Wigginton Oxon 83 J8
Wigginton Staffs 99 G2
Wigginton Bottom Herts 68 B5
Wigglesworth N York 148 E4
Wiggonby Cumb 177 J8
Wiggonholt W Susx 21 H3
Wighill N York 151 G6
Wighton Norfk 121 L3
Wightwick Wolves 97 K4
Wigley Derbys 132 F5
Wigley Hants 34 D7
Wigmore Herefs 80 A2
Wigmore Medway 53 G6
Wigsley Notts 135 G5
Wigsthorpe Nhants 102 A6
Wigston Leics 100 D4
Wigston Fields Leics 100 D3
Wigston Parva Leics 100 A5
Wigthorpe Notts 134 B3
Wigtoft Lincs 119 J4
Wigton Cumb 165 H1
Wigtown D & G 174 C4
Wigtwizzle Sheff 141 L8
Wike Leeds 150 D7
Wilbarston Nhants 101 H5
Wilberfoss E R Yk 151 M5
Wilburton Cambs 103 K8
Wilby Nhants 85 G2
Wilby Norfk 105 L5
Wilby Suffk 90 F1
Wilcot Wilts 47 H6
Wilcott Shrops 112 F7
Wilcrick Newpt 44 E2
Wilday Green Derbys 132 F5
Wildboarclough Ches E 131 K6
Wilden Bed 86 B4
Wilden Worcs 81 J1
Wilde Street Suffk 104 D7
Wildhern Hants 34 D1
Wildhill Herts 69 H5
Wildmanbridge S Lans 209 L8
Wildmoor Worcs 98 B8
Wildsworth Lincs 143 K8
Wilford C Nott 116 F4
Wilford Hill Crematorium
Notts 116 F4
Wilkesley Ches E 113 K3
Wilkhaven Highld 264 E3
Wilkieston W Loth 210 F5
Wilkin's Green Herts 69 G5
Wilksby Lincs 136 E7
Willand Devon 29 J8
Willards Hill E Susx 24 C2
Willaston Ches E 113 L1
Willaston Ches W 129 H4
Willen M Keyn 85 G7
Willenhall Covtry 99 K8
Willenhall Wsall 98 B4
Willerby E R Yk 144 C2
Willerby N York 163 H6
Willersey Gloucs 82 D7
Willersley Herefs 79 K6
Willesborough Kent 40 D7
Willesborough Lees Kent 40 D7
Willesden Gt Lon 51 G2

Willesleigh Devon 27 L4
Willesley Wilts 46 B1
Willett Somset 29 K4
Willey Shrops 96 F3
Willey Warwks 100 B6
Willey Green Surrey 50 B8
Williamscot Oxon 83 L6
Williamstown Rhondd 42 F4
Willian Herts 69 G1
Willicote Warwks 82 E5
Willingale Essex 70 E5
Willingdon E Susx 23 K6
Willingham Cambs 87 H1
Willingham by Stow Lincs 135 H3
Willingham Green Cambs 88 C4
Willington Bed 86 C5
Willington Derbys 116 A6
Willington Dur 169 G4
Willington Kent 39 K3
Willington Warwks 83 G7
Willington Corner Ches W 129 M6
Willington Quay N Tyne 181 H5
Willitoft E R Yk 143 J1
Williton Somset 29 K3
Willoughby Lincs 137 J5
Willoughby Warwks 83 M2
Willoughby Hills Lincs 119 K2
Willoughby-on-the-Wolds Notts 117 H6
Willoughby Waterleys Leics 100 C5
Willoughton Lincs 135 J1
Willow Green Ches W 130 B4
Willows Green Essex 71 H3
Willsbridge S Glos 45 K5
Willsworthy Devon 12 D6
Willtown Somset 30 F6
Wilmcote Warwks 82 E4
Wilmington BaNES 45 K6
Wilmington Devon 14 F3
Wilmington E Susx 23 J6
Wilmington Kent 52 B4
Wilmslow Ches E 131 G3
Wilnecote Staffs 99 G3
Wilpshire Lancs 139 K1
Wilsden C Brad 149 K8
Wilsford Lincs 118 D3
Wilsford Wilts 33 K3
Wilsford Wilts 47 G7
Wilsham Devon 28 D1
Wilshaw Kirk 141 H6
Wilsill N York 150 A3
Wilsley Green Kent 39 K6
Wilsley Pound Kent 39 K6
Wilson Herefs 63 H2
Wilson Leics 116 C6
Wilsontown S Lans 198 F2
Wilstead Bed 85 L6
Wilsthorpe Lincs 102 B1
Wilstone Herts 67 L4
Wilstone Green Herts 67 M4
Wilton Cumb 164 D8
Wilton Herefs 63 H2
Wilton N York 162 F6
Wilton R & Cl 170 D6
Wilton Wilts 33 J4
Wilton Wilts 47 K6
Wilton Dean Border 188 E3
Wimbish Essex 88 B7
Wimbish Green Essex 88 C8
Wimbledon Gt Lon 51 G5
Wimblington Cambs 103 J5
Wimboldsley Ches W 130 D7
Wimborne Minster Dorset 17 K3
Wimborne St Giles Dorset 33 H8
Wimbotsham Norfk 104 C2
Wimpole Cambs 87 G5
Wimpstone Warwks 82 F5
Wincanton Somset 32 B5
Winceby Lincs 136 F6
Wincham Ches W 130 C4
Winchburgh W Loth 210 E4
Winchcombe Gloucs 64 F2
Winchelsea E Susx 25 G4
Winchelsea Beach E Susx 25 G4
Winchester Hants 35 G5
Winchet Hill Kent 39 J5
Winchfield Hants 49 J8
Winchmore Hill Bucks 68 B8
Winchmore Hill Gt Lon 69 J8
Wincle Ches E 131 J6
Wincobank Sheff 133 G1
Winder Cumb 164 D7
Windermere Cumb 156 F3
Winderton Warwks 83 H7
Windhill Highld 250 F2
Windlehurst Stockp 131 J3
Windlesham Surrey 50 A6
Windmill Cnwll 10 B7
Windmill Derbys 132 C4
Windmill Hill E Susx 23 L5
Windmill Hill Somset 30 D7
Windrush Gloucs 65 J4
Windsole Abers 267 L4
Windsor W & M 50 B4
Windsoredge Gloucs 64 B7
Windsor Green Suffk 89 H4
Windy Arbour Warwks 83 G1
Windygates Fife 222 F7
Windyharbour Ches E 131 G5
Windy Hill Wrexhm 129 G8
Wineham W Susx 22 C3
Winestead E R Yk 145 J3
Winewall Lancs 148 F7
Winfarthing Norfk 106 C6
Winford IoW 19 J6
Winford N Som 45 G6
Winforton Herefs 79 K6
Winfrith Newburgh Dorset 16 F5
Wing Bucks 67 L3
Wing Rutlnd 101 K3
Wingate Dur 169 L3
Wingates Bolton 139 K6
Wingates Nthumb 191 G7
Wingerworth Derbys 133 G6
Wingfield C Beds 68 C2
Wingfield Suffk 106 E7
Wingfield Wilts 46 B7
Wingfield Green Suffk 106 E7
Wingham Kent 41 H4
Wingmore Kent 41 G6
Wingrave Bucks 67 L3
Winkburn Notts 134 E7
Winkfield Br For 49 L4
Winkfield Row Br For 49 L5
Winkhill Staffs 115 H1
Winkhurst Green Kent 38 D3
Winkleigh Devon 12 F1
Winksley N York 150 C2
Winkton Dorset 18 B4
Winlaton Gatesd 180 E6
Winlaton Mill Gatesd 180 E6
Winless Highld 280 D5
Winllan Powys 112 C7
Winmarleigh Lancs 147 J6
Winnall Hants 35 G5
Winnersh Wokham 49 J5
Winnington Ches W 130 C5
Winscales Cumb 164 D5
Winscombe N Som 44 E7
Winsford Ches W 130 C6
Winsford Somset 28 F4
Winsham Devon 27 J3
Winsham Somset 15 J2
Winshill Staffs 115 M7
Winshwen Swans 57 J5
Winskill Cumb 166 D4
Winslade Hants 35 K1
Winsley Wilts 46 A6
Winslow Bucks 67 J2
Winson Gloucs 65 G5
Winsor Hants 34 D8
Winster Cumb 156 F4
Winster Derbys 132 E7
Winston Dur 168 F7
Winston Suffk 90 E3
Winstone Gloucs 64 D5
Winswell Devon 27 J8
Winterborne Came Dorset 16 D5
Winterborne Clenston Dorset 17 G2
Winterborne Herringston Dorset 16 D5
Winterborne Houghton Dorset 16 F2
Winterborne Kingston Dorset 17 G3
Winterborne Monkton Dorset 16 C5
Winterborne Stickland Dorset 16 F2
Winterborne Tomson Dorset 17 G3
Winterborne Whitechurch Dorset 17 G3
Winterborne Zelston Dorset 17 H3
Winterbourne S Glos 45 J3
Winterbourne W Berk 48 C4
Winterbourne Abbas Dorset 16 B4
Winterbourne Bassett Wilts 47 G4
Winterbourne Dauntsey Wilts 33 L4
Winterbourne Earls Wilts 33 L4
Winterbourne Gunner Wilts 33 L4
Winterbourne Monkton Wilts 47 G4
Winterbourne Steepleton Dorset 16 B4
Winterbourne Stoke Wilts 33 J3
Winterbrook Oxon 48 F1
Winterburn N York 149 G4
Winteringham N Linc 144 A3
Winterley Ches E 130 E8
Wintersett Wakefd 142 B4
Winterslow Wilts 34 B4
Winterton N Linc 144 A4
Winterton-on-Sea Norfk 123 K7
Winthorpe Lincs 137 K6
Winthorpe Notts 135 G8
Winton Bmouth 17 L4
Winton Cumb 167 H8
Winton E Susx 23 H6
Winton N York 160 F3
Wintringham N York 162 F8
Winwick Cambs 102 B7
Winwick Nhants 100 D8
Winwick Warrtn 130 B1
Wirksworth Derbys 115 M1
Wirswall Ches E 113 J3
Wisbech Cambs 103 J2
Wisbech St Mary Cambs 103 J2
Wisborough Green W Susx 37 G5
Wiseman's Bridge Pembks 55 K5
Wiseton Notts 134 E2
Wishanger Gloucs 64 D5
Wishaw N Lans 209 L7
Wishaw Warwks 98 F4
Wisley Surrey 50 D7
Wispington Lincs 136 D5
Wissenden Kent 40 B7
Wissett Suffk 107 H7
Wissington Norfk 104 D4
Wissington Suffk 89 J8
Wistanstow Shrops 95 K6
Wistanswick Shrops 113 L5
Wistaston Ches E 113 L1
Wistaston Green Ches E 130 D8
Wisterfield Ches E 131 G5
Wiston Pembks 55 H3
Wiston S Lans 198 F6
Wiston W Susx 21 K4
Wistow Cambs 102 F7
Wistow Leics 100 E4
Wistow N York 142 F1
Wiswell Lancs 148 C8
Witcham Cambs 103 J7
Witchampton Dorset 17 J2
Witchford Cambs 103 K7
Witcombe Somset 31 G6
Witham Essex 71 K4
Witham Friary Somset 32 B3
Witham on the Hill Lincs 118 D8
Witham St Hughs Lincs 135 H7
Withcall Lincs 136 E3
Withdean Br & H 22 D5
Witherenden Hill E Susx 23 L2
Witheridge Devon 28 D8
Witherley Leics 99 J4
Withern Lincs 137 H3
Withernsea E R Yk 145 J2
Withernwick E R Yk 153 K7
Withersdale Street Suffk 106 F7
Withersfield Suffk 88 D5
Witherslack Cumb 156 F5
Withiel Cnwll 5 G2
Withiel Florey Somset 29 H4
Withielgoose Cnwll 5 G2
Withington Gloucs 64 F4
Withington Herefs 80 D6
Withington Manch 131 G1
Withington Shrops 96 D1
Withington Staffs 115 G4
Withington Green Ches E 130 F5
Withington Marsh Herefs 80 D6
Withleigh Devon 28 F8
Withnell Lancs 139 J3
Withybed Green Worcs 82 B1
Withybrook Warwks 99 L6
Withycombe Somset 29 J3
Withyham E Susx 38 D6
Withy Mills BaNES 45 K7
Withypool Somset 28 E4
Withywood Bristl 45 H5
Witley Surrey 36 E3
Witnesham Suffk 90 E5
Witney Oxon 65 M5
Wittering C Pete 102 B3
Wittersham Kent 25 G2
Witton Birm 98 D5
Witton Norfk 107 G2
Witton Norfk 123 G5
Witton Gilbert Dur 169 G2
Witton Green Norfk 107 J3
Witton le Wear Dur 168 F4
Witton Park Dur 168 F4
Wiveliscombe Somset 29 K5
Wivelrod Hants 35 K3
Wivelsfield E Susx 22 E3
Wivelsfield Green E Susx 22 E3
Wivelsfield Station W Susx 22 E3
Wivenhoe Essex 72 F3
Wivenhoe Cross Essex 72 F2
Wiveton Norfk 122 A3
Wix Essex 73 H2
Wixford Warwks 82 C4
Wix Green Essex 73 H2
Wixhill Shrops 113 J6
Wixoe Suffk 88 E6
Woburn C Beds 85 J8
Woburn Sands M Keyn 85 H8
Wokefield Park W Berk 49 G6
Woking Surrey 50 C7
Woking Crematorium Surrey 50 B7
Wokingham Wokham 49 K5
Wolborough Devon 13 K8
Woldingham Surrey 51 K7
Wold Newton E R Yk 163 J8
Wold Newton NE Lin 145 G8
Wolfclyde S Lans 199 H6
Wolferlow Herefs 80 F3
Wolferton Norfk 120 E6
Wolfhampcote Warwks 83 M2
Wolfhill P & K 233 H8
Wolf Hills Nthumb 179 G7
Wolf's Castle Pembks 74 F6
Wolfsdale Pembks 54 F3
Wollaston Dudley 97 K6
Wollaston Nhants 85 H3
Wollaston Shrops 95 H1
Wollaton C Nott 116 E4
Wolleigh Devon 13 J6
Wollerton Shrops 113 K5
Wollescote Dudley 97 L6
Wolseley Bridge Staffs 115 G7
Wolsingham Dur 168 D3
Wolstanton Staffs 114 D2
Wolstenholme Rochdl 140 C5
Wolston Warwks 99 L8
Wolsty Cumb 176 E8
Wolvercote Oxon 66 D5
Wolverhampton Wolves 97 K4
Wolverley Shrops 113 G5
Wolverley Worcs 97 J7
Wolverton Hants 48 E7
Wolverton Kent 41 H6
Wolverton M Keyn 84 F7
Wolverton Warwks 82 F3
Wolverton Wilts 32 C4
Wolverton Common Hants 48 E7
Wolvesnewton Mons 62 F7
Wolvey Warwks 99 L6
Wolvey Heath Warwks 99 L5
Wolviston S on T 170 B5
Wombleton N York 161 L6
Wombourne Staffs 97 K5
Wombwell Barns 142 B7
Womenswold Kent 41 H5
Womersley N York 142 E4
Wonastow Mons 62 F5
Wonersh Surrey 36 F2
Wonford Devon 13 L4
Wonson Devon 12 F5
Wonston Dorset 16 E1
Wonston Hants 35 G3
Wooburn Bucks 49 M2
Wooburn Green Bucks 49 M1
Wooburn Moor Bucks 49 M1
Woodacott Devon 11 M1
Woodale N York 159 J6
Woodall Rothm 133 J3
Woodbastwick Norfk 123 G8
Woodbeck Notts 134 F4
Wood Bevington Warwks 82 C4
Woodborough Notts 117 G2
Woodborough Wilts 47 G7
Woodbridge Devon 14 E4
Woodbridge Dorset 32 E7
Woodbridge Suffk 91 G5
Wood Burcote Nhants 84 D6
Woodbury Devon 14 B5
Woodbury Salterton Devon 14 B5
Woodchester Gloucs 64 B6
Woodchurch Kent 40 B8
Woodchurch Wirral 129 G2
Woodcombe Somset 29 G2
Woodcote Gt Lon 51 J6
Woodcote Oxon 48 F3
Woodcote Wrekin 114 B8
Woodcote Green Worcs 81 L1
Woodcott Hants 48 B7
Woodcroft Gloucs 63 G7
Woodcutts Dorset 33 G7
Wood Dalling Norfk 122 B6
Woodditton Cambs 88 D3
Woodeaton Oxon 66 D5
Wood Eaton Staffs 114 C7
Wooden Pembks 55 J6
Wood End Bed 85 K6
Wood End Bed 86 B2
Wood End Cambs 103 H8
Wood End Gt Lon 50 E3
Wood End Herts 69 J2
Woodend Highld 228 B3
Woodend Nhants 84 B5
Woodend Staffs 115 K6
Woodend W Loth 210 B5
Woodend W Susx 20 D5
Wood End Warwks 82 D1

Wood End Warwks 99 H4
Wood End Warwks 99 J6
Wood End Wolves 97 L3
Wood Enderby Lincs 136 E6
Woodend Green Essex 70 E2
Woodfalls Wilts 33 L6
Woodford Cnwll 26 C8
Woodford Devon 8 B5
Woodford Gloucs 63 K7
Woodford Gt Lon 69 L8
Woodford Nhants 101 L8
Woodford Stockp 131 H3
Woodford Bridge Gt Lon 51 L1
Woodford Halse Nhants 84 A5
Woodford Wells Gt Lon 69 L8
Woodgate Birm 98 C6
Woodgate Devon 29 K7
Woodgate Norfk 121 K8
Woodgate Norfk 121 M8
Woodgate W Susx 20 F6
Woodgate Worcs 81 M2
Wood Green Gt Lon 51 J1
Woodgreen Hants 33 L7
Woodgreen Oxon 66 A5
Woodhall N York 159 H4
Woodhall Hill Leeds 141 K1
Woodhall Spa Lincs 136 C7
Woodham Bucks 67 H3
Woodham Dur 169 H5
Woodham Surrey 50 D6
Woodham Ferrers Essex 71 J7
Woodham Mortimer Essex 71 K6
Woodham Walter Essex 71 K5
Wood Hayes Wolves 97 L3
Woodhead Abers 256 E4
Woodhill Shrops 97 G6
Woodhill Somset 30 E5
Woodhorn Nthumb 181 H1
Woodhorn Demesne Nthumb 181 H1
Woodhouse Leeds 141 L1
Woodhouse Leics 116 F8
Woodhouse Sheff 133 H3
Woodhouse Wakefd 142 B3
Woodhouse Eaves Leics 116 F8
Woodhouse Green Staffs 131 H7
Woodhouselee Mdloth 211 H6
Woodhouselees D & G 177 L4
Woodhouse Mill Sheff 133 H3
Woodhouses Cumb 177 K8
Woodhouses Oldham 140 D7
Woodhouses Staffs 98 D2
Woodhouses Staffs 115 J7
Woodhuish Devon 8 D4
Woodhurst Cambs 103 G8
Woodingdean Br & H 22 E6
Woodkirk Leeds 141 L3
Woodland Abers 256 F7
Woodland Devon 7 J4
Woodland Devon 8 B1
Woodland Dur 168 D5
Woodland Kent 40 F7
Woodland S Ayrs 182 F4
Woodland Head Devon 13 H3
Woodlands Abers 245 H4
Woodlands Donc 142 E6
Woodlands Dorset 17 L1
Woodlands Hants 18 E1
Woodlands Kent 52 C6
Woodlands N York 150 D5
Woodlands Somset 29 L3
Woodlands (Coleshill) Crematorium Warwks 98 F5
Woodlands Park W & M 49 L3
Woodlands St Mary W Berk 47 M4
Woodlands (Scarborough) Crematorium N York 163 J5
Woodlands (Scunthorpe) Crematorium N Linc 143 M5
Woodland Street Somset 31 J3
Woodland View Sheff 132 F2
Wood Lane Shrops 112 F5
Wood Lane Staffs 114 C2
Woodleigh Devon 7 L5
Woodlesford Leeds 142 B2
Woodley Stockp 131 J1
Woodley Wokham 49 J4
Woodmancote Gloucs 63 M7
Woodmancote Gloucs 64 E2
Woodmancote Gloucs 64 E5
Woodmancote W Susx 20 C5
Woodmancote W Susx 22 C4
Woodmancote Worcs 81 L6
Woodmancott Hants 35 H2
Woodmansey E R Yk 153 G8
Woodmansgreen W Susx 36 C5
Woodmansterne Surrey 51 H7
Woodmanton Devon 14 B5
Woodmarsh Wilts 46 B7
Woodmill Staffs 115 J7
Woodminton Wilts 33 H6
Woodnesborough Kent 41 J4
Woodnewton Nhants 102 A4
Woodnook Notts 116 D1
Wood Norton Norfk 121 M6
Woodplumpton Lancs 139 G1
Woodrising Norfk 105 K3
Wood Row Leeds 142 B2
Woodrow Worcs 97 K8
Wood's Corner E Susx 24 B3
Woods Eaves Herefs 79 K5
Woodseaves Shrops 113 M5
Woodseaves Staffs 114 B6
Woodsend Wilts 47 J4
Woodsetts Rothm 133 L3
Woodsford Dorset 16 E4
Wood's Green E Susx 39 G6
Woodside Br For 50 B5
Woodside Cumb 164 D4
Woodside Essex 70 C6
Woodside Fife 223 G5
Woodside Gt Lon 51 J5
Woodside Hants 18 E5
Woodside Herts 69 H5
Woodside P & K 233 J7
Woodside Green Kent 40 B4
Woodstock Oxon 66 C4
Woodstock Pembks 75 H7
Woodston C Pete 102 D4
Wood Street Norfk 123 H7
Wood Street Village Surrey 36 E1
Woodthorpe Derbys 133 J5
Woodthorpe Leics 116 F8
Woodthorpe Lincs 137 H4
Woodton Norfk 106 F4
Woodtown Devon 27 G6
Woodvale Sefton 138 C5
Woodvale Crematorium Br & H 22 E6
Woodville Derbys 116 A7
Woodwall Green Staffs 114 B5
Wood Walton Cambs 102 E7
Woodyates Dorset 33 H7
Woody Bay Devon 28 B1
Woofferton Shrops 80 C2
Wookey Somset 31 H2
Wookey Hole Somset 31 H2
Wool Dorset 17 G5
Woolacombe Devon 27 H2
Woolage Green Kent 41 H5
Woolage Village Kent 41 H5
Woolaston Gloucs 63 H7
Woolaston Common Gloucs 63 H6
Woolavington Somset 30 E3
Woolbeding W Susx 36 C6
Woolbrook Devon 14 D5
Woolcotts Somset 29 H4
Wooldale Kirk 141 J6
Wooler Nthumb 202 F7
Woolfardisworthy Devon 13 J1
Woolfardisworthy Devon 26 F6
Woolfold Bury 140 B5
Woolfords S Lans 199 G2
Woolhampton W Berk 48 E5
Woolhope Herefs 80 E8
Woolland Dorset 16 E1
Woollard BaNES 45 J6
Woollensbrook Herts 69 K5
Woolley BaNES 45 L5
Woolley Cambs 102 C8
Woolley Cnwll 26 D7
Woolley Derbys 133 G7
Woolley Wakefd 141 M5
Woolley Bridge Derbys 131 K1
Woolley Green W & M 49 K3
Woolmere Green Worcs 81 M3
Woolmer Green Herts 69 H3
Woolmerston Somset 30 D4
Woolminstone Somset 15 J1
Woolpack Kent 39 L6
Woolpit Suffk 89 K3
Woolpit Green Suffk 89 K3
Woolscott Warwks 83 L2
Woolsgrove Devon 13 J2
Woolsington N u Ty 180 F5
Woolstaston Shrops 95 L4
Woolsthorpe Lincs 117 L5
Woolsthorpe-by-Colsterworth Lincs 118 B6
Woolston C Sotn 19 G2
Woolston Devon 7 L5
Woolston Devon 7 L6
Woolston Shrops 95 K6
Woolston Shrops 112 D6
Woolston Somset 29 K3
Woolston Somset 31 L5
Woolston Warrtn 130 C2
Woolstone Gloucs 64 D1
Woolstone M Keyn 85 G7
Woolstone Oxon 47 L2
Woolston Green Devon 8 A2
Woolton Lpool 129 K2
Woolton Hill Hants 48 B6
Woolverstone Suffk 90 E7
Woolverton Somset 46 A8
Woolwich Gt Lon 51 L3
Woonton Herefs 79 L5
Woonton Herefs 80 D3
Wooperton Nthumb 190 F2
Woore Shrops 114 A3
Wootten Green Suffk 90 F1
Wootton Bed 85 K6
Wootton Hants 18 C4
Wootton Herefs 79 L5
Wootton IoW 19 J5
Wootton Kent 41 H6
Wootton N Linc 144 D4
Wootton Nhants 84 E4
Wootton Oxon 66 B3
Wootton Oxon 66 C6
Wootton Shrops 112 E6
Wootton Staffs 114 C6
Wootton Staffs 115 H3
Wootton Bassett Wilts 46 F3
Wootton Bridge IoW 19 J5
Wootton Broadmead Bed 85 K6
Wootton Common IoW 19 J5
Wootton Courtenay Somset 29 G2
Wootton Fitzpaine Dorset 15 J3
Wootton Rivers Wilts 47 J6
Wootton St Lawrence Hants 48 E8
Wootton Wawen Warwks 82 E3
Worcester Worcs 81 K4
Worcester Park Gt Lon 51 G6
Wordsley Dudley 97 K6
Worfield Shrops 97 G4
Worgret Dorset 17 H5
Workhouse End Bed 86 B5
Workington Cumb 164 D5
Worksop Notts 134 B4
Worlaby Lincs 136 F4
Worlaby N Linc 144 C5
Worlds End Bucks 67 L5
Worlds End Hants 19 L1
World's End W Berk 48 C3
Worlds End W Susx 22 E3
Worle N Som 44 D6
Worleston Ches E 130 C8
Worlingham Suffk 107 J5
Worlington Devon 28 D8
Worlington Suffk 104 D8
Worlingworth Suffk 90 F2
Wormald Green N York 150 D3
Wormbridge Herefs 62 E1
Wormegay Norfk 104 D1
Wormelow Tump Herefs 62 F1
Wormhill Derbys 132 C5
Wormhill Herefs 80 A7
Wormingford Essex 72 D1
Worminghall Bucks 66 F5
Wormington Gloucs 82 B7
Worminster Somset 31 J2
Wormit Fife 223 G2
Wormleighton Warwks 83 K4
Wormley Herts 69 K6
Wormley Surrey 36 E3
Wormleybury Herts 69 K6
Wormley Hill Donc 143 G4
Wormshill Kent 39 M2
Wormsley Herefs 80 A5
Worplesdon Surrey 50 B8
Worrall Sheff 132 F1
Worrall Hill Gloucs 63 J4
Worsbrough Barns 142 A7
Worsbrough Bridge Barns 142 A7
Worsbrough Dale Barns 142 B7
Worsley Salfd 139 M7
Worstead Norfk 122 F6
Worsthorne Lancs 140 C1
Worston Devon 7 H4
Worston Lancs 148 D7
Worth Kent 41 K4
Worth Somset 31 H2
Worth W Susx 37 L4
Wortham Suffk 106 B7
Worthen Shrops 95 H2
Worthenbury Wrexhm 112 F2
Worthing Norfk 121 M7
Worthing W Susx 21 K6
Worthing Crematorium W Susx 21 J5
Worthington Leics 116 C7
Worth Matravers Dorset 17 J7
Worthybrook Mons 62 F5
Worting Hants 48 F8
Wortley Barns 141 M7
Wortley Leeds 141 L1
Worton N York 159 G5
Worton Wilts 46 E7
Wortwell Norfk 106 F6
Wotherton Shrops 95 G3
Wothorpe C Pete 101 M2
Wotter Devon 7 H3
Wotton Surrey 37 H2
Wotton-under-Edge Gloucs 63 M8
Wotton Underwood Bucks 67 G4
Woughton on the Green M Keyn 85 G7
Wouldham Kent 52 F6
Woundale Shrops 97 H5
Wrabness Essex 73 J1
Wrafton Devon 27 J4
Wragby Lincs 136 B4
Wragby Wakefd 142 C4
Wramplingham Norfk 106 C2
Wrangaton Devon 7 K3
Wrangbrook Wakefd 142 D5
Wrangle Lincs 119 M2
Wrangle Common Lincs 119 M1
Wrangle Lowgate Lincs 119 M1
Wrangway Somset 29 L7
Wrantage Somset 30 D6
Wrawby N Linc 144 C6
Wraxall N Som 44 F4
Wraxall Somset 31 K4
Wray Lancs 147 M2
Wray Castle Cumb 156 E3
Wraysbury W & M 50 C4
Wrayton Lancs 147 M2
Wrea Green Lancs 138 E2
Wreaks End Cumb 156 B5
Wreay Cumb 166 B1
Wreay Cumb 166 B6
Wrecclesham Surrey 36 B2
Wrekenton Gatesd 181 G7
Wrelton N York 162 D5
Wrenbury Ches E 113 K2
Wrench Green N York 163 H5
Wreningham Norfk 106 D4
Wrentham Suffk 107 K6
Wrenthorpe Wakefd 141 M3
Wrentnall Shrops 95 K3
Wressle E R Yk 143 H2
Wressle N Linc 144 B6
Wrestlingworth C Beds 86 E5
Wretton Norfk 104 D3
Wrexham Wrexhm 112 E2
Wribbenhall Worcs 97 H8
Wrickton Shrops 96 E6
Wrightington Bar Lancs 139 G5
Wright's Green Essex 70 D4
Wrinehill Staffs 114 B2
Wrington N Som 44 F6
Writhlington BaNES 45 K8
Writtle Essex 71 G6
Wrockwardine Wrekin 96 E1
Wroot N Linc 143 H7
Wrose C Brad 149 L8
Wrotham Kent 52 D7
Wrotham Heath Kent 52 D7
Wrottesley Staffs 97 J3
Wroughton Swindn 47 H3
Wroxall IoW 19 J7
Wroxall Warwks 82 F1
Wroxeter Shrops 96 D2
Wroxham Norfk 122 F8
Wroxton Oxon 83 K7
Wyaston Derbys 115 K3
Wyatt's Green Essex 70 F7
Wyberton East Lincs 119 K3
Wyberton West Lincs 119 J3
Wyboston Bed 86 D4
Wybunbury Ches E 113 M2
Wychbold Worcs 81 L2
Wych Cross E Susx 38 C7
Wychnor Staffs 115 K8
Wyck Hants 35 M3
Wyck Rissington Gloucs 65 J3
Wycliffe Dur 168 E7
Wycoller Lancs 149 G8
Wycomb Leics 117 K6
Wycombe Marsh Bucks 67 L8
Wyddial Herts 69 K1
Wye Kent 40 D6
Wyesham Mons 63 G5
Wyfordby Leics 117 L7
Wyke C Brad 141 J2
Wyke Devon 13 K3
Wyke Devon 15 G3
Wyke Dorset 32 D5
Wyke Shrops 96 E3
Wyke Surrey 50 A8
Wyke Champflower Somset 31 L4
Wykeham N York 163 H6
Wyken Covtry 99 K7
Wyken Shrops 97 H4
Wyke Regis Dorset 16 C7
Wykey Shrops 112 F6
Wykin Leics 99 L4
Wylam Nthumb 180 D6
Wylde Green Birm 98 E4

Wylye Wilts ... 33 H3
Wymeswold Leics ... 117 G6
Wymington Bed ... 85 J2
Wymondham Leics ... 117 M7
Wymondham Norfk ... 106 C3
Wyndham Brdgnd ... 42 E3
Wynford Eagle Dorset ... 16 B3
Wynyard Park S on T ... 169 L5
Wynyard Village S on T ... 169 L5
Wyre Forest Crematorium Worcs ... 97 J8
Wyre Piddle Worcs ... 81 M5
Wysall Notts ... 117 G6
Wyson Herefs ... 80 C2
Wythall Worcs ... 98 D8
Wytham Oxon ... 66 C5
Wythburn Cumb ... 165 K7
Wythenshawe Manch ... 131 G2
Wythop Mill Cumb ... 165 G5
Wyton Cambs ... 86 F1
Wyton E R Yk ... 144 F1
Wyverstone Suffk ... 90 B2
Wyverstone Street Suffk ... 89 L2
Wyville Lincs ... 118 A5

Y

Yaddlethorpe N Linc ... 143 M6
Yafford IoW ... 19 G7
Yafforth N York ... 160 E4
Yalberton Torbay ... 8 C3
Yalding Kent ... 39 H3
Yanwath Cumb ... 166 C5
Yanworth Gloucs ... 65 G4
Yapham E R Yk ... 152 B5
Yapton W Susx ... 21 G6
Yarborough N Som ... 44 D7
Yarbridge IoW ... 19 K6
Yarburgh Lincs ... 136 F1
Yarcombe Devon ... 14 F1
Yard Devon ... 28 D6
Yardley Birm ... 98 E6
Yardley Crematorium Birm ... 98 E6
Yardley Gobion Nhants ... 84 E6
Yardley Hastings Nhants ... 85 G4
Yardley Wood Birm ... 98 E7
Yardro Powys ... 79 J3
Yarford Somset ... 30 B5
Yarkhill Herefs ... 80 E6
Yarley Somset ... 31 H2
Yarlington Somset ... 31 L5
Yarm S on T ... 169 L8
Yarmouth IoW ... 18 E5
Yarnacott Devon ... 27 L5
Yarnbrook Wilts ... 46 C7
Yarner Devon ... 13 H7
Yarnfield Staffs ... 114 D5
Yarnscombe Devon ... 27 K6
Yarnton Oxon ... 66 C5
Yarpole Herefs ... 80 B2
Yarrow Border ... 200 D7
Yarrow Somset ... 30 E2
Yarrow Feus Border ... 200 D7
Yarrowford Border ... 200 E7
Yarsop Herefs ... 80 A6
Yarwell Nhants ... 102 B4
Yate S Glos ... 45 L3
Yateley Hants ... 49 K6
Yatesbury Wilts ... 46 F4
Yattendon W Berk ... 48 E4
Yatton Herefs ... 80 A2
Yatton N Som ... 44 E6
Yatton Keynell Wilts ... 46 C4
Yaverland IoW ... 19 K6
Yawl Devon ... 15 H4
Yawthorpe Lincs ... 135 H1
Yaxham Norfk ... 105 K1
Yaxley Cambs ... 102 D5
Yaxley Suffk ... 106 C8
Yazor Herefs ... 79 M6
Yeading Gt Lon ... 50 E3
Yeadon Leeds ... 150 B7
Yealand Conyers Lancs ... 157 H7
Yealand Redmayne Lancs ... 157 H7
Yealand Storrs Lancs ... 157 H7
Yealmbridge Devon ... 7 H4
Yealmpton Devon ... 7 H4
Yearby R & Cl ... 170 E6
Yearngill Cumb ... 164 F2
Yearsley N York ... 161 J7
Yeaton Shrops ... 113 G7
Yeaveley Derbys ... 115 K3
Yeavering Nthumb ... 202 E7
Yedingham N York ... 162 F6
Yelford Oxon ... 66 A6
Yell Shet ... 281 e3
Yelland Devon ... 27 J4
Yelling Cambs ... 86 F3
Yelvertoft Nhants ... 100 D8
Yelverton Devon ... 7 G1
Yelverton Norfk ... 106 F3
Yenston Somset ... 32 B6
Yeoford Devon ... 13 H3
Yeolmbridge Cnwll ... 11 L5
Yeo Mill Devon ... 28 E5
Yeo Vale Devon ... 27 G6
Yeovil Somset ... 31 J7
Yeovil Crematorium Somset ... 31 H7
Yeovil Marsh Somset ... 31 J7
Yeovilton Somset ... 31 J6
Yerbeston Pembks ... 55 H5
Yesnaby Ork ... 275 b4
Yetlington Nthumb ... 190 E4
Yetminster Dorset ... 31 K8
Yetson Devon ... 8 B4
Yettington Devon ... 14 B5
Yetts o'Muckhart Clacks ... 221 H6
Yews Green C Brad ... 141 H2
Yew Tree Sandw ... 98 C4
Y Felinheli Gwynd ... 125 J6
Y Ferwig Cerdgn ... 75 L2
Y Ffor Gwynd ... 109 G4
Y Gyffylliog Denbgs ... 128 C8
Yielden Bed ... 85 K2
Yieldingtree Worcs ... 97 K7
Yieldshields S Lans ... 198 E3
Yiewsley Gt Lon ... 50 D3
Y Maerdy Conwy ... 111 K3
Y Nant Wrexhm ... 112 D2
Ynysboeth Rhondd ... 43 G3
Ynysddu Caerph ... 43 J3
Ynysforgan Swans ... 57 J5
Ynyshir Rhondd ... 42 F3
Ynyslas Cerdgn ... 92 D5
Ynysmaerdy Rhondd ... 42 F5
Ynysmeudwy Neath ... 57 K4
Ynystawe Swans ... 57 J5
Ynyswen Powys ... 60 C4
Ynyswen Rhondd ... 42 E2
Ynysybwl Rhondd ... 43 G3
Ynysymaengwyn Gwynd ... 92 D3
Yockenthwaite N York ... 158 F6
Yockleton Shrops ... 95 K2
Yokefleet E R Yk ... 143 K3
Yoker C Glas ... 208 E5
York C York ... 151 J5
York Lancs ... 139 L1
York City Crematorium C York ... 151 J6
Yorkletts Kent ... 40 E3
Yorkley Gloucs ... 63 J5
York Town Surrey ... 49 L7
Yorton Heath Shrops ... 113 H7
Youlgreave Derbys ... 132 D6
Youlthorpe E R Yk ... 152 B5
Youlton N York ... 151 G3
Youngsbury Herts ... 69 K3
Young's End Essex ... 71 H3
Yoxall Staffs ... 115 J7
Yoxford Suffk ... 91 J2
Y Rhiw Gwynd ... 108 D6
Ysbyty Cynfyn Cerdgn ... 93 G7
Ysbyty Ifan Conwy ... 110 F2
Ysbyty Ystwyth Cerdgn ... 77 K1
Ysceifiog Flints ... 128 D5
Ysgubor-y-Coed Cerdgn ... 92 E4
Ystalyfera Neath ... 57 L3
Ystrad Rhondd ... 42 F3
Ystrad Aeron Cerdgn ... 76 F4
Ystradfellte Powys ... 60 D4
Ystrad Ffin Carmth ... 77 L6
Ystradgynlais Powys ... 60 B5
Ystrad Meurig Cerdgn ... 77 K2
Ystrad Mynach Caerph ... 43 J3
Ystradowen V Glam ... 42 F6
Ystumtuen Cerdgn ... 92 F7
Ythanbank Abers ... 257 G5
Ythanwells Abers ... 256 B4
Ythsie Abers ... 256 F5

Z

Zeal Monachorum Devon ... 13 G2
Zeals Wilts ... 32 C4
Zelah Cnwll ... 4 C4
Zennor Cnwll ... 2 C3
Zoar Cnwll ... 3 J7
Zouch Notts ... 116 E6

EXCLUSIVE

Better than half-price offer with this atlas

AA DRIVER READY KIT

Only £29.99* (£69.99 RRP)

Includes FREE P&P**

How To Purchase:

Visit **theAA.com/shop/driver** add the kit to your shopping basket, then enter the promotional code: **DRIVER** to receive your discount.

*Terms and conditions
Offer only available at theAA.com/shop/driver in conjunction with AA 2014 Road Atlases and when the promotion code DRIVER has been entered in the shopping basket. Offer only available while stocks last or until 31st December 2014, cannot be used in conjunction with any offer or promotion code. Pictures for illustration purposes only and may be subject to change. The AA reserve the right to replace kit components with other suitable products of the same value at its discretion. Please see website for details on returns and cancellations. **Free standard P&P to the UK mainland and Ireland addresses only. (Usually delivered within 7 working days).

RRP: £9.99

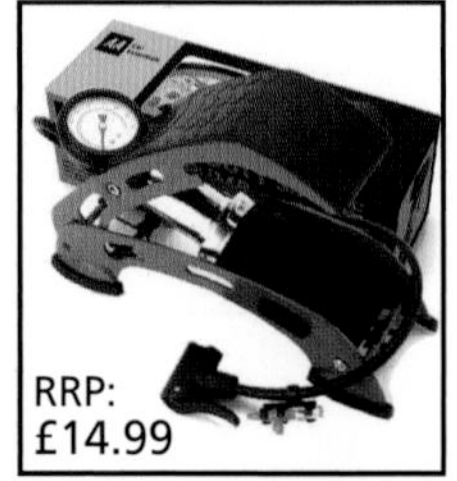
RRP: £14.99

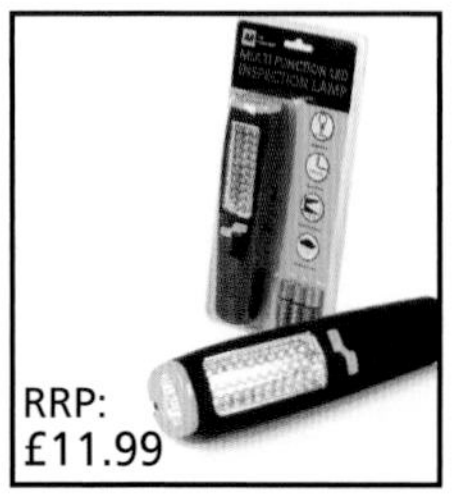
RRP: £11.99

The Driver Ready Kit includes:
Heavy Duty Single Footpump, Booster Cables, Tow Rope, Warning Triangle, High-Visibility Vest Multi-Function Inspection Lamp and Canvas Carry Bag.

RRP: £16.99

RRP: £9.99

RRP: £7.99

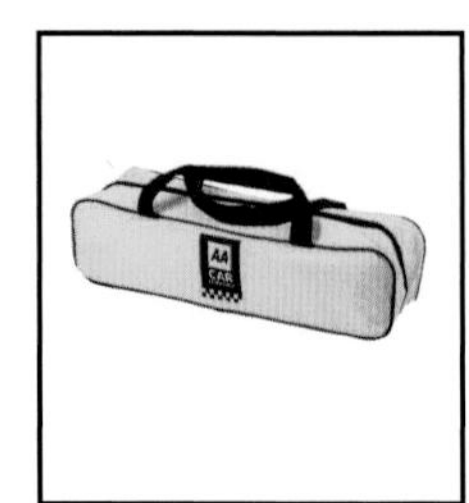

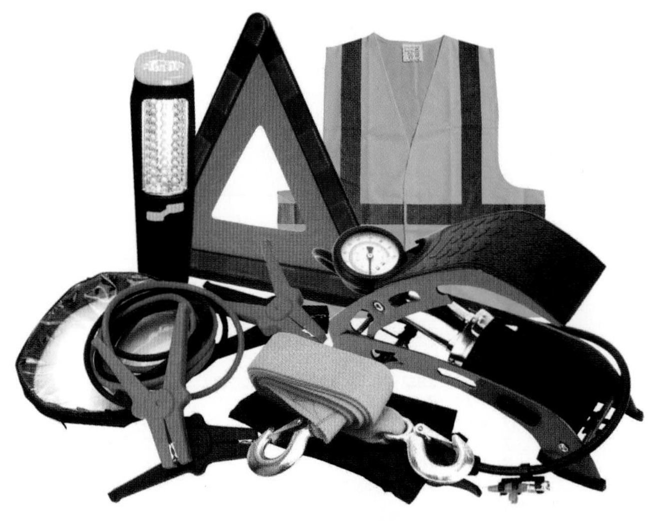

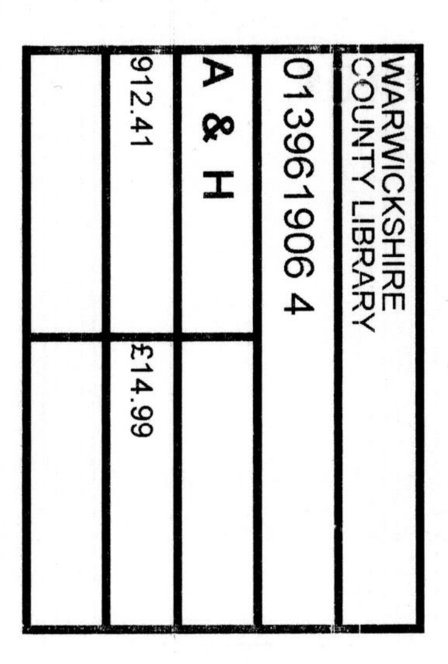

Map pages north

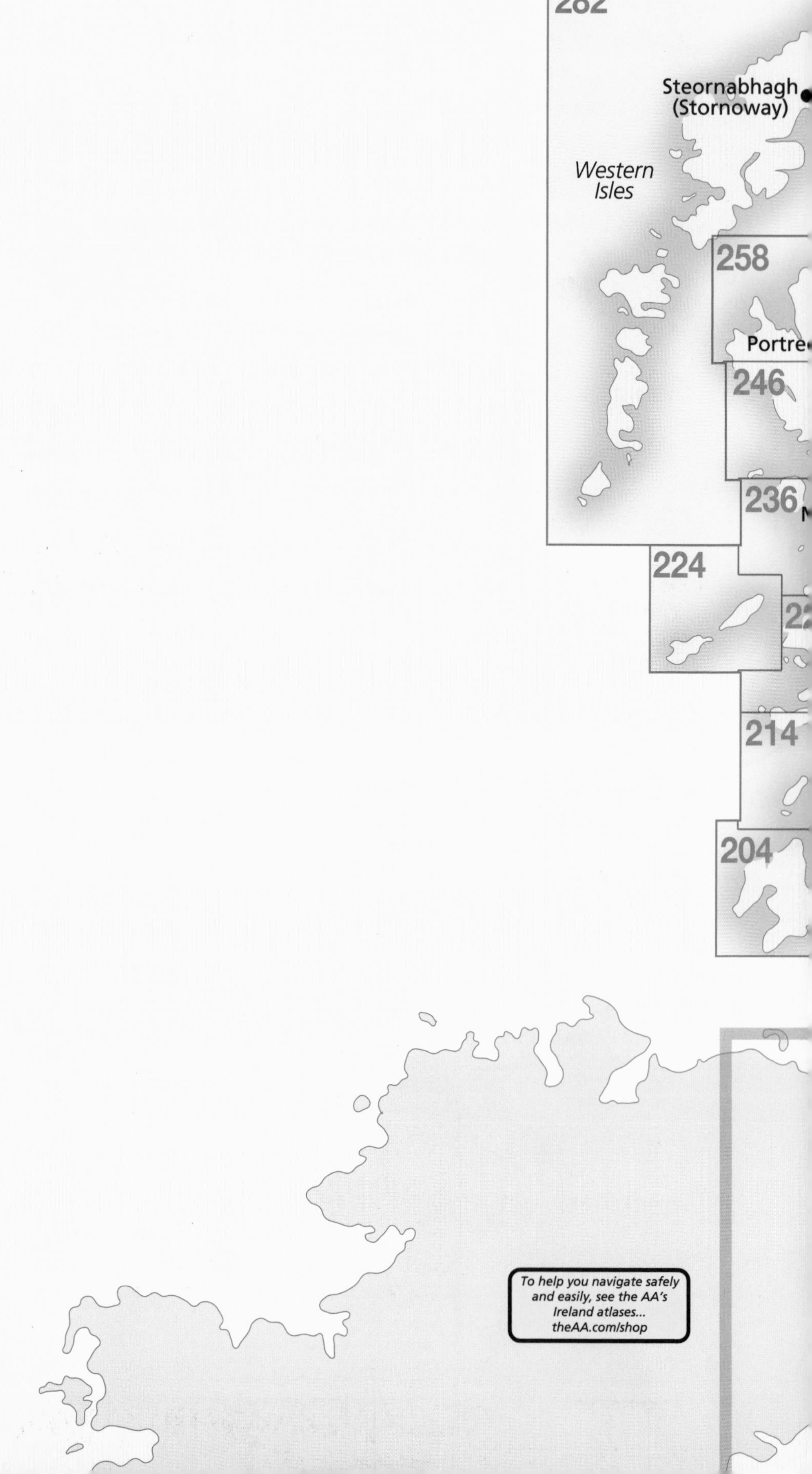